W9-BUV-297

from reviews of the first edition of

APPLIED CRYPTOGRAPHY

Protocols, Algorithms, and Source Code in C

"... the definitive text on the subject. ..."
—*Software Development Magazine*

"... good reading for anyone interested in cryptography."
—*BYTE*

"This book should be on the shelf of any computer professional involved in the use or implementation of cryptography."
—*IEEE Software*

"... dazzling ... fascinating. ... This book *absolutely must* be on your bookshelf ..."
—*PC Techniques*

"... comprehensive ... an encyclopedic work ..."
—*The Cryptogram*

"... a fantastic book on cryptography today. It belongs in the library of anyone interested in cryptography or anyone who deals with information security and cryptographic systems."
—*Computers & Security*

"An encyclopedic survey ... could well have been subtitled 'The Joy of Encrypting' ... a useful addition to the library of any active or would-be security practitioner."
—*Cryptologia*

"... encyclopedic ... readable ... well-informed ... picks up where Dorothy Denning's classic *Cryptography and Data Security* left off a dozen years ago. ... This book would be a bargain at twice the price."
—*;login:*

"This is a marvelous resource—the best book on cryptography and its application available today."
—Dorothy Denning
Georgetown University

"... Schneier's book is an indispensable reference and resource. ... I recommend it highly."
—Martin Hellman
Stanford University

Errata

A list of the errors found in this book along with corresponding corrections is updated periodically. For the most recent electronic version, send email to:

> schneier@counterpane.com

For the most recent printed version, send a stamped, self-addressed envelope to:

> AC Corrections
> Counterpane Systems
> 101 E. Minnekaka Parkway
> Minneapolis, MN 55419

Readers are encouraged to distribute electronic or printed versions of this list to other readers of this book.

APPLIED CRYPTOGRAPHY, SECOND EDITION

PROTOCOLS, ALGORITHMS, AND SOURCE CODE IN C

BRUCE SCHNEIER

John Wiley & Sons, Inc.
New York • Chichester • Brisbane • Toronto • Singapore

Publisher: Katherine Schowalter
Editor: Phil Sutherland
Assistant Editor: Allison Roarty
Managing Editor: Robert Aronds
Text Design & Composition: North Market Street Graphics

Designations used by companies to distinguish their products are often claimed as trademarks. In all instances where John Wiley & Sons, Inc. is aware of a claim, the product names appear in initial capital or all capital letters. Readers, however, should contact the appropriate companies for more complete information regarding trademarks and registration.

This text is printed on acid-free paper.

Copyright © 1996 by Bruce Schneier
Published by John Wiley & Sons, Inc.

All rights reserved. Published simultaneously in Canada.

This publication is designed to provide accurate and authoritative information in regard to the subject matter covered. It is sold with the understanding that the publisher is not engaged in rendering legal, accounting, or other professional service. If legal advice or other expert assistance is required, the services of a competent professional person should be sought.

In no event will the publisher or author be liable for any consequential, incidental, or indirect damages (including damages for loss of business profits, business interruption, loss of business information, and the like) arising from the use or inability to use the protocols and algorithms in this book, even if the publisher or author has been advised of the possibility of such damages.

Some of the protocols and algorithms in this book are protected by patents and copyrights. It is the responsibility of the reader to obtain all necessary patent and copyright licenses before implementing in software any protocol or algorithm in this book. This book does not contain an exhaustive list of all applicable patents and copyrights.

Some of the protocols and algorithms in this book are regulated under the United States Department of State International Traffic in Arms Regulations. It is the responsibility of the reader to obtain all necessary export licenses before implementing in software for export any protocol or algorithm in this book.

Reproduction or translation of any part of this work beyond that permitted by section 107 or 108 of the 1976 United States Copyright Act without the permission of the copyright owner is unlawful. Requests for permission or further information should be addressed to the Permissions Department, John Wiley & Sons, Inc.

Library of Congress Cataloging-in-Publication Data:

Schneier, Bruce
    Applied Cryptography Second Edition : protocols, algorithms, and source code in C
/ Bruce Schneier.
        p.   cm.
    Includes bibliographical references (p. 675).
    ISBN 0-471-12845-7 (cloth : acid-free paper). — ISBN
0-471-11709-9 (paper : acid-free paper)
    1. Computer security.   2. Telecommunication—Security measures.
3. Cryptography. I. Title.
QA76.9.A25S35   1996
005.8'2—dc20   95-12398
                                                                              CIP

Printed in the United States of America
10 9 8

Contents in Brief

Foreword by Whitfield Diffie

Preface

About the Author

1 Foundations

Part I Cryptographic Protocols

2 Protocol Building Blocks

3 Basic Protocols

4 Intermediate Protocols

5 Advanced Protocols

6 Esoteric Protocols

Part II Cryptographic Techniques

7 Key Length

8 Key Management

9 Algorithm Types and Modes

10 Using Algorithms

Part III Cryptographic Algorithms

11 Mathematical Background

12 Data Encryption Standard (DES)

13 Other Block Ciphers

14 Still Other Block Ciphers

15 Combining Block Ciphers

16 Pseudo-Random-Sequence Generators and Stream Ciphers

17 Other Stream Ciphers and Real Random-Sequence Generators

18 One-Way Hash Functions

19 Public-Key Algorithms

20 Public-Key Digital Signature Algorithms

21 Identification Schemes

22 Key-Exchange Algorithms

23 Special Algorithms for Protocols

Part IV The Real World

24 Example Implementations

25 Politics

Afterword by Matt Blaze

Part V Source Code

References

Contents

Foreword by Whitfield Diffie   xv

Preface   xix

   HOW TO READ THIS BOOK   xx

   ACKNOWLEDGMENTS   *xxii*

About the Author   *xxiii*

1 FOUNDATIONS   *1*

1.1   TERMINOLOGY   *1*

1.2   STEGANOGRAPHY   *9*

1.3   SUBSTITUTION CIPHERS AND TRANSPOSITION CIPHERS   *10*

1.4   SIMPLE XOR   *13*

1.5   ONE-TIME PADS   *15*

1.6   COMPUTER ALGORITHMS   *17*

1.7   LARGE NUMBERS   *17*

PART I   CRYPTOGRAPHIC PROTOCOLS

2 PROTOCOL BUILDING BLOCKS   *21*

2.1   INTRODUCTION TO PROTOCOLS   *21*

2.2   COMMUNICATIONS USING SYMMETRIC CRYPTOGRAPHY   *28*

2.3   ONE-WAY FUNCTIONS   *29*

2.4   ONE-WAY HASH FUNCTIONS   *30*

2.5   COMMUNICATIONS USING PUBLIC-KEY CRYPTOGRAPHY   *31*

2.6   DIGITAL SIGNATURES   *34*

2.7   DIGITAL SIGNATURES WITH ENCRYPTION   *41*

2.8   RANDOM AND PSEUDO-RANDOM-SEQUENCE GENERATION   *44*

3 BASIC PROTOCOLS *47*

3.1 KEY EXCHANGE *47*
3.2 AUTHENTICATION *52*
3.3 AUTHENTICATION AND KEY EXCHANGE *56*
3.4 FORMAL ANALYSIS OF AUTHENTICATION AND KEY-EXCHANGE PROTOCOLS *65*
3.5 MULTIPLE-KEY PUBLIC-KEY CRYPTOGRAPHY *68*
3.6 SECRET SPLITTING *70*
3.7 SECRET SHARING *71*
3.8 CRYPTOGRAPHIC PROTECTION OF DATABASES *73*

4 INTERMEDIATE PROTOCOLS *75*

4.1 TIMESTAMPING SERVICES *75*
4.2 SUBLIMINAL CHANNEL *79*
4.3 UNDENIABLE DIGITAL SIGNATURES *81*
4.4 DESIGNATED CONFIRMER SIGNATURES *82*
4.5 PROXY SIGNATURES *83*
4.6 GROUP SIGNATURES *84*
4.7 FAIL-STOP DIGITAL SIGNATURES *85*
4.8 COMPUTING WITH ENCRYPTED DATA *85*
4.9 BIT COMMITMENT *86*
4.10 FAIR COIN FLIPS *89*
4.11 MENTAL POKER *92*
4.12 ONE-WAY ACCUMULATORS *95*
4.13 ALL-OR-NOTHING DISCLOSURE OF SECRETS *96*
4.14 KEY ESCROW *97*

5 ADVANCED PROTOCOLS *101*

5.1 ZERO-KNOWLEDGE PROOFS *101*
5.2 ZERO-KNOWLEDGE PROOFS OF IDENTITY *109*
5.3 BLIND SIGNATURES *112*
5.4 IDENTITY-BASED PUBLIC-KEY CRYPTOGRAPHY *115*
5.5 OBLIVIOUS TRANSFER *116*
5.6 OBLIVIOUS SIGNATURES *117*
5.7 SIMULTANEOUS CONTRACT SIGNING *118*
5.8 DIGITAL CERTIFIED MAIL *122*
5.9 SIMULTANEOUS EXCHANGE OF SECRETS *123*

6 ESOTERIC PROTOCOLS *125*

6.1 SECURE ELECTIONS *125*
6.2 SECURE MULTIPARTY COMPUTATION *134*
6.3 ANONYMOUS MESSAGE BROADCAST *137*
6.4 DIGITAL CASH *139*

PART II CRYPTOGRAPHIC TECHNIQUES

7 KEY LENGTH 151
7.1 SYMMETRIC KEY LENGTH 151
7.2 PUBLIC-KEY KEY LENGTH 158
7.3 COMPARING SYMMETRIC AND PUBLIC-KEY KEY LENGTH 165
7.4 BIRTHDAY ATTACKS AGAINST ONE-WAY HASH FUNCTIONS 165
7.5 HOW LONG SHOULD A KEY BE? 166
7.6 CAVEAT EMPTOR 168

8 KEY MANAGEMENT 169
8.1 GENERATING KEYS 170
8.2 NONLINEAR KEYSPACES 175
8.3 TRANSFERRING KEYS 176
8.4 VERIFYING KEYS 178
8.5 USING KEYS 179
8.6 UPDATING KEYS 180
8.7 STORING KEYS 180
8.8 BACKUP KEYS 181
8.9 COMPROMISED KEYS 182
8.10 LIFETIME OF KEYS 183
8.11 DESTROYING KEYS 184
8.12 PUBLIC-KEY KEY MANAGEMENT 185

9 ALGORITHM TYPES AND MODES 189
9.1 ELECTRONIC CODEBOOK MODE 189
9.2 BLOCK REPLAY 191
9.3 CIPHER BLOCK CHAINING MODE 193
9.4 STREAM CIPHERS 197
9.5 SELF-SYNCHRONIZING STREAM CIPHERS 198
9.6 CIPHER-FEEDBACK MODE 200
9.7 SYNCHRONOUS STREAM CIPHERS 202
9.8 OUTPUT-FEEDBACK MODE 203
9.9 COUNTER MODE 205
9.10 OTHER BLOCK-CIPHER MODES 206
9.11 CHOOSING A CIPHER MODE 208
9.12 INTERLEAVING 210
9.13 BLOCK CIPHERS VERSUS STREAM CIPHERS 210

10 USING ALGORITHMS 213
10.1 CHOOSING AN ALGORITHM 214
10.2 PUBLIC-KEY CRYPTOGRAPHY VERSUS SYMMETRIC CRYPTOGRAPHY 216
10.3 ENCRYPTING COMMUNICATIONS CHANNELS 216
10.4 ENCRYPTING DATA FOR STORAGE 220
10.5 HARDWARE ENCRYPTION VERSUS SOFTWARE ENCRYPTION 223

10.6 COMPRESSION, ENCODING, AND ENCRYPTION *226*
10.7 DETECTING ENCRYPTION *226*
10.8 HIDING CIPHERTEXT IN CIPHERTEXT *227*
10.9 DESTROYING INFORMATION *228*

PART III CRYPTOGRAPHIC ALGORITHMS

11 MATHEMATICAL BACKGROUND *233*
11.1 INFORMATION THEORY *233*
11.2 COMPLEXITY THEORY *237*
11.3 NUMBER THEORY *242*
11.4 FACTORING *255*
11.5 PRIME NUMBER GENERATION *258*
11.6 DISCRETE LOGARITHMS IN A FINITE FIELD *261*

12 DATA ENCRYPTION STANDARD (DES) *265*
12.1 BACKGROUND *265*
12.2 DESCRIPTION OF DES *270*
12.3 SECURITY OF DES *278*
12.4 DIFFERENTIAL AND LINEAR CRYPTANALYSIS *285*
12.5 THE REAL DESIGN CRITERIA *293*
12.6 DES VARIANTS *294*
12.7 HOW SECURE IS DES TODAY? *300*

13 OTHER BLOCK CIPHERS *303*
13.1 LUCIFER *303*
13.2 MADRYGA *304*
13.3 NEWDES *306*
13.4 FEAL *308*
13.5 REDOC *311*
13.6 LOKI *314*
13.7 KHUFU AND KHAFRE *316*
13.8 RC2 *318*
13.9 IDEA *319*
13.10 MMB *325*
13.11 CA-1.1 *327*
13.12 SKIPJACK *328*

14 STILL OTHER BLOCK CIPHERS *331*
14.1 GOST *331*
14.2 CAST *334*
14.3 BLOWFISH *336*
14.4 SAFER *339*
14.5 3-WAY *341*

14.6   CRAB   342
14.7   SXAL8/MBAL   344
14.8   RC5   344
14.9   OTHER BLOCK ALGORITHMS   346
14.10 THEORY OF BLOCK CIPHER DESIGN   346
14.11 USING ONE-WAY HASH FUNCTIONS   351
14.12 CHOOSING A BLOCK ALGORITHM   354

15 COMBINING BLOCK CIPHERS   357
15.1   DOUBLE ENCRYPTION   357
15.2   TRIPLE ENCRYPTION   358
15.3   DOUBLING THE BLOCK LENGTH   363
15.4   OTHER MULTIPLE ENCRYPTION SCHEMES   363
15.5   CDMF KEY SHORTENING   366
15.6   WHITENING   366
15.7   CASCADING MULTIPLE BLOCK ALGORITHMS   367
15.8   COMBINING MULTIPLE BLOCK ALGORITHMS   368

**16 PSEUDO-RANDOM-SEQUENCE
        GENERATORS AND STREAM CIPHERS**   369
16.1   LINEAR CONGRUENTIAL GENERATORS   369
16.2   LINEAR FEEDBACK SHIFT REGISTERS   372
16.3   DESIGN AND ANALYSIS OF STREAM CIPHERS   379
16.4   STREAM CIPHERS USING LFSRs   381
16.5   A5   389
16.6   HUGHES XPD/KPD   389
16.7   NANOTEQ   390
16.8   RAMBUTAN   390
16.9   ADDITIVE GENERATORS   390
16.10 GIFFORD   392
16.11 ALGORITHM M   393
16.12 PKZIP   394

**17 OTHER STREAM CIPHERS AND REAL
        RANDOM-SEQUENCE GENERATORS**   397
17.1   RC4   397
17.2   SEAL   398
17.3   WAKE   400
17.4   FEEDBACK WITH CARRY SHIFT REGISTERS   402
17.5   STREAM CIPHERS USING FCSRs   405
17.6   NONLINEAR-FEEDBACK SHIFT REGISTERS   412
17.7   OTHER STREAM CIPHERS   413
17.8   SYSTEM-THEORETIC APPROACH TO STREAM-CIPHER DESIGN   415
17.9   COMPLEXITY-THEMATIC APPROACH TO STREAM-CIPHER DESIGN   416
17.10 OTHER APPROACHES TO STREAM-CIPHER DESIGN   418

17.11 CASCADING MULTIPLE STREAM CIPHERS *419*
17.12 CHOOSING A STREAM CIPHER *420*
17.13 GENERATING MULTIPLE STREAMS FROM A
SINGLE PSEUDO-RANDOM-SEQUENCE GENERATOR *420*
17.14 REAL RANDOM-SEQUENCE GENERATORS *421*

18 ONE-WAY HASH FUNCTIONS *429*
18.1 BACKGROUND *429*
18.2 SNEFRU *431*
18.3 *N*-HASH *432*
18.4 MD4 *435*
18.5 MD5 *436*
18.6 MD2 *441*
18.7 SECURE HASH ALGORITHM (SHA) *441*
18.8 RIPE-MD *445*
18.9 HAVAL *445*
18.10 OTHER ONE-WAY HASH FUNCTIONS *446*
18.11 ONE-WAY HASH FUNCTIONS USING SYMMETRIC BLOCK ALGORITHMS *446*
18.12 USING PUBLIC-KEY ALGORITHMS *455*
18.13 CHOOSING A ONE-WAY HASH FUNCTION *455*
18.14 MESSAGE AUTHENTICATION CODES *455*

19 PUBLIC-KEY ALGORITHMS *461*
19.1 BACKGROUND *461*
19.2 KNAPSACK ALGORITHMS *462*
19.3 RSA *466*
19.4 POHLIG-HELLMAN *474*
19.5 RABIN *475*
19.6 ELGAMAL *476*
19.7 MCELIECE *479*
19.8 ELLIPTIC CURVE CRYPTOSYSTEMS *480*
19.9 LUC *481*
19.10 FINITE AUTOMATON PUBLIC-KEY CRYPTOSYSTEMS *482*

20 PUBLIC-KEY DIGITAL SIGNATURE ALGORITHMS *483*
20.1 DIGITAL SIGNATURE ALGORITHM (DSA) *483*
20.2 DSA VARIANTS *494*
20.3 GOST DIGITAL SIGNATURE ALGORITHM *495*
20.4 DISCRETE LOGARITHM SIGNATURE SCHEMES *496*
20.5 ONG-SCHNORR-SHAMIR *498*
20.6 ESIGN *499*
20.7 CELLULAR AUTOMATA *500*
20.8 OTHER PUBLIC-KEY ALGORITHMS *500*

21 IDENTIFICATION SCHEMES *503*
21.1 FEIGE-FIAT-SHAMIR *503*

21.2 Guillou-Quisquater *508*
21.3 Schnorr *510*
21.4 Converting Identification Schemes to Signature Schemes *512*

22 KEY-EXCHANGE ALGORITHMS *513*
22.1 Diffie-Hellman *513*
22.2 Station-to-Station Protocol *516*
22.3 Shamir's Three-Pass Protocol *516*
22.4 COMSET *517*
22.5 Encrypted Key Exchange *518*
22.6 Fortified Key Negotiation *522*
22.7 Conference Key Distribution and Secret Broadcasting *523*

23 SPECIAL ALGORITHMS FOR PROTOCOLS *527*
23.1 Multiple-Key Public-Key Cryptography *527*
23.2 Secret-Sharing Algorithms *528*
23.3 Subliminal Channel *531*
23.4 Undeniable Digital Signatures *536*
23.5 Designated Confirmer Signatures *539*
23.6 Computing with Encrypted Data *540*
23.7 Fair Coin Flips *541*
23.8 One-Way Accumulators *543*
23.9 All-or-Nothing Disclosure of Secrets *543*
23.10 Fair and Failsafe Cryptosystems *546*
23.11 Zero-Knowledge Proofs of Knowledge *548*
23.12 Blind Signatures *549*
23.13 Oblivious Transfer *550*
23.14 Secure Multiparty Computation *551*
23.15 Probabilistic Encryption *552*
23.16 Quantum Cryptography *554*

PART IV THE REAL WORLD

24 EXAMPLE IMPLEMENTATIONS *561*
24.1 IBM Secret-Key Management Protocol *561*
24.2 MITRENET *562*
24.3 ISDN *563*
24.4 STU-III *565*
24.5 Kerberos *566*
24.6 KryptoKnight *571*
24.7 SESAME *572*
24.8 IBM Common Cryptographic Architecture *573*
24.9 ISO Authentication Framework *574*
24.10 Privacy-Enhanced Mail (PEM) *577*
24.11 Message Security Protocol (MSP) *584*

24.12 Pretty Good Privacy (PGP)   584
24.13 Smart Cards   587
24.14 Public-Key Cryptography Standards (PKCS)   588
24.15 Universal Electronic Payment System (UEPS)   589
24.16 Clipper   591
24.17 Capstone   593
24.18 AT&T Model 3600 Telephone Security Device (TSD)   594

25 POLITICS   597
25.1   National Security Agency (NSA)   597
25.2   National Computer Security Center (NCSC)   599
25.3   National Institute of Standards and Technology (NIST)   600
25.4   RSA Data Security, Inc.   603
25.5   Public Key Partners   604
25.6   International Association for Cryptographic Research (IACR)   605
25.7   RACE Integrity Primitives Evaluation (RIPE)   605
25.8   Conditional Access for Europe (CAFE)   606
25.9   ISO/IEC 9979   607
25.10 Professional, Civil Liberties, and Industry Groups   608
25.11 Sci.crypt   608
25.12 Cypherpunks   609
25.13 Patents   609
25.14 U.S. Export Rules   610
25.15 Foreign Import and Export of Cryptography   617
25.16 Legal Issues   618

Afterword by Matt Blaze   619

PART V   SOURCE CODE

Source Code   623

References   675

Foreword
By Whitfield Diffie

The literature of cryptography has a curious history. Secrecy, of course, has always played a central role, but until the First World War, important developments appeared in print in a more or less timely fashion and the field moved forward in much the same way as other specialized disciplines. As late as 1918, one of the most influential cryptanalytic papers of the twentieth century, William F. Friedman's monograph *The Index of Coincidence and Its Applications in Cryptography*, appeared as a research report of the private Riverbank Laboratories [577]. And this, despite the fact that the work had been done as part of the war effort. In the same year Edward H. Hebern of Oakland, California filed the first patent for a rotor machine [710], the device destined to be a mainstay of military cryptography for nearly 50 years.

After the First World War, however, things began to change. U.S. Army and Navy organizations, working entirely in secret, began to make fundamental advances in cryptography. During the thirties and forties a few basic papers did appear in the open literature and several treatises on the subject were published, but the latter were farther and farther behind the state of the art. By the end of the war the transition was complete. With one notable exception, the public literature had died. That exception was Claude Shannon's paper "The Communication Theory of Secrecy Systems," which appeared in the *Bell System Technical Journal* in 1949 [1432]. It was similar to Friedman's 1918 paper, in that it grew out of wartime work of Shannon's. After the Second World War ended it was declassified, possibly by mistake.

From 1949 until 1967 the cryptographic literature was barren. In that year a different sort of contribution appeared: David Kahn's history, *The Codebreakers* [794]. It didn't contain any new technical ideas, but it did contain a remarkably complete history of what had gone before, including mention of some things that the government still considered secret. The significance of *The Codebreakers* lay not just in its remarkable scope, but also in the fact that it enjoyed good sales and made tens of thousands of people, who had never given the matter a moment's thought, aware of cryptography. A trickle of new cryptographic papers began to be written.

At about the same time, Horst Feistel, who had earlier worked on identification friend or foe devices for the Air Force, took his lifelong passion for cryptography to the IBM Watson Laboratory in Yorktown Heights, New York. There, he began development of what was to become the U.S. Data Encryption Standard; by the early 1970s several technical reports on this subject by Feistel and his colleagues had been made public by IBM [1482,1484,552].

This was the situation when I entered the field in late 1972. The cryptographic literature wasn't abundant, but what there was included some very shiny nuggets.

Cryptology presents a difficulty not found in normal academic disciplines: the need for the proper interaction of cryptography and cryptanalysis. This arises out of the fact that in the absence of real communications requirements, it is easy to propose a system that appears unbreakable. Many academic designs are so complex that the would-be cryptanalyst doesn't know where to start; exposing flaws in these designs is far harder than designing them in the first place. The result is that the competitive process, which is one strong motivation in academic research, cannot take hold.

When Martin Hellman and I proposed public-key cryptography in 1975 [496], one of the indirect aspects of our contribution was to introduce a problem that does not even appear easy to solve. Now an aspiring cryptosystem designer could produce something that would be recognized as clever—something that did more than just turn meaningful text into nonsense. The result has been a spectacular increase in the number of people working in cryptography, the number of meetings held, and the number of books and papers published.

In my acceptance speech for the Donald E. Fink award—given for the best expository paper to appear in an IEEE journal—which I received jointly with Hellman in 1980, I told the audience that in writing "Privacy and Authentication," I had an experience that I suspected was rare even among the prominent scholars who populate the IEEE awards ceremony: I had written the paper I had wanted to study, but could not find, when I first became seriously interested in cryptography. Had I been able to go to the Stanford bookstore and pick up a modern cryptography text, I would probably have learned about the field years earlier. But the only things available in the fall of 1972 were a few classic papers and some obscure technical reports.

The contemporary researcher has no such problem. The problem now is choosing where to start among the thousands of papers and dozens of books. The contemporary researcher, yes, but what about the contemporary programmer or engineer who merely wants to use cryptography? Where does that person turn? Until now, it has been necessary to spend long hours hunting out and then studying the research literature before being able to design the sort of cryptographic utilities glibly described in popular articles.

This is the gap that Bruce Schneier's *Applied Cryptography* has come to fill. Beginning with the objectives of communication security and elementary examples of programs used to achieve these objectives, Schneier gives us a panoramic view of the fruits of 20 years of public research. The title says it all; from the mundane objective of having a secure conversation the very first time you call someone to the possibilities of digital money and cryptographically secure elections, this is where you'll find it.

Not satisfied that the book was about the real world merely because it went all the way down to the code, Schneier has included an account of the world in which cryptography is developed and applied, and discusses entities ranging from the International Association for Cryptologic Research to the NSA.

When public interest in cryptography was just emerging in the late seventies and early eighties, the National Security Agency (NSA), America's official cryptographic organ, made several attempts to quash it. The first was a letter from a long-time NSA employee allegedly, avowedly, and apparently acting on his own. The letter was sent to the IEEE and warned that the publication of cryptographic material was a violation of the International Traffic in Arms Regulations (ITAR). This viewpoint turned out not even to be supported by the regulations themselves—which contained an explicit exemption for published material—but gave both the public practice of cryptography and the 1977 Information Theory Workshop lots of unexpected publicity.

A more serious attempt occurred in 1980, when the NSA funded the American Council on Education to examine the issue with a view to persuading Congress to give it legal control of publications in the field of cryptography. The results fell far short of NSA's ambitions and resulted in a program of voluntary review of cryptographic papers; researchers were requested to ask the NSA's opinion on whether disclosure of results would adversely affect the national interest before publication.

As the eighties progressed, pressure focused more on the practice than the study of cryptography. Existing laws gave the NSA the power, through the Department of State, to regulate the export of cryptographic equipment. As business became more and more international and the American fraction of the world market declined, the pressure to have a single product in both domestic and offshore markets increased. Such single products were subject to export control and thus the NSA acquired substantial influence not only over what was exported, but also over what was sold in the United States.

As this is written, a new challenge confronts the public practice of cryptography. The government has augmented the widely published and available Data Encryption Standard, with a secret algorithm implemented in tamper-resistant chips. These chips will incorporate a codified mechanism of government monitoring. The negative aspects of this "key-escrow" program range from a potentially disastrous impact on personal privacy to the high cost of having to add hardware to products that had previously encrypted in software. So far key escrow products are enjoying less than stellar sales and the scheme has attracted widespread negative comment, especially from the independent cryptographers. Some people, however, see more future in programming than politicking and have redoubled their efforts to provide the world with strong cryptography that is accessible to public scrutiny.

A sharp step back from the notion that export control law could supersede the First Amendment seemed to have been taken in 1980 when the *Federal Register* announcement of a revision to ITAR included the statement: "... provision has been added to make it clear that the regulation of the export of technical data does not purport to interfere with the First Amendment rights of individuals." But the fact that tension between the First Amendment and the export control laws has not gone away should be evident from statements at a conference held by RSA Data Security. NSA's representative from the export control office expressed the opinion that people who published cryptographic programs were "in a grey area" with respect to the law. If that is so, it is a grey area on which the first edition of this book has shed some light. Export applications for the book itself have been granted, with acknowledgement that published material lay beyond the authority of the Munitions Control Board. Applications to export the enclosed programs on disk, however, have been denied.

The shift in the NSA's strategy, from attempting to control cryptographic research to tightening its grip on the development and deployment of cryptographic products, is presumably due to its realization that all the great cryptographic papers in the world do not protect a single bit of traffic. Sitting on the shelf, this volume may be able to do no better than the books and papers that preceded it, but sitting next to a workstation, where a programmer is writing cryptographic code, it just may.

Whitfield Diffie
Mountain View, CA

Chapters 7 through 10 (Part II) discuss cryptographic techniques. All four chapters in this section are important for even the most basic uses of cryptography. Chapters 7 and 8 are about keys: how long a key should be in order to be secure, how to generate keys, how to store keys, how to dispose of keys, and so on. Key management is the hardest part of cryptography and often the Achilles' heel of an otherwise secure system. Chapter 9 discusses different ways of using cryptographic algorithms, and Chapter 10 gives the odds and ends of algorithms: how to choose, implement, and use algorithms.

Chapters 11 through 23 (Part III) list algorithms. Chapter 11 provides the mathematical background. This chapter is only required if you are interested in public-key algorithms. If you just want to implement DES (or something similar), you can skip ahead. Chapter 12 discusses DES: the algorithm, its history, its security, and some variants. Chapters 13, 14, and 15 discuss other block algorithms; if you want something more secure than DES, skip to the section on IDEA and triple-DES. If you want to read about a bunch of algorithms, some of which may be more secure than DES, read the whole chapter. Chapters 16 and 17 discuss stream algorithms. Chapter 18 focuses on one-way hash functions; MD5 and SHA are the most common, although I discuss many more. Chapter 19 discusses public-key encryption algorithms, Chapter 20 discusses public-key digital signature algorithms, Chapter 21 discusses public-key identification algorithms, and Chapter 22 discusses public-key key exchange algorithms. The important algorithms are RSA, DSA, Fiat-Shamir, and Diffie-Hellman, respectively. Chapter 23 has more esoteric public-key algorithms and protocols; the math in this chapter is quite complicated, so wear your seat belt.

Chapters 24 and 25 (Part IV) turn to the real world of cryptography. Chapter 24 discusses some of the current implementations of these algorithms and protocols, while Chapter 25 touches on some of the political issues surrounding cryptography. These chapters are by no means intended to be comprehensive.

Also included are source code listings for 10 algorithms discussed in Part III. I was unable to include all the code I wanted to due to space limitations, and cryptographic source code cannot otherwise be exported. (Amazingly enough, the State Department allowed export of the first edition of this book with source code, but denied export for a computer disk with the exact same source code on it. Go figure.) An associated source code disk set includes much more source code than I could fit in this book; it is probably the largest collection of cryptographic source code outside a military institution. I can only send source code disks to U.S. and Canadian citizens living in the U.S. and Canada, but hopefully that will change someday. If you are interested in implementing or playing with the cryptographic algorithms in this book, get the disk. See the last page of the book for details.

One criticism of this book is that its encyclopedic nature takes away from its readability. This is true, but I wanted to provide a single reference for those who might come across an algorithm in the academic literature or in a product. For those who are more interested in a tutorial, I apologize. A lot is being done in the field; this is the first time so much of it has been gathered between two covers. Even so, space considerations forced me to leave many things out. I covered topics that I felt were important, practical, or interesting. If I couldn't cover a topic in depth, I gave references to articles and papers that did.

I have done my best to hunt down and eradicate all errors in this book, but many have assured me that it is an impossible task. Certainly, the second edition has far fewer errors than the first. An errata listing is available from me and will be periodically posted to the Usenet newsgroup sci.crypt. If any reader finds an error, please let me know. I'll send the first person to find each error in the book a free copy of the source code disk.

Acknowledgments

The list of people who had a hand in this book may seem unending, but all are worthy of mention. I would like to thank Don Alvarez, Ross Anderson, Dave Balenson, Karl Barrus, Steve Bellovin, Dan Bernstein, Eli Biham, Joan Boyar, Karen Cooper, Whit Diffie, Joan Feigenbaum, Phil Karn, Neal Koblitz, Xuejia Lai, Tom Leranth, Mike Markowitz, Ralph Merkle, Bill Patton, Peter Pearson, Charles Pfleeger, Ken Pizzini, Bart Preneel, Mark Riordan, Joachim Schurman, and Marc Schwartz for reading and editing all or parts of the first edition; Marc Vauclair for translating the first edition into French; Abe Abraham, Ross Anderson, Dave Banisar, Steve Bellovin, Eli Biham, Matt Bishop, Matt Blaze, Gary Carter, Jan Camenisch, Claude Crépeau, Joan Daemen, Jorge Davila, Ed Dawson, Whit Diffie, Carl Ellison, Joan Feigenbaum, Niels Ferguson, Matt Franklin, Rosario Gennaro, Dieter Gollmann, Mark Goresky, Richard Graveman, Stuart Haber, Jingman He, Bob Hogue, Kenneth Iversen, Markus Jakobsson, Burt Kaliski, Phil Karn, John Kelsey, John Kennedy, Lars Knudsen, Paul Kocher, John Ladwig, Xuejia Lai, Arjen Lenstra, Paul Leyland, Mike Markowitz, Jim Massey, Bruce McNair, William Hugh Murray, Roger Needham, Clif Neuman, Kaisa Nyberg, Luke O'Connor, Peter Pearson, René Peralta, Bart Preneel, Yisrael Radai, Matt Robshaw, Michael Roe, Phil Rogaway, Avi Rubin, Paul Rubin, Selwyn Russell, Kazue Sako, Mahmoud Salmasizadeh, Markus Stadler, Dmitry Titov, Jimmy Upton, Marc Vauclair, Serge Vaudenay, Gideon Yuval, Glen Zorn, and several anonymous government employees for reading and editing all or parts of the second edition; Lawrie Brown, Leisa Condie, Joan Daemen, Peter Gutmann, Alan Insley, Chris Johnston, John Kelsey, Xuejia Lai, Bill Leininger, Mike Markowitz, Richard Outerbridge, Peter Pearson, Ken Pizzini, Colin Plumb, RSA Data Security, Inc., Michael Roe, Michael Wood, and Phil Zimmermann for providing source code; Paul MacNerland for creating the figures for the first edition; Karen Cooper for copyediting the second edition; Beth Friedman for proofreading the second edition; Carol Kennedy for indexing the second edition; the readers of sci.crypt and the Cypherpunks mailing list for commenting on ideas, answering questions, and finding errors in the first edition; Randy Seuss for providing Internet access; Jeff Duntemann and Jon Erickson for helping me get started; assorted random Insleys for the impetus, encouragement, support, conversations, friendship, and dinners; and AT&T Bell Labs for firing me and making this all possible. All these people helped to create a far better book than I could have created alone.

Bruce Schneier
Oak Park, Ill.
schneier@counterpane.com

About the Author

BRUCE SCHNEIER is president of Counterpane Systems, an Oak Park, Illinois consulting firm specializing in cryptography and computer security. Bruce is also the author of *E-Mail Security* (John Wiley & Sons, 1995) and *Protect Your Macintosh* (Peachpit Press, 1994); and has written dozens of articles on cryptography for major magazines. He is a contributing editor to *Dr. Dobb's Journal*, where he edits the "Algorithms Alley" column, and a contributing editor to *Computer and Communications Security Reviews*. Bruce serves on the board of directors of the International Association for Cryptologic Research, is a member of the Advisory Board for the Electronic Privacy Information Center, and is on the program committee for the New Security Paradigms Workshop. In addition, he finds time to give frequent lectures on cryptography, computer security, and privacy.

CHAPTER   1

Foundations

1.1 TERMINOLOGY

Sender and Receiver

Suppose a sender wants to send a message to a receiver. Moreover, this sender wants to send the message securely: She wants to make sure an eavesdropper cannot read the message.

Messages and Encryption

A message is **plaintext** (sometimes called cleartext). The process of disguising a message in such a way as to hide its substance is **encryption**. An encrypted message is **ciphertext**. The process of turning ciphertext back into plaintext is **decryption**. This is all shown in Figure 1.1.

(If you want to follow the ISO 7498-2 standard, use the terms "encipher" and "decipher." It seems that some cultures find the terms "encrypt" and "decrypt" offensive, as they refer to dead bodies.)

The art and science of keeping messages secure is **cryptography**, and it is practiced by **cryptographers**. **Cryptanalysts** are practitioners of **cryptanalysis**, the art and science of breaking ciphertext; that is, seeing through the disguise. The branch of mathematics encompassing both cryptography and cryptanalysis is **cryptology** and its practitioners are **cryptologists**. Modern cryptologists are generally trained in theoretical mathematics—they have to be.

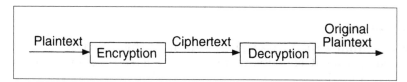

Figure 1.1 *Encryption and Decryption.*

Plaintext is denoted by *M*, for message, or *P*, for plaintext. It can be a stream of bits, a text file, a bitmap, a stream of digitized voice, a digital video image . . . whatever. As far as a computer is concerned, *M* is simply binary data. (After this chapter, this book concerns itself with binary data and computer cryptography.) The plaintext can be intended for either transmission or storage. In any case, *M* is the message to be encrypted.

Ciphertext is denoted by *C*. It is also binary data: sometimes the same size as *M*, sometimes larger. (By combining encryption with compression, *C* may be smaller than *M*. However, encryption does not accomplish this.) The encryption function *E*, operates on *M* to produce *C*. Or, in mathematical notation:

$$E(M) = C$$

In the reverse process, the decryption function *D* operates on *C* to produce *M*:

$$D(C) = M$$

Since the whole point of encrypting and then decrypting a message is to recover the original plaintext, the following identity must hold true:

$$D(E(M)) = M$$

Authentication, Integrity, and Nonrepudiation

In addition to providing confidentiality, cryptography is often asked to do other jobs:

— **Authentication**. It should be possible for the receiver of a message to ascertain its origin; an intruder should not be able to masquerade as someone else.

— **Integrity**. It should be possible for the receiver of a message to verify that it has not been modified in transit; an intruder should not be able to substitute a false message for a legitimate one.

— **Nonrepudiation**. A sender should not be able to falsely deny later that he sent a message.

These are vital requirements for social interaction on computers, and are analogous to face-to-face interactions. That someone is who he says he is . . . that someone's credentials—whether a driver's license, a medical degree, or a passport—are valid . . . that a document purporting to come from a person actually came from that person. . . . These are the things that authentication, integrity, and nonrepudiation provide.

Algorithms and Keys

A **cryptographic algorithm**, also called a **cipher**, is the mathematical function used for encryption and decryption. (Generally, there are two related functions: one for encryption and the other for decryption.)

If the security of an algorithm is based on keeping the way that algorithm works a secret, it is a **restricted** algorithm. Restricted algorithms have historical interest, but are woefully inadequate by today's standards. A large or changing group of users cannot use them, because every time a user leaves the group everyone else must switch to a different algorithm. If someone accidentally reveals the secret, everyone must change their algorithm.

Even more damning, restricted algorithms allow no quality control or standardization. Every group of users must have their own unique algorithm. Such a group can't use off-the-shelf hardware or software products; an eavesdropper can buy the same product and learn the algorithm. They have to write their own algorithms and implementations. If no one in the group is a good cryptographer, then they won't know if they have a secure algorithm.

Despite these major drawbacks, restricted algorithms are enormously popular for low-security applications. Users either don't realize or don't care about the security problems inherent in their system.

Modern cryptography solves this problem with a **key**, denoted by K. This key might be any one of a large number of values. The range of possible values of the key is called the **keyspace**. Both the encryption and decryption operations use this key (i.e., they are dependent on the key and this fact is denoted by the K subscript), so the functions now become:

$$E_K(M) = C$$
$$D_K(C) = M$$

Those functions have the property that (see Figure 1.2):

$$D_K(E_K(M)) = M$$

Some algorithms use a different encryption key and decryption key (see Figure 1.3). That is, the encryption key, K_1, is different from the corresponding decryption key, K_2. In this case:

$$E_{K_1}(M) = C$$
$$D_{K_2}(C) = M$$
$$D_{K_2}(E_{K_1}(M)) = M$$

All of the security in these algorithms is based in the key (or keys); none is based in the details of the algorithm. This means that the algorithm can be published and analyzed. Products using the algorithm can be mass-produced. It doesn't matter if an

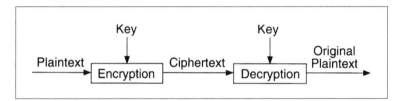

Figure 1.2   Encryption and decryption with a key.

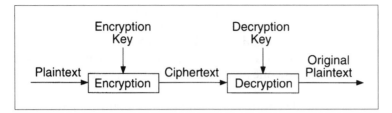

Figure 1.3 Encryption and decryption with two different keys.

eavesdropper knows your algorithm; if she doesn't know your particular key, she can't read your messages.

A **cryptosystem** is an algorithm, plus all possible plaintexts, ciphertexts, and keys.

Symmetric Algorithms

There are two general types of key-based algorithms: symmetric and public-key. **Symmetric algorithms**, sometimes called conventional algorithms, are algorithms where the encryption key can be calculated from the decryption key and vice versa. In most symmetric algorithms, the encryption key and the decryption key are the same. These algorithms, also called secret-key algorithms, single-key algorithms, or one-key algorithms, require that the sender and receiver agree on a key before they can communicate securely. The security of a symmetric algorithm rests in the key; divulging the key means that anyone could encrypt and decrypt messages. As long as the communication needs to remain secret, the key must remain secret.

Encryption and decryption with a symmetric algorithm are denoted by:

$$E_K(M) = C$$
$$D_K(C) = M$$

Symmetric algorithms can be divided into two categories. Some operate on the plaintext a single bit (or sometimes byte) at a time; these are called **stream algorithms** or **stream ciphers**. Others operate on the plaintext in groups of bits. The groups of bits are called **blocks**, and the algorithms are called **block algorithms** or **block ciphers**. For modern computer algorithms, a typical block size is 64 bits—large enough to preclude analysis and small enough to be workable. (Before computers, algorithms generally operated on plaintext one character at a time. You can think of this as a stream algorithm operating on a stream of characters.)

Public-Key Algorithms

Public-key algorithms (also called asymmetric algorithms) are designed so that the key used for encryption is different from the key used for decryption. Furthermore, the decryption key cannot (at least in any reasonable amount of time) be calculated from the encryption key. The algorithms are called "public-key" because the encryption key can be made public: A complete stranger can use the encryption key to encrypt a message, but only a specific person with the corresponding decryption key can decrypt the message. In these systems, the encryption key is often called the **public key**, and the decryption key is often called the **private key**. The private key is sometimes also called the secret key, but to avoid confusion with symmetric algorithms, that tag won't be used here.

Encryption using public key K is denoted by:

$$E_K(M) = C$$

Even though the public key and private key are different, decryption with the corresponding private key is denoted by:

$$D_K(C) = M$$

Sometimes, messages will be encrypted with the private key and decrypted with the public key; this is used in digital signatures (see Section 2.6). Despite the possible confusion, these operations are denoted by, respectively:

$$E_K(M) = C$$
$$D_K(C) = M$$

Cryptanalysis

The whole point of cryptography is to keep the plaintext (or the key, or both) secret from eavesdroppers (also called adversaries, attackers, interceptors, interlopers, intruders, opponents, or simply the enemy). Eavesdroppers are assumed to have complete access to the communications between the sender and receiver.

Cryptanalysis is the science of recovering the plaintext of a message without access to the key. Successful cryptanalysis may recover the plaintext or the key. It also may find weaknesses in a cryptosystem that eventually lead to the previous results. (The loss of a key through noncryptanalytic means is called a **compromise**.)

An attempted cryptanalysis is called an **attack**. A fundamental assumption in cryptanalysis, first enunciated by the Dutchman A. Kerckhoffs in the nineteenth century, is that the secrecy must reside entirely in the key [794]. Kerckhoffs assumes that the cryptanalyst has complete details of the cryptographic algorithm and implementation. (Of course, one would assume that the CIA does not make a habit of telling Mossad about its cryptographic algorithms, but Mossad probably finds out anyway.) While real-world cryptanalysts don't always have such detailed information, it's a good assumption to make. If others can't break an algorithm, even with knowledge of how it works, then they certainly won't be able to break it without that knowledge.

There are four general types of cryptanalytic attacks. Of course, each of them assumes that the cryptanalyst has complete knowledge of the encryption algorithm used:

1. **Ciphertext-only attack**. The cryptanalyst has the ciphertext of several messages, all of which have been encrypted using the same encryption algorithm. The cryptanalyst's job is to recover the plaintext of as many messages as possible, or better yet to deduce the key (or keys) used to

encrypt the messages, in order to decrypt other messages encrypted with the same keys.

Given: $C_1 = E_k(P_1)$, $C_2 = E_k(P_2)$, ... $C_i = E_k(P_i)$

Deduce: Either P_1, P_2, ... P_i; k; or an algorithm
to infer P_{i+1} from $C_{i+1} = E_k(P_{i+1})$

2. **Known-plaintext attack**. The cryptanalyst has access not only to the ciphertext of several messages, but also to the plaintext of those messages. His job is to deduce the key (or keys) used to encrypt the messages or an algorithm to decrypt any new messages encrypted with the same key (or keys).

Given: P_1, $C_1 = E_k(P_1)$, P_2, $C_2 = E_k(P_2)$, ... P_i, $C_i = E_k(P_i)$

Deduce: Either k, or an algorithm
to infer P_{i+1} from $C_{i+1} = E_k(P_{i+1})$

3. **Chosen-plaintext attack**. The cryptanalyst not only has access to the ciphertext and associated plaintext for several messages, but he also chooses the plaintext that gets encrypted. This is more powerful than a known-plaintext attack, because the cryptanalyst can choose specific plaintext blocks to encrypt, ones that might yield more information about the key. His job is to deduce the key (or keys) used to encrypt the messages or an algorithm to decrypt any new messages encrypted with the same key (or keys).

Given: P_1, $C_1 = E_k(P_1)$, P_2, $C_2 = E_k(P_2)$, ... P_i, $C_i = E_k(P_i)$,
where the cryptanalyst gets to choose P_1, P_2, ... P_i

Deduce: Either k, or an algorithm to infer P_{i+1} from $C_{i+1} = E_k(P_{i+1})$

4. **Adaptive-chosen-plaintext attack**. This is a special case of a chosen-plaintext attack. Not only can the cryptanalyst choose the plaintext that is encrypted, but he can also modify his choice based on the results of previous encryption. In a chosen-plaintext attack, a cryptanalyst might just be able to choose one large block of plaintext to be encrypted; in an adaptive-chosen-plaintext attack he can choose a smaller block of plaintext and then choose another based on the results of the first, and so forth.

There are at least three other types of cryptanalytic attack.

5. **Chosen-ciphertext attack**. The cryptanalyst can choose different ciphertexts to be decrypted and has access to the decrypted plaintext. For example, the cryptanalyst has access to a tamperproof box that does automatic decryption. His job is to deduce the key.

Given: C_1, $P_1 = D_k(C_1)$, C_2, $P_2 = D_k(C_2)$, ... C_i, $P_i = D_k(C_i)$

Deduce: k

This attack is primarily applicable to public-key algorithms and will be discussed in Section 19.3. A chosen-ciphertext attack is sometimes effective against a symmetric algorithm as well. (Sometimes a chosen-plaintext attack and a chosen-ciphertext attack are together known as a **chosen-text attack**.)

6. **Chosen-key attack**. This attack doesn't mean that the cryptanalyst can choose the key; it means that he has some knowledge about the relationship between different keys. It's strange and obscure, not very practical, and discussed in Section 12.4.

7. **Rubber-hose cryptanalysis**. The cryptanalyst threatens, blackmails, or tortures someone until they give him the key. Bribery is sometimes referred to as a **purchase-key attack**. These are all very powerful attacks and often the best way to break an algorithm.

Known-plaintext attacks and chosen-plaintext attacks are more common than you might think. It is not unheard-of for a cryptanalyst to get a plaintext message that has been encrypted or to bribe someone to encrypt a chosen message. You may not even have to bribe someone; if you give a message to an ambassador, you will probably find that it gets encrypted and sent back to his country for consideration. Many messages have standard beginnings and endings that might be known to the cryptanalyst. Encrypted source code is especially vulnerable because of the regular appearance of keywords: #define, struct, else, return. Encrypted executable code has the same kinds of problems: functions, loop structures, and so on. Known-plaintext attacks (and even chosen-plaintext attacks) were successfully used against both the Germans and the Japanese during World War II. David Kahn's books [794,795,796] have historical examples of these kinds of attacks.

And don't forget Kerckhoffs's assumption: If the strength of your new cryptosystem relies on the fact that the attacker does not know the algorithm's inner workings, you're sunk. If you believe that keeping the algorithm's insides secret improves the security of your cryptosystem more than letting the academic community analyze it, you're wrong. And if you think that someone won't disassemble your code and reverse-engineer your algorithm, you're naïve. (In 1994 this happened with the RC4 algorithm—see Section 17.1.) The best algorithms we have are the ones that have been made public, have been attacked by the world's best cryptographers for years, and are still unbreakable. (The National Security Agency keeps their algorithms secret from outsiders, but they have the best cryptographers in the world working within their walls—you don't. Additionally, they discuss their algorithms with one another, relying on peer review to uncover any weaknesses in their work.)

Cryptanalysts don't always have access to the algorithms, as when the United States broke the Japanese diplomatic code PURPLE during World War II [794]—but they often do. If the algorithm is being used in a commercial security program, it is simply a matter of time and money to disassemble the program and recover the algorithm. If the algorithm is being used in a military communications system, it is simply a matter of time and money to buy (or steal) the equipment and reverse-engineer the algorithm.

Those who claim to have an unbreakable cipher simply because they can't break it are either geniuses or fools. Unfortunately, there are more of the latter in the world. Beware of people who extol the virtues of their algorithms, but refuse to make them public; trusting their algorithms is like trusting snake oil.

Good cryptographers rely on peer review to separate the good algorithms from the bad.

Security of Algorithms

Different algorithms offer different degrees of security; it depends on how hard they are to break. If the cost required to break an algorithm is greater than the value of the encrypted data, then you're probably safe. If the time required to break an algorithm is longer than the time the encrypted data must remain secret, then you're probably safe. If the amount of data encrypted with a single key is less than the amount of data necessary to break the algorithm, then you're probably safe.

I say "probably" because there is always a chance of new breakthroughs in crypt-analysis. On the other hand, the value of most data decreases over time. It is important that the value of the data always remain less than the cost to break the security protecting it.

Lars Knudsen classified these different categories of breaking an algorithm. In decreasing order of severity [858]:

1. **Total break**. A cryptanalyst finds the key, K, such that $D_K(C) = P$.
2. **Global deduction**. A cryptanalyst finds an alternate algorithm, A, equivalent to $D_K(C)$, without knowing K.
3. **Instance (or local) deduction**. A cryptanalyst finds the plaintext of an intercepted ciphertext.
4. **Information deduction**. A cryptanalyst gains some information about the key or plaintext. This information could be a few bits of the key, some information about the form of the plaintext, and so forth.

An algorithm is **unconditionally secure** if, no matter how much ciphertext a cryptanalyst has, there is not enough information to recover the plaintext. In point of fact, only a one-time pad (see Section 1.5) is unbreakable given infinite resources. All other cryptosystems are breakable in a ciphertext-only attack, simply by trying every possible key one by one and checking whether the resulting plaintext is meaningful. This is called a **brute-force** attack (see Section 7.1).

Cryptography is more concerned with cryptosystems that are computationally infeasible to break. An algorithm is considered **computationally secure** (sometimes called strong) if it cannot be broken with available resources, either current or future. Exactly what constitutes "available resources" is open to interpretation.

You can measure the complexity (see Section 11.1) of an attack in different ways:

1. **Data complexity**. The amount of data needed as input to the attack.
2. **Processing complexity**. The time needed to perform the attack. This is often called the **work factor**.
3. **Storage requirements**. The amount of memory needed to do the attack.

As a rule of thumb, the complexity of an attack is taken to be the minimum of these three factors. Some attacks involve trading off the three complexities: A faster attack might be possible at the expense of a greater storage requirement.

Complexities are expressed as orders of magnitude. If an algorithm has a processing complexity of 2^{128}, then 2^{128} operations are required to break the algorithm. (These operations may be complex and time-consuming.) Still, if you assume that you have enough computing speed to perform a million operations every second and you set a million parallel processors against the task, it will still take over 10^{19} years to recover the key. That's a billion times the age of the universe.

While the complexity of an attack is constant (until some cryptanalyst finds a better attack, of course), computing power is anything but. There have been phenomenal advances in computing power during the last half-century and there is no reason to think this trend won't continue. Many cryptanalytic attacks are perfect for parallel machines: The task can be broken down into billions of tiny pieces and none of the processors need to interact with each other. Pronouncing an algorithm secure simply because it is infeasible to break, given current technology, is dicey at best. Good cryptosystems are designed to be infeasible to break with the computing power that is expected to evolve many years in the future.

Historical Terms

Historically, a **code** refers to a cryptosystem that deals with linguistic units: words, phrases, sentences, and so forth. For example, the word "OCELOT" might be the ciphertext for the entire phrase "TURN LEFT 90 DEGREES," the word "LOL-LIPOP" might be the ciphertext for "TURN RIGHT 90 DEGREES," and the words "BENT EAR" might be the ciphertext for "HOWITZER." Codes of this type are not discussed in this book; see [794,795]. Codes are only useful for specialized circumstances. Ciphers are useful for any circumstance. If your code has no entry for "ANTEATERS," then you can't say it. You can say anything with a cipher.

1.2 STEGANOGRAPHY

Steganography serves to hide secret messages in other messages, such that the secret's very existence is concealed. Generally the sender writes an innocuous message and then conceals a secret message on the same piece of paper. Historical tricks include invisible inks, tiny pin punctures on selected characters, minute differences between handwritten characters, pencil marks on typewritten characters, grilles which cover most of the message except for a few characters, and so on.

More recently, people are hiding secret messages in graphic images. Replace the least significant bit of each byte of the image with the bits of the message. The graphical image won't change appreciably—most graphics standards specify more gradations of color than the human eye can notice—and the message can be stripped out at the receiving end. You can store a 64-kilobyte message in a 1024 × 1024 grey-scale picture this way. Several public-domain programs do this sort of thing.

Peter Wayner's **mimic functions** obfuscate messages. These functions modify a message so that its statistical profile resembles that of something else: the classifieds section of *The New York Times*, a play by Shakespeare, or a newsgroup on the Internet [1584,1585]. This type of steganography won't fool a person, but it might fool some big computers scanning the Internet for interesting messages.

1.3 SUBSTITUTION CIPHERS AND TRANSPOSITION CIPHERS

Before computers, cryptography consisted of character-based algorithms. Different cryptographic algorithms either substituted characters for one another or transposed characters with one another. The better algorithms did both, many times each.

Things are more complex these days, but the philosophy remains the same. The primary change is that algorithms work on bits instead of characters. This is actually just a change in the alphabet size: from 26 elements to two elements. Most good cryptographic algorithms still combine elements of substitution and transposition.

Substitution Ciphers

A **substitution cipher** is one in which each character in the plaintext is substituted for another character in the ciphertext. The receiver inverts the substitution on the ciphertext to recover the plaintext.

In classical cryptography, there are four types of substitution ciphers:

— A **simple substitution cipher**, or **monoalphabetic cipher**, is one in which each character of the plaintext is replaced with a corresponding character of ciphertext. The cryptograms in newspapers are simple substitution ciphers.

— A **homophonic substitution cipher** is like a simple substitution cryptosystem, except a single character of plaintext can map to one of several characters of ciphertext. For example, "A" could correspond to either 5, 13, 25, or 56, "B" could correspond to either 7, 19, 31, or 42, and so on.

— A **polygram substitution cipher** is one in which blocks of characters are encrypted in groups. For example, "ABA" could correspond to "RTQ," "ABB" could correspond to "SLL," and so on.

— A **polyalphabetic substitution cipher** is made up of multiple simple substitution ciphers. For example, there might be five different simple substitution ciphers used; the particular one used changes with the position of each character of the plaintext.

The famous **Caesar Cipher**, in which each plaintext character is replaced by the character three to the right modulo 26 ("A" is replaced by "D," "B" is replaced by "E," . . . , "W" is replaced by "Z," "X" is replaced by "A," "Y" is replaced by "B," and "Z" is replaced by "C") is a simple substitution cipher. It's actually even simpler, because the ciphertext alphabet is a rotation of the plaintext alphabet and not an arbitrary permutation.

ROT13 is a simple encryption program commonly found on UNIX systems; it is also a simple substitution cipher. In this cipher, "A" is replaced by "N," "B" is replaced by "O," and so on. Every letter is rotated 13 places.

Encrypting a file twice with ROT13 restores the original file.

$$P = \text{ROT13}\,(\text{ROT13}\,(P))$$

ROT13 is not intended for security; it is often used in Usenet posts to hide potentially offensive text, to avoid giving away the solution to a puzzle, and so forth.

Simple substitution ciphers can be easily broken because the cipher does not hide the underlying frequencies of the different letters of the plaintext. All it takes is about 25 English characters before a good cryptanalyst can reconstruct the plaintext [1434]. An algorithm for solving these sorts of ciphers can be found in [578,587, 1600,78,1475,1236,880]. A good computer algorithm is [703].

Homophonic substitution ciphers were used as early as 1401 by the Duchy of Mantua [794]. They are much more complicated to break than simple substitution ciphers, but still do not obscure all of the statistical properties of the plaintext language. With a known-plaintext attack, the ciphers are trivial to break. A ciphertext-only attack is harder, but only takes a few seconds on a computer. Details are in [1261].

Polygram substitution ciphers are ciphers in which groups of letters are encrypted together. The Playfair cipher, invented in 1854, was used by the British during World War I [794]. It encrypts pairs of letters together. Its cryptanalysis is discussed in [587,1475,880]. The Hill cipher is another example of a polygram substitution cipher [732]. Sometimes you see Huffman coding used as a cipher; this is an insecure polygram substitution cipher.

Polyalphabetic substitution ciphers were invented by Leon Battista in 1568 [794]. They were used by the Union army during the American Civil War. Despite the fact that they can be broken easily [819,577,587,794] (especially with the help of computers), many commercial computer security products use ciphers of this form [1387,1390,1502]. (Details on how to break this encryption scheme, as used in Word-Perfect, can be found in [135,139].) The Vigenère cipher, first published in 1586, and the Beaufort cipher are also examples of polyalphabetic substitution ciphers.

Polyalphabetic substitution ciphers have multiple one-letter keys, each of which is used to encrypt one letter of the plaintext. The first key encrypts the first letter of the plaintext, the second key encrypts the second letter of the plaintext, and so on. After all the keys are used, the keys are recycled. If there were 20 one-letter keys, then every twentieth letter would be encrypted with the same key. This is called the **period** of the cipher. In classical cryptography, ciphers with longer periods were significantly harder to break than ciphers with short periods. There are computer techniques that can easily break substitution ciphers with very long periods.

A **running-key cipher**—sometimes called a book cipher—in which one text is used to encrypt another text, is another example of this sort of cipher. Even though this cipher has a period the length of the text, it can also be broken easily [576,794].

Transposition Ciphers

In a **transposition cipher** the plaintext remains the same, but the order of characters is shuffled around. In a **simple columnar transposition cipher**, the plaintext is written horizontally onto a piece of graph paper of fixed width and the ciphertext is read off vertically (see Figure 1.4). Decryption is a matter of writing the ciphertext vertically onto a piece of graph paper of identical width and then reading the plaintext off horizontally.

Cryptanalysis of these ciphers is discussed in [587,1475]. Since the letters of the ciphertext are the same as those of the plaintext, a frequency analysis on the ciphertext would reveal that each letter has approximately the same likelihood as in English. This gives a very good clue to a cryptanalyst, who can then use a variety of techniques to determine the right ordering of the letters to obtain the plaintext. Putting the ciphertext through a second transposition cipher greatly enhances security. There are even more complicated transposition ciphers, but computers can break almost all of them.

The German ADFGVX cipher, used during World War I, is a transposition cipher combined with a simple substitution. It was a very complex algorithm for its day but was broken by Georges Painvin, a French cryptanalyst [794].

Although many modern algorithms use transposition, it is troublesome because it requires a lot of memory and sometimes requires messages to be only certain lengths. Substitution is far more common.

Rotor Machines

In the 1920s, various mechanical encryption devices were invented to automate the process of encryption. Most were based on the concept of a **rotor**, a mechanical wheel wired to perform a general substitution.

A **rotor machine** has a keyboard and a series of rotors, and implements a version of the Vigenère cipher. Each rotor is an arbitrary permutation of the alphabet, has 26 positions, and performs a simple substitution. For example, a rotor might be wired

---

Plaintext: COMPUTER GRAPHICS MAY BE SLOW BUT AT LEAST IT'S EXPENSIVE.

```
COMPUTERGR
APHICSMAYB
ESLOWBUTAT
LEASTITSEX
PENSIVE
```

Ciphertext: CAELP OPSEE MHLAN PIOSS UCWTI TSBIV EMUTE RATSG YAERB TX

Figure 1.4 Columnar transposition cipher.

to substitute "F" for "A," "U" for "B," "L" for "C," and so on. And the output pins of one rotor are connected to the input pins of the next.

For example, in a 4-rotor machine the first rotor might substitute "F" for "A," the second might substitute "Y" for "F," the third might substitute "E" for "Y," and the fourth might substitute "C" for "E"; "C" would be the output ciphertext. Then some of the rotors shift, so next time the substitutions will be different.

It is the combination of several rotors and the gears moving them that makes the machine secure. Because the rotors all move at different rates, the period for an n-rotor machine is 26^n. Some rotor machines can also have a different number of positions on each rotor, further frustrating cryptanalysis.

The best-known rotor device is the Enigma. The Enigma was used by the Germans during World War II. The idea was invented by Arthur Scherbius and Arvid Gerhard Damm in Europe. It was patented in the United States by Arthur Scherbius [1383]. The Germans beefed up the basic design considerably for wartime use.

The German Enigma had three rotors, chosen from a set of five, a plugboard that slightly permuted the plaintext, and a reflecting rotor that caused each rotor to operate on each plaintext letter twice. As complicated as the Enigma was, it was broken during World War II. First, a team of Polish cryptographers broke the German Enigma and explained their attack to the British. The Germans modified their Enigma as the war progressed, and the British continued to cryptanalyze the new versions. For explanations of how rotor ciphers work and how they were broken, see [794,86,448,498,446,880,1315,1587,690]. Two fascinating accounts of how the Enigma was broken are [735,796].

Further Reading

This is not a book about classical cryptography, so I will not dwell further on these subjects. Two excellent precomputer cryptology books are [587,1475]; [448] presents some modern cryptanalysis of cipher machines. Dorothy Denning discusses many of these ciphers in [456] and [880] has some fairly complex mathematical analysis of the same ciphers. Another older cryptography text, which discusses analog cryptography, is [99]. An article that presents a good overview of the subject is [579]. David Kahn's historical cryptography books are also excellent [794,795,796].

1.4 SIMPLE XOR

XOR is exclusive-or operation: '^' in C or $\oplus$ in mathematical notation. It's a standard operation on bits:

$$0 \oplus 0 = 0$$
$$0 \oplus 1 = 1$$
$$1 \oplus 0 = 1$$
$$1 \oplus 1 = 0$$

Also note that:

$$a \oplus a = 0$$
$$a \oplus b \oplus b = a$$

The simple-XOR algorithm is really an embarrassment; it's nothing more than a Vigenère polyalphabetic cipher. It's here only because of its prevalence in commercial software packages, at least those in the MS-DOS and Macintosh worlds [1502,1387]. Unfortunately, if a software security program proclaims that it has a "proprietary" encryption algorithm—significantly faster than DES—the odds are that it is some variant of this.

```
/* Usage:  crypto key input_file output_file */

void main (int argc, char *argv[])
{
    FILE *fi, *fo;
    char *cp;
    int c;

    if ((cp = argv[1]) && *cp!='\0')  {
        if ((fi = fopen(argv[2], "rb")) != NULL)  {
            if ((fo = fopen(argv[3], "wb")) != NULL)  {
                while ((c = getc(fi)) != EOF)  {
                    if (!*cp) cp = argv[1];
                    c ^= *(cp++);
                    putc(c,fo);
                }
                fclose(fo);
            }
            fclose(fi);
        }
    }
}
```

This is a symmetric algorithm. The plaintext is being XORed with a keyword to generate the ciphertext. Since XORing the same value twice restores the original, encryption and decryption use exactly the same program:

$$P \oplus K = C$$
$$C \oplus K = P$$

There's no real security here. This kind of encryption is trivial to break, even without computers [587,1475]. It will only take a few seconds with a computer.

Assume the plaintext is English. Furthermore, assume the key length is any small number of bytes. Here's how to break it:

1. Discover the length of the key by a procedure known as **counting coincidences** [577]. XOR the ciphertext against itself shifted various numbers of bytes, and count those bytes that are equal. If the displacement is a multiple of the key length, then something over 6 percent of the bytes will be equal. If it is not, then less than 0.4 percent will be equal (assuming a random key encrypting normal ASCII text; other plaintext will have different numbers). This is called the **index of coincidence**. The smallest displacement that indicates a multiple of the key length is the length of the key.

2. Shift the ciphertext by that length and XOR it with itself. This removes the key and leaves you with plaintext XORed with the plaintext shifted the length of the key. Since English has 1.3 bits of real information per byte (see Section 11.1), there is plenty of redundancy for determining a unique decryption.

Despite this, the list of software vendors that tout this toy algorithm as being "almost as secure as DES" is staggering [1387]. It is the algorithm (with a 160-bit repeated "key") that the NSA finally allowed the U.S. digital cellular phone industry to use for voice privacy. An XOR might keep your kid sister from reading your files, but it won't stop a cryptanalyst for more than a few minutes.

1.5 ONE-TIME PADS

Believe it or not, there is a perfect encryption scheme. It's called a **one-time pad**, and was invented in 1917 by Major Joseph Mauborgne and AT&T's Gilbert Vernam [794]. (Actually, a one-time pad is a special case of a threshold scheme; see Section 3.7.) Classically, a one-time pad is nothing more than a large nonrepeating set of truly random key letters, written on sheets of paper, and glued together in a pad. In its original form, it was a one-time tape for teletypewriters. The sender uses each key letter on the pad to encrypt exactly one plaintext character. Encryption is the addition modulo 26 of the plaintext character and the one-time pad key character.

Each key letter is used exactly once, for only one message. The sender encrypts the message and then destroys the used pages of the pad or used section of the tape. The receiver has an identical pad and uses each key on the pad, in turn, to decrypt each letter of the ciphertext. The receiver destroys the same pad pages or tape section after decrypting the message. New message—new key letters. For example, if the message is:

    ONETIMEPAD

and the key sequence from the pad is

    TBFRGFARFM

then the ciphertext is

    IPKLPSFHGQ

because

$$O + T \bmod 26 = I$$
$$N + B \bmod 26 = P$$
$$E + F \bmod 26 = K$$

etc.

Assuming an eavesdropper can't get access to the one-time pad used to encrypt the message, this scheme is perfectly secure. A given ciphertext message is equally likely to correspond to any possible plaintext message of equal size.

Since every key sequence is equally likely (remember, the key letters are generated randomly), an adversary has no information with which to cryptanalyze the ciphertext. The key sequence could just as likely be:

    POYYAEAAZX

which would decrypt to:

    SALMONEGGS

or

    BXFGBMTMXM

which would decrypt to:

    GREENFLUID

This point bears repeating: Since every plaintext message is equally possible, there is no way for the cryptanalyst to determine which plaintext message is the correct one. A random key sequence added to a nonrandom plaintext message produces a completely random ciphertext message and no amount of computing power can change that.

The caveat, and this is a big one, is that the key letters have to be generated randomly. Any attacks against this scheme will be against the method used to generate the key letters. Using a pseudo-random number generator doesn't count; they always have nonrandom properties. If you use a real random source—this is much harder than it might first appear, see Section 17.14—it's secure.

The other important point is that you can never use the key sequence again, ever. Even if you use a multiple-gigabyte pad, if a cryptanalyst has multiple ciphertexts whose keys overlap, he can reconstruct the plaintext. He slides each pair of ciphertexts against each other and counts the number of matches at each position. If they are aligned right, the proportion of matches jumps suddenly—the exact percentages depend on the plaintext language. From this point cryptanalysis is easy. It's like the index of coincidence, but with just two "periods" to compare [904]. Don't do it.

The idea of a one-time pad can be easily extended to binary data. Instead of a one-time pad consisting of letters, use a one-time pad of bits. Instead of adding the plaintext to the one-time pad, use an XOR. To decrypt, XOR the ciphertext with the same one-time pad. Everything else remains the same and the security is just as perfect.

This all sounds good, but there are a few problems. Since the key bits must be random and can never be used again, the length of the key sequence must be equal to the length of the message. A one-time pad might be suitable for a few short messages, but it will never work for a 1.544 Mbps communications channel. You can store 650 megabytes worth of random bits on a CD-ROM, but there are problems. First, you want exactly two copies of the random bits, but CD-ROMs are economical only for large quantities. And second, you want to be able to destroy the bits already used. CD-ROM has no erase facilities except for physically destroying the entire disk. Digital tape is a much better medium for this sort of thing.

Even if you solve the key distribution and storage problem, you have to make sure the sender and receiver are perfectly synchronized. If the receiver is off by a bit (or if some bits are dropped during the transmission), the message won't make any sense. On the other hand, if some bits are altered during transmission (without any bits being added or removed—something far more likely to happen due to random noise), only those bits will be decrypted incorrectly. But on the other hand, a one-time pad provides no authenticity.

One-time pads have applications in today's world, primarily for ultra-secure low-bandwidth channels. The hotline between the United States and the former Soviet Union was (is it still active?) rumored to be encrypted with a one-time pad. Many Soviet spy messages to agents were encrypted using one-time pads. These messages are still secure today and will remain that way forever. It doesn't matter how long the supercomputers work on the problem. Even after the aliens from Andromeda land with their massive spaceships and undreamed-of computing power, they will not be able to read the Soviet spy messages encrypted with one-time pads (unless they can also go back in time and get the one-time pads).

1.6 COMPUTER ALGORITHMS

There are many cryptographic algorithms. These are three of the most common:

— DES (Data Encryption Standard) is the most popular computer encryption algorithm. DES is a U.S. and international standard. It is a symmetric algorithm; the same key is used for encryption and decryption.

— RSA (named for its creators—Rivest, Shamir, and Adleman) is the most popular public-key algorithm. It can be used for both encryption and digital signatures.

— DSA (Digital Signature Algorithm, used as part of the Digital Signature Standard) is another public-key algorithm. It cannot be used for encryption, but only for digital signatures.

These are the kinds of stuff this book is about.

1.7 LARGE NUMBERS

Throughout this book, I use various large numbers to describe different things in cryptography. Because it is so easy to lose sight of these numbers and what they signify, Table 1.1 gives physical analogues for some of them.

These numbers are order-of-magnitude estimates, and have been culled from a variety of sources. Many of the astrophysics numbers are explained in Freeman

TABLE 1.1
Large Numbers

Physical Analogue	Number
Odds of being killed by lightning (per day)	1 in 9 billion (2^{33})
Odds of winning the top prize in a U.S. state lottery	1 in 4,000,000 (2^{22})
Odds of winning the top prize in a U.S. state lottery and being killed by lightning in the same day	1 in 2^{55}
Odds of drowning (in the U.S. per year)	1 in 59,000 (2^{16})
Odds of being killed in an automobile accident (in the U.S. in 1993)	1 in 6100 (2^{13})
Odds of being killed in an automobile accident (in the U.S. per lifetime)	1 in 88 (2^{7})
Time until the next ice age	14,000 (2^{14}) years
Time until the sun goes nova	10^{9} (2^{30}) years
Age of the planet	10^{9} (2^{30}) years
Age of the Universe	10^{10} (2^{34}) years
Number of atoms in the planet	10^{51} (2^{170})
Number of atoms in the sun	10^{57} (2^{190})
Number of atoms in the galaxy	10^{67} (2^{223})
Number of atoms in the Universe (dark matter excluded)	10^{77} (2^{265})
Volume of the Universe	10^{84} (2^{280}) cm^3
If the Universe is Closed:	
Total lifetime of the Universe	10^{11} (2^{37}) years
	10^{18} (2^{61}) seconds
If the Universe is Open:	
Time until low-mass stars cool off	10^{14} (2^{47}) years
Time until planets detach from stars	10^{15} (2^{50}) years
Time until stars detach from galaxies	10^{19} (2^{64}) years
Time until orbits decay by gravitational radiation	10^{20} (2^{67}) years
Time until black holes decay by the Hawking process	10^{64} (2^{213}) years
Time until all matter is liquid at zero temperature	10^{65} (2^{216}) years
Time until all matter decays to iron	$10^{10^{26}}$ years
Time until all matter collapses to black holes	$10^{10^{76}}$ years

Dyson's paper, "Time Without End: Physics and Biology in an Open Universe," in *Reviews of Modern Physics*, v. 52, n. 3, July 1979, pp. 447–460. Automobile accident deaths are calculated from the Department of Transportation's statistic of 163 deaths per million people in 1993 and an average lifespan of 69.7 years.

PART I

CRYPTOGRAPHIC PROTOCOLS

CHAPTER 2

Protocol Building Blocks

2.1 INTRODUCTION TO PROTOCOLS

The whole point of cryptography is to solve problems. (Actually, that's the whole point of computers—something many people tend to forget.) Cryptography solves problems that involve secrecy, authentication, integrity, and dishonest people. You can learn all about cryptographic algorithms and techniques, but these are academic unless they can solve a problem. This is why we are going to look at protocols first.

A **protocol** is a series of steps, involving two or more parties, designed to accomplish a task. This is an important definition. A "series of steps" means that the protocol has a sequence, from start to finish. Every step must be executed in turn, and no step can be taken before the previous step is finished. "Involving two or more parties" means that at least two people are required to complete the protocol; one person alone does not make a protocol. A person alone can perform a series of steps to accomplish a task (like baking a cake), but this is not a protocol. (Someone else must eat the cake to make it a protocol.) Finally, "designed to accomplish a task" means that the protocol must achieve something. Something that looks like a protocol but does not accomplish a task is not a protocol—it's a waste of time.

Protocols have other characteristics as well:

— Everyone involved in the protocol must know the protocol and all of the steps to follow in advance.

— Everyone involved in the protocol must agree to follow it.

— The protocol must be unambiguous; each step must be well defined and there must be no chance of a misunderstanding.

— The protocol must be complete; there must be a specified action for every possible situation.

The protocols in this book are organized as a series of steps. Execution of the protocol proceeds linearly through the steps, unless there are instructions to branch to another step. Each step involves at least one of two things: computations by one or more of the parties, or messages sent among the parties.

A **cryptographic protocol** is a protocol that uses cryptography. The parties can be friends and trust each other implicitly or they can be adversaries and not trust one another to give the correct time of day. A cryptographic protocol involves some cryptographic algorithm, but generally the goal of the protocol is something beyond simple secrecy. The parties participating in the protocol might want to share parts of their secrets to compute a value, jointly generate a random sequence, convince one another of their identity, or simultaneously sign a contract. The whole point of using cryptography in a protocol is to prevent or detect eavesdropping and cheating. If you have never seen these protocols before, they will radically change your ideas of what mutually distrustful parties can accomplish over a computer network. In general, this can be stated as:

— It should not be possible to do more or learn more than what is specified in the protocol.

This is a lot harder than it looks. In the next few chapters I discuss a lot of protocols. In some of them it is possible for one of the participants to cheat the other. In others, it is possible for an eavesdropper to subvert the protocol or learn secret information. Some protocols fail because the designers weren't thorough enough in their requirements definitions. Others fail because their designers weren't thorough enough in their analysis. Like algorithms, it is much easier to prove insecurity than it is to prove security.

The Purpose of Protocols

In daily life, there are informal protocols for almost everything: ordering goods over the telephone, playing poker, voting in an election. No one thinks much about these protocols; they have evolved over time, everyone knows how to use them, and they work reasonably well.

These days, more and more human interaction takes place over computer networks instead of face-to-face. Computers need formal protocols to do the same things that people do without thinking. If you moved from one state to another and found a voting booth that looked completely different from the ones you were used to, you could easily adapt. Computers are not nearly so flexible.

Many face-to-face protocols rely on people's presence to ensure fairness and security. Would you send a stranger a pile of cash to buy groceries for you? Would you play poker with someone if you couldn't see him shuffle and deal? Would you mail the government your secret ballot without some assurance of anonymity?

It is naïve to assume that people on computer networks are honest. It is naïve to assume that the managers of computer networks are honest. It is even naïve to assume that the designers of computer networks are honest. Most are, but the dishonest few can do a lot of damage. By formalizing protocols, we can examine ways in which dishonest parties can subvert them. Then we can develop protocols that are immune to that subversion.

In addition to formalizing behavior, protocols abstract the process of accomplishing a task from the mechanism by which the task is accomplished. A communications protocol is the same whether implemented on PCs or VAXs. We can examine the protocol without getting bogged down in the implementation details. When we are convinced we have a good protocol, we can implement it in everything from computers to telephones to intelligent muffin toasters.

The Players

To help demonstrate protocols, I have enlisted the aid of several people (see Table 2.1). Alice and Bob are the first two. They will perform all general two-person protocols. As a rule, Alice will initiate all protocols and Bob will respond. If the protocol requires a third or fourth person, Carol and Dave will perform those roles. Other actors will play specialized supporting roles; they will be introduced later.

Arbitrated Protocols

An **arbitrator** is a disinterested third party trusted to complete a protocol (see Figure 2.1a). Disinterested means that the arbitrator has no vested interest in the protocol and no particular allegiance to any of the parties involved. Trusted means that all people involved in the protocol accept what he says as true, what he does as correct, and that he will complete his part of the protocol. Arbitrators can help complete protocols between two mutually distrustful parties.

In the real world, lawyers are often used as arbitrators. For example, Alice is selling a car to Bob, a stranger. Bob wants to pay by check, but Alice has no way of knowing if the check is good. Alice wants the check to clear before she turns the title over to Bob. Bob, who doesn't trust Alice any more than she trusts him, doesn't want to hand over a check without receiving a title.

TABLE 2.1
Dramatis Personae

Alice	First participant in all the protocols
Bob	Second participant in all the protocols
Carol	Participant in the three- and four-party protocols
Dave	Participant in the four-party protocols
Eve	Eavesdropper
Mallory	Malicious active attacker
Trent	Trusted arbitrator
Walter	Warden; he'll be guarding Alice and Bob in some protocols
Peggy	Prover
Victor	Verifier

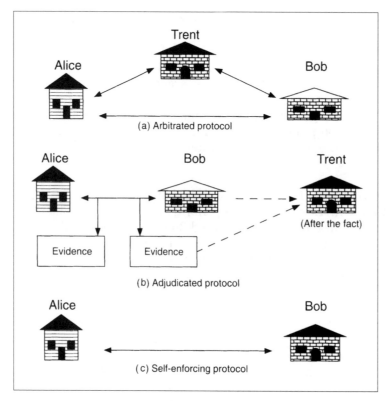

Figure 2.1   *Types of protocols.*

Enter a lawyer trusted by both. With his help, Alice and Bob can use the following protocol to ensure that neither cheats the other:

(1) Alice gives the title to the lawyer.

(2) Bob gives the check to Alice.

(3) Alice deposits the check.

(4) After waiting a specified time period for the check to clear, the lawyer gives the title to Bob. If the check does not clear within the specified time period, Alice shows proof of this to the lawyer and the lawyer returns the title to Alice.

In this protocol, Alice trusts the lawyer not to give Bob the title unless the check has cleared, and to give it back to her if the check does not clear. Bob trusts the lawyer to hold the title until the check clears, and to give it to him once it does. The lawyer doesn't care if the check clears. He will do his part of the protocol in either case, because he will be paid in either case.

In the example, the lawyer is playing the part of an escrow agent. Lawyers also act as arbitrators for wills and sometimes for contract negotiations. The various stock exchanges act as arbitrators between buyers and sellers.

Bankers also arbitrate protocols. Bob can use a certified check to buy a car from Alice:

(1) Bob writes a check and gives it to the bank.

(2) After putting enough of Bob's money on hold to cover the check, the bank certifies the check and gives it back to Bob.

(3) Alice gives the title to Bob and Bob gives the certified check to Alice.

(4) Alice deposits the check.

This protocol works because Alice trusts the banker's certification. Alice trusts the bank to hold Bob's money for her, and not to use it to finance shaky real estate operations in mosquito-infested countries.

A notary public is another arbitrator. When Bob receives a notarized document from Alice, he is convinced that Alice signed the document voluntarily and with her own hand. The notary can, if necessary, stand up in court and attest to that fact.

The concept of an arbitrator is as old as society. There have always been people—rulers, priests, and so on—who have the authority to act fairly. Arbitrators have a certain social role and position in our society; betraying the public trust would jeopardize that. Lawyers who play games with escrow accounts face almost-certain disbarment, for example. This picture of trust doesn't always exist in the real world, but it's the ideal.

This ideal can translate to the computer world, but there are several problems with computer arbitrators:

— It is easier to find and trust a neutral third party if you know who the party is and can see his face. Two parties suspicious of each other are also likely to be suspicious of a faceless arbitrator somewhere else on the network.

— The computer network must bear the cost of maintaining an arbitrator. We all know what lawyers charge; who wants to bear that kind of network overhead?

— There is a delay inherent in any arbitrated protocol.

— The arbitrator must deal with every transaction; he is a bottleneck in large-scale implementations of any protocol. Increasing the number of arbitrators in the implementation can mitigate this problem, but that increases the cost.

— Since everyone on the network must trust the arbitrator, he represents a vulnerable point for anyone trying to subvert the network.

Even so, arbitrators still have a role to play. In protocols using a trusted arbitrator, the part will be played by Trent.

Adjudicated Protocols

Because of the high cost of hiring arbitrators, arbitrated protocols can be subdivided into two lower-level **subprotocols**. One is a nonarbitrated subprotocol, executed every time parties want to complete the protocol. The other is an arbitrated subprotocol, executed only in exceptional circumstances—when there is a dispute. This special type of arbitrator is called an **adjudicator** (see Figure 2.1b).

An adjudicator is also a disinterested and trusted third party. Unlike an arbitrator, he is not directly involved in every protocol. The adjudicator is called in only to determine whether a protocol was performed fairly.

Judges are professional adjudicators. Unlike a notary public, a judge is brought in only if there is a dispute. Alice and Bob can enter into a contract without a judge. A judge never sees the contract until one of them hauls the other into court.

This contract-signing protocol can be formalized in this way:

Nonarbitrated subprotocol (executed every time):

  (1) Alice and Bob negotiate the terms of the contract.
  (2) Alice signs the contract.
  (3) Bob signs the contract.

Adjudicated subprotocol (executed only in case of a dispute):

  (4) Alice and Bob appear before a judge.
  (5) Alice presents her evidence.
  (6) Bob presents his evidence.
  (7) The judge rules on the evidence.

The difference between an adjudicator and an arbitrator (as used in this book) is that the adjudicator is not always necessary. In a dispute, a judge is called in to adjudicate. If there is no dispute, using a judge is unnecessary.

There are adjudicated computer protocols. These protocols rely on the parties to be honest; but if someone suspects cheating, a body of data exists so that a trusted third party could determine if someone cheated. In a good adjudicated protocol, the adjudicator could also determine the cheater's identity. Instead of preventing cheating, adjudicated protocols detect cheating. The inevitability of detection acts as a preventive and discourages cheating.

Self-Enforcing Protocols

A **self-enforcing protocol** is the best type of protocol. The protocol itself guarantees fairness (see Figure 2.1c). No arbitrator is required to complete the protocol. No adjudicator is required to resolve disputes. The protocol is constructed so that there cannot be any disputes. If one of the parties tries to cheat, the other party immediately detects the cheating and the protocol stops. Whatever the cheating party hoped would happen by cheating, doesn't happen.

In the best of all possible worlds, every protocol would be self-enforcing. Unfortunately, there is not a self-enforcing protocol for every situation.

Attacks against Protocols

Cryptographic attacks can be directed against the cryptographic algorithms used in protocols, against the cryptographic techniques used to implement the algorithms and protocols, or against the protocols themselves. Since this section of the book discusses protocols, I will assume that the cryptographic algorithms and techniques are secure. I will only examine attacks against the protocols.

People can try various ways to attack a protocol. Someone not involved in the protocol can eavesdrop on some or all of the protocol. This is called a **passive attack**, because the attacker does not affect the protocol. All he can do is observe the protocol and attempt to gain information. This kind of attack corresponds to a ciphertext-only attack, as discussed in Section 1.1. Since passive attacks are difficult to detect, protocols try to prevent passive attacks rather than detect them. In these protocols, the part of the eavesdropper will be played by Eve.

Alternatively, an attacker could try to alter the protocol to his own advantage. He could pretend to be someone else, introduce new messages in the protocol, delete existing messages, substitute one message for another, replay old messages, interrupt a communications channel, or alter stored information in a computer. These are called **active attacks**, because they require active intervention. The form of these attacks depends on the network.

Passive attackers try to gain information about the parties involved in the protocol. They collect messages passing among various parties and attempt to cryptanalyze them. Active attacks, on the other hand, can have much more diverse objectives. The attacker could be interested in obtaining information, degrading system performance, corrupting existing information, or gaining unauthorized access to resources.

Active attacks are much more serious, especially in protocols in which the different parties don't necessarily trust one another. The attacker does not have to be a complete outsider. He could be a legitimate system user. He could be the system administrator. There could even be many active attackers working together. Here, the part of the malicious active attacker will be played by Mallory.

It is also possible that the attacker could be one of the parties involved in the protocol. He may lie during the protocol or not follow the protocol at all. This type of attacker is called a **cheater**. **Passive cheaters** follow the protocol, but try to obtain more information than the protocol intends them to. **Active cheaters** disrupt the protocol in progress in an attempt to cheat.

It is very difficult to maintain a protocol's security if most of the parties involved are active cheaters, but sometimes it is possible for legitimate parties to detect that active cheating is going on. Certainly, protocols should be secure against passive cheating.

2.2 COMMUNICATIONS USING SYMMETRIC CRYPTOGRAPHY

How do two parties communicate securely? They encrypt their communications, of course. The complete protocol is more complicated than that. Let's look at what must happen for Alice to send an encrypted message to Bob.

(1) Alice and Bob agree on a cryptosystem.

(2) Alice and Bob agree on a key.

(3) Alice takes her plaintext message and encrypts it using the encryption algorithm and the key. This creates a ciphertext message.

(4) Alice sends the ciphertext message to Bob.

(5) Bob decrypts the ciphertext message with the same algorithm and key and reads it.

What can Eve, sitting between Alice and Bob, learn from listening in on this protocol? If all she hears is the transmission in step (4), she must try to cryptanalyze the ciphertext. This passive attack is a ciphertext-only attack; we have algorithms that are resistant (as far as we know) to whatever computing power Eve could realistically bring to bear on the problem.

Eve isn't stupid, though. She also wants to listen in on steps (1) and (2). Then, she would know the algorithm and the key—just as well as Bob. When the message comes across the communications channel in step (4), all she has to do is decrypt it herself.

A good cryptosystem is one in which all the security is inherent in knowledge of the key and none is inherent in knowledge of the algorithm. This is why key management is so important in cryptography. With a symmetric algorithm, Alice and Bob can perform step (1) in public, but they must perform step (2) in secret. The key must remain secret before, during, and after the protocol—as long as the message must remain secret—otherwise the message will no longer be secure. (Public-key cryptography solves this problem another way, and will be discussed in Section 2.5.)

Mallory, an active attacker, could do a few other things. He could attempt to break the communications path in step (4), ensuring that Alice could not talk to Bob at all. Mallory could also intercept Alice's messages and substitute his own. If he knew the key (by intercepting the communication in step (2), or by breaking the cryptosystem), he could encrypt his own message and send it to Bob in place of the intercepted message. Bob would have no way of knowing that the message had not come from Alice. If Mallory didn't know the key, he could only create a replacement message that would decrypt to gibberish. Bob, thinking the message came from Alice, might conclude that either the network or Alice had some serious problems.

What about Alice? What can she do to disrupt the protocol? She can give a copy of the key to Eve. Now Eve can read whatever Bob says. She can reprint his words in *The New York Times*. Although serious, this is not a problem with the protocol. There is nothing to stop Alice from giving Eve a copy of the plaintext at any point during the protocol. Of course, Bob could also do anything that Alice could. This protocol assumes that Alice and Bob trust each other.

In summary, symmetric cryptosystems have the following problems:

— Keys must be distributed in secret. They are as valuable as all the messages they encrypt, since knowledge of the key gives knowledge of all the messages. For encryption systems that span the world, this can be a daunting task. Often couriers hand-carry keys to their destinations.

— If a key is compromised (stolen, guessed, extorted, bribed, etc.), then Eve can decrypt all message traffic encrypted with that key. She can also pretend to be one of the parties and produce false messages to fool the other party.

— Assuming a separate key is used for each pair of users in a network, the total number of keys increases rapidly as the number of users increases. A network of n users requires $n(n-1)/2$ keys. For example, 10 users require 45 different keys to talk with one another and 100 users require 4950 keys. This problem can be minimized by keeping the number of users small, but that is not always possible.

2.3   ONE-WAY FUNCTIONS

The notion of a **one-way function** is central to public-key cryptography. While not protocols in themselves, one-way functions are a fundamental building block for most of the protocols discussed in this book.

One-way functions are relatively easy to compute, but significantly harder to reverse. That is, given x it is easy to compute $f(x)$, but given $f(x)$ it is hard to compute x. In this context, "hard" is defined as something like: It would take millions of years to compute x from $f(x)$, even if all the computers in the world were assigned to the problem.

Breaking a plate is a good example of a one-way function. It is easy to smash a plate into a thousand tiny pieces. However, it's not easy to put all of those tiny pieces back together into a plate.

This sounds good, but it's a lot of smoke and mirrors. If we are being strictly mathematical, we have no proof that one-way functions exist, nor any real evidence that they can be constructed [230,530,600,661]. Even so, many functions look and smell one-way: We can compute them efficiently and, as of yet, know of no easy way to reverse them. For example, in a finite field x^2 is easy to compute, but $x^{1/2}$ is much harder. For the rest of this section, I'm going to pretend that there are one-way functions. I'll talk more about this in Section 11.2.

So, what good are one-way functions? We can't use them for encryption as is. A message encrypted with the one-way function isn't useful; no one could decrypt it. (Exercise: Write a message on a plate, smash the plate into tiny bits, and then give the bits to a friend. Ask your friend to read the message. Observe how impressed he is with the one-way function.) For public-key cryptography, we need something else (although there are cryptographic applications for one-way functions—see Section 3.2).

A **trapdoor one-way function** is a special type of one-way function, one with a secret trapdoor. It is easy to compute in one direction and hard to compute in the other direction. But, if you know the secret, you can easily compute the function in the other direction. That is, it is easy to compute $f(x)$ given x, and hard to compute x given $f(x)$. However, there is some secret information, y, such that given $f(x)$ and y it is easy to compute x.

Taking a watch apart is a good example of a trap-door one-way function. It is easy to disassemble a watch into hundreds of minuscule pieces. It is very difficult to put those tiny pieces back together into a working watch. However, with the secret information—the assembly instructions of the watch—it is much easier to put the watch back together.

2.4 ONE-WAY HASH FUNCTIONS

A **one-way hash function** has many names: compression function, contraction function, message digest, fingerprint, cryptographic checksum, message integrity check (MIC), and manipulation detection code (MDC). Whatever you call it, it is central to modern cryptography. One-way hash functions are another building block for many protocols.

Hash functions have been used in computer science for a long time. A hash function is a function, mathematical or otherwise, that takes a variable-length input string (called a **pre-image**) and converts it to a fixed-length (generally smaller) output string (called a **hash value**). A simple hash function would be a function that takes pre-image and returns a byte consisting of the XOR of all the input bytes.

The point here is to fingerprint the pre-image: to produce a value that indicates whether a candidate pre-image is likely to be the same as the real pre-image. Because hash functions are typically many-to-one, we cannot use them to determine with certainty that the two strings are equal, but we can use them to get a reasonable assurance of accuracy.

A one-way hash function is a hash function that works in one direction: It is easy to compute a hash value from pre-image, but it is hard to generate a pre-image that hashes to a particular value. The hash function previously mentioned is not one-way: Given a particular byte value, it is trivial to generate a string of bytes whose XOR is that value. You can't do that with a one-way hash function. A good one-way hash function is also **collision-free**: It is hard to generate two pre-images with the same hash value.

The hash function is public; there's no secrecy to the process. The security of a one-way hash function is its one-wayness. The output is not dependent on the input in any discernible way. A single bit change in the pre-image changes, on the average, half of the bits in the hash value. Given a hash value, it is computationally unfeasible to find a pre-image that hashes to that value.

Think of it as a way of fingerprinting files. If you want to verify that someone has a particular file (that you also have), but you don't want him to send it to you, then ask him for the hash value. If he sends you the correct hash value, then it is almost certain that he has that file. This is particularly useful in financial transactions, where you don't want a withdrawal of $100 to turn into a withdrawal of $1000 somewhere in the network. Normally, you would use a one-way hash function without a key, so that anyone can verify the hash. If you want only the recipient to be able to verify the hash, then read the next section.

Message Authentication Codes

A **message authentication code** (MAC), also known as a data authentication code (DAC), is a one-way hash function with the addition of a secret key (see Section 18.14). The hash value is a function of both the pre-image and the key. The theory is exactly the same as hash functions, except only someone with the key can verify the hash value. You can create a MAC out of a hash function or a block encryption algorithm; there are also dedicated MACs.

2.5   COMMUNICATIONS USING PUBLIC-KEY CRYPTOGRAPHY

Think of a symmetric algorithm as a safe. The key is the combination. Someone with the combination can open the safe, put a document inside, and close it again. Someone else with the combination can open the safe and take the document out. Anyone without the combination is forced to learn safecracking.

In 1976, Whitfield Diffie and Martin Hellman changed that paradigm of cryptography forever [496]. (The NSA has claimed knowledge of the concept as early as 1966, but has offered no proof.) They described **public-key cryptography**. They used two different keys—one public and the other private. It is computationally hard to deduce the private key from the public key. Anyone with the public key can encrypt a message but not decrypt it. Only the person with the private key can decrypt the message. It is as if someone turned the cryptographic safe into a mailbox. Putting mail in the mailbox is analogous to encrypting with the public key; anyone can do it. Just open the slot and drop it in. Getting mail out of a mailbox is analogous to decrypting with the private key. Generally it's hard; you need welding torches. However, if you have the secret (the physical key to the mailbox), it's easy to get mail out of a mailbox.

Mathematically, the process is based on the trap-door one-way functions previously discussed. Encryption is the easy direction. Instructions for encryption are the public key; anyone can encrypt a message. Decryption is the hard direction. It's made hard enough that people with Cray computers and thousands (even millions) of years couldn't decrypt the message without the secret. The secret, or trapdoor, is the private key. With that secret, decryption is as easy as encryption.

This is how Alice can send a message to Bob using public-key cryptography:

(1) Alice and Bob agree on a public-key cryptosystem.

(2) Bob sends Alice his public key.

(3) Alice encrypts her message using Bob's public key and sends it to Bob.

(4) Bob decrypts Alice's message using his private key.

Notice how public-key cryptography solves the key-management problem with symmetric cryptosystems. Before, Alice and Bob had to agree on a key in secret. Alice could choose one at random, but she still had to get it to Bob. She could hand it to him sometime beforehand, but that requires foresight. She could send it to him by secure courier, but that takes time. Public-key cryptography makes it easy. With no prior arrangements, Alice can send a secure message to Bob. Eve, listening in on the entire exchange, has Bob's public key and a message encrypted in that key, but cannot recover either Bob's private key or the message.

More commonly, a network of users agrees on a public-key cryptosystem. Every user has his or her own public key and private key, and the public keys are all published in a database somewhere. Now the protocol is even easier:

(1) Alice gets Bob's public key from the database.

(2) Alice encrypts her message using Bob's public key and sends it to Bob.

(3) Bob then decrypts Alice's message using his private key.

In the first protocol, Bob had to send Alice his public key before she could send him a message. The second protocol is more like traditional mail. Bob is not involved in the protocol until he wants to read his message.

Hybrid Cryptosystems

The first public-key algorithms became public at the same time that DES was being discussed as a proposed standard. This resulted in some partisan politics in the cryptographic community. As Diffie described it [494]:

> The excitement public key cryptosystems provoked in the popular and scientific press was not matched by corresponding acceptance in the cryptographic establishment, however. In the same year that public key cryptography was discovered, the National Security Agency (NSA), proposed a conventional cryptographic system, designed by International Business Machines (IBM), as a federal *Data Encryption Standard* (DES). Marty Hellman and I criticized the proposal on the ground that its key was too small, but manufacturers were gearing up to support the proposed standard and our criticism was seen by many as an attempt to disrupt the standards-making process to the advantage of our own work. Public key cryptography in its turn was attacked, in sales literature [1125] and technical papers [849,1159] alike, more as though it were a competing product than a recent research discovery. This, however, did not deter the NSA from claiming its share of the credit. Its director, in the words of the *Encyclopedia Britannica* [1461], pointed out that "two-key cryptography had been discovered at the agency a decade earlier," although no evidence for this claim was ever offered publicly.

In the real world, public-key algorithms are not a substitute for symmetric algorithms. They are not used to encrypt messages; they are used to encrypt keys. There are two reasons for this:

1. Public-key algorithms are slow. Symmetric algorithms are generally at least 1000 times faster than public-key algorithms. Yes, computers are getting faster and faster, and in 15 years computers will be able to do public-key cryptography at speeds comparable to symmetric cryptography today. But bandwidth requirements are also increasing, and there will always be the need to encrypt data faster than public-key cryptography can manage.

2. Public-key cryptosystems are vulnerable to chosen-plaintext attacks. If $C = E(P)$, when P is one plaintext out of a set of n possible plaintexts, then a cryptanalyst only has to encrypt all n possible plaintexts and compare the results with C (remember, the encryption key is public). He won't be able to recover the decryption key this way, but he will be able to determine P.

A chosen-plaintext attack can be particularly effective if there are relatively few possible encrypted messages. For example, if P were a dollar amount less than $1,000,000, this attack would work; the cryptanalyst tries all million possible dollar amounts. (Probabilistic encryption solves the problem; see Section 23.15.) Even if P is not as well-defined, this attack can be very effective. Simply knowing that a ciphertext does not correspond to a particular plaintext can be useful information. Symmetric cryptosystems are not vulnerable to this attack because a cryptanalyst cannot perform trial encryptions with an unknown key.

In most practical implementations public-key cryptography is used to secure and distribute **session keys**; those session keys are used with symmetric algorithms to secure message traffic [879]. This is sometimes called a **hybrid cryptosystem**.

(1)   Bob sends Alice his public key.

(2)   Alice generates a random session key, K, encrypts it using Bob's public key, and sends it to Bob.

$$E_B(K)$$

(3)   Bob decrypts Alice's message using his private key to recover the session key.

$$D_B(E_B(K)) = K$$

(4)   Both of them encrypt their communications using the same session key.

Using public-key cryptography for key distribution solves a very important key-management problem. With symmetric cryptography, the data encryption key sits around until it is used. If Eve ever gets her hands on it, she can decrypt messages encrypted with it. With the previous protocol, the session key is created when it is needed to encrypt communications and destroyed when it is no longer needed. This drastically reduces the risk of compromising the session key. Of course, the private key is vulnerable to compromise, but it is at less risk because it is only used once per communication to encrypt a session key. This is further discussed in Section 3.1.

Merkle's Puzzles

Ralph Merkle invented the first construction of public-key cryptography. In 1974 he registered for a course in computer security at the University of California, Berkeley, taught by Lance Hoffman. His term paper topic, submitted early in the term, addressed the problem of "Secure Communication over Insecure Channels" [1064]. Hoffman could not understand Merkle's proposal and eventually Merkle dropped the course. He continued to work on the problem, despite continuing failure to make his results understood.

Merkle's technique was based on "puzzles" that were easier to solve for the sender and receiver than for an eavesdropper. Here's how Alice sends an encrypted message to Bob without first having to exchange a key with him.

(1) Bob generates 2^{20}, or about a million, messages of the form: "This is puzzle number x. This is the secret key number y," where x is a random number and y is a random secret key. Both x and y are different for each message. Using a symmetric algorithm, he encrypts each message with a different 20-bit key and sends them all to Alice.

(2) Alice chooses one message at random and performs a brute-force attack to recover the plaintext. This is a large, but not impossible, amount of work.

(3) Alice encrypts her secret message with the key she recovered and some symmetric algorithm, and sends it to Bob along with x.

(4) Bob knows which secret key y he encrypts in message x, so he can decrypt the message.

Eve can break this system, but she has to do far more work than either Alice or Bob. To recover the message in step (3), she has to perform a brute-force attack against each of Bob's 2^{20} messages in step (1); this attack has a complexity of 2^{40}. The x values won't help Eve either; they were assigned randomly in step (1). In general, Eve has to expend approximately the square of the effort that Alice expends.

This n to n^2 advantage is small by cryptographic standards, but in some circumstances it may be enough. If Alice and Bob can try ten thousand keys per second, it will take them a minute each to perform their steps and another minute to communicate the puzzles from Bob to Alice on a 1.544 MB link. If Eve had comparable computing facilities, it would take her about a year to break the system. Other algorithms are even harder to break.

2.6 DIGITAL SIGNATURES

Handwritten signatures have long been used as proof of authorship of, or at least agreement with, the contents of a document. What is it about a signature that is so compelling [1392]?

1. The signature is authentic. The signature convinces the document's recipient that the signer deliberately signed the document.

2. The signature is unforgeable. The signature is proof that the signer, and no one else, deliberately signed the document.

3. The signature is not reusable. The signature is part of the document; an unscrupulous person cannot move the signature to a different document.

4. The signed document is unalterable. After the document is signed, it cannot be altered.

5. The signature cannot be repudiated. The signature and the document are physical things. The signer cannot later claim that he or she didn't sign it.

In reality, none of these statements about signatures is completely true. Signatures can be forged, signatures can be lifted from one piece of paper and moved to another, and documents can be altered after signing. However, we are willing to live with these problems because of the difficulty in cheating and the risk of detection.

We would like to do this sort of thing on computers, but there are problems. First, computer files are trivial to copy. Even if a person's signature were difficult to forge (a graphical image of a written signature, for example), it would be easy to cut and paste a valid signature from one document to another document. The mere presence of such a signature means nothing. Second, computer files are easy to modify after they are signed, without leaving any evidence of modification.

Signing Documents with Symmetric Cryptosystems and an Arbitrator

Alice wants to sign a digital message and send it to Bob. With the help of Trent and a symmetric cryptosystem, she can.

Trent is a powerful, trusted arbitrator. He can communicate with both Alice and Bob (and everyone else who may want to sign a digital document). He shares a secret key, K_A, with Alice, and a different secret key, K_B, with Bob. These keys have been established long before the protocol begins and can be reused multiple times for multiple signings.

(1) Alice encrypts her message to Bob with K_A and sends it to Trent.

(2) Trent decrypts the message with K_A.

(3) Trent takes the decrypted message and a statement that he has received this message from Alice, and encrypts the whole bundle with K_B.

(4) Trent sends the encrypted bundle to Bob.

(5) Bob decrypts the bundle with K_B. He can now read both the message and Trent's certification that Alice sent it.

How does Trent know that the message is from Alice and not from some imposter? He infers it from the message's encryption. Since only he and Alice share their secret key, only Alice could encrypt a message using it.

Is this as good as a paper signature? Let's look at the characteristics we want:

1. This signature is authentic. Trent is a trusted arbitrator and Trent knows that the message came from Alice. Trent's certification serves as proof to Bob.

2. This signature is unforgeable. Only Alice (and Trent, but everyone trusts him) knows K_A, so only Alice could have sent Trent a message encrypted with K_A. If someone tried to impersonate Alice, Trent would have immediately realized this in step (2) and would not certify its authenticity.

3. This signature is not reusable. If Bob tried to take Trent's certification and attach it to another message, Alice would cry foul. An arbitrator (it could be Trent or it could be a completely different arbitrator with access to the same information) would ask Bob to produce both the message and Alice's encrypted message. The arbitrator would then encrypt the message with K_A and see that it did not match the encrypted message that Bob gave him. Bob, of course, could not produce an encrypted message that matches because he does not know K_A.

4. The signed document is unalterable. Were Bob to try to alter the document after receipt, Trent could prove foul play in exactly the same manner just described.

5. The signature cannot be repudiated. Even if Alice later claims that she never sent the message, Trent's certification says otherwise. Remember, Trent is trusted by everyone; what he says is true.

If Bob wants to show Carol a document signed by Alice, he can't reveal his secret key to her. He has to go through Trent again:

(1) Bob takes the message and Trent's statement that the message came from Alice, encrypts them with K_B, and sends them back to Trent.

(2) Trent decrypts the bundle with K_B.

(3) Trent checks his database and confirms that the original message came from Alice.

(4) Trent re-encrypts the bundle with the secret key he shares with Carol, K_C, and sends it to Carol.

(5) Carol decrypts the bundle with K_C. She can now read both the message and Trent's certification that Alice sent it.

These protocols work, but they're time-consuming for Trent. He must spend his days decrypting and encrypting messages, acting as the intermediary between every pair of people who want to send signed documents to one another. He must keep a database of messages (although this can be avoided by sending the recipient a copy of the sender's encrypted message). He is a bottleneck in any communications system, even if he's a mindless software program.

Harder still is creating and maintaining someone like Trent, someone that everyone on the network trusts. Trent has to be infallible; if he makes even one mistake in a million signatures, no one is going to trust him. Trent has to be completely secure. If his database of secret keys ever got out or if someone managed to modify his programming, everyone's signatures would be completely useless. False documents purported to be signed years ago could appear. Chaos would result. Governments would collapse. Anarchy would reign. This might work in theory, but it doesn't work very well in practice.

Digital Signature Trees

Ralph Merkle proposed a digital signature scheme based on secret-key cryptography, producing an infinite number of one-time signatures using a tree structure [1067,1068]. The basic idea of this scheme is to place the root of the tree in some public file, thereby authenticating it. The root signs one message and authenticates its sub-nodes in the tree. Each of these nodes signs one message and authenticates its sub-nodes, and so on.

Signing Documents with Public-Key Cryptography

There are public-key algorithms that can be used for digital signatures. In some algorithms—RSA is an example (see Section 19.3)—either the public key or the private key can be used for encryption. Encrypt a document using your private key, and you have a secure digital signature. In other cases—DSA is an example (see Section 20.1)—there is a separate algorithm for digital signatures that cannot be used for encryption. This idea was first invented by Diffie and Hellman [496] and further expanded and elaborated on in other texts [1282,1328,1024,1283,426]. See [1099] for a good survey of the field.

The basic protocol is simple:

(1) Alice encrypts the document with her private key, thereby signing the document.

(2) Alice sends the signed document to Bob.

(3) Bob decrypts the document with Alice's public key, thereby verifying the signature.

This protocol is far better than the previous one. Trent is not needed to either sign or verify signatures. (He is needed to certify that Alice's public key is indeed her public key.) The parties do not even need Trent to resolve disputes: If Bob cannot perform step (3), then he knows the signature is not valid.

This protocol also satisfies the characteristics we're looking for:

1. The signature is authentic; when Bob verifies the message with Alice's public key, he knows that she signed it.

2. The signature is unforgeable; only Alice knows her private key.

3. The signature is not reusable; the signature is a function of the document and cannot be transferred to any other document.

4. The signed document is unalterable; if there is any alteration to the document, the signature can no longer be verified with Alice's public key.

5. The signature cannot be repudiated. Bob doesn't need Alice's help to verify her signature.

Signing Documents and Timestamps

Actually, Bob can cheat Alice in certain circumstances. He can reuse the document and signature together. This is no problem if Alice signed a contract (what's another copy of the same contract, more or less?), but it can be very exciting if Alice signed a digital check.

Let's say Alice sends Bob a signed digital check for $100. Bob takes the check to the bank, which verifies the signature and moves the money from one account to the other. Bob, who is an unscrupulous character, saves a copy of the digital check. The following week, he again takes it to the bank (or maybe to a different bank). The bank verifies the signature and moves the money from one account to the other. If Alice never balances her checkbook, Bob can keep this up for years.

Consequently, digital signatures often include timestamps. The date and time of the signature are attached to the message and signed along with the rest of the message. The bank stores this timestamp in a database. Now, when Bob tries to cash Alice's check a second time, the bank checks the timestamp against its database. Since the bank already cashed a check from Alice with the same timestamp, the bank calls the police. Bob then spends 15 years in Leavenworth prison reading up on cryptographic protocols.

Signing Documents with Public-Key Cryptography and One-Way Hash Functions

In practical implementations, public-key algorithms are often too inefficient to sign long documents. To save time, digital signature protocols are often implemented with one-way hash functions [432,433]. Instead of signing a document, Alice signs the hash of the document. In this protocol, both the one-way hash function and the digital signature algorithm are agreed upon beforehand.

(1) Alice produces a one-way hash of a document.

(2) Alice encrypts the hash with her private key, thereby signing the document.

(3) Alice sends the document and the signed hash to Bob.

(4) Bob produces a one-way hash of the document that Alice sent. He then, using the digital signature algorithm, decrypts the signed hash with Alice's public key. If the signed hash matches the hash he generated, the signature is valid.

Speed increases drastically and, since the chances of two different documents having the same 160-bit hash are only one in 2^{160}, anyone can safely equate a signature of the hash with a signature of the document. If a non-one-way hash function were used, it would be an easy matter to create multiple documents that hashed to the same value, so that anyone signing a particular document would be duped into signing a multitude of documents.

This protocol has other benefits. First, the signature can be kept separate from the document. Second, the recipient's storage requirements for the document and signature are much smaller. An archival system can use this type of protocol to verify the existence of documents without storing their contents. The central database could just store the hashes of files. It doesn't have to see the files at all; users submit their hashes to the database, and the database timestamps the submissions and stores them. If there is any disagreement in the future about who created a document and when, the database could resolve it by finding the hash in its files. This system has vast implications concerning privacy: Alice could copyright a document but still keep the document secret. Only if she wished to prove her copyright would she have to make the document public. (See Section 4.1).

Algorithms and Terminology

There are many digital signature algorithms. All of them are public-key algorithms with secret information to sign documents and public information to verify signatures. Sometimes the signing process is called **encrypting with a private key** and the verification process is called **decrypting with a public key**. This is misleading and is only true for one algorithm, RSA. And different algorithms have different implementations. For example, one-way hash functions and timestamps sometimes add extra steps to the process of signing and verifying. Many algorithms can be used for digital signatures, but not for encryption.

In general, I will refer to the signing and verifying processes without any details of the algorithms involved. Signing a message with private key K is:

$$S_K(M)$$

and verifying a signature with the corresponding public key is:

$$V_K(M)$$

The bit string attached to the document when signed (in the previous example, the one-way hash of the document encrypted with the private key) will be called the **digital signature**, or just the **signature**. The entire protocol, by which the receiver of a message is convinced of the identity of the sender and the integrity of the message, is called authentication. Further details on these protocols are in Section 3.2.

Multiple Signatures

How could Alice and Bob sign the same digital document? Without one-way hash functions, there are two options. One is that Alice and Bob sign separate copies of the document itself. The resultant message would be over twice the size of the original document. The second is that Alice signs the document first and then Bob signs Alice's signature. This works, but it is impossible to verify Alice's signature without also verifying Bob's.

With one-way hash functions, multiple signatures are easy:

(1) Alice signs the hash of the document.
(2) Bob signs the hash of the document.
(3) Bob sends his signature to Alice.
(4) Alice sends the document, her signature, and Bob's signature to Carol.
(5) Carol verifies both Alice's signature and Bob's signature.

Alice and Bob can do steps (1) and (2) either in parallel or in series. In step (5), Carol can verify one signature without having to verify the other.

Nonrepudiation and Digital Signatures

Alice can cheat with digital signatures and there's nothing that can be done about it. She can sign a document and then later claim that she did not. First, she signs the document normally. Then, she anonymously publishes her private key, conveniently loses it in a public place, or just pretends to do either one. Alice then claims that her signature has been compromised and that others are using it, pretending to be her. She disavows signing the document and any others that she signed using that private key. This is called repudiation.

Timestamps can limit the effects of this kind of cheating, but Alice can always claim that her key was compromised earlier. If Alice times things well, she can sign a document and then successfully claim that she didn't. This is why there is so much talk about private keys buried in tamper-resistant modules—so that Alice can't get at hers and abuse it.

Although nothing can be done about this possible abuse, one can take steps to guarantee that old signatures are not invalidated by actions taken in disputing new ones. (For example, Alice could "lose" her key to keep from paying Bob for the junk car he sold her yesterday and, in the process, invalidate her bank account.) The solution is for the receiver of a signed document to have it timestamped [453].

The general protocol is given in [28]:

(1) Alice signs a message.
(2) Alice generates a header containing some identifying information. She concatenates the header with the signed message, signs that, and sends it to Trent.
(3) Trent verifies the outside signature and confirms the identifying information. He adds a timestamp to Alice's signed message and the identifying information. Then he signs it all and sends it to both Alice and Bob.
(4) Bob verifies Trent's signature, the identifying information, and Alice's signature.
(5) Alice verifies the message Trent sent to Bob. If she did not originate the message, she speaks up quickly.

Another scheme uses Trent after the fact [209]. After receiving a signed message, Bob can send a copy to Trent for verification. Trent can attest to the validity of Alice's signature.

Applications of Digital Signatures

One of the earliest proposed applications of digital signatures was to facilitate the verification of nuclear test ban treaties [1454,1467]. The United States and the Soviet Union (anyone remember the Soviet Union?) permitted each other to put seismometers on the other's soil to monitor nuclear tests. The problem was that each country needed to assure itself that the host nation was not tampering with the data from the monitoring nation's seismometers. Simultaneously, the host nation needed to assure itself that the monitor was sending only the specific information needed for monitoring.

Conventional authentication techniques can solve the first problem, but only digital signatures can solve both problems. The host nation can read, but not alter, data from the seismometer, and the monitoring nation knows that the data has not been tampered with.

2.7   DIGITAL SIGNATURES WITH ENCRYPTION

By combining digital signatures with public-key cryptography, we develop a protocol that combines the security of encryption with the authenticity of digital signatures. Think of a letter from your mother: The signature provides proof of authorship and the envelope provides privacy.

(1) Alice signs the message with her private key.

$$S_A(M)$$

(2) Alice encrypts the signed message with Bob's public key and sends it to Bob.

$$E_B(S_A(M))$$

(3) Bob decrypts the message with his private key.

$$D_B(E_B(S_A(M))) = S_A(M)$$

(4) Bob verifies with Alice's public key and recovers the message.

$$V_A(S_A(M)) = M$$

Signing before encrypting seems natural. When Alice writes a letter, she signs it and then puts it in an envelope. If she put the letter in the envelope unsigned and then signed the envelope, then Bob might worry if the letter hadn't been covertly replaced. If Bob showed to Carol Alice's letter and envelope, Carol might accuse Bob of lying about which letter arrived in which envelope.

In electronic correspondence as well, signing before encrypting is a prudent practice [48]. Not only is it more secure—an adversary can't remove a signature from an encrypted message and add his own—but there are legal considerations: If the text to be signed is not visible to the signer when he affixes his signature, then the signature may have little legal force [1312]. And there are some cryptanalytic attacks against this technique with RSA signatures (see Section 19.3).

There's no reason Alice has to use the same public-key/private-key key pair for encrypting and signing. She can have two key pairs: one for encryption and the other for signatures. Separation has its advantages: she can surrender her encryption key to the police without compromising her signature, one key can be escrowed (see Section 4.13) without affecting the other, and the keys can have different sizes and can expire at different times.

Of course, timestamps should be used with this protocol to prevent reuse of messages. Timestamps can also protect against other potential pitfalls, such as the one described below.

Resending the Message as a Receipt

Consider an implementation of this protocol, with the additional feature of confirmation messages. Whenever Bob receives a message, he returns it as a confirmation of receipt.

(1) Alice signs a message with her private key, encrypts it with Bob's public key, and sends it to Bob.

$$E_B(S_A(M))$$

(2) Bob decrypts the message with his private key and verifies the signature with Alice's public key, thereby verifying that Alice signed the message and recovering the message.

$$V_A(D_B(E_B(S_A(M)))) = M$$

(3) Bob signs the message with his private key, encrypts it with Alice's public key, and sends it back to Alice.

$$E_A(S_B(M))$$

(4) Alice decrypts the message with her private key and verifies the signature with Bob's public key. If the resultant message is the same one she sent to Bob, she knows that Bob received the message accurately.

If the same algorithm is used for both encryption and digital-signature verification there is a possible attack [506]. In these cases, the digital signature operation is the inverse of the encryption operation: $V_X = E_X$ and $S_X = D_X$.

Assume that Mallory is a legitimate system user with his own public and private key. Now, let's watch as he reads Bob's mail. First, he records Alice's message to Bob in step (1). Then, at some later time, he sends that message to Bob, claiming that it came from him (Mallory). Bob thinks that it is a legitimate message from Mallory, so he decrypts the message with his private key and then tries to verify Mallory's signature by decrypting it with Mallory's public key. The resultant message, which is pure gibberish, is:

$$E_M(D_B(E_B(D_A(M)))) = E_M(D_A(M))$$

Even so, Bob goes on with the protocol and sends Mallory a receipt:

$$E_M(D_B(E_M(D_A(M))))$$

Now, all Mallory has to do is decrypt the message with his private key, encrypt it with Bob's public key, decrypt it again with his private key, and encrypt it with Alice's public key. *Voilà!* Mallory has *M*.

It is not unreasonable to imagine that Bob may automatically send Mallory a receipt. This protocol may be embedded in his communications software, for example, and send receipts automatically. It is this willingness to acknowledge the receipt of gibberish that creates the insecurity. If Bob checked the message for comprehensibility before sending a receipt, he could avoid this security problem.

There are enhancements to this attack that allow Mallory to send Bob a different message from the one he eavesdropped on. Never sign arbitrary messages from other people or decrypt arbitrary messages and give the results to other people.

Foiling the Resend Attack

The attack just described works because the encrypting operation is the same as the signature-verifying operation and the decryption operation is the same as the signature operation. A secure protocol would use even a slightly different operation for encryption and digital signatures. Using different keys for each operation solves the problem, as does using different algorithms for each operation; as do time-stamps, which make the incoming message and the outgoing message different; as do digital signatures with one-way hash functions (see Section 2.6).

In general, then, the following protocol is secure as the public-key algorithm used:

(1) Alice signs a message.

(2) Alice encrypts the message and signature with Bob's public key (using a different encryption algorithm than for the signature) and sends it to Bob.

(3) Bob decrypts the message with his private key.

(4) Bob verifies Alice's signature.

Attacks against Public-Key Cryptography

In all these public-key cryptography protocols, I glossed over how Alice gets Bob's public key. Section 3.1 discusses this in detail, but it is worth mentioning here.

The easiest way to get someone's public key is from a secure database somewhere. The database has to be public, so that anyone can get anyone else's public key. The database also has to be protected from write-access by anyone except Trent; otherwise Mallory could substitute any public key for Bob's. After he did that, Bob couldn't read messages addressed to him, but Mallory could.

Even if the public keys are stored in a secure database, Mallory could still substitute one for another during transmission. To prevent this, Trent can sign each public key with his own private key. Trent, when used in this manner, is often known as a **Key Certification Authority** or **Key Distribution Center** (**KDC**). In practical implementations, the KDC signs a compound message consisting of the user's name, his public key, and any other important information about the user. This signed compound message is stored in the KDC's database. When Alice gets Bob's key, she verifies the KDC's signature to assure herself of the key's validity.

In the final analysis, this is not making things impossible for Mallory, only more difficult. Alice still has the KDC's public key stored somewhere. Mallory would have to substitute his own public key for that key, corrupt the database, and substitute his own keys for the valid keys (all signed with his private key as if he were the KDC), and then he's in business. But, even paper-based signatures can be forged if Mallory goes to enough trouble. Key exchange will be discussed in minute detail in Section 3.1.

2.8   RANDOM AND PSEUDO-RANDOM-SEQUENCE GENERATION

Why even bother with random-number generation in a book on cryptography? There's already a random-number generator built into most every compiler, a mere function call away. Why not use that? Unfortunately, those random-number generators are almost definitely not secure enough for cryptography, and probably not even very random. Most of them are embarrassingly bad.

Random-number generators are not random because they don't have to be. Most simple applications, like computer games, need so few random numbers that they hardly notice. However, cryptography is extremely sensitive to the properties of random-number generators. Use a poor random-number generator and you start getting weird correlations and strange results [1231,1238]. If you are depending on your random-number generator for security, weird correlations and strange results are the last things you want.

The problem is that a random-number generator doesn't produce a random sequence. It probably doesn't produce anything that looks even remotely like a random sequence. Of course, it is impossible to produce something truly random on a computer. Donald Knuth quotes John von Neumann as saying: "Anyone who considers arithmetical methods of producing random digits is, of course, in a state of sin" [863]. Computers are deterministic beasts: Stuff goes in one end, completely predictable operations occur inside, and different stuff comes out the other end. Put the same stuff in on two separate occasions and the same stuff comes out both times. Put the same stuff into two identical computers, and the same stuff comes out of both of them. A computer can only be in a finite number of states (a large finite number, but a finite number nonetheless), and the stuff that comes out will always be a deterministic function of the stuff that went in and the computer's current state. That means that any random-number generator on a computer (at least, on a finite-state machine) is, by definition, periodic. Anything that is periodic is, by definition, predictable. And if something is predictable, it can't be random. A true random-number generator requires some random input; a computer can't provide that.

Pseudo-Random Sequences

The best a computer can produce is a **pseudo-random-sequence generator**. What's that? Many people have taken a stab at defining this formally, but I'll hand-wave here. A pseudo-random sequence is one that looks random. The sequence's period should be long enough so that a finite sequence of reasonable length—that is, one that is actually used—is not periodic. If you need a billion random bits, don't choose a sequence generator that repeats after only sixteen thousand bits. These relatively short nonperiodic subsequences should be as indistinguishable as possible from random sequences. For example, they should have about the same number of ones and zeros, about half the runs (sequences of the same bit) should be of length one, one quarter of length two, one eighth of length three, and so on. They should not be compressible. The distribution of run lengths for zeros and ones should be the same [643,863,99,1357]. These properties can be empirically measured and then compared to statistical expectations using a chi-square test.

For our purposes, a sequence generator is pseudo-random if it has this property:

1. It looks random. This means that it passes all the statistical tests of randomness that we can find. (Start with the ones in [863].)

A lot of effort has gone into producing good pseudo-random sequences on computer. Discussions of generators abound in the academic literature, along with various tests of randomness. All of these generators are periodic (there's no escaping that); but with potential periods of 2^{256} bits and higher, they can be used for the largest applications.

The problem is still those weird correlations and strange results. Every pseudo-random-sequence generator is going to produce them if you use them in a certain way. And that's what a cryptanalyst will use to attack the system.

Cryptographically Secure Pseudo-Random Sequences

Cryptographic applications demand much more of a pseudo-random-sequence generator than do most other applications. Cryptographic randomness doesn't mean just statistical randomness, although that's part of it. For a sequence to be **cryptographically secure pseudo-random**, it must also have this property:

2. It is unpredictable. It must be computationally infeasible to predict what the next random bit will be, given complete knowledge of the algorithm or hardware generating the sequence and all of the previous bits in the stream.

Cryptographically secure pseudo-random sequences should not be compressible . . . unless you know the key. The key is generally the seed used to set the initial state of the generator.

Like any cryptographic algorithm, cryptographically secure pseudo-random-sequence generators are subject to attack. Just as it is possible to break an encryption algorithm, it is possible to break a cryptographically secure pseudo-random-sequence generator. Making generators resistant to attack is what cryptography is all about.

Real Random Sequences

Now we're drifting into the domain of philosophers. Is there such a thing as randomness? What is a random sequence? How do you know if a sequence is random? Is "101110100" more random than "101010101"? Quantum mechanics tells us that there is honest-to-goodness randomness in the real world. But can we preserve that randomness in the deterministic world of computer chips and finite-state machines?

Philosophy aside, from our point of view a sequence generator is **real random** if it has this additional third property:

> 3. It cannot be reliably reproduced. If you run the sequence generator twice with the exact same input (at least as exact as humanly possible), you will get two completely unrelated random sequences.

The output of a generator satisfying these three properties will be good enough for a one-time pad, key generation, and any other cryptographic applications that require a truly random sequence generator. The difficulty is in determining whether a sequence is really random. If I repeatedly encrypt a string with DES and a given key, I will get a nice, random-looking output; you won't be able to tell that it's non-random unless you rent time on the NSA's DES cracker.

CHAPTER 3

Basic Protocols

3.1 KEY EXCHANGE

A common cryptographic technique is to encrypt each individual conversation with a separate key. This is called a session key, because it is used for only one particular communications session. As discussed in Section 8.5, session keys are useful because they only exist for the duration of the communication. How this common session key gets into the hands of the conversants can be a complicated matter.

Key Exchange with Symmetric Cryptography

This protocol assumes that Alice and Bob, users on a network, each share a secret key with the Key Distribution Center (KDC) [1260]—Trent in our protocols. These keys must be in place before the start of the protocol. (The protocol ignores the very real problem of how to distribute these secret keys; just assume they are in place and Mallory has no idea what they are.)

(1) Alice calls Trent and requests a session key to communicate with Bob.

(2) Trent generates a random session key. He encrypts two copies of it: one in Alice's key and the other in Bob's key. Trent sends both copies to Alice.

(3) Alice decrypts her copy of the session key.

(4) Alice sends Bob his copy of the session key.

(5) Bob decrypts his copy of the session key.

(6) Both Alice and Bob use this session key to communicate securely.

This protocol relies on the absolute security of Trent, who is more likely to be a trusted computer program than a trusted individual. If Mallory corrupts Trent, the whole network is compromised. He has all of the secret keys that Trent shares with each of the users; he can read all past communications traffic that he has saved, and all future communications traffic. All he has to do is to tap the communications lines and listen to the encrypted message traffic.

The other problem with this system is that Trent is a potential bottleneck. He has to be involved in every key exchange. If Trent fails, that disrupts the entire system.

Key Exchange with Public-Key Cryptography

The basic hybrid cryptosystem was discussed in Section 2.5. Alice and Bob use public-key cryptography to agree on a session key, and use that session key to encrypt data. In some practical implementations, both Alice's and Bob's signed public keys will be available on a database. This makes the key-exchange protocol even easier, and Alice can send a secure message to Bob even if he has never heard of her:

(1) Alice gets Bob's public key from the KDC.

(2) Alice generates a random session key, encrypts it using Bob's public key, and sends it to Bob.

(3) Bob then decrypts Alice's message using his private key.

(4) Both of them encrypt their communications using the same session key.

Man-in-the-Middle Attack

While Eve cannot do better than try to break the public-key algorithm or attempt a ciphertext-only attack on the ciphertext, Mallory is a lot more powerful than Eve. Not only can he listen to messages between Alice and Bob, he can also modify messages, delete messages, and generate totally new ones. Mallory can imitate Bob when talking to Alice and imitate Alice when talking to Bob. Here's how the attack works:

(1) Alice sends Bob her public key. Mallory intercepts this key and sends Bob his own public key.

(2) Bob sends Alice his public key. Mallory intercepts this key and sends Alice his own public key.

(3) When Alice sends a message to Bob, encrypted in "Bob's" public key, Mallory intercepts it. Since the message is really encrypted with his own public key, he decrypts it with his private key, re-encrypts it with Bob's public key, and sends it on to Bob.

(4) When Bob sends a message to Alice, encrypted in "Alice's" public key, Mallory intercepts it. Since the message is really encrypted with his own public key, he decrypts it with his private key, re-encrypts it with Alice's public key, and sends it on to Alice.

Even if Alice's and Bob's public keys are stored on a database, this attack will work. Mallory can intercept Alice's database inquiry and substitute his own public key for Bob's. He can do the same to Bob and substitute his own public key for Alice's. Or better yet, he can break into the database surreptitiously and substitute his key for both Alice's and Bob's. Then he simply waits for Alice and Bob to talk with each other, intercepts and modifies the messages, and he has succeeded.

This **man-in-the-middle attack** works because Alice and Bob have no way to verify that they are talking to each other. Assuming Mallory doesn't cause any noticeable network delays, the two of them have no idea that someone sitting between them is reading all of their supposedly secret communications.

Interlock Protocol

The **interlock protocol**, invented by Ron Rivest and Adi Shamir [1327], has a good chance of foiling the man-in-the-middle attack. Here's how it works:

(1) Alice sends Bob her public key.

(2) Bob sends Alice his public key.

(3) Alice encrypts her message using Bob's public key. She sends half of the encrypted message to Bob.

(4) Bob encrypts his message using Alice's public key. He sends half of the encrypted message to Alice.

(5) Alice sends the other half of her encrypted message to Bob.

(6) Bob puts the two halves of Alice's message together and decrypts it with his private key. Bob sends the other half of his encrypted message to Alice.

(7) Alice puts the two halves of Bob's message together and decrypts it with her private key.

The important point is that half of the message is useless without the other half; it can't be decrypted. Bob cannot read any part of Alice's message until step (6); Alice cannot read any part of Bob's message until step (7). There are a number of ways to do this:

— If the encryption algorithm is a block algorithm, half of each block (e.g., every other bit) could be sent in each half message.

— Decryption of the message could be dependent on an initialization vector (see Section 9.3), which could be sent with the second half of the message.

— The first half of the message could be a one-way hash function of the encrypted message (see Section 2.4) and the encrypted message itself could be the second half.

To see how this causes a problem for Mallory, let's review his attempt to subvert the protocol. He can still substitute his own public keys for Alice's and Bob's in steps (1) and (2). But now, when he intercepts half of Alice's message in step (3), he cannot decrypt it with his private key and re-encrypt it with Bob's public key. He must invent a totally new message and send half of it to Bob. When he intercepts half of Bob's message to Alice in step (4), he has the same problem. He cannot decrypt it with his private key and re-encrypt it with Alice's public key. He has to invent a totally new message and send half of it to Alice. By the time he intercepts the second halves of the real messages in steps (5) and (6), it is too late for him to change the new messages he invented. The conversation between Alice and Bob will necessarily be completely different.

Mallory could possibly get away with this scheme. If he knows Alice and Bob well enough to mimic both sides of a conversation between them, they might never realize that they are being duped. But surely this is much harder than sitting between the two of them, intercepting and reading their messages.

Key Exchange with Digital Signatures

Implementing digital signatures during a session-key exchange protocol circumvents this man-in-the-middle attack as well. Trent signs both Alice's and Bob's public keys. The signed keys include a signed certification of ownership. When Alice and Bob receive the keys, they each verify Trent's signature. Now they know that the public key belongs to that other person. The key exchange protocol can then proceed.

Mallory has serious problems. He cannot impersonate either Alice or Bob because he doesn't know either of their private keys. He cannot substitute his public key for either of theirs because, while he has one signed by Trent, it is signed as being Mallory's. All he can do is listen to the encrypted traffic go back and forth or disrupt the lines of communication and prevent Alice and Bob from talking.

This protocol uses Trent, but the risk of compromising the KDC is less than the first protocol. If Mallory compromises Trent (breaks into the KDC), all he gets is Trent's private key. This key enables him only to sign new keys; it does not let him decrypt any session keys or read any message traffic. To read the traffic, Mallory has to impersonate a user on the network and trick legitimate users into encrypting messages with his phony public key.

Mallory can launch that kind of attack. With Trent's private key, he can create phony signed keys to fool both Alice and Bob. Then, he can either exchange them in the database for real signed keys, or he can intercept users' database requests and reply with his phony keys. This enables him to launch a man-in-the-middle attack and read people's communications.

This attack will work, but remember that Mallory has to be able to intercept and modify messages. In some networks this is a lot more difficult than passively sitting on a network reading messages as they go by. On a broadcast channel, such as a radio network, it is almost impossible to replace one message with another—although the entire network can be jammed. On computer networks this is easier and seems to be getting easier every day. Consider IP spoofing, router attacks, and so forth; active attacks don't necessarily mean someone down a manhole with a datascope, and they are not limited to three-letter agencies.

Key and Message Transmission

Alice and Bob need not complete the key-exchange protocol before exchanging messages. In this protocol, Alice sends Bob the message, *M*, without any previous key exchange protocol:

(1) Alice generates a random session key, *K*, and encrypts *M* using *K*.

$$E_K(M)$$

(2) Alice gets Bob's public key from the database.

(3) Alice encrypts *K* with Bob's public key.

$$E_B(K)$$

(4) Alice sends both the encrypted message and encrypted session key to Bob.

$$E_K(M), E_B(K)$$

For added security against man-in-the-middle attacks, Alice can sign the transmission.

(5) Bob decrypts Alice's session key, *K*, using his private key.

(6) Bob decrypts Alice's message using the session key.

This hybrid system is how public-key cryptography is most often used in a communications system. It can be combined with digital signatures, timestamps, and any other security protocols.

Key and Message Broadcast

There is no reason Alice can't send the encrypted message to several people. In this example, Alice will send the encrypted message to Bob, Carol, and Dave:

(1) Alice generates a random session key, *K*, and encrypts *M* using *K*.

$$E_K(M)$$

(2) Alice gets Bob's, Carol's, and Dave's public keys from the database.

(3) Alice encrypts *K* with Bob's public key, encrypts *K* with Carol's public key, and then encrypts *K* with Dave's public key.

$$E_B(K), E_C(K), E_D(K)$$

(4) Alice broadcasts the encrypted message and all the encrypted keys to anybody who cares to receive it.

$$E_B(K), E_C(K), E_D(K), E_K(M)$$

(5) Only Bob, Carol, and Dave can decrypt the key, *K*, each using his or her private key.

(6) Only Bob, Carol, and Dave can decrypt Alice's message using *K*.

This protocol can be implemented on a store-and-forward network. A central server can forward Alice's message to Bob, Carol, and Dave along with their particular encrypted key. The server doesn't have to be secure or trusted, since it will not be able to decrypt any of the messages.

3.2 AUTHENTICATION

When Alice logs into a host computer (or an automatic teller, or a telephone banking system, or any other type of terminal), how does the host know who she is? How does the host know she is not Eve trying to falsify Alice's identity? Traditionally, passwords solve this problem. Alice enters her password, and the host confirms that it is correct. Both Alice and the host know this secret piece of knowledge and the host requests it from Alice every time she tries to log in.

Authentication Using One-Way Functions

What Roger Needham and Mike Guy realized is that the host does not need to know the passwords; the host just has to be able to differentiate valid passwords from invalid passwords. This is easy with one-way functions [1599,526,1274,1121]. Instead of storing passwords, the host stores one-way functions of the passwords.

    (1) Alice sends the host her password.

    (2) The host performs a one-way function on the password.

    (3) The host compares the result of the one-way function to the value it previously stored.

Since the host no longer stores a table of everybody's valid password, the threat of someone breaking into the host and stealing the password list is mitigated. The list of passwords operated on by the one-way function is useless, because the one-way function cannot be reversed to recover the passwords.

Dictionary Attacks and Salt

A file of passwords encrypted with a one-way function is still vulnerable. In his spare time, Mallory compiles a list of the 1,000,000 most common passwords. He operates on all 1,000,000 of them with the one-way function and stores the results. If each password is about 8 bytes, the resulting file will be no more than 8 megabytes; it will fit on a few floppy disks. Now, Mallory steals an encrypted password file. He compares that file with his file of encrypted possible passwords and sees what matches.

This is a **dictionary attack**, and it's surprisingly successful (see Section 8.1). **Salt** is a way to make it more difficult. Salt is a random string that is concatenated with passwords before being operated on by the one-way function. Then, both the salt value and the result of the one-way function are stored in a database on the host. If the number of possible salt values is large enough, this practically eliminates a dictionary attack against commonly used passwords because Mallory has to generate the one-way hash for each possible salt value. This is a simple attempt at an initialization vector (see Section 9.3).

The point here is to make sure that Mallory has to do a trial encryption of each password in his dictionary every time he tries to break another person's password, rather than just doing one massive precomputation for all possible passwords.

A lot of salt is needed. Most UNIX systems use only 12 bits of salt. Even with that, Daniel Klein developed a password-guessing program that often cracks 40 percent of the passwords on a given host system within a week [847,848] (see Section 8.1). David Feldmeier and Philip Karn compiled a list of about 732,000 common passwords concatenated with each of 4096 possible salt values. They estimate that 30 percent of passwords on any given host can be broken with this list [561].

Salt isn't a panacea; increasing the number of salt bits won't solve everything. Salt only protects against general dictionary attacks on a password file, not against a concerted attack on a single password. It protects people who have the same password on multiple machines, but doesn't make poorly chosen passwords any better.

SKEY

SKEY is an authentication program that relies on a one-way function for its security. It's easy to explain.

To set up the system, Alice enters a random number, R. The computer computes $f(R)$, $f(f(R))$, $f(f(f(R)))$, and so on, about a hundred times. Call these numbers x_1, x_2, x_3, . . . , x_{100}. The computer prints out this list of numbers, and Alice puts it in her pocket for safekeeping. The computer also stores x_{101}, in the clear, in a login database next to Alice's name.

The first time Alice wants to log in, she types her name and x_{100}. The computer calculates $f(x_{100})$ and compares it with x_{101}; if they match, Alice is authenticated. Then, the computer replaces x_{101} with x_{100} in the database. Alice crosses x_{100} off her list.

Every time Alice logs in, she enters the last uncrossed number on her list: x_i. The computer calculates $f(x_i)$ and compares it with x_{i+1} stored in its database. Eve can't get any useful information because each number is only used once, and the function is one-way. Similarly, the database is not useful to an attacker. Of course, when Alice runs out of numbers on her list, she has to reinitialize the system.

Authentication Using Public-Key Cryptography

Even with salt, the first protocol has serious security problems. When Alice sends her password to her host, anyone who has access to her data path can read it. She might be accessing her host through a convoluted transmission path that passes through four industrial competitors, three foreign countries, and two forward-thinking universities. Eve can be at any one of those points, listening to Alice's login sequence. If Eve has access to the processor memory of the host, she can see the password before the host hashes it.

Public-key cryptography can solve this problem. The host keeps a file of every user's public key; all users keep their own private keys. Here is a naïve attempt at a protocol. When logging in, the protocol proceeds as follows:

(1) The host sends Alice a random string.

(2) Alice encrypts the string with her private key and sends it back to the host, along with her name.

(3) The host looks up Alice's public key in its database and decrypts the message using that public key.

(4) If the decrypted string matches what the host sent Alice in the first place, the host allows Alice access to the system.

No one else has access to Alice's private key, so no one else can impersonate Alice. More important, Alice never sends her private key over the transmission line to the host. Eve, listening in on the interaction, cannot get any information that would enable her to deduce the private key and impersonate Alice.

The private key is both long and non-mnemonic, and will probably be processed automatically by the user's hardware or communications software. This requires an intelligent terminal that Alice trusts, but neither the host nor the communications path needs to be secure.

It is foolish to encrypt arbitrary strings—not only those sent by untrusted third parties, but under any circumstances at all. Attacks similar to the one discussed in Section 19.3 can be mounted. Secure proof-of-identity protocols take the following, more complicated, form:

(1) Alice performs a computation based on some random numbers and her private key and sends the result to the host.

(2) The host sends Alice a different random number.

(3) Alice makes some computation based on the random numbers (both the ones she generated and the one she received from the host) and her private key, and sends the result to the host.

(4) The host does some computation on the various numbers received from Alice and her public key to verify that she knows her private key.

(5) If she does, her identity is verified.

If Alice does not trust the host any more than the host trusts Alice, then Alice will require the host to prove its identity in the same manner.

Step (1) might seem unnecessary and confusing, but it is required to prevent attacks against the protocol. Sections 21.1 and 21.2 mathematically describe several algorithms and protocols for proving identity. See also [935].

Mutual Authentication Using the Interlock Protocol

Alice and Bob are two users who want to authenticate each other. Each of them has a password that the other knows: Alice has P_A and Bob has P_B. Here's a protocol that will *not* work:

(1) Alice and Bob trade public keys.

(2) Alice encrypts P_A with Bob's public key and sends it to him.

(3) Bob encrypts P_B with Alice's public key and sends it to her.

(4) Alice decrypts what she received in step (2) and verifies that it is correct.

(5) Bob decrypts what he received in step (3) and verifies that it is correct.

Mallory can launch a successful man-in-the-middle attack (see Section 3.1):

(1) Alice and Bob trade public keys. Mallory intercepts both messages. He substitutes his public key for Bob's and sends it to Alice. Then he substitutes his public key for Alice's and sends it to Bob.

(2) Alice encrypts P_A with "Bob's" public key and sends it to him. Mallory intercepts the message, decrypts P_A with his private key, re-encrypts it with Bob's public key and sends it on to him.

(3) Bob encrypts P_B with "Alice's" public key and sends it to her. Mallory intercepts the message, decrypts P_B with his private key, re-encrypts it with Alice's public key, and sends it on to her.

(4) Alice decrypts P_B and verifies that it is correct.

(5) Bob decrypts P_A and verifies that it is correct.

Alice and Bob see nothing different. However, Mallory knows both P_A and P_B.

Donald Davies and Wyn Price describe how the interlock protocol (described in Section 3.1) can defeat this attack [435]. Steve Bellovin and Michael Merritt discuss ways to attack this protocol [110]. If Alice is a user and Bob is a host, Mallory can pretend to be Bob, complete the beginning steps of the protocol with Alice, and then drop the connection. True artistry demands Mallory do this by simulating line noise or network failure, but the final result is that Mallory has Alice's password. He can then connect with Bob and complete the protocol, thus getting Bob's password, too.

The protocol can be modified so that Bob gives his password before Alice, under the assumption that the user's password is much more sensitive than the host's password. This falls to a more complicated attack, also described in [110].

SKID

SKID2 and SKID3 are symmetric cryptography identification protocols developed for RACE's RIPE project [1305] (See Section 25.7). They use a MAC (see Section 2.4) to provide security and both assume that both Alice and Bob share a secret key, K.

SKID2 allows Bob to prove his identity to Alice. Here's the protocol:

(1) Alice chooses a random number, R_A. (The RIPE document specifies a 64-bit number). She sends it to Bob.

(2) Bob chooses a random number, R_B. (The RIPE document specifies a 64-bit number). He sends Alice:

$$R_B, H_K(R_A, R_B, B)$$

H_K is the MAC. (The RIPE document suggests the RIPE-MAC function—see Section 18.14.) B is Bob's name.

(3) Alice computes $H_K(R_A,R_B,B)$ and compares it with what she received from Bob. If the results are identical, then Alice knows that she is communicating with Bob.

SKID3 provides mutual authentication between Alice and Bob. Steps (1) through (3) are identical to SKID2, and then the protocol proceeds with:

(4) Alice sends Bob:

$$H_K(R_B,A)$$

A is Alice's name.

(5) Bob computes $H_K(R_B,A)$, and compares it with what he received from Alice. If the results are identical, then Bob knows that he is communicating with Alice.

This protocol is not secure against a man-in-the-middle attack. In general, a man-in-the-middle attack can defeat any protocol that doesn't involve a secret of some kind.

Message Authentication

When Bob receives a message from Alice, how does he know it is authentic? If Alice signed her message, this is easy. Alice's digital signature is enough to convince anyone that the message is authentic.

Symmetric cryptography provides some authentication. When Bob receives a message from Alice encrypted in their shared key, he knows it is from Alice. No one else knows their key. However, Bob has no way of convincing a third party of this fact. Bob can't show the message to Trent and convince him that it came from Alice. Trent can be convinced that the message came from either Alice or Bob (since no one else shared their secret key), but he has no way of knowing which one.

If the message is unencrypted, Alice could also use a MAC. This also convinces Bob that the message is authentic, but has the same problems as symmetric cryptography solutions.

3.3 AUTHENTICATION AND KEY EXCHANGE

These protocols combine authentication with key exchange to solve a general computer problem: Alice and Bob are on opposite ends of a network and want to talk securely. How can Alice and Bob exchange a secret key and at the same time each be sure that he or she is talking to the other and not to Mallory? Most of the protocols assume that Trent shares a different secret key with each participant, and that all of these keys are in place before the protocol begins.

The symbols used in these protocols are summarized in Table 3.1.

Wide-Mouth Frog

The Wide-Mouth Frog protocol [283,284] is probably the simplest symmetric key-management protocol that uses a trusted server. Both Alice and Bob share a secret

TABLE 3.1
Symbols used in authentication and key exchange protocols

A	Alice's name
B	Bob's name
E_A	Encryption with a key Trent shares with Alice
E_B	Encryption with a key Trent shares with Bob
I	Index number
K	A random session key
L	Lifetime
T_A, T_B	A timestamp
R_A, R_B	A random number, sometimes called a **nonce**, chosen by Alice and Bob respectively

key with Trent. The keys are just used for key distribution and not to encrypt any actual messages between users. Just by using two messages, Alice transfers a session key to Bob:

(1) Alice concatenates a timestamp, Bob's name, and a random session key and encrypts the whole message with the key she shares with Trent. She sends this to Trent, along with her name.

$$A, E_A(T_A, B, K)$$

(2) Trent decrypts the message from Alice. Then he concatenates a new timestamp, Alice's name, and the random session key; he encrypts the whole message with the key he shares with Bob. Trent sends to Bob:

$$E_B(T_B, A, K)$$

The biggest assumption made in this protocol is that Alice is competent enough to generate good session keys. Remember that random numbers aren't easy to generate; it might be more than Alice can be trusted to do properly.

Yahalom

In this protocol, both Alice and Bob share a secret key with Trent [283,284].

(1) Alice concatenates her name and a random number, and sends it to Bob.

$$A, R_A$$

(2) Bob concatenates Alice's name, Alice's random number, his own random number, and encrypts it with the key he shares with Trent. He sends this to Trent, along with his name.

$$B, E_B(A, R_A, R_B)$$

(3) Trent generates two messages. The first consists of Bob's name, a random session key, Alice's random number, and Bob's random number, all encrypted with the key he shares with Alice. The second consists of

Alice's name and the random session key, encrypted with the key he shares with Bob. He sends both messages to Alice.

$$E_A(B,K,R_A,R_B),E_B(A,K)$$

(4) Alice decrypts the first message, extracts K, and confirms that R_A has the same value as it did in step (1). Alice sends Bob two messages. The first is the message received from Trent, encrypted with Bob's key. The second is R_B, encrypted with the session key.

$$E_B(A,K),E_K(R_B)$$

(5) Bob decrypts the message encrypted with his key, extracts K, and confirms that R_B has the same value as it did in step (2).

At the end, Alice and Bob are each convinced that they are talking to the other and not to a third party. The novelty here is that Bob is the first one to contact Trent, who only sends one message to Alice.

Needham-Schroeder

This protocol, invented by Roger Needham and Michael Schroeder [1159], also uses symmetric cryptography and Trent.

(1) Alice sends a message to Trent consisting of her name, Bob's name, and a random number.

$$A,B,R_A$$

(2) Trent generates a random session key. He encrypts a message consisting of a random session key and Alice's name with the secret key he shares with Bob. Then he encrypts Alice's random value, Bob's name, the key, and the encrypted message with the secret key he shares with Alice. Finally, he sends her the encrypted message:

$$E_A(R_A,B,K,E_B(K,A))$$

(3) Alice decrypts the message and extracts K. She confirms that R_A is the same value that she sent Trent in step (1). Then she sends Bob the message that Trent encrypted in his key.

$$E_B(K,A)$$

(4) Bob decrypts the message and extracts K. He then generates another random value, R_B. He encrypts the message with K and sends it to Alice.

$$E_K(R_B)$$

(5) Alice decrypts the message with K. She generates $R_B - 1$ and encrypts it with K. Then she sends the message back to Bob.

$$E_K(R_B - 1)$$

(6) Bob decrypts the message with K and verifies that it is $R_B - 1$.

All of this fussing around with R_A and R_B and $R_B - 1$ is to prevent **replay attacks**. In this attack, Mallory can record old messages and then use them later in an attempt to subvert the protocol. The presence of R_A in step (2) assures Alice that

Trent's message is legitimate and not a replay of a response from a previous execution of the protocol. When Alice successfully decrypts R_B and sends Bob $R_B - 1$ in step (5), Bob is ensured that Alice's messages are not replays from an earlier execution of the protocol.

The major security hole in this protocol is that old session keys are valuable. If Mallory gets access to an old K, he can launch a successful attack [461]. All he has to do is record Alice's messages to Bob in step (3). Then, once he has K, he can pretend to be Alice:

(1) Mallory sends Bob the following message:

   $E_B(K,A)$

(2) Bob extracts K, generates R_B, and sends Alice:

   $E_K(R_B)$

(3) Mallory intercepts the message, decrypts it with K, and sends Bob:

   $E_K(R_B - 1)$

(4) Bob verifies that "Alice's" message is $R_B - 1$.

Now, Mallory has Bob convinced that he is Alice.

A stronger protocol, using timestamps, can defeat this attack [461,456]. A timestamp is added to Trent's message in step (2) encrypted with Bob's key: $E_B(K,A,T)$. Timestamps require a secure and accurate system clock—not a trivial problem in itself.

If the key Trent shares with Alice is ever compromised, the consequences are drastic. Mallory can use it to obtain session keys to talk with Bob (or anyone else he wishes to talk to). Even worse, Mallory can continue to do this even after Alice changes her key [90].

Needham and Schroeder attempted to correct these problems in a modified version of their protocol [1160]. Their new protocol is essentially the same as the Otway-Rees protocol, published in the same issue of the same journal.

Otway-Rees

This protocol also uses symmetric cryptography [1224].

(1) Alice generates a message consisting of an index number, her name, Bob's name, and a random number, all encrypted in the key she shares with Trent. She sends this message to Bob along with the index number, her name, and his name:

   $I,A,B,E_A(R_A,I,A,B)$

(2) Bob generates a message consisting of a new random number, the index number, Alice's name, and Bob's name, all encrypted in the key he shares with Trent. He sends it to Trent, along with Alice's encrypted message, the index number, her name, and his name:

   $I,A,B,E_A(R_A,I,A,B),E_B(R_B,I,A,B)$

(3) Trent generates a random session key. Then he creates two messages. One is Alice's random number and the session key, encrypted in the key he shares with Alice. The other is Bob's random number and the session key, encrypted in the key he shares with Bob. He sends these two messages, along with the index number, to Bob:

$I, E_A(R_A, K), E_B(R_B, K)$

(4) Bob sends Alice the message encrypted in her key, along with the index number:

$I, E_A(R_A, K)$

(5) Alice decrypts the message to recover her key and random number. She then confirms that both have not changed in the protocol.

Assuming that all the random numbers match, and the index number hasn't changed along the way, Alice and Bob are now convinced of each other's identity, and they have a secret key with which to communicate.

Kerberos

Kerberos is a variant of Needham-Schroeder and is discussed in detail in Section 24.5. In the basic Kerberos Version 5 protocol, Alice and Bob each share keys with Trent. Alice wants to generate a session key for a conversation with Bob.

(1) Alice sends a message to Trent with her identity and Bob's identity.

A, B

(2) Trent generates a message with a timestamp, a lifetime, L, a random session key, and Alice's identity. He encrypts this in the key he shares with Bob. Then he takes the timestamp, the lifetime, the session key, and Bob's identity, and encrypts these in the key he shares with Alice. He sends both encrypted messages to Alice.

$E_A(T, L, K, B), E_B(T, L, K, A)$

(3) Alice generates a message with her identity and the timestamp, encrypts it in K, and sends it to Bob. Alice also sends Bob the message encrypted in Bob's key from Trent.

$E_K(A, T), E_B(T, L, K, A)$

(4) Bob creates a message consisting of the timestamp plus one, encrypts it in K, and sends it to Alice.

$E_K(T + 1)$

This protocol works, but it assumes that everyone's clocks are synchronized with Trent's clock. In practice, the effect is obtained by synchronizing clocks to within a few minutes of a secure time server and detecting replays within the time interval.

Neuman-Stubblebine

Whether by system faults or by sabotage, clocks can become unsynchronized. If the clocks get out of sync, there is a possible attack against most of these protocols

[644]. If the sender's clock is ahead of the receiver's clock, Mallory can intercept a message from the sender and replay it later when the timestamp becomes current at the receiver's site. This attack is called **suppress-replay** and can have irritating consequences.

This protocol, first presented in [820] and corrected in [1162] attempts to counter the suppress-replay attack. It is an enhancement to Yahalom and is an excellent protocol.

(1) Alice concatenates her name and a random number and sends it to Bob.

$$A, R_A$$

(2) Bob concatenates Alice's name, her random number, and a timestamp, and encrypts with the key he shares with Trent. He sends it to Trent along with his name and a new random number.

$$B, R_B, E_B(A, R_A, T_B)$$

(3) Trent generates a random session key. Then he creates two messages. The first is Bob's name, Alice's random number, a random session key, and the timestamp, all encrypted with the key he shares with Alice. The second is Alice's name, the session key, and the timestamp, all encrypted with the key he shares with Bob. He sends these both to Alice, along with Bob's random number.

$$E_A(B, R_A, K, T_B), E_A(A, K, T_B), R_B$$

(4) Alice decrypts the message encrypted with her key, extracts K, and confirms that R_A has the same value as it did in step (1). Alice sends Bob two messages. The first is the message received from Trent, encrypted with Bob's key. The second is R_B, encrypted with the session key.

$$E_B(A, K, T_B), E_K(R_B)$$

(5) Bob decrypts the message encrypted with his key, extracts K, and confirms that T_B and R_B have the same value they did in step (2).

Assuming both random numbers and the timestamp match, Alice and Bob are convinced of one another's identity and share a secret key. Synchronized clocks are not required because the timestamp is only relative to Bob's clock; Bob only checks the timestamp he generated himself.

One nice thing about this protocol is that Alice can use the message she received from Trent for subsequent authentication with Bob, within some predetermined time limit. Assume that Alice and Bob completed the above protocol, communicated, and then terminated the connection. Alice and Bob can reauthenticate in three steps, without having to rely on Trent.

(1) Alice sends Bob the message Trent sent her in step (3) and a new random number.

$$E_B(A, K, T_B), R'_A$$

(2) Bob sends Alice another new random number, and Alice's new random number encrypted in their session key.

$$R'_B, E_K(R'_A)$$

(3) Alice sends Bob his new random number, encrypted in their session key.

$$E_K(R'_B)$$

The new random numbers prevent replay attacks.

DASS

The Distributed Authentication Security Service (DASS) protocols, developed at Digital Equipment Corporation, also provide for mutual authentication and key exchange [604,1519,1518]. Unlike the previous protocols, DASS uses both public-key and symmetric cryptography. Alice and Bob each have a private key. Trent has signed copies of their public keys.

(1) Alice sends a message to Trent, consisting of Bob's name.

$$B$$

(2) Trent sends Alice Bob's public key, K_B, signed with Trent's private key, T. The signed message includes Bob's name.

$$S_T(B, K_B)$$

(3) Alice verifies Trent's signature to confirm that the key she received is actually Bob's public key. She generates a random session key, and a random public-key/private-key key pair: K_P. She encrypts a timestamp with K. Then she signs a key lifetime, L, her name, and K_P with her private key, K_A. Finally, she encrypts K with Bob's public key, and signs it with K_P. She sends all of this to Bob.

$$E_K(T_A), S_{K_A}(L, A, K_P), S_{K_P}(E_{K_B}(K))$$

(4) Bob sends a message to Trent (this may be a different Trent), consisting of Alice's name.

$$A$$

(5) Trent sends Bob Alice's public key, signed in Trent's private key. The signed message includes Alice's name.

$$S_T(A, K_A)$$

(6) Bob verifies Trent's signature to confirm that the key he received is actually Alice's public key. He then verifies Alice's signature and recovers K_P. He verifies the signature and uses his private key to recover K. Then he decrypts T_A to make sure this is a current message.

(7) If mutual authentication is required, Bob encrypts a new timestamp with K, and sends it to Alice.

$$E_K(T_B)$$

(8) Alice decrypts T_B with K to make sure that the message is current.

SPX, a product by DEC, is based on DASS. Additional information can be found in [34].

Denning-Sacco

This protocol also uses public-key cryptography [461]. Trent keeps a database of everyone's public keys.

(1) Alice sends a message to Trent with her identity and Bob's identity:

A,B

(2) Trent sends Alice Bob's public key, K_B, signed with Trent's private key, T. Trent also sends Alice her own public key, K_A, signed with his private key.

$S_T(B,K_B),S_T(A,K_A)$

(3) Alice sends Bob a random session key and a timestamp, signed in her private key and encrypted in Bob's public key, along with both signed public keys.

$E_B(S_A(K,T_A)),S_T(B,K_B),S_T(A,K_A)$

(4) Bob decrypts Alice's message with his private key and then verifies Alice's signature with her public key. He checks to make sure that the timestamp is still valid.

At this point both Alice and Bob have K, and can communicate securely.

This looks good, but it isn't. After completing the protocol with Alice, Bob can then masquerade as Alice [5]. Watch:

(1) Bob sends his name and Carol's name to Trent

B,C

(2) Trent sends Bob both Bob's and Carol's signed public keys.

$S_T(B,K_B),S_T(C,K_C)$

(3) Bob sends Carol the signed session key and timestamp he previously received from Alice, encrypted with Carol's public key, along with Alice's certificate and Carol's certificate.

$E_C(S_A(K,T_A)),S_T(A,K_A),S_T(C,K_C)$

(4) Carol decrypts Alice's message with her private key and then verifies Alice's signature with her public key. She checks to make sure that the timestamp is still valid.

Carol now thinks she is talking to Alice; Bob has successfully fooled her. In fact, Bob can fool everyone on the network until the timestamp expires.

This is easy to fix. Add the names inside the encrypted message in step (3):

$E_B(S_A(A,B,K,T_A)),S_T(A,K_A),S_T(B,K_B)$

Now Bob can't replay the old message to Carol, because it is clearly meant for communication between Alice and Bob.

Woo-Lam

This protocol also uses public-key cryptography [1610,1611]:

(1) Alice sends a message to Trent with her identity and Bob's identity:

$$A,B$$

(2) Trent sends Alice Bob's public key, K_B, signed with Trent's private key, T.

$$S_T(K_B)$$

(3) Alice verifies Trent's signature. Then she sends Bob her name and a random number, encrypted with Bob's public key.

$$E_{K_B}(A,R_A)$$

(4) Bob sends Trent his name, Alice's name, and Alice's random number encrypted with Trent's public key, K_T.

$$A,B,E_{K_T}(R_A)$$

(5) Trent sends Bob Alice's public key, K_A, signed with Trent's private key. He also sends him Alice's random number, a random session key, Alice's name, and Bob's name, all signed with Trent's private key and encrypted with Bob's public key.

$$S_T(K_A),E_{K_B}(S_T(R_A,K,A,B))$$

(6) Bob verifies Trent's signatures. Then he sends Alice the second part of Trent's message from step (5) and a new random number—all encrypted in Alice's public key.

$$E_{K_A}(S_T(R_A,K,A,B),R_B)$$

(7) Alice verifies Trent's signature and her random number. Then she sends Bob the second random number, encrypted in the session key.

$$E_K(R_B)$$

(8) Bob decrypts his random number and verifies that it unchanged.

Other Protocols

There are many other protocols in the literature. The X.509 protocols are discussed in Section 24.9, KryptoKnight is discussed in Section 24.6, and Encrypted Key Exchange is discussed in Section 22.5.

Another new public-key protocol is Kuperee [694]. And work is being done on protocols that use **beacons**, a trusted node on a network that continuously broadcasts authenticated nonces [783].

Lessons Learned

There are some important lessons in the previous protocols, both those which have been broken and those which have not:

— Many protocols failed because the designers tried to be too clever. They optimized their protocols by leaving out important pieces: names, random numbers, and so on. The remedy is to make everything explicit [43,44].

— Trying to optimize is an absolute tar pit and depends a whole lot on the assumptions you make. For example: If you have authenticated time, you can do a whole lot of things you can't do if you don't.

— The protocol of choice depends on the underlying communications architecture. Do you want to minimize the size of messages or the number of messages? Can all parties talk with each other or can only a few of them?

It's questions like these that led to the development of formal methods for analyzing protocols.

3.4 FORMAL ANALYSIS OF AUTHENTICATION AND KEY-EXCHANGE PROTOCOLS

The problem of establishing secure session keys between pairs of computers (and people) on a network is so fundamental that it has led to a great deal of research. Some of the research focused on the development of protocols like the ones discussed in Sections 3.1, 3.2, and 3.3. This, in turn, has led to a greater and more interesting problem: the formal analysis of authentication and key-exchange protocols. People have found flaws in seemingly secure protocols years after they were proposed, and researchers wanted tools that could prove a protocol's security from the start. Although much of this work can apply to general cryptographic protocols, the emphasis in research is almost exclusively on authentication and key exchange.

There are four basic approaches to the analysis of cryptographic protocols [1045]:

1. Model and verify the protocol using specification languages and verification tools not specifically designed for the analysis of cryptographic protocols.

2. Develop expert systems that a protocol designer can use to develop and investigate different scenarios.

3. Model the requirements of a protocol family using logics for the analysis of knowledge and belief.

4. Develop a formal method based on the algebraic term-rewriting properties of cryptographic systems.

A full discussion on these four approaches and the research surrounding them is well beyond the scope of this book. See [1047,1355] for a good introduction to the topic; I am only going to touch on the major contributions to the field.

The first approach treats a cryptographic protocol as any other computer program and attempts to prove correctness. Some researchers represent a protocol as a finite-state machine [1449,1565], others use extensions of first-order predicate calculus [822], and still others use specification languages to analyze protocols [1566]. However, proving correctness is not the same as proving security and this approach fails to detect many flawed protocols. Although it was widely studied at first, most of the work in this area has been redirected as the third approach gained popularity.

The second approach uses expert systems to determine if a protocol can reach an undesirable state (the leaking of a key, for example). While this approach better identifies flaws, it neither guarantees security nor provides techniques for developing attacks. It is good at determining whether a protocol contains a given flaw, but is unlikely to discover unknown flaws in a protocol. Examples of this approach can be found in [987,1521]; [1092] discusses a rule-based system developed by the U.S. military, called the Interrogator.

The third approach is by far the most popular, and was pioneered by Michael Burrows, Martin Abadi, and Roger Needham. They developed a formal logic model for the analysis of knowledge and belief, called **BAN logic** [283,284]. BAN logic is the most widely used logic for analyzing authentication protocols. It assumes that authentication is a function of integrity and freshness, and uses logical rules to trace both of those attributes through the protocol. Although many variants and extensions have been proposed, most protocol designers still refer back to the original work.

BAN logic doesn't provide a proof of security; it can only reason about authentication. It has a simple, straightforward logic that is easy to apply and still useful for detecting flaws. Some of the statements in BAN logic include:

> Alice believes X. (Alice acts as though X is true.)
>
> Alice sees X. (Someone has sent a message containing X to Alice, who can read and repeat X—possibly after decrypting it.)
>
> Alice said X. (At some time, Alice sent a message that includes the statement X. It is not known how long ago the message was sent or even that it was sent during the current run of the protocol. It is known that Alice believed X when she said it.)
>
> X is fresh. (X has not been sent in a message at any time before the current run of the protocol.)

And so on. BAN logic also provides rules for reasoning about belief in a protocol. These rules can then be applied to the logical statements about the protocol to prove things or answer questions about the protocol. For example, one rule is the message-meaning rule:

> IF Alice believes that Alice and Bob share a secret key, K, and Alice sees X, encrypted under K, and Alice did not encrypt X under K, THEN Alice believes that Bob once said X.

Another rule is the nonce-verification rule:

> IF Alice believes that X could have been uttered only recently and that Bob once said X, THEN Alice believes that Bob believes X.

There are four steps in BAN analysis:

(1) Convert the protocol into idealized form, using the statements previously described.

(2) Add all assumptions about the initial state of the protocol.

(3) Attach logical formulas to the statements: assertions about the state of the system after each statement.

(4) Apply the logical postulates to the assertions and assumptions to discover the beliefs held by the parties in the protocol.

The authors of BAN logic "view the idealized protocols as clearer and more complete specifications than traditional descriptions found in the literature. . . ." [283,284]. Others are not so impressed and criticize this step because it may not accurately reflect the real protocol [1161,1612]. Further debate is in [221,1557]. Other critics try to show that BAN logic can deduce characteristics about protocols that are obviously false [1161]—see [285,1509] for a rebuttal—and that BAN logic deals only with trust and not security [1509]. More debate is in [1488, 706,1002].

Despite these criticisms, BAN logic has been a success. It has found flaws in several protocols, including Needham-Schroeder and an early draft of a CCITT X.509 protocol [303]. It has uncovered redundancies in many protocols, including Yahalom, Needham-Schroeder, and Kerberos. Many published papers use BAN logic to make claims about their protocol's security [40,1162,73].

Other logic systems have been published, some designed as extensions to BAN logic [645,586,1556,828] and others based on BAN to correct perceived weaknesses [1488,1002]. The most successful of these is GNY [645], although it has some shortcomings [40]. Probabalistic beliefs were added to BAN logic, with mixed success, by [292,474]. Other formal logics are [156,798,288]; [1514] attempts to combine the features of several logics. And [1124,1511] present logics where beliefs can change over time.

The fourth approach to the analysis of cryptographic protocols models the protocol as an algebraic system, expresses the state of the participants' knowledge about the protocol, and then analyzes the attainability of certain states. This approach has not received as much attention as formal logics, but that is changing. It was first used by Michael Merritt [1076], who showed that an algebraic model can be used to analyze cryptographic protocols. Other approaches are in [473,1508,1530,1531,1532, 1510,1612].

The Navy Research Laboratory's (NRL) Protocol Analyzer is probably the most successful application of these techniques [1512,823,1046,1513]; it has been used to discover both new and known flaws in a variety of protocols [1044,1045,1047]. The Protocol Analyzer defines the following actions:

— Accept (Bob, Alice, M, N). (Bob accepts the message M as from Alice during Bob's local round N.)

— Learn (Eve, M). (Eve learns M.)

— Send (Alice, Bob, Q, M). (Alice sends M to Bob in response to query, Q.)

— Request (Bob, Alice, Q, N). (Bob sends Q to Alice during Bob's local round N.)

From these actions, requirements can be specified. For example:

— If Bob accepted message M from Alice at some point in the past, then Eve did not learn M at some point in the past.
— If Bob accepted message M from Alice in Bob's local round N, then Alice sent M to Bob as a response to a query in Bob's local round N.

To use the NRL Protocol Analyzer, a protocol must be specified using the previous constructs. Then, there are four phases of analysis: defining transition rules for honest participants, describing operations available to all—honest and dishonest—participants, describing the basic building blocks of the protocol, and describing the reduction rules. The point of all this is to show that a given protocol meets its requirements. Tools like the NRL Protocol Analyzer could eventually lead to a protocol that can be proven secure.

While much of the work in formal methods involves applying the methods to existing protocols, there is some push towards using formal methods to design the protocols in the first place. Some preliminary steps in this direction are [711]. The NRL Protocol Analyzer also attempts to do this [1512,222,1513].

The application of formal methods to cryptographic protocols is still a fairly new idea and it's really hard to figure out where it is headed. At this point, the weakest link seems to be the formalization process.

3.5 MULTIPLE-KEY PUBLIC-KEY CRYPTOGRAPHY

Public-key cryptography uses two keys. A message encrypted with one key can be decrypted with the other. Usually one key is private and the other is public. However, let's assume that Alice has one key and Bob has the other. Now Alice can encrypt a message so that only Bob can decrypt it, and Bob can encrypt a message so that only Alice can read it.

This concept was generalized by Colin Boyd [217]. Imagine a variant of public-key cryptography with three keys: K_A, K_B, and K_C, distributed as shown in Table 3.2.

Alice can encrypt a message with K_A so that Ellen, with K_B and K_C, can decrypt it. So can Bob and Carol in collusion. Bob can encrypt a message so that Frank can read

TABLE 3.2
Three-Key Key Distribution

Alice	K_A
Bob	K_B
Carol	K_C
Dave	K_A and K_B
Ellen	K_B and K_C
Frank	K_C and K_A

it, and Carol can encrypt a message so that Dave can read it. Dave can encrypt a message with K_A so that Ellen can read it, with K_B so that Frank can read it, or with both K_A and K_B so that Carol can read it. Similarly, Ellen can encrypt a message so that either Alice, Dave, or Frank can read it. All the possible combinations are summarized in Table 3.3; there are no other ones.

This can be extended to n keys. If a given subset of the keys is used to encrypt the message, then the other keys are required to decrypt the message.

Broadcasting a Message

Imagine that you have 100 operatives out in the field. You want to be able to send messages to subsets of them, but don't know which subsets in advance. You can either encrypt the message separately for each person or give out keys for every possible combination of people. The first option requires a lot of messages; the second requires a lot of keys.

Multiple-key cryptography is much easier. We'll use three operatives: Alice, Bob, and Carol. You give Alice K_A and K_B, Bob K_B and K_C, and Carol K_C and K_A. Now you can talk to any subset you want. If you want to send a message so that only Alice can read it, encrypt it with K_C. When Alice receives the message, she decrypts it with K_A and then K_B. If you want to send a message so that only Bob can read it, encrypt it with K_A; so that only Carol can read it, with K_B. If you want to send a message so that both Alice and Bob can read it, encrypt it with K_A and K_C, and so on.

This might not seem exciting, but with 100 operatives it is quite efficient. Individual messages mean a shared key with each operative (100 keys total) and each message. Keys for every possible subset means $2^{100} - 2$ different keys (messages to all operatives and messages to no operatives are excluded). This scheme needs only one encrypted message and 100 different keys. The drawback of this scheme is that you also have to broadcast which subset of operatives can read the message, otherwise each operative would have to try every combination of possible keys looking for the correct one. Even just the names of the intended recipients may be significant. At least for the straightforward implementation of this, everyone gets a really large amount of key data.

There are other techniques for message broadcasting, some of which avoid the previous problem. These are discussed in Section 22.7.

TABLE 3.3
Three-Key Message Encryption

Encrypted with Keys:	Must be Decrypted with Keys:
K_A	K_B and K_C
K_B	K_A and K_C
K_C	K_A and K_B
K_A and K_B	K_C
K_A and K_C	K_B
K_B and K_C	K_A

3.6   SECRET SPLITTING

Imagine that you've invented a new, extra gooey, extra sweet, cream filling or a burger sauce that is even more tasteless than your competitors'. This is important; you have to keep it secret. You could tell only your most trusted employees the exact mixture of ingredients, but what if one of them defects to the competition? There goes the secret, and before long every grease palace on the block will be making burgers with sauce as tasteless as yours.

This calls for **secret splitting**. There are ways to take a message and divide it up into pieces [551]. Each piece by itself means nothing, but put them together and the message appears. If the message is the recipe and each employee has a piece, then only together can they make the sauce. If any employee resigns with his single piece of the recipe, his information is useless by itself.

The simplest sharing scheme splits a message between two people. Here's a protocol in which Trent can split a message between Alice and Bob:

(1) Trent generates a random-bit string, R, the same length as the message, M.

(2) Trent XORs M with R to generate S.

$$M \oplus R = S$$

(3) Trent gives R to Alice and S to Bob.

To reconstruct the message, Alice and Bob have only one step to do:

(4) Alice and Bob XOR their pieces together to reconstruct the message:

$$R \oplus S = M$$

This technique, if done properly, is absolutely secure. Each piece, by itself, is absolutely worthless. Essentially, Trent is encrypting the message with a one-time pad and giving the ciphertext to one person and the pad to the other person. Section 1.5 discusses one-time pads; they have perfect security. No amount of computing power can determine the message from one of the pieces.

It is easy to extend this scheme to more people. To split a message among more than two people, XOR more random-bit strings into the mixture. In this example, Trent divides up a message into four pieces:

(1) Trent generates three random-bit strings, R, S, and T, the same length as the message, M.

(2) Trent XORs M with the three strings to generate U:

$$M \oplus R \oplus S \oplus T = U$$

(3) Trent gives R to Alice, S to Bob, T to Carol, and U to Dave.

Alice, Bob, Carol, and Dave, working together, can reconstruct the message:

(4) Alice, Bob, Carol, and Dave get together and compute:

$$R \oplus S \oplus T \oplus U = M$$

This is an adjudicated protocol. Trent has absolute power and can do whatever he wants. He can hand out gibberish and claim that it is a valid piece of the secret; no one will know it until they try to reconstruct the secret. He can hand out a piece to Alice, Bob, Carol, and Dave, and later tell everyone that only Alice, Carol, and Dave are needed to reconstruct the secret, and then fire Bob. But since this is Trent's secret to divide up, this isn't a problem.

However, this protocol has a problem: If any of the pieces gets lost and Trent isn't around, so does the message. If Carol, who has a piece of the sauce recipe, goes to work for the competition and takes her piece with her, the rest of them are out of luck. She can't reproduce the recipe, but neither can Alice, Bob, and Dave working together. Her piece is as critical to the message as every other piece combined. All Alice, Bob, or Dave know is the length of the message—nothing more. This is true because R, S, T, U, and M all have the same length; seeing anyone of them gives the length of M. Remember, M isn't being split in the normal sense of the word; it is being XORed with random values.

3.7 SECRET SHARING

You're setting up a launch program for a nuclear missile. You want to make sure that no single raving lunatic can initiate a launch. You want to make sure that no two raving lunatics can initiate a launch. You want at least three out of five officers to be raving lunatics before you allow a launch.

This is easy to solve. Make a mechanical launch controller. Give each of the five officers a key and require that at least three officers stick their keys in the proper slots before you'll allow them to blow up whomever we're blowing up this week. (If you're really worried, make the slots far apart and require the officers to insert the keys simultaneously—you wouldn't want an officer who steals two keys to be able to vaporize Toledo.)

We can get even more complicated. Maybe the general and two colonels are authorized to launch the missile, but if the general is busy playing golf then five colonels are required to initiate a launch. Make the launch controller so that it requires five keys. Give the general three keys and the colonels one each. The general together with any two colonels can launch the missile; so can the five colonels. However, a general and one colonel cannot; neither can four colonels.

A more complicated sharing scheme, called a **threshold scheme**, can do all of this and more—mathematically. At its simplest level, you can take any message (a secret recipe, launch codes, your laundry list, etc.) and divide it into n pieces, called **shadows** or shares, such that any m of them can be used to reconstruct the message. More precisely, this is called an **(m,n)-threshold scheme**.

With a (3,4)-threshold scheme, Trent can divide his secret sauce recipe among Alice, Bob, Carol, and Dave, such that any three of them can put their shadows together and reconstruct the message. If Carol is on vacation, Alice, Bob, and Dave can do it. If Bob gets run over by a bus, Alice, Carol, and Dave can do it. However, if Bob gets run over by a bus while Carol is on vacation, Alice and Dave can't reconstruct the message by themselves.

General threshold schemes are even more versatile. Any sharing scenario you can imagine can be modeled. You can divide a message among the people in your building so that to reconstruct it, you need seven people from the first floor and five people from the second floor, unless there is someone from the third floor involved, in which case you only need that person and three people from the first floor and two people from the second floor, unless there is someone from the fourth floor involved, in which case you need that person and one person from the third floor, or that person and two people from the first floor and one person from the second floor, unless there is . . . well, you get the idea.

This idea was invented independently by Adi Shamir [1414] and George Blakley [182] and studied extensively by Gus Simmons [1466]. Several different algorithms are discussed in Section 23.2.

Secret Sharing with Cheaters

There are many ways to cheat with a threshold scheme. Here are just a few of them.

Scenario 1: Colonels Alice, Bob, and Carol are in a bunker deep below some isolated field. One day, they get a coded message from the president: "Launch the missiles. We're going to eradicate the last vestiges of neural network research in the country." Alice, Bob, and Carol reveal their shadows, but Carol enters a random number. She's actually a pacifist and doesn't want the missiles launched. Since Carol doesn't enter the correct shadow, the secret they recover is the wrong secret. The missiles stay in their silos. Even worse, no one knows why. Alice and Bob, even if they work together, cannot prove that Carol's shadow is invalid.

Scenario 2: Colonels Alice and Bob are sitting in the bunker with Mallory. Mallory has disguised himself as a colonel and none of the others is the wiser. The same message comes in from the president, and everyone reveals their shadows. "Bwa-ha-ha!" shouts Mallory. "I faked that message from the president. Now I know both of your shadows." He races up the staircase and escapes before anyone can catch him.

Scenario 3: Colonels Alice, Bob, and Carol are sitting in the bunker with Mallory, who is again disguised. (Remember, Mallory doesn't have a valid shadow.) The same message comes in from the president and everyone reveals their shadows. Mallory reveals his shadow only after he has heard the other three. Since only three shadows are needed to reconstruct the secret, he can quickly create a valid shadow and reveals that. Now, not only does he know the secret, but no one realizes that he isn't part of the scheme.

Some protocols that handle these sorts of cheaters are discussed in Section 23.2.

Secret Sharing without Trent

A bank wants its vault to open only if three out of five officers enter their keys. This sounds like a basic (3,5)-threshold scheme, but there's a catch. No one is to know the entire secret. There is no Trent to divide the secret up into five pieces. There are protocols by which the five officers can create a secret and each get a piece, such that none of the officers knows the secret until they all reconstruct it. I'm not going to discuss these protocols in this book; see [756] for details.

Sharing a Secret without Revealing the Shares

These schemes have a problem. When everyone gets together to reconstruct their secret, they reveal their shares. This need not be the case. If the shared secret is a private key (to a digital signature, for example), then n shareholders can each complete a partial signature of the document. After the nth partial signature, the document has been signed with the shared private key and none of the shareholders learns any other shares. The point is that the secret can be reused, and you don't need a trusted processor to handle it. This concept is explored further by Yvo Desmedt and Yair Frankel [483,484].

Verifiable Secret Sharing

Trent gives Alice, Bob, Carol, and Dave each a share or at least he says he does. The only way any of them know if they have a valid share is to try to reconstruct the secret. Maybe Trent sent Bob a bogus share or Bob accidentally received a bad share through communications error. Verifiable secret sharing allows each of them to individually verify that they have a valid share, without having to reconstruct the secret [558,1235].

Secret-Sharing Schemes with Prevention

A secret is divided up among 50 people so that any 10 can get together and reconstruct the secret. That's easy. But, can we implement the same secret-sharing scheme with the added constraint that 20 people can get together and *prevent* the others from reconstructing the secret, no matter how many of them there are? As it turns out, we can [153].

The math is complicated, but the basic idea is that everyone gets two shares: a "yes" share and a "no" share. When it comes time to reconstruct the secret, people submit one of their shares. The actual share they submit depends on whether they wish the secret reconstructed. If there are m or more "yes" shares and fewer than n "no" shares, the secret can be reconstructed. Otherwise, it cannot.

Of course, nothing prevents a sufficient number of "yes" people from going off in a corner without the "no" people (assuming they know who they are) and reconstructing the secret. But in a situation where everyone submits their shares into a central computer, this scheme will work.

Secret Sharing with Disenrollment

You've set up your secret-sharing system and now you want to fire one of your shareholders. You could set up a new scheme without that person, but that's time-consuming. There are methods for coping with this system. They allow a new sharing scheme to be activated instantly once one of the participants becomes untrustworthy [1004].

3.8 CRYPTOGRAPHIC PROTECTION OF DATABASES

The membership database of an organization is a valuable commodity. On the one hand, you want to distribute the database to all members. You want them to communicate with one another, exchange ideas, and invite each other over for cucumber sandwiches. On the other hand, if you distribute the membership database to everyone, copies are bound to fall into the hands of insurance salesmen and other annoying purveyors of junk mail.

Cryptography can ameliorate this problem. We can encrypt the database so that it is easy to extract the address of a single person but hard to extract a mailing list of all the members.

The scheme, from [550,549], is straightforward. Choose a one-way hash function and a symmetric encryption algorithm. Each record of the database has two fields. The index field is the last name of the member, operated on by the one-way hash function. The data field is the full name and address of the member, encrypted using the last name as the key. Unless you know the last name, you can't decrypt the data field.

Searching a specific last name is easy. First, hash the last name and look for the hashed value in the index field of the database. If there is a match, then that last name is in the database. If there are several matches, then there are several people in the database with the last name. Finally, for each matching entry, decrypt the full name and address using the last name as the key.

In [550] the authors use this system to protect a dictionary of 6000 Spanish verbs. They report minimal performance degradation due to the encryption. Additional complications in [549] handle searches on multiple indexes, but the idea is the same. The primary problem with this system is that it's impossible to search for people when you don't know how to spell their name. You can try variant spellings until you find the correct one, but it isn't practical to scan through everyone whose name begins with "Sch" when looking for "Schneier."

This protection isn't perfect. It is possible for a particularly persistent insurance salesperson to reconstruct the membership database through brute-force by trying every possible last name. If he has a telephone database, he can use it as a list of possible last names. This might take a few weeks of dedicated number crunching, but it can be done. It makes his job harder and, in the world of junk mail, "harder" quickly becomes "too expensive."

Another approach, in [185], allows statistics to be compiled on encrypted data.

CHAPTER   4

Intermediate Protocols

4.1 TIMESTAMPING SERVICES

In many situations, people need to certify that a document existed on a certain date. Think about a copyright or patent dispute: The party that produces the earliest copy of the disputed work wins the case. With paper documents, notaries can sign and lawyers can safeguard copies. If a dispute arises, the notary or the lawyer testifies that the letter existed on a certain date.

In the digital world, it's far more complicated. There is no way to examine a digital document for signs of tampering. It can be copied and modified endlessly without anyone being the wiser. It's trivial to change the date stamp on a computer file. No one can look at a digital document and say: "Yes, this document was created before November 4, 1952."

Stuart Haber and W. Scott Stornetta at Bellcore thought about the problem [682, 683,92]. They wanted a digital timestamping protocol with the following properties:

— The data itself must be timestamped, without any regard to the physical medium on which it resides.

— It must be impossible to change a single bit of the document without
   that change being apparent.

— It must be impossible to timestamp a document with a date and time
   different from the present one.

Arbitrated Solution

This protocol uses Trent, who has a trusted timestamping service, and Alice, who wishes to timestamp a document.

(1) Alice transmits a copy of the document to Trent.

(2) Trent records the date and time he received the document and retains a copy of the document for safekeeping.

Now, if anyone calls into question Alice's claim of when the document was created, she just has to call up Trent. He will produce his copy of the document and verify that he received the document on the date and time stamped.

This protocol works, but has some obvious problems. First, there is no privacy. Alice has to give a copy of the document to Trent. Anyone listening in on the communications channel could read it. She could encrypt it, but still the document has to sit in Trent's database. Who knows how secure that database is?

Second, the database itself would have to be huge. And the bandwidth requirements to send large documents to Trent would be unwieldy.

The third problem has to do with the potential errors. An error in transmission, or an electromagnetic bomb detonating somewhere in Trent's central computers, could completely invalidate Alice's claim of a timestamp.

And fourth, there might not be someone as honest as Trent to run the timestamping service. Maybe Alice is using Bob's Timestamp and Taco Stand. There is nothing to stop Alice and Bob from colluding and timestamping a document with any time that they want.

Improved Arbitrated Solution

One-way hash functions and digital signatures can clear up most of these problems easily:

(1) Alice produces a one-way hash of the document.

(2) Alice transmits the hash to Trent.

(3) Trent appends the date and time he received the hash onto the hash and then digitally signs the result.

(4) Trent sends the signed hash with timestamp back to Alice.

This solves every problem but the last. Alice no longer has to worry about revealing the contents of her document; the hash is sufficient. Trent no longer has to store copies of the document (or even of the hash), so the massive storage requirements and security problems are solved (remember, one-way hash functions don't have a key). Alice can immediately examine the signed timestamped hash she receives in step (4), so she will immediately catch any transmission errors. The only problem remaining is that Alice and Trent can still collude to produce any timestamp they want.

Linking Protocol

One way to solve this problem is to link Alice's timestamp with timestamps previously generated by Trent. These timestamps will most probably be generated for people other than Alice. Since the order that Trent receives the different timestamp requests can't be known in advance, Alice's timestamp must have occurred after the previous one. And since the request that came after is linked with Alice's timestamp, then hers must have occurred before. This sandwiches Alice's request in time.

If A is Alice's name, the hash value that Alice wants timestamped is H_n, and the previous time stamp is T_{n-1}, then the protocol is:

(1) Alice sends Trent H_n and A.

(2) Trent sends back to Alice:

$$T_n = S_K(n, A, H_n, t_n, I_{n-1}, H_{n-1}, T_{n-1}, L_n)$$

where L_n consists of the following hashed linking information:

$$L_n = H(I_{n-1}, H_{n-1}, T_{n-1}, L_{n-1})$$

S_K indicates that the message is signed with Trent's private key. Alice's name identifies her as the originator of the request. The parameter n indicates the sequence of the request: This is the nth timestamp Trent has issued. The parameter t_n is the time. The additional information is the identification, original hash, time, and hashed timestamp of the previous document Trent stamped.

(3) After Trent stamps the next document, he sends Alice the identification of the originator of that document: I_{n+1}.

If someone challenges Alice's timestamp, she just contacts the originators of the previous and following documents: I_{n-1} and I_{n+1}. If their documents are called into question, they can get in touch with I_{n-2} and I_{n+2}, and so on. Every person can show that their document was timestamped after the one that came before and before the one that came after.

This protocol makes it very difficult for Alice and Trent to collude and produce a document stamped with a different time than the actual one. Trent cannot forward-date a document for Alice, since that would require knowing in advance what document request came before it. Even if he could fake that, he would have to know what document request came before that, and so on. He cannot back-date a document, because the timestamp must be embedded in the timestamps of the document issued immediately after, and that document has already been issued. The only possible way to break this scheme is to invent a fictitious chain of documents both before and after Alice's document, long enough to exhaust the patience of anyone challenging the timestamp.

Distributed Protocol

People die; timestamps get lost. Many things could happen between the timestamping and the challenge to make it impossible for Alice to get a copy of I_{n-1}'s timestamp. This problem could be alleviated by embedding the previous 10 people's timestamps into Alice's, and then sending Alice the identities of the next 10 people. Alice has a greater chance of finding people who still have their timestamps.

Along a similar line, the following protocol does away with Trent altogether.

(1) Using H_n as input, Alice generates a string of random values using a cryptographically secure pseudo-random-number generator:

$$V_1, V_2, V_3, \ldots V_k$$

(2) Alice interprets each of these values as the identification, I, of another person. She sends H_n to each of these people.

(3) Each of these people attaches the date and time to the hash, signs the result, and sends it back to Alice.

(4) Alice collects and stores all the signatures as the timestamp.

The cryptographically secure pseudo-random-number generator in step (1) prevents Alice from deliberately choosing corrupt Is as verifiers. Even if she makes trivial changes in her document in an attempt to construct a set of corrupt Is, her chances of getting away with this are negligible. The hash function randomizes the Is; Alice cannot force them.

This protocol works because the only way for Alice to fake a timestamp would be to convince all of the k people to cooperate. Since she chose them at random in step (1), the odds against this are very high. The more corrupt society is, the higher a number k should be.

Additionally, there should be some mechanism for dealing with people who can't promptly return the timestamp. Some subset of k is all that would be required for a valid timestamp. The details depend on the implementation.

Further Work

Further improvements to timestamping protocols are presented in [92]. The authors use binary trees to increase the number of timestamps that depend on a given timestamp, reducing even further the possibility that someone could create a chain of fictitious timestamps. They also recommend publishing a hash of the day's timestamps in a public place, such as a newspaper. This serves a function similar to sending the hash to random people in the distributed protocol. In fact, a timestamp has appeared in every Sunday's *New York Times* since 1992.

These timestamping protocols are patented [684,685,686]. A Bellcore spin-off company called Surety Technologies owns the patents and markets a Digital Notary System to support these protocols. In their first version, clients send "certify" requests to a central coordinating server. Following Merkle's technique of using hash functions to build trees [1066], the server builds a tree of hash values whose leaves are all the requests received during a given second, and sends back to each requester the list of hash values hanging off the path from its leaf to the root of the tree. The client software stores this locally, and can issue a Digital Notary "certificate" for any file that has been certified. The sequence of roots of these trees comprises the "Universal Validation Record" that will be available electronically at multiple repository sites (and also published on CD-ROM). The client software also includes a "validate" function, allowing the user to test whether a file has been certified in exactly its current form (by querying a repository for the appropriate tree root and comparing it against a hash value appropriately recomputed from the file and its certificate). For information contact Surety Technologies, 1 Main St., Chatham, NJ, 07928; (201) 701-0600; Fax: (201) 701-0601.

4.2   SUBLIMINAL CHANNEL

Alice and Bob have been arrested and are going to prison. He's going to the men's prison and she's going to the women's prison. Walter, the warden, is willing to let Alice and Bob exchange messages, but he won't allow them to be encrypted. Walter expects them to coordinate an escape plan, so he wants to be able to read everything they say.

Walter also hopes to deceive either Alice or Bob. He wants one of them to accept a fraudulent message as a genuine message from the other. Alice and Bob go along with this risk of deception, otherwise they cannot communicate at all, and they have to coordinate their plans. To do this they have to deceive the warden and find a way of communicating secretly. They have to set up a **subliminal channel**, a covert communications channel between them in full view of Walter, even though the messages themselves contain no secret information. Through the exchange of perfectly innocuous signed messages they will pass secret information back and forth and fool Walter, even though Walter is watching all the communications.

An easy subliminal channel might be the number of words in a sentence. An odd number of words in a sentence might correspond to "1," while an even number of words might correspond to "0." So, while you read this seemingly innocent paragraph, I have sent my operatives in the field the message "101." The problem with this technique is that it is mere steganography (see Section 1.2); there is no key and security depends on the secrecy of the algorithm.

Gustavus Simmons invented the concept of a subliminal channel in a conventional digital signature algorithm [1458,1473]. Since the subliminal messages are hidden in what looks like normal digital signatures, this is a form of obfuscation. Walter sees signed innocuous messages pass back and forth, but he completely misses the information being sent over the subliminal channel. In fact, the subliminal-channel signature algorithm is indistinguishable from a normal signature algorithm, at least to Walter. Walter not only cannot read the subliminal message, but he also has no idea that one is even present.

In general the protocol looks like this:

(1) Alice generates an innocuous message, pretty much at random.

(2) Using a secret key shared with Bob, Alice signs the innocuous message in such a way that she hides her subliminal message in the signature. (This is the meat of the subliminal channel protocol; see Section 23.3.)

(3) Alice sends this signed message to Bob via Walter.

(4) Walter reads the innocuous message and checks the signature. Finding nothing amiss, he passes the signed message to Bob.

(5) Bob checks the signature on the innocuous message, confirming that the message came from Alice.

(6) Bob ignores the innocuous message and, using the secret key he shares with Alice, extracts the subliminal message.

What about cheating? Walter doesn't trust anyone and no one trusts him. He can always prevent communication, but he has no way of introducing phony messages. Since he can't generate any valid signatures, Bob will detect his attempt in step (5). And since he does not know the shared key, he can't read the subliminal messages. Even more important, he has no idea that the subliminal messages are there. Signed messages using a digital signature algorithm look no different from signed messages with subliminal messages embedded in the signature.

Cheating between Alice and Bob is more problematic. In some implementations of a subliminal channel, the secret information Bob needs to read the subliminal message is the same information Alice needs to sign the innocuous message. If this is the case, Bob can impersonate Alice. He can sign messages purporting to come from her, and there is nothing Alice can do about it. If she is to send him subliminal messages, she has to trust him not to abuse her private key.

Other subliminal channel implementations don't have this problem. A secret key shared by Alice and Bob allows Alice to send Bob subliminal messages, but it is not the same as Alice's private key and does not allow Bob to sign messages. Alice need not trust Bob not to abuse her private key.

Applications of Subliminal Channel

The most obvious application of the subliminal channel is in a spy network. If everyone sends and receives signed messages, spies will not be noticed sending subliminal messages in signed documents. Of course, the enemy's spies can do the same thing.

Using a subliminal channel, Alice could safely sign a document under threat. She would, when signing the document, imbed the subliminal message, saying, "I am being coerced." Other applications are more subtle. A company can sign documents and embed subliminal messages, allowing them to be tracked throughout the documents' lifespans. The government can "mark" digital cash. A malicious signature program can leak secret information in its signatures. The possibilities are endless.

Subliminal-Free Signatures

Alice and Bob are sending signed messages to each other, negotiating the terms of a contract. They use a digital signature protocol. However, this contract negotiation has been set up as a cover for Alice's and Bob's spying activities. When they use the digital signature algorithm, they don't care about the messages they are signing. They are using a subliminal channel in the signatures to send secret information to each other. The counterespionage service, however, doesn't know that the contract negotiations and the use of signed messages are just cover-ups. This concern has led people to create **subliminal-free signature schemes**. These digital signature schemes cannot be modified to contain a subliminal channel. See [480,481] for details.

4.3   UNDENIABLE DIGITAL SIGNATURES

Normal digital signatures can be copied exactly. Sometimes this property is useful, as in the dissemination of public announcements. Other times it could be a problem. Imagine a digitally signed personal or business letter. If many copies of that document were floating around, each of which could be verified by anyone, this could lead to embarrassment or blackmail. The best solution is a digital signature that can be proven valid, but that the recipient cannot show to a third party without the signer's consent.

The Alice Software Company distributes DEW (Do-Everything-Word). To ensure that their software is virus-free, they include a digital signature with each copy. However, they want only legitimate buyers of the software, not software pirates, to be able to verify the signature. At the same time, if copies of DEW are found to contain a virus, the Alice Software Company should be unable to deny a valid signature.

Undeniable signatures [343,327] are suited to these sorts of tasks. Like a normal digital signature, an undeniable signature depends on the signed document and the signer's private key. But unlike normal digital signatures, an undeniable signature cannot be verified without the signer's consent. Although a better name for these signatures might be something like "nontransferable signatures," the name comes from the fact that if Alice is forced to either acknowledge or deny a signature—perhaps in court—she cannot falsely deny her real signature.

The mathematics are complicated, but the basic idea is simple:

(1) Alice presents Bob with a signature.

(2) Bob generates a random number and sends it to Alice.

(3) Alice does a calculation using the random number and her private key and sends Bob the result. Alice could only do this calculation if the signature is valid.

(4) Bob confirms this.

There is also an additional protocol so that Alice can prove that she did not sign a document, and cannot falsely deny a signature.

Bob can't turn around and convince Carol that Alice's signature is valid, because Carol doesn't know that Bob's numbers are random. He could have easily worked the protocol backwards on paper, without any help from Alice, and then shown Carol the result. Carol can be convinced that Alice's signature is valid only if she completes the protocol with Alice herself. This might not make much sense now, but it will once you see the mathematics in Section 23.4.

This solution isn't perfect. Yvo Desmedt and Moti Yung show that it is possible, in some applications, for Bob to convince Carol that Alice's signature is valid [489].

For instance, Bob buys a legal copy of DEW. He can validate the signature on the software package whenever he wants. Then, Bob convinces Carol that he's a salesman from the Alice Software Company. He sells her a pirated copy of DEW. When Carol tries to validate the signature with Bob, he simultaneously validates the signature with Alice. When Carol sends him the random number, he then sends it on to Alice. When Alice replies, he then sends the reply on to Carol. Carol is convinced that she is a legitimate buyer of the software, even though she isn't. This attack is an instance of the chess grandmaster problem and is discussed in detail in Section 5.2.

Even so, undeniable signatures have a lot of applications; in many instances Alice doesn't want anyone to be able to verify her signature. She might not want personal correspondence to be verifiable by the press, be shown and verified out of context, or even to be verified after things have changed. If she signs a piece of information she sold, she won't want someone who hasn't paid for the information to be able to verify its authenticity. Controlling who verifies her signature is a way for Alice to protect her personal privacy.

A variant of undeniable signatures separates the relation between signer and message from the relation between signer and signature [910]. In one signature scheme, anyone can verify that the signer actually created the signature, but the cooperation of the signer is required to verify that the signature is valid for the message.

A related notion is an **entrusted undeniable signature** [1229]. Imagine that Alice works for Toxins, Inc., and sends incriminating documents to a newspaper using an undeniable signature protocol. Alice can verify her signature to the newspaper reporter, but not to anyone else. However, CEO Bob suspects that Alice is the source of the documents. He demands that Alice run the disavowal protocol to clear her name, and Alice refuses. Bob maintains that the only reason Alice has to refuse is that she is guilty, and fires her.

Entrusted undeniable signatures are like undeniable signatures, except that the disavowal protocol can only be run by Trent. Bob cannot demand that Alice run the disavowal protocol; only Trent can. And if Trent is the court system, then he will only run the protocol to resolve a formal dispute.

4.4 DESIGNATED CONFIRMER SIGNATURES

The Alice Software Company is doing a booming business selling DEW—so good, in fact, that Alice is spending more time verifying undeniable signatures than writing new features.

Alice would like a way to designate one particular person in the company to be in charge of signature verification for the whole company. Alice, or any other programmer, would be able to sign documents with an undeniable protocol. But the verifications would all be handled by Carol.

As it turns out, this is possible with **designated confirmer signatures** [333,1213]. Alice can sign a document such that Bob is convinced the signature is valid, but he cannot convince a third party; at the same time Alice can designate Carol as the future confirmer of her signature. Alice doesn't even need to ask Carol's permission beforehand; she just has to use Carol's public key. And Carol can still verify Alice's signature if Alice is out of town, has left the company, or just upped and died.

Designated confirmer signatures are kind of a compromise between normal digital signatures and undeniable signatures. There are certainly instances where Alice might want to limit who can verify her signature. On the other hand, giving Alice complete control undermines the enforceability of signatures: Alice might refuse to cooperate in either confirming or denying, she might claim the loss of keys for confirming or denying, or she might just be unavailable. Designated confirmer signatures can give Alice the protection of an undeniable signature while not letting her abuse that protection. Alice might even prefer it that way: Designated confirmer signatures can help prevent false applications, protect her if she actually does lose her key, and step in if she is on vacation, in the hospital, or even dead.

This idea has all sorts of possible applications. Carol can set herself up as a notary public. She can publish her public key in some directory somewhere, and people can designate her as a confirmer for their signatures. She can charge a small fee for confirming signatures for the masses and make a nice living.

Carol can be a copyright office, a government agency, or a host of other things. This protocol allows organizations to separate the people who sign documents from the people who help verify signatures.

4.5 PROXY SIGNATURES

Designated confirmer signatures allows a signer to designate someone else to verify his signature. Alice, for instance, needs to go on a business trip to someplace which doesn't have very good computer network access—to the jungles of Africa, for example. Or maybe she is incapacitated after major surgery. She expects to receive some important e-mail, and has instructed her secretary Bob to respond accordingly. How can Alice give Bob the power to sign messages for her, without giving him her private key?

Proxy signatures is a solution [1001]. Alice can give Bob a proxy, such that the following properties hold:

— *Distinguishability*. Proxy signatures are distinguishable from normal signatures by anyone.

— *Unforgeability.* Only the original signer and the designated proxy signer can create a valid proxy signature.

— *Proxy signer's deviation.* A proxy signer cannot create a valid proxy signature not detected as a proxy signature.

— *Verifiability.* From a proxy signature, a verifier can be convinced of the original signer's agreement on the signed message.

— *Identifiability.* An original signer can determine the proxy signer's identity from a proxy signature.

— *Undeniability.* A proxy signer cannot disavow an accepted proxy signature he created.

In some cases, a stronger form of identifiability is required—that anyone can determine the proxy signer's identity from the proxy signature. Proxy signature schemes, based on different digital signature schemes, are in [1001].

4.6 GROUP SIGNATURES

David Chaum introduces this problem in [330]:

> A company has several computers, each connected to the local network. Each department of that company has its own printer (also connected to the network) and only persons of that department are allowed to use their department's printer. Before printing, therefore, the printer must be convinced that the user is working in that department. At the same time, the company wants privacy; the user's name may not be revealed. If, however, someone discovers at the end of the day that a printer has been used too often, the director must be able to discover who misused that printer, and send him a bill.

The solution to this problem is called a **group signature**. Group signatures have the following properties:

— Only members of the group can sign messages.

— The receiver of the signature can verify that it is a valid signature from the group.

— The receiver of the signature cannot determine which member of the group is the signer.

— In the case of a dispute, the signature can be "opened" to reveal the identity of the signer.

Group Signatures with a Trusted Arbitrator

This protocol uses a trusted arbitrator:

(1) Trent generates a large pile of public-key/private-key key pairs and gives every member of the group a different list of unique private keys. No keys on any list are identical. (If there are n members of the group, and each member gets m key pairs, then there are $n*m$ total key pairs.)

(2) Trent publishes the master list of all public keys for the group, in random order. Trent keeps a secret record of which keys belong to whom.

(3) When group members want to sign a document, he chooses a key at random from his personal list.

(4) When someone wants to verify that a signature belongs to the group, he looks on the master list for the corresponding public key and verifies the signature.

(5) In the event of a dispute, Trent knows which public key corresponds to which group member.

The problem with this protocol is that it requires a trusted party. Trent knows everyone's private keys and can forge signatures. Also, m must be long enough to preclude attempts to analyze which keys each member uses.

Chaum [330] lists a number of other protocols, some in which Trent is unable to fake signatures and others in which Trent is not even required. Another protocol [348] not only hides the identity of the signer, but also allows new members to join the group. Yet another protocol is [1230].

4.7 Fail-Stop Digital Signatures

Let's say Eve is a very powerful adversary. She has vast computer networks and rooms full of Cray computers—orders of magnitude more computing power than Alice. All of these computers chug away, day and night, trying to break Alice's private key. Finally—success. Eve can now impersonate Alice, forging her signature on documents at will.

Fail-stop digital signatures, introduced by Birgit Pfitzmann and Michael Waidner [1240], prevent this kind of cheating. If Eve forges Alice's signatures after a brute-force attack, then Alice can prove they are forgeries. If Alice signs a document and then disavows the signature, claiming forgery, a court can verify that it is not a forgery.

The basic idea behind fail-stop signatures is that for every possible public key, many possible private keys work with it. Each of these private keys yields many different possible signatures. However, Alice has only one private key and can compute just one signature. Alice doesn't know any of the other private keys.

Eve wants to break Alice's private key. (Eve could also be Alice, trying to compute a second private key for herself.) She collects signed messages and, using her array of Cray computers, tries to recover Alice's private key. Even if she manages to recover a valid private key, there are so many possible private keys that it is far more likely that she has a different one. The probability of Eve's recovering the proper private key can be made so small as to be negligible.

Now, when Eve forges a signed document using the private key she generated, it will have a different signature than if Alice signs the document herself. When Alice is hauled off to court, she can produce two different signatures for the same message and public key (corresponding to her private key and to the private key Eve created) to prove forgery. On the other hand, if Alice cannot produce the two different signatures, there is no forgery and Alice is still bound by her signature.

This signature scheme protects against Eve breaking Alice's signature scheme by sheer computational power. It does nothing against Mallory's much more likely attack of breaking into Alice's house and stealing her private key or Alice's attack of signing a document and then conveniently losing her private key. To protect against the former, Alice should buy herself a good guard dog; that kind of thing is beyond the scope of cryptography.

Additional theory and applications of fail-stop signatures can be found in [1239, 1241,730,731].

4.8 Computing with Encrypted Data

Alice wants to know the solution to some function $f(x)$, for some particular value of x. Unfortunately, her computer is broken. Bob is willing to compute $f(x)$ for her, but

Alice isn't keen on letting Bob know her *x*. How can Alice let Bob compute $f(x)$ for her without telling him *x*?

This is the general problem of **computing with encrypted data**, also called **hiding information from an oracle**. (Bob is the oracle; he answers questions.) There are ways to do this for certain functions; they are discussed in Section 23.6.

4.9 BIT COMMITMENT

The Amazing Alice, magician extraordinaire, will now perform a mystifying feat of mental prowess. She will guess the card Bob will choose before he chooses it! Watch as Alice writes her prediction on a piece of paper. Marvel as Alice puts that piece of paper in an envelope and seals it shut. Thrill as Alice hands that sealed envelope to a random member of the audience. "Pick a card, Bob, any card." He looks at it and shows it to Alice and the audience. It's the seven of diamonds. Alice now takes the envelope back from the audience. She rips it open. The prediction, written before Bob chose his card, says "seven of diamonds"! Applause.

To make this work, Alice had to switch envelopes at the end of the trick. However, cryptographic protocols can provide a method immune from any sleight of hand. Why is this useful? Here's a more mundane story:

Stockbroker Alice wants to convince investor Bob that her method of picking winning stocks is sound.

> BOB: "Pick five stocks for me. If they are all winners, I'll give you my business."
> ALICE: "If I pick five stocks for you, you could invest in them without paying me. Why don't I show you the stocks I picked last month?"
> BOB: "How do I know you didn't change last month's picks after you knew their outcome? If you tell me your picks now, I'll know that you can't change them. I won't invest in those stocks until after I've purchased your method. Trust me."
> ALICE: "I'd rather show you my picks from last month. I didn't change them. Trust me."

Alice wants to commit to a prediction (i.e., a bit or series of bits) but does not want to reveal her prediction until sometime later. Bob, on the other hand, wants to make sure that Alice cannot change her mind after she has committed to her prediction.

Bit Commitment Using Symmetric Cryptography

This bit-commitment protocol uses symmetric cryptography:

(1) Bob generates a random-bit string, *R*, and sends it to Alice.

$$R$$

(2) Alice creates a message consisting of the bit she wishes to commit to, *b* (it can actually be several bits), and Bob's random string. She encrypts it with some random key, *K*, and sends the result back to Bob.

$$E_K(R,b)$$

That is the commitment portion of the protocol. Bob cannot decrypt the message, so he does not know what the bit is.

When it comes time for Alice to reveal her bit, the protocol continues:

(3) Alice sends Bob the key.

(4) Bob decrypts the message to reveal the bit. He checks his random string to verify the bit's validity.

If the message did not contain Bob's random string, Alice could secretly decrypt the message she handed Bob with a variety of keys until she found one that gave her a bit other than the one she committed to. Since the bit has only two possible values, she is certain to find one after only a few tries. Bob's random string prevents her from using this attack; she has to find a new message that not only has her bit inverted, but also has Bob's random string exactly reproduced. If the encryption algorithm is good, the chance of her finding this is minuscule. Alice cannot change her bit after she commits to it.

Bit Commitment Using One-Way Functions

This protocol uses one-way functions:

(1) Alice generates two random-bit strings, R_1 and R_2.

R_1, R_2

(2) Alice creates a message consisting of her random strings and the bit she wishes to commit to (it can actually be several bits).

(R_1, R_2, b)

(3) Alice computes the one-way function on the message and sends the result, as well as one of the random strings, to Bob.

$H(R_1, R_2, b), R_1$

This transmission from Alice is evidence of commitment. Alice's one-way function in step (3) prevents Bob from inverting the function and determining the bit.

When it comes time for Alice to reveal her bit, the protocol continues:

(4) Alice sends Bob the original message.

(R_1, R_2, b)

(5) Bob computes the one-way function on the message and compares it and R_1, with the value and random string he received in step (3). If they match, the bit is valid.

The benefit of this protocol over the previous one is that Bob does not have to send any messages. Alice sends Bob one message to commit to a bit and another message to reveal the bit.

Bob's random string isn't required because the result of Alice's commitment is a message operated on by a one-way function. Alice cannot cheat and find another message (R_1, R_2', b'), such that $H(R_1, R_2', b') = H(R_1, R_2, b)$. By sending Bob R_1 she is committing to the value of b. If Alice didn't keep R_2 secret, then Bob could compute both $H(R_1, R_2, b)$ and $H(R_1, R_2, b')$ and see which was equal to what he received from Alice.

Bit Commitment Using Pseudo-Random-Sequence Generators

This protocol is even easier [1137]:

(1) Bob generates a random-bit string and sends it to Alice.

R_B

(2) Alice generates a random seed for a pseudo-random-bit generator. Then, for every bit in Bob's random-bit string, she sends Bob either:

(a) the output of the generator if Bob's bit is 0, or

(b) the XOR of output of the generator and her bit, if Bob's bit is 1.

When it comes time for Alice to reveal her bit, the protocol continues:

(3) Alice sends Bob her random seed.

(4) Bob completes step (2) to confirm that Alice was acting fairly.

If Bob's random-bit string is long enough, and the pseudo-random-bit generator is unpredictable, then there is no practical way Alice can cheat.

Blobs

These strings that Alice sends to Bob to commit to a bit are sometimes called **blobs**. A blob is a sequence of bits, although there is no reason in the protocols why it has to be. As Gilles Brassard said, "They could be made out of fairy dust if this were useful" [236]. Blobs have these four properties:

1. Alice can commit to blobs. By committing to a blob, she is committing to a bit.

2. Alice can open any blob she has committed to. When she opens a blob, she can convince Bob of the value of the bit she committed to when she committed to the blob. Thus, she cannot choose to open any blob as either a zero or a one.

3. Bob cannot learn how Alice is able to open any unopened blob she has committed to. This is true even after Alice has opened other blobs.

4. Blobs do not carry any information other than the bit Alice committed to. The blobs themselves, as well as the process by which Alice commits to and opens them, are uncorrelated to anything else that Alice might wish to keep secret from Bob.

4.10   FAIR COIN FLIPS

It's story time with Joe Kilian [831]:

Alice and Bob wanted to flip a fair coin, but had no physical coin to flip. Alice offered a simple way of flipping a fair coin mentally.

"First, you think up a random bit, then I'll think up a random bit. We'll then exclusive-or the two bits together," she suggested.

"But what if one of us doesn't flip a coin at random?" Bob asked.

"It doesn't matter. As long as one of the bits is truly random, the exclusive-or of the bits should be truly random," Alice replied, and after a moment's reflection, Bob agreed.

A short while later, Alice and Bob happened upon a book on artificial intelligence, lying abandoned by the roadside. A good citizen, Alice said, "One of us must pick this book up and find a suitable waste receptacle." Bob agreed, and suggested they use their coin-flipping protocol to determine who would have to throw the book away.

"If the final bit is a 0, then you will pick the book up, and if it is a 1, then I will," said Alice. "What is your bit?"

Bob replied, "1."

"Why, so is mine," said Alice, slyly, "I guess this isn't your lucky day."

Needless to say, this coin-flipping protocol had a serious bug. While it is true that a truly random bit, x, exclusive-ORed with any independently distributed bit, y, will yield a truly random bit, Alice's protocol did not ensure that the two bits were distributed independently. In fact, it is not hard to verify that no mental protocol can allow two infinitely powerful parties to flip a fair coin. Alice and Bob were in trouble until they received a letter from an obscure graduate student in cryptography. The information in the letter was too theoretical to be of any earthly use to anyone, but the envelope the letter came in was extremely handy.

The next time Alice and Bob wished to flip a coin, they played a modified version of the original protocol. First, Bob decided on a bit, but instead of announcing it immediately, he wrote it down on a piece of paper and placed the paper in the envelope. Next, Alice announced her bit. Finally, Alice and Bob took Bob's bit out of the envelope and computed the random bit. This bit was indeed truly random whenever at least one of them played honestly. Alice and Bob had a working protocol, the cryptographer's dream of social relevance was fulfilled, and they all lived happily ever after.

Those envelopes sound a lot like bit-commitment blobs. When Manuel Blum introduced the problem of flipping a fair coin over a modem [194], he solved it using a bit-commitment protocol:

(1) Alice commits to a random bit, using any of the bit-commitment schemes listed in Section 4.9.

(2) Bob tries to guess the bit.

(3) Alice reveals the bit to Bob. Bob wins the flip if he correctly guessed the bit.

In general, we need a protocol with these properties:

— Alice must flip the coin before Bob guesses.
— Alice must not be able to re-flip the coin after hearing Bob's guess.
— Bob must not be able to know how the coin landed before making his guess.

There are several ways in which we can do this.

Coin Flipping Using One-Way Functions

If Alice and Bob can agree on a one-way function, this protocol is simple:

(1) Alice chooses a random number, x. She computes $y = f(x)$, where $f(x)$ is the one-way function.

(2) Alice sends y to Bob.

(3) Bob guesses whether x is even or odd and sends his guess to Alice.

(4) If Bob's guess is correct, the result of the coin flip is heads. If Bob's guess is incorrect, the result of the coin flip is tails. Alice announces the result of the coin flip and sends x to Bob.

(5) Bob confirms that $y = f(x)$.

The security of this protocol rests in the one-way function. If Alice can find x and x', such that x is even and x' is odd, and $y = f(x) = f(x')$, then she can cheat Bob every time. The least significant bit of $f(x)$ must also be uncorrelated with x. If not, Bob can cheat Alice at least some of the time. For example, if $f(x)$ produces even numbers 75 percent of the time if x is even, Bob has an advantage. (Sometimes the least significant bit is not the best one to use in this application, because it can be easier to compute.)

Coin Flipping Using Public-Key Cryptography

This protocol works with either public-key cryptography or symmetric cryptography. The only requirement is that the algorithm commute. That is:

$$D_{K_1}(E_{K_2}(E_{K_1}(M))) = E_{K_2}(M)$$

In general, this property is not true for symmetric algorithms, but it is true for some public-key algorithms (RSA with identical moduli, for example). This is the protocol:

(1) Alice and Bob each generate a public-key/private-key key pair.

(2) Alice generates two messages, one indicating heads and the other indicating tails. These messages should contain some unique random string, so that

she can verify their authenticity later in the protocol. Alice encrypts both messages with her public key and sends them to Bob in a random order.

$$E_A(M_1), E_A(M_2)$$

(3) Bob, who cannot read either message, chooses one at random. (He can sing "eeny meeny miney moe," engage a malicious computer intent on subverting the protocol, or consult the *I Ching*—it doesn't matter.) He encrypts it with his public key and sends it back to Alice.

$$E_B(E_A(M))$$

M is either M_1 or M_2.

(4) Alice, who cannot read the message sent back to her, decrypts it with her private key and then sends it back to Bob.

$$D_A(E_B(E_A(M))) = E_B(M_1) \text{ if } M = M_1, \text{ or}$$
$$E_B(M_2) \text{ if } M = M_2$$

(5) Bob decrypts the message with his private key to reveal the result of the coin flip. He sends the decrypted message to Alice.

$$D_B(E_B(M_1)) = M_1 \text{ or } D_B(E_B(M_2)) = M_2$$

(6) Alice reads the result of the coin flip and verifies that the random string is correct.

(7) Both Alice and Bob reveal their key pairs so that both can verify that the other did not cheat.

This protocol is self-enforcing. Either party can immediately detect cheating by the other, and no trusted third party is required to participate in either the actual protocol or any adjudication after the protocol has been completed. To see how this works, let's try to cheat.

If Alice wanted to cheat and force heads, she has three potential ways of affecting the outcome. First, she could encrypt two "heads" messages in step (2). Bob would discover this when Alice revealed her keys at step (7). Second, she could use some other key to decrypt the message in step (4). This would result in gibberish, which Bob would discover in step (5). Third, she could lie about the validity of the message in step (6). Bob would also discover this in step (7), when Alice could not prove that the message was not valid. Of course, Alice could refuse to participate in the protocol at any step, at which point Alice's attempted deception would be obvious to Bob.

If Bob wanted to cheat and force "tails," his options are just as poor. He could incorrectly encrypt a message at step (3), but Alice would discover this when she looked at the final message at step (6). He could improperly perform step (5), but this would also result in gibberish, which Alice would discover at step (6). He could claim that he could not properly perform step (5) because of some cheating on the part of Alice, but this form of cheating would be discovered at step (7). Finally, he could send a "tails" message to Alice at step (5), regardless of the message he decrypted, but Alice would immediately be able to check the message for authenticity at step (6).

Flipping Coins into a Well

It is interesting to note that in all these protocols, Alice and Bob don't learn the result of the coin flip at the same time. Each protocol has a point where one of the parties (Alice in the first two protocols and Bob in the last one) knows the result of the coin flip but cannot change it. That party can, however, delay disclosing the result to the other party. This is known as **flipping coins into a well**. Imagine a well. Alice is next to the well and Bob is far away. Bob throws the coin and it lands in the well. Alice can now look into the well and see the result, but she cannot reach down to change it. Bob cannot see the result until Alice lets him come close enough to look.

Key Generation Using Coin Flipping

A real application for this protocol is session-key generation. Coin-flipping protocols allow Alice and Bob to generate a random session key such that neither can influence what the session key will be. And assuming that Alice and Bob encrypt their exchanges, this key generation is secure from eavesdropping as well.

4.11 MENTAL POKER

A protocol similar to the public-key fair coin flip protocol allows Alice and Bob to play poker with each other via electronic mail. Instead of Alice making and encrypting two messages, one for heads and one for tails, she makes 52 messages, M_1, $M_2, \ldots, M_{52}$, one for each card in the deck. Bob chooses five messages at random, encrypts them with his public key, and then sends them back to Alice. Alice decrypts the messages and sends them back to Bob, who decrypts them to determine his hand. He then chooses five more messages at random and sends them back to Alice as he received them; she decrypts these and they become her hand. During the game, additional cards can be dealt to either player by repeating the procedure. At the end of the game, Alice and Bob both reveal their cards and key pairs so that each can be assured that the other did not cheat.

Mental Poker with Three Players

Poker is more fun with more players. The basic mental poker protocol can easily be extended to three or more players. In this case, too, the cryptographic algorithm must be commutative.

(1) Alice, Bob, and Carol each generate a public-key/private-key key pair.

(2) Alice generates 52 messages, one for each card in the deck. These messages should contain some unique random string, so that she can verify their authenticity later in the protocol. Alice encrypts all the messages with her public key and sends them to Bob.

$$E_A(M_n)$$

(3) Bob, who cannot read any of the messages, chooses five at random. He encrypts them with his public key and sends them back to Alice.

$$E_B(E_A(M_n))$$

(4)   Bob sends the other 47 messages to Carol.

$$E_A(M_n)$$

(5)   Carol, who cannot read any of the messages, chooses five at random. She encrypts them with her public key and sends them to Alice.

$$E_C(E_A(M_n))$$

(6)   Alice, who cannot read any of the messages sent back to her, decrypts them with her private key and then sends them back to Bob or Carol (depending on where they came from).

$$D_A(E_B(E_A(M_n))) = E_B(M_n)$$
$$D_A(E_C(E_A(M_n))) = E_C(M_n)$$

(7)   Bob and Carol decrypt the messages with their keys to reveal their hands.

$$D_B(E_B(M_n)) = M_n$$
$$D_C(E_C(M_n)) = M_n$$

(8)   Carol chooses five more messages at random from the remaining 42. She sends them to Alice.

$$E_A(M_n)$$

(9)   Alice decrypts the messages with her private key to reveal her hand.

$$D_A(E_A(M_n)) = M_n$$

(10) At the end of the game Alice, Bob, and Carol all reveal their hands and all of their keys so that everyone can make sure that no one has cheated.

Additional cards can be dealt in the same manner. If Bob or Carol wants a card, either one can take the encrypted deck and go through the protocol with Alice. If Alice wants a card, whoever currently has the deck sends her a random card.

Ideally, step (10) would not be necessary. All players shouldn't be required to reveal their hands at the end of the protocol; only those who haven't folded. Since step (10) is part of the protocol designed only to catch cheaters, perhaps there are improvements.

In poker, one is only interested in whether the winner cheated. Everyone else can cheat as much as they want, as long as they still lose. (Actually, this is not really true. Someone can, while losing, collect data on another player's poker style.) So, let's look at cases in which different players win.

If Alice wins, she reveals her hand and her keys. Bob can use Alice's private key to confirm that Alice performed step (2) correctly—that each of the 52 messages corresponded to a different card. Carol can confirm that Alice is not lying about her hand by encrypting the cards with Alice's public key and verifying that they are the same as the encrypted messages she sent to her in step (8).

If either Bob or Carol wins, the winner reveals his hand and keys. Alice can confirm that the cards are legitimate by checking her random strings. She can also confirm that the cards are the ones dealt by encrypting the cards with the winner's public key and verifying that they are the same as the encrypted messages she received in step (3) or (5).

This protocol isn't secure against collusion among malicious players. Alice and another player can effectively gang up on the third and together swindle that player out of everything without raising suspicion. Therefore, it is important to check all the keys and random strings every time the players reveal their hands. And if you're sitting around the virtual table with two people who never reveal their hands whenever one of them is the dealer (Alice, in the previous protocol), stop playing.

Understand that while this is all interesting theory, actually implementing it on a computer is an arduous task. A Sparc implementation with three players on separate workstations takes eight hours to shuffle a deck of cards, let alone play an actual game [513].

Attacks against Poker Protocols

Cryptographers have shown that a small amount of information is leaked by these poker protocols if the RSA public-key algorithm is used [453,573]. Specifically, if the binary representation of the card is a quadratic residue (see Section 11.3), then the encryption of the card is also a quadratic residue. This property can be used to "mark" some cards—all the aces, for example. This does not reveal much about the hands, but in a game such as poker even a tiny bit of information can be an advantage in the long run.

Shafi Goldwasser and Silvio Micali [624] developed a two-player mental-poker protocol that fixes this problem, although its complexity makes it far more theoretical than practical. A general *n*-player poker protocol that eliminates the problem of information leakage was developed in [389].

Other research on poker protocols can be found in [573,1634,389]. A complicated protocol that allows players to not reveal their hands can be found in [390]. Don Coppersmith discusses two ways to cheat at mental poker using the RSA algorithm [370].

Anonymous Key Distribution

While it is unlikely that anyone is going to use this protocol to play poker via modem, Charles Pfleeger discusses a situation in which this type of protocol would come in handy [1244].

Consider the problem of key distribution. If we assume that people cannot generate their own keys (they might have to be of a certain form, or have to be signed by some organization, or something similar), we have to set up a Key Distribution Center to generate and distribute keys. The problem is that we have to figure out some way of distributing keys such that no one, including the server, can figure out who got which key.

This protocol solves the problem:

(1) Alice generates a public-key/private-key key pair. For this protocol, she keeps both keys secret.

(2) The KDC generates a continuous stream of keys.

(3) The KDC encrypts the keys, one by one, with its own public key.

(4)   The KDC transmits the encrypted keys, one by one, onto the network.

(5)   Alice chooses a key at random.

(6)   Alice encrypts the chosen key with her public key.

(7)   Alice waits a while (long enough so the server has no idea which key she has chosen) and sends the double-encrypted key back to the KDC.

(8)   The KDC decrypts the double-encrypted key with its private key, leaving a key encrypted with Alice's public key.

(9)   The server sends the encrypted key back to Alice.

(10) Alice decrypts the key with her private key.

Eve, sitting in the middle of this protocol, has no idea what key Alice chose. She sees a continuous stream of keys go by in step (4). When Alice sends the key back to the server in step (7), it is encrypted with her public key, which is also secret during this protocol. Eve has no way of correlating it with the stream of keys. When the server sends the key back to Alice in step (9), it is also encrypted with Alice's public key. Only when Alice decrypts the key in step (10) is the key revealed.

If you use RSA, this protocol leaks information at the rate of one bit per message. It's the quadratic residues again. If you're going to distribute keys in this manner, make sure this leakage isn't enough to matter. Also, the stream of keys from the KDC must be great enough to preclude a brute-force attack. Of course, if Alice can't trust the KDC, then she shouldn't be getting keys from it. A malicious KDC could presumably keep records of every key it generates. Then, it could search them all to determine which is Alice's.

This protocol also assumes that Alice is going to act fairly. There are things she can do, using RSA, to get more information than she might otherwise. This is not a problem in our scenario, but can be in other circumstances.

4.12   ONE-WAY ACCUMULATORS

Alice is a member of Cabal, Inc. Occasionally she has to meet with other members in dimly lit restaurants and whisper secrets back and forth. The problem is that the restaurants are so dimly lit that she has trouble knowing if the person across the table from her is also a member.

Cabal Inc. can choose from several solutions. Every member can carry a membership list. This has two problems. One, everyone now has to carry a large database, and two, they have to guard that membership list pretty carefully. Alternatively, a trusted secretary could issue digitally signed ID cards. This has the added advantage of allowing outsiders to verify members (for discounts at the local grocery store, for example), but it requires a trusted secretary. Nobody at Cabal, Inc. can be trusted to that degree.

A novel solution is to use something called a **one-way accumulator** [116]. This is sort of like a one-way hash function, except that it is commutative. That is, it is possible to hash the database of members in any order and get the same value. Moreover, it is possible to add members into the hash and get a new hash, again without regard to order.

So, here's what Alice does. She calculates the accumulation of every member's name other than herself. Then she saves that single value along with her own name. Bob, and every other member, does the same. Now, when Alice and Bob meet in the dimly lit restaurant, they simply trade accumulations and names with each other. Alice confirms that Bob's name added to his accumulation is equal to Alice's name added to her accumulation. Bob does the same. Now they both know that the other is a member. And at the same time, neither can figure out the identities of any other member.

Even better, nonmembers can be given the accumulation of everybody. Now Alice can verify her membership to a nonmember (for membership discounts at their local counterspy shop, perhaps) without the nonmember being able to figure out the entire membership list.

New members can be added just by sending around the new names. Unfortunately, the only way to delete a member is to send everyone a new list and have them recompute their accumulations. But Cabal, Inc. only has to do that if a member resigns; dead members can remain on the list. (Oddly enough, this has never been a problem.)

This is a clever idea, and has applications whenever you want the same effect as digital signatures without a centralized signer.

4.13　ALL-OR-NOTHING DISCLOSURE OF SECRETS

Imagine that Alice is a former agent of the former Soviet Union, now unemployed. In order to make money, Alice sells secrets. Anyone who is willing to pay the price can buy a secret. She even has a catalog. All her secrets are listed by number, with tantalizing titles: "Where is Jimmy Hoffa?", "Who is secretly controlling the Trilateral Commission?", "Why does Boris Yeltsin always look like he swallowed a live frog?", and so on.

Alice won't give away two secrets for the price of one or even partial information about any of the secrets. Bob, a potential buyer, doesn't want to pay for random secrets. He also doesn't want to tell Alice which secrets he wants. It's none of Alice's business, and besides, Alice could then add "what secrets Bob is interested in" to her catalog.

A poker protocol won't work in this case, because at the end of the protocol Alice and Bob have to reveal their hands to each other. There are also tricks Bob can do to learn more than one secret.

The solution is called **all-or-nothing disclosure of secrets (ANDOS)** [246] because, as soon as Bob has gained any information whatsoever about one of Alice's secrets, he has wasted his chance to learn anything about any of the other secrets.

There are several ANDOS protocols in the cryptographic literature. Some of them are discussed in Section 23.9.

4.14   KEY ESCROW

This excerpt is from Silvio Micali's introduction to the topic [1084]:

> Currently, court-authorized line tapping is an effective method for securing crim-
> inals to justice. More importantly, in our opinion, it also prevents the further
> spread of crime by deterring the use of ordinary communication networks for
> unlawful purposes. Thus, there is a legitimate concern that widespread use of
> public-key cryptography may be a big boost for criminal and terrorist organiza-
> tions. Indeed, many bills propose that a proper governmental agency, under cir-
> cumstances allowed by law, should be able to obtain the clear text of any
> communication over a public network. At the present time, this requirement
> would translate into coercing citizens to either (1) *using weak cryptosystems*—
> i.e., cryptosystems that the proper authorities (but also everybody else!) could
> crack with a moderate effort—or (2) *surrendering*, a priori, *their secret key* to the
> authority. It is not surprising that such alternatives have legitimately alarmed
> many concerned citizens, generating as reaction the feeling that privacy should
> come before national security and law enforcement.

Key escrow is the heart of the U.S. government's Clipper program and its Escrowed
Encryption Standard. The challenge here is to develop a cryptosystem that both protects individual privacy but at the same time allows for court-authorized wiretaps.

The Escrowed Encryption Standard gets its security from tamperproof hardware.
Each encryption chip has a unique ID number and secret key. This key is split into
two pieces and stored, along with the ID number, by two different escrow agencies.
Every time the chip encrypts a data file, it first encrypts the session key with this
unique secret key. Then it transmits this encrypted session key and its ID number
over the communications channel. When some law enforcement agency wants to
decrypt traffic encrypted with one of these chips, it listens for the ID number, collects the appropriate keys from the escrow agencies, XORs them together, decrypts
the session key, and then uses the session key to decrypt the message traffic. There
are more complications to make this scheme work in the face of cheaters; see Section 24.16 for details. The same thing can be done in software, using public-key
cryptography [77,1579,1580,1581].

Micali calls his idea **fair cryptosystems** [1084,1085]. (The U.S. government report-
edly paid Micali $1,000,000 for the use of his patents [1086,1087] in their Escrowed
Encryption Standard; Banker's Trust then bought Micali's patent.) In these cryptosystems, the private key is broken up into pieces and distributed to different
authorities. Like a secret sharing scheme, the authorities can get together and reconstruct the private key. However, the pieces have the additional property that they
can be individually verified to be correct, without reconstructing the private key.

Alice can create her own private key and give a piece to each of *n* trustees. None of
these trustees can recover Alice's private key. However, each trustee can verify that
his piece is a valid piece of the private key; Alice cannot send one of the trustees a

random-bit string and hope to get away with it. If the courts authorize a wiretap, the relevant law enforcement authorities can serve a court order on the n trustees to surrender their pieces. With all n pieces, the authorities reconstruct the private key and can wiretap Alice's communications lines. On the other hand, Mallory has to corrupt all n trustees in order to be able to reconstruct Alice's key and violate her privacy.

Here's how the protocol works:

(1) Alice creates her private-key/public-key key pair. She splits the private key into several public pieces and private pieces.

(2) Alice sends a public piece and corresponding private piece to each of the trustees. These messages must be encrypted. She also sends the public key to the KDC.

(3) Each trustee, independently, performs a calculation on its public piece and its private piece to confirm that they are correct. Each trustee stores the private piece somewhere secure and sends the public piece to the KDC.

(4) The KDC performs another calculation on the public pieces and the public key. Assuming that everything is correct, it signs the public key and either sends it back to Alice or posts it in a database somewhere.

If the courts order a wiretap, then each of the trustees surrenders his or her piece to the KDC, and the KDC can reconstruct the private key. Before this surrender, neither the KDC nor any individual trustee can reconstruct the private key; all the trustees are required to reconstruct the key.

Any public-key cryptography algorithm can be made fair in this manner. Some particular algorithms are discussed in Section 23.10. Micali's paper [1084,1085] discusses ways to combine this with a threshold scheme, so that a subset of the trustees (e.g., three out of five) is required to reconstruct the private key. He also shows how to combine this with oblivious transfer (see Section 5.5) so that the trustees do not know whose private key is being reconstructed.

Fair cryptosystems aren't perfect. A criminal can exploit the system, using a subliminal channel (see Section 4.2) to embed another secret key into his piece. This way, he can communicate securely with someone else using this subliminal key without having to worry about court-authorized wiretapping. Another protocol, called **failsafe key escrowing**, solves this problem [946,833]. Section 23.10 describes the algorithm and protocol.

The Politics of Key Escrow

Aside from the government's key-escrow plans, several commercial key-escrow proposals are floating around. This leads to the obvious question: What are the advantages of key-escrow for the user?

Well, there really aren't any. The user gains nothing from key escrow that he couldn't provide himself. He can already back up his keys if he wants (see Section 8.8). Key-escrow guarantees that the police can eavesdrop on his conversations or read his data files even though they are encrypted. It guarantees that the NSA can eavesdrop on his international phone calls—without a warrant—even though they are encrypted. Perhaps he will be allowed to use cryptography in countries that now ban it, but that seems to be the only advantage.

Key escrow has considerable disadvantages. The user has to trust the escrow agents' security procedures, as well as the integrity of the people involved. He has to trust the escrow agents not to change their policies, the government not to change its laws, and those with lawful authority to get his keys to do so lawfully and responsibly. Imagine a major terrorist attack in New York; what sorts of limits on the police would be thrown aside in the aftermath?

It is hard to imagine escrowed encryption schemes working as their advocates imagine without some kind of legal pressure. The obvious next step is a ban on the use of non-escrowed encryption. This is probably the only way to make a commercial system pay, and it's certainly the only way to get technologically sophisticated criminals and terrorists to use it. It's not clear how difficult outlawing non-escrowed cryptography will be, or how it will affect cryptography as an academic discipline. How can I research software-oriented cryptography algorithms without having software non-escrowed encryption devices in my possession; will I need a special license?

And there are legal questions. How do escrowed keys affect users' liability, should some encrypted data get out? If the U.S. government is trying to protect the escrow agencies, will there be the implicit assumption that if the secret was compromised by either the user or the escrow agency, then it must have been the user?

What if a major key-escrow service, either government or commercial, had its entire escrowed key database stolen? What if the U.S. government tried to keep this quiet for a while? Clearly, this would have an impact on users' willingness to use key escrow. If it's not voluntary, a couple of scandals like this would increase political pressure to either make it voluntary, or to add complex new regulations to the industry.

Even more dangerous is a scandal where it becomes public that political opponent of the current administration, or some outspoken critic of some intelligence or police agencies has been under surveillance for years. This could raise public sentiment strongly against escrowed encryption.

If signature keys are escrowed as well as encryption keys, there are additional issues. Is it acceptable for the authorities to use signature keys to run operations against suspected criminals? Will the authenticity of signatures based on escrowed keys be accepted in courts? What recourse do users have if the authorities actually do use their signature keys to sign some unfavorable contract, to help out a state-supported industry, or just to steal money?

The globalization of cryptography raises an additional set of questions. Will key-escrow policies be compatible across national borders? Will multi-national corporations have to keep separate escrowed keys in every country to stay in compliance with the various local laws? Without some kind of compatibility, one of the supposed advantages of key-escrow schemes (international use of strong encryption) falls apart.

What if some countries don't accept the security of escrow agencies on faith? How do users do business there? Are their digital contracts upheld by their courts, or is the fact that their signature key is held in escrow in the U.S. going to allow them to claim in Switzerland that someone else could have signed this electronic contract? Or will there be special waivers for people who do business in such countries?

And what about industrial espionage? There is no reason to believe that countries which currently conduct industrial espionage for their important or state-run companies will refrain from doing so on key-escrowed encryption systems. Indeed, since virtually no country is going to allow other countries to oversee its intelligence operations, widespread use of escrowed encryption will probably increase the use of wiretaps.

Even if countries with good civil rights records use key escrow only for the legitimate pursuit of criminals and terrorists, it's certain to be used elsewhere to keep track of dissidents, blackmail political opponents, and so on. Digital communications offer the opportunity to do a much more thorough job of monitoring citizens' actions, opinions, purchases, and associations than is possible in an analog world.

It's not clear how this will affect commercial key escrow, except that 20 years from now, selling Turkey or China a ready-made key-escrow system may look a lot like selling shock batons to South Africa in 1970, or building a chemical plant for Iraq in 1980. Even worse, effortless and untraceable tapping of communications may tempt a number of governments into tracking many of their citizens' communications, even those which haven't generally tried to do so before. And there's no guarantee that liberal democracies will be immune to this temptation.

CHAPTER 5

Advanced Protocols

5.1 ZERO-KNOWLEDGE PROOFS

Here's another story:

ALICE: "I know the password to the Federal Reserve System computer, the ingredients in McDonald's secret sauce, and the contents of Volume 4 of Knuth."

BOB: "No, you don't."

ALICE: "Yes, I do."

BOB: "Do not!"

ALICE: "Do too!"

BOB: "Prove it!"

ALICE: "All right. I'll tell you." She whispers in Bob's ear.

BOB: "That's interesting. Now I know it, too. I'm going to tell *The Washington Post.*"

ALICE: "Oops."

Unfortunately, the usual way for Alice to prove something to Bob is for Alice to tell him. But then he knows it, too. Bob can then tell anyone else he wants to and Alice can do nothing about it. (In the literature, different characters are often used in these protocols. Peggy is usually cast as the prover and Victor is the verifier. These names appear in the upcoming examples, instead of Alice and Bob.)

Using one-way functions, Peggy could perform a **zero-knowledge proof** [626]. This protocol proves to Victor that Peggy does have a piece of information, but it does not give Victor any way to know what the information is.

These proofs take the form of interactive protocols. Victor asks Peggy a series of questions. If Peggy knows the secret, she can answer all the questions correctly. If she does not, she has some chance—50 percent in the following examples—of answering correctly. After 10 or so questions, Victor will be convinced that Peggy knows the secret. Yet none of the questions or answers gives Victor any information about Peggy's information—only about her knowledge of it.

Basic Zero-Knowledge Protocol

Jean-Jacques Quisquater and Louis Guillou explain zero-knowledge with a story about a cave [1281]. The cave, illustrated in Figure 5.1, has a secret. Someone who knows the magic words can open the secret door between C and D. To everyone else, both passages lead to dead ends.

Peggy knows the secret of the cave. She wants to prove her knowledge to Victor, but she doesn't want to reveal the magic words. Here's how she convinces him:

(1) Victor stands at point A.

(2) Peggy walks all the way into the cave, either to point C or point D.

(3) After Peggy has disappeared into the cave, Victor walks to point B.

(4) Victor shouts to Peggy, asking her either to:
    (a) come out of the left passage or
    (b) come out of the right passage.

(5) Peggy complies, using the magic words to open the secret door if she has to.

(6) Peggy and Victor repeat steps (1) through (5) n times.

Assume that Victor has a camcorder and records everything he sees. He records Peggy disappearing into the cave, he records when he shouts out where he wants Peggy to come out from, and he records Peggy coming out. He records all n trials. If he showed this recording to Carol, would she believe that Peggy knew the magic words to open the door? No. What if Peggy and Victor had agreed beforehand what Victor would call out, and Peggy would make sure that she went into that path. Then she could come out where Victor asked her every time, without knowing the magic words. Or maybe they couldn't do that. Peggy would go into one of the passages and Victor would call out a random request. If Victor guessed right, great; if he didn't, they would edit that trial out of the camcorder recording. Either way, Victor

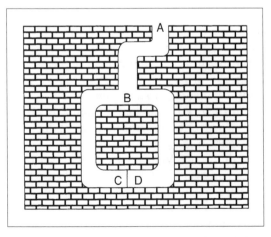

Figure 5.1 *The zero-knowledge cave.*

can get a recording showing exactly the same sequence of events as in a real proof where Peggy knew the magic words.

This shows two things. One, it is impossible for Victor to convince a third party of the proof's validity. And two, it proves that the protocol is zero-knowledge. In the case where Peggy did not know the magic words, Victor will obviously not learn anything from watching the recording. But since there is no way to distinguish a real recording from a faked recording, Victor cannot learn anything from the real proof—it must be zero knowledge.

The technique used in this protocol is called **cut and choose**, because of its similarity to the classic protocol for dividing anything fairly:

(1) Alice cuts the thing in half.

(2) Bob chooses one of the halves for himself.

(3) Alice takes the remaining half.

It is in Alice's best interest to divide fairly in step (1), because Bob will choose whichever half he wants in step (2). Michael Rabin was the first person to use the cut-and-choose technique in cryptography [1282]. The concepts of **interactive protocol** and zero-knowledge were formalized later [626,627].

The cut-and-choose protocol works because there is no way Peggy can repeatedly guess which side Victor will ask her to come out of. If Peggy doesn't know the secret, she can only come out the way she came in. She has a 50 percent chance of guessing which side Victor will ask in each round (sometimes called an **accreditation**) of the protocol, so she has a 50 percent chance of fooling him. The chance of her fooling him in two rounds is 25 percent, and the chance of her fooling him all n times is 1 in 2^n. After 16 rounds, Peggy has a 1 in 65,536 chance of fooling Victor. Victor can safely assume that if all 16 of Peggy's proofs are valid, then she must know the secret words to open the door between points C and D. (The cave analogy isn't perfect. Peggy can simply walk in one side and out the other; there's no need for any cut-and-choose protocol. However, mathematical zero knowledge requires it.)

Assume that Peggy knows some information, and furthermore that the information is the solution to a hard problem. The basic zero-knowledge protocol consists of several rounds.

(1) Peggy uses her information and a random number to transform the hard problem into another hard problem, one that is isomorphic to the original problem. She then uses her information and the random number to solve this new instance of the hard problem.

(2) Peggy commits to the solution of the new instance, using a bit-commitment scheme.

(3) Peggy reveals to Victor the new instance. Victor cannot use this new problem to get any information about the original instance or its solution.

(4) Victor asks Peggy either to:

    (a) prove to him that the old and new instances are isomorphic (i.e., two different solutions to two related problems), or

    (b) open the solution she committed to in step (2) and prove that it is a solution to the new instance.

(5) Peggy complies.

(6) Peggy and Victor repeat steps (1) through (5) n times.

Remember the camcorder in the cave protocol? You can do the same thing here. Victor can make a transcript of the exchange between him and Peggy. He cannot use this transcript to convince Carol, because he can always collude with Peggy to build a simulator that fakes Peggy's knowledge. This argument can be used to prove that the proof is zero-knowledge.

The mathematics behind this type of proof is complicated. The problems and the random transformation must be chosen carefully, so that Victor does not get any information about the solution to the original problem, even after many iterations of the protocol. Not all hard problems can be used for zero-knowledge proofs, but a lot of them can.

Graph Isomorphism

An example might go a long way to explain this concept; this one comes from graph theory [619,622]. A graph is a network of lines connecting different points. If two graphs are identical except for the names of the points, they are called **isomorphic**. For an extremely large graph, finding whether two graphs are isomorphic can take centuries of computer time; it's one of those **NP-complete** problems discussed in Section 11.1.

Assume that Peggy knows the isomorphism between the two graphs, G_1 and G_2. The following protocol will convince Victor of Peggy's knowledge:

(1) Peggy randomly permutes G_1 to produce another graph, H, that is isomorphic to G_1. Because Peggy knows the isomorphism between H and G_1, she also knows the isomorphism between H and G_2. For anyone else, finding an isomorphism between G_1 and H or between G_2 and H is just as hard as finding an isomorphism between G_1 and G_2.

(2) Peggy sends H to Victor.

(3) Victor asks Peggy either to:

    (a) prove that H and G_1 are isomorphic, or

    (b) prove that H and G_2 are isomorphic.

(4) Peggy complies. She either:

    (a) proves that H and G_1 are isomorphic, without proving that H and G_2 are isomorphic, or

    (b) proves that H and G_2 are isomorphic, without proving that H and G_1 are isomorphic.

(5) Peggy and Victor repeat steps (1) through (4) n times.

If Peggy does not know an isomorphism between G_1 and G_2, she cannot create graph H which is isomorphic to both. She can create a graph that is either isomorphic to G_1 or one that is isomorphic to G_2. Like the previous example, she has only a 50 percent chance of guessing which proof Victor will ask her to perform in step (3).

This protocol doesn't give Victor any useful information to aid him in figuring out an isomorphism between G_1 and G_2. Because Peggy generates a new graph H for each round of the protocol, he can get no information no matter how many rounds they go through the protocol. He won't be able to figure out an isomorphism between G_1 and G_2 from Peggy's answers.

In each round, Victor receives a new random permutation of H, along with an isomorphism between H and either G_1 or G_2. Victor could just as well have generated this by himself. Because Victor can create a simulation of the protocol, it can be proven to be zero-knowledge.

Hamiltonian Cycles

A variant of this example was first presented by Manuel Blum [196]. Peggy knows a circular, continuous path along the lines of a graph that passes through each point exactly once. This is called a **Hamiltonian cycle**. Finding a Hamiltonian cycle is another hard problem. Peggy has this piece of information—she probably got it by creating the graph with a certain Hamiltonian cycle—and this is what she wants to convince Victor that she knows.

Peggy knows the Hamiltonian cycle of a graph, G. Victor knows G, but not the Hamiltonian cycle. Peggy wants to prove to Victor that she knows this Hamiltonian cycle without revealing it. This is how she does it:

(1) Peggy randomly permutes G. She moves the points around and changes their labels to make a new graph, H. Since G and H are topologically isomorphic (i.e., the same graph), if she knows the Hamiltonian cycle of G then she can easily find the Hamiltonian cycle of H. If she didn't create H herself, determining the isomorphism between two graphs would be another hard problem; it could also take centuries of computer time. She then encrypts H to get H'. (This has to be a probabilistic encryption of each line in H, that is, an encrypted 0 or an encrypted 1 for each line in H.)

(2) Peggy gives Victor a copy of H'.

(3) Victor asks Peggy either to:
   (a) prove to him that H' is an encryption of an isomorphic copy of G, or
   (b) show him a Hamiltonian cycle for H.

(4) Peggy complies. She either:
   (a) proves that H' is an encryption of an isomorphic copy of G by revealing the permutations and decrypting everything, without showing a Hamiltonian cycle for either G or H, or
   (b) shows a Hamiltonian cycle for H by decrypting only those lines that constitute a Hamiltonian cycle, without proving that G and H are topologically isomorphic.

(5) Peggy and Victor repeat steps (1) through (4) n times.

If Peggy is honest, she can provide either proof in step (4) to Victor. However, if she does not know a Hamiltonian cycle for G, she cannot create an encrypted graph H' which can meet both challenges. The best she can do is to create a graph that is either isomorphic to G or one that has the same number of points and lines and a valid Hamiltonian cycle. While she has a 50 percent chance of guessing which proof Victor will ask her to perform in step (3), Victor can repeat the protocol enough times to convince himself that Peggy knows a Hamiltonian cycle for G.

Parallel Zero-Knowledge Proofs

The basic zero-knowledge protocol involves n exchanges between Peggy and Victor. Why not do them all in parallel:

(1) Peggy uses her information and n random numbers to transform the hard problem into n different isomorphic problems. She then uses her information and the random numbers to solve the n new hard problems.

(2) Peggy commits to the solution of the n new hard problems.

(3) Peggy reveals to Victor the n new hard problems. Victor cannot use these new problems to get any information about the original problems or its solutions.

(4) For each of the n new hard problems, Victor asks Peggy either to:
   (a) prove to him that the old and new problems are isomorphic, or
   (b) open the solution she committed to in step (2) and prove that it is a solution to the new problem.

(5) Peggy complies for each of the n new hard problems.

Unfortunately, it's not that simple. This protocol does not have the same zero-knowledge properties as the previous protocol. In step (4), Victor can choose the challenges as a one-way hash of all the values committed to in the second step, thus making the transcript nonsimulatable. It is still zero-knowledge, but of a different sort. It seems to be secure in practice, but no one knows how to prove it. We do know that in certain circumstances, certain protocols for certain problems can be run in parallel while retaining their zero-knowledge property [247,106,546,616].

Noninteractive Zero-Knowledge Proofs

Carol can't be convinced because the protocol is interactive, and she is not involved in the interaction. To convince Carol, and anyone else who may be interested, we need a noninteractive protocol.

Protocols have been invented for noninteractive zero-knowledge proofs [477, 198,478,197]. These protocols do not require any interaction; Peggy could publish them and thereby prove to anyone who takes the time to check that the proof is valid.

The basic protocol is similar to the parallel zero-knowledge proof, but a one-way hash function takes the place of Victor:

(1) Peggy uses her information and n random numbers to transform the hard problem into n different isomorphic problems. She then uses her information and the random numbers to solve the n new hard problems.

(2) Peggy commits to the solution of the n new hard problems.

(3) Peggy uses all of these commitments together as a single input to a one-way hash function. (After all, the commitments are nothing more than bit strings.) She then saves the first n bits of the output of this one-way hash function.

(4) Peggy takes the n bits generated in step (3). For each ith new hard problem in turn, she takes the ith bit of those n bits and:

   (a) if it is a 0, she proves that the old and new problems are isomorphic, or

   (b) if it is a 1, she opens the solution she committed to in step (2) and proves that it is a solution to the new problem.

(5) Peggy publishes all the commitments from step (2) as well as the solutions in step (4).

(6) Victor or Carol or whoever else is interested, verifies that steps (1) through (5) were executed properly.

This is amazing: Peggy can publish some data that contains no information about her secret, but can be used to convince anyone of the secret's existence. The protocol can also be used for digital signature schemes, if the challenge is set as a one-way hash of both the initial messages and the message to be signed.

This works because the one-way hash function acts as an unbiased random-bit generator. For Peggy to cheat, she has to be able to predict the output of the one-way hash function. (Remember, if she doesn't know the solution to the hard problem, she can do either (a) or (b) of step (4), but not both.) If she somehow knew what the one-way hash function would ask her to do, then she could cheat. However, there is no way for Peggy to force the one-way function to produce certain bits or to guess which bits it will produce. The one-way function is, in effect, Victor's surrogate in the protocol—randomly choosing one of two proofs in step (4).

In a noninteractive protocol, there must be many more iterations of the challenge/reply sequence. Peggy, not Victor, picks the hard problems using random numbers. She can pick different problems, hence different commitment vectors, till the hash function produces something she likes. In an interactive protocol, 10 iterations—a probability of 1 in 2^{10} (1 in 1024) that Peggy can cheat—may be fine. However, that's not enough for noninteractive zero-knowledge proofs. Remember that Mallory can always do either (a) or (b) of step (4). He can try to guess which he will be asked to do, go through steps (1) through (3), and see if he guessed right. If he didn't, he can try again—repeatedly. Making 1024 guesses is easy on a computer. To prevent this brute-force attack, noninteractive protocols need 64 iterations, or even 128 iterations, to be valid.

This is the whole point of using a one-way hash function: Peggy cannot predict the output of the hash function because she cannot predict its input. The commitments which are used as the input are only known after she solves the new problems.

Generalities

Blum proved that any mathematical theorem can be converted into a graph such that the proof of that theorem is equivalent to proving a Hamiltonian cycle in the graph. The general case that any **NP** statement has a zero-knowledge proof, assuming one-way functions and therefore good encryption algorithms, was proved in [620]. Any mathematical proof can be converted into a zero-knowledge proof. Using this technique, a researcher can prove to the world that he knows the proof of a particular theorem without revealing what that solution is. Blum could have published these results without revealing them.

There are also **minimum-disclosure proofs** [590]. In a minimum-disclosure proof, the following properties hold:

1. Peggy cannot cheat Victor. If Peggy does not know the proof, her chances of convincing Victor that she knows the proof are negligible.

2. Victor cannot cheat Peggy. He doesn't get the slightest hint of the proof, apart from the fact that Peggy knows the proof. In particular, Victor cannot demonstrate the proof to anyone else without proving it himself from scratch.

Zero-knowledge proofs have an additional condition:

3. Victor learns nothing from Peggy that he could not learn by himself without Peggy, apart from the fact that Peggy knows the proof.

There is considerable mathematical difference between proofs that are only minimum-disclosure and those that are zero-knowledge. That distinction is beyond the scope of this book, but more sophisticated readers are welcome to peruse the references. The concepts were introduced in [626,619,622]. Further elaboration on their ideas, based on different mathematical assumptions, were developed in [240,319,239].

There are also different kinds of zero-knowledge proofs:

— **Perfect**. There is a simulator that gives transcripts identically distributed to real transcripts (the Hamiltonian cycle and graph isomorphism examples).

— **Statistical**. There is a simulator that gives transcripts identically distributed to real transcripts, except for some constant number of exceptions.

— **Computational**. There is a simulator that gives transcripts indistinguishable from real transcripts.

— **No-use**. A simulator may not exist, but we can prove that Victor will not learn any polynomial amount of information from the proof (the parallel example).

Over the years, extensive work, both theoretical and applied, has been done on minimum-disclosure and zero-knowledge proofs. Mike Burmester and Yvo Desmedt invented **broadcast interactive proofs**, where one prover can broadcast a zero-knowledge interactive proof to a large group of verifiers [280]. Cryptographers proved that *everything* that can be proven with an interactive proof can also be proven with a zero-knowledge interactive proof [753,137].

A good survey article on the topic is [548]. For additional mathematical details, variations, protocols, and applications, consult [590,619,240,319,620,113,241,1528, 660,238,591,617,510,592,214,104,216,832,97,939,622,482,615,618,215,476,71]. *A lot* has been written on this subject.

5.2 ZERO-KNOWLEDGE PROOFS OF IDENTITY

In the real world, we often use physical tokens as proofs of identity: passports, driver's licenses, credit cards, and so on. The token contains something that links it to a person: a picture, usually, or a signature, but it could almost as easily be a thumbprint, a retinal scan, or a dental x-ray. Wouldn't it be nice to do the same thing digitally?

Using zero-knowledge proofs as proofs of identity was first proposed by Uriel Feige, Amos Fiat, and Adi Shamir [566,567]. Alice's private key becomes a function of her "identity." Using a zero-knowledge proof, she proves that she knows her private key and therefore proves her identity. Algorithms for this can be found in Section 23.11.

This idea is quite powerful. It allows a person to prove his identity without any physical token. However, it's not perfect. Here are some abuses.

The Chess Grandmaster Problem

Here's how Alice, who doesn't even know the rules to chess, can defeat a grandmaster. (This is sometimes called the Chess Grandmaster Problem.) She challenges both Gary Kasparov and Anatoly Karpov to a game, at the same time and place, but in separate rooms. She plays white against Kasparov and black against Karpov. Neither grandmaster knows about the other.

Karpov, as white, makes his first move. Alice records the move and walks into the room with Kasparov. Playing white, she makes the same move against Kasparov. Kasparov makes his first move as black. Alice records the move, walks into the room with Karpov, and makes the same move. This continues, until she wins one game and loses the other, or both games end in a draw.

In reality, Kasparov is playing Karpov and Alice is simply acting as the middleman, mimicking the moves of each grandmaster on the other's board. However, if neither Karpov nor Kasparov knows about the other's presence, each will be impressed with Alice's play.

This kind of fraud can be used against zero-knowledge proofs of identity [485,120]. While Alice is proving her identity to Mallory, Mallory can simultaneously prove to Bob that he is Alice.

The Mafia Fraud

When discussing his zero-knowledge identification protocol, Adi Shamir [1424] said: "I could go to a Mafia-owned store a million successive times and they will still not be able to misrepresent themselves as me."

Here's how the Mafia can. Alice is eating at Bob's Diner, a Mafia-owned restaurant. Carol is shopping at Dave's Emporium, an expensive jewelry store. Bob and Carol are both members of the Mafia and are communicating by a secret radio link. Alice and Dave are unaware of the fraud.

At the end of Alice's meal, when she is ready to pay and prove her identity to Bob, Bob signals Carol that the fraud is ready to begin. Carol chooses some expensive diamonds and gets ready to prove her identity to Dave. Now, as Alice proves her identity to Bob, Bob radios Carol and Carol performs the same protocol with Dave. When Dave asks a question in the protocol, Carol radios the question back to Bob, and Bob asks it of Alice. When Alice answers, Bob radios the correct answer to Carol. Actually, Alice is just proving her identity to Dave, and Bob and Carol are simply sitting in the middle of the protocol passing messages back and forth. When the protocol finishes, Alice has proved herself to Dave and has purchased some expensive diamonds (which Carol disappears with).

The Terrorist Fraud

If Alice is willing to collaborate with Carol, they can also defraud Dave. In this protocol, Carol is a well-known terrorist. Alice is helping her enter the country. Dave is the immigration officer. Alice and Carol are connected by a secret radio link.

When Dave asks Carol questions as part of the zero-knowledge protocol, Carol radios them back to Alice, who answers them herself. Carol recites these answers to Dave. In reality, Alice is proving her identity to Dave, with Carol acting as a communications path. When the protocol finishes, Dave thinks that Carol is Alice and lets her into the country. Three days later, Carol shows up at some government building with a minivan full of explosives.

Suggested Solutions

Both the Mafia and Terrorist frauds are possible because the conspirators can communicate via a secret radio. One way to prevent this requires all identifications to take place inside Faraday cages, which block all electromagnetic radiation. In the terrorist example, this assures immigration officer Dave that Carol was not receiving her answers from Alice. In the Mafia example, Bob could simply build a faulty Faraday cage in his restaurant, but jeweler Dave would have a working one; Bob and Carol would not be able to communicate. To solve the Chess Grandmaster Problem, Alice should be forced to sit in her seat until the end of a game.

Thomas Beth and Yvo Desmedt proposed another solution, one using accurate clocks [148]. If each step in the protocol must take place at a given time, no time would be available for the conspirators to communicate. In the Chess Grandmaster Problem, if every move in each game must be made as a clock strikes one minute, then Alice will have no time to run from room to room. In the Mafia story, Bob and Carol will have no time to pass questions and answers to one another.

The Multiple Identity Fraud

There are other possible abuses to zero-knowledge proofs of identity, also discussed in [485,120]. In some implementations, there is no check when an individual registers a public key. Hence, Alice can have several private keys and, therefore, several identities. This can be a great help if she wants to commit tax fraud. Alice can also commit a crime and disappear. First, she creates and publishes several identities. One of them she doesn't use. Then, she uses that identity once and commits a crime so that the person who identifies her is the witness. Then, she immediately stops using that identity. The witness knows the identity of the person who committed the crime, but if Alice never uses that identity again—she's untraceable.

To prevent this, there has to be some mechanism by which each person has only one identity. In [120] the authors suggest the bizarre idea of tamperproof babies who are impossible to clone and contain a unique number as part of their genetic code. They also suggested having each baby apply for an identity at birth. (Actually, the parents would have to do this as the baby would be otherwise occupied.) This could easily be abused; parents could apply for multiple identities at the child's birth. In the end, the uniqueness of an individual is based on trust.

Renting Passports

Alice wants to travel to Zaire, but that government won't give her a visa. Carol offers to rent her identity to Alice. (Bob offered first, but there were some obvious problems.) Carol sells Alice her private key and Alice goes off to Zaire pretending to be Carol.

Carol has not only been paid for her identity, but now she has a perfect alibi. She commits a crime while Alice is in Zaire. "Carol" has proved her identity in Zaire; how could she commit a crime back home?

Of course, Alice is free to commit crimes as well. She does so either before she leaves or after she returns, near Carol's home. First she identifies herself as Carol (she has Carol's private key, so she can easily do that), then she commits a crime and runs away. The police will come looking for Carol. Carol will claim she rented her identity to Alice, but who would believe such a nonsensical story?

The problem is that Alice isn't really proving her identity; she is proving that she knows a piece of secret information. It is the link between that information and the person it belongs to that is being abused. The tamperproof baby solution would protect against this type of fraud, as would a police state where all citizens would have to prove their identity very frequently (at the end of each day, at each street corner, etc.). Biometric methods—fingerprints, retinal scanning, voiceprints, and so on—may help solve this problem.

Proofs of Membership

Alice wants to prove to Bob that she is a member of some super-secret organization, but she does not want to reveal her identity. This problem is similar but different to proving identity, and has also been studied [887,906,907,1201,1445]. Some solutions are related to the problem of group signatures (see Section 4.6).

5.3 BLIND SIGNATURES

An essential feature of digital signature protocols is that the signer knows what he is signing. This is a good idea, except when we want the reverse.

We might want people to sign documents without ever seeing their contents. There are ways that a signer can *almost*, but not exactly, know what he is signing. But first things first.

Completely Blind Signatures

Bob is a notary public. Alice wants him to sign a document, but does not want him to have any idea what he is signing. Bob doesn't care what the document says; he is just certifying that he notarized it at a certain time. He is willing to go along with this.

> (1) Alice takes the document and multiplies it by a random value. This random value is called a **blinding factor**.
>
> (2) Alice sends the blinded document to Bob.
>
> (3) Bob signs the blinded document.
>
> (4) Alice divides out the blinding factor, leaving the original document signed by Bob.

This protocol only works if the signature function and multiplication are commutative. If they are not, there are other ways to modify the document other than by multiplying. Some relevant algorithms appear in Section 23.12. For now, assume that the operation is multiplication and all the math works.

Can Bob cheat? Can he collect any information about the document that he is signing? If the blinding factor is truly random and makes the blinded document truly random, he cannot. The blinded document Bob signs in step (2) looks nothing like the document Alice began with. The blinded document with Bob's signature on it in step (3) looks nothing like the signed document at the end of step (4). Even if Bob got his hands on the document, with his signature, after completing the protocol, he cannot prove (to himself or to anyone else) that he signed it in that particular protocol. He knows that his signature is valid. He can, like anyone else, verify his signature. However, there is no way for him to correlate any information he received during the signing protocol with the signed document. If he signed a million documents using this protocol, he would have no way of knowing in which instance he signed which document.

The properties of completely blind signatures are:

> 1. Bob's signature on the document is valid. The signature is a proof that Bob signed the document. It will convince Bob that he signed the document if it is ever shown to him. It also has all of the other properties of digital signatures discussed in Section 2.6.
>
> 2. Bob cannot correlate the signed document with the act of signing the document. Even if he keeps records of every blind signature he makes, he cannot determine when he signed any given document.

Eve, who is in the middle, watching this protocol, has even less information than Bob.

Blind Signatures

With the completely blind signature protocol, Alice can have Bob sign anything: "Bob owes Alice a million dollars," "Bob owes Alice his first-born child," "Bob owes Alice a bag of chocolates." The possibilities are endless. This protocol isn't useful in many applications.

However, there is a way that Bob can know what he is signing, while still maintaining the useful properties of a blind signature. The heart of this protocol is the cut-and-choose technique. Consider this example. Many people enter this country every day, and the Department of Immigration wants to make sure they are not smuggling cocaine. The officials could search everyone, but instead they use a probabilistic solution. They will search one-tenth of the people coming in. One person in ten has his belongings inspected; the other nine get through untouched. Chronic smugglers will get away with their misdeeds most of the time, but they have a 10 percent chance of getting caught. And if the court system is effective, the penalty for getting caught once will more than wipe out the gains from the other nine times.

If the Department of Immigration wants to increase the odds of catching smugglers, they have to search more people. If they want to decrease the odds, they have to search fewer people. By manipulating the probabilities, they control how successful the protocol is in catching smugglers.

The blind signature protocol works in a similar manner. Bob will be given a large pile of different blinded documents. He will **open**, that is examine, all but one and then sign the last.

Think of the blinded document as being in an envelope. The process of blinding the document is putting the document in an envelope and the process of removing the blinding factor is opening the envelope. When the document is in an envelope, nobody can read it. The document is signed by having a piece of carbon paper in the envelope: When the signer signs the envelope, his signature goes through the carbon paper and signs the document as well.

This scenario involves a group of counterintelligence agents. Their identities are secret; not even the counterintelligence agency knows who they are. The agency's director wants to give each agent a signed document stating: "The bearer of this signed document, (insert agent's cover name here), has full diplomatic immunity." Each of the agents has his own list of cover names, so the agency can't just hand out signed documents. The agents do not want to send their cover names to the agency; the enemy might have corrupted the agency's computer. On the other hand, the agency doesn't want to blindly sign any document an agent gives it. A clever agent might substitute a message like: "Agent (name) has retired and collects a million-dollar-a-year pension. Signed, Mr. President." In this case, blind signatures could be useful.

Assume that all the agents have 10 possible cover names, which they have chosen themselves and which no one else knows. Also assume that the agents don't care under which cover name they are going to get diplomatic immunity. Also assume that the agency's computer is the Agency's Large Intelligent Computing Engine, or ALICE, and that our particular agent is the Bogota Operations Branch: BOB.

(1) BOB prepares n documents, each using a different cover name, giving himself diplomatic immunity.

(2) BOB blinds each of these documents with a different blinding factor.

(3) BOB sends the n blinded documents to ALICE.

(4) ALICE chooses $n - 1$ documents at random and asks BOB for the blinding factors for each of those documents.

(5) BOB sends ALICE the appropriate blinding factors.

(6) ALICE opens (i.e., she removes the blinding factor) $n - 1$ documents and makes sure they are correct—and not pension authorizations.

(7) ALICE signs the remaining document and sends it to BOB.

(8) Agent removes the blinding factor and reads his new cover name: "The Crimson Streak." The signed document gives him diplomatic immunity under that name.

This protocol is secure against BOB cheating. For him to cheat, he would have to predict accurately which document ALICE would not examine. The odds of him doing this are 1 in n—not very good. ALICE knows this and feels confident signing a document that she is not able to examine. With this one document, the protocol is the same as the previous completely blinded signature protocol and maintains all of its properties of anonymity.

There is a trick that makes BOB's chance of cheating even smaller. In step (4), ALICE randomly chooses $n/2$ of the documents to challenge, and BOB sends her the appropriate blinding factors in step (5). In step (7), ALICE multiplies together all of the unchallenged documents and signs the mega-document. In step (8), BOB strips off all the blinding factors. ALICE's signature is acceptable only if it is a valid signature of the product of $n/2$ identical documents. To cheat BOB has to be able to guess exactly which subset ALICE will challenge; the odds are much smaller than the odds of guessing which one document ALICE won't challenge.

BOB has another way to cheat. He can generate two different documents, one that ALICE is willing to sign and one that ALICE is not. Then he can find two different blinding factors that transform each document into the same blinded document. That way, if ALICE asks to examine the document, BOB gives her the blinding factor that transforms it into the benign document. If ALICE doesn't ask to see the document and signs it, he uses the blinding factor that transforms it into the malevolent document. While this is theoretically possible, the mathematics of the particular algorithms involved make the odds of BOB's being able to find such a pair negligibly small. In fact, it can be made as small as the odds of Bob being able to produce the signature on an arbitrary message himself. This issue is discussed further in Section 23.12.

Patents

Chaum has patents for several flavors of blind signatures (see Table 5.1).

5.4 IDENTITY-BASED PUBLIC-KEY CRYPTOGRAPHY

Alice wants to send a secure message to Bob. She doesn't want to get his public key from a key server; she doesn't want to verify some trusted third party's signature on his public-key certificate; and she doesn't even want to store Bob's public key on her own computer. She just wants to send him a secure message.

Identity-based cryptosystems, sometimes called Non-Interactive Key Sharing (NIKS) systems, solve this problem [1422]. Bob's public key is based on his name and network address (or telephone number, or physical street address, or whatever). With normal public-key cryptography, Alice needs a signed certificate that associates Bob's public key with his identity. With identity-based cryptography, Bob's public key *is* his identity. This is a really cool idea, and about as ideal as you can get for a mail system: If Alice knows Bob's address, she can send him secure mail. It makes the cryptography about as transparent as possible.

The system is based on Trent issuing private keys to users based on their identity. If Alice's private key is compromised, she has to change some aspect of her identity to get another one. A serious problem is designing a system in such a way that a collusion of dishonest users cannot forge a key.

A lot of work has been done on the mathematics of these sorts of schemes—most of it in Japan—which turn out to be infuriatingly complicated to make secure. Many of the proposed solutions involve Trent choosing a random number for each user—in my opinion this defeats the real point of the system. Some of the algorithms discussed in Chapters 19 and 20 can be identity-based. For details, algorithms, and cryptanalysis, see [191,1422,891,1022,1515,1202,1196,908,692,674,1131,1023, 1516,1536,1544,63,1210,314,313,1545,1539,1543,933,1517,748,1228]. An algorithm that does not rely on any random numbers is [1035]. The system discussed in [1546,1547,1507] is insecure against a chosen-public-key attack; so is the system proposed as NIKS-TAS [1542,1540,1541,993,375,1538]. Honestly, nothing proposed so far is both practical and secure.

TABLE 5.1
Chaum's Blind Signature Patents

U.S. PATENT #	DATE	TITLE
4,759,063	7/19/88	Blind Signature Systems [323]
4,759,064	7/19/88	Blind Unanticipated Signature Systems [324]
4,914,698	3/3/90	One-Show Blind Signature Systems [326]
4,949,380	8/14/90	Returned-Value Blind Signature Systems [328]
4,991,210	2/5/91	Unpredictable Blind Signature Systems [331]

5.5 OBLIVIOUS TRANSFER

Cryptographer Bob is desperately trying to factor a 500-bit number, n. He knows it's the product of five 100-bit numbers, but nothing more. (This is a problem. If he can't recover the key he'll have to work overtime and he'll miss his weekly mental poker game with Alice.)

What do you know? Here comes Alice now:

> "I happen to know one factor of the number," she says, "and I'll sell it to you for $100. That's a dollar a bit." To show she's serious, she uses a bit-commitment scheme and commits to each bit individually.
>
> Bob is interested, but has only $50. Alice is unwilling to lower her price and offers to sell Bob half the bits for half the price. "It'll save you a considerable amount of work," she says.
>
> "But how do I know that your number is actually a factor of n? If you show me the number and let me verify that it is a factor, then I will agree to your terms," says Bob.
>
> They are at an impasse. Alice cannot convince Bob that her number is a factor of n without revealing it, and Bob is unwilling to buy 50 bits of a number that could very well be worthless.

This story, stolen from Joe Kilian [831], introduces the concept of **oblivious transfer**. Alice transmits a group of messages to Bob. Bob receives some subset of those messages, but Alice has no idea which ones he receives. This doesn't completely solve the problem, however. After Bob has received a random half of the bits, Alice has to convince him that the bits she sent are part of a factor of n, using a zero-knowledge proof.

In the following protocol, Alice will send Bob one of two messages. Bob will receive one, and Alice will not know which.

(1) Alice generates two public-key/private-key key pairs, or four keys in all. She sends both public keys to Bob.

(2) Bob chooses a key in a symmetric algorithm (DES, for example). He chooses one of Alice's public keys and encrypts his DES key with it. He sends the encrypted key to Alice without telling her which of her public keys he used to encrypt it.

(3) Alice decrypts Bob's key twice, once with each of her private keys. In one of the cases, she uses the correct key and successfully decrypts Bob's DES key. In the other case, she uses the wrong key and only manages to generate a meaningless pile of bits that nonetheless look like a random DES key. Since she does not know the correct plaintext, she has no idea which is which.

(4) Alice encrypts both of her messages, each with a different one of the DES keys she generated in the previous step (one real and one meaningless) and sends both of them to Bob.

(5) Bob gets one of Alice's messages encrypted with the proper DES key and the other one encrypted with the gibberish DES key. When Bob decrypts

each of them with his DES key, he can read one of them; the other just looks like gibberish to him.

Bob now has one of the two messages from Alice and Alice does not know which one he was able to read successfully. Unfortunately, if the protocol stopped here it would be possible for Alice to cheat. Another step is necessary.

(6) After the protocol is complete and both possible results of the transfer are known, Alice must give Bob her private keys so that he can verify that she did not cheat. After all, she could have encrypted the same message with both keys in step (4).

At this point, of course, Bob can figure out the second message.

The protocol is secure against an attack by Alice because she has no way of knowing which of the two DES keys is the real one. She encrypts them both, but Bob only successfully recovers one of them—until step (6). It is secure against an attack by Bob because, before step (6), he cannot get Alice's private keys to determine the DES key that the other message was encrypted in. This may still seem like nothing more than a more complicated way to flip coins over a modem, but it has extensive implications when used in more complicated protocols.

Of course, nothing stops Alice from sending Bob two completely useless messages: "Nyah Nyah" and "You sucker." This protocol guarantees that Alice sends Bob one of two messages; it does nothing to ensure that Bob wants to receive either of them.

Other oblivious transfer protocols are found in the literature. Some of them are noninteractive, meaning that Alice can publish her two messages and Bob can learn only one of them. He can do this on his own; he doesn't have to communicate with Alice [105].

No one really cares about being able to do oblivious transfer in practice, but the notion is an important building block for other protocols. Although there are many types of oblivious transfer—I have two secrets and you get one; I have n secrets and you get one; I have one secret which you get with probability $1/2$; and so on—they are all equivalent [245,391,395].

5.6 OBLIVIOUS SIGNATURES

Honestly, I can't think of a good use for these, but there are two kinds [346]:

1. Alice has n different messages. Bob can choose one of the n messages for Alice to sign, and Alice will have no way of knowing which one she signed.
2. Alice has one message. Bob can choose one of n keys for Alice to use in signing the message, and Alice will have no way of knowing which key she used.

It's a neat idea; I'm sure it has a use somewhere.

5.7 SIMULTANEOUS CONTRACT SIGNING

Contract Signing with an Arbitrator

Alice and Bob want to enter into a contract. They've agreed on the wording, but neither wishes to sign unless the other signs as well. Face to face, this is easy: Both sign together. Over a distance, they could use an arbitrator.

(1) Alice signs a copy of the contract and sends it to Trent.

(2) Bob signs a copy of the contract and sends it to Trent.

(3) Trent sends a message to both Alice and Bob indicating that the other has signed the contract.

(4) Alice signs two copies of the contract and sends them to Bob.

(5) Bob signs both copies of the contract, keeps one for himself, and sends the other to Alice.

(6) Alice and Bob both inform Trent that they each have a copy of the contract signed by both of them.

(7) Trent tears up his two copies of the contract with only one signature each.

This protocol works because Trent prevents either of the parties from cheating. If Bob were to refuse to sign the contract in step (5), Alice could appeal to Trent for a copy of the contract already signed by Bob. If Alice were to refuse to sign in step (4), Bob could do the same. When Trent indicates that he received both contracts in step (3), both Alice and Bob know that the other is bound by the contract. If Trent does not receive both contracts in steps (1) and (2), he tears up the one he received and neither party is bound.

Simultaneous Contract Signing without an Arbitrator (Face-to-Face)

If Alice and Bob were sitting face-to-face, they could sign the contract this way [1244]:

(1) Alice signs the first letter of her name and passes the contract to Bob.

(2) Bob signs the first letter of his name and passes the contract to Alice.

(3) Alice signs the second letter of her name and passes the contract to Bob.

(4) Bob signs the second letter of his name and passes the contract to Alice.

(5) This continues until both Alice and Bob have signed their entire names.

If you ignore the obvious problem with this protocol (Alice has a longer name than Bob), it works just fine. After signing only one letter, Alice knows that no judge will bind her to the terms of the contract. But the letter is an act of good faith, and Bob responds with a similar act of good faith.

After each party has signed several letters, a judge could probably be convinced that both parties had signed the contract. The details are murky, though. Surely they are not bound after only the first letter; just as surely they are bound after they sign their entire names. At what point in the protocol do they become bound? After signing one-half of their names? Two-thirds of their names? Three-quarters?

Since neither Alice nor Bob is certain of the exact point at which she or he is bound, each has at least some fear that she or he is bound throughout the protocol. At no point can Bob say: "You signed four letters and I only signed three. You are bound but I am not." Bob has no reason not to continue with the protocol. Furthermore, the longer they continue, the greater the probability that a judge will rule that they are bound. Again, there is no reason not to continue with the protocol. After all, they both wanted to sign the contract; they just didn't want to sign before the other one.

Simultaneous Contract Signing without an Arbitrator (Not Face-to-Face)

This protocol uses the same sort of uncertainty [138]. Alice and Bob alternate taking baby steps toward signing until both have signed.

In the protocol, Alice and Bob exchange a series of signed messages of the form: "I agree that with probability p, I am bound by this contract."

The recipient of this message can take it to a judge and, with probability p, the judge will consider the contract to be signed.

(1) Alice and Bob agree on a date by which the signing protocol should be completed.

(2) Alice and Bob decide on a probability difference that they are willing to live with. For example, Alice might decide that she is not willing to be bound with a greater probability than 2 percent over Bob's probability. Call Alice's difference a; call Bob's difference b.

(3) Alice sends Bob a signed message with $p = a$.

(4) Bob sends Alice a signed message with $p = a + b$.

(5) Let p be the probability of the message Alice received in the previous step from Bob. Alice sends Bob a signed message with $p' = p + a$ or 1, whichever is smaller.

(6) Let p be the probability of the message Bob received in the previous step from Alice. Bob sends Alice a signed message with $p' = p + b$ or 1, whichever is smaller.

(7) Alice and Bob continue alternating steps (5) and (6) until both have received messages with $p = 1$ or until the date agreed to in step (1) has passed.

As the protocol proceeds, both Alice and Bob agree to be bound to the contract with a greater and greater probability. For example, Alice might define her a as 2 percent and Bob might define his b as 1 percent. (It would be nice if they had chosen larger increments; we will be here for a while.) Alice's first message might state that she is bound with 2 percent probability. Bob might respond that he is bound with 3 percent probability. Alice's next message might state that she is bound with 5 percent probability and so on, until both are bound with 100 percent probability.

If both Alice and Bob complete the protocol by the completion date, all is well. Otherwise, either party can take the contract to the judge, along with the other party's last signed message. The judge then randomly chooses a value between 0 and 1 before seeing the contract. If the value is less than the probability the other party signed, then both parties are bound. If the value is greater than the probability, then both parties are not bound. (The judge then saves the value, in case he has to rule on another matter regarding the same contract.) This is what is meant by being bound to the contract with probability p.

That's the basic protocol, but it can have more complications. The judge can rule in the absence of one of the parties. The judge's ruling either binds both or neither party; in no situation is one party bound and the other one not. Furthermore, as long as one party is willing to have a slightly higher probability of being bound than the other (no matter how small), the protocol will terminate.

Simultaneous Contract Signing without an Arbitrator (Using Cryptography)

This cryptographic protocol uses the same baby-step approach [529]. DES is used in the description, although any symmetric algorithm will do.

(1) Both Alice and Bob randomly select $2n$ DES keys, grouped in pairs. The pairs are nothing special; they are just grouped that way for the protocol.

(2) Both Alice and Bob generate n pairs of messages, L_i and R_i: "This is the left half of my ith signature" and "This is the right half of my ith signature," for example. The identifier, i, runs from 1 to n. Each message will probably also include a digital signature of the contract and a timestamp. The contract is considered signed if the other party can produce both halves, L_i and R_i, of a single signature pair.

(3) Both Alice and Bob encrypt their message pairs in each of the DES key pairs, the left message with the left key in the pair and the right message with the right key in the pair.

(4) Alice and Bob send each other their pile of $2n$ encrypted messages, making clear which messages are which halves of which pairs.

(5) Alice and Bob send each other every key pair using the oblivious transfer protocol for each pair. That is, Alice sends Bob either the key used to encrypt the left message or the key used to encrypt the right message, independently, for each of the n pairs. Bob does the same. They can either alternate sending halves or one can send 100 and then the other—it doesn't matter. Now both Alice and Bob have one key in each key pair, but neither knows which halves the other one has.

(6) Both Alice and Bob decrypt the message halves that they can, using the keys they received. They make sure that the decrypted messages are valid.

(7) Alice and Bob send each other the first bits of all $2n$ DES keys.

(8) Alice and Bob repeat step (7) for the second bits of all $2n$ DES keys, the third bits, and so on, until all the bits of all the DES keys have been transferred.

(9) Alice and Bob decrypt the remaining halves of the message pairs and the contract is signed.

(10) Alice and Bob exchange the private keys used during the oblivious transfer protocol in step (5) and each verifies that the other did not cheat.

Why do Alice and Bob have to go through all this work? Let's assume Alice wants to cheat and see what happens. In steps (4) and (5), Alice could disrupt the protocol by sending Bob nonsense bit strings. Bob would catch this in step (6), when he tried to decrypt whatever half he received. Bob could then stop safely, before Alice could decrypt any of Bob's message pairs.

If Alice were very clever, she could only disrupt half the protocol. She could send one half of each pair correctly, but send a gibberish string for the other half. Bob has only a 50 percent chance of receiving the correct half, so half the time Alice could cheat. However, this only works if there is one key pair. If there were only two pairs, this sort of deception would succeed 25 percent of the time. That is why n should be large. Alice has to guess correctly the outcome of n oblivious transfer protocols; she has a 1 in 2^n chance of doing this. If $n = 10$, Alice has a 1 in 1024 chance of deceiving Bob.

Alice could also send Bob random bits in step (8). Perhaps Bob won't know that she is sending him random bits until he receives the whole key and tries to decrypt the message halves. But again, Bob has probability on his side. He has already received half of the keys, and Alice does not know which half. If n is large enough, Alice is sure to send him a nonsense bit to a key he has already received and he will know immediately that she is trying to deceive him.

Maybe Alice will just go along with step (8) until she has enough bits of the keys to mount a brute-force attack and then stop transmitting bits. DES has a 56-bit-long key. If she receives 40 of the 56 bits, she only has to try 2^{16}, or 65,536, keys in order to read the message—a task certainly within the realm of a computer's capabilities. But Bob will have exactly the same number of bits of her keys (or, at worst, one bit less), so he can do the same thing. Alice has no real choice but to continue the protocol.

The basic point is that Alice has to play fairly, because the odds of fooling Bob are just too small. At the end of the protocol, both parties have n signed message pairs, any one of which is sufficient for a valid signature.

There is one way Alice can cheat; she can send Bob identical messages in Step (5). Bob can't detect this until after the protocol is finished, but he can use a transcript of the protocol to convince a judge of Alice's duplicity.

There are two weaknesses with protocols of this type [138]. First, it's a problem if one of the parties has significantly more computing power than the other. If, for example, Alice can mount a brute-force attack faster than Bob can, then she can stop sending bits early in step (8), and figure out Bob's keys herself. Bob, who cannot do the same in a reasonable amount of time, will not be happy.

Second, it's a problem if one of the parties stops the protocol early. If Alice abruptly stops the protocol, both face similar computational efforts, but Bob does not have any real legal recourse. If, for example, the contract specifies that she do something in a week, and Alice terminates the protocol at a point when Bob would have to spend a year's worth of computing power before she is really committed, that's a problem. The real difficulty here is the lack of a near-term deadline by which the process cleanly terminates with either both or neither party bound.

These problems also apply to the protocols in Sections 5.8 and 5.9.

5.8 DIGITAL CERTIFIED MAIL

The same simultaneous oblivious transfer protocol used for contract signing works, with some modifications, for computer certified mail [529]. Suppose Alice wants to send a message to Bob, but she does not want him to read it without signing a receipt. Surly postal workers handle this process in real life, but the same thing can be done with cryptography. Whitfield Diffie first discussed this problem in [490].

At first glance, the simultaneous contract-signing protocol can do this. Alice simply encrypts her message with a DES key. Her half of the protocol can be something like: "This is the left half of the DES key: 32f5," and Bob's half can be something like: "This is the left half of my receipt." Everything else stays the same.

To see why this won't work, remember that the protocol hinges on the fact that the oblivious transfer in step (5) keeps both parties honest. Both of them know that they sent the other party a valid half, but neither knows which. They don't cheat in step (8) because the odds of getting away with it are miniscule. If Alice is sending Bob not a message but half of a DES key, Bob can't check the validity of the DES key in step (6). Alice can still check the validity of Bob's receipt, so Bob is still forced to be honest. Alice can freely send Bob some garbage DES key, and he won't know the difference until she has a valid receipt. Tough luck, Bob.

Getting around this problem requires some adjustment of the protocol:

(1) Alice encrypts her message using a random DES key, and sends the message to Bob.

(2) Alice generates n pairs of DES keys. The first key of each pair is generated at random; the second key of each pair is the XOR of the first key and the message encryption key.

(3) Alice encrypts a dummy message with each of her $2n$ keys.

(4) Alice sends the whole pile of encrypted messages to Bob, making sure he knows which messages are which halves of which pairs.

(5) Bob generates n pairs of random DES keys.

(6) Bob generates a pair of messages that indicates a valid receipt. "This is the left half of my receipt" and "this is the right half of my receipt" are good candidates, with the addition of some kind of random-bit string. He makes n receipt pairs, each numbered. As with the previous protocol, the receipt

is considered valid if Alice can produce both halves of a receipt (with the same number) and all of her encryption keys.

(7) Bob encrypts each of his message pairs with DES key pairs, the ith message pair with the ith key pair, the left message with the left key in the pair, and the right message with the right key in the pair.

(8) Bob sends his pile of message pairs to Alice, making sure that Alice knows which messages are which halves of which pairs.

(9) Alice and Bob send each other every key pair using the oblivious transfer protocol. That is, Alice sends Bob either the key used to encrypt the left message or the key used to encrypt the right message, for each of the n pairs. Bob does the same. They can either alternate sending halves or one can send n and then the other—it doesn't matter. Now both Alice and Bob have one key in each key pair, but neither knows which halves the other has.

(10) Both Alice and Bob decrypt the halves they can and make sure that the decrypted messages are valid.

(11) Alice and Bob send each other the first bits of all $2n$ DES keys. (If they are worried about Eve being able to read these mail messages, then they should encrypt their transmissions to each other.)

(12) Alice and Bob repeat step (11) for the second bits of all $2n$ DES keys, the third bits, and so on, until all the bits of all the DES keys have been transferred.

(13) Alice and Bob decrypt the remaining halves of the message pairs. Alice has a valid receipt from Bob, and Bob can XOR any key pair to get the original message encryption key.

(14) Alice and Bob exchange the private keys used during the oblivious transfer protocol and each verifies that the other did not cheat.

Steps (5) through (8) for Bob, and steps (9) through (12) for both Alice and Bob, are the same as the contract-signing protocol. The twist is all of Alice's dummy messages. They give Bob some way of checking the validity of her oblivious transfer in step (10), which forces her to stay honest during steps (11) through (13). And, as with the simultaneous contract-signing protocol, both a left and a right half of one of Alice's message pairs are required to complete the protocol.

5.9 SIMULTANEOUS EXCHANGE OF SECRETS

Alice knows secret A; Bob knows secret B. Alice is willing to tell Bob A, if Bob tells her B. Bob is willing to tell Alice B, if Alice tells him A. This protocol, observed in a schoolyard, does not work:

(1) Alice: "I'll tell if you tell me first."
(2) Bob: "I'll tell if you tell me first."

(3) Alice: "No, you first."

(4) Bob: "Oh, all right." Bob whispers.

(5) Alice: "Ha! I won't tell you."

(6) Bob: "That's not fair."

Cryptography can make it fair. The previous two protocols are implementations of this more general protocol, one that lets Alice and Bob exchange secrets simultaneously [529]. Rather than repeat the whole protocol, I'll sketch the modifications to the certified mail protocol.

Alice performs steps (1) through (4) using A as the message. Bob goes through similar steps using B as his message. Alice and Bob perform the oblivious transfer in step (9), decrypt the halves they can in step (10), and go through the iterations in steps (11) and (12). If they are concerned about Eve, they should encrypt their messages. Finally, both Alice and Bob decrypt the remaining halves of the message pairs and XOR any key pair to get the original message encryption key.

This protocol allows Alice and Bob to exchange secrets simultaneously, but says nothing about the quality of the secrets exchanged. Alice could promise Bob the solution to the Minotaur's labyrinth, but actually send him a map of Boston's subway system. Bob will get whatever secret Alice sends him. Other protocols are [1286,195,991,1524,705,753,259,358,415].

CHAPTER 6

Esoteric Protocols

6.1 SECURE ELECTIONS

Computerized voting will never be used for general elections unless there is a protocol that both maintains individual privacy and prevents cheating. The ideal protocol has, at the very least, these six requirements:

1. Only authorized voters can vote.
2. No one can vote more than once.
3. No one can determine for whom anyone else voted.
4. No one can duplicate anyone else's vote. (This turns out to be the hardest requirement.)
5. No one can change anyone else's vote without being discovered.
6. Every voter can make sure that his vote has been taken into account in the final tabulation.

Additionally, some voting schemes may have the following requirement:

7. Everyone knows who voted and who didn't.

Before describing the complicated voting protocols with these characteristics, let's look at some simpler protocols.

Simplistic Voting Protocol #1

(1) Each voter encrypts his vote with the public key of a Central Tabulating Facility (CTF).
(2) Each voter sends his vote in to the CTF.
(3) The CTF decrypts the votes, tabulates them, and makes the results public.

This protocol is rife with problems. The CTF has no idea where the votes are from, so it doesn't even know if the votes are coming from eligible voters. It has no idea if eligible voters are voting more than once. On the plus side, no one can change anyone else's vote; but no one would bother trying to modify someone else's vote when it is far easier to vote repeatedly for the result of your choice.

Simplistic Voting Protocol #2

(1) Each voter signs his vote with his private key.

(2) Each voter encrypts his signed vote with the CTF's public key.

(3) Each voter sends his vote to a CTF.

(4) The CTF decrypts the votes, checks the signatures, tabulates the votes, and makes the results public.

This protocol satisfies properties one and two: Only authorized voters can vote and no one can vote more than once—the CTF would record votes received in step (3). Each vote is signed with the voter's private key, so the CTF knows who voted, who didn't, and how often each voter voted. If a vote comes in that isn't signed by an eligible voter, or if a second vote comes in signed by a voter who has already voted, the facility ignores it. No one can change anyone else's vote either, even if they intercept it in step (3), because of the digital signature.

The problem with this protocol is that the signature is attached to the vote; the CTF knows who voted for whom. Encrypting the votes with the CTF's public key prevents anyone from eavesdropping on the protocol and figuring out who voted for whom, but you have to trust the CTF completely. It's analogous to having an election judge staring over your shoulder in the voting booth.

These two examples show how difficult it is to achieve the first three requirements of a secure voting protocol, let alone the others.

Voting with Blind Signatures

We need to somehow dissociate the vote from the voter, while still maintaining authentication. The blind signature protocol does just that.

(1) Each voter generates 10 sets of messages, each set containing a valid vote for each possible outcome (e.g., if the vote is a yes or no question, each set contains two votes, one for "yes" and the other for "no"). Each message also contains a randomly generated identification number, large enough to avoid duplicates with other voters.

(2) Each voter individually blinds all of the messages (see Section 5.3) and sends them, with their blinding factors, to the CTF.

(3) The CTF checks its database to make sure the voter has not submitted his blinded votes for signature previously. It opens nine of the sets to check that they are properly formed. Then it individually signs each message in the set. It sends them back to the voter, storing the name of the voter in its database.

(4) The voter unblinds the messages and is left with a set of votes signed by the CTF. (These votes are signed but unencrypted, so the voter can easily see which vote is "yes" and which is "no.")

(5) The voter chooses one of the votes (ah, democracy) and encrypts it with the CTF's public key.

(6) The voter sends his vote in.

(7) The CTF decrypts the votes, checks the signatures, checks its database for a duplicate identification number, saves the serial number, and tabulates the votes. It publishes the results of the election, along with every serial number and its associated vote.

A malicious voter, call him Mallory, cannot cheat this system. The blind signature protocol ensures that his votes are unique. If he tries to send in the same vote twice, the CTF will notice the duplicate serial number in step (7) and throw out the second vote. If he tries to get multiple votes signed in step (2), the CTF will discover this in step (3). Mallory cannot generate his own votes because he doesn't know the facility's private key. He can't intercept and change other people's votes for the same reason.

The cut-and-choose protocol in step (3) is to ensure that the votes are unique. Without that step, Mallory could create a set of votes that are the same except for the identification number, and have them all validated.

A malicious CTF cannot figure out how individuals voted. Because the blind signature protocol prevents the facility from seeing the serial numbers on the votes before they are cast, the CTF cannot link the blinded vote it signed with the vote eventually cast. Publishing a list of serial numbers and their associated votes allows voters to confirm that their vote was tabulated correctly.

There are still problems. If step (6) is not anonymous and the CTF can record who sent in which vote, then it can figure out who voted for whom. However, if it receives votes in a locked ballot box and then tabulates them later, it cannot. Also, while the CTF may not be able to link votes to individuals, it can generate a large number of signed, valid votes and cheat by submitting those itself. And if Alice discovers that the CTF changed her vote, she has no way to prove it. A similar protocol, which tries to correct these problems, is [1195,1370].

Voting with Two Central Facilities

One solution is to divide the CTF in two. Neither party would have the power to cheat on its own.

The following protocol uses a Central Legitimization Agency (CLA) to certify voters and a separate CTF to count votes [1373].

(1) Each voter sends a message to the CLA asking for a validation number.

(2) The CLA sends the voter back a random validation number. The CLA maintains a list of validation numbers. The CLA also keeps a list of the validation numbers' recipients, in case someone tries to vote twice.

(3) The CLA sends the list of validation numbers to the CTF.

(4) Each voter chooses a random identification number. He creates a message with that number, the validation number he received from the CLA, and his vote. He sends this message to the CTF.

(5) The CTF checks the validation number against the list it received from the CLA in step (3). If the validation number is there, the CTF crosses it off (to prevent someone from voting twice). The CTF adds the identification number to the list of people who voted for a particular candidate and adds one to the tally.

(6) After all votes have been received, the CTF publishes the outcome, as well as the lists of identification numbers and for whom their owners voted.

Like the previous protocol, each voter can look at the lists of identification numbers and find his own. This gives him proof that his vote was counted. Of course, all messages passing among the parties in the protocol should be encrypted and signed to prevent someone from impersonating someone else or intercepting transmissions.

The CTF cannot modify votes because each voter will look for his identification string. If a voter doesn't find his identification string, or finds his identification string in a tally other than the one he voted for, he will immediately know there was foul play. The CTF cannot stuff the ballot box because it is being watched by the CLA. The CLA knows how many voters have been certified and their validation numbers, and will detect any modifications.

Mallory, who is not an eligible voter, can try to cheat by guessing a valid validation number. This threat can be minimized by making the number of possible validation numbers much larger than the number of actual validation numbers: 100-digit numbers for a million voters, for example. Of course, the validation numbers must be generated randomly.

Despite this, the CLA is still a trusted authority in some respects. It can certify ineligible voters. It can certify eligible voters multiple times. This risk could be minimized by having the CLA publish a list of certified voters (but not their validation numbers). If the number of voters on this list is less than the number of votes tabulated, then something is awry. However, if more voters were certified than votes tabulated, it probably means that some certified people didn't bother voting. Many people who are registered to vote don't bother to cast ballots.

This protocol is vulnerable to collusion between the CLA and the CTF. If the two of them got together, they could correlate databases and figure out who voted for whom.

Voting with a Single Central Facility

A more complex protocol can be used to overcome the danger of collusion between the CLA and the CTF [1373]. This protocol is identical to the previous one, with two modifications:

— The CLA and the CTF are one organization, and

— ANDOS (see Section 4.13) is used to anonymously distribute validation numbers in step (2).

Since the anonymous key distribution protocol prevents the CTF from knowing which voter got which validation number, there is no way for the CTF to correlate validation numbers with votes received. The CTF still has to be trusted not to give validation numbers to ineligible voters, though. You can also solve this problem with blind signatures.

Improved Voting with a Single Central Facility

This protocol also uses ANDOS [1175]. It satisfies all six requirements of a good voting protocol. It doesn't satisfy the seventh requirement, but has two properties additional to the six listed at the beginning of the section:

7. A voter can change his mind (i.e., retract his vote and vote again) within a given period of time.
8. If a voter finds out that his vote is miscounted, he can identify and correct the problem without jeopardizing the secrecy of his ballot.

Here's the protocol:

(1) The CTF publishes a list of all legitimate voters.
(2) Within a specified deadline, each voter tells the CTF whether he intends to vote.
(3) The CTF publishes a list of voters participating in the election.
(4) Each voter receives an identification number, I, using an ANDOS protocol.
(5) Each voter generates a public-key/private-key key pair: k, d. If v is the vote, he generates the following message and sends it to the CTF:

$I, E_k(I,v)$

This message must be sent anonymously.
(6) The CTF acknowledges receipt of the vote by publishing:

$E_k(I,v)$

(7) Each voter sends the CTF:

I, d

(8) The CTF decrypts the votes. At the end of the election, it publishes the results of the election and, for each different vote, the list of all $E_k(I,v)$ values that contained that vote.
(9) If a voter observes that his vote is not properly counted, he protests by sending the CTF:

$I, E_k(I,v), d$

(10) If a voter wants to change his vote (possible, in some elections) from v to v', he sends the CTF:

$I, E_k(I,v'), d$

A different voting protocol uses blind signatures instead of ANDOS, but is essentially the same [585]. Steps (1) through (3) are preliminary to the actual voting. Their purpose is to find out and publicize the total number of actual voters. Although some of them probably will not participate, it reduces the ability of the CTF to add fraudulent votes.

In step (4), it is possible for two voters to get the same identification number. This possibility can be minimized by having far more possible identification numbers than actual voters. If two voters submit votes with the same identification tag, the CTF generates a new identification number, I', chooses one of the two votes, and publishes:

$$I', E_k(I, v)$$

The owner of that vote recognizes it and sends in a second vote, by repeating step (5), with the new identification number.

Step (6) gives each voter the capability to check that the CTF received his vote accurately. If his vote is miscounted, he can prove his case in step (9). Assuming a voter's vote is correct in step (6), the message he sends in step (9) constitutes a proof that his vote is miscounted.

One problem with the protocol is that a corrupt CTF could allocate the votes of people who respond in step (2) but who do not actually vote. Another problem is the complexity of the ANDOS protocol. The authors recommend dividing a large population of voters into smaller populations, such as election districts.

Another, more serious problem is that the CTF can neglect to count a vote. This problem cannot be resolved: Alice claims that the CTF intentionally neglected to count her vote, but the CTF claims that the voter never voted.

Voting without a Central Tabulating Facility

The following protocol does away with the CTF entirely; the voters watch each other. Designed by Michael Merritt [452,1076,453], it is so unwieldy that it cannot be implemented practically for more than a handful of people, but it is useful to learn from nevertheless.

Alice, Bob, Carol, and Dave are voting yes or no (0 or 1) on a particular issue. Assume each voter has a public and private key. Also assume that everyone knows everyone else's public keys.

(1) Each voter chooses his vote and does the following:
   (a) He attaches a random string to his vote.
   (b) He encrypts the result of step (a) with Dave's public key.
   (c) He encrypts the result of step (b) with Carol's public key.
   (d) He encrypts the result of step (c) with Bob's public key.
   (e) He encrypts the result of step (d) with Alice's public key.
   (f) He attaches a new random string to the result of step (e) and encrypts it with Dave's public key. He records the value of the random string.
   (g) He attaches a new random string to the result of step (f) and encrypts it with Carol's public key. He records the value of the random string.

(h) He attaches a new random string to the result of step (g) and encrypts it with Bob's public key. He records the value of the random string.

(i) He attaches a new random string to the result of step (h) and encrypts it with Alice's public key. He records the value of the random string.

If E is the encryption function, R_i is a random string, and V is the vote, his message looks like:

$$E_A(R_5,E_B(R_4,E_C(R_3,E_D(R_2,E_A(E_B(E_C(E_D(V,R_1))))))))$$

Each voter saves the intermediate results at each point in the calculation. These results will be used later in the protocol to confirm that his vote is among those being counted.

(2) Each voter sends his message to Alice.

(3) Alice decrypts all of the votes with her private key and then removes all of the random strings at that level.

(4) Alice scrambles the order of all the votes and sends the result to Bob.
    Each vote now looks like this:

$$E_B(R_4,E_C(R_3,E_D(R_2,E_A(E_B(E_C(E_D(V,R_1)))))))$$

(5) Bob decrypts all of the votes with his private key, checks to see that his vote is among the set of votes, removes all the random strings at that level, scrambles all the votes, and then sends the result to Carol.
    Each vote now looks like this:

$$E_C(R_3,E_D(R_2,E_A(E_B(E_C(E_D(V,R_1))))))$$

(6) Carol decrypts all of the votes with her private key, checks to see that her vote is among the set of votes, removes all the random strings at that level, scrambles all the votes, and then sends the result to Dave.
    Each vote now looks like this:

$$E_D(R_2,E_A(E_B(E_C(E_D(V,R_1)))))$$

(7) Dave decrypts all of the votes with his private key, checks to see that his vote is among the set of votes, removes all the random strings at that level, scrambles all the votes, and sends them to Alice.
    Each vote now looks like this:

$$E_A(E_B(E_C(E_D(V,R_1))))$$

(8) Alice decrypts all the votes with her private key, checks to see that her vote is among the set of votes, signs all the votes, and then sends the result to Bob, Carol, and Dave.
    Each vote now looks like this:

$$S_A(E_B(E_C(E_D(V,R_1))))$$

(9) Bob verifies and deletes Alice's signatures. He decrypts all the votes with his private key, checks to see that his vote is among the set of votes, signs all the votes, and then sends the result to Alice, Carol, and Dave.
    Each vote now looks like this:

$$S_B(E_C(E_D(V,R_1)))$$

(10) Carol verifies and deletes Bob's signatures. She decrypts all the votes with her private key, checks to see that her vote is among the set of votes, signs all the votes, and then sends the result to Alice, Bob, and Dave.
Each vote now looks like this:

$$S_C(E_D(V,R_1))$$

(11) Dave verifies and deletes Carol's signatures. He decrypts all the votes with his private key, checks to see that his vote is among the set of votes, signs all the votes, and then sends the result to Alice, Bob, and Carol.
Each vote now looks like this:

$$S_D(V,R_1)$$

(12) All verify and delete Dave's signature. They check to make sure that their vote is among the set of votes (by looking for their random string among the votes).

(13) Everyone removes the random strings from each vote and tallies the votes.

Not only does this protocol work, it is also self-adjudicating. Alice, Bob, Carol, and Dave will immediately know if someone tries to cheat. No CTF or CLA is required. To see how this works, let's try to cheat.

If someone tries to stuff the ballot, Alice will detect the attempt in step (3) when she receives more votes than people. If Alice tries to stuff the ballot, Bob will notice in step (4).

More devious is to substitute one vote for another. Since the votes are encrypted with various public keys, anyone can create as many valid votes as needed. The decryption protocol has two rounds: round one consists of steps (3) through (7), and round two consists of steps (8) through (11). Vote substitution is detected differently in the different rounds.

If someone substitutes one vote for another in round two, his actions are discovered immediately. At every step the votes are signed and sent to all the voters. If one (or more) of the voters noticed that his vote is no longer in the set of votes, he immediately stops the protocol. Because the votes are signed at every step, and because everyone can backtrack through the second round of the protocol, it is easy to detect who substituted the votes.

Substituting one vote for another during round one of the protocol is more subtle. Alice can't do it in step (3), because Bob, Carol, or Dave will detect it in step (5), (6), or (7). Bob could try in step (5). If he replaces Carol's or Dave's vote (remember, he doesn't know which vote corresponds to which voter), Carol or Dave will notice in step (6) or (7). They wouldn't know who tampered with their vote (although it would have had to be someone who had already handled the votes), but they would know that their vote was tampered with. If Bob is lucky and picks Alice's vote to replace, she won't notice until the second round. Then, she will notice her vote missing in step (8). Still, she would not know who tampered with her vote. In the first round, the votes are shuffled from one step to the other and unsigned; it is impossible for anyone to backtrack through the protocol to determine who tampered with the votes.

Another form of cheating is to try to figure out who voted for whom. Because of the scrambling in the first round, it is impossible for someone to backtrack through the protocol and link votes with voters. The removal of the random strings during the first round is also crucial to preserving anonymity. If they are not removed, the scrambling of the votes could be reversed by re-encrypting the emerging votes with the scrambler's public key. As the protocol stands, the confidentiality of the votes is secure.

Even more strongly, because of the initial random string, R_1, even identical votes are encrypted differently at every step of the protocol. No one knows the outcome of the vote until step (11).

What are the problems with this protocol? First, the protocol has an enormous amount of computation. The example described had only four voters and *it* was complicated. This would never work in a real election, with tens of thousands of voters. Second, Dave learns the results of the election before anyone else does. While he still can't affect the outcome, this gives him some power that the others do not have. On the other hand, this is also true with centralized voting schemes.

The third problem is that Alice can copy anyone else's vote, even though she does not know what it is beforehand. To see why this could be a problem, consider a three-person election between Alice, Bob, and Eve. Eve doesn't care about the result of the election, but she wants to know how Alice voted. So she copies Alice's vote, and the result of the election is guaranteed to be equal to Alice's vote.

Other Voting Schemes

Many complex secure election protocols have been proposed. They come in two basic flavors. There are mixing protocols, like "Voting without a Central Tabulating Facility," where everyone's vote gets mixed up so that no one can associate a vote with a voter.

There are also divided protocols, where individual votes are divided up among different tabulating facilities such that no single one of them can cheat the voters [360,359,118,115]. These protocols only protect the privacy of voters to the extent that different "parts" of the government (or whoever is administering the voting) do not conspire against the voter. (This idea of breaking a central authority into different parts, who are only trusted when together, comes from [316].)

One divided protocol is [1371]. The basic idea is that each voter breaks his vote into several shares. For example, if the vote were "yes" or "no," a 1 could indicate "yes" and a 0 could indicate "no"; the voter would then generate several numbers whose sum was either 0 or 1. These shares are sent to tabulating facilities, one to each, and are also encrypted and posted. Each center tallies the shares it receives (there are protocols to verify that the tally is correct) and the final vote is the sum of all the tallies. There are also protocols to ensure that each voter's shares add up to 0 or 1.

Another protocol, by David Chaum [322], ensures that voters who attempt to disrupt the election can be traced. However, the election must then be restarted without the interfering voter; this approach is not practical for large-scale elections.

Another, more complex, voting protocol that solves some of these problems can be found in [770,771]. There is even a voting protocol that uses multiple-key ciphers

[219]. Yet another voting protocol, which claims to be practical for large-scale elections, is in [585]. And [347] allows voters to abstain.

Voting protocols work, but they make it easier to buy and sell votes. The incentives become considerably stronger as the buyer can be sure that the seller votes as promised. Some protocols are designed to be **receipt-free**, so that it is impossible for a voter to prove to someone else that he voted in a certain way [117,1170,1372].

6.2 SECURE MULTIPARTY COMPUTATION

Secure multiparty computation is a protocol in which a group of people can get together and compute any function of many variables in a special way. Each participant in the group provides one or more variables. The result of the function is known to everyone in the group, but no one learns anything about the inputs of any other members other than what is obvious from the output of the function. Here are some examples:

Protocol #1

How can a group of people calculate their average salary without anyone learning the salary of anyone else?

(1) Alice adds a secret random number to her salary, encrypts the result with Bob's public key, and sends it to Bob.

(2) Bob decrypts Alice's result with his private key. He adds his salary to what he received from Alice, encrypts the result with Carol's public key, and sends it to Carol.

(3) Carol decrypts Bob's result with her private key. She adds her salary to what she received from Bob, encrypts the result with Dave's public key, and sends it to Dave.

(4) Dave decrypts Carol's result with his private key. He adds his salary to what he received from Carol, encrypts the result with Alice's public key, and sends it to Alice.

(5) Alice decrypts Dave's result with her private key. She subtracts the random number from step (1) to recover the sum of everyone's salaries.

(6) Alice divides the result by the number of people (four, in this case) and announces the result.

This protocol assumes that everyone is honest; they may be curious, but they follow the protocol. If any participant lies about his salary, the average will be wrong. A more serious problem is that Alice can misrepresent the result to everyone. She can subtract any number she likes in step (5), and no one would be the wiser. Alice could be prevented from doing this by requiring her to commit to her random number using any of the bit-commitment schemes from Section 4.9, but when she revealed her random number at the end of the protocol Bob could learn her salary.

Protocol #2

Alice and Bob are at a restaurant together, having an argument over who is older. They don't, however, want to tell the other their age. They could each whisper their age into the ear of a trusted neutral party (the waiter, for example), who could compare the numbers in his head and announce the result to both Alice and Bob.

The above protocol has two problems. One, your average waiter doesn't have the computational ability to handle situations more complex than determining which of two numbers is greater. And two, if Alice and Bob were really concerned about the secrecy of their information, they would be forced to drown the waiter in a bowl of vichyssoise, lest he tell the wine steward.

Public-key cryptography offers a far less violent solution. There is a protocol by which Alice, who knows a value a, and Bob, who knows a value b, can together determine if $a < b$, so that Alice gets no additional information about b and Bob gets no additional information about a. And, both Alice and Bob are convinced of the validity of the computation. Since the cryptographic algorithm used is an essential part of the protocol, details can be found in Section 23.14.

Of course, this protocol doesn't protect against active cheaters. There's nothing to stop Alice (or Bob, for that matter) from lying about her age. If Bob were a computer program that blindly executed the protocol, Alice could learn his age (is the age of a computer program the length of time since it was written or the length of time since it started running?) by repeatedly executing the protocol. Alice might give her age as 60. After learning that she is older, she could execute the protocol again with her age as 30. After learning that Bob is older, she could execute the protocol again with her age as 45, and so on, until Alice discovers Bob's age to any degree of accuracy she wishes.

Assuming that the participants don't actively cheat, it is easy to extend this protocol to multiple participants. Any number of people can find out the order of their ages by a sequence of honest applications of the protocol; and no participant can learn the age of another.

Protocol #3

Alice likes to do kinky things with teddy bears. Bob has erotic fantasies about marble tables. Both are pretty embarrassed by their particular fetish, but would love to find a mate who shared in their . . . um . . . lifestyle.

Here at the Secure Multiparty Computation Dating Service, we've designed a protocol for people like them. We've numbered an astonishing list of fetishes, from "aardvarks" to "zoot suits." Discreetly separated by a modem link, Alice and Bob can participate in a secure multiparty protocol. Together, they can determine whether they share the same fetish. If they do, they might look forward to a lifetime of bliss together. If they don't, they can part company secure in the knowledge that their particular fetish remains confidential. No one, not even the Secure Multiparty Computation Dating Service, will ever know.

Here's how it works:

(1) Using a one-way function, Alice hashes her fetish into a seven-digit string.

(2) Alice uses the seven-digit string as a telephone number, calls the number,

and leaves a message for Bob. If no one answers or the number is not in service, Alice applies a one-way function to the telephone number until she finds someone who can play along with the protocol.

(3) Alice tells Bob how many times she had to apply the one-way hash function to her fetish.

(4) Bob hashes his fetish the same number of times that Alice did. He also uses the seven-digit string as a telephone number, and asks the person at the other end whether there were any messages for him.

Note that Bob has a chosen-plaintext attack. He can hash common fetishes and call the resulting telephone numbers, looking for messages for him. This protocol only really works if there are enough possible plaintext messages for this to be impractical.

There's also a mathematical protocol, one similar to Protocol #2. Alice knows a, Bob knows b, and together they will determine whether $a = b$, such that Bob does not learn anything additional about a and Alice does not learn anything additional about b. Details are in Section 23.14.

Protocol #4

This is another problem for secure multiparty computation [1373]: A council of seven meets regularly to cast secret ballots on certain issues. (All right, they rule the world—don't tell anyone I told you.) All council members can vote yes or no. In addition, two parties have the option of casting "super votes": S-yes and S-no. They do not have to cast super votes; they can cast regular votes if they prefer. If no one casts any super votes, then the majority of votes decides the issue. In the case of a single or two equivalent super votes, all regular votes are ignored. In the case of two contradicting super votes, the majority of regular votes decides. We want a protocol that securely performs this style of voting.

Two examples should illustrate the voting process. Assume there are five regular voters, N_1 through N_5, and two super voters: S_1 and S_2. Here's the vote on issue #1:

S_1	S_2	N_1	N_2	N_3	N_4	N_5
S-yes	no	no	no	no	yes	yes

In this instance the only vote that matters is S_1's, and the result is "yes."
Here is the vote on issue #2:

S_1	S_2	N_1	N_2	N_3	N_4	N_5
S-yes	S-no	no	no	no	yes	yes

Here the two super votes cancel and the majority of regular "no" votes decide the issue.

If it isn't important to hide the knowledge of whether the super vote or the regular vote was the deciding vote, this is an easy application of a secure voting protocol. Hiding that knowledge requires a more complicated secure multiparty computation protocol.

This kind of voting could occur in real life. It could be part of a corporation's organizational structure, where certain people have more power than others, or it could be part of the United Nations's procedures, where certain nations have more power than others.

Multiparty Unconditionally Secure Protocols

This is just a simple case of a general theorem: Any function of n inputs can be computed by a set of n players in a way that will let all learn the value of the function, but any set of less than $n/2$ players will not get any additional information that does not follow from their own inputs and the value of the output information. For details, see [136,334,1288,621].

Secure Circuit Evaluation

Alice has her input, a. Bob has his input, b. Together they wish to compute some general function, $f(a,b)$, such that Alice learns nothing about Bob's input and Bob learns nothing about Alice's input. The general problem of secure multiparty computation is also called **secure circuit evaluation**. Here, Alice and Bob can create an arbitrary Boolean circuit. This circuit accepts inputs from Alice and from Bob and produces an output. Secure circuit evaluation is a protocol that accomplishes three things:

1. Alice can enter her input without Bob's being able to learn it.
2. Bob can enter his input without Alice's being able to learn it.
3. Both Alice and Bob can calculate the output, with both parties being sure the output is correct and that neither party has tampered with it.

Details on secure circuit evaluation can be found in [831].

6.3 ANONYMOUS MESSAGE BROADCAST

You can't go out to dinner with a bunch of cryptographers without raising a ruckus. In [321], David Chaum introduced the Dining Cryptographers Problem:

> Three cryptographers are sitting down to dinner at their favorite three-star restaurant. Their waiter informs them that arrangements have been made with the maître d'hôtel for the bill to be paid anonymously. One of the cryptographers might be paying for the dinner, or it might have been the NSA. The three cryptographers respect each other's right to make an anonymous payment, but they wonder if the NSA is paying.

How do the cryptographers, named Alice, Bob, and Carol, determine if one of them is paying for dinner, while at the same time preserving the anonymity of the payer? Chaum goes on to solve the problem:

> Each cryptographer flips an unbiased coin behind his menu, between him and the cryptographer to his right, so that only the two of them can see the outcome. Each

cryptographer then states aloud whether the two coins he can see—the one he flipped and the one his left-hand neighbor flipped—fell on the same side or on different sides. If one of the cryptographers is the payer, he states the opposite of what he sees. An odd number of differences uttered at the table indicates that a cryptographer is paying; an even number of differences indicates that NSA is paying (assuming that the dinner was paid for only once). Yet, if a cryptographer is paying, neither of the other two learns anything from the utterances about which cryptographer it is.

To see that this works, imagine Alice trying to figure out which other cryptographer paid for dinner (assuming that neither she nor the NSA paid). If she sees two different coins, then either both of the other cryptographers, Bob and Carol, said, "same" or both said, "different." (Remember, an odd number of cryptographers saying "different" indicates that one of them paid.) If both said, "different," then the payer is the cryptographer closest to the coin that is the same as the hidden coin (the one that Bob and Carol flipped). If both said, "same," then the payer is the cryptographer closest to the coin that is different from the hidden coin. However, if Alice sees two coins that are the same, then either Bob said, "same" and Carol said, "different," or Bob said, "different" and Carol said, "same." If the hidden coin is the same as the two coins she sees, then the cryptographer who said, "different" is the payer. If the hidden coin is different from the two coins she sees, then the cryptographer who said, "same" is the payer. In all of these cases, Alice needs to know the result of the coin flipped between Bob and Carol to determine which of them paid.

This protocol can be generalized to any number of cryptographers; they all sit in a ring and flip coins among them. Even two cryptographers can perform the protocol. Of course, they know who paid, but someone watching the protocol could tell only if one of the two paid or if the NSA paid; they could not tell which cryptographer paid.

The applications of this protocol go far beyond sitting around the dinner table. This is an example of **unconditional sender and recipient untraceability**. A group of users on a network can use this protocol to send anonymous messages.

(1) The users arrange themselves into a circle.
(2) At regular intervals, adjacent pairs of users flip coins between them, using some fair coin flip protocol secure from eavesdroppers.
(3) After every flip, each user announces either "same" or "different."

If Alice wishes to broadcast a message, she simply starts inverting her statement in those rounds corresponding to a 1 in the binary representation of her message. For example, if her message were "1001," she would invert her statement, tell the truth, tell the truth, and then invert her statement. Assuming the result of her flips were "different," "same," "same," "same," she would say "same," "same," "same," "different."

If Alice notices that the overall outcome of the protocol doesn't match the message she is trying to send, she knows that someone else is trying to send a message at the same time. She then stops sending the message and waits some random number of rounds before trying again. The exact parameters have to be worked out based on the amount of message traffic on this network, but the idea should be clear.

To make things even more interesting, these messages can be encrypted in another user's public keys. Then, when everyone receives the message (a real implementation of this should add some kind of standard message-beginning and message-ending strings), only the intended recipient can decrypt and read it. No one else knows who sent it. No one else knows who could read it. Traffic analysis, which traces and compiles patterns of people's communications even though the messages themselves may be encrypted, is useless.

An alternative to flipping coins between adjacent parties would be for them to keep a common file of random bits. Maybe they could keep them on a CD-ROM, or one member of the pair could generate a pile of them and send them to the other party (encrypted, of course). Alternatively, they could agree on a cryptographically secure pseudo-random-number generator between them, and they could each generate the same string of pseudo-random bits for the protocol.

One problem with this protocol is that while a malicious participant cannot read any messages, he can disrupt the system unobserved by lying in step (3). There is a modification to the previous protocol that detects disruption [1578,1242]; the problem is called "The Dining Cryptographers in the Disco."

6.4 Digital Cash

Cash is a problem. It's annoying to carry, it spreads germs, and people can steal it from you. Checks and credit cards have reduced the amount of physical cash flowing through society, but the complete elimination of cash is virtually impossible. It'll never happen; drug dealers and politicians would never stand for it. Checks and credit cards have an audit trail; you can't hide to whom you gave money.

On the other hand, checks and credit cards allow people to invade your privacy to a degree never before imagined. You might never stand for the police following you your entire life, but the police can watch your financial transactions. They can see where you buy your gas, where you buy your food, who you call on the telephone—all without leaving their computer terminals. People need a way to protect their anonymity in order to protect their privacy.

Happily, there is a complicated protocol that allows for authenticated but untraceable messages. Lobbyist Alice can transfer **digital cash** to Congresscritter Bob so that newspaper reporter Eve does not know Alice's identity. Bob can then deposit that electronic money into his bank account, even though the bank has no idea who Alice is. But if Alice tries to buy cocaine with the same piece of digital cash she used to bribe Bob, she will be detected by the bank. And if Bob tries to deposit the same piece of digital cash into two different accounts, he will be detected—but Alice will remain anonymous. Sometimes this is called **anonymous digital cash** to differentiate it from digital money with an audit trail, such as credit cards.

A great social need exists for this kind of thing. With the growing use of the Internet for commercial transactions, there is more call for network-based privacy and anonymity in business. (There are good reasons people are reluctant to send their credit card numbers over the Internet.) On the other hand, banks and governments seem unwilling to give up the control that the current banking system's audit trail provides. They'll have to, though. All it will take for digital cash to catch on is for some trustworthy institution to be willing to convert the digits to real money.

Digital cash protocols are very complex. We'll build up to one, a step at a time. For more formal details, read [318,339,325,335,340]. Realize that this is just one digital cash protocol; there are others.

Protocol #1

The first few protocols are physical analogies of cryptographic protocols. This first protocol is a simplified physical protocol for anonymous money orders:

(1) Alice prepares 100 anonymous money orders for $1000 each.

(2) Alice puts one each, and a piece of carbon paper, into 100 different envelopes. She gives them all to the bank.

(3) The bank opens 99 envelopes and confirms that each is a money order for $1000.

(4) The bank signs the one remaining unopened envelope. The signature goes through the carbon paper to the money order. The bank hands the unopened envelope back to Alice, and deducts $1000 from her account.

(5) Alice opens the envelope and spends the money order with a merchant.

(6) The merchant checks for the bank's signature to make sure the money order is legitimate.

(7) The merchant takes the money order to the bank.

(8) The bank verifies its signature and credits $1000 to the merchant's account.

This protocol works. The bank never sees the money order it signed, so when the merchant brings it to the bank, the bank has no idea that it was Alice's. The bank is convinced that it is valid, though, because of the signature. The bank is confident that the unopened money order is for $1000 (and not for $100,000 or $100,000,000) because of the cut-and-choose protocol (see Section 5.1). It verifies the other 99 envelopes, so Alice has only a 1 percent chance of cheating the bank. Of course, the bank will make the penalty for cheating great enough so that it isn't worth that chance. If the bank refuses to sign the last check (if Alice is caught cheating) without penalizing Alice, she will continue to try until she gets lucky. Prison terms are a better deterrent.

Protocol #2

The previous protocol prevents Alice from writing a money order for more than she claims to, but it doesn't prevent Alice from photocopying the money order and spending it twice. This is called the **double spending problem**; to solve it, we need a complication:

(1) Alice prepares 100 anonymous money orders for $1000 each. On each money order she includes a different random uniqueness string, one long enough to make the chance of another person also using it negligible.

(2) Alice puts one each, and a piece of carbon paper, into 100 different envelopes. She gives them all to the bank.

(3) The bank opens 99 envelopes and confirms that each is a money order for $1000.

(4) The bank signs the one remaining unopened envelope. The signature goes through the carbon paper to the money order. The bank hands the unopened envelope back to Alice and deducts $1000 from her account.

(5) Alice opens the envelope and spends the money order with a merchant.

(6) The merchant checks for the bank's signature to make sure the money order is legitimate.

(7) The merchant takes the money order to the bank.

(8) The bank verifies its signature and checks its database to make sure a money order with the same uniqueness string has not been previously deposited. If it hasn't, the bank credits $1000 to the merchant's account. The bank records the uniqueness string in a database.

(9) If it has been previously deposited, the bank doesn't accept the money order.

Now, if Alice tries to spend a photocopy of the money order, or if the merchant tries to deposit a photocopy of the money order, the bank will know about it.

Protocol #3

The previous protocol protects the bank from cheaters, but it doesn't identify them. The bank doesn't know if the person who bought the money order (the bank has no idea it's Alice) tried to cheat the merchant or if the merchant tried to cheat the bank. This protocol corrects that:

(1) Alice prepares 100 anonymous money orders for $1000 each. On each of the money orders she includes a different random uniqueness string, one long enough to make the chance of another person also using it negligible.

(2) Alice puts one each, and a piece of carbon paper, into 100 different envelopes. She gives them all to the bank.

(3) The bank opens 99 envelopes and confirms that each is a money order for $1000 and that all the random strings are different.

(4) The bank signs the one remaining unopened envelope. The signature goes through the carbon paper to the money order. The bank hands the unopened envelope back to Alice and deducts $1000 from her account.

(5) Alice opens the envelope and spends the money order with a merchant.

(6) The merchant checks for the bank's signature to make sure the money order is legitimate.

(7) The merchant asks Alice to write a random identity string on the money order.

(8) Alice complies.

(9) The merchant takes the money order to the bank.

(10) The bank verifies the signature and checks its database to make sure a money order with the same uniqueness string has not been previously deposited. If it hasn't, the bank credits $1000 to the merchant's account. The bank records the uniqueness string and the identity string in a database.

(11) If the uniqueness string is in the database, the bank refuses to accept the money order. Then, it compares the identity string on the money order with the one stored in the database. If it is the same, the bank knows that the merchant photocopied the money order. If it is different, the bank knows that the person who bought the money order photocopied it.

This protocol assumes that the merchant cannot change the identity string once Alice writes it on the money order. The money order might have a series of little squares, which the merchant would require Alice to fill in with either Xs or Os. The money order might be made out of paper that tears if erased.

Since the interaction between the merchant and the bank takes place after Alice spends the money, the merchant could be stuck with a bad money order. Practical implementations of this protocol might require Alice to wait near the cash register during the merchant-bank interaction, much the same way as credit-card purchases are handled today.

Alice could also frame the merchant. She could spend a copy of the money order a second time, giving the same identity string in step (7). Unless the merchant keeps a database of money orders it already received, he would be fooled. The next protocol eliminates that problem.

Protocol #4

If it turns out that the person who bought the money order tried to cheat the merchant, the bank would want to know who that person was. To do that requires moving away from a physical analogy and into the world of cryptography.

The technique of secret splitting can be used to hide Alice's name in the digital money order.

(1) Alice prepares n anonymous money orders for a given amount.

    Each of the money orders contains a different random uniqueness string, X, one long enough to make the chance of two being identical negligible.

    On each money order, there are also n pairs of identity bit strings, I_1, $I_2, \ldots, I_n$. (Yes, that's n different pairs on *each* check.) Each of these pairs is generated as follows: Alice creates a string that gives her name, address, and any other piece of identifying information that the bank wants to see. Then, she splits it into two pieces using the secret splitting protocol (see Section 3.6). Then, she commits to each piece using a bit-commitment protocol.

For example, I_{37} consists of two parts: I_{37_L} and I_{37_R}. Each part is a bit-committed packet that Alice can be asked to open and whose proper opening can be instantly verified. Any pair (e.g., I_{37_L} and I_{37_R}, but not I_{37_L} and I_{38_R}), reveals Alice's identity.

Each of the money orders looks like this:

```
Amount
Uniqueness String: X
Identity Strings:  I₁ = (I₁ᴸ, I₁ᴿ)
                   I₂ = (I₂ᴸ, I₂ᴿ)
                   ....
                   Iₙ = (Iₙᴸ, Iₙᴿ)
```

(2) Alice blinds all n money orders, using a blind signature protocol. She gives them all to the bank.

(3) The bank asks Alice to unblind $n - 1$ of the money orders at random and confirms that they are all well formed. The bank checks the amount, the uniqueness string, and asks Alice to reveal all of the identity strings.

(4) If the bank is satisfied that Alice did not make any attempts to cheat, it signs the one remaining blinded money order. The bank hands the blinded money order back to Alice and deducts the amount from her account.

(5) Alice unblinds the money order and spends it with a merchant.

(6) The merchant verifies the bank's signature to make sure the money order is legitimate.

(7) The merchant asks Alice to randomly reveal either the left half or the right half of each identity string on the money order. In effect, the merchant gives Alice a random n-bit **selector string**, $b_1, b_2, \ldots, b_n$. Alice opens either the left or right half of I_i, depending on whether b_i is a 0 or a 1.

(8) Alice complies.

(9) The merchant takes the money order to the bank.

(10) The bank verifies the signature and checks its database to make sure a money order with the same uniqueness string has not been previously deposited. If it hasn't, the bank credits the amount to the merchant's account. The bank records the uniqueness string and all of the identity information in a database.

(11) If the uniqueness string is in the database, the bank refuses to accept the money order. Then, it compares the identity string on the money order with the one stored in the database. If it is the same, the bank knows that the merchant copied the money order. If it is different, the bank knows that the person who bought the money order photocopied it. Since the second merchant who accepted the money order handed Alice a different selector string than did the first merchant, the bank finds a bit position where one merchant had Alice open the left half and the other merchant had Alice open the right half. The bank XORs the two halves together to reveal Alice's identity.

This is quite an amazing protocol, so let's look at it from various angles.

Can Alice cheat? Her digital money order is nothing more than a string of bits, so she can copy it. Spending it the first time won't be a problem; she'll just complete the protocol and everything will go smoothly. The merchant will give her a random n-bit selector string in step (7) and Alice will open either the left half or right half of each I_i in step (8). In step (10), the bank will record all of this data, as well as the money order's uniqueness string.

When she tries to use the same digital money order a second time, the merchant (either the same merchant or a different merchant) will give her a different random selector string in step (7). Alice must comply in step (8); not doing so will immediately alert the merchant that something is suspicious. Now, when the merchant brings the money order to the bank in step (10), the bank would immediately notice that a money order with the same uniqueness string was already deposited. The bank then compares the opened halves of the identity strings. The odds that the two random selector strings are the same is 1 in 2^n; it isn't likely to happen before the next ice age. Now, the bank finds a pair with one half opened the first time and the other half opened the second time. It XORs the two halves together, and out pops Alice's name. The bank knows who tried to spend the money order twice.

Note that this protocol doesn't keep Alice from trying to cheat; it detects her cheating with almost certainty. Alice can't prevent her identity from being revealed if she cheats. She can't change either the uniqueness string or any of the identity strings, because then the bank's signature will no longer be valid. The merchant will immediately notice that in step (6).

Alice could try to sneak a bad money order past the bank, one on which the identity strings don't reveal her name; or better yet, one whose identity strings reveal someone else's name. The odds of her getting this ruse past the bank in step (3) are 1 in n. These aren't impossible odds, but if you make the penalty severe enough, Alice won't try it. Or, you could increase the number of redundant money orders that Alice makes in step (1).

Can the merchant cheat? His chances are even worse. He can't deposit the money order twice; the bank will notice the repeated use of the selector string. He can't fake blaming Alice; only she can open any of the identity strings.

Even collusion between Alice and the merchant can't cheat the bank. As long as the bank signs the money order with the uniqueness string, the bank is assured of only having to make good on the money order once.

What about the bank? Can it figure out that the money order it accepted from the merchant was the one it signed for Alice? Alice is protected by the blind signature protocol in steps (2) through (5). The bank cannot make the connection, even if it keeps complete records of every transaction. Even more strongly, there is no way for the bank and the merchant to get together to figure out who Alice is. Alice can walk in the store and, completely anonymously, make her purchase.

Eve can cheat. If she can eavesdrop on the communication between Alice and the merchant, and if she can get to the bank before the merchant does, she can deposit the digital cash first. The bank will accept it and, even worse, when the merchant tries to deposit the cash he will be identified as a cheater. If Eve steals and spends

Alice's cash before Alice can, then Alice will be identified as a cheater. There's no way to prevent this; it is a direct result of the anonymity of the cash. Both Alice and the merchant have to protect their bits as they would paper money.

This protocol lies somewhere between an arbitrated protocol and a self-enforcing protocol. Both Alice and the merchant trust the bank to make good on the money orders, but Alice does not have to trust the bank with knowledge of her purchases.

Digital Cash and the Perfect Crime

Digital cash has its dark side, too. Sometimes people don't want so much privacy. Watch Alice commit the perfect crime [1575]:

(1) Alice kidnaps a baby.
(2) Alice prepares 10,000 anonymous money orders for $1000 (or as many as she wants for whatever denomination she wants).
(3) Alice blinds all 10,000 money orders, using a blind signature protocol. She sends them to the authorities with the threat to kill the baby unless the following instructions are met:
   (a) Have a bank sign all 10,000 money orders.
   (b) Publish the results in a newspaper.
(4) The authorities comply.
(5) Alice buys a newspaper, unblinds the money orders, and starts spending them. There is no way for the authorities to trace the money orders to her.
(6) Alice frees the baby.

Note that this situation is much worse than any involving physical tokens—cash, for example. Without physical contact, the police have less opportunity to apprehend the kidnapper.

In general, though, digital cash isn't a good deal for criminals. The problem is that the anonymity only works one way: The spender is anonymous, but the merchant is not. Moreover, the merchant cannot hide the fact that he received money. Digital cash will make it easy for the government to determine how much money you made, but impossible to determine what you spent it on.

Practical Digital Cash

A Dutch company, DigiCash, owns most of the digital cash patents and has implemented digital cash protocols in working products. Anyone interested should contact DigiCash BV, Kruislaan 419, 1098 VA Amsterdam, Netherlands.

Other Digital Cash Protocols

There are other digital cash protocols; see [707,1554,734,1633,973]. Some of them involve some pretty complicated mathematics. Generally, the various digital cash protocols can be divided into various categories. **On-line** systems require the merchant to communicate with the bank at every sale, much like today's credit-card protocols. If there is a problem, the bank doesn't accept the cash and Alice cannot cheat.

Off-line systems, like Protocol #4, require no communication between the merchant and the bank until after the transaction between the merchant and the customer. These systems do not prevent Alice from cheating, but instead detect her cheating. Protocol #4 detected her cheating by making Alice's identity known if she tried to cheat. Alice knows that this will happen, so she doesn't cheat.

Another way is to create a special smart card (see Section 24.13) containing a tamperproof chip called an **observer** [332,341,387]. The observer chip keeps a mini database of all the pieces of digital cash spent by that smart card. If Alice attempts to copy some digital cash and spend it twice, the imbedded observer chip would detect the attempt and would not allow the transaction. Since the observer chip is tamperproof, Alice cannot erase the mini-database without permanently damaging the smart card. The cash can wend its way through the economy; when it is finally deposited, the bank can examine the cash and determine who, if anyone, cheated.

Digital cash protocols can also be divided along another line. **Electronic coins** have a fixed value; people using this system will need several coins in different denominations. **Electronic checks** can be used for any amount up to a maximum value and then returned for a refund of the unspent portion.

Two excellent and completely different off-line electronic coin protocols are [225,226,227] and [563,564,565]. A system called NetCash, with weaker anonymity properties, has also been proposed [1048,1049]. Another new system is [289].

In [1211], Tatsuaki Okamoto and Kazuo Ohta list six properties of an ideal digital cash system:

1. Independence. The security of the digital cash is not dependent on any physical location. The cash can be transferred through computer networks.

2. Security. The digital cash cannot be copied and reused.

3. Privacy (Untraceability). The privacy of the user is protected; no one can trace the relationship between the user and his purchases.

4. Off-line Payment. When a user pays for a purchase with electronic cash, the protocol between the user and the merchant is executed off-line. That is, the shop does not need to be linked to a host to process the user's payment.

5. Transferability. The digital cash can be transferred to other users.

6. Divisibility. A piece of digital cash in a given amount can be subdivided into smaller pieces of cash in smaller amounts. (Of course, everything has to total up properly in the end.)

The protocols previously discussed satisfy properties 1, 2, 3, and 4, but not 5 and 6. Some on-line digital cash systems satisfy all properties except 4 [318,413, 1243]. The first off-line digital cash system that satisfies properties 1, 2, 3, and 4, similar to the one just discussed, was proposed in [339]. Okamoto and Ohta proposed a system that satisfies properties 1 through 5 [1209]; they also proposed a system that satisfies properties 1 through 6 as well, but the data requirement for a single purchase is approximately 200 megabytes. Another off-line divisible coin system is described in [522].

The digital cash scheme proposed in [1211], by the same authors, satisfies properties 1 through 6, without the enormous data requirements. The total data transfer for a payment is about 20 kilobytes, and the protocol can be completed in several seconds. The authors consider this the first ideal untraceable electronic cash system.

Anonymous Credit Cards

This protocol [988] uses several different banks to protect the identity of the customer. Each customer has an account at two different banks. The first bank knows the person's identity and is willing to extend him credit. The second bank knows the customer only under a pseudonym (similar to a numbered Swiss bank account).

The customer can withdraw funds from the second bank by proving that the account is his. However, the bank does not know the person and is unwilling to extend him credit. The first bank knows the customer and transfers funds to the second bank—without knowing the pseudonym. The customer then spends these funds anonymously. At the end of the month, the second bank gives the first bank a bill, which it trusts the bank to pay. The first bank passes the bill on to the customer, which it trusts the customer to pay. When the customer pays, the first bank transfers additional funds to the second bank. All transactions are handled through an intermediary, which acts sort of like an electronic Federal Reserve: settling accounts among banks, logging messages, and creating an audit trail.

Exchanges between the customer, merchant, and various banks are outlined in [988]. Unless everyone colludes against the customer, his anonymity is assured. However, this is not digital cash; it is easy for the bank to cheat. The protocol allows customers to keep the advantages of credit cards without giving up their privacy.

PART II

CRYPTOGRAPHIC TECHNIQUES

CHAPTER   **7**

Key Length

7.1   Symmetric Key Length

The security of a symmetric cryptosystem is a function of two things: the strength of the algorithm and the length of the key. The former is more important, but the latter is easier to demonstrate.

Assume that the strength of the algorithm is perfect. This is extremely difficult to achieve in practice, but easy enough for this example. By perfect, I mean that there is no better way to break the cryptosystem other than trying every possible key in a brute-force attack.

To launch this attack, a cryptanalyst needs a small amount of ciphertext and the corresponding plaintext; a brute-force attack is a known-plaintext attack. For a block cipher, the cryptanalyst would need a block of ciphertext and corresponding plaintext: generally 64 bits. Getting this plaintext and ciphertext is easier than you might imagine. A cryptanalyst might get a copy of a plaintext message by some means and intercept the corresponding ciphertext. He may know something about the format of the ciphertext: For example, it is a WordPerfect file, it has a standard electronic-mail message header, it is a UNIX directory file, it is a TIFF image, or it is a standard record in a customer database. All of these formats have some predefined bytes. The cryptanalyst doesn't need much plaintext to launch this attack.

Calculating the complexity of a brute-force attack is easy. If the key is 8 bits long, there are 2^8, or 256, possible keys. Therefore, it will take 256 attempts to find the correct key, with a 50 percent chance of finding the key after half of the attempts. If the key is 56 bits long, then there are 2^{56} possible keys. Assuming a supercomputer can try a million keys a second, it will take 2285 years to find the correct key. If the key is 64 bits long, then it will take the same supercomputer about 585,000 years to find the correct key among the 2^{64} possible keys. If the key is 128 bits long, it will take 10^{25} years. The universe is only 10^{10} years old, so 10^{25} years is a long time. With a 2048-bit key, a million million-attempts-per-second computers working in parallel will spend 10^{597} years finding the key. By that time the universe will have long collapsed or expanded into nothingness.

Before you rush to invent a cryptosystem with an 8-kilobyte key, remember the other side to the strength question: The algorithm must be so secure that there is no better way to break it than with a brute-force attack. This is not as easy as it might seem. Cryptography is a subtle art. Cryptosystems that look perfect are often extremely weak. Strong cryptosystems, with a couple of minor changes, can become weak. The warning to the amateur cryptographer is to have a healthy, almost paranoid, suspicion of any new algorithm. It is best to trust algorithms that professional cryptographers have scrutinized for years without cracking them and to be suspicious of algorithm designers' grandiose claims of security.

Recall an important point from Section 1.1: The security of a cryptosystem should rest in the key, not in the details of the algorithm. Assume that any cryptanalyst has access to all the details of your algorithm. Assume he has access to as much ciphertext as he wants and can mount an intensive ciphertext-only attack. Assume that he can mount a plaintext attack with as much data as he needs. Even assume that he can mount a chosen-plaintext attack. If your cryptosystem can remain secure, even in the face of all that knowledge, then you've got something.

That warning aside, there is still plenty of room in cryptography to maneuver. In reality, this kind of security isn't really necessary in many situations. Most adversaries don't have the knowledge and computing resources of a major government, and even the ones who do probably aren't that interested in breaking your cryptosystem. If you're plotting to overthrow a major government, stick with the tried and true algorithms in the back of the book. The rest of you, have fun.

Time and Cost Estimates for Brute-Force Attack

Remember that a brute-force attack is typically a known-plaintext attack; it requires a small amount of ciphertext and corresponding plaintext. If you assume that a brute-force attack is the most efficient attack possible against an algorithm—a big assumption—then the key must be long enough to make the attack infeasible. How long is that?

Two parameters determine the speed of a brute-force attack: the number of keys to be tested and the speed of each test. Most symmetric algorithms accept any fixed-length bit pattern as the key. DES has a 56-bit key; it has 2^{56} possible keys. Some algorithms discussed in this book have a 64-bit key; these have 2^{64} possible keys. Others have a 128-bit key.

The speed at which each possible key can be tested is also a factor, but a less important one. For the purposes of this analysis, I will assume that each different algorithm can be tested in the same amount of time. The reality may be that one algorithm may be tested two, three, or even ten times faster than another. But since we are looking for key lengths that are millions of times more difficult to crack than would be feasible, small differences due to test speed are irrelevant.

Most of the debate in the cryptologic community about the efficiency of brute-force attacks has centered on the DES algorithm. In 1977, Whitfield Diffie and Martin Hellman [497] postulated the existence of a special-purpose DES-cracking machine. This machine consisted of a million chips, each capable of testing a million keys per second. Such a machine could test 2^{56} keys in 20 hours. If built to attack an algorithm with a 64-bit key, it could test all 2^{64} keys in 214 days.

A brute-force attack is tailor-made for parallel processors. Each processor can test a subset of the keyspace. The processors do not have to communicate among themselves; the only communication required at all is a single message signifying success. There are no shared memory requirements. It is easy to design a machine with a million parallel processors, each working independent of the others.

More recently, Michael Wiener decided to design a brute-force cracking machine [1597,1598]. (He designed the machine for DES, but the analysis holds for most any algorithm.) He designed specialized chips, boards, and racks. He estimated prices. And he discovered that for $1 million, someone could build a machine that could crack a 56-bit DES key in an average of 3.5 hours (results guaranteed in 7 hours). And that the price/speed ratio is linear. Table 7.1 generalizes these numbers to a variety of key lengths. Remember Moore's Law: Computing power doubles approximately every 18 months. This means costs go down a factor of 10 every five years; what cost $1 million to build in 1995 will cost a mere $100,000 in the year 2000. Pipelined computers might do even better [724].

For 56-bit keys, these numbers are within the budgets of most large companies and many criminal organizations. The military budgets of most industrialized nations can afford to break 64-bit keys. Breaking an 80-bit key is still beyond the realm of possibility, but if current trends continue that will change in only 30 years.

Of course, it is ludicrous to estimate computing power 35 years in the future. Breakthroughs in some science-fiction technology could make these numbers look like a joke. Conversely, physical limitations unknown at the present time could make them unrealistically optimistic. In cryptography it is wise to be pessimistic. Fielding an algorithm with an 80-bit key seems extremely short-sighted. Insist on at least 112-bit keys.

Table 7.1
Average Time Estimates for a Hardware Brute-Force Attack in 1995

Cost	40	56	64	80	112	128
	\multicolumn{6}{c}{LENGTH OF KEY IN BITS}					
$100 K	2 seconds	35 hours	1 year	70,000 years	10^{14} years	10^{19} years
$1 M	.2 seconds	3.5 hours	37 days	7000 years	10^{13} years	10^{18} years
$10 M	.02 seconds	21 minutes	4 days	700 years	10^{12} years	10^{17} years
$100 M	2 milliseconds	2 minutes	9 hours	70 years	10^{11} years	10^{16} years
$1 G	.2 milliseconds	13 seconds	1 hour	7 years	10^{10} years	10^{15} years
$10 G	.02 milliseconds	1 second	5.4 minutes	245 days	10^{9} years	10^{14} years
$100 G	2 microseconds	.1 second	32 seconds	24 days	10^{8} years	10^{13} years
$1 T	.2 microseconds	.01 second	3 seconds	2.4 days	10^{7} years	10^{12} years
$10 T	.02 microseconds	1 millisecond	.3 second	6 hours	10^{6} years	10^{11} years

If an attacker wants to break a key badly enough, all he has to do is spend money. Consequently, it seems prudent to try to estimate the minimum "value" of a key: How much value can be trusted to a single key before it makes economic sense to try to break? To give an extreme example, if an encrypted message is worth $1.39, then it wouldn't make much financial sense to set a $10-million cracker to the task of recovering the key. On the other hand, if the plaintext message is worth $100 million, then decrypting that single message would justify the cost of building the cracker. Also, the value of some messages decreases rapidly with time.

Software Crackers

Without special-purpose hardware and massively parallel machines, brute-force attacks are significantly harder. A software attack is about a thousand times slower than a hardware attack.

The real threat of a software-based brute-force attack is not that it is certain, but that it is "free." It costs nothing to set up a microcomputer to test possible keys whenever it is idle. If it finds the correct key—great. If it doesn't, then nothing is lost. It costs nothing to set up an entire microcomputer network to do that. A recent experiment with DES used the collective idle time of 40 workstations to test 2^{34} keys in a single day [603]. At this speed, it will take four million days to test all keys, but if enough people try attacks like this, then someone somewhere will get lucky. As was said in [603]:

> The crux of the software threat is sheer bad luck. Imagine a university computer network of 512 workstations, networked together. On some campuses this would be a medium-sized network. They could even be spread around the world, coordinating their activity through electronic mail. Assume each workstation is capable of running [the algorithm] at a rate of 15,000 encryptions per second. . . . Allowing for the overhead of testing and changing keys, this comes down to . . . 8192 tests per second per machine. To exhaust [a 56-bit] keyspace with this setup would take 545 years (assuming the network was dedicated to the task twenty-four hours per day). Notice, however, that the same calculations give our hypothetical student hackers one chance in 200,000 of cracking a key in one day. Over a long weekend their odds increase to one chance in sixty-six thousand. The faster their hardware, or the more machines involved, the better their chance becomes. These are not good odds for earning a living from horse racing, but they're not the stuff of good press releases either. They are much better odds than the Government gives on its lotteries, for instance. "One-in-a-million"? "Couldn't happen again in a thousand years"? It is no longer possible to say such things honestly. Is this an acceptable ongoing risk?

Using an algorithm with a 64-bit key instead of a 56-bit key makes this attack 256 times more difficult. With a 40-bit key, the picture is far more bleak. A network of 400 computers, each capable of performing 32,000 encryptions per second, can complete a brute-force attack against a 40-bit key in a single day. (In 1992, the RC2 and RC4 algorithms were approved for export with a 40-bit key—see Section 13.8.)

A 128-bit key makes a brute-force attack ridiculous even to contemplate. Industry experts estimate that by 1996 there will be 200 million computers in use worldwide. This estimate includes everything from giant Cray mainframes to subnotebooks. If every one of those computers worked together on this brute-force attack, and each computer performed a million encryptions per second every second, it would still take a million times the age of the universe to recover the key.

Neural Networks

Neural nets aren't terribly useful for cryptanalysis, primarily because of the shape of the solution space. Neural nets work best with problems that have a continuity of solutions, some better than others. This allows a neural net to learn, proposing better and better solutions as it does. Breaking an algorithm provides for very little in the way of learning opportunities: You either recover the key or you don't. (At least this is true if the algorithm is any good.) Neural nets work well in structured environments where there is something to learn, but not in the high-entropy, seemingly random world of cryptography.

Viruses

The greatest difficulty in getting millions of computers to work on a brute-force attack is convincing millions of computer owners to participate. You could ask politely, but that's time-consuming and they might say no. You could try breaking into their machines, but that's even more time-consuming and you might get arrested. You could also use a computer virus to spread the cracking program more efficiently over as many computers as possible.

This is a particularly insidious idea, first presented in [1593]. The attacker writes and lets loose a computer virus. This virus doesn't reformat the hard drive or delete files; it works on a brute-force cryptanalysis problem whenever the computer is idle. Various studies have shown that microcomputers are idle between 70 percent and 90 percent of the time, so the virus shouldn't have any trouble finding time to work on its task. If it is otherwise benign, it might even escape notice while it does its work.

Eventually, one machine will stumble on the correct key. At this point there are two ways of proceeding. First, the virus could spawn a different virus. It wouldn't do anything but reproduce and delete any copies of the cracking virus it finds but would contain the information about the correct key. This new virus would simply propagate through the computer world until it lands on the computer of the person who wrote the original virus.

A second, sneakier approach would be for the virus to display this message on the screen:

```
There is a serious bug in this computer.
Please call 1-800-123-4567 and read the
following 64-bit number to the operator:

xxxx xxxx xxxx xxxx

There is a $100 reward for the first
person to report this bug.
```

How efficient is this attack? Assume the typical infected computer tries a thousand keys per second. This rate is far less than the computer's maximum potential, because we assume it will be doing other things occasionally. Also assume that the typical virus infects 10 million machines. This virus can break a 56-bit key in 83 days and a 64-bit key in 58 years. You might have to bribe the antiviral software makers, but that's your problem. Any increase in computer speeds or the virus infection rate would, of course, make this attack more efficient.

The Chinese Lottery

The Chinese Lottery is an eclectic, but possible, suggestion for a massively parallel cryptanalysis machine [1278]. Imagine that a brute-force, million-test-per-second cracking chip was built into every radio and television sold. Each chip is programmed to test a different set of keys automatically upon receiving a plaintext/ciphertext pair over the airwaves. Every time the Chinese government wants to break a key, it broadcasts the data. All the radios and televisions in the country start chugging away. Eventually, the correct key will appear on someone's display, somewhere in the country. The Chinese government pays a prize to that person; this makes sure that the result is reported promptly and properly, and also helps the sale of radios and televisions with the cracking chips.

If every man, woman, and child in China owns a radio or television, then the correct key to a 56-bit algorithm will appear in 61 seconds. If only 1 in 10 Chinese owns a radio or television—closer to reality—the correct key will appear in 10 minutes. The correct key for a 64-bit algorithm will appear in 4.3 hours—43 hours if only 1 in 10 owns a radio or television.

Some modifications are required to make this attack practical. First, it would be easier to have each chip try random keys instead of a unique set of keys. This would make the attack about 39 percent slower—not much in light of the numbers we're working with. Also, the Chinese Communist party would have to mandate that every person listen to or watch a certain show at a certain time, just to make sure that all of the radios and televisions are operating when the plaintext/ciphertext pair is broadcast. Finally, everyone would have to be instructed to call a Central-Party-Whatever-It's-Called if a key ever shows up on their screen, and then to read off the string of numbers appearing there.

Table 7.2 shows the effectiveness of the Chinese Lottery for different countries and different key lengths. China would clearly be in the best position to launch such an attack if they have to outfit every man, woman, and child with their own television or radio. The United States has fewer people but a lot more equipment per capita. The state of Wyoming could break a 56-bit key all by itself in less than a day.

Biotechnology

If biochips are possible, then it would be foolish not to use them as a distributed brute-force cryptanalysis tool. Consider a hypothetical animal, unfortunately called a "DESosaur" [1278]. It consists of biological cells capable of testing possible keys. The plaintext/ciphertext pair is broadcast to the cells via some optical channel (these cells are transparent, you see). Solutions are carried to the DESosaur's speech organ via special cells that travel through the animal's circulatory system.

The typical dinosaur had about 10^{14} cells (excluding bacteria). If each of them can perform a million encryptions per second (granted, this is a big if), breaking a 56-bit

Table 7.2
Brute-Force Cracking Estimates for Chinese Lottery

Country	Population	# of Televisions/Radios	TIME TO BREAK 56-bit	TIME TO BREAK 64-bit
China	1,190,431,000	257,000,000	280 seconds	20 hours
U.S.	260,714,000	739,000,000	97 seconds	6.9 hours
Iraq	19,890,000	4,730,000	4.2 hours	44 days
Israel	5,051,000	3,640,000	5.5 hours	58 days
Wyoming	470,000	1,330,000	15 hours	160 days
Winnemucca, NV	6,100	17,300	48 days	34 years

(All data is from the *1995 World Almanac and Book of Facts*.)

key would take seven ten-thousandths of a second. Breaking a 64-bit key would take less than two tenths of a second. Breaking a 128-bit key would still take 10^{11} years, though.

Another biological approach is to use genetically engineered cryptanalytic algae that are capable of performing brute-force attacks against cryptographic algorithms [1278]. These organisms would make it possible to construct a distributed machine with more processors because they could cover a larger area. The plaintext/ciphertext pair could be broadcast by satellite. If an organism found the result, it could induce the nearby cells to change color to communicate the solution back to the satellite.

Assume the typical algae cell is the size of a cube 10 microns on a side (this is probably a large estimate), then 10^{15} of them can fill a cubic meter. Pump them into the ocean and cover 200 square miles (518 square kilometers) of water to a meter deep (you figure out how to do it—I'm just the idea man), and you'd have 10^{23} (over a hundred billion gallons) of them floating in the ocean. (For comparison, the Exxon *Valdez* spilled 10 million gallons of oil.) If each of them can try a million keys per second, they will recover the key for a 128-bit algorithm in just over 100 years. (The resulting algae bloom is your problem.) Breakthroughs in algae processing speed, algae diameter, or even the size puddle one could spread across the ocean, would reduce these numbers significantly.

Don't even ask me about nanotechnology.

Thermodynamic Limitations

One of the consequences of the second law of thermodynamics is that a certain amount of energy is necessary to represent information. To record a single bit by changing the state of a system requires an amount of energy no less than kT, where T is the absolute temperature of the system and k is the Boltzman constant. (Stick with me; the physics lesson is almost over.)

Given that k = $1.38 \cdot 10^{-16}$ erg/°Kelvin, and that the ambient temperature of the universe is 3.2°K, an ideal computer running at 3.2°K would consume $4.4 \cdot 10^{-16}$ ergs every time it set or cleared a bit. To run a computer any colder than the cosmic background radiation would require extra energy to run a heat pump.

Now, the annual energy output of our sun is about $1.21 * 10^{41}$ ergs. This is enough to power about $2.7 * 10^{56}$ single bit changes on our ideal computer; enough state changes to put a 187-bit counter through all its values. If we built a Dyson sphere around the sun and captured all of its energy for 32 years, without any loss, we could power a computer to count up to 2^{192}. Of course, it wouldn't have the energy left over to perform any useful calculations with this counter.

But that's just one star, and a measly one at that. A typical supernova releases something like 10^{51} ergs. (About a hundred times as much energy would be released in the form of neutrinos, but let them go for now.) If all of this energy could be channeled into a single orgy of computation, a 219-bit counter could be cycled through all of its states.

These numbers have nothing to do with the technology of the devices; they are the maximums that thermodynamics will allow. And they strongly imply that brute-force attacks against 256-bit keys will be infeasible until computers are built from something other than matter and occupy something other than space.

7.2   PUBLIC-KEY KEY LENGTH

One-way functions were discussed in Section 2.3. Multiplying two large primes is a one-way function; it's easy to multiply the numbers to get a product but hard to factor the product and recover the two large primes (see Section 11.3). Public-key cryptography uses this idea to make a trap-door one-way function. Actually, that's a lie; factoring is *conjectured to be* a hard problem (see Section 11.4). As far as anyone knows, it seems to be. Even if it is, no one can prove that hard problems are actually hard. Most everyone assumes that factoring is hard, but it has never been mathematically proven one way or the other.

This is worth dwelling on. It is easy to imagine that 50 years in the future we will all sit around, reminiscing about the good old days when people used to think factoring was hard, cryptography was based on factoring, and companies actually made money from this stuff. It is easy to imagine that future developments in number theory will make factoring easier or that developments in complexity theory will make factoring trivial. There's no reason to believe this will happen—and most people who know enough to have an opinion will tell you that it is unlikely—but there's also no reason to believe it won't.

In any case, today's dominant public-key encryption algorithms are based on the difficulty of factoring large numbers that are the product of two large primes. (Other algorithms are based on something called the Discrete Logarithm Problem, but for the moment assume the same discussion applies.) These algorithms are also susceptible to a brute-force attack, but of a different type. Breaking these algorithms does not involve trying every possible key; breaking these algorithms involves trying to factor the large number (or taking discrete logarithms in a very large finite field—a similar problem). If the number is too small, you have no security. If the number is large enough, you have security against all the computing power in the world working from now until the sun goes nova—given today's understanding of the mathematics. Section 11.3 discusses factoring in more mathematical detail; here I will limit the discussion to how long it takes to factor numbers of various lengths.

Factoring large numbers is hard. Unfortunately for algorithm designers, it is getting easier. Even worse, it is getting easier faster than mathematicians expected. In 1976 Richard Guy wrote: "I shall be surprised if anyone regularly factors numbers of size 10^{80} without special form during the present century" [680]. In 1977 Ron Rivest said that factoring a 125-digit number would take 40 quadrillion years [599]. In 1994 a 129-digit number was factored [66]. If there is any lesson in all this, it is that making predictions is foolish.

Table 7.3 shows factoring records over the past dozen years. The fastest factoring algorithm during the time was the quadratic sieve (see Section 11.3).

These numbers are pretty frightening. Today it is not uncommon to see 512-bit numbers used in operational systems. Factoring them, and thereby completely compromising their security, is well in the range of possibility: A weekend-long worm on the Internet could do it.

Computing power is generally measured in mips-years: a one-million-instruction-per-second (mips) computer running for one year, or about $3*10^{13}$ instructions. By convention, a 1-mips machine is equivalent to the DEC VAX 11/780. Hence, a mips-year is a VAX 11/780 running for a year, or the equivalent. (A 100 MHz Pentium is about a 50 mips machine; a 1800-node Intel Paragon is about 50,000.)

The 1983 factorization of a 71-digit number required 0.1 mips-years; the 1994 factorization of a 129-digit number required 5000. This dramatic increase in computing power resulted largely from the introduction of distributed computing, using the idle time on a network of workstations. This trend was started by Bob Silverman and fully developed by Arjen Lenstra and Mark Manasse. The 1983 factorization used 9.5 CPU hours on a single Cray X-MP; the 1994 factorization took 5000 mips-years and used the idle time on 1600 computers around the world for about eight months. Modern factoring methods lend themselves to this kind of distributed implementation.

The picture gets even worse. A new factoring algorithm has taken over from the quadratic sieve: the general number field sieve. In 1989 mathematicians would have

Table 7.3
Factoring Using the Quadratic Sieve

Year	# of decimal digits factored	How many times harder to factor a 512-bit number
1983	71	>20 million
1985	80	>2 million
1988	90	250,000
1989	100	30,000
1993	120	500
1994	129	100

told you that the general number field sieve would never be practical. In 1992 they would have told you that it was practical, but only faster than the quadratic sieve for numbers greater than 130 to 150 digits or so. Today it is known to be faster than the quadratic sieve for numbers well below 116 digits [472,635]. The general number field sieve can factor a 512-bit number over 10 times faster than the quadratic sieve. The algorithm would require less than a year to run on an 1800-node Intel Paragon. Table 7.4 gives the number of mips-years required to factor numbers of different sizes, given current implementations of the general number field sieve [1190].

And the general number field sieve is still getting faster. Mathematicians keep coming up with new tricks, new optimizations, new techniques. There's no reason to think this trend won't continue. A related algorithm, the special number field sieve, can already factor numbers of a certain specialized form—numbers not generally used for cryptography—much faster than the general number field sieve can factor general numbers of the same size. It is not unreasonable to assume that the general number field sieve can be optimized to run this fast [1190]; it is possible that the NSA already knows how to do this. Table 7.5 gives the number of mips-years required for the special number field sieve to factor numbers of different lengths [1190].

At a European Institute for System Security workshop in 1991, the participants agreed that a 1024-bit modulus should be sufficient for long-term secrets through 2002 [150]. However, they warned: "Although the participants of this workshop feel best qualified in their respective areas, this statement [with respect to lasting security] should be taken with caution." This is good advice.

The wise cryptographer is ultra-conservative when choosing public-key key lengths. To determine how long a key you need requires you to look at both the intended security and lifetime of the key, and the current state-of-the-art of factoring. Today you need a 1024-bit number to get the level of security you got from a 512-bit number in the early 1980s. If you want your keys to remain secure for 20 years, 1024 bits is likely too short.

Even if your particular secrets aren't worth the effort required to factor your modulus, you may be at risk. Imagine an automatic banking system that uses RSA for security. Mallory can stand up in court and say: "Did you read in the newspaper in 1994 that RSA-129 was broken, and that 512-bit numbers can be factored by any

Table 7.4
Factoring Using the General
Number Field Sieve

# of bits	Mips-years required to factor
512	30,000
768	$2*10^8$
1024	$3*10^{11}$
1280	$1*10^{14}$
1536	$3*10^{16}$
2048	$3*10^{20}$

Table 7.5
Factoring Using the Special
Number Field Sieve

# of bits	Mips-years required to factor
512	<200
768	100,000
1024	$3*10^7$
1280	$3*10^9$
1536	$2*10^{11}$
2048	$4*10^{14}$

organization willing to spend a few million dollars and wait a few months? My bank uses 512-bit numbers for security and, by the way, I didn't make these seven withdrawals." Even if Mallory is lying, the judge will probably put the onus on the bank to prove it.

Why not use 10,000-bit keys? You can, but remember that you pay a price in computation time as your keys get longer. You want a key long enough to be secure, but short enough to be computationally usable.

Earlier in this section I called making predictions foolish. Now I am about to make some. Table 7.6 gives my recommendations for public-key lengths, depending on how long you require the key to be secure. There are three key lengths for each year, one secure against an individual, one secure against a major corporation, and the third secure against a major government.

Here are some assumptions from [66]:

> We believe that we could acquire 100 thousand machines without superhuman or unethical efforts. That is, we would *not* set free an Internet worm or virus to find resources for us. Many organizations have several thousand machines each on the net. Making use of their facilities would require skillful diplomacy, but should not be impossible. Assuming the 5 mips average power, and one year elapsed time, it is not too unreasonable to embark on a project which would require half a million mips years.

The project to factor the 129-digit number harnessed an estimated 0.03 percent of the total computing power of the Internet [1190], and they didn't even try very hard. It isn't unreasonable to assume that a well-publicized project can harness 2 percent of the world's computing power for a year.

Assume a dedicated cryptanalyst can get his hands on 10,000 mips-years, a large corporation can get 10^7 mips-years, and that a large government can get 10^9 mips-years. Also assume that computing power will increase by a factor of 10 every five years. And finally, assume that advances in factoring mathematics allow us to factor general numbers at the speeds of the special number field sieve. (This isn't possible yet, but the breakthrough could occur at any time.) Table 7.6 recommends different key lengths for security during different years.

Table 7.6
Recommended Public-key Key Lengths (in bits)

Year	vs. Individual	vs. Corporation	vs. Government
1995	768	1280	1536
2000	1024	1280	1536
2005	1280	1536	2048
2010	1280	1536	2048
2015	1536	2048	2048

Remember to take the value of the key into account. Public keys are often used to secure things of great value for a long time: the bank's master key for a digital cash system, the key the government uses to certify its passports, or a notary public's digital signature key. It probably isn't worth the effort to spend months of computing time to break an individual's private key, but if you can print your own money with a broken key the idea becomes more attractive. A 1024-bit key is long enough to sign something that will be verified within the week, or month, or even a few years. But you don't want to stand up in court 20 years from now with a digitally signed document and have the opposition demonstrate how to forge documents with the same signature.

Making predictions beyond the near future is even more foolish. Who knows what kind of advances in computing, networking, and mathematics are going to happen by 2020? However, if you look at the broad picture, in every decade we can factor numbers twice as long as in the previous decade. This leads to Table 7.7.

On the other hand, factoring technology may reach its Omega point long before 2045. Twenty years from now, we may be able to factor anything. I think that is unlikely, though.

Not everyone will agree with my recommendations. The NSA has mandated 512-bit to 1024-bit keys for their Digital Signature Standard (see Section 20.1)—far less than I recommend for long-term security. Pretty Good Privacy (see Section 24.12) has a maximum RSA key length of 2047 bits. Arjen Lenstra, the world's most suc-

Table 7.7
Long-range
Factoring Predictions

Year	Key Length (in bits)
1995	1024
2005	2048
2015	4096
2025	8192
2035	16,384
2045	32,768

cessful factorer, refuses to make predictions past 10 years [949]. Table 7.8 gives Ron Rivest's key-length recommendations, originally made in 1990, which I consider much too optimistic [1323]. While his analysis looks fine on paper, recent history illustrates that surprises regularly happen. It makes sense to choose your keys to be resilient against future surprises.

Low estimates assume a budget of $25,000, the quadratic sieve algorithm, and a technology advance of 20 percent per year. Average estimates assume a budget of $25 million, the general number field sieve algorithm, and a technology advance of 33 percent per year. High estimates assume a budget of $25 billion, a general quadratic sieve algorithm running at the speed of the special number field sieve, and a technology advance of 45 percent per year.

There is always the possibility that an advance in factoring will surprise me as well, but I factored that into my calculations. But why trust me? I just proved my own foolishness by making predictions.

DNA Computing

Now it gets weird. In 1994 Leonard M. Adleman actually demonstrated a method for solving an **NP-complete** problem (see Section 11.2) in a biochemistry laboratory, using DNA molecules to represent guesses at solutions to the problem [17]. (That's "solutions" meaning "answers," not meaning "liquids containing solutes." Terminology in this field is going to be awkward.) The problem that Adleman solved was an instance of the Directed Hamiltonian Path problem: Given a map of cities connected by one-way roads, find a path from City A to City Z that passes exactly once through all other cities on the map. Each city was represented by a different random 20-base string of DNA; with conventional molecular biology techniques, Adleman synthesized 50 picomols (30 million million molecules) of the DNA string representing each city. Each road was also represented by a 20-base DNA string, but these strings were not chosen randomly: They were cleverly chosen so that the "beginning" end of the DNA string representing the road from City P to City K ("Road PK") would tend to stick to the DNA string representing City P, and the end of Road PK would tend to stick to City K.

Table 7.8
Rivest's Optimistic Key-length
Recommendations (in bits)

Year	Low	Average	High
1990	398	515	1289
1995	405	542	1399
2000	422	572	1512
2005	439	602	1628
2010	455	631	1754
2015	472	661	1884
2020	489	677	2017

Adleman synthesized 50 picomols of the DNA representing each road, mixed them all together with the DNA representing all the cities, and added a ligase enzyme, which links together the ends of DNA molecules. The clever relationship between the road DNA strings and the city DNA strings causes the ligase to link the road DNA strings together in a legal fashion. That is, the "exit" end of the road from P to K will always be linked to the "entrance" end of some road that originates at City K, never to the "exit" end of any road and never to the "entrance" end of a road that originates at some city other than K. After a carefully limited reaction time, the ligase has built a large number of DNA strings representing legal but otherwise random multiroad paths within the map.

From this soup of random paths, Adleman can find the tiniest trace—perhaps even a single molecule—of the DNA that represents the answer to the problem. Using common techniques of molecular biology, he discards all the DNA strings representing paths that are too long or too short. (The number of roads in the desired path must equal the number of cities minus one.) Next he discards all the DNA strings that do not pass through City A, then those that miss City B, and so forth. If any DNA survives this screening, it is examined to find the sequence of roads that it represents: This is the solution to the directed Hamiltonian path problem.

By definition, an instance of any **NP-complete** problem can be transformed, in polynomial time, into an instance of any other **NP-complete** problem, and therefore into an instance of the directed Hamiltonian path problem. Since the 1970s, cryptologists have been trying to use **NP-complete** problems for public-key cryptography.

While the instance that Adleman solved was very modest (seven cities on his map, a problem that can be solved by inspection in a few minutes), the technique is in its infancy and has no forbidding obstacles keeping it from being extended to larger problems. Thus, arguments about the security of cryptographic protocols based on **NP-complete** problems, arguments that heretofore have begun, "Suppose an adversary has a million processors, each of which can perform a million tests each second," may soon have to be replaced with, "Suppose an adversary has a thousand fermentation vats, each 20,000 liters in capacity."

Quantum Computing

Now, it gets even weirder. The underlying principle behind quantum computing involves Einstein's wave-particle duality. A photon can simultaneously exist in a large number of states. A classic example is that a photon behaves like a wave when it encounters a partially silvered mirror; it is both reflected and transmitted, just as an ocean wave striking a seawall with a small opening in it will both reflect off the wall and pass through it. However, when a photon is measured, it behaves like a particle and only a single state can be detected.

In [1443], Peter Shor outlines a design for a factoring machine based on quantum mechanical principles. Unlike a classical computer, which can be thought of as having a single, fixed state at a given time, a quantum computer has an internal wave function, which is a superposition of a combination of the possible basis states. Computations transform the wave function, altering the entire set of states in a single operation. In this way, a quantum computer is an improvement over classical finite-state automata: It uses quantum properties to allow it to factor in polynomial time, theoretically allowing one to break cryptosystems based on factoring or the discrete logarithm problem.

The consensus is that quantum computers are compatible with the fundamental laws of quantum mechanics. However, it is unlikely that a quantum factoring machine will be built in the foreseeable future . . . if ever. One major obstacle is the problem of decoherence, which causes superimposed waveforms to lose their distinctness and makes the computer fail. Decoherence will make a quantum computer running at 1° Kelvin fail after just one nanosecond. Additionally, an enormous number of gates would be required to build a quantum factoring device; this may render the machine impossible to build. Shor's design requires a complete modular exponentiator. No internal clock can be used, so millions or possibly billions of individual gates would be required to factor cryptographically significant numbers. If n quantum gates have some minimum probability p of failure, the average number of trials required per successful run is $(1/(1 - p))^n$. The number of gates required presumably grows polynomially with the length (in bits) of the number, so the number of trials required would be superexponential with the length of the numbers used—worse than factoring by trial division!

So, while quantum factorization is an area of great academic excitement, it is extremely unlikely that it will be practical in the foreseeable future. But don't say I didn't warn you.

7.3 COMPARING SYMMETRIC AND PUBLIC-KEY KEY LENGTH

A system is going to be attacked at its weakest point. If you are designing a system that uses both symmetric and public-key cryptography, the key lengths for each type of cryptography should be chosen so that it is equally difficult to attack the system via each mechanism. It makes no sense to use a symmetric algorithm with a 128-bit key together with a public-key algorithm with a 386-bit key, just as it makes no sense to use a symmetric algorithm with a 56-bit key together with a public-key algorithm with a 1024-bit key.

Table 7.9 lists public-key modulus lengths whose factoring difficulty roughly equals the difficulty of a brute-force attack for popular symmetric key lengths.

This table says that if you are concerned enough about security to choose a symmetric algorithm with a 112-bit key, you should choose a modulus length for your public-key algorithm of about 1792 bits. In general, though, you should choose a public-key length that is more secure than your symmetric-key length. Public keys generally stay around longer, and are used to protect more information.

7.4 BIRTHDAY ATTACKS AGAINST ONE-WAY HASH FUNCTIONS

There are two brute-force attacks against a one-way hash function. The first is the most obvious: Given the hash of message, $H(M)$, an adversary would like to be able to create another document, M', such that $H(M) = H(M')$. The second attack is more

Table 7.9
Symmetric and Public-key Key Lengths
with Similar Resistances to Brute-Force Attacks

Symmetric Key Length	Public-key Key Length
56 bits	384 bits
64 bits	512 bits
80 bits	768 bits
112 bits	1792 bits
128 bits	2304 bits

subtle: An adversary would like to find two random messages, M, and M', such that $H(M) = H(M')$. This is called a **collision**, and it is a far easier attack than the first one.

The birthday paradox is a standard statistics problem. How many people must be in a room for the chance to be greater than even that one of them shares your birthday? The answer is 253. Now, how many people must there be for the chance to be greater than even that at least two of them will share the same birthday? The answer is surprisingly low: 23. With only 23 people in the room, there are still 253 different *pairs* of people in the room.

Finding someone with a specific birthday is analogous to the first attack; finding two people with the same random birthday is analogous to the second attack. The second attack is commonly known as a **birthday attack**.

Assume that a one-way hash function is secure and the best way to attack it is by using brute force. It produces an m-bit output. Finding a message that hashes to a given hash value would require hashing 2^m random messages. Finding two messages that hash to the same value would only require hashing $2^{m/2}$ random messages. A machine that hashes a million messages per second would take 600,000 years to find a second message that matched a given 64-bit hash. The same machine could find a pair of messages that hashed to the same value in about an hour.

This means that if you are worried about a birthday attack, you should choose a hash-value twice as long as you otherwise might think you need. For example, if you want to drop the odds of someone breaking your system to less than 1 in 2^{80}, use a 160-bit one-way hash function.

7.5 How Long Should a Key Be?

There's no single answer to this question; it depends on the situation. To determine how much security you need, you must ask yourself some questions. How much is your data worth? How long does it need to be secure? What are your adversaries' resources?

A customer list might be worth $1000. Financial data for an acrimonious divorce case might be worth $10,000. Advertising and marketing data for a large corporation might be worth $1 million. The master keys for a digital cash system might be worth billions.

In the world of commodities trading, secrets only need to be kept for minutes. In the newspaper business, today's secrets are tomorrow's headlines. Product development information might need to remain secret for a year or two. U.S. Census data are required by law to remain secret for 100 years.

The guest list for your sister's surprise birthday party is only interesting to your nosy relatives. Corporate trade secrets are interesting to rival companies. Military secrets are interesting to rival militaries.

You can even specify security requirements in these terms. For example:

> The key length must be such that there is a probability of no more than 1 in 2^{32} that an attacker with $100 million to spend could break the system within one year, even assuming technology advances at a rate of 30 percent per annum over the period.

Table 7.10, taken partially from [150], estimates the secrecy requirements for several kinds of information:

Future computing power is harder to estimate, but here is a reasonable rule of thumb: The efficiency of computing equipment divided by price doubles every 18 months and increases by a factor of 10 every five years. Thus, in 50 years the fastest computers will be 10 billion times faster than today's! Remember, too, that these numbers only relate to general-purpose computers; who knows what kind of specialized cryptosystem-breaking equipment will be developed in the next 50 years?

Assuming that a cryptographic algorithm will be in use for 30 years, you can get some idea how secure it must be. An algorithm designed today probably will not see general use until 2000, and will still be used in 2025 to encrypt messages that must remain secret until 2075 or later.

Table 7.10
Security Requirements for Different Information

Type of Traffic	Lifetime	Minimum Key Length
Tactical military information	minutes/hours	56–64 bits
Product announcements, mergers, interest rates	days/weeks	64 bits
Long-term business plans	years	64 bits
Trade secrets (e.g., recipe for Coca-Cola)	decades	112 bits
H-bomb secrets	>40 years	128 bits
Identities of spies	>50 years	128 bits
Personal affairs	>50 years	128 bits
Diplomatic embarrassments	>65 years	at least 128 bits
U.S. census data	100 years	at least 128 bits

7.6 CAVEAT EMPTOR

This entire chapter is a whole lot of nonsense. The very notion of predicting computing power 10 years in the future, let alone 50 years is absolutely ridiculous. These calculations are meant to be a guide, nothing more. If the past is any guide, the future will be vastly different from anything we can predict.

Be conservative. If your keys are longer than you imagine necessary, then fewer technological surprises can harm you.

CHAPTER 8

Key Management

Alice and Bob have a secure communications system. They play mental poker, simultaneously sign contracts, even exchange digital cash. Their protocols are secure. Their algorithms are top-notch. Unfortunately, they buy their keys from Eve's "Keys-R-Us," whose slogan is "You can trust us: Security is the middle name of someone our ex-mother-in-law's travel agent met at the Kwik-E-Mart."

Eve doesn't have to break the algorithms. She doesn't have to rely on subtle flaws in the protocols. She can use their keys to read all of Alice's and Bob's message traffic without lifting a cryptanalytic finger.

In the real world, key management is the hardest part of cryptography. Designing secure cryptographic algorithms and protocols isn't easy, but you can rely on a large body of academic research. Keeping the keys secret is much harder.

Cryptanalysts often attack both symmetric and public-key cryptosystems through their key management. Why should Eve bother going through all the trouble of trying to break the cryptographic algorithm if she can recover the key because of sloppy key storage procedures? Why should she spend $10 million building a cryptanalysis machine if she can spend $1000 bribing a clerk? Spending a million dollars to buy a well-placed communications clerk in a diplomatic embassy can be a bargain. The Walkers sold U.S. Navy encryption keys to the Soviets for years. The CIA's director of counterintelligence went for less than $2 million, wife included. That's far cheaper than building massive cracking machines and hiring brilliant cryptanalysts. Eve can steal the keys. She can arrest or abduct someone who knows the keys. She can seduce someone and get the keys that way. (The Marines who guarded the U.S. Embassy in Moscow were not immune to that attack.) It's a whole lot easier to find flaws in people than it is to find them in cryptosystems.

Alice and Bob must protect their key to the same degree as all the data it encrypts. If a key isn't changed regularly, this can be an enormous amount of data. Unfortunately, many commercial products simply proclaim "We use DES" and forget about everything else. The results are not very impressive.

For example, the DiskLock program for Macintosh (version 2.1), sold at most software stores, claims the security of DES encryption. It encrypts files using DES. Its implementation of the DES algorithm is correct. However, DiskLock stores the DES key with the encrypted file. If you know where to look for the key, and want to read a file encrypted with DiskLock's DES, recover the key from the encrypted file and then decrypt the file. It doesn't matter that this program uses DES encryption—the implementation is completely insecure.

Further information on key management can be found in [457,98,1273,1225, 775,357]. The following sections discuss some of the issues and solutions.

8.1 GENERATING KEYS

The security of an algorithm rests in the key. If you're using a cryptographically weak process to generate keys, then your whole system is weak. Eve need not cryptanalyze your encryption algorithm; she can cryptanalyze your key generation algorithm.

Reduced Keyspaces

DES has a 56-bit key. Implemented properly, any 56-bit string can be the key; there are 2^{56} (10^{16}) possible keys. Norton Discreet for MS-DOS (versions 8.0 and earlier) only allows ASCII keys, forcing the high-order bit of each byte to be zero. The program also converts lowercase letters to uppercase (so the fifth bit of each byte is always the opposite of the sixth bit) and ignores the low-order bit of each byte, resulting in only 2^{40} possible keys. These poor key generation procedures have made its DES ten thousand times easier to break than a proper implementation.

Table 8.1 gives the number of possible keys with various constraints on the input strings. Table 8.2 gives the time required for an exhaustive search through all of those keys, given a million attempts per second. Remember, there is very little time differential between an exhaustive search for 8-byte keys and an exhaustive search of 4-, 5-, 6-, 7-, and 8-byte keys.

All specialized brute-force hardware and parallel implementations will work here. Testing a million keys per second (either with one machine or with multiple machines in parallel), it is feasible to crack lowercase-letter and lowercase-letter-

Table 8.1
Number of Possible Keys of Various Keyspaces

	4-Byte	5-Byte	6-Byte	7-Byte	8-Byte
Lowercase letters (26):	460,000	$1.2 \cdot 10^7$	$3.1 \cdot 10^8$	$8.0 \cdot 10^9$	$2.1 \cdot 10^{11}$
Lowercase letters and digits (36):	1,700,000	$6.0 \cdot 10^7$	$2.2 \cdot 10^9$	$7.8 \cdot 10^{10}$	$2.8 \cdot 10^{12}$
Alphanumeric characters (62):	$1.5 \cdot 10^7$	$9.2 \cdot 10^8$	$5.7 \cdot 10^{10}$	$3.5 \cdot 10^{12}$	$2.2 \cdot 10^{14}$
Printable characters (95):	$8.1 \cdot 10^7$	$7.7 \cdot 10^9$	$7.4 \cdot 10^{11}$	$7.0 \cdot 10^{13}$	$6.6 \cdot 10^{15}$
ASCII characters (128):	$2.7 \cdot 10^8$	$3.4 \cdot 10^{10}$	$4.4 \cdot 10^{12}$	$5.6 \cdot 10^{14}$	$7.2 \cdot 10^{16}$
8-bit ASCII characters (256):	$4.3 \cdot 10^9$	$1.1 \cdot 10^{12}$	$2.8 \cdot 10^{14}$	$7.2 \cdot 10^{16}$	$1.8 \cdot 10^{19}$

Table 8.2
Exhaustive Search of Various Keyspaces (assume one million attempts per second)

	4-Byte	5-Byte	6-Byte	7-Byte	8-Byte
Lowercase letters (26):	.5 seconds	12 seconds	5 minutes	2.2 hours	2.4 days
Lowercase letters and digits (36):	1.7 seconds	1 minute	36 minutes	22 hours	33 days
Alphanumeric characters (62):	15 seconds	15 minutes	16 hours	41 days	6.9 years
Printable characters (95):	1.4 minutes	2.1 hours	8.5 days	2.2 years	210 years
ASCII characters (128):	4.5 minutes	9.5 hours	51 days	18 years	2300 years
8-bit ASCII characters (256):	1.2 hours	13 days	8.9 years	2300 years	580,000 years

and-number keys up to 8 bytes long, alphanumeric-character keys up to 7 bytes long, printable character and ASCII-character keys up to 6 bytes long, and 8-bit-ASCII-character keys up to 5 bytes long.

And remember, computing power doubles every 18 months. If you expect your keys to stand up against brute-force attacks for 10 years, you'd better plan accordingly.

Poor Key Choices

When people choose their own keys, they generally choose poor ones. They're far more likely to choose "Barney" than "*9 (hH/A." This is not always due to poor security practices; "Barney" is easier to remember than "*9 (hH/A." The world's most secure algorithm won't help much if the users habitually choose their spouse's names for keys or write their keys on little pieces of paper in their wallets. A smart brute-force attack doesn't try all possible keys in numerical order; it tries the obvious keys first.

This is called a **dictionary attack**, because the attacker uses a dictionary of common keys. Daniel Klein was able to crack 40 percent of the passwords on the average computer using this system [847,848]. No, he didn't try one password after another, trying to login. He copied the encrypted password file and mounted the attack offline. Here's what he tried:

1. The user's name, initials, account name, and other relevant personal information as a possible password. All in all, up to 130 different passwords were tried based on this information. For an account name **klone** with a user named "Daniel V. Klein," some of the passwords that would be tried were: klone, klone0, klone1, klone123, dvk, dvkdvk, dklein, DKlein leinad, nielk, dvklein, danielk, DvkkvD, DANIEL-KLEIN, (klone), KleinD, and so on.

2. Words from various databases. These included lists of men's and women's names (some 16,000 in all); places (including variations so that "spain," "spanish," and "spaniard" would all be considered); names of famous people; cartoons and cartoon characters; titles, characters, and locations from films and science fiction stories; mythical creatures (garnered from *Bullfinch's Mythology* and dictionaries of mythical beasts); sports (includ-

ing team names, nicknames, and specialized terms); numbers (both as numerals—"2001," and written out—"twelve"); strings of letters and numbers ("a," "aa," "aaa," "aaaa," etc.); Chinese syllables (from the Pinyin Romanization of Chinese, an international standard system of writing Chinese on an English keyboard); the King James Bible; biological terms; colloquial and vulgar phrases (such as "fuckyou," "ibmsux," and "deadhead"); keyboard patterns (such as "qwerty," "asdf," and "zxcvbn"); abbreviations (such as "roygbiv"—the colors in the rainbow, and "ooottafagvah"—a mnemonic for remembering the 12 cranial nerves); machine names (acquired from */etc/hosts*); characters, plays, and locations from Shakespeare; common Yiddish words; the names of asteroids; and a collection of words from various technical papers Klein previously published. All told, more than 60,000 separate words were considered per user (with any inter- and intra-dictionary duplicates being discarded).

3. Variations on the words from step 2. This included making the first letter uppercase or a control character, making the entire word uppercase, reversing the word (with and without the aforementioned capitalization), changing the letter 'o' to the digit '0' (so that the word "scholar" would also be checked as "sch0lar"), changing the letter 'l' to the digit '1' (so that the word "scholar" would also be checked as "scho1ar"), and performing similar manipulation to change the letter 'z' into the digit '2', and the letter 's' into the digit '5'. Another test was to make the word into a plural (irrespective of whether the word was actually a noun), with enough intelligence built in so that "dress" became "dresses," "house" became "houses," and "daisy" became "daisies." Klein did not consider pluralization rules exclusively, though, so that "datum" forgivably became "datums" (not "data"), while "sphynx" became "sphynxs" (and not "sphynges"). Similarly, the suffixes "-ed," "-er," and "-ing" were added to transform words like "phase" into "phased," "phaser," and "phasing." These additional tests added another 1,000,000 words to the list of possible passwords that were tested for each user.

4. Various capitalization variations on the words from step 2 that were not considered in step 3. This included all single-letter capitalization variations (so that "michael" would also be checked as "mIchael," "miChael," "micHael," "michAel," etc.), double-letter capitalization variations ("MIchael," "MiChael," "MicHael," ..., "mIChael," "mIcHael," etc.), triple-letter variations, etc. The single-letter variations added roughly another 400,000 words to be checked per user, while the double-letter variations added another 1,500,000 words. Three-letter variations would have added at least another 3,000,000 words per user had there been enough time to complete the tests. Tests of four-, five-, and six-letter variations were deemed to be impracticable without much more computational horsepower to carry them out.

5. Foreign language words on foreign users. The specific test that was performed was to try Chinese language passwords on users with Chinese

names. The Pinyin Romanization of Chinese syllables was used, combining syllables together into one-, two-, and three-syllable words. Because no tests were done to determine whether the words actually made sense, an exhaustive search was initiated. Since there are 298 Chinese syllables in the Pinyin system, there are 158,404 two-syllable words, and slightly more than 16,000,000 three-syllable words. A similar mode of attack could as easily be used with English, using rules for building pronounceable nonsense words.

6. Word pairs. The magnitude of an exhaustive test of this nature is staggering. To simplify the test, only words of three or four characters in length from /usr/dict/words were used. Even so, the number of word pairs is about ten million.

A dictionary attack is much more powerful when it is used against a file of keys and not a single key. A single user may be smart enough to choose good keys. If a thousand people each choose their own key as a password to a computer system, the odds are excellent that at least one person will choose a key in the attacker's dictionary.

Random Keys

Good keys are random-bit strings generated by some automatic process. If the key is 64 bits long, every possible 64-bit key must be equally likely. Generate the key bits from either a reliably random source (see Section 17.14) or a cryptographically secure pseudo-random-bit generator (see Chapters 16 and 17.) If these automatic processes are unavailable, flip a coin or roll a die.

This is important, but don't get too caught up in arguing about whether random noise from audio sources is more random than random noise from radioactive decay. None of these random-noise sources will be perfect, but they will probably be good enough. It is important to use a good random-number generator for key generation, but it is far more important to use good encryption algorithms and key management procedures. If you are worried about the randomness of your keys, use the key-crunching technique described below.

Some encryption algorithms have weak keys: specific keys that are less secure than the other keys. I advise testing for these weak keys and generating a new one if you discover one. DES has only 16 weak keys out of 2^{56}, so the odds of generating any of these keys are incredibly small. It has been argued that a cryptanalyst would have no idea that a weak key is being used and therefore gains no advantage from their accidental use. It has also been argued that not using weak keys gives a cryptanalyst information. However, testing for the few weak keys is so easy that it seems imprudent not to do so.

Generating keys for public-key cryptography systems is harder, because often the keys must have certain mathematical properties (they may have to be prime, be a quadratic residue, etc.). Techniques for generating large random prime numbers are discussed in Section 11.5. The important thing to remember from a key management point of view is that the random seeds for those generators must be just that: random.

Generating a random key isn't always possible. Sometimes you need to remember your key. (See how long it takes you to remember 25e8 56f2 e8ba c820). If you have to generate an easy-to-remember key, make it obscure. The ideal would be something easy to remember, but difficult to guess. Here are some suggestions:

— Word pairs separated by a punctuation character, for example "turtle*moose" or "zorch!splat"

— Strings of letters that are an acronym of a longer phrase; for example, "Mein Luftkissenfahrzeug ist voller Aale!" generates the key "MLivA!"

Pass Phrases

A better solution is to use an entire phrase instead of a word, and to convert that phrase into a key. These phrases are called **pass phrases**. A technique called **key crunching** converts the easy-to-remember phrases into random keys. Use a one-way hash function to transform an arbitrary-length text string into a pseudo-random-bit string.

For example, the easy-to-remember text string:

```
My name is Ozymandias, king of kings. Look on my works, ye mighty, and despair.
```

might crunch into this 64-bit key:

```
e6c1 4398 5ae9 0a9b
```

Of course, it can be difficult to type an entire phrase into a computer with the echo turned off. Clever suggestions to solve this problem would be appreciated.

If the phrase is long enough, the resulting key will be random. Exactly what "long enough" means is open to interpretation. Information theory tells us that standard English has about 1.3 bits of information per character (see Section 11.1). For a 64-bit key, a pass phrase of about 49 characters, or 10 normal English words, should be sufficient. As a rule of thumb, figure that you need five words for each 4 bytes of key. That's a conservative assumption, since it doesn't take into account case, spacing, and punctuation.

This technique can even be used to generate private keys for public-key cryptography systems: The text string could be crunched into a random seed, and that seed could be fed into a deterministic system that generates public-key/private-key key pairs.

If you are choosing a pass phrase, choose something unique and easy-to-remember. Don't choose phrases from literature—the example from "Ozymandias" is a bad one. Both the complete works of Shakespeare and the dialogue from *Star Wars* are available on-line and can be used in a dictionary attack. Choose something obscure, but personal. Include punctuation and capitalization; if you can, include numbers and non-alphanumeric symbols. Poor or improper English, or even a foreign language, makes the pass phrase less susceptible to a dictionary attack. One suggestion is to use a phrase that is "shocking nonsense": something offensive enough that you are likely to remember and unlikely to write down.

Despite everything written here, obscurity is no substitute for true randomness. The best keys are random keys, difficult as they are to remember.

X9.17 Key Generation

The ANSI X9.17 standard specifies a method of key generation (see Figure 8.1) [55]. This does not generate easy-to-remember keys; it is more suitable for generating session keys or pseudo-random numbers within a system. The cryptographic algorithm used to generate keys is triple-DES, but it could just as easily be any algorithm.

Let $E_K(X)$ be triple-DES encryption of X with key K. This is a special key reserved for secret key generation. V_0 is a secret 64-bit seed. T is a timestamp. To generate the random key R_i, calculate:

$$R_i = E_K(E_K(T_i) \oplus V_i)$$

To generate V_{i+1}, calculate:

$$V_{i+1} = E_K(E_K(T_i) \oplus R_i)$$

To turn R_i into a DES key, simply adjust every eighth bit for parity. If you need a 64-bit key, use it as is. If you need a 128-bit key, generate a pair of keys and concatenate them together.

DoD Key Generation

The U.S. Department of Defense recommends using DES in OFB mode (see Section 9.8) to generate random keys [1144]. Generate a DES key from system interrupt vectors, system status registers, and system counters. Generate an initialization vector from the system clock, system ID, and date and time. For the plaintext, use an externally generated 64-bit quantity: eight characters typed in by a system administrator, for example. Use the output as your key.

8.2 NONLINEAR KEYSPACES

Imagine that you are a military cryptography organization, building a piece of cryptography equipment for your troops. You want to use a secure algorithm, but you are

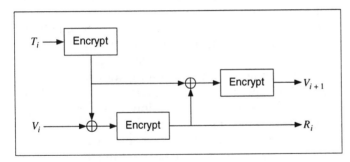

Figure 8.1   ANSI X9.17 key generation.

worried about the equipment falling into enemy hands. The last thing you want is for your enemy to be able to use the equipment to protect *their* secrets.

If you can put your algorithm in a tamperproof module, here's what you can do. You can require keys of a special and secret form; all other keys will cause the module to encrypt and decrypt using a severely weakened algorithm. You can make it so that the odds of someone, not knowing this special form but accidentally stumbling on a correct key, are vanishingly small.

This is called a **nonlinear keyspace**, because all the keys are not equally strong. (The opposite is a linear, or **flat**, keyspace.) An easy way to do this is to create the key as two parts: the key itself and some fixed string encrypted with that key. The module decrypts the string with the key; if it gets the fixed string it uses the key normally, if not it uses a different, weak algorithm. If the algorithm has a 128-bit key and a 64-bit block size, the overall key is 192 bits; this gives the algorithm an effective key of 2^{128}, but makes the odds of randomly choosing a good key one in 2^{64}.

You can be even subtler. You can design an algorithm such that certain keys are stronger than others. An algorithm can have no weak keys—keys that are obviously very poor—and can still have a nonlinear keyspace.

This only works if the algorithm is secret and the enemy can't reverse-engineer it, or if the difference in key strength is subtle enough that the enemy can't figure it out. The NSA did this with the secret algorithms in their Overtake modules (see Section 25.1). Did they do the same thing with Skipjack (see Section 13.12)? No one knows.

8.3   TRANSFERRING KEYS

Alice and Bob are going to use a symmetric cryptographic algorithm to communicate securely; they need the same key. Alice generates a key using a random-key generator. Now she has to give it to Bob—securely. If Alice can meet Bob somewhere (a back alley, a windowless room, or one of Jupiter's moons), she can give him a copy of the key. Otherwise, they have a problem. Public-key cryptography solves the problem nicely and with a minimum of prearrangement, but these techniques are not always available (see Section 3.1). Some systems use alternate channels known to be secure. Alice could send Bob the key with a trusted messenger. She could send it by certified mail or via an overnight delivery service. She could set up another communications channel with Bob and hope no one is eavesdropping on that one.

Alice could send Bob the symmetric key over their communications channel—the one they are going to encrypt. This is foolish; if the channel warrants encryption, sending the encryption key in the clear over the same channel guarantees that anyone eavesdropping on the channel can decrypt all communications.

The X9.17 standard [55] specifies two types of keys: key-encryption keys and data keys. **Key-Encryption Keys** encrypt other keys for distribution. **Data Keys** encrypt message traffic. These key-encrypting keys have to be distributed manually (although they can be secured in a tamperproof device, like a smart card), but only seldomly. Data keys are distributed more often. More details are in [75]. This two-tiered key concept is used a lot in key distribution.

Another solution to the distribution problem splits the key into several different parts (see Section 3.6) and sends each of those parts over a different channel. One part could be sent over the telephone, one by mail, one by overnight delivery service, one by carrier pigeon, and so on. (see Figure 8.2). Since an adversary could collect all but one of the parts and still have no idea what the key is, this method will work in all but extreme cases. Section 3.6 discusses schemes for splitting a key into several parts. Alice could even use a secret sharing scheme (see Section 3.7), allowing Bob to reconstruct the key if some of the shares are lost in transmission.

Alice sends Bob the key-encryption key securely, either by a face-to-face meeting or the splitting technique just discussed. Once Alice and Bob both have the key-encryption key, Alice can send Bob daily data keys over the same communications channel. Alice encrypts each data key with the key-encryption key. Since the amount of traffic being encrypted with the key-encryption key is low, it does not have to be changed as often. However, since compromise of the key-encryption key could compromise every message encrypted with every key that was encrypted with the key-encryption key, it must be stored securely.

Key Distribution in Large Networks

Key-encryption keys shared by pairs of users work well in small networks, but can quickly get cumbersome if the networks become large. Since every pair of users must exchange keys, the total number of key exchanges required in an n-person network is $n(n - 1)/2$.

In a six-person network, 15 key exchanges are required. In a 1000-person network, nearly 500,000 key exchanges are required. In these cases, creating a central key server (or servers) makes the operation much more efficient.

Alternatively, any of the symmetric-cryptography or public-key-cryptography protocols in Section 3.1 provides for secure key distribution.

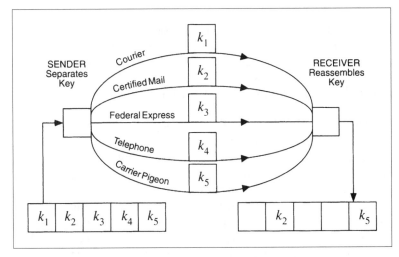

Figure 8.2   Key distribution via parallel channels.

8.4 VERIFYING KEYS

When Bob receives a key, how does he know it came from Alice and not from someone pretending to be Alice? If Alice gives it to him when they are face-to-face, it's easy. If Alice sends her key via a trusted courier, then Bob has to trust the courier. If the key is encrypted with a key-encryption key, then Bob has to trust the fact that only Alice has that key. If Alice uses a digital signature protocol to sign the key, Bob has to trust the public-key database when he verifies that signature. (He also has to trust that Alice has kept her key secure.) If a Key Distribution Center (KDC) signs Alice's public key, Bob has to trust that his copy of the KDC's public key has not been tampered with.

In the end, someone who controls the entire network around Bob can make him think whatever he likes. Mallory could send an encrypted and signed message purporting to be from Alice. When Bob tried to access the public-key database to verify Alice's signature, Mallory could substitute his own public key. Mallory could invent his own false KDC and exchange the real KDC's public key for his own creation. Bob wouldn't be the wiser.

Some people have used this argument to claim that public-key cryptography is useless. Since the only way for Alice and Bob to ensure that their keys have not been tampered with is to meet face-to-face, public-key cryptography doesn't enhance security at all.

This view is naïve. It is theoretically true, but reality is far more complicated. Public-key cryptography, used with digital signatures and trusted KDCs, makes it much more difficult to substitute one key for another. Bob can never be absolutely certain that Mallory isn't controlling his entire reality, but Bob can be confident that doing so requires more resources than most real-world Mallorys have access to.

Bob could also verify Alice's key over the telephone, where he can hear her voice. Voice recognition is a really good authentication scheme. If it's a public key, he can safely recite it in public. If it's a secret key, he can use a one-way hash function to verify the key. Both PGP (see Section 24.12) and the AT&T TSD (see Section 24.18) use this kind of key verification.

Sometimes, it may not even be important to verify exactly whom a public key belongs to. It may be necessary to verify that it belongs to the same person to whom it belonged last year. If someone sends a signed withdrawal message to a bank, the bank does not have to be concerned with who withdraws the money, only whether it is the same person who deposited the money in the first place.

Error Detection during Key Transmission

Sometimes keys get garbled in transmission. Since a garbled key can mean megabytes of undecryptable ciphertext, this is a problem. All keys should be transmitted with some kind of error detection and correction bits. This way errors in transmission can be easily detected and, if required, the key can be resent.

One of the most widely used methods is to encrypt a constant value with the key, and to send the first 2 to 4 bytes of that ciphertext along with the key. At the receiving end, do the same thing. If the encrypted constants match, then the key has been transmitted without error. The chance of an undetected error ranges from one in 2^{16} to one in 2^{32}.

Key-error Detection during Decryption

Sometimes the receiver wants to check if a particular key he has is the correct symmetric decryption key. If the plaintext message is something like ASCII, he can try to decrypt and read the message. If the plaintext is random, there are other tricks.

The naïve approach is to attach a **verification block**: a known header to the plaintext message before encryption. At the receiving end, Bob decrypts the header and verifies that it is correct. This works, but it gives Eve a known plaintext to help cryptanalyze the system. It also makes attacks against short-key ciphers like DES and all exportable ciphers easy. Precalculate the checksum once for each key, then use that checksum to determine the key in any message you intercept after that. This is a feature of *any* key checksum that doesn't include random or at least different data in each checksum. It's very similar in concept to using salt when generating keys from passphrases.

Here's a better way to do this [821]:

(1) Generate an IV (not the one used for the message).
(2) Use that IV to generate a large block of bits: say, 512.
(3) Hash the result.
(4) Use the same fixed bits of the hash, say 32, for the key checksum.

This gives Eve some information, but very little. If she tries to use the low 32 bits of the final hash value to mount a brute-force attack, she has to do multiple encryptions plus a hash per candidate key; brute-force on the key itself would be quicker.

She also gets no known-plaintext values to try out, and even if she manages to choose our random value for us, she never gets a chosen-plaintext out of us, since it goes through the hash function before she sees it.

8.5 Using Keys

Software encryption is scary. Gone are the days of simple microcomputers under the control of single programs. Now there's Macintosh System 7, Windows NT, and UNIX. You can't tell when the operating system will suspend the encryption application in progress, write everything to disk, and take care of some pressing task. When the operating system finally gets back to encrypting whatever is being encrypted, everything will look just fine. No one will ever realize that the operating system wrote the encryption application to disk, and that it wrote the key along with it. The key will sit on the disk, unencrypted, until the computer writes over that area of memory again. It could be minutes or it could be months. It could even be never; the key could still be sitting there when an adversary goes over the hard drive with a fine-tooth comb. In a preemptive, multitasking environment, you can set your encryption operation to a high enough priority so it will not be interrupted. This would mitigate the risk. Even so, the whole thing is dicey at best.

Hardware implementations are safer. Many encryption devices are designed to erase the key if tampered with. For example, the IBM PS/2 encryption card has an epoxy unit containing the DES chip, battery, and memory. Of course, you have to trust the hardware manufacturer to implement the feature properly.

Some communications applications, such as telephone encryptors, can use **session keys**. A session key is a key that is just used for one communications session—a single telephone conversation—and then discarded. There is no reason to store the key after it has been used. And if you use some key-exchange protocol to transfer the key from one conversant to the other, the key doesn't have to be stored before it is used either. This makes it far less likely that the key might be compromised.

Controlling Key Usage

In some applications it may be desirable to control how a session key is used. Some users may need session keys only for encryption or only for decryption. Session keys might only be authorized for use on a certain machine or at a certain time. One scheme to handle these sorts of restrictions attaches a **Control Vector** (CV) to the key; the control vector specifies the uses and restrictions for that key (see Section 24.1) [1025,1026]. This CV is hashed and XORed with a master key; the result is used as an encryption key to encrypt the session key. The resultant encrypted session key is then stored with the CV. To recover the session key, hash the CV and XOR it with the master key, and use the result to decrypt the encrypted session key.

The advantages of this scheme are that the CV can be of arbitrary length and that it is always stored in the clear with the encrypted key. This scheme assumes quite a bit about tamperproof hardware and the inability of users to get at the keys directly. This system is discussed further in Sections 24.1 and 24.8.

8.6 UPDATING KEYS

Imagine an encrypted data link where you want to change keys daily. Sometimes it's a pain to distribute a new key every day. An easier solution is to generate a new key from the old key; this is sometimes called **key updating**.

All it takes is a one-way function. If Alice and Bob share the same key and they both operate on it using the same one-way function, they will get the same result. Then they can take the bits they need from the results to create the new key.

Key updating works, but remember that the new key is only as secure as the old key was. If Eve managed to get her hands on the old key, she can perform the key updating function herself. However, if Eve doesn't have the old key and is trying a ciphertext-only attack on the encrypted traffic, this is a good way for Alice and Bob to protect themselves.

8.7 STORING KEYS

The least complex key storage problem is that of a single user, Alice, encrypting files for later use. Since she is the only person involved, she is the only person responsible for the key. Some systems take the easy approach: The key is stored in Alice's brain and never on the system. Alice is responsible for remembering the key and entering it every time she needs a file encrypted or decrypted.

An example of this system is IPS [881]. Users can either directly enter the 64-bit key or enter the key as a longer character string. The system then generates a 64-bit key from the character string using a key-crunching technique.

Another solution is to store the key in a magnetic stripe card, plastic key with an embedded ROM chip (called a **ROM key**), or smart card [556,557,455]. A user could then enter his key into the system by inserting the physical token into a special reader in his encryption box or attached to his computer terminal. While the user can use the key, he does not know it and cannot compromise it. He can use it only in the way and for the purposes indicated by the control vector.

A ROM key is a very clever idea. People understand physical keys, what they signify and how to protect them. Putting a cryptographic key in the same physical form makes storing and protecting that key more intuitive.

This technique is made more secure by splitting the key into two halves, storing one half in the terminal and the other half in the ROM key. The U.S. government's STU-III secure telephone works this way. Losing the ROM key does not compromise the cryptographic key—change that key and everything is back to normal. The same is true with the loss of the terminal. This way, compromising either the ROM key or the system does not compromise the cryptographic key—an adversary must have both parts.

Hard-to-remember keys can be stored in encrypted form, using something similar to a key-encryption key. For example, an RSA private key could be encrypted with a DES key and stored on disk. To recover the RSA key, the user has to type in the DES key to a decryption program.

If the keys are generated deterministically (with a cryptographically secure pseudo-random-sequence generator), it might be easier to regenerate the keys from an easy-to-remember password every time they are required.

Ideally, a key should never appear unencrypted outside the encryption device. This isn't always possible, but it is a worthy goal.

8.8   Backup Keys

Alice is the chief financial officer at Secrets, Ltd.—"We don't tell you our motto." Like any good corporate officer, she follows the company's security guidelines and encrypts all her data. Unfortunately, she ignores the company's street-crossing guidelines and gets hit by a truck. What does the company's president, Bob, do?

Unless Alice left a copy of her key, he's in deep trouble. The whole point of encryption is to make files unrecoverable without the key. Unless Alice was a moron and used lousy encryption software, her files are gone forever.

Bob can avoid this in several ways. The simplest is sometimes called **key escrow** (see Section 4.14): He requires all employees to write their keys on paper and give them to the company's security officer, who will lock them in a safe somewhere (or encrypt them all with a master key). Now, when Alice is bowled over on the Interstate, Bob can ask his security officer for her key. Bob should make sure to have the combination to the safe himself as well; otherwise, if the security officer is run over by another truck, Bob will be out of luck again.

The problem with this key management system is that Bob has to trust his security officer not to misuse everyone's keys. Even more significantly, all the employees have to trust the security officer not to misuse their keys. A far better solution is to use a secret-sharing protocol (see Section 3.7).

When Alice generates a key, she also divides up that key into some number of pieces. She then sends each piece—encrypted, of course—to a different company officer. None of those pieces alone is the key, but someone can gather all the pieces together and reconstruct the key. Now Alice is protected against any one malicious person, and Bob is protected against losing all of Alice's data after her run-in with the truck. Or, she could just store the different pieces, encrypted with each of the officer's different public keys, on her own hard disk. That way, no one gets involved with key management until it becomes necessary.

Another backup scheme [188] uses smart cards (see Section 24.13) for the temporary escrow of keys. Alice can put the key to secure her hard drive onto the smart card and give it to Bob while she is away. Bob can use the card to get into Alice's hard drive, but because the key is stored in the card Bob cannot learn it. And the system is bilaterally auditable: Bob can verify that the key will open Alice's drive, and when Alice returns she can verify if Bob has used the key and how many times.

Such a scheme makes no sense for data transmission. On a secure telephone, the key should exist for the length of the call and no longer. For data storage, as just described, key escrow can be a good idea. I've lost about one key every five years, and my memory is better than most. If 200 million people were using cryptography, that same rate would equal 40 million lost keys per year. I keep copies of my house keys with a neighbor because I may lose mine. If house keys were like cryptographic keys, and I lost them, I could never get inside and recover my possessions, ever again. Just as I keep off-site backups of my data, it makes sense to keep backups of my data-encryption keys.

8.9 COMPROMISED KEYS

All of the protocols, techniques, and algorithms in this book are secure only if the key (the private key in a public-key system) remains secret. If Alice's key is lost, stolen, printed in the newspaper, or otherwise compromised, then all her security is gone.

If the compromised key was for a symmetric cryptosystem, Alice has to change her key and hope the actual damage was minimal. If it was a private key, she has bigger problems; her public key is probably on servers all over the network. And if Eve gets access to Alice's private key, she can impersonate her on the network: reading encrypted mail, signing correspondence, entering into contracts, and so forth. Eve can, effectively, become Alice.

It is vital that news of a private key's compromise propagate quickly throughout the network. Any databases of public keys must immediately be notified that a particular private key has been compromised, lest some unsuspecting person encrypt a message in that compromised key.

One hopes Alice knows when her key was compromised. If a KDC is managing the keys, Alice should notify it that her key has been compromised. If there is no KDC, then she should notify all correspondents who might receive messages from her. Someone should publicize the fact that any message received after her key was lost is suspect, and that no one should send messages to Alice with the associated public key. The application should be using some sort of timestamp, and then users can determine which messages are legitimate and which are suspect.

If Alice doesn't know exactly when her key was compromised, things are more difficult. Alice may want to back out of a contract because the person who stole the key signed it instead of her. If the system allows this, then anyone can back out of a contract by claiming that his key was compromised before it was signed. It has to be a matter for an adjudicator to decide.

This is a serious problem and brings to light the dangers of Alice tying all of her identity to a single key. It would be better for Alice to have different keys for different applications—just as she has different physical keys in her pocket for different locks. Other solutions to this problem involve biometrics, limits on what can be done with a key, time delays, and countersigning.

These procedures and tips are hardly optimal, but are the best we can do. The moral of the story is to protect keys, and protect private keys above all else.

8.10 LIFETIME OF KEYS

No encryption key should be used for an indefinite period. It should expire automatically like passports and licenses. There are several reasons for this:

— The longer a key is used, the greater the chance that it will be compromised. People write keys down; people lose them. Accidents happen. If you use the same key for a year, there's a far greater chance of compromise than if you use it for a day.

— The longer a key is used, the greater the loss if the key is compromised. If a key is used only to encrypt a single budgetary document on a file server, then the loss of the key means only the compromise of that document. If the same key is used to encrypt all the budgetary information on the file server, then its loss is much more devastating.

— The longer a key is used, the greater the temptation for someone to spend the effort necessary to break it—even if that effort is a brute-force attack. Breaking a key shared between two military units for a day would enable someone to read and fabricate messages between those units for that day. Breaking a key shared by an entire military command structure for a year would enable that same person to read and fabricate messages throughout the world for a year. In our budget-conscious, post-Cold War world, which key would you choose to attack?

— It is generally easier to do cryptanalysis with more ciphertext encrypted with the same key.

For any cryptographic application, there must be a policy that determines the permitted lifetime of a key. Different keys may have different lifetimes. For a connection-based system, like a telephone, it makes sense to use a key for the length of the telephone call and to use a new one with each call.

Systems on dedicated communications channels are not as obvious. Keys should have relatively short lifetimes, depending on the value of the data and the amount of data encrypted during a given period. The key for a gigabit-per-second communications link might have to be changed more often than the key for a 9600-baud modem link. Assuming there is an efficient method of transferring new keys, session keys should be changed at least daily.

Key-encryption keys don't have to be replaced as frequently. They are used only occasionally (roughly once per day) for key exchange. This generates little ciphertext for a cryptanalyst to work with, and the corresponding plaintext has no particular form. However, if a key-encryption key is compromised, the potential loss is extreme: all communications encrypted with every key encrypted with the key-encryption key. In some applications, key-encryption keys are replaced only once a month or once a year. You have to balance the inherent danger in keeping a key around for a while with the inherent danger in distributing a new one.

Encryption keys used to encrypt data files for storage cannot be changed often. The files may sit encrypted on disk for months or years before someone needs them again. Decrypting them and re-encrypting them with a new key every day doesn't enhance security in any way; it just gives a cryptanalyst more to work with. One solution might be to encrypt each file with a unique file key, and then encrypt all the file keys with a key-encryption key. The key-encryption key should then be either memorized or stored in a secure location, perhaps in a safe somewhere. Of course, losing this key would mean losing all the individual file keys.

Private keys for public-key cryptography applications have varying lifetimes, depending on the application. Private keys used for digital signatures and proofs of identity may have to last years (even a lifetime). Private keys used for coin-flipping protocols can be discarded immediately after the protocol is completed. Even if a key's security is expected to last a lifetime, it may be prudent to change the key every couple of years. The private keys in many networks are good only for two years; after that the user must get a new private key. The old key would still have to remain secret, in case the user needed to verify a signature from that period. But the new key would be used to sign new documents, reducing the number of signed documents a cryptanalyst would have for an attack.

8.11 DESTROYING KEYS

Given that keys must be replaced regularly, old keys must be destroyed. Old keys are valuable, even if they are never used again. With them, an adversary can read old messages encrypted with those keys [65].

Keys must be destroyed securely (see Section 10.9). If the key is written on paper, the paper should be shredded or burned. Be careful to use a high-quality shredder; many lousy shredders are on the market. Algorithms in this book are secure against brute-force attacks costing millions of dollars and taking millions of years. If an adversary can recover your key by taking a bag of shredded documents from your trash and paying 100 unemployed workers in some backwater country ten cents per hour for a year to piece the shredded pages together, that would be $26,000 well spent.

If the key is in a hardware EEPROM, the key should be overwritten multiple times. If the key is in a hardware EPROM or PROM, the chip should be smashed into tiny bits and scattered to the four winds. If the key is stored on a computer disk, the actual bits of the storage should be overwritten multiple times (see Section 10.9) or the disk should be shredded.

A potential problem is that, in a computer, keys can be easily copied and stored in multiple locations. Any computer that does its own memory management, constantly swapping programs in and out of memory, exacerbates the problem. There is no way to ensure that successful key erasure has taken place in the computer, especially if the computer's operating system controls the erasure process. The more paranoid among you should consider writing a special erasure program that scans all disks looking for copies of the key's bit pattern on unused blocks and then erases those blocks. Also remember to erase the contents of any temporary, or "swap," files.

8.12 PUBLIC-KEY KEY MANAGEMENT

Public-key cryptography makes key management easier, but it has its own unique problems. Each person has only one public key, regardless of the number of people on the network. If Alice wants to send a message to Bob, she has to get Bob's public key. She can go about this several ways:

— She can get it from Bob.

— She can get it from a centralized database.

— She can get it from her own private database.

Section 2.5 discussed a number of possible attacks against public-key cryptography, based on Mallory substituting his key for Bob's. The scenario is that Alice wants to send a message to Bob. She goes to the public-key database and gets Bob's public key. But Mallory, who is sneaky, has substituted his own key for Bob's. (If Alice asks Bob directly, Mallory has to intercept Bob's transmission and substitute his key for Bob's.) Alice encrypts her message in Mallory's key and sends it to Bob. Mallory intercepts the message, decrypts it, and reads it. He re-encrypts it with Bob's real key and sends it on to Bob. Neither Alice nor Bob is the wiser.

Public-key Certificates

A **public-key certificate** is someone's public key, signed by a trustworthy person. Certificates are used to thwart attempts to substitute one key for another [879]. Bob's certificate, in the public-key database, contains a lot more than his public key. It contains information about Bob—his name, address, and so on—and it is signed by someone Alice trusts: Trent (usually known as a **certification authority**, or CA). By signing both the key and the information about Bob, Trent certifies that the information about Bob is correct and that the public key belongs to Bob. Alice checks Trent's signature and then uses the public key, secure in the knowledge that it is Bob's and no one else's. Certificates play an important role in a number of public-key protocols such as PEM [825] (see Section 24.10) and X.509 [304] (see Section 24.9).

A complicated noncryptographic issue surrounds this type of system. What is the meaning of certification? Or, to put it another way, who is trusted to issue certificates to whom? Anyone may sign anyone else's certificate, but there needs to be some way to filter out questionable certificates: for example, certificates for employees of one company signed by the CA of another company. Normally, a certification chain transfers trust: A single trusted entity certifies trusted agents, trusted agents certify company CAs, and company CAs certify their employees.

Here are some more things to think about:

— What level of trust in someone's identity is implied by his certificate?
— What are the relationships between a person and the CA that certified his public key, and how can those relationships be implied by the certificate?
— Who can be trusted to be the "single trusted entity" at the top of the certification chain?
— How long can a certification chain be?

Ideally, Bob would follow some kind of authentication procedure before the CA signs his certificate. Additionally, some kind of timestamp or an indication of the certificate's validity period is important to guard against compromised keys [461].

Timestamping is not enough. Keys may be invalidated before they have expired, either through compromise or for administrative reasons. Hence, it is important the CA keep a list of invalid certificates, and for users to regularly check that list. This key revocation problem is still a difficult one to solve.

And one public-key/private-key pair is not enough. Certainly any good implementation of public-key cryptography needs separate keys for encryption and digital signatures. This separation allows for different security levels, expiration times, backup procedures, and so on. Someone might sign messages with a 2048-bit key stored on a smart card and good for twenty years, while they might use a 768-bit key stored in the computer and good for six months for encryption.

And a single pair of encryption and signature keys isn't enough, either. A private key authenticates a relationship as well as an identity, and people have more than one relationship. Alice might want to sign one document as Alice the individual, another as Alice, vice-president of Monolith, Inc., and a third as Alice, president of her community organization. Some of these keys are more valuable than others, so they can be better protected. Alice might have to store a backup of her work key with the company's security officer; she doesn't want the company to have a copy of the key she signed her mortgage with. Just as Alice has multiple physical keys in her pocket, she is going to have multiple cryptographic keys.

Distributed Key Management

In some situations, this sort of centralized key management will not work. Perhaps there is no CA whom Alice and Bob both trust. Perhaps Alice and Bob trust only their friends. Perhaps Alice and Bob trust no one.

Distributed key management, used in PGP (see Section 24.12), solves this problem with **introducers**. Introducers are other users of the system who sign their friends' public keys. For example, when Bob generates his public key, he gives copies to his friends: Carol and Dave. They know Bob, so they each sign Bob's key and give Bob a copy of the signature. Now, when Bob presents his key to a stranger, Alice, he presents it with the signatures of these two introducers. If Alice also knows and trusts Carol, she has reason to believe that Bob's key is valid. If she knows and trusts Carol and Dave a little, she has reason to believe that Bob's key is valid. If she doesn't know either Carol or Dave, she has no reason to trust Bob's key.

Over time, Bob will collect many more introducers. If Alice and Bob travel in similar circles, the odds are good that Alice will know one of Bob's introducers. To prevent against Mallory's substituting one key for another, an introducer must be sure that Bob's key belongs to Bob before he signs it. Perhaps the introducer should require the key be given face-to-face or verified over the telephone.

The benefit of this mechanism is that there is no CA that everyone has to trust. The down side is that when Alice receives Bob's public key, she has no guarantee that she will know any of the introducers and therefore no guarantee that she will trust the validity of the key.

CHAPTER 9

Algorithm Types and Modes

There are two basic types of symmetric algorithms: block ciphers and stream ciphers. **Block ciphers** operate on blocks of plaintext and ciphertext—usually of 64 bits but sometimes longer. **Stream ciphers** operate on streams of plaintext and ciphertext one bit or byte (sometimes even one 32-bit word) at a time. With a block cipher, the same plaintext block will always encrypt to the same ciphertext block, using the same key. With a stream cipher, the same plaintext bit or byte will encrypt to a different bit or byte every time it is encrypted.

A cryptographic **mode** usually combines the basic cipher, some sort of feedback, and some simple operations. The operations are simple because the security is a function of the underlying cipher and not the mode. Even more strongly, the cipher mode should not compromise the security of the underlying algorithm.

There are other security considerations: Patterns in the plaintext should be concealed, input to the cipher should be randomized, manipulation of the plaintext by introducing errors in the ciphertext should be difficult, and encryption of more than one message with the same key should be possible. These will be discussed in detail in the next sections.

Efficiency is another consideration. The mode should not be significantly less efficient than the underlying cipher. In some circumstances it is important that the ciphertext be the same size as the plaintext.

A third consideration is fault-tolerance. Some applications need to parallelize encryption or decryption, while others need to be able to preprocess as much as possible. In still others it is important that the decrypting process be able to recover from bit errors in the ciphertext stream, or dropped or added bits. As we will see, different modes have different subsets of these characteristics.

9.1 ELECTRONIC CODEBOOK MODE

Electronic codebook (ECB) mode is the most obvious way to use a block cipher: A block of plaintext encrypts into a block of ciphertext. Since the same block of plaintext always encrypts to the same block of ciphertext, it is theoretically possible to create a code book of plaintexts and corresponding ciphertexts. However, if the block size is 64 bits, the code book will have 2^{64} entries—much too large to pre-compute and store. And remember, every key has a different code book.

This is the easiest mode to work with. Each plaintext block is encrypted independently. You don't have to encrypt a file linearly; you can encrypt the 10 blocks in the middle first, then the blocks at the end, and finally the blocks in the beginning. This is important for encrypted files that are accessed randomly, like a database. If a database is encrypted with ECB mode, then any record can be added, deleted, encrypted, or decrypted independently of any other record—assuming that a record consists of a discrete number of encryption blocks. And processing is parallelizeable; if you have multiple encryption processors, they can encrypt or decrypt different blocks without regard for each other.

The problem with ECB mode is that if a cryptanalyst has the plaintext and ciphertext for several messages, he can start to compile a code book without knowing the key. In most real-world situations, fragments of messages tend to repeat. Different messages may have bit sequences in common. Computer-generated messages, like electronic mail, may have regular structures. Messages may be highly redundant or have long strings of zeros or spaces.

If a cryptanalyst learns that the plaintext block "5e081bc5" encrypts to the cipher-text block "7ea593a4," he can immediately decrypt that ciphertext block whenever it appears in another message. If the encrypted messages have a lot of redundancies, and these tend to show up in the same places in different messages, a cryptanalyst can get a lot of information. He can mount statistical attacks on the underlying plaintext, irrespective of the strength of the block cipher.

This vulnerability is greatest at the beginning and end of messages, where well-defined headers and footers contain information about the sender, receiver, date, and so on. This problem is sometimes called **stereotyped beginnings** and **stereotyped endings**.

On the plus side, there is no security risk in encrypting multiple messages with the same key. In fact, each block can be looked at as a separate message encrypted with the same key. Bit errors in the ciphertext, when decrypted, will cause the entire plaintext block to decrypt incorrectly but will not affect the rest of the plaintext. However, if a ciphertext bit is accidentally lost or added, all subsequent ciphertext will decrypt incorrectly unless there is some kind of frame structure to realign the block boundaries.

Padding

Most messages don't divide neatly into 64-bit (or whatever size) encryption blocks; there is usually a short block at the end. ECB requires 64-bit blocks. **Padding** is the way to deal with this problem.

Pad the last block with some regular pattern—zeros, ones, alternating ones and zeros—to make it a complete block. If you need to delete the padding after decryption, add the number of padding bytes as the last byte of the last block. For example, assume the block size is 64 bits and the last block consists of 3 bytes (24 bits). Five bytes of padding are required to make the last block 64 bits; add 4 bytes of zeros and a final byte with the number 5. After decryption, delete the last 5 bytes of the last decryption block. For this method to work correctly, every message must be padded. Even if the plaintext ends on a block boundary, you have to pad one complete block. Otherwise, you can use an end-of-file character to denote the final plaintext byte, and then pad after that character.

Figure 9.1 is an alternative, called **ciphertext stealing** [402]. P_{n-1} is the last full plaintext block and P_n is the final, short, plaintext block. C_{n-1} is the last full ciphertext block and C_n is the final, short, ciphertext block. C' is just an intermediate result and is not part of the transmitted ciphertext.

9.2   BLOCK REPLAY

A more serious problem with ECB mode is that an adversary could modify encrypted messages without knowing the key, or even the algorithm, in such a way as to fool the intended recipient. This problem was first discussed in [291].

To illustrate the problem, consider a money transfer system that moves money between accounts in different banks. To make life easier for the bank's computer systems, banks agree on a standard message format for money transfer that looks like this:

```
Bank One: Sending          1.5 blocks
Bank Two: Receiving         1.5 blocks
Depositor's Name           6 blocks
Depositor's Account        2 blocks
Amount of Deposit          1 block
```

A block corresponds to an 8-byte encryption block. The messages are encrypted using some block algorithm in ECB mode.

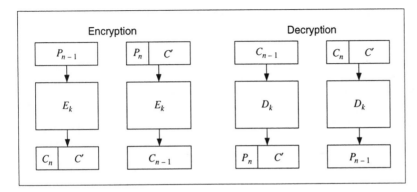

Figure 9.1   Ciphertext stealing in ECB mode.

Mallory, who is listening on the communications line between two banks, Bank of Alice and Bank of Bob, can use this information to get rich. First, he sets up his computer to record all of the encrypted messages from Bank of Alice to Bank of Bob. Then, he transfers $100 from Bank of Alice to his account in Bank of Bob. Later, he does it again. Using his computer, he examines the recorded messages looking for a pair of identical messages. These messages are the ones authorizing the $100 transfers to his account. If he finds more than one pair of identical messages (which is most likely in real life), he does another money transfer and records those results. Eventually he can isolate the message that authorized his money transaction.

Now he can insert that message into the communications link at will. Every time he sends the message to Bank of Bob, another $100 will be credited to his account. When the two banks reconcile their transfers (probably at the end of the day), they will notice the phantom transfer authorizations; but if Mallory is clever, he will have already withdrawn the money and headed for some banana republic without extradition laws. And he probably did his scam with dollar amounts far larger than $100, and with lots of different banks.

At first glance, the banks could easily prevent this by adding a timestamp to their messages.

```
Date/Time Stamp:        1 block
Bank One: Sending       1.5 blocks
Bank Two: Receiving     1.5 blocks
Depositor's Name        6 blocks
Depositor's Account     2 blocks
Amount of Deposit       1 block
```

Two identical messages would be easy to spot using this system. Still, using a technique called **block replay**, Mallory can still get rich. Figure 9.2 shows that Mallory can pick out the eight ciphertext blocks that correspond to his own name and account number: blocks 5 through 12. A diabolical laugh is appropriate at this point, because Mallory is now ready.

He intercepts random messages from Bank of Alice to Bank of Bob and replaces blocks 5 through 12 in the message with the bytes that correspond to his name and

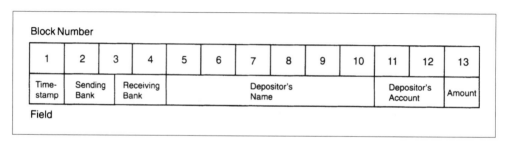

Figure 9.2   Encryption blocks for an example record.

account number. Then he sends them on to Bank of Bob. He doesn't have to know who the original depositor was; he doesn't even have to know what the amount was (although, he could correlate the messages he doctored with the various deposits into his account and determine the encrypted blocks corresponding to some dollar amount). He simply changes the name and account numbers to his own and watches his account balance grow. (I suppose Mallory has to be careful not to modify a withdrawal message, but assume for the moment that each is a different length or something.)

This will take longer than a day for the banks to catch. When they reconcile their transfers at the end of the day, everything will match. It probably won't be until one of the legitimate depositors notices that his deposits are not being credited, or when someone flags unusual activity in Mallory's account, that the banks will figure out the scam. Mallory isn't stupid, and by then he will have closed his account, changed his name, and bought a villa in Argentina.

Banks can minimize the problem by changing their keys frequently, but this only means that Mallory is going to have to work more quickly. Adding a MAC, however, will also solve the problem. Even so, this is a fundamental problem with ECB mode. Mallory can remove, repeat, or interchange blocks at will. The solution is a technique called **chaining**.

9.3 CIPHER BLOCK CHAINING MODE

Chaining adds a **feedback** mechanism to a block cipher: The results of the encryption of previous blocks are fed back into the encryption of the current block. In other words, each block is used to modify the encryption of the next block. Each ciphertext block is dependent not just on the plaintext block that generated it but on all the previous plaintext blocks.

In **cipher block chaining** (**CBC**) mode, the plaintext is XORed with the previous ciphertext block before it is encrypted. Figure 9.3a shows CBC encryption in action. After a plaintext block is encrypted, the resulting ciphertext is also stored in a feedback register. Before the next plaintext block is encrypted, it is XORed with the feedback register to become the next input to the encrypting routine. The resulting ciphertext is again stored in the feedback register, to be XORed with the next plaintext block, and so on until the end of the message. The encryption of each block depends on all the previous blocks.

Decryption is just as straightforward (see Figure 9.3b). A ciphertext block is decrypted normally and also saved in a feedback register. After the next block is decrypted, it is XORed with the results of the feedback register. Then the next ciphertext block is stored in the feedback register, and so on, until the end of the message.

Mathematically, this looks like:

$$C_i = E_K(P_i \oplus C_{i-1})$$
$$P_i = C_{i-1} \oplus D_K(C_i)$$

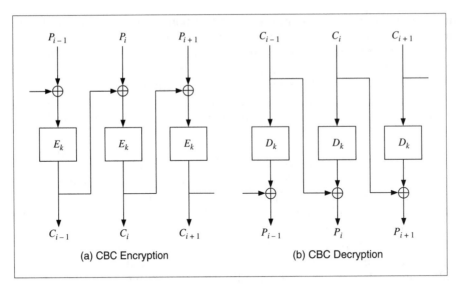

Figure 9.3   *Cipher block chaining mode.*

Initialization Vector

CBC mode forces identical plaintext blocks to encrypt to different ciphertext blocks only when some previous plaintext block is different. Two identical messages will still encrypt to the same ciphertext. Even worse, two messages that begin the same will encrypt in the same way up to the first difference.

Some messages have a common header: a letterhead, or a "From" line, or whatever. While block replay would still be impossible, this identical beginning might give a cryptanalyst some useful information.

Prevent this by encrypting random data as the first block. This block of random data is called the **initialization vector** (**IV**), initializing variable, or initial chaining value. The IV has no meaning; it's just there to make each message unique. When the receiver decrypts this block, he just uses it to fill the feedback register and otherwise ignores it. A timestamp often makes a good IV. Otherwise, use some random bits from someplace.

With the addition of IVs, identical plaintext messages encrypt to different ciphertext messages. Thus, it is impossible for an eavesdropper to attempt block replay, and more difficult for him to build a code book. While the IV should be unique for each message encrypted with the same key, it is not an absolute requirement.

The IV need not be secret; it can be transmitted in the clear with the ciphertext. If this seems wrong, consider the following argument. Assume that we have a message of several blocks: $B_1, B_2, \ldots, B_i$. B_1 is encrypted with the IV. B_2 is encrypted using the ciphertext of B_1 as the IV. B_3 is encrypted using the ciphertext of B_2 as the IV, and so on. So, if there are n blocks, there are n-1 exposed "IVs," even if the original IV is kept secret. So there's no reason to keep the IV secret; the IV is just a dummy ciphertext block—you can think of it as B_0 to start the chaining.

Padding

Padding works just like ECB mode, but in some applications the ciphertext has to be exactly the same size as the plaintext. Perhaps a plaintext file has to be encrypted and then replaced in the exact same memory location. In this case, you have to encrypt the last short block differently. Assume the last block has j bits. After encrypting the last full block, encrypt the ciphertext again, select the left-most j bits of the encrypted ciphertext, and XOR that with the short block to generate the ciphertext. Figure 9.4 illustrates this.

The weakness here is that while Mallory cannot recover the last plaintext block, he can change it systematically by changing individual bits in the ciphertext. If the last few bits of the ciphertext contain essential information, this is a weakness. If the last bits simply contain housekeeping information, it isn't a problem.

Ciphertext stealing is a better way (see Figure 9.5) [402]. P_{n-1} is the last full plaintext block, and P_n is the final, short, plaintext block. C_{n-1} is the last full ciphertext block, and C_n is the final, short, ciphertext block. C' is just an intermediate result and is not part of the transmitted ciphertext. The benefit of this method is that all the bits of the plaintext message go through the encryption algorithm.

Error Propagation

CBC mode can be characterized as **feedback** of the ciphertext at the encryption end and **feedforward** of the ciphertext at the decryption end. This has implications having to do with errors. A single bit error in a plaintext block will affect that ciphertext block and all subsequent ciphertext blocks. This isn't significant because decryption will reverse that effect, and the recovered plaintext will have the same single error.

Ciphertext errors are more common. They can easily result from a noisy communications path or a malfunction in the storage medium. In CBC mode, a single-bit error in the ciphertext affects one block and one bit of the recovered plaintext. The

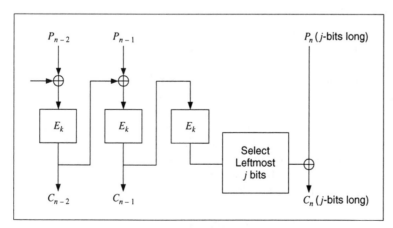

Figure 9.4   Encrypting the last short block in CBC mode.

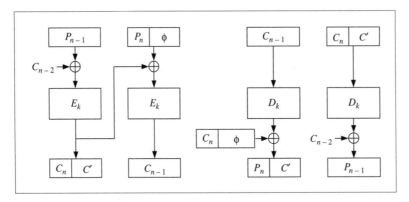

Figure 9.5   Ciphertext stealing in CBC mode.

block containing the error is completely garbled. The subsequent block has a 1-bit error in the same bit position as the error.

This property of taking a small ciphertext error and converting it into a large plaintext error is called **error extension**. It is a major annoyance. Blocks after the second are not affected by the error, so CBC mode is **self-recovering**. Two blocks are affected by an error, but the system recovers and continues to work correctly for all subsequent blocks. CBC is an example of a block cipher being used in a self-synchronizing manner, but only at the block level.

While CBC mode recovers quickly from bit errors, it doesn't recover at all from synchronization errors. If a bit is added or lost from the ciphertext stream, then all subsequent blocks are shifted one bit out of position and decryption will generate garbage indefinitely. Any cryptosystem that uses CBC mode must ensure that the block structure remains intact, either by framing or by storing data in multiple-block-sized chunks.

Security Problems

Some potential problems are caused by the structure of CBC. First, because a ciphertext block affects the following block in a simple way, Mallory can add blocks to the end of an encrypted message without being detected. Sure, it will probably decrypt to gibberish, but in some situations this is undesirable.

If you are using CBC, you should structure your plaintext so that you know where the message ends and can detect the addition of extra blocks.

Second, Mallory can alter a ciphertext block to introduce controlled changes in the following decrypted plaintext block. For example, if Mallory toggles a single ciphertext bit, the entire block will decrypt incorrectly, but the following block will have a 1-bit error in the corresponding bit position. There are situations where this is desirable. The entire plaintext message should include some kind of controlled redundancy or authentication.

Finally, although plaintext patterns are concealed by chaining, very long messages will still have patterns. The birthday paradox predicts that there will be identical blocks after $2^{m/2}$ blocks, where m is the block size. For a 64-bit block size, that's about 34 gigabytes. A message has to be pretty long before this is a problem.

9.4   STREAM CIPHERS

Stream ciphers convert plaintext to ciphertext 1 bit at a time. The simplest implementation of a stream cipher is shown in Figure 9.6. A **keystream generator** (sometimes called a running-key generator) outputs a stream of bits: $k_1, k_2, k_3, \ldots, k_i$. This keystream (sometimes called a running key) is XORed with a stream of plaintext bits, $p_1, p_2, p_3, \ldots, p_i$, to produce the stream of ciphertext bits.

$$c_i = p_i \oplus k_i$$

At the decryption end, the ciphertext bits are XORed with an identical keystream to recover the plaintext bits.

$$p_i = c_i \oplus k_i$$

Since

$$p_i \oplus k_i \oplus k_i = p_i$$

this works nicely.

The system's security depends entirely on the insides of the keystream generator. If the keystream generator outputs an endless stream of zeros, the ciphertext will equal the plaintext and the whole operation will be worthless. If the keystream generator spits out a repeating 16-bit pattern, the algorithm will be a simple XOR with negligible security (see Section 1.4). If the keystream generator spits out an endless stream of random (not pseudo-random, but real random—see Section 2.8) bits, you have a one-time pad and perfect security.

The reality of stream cipher security lies somewhere between the simple XOR and the one-time pad. The keystream generator generates a bit stream that looks random, but is actually a deterministic stream that can be flawlessly reproduced at decryption time. The closer the keystream generator's output is to random, the harder time a cryptanalyst will have breaking it.

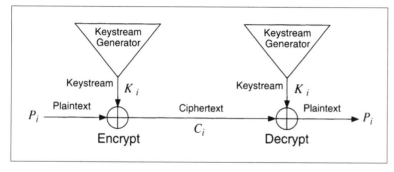

Figure 9.6   Stream cipher.

If, however, the keystream generator produces the same bit stream every time it is turned on, the resulting cryptosystem will be trivial to break. An example will show why.

If Eve has a ciphertext and associated plaintext, she can XOR the plaintext and the ciphertext to recover the keystream. Or, if she has two different ciphertexts encrypted with the same keystream, she can XOR them together and get two plaintext messages XORed with each other. This is easy to break, and then she can XOR one of the plaintexts with the ciphertext to get the keystream.

Now, whenever she intercepts another ciphertext message, she has the keystream bits necessary to decrypt it. In addition, she can decrypt and read any old ciphertext messages she has previously intercepted. When Eve gets a single plaintext/ciphertext pair, she can read everything.

This is why all stream ciphers have keys. The output of the keystream generator is a function of the key. Now, if Eve gets a plaintext/ciphertext pair, she can only read messages encrypted with a single key. Change the key, and the adversary is back to square one. Stream ciphers are especially useful to encrypt never-ending streams of communications traffic: a T-1 link between two computers, for example.

A keystream generator has three basic parts (see Figure 9.7). The internal state describes the current state of the keystream generator. Two keystream generators, with the same key and the same internal state, will produce the same keystream. The output function takes the internal state and generates a keystream bit. The next-state function takes the internal state and generates a new internal state.

9.5 Self-Synchronizing Stream Ciphers

For a **self-synchronizing stream cipher**, each keystream bit is a function of a fixed number of previous ciphertext bits [1378]. The military calls this **ciphertext auto key** (CTAK). The basic idea was patented in 1946 [667].

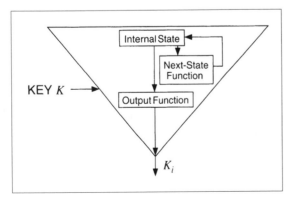

Figure 9.7   Inside a keystream generator.

Figure 9.8 shows a self-synchronizing stream cipher. The internal state is a function of the previous n ciphertext bits. The cryptographic complexity is in the output function, which takes the internal state and generates a keystream bit.

Since the internal state depends wholly on the previous n ciphertext bits, the decryption keystream generator will automatically synchronize with the encryption keystream generator after receiving n ciphertext bits.

In smart implementations of this mode, each message begins with a random header n bits long. That header is encrypted, transmitted, and then decrypted. The decryption will be incorrect, but after those n bits both keystream generators will be synchronized.

The down side of a self-synchronizing stream cipher is error propagation. For each ciphertext bit garbled in transmission, the decryption keystream generator will incorrectly produce n keystream bits. Therefore, for each ciphertext error, there will be n corresponding plaintext errors, until the garbled bit works its way out of the internal state.

Security Problems

Self-synchronizing stream ciphers are also vulnerable to a playback attack. First Mallory records some ciphertext bits. Then, at a later time, he substitutes this recording into current traffic. After some initial garbage while the receiving end resynchronizes, the old ciphertext will decrypt as normal. The receiving end has no way of knowing that this is not current data, but old data being replayed. Unless timestamps are used, Mallory can convince a bank to credit his account again and again, by replaying the same message (assuming the key hasn't been changed, of course). Other weaknesses in this type of scheme could be exploited in the cases of very frequent resynchronization [408].

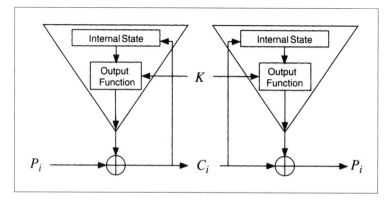

Figure 9.8   A self-synchronizing keystream generator.

9.6 CIPHER-FEEDBACK MODE

Block ciphers can also be implemented as a self-synchronizing stream cipher; this is called **cipher-feedback (CFB)** mode. With CBC mode, encryption cannot begin until a complete block of data is received. This is a problem in some network applications. In a secure network environment, for example, a terminal must be able to transmit each character to the host as it is entered. When data has to be processed in byte-sized chunks, CBC mode just won't do.

In CFB mode, data can be encrypted in units smaller than the block size. The following example will encrypt one ASCII character at a time (this is called **8-bit CFB**), but nothing is sacred about the number eight. You can encrypt data one bit at a time using 1-bit CFB, although using one complete encryption of a block cipher for a single bit seems like a whole lot of work; a stream cipher might be a better idea. (Reducing the number of rounds of the block cipher to speed things up is not recommended [1269].) You can also use 64-bit CFB, or any n-bit CFB where n is less than or equal to the block size.

Figure 9.9 shows 8-bit CFB mode working with a 64-bit block algorithm. A block algorithm in CFB mode operates on a queue the size of the input block. Initially, the queue is filled with an IV, as in CBC mode. The queue is encrypted and the left-most eight bits of the result are XORed with the first 8-bit character of the plaintext to become the first 8-bit character of the ciphertext. This character can now be transmitted. The same eight bits are also moved to the right-most eight bit positions of the queue, and all the other bits move eight to the left. The eight left-most bits are discarded. Then the next plaintext character is encrypted in the same manner. Decryption is the reverse of this process. On both the encryption and the decryption side, the block algorithm is used in its encryption mode.

If the block size of the algorithm is n, then n-bit CFB looks like (see Figure 9.10):

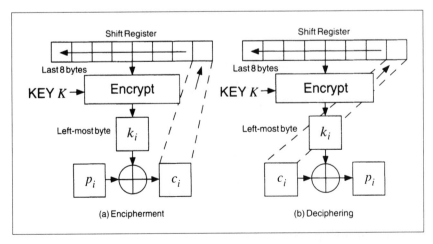

Figure 9.9   *8-bit cipher-feedback mode.*

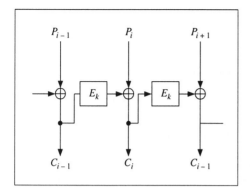

Figure 9.10 n-bit CFB with an n-bit algorithm.

$$C_i = P_i \oplus E_K(C_{i-1})$$
$$P_i = C_i \oplus E_K(C_{i-1})$$

Like CBC mode, CFB mode links the plaintext characters together so that the ciphertext depends on all the preceding plaintext.

Initialization Vector

To initialize the CFB process, the input to the block algorithm must be initialized with an IV. Like the IV used in CBC mode, it need not be secret.

The IV must be unique, though. (This is different from the IV in CBC mode, which should be unique but does not have to be.) If the IV in CFB is not unique, a cryptanalyst can recover the corresponding plaintext. The IV must be changed with every message. It can be a serial number, which increments after each message and does not repeat during the lifetime of the key. For data encrypted for storage, it can be a function of the index used to look up the data.

Error Propagation

With CFB mode, an error in the plaintext affects all subsequent ciphertext and reverses itself at decryption. An error in the ciphertext is more interesting. The first effect of a single-bit error in the ciphertext is to cause a single error in the plaintext. After that, the error enters the shift register, where it causes ciphertext to be garbled until it falls off the other end of the register. In 8-bit CFB mode, 9 bytes of decrypted plaintext are garbled by a single-bit error in the ciphertext. After that, the system recovers and all subsequent ciphertext is decrypted correctly. In general, in n-bit CFB a single ciphertext error will affect the decryption of the current and following m/n-1 blocks, where m is the block size.

One subtle problem with this kind of error propagation is that if Mallory knows the plaintext of a transmission, he can toggle bits in a given block and make it decrypt to whatever he wants. The *next* block will decrypt to garbage, but the damage may already be done. And he can change the final bits of a message without detection.

CFB is self-recovering with respect to synchronization errors as well. The error enters the shift register, where it garbles 8 bytes of data until it falls off the other end. CFB is an example of block cipher being used as a self-synchronizing stream cipher (at the block level).

9.7 SYNCHRONOUS STREAM CIPHERS

In a **synchronous stream cipher** the keystream is generated independent of the message stream. The military calls this **Key Auto-Key** (KAK). On the encryption side, a keystream generator spits out keystream bits, one after the other. On the decryption side, another keystream generator spits out the identical keystream bits, one after the other. This works, as long as the two keystream generators are synchronized. If one of them skips a cycle or if a ciphertext bit gets lost during transmission, then every ciphertext character after the error will decrypt incorrectly.

If this happens, the sender and receiver must resynchronize their keystream generators before they can proceed. Frustrating matters even further, they must do this in such a way as to ensure that no part of the keystream is repeated, so the obvious solution of resetting the keystream generator to an earlier state won't work.

On the plus side, synchronous ciphers do not propagate transmission errors. If a bit is garbled during transmission, which is far more likely than a bit being lost altogether, then only the garbled bit will be decrypted incorrectly. All preceding and subsequent bits will be unaffected.

Since a keystream generator must generate the same output on both the encryption and decryption ends, it must be deterministic. Because it is implemented in a finite-state machine (i.e., a computer), the sequence will eventually repeat. These keystream generators are called **periodic**. Except for one-time pads, all keystream generators are periodic.

The keystream generator must have a long period, one far longer than the number of bits the generator will output between key changes. If the period is less than the plaintext, then different parts of the plaintext will be encrypted the same way—a severe weakness. If a cryptanalyst knows a piece of the plaintext, he can recover a piece of the keystream and use that to recover more of the plaintext. Even if the analyst only has the ciphertext, he can XOR the sections encrypted with the same keystream and get the XOR of plaintext with plaintext. This is just the simple XOR algorithm with a very long key.

How long a period is long enough depends on the application. A keystream generator encrypting a continuous T-1 link will encrypt 2^{37} bits per day. The keystream generator's period must be orders of magnitude larger than that, even if the key is changed daily. If the period is long enough, you might only have to change the key weekly or even monthly.

Synchronous stream ciphers also protect against any insertions and deletions in the ciphertext, because these cause a loss of synchronization and will be immediately detected. They do not, however, fully protect against bit toggling. Like block ciphers in CFB mode, Mallory can toggle individual bits in the stream. If he knows the plaintext, he can make those bits decrypt to whatever he wants. Subsequent bits will decrypt correctly, so in certain applications Mallory can still do considerable damage.

Insertion Attack

Synchronous stream ciphers are vulnerable to an **insertion attack** [93]. Mallory has recorded a ciphertext stream, but does not know the plaintext or the keystream used to encrypt the plaintext.

```
Original plaintext:     p₁ p₂ p₃ p₄ ...
Original keystream:     k₁ k₂ k₃ k₄ ...
Original ciphertext:    c₁ c₂ c₃ c₄ ...
```

Mallory inserts a single known bit, p', into the plaintext after p_1 and then manages to get the modified plaintext encrypted with the same keystream. He records the resultant new ciphertext:

```
New plaintext:          p₁ p' p₂ p₃ p₄ ...
Original keystream:     k₁ k₂ k₃ k₄ k₅ ...
Updated ciphertext:     c₁ c'₂ c'₃ c'₄ c'₅ ...
```

Assuming he knows the value of p', he can determine the entire plaintext after that bit from the original ciphertext and new ciphertext:

```
k₂ = c'₂ ⊕ p', and then p₂ = c₂ ⊕ k₂
k₃ = c'₃ ⊕ p₂, and then p₃ = c₃ ⊕ k₃
k₄ = c'₄ ⊕ p₃, and then p₄ = c₄ ⊕ k₄
```

Mallory doesn't even have to know the exact position in which the bit was inserted; he can just compare the original and updated ciphertexts to see where they begin to differ. To protect against this attack, never use the same keystream to encrypt two different messages.

9.8   OUTPUT-FEEDBACK MODE

Output-feedback (OFB) mode is a method of running a block cipher as a synchronous stream cipher. It is similar to CFB mode, except that n bits of the previous output block are moved into the right-most positions of the queue (see Figure 9.11). Decryption is the reverse of this process. This is called n-bit OFB. On both the encryption and the decryption sides, the block algorithm is used in its encryption mode. This is sometimes called **internal feedback**, because the feedback mechanism is independent of both the plaintext and the ciphertext streams [291].

If n is the block size of the algorithm, then n-bit OFB looks like (see Figure 9.12):

$$C_i = P_i \oplus S_i;\ S_i = E_K(S_{i-1})$$
$$P_i = C_i \oplus S_i;\ S_i = E_K(S_{i-1})$$

S_i is the state, which is independent of either the plaintext or the ciphertext.

One nice feature of OFB mode is that most of the work can occur offline, before the plaintext message even exists. When the message finally arrives, it can be XORed with the output of the algorithm to produce the ciphertext.

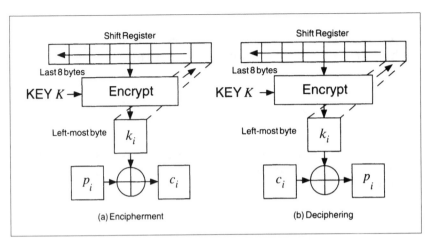

Figure 9.11   8-bit output-feedback mode.

Initialization Vector

The OFB shift register must also be initially loaded with an IV. It should be unique but does not have to be secret.

Error Propagation

OFB mode has no error extension. A single-bit error in the ciphertext causes a single-bit error in the recovered plaintext. This can be useful in some digitized analog transmissions, like digitized voice or video, where the occasional single-bit error can be tolerated but error extension cannot.

On the other hand, a loss of synchronization is fatal. If the shift registers on the encryption end and the decryption end are not identical, then the recovered plaintext will be gibberish. Any system that uses OFB mode must have a mechanism for detecting a synchronization loss and a mechanism to fill both shift registers with a new (or the same) IV to regain synchronization.

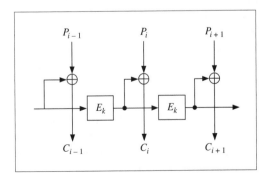

Figure 9.12   n-bit OFB with an n-bit algorithm.

Security Problems with OFB

An analysis of OFB mode [588,430,431,789] demonstrates that OFB should be used only when the feedback size is the same as the block size. For example, you should only use a 64-bit algorithm in 64-bit OFB mode. Even though the U.S. government authorizes other feedback sizes for DES [1143], avoid them.

OFB mode XORs a keystream with the text. This keystream will eventually repeat. It is important that it does not repeat with the same key; otherwise, there is no security. When the feedback size equals the block size, the block cipher acts as a permutation of m-bit values (where m is the block length) and the average cycle length is $2^m - 1$. For a 64-bit block length, this is a very long number. When the feedback size n is less than the block length, the average cycle length drops to around $2^{m/2}$. For a 64-bit block cipher, this is only 2^{32}—not long enough.

Stream Ciphers in OFB

A stream cipher can also run in OFB mode. In this case, the key affects the next-state function (see Figure 9.13). The output function does not depend on the key; very often it is something simple like a single bit of the internal state or the XOR of multiple bits of the internal state. The cryptographic complexity is in the next-state function; this function is key-dependent. This method is also called internal feedback [291], because the feedback mechanism is internal to the key generation algorithm.

In a variant of this mode, the key determines just the initial state of the keystream generator. After the key sets the internal state of the generator, the generator runs undisturbed from then on.

9.9 Counter Mode

Block ciphers in **counter mode** use sequence numbers as the input to the algorithm [824,498,715]. Instead of using the output of the encryption algorithm to fill the register, the input to the register is a counter. After each block encryption, the counter

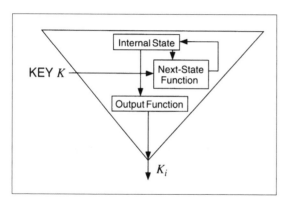

Figure 9.13 A keystream generator in output-feedback mode.

increments by some constant, typically one. The synchronization and error propagation characteristics of this mode are identical to those of OFB. Counter mode solves the OFB mode problem of n-bit output where n is less than the block length.

Nothing is sacred about the counter; it does not have to count through all the possible inputs in order. You can use any of the random-sequence generators in Chapters 16 and 17, whether cryptographically secure or not, as input to the block algorithm.

Stream Ciphers in Counter Mode

Stream ciphers in counter mode have simple next-state functions and complicated output functions dependent on the key. This technique, illustrated in Figure 9.14, was suggested in [498,715]. The next-state function can be something as simple as a counter, adding one to the previous state.

With a counter mode stream cipher, it is possible to generate the ith key bit, k_i, without first generating all the previous key bits. Simply set the counter manually to the ith internal state and generate the bit. This is useful to secure random-access data files; you can decrypt a specific block of data without decrypting the entire file.

9.10 OTHER BLOCK-CIPHER MODES

Block Chaining Mode

To use a block algorithm in **block chaining (BC)** mode, simply XOR the input to the block cipher with the XOR of all the previous ciphertext blocks. As with CBC, an IV starts the process.

Mathematically, this looks like:

$$C_i = E_K(P_i \oplus F_i); \ F_{i+1} = F_i \oplus C_i$$
$$P_i = F_i \oplus D_K(C_i); \ F_{i+1} = F_i \oplus C_i$$

Like CBC, BC's feedback process extends errors in the plaintext. The primary problem with BC is that because the decryption of a ciphertext block depends on all

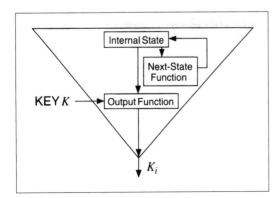

Figure 9.14 A keystream generator in counter mode.

the previous ciphertext blocks, a single error in the ciphertext will result in the incorrect decryption of all subsequent ciphertext blocks.

Propagating Cipher Block Chaining Mode

Propagating cipher block chaining (PCBC) [1080] mode is similar to CBC mode, except that both the previous plaintext block and the previous ciphertext block are XORed with the current plaintext block before encryption (or after decryption) (see Figure 9.15).

$$C_i = E_K(P_i \oplus C_{i-1} \oplus P_{i-1})$$
$$P_i = C_{i-1} \oplus P_{i-1} \oplus D_K(C_i)$$

PCBC was used in Kerberos version 4 (see Section 24.5) to perform both encryption and integrity checking in one pass. In PCBC mode, an error in the ciphertext will result in incorrect decryption of all blocks that follow. This means that checking a standard block at the end of a message will ensure the integrity of the entire message.

Unfortunately, there is a problem with this mode [875]. Swapping two ciphertext blocks results in the incorrect decryption of the two corresponding plaintext blocks, but due to the nature of the XOR with the plaintext and the ciphertext, the errors cancel. So if the integrity checker looks only at the last few blocks of the decrypted plaintext, it could be fooled into accepting a partially garbled message. Although no one has figured out how to exploit this weakness, Kerberos version 5 switched to CBC mode after the flaw was discovered.

Cipher Block Chaining with Checksum

Cipher block chaining with checksum (CBCC) is a CBC variant [1618]. Keep a running XOR of all the plaintext blocks, and XOR that with the last plaintext block before encryption. CBCC ensures that any change made to any ciphertext block

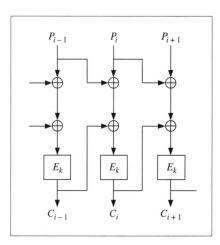

Figure 9.15   Propagating cipher block chaining mode.

changes the decrypted output of the last block. If the last block contains any sort of integrity check or a constant, then the integrity of the decrypted plaintext can be checked with very little additional overhead.

Output Feedback with a Nonlinear Function

Output feedback with a nonlinear function (OFBNLF) [777] is a variant of both OFB and ECB where the key changes with every block:

$$C_i = E_{K_i}(P_i); \; K_i = E_K(K_{i-1})$$
$$P_i = D_{K_i}(C_i); \; K_i = E_K(K_{i-1})$$

A single bit error in the ciphertext propagates to only one plaintext block. However, if a single bit is lost or added, then there is infinite error extension. With a block algorithm that has a complicated key scheduling algorithm, like DES, this mode is slow. I know of no cryptanalysis of this mode.

More Modes

Other modes are possible, although they are not extensively used. **Plaintext block chaining (PBC)** is like CBC except the previous plaintext block is XORed with the plaintext block instead of with the ciphertext block. **Plaintext feedback (PFB)** is like CFB, except the plaintext, not the ciphertext, is used for feedback. These two modes allow chosen-plaintext attacks in order to resist known-plaintext attacks. There is also **cipher block chaining of plaintext difference (CBCPD)**. I'm sure it gets even weirder.

If a cryptanalyst has a brute-force keysearch machine, then he can recover the key if he can guess one of the plaintext blocks. Some of these stranger modes amount to light encryption before applying the encryption algorithm: for example, XORing the text with a fixed secret string or permuting the text. Almost anything nonstandard will frustrate this sort of cryptanalysis.

9.11 CHOOSING A CIPHER MODE

If simplicity and speed are your main concerns, ECB is the easiest and fastest mode to use a block cipher. It is also the weakest. Besides being vulnerable to replay attacks, an algorithm in ECB mode is the easiest to cryptanalyze. I don't recommend ECB for message encryption.

For encrypting random data, such as other keys, ECB is a good mode to use. Since the data is short and random, none of the shortcomings of ECB matter for this application.

For normal plaintext, use CBC, CFB, or OFB. Which mode you choose depends on your specific requirements. Table 9.1 gives a summary of the security and efficiency of the various modes.

CBC is generally best for encrypting files. The increase in security is significant; and while there are sometimes bit errors in stored data, there are almost never synchronization errors. If your application is software-based, CBC is almost always the best choice.

Table 9.1
Summary of Block Cipher Modes

ECB:	CBC:
Security:	***Security:***
– Plaintext patterns are not concealed.	+ Plaintext patterns are concealed by XORing with previous ciphertext block.
– Input to the block cipher is not randomized; it is the same as the plaintext.	+ Input to the block cipher is randomized by XORing with the previous ciphertext block.
+ More than one message can be encrypted with the same key.	+ More than one message can be encrypted with the same key.
– Plaintext is easy to manipulate; blocks can be removed, repeated, or interchanged.	+/– Plaintext is somewhat difficult to manipulate; blocks can be removed from the beginning and end of the message, bits of the first block can be changed, and repetition allows some controlled changes.
Efficiency:	***Efficiency:***
+ Speed is the same as the block cipher.	+ Speed is the same as the block cipher.
– Ciphertext is up to one block longer than the plaintext, due to padding.	– Ciphertext is up to one block longer than the plaintext, not counting the IV.
– No preprocessing is possible.	– No preprocessing is possible.
+ Processing is parallelizable.	+/– Encryption is not parallelizable; decryption is parallelizable and has a random-access property.
Fault-tolerance:	***Fault-tolerance:***
– A ciphertext error affects one full block of plaintext.	– A ciphertext error affects one full block of plaintext and the corresponding bit in the next block.
– Synchronization error is unrecoverable.	– Synchronization error is unrecoverable.

CFB:	OFB/Counter:
Security:	***Security:***
+ Plaintext patterns are concealed.	+ Plaintext patterns are concealed.
+ Input to the block cipher is randomized.	+ Input to the block cipher is randomized.
+ More than one message can be encrypted with the same key, provided that a different IV is used.	+ More than one message can be encrypted with the same key, provided that a different IV is used.
+/– Plaintext is somewhat difficult to manipulate; blocks can be removed from the beginning and end of the message, bits of the first block can be changed, and repetition allows some controlled changes.	– Plaintext is very easy to manipulate; any change in ciphertext directly affects the plaintext.
Efficiency:	***Efficiency:***
+ Speed is the same as the block cipher.	+ Speed is the same as the block cipher.
– Ciphertext is the same size as the plaintext, not counting the IV.	– Ciphertext is the same size as the plaintext, not counting the IV.
+/– Encryption is not parallelizable; decryption is parallelizable and has a random-access property.	+ Processing is possible before the message is seen.
– Some preprocessing is possible before a block is seen; the previous ciphertext block can be encrypted.	–/+ OFB processing is not parallelizable; counter processing is parallelizable.
+/– Encryption is not parallelizable; decryption is parallelizable and has a random-access property.	***Fault-tolerance:***
Fault-tolerance:	+ A ciphertext error affects only the corresponding bit of plaintext.
– A ciphertext error affects the corresponding bit of plaintext and the next full block.	– Synchronization error is unrecoverable.
+ Synchronization errors of full block sizes are recoverable. 1-bit CFB can recover from the addition or loss of single bits.	

CFB—specifically 8-bit CFB—is generally the mode of choice for encrypting streams of characters when each character has to be treated individually, as in a link between a terminal and a host. OFB is most often used in high-speed synchronous systems where error propagation is intolerable. OFB is also the mode of choice if preprocessing is required.

OFB is the mode of choice in a error-prone environment, because it has no error extension.

Stay away from the weird modes. One of the four basic modes—ECB, CBC, OFB, and CFB—is suitable for almost any application. These modes are not overly complex and probably do not reduce the security of the system. While it is possible that a complicated mode might increase the security of a system, most likely it just increases the complexity. None of the weird modes has any better error propagation or error recovery characteristics.

9.12 INTERLEAVING

With most modes, encryption of a bit (or block) depends on the encryption of the previous bits (or blocks). This can often make it impossible to parallelize encryption. For example, consider a hardware box that does encryption in CBC mode. Even if the box contains four encryption chips, only one can work at any time. The next chip needs the results of the previous chip before it starts working.

The solution is to **interleave** multiple encryption streams. (This is not multiple encryption; that's covered in Sections 15.1 and 15.2). Instead of a single CBC chain, use four. The first, fifth, and every fourth block thereafter are encrypted in CBC mode with one IV. The second, sixth, and every fourth block thereafter are encrypted in CBC mode with another IV, and so on. The total IV is much longer than it would have been without interleaving.

Think of it as encrypting four different messages with the same key and four different IVs. These messages are all interleaved.

This trick can also be used to increase the overall speed of hardware encryption. If you have three encryption chips, each capable of encrypting data at 33 megabits/second, you can interleave them to encrypt a single 100 megabit/second data channel.

Figure 9.16 shows three parallel streams interleaved in CFB mode. The idea can also work in CBC and OFB modes, and with any number of parallel streams. Just remember that each stream needs its own IV. Don't share.

9.13 BLOCK CIPHERS VERSUS STREAM CIPHERS

Although block and stream ciphers are very different, block ciphers can be implemented as stream ciphers and stream ciphers can be implemented as block ciphers. The best definition of the difference I've found is from Rainer Rueppel [1362]:

> Block ciphers operate on data with a fixed transformation on large blocks of plaintext data; stream ciphers operate with a time-varying transformation on individual plaintext digits.

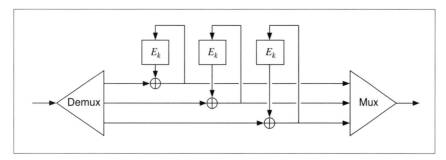

Figure 9.16   Interleaving three CFB encryptions.

In the real world, block ciphers seem to be more general (i.e., they can be used in any of the four modes) and stream ciphers seem to be easier to analyze mathematically. There is a large body of theoretical work on the analysis and design of stream ciphers—most of it done in Europe, for some reason. They have been used by the world's militaries since the invention of electronics. This seems to be changing; recently a whole slew of theoretical papers have been written on block cipher design. Maybe soon there will be a theory of block cipher design as rich as our current theory of stream cipher design.

Otherwise, the differences between stream ciphers and block ciphers are in the implementation. Stream ciphers that only encrypt and decrypt data one bit at a time are not really suitable for software implementation. Block ciphers can be easier to implement in software, because they often avoid time-consuming bit manipulations and they operate on data in computer-sized blocks. On the other hand, stream ciphers can be more suitable for hardware implementation because they can be implemented very efficiently in silicon.

These are important considerations. It makes sense for a hardware encryption device on a digital communications channel to encrypt the individual bits as they go by. This is what the device sees. On the other hand, it makes no sense for a software encryption device to encrypt each individual bit separately. There are some specific instances where bit- and byte-wise encryption might be necessary in a computer system—encrypting the link between the keyboard and the CPU, for example—but generally the encryption block should be at least the width of the data bus.

CHAPTER 10

Using Algorithms

Think of security—data security, communications security, information security, whatever—as a chain. The security of the entire system is only as strong as the weakest link. Everything has to be secure: cryptographic algorithms, protocols, key management, and more. If your algorithms are great but your random-number generator stinks, any smart cryptanalyst is going to attack your system through the random-number generation. If you patch that hole but forget to securely erase a memory location that contains the key, a cryptanalyst will break your system via that route. If you do everything right and accidentally e-mail a copy of your secure files to *The Wall Street Journal*, you might as well not have bothered.

It's not fair. As the designer of a secure system, you have to think of every possible means of attack and protect against them all, but a cryptanalyst only has to find one hole in your security and exploit it.

Cryptography is only a part of security, and often a very small part. It is the mathematics of making a system secure, which is different from actually making a system secure. Cryptography has its "size queens": people who spend so much time arguing about how long a key should be that they forget about everything else. If the secret police want to know what is on your computer, it is far easier for them to break into your house and install a camera that can record what is on your computer screen than it is for them to cryptanalze your hard drive.

Additionally, the traditional view of computer cryptography as "spy versus spy" technology is becoming increasingly inappropriate. Over 99 percent of the cryptography used in the world is not protecting military secrets; it's in applications such as bank cards, pay-TV, road tolls, office building and computer access tokens, lottery terminals, and prepayment electricity meters [43,44]. In these applications, the role of cryptography is to make petty crime slightly more difficult; the paradigm of the well-funded adversary with a rabbit warren of cryptanalysts and roomsful of computers just doesn't apply.

Most of those applications have used lousy cryptography, but successful attacks against them had nothing to do with cryptanalysis. They involved crooked employees, clever sting operations, stupid implementations, integration blunders, and random idiocies. (I strongly recommend Ross Anderson's paper, "Why Cryptosytems Fail" [44]; it should be required reading for anyone involved in this field.) Even the NSA has admitted that most security failures in its area of interest are due to failures in implementation, and not failures in algorithms or protocols [1119]. In these instances it didn't matter how good the cryptography was; the successful attacks bypassed it completely.

10.1 CHOOSING AN ALGORITHM

When it comes to evaluating and choosing algorithms, people have several alternatives:

— They can choose a published algorithm, based on the belief that a published algorithm has been scrutinized by many cryptographers; if no one has broken the algorithm yet, then it must be pretty good.

— They can trust a manufacturer, based on the belief that a well-known manufacturer has a reputation to uphold and is unlikely to risk that reputation by selling equipment or programs with inferior algorithms.

— They can trust a private consultant, based on the belief that an impartial consultant is best equipped to make a reliable evaluation of different algorithms.

— They can trust the government, based on the belief that the government is trustworthy and wouldn't steer its citizens wrong.

— They can write their own algorithms, based on the belief that their cryptographic ability is second-to-none and that they should trust nobody but themselves.

Any of these alternatives is problematic, but the first seems to be the most sensible. Putting your trust in a single manufacturer, consultant, or government is asking for trouble. Most people who call themselves security consultants (even those from big-name firms) usually don't know anything about encryption. Most security product manufacturers are no better. The NSA has some of the world's best cryptographers working for it, but they're not telling all they know. They have their own interests to further which are not congruent with those of their citizens. And even if you're a genius, writing your own algorithm and then using it without any peer review is just plain foolish.

The algorithms in this book are public. Most have appeared in the open literature and many have been cryptanalyzed by experts in the field. I list all published results, both positive and negative. I don't have access to the cryptanalysis done by any of the myriad military security organizations in the world (which are probably better than the academic institutions—they've been doing it longer and are better funded), so it is possible that these algorithms are easier to break than it appears. Even so, it is far more likely that they are more secure than an algorithm designed and implemented in secret in some corporate basement.

The hole in all this reasoning is that we don't know the abilities of the various military cryptanalysis organizations.

What algorithms can the NSA break? For the majority of us, there's really no way of knowing. If you are arrested with a DES-encrypted computer hard drive, the FBI is unlikely to introduce the decrypted plaintext at your trial; the fact that they can break an algorithm is often a bigger secret than any information that is recovered. During WWII, the Allies were forbidden from using decrypted German Ultra traffic unless they could have plausibly gotten the information elsewhere. The only way to get the NSA to admit to the ability to break a given algorithm is to encrypt something so valuable that its public dissemination is worth the admission. Or, better yet, create a really funny joke and send it via encrypted e-mail to shady characters in shadowy countries. NSA employees are people, too; I doubt even they can keep a good joke secret.

A good working assumption is that the NSA can read any message that it chooses, but that it cannot read all messages that it chooses. The NSA is limited by resources, and has to pick and choose among its various targets. Another good assumption is that they prefer breaking knuckles to breaking codes; this preference is so strong that they will only resort to breaking codes when they wish to preserve the secret that they have read the message.

In any case, the best most of us can do is to choose among public algorithms that have withstood a reasonable amount of public scrutiny and cryptanalysis.

Algorithms for Export

Algorithms for export out of the United States must be approved by the U.S. government (actually, by the NSA—see Section 25.1). It is widely believed that these export-approved algorithms can be broken by the NSA. Although no one has admitted this on the record, these are some of the things the NSA is rumored to privately suggest to companies wishing to export their cryptographic products:

— Leak a key bit once in a while, embedded in the ciphertext.

— "Dumb down" the effective key to something in the 30-bit range. For example, while the algorithm might accept a 100-bit key, most of those keys might be equivalent.

— Use a fixed IV, or encrypt a fixed header at the beginning of each encrypted message. This facilitates a known-plaintext attack.

— Generate a few random bytes, encrypt them with the key, and then put both the plaintext and the ciphertext of those random bytes at the beginning of the encrypted message. This also facilitates a known-plaintext attack.

NSA gets a copy of the source code, but the algorithm's details remain secret from everyone else. Certainly no one advertises any of these deliberate weaknesses, but beware if you buy a U.S. encryption product that has been approved for export.

10.2 PUBLIC-KEY CRYPTOGRAPHY VERSUS SYMMETRIC CRYPTOGRAPHY

Which is better, public-key cryptography or symmetric cryptography? This question doesn't make any sense, but has been debated since public-key cryptography was invented. The debate assumes that the two types of cryptography can be compared on an equal footing. They can't.

Needham and Schroeder [1159] pointed out that the number and length of messages are far greater with public-key algorithms than with symmetric algorithms. Their conclusion was that the symmetric algorithm was more efficient than the public-key algorithm. While true, this analysis overlooks the significant security benefits of public-key cryptography.

Whitfield Diffie writes [492,494]:

> In viewing public-key cryptography as a new form of cryptosystem rather than a new form of key management, I set the stage for criticism on grounds of both security and performance. Opponents were quick to point out that the RSA system ran about one-thousandth as fast as DES and required keys about ten times as large. Although it had been obvious from the beginning that the use of public key systems could be limited to exchanging keys for conventional [symmetric] cryptography, it was not immediately clear that this was necessary. In this context, the proposal to build *hybrid* systems [879] was hailed as a discovery in its own right.

Public-key cryptography and symmetric cryptography are different sorts of animals; they solve different sorts of problems. Symmetric cryptography is best for encrypting data. It is orders of magnitude faster and is not susceptible to chosen-ciphertext attacks. Public-key cryptography can do things that symmetric cryptography can't; it is best for key management and a myriad of protocols discussed in Part I.

Other primitives were discussed in Part I: one-way hash functions, message authentication codes, and so on. Table 10.1 lists different types of algorithms and their properties [804].

10.3 ENCRYPTING COMMUNICATIONS CHANNELS

This is the classic Alice and Bob problem: Alice wants to send Bob a secure message. What does she do? She encrypts the message.

In theory, this encryption can take place at any layer in the OSI (Open Systems Interconnect) communications model. (See the OSI security architecture standard for more information [305].) In practice, it takes place either at the lowest layers (one and two) or at higher layers. If it takes place at the lowest layers, it is called **link-by-link**

Table 10.1
Classes of Algorithms

Algorithm	Confidentiality	Authentication	Integrity	Key Management
Symmetric encryption algorithms	Yes	No	No	Yes
Public-key encryption algorithms	Yes	No	No	Yes
Digital signature algorithms	No	Yes	Yes	No
Key-agreement algorithms	Yes	Optional	No	Yes
One-way hash functions	No	No	Yes	No
Message authentication codes	No	Yes	Yes	No

encryption; everything going through a particular data link is encrypted. If it takes place at higher layers, it is called **end-to-end encryption**; the data are encrypted selectively and stay encrypted until they are decrypted by the intended final recipient. Each approach has its own benefits and drawbacks.

Link-by-Link Encryption

The easiest place to add encryption is at the physical layer (see Figure 10.1). This is called link-by-link encryption. The interfaces to the physical layer are generally standardized and it is easy to connect hardware encryption devices at this point. These devices encrypt all data passing through them, including data, routing information, and protocol information. They can be used on any type of digital communication link. On the other hand, any intelligent switching or storing nodes between the sender and the receiver need to decrypt the data stream before processing it.

This type of encryption is very effective. Because everything is encrypted, a cryptanalyst can get no information about the structure of the information. He has no idea who is talking to whom, how long the messages they are sending are, what times of day they communicate, and so on. This is called **traffic-flow security**: the enemy is not only denied access to the information, but also access to the knowledge of where and how much information is flowing.

Security does not depend on any traffic management techniques. Key management is also simple; only the two endpoints of the line need a common key, and they can change their key independently from the rest of the network.

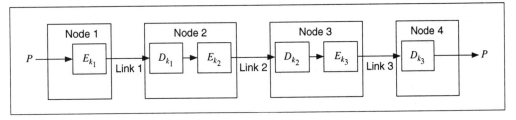

Figure 10.1   Link encryption.

Imagine a synchronous communications line, encrypted using 1-bit CFB. After initialization, the line can run indefinitely, recovering automatically from bit or synchronization errors. The line encrypts whenever messages are sent from one end to the other; otherwise it just encrypts and decrypts random data. Eve has no idea when messages are being sent and when they are not; she has no idea when messages begin and end. All she sees is an endless stream of random-looking bits.

If the communications line is asynchronous, the same 1-bit CFB mode can be used. The difference is that the adversary can get information about the rate of transmission. If this information must be concealed, make some provision for passing dummy messages during idle times.

The biggest problem with encryption at the physical layer is that each physical link in the network needs to be encrypted: Leaving any link unencrypted jeopardizes the security of the entire network. If the network is large, the cost may quickly become prohibitive for this kind of encryption.

Additionally, every node in the network must be protected, since it processes unencrypted data. If all the network's users trust one another, and all nodes are in secure locations, this may be tolerable. But this is unlikely. Even in a single corporation, information might have to be kept secret within a department. If the network accidentally misroutes information, anyone can read it. Table 10.2 summarizes the pros and cons of link-by-link encryption.

End-to-End Encryption

Another approach is to put encryption equipment between the network layer and the transport layer. The encryption device must understand the data according to the protocols up to layer three and encrypt only the transport data units, which are then recombined with the unencrypted routing information and sent to lower layers for transmission.

This approach avoids the encryption/decryption problem at the physical layer. By providing end-to-end encryption, the data remains encrypted until it reaches its final destination (see Figure 10.2). The primary problem with end-to-end encryption is that the routing information for the data is not encrypted; a good cryptanalyst can

Table 10.2
Link-by-Link Encryption: Advantages and Disadvantages

Advantages:
Easier operation, since it can be made transparent to the user. That is, everything is encrypted before being sent over the link.
Only one set of keys per link is required.
Provides traffic-flow security, since any routing information is encrypted.
Encryption is online.

Disadvantages:
Data is exposed in the intermediate nodes.

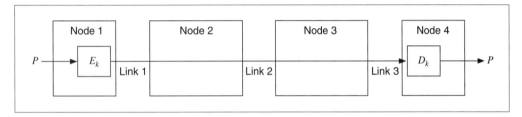

Figure 10.2   End-to-end encryption.

learn much from who is talking to whom, at what times and for how long, without ever knowing the contents of those conversations. Key management is also more difficult, since individual users must make sure they have common keys.

Building end-to-end encryption equipment is difficult. Each particular communications system has its own protocols. Sometimes the interfaces between the levels are not well-defined, making the task even more difficult.

If encryption takes place at a high layer of the communications architecture, like the applications layer or the presentation layer, then it can be independent of the type of communication network used. It is still end-to-end encryption, but the encryption implementation does not have to bother about line codes, synchronization between modems, physical interfaces, and so forth. In the early days of electromechanical cryptography, encryption and decryption took place entirely offline; this is only one step removed from that.

Encryption at these high layers interacts with the user software. This software is different for different computer architectures, and so the encryption must be optimized for different computer systems. Encryption can occur in the software itself or in specialized hardware. In the latter case, the computer will send the data to the specialized hardware for encryption before sending it to lower layers of the communication architecture for transmission. This process requires some intelligence and is not suitable for dumb terminals. Additionally, there may be compatibility problems with different types of computers.

The major disadvantage of end-to-end encryption is that it allows **traffic analysis**. Traffic analysis is the analysis of encrypted messages: where they come from, where they go to, how long they are, when they are sent, how frequent or infrequent they are, whether they coincide with outside events like meetings, and more. A lot of good information is buried in that data, and a cryptanalyst will want to get his hands on it. Table 10.3 presents the positive and negative aspects of end-to-end encryption.

Combining the Two

Table 10.4, primarily from [1244], compares link-by-link and end-to-end encryption. Combining the two, while most expensive, is the most effective way of securing a network. Encryption of each physical link makes any analysis of the routing information impossible, while end-to-end encryption reduces the threat of unencrypted data at the various nodes in the network. Key management for the two

Table 10.3
End-to-End Encryption: Advantages and Disadvantages

Advantages:
Higher secrecy level.

Disadvantages:
Requires a more complex key-management system.
Traffic analysis is possible, since routing information is not encrypted.
Encryption is offline.

schemes can be completely separate: The network managers can take care of encryption at the physical level, while the individual users have responsibility for end-to-end encryption.

10.4 ENCRYPTING DATA FOR STORAGE

Encrypting data for storage and later retrieval can also be thought of in the Alice and Bob model. Alice is still sending a message to Bob, but in this case "Bob" is Alice at some future time. However, the problem is fundamentally different.

In communications channels, messages in transit have no intrinsic value. If Bob doesn't receive a particular message, Alice can always resend it. This is not true for data encrypted for storage. If Alice can't decrypt her message, she can't go back in time and re-encrypt it. She has lost it forever. This means that encryption applications for data storage should have some mechanisms to prevent unrecoverable errors from creeping into the ciphertext.

The encryption key has the same value as the message, only it is smaller. In effect, cryptography converts large secrets into smaller ones. Being smaller, they can be easily lost. Key management procedures should assume that the same keys will be used again and again, and that data may sit on a disk for years before being decrypted.

Furthermore, the keys will be around for a long time. A key used on a communications link should, ideally, exist only for the length of the communication. A key used for data storage might be needed for years, and hence must be stored securely for years.

Other problems particular to encrypting computer data for storage were listed in [357]:

— The data may also exist in plaintext form, either on another disk, in another computer, or on paper. There is much more opportunity for a cryptanalyst to perform a known-plaintext attack.

— In database applications, pieces of data may be smaller than the block size of most algorithms. This will cause the ciphertext to be considerably larger than the plaintext.

Table 10.4
Comparing Link-by-Link and End-to-End Encryption

LINK-BY-LINK ENCRYPTION	END-TO-END ENCRYPTION
Security within Hosts	
Message exposed in sending host	Message encrypted in sending host
Message exposed in intermediate nodes	Message encrypted in intermediate nodes
Role of User	
Applied by sending host	Applied by sending process
Invisible to user	User applies encryption
Host maintains encryption	User must find algorithm
One facility for all users	User selects encryption
Can be done in hardware	More easily done in software
All or no messages encrypted	User chooses to encrypt or not, for each message
Implementation Concerns	
Requires one key per host pair	Requires one key per user pair
Requires encryption hardware or software at each host	Requires encryption hardware or software at each node
Provides node authentication	Provides user authentication

— The speed of I/O devices demands fast encryption and decryption, and will probably require encryption hardware. In some applications, special high-speed algorithms may be required.

— Safe, long-term storage for keys is required.

— Key management is much more complicated, since different people need access to different files, different portions of the same file, and so forth.

If the encrypted files are not structured as records and fields, such as text files, retrieval is easier: The entire file is decrypted before use. If the encrypted files are database files, this solution is problematic. Decrypting the entire database to access a single record is inefficient, but encrypting records independently might be susceptible to a block-replay kind of attack.

In addition, you must make sure the unencrypted file is erased after encryption (see Section 10.9). For further details and insights, consult [425,569].

Dereferencing Keys

When encrypting a large hard drive, you have two options. You can encrypt all the data using a single key. This gives a cryptanalyst a large amount of ciphertext to analyze and makes it impossible to allow multiple users to see only parts of the drive. Or, you can encrypt each file with a different key, forcing users to memorize a different key for each file.

The solution is to encrypt each file with a separate key, and to encrypt the keys with another key known by the users. Each user only has to remember that one key. Different users can have different subsets of the file-encryption keys encrypted with their key. And there can even be a master key under which every file-encryption key is encrypted. This is even more secure because the file-encryption keys are random and less susceptible to a dictionary attack.

Driver-Level vs. File-Level Encryption

There are two ways to encrypt a hard drive: at the file level and at the driver level. Encryption at the file level means that every file is encrypted separately. To use a file that's been encrypted, you must first decrypt the file, then use it, and then re-encrypt it.

Driver-level encryption maintains a logical drive on the user's machine that has all data on it encrypted. If done well, this can provide security that, beyond choosing good passwords, requires little worry on the part of the user. The driver must be considerably more complex than a simple file-encryption program, however, because it must deal with the issues of being an installed device driver, allocation of new sectors to files, recycling of old sectors from files, random-access read and update requests for any data on the logical disk, and so on.

Typically, the driver prompts the user for a password before starting up. This is used to generate the master decryption key, which may then be used to decrypt actual decryption keys used on different data.

Providing Random Access to an Encrypted Drive

Most systems expect to be able to access individual disk sectors randomly. This adds some complication for using many stream ciphers and block ciphers in any chaining mode. Several solutions are possible.

Use the sector address to generate a unique IV for each sector being encrypted or decrypted. The drawback is that each sector will always be encrypted with the same IV. Make sure this is not a security problem.

For the master key, generate a pseudo-random block as large as one sector. (You can do this by running an algorithm in OFB mode, for example.) To encrypt any sector, first XOR in this pseudo-random block, then encrypt normally with a block cipher in ECB mode. This is called ECB+OFB (see Section 15.4).

Since CBC and CFB are error-recovering modes, you can use all but the first block or two in the sector to generate the IV for that sector. For example, the IV for sector 3001 may be the hash of the all but the first 128 bits of the sector's data. After generating the IV, encrypt normally in CBC mode. To decrypt the sector, you use the second 64-bit block of the sector as an IV, and decrypt the remainder of the sector. Then, using the decrypted data, you regenerate the IV and decrypt the first 128 bits.

You can use a block cipher with a large enough block size that it can encrypt the whole sector at once. Crab (see Section 14.6) is an example.

10.5 HARDWARE ENCRYPTION VERSUS SOFTWARE ENCRYPTION

Hardware

Until very recently, all encryption products were in the form of specialized hardware. These encryption/decryption boxes plugged into a communications line and

Table 10.5
Comparing File-Level and Driver-Level Encryption

FILE-LEVEL ENCRYPTION	DRIVER-LEVEL ENCRYPTION
Benefits:	
Ease of implementation and use.	Temporary files, work files, and so forth can be kept on the secure drive.
Flexible.	
Relatively small performance penalty.	
Users can move files between different machines without problems.	It's harder to forget to re-encrypt something on this kind of system.
Users can back files up without problems.	
Security Issues:	
Potential leakage through security-unconscious programs. (Program may write file to disk for temporary storage, for example.)	Lots of things can go wrong with a device-driver or memory-resident program.
Bad implementations may always re-encrypt with same key for same password.	Bad implementations will allow chosen-plaintext, or even chosen-ciphertext attacks.
	If whole system is master-keyed under one password, loss of that password means that the attacker gets everything.
	A more limited set of ciphers can reasonably be used for this kind of application. For example, OFB stream ciphers would not work.
Usability Problems:	
User has to figure out what to do.	There will be a performance penalty.
There may be different passwords for different files.	The driver may interact in weird ways with Windows, OS/2 DOS emulation, device drivers, and so on.
Manual encryption of selected files is the only access control.	

encrypted all the data going across that line. Although software encryption is becoming more prevalent today, hardware is still the embodiment of choice for military and serious commercial applications. The NSA, for example, only authorizes encryption in hardware. There are several reasons why this is so.

The first is speed. As we will see in Part III, encryption algorithms consist of many complicated operations on plaintext bits. These are not the sorts of operations that are built into your run-of-the-mill computer. The two most common encryption algorithms, DES and RSA, run inefficiently on general-purpose processors. While some cryptographers have tried to make their algorithms more suitable for software implementation, specialized hardware will always win a speed race.

Additionally, encryption is often a computation-intensive task. Tying up the computer's primary processor for this is inefficient. Moving encryption to another chip, even if that chip is just another processor, makes the whole system faster.

The second reason is security. An encryption algorithm running on a generalized computer has no physical protection. Mallory can go in with various debugging tools and surreptitiously modify the algorithm without anyone ever realizing it. Hardware encryption devices can be securely encapsulated to prevent this. Tamper-proof boxes can prevent someone from modifying a hardware encryption device. Special-purpose VLSI chips can be coated with a chemical such that any attempt to access their interior will result in the destruction of the chip's logic. The U.S. government's Clipper and Capstone chips (see Sections 24.16 and 24.17) are designed to be tamperproof. The chips can be designed so that it is impossible for Mallory to read the unencrypted key.

IBM developed a cryptographic system for encrypting data and communications on mainframe computers [515,1027]. It includes tamper-resistant modules to hold keys. This system is discussed in Section 24.1.

Electromagnetic radiation can sometimes reveal what is going on inside a piece of electronic equipment. Dedicated encryption boxes can be shielded, so that they leak no compromising information. General-purpose computers can be shielded as well, but it is a far more complex problem. The U.S. military calls this **TEMPEST**; it's a subject well beyond the scope of this book.

The final reason for the prevalence of hardware is the ease of installation. Most encryption applications don't involve general-purpose computers. People may wish to encrypt their telephone conversations, facsimile transmissions, or data links. It is cheaper to put special-purpose encryption hardware in the telephones, facsimile machines, and modems than it is to put in a microprocessor and software.

Even when the encrypted data comes from a computer, it is easier to install a dedicated hardware encryption device than it is to modify the computer's system software. Encryption should be invisible; it should not hamper the user. The only way to do this in software is to write encryption deep into the operating system. This isn't easy. On the other hand, even a computer neophyte can plug an encryption box between his computer and his external modem.

The three basic kinds of encryption hardware on the market today are: self-contained encryption modules (that perform functions such as password verification and key management for banks), dedicated encryption boxes for communications links, and boards that plug into personal computers.

Some encryption boxes are designed for certain types of communications links, such as T-1 encryption boxes that are designed not to encrypt synchronization bits. There are different boxes for synchronous and asynchronous communications lines. Newer boxes tend to accept higher bit rates and are more versatile.

Even so, many of these devices have some incompatibilities. Buyers should be aware of this and be well-versed in their particular needs, lest they find themselves the owners of encryption equipment unable to perform the task at hand. Pay attention to restrictions in hardware type, operating system, applications software, network, and so forth.

PC-board encryptors usually encrypt everything written to the hard disk and can be configured to encrypt everything sent to the floppy disk and serial port as well. These boards are not shielded against electromagnetic radiation or physical interference, since there would be no benefit in protecting the boards if the computer remained unaffected.

More companies are starting to put encryption hardware into their communications equipment. Secure telephones, facsimile machines, and modems are all available.

Internal key management for these devices is generally secure, although there are as many different schemes as there are equipment vendors. Some schemes are more suited for one situation than another, and buyers should know what kind of key management is incorporated into the encryption box and what they are expected to provide themselves.

Software

Any encryption algorithm can be implemented in software. The disadvantages are in speed, cost, and ease of modification (or manipulation). The advantages are in flexibility and portability, ease of use, and ease of upgrade. The algorithms written in C at the end of this book can be implemented, with little modification, on any computer. They can be inexpensively copied and installed on many machines. They can be incorporated into larger applications, such as communications programs or word processors.

Software encryption programs are popular and are available for all major operating systems. These are meant to protect individual files; the user generally has to manually encrypt and decrypt specific files. It is important that the key management scheme be secure: The keys should not be stored on disk anywhere (or even written to a place in memory from where the processor swaps out to disk). Keys and unencrypted files should be erased after encryption. Many programs are sloppy in this regard, and a user has to choose carefully.

Of course, Mallory can always replace the software encryption algorithm with something lousy. But for most users, that isn't a problem. If Mallory can break into our office and modify our encryption program, he can also put a hidden camera on the wall, a wiretap on the telephone, and a TEMPEST detector down the street. If Mallory is that much more powerful than the user, the user has lost the game before it starts.

10.6   COMPRESSION, ENCODING, AND ENCRYPTION

Using a data compression algorithm together with an encryption algorithm makes sense for two reasons:

> Cryptanalysis relies on exploiting redundancies in the plaintext; compressing a file before encryption reduces these redundancies.

> Encryption is time-consuming; compressing a file before encryption speeds up the entire process.

The important thing to remember is to compress before encryption. If the encryption algorithm is any good, the ciphertext will not be compressible; it will look like random data. (This makes a reasonable test of an encryption algorithm; if the ciphertext can be compressed, then the algorithm probably isn't very good.)

If you are going to add any type of transmission encoding or error detection and recovery, remember to add that after encryption. If there is noise in the communications path, decryption's error-extension properties will only make that noise worse. Figure 10.3 summarizes these steps.

10.7   DETECTING ENCRYPTION

How does Eve detect an encrypted file? Eve is in the spy business, so this is an important question. Imagine that she's eavesdropping on a network where messages are flying in all directions at high speeds; she has to pick out the interesting ones. Encrypted files are certainly interesting, but how does she know they are encrypted?

Generally, she relies on the fact that most popular encryption programs have well-defined headers. Electronic-mail messages encrypted with either PEM or PGP (see Sections 24.10 and 24.12) are easy to identify for that reason.

Other file encryptors just produce a ciphertext file of seemingly random bits. How can she distinguish it from any other file of seemingly random bits? There is no sure way, but Eve can try a number of things:

— Examine the file. ASCII text is easy to spot. Other file formats, such as TIFF, T$_e$X, C, Postscript, G3 facsimile, or Microsoft Excel, have stan-

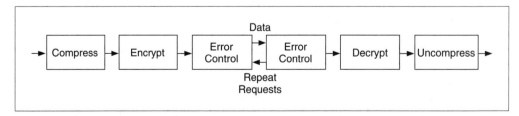

Figure 10.3   Encryption with compression and error control.

dard identifying characteristics. Executable code is detectable, as well. UNIX files often have "magic numbers" that can be detected.

— Try to uncompress the file, using the major compression algorithms. If the file is compressed (and not encrypted), this should yield the original file.

— Try to compress the file. If the file is ciphertext (and the algorithm is good), then the probability that the file can be appreciably compressed by a general-purpose compression routine is small. (By appreciably, I mean more than 1 or 2 percent.) If it is something else (a binary image or a binary data file, for example) it probably can be compressed.

Any file that cannot be compressed and is not already compressed is probably ciphertext. (Of course, it is possible to specifically make ciphertext that is compressible.) Identifying the algorithm is a whole lot harder. If the algorithm is good, you can't. If the algorithm has some slight biases, it might be possible to recognize those biases in the file. However, the biases have to be pretty significant or the file has to be pretty big in order for this to work.

10.8 HIDING CIPHERTEXT IN CIPHERTEXT

Alice and Bob have been sending encrypted messages to each other for the past year. Eve has been collecting them all, but she cannot decrypt any of them. Finally, the secret police tire of all this unreadable ciphertext and arrest the pair. "Give us your encryption keys," they demand. Alice and Bob refuse, but then they notice the thumbscrews. What can they do?

Wouldn't it be nice to be able to encrypt a file such that there are two possible decryptions, each with a different key. Alice could encrypt a real message to Bob in one of the keys and some innocuous message in the other key. If Alice were caught, she could surrender the key to the innocuous message and keep the real key secret.

The easiest way to do this is with one-time pads. Let P be the plaintext, D the dummy plaintext, C the ciphertext, K the real key, and K' the dummy key. Alice encrypts P:

$$P \oplus K = C$$

Alice and Bob share K, so Bob can decrypt C:

$$C \oplus K = P$$

If the secret police ever force them to surrender their key, they don't surrender K, but instead surrender:

$$K' = C \oplus D$$

The police then recover the dummy plaintext:

$$C \oplus K' = D$$

Since these are one-time pads and K is completely random, there is no way to prove that K' was not the real key. To make matters more convincing, Alice and Bob should concoct some mildly incriminating dummy messages to take the place of the really incriminating real messages. A pair of Israeli spies once did this.

Alice could take P and encrypt it with her favorite algorithm and key K to get C. Then she takes C and XORs it with some piece of mundane plaintext—*Pride and Prejudice* for example, to get K'. She stores both C and the XOR on her hard disk. Now, when the secret police interrogate her, she can explain that she is an amateur cryptographer and that K' is a merely one-time pad for C. The secret police might suspect something, but unless they know K they cannot prove that Alice's explanation isn't valid.

Another method is to encrypt P with a symmetric algorithm and K, and D with K'. Intertwine bits (or bytes) of the ciphertext to make the final ciphertexts. If the secret police demand the key, Alice gives them K' and says that the alternating bits (or bytes) are random noise designed to frustrate cryptanalysis. The trouble is the explanation is so implausible that the secret police will probably not believe her (especially considering it is suggested in this book).

A better way is for Alice to create a dummy message, D, such that the concatenation of P and D, compressed, is about the same size as D. Call this concatenation P'. Alice then encrypts P' with whatever algorithm she and Bob share to get C. Then she sends C to Bob. Bob decrypts C to get P', and then P and D. Then they both compute $C \oplus D = K'$. This K' becomes the dummy one-time pad they use in case the secret police break their doors down. Alice has to transmit D so that hers and Bob's alibis match.

Another method is for Alice to take an innocuous message and run it through some error-correcting code. Then she can introduce errors that correspond to the secret encrypted message. On the receiving end, Bob can extract the errors to reconstruct the secret message and decrypt it. He can also use the error-correcting code to recover the innocuous message. Alice and Bob might be hard pressed to explain to the secret police why they consistently get a 30 percent bit-error rate on an otherwise noise-free computer network, but in some circumstances this scheme can work.

Finally, Alice and Bob can use the subliminal channels in their digital signature algorithms (see Sections 4.2 and 23.3). This is undetectable, works great, but has the drawback of only allowing 20 or so characters of subliminal text to be sent per signed innocuous message. It really isn't good for much more than sending keys.

10.9 DESTROYING INFORMATION

When you delete a file on most computers, the file isn't really deleted. The only thing deleted is an entry in the disk's index file, telling the machine that the file is there. Many software vendors have made a fortune selling file-recovery software that recovers files after they have been deleted.

And there's yet another worry: Virtual memory means your computer can read and write memory to disk any time. Even if you don't save it, you never know when a sensitive document you are working on is shipped off to disk. This means that even if you never save your plaintext data, your computer might do it for you. And driver-level compression programs like Stacker and DoubleSpace can make it even harder to predict how and where information is stored on a disk.

To erase a file so that file-recovery software cannot read it, you have to physically write over all of the file's bits on the disk. According to the National Computer Security Center [1148]:

> Overwriting is a process by which unclassified data are written to storage locations that previously held sensitive data. . . . To purge the . . . storage media, the DoD requires overwriting with a pattern, then its complement, and finally with another pattern; e.g., overwrite first with 0011 0101, followed by 1100 1010, then 1001 0111. The number of times an overwrite must be accomplished depends on the storage media, sometimes on its sensitivity, and sometimes on different DoD component requirements. In any case, a purge is not complete until a final overwrite is made using unclassified data.

You may have to erase files or you may have to erase entire drives. You should also erase all unused space on your hard disk.

Most commercial programs that claim to implement the DoD standard overwrite three times: first with all ones, then with all zeros, and finally with a repeating one-zero pattern. Given my general level of paranoia, I recommend overwriting a deleted file seven times: the first time with all ones, the second time with all zeros, and five times with a cryptographically secure pseudo-random sequence. Recent developments at the National Institute of Standards and Technology with electron-tunneling microscopes suggest even that might not be enough. Honestly, if your data is sufficiently valuable, assume that it is *impossible* to erase data completely off magnetic media. Burn or shred the media; it's cheaper to buy media new than to lose your secrets.

PART III

CRYPTOGRAPHIC

ALGORITHMS

Chapter 11

Mathematical Background

11.1 Information Theory

Modern information theory was first published in 1948 by Claude Elmwood Shannon [1431,1432]. (His papers have been reprinted by the IEEE Press [1433].) For a good mathematical treatment of the topic, consult [593]. In this section, I will just sketch some important ideas.

Entropy and Uncertainty

Information theory defines the **amount of information** in a message as the minimum number of bits needed to encode all possible meanings of that message, assuming all messages are equally likely. For example, the day-of-the-week field in a database contains no more than 3 bits of information, because the information can be encoded with 3 bits:

```
000 = Sunday
001 = Monday
010 = Tuesday
011 = Wednesday
100 = Thursday
101 = Friday
110 = Saturday
111 is unused
```

If this information were represented by corresponding ASCII character strings, it would take up more memory space but would not contain any more information. Similarly, the "sex" field of a database contains only 1 bit of information, even though it might be stored as one of two 6-byte ASCII strings: "MALE" or "FEMALE."

Formally, the amount of information in a message M is measured by the **entropy** of a message, denoted by $H(M)$. The entropy of a message indicating sex is 1 bit; the entropy of a message indicating the day of the week is slightly less than 3 bits. In general, the entropy of a message measured in bits is $\log_2 n$, in which n is the number of possible meanings. This assumes that each meaning is equally likely.

The entropy of a message also measures its **uncertainty**. This is the number of plaintext bits needed to be recovered when the message is scrambled in ciphertext in order to learn the plaintext. For example, if the ciphertext block "QHP*5M" is either "MALE" or "FEMALE," then the uncertainty of the message is 1. A cryptanalyst has to learn only one well-chosen bit to recover the message.

Rate of a Language

For a given language, the **rate of the language** is

$$r = H(M)/N$$

in which N is the length of the message. The rate of normal English takes various values between 1.0 bits/letter and 1.5 bits/letter, for large values of N. Shannon, in [1434], said that the entropy depends on the length of the text. Specifically he indicated a rate of 2.3 bits/letter for 8-letter chunks, but the rate drops to between 1.3 and 1.5 for 16-letter chunks. Thomas Cover used a gambling estimating technique and found an entropy of 1.3 bits/character [386]. (I'll use 1.3 in this book.) The **absolute rate** of a language is the maximum number of bits that can be coded in each character, assuming each character sequence is equally likely. If there are L characters in a language, the absolute rate is:

$$R = \log_2 L$$

This is the maximum entropy of the individual characters.

For English, with 26 letters, the absolute rate is $\log_2 26$, or about 4.7 bits/letter. It should come as no surprise to anyone that the actual rate of English is much less than the absolute rate; natural language is highly redundant.

The **redundancy** of a language, denoted D, is defined by:

$$D = R - r$$

Given that the rate of English is 1.3, the redundancy is 3.4 bits/letter. This means that each English character carries 3.4 bits of redundant information.

An ASCII message that is nothing more than printed English has 1.3 bits of information per byte of message. This means it has 6.7 bits of redundant information, giving it an overall redundancy of 0.84 bits of information per bit of ASCII text, and an entropy of 0.16 bits of information per bit of ASCII text. The same message in BAUDOT, at 5 bits per character, has a redundancy of 0.74 bits per bit and an entropy of 0.26 bits per bit. Spacing, punctuation, numbers, and formatting modify these results.

Security of a Cryptosystem

Shannon defined a precise mathematical model of what it means for a cryptosystem to be secure. The goal of a cryptanalyst is to determine the key K, the plaintext P, or both. However, he may be satisfied with some probabilistic information about P: whether it is digitized audio, German text, spreadsheet data, or something else.

In most real-world cryptanalysis, the cryptanalyst has some probabilistic information about P before he even starts. He probably knows the language of the plaintext. This language has a certain redundancy associated with it. If it is a message to Bob, it probably begins with "Dear Bob." Certainly "Dear Bob" is more probable than "e8T&g [,m." The purpose of cryptanalysis is to modify the probabilities associated with each possible plaintext. Eventually one plaintext will emerge from the pile of possible plaintexts as certain (or at least, very probable).

There is such a thing as a cryptosystem that achieves **perfect secrecy**: a cryptosystem in which the ciphertext yields no possible information about the plaintext (except possibly its length). Shannon theorized that it is only possible if the number of possible keys is at least as large as the number of possible messages. In other words, the key must be at least as long as the message itself, and no key can be reused. In still other words, the one-time pad (see Section 1.5) is the only cryptosystem that achieves perfect secrecy.

Perfect secrecy aside, the ciphertext unavoidably yields some information about the corresponding plaintext. A good cryptographic algorithm keeps this information to a minimum; a good cryptanalyst exploits this information to determine the plaintext.

Cryptanalysts use the natural redundancy of language to reduce the number of possible plaintexts. The more redundant the language, the easier it is to cryptanalyze. This is the reason that many real-world cryptographic implementations use a compression program to reduce the size of the text before encrypting it. Compression reduces the redundancy of a message as well as the work required to encrypt and decrypt.

The entropy of a cryptosystem is a measure of the size of the keyspace, K. It is approximated by the base two logarithm of the number of keys:

$$H(K) = \log_2 K$$

A cryptosystem with a 64-bit key has an entropy of 64 bits; a cryptosystem with a 56-bit key has an entropy of 56 bits. In general, the greater the entropy, the harder it is to break a cryptosystem.

Unicity Distance

For a message of length n, the number of different keys that will decipher a ciphertext message to some intelligible plaintext in the same language as the original plaintext (such as an English text string) is given by the following formula [712,95]:

$$2^{H(K) - nD} - 1$$

Shannon [1432] defined the **unicity distance**, U, also called the unicity point, as an approximation of the amount of ciphertext such that the sum of the real information (entropy) in the corresponding plaintext plus the entropy of the encryption key equals the number of ciphertext bits used. He then went on to show that ciphertexts longer than this distance are reasonably certain to have only one meaningful decryption. Ciphertexts significantly shorter than this are likely to have multiple, equally valid decryptions and therefore gain security from the opponent's difficulty in choosing the correct one.

For most symmetric cryptosystems, the unicity distance is defined as the entropy of the cryptosystem divided by the redundancy of the language.

$$U = H(K)/D$$

Unicity distance does not make deterministic predictions, but gives probabilistic results. Unicity distance estimates the minimum amount of ciphertext for which it is likely that there is only a single intelligible plaintext decryption when a brute-force attack is attempted. Generally, the longer the unicity distance, the better the cryptosystem. For DES, with a 56-bit key, and an ASCII English message, the unicity distance is about 8.2 ASCII characters or 66 bits. Table 11.1 gives the unicity distances for varying key lengths. The unicity distances for some classical cryptosystems are found in [445].

Unicity distance is not a measure of how much ciphertext is required for cryptanalysis, but how much ciphertext is required for there to be only one reasonable solution for cryptanalysis. A cryptosystem may be computationally infeasible to break even if it is theoretically possible to break it with a small amount of ciphertext. (The largely esoteric theory of relativized cryptography is relevant here [230,231,232,233,234,235].) The unicity distance is inversely proportional to the redundancy. As redundancy approaches zero, even a trivial cipher can be unbreakable with a ciphertext-only attack.

Shannon defined a cryptosystem whose unicity distance is infinite as one that has **ideal secrecy**. Note that an ideal cryptosystem is not necessarily a perfect cryptosystem, although a perfect cryptosystem would necessarily be an ideal cryptosystem. If a cryptosystem has ideal secrecy, even successful cryptanalysis will leave some uncertainty about whether the recovered plaintext is the real plaintext.

Information Theory in Practice

While these concepts have great theoretical value, actual cryptanalysis seldom proceeds along these lines. Unicity distance guarantees insecurity if it's too small but does not guarantee security if it's high. Few practical algorithms are absolutely impervious to analysis; all manner of characteristics might serve as entering wedges

Table 11.1
Unicity Distances of ASCII Text Encrypted
with Algorithms with Varying Key Lengths

Key Length (in bits)	Unicity Distance (in characters)
40	5.9
56	8.2
64	9.4
80	11.8
128	18.8
256	37.6

to crack some encrypted messages. However, similar information theory considerations are occasionally useful, for example, to determine a recommended key change interval for a particular algorithm. Cryptanalysts also employ a variety of statistical and information theory tests to help guide the analysis in the most promising directions. Unfortunately, most literature on applying information theory to cryptanalysis remains classified, including the seminal 1940 work of Alan Turing.

Confusion and Diffusion

The two basic techniques for obscuring the redundancies in a plaintext message are, according to Shannon, confusion and diffusion [1432].

Confusion obscures the relationship between the plaintext and the ciphertext. This frustrates attempts to study the ciphertext looking for redundancies and statistical patterns. The easiest way to do this is through substitution. A simple substitution cipher, like the Caesar Cipher, is one in which every identical letter of plaintext is substituted for a single letter of ciphertext. Modern substitution ciphers are more complex: A long block of plaintext is substituted for a different block of ciphertext, and the mechanics of the substitution change with each bit in the plaintext or key. This type of substitution is not necessarily enough; the German Enigma is a complex substitution algorithm that was broken during World War II.

Diffusion dissipates the redundancy of the plaintext by spreading it out over the ciphertext. A cryptanalyst looking for those redundancies will have a harder time finding them. The simplest way to cause diffusion is through transposition (also called **permutation**). A simple transposition cipher, like columnar transposition, simply rearranges the letters of the plaintext. Modern ciphers do this type of permutation, but they also employ other forms of diffusion that can diffuse parts of the message throughout the entire message.

Stream ciphers rely on confusion alone, although some feedback schemes add diffusion. Block algorithms use both confusion and diffusion. As a general rule, diffusion alone is easily cracked (although double transposition ciphers hold up better than many other pencil-and-paper systems).

11.2   COMPLEXITY THEORY

Complexity theory provides a methodology for analyzing the **computational complexity** of different cryptographic techniques and algorithms. It compares cryptographic algorithms and techniques and determines their security. Information theory tells us that all cryptographic algorithms (except one-time pads) can be broken. Complexity theory tells us whether they can be broken before the heat death of the universe.

Complexity of Algorithms

An algorithm's complexity is determined by the computational power needed to execute it. The computational complexity of an algorithm is often measured by two variables: T (for **time complexity**) and S (for **space complexity**, or memory requirement). Both T and S are commonly expressed as functions of n, where n is the size of the input. (There are other measures of complexity: the number of random bits, the communications bandwidth, the amount of data, and so on.)

Generally, the computational complexity of an algorithm is expressed in what is called "big O" notation: the order of magnitude of the computational complexity. It's just the term of the complexity function which grows the fastest as n gets larger; all lower-order terms are ignored. For example, if the time complexity of a given algorithm is $4n^2 + 7n + 12$, then the computational complexity is on the order of n^2, expressed $O(n^2)$.

Measuring time complexity this way is system-independent. You don't have to know the exact timings of various instructions or the number of bits used to represent different variables or even the speed of the processor. One computer might be 50 percent faster than another and a third might have a data path twice as wide, but the order-of-magnitude complexity of an algorithm remains the same. This isn't cheating; when you're dealing with algorithms as complex as the ones presented here, the other stuff is negligible (is a constant factor) compared to the order-of-magnitude complexity.

This notation allows you to see how the input size affects the time and space requirements. For example, if $T = O(n)$, then doubling the input size doubles the running time of the algorithm. If $T = O(2^n)$, then adding one bit to the input size doubles the running time of the algorithm (within a constant factor).

Generally, algorithms are classified according to their time or space complexities. An algorithm is **constant** if its complexity is independent of n: $O(1)$. An algorithm is **linear**, if its time complexity is $O(n)$. Algorithms can also be **quadratic**, **cubic**, and so on. All these algorithms are **polynomial**; their complexity is $O(n^m)$, when m is a constant. The class of algorithms that have a polynomial time complexity are called **polynomial-time** algorithms.

Algorithms whose complexities are $O(t^{f(n)})$, where t is a constant greater than 1 and $f(n)$ is some polynomial function of n, are called **exponential**. The subset of exponential algorithms whose complexities are $O(c^{f(n)})$, where c is a constant and $f(n)$ is more than constant but less than linear, is called **superpolynomial**.

Ideally, a cryptographer would like to be able to say that the best algorithm to break this encryption algorithm is of exponential-time complexity. In practice, the strongest statements that can be made, given the current state of the art of computational complexity theory, are of the form "all known cracking algorithms for this cryptosystem are of superpolynomial-time complexity." That is, the cracking algorithms that we know are of superpolynomial-time complexity, but it is not yet possible to prove that no polynomial-time cracking algorithm could ever be discovered. Advances in computational complexity may some day make it possible to design algorithms for which the existence of polynomial-time cracking algorithms can be ruled out with mathematical certainty.

As n grows, the time complexity of an algorithm can make an enormous difference in whether the algorithm is practical. Table 11.2 shows the running times for different algorithm classes in which n equals one million. The table ignores constants, but also shows why ignoring constants is reasonable.

Table 11.2
Running Times of Different Classes of Algorithms

Class	Complexity	# of Operations for $n = 10^6$	Time at 10^6 O/S
Constant	$O(1)$	1	1 μsec.
Linear	$O(n)$	10^6	1 sec.
Quadratic	$O(n^2)$	10^{12}	11.6 days
Cubic	$O(n^3)$	10^{18}	32,000 yrs.
Exponential	$O(2^n)$	$10^{301,030}$	$10^{301,006}$ times the age of the universe

Assuming that the unit of "time" for our computer is a microsecond, the computer can complete a constant algorithm in a microsecond, a linear algorithm in a second, and a quadratic algorithm in 11.6 days. It would take 32,000 years to complete a cubic algorithm; not terribly practical, but a computer built to withstand the next ice age would deliver a solution eventually. Performing the exponential algorithm is futile, no matter how well you extrapolate computing power, parallel processing, or contact with superintelligent aliens.

Look at the problem of a brute-force attack against an encryption algorithm. The time complexity of this attack is proportional to the number of possible keys, which is an exponential function of the key length. If n is the length of the key, then the complexity of a brute-force attack is $O(2^n)$. Section 12.3 discusses the controversy surrounding a 56-bit key for DES instead of a 112-bit key. The complexity of a brute-force attack against a 56-bit key is 2^{56}; against a 112-bit key the complexity is 2^{112}. The former is possible; the latter isn't.

Complexity of Problems

Complexity theory also classifies the inherent complexity of problems, not just the complexity of particular algorithms used to solve problems. (Excellent introductions to this topic are [600,211,1226]; see also [1096,27,739].) The theory looks at the minimum time and space required to solve the hardest instance of a problem on a theoretical computer known as a **Turing machine**. A Turing machine is a finite-state machine with an infinite read-write memory tape. It turns out that a Turing machine is a realistic model of computation.

Problems that can be solved with polynomial-time algorithms are called **tractable**, because they can usually be solved in a reasonable amount of time for reasonable-sized inputs. (The exact definition of "reasonable" depends on the circumstance.) Problems that cannot be solved in polynomial time are called **intractable**, because calculating their solution quickly becomes infeasible. Intractable problems are sometimes just called **hard**. Problems that can only be solved with algorithms that are superpolynomial are computationally intractable, even for relatively small values of n.

It gets worse. Alan Turing proved that some problems are **undecidable**. It is impossible to devise any algorithm to solve them, regardless of the algorithm's time complexity.

Problems can be divided into complexity classes, which depend on the complexity of their solutions. Figure 11.1 shows the more important complexity classes and their presumed relationships. (Unfortunately, not much about this material has been proved mathematically.)

On the bottom, the class **P** consists of all problems that can be solved in polynomial time. The class **NP** consists of all problems that can be solved in polynomial time only on a nondeterministic Turing machine: a variant of a normal Turing machine that can make guesses. The machine guesses the solution to the problem—either by making "lucky guesses" or by trying all guesses in parallel—and checks its guess in polynomial time.

NP's relevance to cryptography is this: Many symmetric algorithms and all public-key algorithms can be cracked in nondeterministic polynomial time. Given a ciphertext C, the cryptanalyst simply guesses a plaintext, X, and a key, k, and in polynomial time runs the encryption algorithm on inputs X and k and checks whether the result is equal to C. This is important theoretically, because it puts an upper bound on the complexity of cryptanalysis for these algorithms. In practice, of course, it is a deterministic polynomial-time algorithm that the cryptanalyst seeks. Furthermore, this argument is not applicable to all classes of ciphers; in particular, it is not applicable to one-time pads—for any C, there are many X, k pairs that yield C when run through the encryption algorithm, but most of these Xs are nonsense, not legitimate plaintexts.

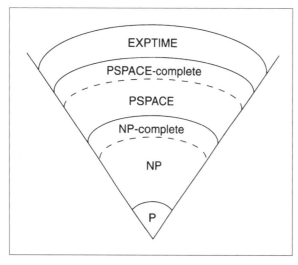

Figure 11.1   Complexity classes.

The class **NP** includes the class **P**, because any problem solvable in polynomial time on a deterministic Turing machine is also solvable in polynomial time on a nondeterministic Turing machine; the guessing stage can simply be omitted.

If all **NP** problems are solvable in polynomial time on a deterministic machine, then **P** = **NP**. Although it seems obvious that some **NP** problems are much harder than others (a brute-force attack against an encryption algorithm versus encrypting a random block of plaintext), it has never been proven that **P** ≠ **NP** (or that **P** = **NP**). However, most people working in complexity theory believe that they are unequal.

Stranger still, specific problems in **NP** can be proven to be as difficult as any problem in the class. Steven Cook [365] proved that the Satisfiability problem (given a propositional Boolean formula, is there a way to assign truth values to the variables that makes the formula true?) is **NP-complete**. This means that, if Satisfiability is solvable in polynomial time, then **P** = **NP**. Conversely, if any problem in **NP** can be proven not to have a deterministic polynomial-time algorithm, the proof will show that Satisfiability does not have a deterministic polynomial-time algorithm either. No problem is harder than Satisfiability in **NP**.

Since Cook's seminal paper was published, a huge number of problems have been shown to be equivalent to Satisfiability; hundreds are listed in [600], and some examples follow. By equivalent, I mean that these problems are also **NP-complete**; they are in **NP** and also as hard as any problem in **NP**. If their solvability in deterministic polynomial time were resolved, the **P** versus **NP** question would be solved. The question of whether **P** = **NP** is the central unsolved question of computational complexity theory, and no one expects it to be solved anytime soon. If someone showed that **P** = **NP**, then most of this book would be irrelevant: As previously explained, many classes of ciphers are trivially breakable in nondeterministic polynomial time. If **P** = **NP**, they are breakable by feasible, deterministic algorithms.

Further out in the complexity hierarchy is **PSPACE**. Problems in **PSPACE** can be solved in polynomial space, but not necessarily polynomial time. **PSPACE** includes **NP**, but some problems in **PSPACE** are thought to be harder than **NP**. Of course, this isn't proven either. There is a class of problems, the so-called **PSPACE-complete** problems, with the property that, if any one of them is in **NP** then **PSPACE** = **NP** and if any one of them is in **P** then **PSPACE** = **P**.

And finally, there is the class of problems called **EXPTIME**. These problems are solvable in exponential time. The **EXPTIME-complete** problems can actually be proven not to be solvable in deterministic polynomial time. It has been shown that **P** does not equal **EXPTIME**.

NP-Complete Problems

Michael Garey and David Johnson compiled a list of over 300 **NP-complete** problems [600]. Here are just a few of them:

— Traveling Salesman Problem. A traveling salesman has to visit n different cities using only one tank of gas (there is a maximum distance he can travel). Is there a route that allows him to visit each city exactly once on that single tank of gas? (This is a generalization of the Hamiltonian Cycle problem—see Section 5.1.)

— Three-Way Marriage Problem. In a room are n men, n women, and n clergymen (priests, rabbis, whatever). There is also a list of acceptable marriages, which consists of one man, one woman, and one clergyman willing to officiate. Given this list of possible triples, is it possible to arrange n marriages such that everyone is either marrying one person or officiating at one marriage?

— Three-Satisfiability. There is a list of n logical statements, each with three variables. For example: if (x and y) then z, (x and w) or (not z), if ((not u and not x) or (z and (u or not x))) then (not z and u) or x, and so on. Is there a truth assignment for all the variables that satisfies all the statements? (This is a special case of the Satisfiability problem previously mentioned.)

11.3 NUMBER THEORY

This isn't a book on number theory, so I'm just going to sketch a few ideas that apply to cryptography. If you want a detailed mathematical text on number theory, consult one of these books: [1430,72,1171,12,959,681,742,420]. My two favorite books on the mathematics of finite fields are [971,1042]. See also [88,1157, 1158,1060].

Modular Arithmetic

You all learned modular arithmetic in school; it was called "clock arithmetic." Remember these word problems? If Mildred says she'll be home by 10:00, and she's 13 hours late, what time does she get home and for how many years does her father ground her? That's arithmetic modulo 12. Twenty-three modulo 12 equals 11.

$$(10 + 13) \bmod 12 = 23 \bmod 12 = 11 \bmod 12$$

Another way of writing this is to say that 23 and 11 are equivalent, modulo 12:

$$23 \equiv 11 \pmod{12}$$

Basically, $a \equiv b \pmod n$ if $a = b + kn$ for some integer k. If a is non-negative and b is between 0 and n, you can think of b as the remainder of a when divided by n. Sometimes, b is called the **residue** of a, modulo n. Sometimes a is called **congruent** to b, modulo n (the triple equals sign, $\equiv$, denotes congruence). These are just different ways of saying the same thing.

The set of integers from 0 to $n - 1$ form what is called a **complete set of residues** modulo n. This means that, for every integer a, its residue modulo n is some number from 0 to $n - 1$.

The operation $a \bmod n$ denotes the residue of a, such that the residue is some integer from 0 to $n - 1$. This operation is **modular reduction**. For example, $5 \bmod 3 = 2$.

This definition of mod may be different from the definition used in some programming languages. For example, PASCAL's modulo operator sometimes returns a negative number. It returns a number between $-(n-1)$ and $n-1$. In C, the % operator returns the remainder from the division of the first expression by the second; this can be a negative number if either operand is negative. For all the algorithms in this book, make sure you add n to the result of the modulo operator if it returns a negative number.

Modular arithmetic is just like normal arithmetic: It's commutative, associative, and distributive. Also, reducing each intermediate result modulo n yields the same result as doing the whole calculation and then reducing the end result modulo n.

$$(a + b) \bmod n = ((a \bmod n) + (b \bmod n)) \bmod n$$
$$(a - b) \bmod n = ((a \bmod n) - (b \bmod n)) \bmod n$$
$$(a * b) \bmod n = ((a \bmod n) * (b \bmod n)) \bmod n$$
$$(a * (b + c)) \bmod n = (((a * b) \bmod n) + ((a * c) \bmod n)) \bmod n$$

Cryptography uses computation mod n a lot, because calculating discrete logarithms and square roots mod n can be hard problems. Modular arithmetic is also easier to work with on computers, because it restricts the range of all intermediate values and the result. For a k-bit modulus, n, the intermediate results of any addition, subtraction, or multiplication will not be more than $2k$-bits long. So we can perform exponentiation in modular arithmetic without generating huge intermediate results. Calculating the power of some number modulo some number,

$a^x \bmod n,$

is just a series of multiplications and divisions, but there are speedups. One kind of speedup aims to minimize the number of modular multiplications; another kind aims to optimize the individual modular multiplications. Because the operations are distributive, it is faster to do the exponentiation as a stream of successive multiplications, taking the modulus every time. It doesn't make much difference now, but it will when you're working with 200-bit numbers.

For example, if you want to calculate $a^8 \bmod n$, don't use the naïve approach and perform seven multiplications and one huge modular reduction:

$(a * a * a * a * a * a * a * a) \bmod n$

Instead, perform three smaller multiplications and three smaller modular reductions:

$((a^2 \bmod n)^2 \bmod n)^2 \bmod n$

By the same token,

$a^{16} \bmod n = (((a^2 \bmod n)^2 \bmod n)^2 \bmod n)^2 \bmod n$

Computing $a^x \bmod n$, where x is not a power of 2, is only slightly harder. Binary notation expresses x as a sum of powers of 2: 25 is 11001 in binary, so $25 = 2^4 + 2^3 + 2^0$. So

$$a^{25} \bmod n = (a * a^{24}) \bmod n = (a * a^8 * a^{16}) \bmod n$$
$$= (a * ((a^2)^2)^2 * (((a^2)^2)^2)^2) \bmod n = ((((a^2 * a)^2)^2)^2 * a) \bmod n$$

With judicious storing of intermediate results, you only need six multiplications:

$$(((((((a^2 \bmod n) \ast a) \bmod n)^2 \bmod n)^2 \bmod n)^2 \bmod n) \ast a) \bmod n$$

This is called **addition chaining** [863], or the binary square and multiply method. It uses a simple and obvious addition chain based on the binary representation. In C, it looks like:

```
unsigned long qe2(unsigned long x, unsigned long y, unsigned long n) {
        unsigned long s,t,u;
        int i;

        s = 1; t = x; u = y;

        while(u) {
                if(u&1) s = (s*t)%n;
                u>>=1;
                t = (t*t)%n;
        }
        return(s);
}
```

Another, recursive, algorithm is:

```
unsigned long fast_exp(unsigned long x, unsigned long y, unsigned long N) {
        unsigned long tmp;
    if(y==1) return(x % N);
    if ((y&1)==0) {
        tmp = fast_exp(x,y/2,N);
        return ((tmp*tmp)%N);
    }
    else {
        tmp = fast_exp(x,(y-1)/2,N);
        tmp = (tmp*tmp)%N;
        tmp = (tmp*x)%N;
        return (tmp);
    }
}
```

This technique reduces the operation to, on the average, $1.5 \ast k$ operations, if k is the length of the number x in bits. Finding the calculation with the fewest operations is a hard problem (it has been proven that the sequence must contain at least $k - 1$ operations), but it is not too hard to get the number of operations down to $1.1 \ast k$ or better, as k grows.

An efficient way to do modular reductions many times using the same n is **Montgomery's method** [1111]. Another method is called **Barrett's algorithm** [87]. The software performance of these two algorithms and the algorithm previously discussed is in [210]: The algorithm I've discussed is the best choice for singular modular reductions; Barrett's algorithm is the best choice for small arguments; and Montgomery's method is the best choice for general modular exponentiations. (Montgomery's method can also take advantage of small exponents, using something called mixed arithmetic.)

The inverse of exponentiation modulo n is calculating a **discrete logarithm**. I'll discuss this shortly.

Prime Numbers

A **prime** number is an integer greater than 1 whose only factors are 1 and itself: No other number evenly divides it. Two is a prime number. So are 73, 2521, 2365347734339, and $2^{756839} - 1$. There are an infinite number of primes. Cryptography, especially public-key cryptography, uses large primes (512 bits and even larger) often.

Evangelos Kranakis wrote an excellent book on number theory, prime numbers, and their applications to cryptography [896]. Paulo Ribenboim wrote two excellent references on prime numbers in general [1307,1308].

Greatest Common Divisor

Two numbers are **relatively prime** when they share no factors in common other than 1. In other words, if the **greatest common divisor** of a and n is equal to 1. This is written:

$$\gcd(a,n) = 1$$

The numbers 15 and 28 are relatively prime, 15 and 27 are not, and 13 and 500 are. A prime number is relatively prime to all other numbers except its multiples.

One way to compute the greatest common divisor of two numbers is with **Euclid's algorithm**. Euclid described the algorithm in his book, *Elements*, written around 300 B.C. He didn't invent it. Historians believe the algorithm could be 200 years older. It is the oldest nontrivial algorithm that has survived to the present day, and it is still a good one. Knuth describes the algorithm and some modern modifications [863].

In C:

```c
/* returns gcd of x and y */

int gcd (int x, int y)
{
    int g;

    if (x < 0)
        x = -x;
    if (y < 0)
        y = -y;
    if (x + y == 0)
        ERROR;
    g = y;
    while (x > 0) {
        g = x;
        x = y % x;
        y = g;
    }
    return g;
}
```

This algorithm can be generalized to return the gcd of an array of *m* numbers:

```
/* returns the gcd of x1, x2...xm */

int multiple_gcd (int m, int *x)
{
    size_t i;
    int g;

    if (m < 1)
        return 0;
    g = x[0];
    for (i=1; i<m; ++i) {
        g = gcd(g, x[i]);
/* optimization, since for random x[i], g==1 60% of the time: */
        if (g == 1)
            return 1;
    }
    return g;
}
```

Inverses Modulo a Number

Remember inverses? The multiplicative inverse of 4 is 1/4, because $4*1/4 = 1$. In the modulo world, the problem is more complicated:

$$4*x \equiv 1 \;(\text{mod } 7)$$

This equation is equivalent to finding an *x* and *k* such that

$$4x = 7k + 1$$

where both *x* and *k* are integers.

The general problem is finding an *x* such that

$$1 = (a*x) \bmod n$$

This is also written as

$$a^{-1} \equiv x \;(\text{mod } n)$$

The modular inverse problem is a lot more difficult to solve. Sometimes it has a solution, sometimes not. For example, the inverse of 5, modulo 14, is 3. On the other hand, 2 has no inverse modulo 14.

In general, $a^{-1} \equiv x \;(\text{mod } n)$ has a unique solution if *a* and *n* are relatively prime. If *a* and *n* are not relatively prime, then $a^{-1} \equiv x \;(\text{mod } n)$ has no solution. If *n* is a prime number, then every number from 1 to $n - 1$ is relatively prime to *n* and has exactly one inverse modulo *n* in that range.

So far, so good. Now, how do you go about finding the inverse of *a* modulo *n*? There are a couple of ways. Euclid's algorithm can also compute the inverse of a number modulo *n*. Sometimes this is called the **extended Euclidean algorithm**.

Here's the algorithm in C++:

```
#define isEven(x)   ((x & 0x01) == 0)
```

```cpp
#define isOdd(x)     (x & 0x01)
#define swap(x,y)    (x ^= y, y ^= x, x ^= y)

void ExtBinEuclid(int *u, int *v, int *u1, int *u2, int *u3)
{
    // warning: u and v will be swapped if u < v
    int k, t1, t2, t3;

    if ( *u < *v ) swap(*u,*v);
    for (k = 0; isEven(*u) && isEven(*v); ++k) {
        *u >>= 1; *v >>= 1;
    }
    *u1 = 1; *u2 = 0; *u3 = *u; t1 = *v; t2 = *u-1; t3 = *v;
    do {
        do {
            if (isEven(*u3)) {
                if (isOdd(*u1) || isOdd(*u2)) {
                    *u1 += *v; *u2 += *u;
                }
                *u1 >>= 1; *u2 >>= 1; *u3 >>= 1;
            }
            if (isEven(t3) || *u3 < t3) {
                swap(*u1,t1); swap(*u2,t2); swap(*u3,t3);
            }
        } while (isEven(*u3));
        while (*u1 < t1 || *u2 < t2) {
            *u1 += *v; *u2 += *u;
        }
        *u1 -= t1; *u2 -= t2; *u3 -= t3;
    } while (t3 > 0);
    while (*u1 >= *v && *u2 >= *u) {
        *u1 -= *v; *u2 -= *u;
    }
    *u1 <<= k; *u2 <<= k; *u3 <<= k;
}

main(int argc, char **argv) {
    int a, b, gcd;

    if ( argc < 3 ) {
        cerr << "Usage: xeuclid u v" << endl;
        return -1;
    }
    int u = atoi(argv[1]);
    int v = atoi(argv[2]);
    if ( u <= 0 || v <= 0 ) {
        cerr << "Arguments must be positive!" << endl;
        return -2;
    }
    // warning: u and v will be swapped if u < v
    ExtBinEuclid(&u, &v, &a, &b, &gcd);
    cout << a << " * " << u << " + (-"
        << b << ") * " << v << " = " << gcd << endl;
    if ( gcd == 1 )
```

```
        cout << "the inverse of " << v << " mod " << u << " is: "
            << u - b << endl;
    return 0;
}
```

I'm not going to prove that it works or give the theory behind it. Details can be found in [863], or in any of the number theory texts previously listed.

The algorithm is iterative and can be slow for large numbers. Knuth showed that the average number of divisions performed by the algorithm is:

$$.843*\log_2{(n)} + 1.47$$

Solving for Coefficients

Euclid's algorithm can be used to solve this class of problems: Given an array of m variables $x_1, x_2, \ldots x_m$, find an array of m coefficients, $u_1, u_2 \ldots u_m$, such that

$$u_1*x_1 + \ldots + u_m*x_m = 1$$

Fermat's Little Theorem

If m is a prime, and a is not a multiple of m, then **Fermat's little theorem** says

$$a^{m-1} \equiv 1 \pmod{m}$$

(Pierre de Fermat, pronounced "Fair-ma," was a French mathematician who lived from 1601 to 1665. This theorem has nothing to do with his last theorem.)

The Euler Totient Function

There is another method for calculating the inverse modulo n, but it's not always possible to use it. The **reduced set of residues** mod n is the subset of the complete set of residues that is relatively prime to n. For example, the reduced set of residues mod 12 is $\{1,5,7,11\}$. If n is prime, then the reduced set of residues mod n is the set of all numbers from 1 to $n-1$. The number 0 is never part of the reduced set of residues for any n not equal to 1.

The **Euler totient function**, also called the Euler phi function and written as $\phi(n)$, is the number of elements in the reduced set of residues modulo n. In other words, $\phi(n)$ is the number of positive integers less than n that are relatively prime to n (for any n greater than 1). (Leonhard Euler, pronounced "Oiler," was a Swiss mathematician who lived from 1707 to 1783.)

If n is prime, then $\phi(n) = n - 1$. If $n = pq$, where p and q are prime, then $\phi(n) = (p-1)(q-1)$. These numbers appear in some public-key algorithms; this is why.

According to **Euler's generalization of Fermat's little theorem**, if $\gcd(a,n) = 1$, then

$$a^{\phi(n)} \bmod n = 1$$

Now it is easy to compute $a^{-1} \bmod n$:

$$x = a^{\phi(n)-1} \bmod n$$

For example, what is the inverse of 5, modulo 7? Since 7 is prime, $\phi(7) = 7 - 1 = 6$. So, the inverse of 5, modulo 7, is

$$5^{6-1} \bmod 7 = 5^5 \bmod 7 = 3$$

Both methods for calculating inverses can be extended to solve for x in the general problem (if $\gcd(a,n) = 1$):

$$(a \star x) \bmod n = b$$

Using Euler's generalization, solve

$$x = (b \star a^{\phi(n)-1}) \bmod n$$

Using Euclid's algorithm, solve

$$x = (b \star (a^{-1} \bmod n)) \bmod n$$

In general, Euclid's algorithm is faster than Euler's generalization for calculating inverses, especially for numbers in the 500-bit range. If $\gcd(a,n) \neq 1$, all is not lost. In this general case, $(a \star x) \bmod n = b$, can have multiple solutions or no solution.

Chinese Remainder Theorem

If you know the prime factorization of n, then you can use something called the **Chinese remainder theorem** to solve a whole system of equations. The basic version of this theorem was discovered by the first-century Chinese mathematician, Sun Tse.

In general, if the prime factorization of n is $p_1 \star p_2 \star \ldots \star p_t$, then the system of equations

$$(x \bmod p_i) = a_i, \text{ where } i = 1, 2, \ldots, t$$

has a unique solution, x, where x is less than n. (Note that some primes can appear more than once. For example, p_1 might be equal to p_2.) In other words, a number (less than the product of some primes) is uniquely identified by its residues mod those primes.

For example, use 3 and 5 as primes, and 14 as the number. 14 mod 3 = 2, and 14 mod 5 = 4. There is only one number less than 3 $\star$ 5 = 15 which has those residues: 14. The two residues uniquely determine the number.

So, for an arbitrary $a < p$ and $b < q$ (where p and q are prime), there exists a unique x, where x is less than pq, such that

$$x \equiv a \pmod p, \text{ and } x \equiv b \pmod q$$

To find this x, first use Euclid's algorithm to find u, such that

$$u \star q \equiv 1 \pmod p$$

Then compute:

$$x = (((a - b) \star u) \bmod p) \star q + b$$

Here is the Chinese remainder theorem in C:

```
/* r is the number of elements in arrays m and u;
m is the array of (pairwise relatively prime) moduli
u is the array of coefficients
```

```
return value is n such than n == u[k]%m[k] (k=0..r-1) and
  n < m[0]*m[1]*...*m[r-1]
*/

/* totient() is left as an exercise to the reader. */

int chinese_remainder (size_t r, int *m, int *u)
{
    size_t i;
    int modulus;
    int n;

    modulus = 1;
    for (i=0; i<r; ++i)
        modulus *= m[i];

    n = 0;
    for (i=0; i<r; ++i) {
        n += u[i] * modexp(modulus / m[i], totient(m[i]),
    m[i]);
        n %= modulus;
    }

    return n;
}
```

The converse of the Chinese remainder theorem can also be used to find the solution to the problem: if p and q are primes, and p is less than q, then there exists a unique x less than pq, such that

$$a \equiv x \; (\text{mod } p), \text{ and } b \equiv x \; (\text{mod } q)$$

If $a \geq b \text{ mod } p$, then

$$x = (((a - (b \text{ mod } p))*u) \text{ mod } p)*q + b$$

If $a < b \text{ mod } p$, then

$$x = (((a + p - (b \text{ mod } p))*u) \text{ mod } p)*q + b$$

Quadratic Residues

If p is prime, and a is greater than 0 and less than p, then a is a **quadratic residue** mod p if

$$x^2 \equiv a \; (\text{mod } p), \text{ for some } x$$

Not all values of a satisfy this property. For a to be a quadratic residue modulo n, it must be a quadratic residue modulo all the prime factors of n. For example, if $p = 7$, the quadratic residues are 1, 2, and 4:

$$1^2 = 1 \equiv 1 \; (\text{mod } 7)$$
$$2^2 = 4 \equiv 4 \; (\text{mod } 7)$$
$$3^2 = 9 \equiv 2 \; (\text{mod } 7)$$

$$4^2 = 16 \equiv 2 \; (\text{mod } 7)$$
$$5^2 = 25 \equiv 4 \; (\text{mod } 7)$$
$$6^2 = 36 \equiv 1 \; (\text{mod } 7)$$

Note that each quadratic residue appears twice on this list.

There are no values of x which satisfy any of these equations:

$$x^2 \equiv 3 \; (\text{mod } 7)$$
$$x^2 \equiv 5 \; (\text{mod } 7)$$
$$x^2 \equiv 6 \; (\text{mod } 7)$$

The **quadratic nonresidues** modulo 7, the numbers that are not quadratic residues, are 3, 5, and 6.

Although I will not do so here, it is easy to prove that, when p is odd, there are exactly $(p - 1)/2$ quadratic residues mod p and the same number of quadratic nonresidues mod p. Also, if a is a quadratic residue mod p, then a has exactly two square roots, one of them between 0 and $(p - 1)/2$, and the other between $(p - 1)/2$ and $(p - 1)$. One of these square roots is also a quadratic residue mod p; this is called the **principal square root**.

If n is the product of two primes, p and q, there are exactly $(p - 1)(q - 1)/4$ quadratic residues mod n. A quadratic residue mod n is a perfect square modulo n. This is because to be a square mod n, the residue must be a square mod p and a square mod q. For example, there are 11 quadratic residues mod 35: 1, 4, 9, 11, 14, 15, 16, 21, 25, 29, and 30. Each quadratic residue has exactly four square roots.

Legendre Symbol

The **Legendre symbol**, written $L(a,p)$, is defined when a is any integer and p is a prime greater than 2. It is equal to 0, 1, or –1.

$L(a,p) = 0$ if a is divisible by p.

$L(a,p) = 1$ if a is a quadratic residue mod p.

$L(a,p) = -1$ is a is a quadratic nonresidue mod p.

One way to calculate $L(a,p)$ is:

$$L(a,p) = a^{(p - 1)/2} \bmod p$$

Or you can use the following algorithm:

1. If $a = 1$, then $L(a,p) = 1$
2. If a is even, then $L(a,p) = L(a/2,p) \cdot (-1)^{(p^2 - 1)/8}$
3. If a is odd (and $\neq 1$), then $L(a,p) = L(p \bmod a, a) \cdot (-1)^{(a - 1) \cdot (p - 1)/4}$

Note that this is also an efficient way to determine whether a is a quadratic residue mod p (when p is prime).

Jacobi Symbol

The **Jacobi symbol**, written $J(a,n)$, is a generalization of the Legendre symbol to composite moduli; it is defined for any integer a and any odd integer n. The function shows up in primality testing. The Jacobi symbol is a function on the set of reduced residues of the divisors of n and can be calculated by several formulas [1412]. This is one method:

Definition 1: $J(a,n)$ is only defined if n is odd.

Definition 2: $J(0,n) = 0$.

Definition 3: If n is prime, then the Jacobi symbol $J(a,n) = 0$ if n divides a.

Definition 4: If n is prime, then the Jacobi symbol $J(a,n) = 1$ if a is a quadratic residue modulo n.

Definition 5: If n is prime, then the Jacobi symbol $J(a,n) = -1$ if a is a quadratic nonresidue modulo n.

Definition 6: If n is composite, then the Jacobi symbol $J(a,n) = J(a,p_1)$ $* \ldots * J(a,p_m)$, where $p_1 \ldots p_m$ is the prime factorization of n.

The following algorithm computes the Jacobi symbol recursively:

Rule 1: $J(1,n) = 1$

Rule 2: $J(a*b,n) = J(a,n)*J(b,n)$

Rule 3: $J(2,n) = 1$ if $(n^2 - 1)/8$ is even, and -1 otherwise

Rule 4: $J(a,n) = J((a \bmod n),n)$

Rule 5: $J(a,b_1*b_2) = J(a,b_1)*J(a,b_2)$

Rule 6: If the greatest common divisor of a and $b = 1$, and a and b are odd:

Rule 6a: $J(a,b) = J(b,a)$ if $(a - 1)(b - 1)/4$ is even

Rule 6b: $J(a,b) = -J(b,a)$ if $(a - 1)(b - 1)/4$ is odd

Here is the algorithm in C:

```
/* This algorithm computes the Jacobi symbol recursively */

int jacobi(int a, int b)
{
int g;

    assert(odd(b));

    if (a >= b) a %= b;     /* by Rule 4 */
    if (a == 0) return 0;  /* by Definition 2 */
    if (a == 1) return 1;  /* by Rule 1 */

    if (a < 0)
        if (((b-1)/2 % 2 == 0)
```

```
            return jacobi(-a,b);
        else
            return -jacobi(-a,b);

    if (a % 2 == 0) /* a is even */
        if (((b*b - 1)/8) % 2 == 0)
            return +jacobi(a/2, b)
        else
            return -jacobi(a/2, b) /* by Rule 3 and Rule 2 */
    g = gcd(a,b);

    assert(odd(a)); /* this is guaranteed by the (a % 2 == 0)
test */

    if (g == a) /* a exactly divides b */
        return 0; /* by Rules 5 and 4, and Definition 2 */
    else if (g != 1)
        return jacobi(g,b) * jacobi(a/g, b); /* by Rule 2 */
    else if (((a-1)*(b-1)/4) % 2 == 0)
        return +jacobi(b,a);        /* by Rule 6a */
    else
        return -jacobi(b,a);        /* by Rule 6b */
}
```

If n is known to be prime beforehand, simply compute $a^{((n-1)/2)}$ mod n instead of running the previous algorithm; in this case $J(a,n)$ is equivalent to the Legendre symbol.

The Jacobi symbol cannot be used to determine whether a is a quadratic residue mod n (unless n is prime, of course). Note that, if $J(a,n) = 1$ and n is composite, it is not necessarily true that a is a quadratic residue modulo n. For example:

$$J(7,143) = J(7,11) \cdot J(7,13) = (-1)(-1) = 1$$

However, there is no integer x such that $x^2 \equiv 7 \pmod{143}$.

Blum Integers

If p and q are two primes, and both are congruent to 3 modulo 4, then $n = pq$ is sometimes called a **Blum integer**. If n is a Blum integer, each quadratic residue has exactly four square roots, one of which is also a square; this is the principal square root. For example, the principal square root of 139 mod 437 is 24. The other three square roots are 185, 252, and 413.

Generators

If p is a prime, and g is less than p, then g is a **generator** mod p if

for each b from 1 to $p - 1$, there exists some a where $g^a \equiv b \pmod{p}$.

Another way of saying this is that g is **primitive** with respect to p.
For example, if $p = 11$, 2 is a generator mod 11:

$$2^{10} = 1024 \equiv 1 \pmod{11}$$
$$2^1 = 2 \equiv 2 \pmod{11}$$

$$2^8 = 256 \equiv 3 \pmod{11}$$
$$2^2 = 4 \equiv 4 \pmod{11}$$
$$2^4 = 16 \equiv 5 \pmod{11}$$
$$2^9 = 512 \equiv 6 \pmod{11}$$
$$2^7 = 128 \equiv 7 \pmod{11}$$
$$2^3 = 8 \equiv 8 \pmod{11}$$
$$2^6 = 64 \equiv 9 \pmod{11}$$
$$2^5 = 32 \equiv 10 \pmod{11}$$

Every number from 1 to 10 can be expressed as $2^a \pmod{p}$.

For $p = 11$, the generators are 2, 6, 7, and 8. The other numbers are not generators. For example, 3 is not a generator because there is no solution to

$$3^a \equiv 2 \pmod{11}$$

In general, testing whether a given number is a generator is not an easy problem. It is easy, however, if you know the factorization of $p - 1$. Let $q_1, q_2, \ldots, q_n$ be the distinct prime factors of $p - 1$. To test whether a number g is a generator mod p, calculate

$$g^{(p-1)/q} \bmod p$$

for all values of $q = q_1, q_2, \ldots, q_n$.

If that number equals 1 for some value of q, then g is not a generator. If that value does not equal 1 for any values of q, then g is a generator.

For example, let $p = 11$. The prime factors of $p - 1 = 10$ are 2 and 5. To test whether 2 is a generator:

$$2^{(11-1)/5} \pmod{11} = 4$$
$$2^{(11-1)/2} \pmod{11} = 10$$

Neither result is 1, so 2 is a generator.

To test whether 3 is a generator:

$$3^{(11-1)/5} \pmod{11} = 9$$
$$3^{(11-1)/2} \pmod{11} = 1$$

Therefore, 3 is not a generator.

If you need to find a generator mod p, simply choose a random number from 1 to $p - 1$ and test whether it is a generator. Enough of them will be, so you'll probably find one fast.

Computing in a Galois Field

Don't be alarmed; that's what we were just doing. If n is prime or the power of a large prime, then we have what mathematicians call a **finite field**. In honor of that fact, we use p instead of n. In fact, this type of finite field is so exciting that mathematicians gave it its own name: a **Galois field**, denoted as GF(p). (Évariste Galois was a French mathematician who lived in the early nineteenth century and did a lot of work in number theory before he was killed at age 20 in a duel.)

In a Galois field, addition, subtraction, multiplication, and division by nonzero elements are all well-defined. There is an additive identity, 0, and a multiplicative identity, 1. Every nonzero number has a unique inverse (this would not be true if p were not prime). The commutative, associative, and distributive laws are true.

Arithmetic in a Galois field is used a great deal in cryptography. All of the number theory works; it keeps numbers a finite size, and division doesn't have any rounding errors. Many cryptosystems are based on GF(p), where p is a large prime.

To make matters even more complicated, cryptographers also use arithmetic modulo **irreducible** polynomials of degree n whose coefficients are integers modulo q, where q is prime. These fields are called GF(q^n). All arithmetic is done modulo $p(x)$, where $p(x)$ is an irreducible polynomial of degree n.

The mathematical theory behind this is far beyond the scope of the book, although I will describe some cryptosystems that use it. If you want to try to work more with this, GF(2^3) has the following elements: 0, 1, x, $x + 1$, x^2, $x^2 + 1$, $x^2 + x$, $x^2 + x + 1$. There is an algorithm for computing inverses in GF(2^n) that is suitable for parallel implementation [421].

When talking about polynomials, the term "prime" is replaced by "irreducible." A polynomial is irreducible if it cannot be expressed as the product of two other polynomials (except for 1 and itself, of course). The polynomial $x^2 + 1$ is irreducible over the integers. The polynomial $x^3 + 2x^2 + x$ is not; it can be expressed as $x(x + 1)(x + 1)$.

A polynomial that is a generator in a given field is called primitive; all its coefficients are relatively prime. We'll see primitive polynomials again when we talk about linear-feedback shift registers (see Section 16.2).

Computation in GF(2^n) can be quickly implemented in hardware with linear-feedback shift registers. For that reason, computation over GF(2^n) is often quicker than computation over GF(p). Just as exponentiation is much more efficient in GF(2^n), so is calculating discrete logarithms [180,181,368,379]. If you want to learn more about this, read [140].

For a Galois field GF(2^n), cryptographers like to use the trinomial $p(x) = x^n + x + 1$ as the modulus, because the long string of zeros between the x^n and x coefficients makes it easy to implement a fast modular multiplication [183]. The trinomial must be primitive, otherwise the math does not work. Values of n less than 1000 [1649,1648] for which $x^n + x + 1$ is primitive are:

> 1, 3, 4, 6, 9, 15, 22, 28, 30, 46, 60, 63, 127, 153, 172, 303, 471, 532, 865, 900

There exists a hardware implementation of GF(2^{127}) where $p(x) = x^{127} + x + 1$ [1631,1632,1129]. Efficient hardware architectures for implementing exponentiation in GF(2^n) are discussed in [147].

11.4 FACTORING

Factoring a number means finding its prime factors.

$$10 = 2 \ast 5$$
$$60 = 2 \ast 2 \ast 3 \ast 5$$

$$252601 = 41*61*101$$
$$2^{113} - 1 = 3391*23279*65993*1868569*1066818132868207$$

The factoring problem is one of the oldest in number theory. It's simple to factor a number, but it's time-consuming. This is still true, but there have been some major advances in the state of the art.

Currently, the best factoring algorithm is:

Number field sieve (NFS) [953] (see also [952,16,279]). The **general number field sieve** is the fastest-known factoring algorithm for numbers larger than 110 digits or so [472,635]. It was impractical when originally proposed, but that has changed due to a series of improvements over the last few years [953]. The NFS is still too new to have broken any factoring records, but this will change soon. An early version was used to factor the ninth Fermat number: $2^{512} + 1$ [955,954].

Other factoring algorithms have been supplanted by the NFS:

Quadratic sieve (QS) [1257,1617,1259]. This is the fastest-known algorithm for numbers less than 110 decimal digits long and has been used extensively [440]. A faster version of this algorithm is called the multiple polynomial quadratic sieve [1453,302]. The fastest version of this algorithm is called the double large prime variation of the multiple polynomial quadratic sieve.

Elliptic curve method (ECM) [957,1112,1113]. This method has been used to find 43-digit factors, but nothing larger.

Pollard's Monte Carlo algorithm [1254,248]. (This algorithm also appears in volume 2, page 370 of Knuth [863].)

Continued fraction algorithm. See [1123,1252,863]. This algorithm isn't even in the running.

Trial division. This is the oldest factoring algorithm and consists of testing every prime number less than or equal to the square root of the candidate number.

See [251] for a good introduction to these different factoring algorithms, except for the NFS. The best discussion of the NFS is [953]. Other, older references are [505, 1602,1258]. Information on parallel factoring can be found in [250].

If n is the number being factored, the fastest QS variants have a heuristic asymptotic run time of:

$$e^{(1 + o(1))(\ln (n))^{(1/2)}(\ln (\ln (n)))^{(1/2)}}$$

The NFS is much faster, with a heuristic asymptotic time estimate of:

$$e^{(1.923 + o(1))(\ln (n))^{(1/3)}(\ln (\ln (n)))^{(2/3)}}$$

In 1970, the big news was the factoring of a 41-digit hard number [1123]. (A "hard" number is one that does not have any small factors and is not of a special form that allows it to be factored more easily.) Ten years later, factoring hard numbers twice that size took a Cray computer just a few hours [440].

In 1988, Carl Pomerance designed a modular factoring machine, using custom VLSI chips [1259]. The size of the number you would be able to factor depends on how large a machine you can afford to build. He never built it.

In 1993, a 120-digit hard number was factored using the quadratic sieve; the calculation took 825 mips-years and was completed in three months real time [463]. Other results are [504].

Today's factoring attempts use computer networks [302,955]. In factoring a 116-digit number, Arjen Lenstra and Mark Manasse used 400 mips-years—the spare time on an array of computers around the world for a few months.

In March 1994, a 129-digit (428-bit) number was factored using the double large prime variation of the multiple polynomial QS [66] by a team of mathematicians led by Lenstra. Volunteers on the Internet carried out the computation: 600 people and 1600 machines over the course of eight months, probably the largest ad hoc multiprocessor ever assembled. The calculation was the equivalent of 4000 to 6000 mips-years. The machines communicated via electronic mail, sending their individual results to a central repository where the final steps of analysis took place. This computation used the QS and five-year-old theory; it would have taken one-tenth the time using the NFS [949]. According to [66]: "We conclude that commonly used 512-bit RSA moduli are vulnerable to any organization prepared to spend a few million dollars and to wait a few months." They estimate that factoring a 512-bit number would be 100 times harder using the same technology, and only 10 times harder using the NFS and current technology [949].

To keep up on the state of the art of factoring, RSA Data Security, Inc. set up the RSA Factoring Challenge in March 1991 [532]. The challenge consists of a list of hard numbers, each the product of two primes of roughly equal size. Each prime was chosen to be congruent to 2 modulo 3. There are 42 numbers in the challenge, one each of length 100 digits through 500 digits in steps of 10 digits (plus one additional number, 129 digits long). At the time of writing, RSA-100, RSA-110, RSA-120, and RSA-129 have been factored, all using the QS. RSA-130 might be next (using the NFS), or the factoring champions might skip directly to RSA-140.

This is a fast-moving field. It is difficult to extrapolate factoring technology because no one can predict advances in mathematical theory. Before the NFS was discovered, many people conjectured that the QS was asymptotically as fast as any factoring method could be. They were wrong.

Near-term advances in the NFS are likely to come in the form of bringing down the constant: 1.923. Some numbers of a special form, like Fermat numbers, have a constant more along the lines of 1.5 [955,954]. If the hard numbers used in public-key cryptography had that kind of constant, 1024-bit numbers could be factored today. One way to lower the constant is to find better ways of representing numbers as polynomials with small coefficients. The problem hasn't been studied very extensively yet, but it is probable that advances are coming [949].

For the most current results from the RSA Factoring Challenge, send e-mail to challenge-info@rsa.com.

Square Roots Modulo n

If n is the product of two primes, then the ability to calculate square roots mod n is computationally equivalent to the ability to factor n [1283,35,36,193]. In other words, someone who knows the prime factors of n can easily compute the square roots of a number mod n, but for everyone else the computation has been proven to be as hard as computing the prime factors of n.

11.5   PRIME NUMBER GENERATION

Public-key algorithms need prime numbers. Any reasonably sized network needs lots of them. Before discussing the mathematics of prime number generation, I will answer a few obvious questions.

1. If everyone needs a different prime number, won't we run out? No. In fact, there are approximately 10^{151} primes 512 bits in length or less. For numbers near n, the probability that a random number is prime is approximately one in $\ln n$. So the total number of primes less than n is $n/(\ln n)$. There are only 10^{77} atoms in the universe. If every atom in the universe needed a billion new primes every microsecond from the beginning of time until now, you would only need 10^{109} primes; there would still be approximately 10^{151} 512-bit primes left.

2. What if two people accidentally pick the same prime number? It won't happen. With over 10^{151} prime numbers to choose from, the odds of that happening are significantly less than the odds of your computer spontaneously combusting at the exact moment you win the lottery.

3. If someone creates a database of all primes, won't he be able to use that database to break public-key algorithms? Yes, but he can't do it. If you could store one gigabyte of information on a drive weighing one gram, then a list of just the 512-bit primes would weigh so much that it would exceed the Chandrasekhar limit and collapse into a black hole . . . so you couldn't retrieve the data anyway.

But if factoring numbers is so hard, how can generating prime numbers be easy? The trick is that the yes/no question, "Is n prime?" is a much easier question to answer than the more complicated question, "What are the factors of n?"

The wrong way to find primes is to generate random numbers and then try to factor them. The right way is to generate random numbers and test if they are prime. There are several probabilistic primality tests; tests that determine whether a number is prime with a given degree of confidence. Assuming this "degree of confidence" is large enough, these sorts of tests are good enough. I've heard primes generated in this manner called "industrial-grade primes": These are numbers that are probably prime with a controllably small chance of error.

Assume a test is set to fail once in 2^{50} tries. This means that there is a 1 in 10^{15} chance that the test falsely indicates that a composite number is prime. (The test will never falsely indicate that a prime number is composite.) If for some reason you need more confidence that the number is prime, you can set the failure level even lower. On the other hand, if you consider that the odds of the number being composite are 300 million times less than the odds of winning top prize in a state lottery, you might not worry about it so much.

Overviews of recent developments in the field can be found in [1256,206]. Other important papers are [1490,384,11,19,626,651,911].

Solovay-Strassen

Robert Solovay and Volker Strassen developed a probabilistic primality testing algorithm [1490]. Their algorithm uses the Jacobi symbol to test if p is prime:

(1) Choose a random number, a, less than p.

(2) If the $\gcd(a,p) \neq 1$, then p fails the test and is composite.

(3) Calculate $j = a^{(p-1)/2} \bmod p$.

(4) Calculate the Jacobi symbol $J(a,p)$.

(5) If $j \neq J(a,p)$, then p is definitely not prime.

(6) If $j = J(a,p)$, then the likelihood that p is not prime is no more than 50 percent.

A number a that does not indicate that p is definitely not prime is called a **witness**. If p is composite, the odds of a random a being a witness is no less than 50 percent. Repeat this test t times, with t different random values for a. The odds of a composite number passing all t tests is no more than one in 2^t.

Lehmann

Another, simpler, test was developed independently by Lehmann [945]. Here it tests if p is prime:

(1) Choose a random number a less than p.

(2) Calculate $a^{(p-1)/2} \bmod p$.

(3) If $a^{(p-1)/2} \not\equiv 1$ or $-1 \pmod p$, then p is definitely not prime.

(4) If $a^{(p-1)/2} \equiv 1$ or $-1 \pmod p$, then the likelihood that p is not prime is no more than 50 percent.

Again, the odds of a random a being a witness to p's compositeness is no less than 50 percent. Repeat this test t times. If the calculation equals 1 or -1, but does not always equal 1, then p is probably prime with an error rate of 1 in 2^t.

Rabin-Miller

The algorithm everyone uses—it's easy—was developed by Michael Rabin, based in part on Gary Miller's ideas [1093,1284]. Actually, this is a simplified version of the algorithm recommended in the DSS proposal [1149,1154].

Choose a random number, p, to test. Calculate b, where b is the number of times 2 divides $p - 1$ (i.e., 2^b is the largest power of 2 that divides $p - 1$). Then calculate m, such that $p = 1 + 2^b {}^* m$.

(1) Choose a random number, a, such that a is less than p.

(2) Set $j = 0$ and set $z = a^m \bmod p$.

(3) If $z = 1$, or if $z = p - 1$, then p passes the test and may be prime.

(4) If $j > 0$ and $z = 1$, then p is not prime.

(5) Set $j = j + 1$. If $j < b$ and $z \neq p - 1$, set $z = z^2 \bmod p$ and go back to step (4). If $z = p - 1$, then p passes the test and may be prime.

(6) If $j = b$ and $z \neq p - 1$, then p is not prime.

The odds of a composite passing decreases faster with this test than with previous ones. Three-quarters of the possible values of a are guaranteed to be witnesses. This means that a composite number will slip through t tests no more than $\frac{1}{4}^t$ of the time, where t is the number of iterations. Actually, these numbers are very pessimistic. For most random numbers, something like 99.9 percent of the possible a values are witnesses [96].

There are even better estimations [417]. For n-bit candidate primes (where n is more than 100), the odds of error in one test are less than 1 in $4n2^{(k/2)^{(1/2)}}$. And for a 256-bit n, the odds of error in six tests are less than 1 in 2^{51}. More theory is in [418].

Practical Considerations

In real-world implementations, prime generation goes quickly.

(1) Generate a random n-bit number, p.

(2) Set the high-order and low-order bit to 1. (The high-order bit ensures that the prime is of the required length and the low-order bit ensures that it is odd.)

(3) Check to make sure p is not divisible by any small primes: 3, 5, 7, 11, and so on. Many implementations test p for divisibility by all primes less than 256. The most efficient is to test for divisibility by all primes less than 2000 [949]. You can do this efficiently using a wheel [863].

(4) Perform the Rabin-Miller test for some random a. If p passes, generate another random a and go through the test again. Choose a small value of a to make the calculations go quicker. Do five tests [651]. (One might seem like enough, but do five.) If p fails one of the tests, generate another p and try again.

Another option is not to generate a random p each time, but to incrementally search through numbers starting at a random point until you find a prime.

Step (3) is optional, but it is a good idea. Testing a random odd p to make sure it is not divisible by 3, 5, and 7 eliminates 54 percent of the odd numbers before you get to step (4). Testing against all primes less than 100 eliminates 76 percent of the odd numbers; testing against all primes less than 256 eliminates 80 percent. In general, the fraction of odd candidates that is not a multiple of any prime less than n is $1.12/\ln n$. The larger the n you test up to, the more precomputation is required before you get to the Rabin-Miller test.

One implementation of this method on a Sparc II was able to find 256-bit primes in an average of 2.8 seconds, 512-bit primes in an average of 24.0 seconds, 768-bit primes in an average of 2.0 minutes, and 1024-bit primes in an average of 5.1 minutes [918].

Strong Primes

If n is the product of two primes, p and q, it may be desirable to use **strong primes** for p and q. These are prime numbers with certain properties that make the product n difficult to factor by specific factoring methods. Among the properties suggested have been [1328,651]:

>   The greatest common divisor of $p - 1$ and $q - 1$ should be small.
>
>   Both $p - 1$ and $q - 1$ should have large prime factors, respectively p' and q'.
>
>   Both $p' - 1$ and $q' - 1$ should have large prime factors.
>
>   Both $p + 1$ and $q + 1$ should have large prime factors.
>
>   Both $(p - 1)/2$ and $(q - 1)/2$ should be prime [182]. (Note that if this condition is true, then so are the first two.)

Whether strong primes are necessary is a subject of debate. These properties were designed to thwart some older factoring algorithms. However, the fastest factoring algorithms have as good a chance of factoring numbers that meet these criteria as they do of factoring numbers that do not [831].

I recommend against specifically generating strong primes. The length of the primes is much more important than the structure. Moreover, structure may be damaging because it is less random.

This may change. New factoring techniques may be developed that work better on numbers with certain properties than on numbers without them. If so, strong primes may be required once again. Check current theoretical mathematics journals for updates.

11.6   Discrete Logarithms in a Finite Field

Modular exponentiation is another one-way function used frequently in cryptography. Evaluating this expression is easy:

$$a^x \bmod n$$

The inverse problem of modular exponentiation is that of finding the discrete logarithm of a number. This is a hard problem:

Find x where $a^x \equiv b \pmod{n}$.

For example:

If $3^x \equiv 15 \bmod 17$, then $x = 6$

Not all discrete logarithms have solutions (remember, the only valid solutions are integers). It's easy to see that there is no solution, x, to the equation

$$3^x \equiv 7 \pmod{13}$$

It's far more difficult to solve these problems using 1024-bit numbers.

Calculating Discrete Logarithms in a Finite Group

There are three main groups whose discrete logarithms are of interest to cryptographers:

— The multiplicative group of prime fields: $GF(p)$
— The multiplicative group of finite fields of characteristic 2: $GF(2^n)$
— Elliptic curve groups over finite fields F: $EC(F)$

The security of many public-key algorithms is based on the problem of finding discrete logarithms, so the problem has been extensively studied. A good comprehensive overview of the problem, and the best solutions at the time, can be found in [1189,1039]. The best current article on the topic is [934].

If p is the modulus and is prime, then the complexity of finding discrete logarithms in $GF(p)$ is essentially the same as factoring an integer n of about the same size, when n is the product of two approximately equal-length primes [1378,934]. This is:

$$e^{(1 + 0(1))(\ln (p))^{(1/2)}(\ln (\ln (p)))^{(1/2)}}$$

The number field sieve is faster, with an heuristic asymptotic time estimate of

$$e^{(1.923 + 0(1))(\ln (p))^{(1/3)}(\ln (\ln (p)))^{(2/3)}}$$

Stephen Pohlig and Martin Hellman found a fast way of computing discrete logarithms in $GF(p)$ if $p - 1$ has only small prime factors [1253]. For this reason, only fields where $p - 1$ has at least one large factor are used in cryptography. Another algorithm [14] computes discrete logarithms at a speed comparable to factoring; it has been expanded to fields of the form $GF(p^n)$ [716]. This algorithm was criticized [727] for having some theoretical problems. Other articles [1588] show how difficult the problem really is.

Computing discrete logarithms is closely related to factoring. If you can solve the discrete logarithm problem, then you can factor. (The converse has never been proven to be true.) Currently, there are three methods for calculating discrete logarithms in a prime field [370,934,648]: the linear sieve, the Gaussian integer scheme, and the number field sieve.

The preliminary, extensive computing has to be done only once per field. Afterward, individual logarithms can be quickly calculated. This can be a security disadvantage for systems based on these fields. It is important that different applications use different prime fields. Multiple users in the same application can use a common field, though.

In the world of extension fields, $GF(2^n)$ hasn't been ignored by researchers. An algorithm was proposed in [727]. Coppersmith's algorithm makes finding discrete logarithms in fields such as $GF(2^{127})$ reasonable and finding them in fields around $GF(2^{400})$ possible [368]. This was based on work in [180]. The precomputation stage of this algorithm is enormous, but otherwise it is nice and efficient. A practical implementation of a less efficient version of the same algorithm, after a seven-hour precomputation period, found discrete logs in $GF(2^{127})$ in several seconds each [1130,180]. (This particular field, once used in some cryptosystems [142,1631,1632], is insecure.) For surveys of some of these results, consult [1189,1039].

More recently, the precomputations for $GF(2^{227})$, $GF(2^{313})$, and $GF(2^{401})$ are done, and significant progress has been made towards $GF(2^{503})$. These calculations are being executed on an nCube-2 massively parallel computer with 1024 processors [649,650]. Computing discrete logarithms in $GF(2^{593})$ is still barely out of reach.

Like discrete logarithms in a prime field, the precomputation required to calculate discrete logarithms in a polynomial field has to be done only once. Taher ElGamal [520] gives an algorithm for calculating discrete logs in the field $GF(p^2)$.

CHAPTER   12

Data Encryption Standard (DES)

12.1   BACKGROUND

The Data Encryption Standard (DES), known as the Data Encryption Algorithm (DEA) by ANSI and the DEA-1 by the ISO, has been a worldwide standard for 20 years. Although it is showing signs of old age, it has held up remarkably well against years of cryptanalysis and is still secure against all but possibly the most powerful of adversaries.

Development of the Standard

In the early 1970s, nonmilitary cryptographic research was haphazard. Almost no research papers were published in the field. Most people knew that the military used special coding equipment to communicate, but few understood the science of cryptography. The National Security Agency (NSA) had considerable knowledge, but they did not even publicly admit their own existence.

Buyers didn't know what they were buying. Several small companies made and sold cryptographic equipment, primarily to overseas governments. The equipment was all different and couldn't interoperate. No one really knew if any of it was secure; there was no independent body to certify the security. As one government report said [441]:

> The intricacies of relating key variations and working principles to the real strength of the encryption/decryption equipment were, and are, virtually unknown to almost all buyers, and informed decisions as to the right type of on-line, off-line, key generation, etc., which will meet buyers' security needs, have been most difficult to make.

In 1972, the National Bureau of Standards (NBS), now the National Institute of Standards and Technology (NIST), initiated a program to protect computer and communications data. As part of that program, they wanted to develop a single, standard cryptographic algorithm. A single algorithm could be tested and certified, and different cryptographic equipment using it could interoperate. It would also be cheaper to implement and readily available.

In the May 15, 1973 *Federal Register*, the NBS issued a public request for proposals for a standard cryptographic algorithm. They specified a series of design criteria:

— The algorithm must provide a high level of security.

— The algorithm must be completely specified and easy to understand.

— The security of the algorithm must reside in the key; the security should not depend on the secrecy of the algorithm.

— The algorithm must be available to all users.

— The algorithm must be adaptable for use in diverse applications.

— The algorithm must be economically implementable in electronic devices.

— The algorithm must be efficient to use.

— The algorithm must be able to be validated.

— The algorithm must be exportable.

Public response indicated that there was considerable interest in a cryptographic standard, but little public expertise in the field. None of the submissions came close to meeting the requirements.

The NBS issued a second request in the August 27, 1974 *Federal Register*. Eventually they received a promising candidate: an algorithm based on one developed by IBM during the early 1970s, called Lucifer (see Section 13.1). IBM had a team working on cryptography at both Kingston and Yorktown Heights, including Roy Adler, Don Coppersmith, Horst Feistel, Edna Grossman, Alan Konheim, Carl Meyer, Bill Notz, Lynn Smith, Walt Tuchman, and Bryant Tuckerman.

The algorithm, although complicated, was straightforward. It used only simple logical operations on small groups of bits and could be implemented fairly efficiently in hardware.

The NBS requested the NSA's help in evaluating the algorithm's security and determining its suitability as a federal standard. IBM had already filed for a patent [514], but was willing to make its intellectual property available to others for manufacture, implementation, and use. Eventually, the NBS worked out the terms of agreement with IBM and received a nonexclusive, royalty-free license to make, use, and sell equipment that implemented the algorithm.

Finally, in the March 17, 1975 *Federal Register*, the NBS published both the details of the algorithm and IBM's statement granting a nonexclusive, royalty-free license for the algorithm, and requested comment [536]. Another notice, in the August 1, 1975 *Federal Register*, again requested comments from agencies and the general public.

And there were comments [721,497,1120]. Many were wary of the NSA's "invisible hand" in the development of the algorithm. They were afraid that the NSA had modified the algorithm to install a trapdoor. They complained that the NSA reduced the key size from the original 128-bits to 56-bits (see Section 13.1). They complained about the inner workings of the algorithm. Much of NSA's reasoning became clear in the early 1990s, but in the 1970s this seemed mysterious and worrisome.

In 1976, the NBS held two workshops to evaluate the proposed standard. The first workshop discussed the mathematics of the algorithm and the possibility of a trapdoor [1139]. The second workshop discussed the possibility of increasing the algorithm's key length [229]. The algorithm's designers, evaluators, implementors, vendors, users, and critics were invited. From all reports, the workshops were lively [1118].

Despite criticism, the Data Encryption Standard was adopted as a federal standard on November 23, 1976 [229] and authorized for use on all unclassified government communications. The official description of the standard, FIPS PUB 46, "Data Encryption Standard," was published on January 15, 1977 and became effective six months later [1140]. FIPS PUB 81, "DES Modes of Operation," was published in 1980 [1143]. FIPS PUB 74, "Guidelines for Implementing and Using the NBS Data Encryption Standard," was published in 1981 [1142]. NBS also published FIPS PUB 112, specifying DES for password encryption [1144], and FIPS PUB 113, specifying DES for computer data authentication [1145]. (FIPS stands for Federal Information Processing Standard.)

These standards were unprecedented. Never before had an NSA-evaluated algorithm been made public. This was probably the result of a misunderstanding between NSA and NBS. The NSA thought DES was hardware-only. The standard mandated a hardware implementation, but NBS published enough details so that people could write DES software. Off the record, NSA has characterized DES as one of their biggest mistakes. If they knew the details would be released so that people could write software, they would never have agreed to it. DES did more to galvanize the field of cryptanalysis than anything else. Now there was an algorithm to study: one that the NSA said was secure. It is no accident that the next government standard algorithm, Skipjack (see Section 13.12), was classified.

Adoption of the Standard

The American National Standards Institute (ANSI) approved DES as a private-sector standard in 1981 (ANSI X3.92) [50]. They called it the Data Encryption Algorithm (DEA). ANSI published a standard for DEA modes of operation (ANSI X3.106) [52], similar to the NBS document, and a standard for network encryption that uses DES (ANSI X3.105) [51].

Two other groups within ANSI, representing retail and wholesale banking, developed DES-based standards. Retail banking involves transactions between financial institutions and private individuals, and wholesale banking involves transactions between financial institutions.

ANSI's Financial Institution Retail Security Working Group developed a standard for the management and security of PINs (ANSI X9.8) [53] and another DES-based standard for the authentication of retail financial messages (ANSI X9.19) [56]. The group has a draft standard for secure key distribution (ANSI X9.24) [58].

ANSI's Financial Institution Wholesale Security Working Group developed its own set of standards for message authentication (ANSI X9.9) [54], key management (ANSI X9.17) [55,1151], encryption (ANSI X9.23) [57], and secure personal and node authentication (ANSI X9.26) [59].

The American Bankers Association develops voluntary standards for the financial industry. They published a standard recommending DES for encryption [1], and another standard for managing cryptographic keys [2].

Before the Computer Security Act of 1987, the General Services Administration (GSA) was responsible for developing federal telecommunications standards. Since then, that responsibility transferred to NIST. The GSA published three standards that used DES: two for general security and interoperability requirements (Federal Standard 1026 [662] and Federal Standard 1027 [663]), and one for Group 3 facsimile equipment (Federal Standard 1028) [664].

The Department of the Treasury wrote policy directives requiring that all electronic-funds transfer messages be authenticated with DES [468,470]. They also wrote DES-based criteria that all authentication devices must meet [469].

The ISO first voted to approve DES—they called it the DEA-1—as an international standard, then decided not to play a role in the standardization of cryptography. However, in 1987 the International Wholesale Financial Standards group of ISO used DES in an international authentication standard [758] and for key management [761]. DES is also specified in an Australian banking standard [1497].

Validation and Certification of DES Equipment

As part of the DES standard, NIST validates implementations of DES. This validation confirms that the implementation follows the standard. Until 1994, NIST only validated hardware and firmware implementations—until then the standard prohibited software implementations. As of March 1995, 73 different implementations had been validated.

NIST also developed a program to certify that authentication equipment conformed to ANSI X9.9 and FIPS 113. As of March, 1995, 33 products had been validated. The Department of the Treasury has an additional certification procedure. NIST also has a program to confirm that equipment conforms to ANSI X9.17 for wholesale key management [1151]; four products have been validated as of March, 1995.

1987

The terms of the DES standard stipulate that it be reviewed every five years. In 1983 DES was recertified without a hitch. In the March 6, 1987 *Federal Register*, NBS published a request for comments on the second five-year review. NBS offered three alternatives for consideration [1480,1481]: reaffirm the standard for another five years, withdraw the standard, or revise the applicability of the standard.

NBS and NSA reviewed the standard. NSA was more involved this time. Because of an executive directive called NSDD-145, signed by Reagan, NSA had veto power over the NBS in matters of cryptography. Initially, the NSA announced that it would not recertify the standard. The problem was not that DES had been broken, or even that it was suspected of having been broken. It was simply increasingly likely that it would soon be broken.

In its place, the NSA proposed the Commercial COMSEC Endorsement Program (CCEP), which would eventually provide a series of algorithms to replace DES [85]. These NSA-designed algorithms would not be made public, and would only be available in tamper-proof VLSI chips (see Section 25.1).

This announcement wasn't well received. People pointed out that business (especially the financial industry) uses DES extensively, and that no adequate alternative is available. Withdrawal of the standard would leave many organizations with no data protection. After much debate, DES was reaffirmed as a U.S. government standard until 1992 [1141]. According to the NBS, DES would not be certified again [1480].

1993

Never say "not." In 1992, there was still no alternative for DES. The NBS, now called NIST, again solicited comments on DES in the *Federal Register* [540]:

> The purpose of this notice is to announce the review to assess the continued adequacy of the standard to protect computer data. Comments from industry and the public are invited on the following alternatives for FIPS 46-1. The costs (impacts) and benefits of these alternatives should be included in the comments:
>
> —Reaffirm the standard for another five (5) years. The National Institute of Standards and Technology would continue to validate equipment that implements the standard. FIPS 46-1 would continue to be the only approved method for protecting unclassified computer data.
>
> —Withdraw the standard. The National Institute of Standards and Technology would no longer continue to support the standard. Organizations could continue to utilize existing equipment that implements the standard. Other standards could be issued by NIST as a replacement for the DES.
>
> —Revise the applicability and/or implementation statements for the standard. Such revisions could include changing the standard to allow the use of implementations of the DES in software as well as hardware; to allow the iterative use of the DES in specific applications; to allow the use of alternative algorithms that are approved and registered by NIST.

The comment period closed on December 10, 1992. According to Raymond Kammer, then the acting director of NIST [813]:

> Last year, NIST formally solicited comments on the recertification of DES. After reviewing those comments, and the other technical inputs that I have received, I plan to recommend to the Secretary of Commerce that he recertify DES for another five years. I also plan to suggest to the Secretary that when we announce the recertification we state our intention to consider alternatives to it over the next five years. By putting that announcement on the table, we hope to give people an opportunity to comment on orderly technological transitions. In the meantime, we need to consider the large installed base of systems that rely upon this proven standard.

Even though the Office of Technology Assessment quoted NIST's Dennis Branstead as saying that the useful lifetime of DES would end in the late 1990s

[1191], the algorithm was recertified for another five years [1150]. Software implementations of DES were finally allowed to be certified.

Anyone want to guess what will happen in 1998?

12.2   DESCRIPTION OF DES

DES is a block cipher; it encrypts data in 64-bit blocks. A 64-bit block of plaintext goes in one end of the algorithm and a 64-bit block of ciphertext comes out the other end. DES is a symmetric algorithm: The same algorithm and key are used for both encryption and decryption (except for minor differences in the key schedule).

The key length is 56 bits. (The key is usually expressed as a 64-bit number, but every eighth bit is used for parity checking and is ignored. These parity bits are the least-significant bits of the key bytes.) The key can be any 56-bit number and can be changed at any time. A handful of numbers are considered weak keys, but they can easily be avoided. All security rests within the key.

At its simplest level, the algorithm is nothing more than a combination of the two basic techniques of encryption: confusion and diffusion. The fundamental building block of DES is a single combination of these techniques (a substitution followed by a permutation) on the text, based on the key. This is known as a **round**. DES has 16 rounds; it applies the same combination of techniques on the plaintext block 16 times (see Figure 12.1).

The algorithm uses only standard arithmetic and logical operations on numbers of 64 bits at most, so it was easily implemented in late 1970s hardware technology. The repetitive nature of the algorithm makes it ideal for use on a special-purpose chip. Initial software implementations were clumsy, but current implementations are better.

Outline of the Algorithm

DES operates on a 64-bit block of plaintext. After an initial permutation, the block is broken into a right half and a left half, each 32 bits long. Then there are 16 rounds of identical operations, called Function f, in which the data are combined with the key. After the sixteenth round, the right and left halves are joined, and a final permutation (the inverse of the initial permutation) finishes off the algorithm.

In each round (see Figure 12.2), the key bits are shifted, and then 48 bits are selected from the 56 bits of the key. The right half of the data is expanded to 48 bits via an expansion permutation, combined with 48 bits of a shifted and permuted key via an XOR, sent through 8 S-boxes producing 32 new bits, and permuted again. These four operations make up Function f. The output of Function f is then combined with the left half via another XOR. The result of these operations becomes the new right half; the old right half becomes the new left half. These operations are repeated 16 times, making 16 rounds of DES.

If B_i is the result of the ith iteration, L_i and R_i are the left and right halves of B_i, K_i is the 48-bit key for round i, and f is the function that does all the substituting and permuting and XORing with the key, then a round looks like:

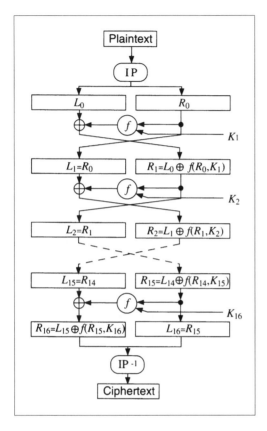

Figure 12.1   DES.

$$L_i = R_{i-1}$$
$$R_i = L_{i-1} \oplus f\left(R_{i-1}, K_i\right)$$

The Initial Permutation

The initial permutation occurs before round 1; it transposes the input block as described in Table 12.1. This table, like all the other tables in this chapter, should be read left to right, top to bottom. For example, the initial permutation moves bit 58 of the plaintext to bit position 1, bit 50 to bit position 2, bit 42 to bit position 3, and so forth.

The initial permutation and the corresponding final permutation do not affect DES's security. (As near as anyone can tell, its primary purpose is to make it easier to load plaintext and ciphertext data into a DES chip in byte-sized pieces. Remember that DES predates 16-bit or 32-bit microprocessor busses.) Since this bit-wise permutation is difficult in software (although it is trivial in hardware), many software implementations of DES leave out both the initial and final permutations. While this new algorithm is no less secure than DES, it does not follow the DES standard and should not be called DES.

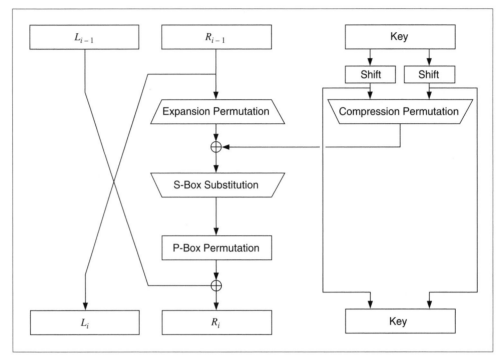

Figure 12.2   One round of DES.

The Key Transformation

Initially, the 64-bit DES key is reduced to a 56-bit key by ignoring every eighth bit. This is described in Table 12.2. These bits can be used as parity check to ensure the key is error-free. After the 56-bit key is extracted, a different 48-bit **subkey** is generated for each of the 16 rounds of DES. These subkeys, K_i, are determined in the following manner.

First, the 56-bit key is divided into two 28-bit halves. Then, the halves are circularly shifted left by either one or two bits, depending on the round. This shift is given in Table 12.3.

Table 12.1
Initial Permutation

58,	50,	42,	34,	26,	18,	10,	2,	60,	52,	44,	36,	28,	20,	12,	4,
62,	54,	46,	38,	30,	22,	14,	6,	64,	56,	48,	40,	32,	24,	16,	8,
57,	49,	41,	33,	25,	17,	9,	1,	59,	51,	43,	35,	27,	19,	11,	3,
61,	53,	45,	37,	29,	21,	13,	5,	63,	55,	47,	39,	31,	23,	15,	7

Table 12.2
Key Permutation

57,	49,	41,	33,	25,	17,	9,	1,	58,	50,	42,	34,	26,	18,
10,	2,	59,	51,	43,	35,	27,	19,	11,	3,	60,	52,	44,	36,
63,	55,	47,	39,	31,	23,	15,	7,	62,	54,	46,	38,	30,	22,
14,	6,	61,	53,	45,	37,	29,	21,	13,	5,	28,	20,	12,	4

After being shifted, 48 out of the 56 bits are selected. Because this operation permutes the order of the bits as well as selects a subset of bits, it is called a **compression permutation**. This operation provides a subset of 48 bits. Table 12.4 defines the compression permutation (also called the permuted choice). For example, the bit in position 33 of the shifted key moves to position 35 of the output, and the bit in position 18 of the shifted key is ignored.

Because of the shifting, a different subset of key bits is used in each subkey. Each bit is used in approximately 14 of the 16 subkeys, although not all bits are used exactly the same number of times.

The Expansion Permutation

This operation expands the right half of the data, R_i, from 32 bits to 48 bits. Because this operation changes the order of the bits as well as repeating certain bits, it is known as an **expansion permutation**. This operation has two purposes: It makes the right half the same size as the key for the XOR operation and it provides a longer result that can be compressed during the substitution operation. However, neither of those is its main cryptographic purpose. By allowing one bit to affect two substitutions, the dependency of the output bits on the input bits spreads faster. This is called an **avalanche effect**. DES is designed to reach the condition of having every bit of the ciphertext depend on every bit of the plaintext and every bit of the key as quickly as possible.

Figure 12.3 defines the expansion permutation. This is sometimes called the **E-box**. For each 4-bit input block, the first and fourth bits each represent two bits of the output block, while the second and third bits each represent one bit of the output block. Table 12.5 shows which output positions correspond to which input positions. For example, the bit in position 3 of the input block moves to position 4 of the output block, and the bit in position 21 of the input block moves to positions 30 and 32 of the output block.

Although the output block is larger than the input block, each input block generates a unique output block.

Table 12.3
Number of Key Bits Shifted per Round

Round	1	2	3	4	5	6	7	8	9	10	11	12	13	14	15	16
Number	1	1	2	2	2	2	2	2	1	2	2	2	2	2	2	1

Table 12.4
Compression Permutation

14,	17,	11,	24,	1,	5,	3,	28,	15,	6,	21,	10,
23,	19,	12,	4,	26,	8,	16,	7,	27,	20,	13,	2,
41,	52,	31,	37,	47,	55,	30,	40,	51,	45,	33,	48,
44,	49,	39,	56,	34,	53,	46,	42,	50,	36,	29,	32

The S-Box Substitution

After the compressed key is XORed with the expanded block, the 48-bit result moves to a substitution operation. The substitutions are performed by eight **substitution boxes**, or **S-boxes**. Each S-box has a 6-bit input and a 4-bit output, and there are eight different S-boxes. (The total memory requirement for the eight DES S-boxes is 256 bytes.) The 48 bits are divided into eight 6-bit sub-blocks. Each separate block is operated on by a separate S-box: The first block is operated on by S-box 1, the second block is operated on by S-box 2, and so on. See Figure 12.4.

Each S-box is a table of 4 rows and 16 columns. Each entry in the box is a 4-bit number. The 6 input bits of the S-box specify under which row and column number to look for the output. Table 12.6 shows all eight S-boxes.

The input bits specify an entry in the S-box in a very particular manner. Consider an S-box input of 6 bits, labeled b_1, b_2, b_3, b_4, b_5, and b_6. Bits b_1 and b_6 are combined to form a 2-bit number, from 0 to 3, which corresponds to a row in the table. The middle 4 bits, b_2 through b_5, are combined to form a 4-bit number, from 0 to 15, which corresponds to a column in the table.

For example, assume that the input to the sixth S-box (i.e., bits 31 through 36 of the XOR function) is 110011. The first and last bits combine to form 11, which cor-

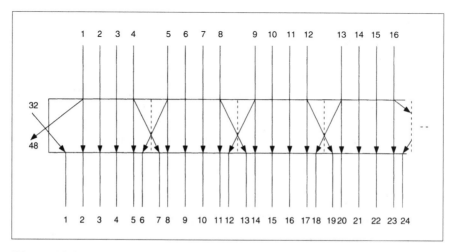

Figure 12.3 Expansion permutation.

Table 12.5
Expansion Permutation

32,	1,	2,	3,	4,	5,	4,	5,	6,	7,	8,	9,
8,	9,	10,	11,	12,	13,	12,	13,	14,	15,	16,	17,
16,	17,	18,	19,	20,	21,	20,	21,	22,	23,	24,	25,
24,	25,	26,	27,	28,	29,	28,	29,	30,	31,	32,	1

responds to row 3 of the sixth S-box. The middle 4 bits combine to form 1001, which corresponds to the column 9 of the same S-box. The entry under row 3, column 9 of S-box 6 is 14. (Remember to count rows and columns from 0 and not from 1.) The value 1110 is substituted for 110011.

It is, of course, far easier to implement the S-boxes in software as 64-entry arrays. It takes some rearranging of the entries to do this, but that's not hard. (Don't just change the indexing without rearranging the entries. The S-boxes are designed very carefully.) However, this way of describing the S-boxes helps visualize how they work. Each S-box can be viewed as a substitution function on a 4-bit entry: b_2 through b_5 go in, and a 4-bit result comes out. Bits b_1 and b_6 come from neighboring blocks; they select one out of four substitution functions available in the particular S-box.

The S-box substitution is the critical step in DES. The algorithm's other operations are linear and easy to analyze. The S-boxes are nonlinear and, more than anything else, give DES its security.

The result of this substitution phase is eight 4-bit blocks which are recombined into a single 32-bit block. This block moves to the next step: the P-box permutation.

The P-Box Permutation

The 32-bit output of the S-box substitution is permuted according to a **P-box**. This permutation maps each input bit to an output position; no bits are used twice and no bits are ignored. This is called a **straight permutation** or just a permutation. Table 12.7 shows the position to which each bit moves. For example, bit 21 moves to bit 4, while bit 4 moves to bit 31.

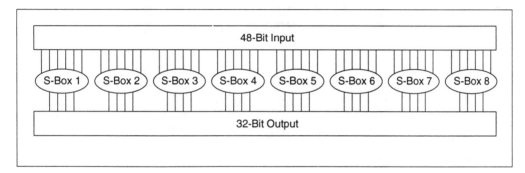

Figure 12.4   S-box substitution.

Table 12.6
S-Boxes

S-box 1:

14,	4,	13,	1,	2,	15,	11,	8,	3,	10,	6,	12,	5,	9,	0,	7,
0,	15,	7,	4,	14,	2,	13,	1,	10,	6,	12,	11,	9,	5,	3,	8,
4,	1,	14,	8,	13,	6,	2,	11,	15,	12,	9,	7,	3,	10,	5,	0,
15,	12,	8,	2,	4,	9,	1,	7,	5,	11,	3,	14,	10,	0,	6,	13,

S-box 2:

15,	1,	8,	14,	6,	11,	3,	4,	9,	7,	2,	13,	12,	0,	5,	10,
3,	13,	4,	7,	15,	2,	8,	14,	12,	0,	1,	10,	6,	9,	11,	5,
0,	14,	7,	11,	10,	4,	13,	1,	5,	8,	12,	6,	9,	3,	2,	15,
13,	8,	10,	1,	3,	15,	4,	2,	11,	6,	7,	12,	0,	5,	14,	9,

S-box 3:

10,	0,	9,	14,	6,	3,	15,	5,	1,	13,	12,	7,	11,	4,	2,	8,
13,	7,	0,	9,	3,	4,	6,	10,	2,	8,	5,	14,	12,	11,	15,	1,
13,	6,	4,	9,	8,	15,	3,	0,	11,	1,	2,	12,	5,	10,	14,	7,
1,	10,	13,	0,	6,	9,	8,	7,	4,	15,	14,	3,	11,	5,	2,	12,

S-box 4:

7,	13,	14,	3,	0,	6,	9,	10,	1,	2,	8,	5,	11,	12,	4,	15,
13,	8,	11,	5,	6,	15,	0,	3,	4,	7,	2,	12,	1,	10,	14,	9,
10,	6,	9,	0,	12,	11,	7,	13,	15,	1,	3,	14,	5,	2,	8,	4,
3,	15,	0,	6,	10,	1,	13,	8,	9,	4,	5,	11,	12,	7,	2,	14,

S-box 5:

2,	12,	4,	1,	7,	10,	11,	6,	8,	5,	3,	15,	13,	0,	14,	9,
14,	11,	2,	12,	4,	7,	13,	1,	5,	0,	15,	10,	3,	9,	8,	6,
4,	2,	1,	11,	10,	13,	7,	8,	15,	9,	12,	5,	6,	3,	0,	14,
11,	8,	12,	7,	1,	14,	2,	13,	6,	15,	0,	9,	10,	4,	5,	3,

S-box 6:

12,	1,	10,	15,	9,	2,	6,	8,	0,	13,	3,	4,	14,	7,	5,	11,
10,	15,	4,	2,	7,	12,	9,	5,	6,	1,	13,	14,	0,	11,	3,	8,
9,	14,	15,	5,	2,	8,	12,	3,	7,	0,	4,	10,	1,	13,	11,	6,
4,	3,	2,	12,	9,	5,	15,	10,	11,	14,	1,	7,	6,	0,	8,	13,

S-box 7:

4,	11,	2,	14,	15,	0,	8,	13,	3,	12,	9,	7,	5,	10,	6,	1,
13,	0,	11,	7,	4,	9,	1,	10,	14,	3,	5,	12,	2,	15,	8,	6,
1,	4,	11,	13,	12,	3,	7,	14,	10,	15,	6,	8,	0,	5,	9,	2,
6,	11,	13,	8,	1,	4,	10,	7,	9,	5,	0,	15,	14,	2,	3,	12,

S-box 8:

13,	2,	8,	4,	6,	15,	11,	1,	10,	9,	3,	14,	5,	0,	12,	7,
1,	15,	13,	8,	10,	3,	7,	4,	12,	5,	6,	11,	0,	14,	9,	2,
7,	11,	4,	1,	9,	12,	14,	2,	0,	6,	10,	13,	15,	3,	5,	8,
2,	1,	14,	7,	4,	10,	8,	13,	15,	12,	9,	0,	3,	5,	6,	11

Table 12.7
P-Box Permutation

16,	7,	20,	21,	29,	12,	28,	17,	1,	15,	23,	26,	5,	18,	31,	10,
2,	8,	24,	14,	32,	27,	3,	9,	19,	13,	30,	6,	22,	11,	4,	25

Finally, the result of the P-box permutation is XORed with the left half of the initial 64-bit block. Then the left and right halves are switched and another round begins.

The Final Permutation

The final permutation is the inverse of the initial permutation and is described in Table 12.8. Note that the left and right halves are not exchanged after the last round of DES; instead the concatenated block $R_{16}L_{16}$ is used as the input to the final permutation. There's nothing going on here; exchanging the halves and shifting around the permutation would yield exactly the same result. This is so that the algorithm can be used to both encrypt and decrypt.

Decrypting DES

After all the substitutions, permutations, XORs, and shifting around, you might think that the decryption algorithm is completely different and just as confusing as the encryption algorithm. On the contrary, the various operations were chosen to produce a very useful property: The same algorithm works for both encryption and decryption.

With DES it is possible to use the same function to encrypt or decrypt a block. The only difference is that the keys must be used in the reverse order. That is, if the encryption keys for each round are K_1, K_2, K_3, ... , K_{16}, then the decryption keys are K_{16}, K_{15}, K_{14}, ... , K_1. The algorithm that generates the key used for each round is circular as well. The key shift is a right shift and the number of positions shifted is 0,1,2,2,2,2,2,2,1,2,2,2,2,2,2,1.

Modes of DES

FIPS PUB 81 specifies four modes of operation: ECB, CBC, OFB, and CFB (see Chapter 9) [1143]. The ANSI banking standards specify ECB and CBC for encryption, and CBC and n-bit CFB for authentication [52].

In the software world, certification is usually not an issue. Because of its simplicity, ECB is most often used in off-the-shelf commercial software products, although

Table 12.8
Final Permutation

40,	8,	48,	16,	56,	24,	64,	32,	39,	7,	47,	15,	55,	23,	63,	31,
38,	6,	46,	14,	54,	22,	62,	30,	37,	5,	45,	13,	53,	21,	61,	29,
36,	4,	44,	12,	52,	20,	60,	28,	35,	3,	43,	11,	51,	19,	59,	27,
34,	2,	42,	10,	50,	18,	58,	26,	33,	1,	41,	9,	49,	17,	57,	25

it is the most vulnerable to attack. CBC is used occasionally, even though it is just slightly more complicated than ECB and provides much more security.

Hardware and Software Implementations of DES

Much has been written on efficient hardware and software implementations of the algorithm [997,81,533,534,437,738,1573,176,271,1572]. At this writing, the recordholder for the fastest DES chip is a prototype developed at Digital Equipment Corporation [512]. It supports ECB and CBC modes and is based on a GaAs gate array of 50,000 transistors. Data can be encrypted and decrypted at a rate of 1 gigabit per second, which translates to 16.8 million blocks per second. This is impressive. Table 12.9 gives the specifications for some commercial DES chips. Seeming discrepancies between clock speed and data rate are due to pipelining within the chip; a chip might have multiple DES engines working in parallel.

The most impressive DES chip is VLSI's 6868 (formerly called "Gatekeeper"). Not only can it perform DES encryption in only 8 clock cycles (prototypes in the lab can do it in 4 clock cycles), but it can also do ECB triple-DES in 25 clock cycles, and OFB or CBC triple-DES in 35 clock cycles. This sounds impossible to me, too, but I assure you it works.

A software implementation of DES on an IBM 3090 mainframe can perform 32,000 DES encryptions per second. Most microcomputers are slower, but impressive nonetheless. Table 12.10 [603,793] gives actual results and estimates for various Intel and Motorola microprocessors.

12.3 SECURITY OF DES

People have long questioned the security of DES [458]. There has been much speculation on the key length, number of iterations, and design of the S-boxes. The S-boxes were particularly mysterious—all those constants, without any apparent reason as to why or what they're for. Although IBM claimed that the inner workings were the result of 17 man-years of intensive cryptanalysis, some people feared that the NSA embedded a trapdoor into the algorithm so they would have an easy means of decrypting messages.

The U.S. Senate Select Committee on Intelligence, with full top-secret clearances, investigated the matter in 1978. The findings of the committee are classified, but an unclassified summary of those findings exonerated the NSA from any improper involvement in the algorithm's design [1552]. "It was said to have convinced IBM that a shorter key was adequate, to have indirectly assisted in the development of the S-box structures and to have certified that the final DES algorithm was, to the best of their knowledge, free of any statistical or mathematical weaknesses" [435]. However, since the government never made the details of the investigation public, many people remained unconvinced.

Tuchman and Meyer, two of the IBM cryptographers who designed DES, said the NSA did not alter the design [841]:

> Their basic approach was to look for strong substitution, permutation, and key scheduling functions. . . . IBM has classified the notes containing the selection

Table 12.9
Commercial DES Chips

Manufacturer	Chip	Year	Clock	Data Rate	Availability
AMD	Am9518	1981	3 MHz	1.3 MByte/s	N
AMD	Am9568	?	4 MHz	1.5 MByte/s	N
AMD	AmZ8068	1982	4 MHz	1.7 MByte/s	N
AT&T	T7000A	1985	?	1.9 MByte/s	N
CE-Infosys	SuperCrypt CE99C003	1992	20 MHz	12.5 MByte/s	Y
CE-Infosys	SuperCrypt CE99C003A	1994	30 MHz	20.0 MByte/s	Y
Cryptech	Cry12C102	1989	20 MHz	2.8 MByte/s	Y
Newbridge	CA20C03A	1991	25 MHz	3.85 MByte/s	Y
Newbridge	CA20C03W	1992	8 MHz	0.64 MByte/s	Y
Newbridge	CA95C68/18/09	1993	33 MHz	14.67 MByte/s	Y
Pijnenburg	PCC100	?	?	2.5 MByte/s	Y
Semaphore Communications	Roadrunner284	?	40 MHz	35.5 MByte/s	Y
VLSI Technology	VM007	1993	32 MHz	200.0 MByte/s	Y
VLSI Technology	VM009	1993	33 MHz	14.0 MByte/s	Y
VLSI Technology	6868	1995	32 MHz	64.0 MByte/s	Y
Western Digital	WD2001/2002	1984	3 MHz	0.23 MByte/s	N

Table 12.10
DES Speeds on Different Microprocessors and Computers

Processor	Speed (in MHz)	DES Blocks (per second)
8088	4.7	370
68000	7.6	900
80286	6	1,100
68020	16	3,500
68030	16	3,900
80386	25	5,000
68030	50	10,000
68040	25	16,000
68040	40	23,000
80486	66	43,000
Sun ELC		26,000
HyperSparc		32,000
RS6000-350		53,000
Sparc 10/52		84,000
DEC Alpha 4000/610		154,000
HP 9000/887	125	196,000

criteria at the request of the NSA. . . . "The NSA told us we had inadvertently reinvented some of the deep secrets it uses to make its own algorithms," explains Tuchman.

Later in the article, Tuchman is quoted: "We developed the DES algorithm entirely within IBM using IBMers. The NSA did not dictate a single wire!" Tuchman reaffirmed this when he spoke on the history of DES at the 1992 National Computer Security Conference.

On the other hand, Coppersmith wrote [373,374]: "The National Security Agency (NSA) also provided technical advice to IBM." And Konheim has been quoted as saying: "We sent the S-boxes off to Washington. They came back and were all different. We ran our tests and they passed." People have pointed to this as evidence that the NSA put a trapdoor in DES.

NSA, when questioned regarding any imposed weakness in DES, said [363]:

> Regarding the Data Encryption Standard (DES), we believe that the public record from the Senate Committee for Intelligence's investigation in 1978 into NSA's role in the development of the DES is responsive to your question. That committee report indicated that NSA did not tamper with the design of the algorithm in any way and that the security afforded by the DES was more than adequate for at least a 5–10 year time span for the unclassified data for which it was intended. In short, NSA did not impose or attempt to impose any weakness on the DES.

Then why did they modify the S-boxes? Perhaps it was to ensure that IBM did not put a trapdoor in DES. The NSA had no reason to trust IBM's researchers, and would be lax in their duty if they did not make absolutely sure that DES was free of trapdoors. Dictating the S-boxes is one way they could make sure.

Very recently some new cryptanalysis results have shed some light on this issue, but for many years this has been the subject of much speculation.

Weak Keys

Because of the way the initial key is modified to get a subkey for each round of the algorithm, certain initial keys are **weak keys** [721,427]. Remember that the initial value is split into two halves, and each half is shifted independently. If all the bits in each half are either 0 or 1, then the key used for any cycle of the algorithm is the same for all the cycles of the algorithm. This can occur if the key is entirely 1s, entirely 0s, or if one half of the key is entirely 1s and the other half is entirely 0s. Also, two of the weak keys have other properties that make them less secure [427].

The four weak keys are shown in hexadecimal notation in Table 12.11. (Remember that every eighth bit is a parity bit.)

Additionally, some pairs of keys encrypt plaintext to the identical ciphertext. In other words, one key in the pair can decrypt messages encrypted with the other key in the pair. This is due to the way in which DES generates subkeys; instead of generating 16 different subkeys, these keys generate only two different subkeys. Each of these subkeys is used eight times in the algorithm. These keys are called **semiweak keys**, and are shown in hexadecimal notation in Table 12.12.

Table 12.11
DES Weak Keys

Weak Key Value (with parity bits)				Actual Key
0101	0101	0101	0101	0000000 0000000
1F1F	1F1F	0E0E	0E0E	0000000 FFFFFFF
E0E0	E0E0	F1F1	F1F1	FFFFFFF 0000000
FEFE	FEFE	FEFE	FEFE	FFFFFFF FFFFFFF

Some keys produce only four subkeys, each used four times in the algorithm. These **possibly weak** keys are listed in Table 12.13.

Before condemning DES for having weak keys, consider that this list of 64 keys is minuscule compared to the total set of 72,057,594,037,927,936 possible keys. If you select a random key, the odds of picking one of these keys is negligible. If you are truly paranoid, you could always check for weak keys during key generation. Some people don't think it's worth the bother. Others say that it's so easy to check, there's no reason not to.

There is further analysis on weak and semiweak keys in [1116], and additional key patterns have been investigated for weaknesses. None have been found.

Complement Keys

Take the bit-wise complement of a key; that is, replace all the 0s with 1s and the 1s with 0s. Now, if the original key encrypts a block of plaintext, then the complement of the key will encrypt the complement of the plaintext block into the complement of the ciphertext block.

If x' is the complement of x, then the identity is as follows:

$$E_K(P) = C$$
$$E_{K'}(P') = C'$$

This isn't anything mysterious. The subkeys are XORed with the right half after the expansion permutation in every round. This **complementation property** is a direct result of that fact.

Table 12.12
DES Semiweak Key Pairs

01FE	01FE	01FE	01FE	and	FE01	FE01	FE01	FE01
1FE0	1FE0	0EF1	0EF1	and	E01F	E01F	F10E	F10E
01E0	01E0	01F1	01F1	and	E001	E001	F101	F101
1FFE	1FFE	0EFE	0EFE	and	FE1F	FE1F	FE0E	FE0E
011F	011F	010E	010E	and	1F01	1F01	0E01	0E01
E0FE	E0FE	F1FE	F1FE	and	FEE0	FEE0	FEF1	FEF1

Table 12.13
DES Possibly Weak Keys

1F	1F	01	01	0E	0E	01	01	E0	01	01	E0	F1	01	01	F1
01	1F	1F	01	01	0E	0E	01	FE	1F	01	E0	FE	0E	01	F1
1F	01	01	1F	0E	01	01	0E	FE	01	1F	E0	FE	01	0E	F1
01	01	1F	1F	01	01	0E	0E	E0	1F	1F	E0	F1	0E	0E	F1
E0	E0	01	01	F1	F1	01	01	FE	01	01	FE	FE	01	01	FE
FE	FE	01	01	FE	FE	01	01	E0	1F	01	FE	F1	0E	01	FE
FE	E0	1F	01	FE	F1	0E	01	E0	01	1F	FE	F1	01	0E	FE
E0	FE	1F	01	F1	FE	0E	01	FE	1F	1F	FE	FE	0E	0E	FE
FE	E0	01	1F	FE	F1	01	0E	1F	FE	01	E0	0E	FE	01	F1
E0	FE	01	1F	F1	FE	01	0E	01	FE	1F	E0	01	FE	0E	F1
E0	E0	1F	1F	F1	F1	0E	0E	1F	E0	01	FE	0E	F1	01	FE
FE	FE	1F	1F	FE	FE	0E	0E	01	E0	1F	FE	01	F1	0E	FE
FE	1F	E0	01	FE	0E	F1	01	01	01	E0	E0	01	01	F1	F1
E0	1F	FE	01	F1	0E	FE	01	1F	1F	E0	E0	0E	0E	F1	F1
FE	01	E0	1F	FE	01	F1	0E	1F	01	FE	E0	0E	01	FE	F1
E0	01	FE	1F	F1	01	FE	0E	01	1F	FE	E0	01	0E	FE	F1
01	E0	E0	01	01	F1	F1	01	1F	01	E0	FE	0E	01	F1	FE
1F	FE	E0	01	0E	FE	F0	01	01	1F	E0	FE	01	0E	F1	FE
1F	E0	FE	01	0E	F1	FE	01	01	01	FE	FE	01	01	FE	FE
01	FE	FE	01	01	FE	FE	01	1F	1F	FE	FE	0E	0E	FE	FE
1F	E0	E0	1F	0E	F1	F1	0E	FE	FE	E0	E0	FE	FE	F1	F1
01	FE	E0	1F	01	FE	F1	0E	E0	FE	FE	E0	F1	FE	FE	F1
01	E0	FE	1F	01	F1	FE	0E	FE	E0	E0	FE	FE	F1	F1	FE
1F	FE	FE	1F	0E	FE	FE	0E	E0	E0	FE	FE	F1	F1	FE	FE

What this means is that a chosen-plaintext attack against DES only has to test half the possible keys: 2^{55} keys instead of 2^{56} [1080]. Eli Biham and Adi Shamir showed [172] that there is a known-plaintext attack of the same complexity, requiring at least 2^{33} known plaintexts.

It is questionable whether this is a weakness, since most messages don't have complement blocks of plaintext (in random plaintext, the odds against it are extremely high) and users can be warned not to use complement keys.

Algebraic Structure

All possible 64-bit plaintext blocks can be mapped onto all possible 64-bit cipher-text blocks in $2^{64}!$ different ways. The DES algorithm, with its 56-bit key, gives us 2^{56} (approximately 10^{17}) of these mappings. Using multiple encryption, it seems possible to reach a larger portion of those possible mappings. However, this is only true if the DES operation does not have certain algebraic structures.

If DES were **closed**, then for any K_1 and K_2 there would always be a K_3 such that

$$E_{K_2}(E_{K_1}(P)) = E_{K_3}(P)$$

In other words, the DES encryption operation would form a group, and encrypting a set of plaintext blocks with K_1 followed by K_2 would be identical to encrypting the blocks with K_3. Even worse, DES would be vulnerable to a meet-in-the-middle known-plaintext attack that runs in only 2^{28} steps [807].

If DES were **pure**, then for any K_1, K_2, and K_3 there would always be a K_4 such that

$$E_{K_3}(E_{K_2}(E_{K_1}(P))) = E_{K_4}(P)$$

Triple encryption would be useless. (Note that a closed cipher is necessarily pure, but a pure cipher is not necessarily closed.)

An early theoretical paper by Don Coppersmith gave some hints, but it wasn't enough [377]. Various cryptographers wrestled with this question [588,427,431, 527,723,789]. Cycling experiments gathered "overwhelming evidence" that DES is not a group [807,371,808,1116,809], but it wasn't until 1992 that cryptographers proved that DES is not a group [293]. Coppersmith said that the IBM team knew it all along.

Key Length

IBM's original submission to NBS had a 112-bit key. By the time the DES became a standard, that was reduced to a 56-bit key. Many cryptographers argued for the longer key. Their arguments centered on the possibility of a brute-force attack (see Section 7.1).

In 1976 and 1977, Diffie and Hellman argued that a special-purpose DES-cracking parallel computer could recover the key in a day and cost $20 million. In 1981, Diffie upped this to a two-day search time and a cost of $50 million [491]. Diffie and Hellman argued then that this was out of reach for everybody except organizations like the NSA, but that by 1990 DES would be totally insecure [714].

Hellman [716] presented another argument against the small key size: By trading memory space for time, it would be possible to speed up the searching process. He suggested the possibility of computing and storing 2^{56} possible results of encrypting a single plaintext block under every possible key. Then, to break an unknown key, all that would be required would be for the cryptanalyst to insert the plaintext block into the encryption stream, recover the resulting ciphertext, and look the key up. Hellman pegged the cost of this cracking machine at $5 million.

Arguments for and against the existence of a DES-cracker lurking in some government basement somewhere have continued. Several people pointed out that the mean time between failures for the DES chips would never be high enough to ensure that the machine would work. This objection was shown to be superfluous in [1278]. Others suggested ways to speed the process even further and to reduce the effects of chip failures.

Meanwhile, hardware implementations of DES slowly approached the million-encryptions-per-second requirement of Diffie and Hellman's special-purpose machine. In 1984 DES chips capable of performing 256,000 encryptions per second had been produced [533,534]. By 1987 chips performing 512,000 encryptions per second were being developed, and a version capable of checking over a million keys per second was feasible [738,1573]. And in 1993 Michael Wiener designed a $1 million machine that could complete a brute-force attack against DES in an average of 3.5 hours (see Section 7.1).

No one has publicly admitted building this machine, although it is a reasonable assumption that someone has. A million dollars is not a lot of money to a large—or even a medium-sized—country.

It was not until 1990 that two Israeli mathematicians, Biham and Shamir, discovered **differential cryptanalysis**, a technique that put to rest the question of key length. Before we discuss that technique, let's turn to some other design criticisms of DES.

Number of Rounds

Why 16 rounds? Why not 32? After five rounds every ciphertext bit is a function of every plaintext bit and every key bit [1078,1080], and after eight rounds the ciphertext was essentially a random function of every plaintext bit and every key bit [880]. (This is called the avalanche effect.) So why not stop after eight rounds?

Over the years, variants of DES with a reduced number of rounds have been successfully attacked. DES with three or four rounds was easily broken in 1982 [49]. DES with six rounds fell some years later [336]. Biham and Shamir's differential cryptanalysis explained this as well: DES with any number of rounds fewer than 16 could be broken with a known-plaintext attack more efficiently than by a brute-force attack. Certainly brute-force is a much more likely attack, but it is interesting that the algorithm has exactly 16 rounds.

Design of the S-Boxes

In addition to being accused of reducing the key length, NSA was also accused of modifying the contents of the S-boxes. When pressed for design justification for the S-boxes, the NSA indicated that elements of the algorithm's design were "sensitive" and would not be made public. Many cryptographers were concerned that the NSA-designed S-boxes hid a trapdoor, making it possible for them to easily cryptanalyze the algorithm.

Since then, considerable effort has gone into analyzing the design and operation of the S-boxes. In the mid-1970s, Lexar Corporation [961,721] and Bell Laboratories [1120] examined the operation of the S-boxes. Neither analysis revealed any weaknesses, although both found inexplicable features. The S-boxes had more features in common with a linear transformation than one would expect if they were chosen at random. The Bell Laboratories team stated that the S-boxes may have hidden trapdoors, and the Lexar report concluded with:

> Structures have been found in DES that were undoubtedly inserted to strengthen the system against certain types of attack. Structures have also been found that appear to weaken the system.

On the other hand, this report also warned:

> . . . the problem [of the search for structure in the S-boxes] is complicated by the ability of the human mind to find apparent structure in random data, which is really not structure at all.

At the second workshop on DES, the National Security Agency revealed several design criteria behind the S-boxes [229]. This did nothing to quell people's suspicions, and the debate continued [228,422,714,1506,1551].

Various oddities about the S-boxes appeared in the literature. The last three output bits of the fourth S-box can be derived in the same way as the first by complementing some of the input bits [436,438]. Two different, but carefully chosen, inputs to S-boxes can produce the same output [436]. It is possible to obtain the same output of a single DES round by changing bits in only three neighboring S-boxes [487]. Shamir noticed that the S-boxes entries appeared to be somewhat imbalanced, but wasn't about to turn that imbalance into an attack [1423]. (He mentioned a feature of the fifth S-box, but it took another eight years before linear cryptanalysis exploited that feature.) Other researchers showed that publicly known design principles could be used to generate S-boxes with the observed characteristics [266].

Additional Results

There were other attempts to cryptanalyze DES. One cryptographer looked at nonrandomness based on spectral tests [559]. Others analyzed sequences of linear factors, but their attack failed after eight rounds [1297,336,531]. A 1987 unpublished attack by Donald Davies exploited the way the expansion permutation repeats bits into adjacent S-boxes; this attack is also impractical after eight rounds [172,429].

12.4 DIFFERENTIAL AND LINEAR CRYPTANALYSIS

Differential Cryptanalysis

In 1990, Eli Biham and Adi Shamir introduced **differential cryptanalysis** [167,168, 171,172]. This is a new method of cryptanalysis, heretofore unknown to the public. Using this method, Biham and Shamir found a chosen-plaintext attack against DES that was more efficient than brute force.

Differential cryptanalysis looks specifically at **ciphertext pairs**: pairs of ciphertexts whose plaintexts have particular differences. It analyzes the evolution of these differences as the plaintexts propagate through the rounds of DES when they are encrypted with the same key.

Simply, choose pairs of plaintexts with a fixed difference. The two plaintexts can be chosen at random, as long as they satisfy particular difference conditions; the cryptanalyst does not even have to know their values. (For DES, the term "difference" is defined using XOR. This can be different for different algorithms.) Then, using the differences in the resulting ciphertexts, assign different probabilities to different keys. As you analyze more and more ciphertext pairs, one key will emerge as the most probable. This is the correct key.

The details are more complicated. Figure 12.5 is the DES round function. Imagine a pair of inputs, X and X', that have the difference ΔX. The outputs, Y and Y' are known, and therefore so is the difference, ΔY. Both the expansion permutation and the P-box are known, so ΔA and ΔC are known. B and B' are not known, but their difference ΔB is known and equal to ΔA. (When looking at the difference, the XOR-ing of K_i with A and A' cancels out.) So far, so good. Here's the trick: For any given ΔA, not all values of ΔC are equally likely. The combination of ΔA and ΔC suggests values for bits of A XOR K_i and A' XOR K_i. Since A and A' are known, this gives us information about K_i.

Look at the last round of DES. (Differential cryptanalysis ignores the initial and final permutation. They have no effect on the attack, except to make it harder to explain.) If we can identify K_{16}, then we have 48 bits of the key. (Remember, the sub-key in each round consists of 48 bits of the 56-bit key.) The other 8 bits we can get by brute force. Differential cryptanalysis will get us K_{16}.

Certain differences in plaintext pairs have a high probability of causing certain differences in the resulting ciphertext pairs. These are called **characteristics**. Characteristics extend over a number of rounds and essentially define a path through these rounds. There is an input difference, a difference at each round, and an output difference—with a specific probability.

You can find these characteristics by generating a table where the rows represent the possible input XORs (the XOR of two different sets of input bits), the columns

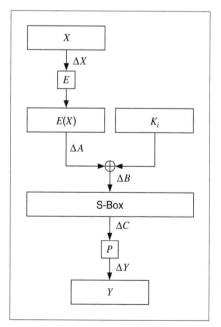

Figure 12.5   DES round function.

represent the possible output XORs, and the entries represent the number of times a particular output XOR occurs for a given input XOR. You can generate such a table for each of DES's eight S-boxes.

For example, Figure 12.6a is a one-round characteristic. The input difference of the left side is L; it could be anything. The input difference of the right side is 0. (The two inputs have the same right-hand side, so their difference is 0.) Since there is no difference going in to the round function, then there is no difference coming out of the round function. Therefore, the output difference of the left side is $L \oplus 0 = L$, and the output difference of the right side is 0. This is a trivial characteristic, and is true with probability 1.

Figure 12.6b is a less obvious characteristic. Again, the input difference to the left side is arbitrary: L. The input difference to the right side is 0x60000000; the two inputs differ in only the second and third bits. With a probability of $^{14}/_{64}$, the output difference of the round function is $L \oplus 0x00808200$. This means that the output difference of the left side is $L \oplus 0x00808200$ and the output difference of the right side is 0x60000000—with probability $^{14}/_{64}$.

Different characteristics can be joined. And, assuming the rounds are independent, the probabilities can be multiplied. Figure 12.7 joins the two characteristics previously described. The input difference to the left side is 0x00808200 and the input difference to the right side is 0x60000000. At the end of the first round the input difference and the output of the round function cancel out, leaving an output difference of 0. This feeds into the second round; the final output difference of the left side is 0x60000000 and the final output difference of the right side is 0. This two-round characteristic has a probability of $^{14}/_{64}$.

A plaintext pair that satisfies the characteristic is a **right pair**. A plaintext pair which does not is a **wrong pair**. A right pair will suggest the correct round key (for the last round of the characteristic); a wrong pair will suggest a random round key.

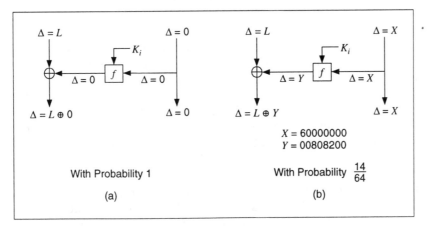

Figure 12.6   *DES characteristics.*

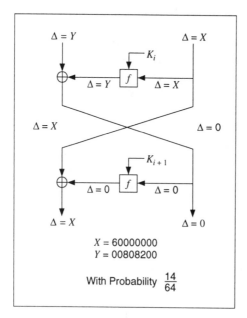

$X = 60000000$
$Y = 00808200$

With Probability $\frac{14}{64}$

Figure 12.7   A two-round DES character-istic.

To find the correct round key, simply collect enough guesses so that one subkey is suggested more often than all the others. In effect, the correct subkey will rise out of all the random alternatives.

So, the basic differential attack on *n*-round DES will recover the 48-bit subkey used in round *n*, and the remaining 8 key bits are obtained by brute-force guessing.

There are still considerable problems. First, there is a negligible chance of success until you reach some threshold. That is, until you accumulate sufficient data you can't tell the correct subkey from all the noise. And the attack isn't practical: You have to use counters to assign different probabilities to 2^{48} possible subkeys, and too much data is required to make this work.

At this point, Biham and Shamir tweaked their attack. Instead of a using a 15-round characteristic on 16-round DES, they used a 13-round characteristic and some tricks to get the last few rounds. A shorter characteristic with a higher probability worked better. And they used some clever mathematics to obtain 56-bit key candidates which could be tested immediately, eliminating the need for counters. This attack succeeds as soon as a right pair is found; this avoids the threshold and gives a linear success probability. If you have 1000 times fewer pairs, then you have 1000 times smaller chance of success. This sounds terrible, but it is a lot better than the threshold. There is always some chance of immediate success.

The results are most interesting. Table 12.14 is a summary of the best differential attack against DES with varying numbers of rounds [172]. The first column is the number of rounds. The next two columns are the numbers of chosen plaintexts or known plaintexts that must be examined for the attack, and the fourth column is

Table 12.14
Differential Cryptanalysis Attacks against DES

No. of Rounds	Chosen Plaintexts	Known Plaintexts	Analyzed Plaintexts	Complexity of Analysis
8	2^{14}	2^{38}	4	2^{9}
9	2^{24}	2^{44}	2	$2^{32\dagger}$
10	2^{24}	2^{43}	2^{14}	2^{15}
11	2^{31}	2^{47}	2	$2^{32\dagger}$
12	2^{31}	2^{47}	2^{21}	2^{21}
13	2^{39}	2^{52}	2	$2^{32\dagger}$
14	2^{39}	2^{51}	2^{29}	2^{29}
15	2^{47}	2^{56}	2^{7}	2^{37}
16	2^{47}	2^{55}	2^{36}	2^{37}

†The complexity of the analysis can be greatly reduced for these variants by using about four times as many plaintexts with the clique method.

the number of those plaintexts actually analyzed. The last column is the complexity of analysis, after the required plaintexts are found.

The best attack against full 16-round DES requires 2^{47} chosen plaintexts. This can be converted to a known plaintext attack, but that requires 2^{55} known plaintexts. And 2^{37} DES operations are required during analysis.

Differential cryptanalysis works against DES and other similar algorithms with constant S-boxes. The attack is heavily dependent on the structure of the S-boxes; the ones in DES just happen to be optimized against differential cryptanalysis. And the attack works against DES in any of its operating modes—ECB, CBC, CFB, and OFB—with the same complexity [172].

DES's resistance can be improved by increasing the number of rounds. Chosen-plaintext differential cryptanalysis DES with 17 or 18 rounds takes about the same time as a brute-force search [160]. At 19 rounds or more, differential cryptanalysis becomes impossible because it requires more than 2^{64} chosen plaintexts: Remember, DES has a 64-bit block size, so it only *has* 2^{64} possible plaintext blocks. (In general, you can prove that an algorithm is resistant to differential cryptanalysis by showing that the amount of plaintext required to mount such an attack is greater than the amount of plaintext possible.)

Here are a few important points. First, this attack is largely theoretical. The enormous time and data requirements to mount a differential cryptanalytic attack put it beyond the reach of almost everyone. To get the requisite data for this attack against a full DES, you have to encrypt a 1.5 megabits-per-second data stream of *chosen plaintext* for almost three years. Second, this is primarily a chosen-plaintext attack. It can be converted to a known-plaintext attack, but you have to sift through all of the plaintext-ciphertext pairs looking for the useful ones. For full 16-round DES, this makes the attack slightly less efficient than brute force (the differential cryptanalytic attack requires $2^{55.1}$ operations, and brute force requires 2^{55}). The consensus is that DES, when implemented properly, is still secure against differential cryptanalysis.

Why is DES so resistant to differential cryptanalysis? Why are the S-boxes optimized to make this attack as difficult as possible? Why are there as many rounds as required, but no more? Because the designers knew about it. IBM's Don Coppersmith recently wrote [373,374]:

> The design took advantage of certain cryptanalytic techniques, most prominently the technique of "differential cryptanalysis," which were not known in the published literature. After discussions with NSA, it was decided that disclosure of the design consideration would reveal the technique of differential cryptanalysis, a powerful technique that can be used against many ciphers. This in turn would weaken the competitive advantage the United States enjoyed over other countries in the field of cryptography.

Adi Shamir responded to this, challenging Coppersmith to say that he hadn't found any stronger attacks against DES since then. Coppersmith has chosen to remain silent on that question [1426].

Related-Key Cryptanalysis

Table 12.3 showed the number of bits the DES key is rotated after each round: 2 bits after each round, except for 1 bit after rounds 1, 2, 9, and 16. Why?

Related-key cryptanalysis is similar to differential cryptanalysis, but it examines the difference between keys. The attack is different from any previously discussed: The cryptanalyst chooses a relationship between a pair of keys, but does not know the keys themselves. Data is encrypted with both keys. In the known-plaintext version, the cryptanalyst knows the plaintext and ciphertext of data encrypted with the two keys. In the chosen-plaintext version, the cryptanalyst gets to choose the plaintext encrypted with the two keys.

A modified DES, where the key is rotated two bits after every round, is less secure. Related-key cryptanalysis can break that variant using 2^{17} chosen-key chosen plaintexts or 2^{33} chosen-key known plaintexts [158,163].

This attack is not at all practical, but it is interesting for three reasons. One, it is the first cryptanalytic attack against DES's subkey-generation algorithm. Two, this attack is independent of the number of rounds of the cryptographic algorithm; it's just as effective against DES with 16 rounds, 32 rounds, or 1000 rounds. And three, DES is impervious to this attack. The variability in the rotation thwarts related-key cryptanalysis.

Linear Cryptanalysis

Linear cryptanalysis is another type of cryptanalytic attack, invented by Mitsuru Matsui [1016,1015,1017]. This attack uses linear approximations to describe the action of a block cipher (in this case, DES.)

This means that if you XOR some of the plaintext bits together, XOR some ciphertext bits together, and then XOR the result, you will get a single bit that is the

XOR of some of the key bits. This is a linear approximation and will hold with some probability p. If $p \neq \frac{1}{2}$, then this bias can be exploited. Use collected plaintexts and associated ciphertexts to guess the values of the key bits. The more data you have, the more reliable the guess. The greater the bias, the greater the success rate with the same amount of data.

How do you identify good linear approximations for DES? Find good 1-round linear approximations and join them together. (Again, ignore the initial and final permutations; they don't affect the attack.) Look at the S-boxes. There are 6 input bits and 4 output bits. The input bits can be combined using XOR in 63 useful ways $(2^6 - 1)$, and the output bits can be combined in 15 useful ways. Now, for each S-box you can evaluate the probability that for a randomly chosen input, an input XOR combination equals some output XOR combination. If there is a combination with a high enough bias, then linear cryptanalysis may work.

If the linear approximations are unbiased, then they would hold for 32 of the 64 possible inputs. I'll spare you the pages of tables, but the most biased S-box is S-box 5. In fact, the second input bit is equal to the XOR of all 4 output bits for only 12 inputs. This translates to a probability of $\frac{3}{16}$, or a bias of $\frac{5}{16}$, and is the most extreme bias in all the S-boxes. (Shamir noted this in [1423], but could not find a way to exploit it.)

Figure 12.8 shows how to turn this into an attack against the DES round function. The input bit into S-box 5 is b_{26}. (I am numbering the bits from left to right and from 1 to 64. Matsui ignores this convention with DES and numbers his bits from right

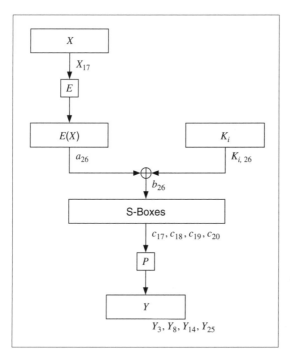

Figure 12.8 A 1-round linear approximation for DES.

to left and from 0 to 63. It's enough to drive you mad.) The 4 output bits from S-box 5 are c_{17}, c_{18}, c_{19}, and c_{20}. We can trace b_{26} backwards from the input to the S-box. The bit a_{26} is XORed with a bit from the subkey $K_{i,26}$ to obtain b_{26}. And bit X_{17} goes through the expansion permutation to become a_{26}. After the S-box, the 4 output bits go through the P-box to become 4 output bits of the round function: Y_3, Y_8, Y_{14}, and Y_{25}. This means that with probability $\frac{1}{2} - \frac{5}{16}$:

$$X_{17} \oplus Y_3 \oplus Y_8 \oplus Y_{14} \oplus Y_{25} = K_{i,26}$$

Linear approximations for different rounds can be joined in a manner similar to that discussed under differential cryptanalysis. Figure 12.9 is a 3-round approximation with a probability of $\frac{1}{2} + .0061$. The individual approximations are of varying quality: The last is very good, the first is pretty good, and the middle is bad. But together the three 1-round approximations give a very good three-round approximation.

The basic attack is to use the best linear approximation for 16-round DES. It requires 2^{47} known plaintext blocks, and will result in 1 key bit. That's not very useful. If you interchange the role of plaintext and ciphertext and use decryption as well as encryption, you can get 2 key bits. That's still not very useful.

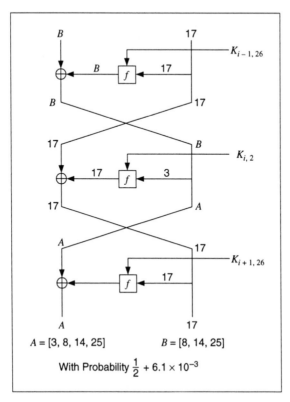

Figure 12.9   A 3-round linear approximation for DES.

There are refinements. Use a 14-round linear approximation for rounds 2 through 15. Guess the 6 subkey bits relevant to S-box 5 for the first and last rounds (12 key bits in all). Effectively you are doing 2^{12} linear cryptanalyses in parallel and picking the correct one based on probabilities. This recovers the 12 bits plus the b_{26}, and reversing plaintext and ciphertext recovers another 13 bits. To get the remaining 30 bits, use exhaustive search. There are other tricks, but that's basically it.

Against full 16-round DES, this attack can recover the key with an average of 2^{43} known plaintexts. A software implementation of this attack recovered a DES key in 50 days using 12 HP9000/735 workstations [1019]. That is the most effective attack against DES at the time of this writing.

Linear cryptanalysis is heavily dependent on the structure of the S-boxes and the S-boxes in DES are not optimized against this attack. In fact, the ordering of the S-boxes chosen for DES lies among the 9 percent to 16 percent that offer the least protection against linear cryptanalysis [1018]. According to Don Coppersmith [373,374], resistance to linear cryptanalysis "was not part of the design criteria of DES." Either they didn't know about linear cryptanalysis or they knew about something else even more powerful whose resistance criteria took precedence.

Linear cryptanalysis is newer than differential cryptanalysis, and there may be more performance improvements in the coming years. Some ideas are proposed in [1270,811], but it is not clear that they can be used effectively against full DES. They work very well against reduced round variants, however.

Future Directions

Some work has been done to try to extend the concept of differential cryptanalysis to higher-order differentials [702,161,927,858,860]. Lars Knudsen uses something called partial differentials to attack 6-round DES; it requires 32 chosen plaintexts and 20,000 encryptions [860]. It is still too new to know if these extensions will make it easier to attack full 16-round DES.

Another avenue of attack is **differential-linear cryptanalysis**: combining differential and linear cryptanalysis. Susan Langford and Hellman have an attack on 8-round DES that recovers 10 key bits with an 80 percent probability of success with 512 chosen plaintexts and a 95 percent probability of success with 768 chosen plaintexts [938]. After the attack, a brute-force search of the remaining keyspace (2^{46} possible keys) is required. While this attack is comparable in time to previous attacks, it requires far less plaintext. However, it doesn't seem to extend easily to more rounds.

But this attack is still new and work continues. It is possible that there may be a breakthrough some time during the next few years. Maybe there are benefits in combining this attack with higher-order differential cryptanalysis. Who knows?

12.5   THE REAL DESIGN CRITERIA

After differential cryptanalysis became public, IBM published the design criteria for the S-boxes and the P-box [373,374]. The criteria for the S-boxes are:

— Each S-box has 6 input bits and 4 output bits. (This was the largest size that could be accommodated in a single chip with 1974 technology.)

— No output bit of an S-box should be too close to a linear function of the input bits.

— If you fix the left-most and right-most bits of an S-box and vary the 4 middle bits, each possible 4-bit output is attained exactly once.

— If two inputs to an S-box differ in exactly 1 bit, the outputs must differ in at least 2 bits.

— If two inputs to an S-box differ in the 2 middle bits exactly, the outputs must differ in at least 2 bits.

— If two inputs to an S-box differ in their first 2 bits and are identical in their last 2 bits, the two outputs must not be the same.

— For any nonzero 6-bit difference between inputs, no more than 8 of the 32 pairs of inputs exhibiting that difference may result in the same output difference.

— A criterion similar to the previous one, but for the case of three active S-boxes.

The criteria for the P-box are:

— The 4 output bits from each S-box in round i are distributed so that 2 of them affect the middle-bits of S-boxes at round $i + 1$ and the other 2 affect end bits.

— The 4 output bits from each S-box affect six different S-boxes; no 2 affect the same S-box.

— If the output bit from one S-box affects a middle bit of another S-box, then an output bit from that other S-box cannot affect a middle bit of the first S-box.

The paper goes on to discuss the criteria. Generating S-boxes is pretty easy today, but was a complicated task in the early 1970s. Tuchman has been quoted as saying that they ran computer programs for months cooking up the S-boxes.

12.6 DES VARIANTS

Multiple DES

Some DES implementations use triple-DES (see Figure 12.10) [55]. Since DES is not a group, then the resultant ciphertext is much harder to break using exhaustive search: 2^{112} attempts instead of 2^{56} attempts. See Section 15.2 for more details.

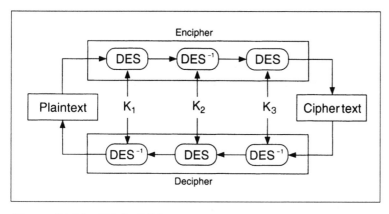

Figure 12.10   Triple-DES.

DES with Independent Subkeys

Another variation is to use a different subkey for each round, instead of generating them from a single 56-bit key [851]. Since 48 key bits are used in each of 16 rounds, this means that the key length for this variant is 768 bits. This variant would drastically increase the difficulty of a brute-force attack against the algorithm; that attack would have a complexity of 2^{768}.

However, a meet-in-the-middle attack (see Section 15.1) would be possible. This would reduce the complexity of attack to 2^{384}; still long enough for any conceivable security needs.

Although independent subkeys foil linear cryptanalysis, this variant is susceptible to differential cryptanalysis and can be broken with 2^{61} chosen plaintexts (see Table 12.15) [167,172]. It would seem that any modification of the key schedule cannot make DES much stronger.

DESX

DESX is a DES variant from RSA Data Security, Inc. that has been included in the MailSafe electronic mail security program since 1986 and the BSAFE toolkit since 1987. DESX uses a technique called whitening (see Section 15.6) to obscure the inputs and outputs to DES. In addition to a 56-bit DES key, DESX has an additional 64-bit whitening key. These 64 bits are XORed to the plaintext before the first round of DES. An additional 64 bits, computed as a one-way function of the entire 120-bit DES key, is XORed to the ciphertext after the last round [155]. Whitening makes DESX much stronger than DES against a brute-force attack; the attack requires $(2^{120})/n$ operations with n known plaintexts. It also improves security against differential and linear cryptanalysis; the attacks require 2^{61} chosen plaintexts and 2^{60} known plaintexts, respectively [1338].

CRYPT(3)

CRYPT(3) is a DES variant found on UNIX systems. It is primarily used as a one-way function for passwords, but sometimes can also be used for encryption. The difference between CRYPT(3) and DES is that CRYPT(3) has a key-dependent expansion permutation with 2^{12} possible permutations. This was done primarily so that off-the-shelf DES chips could not be used to construct a hardware password-cracker.

Generalized DES

Generalized DES (GDES) was designed both to speed up DES and to strengthen the algorithm [1381,1382]. The overall block size increases while the amount of computation remains constant.

Figure 12.11 is a block diagram of GDES. GDES operates on variable-sized blocks of plaintext. Encryption blocks are divided up into q 32-bit sub-blocks; the exact number depends on the total block size (this was variable in the design, but must be fixed for each implementation). In general, q equals the block size divided by 32.

Function f is calculated once per round on the right-most block. The result is XORed with all the other parts, which are then rotated to the right. GDES has a variable number of rounds, n. There is a slight modification to the last round, so that the encryption and decryption processes differ only in the order of the subkeys (just like DES). In fact, if $q = 2$ and $n = 16$, this *is* DES.

Biham and Shamir [167,168] showed that, using differential cryptanalysis, GDES with $q = 8$ and $n = 16$ is breakable with only six chosen plaintexts. If independent subkeys are also used, 16 chosen plaintexts are required. GDES with $q = 8$ and $n = 22$ is breakable with 48 chosen plaintexts, and GDES with $q = 8$ and $n = 31$ requires only 500,000 chosen plaintexts to break. Even GDES with $q = 8$ and $n = 64$ is weaker than DES; 2^{49} chosen plaintexts are required to break it. In fact, any GDES scheme that is faster than DES is also less secure (see Table 12.15).

A variant of this scheme recently appeared [1591]. It is probably no more secure than the original GDES. In general, any large block DES variant that is faster than DES is probably also less secure than DES.

DES with Alternate S-Boxes

Other DES modifications centered around the S-boxes. Some designs made the order of the S-boxes variable. Other designers varied the contents of the S-boxes themselves. Biham and Shamir showed [170,172] that the design of the S-boxes, and even the order of the S-boxes themselves, were optimized against differential cryptanalysis:

> The replacement of the order of the eight DES S-boxes (without changing their value) also makes DES much weaker: DES with 16 rounds of a particular replaced order is breakable in about 2^{38} steps. . . . DES with random S-boxes is shown to be very easy to break. Even a minimal change of one entry of one of the DES S-boxes can make DES easier to break.

The DES S-boxes were not optimized against linear cryptanalysis. There are better S-boxes than the ones that come with DES, but blindly choosing new S-boxes isn't a good idea.

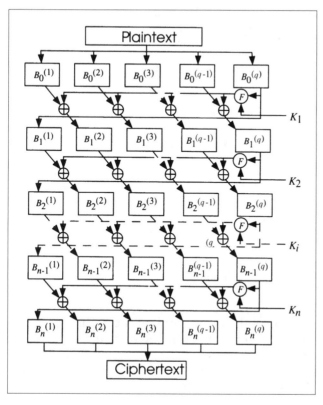

Figure 12.11   GDES.

Table 12.15 [167,169] lists some modifications to DES and the number of chosen plaintexts required for differential cryptanalysis. One change not listed, combining the left and right halves using addition mod 2^4 instead of XOR, is 2^{17} times harder to break than DES [689].

RDES

RDES is a variant that replaces swapping the left and right halves at the end of each round with a key-dependent swap [893]. The swappings are fixed, depending solely on the key. This means that the 15 key-dependent swaps occur with 2^{15} possible instances, and that the variant is not resistant to differential cryptanalysis [816,894,112]. RDES has a large number of weak keys. In fact, almost every key is weaker than a typical DES key. This variant should not be used.

A better idea is to swap only within the right half, at the beginning of each round. Another better idea is to make the swapping dependent on the input data and not a static function of the key. There are a number of possible variants [813,815]. In

Table 12.15
Differential Cryptanalysis Attacks against DES Variants

Modified Operation	Chosen Plaintexts
Full DES (no modification)	2^{47}
P permutation	Cannot strengthen
Identity permutation	2^{19}
Order of S-boxes	2^{38}
Replace XORs by additions	$2^{39}, 2^{31}$
S-boxes:	
Random	2^{18}–2^{20}
Random permutations	2^{33}–2^{41}
One entry	2^{33}
Uniform tables	2^{26}
Elimination of the E Expansion	2^{26}
Order of E and subkey XOR	2^{44}
GDES (width q = 8):	
16 rounds	6, 16
64 rounds	2^{49} (independent key)

RDES-1, there is a data-dependent swap of the 16-bit words at the beginning of each round. In RDES-2, there is a data-dependent swap of the bytes at the beginning of each round after the 16-bit swappings as in RDES-1. And so on through RDES-4. RDES-1 is secure against both differential cryptanalysis [815] and linear cryptanalysis [1136]. Presumably RDES-2 and greater are as well.

sⁿDES

A group of Korean researchers, led by Kwangjo Kim, has attempted to find a set of S-boxes that are optimally secure against both linear and differential cryptanalysis. Their first attempt, known as s^2DES, was presented in [834] and shown to be worse than DES against differential cryptanalysis in [855,858]. Their next attempt, s^3DES, was presented in [839] and shown to be worse than DES against linear cryptanalysis [856,1491,1527,858,838]. Biham suggested a minor change to make s^3DES secure against both linear and differential cryptanalysis [165]. The group went back to their computers and developed better techniques for S-box design [835,837]. They proposed s^4DES [836] and then s^5DES [838,944].

Table 12.16 gives the s^3DES S-boxes with S-box 1 and S-box 2 reversed, which are secure against both differential and linear cryptanalysis. Sticking this variant in a triple-DES mix is sure to irritate cryptanalysts.

DES with Key-Dependent S-Boxes

Linear and differential cryptanalysis work only if the analyst knows the composition of the S-boxes. If the S-boxes are key-dependent and chosen by a cryptographically strong method, then linear and differential cryptanalysis are much more difficult. Remember though, that randomly generated S-boxes have very poor differential and linear characteristics; even if they are secret.

Table 12.16
s³DES S-Boxes (with S-box 1 and S-box 2 reversed)

S-box 1:

13	14	0	3	10	4	7	9	11	8	12	6	1	15	2	5
8	2	11	13	4	1	14	7	5	15	0	3	10	6	9	12
14	9	3	10	0	7	13	4	8	5	6	15	11	12	1	2
1	4	14	7	11	13	8	2	6	3	5	10	12	0	15	9

S-box 2:

15	8	3	14	4	2	9	5	0	11	10	1	13	7	6	12
6	15	9	5	3	12	10	0	13	8	4	11	14	2	1	7
9	14	5	8	2	4	15	3	10	7	6	13	1	11	12	0
10	5	3	15	12	9	0	6	1	2	8	4	11	14	7	13

S-box 3:

13	3	11	5	14	8	0	6	4	15	1	12	7	2	10	9
4	13	1	8	7	2	14	11	15	10	12	3	9	5	0	6
6	5	8	11	13	14	3	0	9	2	4	1	10	7	15	12
1	11	7	2	8	13	4	14	6	12	10	15	3	0	9	5

S-box 4:

9	0	7	11	12	5	10	6	15	3	1	14	2	8	4	13
5	10	12	6	0	15	3	9	8	13	11	1	7	2	14	4
10	7	9	12	5	0	6	11	3	14	4	2	8	13	15	1
3	9	15	0	6	10	5	12	14	2	1	7	13	4	8	11

S-box 5:

5	15	9	10	0	3	14	4	2	12	7	1	13	6	8	11
6	9	3	15	5	12	0	10	8	7	13	4	2	11	14	1
15	0	10	9	3	5	4	14	8	11	1	7	6	12	13	2
12	5	0	6	15	10	9	3	7	2	14	11	8	1	4	13

S-box 6:

4	3	7	10	9	0	14	13	15	5	12	6	2	11	1	8
14	13	11	4	2	7	1	8	9	10	5	3	15	0	12	6
13	0	10	9	4	3	7	14	1	15	6	12	8	5	11	2
1	7	4	14	11	8	13	2	10	12	3	5	6	15	0	9

S-box 7:

4	10	15	12	2	9	1	6	11	5	0	3	7	14	13	8
10	15	6	0	5	3	12	9	1	8	11	13	14	4	7	2
2	12	9	6	15	10	4	1	5	11	3	0	8	7	14	13
12	6	3	9	0	5	10	15	2	13	4	14	7	11	1	8

S-box 8:

13	10	0	7	3	9	14	4	2	15	12	1	5	6	11	8
2	7	13	1	4	14	11	8	15	12	6	10	9	5	0	3
4	13	14	0	9	3	7	10	1	8	2	11	15	5	12	6
8	11	7	14	2	4	13	1	6	5	9	0	12	15	3	10

Here is a method to use 48 additional key bits to generate S-boxes that are resistant to both linear and differential cryptanalysis [165].

(1) Rearrange the DES S-boxes: 24673158.

(2) Select 16 of the remaining key bits. If the first bit is 1, swap the first two rows of S-box 1 with the last two rows of S-box 1. If the second bit is a 1, swap the first eight columns of S-box 1 with the second eight columns of S-box 1. Do the same to S-box 2 with the third and fourth key bits. Do the same with S-boxes 3 through 8.

(3) Take the remaining 32 key bits. XOR the first four with every entry of S-box 1, the second four with every entry of S-box 2, and so on.

The complexity of a differential cryptanalysis attack against this system is 2^{51}; the complexity of a linear cryptanalysis attack is 2^{53}. The complexity of exhaustive search is 2^{102}.

What is neat about this DES variant is that it can be implemented in existing hardware. Several DES chip vendors sell DES chips with loadable S-boxes. This S-box generation method can be done outside the chip and then loaded in. Differential and linear cryptanalysis require so much known or chosen plaintext as to be unworkable, and a brute-force attack is inconceivable—with no speed penalties.

12.7 How Secure Is DES Today?

The answer is both easy and hard. The easy answer just looks at key length (see Section 7.1). A brute-force DES-cracking machine that can find a key in an average of 3.5 hours cost only $1 million in 1993 [1597,1598]. DES is so widespread that it is naïve to pretend that the NSA and its counterparts haven't built such a machine. And remember, that cost will drop by a factor of 5 every 10 years. DES will only become less secure as time goes on.

The hard answer tries to estimate cryptanalytic techniques. Differential cryptanalysis was known by the NSA long before the mid-1970s, when DES first became a standard. It is naïve to pretend that the NSA theoreticians have been idle since then; almost certainly they have developed newer cryptanalytic techniques that can be applied against DES. But there are no facts, only rumors.

Winn Schwartau writes that the NSA had built a massively parallel DES-cracking machine as early as the mid-1980s [1404]. At least one such machine was built by Harris Corp. with a Cray Y-MP as a front end. Supposedly there are a series of algorithms that can reduce the complexity of a DES brute-force search by several orders of magnitude. Contextual algorithms, based on the inner workings of DES, can scrap sets of possible keys based on partial solutions. Statistical algorithms reduce the effective key size even further. And other algorithms choose likely keys—words, printable ASCII, and so on (see Section 8.1)—to test. The rumor is that the NSA can crack DES in 3 to 15 minutes, depending on how much preprocessing they can do. And these machines cost only $50,000 each, in quantity.

A different rumor is that if the NSA has a large amount of plaintext and ciphertext, its experts can perform some kind of statistical calculation and then go out to an array of optical disks and retrieve the key.

These are just rumors, but they don't give me a warm, fuzzy feeling about DES. It has just been too big a target for too long. Almost any change to DES will be more annoying; maybe the resultant cipher will be easier to break, but the NSA might not have the resources to devote to the problem.

My recommendation is to use Biham's construction for key-dependent S-boxes. It is easy to implement in software and in hardware chips that have loadable S-boxes, and has no performance penalty over DES. It increases the algorithm's resistance to a brute-force attack, makes differential and linear cryptanalysis harder, and gives the NSA something at least as strong as DES—but different—to worry about.

CHAPTER   13

Other Block Ciphers

13.1 LUCIFER

In the late 1960s, led by Horst Feistel and later by Walt Tuchman, IBM initiated a research program in computer cryptography called Lucifer. Lucifer is also the name of a block algorithm that came out of that program in the early 1970s [1482,1484]. In fact, there are at least two different algorithms with that name [552,1492]. And [552] leaves some gaps in the specification of the algorithm. All this has led to more than a little confusion.

Lucifer is a substitution-permutation network, with building blocks similar to DES. In DES, the output of the function f is XORed with the input of the previous round to form the input of the next round. Lucifer's S-boxes have 4-bit inputs and 4-bit outputs; the input of the S-boxes is the bit-permuted output of the S-boxes of the previous round; the input of the S-boxes of the first round is the plaintext. A key bit is used to choose the actual S-box from two possible S-boxes. (Lucifer represents this as a single T-box with 9 bits in and 8 bits out.) Unlike DES, there is no swapping between rounds and no block halves are used. Lucifer has 16 rounds, 128-bit blocks, and a key schedule simpler than DES.

Using differential cryptanalysis against the first incarnation of Lucifer, Biham and Shamir [170,172] showed that Lucifer, with 32-bit blocks and 8 rounds, can be broken with 40 chosen plaintexts and 2^{29} steps; the same attack can break Lucifer with 128-bit blocks and 8 rounds with 60 chosen plaintexts and 2^{53} steps. Another differential cryptanalytic attack breaks 18-round, 128-bit Lucifer with 24 chosen plaintexts in 2^{21} steps. All of these attacks used the strong DES S-boxes. Using differential cryptanalysis against the second incarnation, they found the S-boxes to be much weaker than DES. Further analysis showed that over half the possible keys are insecure [112]. Related-key cryptanalysis can break 128-bit Lucifer, with any number of rounds, with 2^{33} chosen-key chosen plaintexts, or with 2^{65} chosen-key known plaintexts [158]. The second incarnation of Lucifer is even weaker [170,172,112].

Some people feel that Lucifer is more secure than DES because of the longer key length and lack of published results. This is clearly not the case.

Lucifer is the subject of several U.S. patents: [553,554,555,1483]. They have all expired.

13.2 MADRYGA

W. E. Madryga proposed this block algorithm in 1984 [999]. It is efficient for software: It has no irritating permutations and all its operations work on bytes.

His design objectives are worth repeating:

1. The plaintext cannot be derived from the ciphertext without using the key. (This just means that the algorithm is secure.)

2. The number of operations required to determine the key from a sample of plaintext and ciphertext should be statistically equal to the product of the operations in an encryption times the number of possible keys. (This means that no plaintext attack should be better than brute force.)

3. Knowledge of the algorithm should not defeat the strength of the cipher. (All the security should rest in the key.)

4. A one-bit change of the key should produce a radical change in the ciphertext using the same plaintext, and a 1-bit change of the plaintext should produce a radical change in the ciphertext using the same key. (This is the avalanche effect.)

5. The algorithm should contain a noncommutative combination of substitution and permutation.

6. The algorithm should include substitutions and permutations under the control of both the input data and the key.

7. Redundant bit groups in the plaintext should be totally obscured in the ciphertext.

8. The length of the ciphertext should be the same length as the plaintext.

9. There should be no simple relationships between any possible keys and ciphertext effects.

10. Any possible key should produce a strong cipher. (There should be no weak keys.)

11. The length of the key and the text should be adjustable to meet varying security requirements.

12. The algorithm should be efficiently implementable in software on large mainframes, minicomputers, and microcomputers, and in discrete logic. (In fact, the functions used in the algorithm are limited to XOR and bit-shifting.)

DES had already met objectives one through nine, but the next three were new. Assuming that the best way to break the algorithm was through brute force, a variable-length key would surely silence those who thought 56 bits was too low. They could implement this algorithm with any key length they desired. And, for anyone who has ever attempted to implement DES in software, an algorithm that took software implementations into account would be welcomed.

Description of Madryga

Madryga consists of two nested cycles. The outer cycle repeats eight times (although this could be increased if security warrants) and consists of an application of the inner cycle to the plaintext. The inner cycle transforms plaintext to ciphertext and repeats once for each 8-bit block (byte) of the plaintext. Thus, the algorithm passes through the entire plaintext eight successive times.

An iteration of the inner cycle operates on a 3-byte window of data, called the working frame (see Figure 13.1). This window advances 1 byte for each iteration. (The data are considered circular when dealing with the last 2 bytes.) The first 2 bytes of the working frame are together rotated a variable number of positions, while the last byte is XORed with some key bits. As the working frame advances, all bytes are successively rotated and XORed with key material. Successive rotations overlap the results of a previous XOR and rotation, and data from the XOR is used to influence the rotation. This makes the entire process reversible.

Because every byte of data influences the 2 bytes to its left and the 1 byte to its right, after eight passes every byte of the ciphertext is dependent on 16 bytes to the left and 8 bytes to the right.

When encrypting, each iteration of the inner cycle starts the working frame at the next-to-last byte of the plaintext and advances circularly through to the third-to-last

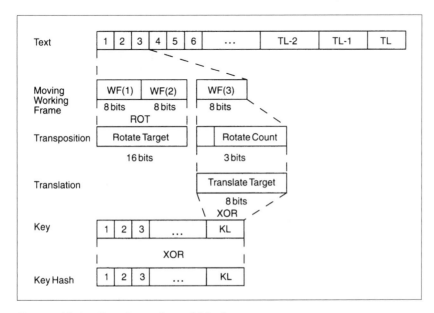

Figure 13.1   One iteration of Madryga.

byte of the plaintext. First, the entire key is XORed with a random constant and then rotated to the left 3 bits. The low-order 3 bits of the low-order byte of the working frame are saved; they will control the rotation of the other 2 bytes. Then, the low-order byte of the working frame is XORed with the low-order byte of the key. Next, the concatenation of the 2 high-order bytes are rotated to the left the variable number of bits (0 to 7). Finally, the working frame is shifted to the right 1 byte and the whole process repeats.

The point of the random constant is to turn the key into a pseudo-random sequence. The length of this constant must be equal to the length of the key and must be the same for everyone who wishes to communicate with one another. For a 64-bit key, Madryga recommends the constant 0x0f1e2d3c4b5a6978.

Decryption reverses this process. Each iteration of the inner cycle starts the working frame at the third-to-last byte of the ciphertext and advances in the reverse direction circularly through to the second-to-last byte of the ciphertext. Both the key and the 2 ciphertext bytes are shifted to the right. And the XOR is done before the rotations.

Cryptanalysis of Madryga

Researchers at Queensland University of Technology [675] examined Madryga, along with several other block ciphers. They observed that the algorithm didn't exhibit the plaintext-ciphertext avalanche effect. Additionally, many ciphertexts had a higher percentage of ones than zeros.

Although I know of no formal analysis of the algorithm, it doesn't look terribly secure. A cursory review by Eli Biham led to the following observations [160]:

> The algorithm consists only of linear operations (rotations and XOR), which are slightly modified depending on the data.
>
> There is nothing like the strength of DES's S-boxes.
>
> The parity of all the bits of the plaintext and the ciphertext is a constant, depending only on the key. So, if you have one plaintext and its corresponding ciphertext, you can predict the parity of the ciphertext for any plaintext.

None of this is damning in itself, but it doesn't leave me with a good feeling about the algorithm. I do not recommend Madryga.

13.3 NewDES

NewDES was designed in 1985 by Robert Scott as a possible DES replacement [1405,364]. The algorithm is not a DES variant, as its name might imply. It operates on 64-bit blocks of plaintext, but it has a 120-bit key. NewDES is simpler than DES, with no initial or final permutations. All operations are on entire bytes. (Actually, NewDES isn't anything like a new version of DES; the name is unfortunate.)

The plaintext block is divided into eight 1-byte sub-blocks: B_0, B_1, . . . , B_6, B_7. Then the sub-blocks go through 17 rounds. Each round has eight steps. In each step, one of the sub-blocks is XORed with some key material (there is one exception), substituted with another byte via an f function, and then XORed with another sub-block to become that sub-block. The 120-bit key is divided into 15 key sub-blocks: $K_0, K_1, \ldots, K_{13}, K_{14}$. The process is easier to understand visually than to describe. Figure 13.2 shows the NewDES encryption algorithm.

The f-function is derived from the Declaration of Independence. See [1405] for details.

Scott showed that every bit of the plaintext block affects every bit of the cipher-text block after only 7 rounds. He also analyzed the f function and found no obvious problems. NewDES has the same complementation property that DES has [364]: If

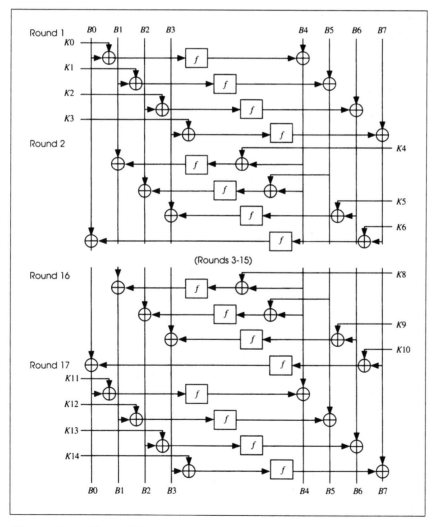

Figure 13.2   NewDES.

$E_K(P) = C$, then $E_{K'}(P') = C'$. This reduces the work required for a brute-force attack from 2^{120} steps to 2^{119} steps. Biham noticed that any change of a full byte, applied to all the key and data bytes, leads to another complementation property [160]. This reduces a brute-force attack further to 2^{112} steps.

This is not damning, but Biham's related-key cryptanalytic attack can break NewDES with 2^{33} chosen-key chosen-plaintexts in 2^{48} steps [160]. While this attack is time-consuming and largely theoretical, it shows that NewDES is weaker than DES.

13.4 FEAL

FEAL was designed by Akihiro Shimizu and Shoji Miyaguchi from NTT Japan [1435]. It uses a 64-bit block and a 64-bit key. The idea was to make a DES-like algorithm with a stronger round function. Needing fewer rounds, the algorithm would run faster. Unfortunately, reality fell far short of the design goals.

Description of FEAL

Figure 13.3 is a block diagram of one round of FEAL. The encryption process starts with a 64-bit block of plaintext. First, the data block is XORed with 64 key bits. The

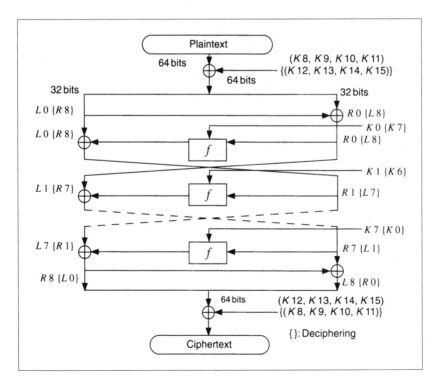

Figure 13.3   One round of FEAL.

data block is then split into a left half and a right half. The left half is XORed with the right half to form a new right half. The left and new right halves go through n rounds (four, initially). In each round the right half is combined with 16 bits of key material (using function f) and XORed with the left half to form the new right half. The original right half (before the round) forms the new left half. After n rounds (remember not to switch the left and right halves after the nth round) the left half is again XORed with the right half to form a new right half, and then the left and right halves are concatenated together to form a 64-bit whole. The data block is XORed with another 64 bits of key material, and the algorithm terminates.

Function f takes the 32 bits of data and 16 bits of key material and mixes them together. First the data block is broken up into 8-bit chunks, then the chunks are XORed and substituted with each other. Figure 13.4 is a block diagram of function f. The two functions S_0 and S_1, are defined as:

$$S_0(a,b) = \text{rotate left two bits } ((a + b) \bmod 256)$$
$$S_1(a,b) = \text{rotate left two bits } ((a + b + 1) \bmod 256)$$

The same algorithm can be used for decryption. The only difference is: When decrypting, the key material must be used in the reverse order.

Figure 13.5 is a block diagram of the key-generating function. First the 64-bit key is divided into two halves. The halves are XORed and operated on by function f_k, as indicated in the diagram. Figure 13.6 is a block diagram of function f_k. The two 32-bit inputs are broken up into 8-bit blocks and combined and substituted as shown. S_0 and S_1 are defined as just shown. The 16-bit key blocks are then used in the encryption/decryption algorithm.

On a 10 megahertz 80286 microprocessor, an assembly-language implementation of FEAL-32 can encrypt data at a speed of 220 kilobits per second. FEAL-64 can encrypt data at a speed of 120 kilobits per second [1104].

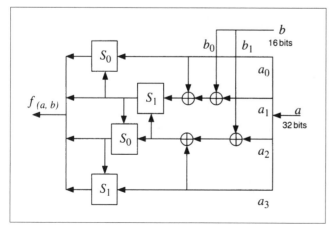

Figure 13.4   Function f.

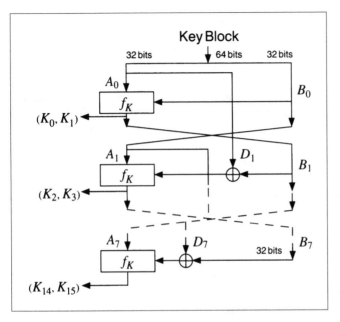

Figure 13.5   *Key processing part of FEAL.*

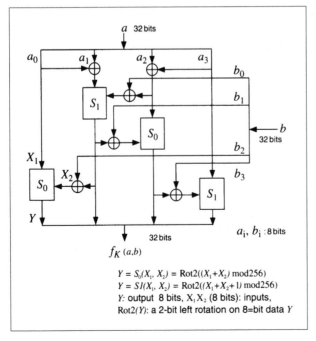

Figure 13.6   *Function f_K.*

Cryptanalysis of FEAL

FEAL-4, FEAL with four rounds, was successfully cryptanalyzed with a chosen-plaintext attack in [201] and later demolished in [1132]. This latter attack, by Sean Murphy, was the first published differential-cryptanalysis attack and required only 20 chosen plaintexts. The designers retaliated with 8-round FEAL [1436,1437,1108] which Biham and Shamir cryptanalyzed at the SECURICOM '89 conference [1424]. Another chosen-plaintext attack, using only 10,000 blocks, against FEAL-8 [610] forced the designers to throw up their hands and define FEAL-*N* [1102,1104], with a variable number of rounds (greater than 8, of course).

Biham and Shamir used differential cryptanalysis against FEAL-*N*; they could break it more quickly than by brute force (with fewer than 2^{64} chosen plaintext encryptions) for *N* less than 32 [169]. FEAL-16 required 2^{28} chosen plaintexts or $2^{46.5}$ known plaintexts to break. FEAL-8 required 2000 chosen plaintexts or $2^{37.5}$ known plaintexts to break. FEAL-4 could be broken with just eight carefully selected chosen plaintexts.

The FEAL designers also defined FEAL-*NX*, a modification of FEAL, that accepts 128-bit keys (see Figure 13.7) [1103,1104]. Biham and Shamir showed that FEAL-*NX* with a 128-bit key is just as easy to break as FEAL-*N* with a 64-bit key, for any value of *N* [169]. Recently FEAL-*N*(X)S has been proposed, which strengthens FEAL with a dynamic swapping function [1525].

There's more. Another attack against FEAL-4, requiring only 1000 known plaintexts, and against FEAL-8, requiring only 20,000 known plaintexts, was published in [1520]. Other attacks are in [1549,1550]. The best attack is by Mitsuru Matsui and Atshuiro Yamagishi [1020]. This is the first use of linear cryptanalysis, and can break FEAL-4 with 5 known plaintexts, FEAL-6 with 100 known plaintexts and FEAL-8 with 2^{15} known plaintexts. Further refinements are in [64]. Differential-linear cryptanalysis can break FEAL-8 with only 12 chosen plaintexts [62]. Whenever someone discovers a new cryptanalytic attack, he always seems to try it out on FEAL first.

Patents

FEAL is patented in the United States [1438] and has patents pending in England, France, and Germany. Anyone wishing to license the algorithm should contact the Intellectual Property Department, NTT, 1-6 Uchisaiwai-cho, 1-chome, Chiyoda-ku, 100 Japan.

13.5 REDOC

REDOC II is another block algorithm, designed by Michael Wood for Cryptech, Inc. [1613,400]. It has a 20-byte (160-bit) key and an 80-bit block.

REDOC II performs all of its manipulations—permutations, substitutions, and key XORs—on bytes; the algorithm is efficient in software. REDOC II uses variable function tables. Unlike DES, which has a fixed (albeit optimized for security) set of permutation and substitution tables, REDOC II uses a key-dependent and plaintext-dependent set of tables (S-boxes, actually). REDOC II has 10 rounds; each round is a complicated series of manipulations on the block.

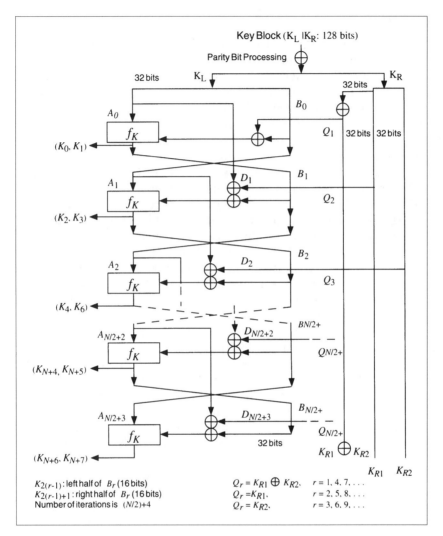

Figure 13.7   FEAL-NX key schedule.

Another unique feature in the design is the use of **masks**. These are numbers derived from the key table that are used to select the tables in a given function within a given round. Both the value of the data and the masks are used together to select the function tables.

Assuming that brute force is the most efficient means of attack, REDOC II is very secure: 2^{160} operations are required to recover the key. Thomas Cusick cryptanalyzed 1 round of REDOC II, but he was unable to extend the attack to multiple rounds [400]. Using differential cryptanalysis, Biham and Shamir were able to successfully cryptanalyze 1 round of REDOC II with 2300 chosen-plaintexts [170]. This attack cannot be extended to multiple rounds, but they were able to obtain three mask values after 4 rounds. I know of no other cryptanalysis.

REDOC III

REDOC III is a streamlined version of REDOC II, also designed by Michael Wood [1615]. It operates on an 80-bit block. The key length is variable and can be as large as 2560 bytes (20,480 bits). The algorithm consists solely of XORing key bytes with message bytes; there are no permutations or substitutions.

(1) Create a key table of 256 10-byte keys, using the secret key.
(2) Create two 10-byte mask blocks, M_1 and M_2. M_1 is the XOR of the first 128 10-byte keys; M_2 is the XOR of the second 128 10-byte keys.
(3) To encrypt a 10-byte block:

    (a) XOR the first byte of the data block with the first byte of M_1. Select a key from the key table computed in step (1). Use the computed XOR as the index into the table. XOR each byte in the data block with the corresponding byte in the chosen key, except for the first data byte.

    (b) XOR the second byte of the data block with the second byte of M_1. Select a key from the key table computed in step (1). Use the computed XOR as the index into the table. XOR each byte in the data block with the corresponding byte in the chosen key, except for the second data byte.

    (c) Continue with the entire block (bytes 3 through 10), until each byte has been used to select a key from the key table after XORing it with the corresponding M_1 value. Then XOR each byte with the key except for the byte used to select the key.

    (d) Repeat steps (a) through (c) with M_2.

The algorithm is easy and fast. On a 33 megahertz 80386, the algorithm encrypts data at 2.75 megabits per second. Wood estimates that a VLSI-pipelined design, with a 64-bit data path, woud encrypt data at over 1.28 gigabits per second with a 20 megahertz clock.

REDOC III is not secure [1440]. It is vulnerable to differential cryptanalysis. Only about 2^{23} chosen plaintexts are required to reconstruct both masks.

Patents and Licenses

Both REDOC versions are patented in the United States [1614]. Foreign patents are pending. Anyone interested in licensing either REDOC II or REDOC III should contact Michael C. Wood, Delta Computec, Inc., 6647 Old Thompson Rd., Syracuse, NY 13211.

13.6 LOKI

LOKI is Australian and was first presented in 1990 as a potential alternative to DES [273]. It uses a 64-bit block and a 64-bit key. The general structure of the algorithm and key schedule were based on [274,275], and the design of the S-boxes was based on [1247].

Using differential cryptanalysis, Biham and Shamir were able to break LOKI with 11 or fewer rounds faster than by brute force [170]. Furthermore, there is an 8-bit complementation property, which reduces the complexity of a brute-force attack by a factor of 256 [170,916,917].

Lars Knudsen showed that LOKI, with 14 rounds or fewer, is vulnerable to differential cryptanalysis [852,853]. Additionally, if LOKI is implemented with alternate S-boxes, the resulting cipher will probably be vulnerable to differential cryptanalysis.

LOKI91

In response to these attacks, LOKI's designers went back to the drawing board and revised their algorithm. The result is LOKI91 [272]. (The previous version of LOKI was renamed LOKI89.)

To make the algorithm more resistant to differential cryptanalysis and to remove the complementation property, the following changes were made to the original design:

1. The subkey generation algorithm was changed so that the halves were swapped every second round, not every round.
2. The subkey generation algorithm was changed so that the rotation of the left subkey alternated between 12 and 13 bits to the left.
3. The initial and final XOR of the block with the key were eliminated.
4. The S-box function was altered to flatten out their XOR profile (to improve their resistance to differential cryptanalysis), and to eliminate any value of x such that f(x) = 0, where f is the combination of the E-, S-, and P-boxes.

Description of LOKI91

The mechanics of LOKI91 are similar to DES (see Figure 13.8). The data block is then divided into a left half and a right half and goes through 16 rounds, much like DES. In each round, the right half is first XORed with a piece of the key, then sent through an expansion permutation (see Table 13.1).

The 48-bit output is divided into four 12-bit blocks, and each block is sent through an S-box substitution. The S-box substitution is as follows: Take each 12-bit input; use the 2 left-most bits and the 2 right-most bits to form the number r, and the 8 innermost bits and form the number c. The output of the S-box, O, is as follows:

$$O(r,c) = (c + ((r \star 17) \oplus \text{0xff}) \, \& \, \text{0xff})^{31} \bmod P_r$$

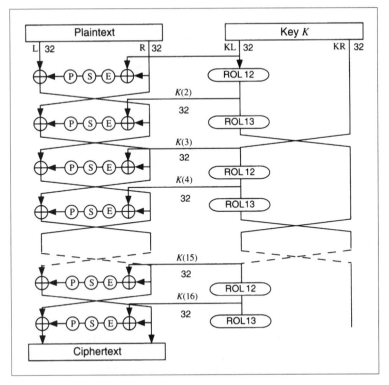

Figure 13.8   LOKI91.

P_r is given in Table 13.2.

Then, the four 8-bit outputs are recombined to form a single 32-bit number and sent through the permutation described in Table 13.3. Finally, the right half is XORed with the left half to become the new left half, and the left half becomes the new right half. After 16 rounds, the block is again XORed with the key to produce the ciphertext.

The subkeys are generated from the key in a straightforward manner. The 64-bit key is split into a left half and a right half. In each round, the subkey is the left half. This left half is then rotated 12 or 13 bits to the left, and then every two rounds the left and right halves are exchanged. As with DES, the same algorithm can be used for both encryption and decryption, with some modification in how the subkeys are used.

Table 13.1
Expansion Permutation

4,	3,	2,	1,	32,	31,	20,	29,	28,	27,	26,	25,
28,	27,	26,	25,	24,	23,	22,	21,	20,	19,	18,	17,
20,	19,	18,	17,	16,	15,	14,	13,	12,	11,	10,	9,
12,	11,	10,	9,	8,	7,	6,	5,	4,	3,	2,	1

Table 13.2
$$P_r$$

r:	1,	2,	3,	4,	5,	6,	7,	8,	9,	10,	11,	12,	13,	14,	15,	16
P_r:	375,	379,	391,	395,	397,	415,	419,	425,	433,	445,	451,	463,	471,	477,	487,	499

Cryptanalysis of LOKI91

Knudsen attempted to cryptanalyze LOKI91 [854,858], but found it secure against differential cryptanalysis. However, he found a related-key chosen-plaintext attack that reduces the complexity of a brute-force search by almost a factor of four. This attack exploits a weakness in the key schedule and may also apply if the algorithm is used as a one-way hash function (see Section 18.11).

Another attack on related keys can break LOKI91 with 2^{32} chosen-key chosen plaintexts, or 2^{48} chosen-key known plaintexts [158]. The attack is independent of the number of rounds of the algorithm. (In the same paper, Biham breaks LOKI89 with 2^{17} chosen-key chosen plaintexts or 2^{33} known-key known plaintexts using related-key cryptanalysis.) It's easy to make LOKI91 resistant to this attack; avoid the simple key schedule.

Patents and Licenses

LOKI is not patented. Anyone can implement the algorithm and use it. The source code implementation in this book is copyrighted by the University of New South Wales. Anyone interested in using this implementation (or their other implementation, which is several orders of magnitude faster) in a commercial product should contact Director CITRAD, Department of Computer Science, University College, UNSW, Australian Defense Force Academy, Canberra ACT 2600, Australia; FAX: +61 6 268 8581.

13.7 KHUFU AND KHAFRE

In 1990 Ralph Merkle proposed two algorithms. The basic design principles behind them are [1071]:

1. DES's 56-bit key size is too small. Considering the negligible cost of increasing the key size (computer memory is cheap and plentiful), it should be increased.

2. DES's extensive use of permutations, while suitable for hardware implementations, is very difficult to implement in software. The faster software

Table 13.3
P-Box Permutation

32,	24,	16,	8,	31,	23,	15,	7,	30,	22,	14,	6,	29,	21,	13,	5,
28,	20,	12,	4,	27,	19,	11,	3,	26,	18,	10,	2,	25,	17,	9,	1

implementations of DES implement the permutations by table lookup. Table lookup can provide the same "diffusion" characteristics as permutation and can be much more flexible.

3. The S-boxes in DES are small, with only 64 4-bit entries per box. Now that memory is larger, S-boxes should grow. Moreover, all eight S-boxes are used simultaneously. While this is suitable for hardware, it seems like an unreasonable restriction in software. A larger S-box size and sequential (rather than parallel) S-box usage should be employed.

4. The initial and final permutations in DES are widely viewed as cryptographically pointless and should be discarded.

5. All the faster implementations of DES precompute the keys for each round. Given this fact, there is no reason not to make this computation more complicated.

6. Unlike DES, the S-box design criteria should be public.

To this list, Merkle would probably now add "resistant to differential cryptanalysis and to linear attacks," but those attacks were still unknown at the time.

Khufu

Khufu is a 64-bit block cipher. The 64-bit plaintext is first divided into two 32-bit halves, L and R. First, both halves are XORed with some key material. Then, they are subjected to a series of rounds similar to DES. In each round, the least significant byte of L is used as the input to an S-box. Each S-box has 8 input bits and 32 output bits. The selected 32-bit entry in the S-box is then XORed with R. L is then rotated some multiple of 8 bits, L and R are swapped, and the round ends. The S-box itself is not static, but changes every 8 rounds. Finally, after the last round, L and R are XORed with more key material, and then combined to form the ciphertext block.

Although parts of the key are XORed with the encryption block at the beginning and end of the algorithm, the primary purpose of the key is to generate the S-boxes. These S-boxes are secret and, in essence, part of the key. Khufu calls for a total key size of 512 bits (64 bytes) and gives an algorithm for generating S-boxes from the key. The number of rounds for the algorithm is left open. Merkle mentioned that 8-round Khufu is susceptible to a chosen-plaintext attack and recommended 16, 24, or 32 rounds [1071]. (He restricted the choice of rounds to a multiple of eight.)

Because Khufu has key-dependent and secret S-boxes, it is resistant to differential cryptanalysis. There is a differential attack against 16-round Khufu that recovers the key after 2^{31} chosen plaintexts [611], but it cannot be extended to more rounds. If brute-force is the best way to attack Khufu, it is impressively secure. A 512-bit key gives a complexity of 2^{512}—inconceivable under any circumstances.

Khafre

Khafre is the second of two cryptosystems proposed by Merkle [1071]. (Khufu and Khafre are names of Egyptian pharaohs.) It is similar in design to Khufu, except that it was designed for applications without precomputation time. The S-boxes are not key-dependent. Instead, Khafre uses fixed S-boxes. And the key is XORed with the encryption block not only before the first round and after the last round, but also after every 8 rounds of encryption.

Merkle speculated that key sizes of 64- or 128-bits would be used for Khafre and that more rounds of encryption would be required for Khafre than for Khufu. This, combined with the fact that each round of Khafre is more complex than for Khufu, makes Khafre slower. In compensation, Khafre does not require any precomputation and will encrypt small amounts of data more quickly.

In 1990 Biham and Shamir turned their differential cryptanalysis techniques against Khafre [170]. They were able to break 16-round Khafre with a chosen-plaintext attack using about 1500 different encryptions. It took about an hour, using their personal computer. Converting that to a known-plaintext attack would require about 2^{38} encryptions. Khafre with 24 rounds can be broken by a chosen-plaintext attack using 2^{53} encryptions, and a known-plaintext attack using 2^{59} encryptions.

Patents

Both Khufu and Khafre are patented [1072]. Source code for the algorithms are in the patent. Anyone interested in licensing either or both algorithms should contact Director of Licensing, Xerox Corporation, P.O. Box 1600, Stamford, CT, 06904-1600.

13.8 RC2

RC2 is a variable-key-size encryption algorithm designed by Ron Rivest for RSA Data Security, Inc. (RSADSI). Apparently, "RC" stands for "Ron's Code," although it officially stands for "Rivest Cipher." (RC3 was broken at RSADSI during development; RC1 never got further than Rivest's notebook.) It is proprietary, and its details have not been published. Don't think for a minute that this helps security. RC2 has already appeared in commercial products. As far as I know, RC2 has not been patented and is only protected as a trade secret.

RC2 is a variable-key-size 64-bit block cipher, designed to be a replacement for DES. According to the company, software implementations of RC2 are three times faster than DES. The algorithm accepts a variable-length key, from 0 bytes to the maximum string length the computer system supports; encryption speed is independent of key size. This key is preprocessed to yield a key-dependent table of 128 bytes. So the number of effectively different keys is 2^{1024}. RC2 has no S-boxes [805]; the two operations are "mix" and "mash," and one is chosen in each round. According to their literature [1334]:

> ... RC2 is not an iterative block cipher. This suggests that RC2 offers more protection against differential and linear cryptanalysis than other block ciphers which have relied for their security on copying the design of DES.

RSADSI's refusal to make RC2 public casts doubt on their claims. They are willing to provide details of the algorithm to most anyone willing to sign a nondisclosure agreement, and have claimed to allow cryptanalysts to publish any negative results they find. I don't know of any cryptanalyst outside the employ of the company who studied it, since it would amount to doing their analysis work for them.

Still, Ron Rivest is not the usual snake-oil peddler. He's a respected and competent cryptographer. I would put a fair degree of trust in the algorithm, even though I haven't personally inspected the code. RC4, once the proprietary intellectual property of RSADSI, was posted to the Internet (see Section 17.1), and it's probably just a matter of time before RC2 is posted as well.

An agreement between the Software Publishers Association (SPA) and the U.S. government gave RC2 and RC4 (see Section 17.1) special export status (see Section 25.14). Products that implement one of these two algorithms have a much simpler export approval process, provided that the keys are no more than 40 bits long.

Is a 40-bit key enough? There are a total of one trillion possible keys. Assuming that brute force is the most efficient method of cryptanalysis (a big assumption, considering that the algorithm has never been published), and assuming that a brute-force cryptanalysis chip can test one million keys per second, it will take him 12.7 days to find the correct key. One thousand machines working in parallel can produce the key in twenty minutes.

RSA Data Security, Inc., maintains that while encryption and decryption are quick, exhaustive key search is not. A significant amount of time is spent setting up the key schedule. While this time is negligible when encrypting and decrypting messages, it is not when trying every possible key.

The U.S. government would never allow export of any algorithm it couldn't, at least in theory, break. They could create a magnetic tape or CD of a specific plaintext block encrypted with every possible key. To break a given message, they could just run the tape and compare the ciphertext blocks in the message with the ciphertext blocks on the tape. If there is a match, they could try the candidate key and see if the message makes any sense. If they choose a common plaintext block (all zeros, the ASCII characters for a space, etc.), this method should work. The storage requirement for a 64-bit plaintext block encrypted with all 10^{12} possible keys is 8 terabytes—certainly possible.

For information on licensing RC2, contact RSADSI (see Section 25.4).

13.9 IDEA

The first incarnation of the IDEA cipher, by Xuejia Lai and James Massey, surfaced in 1990 [929]. It was called PES (Proposed Encryption Standard). The next year, after Biham and Shamir's demonstrated differential cryptanalysis, the authors strengthened their cipher against the attack and called the new algorithm IPES (Improved Proposed Encryption Standard) [931,924]. IPES changed its name to IDEA (International Data Encryption Algorithm) in 1992 [925].

IDEA is based on some impressive theoretical foundations and, although cryptanalysis has made some progress against reduced-round variants, the algorithm still seems strong. In my opinion, it is the best and most secure block algorithm available to the public at this time.

The future of IDEA is not yet clear. There has been no rush to adopt it as a replacement to DES, partly because it is patented and must be licensed for commercial applications, and partly because people are still waiting to see how well the algorithm fares during the coming years of cryptanalysis. Its current claim to fame is that it is part of PGP (see Section 24.12).

Overview of IDEA

IDEA is a block cipher; it operates on 64-bit plaintext blocks. The key is 128 bits long. The same algorithm is used for both encryption and decryption.

As with all the other block ciphers we've seen, IDEA uses both confusion and diffusion. The design philosophy behind the algorithm is one of "mixing operations from different algebraic groups." Three algebraic groups are being mixed, and they are all easily implemented in both hardware and software:

— XOR
— Addition modulo 2^{16}
— Multiplication modulo $2^{16} + 1$. (This operation can be viewed as IDEA's S-box.)

All these operations (and these are the only operations in the algorithm—there are no bit-level permutations) operate on 16-bit sub-blocks. This algorithm is even efficient on 16-bit processors.

Description of IDEA

Figure 13.9 is an overview of IDEA. The 64-bit data block is divided into four 16-bit sub-blocks: X_1, X_2, X_3, and X_4. These four sub-blocks become the input to the first round of the algorithm. There are eight rounds total. In each round the four sub-blocks are XORed, added, and multiplied with one another and with six 16-bit sub-keys. Between rounds, the second and third sub-blocks are swapped. Finally, the four sub-blocks are combined with four subkeys in an output transformation.

In each round, the sequence of events is as follows:

(1) Multiply X_1 and the first subkey.
(2) Add X_2 and the second subkey.
(3) Add X_3 and the third subkey.
(4) Multiply X_4 and the fourth subkey.
(5) XOR the results of steps (1) and (3).
(6) XOR the results of steps (2) and (4).
(7) Multiply the results of step (5) with the fifth subkey.
(8) Add the results of steps (6) and (7).
(9) Multiply the results of step (8) with the sixth subkey.
(10) Add the results of steps (7) and (9).

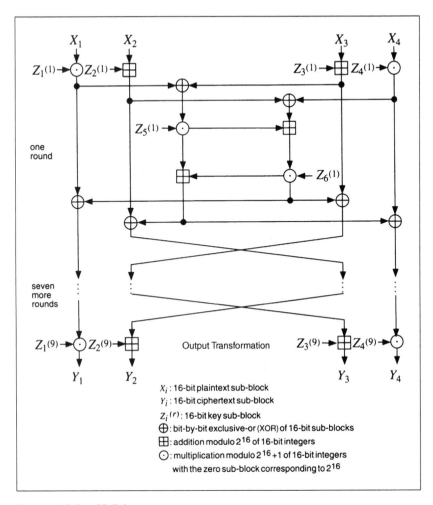

Figure 13.9   IDEA.

(11) XOR the results of steps (1) and (9).

(12) XOR the results of steps (3) and (9).

(13) XOR the results of steps (2) and (10).

(14) XOR the results of steps (4) and (10).

The output of the round is the four sub-blocks that are the results of steps (11), (12), (13), and (14). Swap the two inner blocks (except for the last round) and that's the input to the next round.

After the eighth round, there is a final output transformation:

(1) Multiply X_1 and the first subkey.

(2) Add X_2 and the second subkey.

(3) Add X_3 and the third subkey.

(4) Multiply X_4 and the fourth subkey.

Finally, the four sub-blocks are reattached to produce the ciphertext.

Creating the subkeys is also easy. The algorithm uses 52 of them (six for each of the eight rounds and four more for the output transformation). First, the 128-bit key is divided into eight 16-bit subkeys. These are the first eight subkeys for the algorithm (the six for the first round, and the first two for the second round). Then, the key is rotated 25 bits to the left and again divided into eight subkeys. The first four are used in round 2; the last four are used in round 3. The key is rotated another 25 bits to the left for the next eight subkeys, and so on until the end of the algorithm.

Decryption is exactly the same, except that the subkeys are reversed and slightly different. The decryption subkeys are either the additive or multiplicative inverses of the encryption subkeys. (For the purposes of IDEA, the all-zero sub-block is considered to represent $2^{16} = -1$ for multiplication modulo $2^{16} + 1$; thus the multiplicative inverse of 0 is 0.) Calculating these takes some doing, but you only have to do it once for each decryption key. Table 13.4 shows the encryption subkeys and the corresponding decryption subkeys.

Speed of IDEA

Current software implementations of IDEA are about twice as fast as DES. IDEA on a 33 megahertz 386 machine encrypts data at 880 kilobits per second, and 2400 kilobits per second on a 66 megahertz 486 machine. You might think IDEA should be faster, but multiplications aren't cheap. To multiply two 32-bit numbers on a 486 requires 40 clock cycles (10 on a Pentium).

A VLSI implementation of PES encrypts data at 55 megabits per second at 25 megahertz [208,398]. Another VLSI chip developed at ETH Zurich, consisting of 251,000 transistors on a chip 107.8 square millimeters, encrypts data using the

Table 13.4
IDEA Encryption and Decryption Subkeys

Round	Encryption Subkeys	Decryption Subkeys
1st	$Z_1^{(1)}\, Z_2^{(1)}\, Z_3^{(1)}\, Z_4^{(1)}\, Z_5^{(1)}\, Z_6^{(1)}$	$Z_1^{(9)-1}\, -Z_2^{(9)}\, -Z_3^{(9)}\, Z_4^{(9)-1}\, Z_5^{(8)}\, Z_6^{(8)}$
2nd	$Z_1^{(2)}\, Z_2^{(2)}\, Z_3^{(2)}\, Z_4^{(2)}\, Z_5^{(2)}\, Z_6^{(2)}$	$Z_1^{(8)-1}\, -Z_3^{(8)}\, -Z_2^{(8)}\, Z_4^{(8)-1}\, Z_5^{(7)}\, Z_6^{(7)}$
3rd	$Z_1^{(3)}\, Z_2^{(3)}\, Z_3^{(3)}\, Z_4^{(3)}\, Z_5^{(3)}\, Z_6^{(3)}$	$Z_1^{(7)-1}\, -Z_3^{(7)}\, -Z_2^{(7)}\, Z_4^{(7)-1}\, Z_5^{(6)}\, Z_6^{(6)}$
4th	$Z_1^{(4)}\, Z_2^{(4)}\, Z_3^{(4)}\, Z_4^{(4)}\, Z_5^{(4)}\, Z_6^{(4)}$	$Z_1^{(6)-1}\, -Z_3^{(6)}\, -Z_2^{(6)}\, Z_4^{(6)-1}\, Z_5^{(5)}\, Z_6^{(5)}$
5th	$Z_1^{(5)}\, Z_2^{(5)}\, Z_3^{(5)}\, Z_4^{(5)}\, Z_5^{(5)}\, Z_6^{(5)}$	$Z_1^{(5)-1}\, -Z_3^{(5)}\, -Z_2^{(5)}\, Z_4^{(5)-1}\, Z_5^{(4)}\, Z_6^{(4)}$
6th	$Z_1^{(6)}\, Z_2^{(6)}\, Z_3^{(6)}\, Z_4^{(6)}\, Z_5^{(6)}\, Z_6^{(6)}$	$Z_1^{(4)-1}\, -Z_3^{(4)}\, -Z_2^{(4)}\, Z_4^{(4)-1}\, Z_5^{(3)}\, Z_6^{(3)}$
7th	$Z_1^{(7)}\, Z_2^{(7)}\, Z_3^{(7)}\, Z_4^{(7)}\, Z_5^{(7)}\, Z_6^{(7)}$	$Z_1^{(3)-1}\, -Z_3^{(3)}\, -Z_2^{(3)}\, Z_4^{(3)-1}\, Z_5^{(2)}\, Z_6^{(2)}$
8th	$Z_1^{(8)}\, Z_2^{(8)}\, Z_3^{(8)}\, Z_4^{(8)}\, Z_5^{(8)}\, Z_6^{(8)}$	$Z_1^{(2)-1}\, -Z_3^{(2)}\, -Z_2^{(2)}\, Z_4^{(2)-1}\, Z_5^{(1)}\, Z_6^{(1)}$
output transformation	$Z_1^{(9)}\, Z_2^{(9)}\, Z_3^{(9)}\, Z_4^{(9)}$	$Z_1^{(1)-1}\, -Z_2^{(1)}\, -Z_3^{(1)}\, Z_4^{(1)-1}$

IDEA algorithm at a 177 megabit-per-second data rate when clocked at 25 megahertz [926,207,397].

Cryptanalysis of IDEA

IDEA's key length is 128 bits—over twice as long as DES. Assuming that a brute-force attack is the most efficient, it would require 2^{128} (10^{38}) encryptions to recover the key. Design a chip that can test a billion keys per second and throw a billion of them at the problem, and it will still take 10^{13} years—that's longer than the age of the universe. An array of 10^{24} such chips can find the key in a day, but there aren't enough silicon atoms in the universe to build such a machine. Now we're getting somewhere—although I'd keep my eye on the dark matter debate.

Perhaps brute force isn't the best way to attack IDEA. The algorithm is still too new for any definitive cryptanalytic results. The designers have done their best to make the algorithm immune to differential cryptanalysis; they defined the concept of a Markov cipher and showed that resistance to differential cryptanalysis can be modeled and quantified [931,925]. (Figure 13.10 shows the original PES algorithm to be contrasted with the IDEA algorithm of Figure 13.9 which was strengthened against differential cryptanalysis. It's amazing how a few subtle changes can make such a big difference.) In [925], Lai argued (he gave evidence, not a proof) that IDEA is immune to differential cryptanalysis after only 4 of its 8 rounds. According to Biham, his related-key cryptanalytic attack doesn't work against IDEA, either [160].

Willi Meier examined the three algebraic operations of IDEA, and pointed out that while they are incompatible, there are instances where they can be simplified in such a way as to facilitate cryptanalysis some percentage of the time [1050]. His attack is more efficient than brute-force for 2-round IDEA (2^{42} operations), but less efficient for 3-round IDEA or higher. Normal IDEA, with 8 rounds, is safe.

Joan Daemen discovered a class of weak keys for IDEA [406,409]. These are not weak keys in the sense of the DES weak keys; that is, the encryption function is self-inverse. They are weak in the sense that if they are used, an attacker can easily identify them in a chosen-plaintext attack. For example, a weak key is (in hex):

$$0000,0000,0x00,0000,0000,000x,xxxx,x000$$

The number at the positions of "*x*" can be any number. If this key is used, the bit-wise XOR of certain plaintext pairs guarantees the bit-wise XOR of the resultant ciphertext pairs.

In any case, the chance of accidentally generating one of these weak keys is very small: one in 2^{96}. There is no danger if you choose keys at random. And it is easy to modify IDEA so that it doesn't have any weak keys: XOR every subkey with the value 0x0dae [409].

I know of no other cryptanalytic results against IDEA, although many people have tried.

IDEA Modes of Operation and Variants

IDEA can work within any block cipher mode discussed in Chapter 9. Any double-IDEA implementation would be susceptible to the same meet-in-the-middle

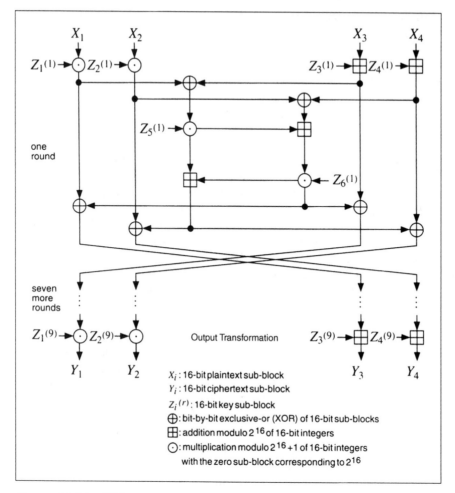

Figure 13.10 PES.

attack as DES (see Section 15.1). However, because IDEA's key length is more than double DES's, the attack is impractical. It would require a storage space of $64*2^{128}$ bits, or 10^{39} bytes. Maybe there's enough matter in the universe to create a memory device that large, but I doubt it.

If you're worried about parallel universes as well, use a triple-IDEA implementation (see Section 15.2):

$$C = E_{K_3}(D_{K_2}(E_{K_1}(P)))$$

It is immune to the meet-in-the-middle attack.

There's also no reason why you can't implement IDEA with independent subkeys, especially if you have key-management tools to handle the longer key. IDEA needs a total of 52 16-bit keys, for a total key length of 832 bits. This variant is definitely more secure, but no one knows by how much.

A naïve variation might double the block size. The algorithm would work just as well with 32-bit sub-blocks instead of 16-bit sub-blocks, and a 256-bit key. Encryption would be quicker and security would increase 2^{32} times. Or would it? The theory behind the algorithm hinges on the fact that $2^{16} + 1$ is prime; $2^{32} + 1$ is not. Perhaps the algorithm could be modified to work, but it would have very different security properties. Lai says it would be difficult to make it work [926].

While IDEA appears to be significantly more secure than DES, it isn't always easy to substitute one for the other in an existing application. If your database and message templates are hardwired to accept a 64-bit key, it may be impossible to implement IDEA's 128-bit key.

For those applications, generate a 128-bit key by concatenating the 64-bit key with itself. Remember that IDEA is weakened considerably by this modification.

If you are more concerned with speed than security, you might consider a variant of IDEA with fewer rounds. Currently the best attack against IDEA is faster than brute force only for 2.5 rounds or less [1050]; 4 round IDEA would be twice as fast and, as far as I know, just as secure.

Caveat Emptor

IDEA is a relatively new algorithm, and many questions remain. Is IDEA a group? (Lai thinks not [926].) Are there any still-undiscovered ways of breaking this cipher? IDEA has a firm theoretical basis, but time and time again secure-looking algorithms have fallen to new forms of cryptanalysis. Several academic and military groups have cryptanalyzed IDEA. None of them has gone public about any successes they might have had. One might—someday.

Patents and Licenses

IDEA is patented in Europe and the United States [1012,1013]. The patent is held by Ascom-Tech AG. No license fee is required for non-commercial use. Commercial users interested in licensing the algorithm should contact Ascom Systec AG, Dept CMVV, Gewerbepark, CH-5506, Mägenwil, Switzerland; +41 64 56 59 83; Fax: +41 64 56 59 90; idea@ascom.ch.

13.10 MMB

A complaint against IDEA, that it uses a 64-bit encryption block, was addressed by Joan Daemen in an algorithm called MMB (Modular Multiplication-based Block cipher) [385,405,406]. MMB is based on the same basic theory as IDEA: mixing operations of different algebraic groups. MMB is an iterative algorithm that mainly consists of linear steps (XOR and key applications) and the parallel applications of four large nonlinear invertible substitutions. These substitutions are determined by a multiplication modulo $2^{32} - 1$ with constant factors. The result is an algorithm that has both a 128-bit key and a 128-bit block size.

MMB operates on 32-bit sub-blocks of text (x_0, x_1, x_2, x_3) and 32-bit sub-blocks of key (k_0, k_1, k_2, k_3). This makes the algorithm well suited for implementation on modern, 32-bit processors. A nonlinear function, f, is applied six times alternating with XORing. Here it is (all index operations are mod 4):

$$x_i = x_i \oplus k_i, \text{ for } i = 0 \text{ to } 3$$
$$f(x_0, x_1, x_2, x_3)$$
$$x_i = x_i \oplus k_{i+1}, \text{ for } i = 0 \text{ to } 3$$
$$f(x_0, x_1, x_2, x_3)$$
$$x_i = x_i \oplus k_{i+2}, \text{ for } i = 0 \text{ to } 3$$
$$f(x_0, x_1, x_2, x_3)$$
$$x_i = x_i \oplus k_i, \text{ for } i = 0 \text{ to } 3$$
$$f(x_0, x_1, x_2, x_3)$$
$$x_i = x_i \oplus k_{i+1}, \text{ for } i = 0 \text{ to } 3$$
$$f(x_0, x_1, x_2, x_3)$$
$$x_i = x_i \oplus k_{i+2}, \text{ for } i = 0 \text{ to } 3$$
$$f(x_0, x_1, x_2, x_3)$$

The function f has three steps:

(1) $x_i = c_i * x_i$, for $i = 0$ to 3 (If the input to the multiplication is all 1s, the output is also all 1s.)

(2) If the least significant bit of $x_0 = 1$, then $x_0 = x_0 \oplus C$. If the least significant byte of $x_3 = 0$, then $x_3 = x_3 \oplus C$.

(3) $x_i = x_{i-1} \oplus x_i \oplus x_{i+1}$, for $i = 0$ to 3

All index operations are mod 4. The multiplication operation in step (1) is modulo $2^{32} - 1$. For the purposes of the algorithm, if the second operand is $2^{32} - 1$, then the result is $2^{32} - 1$. The various constants are:

$$C = \text{2aaaaaaa}$$
$$c_0 = \text{025f1cdb}$$
$$c_1 = 2 * c_0$$
$$c_2 = 2^3 * c_0$$
$$c_3 = 2^7 * c_0$$

The constant C is the "simplest" constant with a high ternary weight, a least-significant bit of zero, and no circular symmetry. The constant c_0 has certain other characteristics. The constants c_1, c_2, and c_3 are shifted versions of c_0, preventing attacks based on symmetry. See [405] for more details.

Decryption is the reverse process. Steps (2) and (3) are their own inverse. Step (1) uses c_i^{-1} instead of c_i. The value of c_0^{-1} is 0dad4694.

Security of MMB

The design of MMB ensures that each round has considerable diffusion independent of the key. In IDEA, the amount of diffusion is to some extent dependent on the particular subkeys. MMB was also designed not to have any weak keys as IDEA has.

MMB is dead [402]. Although no cryptanalysis has been published, this is true for several reasons. First, it was not designed to be resistant to linear cryptanalysis. The multiplication factors were chosen to be resistant to differential cryptanalysis, but the algorithm's authors were unaware of linear cryptanalysis.

Second, Eli Biham has an effective chosen-key attack [160], which exploits the fact that all rounds are identical and that the key schedule is just a cyclic shift by 32 bits. Third, even though MMB would be very efficient in software, the algorithm would be less efficient than DES in hardware.

Daemen suggests that anyone interested in improving MMB should first do an analysis of modular multiplication with respect to linear cryptanalysis and choose a new multiplication factor, and then make the constant C different for each round [402]. Then, improve the key scheduling by adding constants to the round keys to remove the bias. He's not going to do it; he designed 3-Way instead (see Section 14.5).

13.11   CA-1.1

CA is a block cipher built on cellular automata, designed by Howard Gutowitz [677,678,679]. It encrypts plaintext in 384-bit blocks and has a 1088-bit key (it's really two keys, a 1024-bit key and a 64-bit key). Because of the nature of cellular automata, the algorithm is most efficient when implemented in massively parallel integrated circuits.

CA-1.1 uses both reversible and irreversible cellular automaton rules. Under a reversible rule, each state of the lattice comes from a unique predecessor state, while under an irreversible rule, each state can have many predecessor states. During encryption, irreversible rules are iterated backward in time. To go backward from a given state, one of the possible predecessor states is selected at random. This process can be repeated many times. Backward iteration thus serves to mix random information with the message information. CA-1.1 uses a particular kind of partially linear irreversible rule, which is such that a random predecessor state for any given state can be rapidly built. Reversible rules are also used for some stages of encryption.

The reversible rules (simple parallel permutations on sub-blocks of the state) are nonlinear. The irreversible rules are derived entirely from information in the key, while the reversible rules depend both on key information and on the random information inserted during the stages of encryption with irreversible rules.

CA-1.1 is built around a block-link structure. That is, the processing of the message block is partially segregated from the processing of the stream of random information inserted during encryption. This random information serves to link stages of encryption together. It can also be used to chain together a ciphertext stream. The information in the link is generated as part of encryption.

Because CA-1.1 is a new algorithm, it is too early to make any pronouncements on its security. Gutowitz discusses some possible attacks, including differential cryptanalysis, but is unable to break the algorithm. As an incentive, Gutowitz has offered a $1000 prize to "the first person who develops a tractable procedure to break CA-1.1."

CA-1.1 is patented [678], but is available free for non-commercial use. Anyone interested in either licensing the algorithm or in the cryptanalysis prize should contact Howard Gutowitz, ESPCI, Laboratoire d'Électronique, 10 rue Vauquelin, 75005 Paris, France.

13.12 SKIPJACK

Skipjack is the NSA-developed encryption algorithm for the Clipper and Capstone chips (see Sections 24.16 and 24.17). Since the algorithm is classified Secret, its details have never been published. It will only be implemented in tamperproof hardware.

The algorithm is classified Secret, not because that enhances its security, but because the NSA doesn't want Skipjack being used without the Clipper key-escrow mechanism. They don't want the algorithm implemented in software and spread around the world.

Is Skipjack secure? If the NSA wants to produce a secure algorithm, they presumably can. On the other hand, if the NSA wants to design an algorithm with a trapdoor, they can do that as well.

Here's what has been published [1154,462].

— It's an iterative block cipher.
— The block size is 64 bits.
— It has an 80-bit key.
— It can be used in ECB, CBC, 64-bit OFB, or 1-, 8-, 16-, 32- or 64-bit CFB modes.
— There are 32 rounds of processing per single encrypt or decrypt operation.
— NSA started the design in 1985 and completed the evaluation in 1990.

The documentation for the Mykotronx Clipper chip says that the latency for the Skipjack algorithm is 64 clock cycles. This means that each round consists of two clock cycles: presumably one for the S-box substitution and another for the final XOR at the end of the round. (Remember: permutations take no time in hardware.) The Mykotronx documentation calls this two-clock-cycle operation a "G-box," and the whole thing a "shift." (Some part of the G-box is called an "F-table," probably a table of constants but maybe a table of functions.)

I heard a rumor that Skipjack uses 16 S-boxes, and another that the total memory requirement for storing the S-boxes is 128 bytes. It is unlikely that both of these rumors are true.

Another rumor implies that Skipjack's rounds, unlike DES's, do not operate on half of the block size. This, combined with the notion of "shifts," an inadvertent statement made at Crypto '94 that Skipjack has "a 48-bit internal structure," implies that it is similar in design to SHA (see Section 18.7) but with four 16-bit sub-blocks: three sub-blocks go through a key-dependent one-way function to produce

16 bits, which are XORed with the remaining sub-block; then the whole block is circularly shifted 16 bits to become the input to the next round, or shift. This also implies 128 bytes of S-box data. I suspect that the S-boxes are key-dependent.

The structure of Skipjack is probably similar to DES. The NSA realizes that their tamperproof hardware will be reverse-engineered eventually; they won't risk any advanced cryptographic techniques.

The fact that the NSA is planning to use the Skipjack algorithm to encrypt their Defense Messaging System (DMS) implies that the algorithm is secure. To convince the skeptics, NIST allowed a panel of "respected experts from outside the government . . . access to the confidential details of the algorithm to assess its capabilities and publicly report its findings" [812].

The preliminary report of these experts [262] (there never was a final report, and probably never will be) concluded that:

> Under an assumption that the cost of processing power is halved every 18 months, it will be 36 years before the difficulty of breaking Skipjack by exhaustive search will be equal to the difficulty of breaking DES today. Thus, there is no significant risk that Skipjack will be broken by exhaustive search in the next 30–40 years.
>
> There is no significant risk that Skipjack can be broken through a shortcut method of attack, including differential cryptanalysis. There are no weak keys; there is no complementation property. The experts, not having time to evaluate the algorithm to any great extent, instead evaluated NSA's own design and evaluation process.
>
> The strength of Skipjack against a cryptanalytic attack does not depend on the secrecy of the algorithm.

Of course, the panelists did not look at the algorithm long enough to come to any conclusions themselves. All they could do was to look at the results that the NSA showed to them.

One unanswered question is whether the Skipjack keyspace is flat (see Section 8.2). Even if Skipjack has no weak keys in the DES sense, some artifact of the key-scheduling process could make some keys stronger than others. Skipjack could have 2^{70} strong keys, far more than DES; the odds of choosing one of those strong keys at random would still be about 1 in 1000. Personally, I think the Skipjack keyspace is flat, but the fact that no one has ever said this publicly is worrisome.

Skipjack is patented, but the patent is being withheld from distribution by a patent secrecy agreement [1122]. The patent will only be issued when and if the Skipjack algorithm is successfully reverse-engineered. This gives the government the best of both worlds: the protection of a patent and the confidentiality of a trade secret.

CHAPTER 14

Still Other Block Ciphers

14.1 GOST

GOST is a block algorithm from the former Soviet Union [655,1393]. "GOST" is an acronym for "Gosudarstvennyi Standard," or Government Standard, sort of similar to a FIPS, except that it can (and does) refer to just about any kind of standard. (Actually, the full name is Gosudarstvennyi Standard Soyuza SSR, or Government Standard of the Union of Soviet Socialist Republics.) This standard is number 28147-89. The Government Committee for Standards of the USSR authorized the standard, whoever they were.

I don't know whether GOST 28147-89 was used for classified traffic or just for civilian encryption. A remark at its beginning states that the algorithm "satisfies all cryptographic requirements and not limits the grade of information to be protected." I have heard claims that it was initially used for very high-grade communications, including classified military communications, but I have no confirmation.

Description of GOST

GOST is a 64-bit block algorithm with a 256-bit key. GOST also has some additional key material that will be discussed later. The algorithm iterates a simple encryption algorithm for 32 rounds.

To encrypt, first break the text up into a left half, L, and a right half, R. The subkey for round i is K_i. A round, i, of GOST is:

$$L_i = R_{i-1}$$
$$R_i = L_{i-1} \oplus f(R_{i-1}, K_i)$$

Figure 14.1 is a single round of GOST. Function f is straightforward. First, the right half and the ith subkey are added modulo 2^{32}. The result is broken into eight 4-bit chunks, and each chunk becomes the input to a different S-box. There are eight different S-boxes in GOST; the first 4 bits go into the first S-box, the second 4 bits go

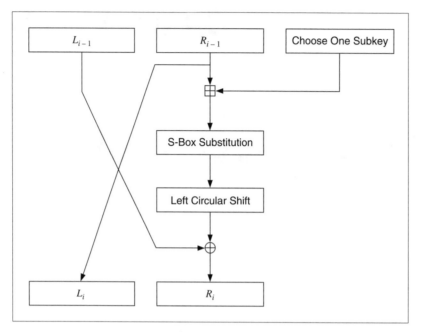

Figure 14.1   One round of GOST.

into the second S-box, and so on. Each S-box is a permutation of the numbers 0 through 15. For example, an S-box might be:

$$7, 10, 2, 4, 15, 9, 0, 3, 6, 12, 5, 13, 1, 8, 11$$

In this case, if the input to the S-box is 0, the output is 7. If the input is 1, the output is 10, and so on. All eight S-boxes are different; these are considered additional key material. The S-boxes are to be kept secret.

The outputs of the eight S-boxes are recombined into a 32-bit word, then the entire word undergoes an 11-bit left circular shift. Finally, the result XORed to the left half to become the new right half, and the right half becomes the new left half. Do this 32 times and you're done.

The subkeys are generated simply. The 256-bit key is divided into eight 32-bit blocks: $k_1, k_2, \ldots, k_8$. Each round uses a different subkey, as shown in Table 14.1. Decryption is the same as encryption with the order of the k_is reversed.

The GOST standard does not discuss how to generate the S-boxes, only that they are somehow supplied [655]. This has led to speculation that some Soviet organization would supply good S-boxes to those organizations it liked and bad S-boxes to those organizations it wished to eavesdrop on. This may very well be true, but further conversations with a GOST chip manufacturer within Russia offered another alternative. He generated the S-box permutations himself, using a random-number generator.

Table 14.1
Use of GOST Subkeys in Different Rounds

Round:	1	2	3	4	5	6	7	8	9	10	11	12	13	14	15	16
Subkey:	1	2	3	4	5	6	7	8	1	2	3	4	5	6	7	8
Round:	17	18	19	20	21	22	23	24	25	26	27	28	29	30	31	32
Subkey:	1	2	3	4	5	6	7	8	8	7	6	5	4	3	2	1

More recently, a set of S-boxes used in an application for the Central Bank of the Russian Federation surfaced. These S-boxes are also used in the GOST one-way hash function (see section 18.11) [657]. They are listed in Table 14.2.

Cryptanalysis of GOST

These are the major differences between DES and GOST.

— DES has a complicated procedure for generating the subkeys from the keys. GOST has a very simple procedure.

— DES has a 56-bit key; GOST has a 256-bit key. If you add in the secret S-box permutations, GOST has a total of about 610 bits of secret information.

Table 14.2
GOST S-Boxes

S-box 1:

4	10	9	2	13	8	0	14	6	11	1	12	7	15	5	3

S-box 2:

14	11	4	12	6	13	15	10	2	3	8	1	0	7	5	9

S-box 3:

5	8	1	13	10	3	4	2	14	15	12	7	6	0	9	11

S-box 4:

7	13	10	1	0	8	9	15	14	4	6	12	11	2	5	3

S-box 5:

6	12	7	1	5	15	13	8	4	10	9	14	0	3	11	2

S-box 6:

4	11	10	0	7	2	1	13	3	6	8	5	9	12	15	14

S-box 7:

13	11	4	1	3	15	5	9	0	10	14	7	6	8	2	12

S-box 8:

1	15	13	0	5	7	10	4	9	2	3	14	6	11	8	12

— The S-boxes in DES have 6-bit inputs and 4-bit outputs; the S-boxes in GOST have 4-bit inputs and outputs. Both algorithms have eight S-boxes, but an S-box in GOST is one-fourth the size of an S-box in DES.

— DES has an irregular permutation, called a P-box; GOST uses an 11-bit left circular shift.

— DES has 16 rounds; GOST has 32 rounds.

If there is no better way to break GOST other than brute force, it is a very secure algorithm. GOST has a 256-bit key—longer if you count the secret S-boxes. Against differential and linear cryptanalysis, GOST is probably stronger than DES. Although the random S-boxes in GOST are probably weaker than the fixed S-boxes in DES, their secrecy adds to GOST's resistance against differential and linear attacks. Also, both of these attacks depend on the number of rounds: the more rounds, the more difficult the attack. GOST has twice as many rounds as DES; this alone probably makes both differential and linear cryptanalysis infeasible.

The other parts of GOST are either on par or worse than DES. GOST doesn't have the same expansion permutation that DES has. Deleting this permutation from DES weakens it by reducing the avalanche effect; it is reasonable to believe that GOST is weaker for not having it. GOST's use of addition instead is no less secure than DES's XOR.

The greatest difference between them seems to be GOST's cyclic shift instead of a permutation. The DES permutation increases the avalanche effect. In GOST a change in one input bit affects one S-box in one round, which then affects two S-boxes in the next round, three the round after that, and so on. GOST requires 8 rounds before a single change in an input affects every output bit; DES only requires 5 rounds. This is certainly a weakness. But remember: GOST has 32 rounds to DES's 16.

GOST's designers tried to achieve a balance between efficiency and security. They modified DES's basic design to create an algorithm that is better suited for software implementation. They seem to have been less sure of their algorithm's security, and have tried to compensate by making the key length very large, keeping the S-boxes secret, and doubling the number of iterations. Whether their efforts have resulted in an algorithm more secure than DES remains to be seen.

14.2 CAST

CAST was designed in Canada by Carlisle Adams and Stafford Tavares [10,7]. They claim that the name refers to their design procedure and should conjure up images of randomness, but note the authors' initials. The example CAST algorithm uses a 64-bit block size and a 64-bit key.

The structure of CAST should be familiar. The algorithm uses six S-boxes with an 8-bit input and a 32-bit output. Construction of these S-boxes is implementation-dependent and complicated; see the references for details.

To encrypt, first divide the plaintext block into a left half and a right half. The algorithm has 8 rounds. In each round the right half is combined with some key material using function f and then XORed with the left half to form the new right half. The original right half (before the round) becomes the new left half. After 8 rounds (don't switch the left and right halves after the eighth round), the two halves are concatenated to form the ciphertext.

Function f is simple:

(1)   Divide the 32-bit input into four 8-bit quarters: a, b, c, d.

(2)   Divide the 16-bit subkey into two 8-bit halves: e, f.

(3)   Process a through S-box 1, b through S-box 2, c through S-box 3, d through S-box 4, e through S-box 5, and f through S-box 6.

(4)   XOR the six S-box outputs together to get the final 32-bit output.

Alternatively, the 32-bit input can be XORed with 32 bits of key, divided into four 8-bit quarters, processed through the S-boxes, and then XORed together [7]. N rounds of this appears to be as secure as $N + 2$ rounds of the other option.

The 16-bit subkey for each round is easily calculated from the 64-bit key. If k_1, $k_2, \ldots, k_8$ are the 8 bytes of the key, then the subkeys for each round are:

Round 1: k_1, k_2

Round 2: k_3, k_4

Round 3: k_5, k_6

Round 4: k_7, k_8

Round 5: k_4, k_3

Round 6: k_2, k_1

Round 7: k_8, k_7

Round 8: k_6, k_5

The strength of this algorithm lies in its S-boxes. CAST does not have fixed S-boxes; new ones are constructed for each application. Design criteria are in [10]; bent functions are the S-box columns, selected for a number of desirable S-box properties (see Section 14.10). Once a set of S-boxes has been constructed for a given implementation of CAST, they are fixed for all time. The S-boxes are implementation-dependent, but not key-dependent.

It was shown in [10] that CAST is resistant to differential cryptanalysis and in [728] that CAST is resistant to linear cryptanalysis. There is no known way to break CAST other than brute force.

Northern Telecom is using CAST in their Entrust security software package for Macintoshes, PCs, and UNIX workstations. The particular S-boxes they chose are not public. The Canadian government is evaluating CAST as a new encryption standard. CAST is patent-pending.

14.3 BLOWFISH

Blowfish is an algorithm of my own design, intended for implementation on large microprocessors [1388,1389]. The algorithm is unpatented, and the C code in the back of this book is in the public domain. I designed Blowfish to meet the following design criteria.

1. Fast. Blowfish encrypts data on 32-bit microprocessors at a rate of 26 clock cycles per byte.
2. Compact. Blowfish can run in less than 5K of memory.
3. Simple. Blowfish uses only simple operations: addition, XORs, and table lookups on 32-bit operands. Its design is easy to analyze which makes it resistant to implementation errors [1391].
4. Variably Secure. Blowfish's key length is variable and can be as long as 448 bits.

Blowfish is optimized for applications where the key does not change often, like a communications link or an automatic file encryptor. It is significantly faster than DES when implemented on 32-bit microprocessors with large data caches, such as the Pentium and the PowerPC. Blowfish is not suitable for applications, such as packet switching, with frequent key changes, or as a one-way hash function. Its large memory requirement makes it infeasible for smart card applications.

Description of Blowfish

Blowfish is a 64-bit block cipher with a variable-length key. The algorithm consists of two parts: key expansion and data encryption. Key expansion converts a key of up to 448 bits into several subkey arrays totaling 4168 bytes.

Data encryption consists of a simple function iterated 16 times. Each round consists of a key-dependent permutation, and a key- and data-dependent substitution. All operations are additions and XORs on 32-bit words. The only additional operations are four indexed array data lookups per round.

Blowfish uses a large number of subkeys. These keys must be precomputed before any data encryption or decryption.

The P-array consists of 18 32-bit subkeys:

$$P_1, P_2, \ldots, P_{18}$$

Four 32-bit S-boxes have 256 entries each:

$$S_{1,0}, S_{1,1}, \ldots, S_{1,255}$$
$$S_{2,0}, S_{2,1}, \ldots, S_{2,255}$$
$$S_{3,0}, S_{3,1}, \ldots, S_{3,255}$$
$$S_{4,0}, S_{4,1}, \ldots, S_{4,255}$$

The exact method used to calculate these subkeys will be described later in this section.

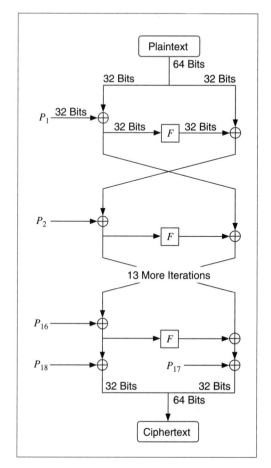

Figure 14.2   Blowfish.

Blowfish is a Feistel network (see Section 14.10) consisting of 16 rounds. The input is a 64-bit data element, x. To encrypt:

Divide x into two 32-bit halves: x_L, x_R

For $i = 1$ to 16:

$\quad x_L = x_L \oplus P_i$

$\quad x_R = F(x_L) \oplus x_R$

$\quad$ Swap x_L and x_R

Swap x_L and x_R (Undo the last swap.)

$x_R = x_R \oplus P_{17}$

$x_L = x_L \oplus P_{18}$

Recombine x_L and x_R

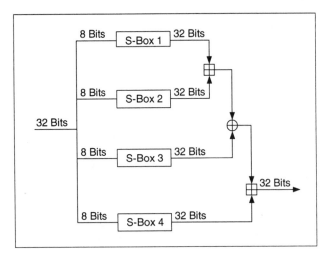

Figure 14.3   Function F.

Function F is as follows (see Figure 14.3):

Divide x_L into four eight-bit quarters:
a, b, c, and d $F(x_L) = ((S_{1,a} + S_{2,b} \bmod 2^{32}) \oplus S_{3,c}) + S_{4,d} \bmod 2^{32}$

Decryption is exactly the same as encryption, except that $P_1, P_2, \ldots, P_{18}$ are used in the reverse order.

Implementations of Blowfish that require the fastest speeds should unroll the loop and ensure that all subkeys are stored in cache. See [568] for details.

The subkeys are calculated using the Blowfish algorithm. The exact method follows.

(1) Initialize first the P-array and then the four S-boxes, in order, with a fixed string. This string consists of the hexadecimal digits of π.

(2) XOR P_1 with the first 32 bits of the key, XOR P_2 with the second 32-bits of the key, and so on for all bits of the key (up to P_{18}). Repeatedly cycle through the key bits until the entire P-array has been XORed with key bits.

(3) Encrypt the all-zero string with the Blowfish algorithm, using the subkeys described in steps (1) and (2).

(4) Replace P_1 and P_2 with the output of step (3).

(5) Encrypt the output of step (3) using the Blowfish algorithm with the modified subkeys.

(6) Replace P_3 and P_4 with the output of step (5).

(7) Continue the process, replacing all elements of the P-array, and then all four S-boxes in order, with the output of the continuously changing Blowfish algorithm.

In total, 521 iterations are required to generate all required subkeys. Applications can store the subkeys—there's no need to execute this derivation process multiple times.

Security of Blowfish

Serge Vaudenay examined Blowfish with known S-boxes and r rounds; a differential attack can recover the P-array with 2^{8r+1} chosen plaintexts [1568]. For certain weak keys that generate bad S-boxes (the odds of getting them randomly are 1 in 2^{14}), the same attack requires only 2^{4r+1} chosen plaintexts to recover the P-array. With unknown S-boxes this attack can detect whether a weak key is being used, but cannot determine what it is (neither the S-boxes nor the P-array). This attack only works against reduced-round variants; it is completely ineffective against 16-round Blowfish.

Of course, the discovery of weak keys is significant, even though they seem impossible to exploit. A weak key is one in which two entries for a given S-box are identical. There is no way to check for weak keys before doing the key expansion. If you are worried, you have to do the key expansion and check for identical S-box entries. I don't think this is necessary, though.

I know of no successful cryptanalysis against Blowfish. To be safe, do not implement Blowfish with a reduced number of rounds.

Kent Marsh Ltd. has incorporated Blowfish in their FolderBolt security product for Microsoft Windows and Macintosh. It is also part of Nautilus and PGPfone.

14.4 SAFER

SAFER K-64 stands for Secure And Fast Encryption Routine with a Key of 64 bits [1009]. James Massey produced this nonproprietary algorithm for Cylink Corp. and it is incorporated into some of their products. The government of Singapore is planning to use this algorithm—with a 128-bit key [1010]—for a wide variety of applications. There are no patent, copyright, or other restrictions on its use.

The algorithm has a block and key size of 64 bits. It is not a Feistel network like DES (see Section 14.10), but an iterated block cipher: The same function is applied for some number of rounds. Each round uses two 64-bit subkeys, and the algorithm only uses operations on bytes.

Description of SAFER K-64

The plaintext block is divided into eight byte-length sub-blocks: $B_1, B_2, \ldots, B_7, B_8$. Then the sub-blocks go through r rounds. Finally, an output transformation is applied to the sub-blocks. Each round uses two subkeys: K_{2i-1} and K_{2i}.

Figure 14.4 shows one round of SAFER K-64. First, sub-blocks are either XORed or added with bytes of subkey K_{2i-1}. Then, the eight sub-blocks are subjected to one of two nonlinear transformations:

$$y = 45^x \bmod 257. \text{ (If } x = 128, \text{ then } y = 0.)$$
$$y = \log_{45} x. \text{ (If } x = 0, \text{ then } y = 128.)$$

These are operations in the finite field GF(257), and 45 is a primitive element in that field. In practical implementations of SAFER K-64, it is quicker to implement this in a lookup table than to calculate new results all the time.

Then, sub-blocks are either XORed or added with bytes of subkey K_{2r}. The results of this operation are fed through three layers of linear operations designed to increase the avalanche effect. Each operation is called a Pseudo-Hadamard Transform (PHT). If the inputs to a PHT are a_1 and a_2, then the outputs are:

$$b_1 = (2a_1 + a_2) \bmod 256$$
$$b_2 = (a_1 + a_2) \bmod 256$$

After r rounds, there is a final output transformation. This is the same as the first step of each round. B_1, B_4, B_5, and B_8 are XORed with the corresponding bytes of the last subkey, and B_2, B_3, B_6, and B_7 are added to the corresponding bytes of the last subkey. The result is the ciphertext.

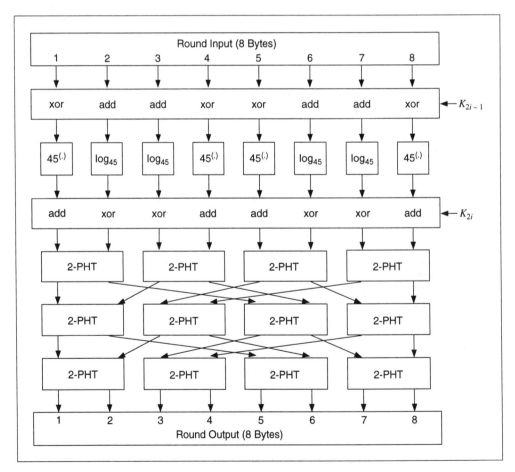

Figure 14.4   One round of SAFER.

Decryption is the reverse process: the output transformation (with subtraction instead of addition), then *r* reverse rounds. The Inverse PHT (IPHT) is:

$$a_1 = (b_1 - b_2) \bmod 256$$
$$a_2 = (-b_1 + 2b_2) \bmod 256$$

Massey recommends 6 rounds, but you can increase that if you want greater security.

Generating subkeys is easy. The first subkey, K_1, is simply the user key. Subsequent subkeys are generated by the following procedure:

$$K_{i+1} = (K_1 <<< 3i) + c_i$$

The symbol "$<<<$" is a left circular shift or a left rotation. The rotation is byte by byte, and c_i is a round constant. If c_{ij} is the *j*th byte of the *i*th round constant, then you can calculate all of the round constants by the formula

$$c_{ij} = 45^{45^{((9i + j) \bmod 256) \bmod 257}} \bmod 257$$

Generally, these values are stored in a table.

SAFER K-128

This alternate key schedule was developed by the Ministry of Home Affairs in Singapore, and then incorporated into SAFER by Massey [1010]. It uses two keys, K_a and K_b, each 64-bits long. The trick is to generate two subkey sequences in parallel, and then alternate subkeys from each sequence. This means that if you choose $K_a = K_b$, then the 128-bit key is compatible with the 64-bit key K_a.

Security of SAFER K-64

Massey showed that SAFER K-64 is immune to differential cryptanalysis after 8 rounds and is adequately secure against the attack after 6 rounds. After only 3 rounds linear cryptanalysis is ineffective against this algorithm [1010].

Knudsen found a weakness in the key schedule: For virtually every key, there exists at least one (and sometimes as many as nine) other key that encrypts some different plaintext to identical ciphertexts [862]. The number of different plaintexts that encrypt to identical ciphertexts after 6 rounds is anywhere from 2^{22} to 2^{28}. While this attack may not impact SAFER's security when used as an encryption algorithm, it greatly reduces its security when used as a one-way hash function. In any case, Knudsen recommends at least 8 rounds.

SAFER was designed for Cylink, and Cylink is tainted by the NSA [80]. I recommend years of intense cryptanalysis before using SAFER in any form.

14.5   3-WAY

3-Way is a block cipher designed by Joan Daemen [402,410]. It has a 96-bit block length and key length, and is designed to be very efficient in hardware.

3-Way is not a Feistel network, but it is an iterated block cipher. 3-Way can have n rounds; Daemen recommends 11.

Description of 3-Way

The algorithm is simple to describe. To encrypt a plaintext block, x:

> For $i = 0$ to $n - 1$
> $x = x$ XOR K_i
> $x =$ theta (x)
> $x =$ pi $- 1$ (x)
> $x =$ gamma (x)
> $x =$ pi $- 2$ (x)
> $x = x \oplus K_n$
> $x =$ theta (x)

The functions are:

— theta(x) is a linear substitution function—basically a bunch of circular shifts and XORs.

— pi–1(x) and pi–2(x) are simple permutations.

— gamma(x) is a nonlinear substitution function. This is the step that gives 3-Way its name; it is the parallel execution of the substitution step on 3-bit blocks of the input.

Decryption is similar to encryption, except that the bits of the input have to be reversed and the bits of the output have to be reversed. Code to implement 3-Way can be found in the back of this book.

So far, there has been no successful cryptanalysis of 3-Way. The algorithm is unpatented.

14.6 CRAB

This algorithm was developed by Burt Kaliski and Matt Robshaw of RSA Laboratories [810]. The idea behind Crab is to use techniques from one-way hash functions to make a fast encryption algorithm. Hence, Crab is very similar to MD5, and this section assumes you are familiar with Section 18.5.

Crab has a very large block: 1024 bytes. Since Crab is presented more as a research contribution than a real algorithm, no definitive key-generation routines are presented. The authors suggest a method that could turn an 80-bit key into three requisite subkeys, although the algorithm could easily accept variable-length keys. Crab uses two sets of large subkeys:

A permutation of the numbers 0 through 255: $P_0, P_1, P_2, \ldots, P_{255}$.

A 2048-entry array of 32-bit numbers: $S_0, S_1, S_2, \ldots, S_{2047}$.

These subkeys must all be calculated before encryption or decryption.
To encrypt a 1024-byte block X:

(1) Divide X into 256 32-bit sub-blocks: $X_0, X_1, X_2, \ldots, X_{255}$.

(2) Permute the sub-blocks of X according to P.

(3) For $r = 0$ to 3
  For $g = 0$ to 63

$$A = X_{(4g)} \lll 2r$$
$$B = X_{(4g + 1)} \lll 2r$$
$$C = X_{(4g + 2)} \lll 2r$$
$$D = X_{(4g + 3)} \lll 2r$$

For step $s = 0$ to 7

$$A = A \oplus (B + f_r(B,C,D) + S_{512r + 8g + s})$$
$$TEMP = D$$
$$D = C$$
$$C = B$$
$$B = A \lll 5$$
$$A = TEMP$$

$$X_{(4g)} \lll 2r = A$$
$$X_{(4g + 1)} \lll 2r = B$$
$$X_{(4g + 2)} \lll 2r = C$$
$$X_{(4g + 3)} \lll 2r = D$$

(4) Recombine $X_0, X_1, X_2, \ldots, X_{255}$ to form the ciphertext.

The functions $f_r(B,C,D)$ are similar to those used in MD5:

$$f_0(B,C,D) = (B \wedge C) \vee ((\neg B) \wedge D)$$
$$f_1(B,C,D) = (B \wedge D) \vee (C \wedge (\neg D))$$
$$f_2(B,C,D) = B \oplus C \oplus D$$
$$f_3(B,C,D) = C \oplus (B \vee (\neg D))$$

Decryption is the reverse process.

Generating the subkeys is a large task. Here is how the permutation array, P, could be generated from an 80-bit key, K.

(1) Initialize $K_0, K_1, K_2, \ldots, K_9$ with the 10 bytes of K.

(2) For $i = 10$ to 255

$$K_i = K_{i-2} \oplus K_{i-6} \oplus K_{i-7} \oplus K_{i-10}$$

(3) For $i = 0$ to 255, $P_i = i$

(4) $m = 0$

(5) For $j = 0$ to 1

> For $i = 256$ to 1 step -1
>
> $m = (K_{256 - i} + K_{257 - i}) \bmod i$
>
> $K_{257 - i} = K_{257 - i} <<< 3$
>
> Swap P_i and $P_{i - 1}$

The S-array of 2048 32-bit words could be generated in a similar manner, either from the same 80-bit key or from another key. The authors caution that these details should "be viewed as motivational; there may very well be alternative schemes which are both more efficient and offer improved security" [810].

Crab was proposed as a testbed of new ideas and not as a working algorithm. It uses many of the same techniques as MD5. Biham has argued that a very large block size makes an algorithm easier to cryptanalyze [160]. On the other hand, Crab may make efficient use of a very large key. In such a case, "easier to cryptanalyze" might not mean much.

14.7 SXAL8/MBAL

This is a 64-bit block algorithm from Japan [769]. SXAL8 is the basic algorithm; MBAL is an expanded version with a variable block length. Since MBAL does some clever things internally, the authors claim that they can get adequate security with only a few rounds. With a block length of 1024 bytes, MBAL is about 70 times faster than DES. Unfortunately, [1174] shows that MBAL is susceptible to differential cryptanalysis, and [865] shows that it is susceptible to linear cryptanalysis.

14.8 RC5

RC5 is a block cipher with a variety of parameters: block size, key size, and number of rounds. It was invented by Ron Rivest and analyzed by RSA Laboratories [1324,1325].

There are three operations: XOR, addition, and rotations. Rotations are constant-time operations on most processors and variable rotations are a nonlinear function. These rotations, which depend on both the key and the data, are the interesting operation.

RC5 has a variable-length block, but this example will focus on a 64-bit data block. Encryption uses $2r + 2$ key-dependent 32-bit words—$S_0, S_1, S_2, \ldots, S_{2r + 1}$—where r is the number of rounds. We'll generate those words later. To encrypt, first divide the plaintext block into two 32-bit words: A and B. (RC5 assumes a little-endian convention for packing bytes into words: The first byte goes into the low-order bit positions of register A, etc.) Then:

$$A = A + S_0$$
$$B = B + S_1$$

For $i = 1$ to r:
$$A = ((A \oplus B) <<< B) + S_{2i}$$
$$B = ((B \oplus A) <<< A) + S_{2i + 1}$$

The output is in the registers A and B.

Decryption is just as easy. Divide the plaintext block into two words, A and B, and then:

For $i = r$ down to 1:
$$B = ((B - S_{2i + 1}) >>> A) \oplus A$$
$$A = ((A - S_{2i}) >>> B) \oplus B$$
$$B = B - S_1$$
$$A = A - S_0$$

The symbol ">>>" is a right circular shift. Of course, all addition and subtraction are mod 2^{32}.

Creating the array of keys is more complicated, but also straightforward. First, copy the bytes of the key into an array, L, of c 32-bit words, padding the final word with zeros if necessary. Then, initialize an array, S, using a linear congruential generator mod 2^{32}:

$$S_0 = P$$
for $i = 1$ to $2(r + 1) - 1$:
$$S_i = (S_{i - 1} + Q) \bmod 2^{32}$$

$P = 0xb7e15163$ and $Q = 0x9e3779b9$; these constants are based on the binary representation of e and phi.

Finally, mix L into S:

$$i = j = 0$$
$$A = B = 0$$
do $3n$ times (where n is the maximum of $2(r + 1)$ and c):
$$A = S_i = (S_i + A + B) <<< 3$$
$$B = L_j = (L_j + A + B) <<< (A + B)$$
$$i = (i + 1) \bmod 2(r + 1)$$
$$j = (j + 1) \bmod c$$

RC5 is actually a family of algorithms. We just defined RC5 with a 32-bit word size and 64-bit block; there's no reason why the same algorithm can't have a 64-bit word size and 128-bit block size. For $w = 64$, P and Q are 0xb7e151628aed2a6b and 0x9e3779b97f4a7c15, respectively. Rivest designates particular implementations of RC5 as RC5-$w/r/b$, where w is the word size, r is the number of rounds, and b is the length of the key in bytes.

RC5 is new, but RSA Laboratories has spent considerable time analyzing it with a 64-bit block. After 5 rounds, the statistics look very good. After 8 rounds, every plaintext bit affects at least one rotation. There is a differential attack that requires 2^{24} chosen plaintexts for 5 rounds, 2^{45} for 10 rounds, 2^{53} for 12 rounds, and 2^{68} for 15 rounds. Of course, there are only 2^{64} possible chosen plaintexts, so this attack won't work for 15 or more rounds. Linear cryptanalysis estimates indicate that it is secure after 6 rounds. Rivest recommends at least 12 rounds, and possibly 16 [1325]. This number may change.

RSADSI is in the process of patenting RC5, and the name is trademarked. The company claims that license fees will be very small, but you'd better check with them.

14.9 OTHER BLOCK ALGORITHMS

There is an algorithm called CRYPTO-MECCANO in the literature [301]; it is insecure. Four Japanese cryptographers presented an algorithm based on chaotic maps at Eurocrypt '91 [687,688]; Biham cryptanalyzed the algorithm at the same conference [157]. Another algorithm relies on subsets of a particular set of random codes [693]. There are several algorithms based on the theory of error-correcting codes: a variant of the McEliece algorithm (see Section 19.7) [786,1290], the Rao-Nam algorithm [1292,733,1504,1291,1056,1057,1058,1293], variants of the Rao-Nam algorithm [464,749,1503], and the Li-Wang algorithm [964,1561]—they are all insecure. CALC is insecure [1109]. An algorithm called TEA, for Tiny Encryption Algorithm, is too new to comment on [1592]. Vino is another algorithm [503]. MacGuffin, a block algorithm by Matt Blaze and me, is also insecure [189]; it was broken at the same conference it was proposed. BaseKing, similar in design philosophy as 3-way but with a 192-bit block [402], is too new to comment on.

There are many more block algorithms outside the cryptology community. Some are used by various government and military organizations. I have no information about any of those. There are also dozens of proprietary commercial algorithms. Some might be good; most are probably not. If companies do not feel that their interests are served by making their algorithms public, it is best to assume they're right and avoid the algorithm.

14.10 THEORY OF BLOCK CIPHER DESIGN

In Section 11.1, I described Shannon's principles of confusion and diffusion. Fifty years after these principles were first written, they remain the cornerstone of good block cipher design.

Confusion serves to hide any relationship between the plaintext, the ciphertext, and the key. Remember how linear and differential cryptanalysis can exploit even a slight relationship between these three things? Good confusion makes the relationship statistics so complicated that even these powerful cryptanalytic tools won't work.

Diffusion spreads the influence of individual plaintext or key bits over as much of the ciphertext as possible. This also hides statistical relationships and makes cryptanalysis more difficult.

Confusion alone is enough for security. An algorithm consisting of a single key-dependent lookup table of 64 bits of plaintext to 64 bits of ciphertext would be plenty strong. The problem is that large lookup tables require lots of memory to implement: 10^{20} bytes of memory for the table just mentioned. The whole point of block cipher design is to create something that looks like a large lookup table, but with much smaller memory requirements.

The trick is to repeatedly mix confusion (with much smaller tables) and diffusion in a single cipher in different combinations. This is called a **product cipher**. Sometimes a block cipher that incorporates layers of substitution and permutation is called a **substitution-permutation network**, or even an **SP network**.

Look back at function f of DES. The expansion permutation and P-box perform diffusion; the S-boxes perform confusion. The expansion permutation and P-box are linear; the S-boxes are nonlinear. Each operation is pretty simple on its own; together they work pretty well.

DES also illustrates a few more principles of block cipher design. The first is the idea of an **iterated block cipher**. This simply means taking a simple round function and iterating it multiple times. Two-round DES isn't very strong; it takes 5 rounds before all of the output bits are dependent on all of the input bits and all of the key bits [1078,1080]. Sixteen-round DES is strong; 32-round DES is even stronger.

Feistel Networks

Most block algorithms are **Feistel networks**. This idea dates from the early 1970s [552,553]. Take a block of length n and divide it into two halves of length $n/2$: L and R. Of course, n must be even. You can define an iterated block cipher where the output of the ith round is determined from the output of the previous round:

$$L_i = R_{i-1}$$
$$R_i = L_{i-1} \oplus f(R_{i-1}, K_i)$$

K_i is the subkey used in the ith round and f is an arbitrary round function.

You've seen this concept in DES, Lucifer, FEAL, Khufu, Khafre, LOKI, GOST, CAST, Blowfish, and others. Why is it such a big deal? The function is guaranteed to be reversible. Because XOR is used to combine the left half with the output of the round function, it is necessarily true that

$$L_{i-1} \oplus f(R_{i-1}, K_i) \oplus f(R_{i-1}, K_i) = L_{i-1}$$

A cipher that uses this construction is guaranteed to be invertible as long as the inputs to f in each round can be reconstructed. It doesn't matter what f is; f need not be invertible. We can design f to be as complicated as we please, and we don't have to implement two different algorithms—one for encryption and another for decryption. The structure of a Feistel network takes care of all this automatically.

Simple Relations

DES has the property that if $E_K(P) = C$, then $E_{K'}(P') = C'$, where P', C', and K' are the bit-wise complements of P, C, and K. This property reduces the complexity of a brute-force attack by a factor of two. LOKI has complementation properties that reduce the complexity of a brute-force attack by a factor of 256.

A **simple relation** can be defined as [857]:

$$\text{If } E_K(P) = C, \text{ then } E_{f(K)}(g(P,K)) = h(C,K)$$

where f, g, and h are simple functions. By simple I mean that they are easy to compute, much easier than an iteration of the block cipher. In DES, f is the bit-wise complement of K, g is the bit-wise complement of P, and h is the bit-wise complement of C. This is a result of XORing the key into part of the text.

In a good block cipher, there are no simple relations. Methods for finding some of these weaknesses are in [917].

Group Structure

When discussing an algorithm, the question of whether it is a group arises. The elements of the group are the ciphertext blocks with each possible key, and the group operation is composition. Looking at an algorithm's group structure is an attempt to get a handle on just how much extra scrambling happens under multiple encryption.

The useful question is, however, not whether an algorithm is actually a group, but just how close to a group it is. If it were only lacking one element, it wouldn't be a group; but double encryption would be—statistically speaking—a waste of time. The work on DES showed that DES is very far away from being a group. There are still some interesting questions about the semigroup that DES encryption generates. Does it contain the identity: That is, does it even generate a group? To put it another way, does some combination of encryption (not decryption) operations eventually generate the identity function? If so, how long is the shortest such combination?

The goal is to estimate the size of the keyspace for a theoretical brute-force attack, and the result is a greatest lower bound on the keyspace entropy.

Weak Keys

In a good block cipher, all keys are equally strong. Algorithms with a small number of weak keys, like DES, are generally no problem. The odds of picking one at random are very small, and it's easy to test for and discard them. However, these weak keys can sometimes be exploited if the block cipher is used as a one-way hash function (see Section 18.11).

Strength against Differential and Linear Cryptanalysis

The study of differential and linear cryptanalysis has shed significant light on the theory of good block cipher design. The inventors of IDEA introduced the concept of **differentials**, a generalization of the basic idea of characteristics [931]. They argued that block ciphers can be designed to resist this attack; IDEA is the result of that work [931]. This concept was further formalized in [1181,1182], when Kaisa Nyberg and Lars Knudsen showed how to make block ciphers provably secure against differential cryptanalysis. This theory has extensions to higher-order differentials [702,161,927,858,860] and partial differentials [860]. Higher-order differentials seem to apply only to ciphers with a small number of rounds, but partial differentials combine nicely with differentials.

Linear cryptanalysis is newer, and is still being improved. Notions of key ranking [1019] and multiple approximations [811,812] have been defined. Other work that extends the idea of linear cryptanalysis can be found in [1270]; [938] tries to combine linear and differential cryptanalysis into one attack. It is unclear what design techniques will protect against these sorts of attacks.

Knudsen has made some progress, considering some necessary (but not perhaps sufficient) criteria for what he calls **practically secure Feistel networks**: ciphers that resist both linear and differential cryptanalysis [857]. Nyberg introduced in linear cryptanalysis an analogy to the concept of differentials from differential cryptanalysis [1180].

Interestingly enough, there seems to be a duality between differential and linear cryptanalysis. This duality becomes apparent both in the design of techniques to construct good differential characteristics and linear approximations [164,1018], and also in the design criteria for making algorithms that are secure against both attacks [307]. Exactly where this line of research will lead is still unknown. As a start, Daemen has developed an algorithm-design strategy based on linear and differential cryptanalysis [402].

S-Box Design

The strength of various Feistel networks—and specifically their resistance to differential and linear cryptanalysis—is tied directly to their S-boxes. This has prompted a spate of research on what constitutes a good S-box.

An S-box is simply a substitution: a mapping of m-bit inputs to n-bit outputs. Previously I talked about one large lookup table of 64-bit inputs to 64-bit outputs; that would be a 64*64-bit S-box. An S-box with an m-bit input and an n-bit output is called a ***m*n*-bit S-box**. S-boxes are generally the only nonlinear step in an algorithm; they are what give a block cipher its security. In general, the bigger they are, the better.

DES has eight different 6*4-bit S-boxes. Khufu and Khafre have a single 8*32-bit S-box, LOKI has a 12*8-bit S-box, and both Blowfish and CAST have 8*32-bit S-boxes. In IDEA the modular multiplication step is effectively the S-box; it is a 16*16-bit S-box. The larger this S-box, the harder it is to find useful statistics to attack using either differential or linear cryptanalysis [653,729,1626]. Also, while random S-boxes are usually not optimal to protect against differential and linear attacks, it is easier to find strong S-boxes if the S-boxes are larger. Most random S-boxes are nonlinear, nondegenerate, and have strong resistance to linear cryptanalysis—and the fraction that does not goes down rapidly as the number of input bits decreases [1185,1186,1187].

The size of m is more important than the size of n. Increasing the size of n reduces the effectiveness of differential cryptanalysis, but greatly increases the effectiveness of linear cryptanalysis. In fact, if $n \geq 2^m - m$, then there is definitely a linear relation of the input and output bits of the S-box. And if $n \geq 2^m$, then there is a linear relation of only the output bits [164].

Much of this work involves the study of **Boolean functions** [94,1098,1262,1408]. In order to be secure, the Boolean functions used in S-boxes must satisfy specific conditions. They should not be linear or affine, nor even close to linear or affine [9,1177,1178,1188]. There should be a balance of zeros and ones, and no correlations between different combinations of bits. The output bits should behave independently when any single input bit is complemented. These design criteria are also related to the study of **bent functions**: functions which can be shown to be optimally nonlinear. Although their definition is simple and natural, their study is very complicated [1344,1216,947,905,1176,1271,295,296,297,149,349,471,298].

One property that seems very important is the avalanche effect: how many output bits of an S-box change when some subset of the input bits are changed. It's easy to impose conditions on Boolean functions so that they satisfy certain avalanche criteria, but constructing them is a harder task. The **strict avalanche criteria** (**SAC**) guarantees that exactly half of the output bits change when one input bit changes [1586]. See also [982,571,1262,399]. One paper attempts to look at all these criteria in terms of information leakage [1640].

A few years ago cryptographers proposed choosing S-boxes so that the difference distribution table for each S-box is uniform. This would provide immunity against differential cryptanalysis by smoothing out the differentials in any particular round [6,443,444,1177]. LOKI is an example of this design. However, this approach can sometimes aid in differential cryptanalysis [172]. Actually, a better approach is making sure that the maximum differential is as small as possible. Kwangjo Kim proposed five criteria for the construction of S-boxes [834], similar to the design criteria for the DES S-boxes.

Choosing good S-boxes is not an easy task; there are many competing ideas on how to do it. Four general approaches can be identified.

1. Choose randomly. It is clear that small random S-boxes are insecure, but large random S-boxes may be good enough. Random S-boxes with eight or more inputs are quite strong [1186,1187]. Twelve-bit S-boxes are better. Even more strength is added if the S-boxes are both random and key-dependent. IDEA uses both large and key-dependent S-boxes.

2. Choose and test. Some ciphers generate random S-boxes and then test them for the requisite properties. See [9,729] for examples of this approach.

3. Man-made. This technique uses little mathematics: S-boxes are generated using more intuitive techniques. Bart Preneel stated that "... theoretically interesting criteria are not sufficient [for choosing Boolean functions for S-boxes] ..." and that "... ad hoc design criteria are required" [1262].

4. Math-made. Generate S-boxes according to mathematical principles so that they have proven security against differential and linear cryptanalysis, and good diffusive properties. See [1179] for an excellent example of this approach.

There has been some call for a combination of the "math-made" and "man-made" approaches [1334], but the real debate seems to be between randomly chosen

S-boxes and S-boxes with certain properties. Certainly the latter approach has the advantage of being optimal against known attacks—linear and differential crypt-analysis—but it offers unknown protection against unknown attacks. The designers of DES knew about differential cryptanalysis, and its S-boxes were optimized against it. They did not seem to know about linear cryptanalysis, and the DES S-boxes are very weak against it [1018]. Randomly selected S-boxes in DES would be weaker against differential cryptanalysis and stronger against linear cryptanalysis.

On the other hand, random S-boxes may not be optimal against these attacks, but they can be made sufficiently large and therefore sufficiently resistant. Also, they are more likely to be sufficiently resistant against unknown attacks. The debate is still raging, but my personal feeling is that S-boxes should be as large as possible, random, and key-dependent.

Designing a Block Cipher

It is easy to design a block cipher. If you think of a 64-bit block cipher as a permutation of the 64-bit numbers, it is clear that almost all of those permutations are secure. What is difficult is to design a block cipher that is not only secure, but can also be easily described and simply implemented.

It's easy to design a block cipher if you have sufficient memory for $48 * 32$ S-boxes. It's hard to design an insecure DES variant if you iterate it for 128 rounds. If the length of your key is 512 bits, you really don't care if there are key-complementation properties.

The real trick—and the reason that real-world block cipher design is very difficult—is to design a block cipher with the smallest possible key, the smallest possible memory requirement, and the fastest possible running time.

14.11 USING ONE-WAY HASH FUNCTIONS

The simplest way to encrypt with a one-way function is to hash the previous ciphertext block concatenated with the key, then XOR the result with the current plaintext block:

$$C_i = P_i \oplus H(K, C_{i-1})$$
$$P_i = C_i \oplus H(K, C_{i-1})$$

Set the block length equal to the output of the one-way hash function. This, in effect uses the one-way function as a block cipher in CFB mode. A similar construction can use the one-way function in OFB mode:

$$C_i = P_i \oplus S_i; \; S_i = H(K, C_{i-1})$$
$$P_i = C_i \oplus S_i; \; S_i = H(K, C_{i-1})$$

The security of this scheme depends on the security of the one-way function.

Karn

This method, invented by Phil Karn and placed in the public domain, makes an invertible encryption algorithm out of certain one-way hash functions.

The algorithm operates on plaintext and ciphertext in 32-byte blocks. The key can be any length, although certain key lengths will be more efficient for certain one-way hash functions. For the one-way hash functions MD4 and MD5, 96-byte keys work best.

To encrypt, first split the plaintext into two 16-byte halves: P_l and P_r. Then, split the key into two 48-byte halves: K_l and K_r.

$$P = P_l, P_r$$
$$K = K_l, K_r$$

Append K_l to P_l and hash it with a one-way hash function, then XOR the result of the hash with P_r to produce C_r, the right half of the ciphertext. Then, append K_r to C_r and hash it with the one-way hash function. XOR the result with P_l to produce C_l. Finally, append C_r to C_l to produce the ciphertext.

$$C_r = P_r \oplus H(P_l, K_l)$$
$$C_l = P_l \oplus H(C_r, K_r)$$
$$C = C_l, C_r$$

To decrypt, simply reverse the process. Append K_r to C_r, hash and XOR with C_l to produce P_l. Append K_l to P_l, hash and XOR with C_r to produce P_r.

$$P_l = C_l \oplus H(C_r, K_r)$$
$$P_r = C_r \oplus H(P_l, K_l)$$
$$P = P_l, P_r$$

The overall structure of Karn is the same as many of the other block algorithms discussed in this section. It has only two rounds, because the complexity of the algorithm is embedded in the one-way hash function. And since the key is used only as the input to the hash function, it cannot be recovered even using a chosen-plaintext attack—assuming, of course, that the one-way hash function is secure.

Luby-Rackoff

Michael Luby and Charles Rackoff showed that Karn is not secure [992]. Consider two single-block messages: *AB* and *AC*. If a cryptanalyst knows both the plaintext and the ciphertext of the first message, and knows the first half of the plaintext of the second message, then he can easily compute the entire second message. This known-plaintext attack is useful only in certain circumstances, but it is a major security problem.

A three-round encryption algorithm avoids this problem [992,1643,1644]. It uses three different hash functions: H_1, H_2, and H_3. Further work shows that H_1 can equal H_2, or that H_2 can equal H_3, but not both [1193]. Also, H_1, H_2, and H_3 cannot be based on iterating the same basic function [1643]. Anyway, assuming that $H(k,x)$ behaves like a pseudo-random function, here is a three-round version:

(1) Divide the key into two halves: K_l and K_r.
(2) Divide the plaintext block into two halves: L_0 and R_0.

(3) Append K_l to L_0 and hash it. XOR the result of the hash with R_0 to produce R_1:

$$R_1 = R_0 \oplus H(K_l,L_0)$$

(4) Append K_r to R_1 and hash it. XOR the result of the hash with L_0 to produce L_1:

$$L_1 = L_0 \oplus H(K_r,R_1)$$

(5) Append K_l to L_1 and hash it. XOR the result of the hash with R_1 to produce R_2:

$$R_2 = R_1 \oplus H(K_l,L_1)$$

(6) Append L_1 to R_2 to generate the message.

Message Digest Cipher (MDC)

MDC, invented by Peter Gutmann [676], is a means of turning one-way hash functions into a block cipher that runs in CFB mode. The cipher runs almost as fast as the hash function and is at least as secure as the hash function. The rest of this section assumes you are familiar with Chapter 18.

Hash functions such as MD5 and SHA use a 512-bit text block to transform an input value (128 bits with MD5, and 160 bits with SHA) into an output value of equal size. This transformation is not reversible, but it is perfect for CFB mode: The same operation is used for both encryption and decryption.

Let's look at MDC with SHA. MDC has a 160-bit block size and a 512-bit key. The hash function is run "sideways," with the old hash state as the input plaintext block (160 bits) and the 512-bit hash input as a key (see Figure 14.5). Normally, when using the hash to simply hash some input, the 512-bit input to the hash is varied as each new 512-bit block is hashed. But in this case the 512-bit input becomes an unchanging key.

MDC can be used with any one-way hash function: MD4, MD5, Snefru, and others. It is unpatented. Anyone can use it at any time, in any way, royalty-free [676].

However, I don't trust this construction. It is possible to attack the hash function in a way that hash functions are not designed to withstand. It is not important for hash functions to be able to resist a chosen-plaintext attack, where a cryptanalyst chooses several of those starting 160-bit values, has them "encrypted" by the same 512-bit "key," and uses this to learn some information about the 512-bit key used. Since the designers didn't have to worry about this, it seems like a bad idea to count on your cipher being able to resist this attack.

Security of Ciphers Based on One-Way Hash Functions

While these constructions can be secure, they depend on the choice of the underlying one-way hash function. A good one-way hash function doesn't necessarily make a secure encryption algorithm. Cryptographic requirements are different. For example, linear cryptanalysis is not a viable attack against one-way hash functions, but works against encryption algorithms. A one-way hash function such as SHA could have linear characteristics which, while not affecting its security as a one-

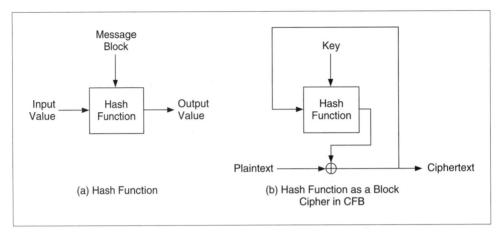

Figure 14.5   Message Digest Cipher (MDC).

way hash function, could make it insecure in an encryption algorithm such as MDC. I know of no cryptanalytic analysis of particular one-way hash functions as block ciphers; wait for such analysis before you trust any of them.

14.12 CHOOSING A BLOCK ALGORITHM

It's a tough decision. DES is almost certainly insecure against the major governments of the world unless you only encrypt very small chunks of data for a single key. It's probably all right against anyone else, but that is changing soon. Brute-force DES key search machines will quickly become economical for all sorts of organizations.

Biham's key-dependent S-boxes for DES should be secure for at least a few years against all but the most well-funded adversaries, and possibly even from them. If you need security that lasts decades or fear the cryptanalytic efforts of major governments, use triple-DES with three independent keys.

The other algorithms aren't worthless. I like Blowfish because it is fast and I wrote it. 3-WAY looks good, and GOST is probably okay. The problem with any recommendation is that the NSA almost certainly has an array of impressive cryptanalytic techniques that are still classified, and I don't know which algorithms they can break with them. Table 14.3 gives timing measurements for some algorithms. These are meant for comparison purposes only.

My favorite algorithm is IDEA. Its 128-bit key, combined with its resistance to any public means of cryptanalysis, gives me a warm, fuzzy feeling about the algorithm. The algorithm has been analyzed by a lot of different groups, and no serious results have been announced yet. Barring extraordinary cryptanalytic news tomorrow, I am betting on IDEA today.

Table 14.3
Encryption Speeds of Some Block Ciphers on a 33 MHz 486SX

Algorithm	Encryption Speed (Kilobytes/second)	Algorithm	Encryption Speed (Kilobytes/second)
Blowfish (12 rounds)	182	MDC (using MD4)	186
Blowfish (16 rounds)	135	MDC (using MD5)	135
Blowfish (20 rounds)	110	MDC (using SHA)	23
DES	35	NewDES	233
FEAL-8	300	REDOC II	1
FEAL-16	161	REDOC III	78
FEAL-32	91	RC5-32/8	127
GOST	53	RC5-32/12	86
IDEA	70	RC5-32/16	65
Khufu (16 rounds)	221	RC5-32/20	52
Khufu (24 rounds)	153	SAFER (6 rounds)	81
Khufu (32 rounds)	115	SAFER (8 rounds)	61
Luby-Rackoff (using MD4)	47	SAFER (10 rounds)	49
Luby-Rackoff (using MD5)	34	SAFER (12 rounds)	41
Luby-Rackoff (using SHA)	11	3-Way	25
Lucifer	52	Triple-DES	12

CHAPTER 15

Combining Block Ciphers

There are many ways to combine block algorithms to get new algorithms. The impetus behind these schemes is to try to increase security without going through the trouble of designing a new algorithm. DES is a secure algorithm; it has been cryptanalyzed for a good 20 years and the most practical way to break it is still brute force. However, the key is too short. Wouldn't it be nice to use DES as a building block for another algorithm with a longer key? We'd have the best of both worlds: the assurance of two decades of cryptanalysis plus a long key.

Multiple encryption is one combination technique: using an algorithm to encrypt the same plaintext block multiple times with multiple keys. Cascading is like multiple encryption, but uses different algorithms. There are other techniques.

Encrypting a plaintext block twice with the same key, whether with the same algorithm or a different one, is not smart. For the same algorithm, it does not affect the complexity of a brute-force search. (Remember, you assume a cryptanalyst knows the algorithm including the number of encryptions used.) For different algorithms, it may or may not. If you are going to use any of the techniques in this chapter, make sure the multiple keys are different and independent.

15.1 DOUBLE ENCRYPTION

A naïve way of improving the security of a block algorithm is to encrypt a block twice with two different keys. First encrypt a block with the first key, then encrypt the resulting ciphertext with the second key. Decryption is the reverse process.

$$C = E_{K_2}(E_{K_1}(P))$$
$$P = D_{K_1}(D_{K_2}(C))$$

If the block algorithm is a group (see Section 11.3), then there is always a K_3 such that

$$C = E_{K_2}(E_{K_1}(P)) = E_{K_3}(P)$$

If this is not the case, the resultant doubly-encrypted ciphertext block should be much harder to break using an exhaustive search. Instead of 2^n attempts (where n is the bit length of the key), it would require 2^{2n} attempts. If the algorithm is a 64-bit algorithm, the doubly-encrypted ciphertext would require 2^{128} attempts to find the key.

This turns out not to be true for a known-plaintext attack. Merkle and Hellman [1075] developed a time-memory trade-off that could break this double-encryption scheme in 2^{n+1} encryptions, not in 2^{2n} encryptions. (They showed this for DES, but the result can be generalized to any block algorithm.) The attack is called a **meet-in-the-middle attack**; it works by encrypting from one end, decrypting from the other, and matching the results in the middle.

In this attack, the cryptanalyst knows P_1, C_1, P_2, and C_2, such that

$$C_1 = E_{K_2}(E_{K_1}(P_1))$$
$$C_2 = E_{K_2}(E_{K_1}(P_2))$$

For each possible K, he computes $E_K(P_1)$ and stores the result in memory. After collecting them all, he computes $D_K(C_1)$ for each K and looks for the same result in memory. If he finds it, it is possible that the current key is K_2 and the key in memory is K_1. He tries encrypting P_2 with K_1 and K_2; if he gets C_2 he can be pretty sure (with a probability of success of 1 in 2^{2m-2n}, where m is the block size) that he has both K_1 and K_2. If not, he keeps looking. The maximum number of encryption trials he will probably have to run is $2 * 2^n$, or 2^{n+1}. If the probability of error is too large, he can use a third ciphertext block to get a probability of success of 1 in 2^{3m-2n}. There are still other optimizations [912].

This attack requires a lot of memory: 2^n blocks. For a 56-bit algorithm, this translates to 2^{56} 64-bit blocks, or 10^{17} bytes. This is still considerably more memory storage than one could comfortably comprehend, but it's enough to convince the most paranoid of cryptographers that double encryption is not worth anything.

For a 128-bit key, the amount of memory required is an enormous 10^{39} bytes. If we assume that a way exists to store a bit of information on a single atom of aluminum, the memory device required to launch this attack would be a cube of solid aluminum over a kilometer on a side. And then you need some place to put it! The meet-in-the middle attack seems infeasible for keys this size.

Another double-encryption method, sometimes called **Davies-Price**, is a variant of CBC [435].

$$C_i = E_{K_1}(P_i \oplus E_{K_2}(C_{i-1}))$$
$$P_i = D_{K_1}(C_i) \oplus E_{K_2}(C_{i-1})$$

They claim "no special virtue of this mode," but it seems to be vulnerable to the same meet-in-the-middle attacks as other double-encryption modes.

15.2 TRIPLE ENCRYPTION

Triple Encryption with Two Keys

A better idea, proposed by Tuchman in [1551], operates on a block three times with two keys: with the first key, then with the second key, and finally with the first key again. He suggested that the sender first encrypt with the first key, then decrypt with the second key, and finally encrypt with the first key. The receiver decrypts with the first key, then encrypts with the second key, and finally decrypts with the first key.

$$C = E_{K_1}(D_{K_2}(E_{K_1}(P)))$$
$$P = D_{K_1}(E_{K_2}(D_{K_1}(C)))$$

This is sometimes called **encrypt-decrypt-encrypt (EDE)** mode [55]. If the block algorithm has an n-bit key, then this scheme has a $2n$-bit key. The curious encrypt-decrypt-encrypt pattern was designed by IBM to preserve compatibility with conventional implementations of the algorithm: Setting the two keys equal to each other is identical to encrypting once with the key. There is no security inherent in the encrypt-decrypt-encrypt pattern, but this mode has been adopted to improve the DES algorithm in the X9.17 and ISO 8732 standards [55,761].

K_1 and K_2 alternate to prevent the meet-in-the-middle attack previously described. If $C = E_{K_2}(E_{K_1}(E_{K_1}(P)))$, then a cryptanalyst could precompute $E_{K_1}(E_{K_1}(P)))$ for every possible K_1 and then proceed with the attack. It only requires 2^{n+2} encryptions.

Triple encryption with two keys is not susceptible to the same meet-in-the-middle attack described earlier. But Merkle and Hellman developed another time-memory trade-off that could break this technique in 2^{n-1} steps using 2^n blocks of memory [1075].

For each possible K_2, decrypt 0 and store the result in memory. Then, decrypt 0 with each possible K_1 to get P. Triple-encrypt P to get C, and then decrypt C with K_1. If that decryption is a decryption of 0 with a K_2 (stored in memory), the $K_1 K_2$ pair is a possible candidate. Check if it is right. If it's not, keep looking.

This is a chosen-plaintext attack, requiring an enormous amount of chosen plaintext to mount. It requires 2^n time and memory, and 2^m chosen plaintexts. It is not very practical, but it is a weakness.

Paul van Oorschot and Michael Wiener converted this to a known-plaintext attack, requiring p known plaintexts. This example assumes EDE mode.

(1) Guess the first intermediate value, a.

(2) Tabulate, for each possible K_1, the second intermediate value, b, when the first intermediate value is a, using known plaintext:

$$b = D_{K_1}(C)$$

where C is the resulting ciphertext from a known plaintext.

(3) Look up in the table, for each possible K_2, elements with a matching second intermediate value, b:

$$b = E_{K_2}(a)$$

(4) The probability of success is p/m, where p is the number of known plaintexts and m is the block size. If there is no match, try another a and start again.

The attack requires $2^{n+m}/p$ time and p memory. For DES, this is $2^{120}/p$ [1558]. For p greater than 256, this attack is faster than exhaustive search.

Triple Encryption with Three Keys

If you are going to use triple encryption, I recommend three different keys. The key length is longer, but key storage is usually not a problem. Bits are cheap.

$$C = E_{K_3}(D_{K_2}(E_{K_1}(P)))$$
$$P = D_{K_1}(E_{K_2}(D_{K_3}(C)))$$

The best time-memory trade-off attack takes 2^{2n} steps and requires 2^n blocks of memory; it's a meet-in-the-middle attack [1075]. Triple encryption, with three independent keys, is as secure as one might naïvely expect double encryption to be.

Triple Encryption with Minimum Key (TEMK)

There is a secure way of using triple encryption with two keys that prevents the previous attack, called Triple Encryption with Minimum Key (TEMK) [858]. The trick is to derive three keys from two: X_1 and X_2:

$$K_1 = E_{X_1}(D_{X_2}(E_{X_1}(T_1)))$$
$$K_2 = E_{X_1}(D_{X_2}(E_{X_1}(T_2)))$$
$$K_3 = E_{X_1}(D_{X_2}(E_{X_1}(T_3)))$$

T_1, T_2, and T_3 are constants, which do not have to be secret. This is a special construction that guarantees that for any particular pair of keys, the best attack is a known-plaintext attack.

Triple-Encryption Modes

It's not enough to just specify triple encryption; there are several ways to do it. The decision of which to use affects both security and efficiency.

Here are two possible triple-encryption modes:

Inner-CBC: Encrypt the entire file in CBC mode three different times (see Figure 15.1a). This requires three different IVs.

$$C_i = E_{K_3}(S_i \oplus C_{i-1}); \ S_i = D_{K_2}(T_i \oplus S_{i-1}); \ T_i = E_{K_1}(P_i \oplus T_{i-1})$$
$$P_i = T_{i-1} \oplus D_{K_1}(T_i); \ T_i = S_{i-1} \oplus E_{K_2}(S_i); \ S_i = C_{i-1} \oplus D_{K_3}(C_i)$$

C_0, S_0, and T_0 are IVs.

Outer-CBC: Triple-encrypt the entire file in CBC mode (see Figure 15.1b). This requires one IV.

$$C_i = E_{K_3}(D_{K_2}(E_{K_1}(P_i \oplus C_{i-1})))$$
$$P_i = C_{i-1} \oplus D_{K_1}(E_{K_2}(D_{K_3}(C_i)))$$

Both modes require more resources than single encryption: more hardware or more time. However, given three encryption chips, the throughput of inner-CBC is no slower than single encryption. Since the three CBC encryptions are independent, three chips can be kept busy all the time, each feeding back into itself.

On the other hand, outer-CBC feedback is outside the three encryptions. This means that even with three chips, the throughput is only one-third that of single

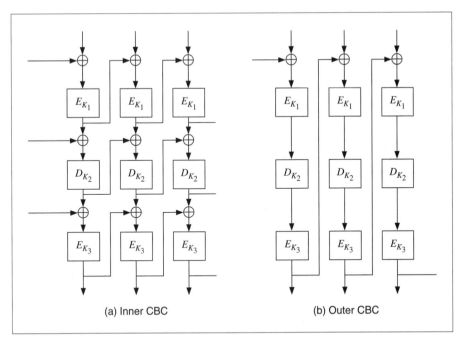

Figure 15.1   Triple encryption in CBC mode.

encryption. To get the same throughput with outer-CBC, you need to interleave IVs (see Section 9.12):

$$C_i = E_{K_3}(D_{K_2}(E_{K_1}(P_i \oplus C_{i-3})))$$

In this case C_0, C_{-1}, and C_{-2} are IVs. This doesn't help software implementations any, unless you have a parallel machine.

Unfortunately, the simpler mode is also the least secure. Biham analyzed various modes with respect to chosen-ciphertext differential cryptanalysis and found that inner-CBC is only slightly more secure than single encryption against a differential attack. If you think of triple encryption as a single larger algorithm, then inner feedbacks allow the introduction of external and known information into the inner workings of the algorithm; this facilitates cryptanalysis. The differential attacks require enormous amounts of chosen ciphertext to mount and are not very practical, but the results should be enough to give the most paranoid pause. Another analysis against meet-in-the-middle and brute-force attacks concludes that they are all equally secure [806].

There are other modes, as well. You can encrypt the entire file once in ECB, then twice in CBC; or once in CBC, once in ECB, and once in CBC; or twice in CBC and once in ECB. Biham showed that these variants are no more secure than single DES against a chosen-plaintext differential cryptanalysis attack [162]. And he doesn't have high hopes for any other variants. If you are going to use triple encryption, use modes with outer feedback.

Variants on Triple Encryption

Before there were proofs that DES does not form a group, several schemes were proposed for multiple encryption. One way to guarantee that triple encryption doesn't reduce to single encryption is to change the effective block size. One simple method is to add a bit of padding. Pad the text with a string of random bits, half a block in length, between the first and second and between the second and third encryptions (see Figure 15.2). If p is the padding function, then:

$$C = E_{K_3}(p(E_{K_2}(p(E_{K_1}(P)))))$$

This padding not only disrupts patterns, but also overlaps encrypted blocks like bricks. It only adds one block to the length of the message.

Another technique, proposed by Carl Ellison, is to use some kind of keyless permutation function between the three encryptions. The permutation could work on large blocks—8 kilobytes or so—and would effectively give this variant a block size of 8 kilobytes. Assuming that the permutation is fast, this variant is not much slower than basic triple encryption.

$$C = E_{K_3}(T(E_{K_2}(T(E_{K_1}(P)))))$$

T collects a block of input (up to 8 kilobytes in length) and uses a pseudo-random-number generator to transpose it. A 1-bit change in the input causes 8 changed output bytes after the first encryption, up to 64 changed output bytes after the second encryption, and up to 512 changed output bytes after the third encryption. If each block algorithm is in CBC mode, as originally proposed, then the effect of a single

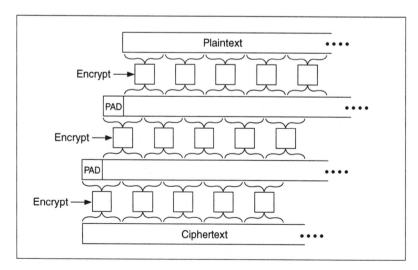

Figure 15.2   Triple encryption with padding.

changed input bit is likely to be the entire 8 kilobyte block, even in blocks other than the first.

The most recent variant of this scheme responded to Biham's attack on inner-CBC by including a whitening pass to hide plaintext patterns. That pass is a stream XOR with a cryptographically secure random-number generator called R below. The T on either side of it prevents the cryptanalyst from knowing *a priori* which key was used to encrypt any given byte on input to the last encryption. The second encryption is labelled nE (encryption with one of n different keys, used cyclically):

$$C = E_{K_3}(R(T(nE_{K_2}(T(E_{K_1}(R))))))$$

All encryptions are in ECB mode and keys are provided at least for the $n + 2$ encryption keys and the cryptographically secure random-number generator.

This scheme was proposed with DES, but works with any block algorithm. I know of no analysis of the security of this scheme.

15.3   DOUBLING THE BLOCK LENGTH

There is some argument in the academic community whether a 64-bit block is long enough. On the one hand, a 64-bit block length only diffuses plaintext over 8 bytes of ciphertext. On the other hand, a longer block length makes it harder to hide patterns securely; there is more room to make mistakes.

Some propose doubling the block length of an algorithm using multiple encryptions [299]. Before implementing any of these, look for the possibility of meet-in-the-middle attacks. Richard Outerbridge's scheme [300], illustrated in Figure 15.3, is no more secure than single-block, two-key triple encryption [859].

However, I advise against this sort of thing. It isn't faster than conventional triple encryption: six encryptions are still required to encrypt two blocks of data. We know the characteristics of triple encryption; constructions like this often have hidden problems.

15.4   OTHER MULTIPLE ENCRYPTION SCHEMES

The problem with two-key triple encryption is that it only doubles the size of the keyspace, but it requires three encryptions per block of plaintext. Wouldn't it be nice to find some clever way of combining two encryptions that would double the size of the keyspace?

Double OFB/Counter

This method uses a block algorithm to generate two keystreams, which are then used to encrypt the plaintext.

$$S_i = E_{K_1}(S_{i-1} \oplus I_1); I_1 = I_1 + 1$$
$$T_i = E_{K_2}(T_{i-1} \oplus I_2); I_2 = I_2 + 1$$
$$C_i = P_i \oplus S_i \oplus T_i$$

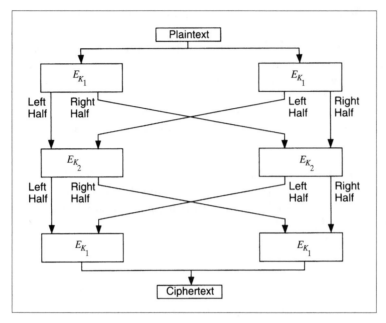

Figure 15.3   Doubling the block length.

S_i and T_i are internal variables, and I_1 and I_2 are counters. Two copies of the block algorithm run in a kind of hybrid OFB/counter mode, and the plaintext, S_i, and T_i are XORed together. The two keys, K_1 and K_2, are independent. I know of no cryptanalysis of this variant.

ECB + OFB

This method was designed for encrypting multiple messages of a fixed length, for example, disk blocks [186,188]. Use two keys: K_1 and K_2. First, use the algorithm and K_1 to generate a mask of the required block length. This mask will be used repeatedly to encrypt messages with the same keys. Then, XOR the plaintext message with the mask. Finally, encrypt the XORed plaintext with the algorithm and K_2 in ECB mode.

This mode has not been analyzed outside the paper in which it was proposed. Clearly it is at least as strong as a single ECB encryption and may be as strong as two passes with the algorithm. Possibly, a cryptanalyst could search for the two keys independently, if several known plaintext files are encrypted with the same key.

To thwart analysis of identical blocks in the same positions of different messages, you can add an IV. Unlike an IV in any other mode, here the IV is XORed with every block of the message before ECB encryption.

Matt Blaze designed this mode for his UNIX Cryptographic File System (CFS). It is a nice mode because the latency is only one encryption in ECB mode; the mask can be generated once and stored. In CFS, DES is the block algorithm.

xDESⁱ

In [1644,1645], DES is used as a building block for a series of block algorithms with both larger key sizes and larger block sizes. These constructions do not depend on DES in any way and can be used with any block algorithm.

The first, xDES[1], is simply a Luby-Rackoff construction with the block cipher as the underlying function (see Section 14.11). The block size is twice the size of the underlying block cipher and the key size is three times the size of the underlying block cipher. In each of 3 rounds, encrypt the right half with the block algorithm and one of the keys, XOR the result with the left half, and swap the two halves.

This is faster than conventional triple encryption, since three encryptions encrypt a block twice as large as the underlying algorithm. But there is also a simple meet-in-the-middle attack that finds the key with a table the size of 2^k, where k is the key size of the underlying algorithm. Encrypt the right half of a plaintext block with all possible values of K_1, XOR the left half of the plaintext, and store these values in a table. Then, encrypt the right half of the ciphertext with all possible values of K_3 and look for a match in the table. If you find one, the key pair K_1 and K_3 are possible candidates for the right key. Repeat the attack a few times, and only one candidate will remain. This shows that xDES[1] is not an ideal solution. Even worse, there is a chosen plaintext attack that proves xDES[1] is not much stronger than the underlying block cipher [858].

xDES[2] extends this idea to a 5-round algorithm with a block size 4 times that of the underlying block cipher and a key size 10 times that of the underlying block cipher. Figure 15.4 is one round of xDES[2]; each of the four sub-blocks are the size of the underlying block ciphers and all 10 keys are independent.

This scheme is also faster than triple encryption: Ten encryptions are used to encrypt a block four times the size of the underlying block cipher. However, it is vulnerable to differential cryptanalysis [858] and should not be used. The scheme is even vulnerable if DES with independent round keys is used.

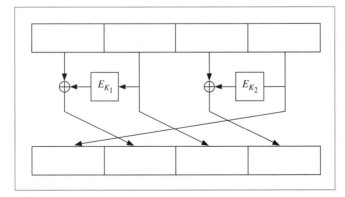

Figure 15.4   One round of xDES².

For $i \geq 3$, $xDES^i$ is probably too big to be useful as a block algorithm. For example, the block size for $xDES^3$ is 6 times that of the underlying cipher, the key size is 21 times, and 21 encryptions are required to encrypt a block 6 times that of the underlying block cipher. Triple encryption is faster.

Quintuple Encryption

If triple encryption isn't secure enough—perhaps you need to encrypt triple-encryption keys using an even stronger algorithm—then higher multiples might be in order. Quintuple encryption is very strong against meet-in-the-middle attacks. (Similar arguments to the ones used with double encryption can show that quadruple encryption provides minimal security improvements over triple encryption.)

$$C = E_{K_1}(D_{K_2}(E_{K_3}(D_{K_2}(E_{K_1}(P)))))$$
$$P = D_{K_1}(E_{K_2}(D_{K_3}(E_{K_2}(D_{K_1}(C)))))$$

This construction is backwards compatible with triple encryption if $K_2 = K_3$, and is backwards compatible with single encryption if $K_1 = K_2 = K_3$. Of course, it would be even stronger if all five keys were independent.

15.5 CDMF Key Shortening

This method was designed by IBM for their Commercial Data Masking Facility or CDMF (see Section 24.8) to shrink a 56-bit DES key to a 40-bit key suitable for export [785]. It assumes that the original DES key includes the parity bits.

(1) Zero the parity bits: bits 8, 16, 24, 32, 40, 48, 56, 64.

(2) Encrypt the output of step (1) with DES and the key 0xc408b0540ba1e0ae, and XOR the result with the output of step (1).

(3) Take the output of step (2) and zero the following bits: 1, 2, 3, 4, 8, 16, 17, 18, 19, 20, 24, 32, 33, 34, 35, 36, 40, 48, 49, 50, 51, 52, 56, 64.

(4) Encrypt the output of step (3) with DES and the following key: 0xef2c041ce6382fe6. This key is then used for message encryption.

Remember that this method shortens the key length, and thereby weakens the algorithm.

15.6 Whitening

Whitening is the name given to the technique of XORing some key material with the input to a block algorithm, and XORing some other key material with the output. This was first done in the DESX variant developed by RSA Data Security, Inc., and then (presumably independently) in Khufu and Khafre. (Rivest named this technique; it's a nonstandard usage of the word.)

The idea is to prevent a cryptanalyst from obtaining a plaintext/ciphertext pair for the underlying algorithm. The technique forces a cryptanalyst to guess not only the algorithm key, but also one of the whitening values. Since there is an XOR both before and after the block algorithm, this technique is not susceptible to a meet-in-the-middle attack.

$$C = K_3 \oplus E_{K_2}(P \oplus K_1)$$
$$P = K_1 \oplus D_{K_2}(C \oplus K_3)$$

If $K_1 = K_3$, then a brute-force attack requires $2^{n + m/p}$ operations, where n is the key size, m is the block size, and p is the number of known plaintexts. If K_1 and K_3 are different, then a brute-force attack requires $2^{n + m + 1}$ operations with three known plaintexts. Against differential and linear cryptanalysis, these measures only provide a few key bits of protection. But computationally this is a very cheap way to increase the security of a block algorithm.

15.7 CASCADING MULTIPLE BLOCK ALGORITHMS

What about encrypting a message once with Algorithm A and key K_A, then again with Algorithm B and key K_B? Maybe Alice and Bob have different ideas about which algorithms are secure: Alice wants to use Algorithm A and Bob wants to use Algorithm B. This technique is sometimes called **cascading**, and can be extended far beyond only two algorithms and keys.

Pessimists have said that there is no guarantee that the two algorithms will work together to increase security. There may be subtle interactions between the two algorithms that actually *decrease* security. Even triple encryption with three different algorithms may not be as secure as you think. Cryptography is a black art; if you don't know what you are doing, you can easily get into trouble.

Reality is much rosier. The previous warnings are true only if the different keys are related to each other. If all of the multiple keys are independent, then the resultant cascade is at least as difficult to break as the first algorithm in the cascade [1033]. If the second algorithm is vulnerable to a chosen-plaintext attack, then the first algorithm might facilitate that attack and make the second algorithm vulnerable to a known-plaintext attack when used in a cascade. This potential attack is not limited to encryption algorithms: If you let someone else specify any algorithm which is used on your message before encryption, then you had better be sure that your encryption will withstand a chosen-plaintext attack. (Note that the most common algorithm used for compressing and digitizing speech to modem speeds, used before any encryption, is CELP—designed by the NSA.)

This can be better phrased: Using a chosen-plaintext attack, a cascade of ciphers is at least as hard to break as any of its component ciphers [858]. A previous result showed that the cascade is at least as difficult to break as the strongest algorithm, but that result is based on some unstated assumptions [528]. Only if the algorithms commute, as they do in the case of cascaded stream ciphers (or block ciphers in OFB mode), is the cascade at least as strong as the strongest algorithm.

If Alice and Bob do not trust each other's algorithms, they can use a cascade. If these are stream algorithms, the order doesn't matter. If they are block algorithms, Alice can first use Algorithm A and then use Algorithm B. Bob, who trusts Algorithm B more, can use Algorithm B followed by Algorithm A. They might even add a good stream cipher between the two algorithms; it can't hurt and could very well increase security.

Remember that the keys for each algorithm in the cascade must be independent. If Algorithm A has a 64-bit key and Algorithm B has a 128-bit key, then the resultant cascade must have a 192-bit key. If you don't use independent keys, then the pessimists are much more likely to be right.

15.8 COMBINING MULTIPLE BLOCK ALGORITHMS

Here's another way to combine multiple block algorithms, one that is guaranteed to be at least as secure as both algorithms. With two algorithms (and two independent keys):

(1) Generate a random-bit string, R, the same size as the message M.

(2) Encrypt R with the first algorithm.

(3) Encrypt $M \oplus R$ with the second algorithm.

(4) The ciphertext message is the results of steps (2) and (3).

Assuming the random-bit string is indeed random, this method encrypts M with a one-time pad and then encrypts both the pad and the encrypted message with each of the two algorithms. Since both are required to reconstruct M, a cryptanalyst must break both algorithms. The drawback is that the ciphertext is twice the size of the plaintext.

This method can be extended to multiple algorithms, but the ciphertext expands with each additional algorithm. It's a good idea, but I don't think it's very practical.

CHAPTER 16

Pseudo-Random-Sequence Generators and Stream Ciphers

16.1 LINEAR CONGRUENTIAL GENERATORS

Linear congruential generators are pseudo-random-sequence generators of the form

$$X_n = (aX_{n-1} + b) \bmod m$$

in which X_n is the nth number of the sequence, and X_{n-1} is the previous number of the sequence. The variables a, b, and m are constants: a is the **multiplier**, b is the **increment**, and m is the modulus. The key, or seed, is the value of X_0.

This generator has a period no greater than m. If a, b, and m are properly chosen, then the generator will be a **maximal period generator** (sometimes called maximal length) and have period of m. (For example, b should be relatively prime to m.) Details on choosing constants to ensure maximal period can be found in [863,942]. Another good article on linear congruential generators and their theory is [1446].

Table 16.1, taken from [1272], gives a list of good constants for linear congruential generators. They all produce maximal period generators and even more important, pass the spectral test for randomness for dimensions 2, 3, 4, 5, and 6 [385,863]. They are organized by the largest product that does not overflow a specific word length.

The advantage of linear congruential generators is that they are fast, requiring few operations per bit.

Unfortunately, linear congruential generators cannot be used for cryptography; they are predictable. Linear congruential generators were first broken by Jim Reeds [1294,1295,1296] and then by Joan Boyar [1251]. She also broke quadratic generators:

$$X_n = (aX_{n-1}^2 + bX_{n-1} + c) \bmod m$$

and cubic generators:

$$X_n = (aX_{n-1}^3 + bX_{n-1}^2 + cX_{n-1} + d) \bmod m$$

Other researchers extended Boyar's work to break any polynomial congruential generator [923,899,900]. Truncated linear congruential generators were also broken

Table 16.1
Constants for Linear Congruential Generators

Overflow At:	a	b	m
2^{20}	106	1283	6075
2^{21}	211	1663	7875
2^{22}	421	1663	7875
2^{23}	430	2531	11979
	936	1399	6655
	1366	1283	6075
2^{24}	171	11213	53125
	859	2531	11979
	419	6173	29282
	967	3041	14406
2^{25}	141	28411	134456
	625	6571	31104
	1541	2957	14000
	1741	2731	12960
	1291	4621	21870
	205	29573	139968
2^{26}	421	17117	81000
	1255	6173	29282
	281	28411	134456
2^{27}	1093	18257	86436
	421	54773	259200
	1021	24631	116640
	1021	25673	121500
2^{28}	1277	24749	117128
	741	66037	312500
	2041	25673	121500
2^{29}	2311	25367	120050
	1807	45289	214326
	1597	51749	244944
	1861	49297	233280
	2661	36979	175000
	4081	25673	121500
	3661	30809	145800
2^{30}	3877	29573	139968
	3613	45289	214326
	1366	150889	714025
2^{31}	8121	28411	134456
	4561	51349	243000
	7141	54773	259200
2^{32}	9301	49297	233280
	4096	150889	714025
2^{33}	2416	374441	1771875
2^{34}	17221	107839	510300
	36261	66037	312500
2^{35}	84589	45989	217728

[581,705,580], as were truncated linear congruential generators with unknown parameters [1500,212]. The preponderance of evidence is that congruential generators aren't useful for cryptography.

Linear congruential generators remain useful for noncryptographic applications, however, such as simulations. They are efficient and show good statistical behavior with respect to most reasonable empirical tests. Considerable information on linear congruential generators and their implementations can be found in [942].

Combining Linear Congruential Generators

Various people examined the combination of linear congruential generators [1595,941]. The results are no more cryptographically secure, but the combinations have longer periods and perform better in some randomness tests.

Use this generator for 32-bit computers [941]:

```
static long s1 = 1 ; /* A "long" must be 32 bits long. */ static long s2 = 1 ;

#define MODMULT(a,b,c,m,s) q = s/a; s = b*(s-a*q) - c*q; if (s<0) s+=m  ;
/* MODMULT(a,b,c,m,s) computes s*b mod m, provided that m=a*b+c and 0 <= c <
m. */

/* combinedLCG returns a pseudorandom real value in the range
 * (0,1). It combines linear congruential generators with
 * periods of 2^31-85 and 2^31-249, and has a period that is the
 * product of these two prime numbers. */

double combinedLCG ( void )
{
  long q ;
  long z ;

  MODMULT ( 53668, 40014, 12211, 2147483563L, s1 )
  MODMULT ( 52774, 40692, 3791, 2147483399L, s2 )
  z = s1 - s2 ;
  if ( z < 1 )
    z += 2147483562 ;
  return z * 4.656613e-10 ;
}

/* In general, call initLCG before using combinedLCG. */
void initLCG ( long InitS1, long InitS2 )
{
  s1 = InitS1 ;
  s2 = InitS2 ;
}
```

This generator works as long as the machine can represent all integers between $-2^{31} + 85$ and $2^{31} - 85$. The variables, s_1 and s_2, are global; they hold the current state of the generator. Before the first call, they must be initialized. The variable s_1 needs an initial value between 1 and 2147483562; the variable s_2 needs an initial value between 1 and 2147483398. The generator has a period somewhere in the neighborhood of 10^{18}.

If you only have a 16-bit computer, use this generator instead:

```
static int s1 = 1 ; /* An "int" must be 16 bits long. */
static int s2 = 1 ;
static int s3 = 1 ;

#define MODMULT(a,b,c,m,s) q = s/a; s = b*(s-a*q) - c*q; if
(s<0) s+=m  ;

/* combined LCG returns a pseudorandom real value in the
range
* (0,1). It combines linear congruential generators with
* periods of 2^15-405, 2^15-1041, and 2^15-1111, and has a period
* that is the product of these three prime numbers. */

double combinedLCG ( void )
{
  int q ;
  int z ;

  MODMULT ( 206, 157, 21, 32363, s1 )
  MODMULT ( 217, 146, 45, 31727, s2 )
  MODMULT ( 222, 142, 133, 31657, s3 )
  z = s1 - s2 ;
  if ( z > 706 )
    z -= 32362 ;
  z += s3 ;
  if ( z < 1 )
    z += 32362 ;
  return z * 3.0899e-5 ;
}

/* In general, call initLCG before using combinedLCG. */
void initLCG ( int InitS1, int InitS2, InitS3 )
{
  s1 = InitS1 ;
  s2 = InitS2 ;
  s3 = InitS3 ;
}
```

This generator works as long as the machine can represent all integers between -32363 and 32363. The variables, s_1, s_2, and s_3, are global; they hold the current state of the generator. Before the first call, they must be initialized. The variable s_1 needs an initial value between 1 and 32362. The variable s_2 needs an initial value between 1 and 31726. The variable s_3 needs an initial value between 1 and 31656. This generator has a period of $1.6*10^{13}$.

For both of these generators, the constant term b in the linear congruence is 0.

16.2 LINEAR FEEDBACK SHIFT REGISTERS

Shift register sequences are used in both cryptography and coding theory. There is a wealth of theory about them; stream ciphers based on shift registers have been the workhorse of military cryptography since the beginnings of electronics.

A **feedback shift register** is made up of two parts: a shift register and a **feedback function** (see Figure 16.1). The shift register is a sequence of bits. (The **length** of a shift register is figured in bits; if it is n bits long, it is called an n-bit shift register.) Each time a bit is needed, all of the bits in the shift register are shifted 1 bit to the right. The new left-most bit is computed as a function of the other bits in the register. The output of the shift register is 1 bit, often the least significant bit. The **period** of a shift register is the length of the output sequence before it starts repeating.

Cryptographers have liked stream ciphers made up of shift registers: They are easily implemented in digital hardware. I will only touch on the mathematical theory. Ernst Selmer, the Norwegian government's chief cryptographer, worked out the theory of shift register sequences in 1965 [1411]. Solomon Golomb, an NSA mathematician, wrote a book with Selmer's results and some of his own [643]. See also [970,971,1647].

The simplest kind of feedback shift register is a **linear feedback shift register**, or LFSR (see Figure 16.2). The feedback function is simply the XOR of certain bits in the register; the list of these bits is called a **tap sequence**. Sometimes this is called a **Fibonacci configuration**. Because of the simple feedback sequence, a large body of mathematical theory can be applied to analyzing LFSRs. Cryptographers like to analyze sequences to convince themselves that they are random enough to be secure. LFSRs are the most common type of shift registers used in cryptography.

Figure 16.3 is a 4-bit LFSR tapped at the first and fourth bit. If it is initialized with the value 1111, it produces the following sequence of internal states before repeating:

$$1\ 1\ 1\ 1$$
$$0\ 1\ 1\ 1$$
$$1\ 0\ 1\ 1$$
$$0\ 1\ 0\ 1$$
$$1\ 0\ 1\ 0$$
$$1\ 1\ 0\ 1$$
$$0\ 1\ 1\ 0$$
$$0\ 0\ 1\ 1$$
$$1\ 0\ 0\ 1$$

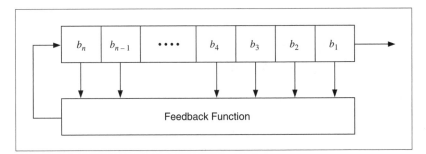

Figure 16.1   Feedback shift register.

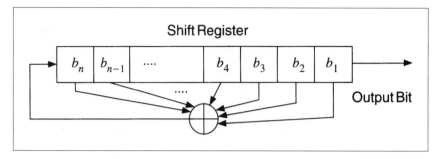

Figure 16.2   Linear feedback shift register.

$$0\ 1\ 0\ 0$$
$$0\ 0\ 1\ 0$$
$$0\ 0\ 0\ 1$$
$$1\ 0\ 0\ 0$$
$$1\ 1\ 0\ 0$$
$$1\ 1\ 1\ 0$$

The output sequence is the string of least significant bits:

$$1\ 1\ 1\ 1\ 0\ 1\ 0\ 1\ 1\ 0\ 0\ 1\ 0\ 0\ 0.\ .\ .\ .$$

An n-bit LFSR can be in one of $2^n - 1$ internal states. This means that it can, in theory, generate a $2^n - 1$-bit-long pseudo-random sequence before repeating. (It's $2^n - 1$ and not 2^n because a shift register filled with zeros will cause the LFSR to output a neverending stream of zeros—this is not particularly useful.) Only LFSRs with certain tap sequences will cycle through all $2^n - 1$ internal states; these are the maximal-period LFSRs. The resulting output sequence is called an **m-sequence**.

In order for a particular LFSR to be a maximal-period LFSR, the polynomial formed from a tap sequence plus the constant 1 must be a primitive polynomial mod 2. The **degree** of the polynomial is the length of the shift register. A primitive polynomial of degree n is an irreducible polynomial that divides $x^{2^n - 1} + 1$, but not $x^d + 1$ for any d that divides $2^n - 1$ (see Section 11.3). For the mathematical theory behind all this, consult [643,1649,1648].

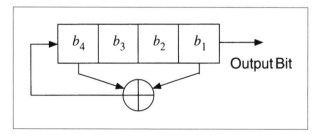

Figure 16.3   4-bit LFSR.

In general, there is no easy way to generate primitive polynomials mod 2 for a given degree. The easiest way is to choose a random polynomial and test whether it is primitive. This is complicated—something like testing random numbers for primality—but many mathematical software packages do this. See [970,971] for some methods.

Table 16.2 lists some, but by no means all, primitive polynomials mod 2 of varying degrees [1583,643,1649,1648,1272,691]. For example, the listing (32, 7, 5, 3, 2, 1, 0) means that the following polynomial is primitive modulo 2:

$$x^{32} + x^7 + x^5 + x^3 + x^2 + x + 1$$

It's easy to turn this into a maximal-period LFSR. The first number is the length of the LFSR. The last number is always 0 and can be ignored. All the numbers, except the 0, specify the tap sequence, counting from the left of the shift register. That is, low degree terms in the polynomial correspond to taps near the left-hand side of the register.

To continue the example, the listing (32, 7, 5, 3, 2, 1, 0) means that if you take a 32-bit shift register and generate the new bit by XORing the thirty-second, seventh, fifth, third, second, and first bits together (see Figure 16.4), the resultant LFSR will be maximal length; it will cycle through $2^{32} - 1$ values before repeating.

The C code for this LFSR looks like:

```
int LFSR () {
    static unsigned long ShiftRegister = 1;
    /* Anything but 0. */
    ShiftRegister = (((((ShiftRegister >> 31)
            ^ (ShiftRegister >> 6)
            ^ (ShiftRegister >> 4)
            ^ (ShiftRegister >> 2)
            ^ (ShiftRegister >> 1)
            ^ ShiftRegister))
            & 0x00000001)
            << 31)
            | (ShiftRegister >> 1) ;
    return ShiftRegister & 0x00000001;
}
```

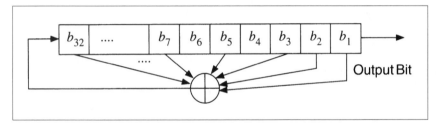

Figure 16.4   *32-bit long maximal-length LFSR.*

Table 16.2
Some Primitive Polynomials Mod 2

(1, 0)	(36, 11, 0)	(68, 9, 0)	(97, 6, 0)
(2, 1, 0)	(36, 6, 5, 4, 2, 1, 0)	(68, 7, 5, 1, 0)	(98, 11, 0)
(3, 1, 0)	(37, 6, 4, 1, 0)	(69, 6, 5, 2, 0)	(98, 7, 4, 3, 1, 0)
(4, 1, 0)	(37, 5, 4, 3, 2, 1, 0)	(70, 5, 3, 1, 0)	(99, 7, 5, 4, 0)
(5, 2, 0)	(38, 6, 5, 1, 0)	(71, 6, 0)	(100, 37, 0)
(6, 1, 0)	(39, 4, 0)	(71, 5, 3, 1, 0)	(100, 8, 7, 2, 0)
(7, 1, 0)	(40, 5, 4, 3, 0)	(72, 10, 9, 3, 0)	(101, 7, 6, 1, 0)
(7, 3, 0)	(41, 3, 0)	(72, 6, 4, 3, 2, 1, 0)	(102, 6 5 3 0)
(8, 4, 3, 2, 0)	(42, 7, 4, 3, 0)	(73, 25, 0)	(103, 9, 9)
(9, 4, 0)	(42, 5, 4, 3, 2, 1, 0)	(73, 4, 3, 2, 0)	(104, 11, 10, 1, 0)
(10, 3, 0)	(43, 6, 4, 3, 0)	(74, 7, 4, 3, 0)	(105, 16, 0)
(11, 2, 0)	(44, 6, 5, 2, 0)	(75, 6, 3, 1, 0)	(106, 15, 0)
(12, 6, 4, 1, 0)	(45, 4, 3, 1, 0)	(76, 5, 4, 2, 0)	(107, 9, 7, 4, 0)
(13, 4, 3, 1, 0)	(46, 8, 7, 6, 0)	(77, 6, 5, 2, 0)	(108, 31, 0)
(14, 5, 3, 1, 0)	(46, 8, 5, 3, 2, 1, 0)	(78, 7, 2, 1, 0)	(109, 5, 4, 2, 0)
(15, 1, 0)	(47, 5, 0)	(79, 9, 0)	(110, 6, 4, 1, 0)
(16, 5, 3, 2, 0)	(48, 9, 7, 4, 0)	(79, 4, 3, 2, 0)	(111, 10, 0)
(17, 3, 0)	(48, 7, 5, 4, 2, 1, 0)	(80, 9, 4, 2, 0)	(111, 49, 0)
(17, 5, 0)	(49, 9, 0)	(80, 7, 5, 3, 2, 1, 0)	(113, 9, 0)
(17, 6, 0)	(49, 6, 5, 4, 0)	(81, 4, 0)	(113, 15, 0)
(18, 7, 0)	(50, 4, 3, 2, 0)	(82, 9, 6, 4, 0)	(113, 30, 0)
(18, 5, 2, 1, 0)	(51, 6, 3, 1, 0)	(82, 8, 7, 6, 1, 0)	(114, 11, 2, 1, 0)
(19, 5, 2, 1, 0)	(52, 3, 0)	(83, 7, 4, 2, 0)	(115, 8, 7, 5, 0)
(20, 3, 0)	(53, 6, 2, 1, 0)	(84, 13, 0)	(116, 6, 5, 2, 0)
(21, 2, 0)	(54, 8, 6, 3, 0)	(84, 8, 7, 5, 3, 1, 0)	(117, 5, 2, 1, 0)
(22, 1, 0)	(54, 6, 5, 4, 3, 2, 0)	(85, 8, 2, 1, 0)	(118, 33, 0)
(23, 5, 0)	(55, 24, 0)	(86, 6, 5, 2, 0)	(119, 8, 0)
(24, 4, 3, 1, 0)	(55, 6, 2, 1, 0)	(87, 13, 0)	(119, 45, 0)
(25, 3, 0)	(56, 7, 4, 2, 0)	(87, 7, 5, 1, 0)	(120, 9, 6, 2, 0)
(26, 6, 2, 1, 0)	(57, 7, 0)	(88, 11, 9, 8, 0)	(121, 18, 0)
(27, 5, 2, 1, 0)	(57, 5, 3, 2, 0)	(88, 8, 5, 4, 3, 1, 0)	(122, 6, 2, 1, 0)
(28, 3, 0)	(58, 19, 0)	(89, 38, 0)	(123, 2, 0)
(29, 2, 0)	(58, 6, 5, 1, 0)	(89, 51, 0)	(124, 37, 0)
(30, 6, 4, 1, 0)	(59, 7, 4, 2, 0)	(89, 6, 5, 3, 0)	(125, 7, 6, 5, 0)
(31, 3, 0)	(59, 6, 5, 4, 3, 1, 0)	(90, 5, 3, 2, 0)	(126, 7, 4, 2, 0)
(31, 6, 0)	(60, 1, 0)	(91, 8, 5, 1, 0)	(127, 1, 0)
(31, 7, 0)	(61, 5, 2, 1, 0)	(91, 7, 6, 5, 3, 2, 0)	(127, 7, 0)
(31, 13, 0)	(62, 6, 5, 3, 0)	(92, 6, 5, 2, 0)	(127, 63, 0)
(32, 7, 6, 2, 0)	(63, 1, 0)	(93, 2, 0)	(128, 7, 2, 1, 0)
(32, 7, 5, 3, 2, 1, 0)	(64, 4, 3, 1, 0)	(94, 21, 0)	(129, 5, 0)
(33, 13, 0)	(65, 18, 0)	(94, 6, 5, 1, 0)	(130, 3, 0)
(33, 16, 4, 1, 0)	(65, 4, 3, 1, 0)	(95, 11, 0)	(131, 8, 3, 2, 0)
(34, 8, 4, 3, 0)	(66, 9, 8, 6, 0)	(95, 6, 5, 4, 2, 1, 0)	(132, 29, 0)
(34, 7, 6, 5, 2, 1, 0)	(66, 8, 6, 5, 3, 2, 0)	(96, 10, 9, 6, 0)	(133, 9, 8, 2, 0)
(35, 2, 0)	(67, 5, 2, 1, 0)	(96, 7, 6, 4, 3, 2, 0)	(134, 57, 0)

Table 16.2 (*Cont.*)
Some Primitive Polynomials Mod 2

(135, 11, 0)	(152, 6, 3, 2, 0)	(178, 87, 0)	(270, 133, 0)
(135, 16, 0)	(153, 1, 0)	(183, 56, 0)	(282, 35, 0)
(135, 22, 0)	(153, 8, 0)	(194, 87, 0)	(282, 43, 0)
(136, 8, 3, 2, 0)	(154, 9, 5, 1, 0)	(198, 65, 0)	(286, 69, 0)
(137, 21, 0)	(155, 7, 5, 4, 0)	(201, 14, 0)	(286, 73, 0)
(138, 8, 7, 1, 0)	(156, 9, 5, 3, 0)	(201, 17, 0)	(294, 61, 0)
(139, 8, 5, 3, 0)	(157, 6, 5, 2, 0)	(201, 59, 0)	(322, 67, 0)
(140, 29, 0)	(158, 8, 6, 5, 0)	(201, 79, 0)	(333, 2, 0)
(141, 13, 6, 1, 0)	(159, 31, 0)	(202, 55, 0)	(350, 53, 0)
(142, 21, 0)	(159, 34, 0)	(207, 43, 0)	(366, 29, 0)
(143, 5, 3, 2, 0)	(159, 40, 0)	(212, 105, 0)	(378, 43, 0)
(144, 7, 4, 2, 0)	(160, 5, 3, 2, 0)	(218, 11, 0)	(378, 107, 0)
(145, 52, 0)	(161, 18, 0)	(218, 15, 0)	(390, 89, 0)
(145, 69, 0)	(161, 39, 0)	(218, 71, 0)	(462, 73, 0)
(146, 5, 3, 2, 0)	(161, 60, 0)	(218, 83, 0)	(521, 32, 0)
(147, 11, 4, 2, 0)	(162, 8, 7, 4, 0)	(225, 32, 0)	(521, 48, 0)
(148, 27, 0)	(163, 7, 6, 3, 0)	(225, 74, 0)	(521, 158, 0)
(149, 10, 9, 7, 0)	(164, 12, 6, 5, 0)	(225, 88, 0)	(521, 168, 0)
(150, 53, 0)	(165, 9, 8, 3, 0)	(225, 97, 0)	(607, 105, 0)
(151, 3, 0)	(166, 10, 3, 2, 0)	(225, 109, 0)	(607, 147, 0)
(151, 9, 0)	(167, 6, 0)	(231, 26, 0)	(607, 273, 0)
(151, 15, 0)	(170, 23, 0)	(231, 34, 0)	(1279, 216, 0)
(151, 31, 0)	(172, 2, 0)	(234, 31, 0)	(1279, 418, 0)
(151, 39, 0)	(174, 13, 0)	(234, 103, 0)	(2281, 715, 0)
(151, 43, 0)	(175, 6, 0)	(236, 5, 0)	(2281, 915, 0)
(151, 46, 0)	(175, 16, 0)	(250, 103, 0)	(2281, 1029, 0)
(151, 51, 0)	(175, 18, 0)	(255, 52, 0)	(3217, 67, 0)
(151, 63, 0)	(175, 57, 0)	(255, 56, 0)	(3217, 576, 0)
(151, 66, 0)	(177, 8, 0)	(255, 82, 0)	(4423, 271, 0)
(151, 67, 0)	(177, 22, 0)	(258, 83, 0)	(9689, 84, 0)
(151, 70, 0)	(177, 88, 0)	(266, 47, 0)	

The code is a little more complicated when the shift register is longer than the computer's word size, but not significantly so.

Note that all of these listings have an odd number of coefficients. I have provided such a large table because LFSRs are often used for stream-cipher cryptography and I wanted many examples so that different people would pick different primitive polynomials. Since, if $p(x)$ is primitive, then so is $x^n p(1/x)$; each entry on the table is actually two primitive polynomials.

For example, if $(a, b, 0)$ is primitive, then $(a, a - b, 0)$ is also primitive. If $(a, b, c, d, 0)$ is primitive, then $(a, a - d, a - c, a - b, 0)$ is also primitive. Mathematically:

$$\text{if } x^a + x^b + 1 \text{ is primitive, so is } x^a + x^{a-b} + 1$$
$$\text{if } x^a + x^b + x^c + x^d + 1 \text{ is primitive, so is } x^a + x^{a-d} + x^{a-c} + x^{a-b} + 1$$

Primitive trinomials are fastest in software, because only two bits of the shift register have to be XORed to generate each new bit. Actually, all the feedback polynomials listed in Table 16.2 are **sparse**, meaning that they only have a few coefficients. Sparseness is always a source of weakness, sometimes enough to break the algorithm. It is far better to use **dense** primitive polynomials, those with a lot of coefficients, for cryptographic applications. If you use dense polynomials, and especially if you make them part of the key, you can live with much shorter LFSRs.

Generating dense primitive polynomials modulo 2 is not easy. In general, to generate primitive polynomials of degree k you need to know the factorization of $2^k - 1$. Three good references for finding primitive polynomials are [652,1285,1287].

LFSRs are competent pseudo-random-sequence generators all by themselves, but they have some annoying nonrandom properties. Sequential bits are linear, which makes them useless for encryption. For an LFSR of length n, the internal state is the next n output bits of the generator. Even if the feedback scheme is unknown, it can be determined from only $2n$ output bits of the generator, by using the highly efficient Berlekamp-Massey algorithm [1082,1083]: see Section 16.3.

Also, large random numbers generated from sequential bits of this sequence are highly correlated and, for certain types of applications, not very random at all. Even so, LFSRs are often used as building blocks in encryption algorithms.

LFSRs in Software

LFSRs are slow in software, but they're faster in assembly language than in C. One solution is to run 16 LFSRs (or 32, depending on your computer's word size) in parallel. This scheme uses an array of words that is the length of the LFSR, with each bit position in the words representing a different LFSR. Assuming all the feedback polynomials are the same, this can run pretty quickly. In general, the best way to update shift registers is to multiply the current state by suitable binary matrices [901].

It is also possible to modify the LFSR's feedback scheme. The resultant generator is no better cryptographically, but it still has a maximal period and is easy to implement in software [1272]. Instead of using the bits in the tap sequence to generate the new left-most bit, each bit in the tap sequence is XORed with the output of the generator and replaced; then the output of the generator becomes the new left-most bit (see Figure 16.5). This is sometimes called a **Galois configuration**.

In C, this looks like:

```
#define mask 0x80000057

static unsigned long ShiftRegister=1;
void seed_LFSR (unsigned long seed)
{
     if (seed == 0) /* avoid calamity */
          seed = 1;
     ShiftRegister = seed;
}

int modified_LFSR (void)
{
```

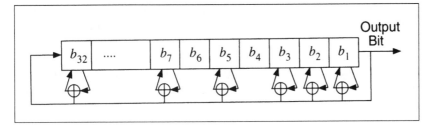

Figure 16.5   Galois LFSR.

```
if (ShiftRegister & 0x00000001) {
    ShiftRegister = ((ShiftRegister ^ mask >> 1) |
0x8000000;
    return 1;
} else {
    ShiftRegister >>= 1;
    return 0;
}
}
```

The savings here is that all the XORs can be done as a single operation. This can also be parallelized, and the different feedback polynomials can be different. The Galois configuration can also be faster in hardware, especially in custom VLSI implementations. In general, if you are using hardware that is good at shifts, use a Fibonacci configuration; if you can exploit parallelism, use a Galois configuration.

16.3   DESIGN AND ANALYSIS OF STREAM CIPHERS

Most practical stream-cipher designs center around LFSRs. In the early days of electronics, they were very easy to build. A shift register is nothing more than an array of bit memories and the feedback sequence is just a series of XOR gates. Even in VLSI circuitry, a LFSR-based stream cipher can give you a lot of security with only a few logic gates.

The problem with LFSRs is that they are very inefficient in software. You want to avoid sparse feedback polynomials—they facilitate correlation attacks [1051,1090, 350]—and dense feedback polynomials are inefficient. Any stream cipher outputs a bit at a time; you have to iterate the algorithm 64 times to encrypt what a single iteration of DES can encrypt. In fact, a simple LFSR algorithm like the shrinking generator described later is no faster in software than DES.

This branch of cryptography is fast-paced and very politically charged. Most designs are secret; a majority of military encryptions systems in use today are based on LFSRs. In fact, most Cray computers (Cray 1, Cray X-MP, Cray Y-MP) have a rather curious instruction generally known as "population count." It counts the 1 bits in a register and can be used both to efficiently calculate the Hamming distance between two binary words and to implement a vectorized version of a LFSR. I've heard this called the canonical NSA instruction, demanded by almost all computer contracts.

On the other hand, an astonishingly large number of seemingly complex shift-register-based generators have been cracked. And certainly military cryptanalysis institutions such as the NSA have cracked a lot more. Sometimes it's amazing to see the simple ones proposed again and again.

Linear Complexity

Analyzing stream ciphers is often easier than analyzing block ciphers. For example, one important metric used to analyze LFSR-based generators is **linear complexity**, or linear span. This is defined as the length, n, of the shortest LFSR that can mimic the generator output. Any sequence generated by a finite-state machine over a finite field has a finite linear complexity [1006]. Linear complexity is important because a simple algorithm, called the **Berlekamp-Massey algorithm**, can generate this LFSR after examining only $2n$ bits of the keystream [1005]. Once you've generated this LFSR, you've broken the stream cipher.

This idea has extensions from fields to rings [1298], and when the output sequence is viewed as numbers over fields of odd characteristic [842]. A further enhancement is the notion of a **linear complexity profile**, which measures the linear complexity of the sequence as it gets longer and longer [1357,1168,411,1582]. Another algorithm for computing linear complexity is useful only in very specialized circumstances [597,595,596,1333]. A generalization of linear complexity is in [776]. There is also the notion of sphere complexity [502] and 2-adic complexity [844].

In any case, remember that a high linear complexity does not necessarily indicate a secure generator, but a low linear complexity indicates an insecure one [1357,1249].

Correlation Immunity

Cryptographers try to get a high linear complexity by combining the output of several output sequences in some nonlinear manner. The danger here is that one or more of the internal output sequences—often just outputs of individual LFSRs—can be correlated with the combined keystream and attacked using linear algebra. Often this is called a **correlation attack** or a divide-and-conquer attack. Thomas Siegenthaler has shown that **correlation immunity** can be precisely defined, and that there is a trade-off between correlation immunity and linear complexity [1450].

The basic idea behind a correlation attack is to identify some correlation between the output of the generator and the output of one of its internal pieces. Then, by observing the output sequence, you can obtain information about that internal output. Using that information and other correlations, collect information about the other internal outputs until the entire generator is broken.

Correlation attacks and variations such as fast correlation attacks—these offer a trade-off between computational complexity and effectiveness—have been successfully applied to a number of LFSR-based keystream generators [1451,278,1452,572, 1636,1051,1090,350,633,1054,1089,995]. Some interesting new ideas along these lines are in [46,1641].

Other Attacks

There are other general attacks against keystream generators. The **linear consistency test** attempts to identify some subset of the encryption key using matrix techniques [1638]. There is also the **meet-in-the-middle consistency attack** [39,41]. The **linear syndrome algorithm** relies on being able to write a fragment of the output sequence as a linear equation [1636,1637]. There is the **best affine approximation attack** [502] and the **derived sequence attack** [42]. The techniques of differential cryptanalysis have even been applied to stream ciphers [501], as has linear cryptanalysis [631].

16.4 STREAM CIPHERS USING LFSRs

The basic approach to designing a keystream generator using LFSRs is simple. First you take one or more LFSRs, generally of different lengths and with different feedback polynomials. (If the lengths are all relatively prime and the feedback polynomials are all primitive, the whole generator is maximal length.) The key is the initial state of the LFSRs. Every time you want a bit, shift the LFSRs once (this is sometimes called **clocking**). The output bit is a function, preferably a nonlinear function, of some of the bits of the LFSRs. This function is called the **combining function**, and the whole generator is called a **combination generator**. (If the output bit is a function of a single LFSR, the generator is called a **filter generator**.) Much of the theoretical background for this kind of thing was laid down by Selmer and Neal Zierler [1647].

Complications have been added. Some generators have LFSRs clocked at different rates; sometimes the clocking of one generator depends on the output of another. These are all electronic versions of pre-WWII cipher machine ideas, and are called **clock-controlled generators** [641]. Clock control can be feedforward, where the output of one LFSR controls the clocking of another, or feedback, where the output of one LFSR controls its own clocking.

Although these generators are, at least in theory, susceptible to embedding and probabilistic correlation attacks [634,632], many are secure for now. Additional theory on clock-controlled shift registers is in [89].

Ian Cassells, once the head of pure mathematics at Cambridge and a former Bletchly Park cryptanalyst, said that "cryptography is a mixture of mathematics and muddle, and without the muddle the mathematics can be used against you." What he meant was that in stream ciphers, you need some kind of mathematical structure—such as a LFSR—to guarantee maximal-length and other properties, and then some complicated nonlinear muddle to stop someone from getting at the register and solving it. This advice also holds true for block algorithms.

What follows is a smattering of LFSR-based keystream generators that have appeared in the literature. I don't know if any of them have been used in actual cryptographic products. Most of them are of theoretical interest only. Some have been broken; some may still be secure.

Since LFSR-based ciphers are generally implemented in hardware, electronics logic symbols will be used in the figures. In the text, $\oplus$ is XOR, $\wedge$ is AND, $\vee$ is OR, and $\neg$ is NOT.

Geffe Generator

This keystream generator uses three LFSRs, combined in a nonlinear manner (see Figure 16.6) [606]. Two of the LFSRs are inputs into a multiplexer, and the third LFSR controls the output of the multiplexer. If a_1, a_2, and a_3 are the outputs of the three LFSRs, the output of the Geffe generator can be described by:

$$b = (a_1 \wedge a_2) \oplus ((\neg\, a_1) \wedge a_3)$$

If the LFSRs have lengths n_1, n_2, and n_3, respectively, then the linear complexity of the generator is

$$(n_1 + 1)n_2 + n_1 n_3$$

The period of the generator is the least common multiple of the periods of the three generators. Assuming the degrees of the three primitive feedback polynomials are relatively prime, the period of this generator is the product of the periods of the three LFSRs.

Although this generator looks good on paper, it is cryptographically weak and falls to a correlation attack [829,1638]. The output of the generator equals the output of LFSR-2 75 percent of the time. So, if the feedback taps are known, you can guess the initial value for LFSR-2 and generate the output sequence of that register. Then you can count the number of times the output of the LFSR-2 agrees with the output of the generator. If you guessed wrong, the two sequences will agree about 50 percent of the time; if you guessed right, the two sequences will agree about 75 percent of the time.

Similarly, the output of the generator equals the output of LFSR-3 about 75 percent of the time. With those correlations, the keystream generator can be easily cracked. For example, if the primitive polynomials only have three terms each, and the largest LFSR is of length n, it only takes a segment of the output sequence $37n$-bits long to reconstruct the internal states of all three LFSRs [1639].

Generalized Geffe Generator

Instead of choosing between two LFSRs, this scheme chooses between k LFSRs, as long as k is a power of 2. There are $k + 1$ LFSRs total (see Figure 16.7). LFSR-1 must be clocked $\log_2 k$ times faster than the other k LFSRs.

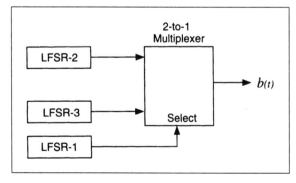

Figure 16.6   Geffe generator.

Even though this scheme is more complex than the Geffe generator, the same kind of correlation attack is possible. I don't recommend this generator.

Jennings Generator

This scheme uses a multiplexer to combine two LFSRs [778,779,780]. The multiplexer, controlled by LFSR-1, selects 1 bit of LFSR-2 for each output bit. There is also a function that maps the output of LFSR-2 to the input of the multiplexer (see Figure 16.8).

The key is the initial state of the two LFSRs and the mapping function. Although this generator has great statistical properties, it fell to Ross Anderson's meet-in-the-middle consistency attack [39] and the linear consistency attack [1638,442]. Don't use this generator.

Beth-Piper Stop-and-Go Generator

This generator, shown in Figure 16.9, uses the output of one LFSR to control the clock of another LFSR [151]. The clock input of LFSR-2 is controlled by the output of LFSR-1, so that LFSR-2 can change its state at time t only if the output of LFSR-1 was 1 at time $t - 1$.

No one has been able to prove results about this generator's linear complexity in the general case. However, it falls to a correlation attack [1639].

Alternating Stop-and-Go Generator

This generator uses three LFSRs of different length. LFSR-2 is clocked when the output of LFSR-1 is 1; LFSR-3 is clocked when the output of LFSR-1 is 0. The output of the generator is the XOR of LFSR-2 and LFSR-3 (see Figure 16.10) [673].

This generator has a long period and large linear complexity. The authors found a correlation attack against LFSR-1, but it does not substantially weaken the generator. There have been other attempts at keystream generators along these lines [1534, 1574,1477].

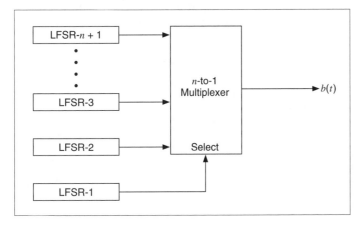

Figure 16.7   Generalized Geffe generator.

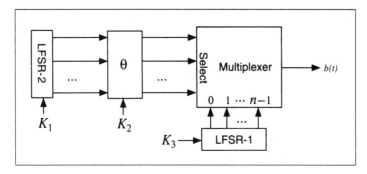

Figure 16.8   Jennings generator.

Bilateral Stop-and-Go Generator

This generator uses two LFSRs, both of length n (see Figure 16.11) [1638]. The output of the generator is the XOR of the outputs of each LFSR. If the output of LFSR-2 at time $t - 1$ is 0 and the output at time $t - 2$ is 1, then LFSR-2 does not clock at time t. Conversely, if the output of LFSR-1 at time $t - 1$ is 0 and the output at $t - 2$ is 1, and if LFSR-1 clocked at time t, then LFSR-2 does not clock at time t.

The linear complexity of this system is roughly equal to the period. According to [1638], "no evident key redundancy has been observed in this system."

Threshold Generator

This generator tries to get around the security problems of the previous generators by using a variable number of LFSRs [277]. The theory is that if you use a lot of LFSRs, it's harder to break the cipher.

This generator is illustrated in Figure 16.12. Take the output of a large number of LFSRs (use an odd number of them). Make sure the lengths of all the LFSRs are relatively prime and all the feedback polynomials are primitive: maximize the period. If more than half the output bits are 1, then the output of the generator is 1. If more than half the output bits are 0, then the output of the generator is 0.

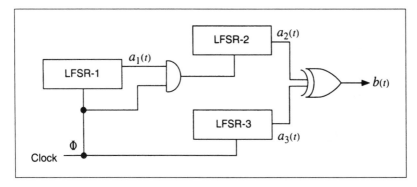

Figure 16.9   Beth-Piper stop-and-go generator.

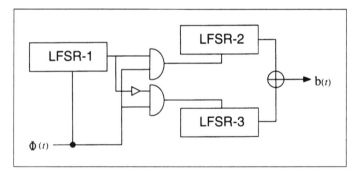

Figure 16.10   Alternating stop-and-go generator.

With three LFSRs, the output generator can be written as:

$$b = (a_1 \wedge a_2) \oplus (a_1 \wedge a_3) \oplus (a_2 \wedge a_3)$$

This is very similar to the Geffe generator, except that it has a larger linear complexity of

$$n_1n_2 + n_1n_3 + n_2n_3$$

where n_1, n_2, and n_3 are the lengths of the first, second, and third LFSRs.

This generator isn't great. Each output bit of the generator yields some information about the state of the LFSRs—0.189 bit to be exact—and the whole thing falls to a correlation attack. I don't recommend using it.

Self-Decimated Generators

Self-decimated generators are generators that control their own clock. Two have been proposed, one by Rainer Rueppel (see Figure 16.13) [1359] and another by Bill

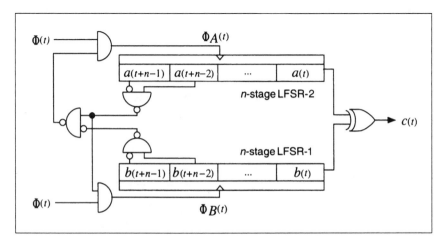

Figure 16.11   Bilateral stop-and-go generator.

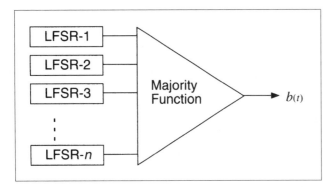

Figure 16.12   Threshold generator.

Chambers and Dieter Gollmann [308] (see Figure 16.14). In Rueppel's generator, when the output of the LFSR is 0, the LFSR is clocked d times. When the output of the LFSR is 1, the LFSR is clocked k times. Chambers's and Gollmann's generator is more complicated, but the idea is the same. Unfortunately, both generators are insecure [1639], although some modifications have been proposed that may correct the problems [1362].

Multispeed Inner-Product Generator

This generator, by Massey and Rueppel [1014], uses two LFSRs clocked at two different speeds (see Figure 16.15). LFSR-2 is clocked d times as fast as LFSR-1. The individual bits of the two LFSRs are ANDed together and then XORed with each other to produce the final output bit of the generator.

Although this generator has high linear complexity and it possesses excellent statistical properties, it still falls to a linear consistency attack [1639]. If n_1 is the length of LFSR-1, n_2 is the length of the LFSR-2, and d is the speed multiple between the two, then the internal state of the generator can be recovered from an output sequence of length

$$n_1 + n_2 + \log_2 d$$

Summation Generator

More work by Rainer Rueppel, this generator adds the output of two LFSRs (with carry) [1358,1357]. This operation is highly nonlinear. Through the late 1980s, this

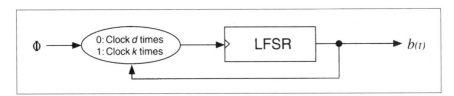

Figure 16.13   Rueppel's self-decimated generator.

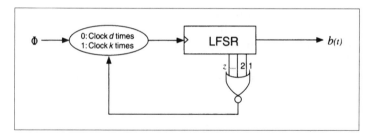

Figure 16.14   Chambers's and Gollmann's self-decimated generator.

generator was the security front-runner, but it fell to a correlation attack [1053, 1054,1091]. And it has been shown that this is an example of a feedback with carry shift register (see Section 17.4), and can be broken [844].

DNRSG

That stands for "dynamic random-sequence generator" [1117]. The idea is to have two different filter generators—threshold, summation, or whatever—fed by a single set of LFSRs and controlled by another LFSR.

First clock all the LFSRs. If the output of LFSR-0 is 1, then compute the output of the first filter generator. If the output of LFSR-0 is 0, then compute the output of the second filter generator. The final output is the first output XOR the second.

Gollmann Cascade

The Gollmann cascade (see Figure 16.16), described in [636,309], is a strengthened version of a stop-and-go generator. It consists of a series of LFSRs, with the clock of each controlled by the previous LFSR. If the output of LFSR-1 is 1 at time $t - 1$, then LFSR-2 clocks. If the output of LFSR-2 is 1 at time $t - 1$, then LFSR-3 clocks, and so on. The output of the final LFSR is the output of the generator. If all the LFSRs have the same length, n, the linear complexity of a system with k LFSRs is

$$n(2^n - 1)^{k-1}$$

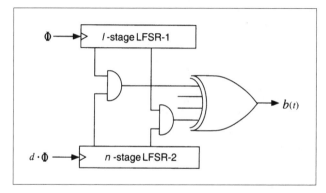

Figure 16.15   Multispeed inner-product generator.

Cascades are a cool idea: They are conceptually very simple and they can be used to generate sequences with huge periods, huge linear complexities, and good statistical properties. They are vulnerable to an attack called **lock-in** [640]. This is a technique by which a cryptanalyst reconstructs the input to the last shift register in the cascade, then proceeds to break the cascade register by register. This is a serious problem in some situations and weakens the effective key length of the algorithm, but precautions can be taken to minimize the attack.

Further analysis has indicated that the sequence approaches random as k gets larger [637,638,642,639]. Based on recent attacks on short Gollmann cascades [1063], I recommend using a k of at least 15. You're better off using more LFSRs of shorter length than fewer LFSRs of longer length.

Shrinking Generator

The shrinking generator [378] uses a different form of clock control than the previous generators. Take two LFSRs: LFSR-1 and LFSR-2. Clock both of them. If the output of LFSR-1 is 1, then the output of the generator is LFSR-2. If the output of LFSR-1 is 0, discard the two bits, clock both LFSRs, and try again.

This idea is simple, reasonably efficient, and looks secure. If the feedback polynomials are sparse, the generator is vulnerable, but no other problems have been found. Even so, it's new. One implementation problem is that the output rate is not regular; if LFSR-1 has a long string of zeros then the generator outputs nothing. The authors suggest buffering to solve this problem [378]. Practical implementation of the shrinking generator is discussed in [901].

Self-Shrinking Generator

The self-shrinking generator [1050] is a variant of the shrinking generator. Instead of using two LFSRs, use pairs of bits from a single LFSR. Clock a LFSR twice. If the first bit in the pair is 1, the output of the generator is the second bit. If the first bit is 0, discard both bits and try again. While the self-shrinking generator requires about half the memory space as the shrinking generator, it is also half the speed.

While the self-shrinking generator also seems secure, it still has some unexplained behavior and unknown properties. This is a very new generator; give it some time.

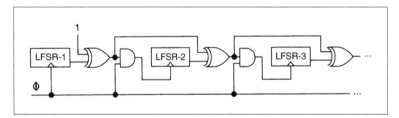

Figure 16.16   Gollmann cascade.

16.5   A5

A5 is the stream cipher used to encrypt GSM (Group Special Mobile). That's the non-American standard for digital cellular mobile telephones. It is used to encrypt the link from the telephone to the base station. The rest of the link is unencrypted; the telephone company can easily eavesdrop on your conversations.

A lot of strange politics surrounds this one. Originally it was thought that GSM's cryptography would prohibit export of the phones to some countries. Now some officials are discussing whether A5 might harm export sales, implying that it is so weak as to be an embarrassment. Rumor has it that the various NATO intelligence agencies had a catfight in the mid-1980s over whether GSM encryption should be strong or weak. The Germans wanted strong cryptography, as they were sitting near the Soviet Union. The other countries overruled them, and A5 is a French design.

We know most of the details. A British telephone company gave all the documentation to Bradford University without remembering to get them to sign a nondisclosure agreement. It leaked here and there, and was eventually posted to the Internet. A paper describing A5 is [1622]; there is also code at the back of this book.

A5 consists of three LFSRs; the register lengths are 19, 22, and 23; all the feedback polynomials are sparse. The output is the XOR of the three LFSRs. A5 uses variable clock control. Each register is clocked based on its own middle bit, XORed with the inverse threshold function of the middle bits of all three registers. Usually, two of the LFSRs clock in each round.

There is a trivial attack requiring 2^{40} encryptions: Guess the contents of the first two LFSRs, then try to determine the third LFSR from the keystream. (Whether this attack is actually feasible is under debate, but a hardware key search machine currently under design should resolve the matter soon [45].)

Nonetheless, it is becoming clear that the basic ideas behind A5 are good. It is very efficient. It passes all known statistical tests; its only known weakness is that its registers are short enough to make exhaustive search feasible. Variants of A5 with longer shift registers and denser feedback polynomials should be secure.

16.6   HUGHES XPD/KPD

This algorithm is brought to you by Hughes Aircraft Corp. They put it in army tactical radios and direction-finding equipment for sale to foreign militaries. It was designed in 1986 and called XPD, for Exportable Protection Device. Later it was renamed KPD—Kinetic Protection Device—and declassified [1037,1036].

The algorithm uses a 61-bit LFSR. There are 2^{10} different primitive feedback polynomials, which were approved by the NSA. The key selects one of these polynomials (they are all stored in ROM somewhere), as well as the initial state of the LFSR.

It has eight different nonlinear filters, each of which has six taps from the LFSR and which produces 1 bit. The bits combine to generate a byte, which is used to encrypt or decrypt the datastream.

This algorithm looks pretty impressive, but I doubt it is. The NSA allows export, so there must be some attack on the order of 2^{40} or less. What is it?

16.7 NANOTEQ

Nanoteq is a South African electronics company. This is their algorithm that has been fielded by the South African police to encrypt their fax transmissions, and presumably for other uses as well.

The algorithm is described, more or less, in [902,903]. It uses a 127-bit LFSR with a fixed feedback polynomial; the key is the initial state of the feedback register. The 127 bits of the register are reduced to a single keystream bit using 25 primitive cells. Each cell has five inputs and one output:

$$f(x_1,x_2,x_3,x_4,x_5) = x_1 + x_2 + (x_1 + x_3)(x_2 + x_4 + x_5) + (x_1 + x_4)(x_2 + x_3) + x_5$$

Each input of the function is XORed with some bit of the key. There is also a secret permutation that depends on the particular implementation, and is not detailed in the papers. This algorithm is only available in hardware.

Is this algorithm secure? I doubt it. During the transition to majority rule, embarrassing faxes from one police station to another would sometimes turn up in the liberal newspapers. These could easily have been the results of U.S., U.K., or Soviet intelligence efforts. Ross Anderson took some initial steps towards cryptanalyzing this algorithm in [46]; I expect more results to come soon.

16.8 RAMBUTAN

Rambutan is a British algorithm, designed by the Communications Electronics Security Group (one of the aliases used by GCHQ). It is only sold as a hardware module and is approved for the protection of classified material up to "Confidential." The algorithm itself is secret, and the chip is not generally commercially available.

Rambutan has a 112-bit key (plus parity bits) and can operate in three modes: ECB, CBC, and 8-bit CFB. This strongly indicates that it is a block algorithm, but rumors point elsewhere. Supposedly, it is a LFSR stream cipher. It has five shift registers, each one of a different length around 80 bits. The feedback polynomials are fairly sparse, with only about 10 taps each. Each shift register provides four inputs to a very large and complex nonlinear function which eventually spits out a single bit.

Why call it Rambutan? Perhaps, like the fruit, it's spiny and forbidding on the outside but soft and yielding inside. On the other hand, maybe that's not the reason.

16.9 ADDITIVE GENERATORS

Additive generators (sometimes called lagged Fibonacci generators) are extremely efficient because they produce random words instead of random bits [863]. They are not secure on their own, but can be used as building blocks for secure generators.

The initial state of the generator is an array of n-bit words: 8-bit words, 16-bit words, 32-bit words, whatever: $X_1, X_2, X_3, \ldots, X_m$. This initial state is the key. The ith word of the generator is

$$X_i = (X_{i-a} + X_{i-b} + X_{i-c} + \ldots + X_{i-m}) \bmod 2^n$$

If the coefficients $a, b, c, \ldots, m$ are chosen right, the period of this generator is at least $2^n - 1$. One of the requirements on the coefficients is that the least significant bit forms a maximal-length LFSR.

For example, (55,24,0) is a primitive polynomial mod 2 from Table 16.2. This means that the following additive generator is maximal length.

$$X_i = (X_{i-55} + X_{i-24}) \bmod 2^n$$

This works because the primitive polynomial has three coefficients. If it has more than three, you need some additional requirements to make it maximal length. See [249] for details.

Fish

Fish is an additive generator based on techniques used in the shrinking generator [190]. It produces a stream of 32-bit words which can be XORed with a plaintext stream to produce ciphertext, or XORed with a ciphertext stream to produce plaintext. The algorithm is named as it is because it is a Fibonacci shrinking generator.

First, use these two additive generators. The key is the initial values of these generators.

$$A_i = (A_{i-55} + A_{i-24}) \bmod 2^{32}$$
$$B_i = (B_{i-52} + B_{i-19}) \bmod 2^{32}$$

These sequences are shrunk, as a pair, depending on the least significant bit of B_i: if it is 1, use the pair; if it is 0, ignore the pair. C_i is the sequence of used words from A_i, and D_i is the sequence of used words from B_i. These words are used in pairs—C_{2j}, C_{2j+1}, D_{2j}, and D_{2j+1}—to generate two 32-bit output words: K_{2j} and K_{2j+1}.

$$E_{2j} = C_{2j} \oplus (D_{2j} \wedge D_{2j+1})$$
$$F_{2j} = D_{2j+1} \wedge (E_{2j} \wedge C_{2j+1})$$
$$K_{2j} = E_{2j} \oplus F_{2j}$$
$$K_{2i+1} = C_{2i+1} \oplus F_{2j}$$

This algorithm is fast. On a 33 megahertz 486, a C implementation of Fish encrypts data at 15 megabits per second. Unfortunately, it is also insecure; an attack has a work factor of about 2^{40} [45].

Pike

Pike is a leaner, meaner version of Fish, brought to you by Ross Anderson, the man who broke Fish [45]. It uses three additive generators. For example:

$$A_i = (A_{i-55} + A_{i-24}) \bmod 2^{32}$$

$$B_i = (B_{i-57} + B_{i-7}) \bmod 2^{32}$$
$$C_i = (C_{i-58} + C_{i-19}) \bmod 2^{32}$$

To generate the keystream word, look at the addition carry bits. If all three agree (all are 0 or all are 1), then clock all three generators. If they do not, just clock the two generators that agree. Save the carry bits for next time. The final output is the XOR of the three generators.

Pike is faster than Fish, since on the average 2.75 steps will be required per output rather than 3. It is far too new to trust, but looks good so far.

Mush

Mush is a mutual shrinking generator. It's easy to explain [1590]. Take two additive generators: A and B. If the carry bit of A is set, clock B. If the carry bit of B is set, clock A. Clock A, and set the carry bit if there is a carry. Clock B, and set the carry bit if there is a carry. The final output is the XOR of the output of A and B.

The easiest generators to use are the ones from Fish:

$$A_i = (A_{i-55} + A_{i-24}) \bmod 2^{32}$$
$$B_i = (B_{i-52} + B_{i-19}) \bmod 2^{32}$$

On the average, three generator iterations are required to produce one output word. And if the coefficients of the additive generators are chosen correctly and are relatively prime, the output sequence will be maximal length. I know of no successful attacks, but remember that this algorithm is very new.

16.10 GIFFORD

David Gifford invented a stream cipher and used it to encrypt news wire reports in the Boston area from 1984 until 1988 [608,607,609]. The algorithm has a single 8-byte register: $b_0, b_1, \ldots, b_7$. The key is the initial state of the register. The algorithm works in OFB; the plaintext does not affect the algorithm at all. (See Figure 16.17).

To generate a key byte k_i, concatenate b_0 and b_2 and concatenate b_4 and b_7. Multiply the two together to get a 32-bit number. The third byte from the left is k_i.

To update the register, take b_1 and sticky right shift it 1 bit. This means the left-most bit is both shifted and also remains in place. Take b_7 and shift it 1 bit to the left; there should be a 0 in the right-most bit position. Take the XOR of the modified b_1, the modified b_7, and b_0. Shift the original register 1 byte to the right and put this byte in the left-most position.

This algorithm remained secure throughout its life, but was broken in 1994 [287]. It turns out that the feedback polynomial isn't primitive and can be attacked that way—oops.

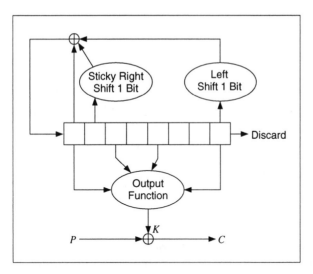

Figure 16.17   Gifford.

16.11   ALGORITHM M

The name is from Knuth [863]. It's a method for combining multiple pseudo-random streams that increases their security. One generator's output is used to select a delayed output from the other generator [996,1003]. In C:

```
#define ARR_SIZE (8192) /* for example - the larger the better
*/

static unsigned char delay[ ARR_SIZE ] ;

unsigned char prngA( void ) ;
long prngB( void ) ;

void init_algM( void )
{
  long i ;

  for ( i = 0 ; i < ARR_SIZE ; i++ )
    delay[i] = prngA() ;

} /* init_algM */

unsigned char algM( void )
{
  long j,v ;
```

```
        j = prngB() % ARR_SIZE ;     /* get the delay[] index */
        v = delay[j] ;               /* get the value to return */
        delay[j] = prngA() ;         /* replace it */

        return ( v ) ;
} /* algM */
```

This has strength in that if prngA were truly random, one could not learn anything about prngB (and could therefore not cryptanalyze it). If prngA were of the form that it could be cryptanalyzed only if its output were available in order (i.e., only if prngB were cryptanalyzed first) and otherwise it was effectively truly random, then the combination would be secure.

16.12 PKZIP

Roger Schlafly designed the encryption algorithm built into the PKZIP data compression program. It's a stream cipher that encrypts data one byte at a time. At least, this is the algorithm in version 2.04g. I can't speak for later versions, but unless there is some announcement you can probably assume that they are identical.

The algorithm uses three 32-bit variables, initialized as follows:

$$K_0 = 305419896$$
$$K_1 = 591751049$$
$$K_2 = 878082192$$

It has an 8-bit key, K_3, derived from K_2. Here is the algorithm (all symbols are standard C notation):

$$C_i = P_i \wedge K_3$$
$$K_0 = \text{crc32} (K_0, P_i)$$
$$K_1 = K_1 + (K_0 \,\&\, 0\text{x}000000\text{ff})$$
$$K_1 = K_1 * 134775813 + 1$$
$$K_2 = \text{crc32} (K_2, K_1 >> 24)$$
$$K_3 = ((K_2 \,|\, 2) * ((K_2 \,|\, 2) \wedge 1)) >> 8$$

The function crc32 takes the previous value and a byte, XORs them, and calculates the next value by the CRC polynomial denoted by 0xedb88320. In practice, a 256-entry table can be precomputed and the crc32 calculation becomes:

$$\text{crc32} (a, b) = (a >> 8) \wedge \text{table} [(a \,\&\, 0\text{xff}) \oplus b]$$

The table is precomputed by the original definition of crc32:

$$\text{table} [i] = \text{crc32} (i, 0)$$

To encrypt a plaintext stream, first loop the key bytes through the encryption algorithm to update the keys. Ignore the ciphertext output in this step. Then encrypt the plaintext, one byte at a time. Twelve random bytes are prepended to the plaintext, but that's not really important. Decryption is similar to encryption, except that C_i is used in the second step of the algorithm instead of P_i.

Security of PKZIP

Unfortunately, it's not that great. An attack requires 40 to 200 bytes of known plaintext and has a time complexity of about 2^{27} [166]. You can do it in a few hours on your personal computer. If the compressed file has any standard headers, getting the known plaintext is no problem. Don't use the built-in encryption in PKZIP.

CHAPTER 17

Other Stream Ciphers and Real Random-Sequence Generators

17.1 RC4

RC4 is a variable-key-size stream cipher developed in 1987 by Ron Rivest for RSA Data Security, Inc. For seven years it was proprietary, and details of the algorithm were only available after signing a nondisclosure agreement.

In September, 1994 someone posted source code to the Cypherpunks mailing list—anonymously. It quickly spread to the Usenet newsgroup sci.crypt, and via the Internet to ftp sites around the world. Readers with legal copies of RC4 confirmed compatibility. RSA Data Security, Inc. tried to put the genie back into the bottle, claiming that it was still a trade secret even though it was public; it was too late. It has since been discussed and dissected on Usenet, distributed at conferences, and taught in cryptography courses.

RC4 is simple to describe. The algorithm works in OFB: The keystream is independent of the plaintext. It has a $8 * 8$ S-box: $S_0, S_1, \ldots, S_{255}$. The entries are a permutation of the numbers 0 through 255, and the permutation is a function of the variable-length key. It has two counters, i and j, initialized to zero.

To generate a random byte, do the following:

$$i = (i + 1) \bmod 256$$
$$j = (j + S_i) \bmod 256$$
$$\text{swap } S_i \text{ and } S_j$$
$$t = (S_i + S_j) \bmod 256$$
$$K = S_t$$

The byte K is XORed with the plaintext to produce ciphertext or XORed with the ciphertext to produce plaintext. Encryption is fast—about 10 times faster than DES.

Initializing the S-box is also easy. First, fill it linearly: $S_0 = 0, S_1 = 1, \ldots, S_{255} = 255$. Then fill another 256-byte array with the key, repeating the key as necessary to fill the entire array: $K_0, K_1, \ldots, K_{255}$. Set the index j to zero. Then:

for $i = 0$ to 255:

$\quad j = (j + S_i + K_i)$ mod 256

$\quad$ swap S_i and S_j

And that's it. RSADSI claims that the algorithm is immune to differential and linear cryptanalysis, doesn't seem to have any small cycles, and is highly non-linear. (There are no public cryptanalytic results. RC4 can be in about 2^{1700} $(256! \times 256^2)$ possible states: an enormous number.) The S-box slowly evolves with use: i ensures that every element changes and j ensures that the elements change randomly. The algorithm is simple enough that most programmers can quickly code it from memory.

It should be possible to generalize this idea to larger S-boxes and word sizes. The previous version is 8-bit RC4. There's no reason why you can't define 16-bit RC4 with a 16 * 16 S-box (100K of memory) and a 16-bit word. You'd have to iterate the initial setup a lot more times—65,536 to keep with the stated design—but the resulting algorithm should be faster.

RC4 has special export status if its key length is 40 bits or under (see Section 13.8). This special export status has nothing to do with the secrecy of the algorithm, although RSA Data Security, Inc. has hinted for years that it does. The name is trademarked, so anyone who writes his own code has to call it something else. Various internal documents by RSA Data Security, Inc. have not yet been made public [1320,1337].

So, what's the deal with RC4? It's no longer a trade secret, so presumably anyone can use it. However, RSA Data Security, Inc. will almost certainly sue anyone who uses unlicensed RC4 in a commercial product. They probably won't win, but they will certainly make it cheaper for a company to license than fight.

RC4 is in dozens of commercial cryptography products, including Lotus Notes, Apple Computer's AOCE, and Oracle Secure SQL. It is part of the Cellular Digital Packet Data specification [37].

17.2 SEAL

SEAL is a software-efficient stream cipher designed at IBM by Phil Rogaway and Don Coppersmith [1340]. The algorithm was optimized for 32-bit processors: To run well it needs eight 32-bit registers and a cache of a few kilobytes. Using a relatively slow operation, SEAL preprocesses the key operation into a set of tables. These tables are then used to speed up encryption and decryption.

Pseudo-random Function Family

One novel feature of SEAL is that is isn't really a traditional stream cipher: it is a **pseudo-random function family**. Given a 160-bit key k, and a 32-bit n, SEAL stretches n into an L-bit string $k(n)$. L can take any value less than 64 kilobytes. SEAL is supposed to enjoy the property that if k is selected at random, then $k(n)$ should be computationally indistinguishable from a random L-bit function of n.

The practical effect of SEAL being a pseudo-random function family is that it is useful in applications where traditional stream ciphers are not. With most stream ciphers you generate a sequence of bits in one direction: Knowing the key and a position i, the only way to determine the ith bit generated is to generate all the bits up until the ith one. But a pseudo-random function family is different: You get easy access at any desired position in the key stream. This is very useful.

Imagine you need to secure a hard drive. You want to encrypt each and every 512-byte sector. With a pseudo-random function family like SEAL, you can encrypt the contents of sector n by XORing it with $k(n)$. It is as though the entire disk is XORed with a long pseudo-random string, where any piece of that long string can be computed without any trouble.

A pseudo-random function family also simplifies the synchronization problem encountered with standard stream ciphers. Suppose you send encrypted messages over a channel that sometimes drops messages. With a pseudo-random function family, you can encrypt under k the nth message you transmit, x_n, as n together with the XOR of x_n and $k(n)$. The receiver doesn't need to store any state to recover x_n, nor does he need to worry about lost messages affecting the message decryption process.

Description of SEAL

The inner loop of SEAL is shown by Figure 17.1. Three key-derived tables, called R, S, and T, drive the algorithm. The preprocessing step maps the key k, to these tables using a procedure based on SHA (see Section 18.7). The 2-kilobyte table, T, is a $9 * 32$ bit S-box.

SEAL also uses four 32-bit registers, A, B, C, and D, whose initial values are determined by n and the k-derived tables R and T. These registers get modified over several iterations, each one involving 8 rounds. In each round 9 bits of a first register (either A, B, C, or D) are used to index into table T. The value retrieved from T is then added to or XORed with the contents of a second register: again one of A, B, C, or D. The first register is then circularly shifted by nine positions. In some rounds the second register is further modified by adding or XORing it with the (now shifted) first register. After 8 rounds of this, A, B, C, and D are added to the keystream, each masked first by adding or XORing it with a certain word from S. The iteration is completed by adding to A and C additional values dependent on n, n_1, n_2, n_3, n_4; exactly which one depends on the parity of the iteration number.

The important ideas in this design seem to be:

1. Use a large, secret, key-derived S-box (T).

2. Alternate arithmetic operations which don't commute (addition and XOR).

3. Use an internal state maintained by the cipher which is not directly manifest in the data stream (the n_i values which modify A and C at the end of each iteration).

4. Vary the round function according to the round number, and vary the iteration function according to the iteration number.

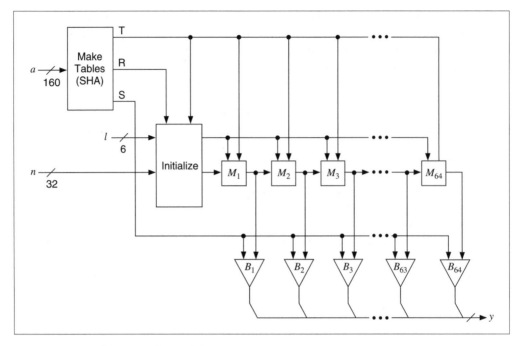

Figure 17.1   The inner loop of SEAL.

SEAL requires about five elementary machine operations to encrypt each byte of text. It runs at 58 megabits per second on a 50 megahertz 486 machine. This is probably the fastest software algorithm in the book.

On the other hand, SEAL must preprocess its key into internal tables. These tables total roughly 3 kilobytes in size, and their calculation takes about 200 SHA computations. Thus, SEAL is not appropriate to use in situations where you don't have the time to perform the key setup or you don't have the memory to store the tables.

Security of SEAL

SEAL is a new algorithm and has yet to be subjected to any published cryptanalysis. This suggests caution. However, SEAL seems to be well thought through. Its peculiarities do, in the end, make a good deal of sense. And Don Coppersmith is generally regarded as the world's cleverest cryptanalyst.

Patents and Licenses

SEAL is being patented [380]. Anyone wishing to license SEAL should contact the Director of Licenses, IBM Corporation, 500 Columbus Ave., Thurnwood, NY, 10594.

17.3 WAKE

WAKE is the Word Auto Key Encryption algorithm, invented by David Wheeler [1589]. It produces a stream of 32-bit words which can be XORed with a plaintext stream to produce ciphertext, or XORed with a ciphertext stream to produce plain-text. And it's fast.

WAKE works in CFB; the previous ciphertext word is used to generate the next key word. It also uses an S-box of 256 32-bit values. This S-box has a special prop-erty: The high-order byte of all the entries is a permutation of all possible bytes, and the low-order 3 bytes are random.

First, generate the S-box entries, S_i, from the key. Then initialize four registers with the key (or with another key): a_0, b_0, c_0, and d_0. To generate a 32-bit keystream word, K_i:

$$K_i = d_i$$

The ciphertext word C_i, is the plaintext word, P_i XORed with K_i.

Then, update the four registers:

$$a_{i+1} = M(a_i, d_i)$$
$$b_{i+1} = M(b_i, a_{i+1})$$
$$c_{i+1} = M(c_i, b_{i+1})$$
$$d_{i+1} = M(d_i, c_{i+1})$$

Function M is

$$M(x,y) = (x+y) >> 8 \oplus S_{(x+y) \wedge 255}$$

This is shown in Figure 17.2. The operation >> is a right shift, not a rotation. The low-order 8 bits of $x + y$ are the input into the S-box. Wheeler gives a procedure for

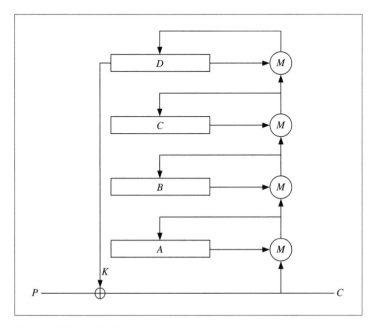

Figure 17.2   Wake.

generating the S-box, but it isn't really complete. Any algorithm to generate random bytes and a random permutation will work.

WAKE's biggest asset is that it is fast. However, it's insecure against a chosen-plaintext or chosen-ciphertext attack. It is being used in the current version of Dr. Solomon's Anti-Virus program.

17.4 FEEDBACK WITH CARRY SHIFT REGISTERS

A feedback with carry shift register, or FCSR, is similar to a LFSR. Both have a shift register and a feedback function; the difference is that a FCSR also has a carry register (see Figure 17.3). Instead of XORing all the bits in the tap sequence, add the bits together and add in the contents of the carry register. The result mod 2 becomes the new bit. The result divided by 2 becomes the new content of the carry register.

Figure 17.4 is an example of a 3-bit FCSR tapped at the first and second bit. Its initial value is 001, and the initial contents of the carry register is 0. The output bit is the right-most bit of the shift register.

Shift Register	Carry Register
0 0 1	0
1 0 0	0
0 1 0	0
1 0 1	0
1 1 0	0
1 1 1	0
0 1 1	1

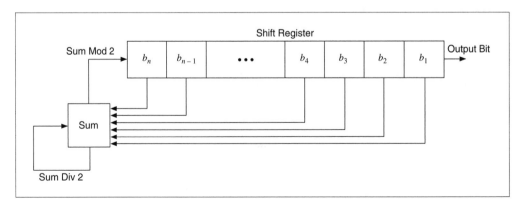

Figure 17.3   *Feedback with carry shift register.*

1 0 1	1
0 1 0	1
0 0 1	1
0 0 0	1
1 0 0	0

Note that the final internal state (including the contents of the carry register) is the same as the second internal state. The sequence cycles at this point, and has a period of 10.

There are a few things to note here. First, the carry register is not a single bit; it is a number. The size of the carry register must be at least $\log_2 t$, where t is the number of taps. There are only two taps in the previous example, so the carry register only has to be 1 bit wide. If there were four taps, the carry register would have to be 2 bits wide, and could be either 0, 1, 2, or 3.

Second, there is an initial transient before the FCSR settles down into its repeating period. In the previous example, only one state never repeated. For larger and more complicated FCSRs, there may be more.

Third, the maximum period of a FCSR is not $2^n - 1$, where n is the length of the shift register. The maximum period is $q - 1$, where q is the **connection integer**. This number gives the taps and is defined by:

$$q = 2q_1 + 2^2q_2 + 2^4q_4 + \ldots + 2^nq_n - 1$$

(Yes, the q_is are numbered from left to right.) And even worse, q has to be a prime for which 2 is a primitive root. The rest of this discussion assumes q is of this form.

In this example, $q = 2*0 + 4*1 + 8*1 - 1 = 11$. And 11 is a prime with 2 as a primitive root. So the maximum period is 10.

Not all initial states give you the maximum period. For example, look at the FCSR when the initial value is 101 and the carry register is set to 4.

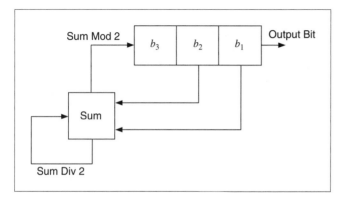

Figure 17.4   3-bit FCSR.

Shift Register	Carry Register
1 0 1	4
1 1 0	2
1 1 1	1
1 1 1	1

At this point the register spits out a neverending stream of 1s.

Any initial state will result in one of four things. First, it is part of the maximum period. Second, it will fall into the maximum period after an initial transient. Third, it will fall into a sequence of all zeros after an initial transient. Fourth, it will fall into a sequence of all ones after an initial transient.

There is a mathematical formula for determining what will happen to a given initial state, but it's much easier to just test it. Run the FCSR for a while. (If m is the initial memory, and t is the number of taps, then $\log_2(t) + \log_2(m) + 1$ steps are enough.) If it degenerates into a neverending stream of 0s or 1s within n bits, where n is the length of the FCSR, don't use it. If it doesn't, then use it. Since the initial state of a FCSR corresponds to the key of the stream cipher, this means that a FCSR-based generator will have a set of weak keys.

Table 17.1 lists all connection integers less than 10,000 for which 2 is a primitive root. These all have maximum period $q - 1$. To turn one of these numbers into a tap sequence, calculate the binary expansion of $q + 1$. For example, 9949 would translate to taps on bits 1, 2, 3, 4, 6, 7, 9, 10, and 13, because

$$9950 = 2^{13} + 2^{10} + 2^9 + 2^7 + 2^6 + 2^4 + 2^3 + 2^2 + 2^1$$

Table 17.2 lists *all* the 4-tap tap sequences that result in a maximal-length FCSR for shift register lengths of 32 bits, 64 bits, and 128 bits. Each of the four values, a, b, c, and d, combine to generate q, a prime for which 2 is primitive.

$$q = 2^a + 2^b + 2^c + 2^d - 1$$

Any of these tap sequences can be used to create a FCSR with period $q - 1$.

The idea of using FCSRs for cryptography is still very new; it is being pioneered by Andy Klapper and Mark Goresky [844,845,654,843,846]. Just as the analysis of LFSRs is based on the addition of primitive polynomials mod 2, analysis of FCSRs is based on addition over something called the **2-adic** numbers. The theory is well beyond the scope of this book, but there seems to be a 2-adic analog for everything. Just as you can define linear complexity, you can define 2-adic complexity. There is even a 2-adic analog to the Berlekamp-Massey algorithm. What this means is that the list of potential stream ciphers has just doubled—at least. Anything you can do with a LFSR you can do with a FCSR.

There are further enhancements to this sort of idea, ones that involve multiple carry registers. The analysis of these sequence generators is based on addition over the ramified extensions of the 2-adic numbers [845,846].

17.5 STREAM CIPHERS USING FCSRS

There aren't any FCSR stream ciphers in the literature; the theory is still too new. In the interests of getting the ball rolling, I propose some here. I am taking two different tacks: I am proposing FCSR stream ciphers that are identical to previously proposed LFSR generators, and I am proposing stream ciphers that use both FCSRs and LFSRs. The security of the former can probably be analyzed using 2-adic numbers; the latter cannot be analyzed using algebraic techniques—they can probably only be analyzed indirectly. In any case, it is important to choose LFSRs and FCSRs whose periods are relatively prime.

All this will come later. Right now I know of no implementation or analysis of any of these ideas. Wait some years and scan the literature before you trust any of them.

Cascade Generators

There are two ways to use FCSRs in a cascade generator:

— FCSR Cascade. The Gollmann cascade with FCSRs instead of LFSRs.
— LFSR/FCSR Cascade. The Gollmann cascade with the generators alternating between LFSRs and FCSRs.

FCSR Combining Generators

These generators use a variable number of LFSRs and/or FCSRs, and a variety of functions to combine them. The XOR operation destroys the algebraic properties of FCSRs, so it makes sense to use it to combine them. The generator, shown in Figure 17.5, uses a variable number of FCSRs. Its output is the XOR of the outputs of the individual FCSRs.

Other generators along similar lines are:

— FCSR Parity Generator. All registers are FCSRs and the combining function is XOR.
— LFSR/FCSR Parity Generator. Registers are a mix of LFSRs and FCSRs and the combining function is XOR.
— FCSR Threshold Generator. All registers are FCSRs and the combining function is the majority function.
— LFSR/FCSR Threshold Generator. Registers are a mix of LFSRs and FCSRs and the combining function is the majority function.
— FCSR Summation Generator. All registers are FCSRs and the combining function is addition with carry.
— LFSR/FCSR Summation Generator. Registers are a mix of LFSRs and FCSRs and the combining function is addition with carry.

Table 17.1
Connection Integers for Maximal-period FCSRs

2	653	1549	2477	3539
5	659	1571	2531	3547
11	661	1619	2539	3557
13	677	1621	2549	3571
19	701	1637	2557	3581
29	709	1667	2579	3613
37	757	1669	2621	3637
53	773	1693	2659	3643
59	787	1733	2677	3659
61	797	1741	2683	3677
67	821	1747	2693	3691
83	827	1787	2699	3701
101	829	1861	2707	3709
107	853	1867	2741	3733
131	859	1877	2789	3779
139	877	1901	2797	3797
149	883	1907	2803	3803
163	907	1931	2819	3851
173	941	1949	2837	3853
179	947	1973	2843	3877
181	1019	1979	2851	3907
197	1061	1987	2861	3917
211	1091	1997	2909	3923
227	1109	2027	2939	3931
269	1117	2029	2957	3947
293	1123	2053	2963	3989
317	1171	2069	3011	4003
347	1187	2083	3019	4013
349	1213	2099	3037	4019
373	1229	2131	3067	4021
379	1237	2141	3083	4091
389	1259	2213	3187	4093
419	1277	2221	3203	4099
421	1283	2237	3253	4133
443	1291	2243	3299	4139
461	1301	2267	3307	4157
467	1307	2269	3323	4219
491	1373	2293	3347	4229
509	1381	2309	3371	4243
523	1427	2333	3413	4253
541	1451	2339	3461	4259
547	1453	2357	3467	4261
557	1483	2371	3469	4283
563	1493	2389	3491	4349
587	1499	2437	3499	4357
613	1523	2459	3517	4363
619	1531	2467	3533	4373

Table 17.1 (*Cont.*)
Connection Integers for Maximal-period FCSRs

4397	5693	6781	7717	8861
4451	5701	6803	7757	8867
4483	5717	6827	7789	8923
4493	5741	6829	7829	8933
4507	5749	6869	7853	8963
4517	5779	6883	7877	8971
4547	5813	6899	7883	9011
4603	5827	6907	7901	9029
4621	5843	6917	7907	9059
4637	5851	6947	7933	9173
4691	5869	6949	7949	9181
4723	5923	6971	8053	9203
4787	5939	7013	8069	9221
4789	5987	7019	8093	9227
4813	6011	7027	8117	9283
4877	6029	7043	8123	9293
4933	6053	7069	8147	9323
4957	6067	7109	8171	9341
4973	6101	7187	8179	9349
4987	6131	7211	8219	9371
5003	6173	7219	8221	9397
5011	6197	7229	8237	9419
5051	6203	7237	8243	9421
5059	6211	7243	8269	9437
5077	6229	7253	8291	9467
5099	6269	7283	8293	9491
5107	6277	7307	8363	9533
5147	6299	7331	8387	9539
5171	6317	7349	8429	9547
5179	6323	7411	8443	9587
5189	6373	7451	8467	9613
5227	6379	7459	8539	9619
5261	6389	7477	8563	9629
5309	6397	7499	8573	9643
5333	6469	7507	8597	9661
5387	6491	7517	8627	9677
5443	6547	7523	8669	9733
5477	6619	7541	8677	9749
5483	6637	7547	8693	9803
5501	6653	7549	8699	9851
5507	6659	7573	8731	9859
5557	6691	7589	8741	9883
5563	6701	7603	8747	9901
5573	6709	7621	8803	9907
5651	6733	7643	8819	9923
5659	6763	7669	8821	9941
5683	6779	7691	8837	9949

Table 17.2
Tap Sequences for Maximal-length FCSRs

(32, 6, 3, 2)	(64, 24, 19, 2)	(64, 59, 28, 2)	(96, 55, 53, 2)
(32, 7, 5, 2)	(64, 25, 3, 2)	(64, 59, 38, 2)	(96, 56, 9, 2)
(32, 8, 3, 2)	(64, 25, 4, 2)	(64, 59, 44, 2)	(96, 56, 51, 2)
(32, 13, 8, 2)	(64, 25, 11, 2)	(64, 60, 49, 2)	(96, 57, 3, 2)
(32, 13, 12, 2)	(64, 25, 19, 2)	(64, 61, 51, 2)	(96, 57, 17, 2)
(32, 15, 6, 2)	(64, 27, 5, 2)	(64, 63, 8, 2)	(96, 57, 47, 2)
(32, 16, 2, 1)	(64, 27, 16, 2)	(64, 63, 13, 2)	(96, 58, 35, 2)
(32, 16, 3, 2)	(64, 27, 22, 2)	(64, 63, 61, 2)	(96, 59, 46, 2)
(32, 16, 5, 2)	(64, 28, 19, 2)		(96, 60, 29, 2)
(32, 17, 5, 2)	(64, 28, 25, 2)	(96, 15, 5, 2)	(96, 60, 41, 2)
(32, 19, 2, 1)	(64, 29, 16, 2)	(96, 21, 17, 2)	(96, 60, 45, 2)
(32, 19, 5, 2)	(64, 29, 28, 2)	(96, 25, 19, 2)	(96, 61, 17, 2)
(32, 19, 9, 2)	(64, 31, 12, 2)	(96, 25, 20, 2)	(96, 63, 20, 2)
(32, 19, 12, 2)	(64, 32, 21, 2)	(96, 29, 15, 2)	(96, 65, 12, 2)
(32, 19, 17, 2)	(64, 35, 29, 2)	(96, 29, 17, 2)	(96, 65, 39, 2)
(32, 20, 17, 2)	(64, 36, 7, 2)	(96, 30, 3, 2)	(96, 65, 51, 2)
(32, 21, 9, 2)	(64, 37, 2, 1)	(96, 32, 21, 2)	(96, 67, 5, 2)
(32, 21, 15, 2)	(64, 37, 11, 2)	(96, 32, 27, 2)	(96, 67, 25, 2)
(32, 23, 8, 2)	(64, 39, 4, 2)	(96, 33, 5, 2)	(96, 67, 34, 2)
(32, 23, 21, 2)	(64, 39, 25, 2)	(96, 35, 17, 2)	(96, 68, 5, 2)
(32, 25, 5, 2)	(64, 41, 5, 2)	(96, 35, 33, 2)	(96, 68, 19, 2)
(32, 25, 12, 2)	(64, 41, 11, 2)	(96, 39, 21, 2)	(96, 69, 17, 2)
(32, 27, 25, 2)	(64, 41, 27, 2)	(96, 40, 25, 2)	(96, 69, 36, 2)
(32, 29, 19, 2)	(64, 43, 21, 2)	(96, 41, 12, 2)	(96, 70, 23, 2)
(32, 29, 20, 2)	(64, 43, 28, 2)	(96, 41, 27, 2)	(96, 71, 6, 2)
(32, 30, 3, 2)	(64, 45, 28, 2)	(96, 41, 35, 2)	(96, 71, 40, 2)
(32, 30, 7, 2)	(64, 45, 41, 2)	(96, 42, 35, 2)	(96, 72, 53, 2)
(32, 31, 5, 2)	(64, 47, 5, 2)	(96, 43, 14, 2)	(96, 73, 32, 2)
(32, 31, 9, 2)	(64, 47, 21, 2)	(96, 44, 23, 2)	(96, 77, 27, 2)
(32, 31, 30, 2)	(64, 47, 30, 2)	(96, 45, 41, 2)	(96, 77, 31, 2)
	(64, 49, 19, 2)	(96, 47, 36, 2)	(96, 77, 32, 2)
(64, 3, 2, 1)	(64, 49, 20, 2)	(96, 49, 31, 2)	(96, 77, 33, 2)
(64, 14, 3, 2)	(64, 52, 29, 2)	(96, 51, 30, 2)	(96, 77, 71, 2)
(64, 15, 8, 2)	(64, 53, 8, 2)	(96, 53, 17, 2)	(96, 78, 39, 2)
(64, 17, 2, 1)	(64, 53, 43, 2)	(96, 53, 19, 2)	(96, 79, 4, 2)
(64, 17, 9, 2)	(64, 56, 39, 2)	(96, 53, 32, 2)	(96, 81, 80, 2)
(64, 17, 16, 2)	(64, 56, 45, 2)	(96, 53, 48, 2)	(96, 83, 14, 2)
(64, 19, 2, 1)	(64, 59, 5, 2)	(96, 54, 15, 2)	(96, 83, 26, 2)
(64, 19, 18, 2)	(64, 59, 8, 2)	(96, 55, 44, 2)	(96, 83, 54, 2)

Table 17.2 (*Cont.*)
Tap Sequences for Maximal-length FCSRs

(96, 83, 60, 2)	(128, 31, 25, 2)	(128, 81, 55, 2)	(128, 105, 11, 2)
(96, 83, 65, 2)	(128, 33, 21, 2)	(128, 82, 67, 2)	(128, 105, 31, 2)
(96, 83, 78, 2)	(128, 35, 22, 2)	(128, 83, 60, 2)	(128, 105, 48, 2)
(96, 84, 65, 2)	(128, 37, 8, 2)	(128, 83, 61, 2)	(128, 107, 40, 2)
(96, 85, 17, 2)	(128, 41, 12, 2)	(128, 83, 77, 2)	(128, 107, 62, 2)
(96, 85, 31, 2)	(128, 42, 35, 2)	(128, 84, 15, 2)	(128, 107, 102, 2)
(96, 85, 76, 2)	(128, 43, 25, 2)	(128, 84, 43, 2)	(128, 108, 35, 2)
(96, 85, 79, 2)	(128, 43, 42, 2)	(128, 85, 63, 2)	(128, 108, 73, 2)
(96, 86, 39, 2)	(128, 45, 17, 2)	(128, 87, 57, 2)	(128, 108, 75, 2)
(96, 86, 71, 2)	(128, 45, 27, 2)	(128, 87, 81, 2)	(128, 108, 89, 2)
(96, 87, 9, 2)	(128, 49, 9, 2)	(128, 89, 81, 2)	(128, 109, 11, 2)
(96, 87, 44, 2)	(128, 51, 9, 2)	(128, 90, 43, 2)	(128, 109, 108, 2)
(96, 87, 45, 2)	(128, 54, 51, 2)	(128, 91, 9, 2)	(128, 110, 23, 2)
(96, 88, 19, 2)	(128, 55, 45, 2)	(128, 91, 13, 2)	(128, 111, 61, 2)
(96, 88, 35, 2)	(128, 56, 15, 2)	(128, 91, 44, 2)	(128, 113, 59, 2)
(96, 88, 43, 2)	(128, 56, 19, 2)	(128, 92, 35, 2)	(128, 114, 83, 2)
(96, 88, 79, 2)	(128, 56, 55, 2)	(128, 95, 94, 2)	(128, 115, 73, 2)
(96, 89, 35, 2)	(128, 57, 21, 2)	(128, 96, 23, 2)	(128, 117, 105, 2)
(96, 89, 51, 2)	(128, 57, 37, 2)	(128, 96, 61, 2)	(128, 119, 30, 2)
(96, 89, 69, 2)	(128, 59, 29, 2)	(128, 97, 25, 2)	(128, 119, 101, 2)
(96, 89, 87, 2)	(128, 59, 49, 2)	(128, 97, 68, 2)	(128, 120, 9, 2)
(96, 92, 51, 2)	(128, 60, 57, 2)	(128, 97, 72, 2)	(128, 120, 27, 2)
(96, 92, 71, 2)	(128, 61, 9, 2)	(128, 97, 75, 2)	(128, 120, 37, 2)
(96, 93, 32, 2)	(128, 61, 23, 2)	(128, 99, 13, 2)	(128, 120, 41, 2)
(96, 93, 39, 2)	(128, 61, 52, 2)	(128, 99, 14, 2)	(128, 120, 79, 2)
(96, 94, 35, 2)	(128, 63, 40, 2)	(128, 99, 26, 2)	(128, 120, 81, 2)
(96, 95, 4, 2)	(128, 63, 62, 2)	(128, 99, 54, 2)	(128, 121, 5, 2)
(96, 95, 16, 2)	(128, 67, 41, 2)	(128, 99, 56, 2)	(128, 121, 67, 2)
(96, 95, 32, 2)	(128, 69, 33, 2)	(128, 99, 78, 2)	(128, 121, 95, 2)
(96, 95, 44, 2)	(128, 71, 53, 2)	(128, 100, 13, 2)	(128, 121, 96, 2)
(96, 95, 45, 2)	(128, 72, 15, 2)	(128, 100, 39, 2)	(128, 123, 40, 2)
	(128, 72, 41, 2)	(128, 101, 44, 2)	(128, 123, 78, 2)
(128, 5, 4, 2)	(128, 73, 5, 2)	(128, 101, 97, 2)	(128, 124, 41, 2)
(128, 15, 4, 2)	(128, 73, 65, 2)	(128, 103, 46, 2)	(128, 124, 69, 2)
(128, 21, 19, 2)	(128, 73, 67, 2)	(128, 104, 13, 2)	(128, 124, 81, 2)
(128, 25, 5, 2)	(128, 75, 13, 2)	(128, 104, 19, 2)	(128, 125, 33, 2)
(128, 26, 11, 2)	(128, 80, 39, 2)	(128, 104, 35, 2)	(128, 125, 43, 2)
(128, 27, 25, 2)	(128, 80, 53, 2)	(128, 105, 7, 2)	(128, 127, 121, 2)

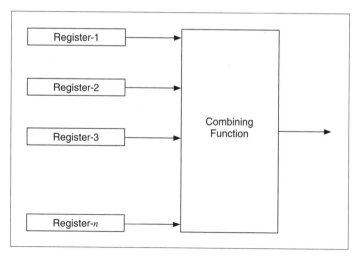

Figure 17.5   Combining Generators.

LFSR/FCSR Summation/Parity Cascade

The theory is that addition with carry destroys the algebraic properties of LFSRs, and that XOR destroys the algebraic properties of FCSRs. This generator combines those ideas, as used in the LFSR/FCSR Summation Generator and the LFSR/FCSR Parity Generator just listed, with the Gollmann cascade.

The generator is a series of arrays of registers, with the clock of each array controlled by the output of the previous array. Figure 17.6 is one stage of this generator. The first array of LFSRs is clocked and the results are combined using addition with carry. If the output of this combining function is 1, then the next array (of FCSRs) is clocked and the output of those FCSRs is combined with the output of the previous combining function using XOR. If the output of the first combining function is 0, then the array of FCSRs is not clocked and the output is simply added to the carry from the previous round. If the output of this second combining function is 1, then the third array of LFSRs is clocked, and so on.

This generator uses a lot of registers: $n*m$, where n is the number of stages and m is the number of registers per stage. I recommend $n = 10$ and $m = 5$.

Alternating Stop-and-Go Generators

These generators are stop-and-go generators with FCSRs instead of some LFSRs. Additionally, the XOR operation can be replaced with an addition with carry (see Figure 17.7).

— FCSR Stop-and-Go Generator. Register-1, Register-2, and Register-3 are FCSRs. The combining operation is XOR.

— FCSR/LFSR Stop-and-Go Generator. Register-1 is a FCSR, and Registers-2 and -3 are LFSRs. The combining operation is addition with carry.

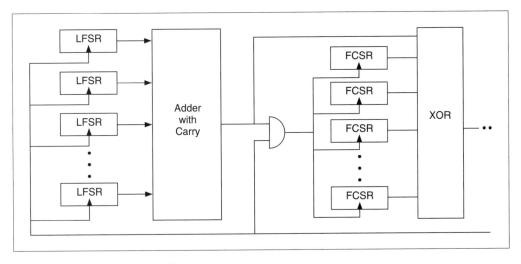

Figure 17.6   Concoction Generator.

— LFSR/FCSR Stop-and-Go Generator. Register-1 is a LFSR, and Regis-
ters-2 and -3 are FCSRs. The combining operation is XOR.

Shrinking Generators

There are four basic generator types using FCSRs:

— FCSR Shrinking Generator. A shrinking generator with FCSRs
instead of LFSRs.
— FCSR/LFSR Shrinking Generator. A shrinking generator with a LFSR
shrinking a FCSR.
— LFSR/FCSR Shrinking Generator: A shrinking generator with a FCSR
shrinking a LFSR.

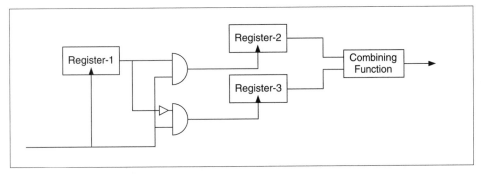

Figure 17.7   Alternating stop-and-go generators.

— FCSR Self-Shrinking Generator. A self-shrinking generator with a FCSR instead of a LFSR.

17.6 NONLINEAR-FEEDBACK SHIFT REGISTERS

It is easy to imagine a more complicated feedback sequence than the ones used in LFSRs or FCSRs. The problem is that there isn't any mathematical theory that can analyze them. You'll get something, but who knows what it is? In particular, here are some problems with nonlinear-feedback shift register sequences.

— There may be biases, such as more ones than zeros or fewer runs than expected, in the output sequence.
— The maximum period of the sequence may be much lower than expected.
— The period of the sequence might be different for different starting values.
— The sequence may appear random for a while, but then "dead end" into a single value. (This can easily be solved by XORing the nonlinear function with the rightmost bit.)

On the plus side, if there is no theory to analyze nonlinear-feedback shift registers for security, there are few tools to cryptanalyze stream ciphers based on them. We can use nonlinear-feedback shift registers in stream-cipher design, but we have to be careful.

In a nonlinear-feedback shift register, the feedback function can be anything you want (see Figure 17.8).

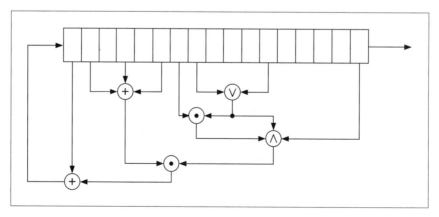

Figure 17.8   A nonlinear-feedback shift register (probably insecure).

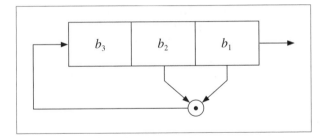

Figure 17.9   3-bit nonlinear feedback shift register.

Figure 17.9 is a 3-bit shift register with the following feedback function: The new bit is the first bit times the second bit. If it is initialized with the value 110, it produces the following sequence of internal states:

$$
\begin{array}{c}
1\ 1\ 0 \\
0\ 1\ 1 \\
1\ 0\ 1 \\
0\ 1\ 0 \\
0\ 0\ 1 \\
0\ 0\ 0 \\
0\ 0\ 0
\end{array}
$$

And so on forever.

The output sequence is the string of least significant bits:

$$0\ 1\ 1\ 0\ 1\ 0\ 0\ 0\ 0\ 0\ 0\ 0\ldots.$$

This isn't terribly useful.

It gets even worse. If the initial value is 100, it produces 010, 001, then repeats forever at 000. If the initial value is 111, it repeats itself forever right from the start.

Some work has been done on computing the linear complexity of the product of two LFSRs [1650,726,1364,630,658,659]. A construction that involved computing LFSRs over a field of odd characteristic [310] is insecure [842].

17.7 OTHER STREAM CIPHERS

Many other stream ciphers have appeared in the literature here and there. Here are some of them.

Pless Generator

This generator is designed around the capabilities of the J-K flip-flop [1250]. Eight LFSRs drive four J-K flip-flops; each flip-flop acts as a nonlinear combiner for two of the LFSRs. To avoid the problem that knowledge of an output of the flip-flop identifies both the source and value of the next output bit, clock the four flip-flops and then interleave the outputs to yield the final keystream.

This algorithm has been cryptanalyzed by attacking each of the four flip-flops independently [1356]. Additionally, combining J-K flip-flops is cryptographically weak; generators of this type succumb to correlation attacks [1451].

Cellular Automaton Generator

In [1608,1609], Steve Wolfram proposed using a one-dimensional cellular automaton as a pseudo-random-number generator. Cellular automata is not the subject of this book, but Wolfram's generator consisted of a one-dimensional array of bits, a_1, a_2, a_3, ..., a_k, ..., a_n, and an update function:

$$a_k' = a_{k-1} \oplus (a_k \vee a_{k+1})$$

The bit is extracted from one of the a_k values; which one really doesn't matter.

The generator's behavior appears to be quite random. However, there is a known-plaintext attack against these generators [1052]. This attack works on a PC with values of n up to 500 bits. Additionally, Paul Bardell proved that the output of a cellular automaton can also be generated by a linear-feedback shift register of equal length and is therefore no more secure [83].

1/p Generator

This generator was proposed, and then cryptanalyzed, in [193]. If the internal state of the generator at time t is x_t, then

$$x_{t+1} = bx_t \bmod p$$

The output of the generator is the least significant bit of x_t div p, where div is the truncated integer division. For maximum period, the constants b and p should be chosen so that p is prime and b is a primitive root mod p. Unfortunately, this generator isn't secure. (Note that for $b = 2$, an FCSR with a connection integer p outputs the reverse of this sequence.)

crypt(1)

The original UNIX encryption algorithm, crypt(1), is a stream cipher based on the same ideas as the Enigma. This is a 256-element, single-rotor substitution cipher with a reflector. Both the rotor and the reflector are generated from the key. This algorithm is far simpler than the World War II German Enigma and, for a skilled cryptanalyst, very easy to break [1576,1299]. A public-domain UNIX program, called Crypt Breakers Workbench (CBW), can be used to break files encrypted with crypt(1).

Other Schemes

Another generator is based on the knapsack problem (see Section 19.2) [1363]. CRYPTO-LEGGO is insecure [301]. Joan Daemen has developed SubStream, Jam, and StepRightUp [402]; they are all too new to comment on. Many other algorithms are described in the literature, and even more are kept secret and incorporated into equipment.

17.8 SYSTEM-THEORETIC APPROACH TO STREAM-CIPHER DESIGN

In practice, stream-cipher design is a lot like block-cipher design. It involves more mathematical theory, but in the end a cryptographer proposes a design and then tries to analyze it.

According to Rainer Rueppel, there are four different approaches to the construction of stream ciphers [1360,1362]:

— System-theoretic approach. Try to make sure that each design creates a difficult and unknown problem for the cryptanalyst, using a set of fundamental design principles and criteria.

— Information-theoretic approach. Try to keep the cryptanalyst in the dark about the plaintext. No matter how much work the cryptanalyst invests, he will never get a unique solution.

— Complexity-theoretic approach. Try to base the cryptosystem on, or make it equivalent to, some known and difficult problem such as factoring or taking discrete logarithms.

— Randomized approach. Try to generate an unmanageably large problem by forcing the cryptanalyst to examine lots of useless data in his attempts at cryptanalysis.

The approaches differ in their assumptions about the capabilities and opportunities of the cryptanalyst, the definition of cryptographic success, and the notion of security. Most of the research in this field is theoretical, but there are some good stream ciphers among the impractical ones.

The system-theoretic approach was used in all the stream ciphers previously listed; it produces most of the stream ciphers that are practical enough to be used in the real world. A cryptographer designs keystream generators that have testable security properties—period, distribution of bit patterns, linear complexity, and so on—and not ciphers based on mathematical theory. The cryptographer also studies various cryptanalytic techniques against these generators and makes sure the generators are immune to these attacks.

Over the years, the approach has resulted in a set of design criteria for stream ciphers [1432,99,1357,1249]. These were discussed by Rueppel in [1362], in which he details the theory behind them.

— Long period, no repetitions.
— Linear complexity criteria—large linear complexity, linear complexity profile, local linear complexity, and so forth.

— Statistical criteria such as ideal k-tuple distributions.

— Confusion—every keystream bit must be a complex transformation of all or most of the key bits.

— Diffusion—redundancies in substructures must be dissipated into long-range statistics.

— Nonlinearity criteria for Boolean functions like mth-order correlation immunity, distance to linear functions, avalanche criterion, and so on.

This list of design criteria is not unique for stream ciphers designed by the system-theoretic approach; it is true for all stream ciphers. It is even true for all block ciphers. The unique point about the system-theoretic approach is that stream ciphers are designed to satisfy these goals directly.

The major problem with these cryptosystems is that nothing can be proven about their security; the design criteria have never been proved to be either necessary or sufficient for security. A keystream generator may satisfy all the design principles, but could still turn out to be insecure. Another could turn out to be secure. There is still some magic to the process.

On the other hand, breaking each of these keystream generators is a different problem for a cryptanalyst. If enough different generators are out there, it may not be worth the cryptanalyst's time to try to break each one. He may better achieve fame and glory by figuring out better ways to factor large numbers or calculating discrete logarithms.

17.9 COMPLEXITY-THEORETIC APPROACH TO STREAM-CIPHER DESIGN

Rueppel also delineated a complexity-theoretic approach to stream-cipher design. Here, a cryptographer attempts to use complexity theory to prove that his generators are secure. Consequently, the generators tend to be more complicated, based on the same sorts of hard problems as public-key cryptography. And like public-key algorithms, they tend to be slow and cumbersome.

Shamir's Pseudo-Random-Number Generator

Adi Shamir used the RSA algorithm as a pseudo-random-number generator [1417]. While Shamir showed that predicting the output of the pseudo-random-number generator is equivalent to breaking RSA, potential biases in the output were demonstrated in [1401,200].

Blum-Micali Generator

This generator gets its security from the difficulty of computing discrete logarithms [200]. Let g be a prime and p be an odd prime. A key x_0, starts off the process:

$$x_{i+1} = g^{x_i} \bmod p$$

The output of the generator is 1 if $x_i < (p-1)/2$, and 0 otherwise.

If p is large enough so that computing discrete logarithms mod p is infeasible, then this generator is secure. Additional theoretical results can be found in [1627, 986,985,1237,896,799].

RSA

This RSA generator [35,36] is a modification of [200]. The initial parameters are a modulus N which is the product of two large primes p and q, an integer e which is relatively prime to $(p-1)(q-1)$, and a random seed x_0, where x_0 is less than N.

$$x_{i+1} = x_i^e \bmod N$$

The output of the generator is the least significant bit of x_i. The security of this generator is based on the difficulty of breaking RSA. If N is large enough, then the generator is secure. Additional theory can be found in [1569,1570,1571,30,354].

Blum, Blum, and Shub

The simplest and most efficient complexity-theoretic generator is called the Blum, Blum, and Shub generator, after its inventors. Mercifully, we shall abbreviate it to BBS, although it is sometimes called the quadratic residue generator [193].

The theory behind the BBS generator has to do with quadratic residues modulo n (see Section 11.3). Here's how it works.

First find two large prime numbers, p and q, which are congruent to 3 modulo 4. The product of those numbers, n, is a Blum integer. Choose another random integer, x, which is relatively prime to n. Compute

$$x_0 = x^2 \bmod n$$

That's the seed for the generator.

Now you can start computing bits. The ith pseudo-random bit is the least significant bit of x_i, where

$$x_i = x_{i-1}^2 \bmod n$$

The most intriguing property of this generator is that you don't have to iterate through all $i-1$ bits to get the ith bit. If you know p and q, you can compute the ith bit directly.

$$b_i \text{ is the least significant bit of } x_i, \text{ where } x_i = x_0^{(2^i) \bmod ((p-1)(q-1))}$$

This property means you can use this cryptographically strong pseudo-random-bit generator as a stream cryptosystem for a random-access file.

The security of this scheme rests on the difficulty of factoring n. You can make n public, so anyone can generate bits using the generator. However, unless a cryptanalyst can factor n, he can never predict the output of the generator—not even with a statement like: "The next bit has a 51 percent chance of being a 1."

More strongly, the BBS generator is **unpredictable to the left** and **unpredictable to the right**. This means that given a sequence generated by the generator, a cryptanalyst cannot predict the next bit in the sequence nor the previous bit in the sequence. This is not security based on some complicated bit generator that no one understands, but the mathematics behind factoring n.

This algorithm is slow, but there are speedups. As it turns out, you can use more than the least significant bit of each x_i as a pseudo-random bit. According to [1569, 1570,1571,35,36], if n is the length of x_i, the least significant $\log_2 n$ bits of x_i can be used. The BBS generator is comparatively slow and isn't useful for stream ciphers. However, for high-security applications, such as key generation, this generator is the best of the lot.

17.10 OTHER APPROACHES TO STREAM-CIPHER DESIGN

In an information-theoretic approach to stream ciphers, the cryptanalyst is assumed to have unlimited time and computing power. The only practical stream cipher that is secure against an adversary like this is a one-time pad (see Section 1.5). Since bits would be impractical on a pad, this is sometimes called a **one-time tape**. Two magnetic tapes, one at the encryption end and the other at the decryption end, would have the same random keystream on them. To encrypt, simply XOR the plaintext with the bits on the tape. To decrypt, XOR the ciphertext with the bits on the other, identical, tape. You never use the same keystream bits twice. Since the keystream bits are truly random, no one can predict the keystream. If you burn the tapes when you are through with them, you've got perfect secrecy (assuming no one else has copies of the tape).

Another information-theoretic stream cipher, developed by Claus Schnorr, assumes that the cryptanalyst only has access to a limited number of ciphertext bits [1395]. The results are highly theoretical and have no practical value, at least not yet. For more details, consult [1361,1643,1193].

In a randomized stream cipher, the cryptographer tries to ensure that the cryptanalyst has an infeasibly large problem to solve. The objective is to increase the number of bits the cryptanalyst has to work with, while keeping the secret key small. This can be done by making use of a large public random string for encryption and decryption. The key would specify which parts of the large random string are to be used for encryption and decryption. The cryptanalyst, not knowing the key, is forced to pursue a brute-force search through the random string. The security of this sort of cipher can be expressed by the average number of bits a cryptanalyst must examine before the chances of determining the key improve over pure guessing.

Rip van Winkle Cipher

James Massey and Ingemar Ingemarsson proposed the Rip van Winkle cipher [1011], so named because the receiver has to receive 2^n bits of ciphertext before attempting decryption. The algorithm, illustrated in Figure 17.10, is simple to implement, provably secure, and completely impractical. Simply XOR the plaintext with the keystream, and delay the keystream by 0 to 20 years—the exact delay is part of the key. In Massey's words: "One can easily guarantee that the enemy cryptanalyst will need thousands of years to break the cipher, if one is willing to wait millions of years to read the plaintext." Further work on this idea can be found in [1577,755].

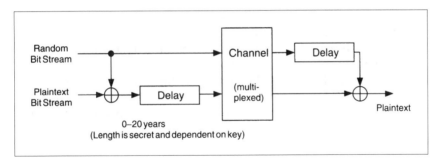

Figure 17.10   Rip van Winkle cipher.

Diffie's Randomized Stream Cipher

This scheme was first proposed by Whitfield Diffie [1362]. The data are 2^n random sequences. The key is k, a random n-bit string. To encrypt a message, Alice uses the kth random string as a one-time pad. She then sends the ciphertext plus the 2^n random strings over $2^n + 1$ different communications channels.

Bob knows k, so he can easily choose which one-time pad to decrypt the message with. Eve has no choice but to examine the random sequences one at a time until she finds the correct one-time pad. Any attack must examine an expected number of bits which is in $O(2^n)$. Rueppel points out that if you send n random strings instead of 2^n, and if the key is used to specify a linear combination of those random strings, the security is the same.

Maurer's Randomized Stream Cipher

Ueli Maurer described a scheme based on XORing the plaintext with several large public random-bit sequences [1034,1029,1030]. The key is the set of starting positions within each sequence. This turns out to be provably almost secure, with a calculable probability of being broken based on how much memory the attacker has at his disposal, without regard to the amount of computing power he has. Maurer claims that this scheme would be practical with about 100 different sequences of 10^{20} random bits each. Digitizing the face of the moon might be one way to get this many bits.

17.11 CASCADING MULTIPLE STREAM CIPHERS

If performance is no issue, there's no reason not to choose multiple stream ciphers and cascade them. Simply XOR the output of each generator with the plaintext to get the ciphertext. Ueli Maurer's result (see Section 15.7) says that if the generators have independent keys, then the security of the cascade is at least as secure as the strongest algorithm in the cascade. It is probably much more secure than that.

Stream ciphers can be combined in all the same ways as block ciphers (see Chapter 15). Stream ciphers can be cascaded (see Section 15.7) with other stream ciphers, or together with block ciphers.

A clever trick is to use one algorithm, either a block or stream algorithm, to frequently rekey a fast stream algorithm (which could even be a block algorithm in OFB mode). The fast algorithm could be weak, since a cryptanalyst would never see very much plaintext encrypted with any one key.

There's a trade-off between the size of the fast algorithm's internal state (which may impact security) and how often you can afford to rekey. The rekey needs to be relatively fast; algorithms that have a long key setup routine aren't suitable for this kind of application. And the rekeying should be independent of the internal state of the fast algorithm.

17.12 CHOOSING A STREAM CIPHER

If the study of stream ciphers offers any lessons, it's that new types of attacks are invented with alarming regularity. Classically, stream ciphers have been based on considerable mathematical theory. This theory can be used to prove good properties about the cipher, but can also be used to find new attacks against the cipher. I worry about any stream cipher based solely on LFSRs for this reason.

I prefer stream ciphers that are designed more along the lines of block ciphers: nonlinear transformations, large S-boxes, and so on. RC4 is my favorite, and SEAL is a close second. I would be very interested in seeing cryptanalytic results against my generators that combine LFSRs and FCSRs; this seems to be a very fruitful area of stream-cipher research to mine for actual designs. Or, you can use a block cipher in OFB or CFB to get a stream cipher.

Table 17.3 gives some timing measurements for some algorithms. These are meant for comparison purposes only.

17.13 GENERATING MULTIPLE STREAMS FROM A SINGLE PSEUDO-RANDOM-SEQUENCE GENERATOR

If you need to encrypt multiple channels of communications in a single box—a multiplexer, for example—the easy solution is to use a different pseudo-random-sequence generator for each stream. This has two problems: It requires more hardware, and all the different generators have to be synchronized. It would be simpler to use a single generator.

Table 17.3
Encryption Speeds of Some
Stream Ciphers on a 33MHz 486SX

Algorithm	Encryption Speed (Kilobytes/Second)
A5	5
PIKE	62
RC4	164
SEAL	381

One solution is to clock the generator multiple times. If you want three independent streams, clock the generator three times and send 1 bit into each stream. This technique works, but you may have trouble clocking the generator as fast as you would like. For example, if you can only clock the generator three times as fast as the data stream, you can only create three streams. Another way is to use the same sequence for each channel—perhaps with a variable time delay. This is insecure.

A really clever idea [1489], patented by the NSA, is shown in Figure 17.11. Dump the output of your favorite generator into an *m*-bit simple shift register. At each clock pulse, shift the register one to the right. Then, for each output stream, AND the register with a different *m*-bit control vector viewed as a unique identifier for the desired output stream, then XOR all the bits together to get the output bit for that stream. If you want several output streams in parallel, you need a separate control vector and an XOR/AND logic array for each output stream.

There are some things to watch out for. If any of the streams are linear combinations of other streams, then the system can be broken. But if you are clever, this is an easy and secure way to solve the problem.

17.14   REAL RANDOM-SEQUENCE GENERATORS

Sometimes cryptographically secure pseudo-random numbers are not good enough. Many times in cryptography, you want real random numbers. Key generation is a prime example. It's fine to generate random cryptographic keys based on a pseudo-

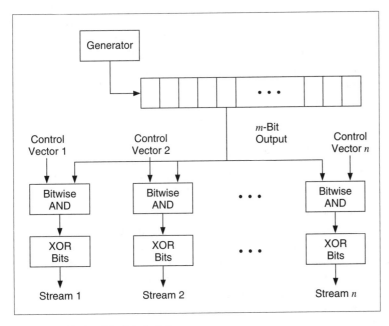

Figure 17.11   Multiple-bit generator.

random sequence generator, but if an adversary gets a copy of that generator and the master key, the adversary can create the same keys and break your cryptosystem, no matter how secure your algorithms are. A random-sequence generator's sequences cannot be reproduced. No one, not even you, can reproduce the bit sequence out of those generators.

There is a large philosophical debate over whether any of these techniques actually produces real random bits. I am not going to address that debate. The point here is to produce bits that have the same statistical properties as random bits and are not reproducible.

The important thing about any real random-sequence generator is that it be tested. There is a wealth of literature on this topic. Tests of randomness can be found in [863,99]. Maurer showed that all these tests can be derived from trying to compress the sequence [1031,1032]. If you can compress a random sequence, then it is not truly random.

Anyhow, what we have here is a whole lot of black magic. The primary point is to generate a sequence of bits that your adversary is unlikely to guess. It doesn't sound like much, but it's harder than you think. I can't prove that any of these techniques generates random bits. These techniques produce a sequence of bits that cannot be easily reproduced. For some details, see [1375,1376,511].

RAND Tables

Back in 1955, when computers were still new, the Rand Corporation published a book that contained a million random digits [1289]. Their method is described in the book:

> The random digits in the book were produced by rerandomization of a basic table generated by an electronic roulette wheel. Briefly, a random frequency pulse source, providing on the average about 100,000 pulses per second, was gated about once per second by a constant frequency pulse. Pulse standardization circuits passed the pulses through a 5-place binary counter. In principle the machine was a 32-place roulette wheel which made, on the average, about 3000 revolutions per trial and produced one number per second. A binary-to-decimal converter was used which converted 20 of the 32 numbers (the other twelve were discarded) and retained only the final digit of two-digit numbers; this final digit was fed into an IBM punch to produce finally a punched card table of random digits.

The book goes on to discuss the results of various randomness tests on the data. It also suggests how to use the book to find a random number:

> The lines of the digit table are numbered from 00000 to 19999. In any use of the table, one should first find a random starting position. A common procedure for doing this is to open the book to an unselected page of the digit table and blindly choose a five-digit number; this number with the first digit reduced modulo 2 determines the starting line; the two digits to the right of the initially selected five-digit number are reduced modulo 50 to determine the starting column in the starting line. To guard against the tendency of books to open repeatedly at the same page and the natural tendency of a person to choose a number toward the center of the

page: every five-digit number used to determine a starting position should be marked and not used a second time for this purpose.

The meat of the book is the "Table of Random Digits." It lists them in 5-digit groups—"10097 32533 76520 13586 . . ."—50 on a line and 50 lines on a page. The table goes on for 400 pages and, except for a particularly racy section on page 283 which reads "69696," makes for a boring read. The book also includes a table of 100,000 normal deviates.

The interesting thing about the RAND book is not its million random digits, but that they were created before the computer revolution. Many cryptographic algorithms use arbitrary constants—so-called "magic numbers." Choosing magic numbers from the RAND tables ensures that they haven't been specially chosen for some nefarious reason. Khafre does this, for example.

Using Random Noise

The best way to collect a large number of random bits is to tap the natural randomness of the real world. Often this method requires specialized hardware, but you can play tricks with computers.

Find an event that happens regularly but randomly: atmospheric noise peaking at a certain threshold, a toddler falling while learning to walk, or some such. Measure the time interval between one event and the next event. Record it. Measure the time interval between the second event and the third event. Record it as well. If the first time interval is greater than the second, output 1 as the bit. If the second time interval is greater than the first, output 0 as the event. Do it again for the next event.

Throw a dart at the New York Stock Exchange closing prices in your local newspaper. Compare the closing price of the stock you hit with the closing price of the stock directly above it. If the one you hit is more, output 0; if it less, output 1.

Hook a Geiger counter up to your computer, count emissions over a fixed time interval, and keep the least significant bit. Or measure the time between successive ticks. (Since the radioactive source is decaying, the average time between successive ticks is continuously getting longer. You want to choose a source with the half life long enough to make this negligible—like plutonium. Or, if you're worried about your health, you can apply appropriate statistical corrections.)

G. B. Agnew proposed a real random-bit generator, suitable for integration into a VLSI device [21]. It is a metal insulator semiconduction capacitor (MISC). Two of them are placed in close proximity, and the random bit is a function of the difference in charge between the two. Another random-number generator generates a random-bit stream based on the frequency instability in a free-running oscillator [535]. A commercial chip from AT&T generates random numbers from the same phenomenon [67]. M. Gude built a random-number generator that collected random bits from physical phenomena, such as radioactive decay [668,669]. Manfield Richter developed a random-number generator based on thermal noise from a semiconductor diode [1309].

Supposedly the time intervals between successive 2e4 light emissions from a trapped mercury atom are random. Use that. Better yet, find a semiconductor company that makes random-number-generation chips; they are out there.

There is also a random-number generator that uses the computer's disk drive [439]. It measures the time required to read a disk block and uses the variation in that time as a random number source. It filters the timing data to remove structure that comes from quantization, then applies a fast Fourier transform to vectors of the numbers. This removes bias and correlation. Finally, it uses the spectral angles for frequencies in $(0, \pi)$, normalized to the unit interval, as the random bits. A large part of the variation in disk rotation speed is caused by air turbulence, so there is randomness in the system. There are caveats, though. If you keep too many bits of the output, you are using the fast Fourier transform as a random-number generator and risk predictability. And it's best to read the same disk block over and over, so that your filtering doesn't have to remove structure that comes from the disk-scheduler. An implementation of this system was able to collect about 100 bits per minute [439].

Using the Computer's Clock

If you want a single random bit (or even a few), take the least significant bit from any clock register. This might not be terribly random in a UNIX system because of various potential synchronizations, but it works on some personal computers.

Beware of getting too many bits this way. Executing the same subroutine several times in succession could easily skew bits generated in this manner. For example, if each bit generation subroutine takes an even number of clock ticks to execute, you will get an endless stream of the same bit out of the generator. If each subroutine takes an odd number of clock ticks to execute, you will get an endless stream of alternating bits out of the generator. Even if the resonance isn't this obvious, the resultant bit stream will be far from random.

One random-number generator works this way [918]:

> Our truly random number generator . . . works by setting an alarm and then incrementing a counter register rapidly in the CPU until an interrupt occurs. The contents of the register are then XORed with the contents of an output buffer byte (truncating the register's data to 8 bits). After each byte of the output buffer is filled, the buffer is further processed by doing a right, circular shift of each character by 2 bits. This has the effect of moving the most active (and random) least significant bits into the most significant positions. The entire process is then repeated 3 times. Finally each character of the buffer has been touched by the two most random bits of the counter register after interrupts. That is $4n$ interrupts have occurred where n is the number of desired random bytes.

This method is very sensitive to the randomness of system interrupts and the granularity of the clock. The output looked pretty good when tested on real UNIX machines.

Measuring Keyboard Latency

People's typing patterns are both random and nonrandom. They are nonrandom enough that they can be used as a means of identification, but they are random enough that they can be used to generate random bits. Measure the time between successive keystrokes, then take the least significant bits of those measurements. These bits are going to be pretty random. This technique may not work on a UNIX terminal, since the keystrokes pass through filters and other mechanisms before they get to your program, but it will work on most personal computers.

Ideally, you only want to collect one random bit per keystroke. Collecting more may skew the results, depending on how good a typist is sitting at the keyboard. This technique is limited, though. While it's easy to have someone type 100 words or so when it is time to generate a key, it isn't reasonable to ask the typist to type a 100,000-word essay to generate a keystream for a one-time pad.

Biases and Correlations

A major problem with all these systems is that there could be nonrandomness in the generated sequence. The underlying physical processes might be random, but many kinds of measuring instruments are between the digital part of the computer and the physical process. Those instruments could easily introduce problems.

A way to eliminate **bias**, or skew, is to XOR several bits together. If a random bit is biased toward 0 by a factor e, then the probability of 0 can be written as:

$$P(0) = .5 + e$$

XORing two of these bits together yields:

$$P(0) = (.5 + e)^2 + (.5 - e)^2 = .5 + 2e^2$$

By the same calculation, XORing 4 bits together yields:

$$P(0) = .5 + 8e^4$$

XORing m bits will exponentially converge to an equal probability of 0 and 1. If you know the maximum bias you are willing to accept for your application, you can calculate how many bits you need to XOR together to get random bits below that bias.

An even better method is to look at the bits in pairs. If the 2 bits are the same, discard them and look at the next pair. If the 2 bits are different, take the first bit as the output of the generator. This eliminates bias completely. Other techniques for reducing bias use transition mappings, compression, and fast Fourier transforms [511].

The potential problem with both methods is that if there is a **correlation** between adjacent bits, then these methods will increase the bias. One way to correct this is to use multiple random sources. Take four different random sources and XOR the bits together; or take two random sources, and look at those bits in pairs.

For example, take a radioactive source and hook a Geiger counter to your computer. Take a pair of noisy diodes and record as an event every time the noise exceeds a certain peak. Measure atmospheric noise. Get a random bit from each and XOR them together to produce the random bit. The possibilities are endless.

The mere fact that a random-number generator has a bias does not necessarily mean that it is unusable. It just means that it is less secure. For example, consider the problem of Alice generating a triple-DES 168-bit key. All she has is a random-bit generator with a bias toward 0: It produces 55 percent 0s and 45 percent 1s. This means that there are only 0.99277 bits of entropy per key bit, as opposed to 1 bit of entropy if the generator were perfect. Mallory, trying to break the key, can optimize his brute-force search to try the most probable key first (000 . . . 0), and work toward the least probable key (111 . . . 1). Because of the bias, Mallory can expect to find the key in 2^{109} attempts. If there were no bias, Mallory would expect to make 2^{111} attempts. The resultant key is less secure, but not appreciably so.

Distilling Randomness

In general, the best way to generate random numbers is to find a whole lot of seemingly random events and distill randomness from them. This randomness can then be stored in a pool or reservoir that applications can draw on as needed. One-way hash functions are ready-made for the job; they're fast, so you can shovel quite a bit through them without worrying too much about performance or the actual randomness of each observation. Hash almost anything you can find that has at least some randomness. Try:

— A copy of every keystroke

— Mouse commands

— The sector number, time of day, and seek latency for every disk operation

— Actual mouse position

— Number of current scanline of monitor

— Contents of the actually displayed image

— Contents of FATs, kernel tables, and so on

— Access/modify times of /dev/tty

— CPU load

— Arrival times of network packets

— Input from a microphone

— /dev/audio without a microphone attached

If your system uses separate crystal oscillators for its CPU and time-of-day clocks, try reading the time of day in a tight loop. On some (but not all) systems this will reflect the random phase jitter between the two oscillators.

Since much of the randomness in these events is in their timing, use the most finely grained time-of-day clock you can find. A standard PC uses an Intel 8254 clock chip (or equivalent) driven at 1.1931818 megahertz, so reading the counter register directly gives you 838-nanosecond resolution. To avoid skewing the results, avoid taking your event samples on a timer interrupt.

Here is the process in C with MD5 (see Section 18.5) as the hash function:

```
char Randpool[16];

/* Call early and call often on a wide variety of random or semi-
 * random system events to churn the randomness pool.
```

```
     * The exact format and length of randevent doesn't matter as long as
     * its contents are at least somewhat unpredictable.
     */
    void churnrand(char *randevent,unsigned int randlen)
    {
          MD5_CTX md5;
          MD5Init(&md5);
          MD5Update(&md5,Randpool,sizeof(Randpool));
          MD5Update(&md5,randevent,randlen);
          MD5Final(Randpool,&md5);
    }
```

After calling churnrand() enough to build up sufficient randomness in Randpool, you can now generate random bits from it. MD5 again comes in handy, this time as a counter-mode pseudo-random byte-stream generator.

```
    long Randcnt;
    void genrand(char *buf,unsigned int buflen)
    {
          MD5_CTX md5;
          char tmp[16];
          unsigned int n;

          while(buflen != 0) {
                /* Hash the pool with a counter */
                MD5Init(&md5);
                MD5Update(&md5,Randpool,sizeof(Randpool));
                MD5Update(&md5,(unsigned char *)&Randcnt,sizeof(Randcnt));
                MD5Final(tmp,&md5);
                Randcnt++; /* Increment counter */

                /* Copy 16 bytes or requested amount, whichever is less,
                 * to the user's buffer */
                n = (buflen < 16) ? buflen : 16;
                memcpy(buf,tmp,n);
                buf += n;
                buflen -= n;
          }
    }
```

The hash function is crucial here for several reasons. First, it provides an easy way to generate an arbitrary amount of pseudo-random data without having to call churnrand() each time. In effect, the system degrades gracefully from perfect to practical randomness when the demand exceeds the supply. In this case it becomes *theoretically* possible to use the result from one genrand() call to determine a previous or subsequent result. But this requires inverting MD5, which is computationally infeasible.

This is important since the routine doesn't know what each caller will do with the random data it returns. One call might generate a random number for a protocol that is sent in the clear, perhaps in response to a direct request by an attacker. The very next call might generate a secret key for an unrelated session that the attacker wishes to penetrate. Obviously, it is very important that an attacker not be able to deduce the secret key from the nonce.

One problem remains. There must be sufficient randomness in the Randpool[] array before the first call to genrand(). If the system has been running for a while with a local user typing on the keyboard, no problem. But what about a standalone system that reboots automatically without seeing any keyboard or mouse input?

This is a tough one. A partial solution would require the operator to type for a while after the very first reboot, and to create a seed file on disk before shutting down to carry the randomness in Randseed[] across reboots. But do not save the Randseed[] array directly. An attacker who steals this file could determine all of the results from genrand() after the last call to churnrand() prior to the file being created.

The fix to this problem is to hash the Randseed[] array before storing it, perhaps by just calling genrand(). When the system reboots, you read in the seed file, pass it to churnrand(), then promptly destroy it. Unfortunately, this does not deal with the threat of someone stealing the seed file between reboots and using it to guess future values of the genrand() function. I see no solution to this problem other than to wait until enough external random events have taken place after a reboot before allowing genrand() to produce results.

CHAPTER 18

One-Way Hash Functions

18.1 Background

A one-way hash function, $H(M)$, operates on an arbitrary-length pre-image message, M. It returns a fixed-length hash value, h.

$$h = H(M), \text{ where } h \text{ is of length } m$$

Many functions can take an arbitrary-length input and return an output of fixed length, but one-way hash functions have additional characteristics that make them one-way [1065]:

Given M, it is easy to compute h.

Given h, it is hard to compute M such that $H(M) = h$.

Given M, it is hard to find another message, M', such that $H(M) = H(M')$.

If Mallory could do the hard things, he would undermine the security of every protocol that uses the one-way hash function. The whole point of the one-way hash function is to provide a "fingerprint" of M that is unique. If Alice signed M by using a digital signature algorithm on $H(M)$, and Bob could produce M', another message different from M where $H(M) = H(M')$, then Bob could claim that Alice signed M'.

In some applications, one-wayness is insufficient; we need an additional requirement called **collision-resistance**.

It is hard to find two random messages, M and M', such that $H(M) = H(M')$.

Remember the birthday attack from Section 7.4? It is not based on finding another message M', such that $H(M) = H(M')$, but based on finding two random messages, M and M', such that $H(M) = H(M')$.

The following protocol, first described by Gideon Yuval [1635], shows how—if the previous requirement were not true—Alice could use the birthday attack to swindle Bob.

(1) Alice prepares two versions of a contract: one is favorable to Bob; the other bankrupts him.

(2) Alice makes several subtle changes to each document and calculates the hash value for each. (These changes could be things like: replacing SPACE with SPACE-BACKSPACE-SPACE, putting a space or two before a carriage return, and so on. By either making or not making a single change on each of 32 lines, Alice can easily generate 2^{32} different documents.)

(3) Alice compares the hash values for each change in each of the two documents, looking for a pair that matches. (If the hash function only outputs a 64-bit value, she would usually find a matching pair with 2^{32} versions of each.) She reconstructs the two documents that hash to the same value.

(4) Alice has Bob sign the version of the contract that is favorable to him, using a protocol in which he only signs the hash value.

(5) At some time in the future, Alice substitutes the contract Bob signed with the one that he didn't. Now she can convince an adjudicator that Bob signed the other contract.

This is a big problem. (One moral is to always make a cosmetic change to any document you sign.)

Other similar attacks could be mounted assuming a successful birthday attack. For example, an adversary could send an automated control system (on a satellite, perhaps) random message strings with random signature strings. Eventually, one of those random messages will have a valid signature. The adversary would have no idea what the command would do, but if his only objective was to tamper with the satellite, this would do it.

Length of One-Way Hash Functions

Hash functions of 64 bits are just too small to survive a birthday attack. Most practical one-way hash functions produce 128-bit hashes. This forces anyone attempting the birthday attack to hash 2^{64} random documents to find two that hash to the same value, not enough for lasting security. NIST, in its Secure Hash Standard (SHS), uses a 160-bit hash value. This makes the birthday attack even harder, requiring 2^{80} random hashes.

The following method has been proposed to generate a longer hash value than a given hash function produces.

(1) Generate the hash value of a message, using a one-way hash function listed in this book.

(2) Prepend the hash value to the message.

(3) Generate the hash value of the concatenation of the message and the hash value.

(4) Create a larger hash value consisting of the hash value generated in step (1) concatenated with the hash value generated in step (3).

(5) Repeat steps (1) through (3) as many times as you wish, concatenating as you go.

Although this method has never been proved to be either secure or insecure, various people have some serious reservations about it [1262,859].

Overview of One-Way Hash Functions

It's not easy to design a function that accepts an arbitrary-length input, let alone make it one-way. In the real world, one-way hash functions are built on the idea of a **compression function**. This one-way function outputs a hash value of length n given an input of some larger length m [1069,414]. The inputs to the compression function are a message block and the output of the previous blocks of text (see Figure 18.1). The output is the hash of all blocks up to that point. That is, the hash of block M_i is

$$h_i = f(M_i, h_{i-1})$$

This hash value, along with the next message block, becomes the next input to the compression function. The hash of the entire message is the hash of the last block.

The pre-image should contain some kind of binary representation of the length of the entire message. This technique overcomes a potential security problem resulting from messages with different lengths possibly hashing to the same value [1069,414]. This technique is sometimes called **MD-strengthening** [930].

Various researchers have theorized that if the compression function is secure, then this method of hashing an arbitrary-length pre-image is also secure—but nothing has been proved [1138,1070,414].

A lot has been written on the design of one-way hash functions. For more mathematical information, consult [1028,793,791,1138,1069,414,91,858,1264]. Bart Preneel's thesis [1262] is probably the most comprehensive treatment of one-way hash functions.

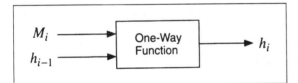

Figure 18.1   *One-way function.*

18.2 SNEFRU

Snefru is a one-way hash function designed by Ralph Merkle [1070]. (Snefru, like Khufu and Khafre, was an Egyptian pharaoh.) Snefru hashes arbitrary-length messages into either 128-bit or 256-bit values.

First the message is broken into chunks, each $512-m$ in length. (The variable m is the length of the hash value.) If the output is a 128-bit hash value, then the chunks are each 384 bits long; if the output is a 256-bit hash value, then the chunks are each 256 bits long.

The heart of the algorithm is function H, which hashes a 512-bit value into an m-bit value. The first m bits of H's output are the hash of the block; the rest are discarded. The next block is appended to the hash of the previous block and hashed again. (The initial block is appended to a string of zeros.) After the last block (if the message isn't an integer number of blocks long, zeros are used to pad the last block), the first m bits are appended to a binary representation of the length of the message and hashed one final time.

Function H is based on E, which is a reversible block-cipher function that operates on 512-bit blocks. H is the last m bits of the output of E XORed with the first m bits of the input of E.

The security of Snefru resides in function E, which randomizes data in several passes. Each pass is composed of 64 randomizing rounds. In each round a different byte of the data is used as an input to an S-box; the output word of the S-box is XORed with two neighboring words of the message. The S-boxes are constructed in a manner similar to those in Khafre (see Section 13.7). Some rotations are thrown in, too. Originally Snefru was designed with two passes.

Cryptanalysis of Snefru

Using differential cryptanalysis, Biham and Shamir demonstrated the insecurity of two-pass Snefru (128-bit hash value) [172]. Their attack finds pairs of messages that hash to the same value within minutes.

On 128-bit Snefru, their attacks work better than brute force for four passes or less. A birthday attack against Snefru takes 2^{64} operations; differential cryptanalysis can find a pair of messages that hash to the same value in $2^{28.5}$ operations for three-pass Snefru and $2^{44.5}$ operations for four-pass Snefru. Finding a message that hashes to a given value by brute force requires 2^{128} operations; differential cryptanalysis takes 2^{56} operations for three-pass Snefru and 2^{88} operations for four-pass Snefru.

Although Biham and Shamir didn't analyze 256-bit hash values, they extended their analysis to 224-bit hash values. Compared to a birthday attack that requires 2^{112} operations, they can find messages that hash to the same value in $2^{12.5}$ operations for two-pass Snefru, 2^{33} operations for three-pass Snefru, and 2^{81} operations for four-pass Snefru.

Currently, Merkle recommends using Snefru with at least eight passes [1073]. However, with this many passes the algorithm is significantly slower than either MD5 or SHA.

18.3 N-HASH

N-Hash is an algorithm invented by researchers at Nippon Telephone and Telegraph, the same people who invented FEAL, in 1990 [1105,1106]. N-Hash uses 128-bit message blocks, a complicated randomizing function similar to FEAL's, and produces a 128-bit hash value.

The hash of each 128-bit block is a function of the block and the hash of the previous block.

$$H_0 = I, \text{ where } I \text{ is a random initial value}$$
$$H_i = g(M_i, H_{i-1}) \oplus M_i \oplus H_{i-1}$$

The hash of the entire message is the hash of the last message block. The random initial value, I, can be any value determined by the user (even all zeros).

The function g is a complicated one. Figure 18.2 is an overview of the algorithm. Initially, the 128-bit hash of the previous message block, H_{i-1}, has its 64-bit left half

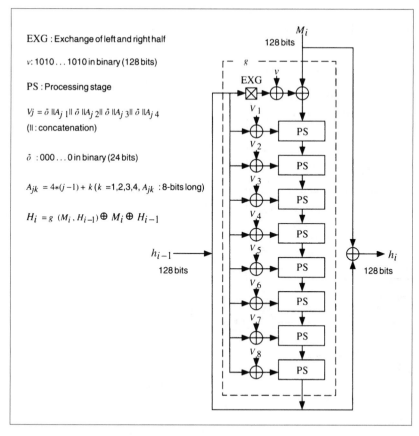

Figure 18.2   Outline of N-Hash.

and 64-bit right half swapped; it is then XORed with a repeating one/zero pattern (128 bits worth), and then XORed with the current message block, M_i. This value then cascades into N ($N = 8$ in the figures) processing stages. The other input to the processing stage is the previous hash value XORed with one of eight binary constant values.

One processing stage is given in Figure 18.3. The message block is broken into four 32-bit values. The previous hash value is also broken into four 32-bit values. The function f is given in Figure 18.4. Functions S_0 and S_1 are the same as they were in FEAL.

$$S_0(a,b) = \text{rotate left two bits } ((a + b) \bmod 256)$$
$$S_1(a,b) = \text{rotate left two bits } ((a + b + 1) \bmod 256)$$

The output of one processing stage becomes the input to the next processing stage. After the last processing stage, the output is XORed with the M_i and H_{i-1}, and then the next block is ready to be hashed.

Cryptanalysis of N-Hash

Bert den Boer discovered a way to produce collisions in the round function of N-Hash [1262]. Biham and Shamir used differential cryptanalysis to break 6-round

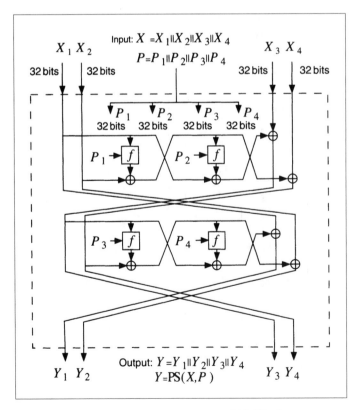

Figure 18.3   *One processing stage of* N-Hash.

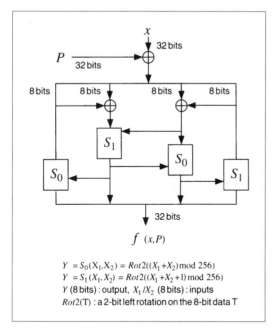

Figure 18.4   Function f.

N-Hash [169,172]. Their particular attack (there certainly could be others) works for any N that is divisible by 3, and is more efficient than the birthday attack for any N less than 15.

The same attack can find pairs of messages that hash to the same value for 12-round N-Hash in 2^{56} operations, compared to 2^{64} operations for a brute-force attack. N-hash with 15 rounds is safe from differential cryptanalysis: The attack requires 2^{72} operations.

The algorithm's designers recommend using N-Hash with at least 8 rounds [1106]. Given the proven insecurity of N-Hash and FEAL (and its speed with 8 rounds), I recommend using another algorithm entirely.

18.4   MD4

MD4 is a one-way hash function designed by Ron Rivest [1318,1319,1321]. MD stands for **Message Digest**; the algorithm produces a 128-bit hash, or message digest, of the input message.

In [1319], Rivest outlined his design goals for the algorithm:

> *Security.* It is computationally infeasible to find two messages that hashed to the same value. No attack is more efficient than brute force.
> *Direct Security.* MD4's security is not based on any assumption, like the difficulty of factoring.

Speed. MD4 is suitable for high-speed software implementations. It is based on a simple set of bit manipulations on 32-bit operands.

Simplicity and Compactness. MD4 is as simple as possible, without large data structures or a complicated program.

Favor Little-Endian Architectures. MD4 is optimized for microprocessor architectures (specifically Intel microprocessors); larger and faster computers make any necessary translations.

After the algorithm was first introduced, Bert den Boer and Antoon Bosselaers successfully cryptanalyzed the last two of the algorithm's three rounds [202]. In an unrelated cryptanalytic result, Ralph Merkle successfully attacked the first two rounds [202]. Eli Biham discussed a differential cryptanalysis attack against the first two rounds of MD4 [159]. Even though these attacks could not be extended to the full algorithm, Rivest strengthened the algorithm. The result is MD5.

18.5 MD5

MD5 is an improved version of MD4 [1386,1322]. Although more complex than MD4, it is similar in design and also produces a 128-bit hash.

Description of MD5

After some initial processing, MD5 processes the input text in 512-bit blocks, divided into 16 32-bit sub-blocks. The output of the algorithm is a set of four 32-bit blocks, which concatenate to form a single 128-bit hash value.

First, the message is padded so that its length is just 64 bits short of being a multiple of 512. This padding is a single 1-bit added to the end of the message, followed by as many zeros as are required. Then, a 64-bit representation of the message's length (before padding bits were added) is appended to the result. These two steps serve to make the message length an exact multiple of 512 bits in length (required for the rest of the algorithm), while ensuring that different messages will not look the same after padding.

Four 32-bit variables are initialized:

$$A = 0x01234567$$
$$B = 0x89abcdef$$
$$C = 0xfedcba98$$
$$D = 0x76543210$$

These are called **chaining variables**.

Now, the main loop of the algorithm begins. This loop continues for as many 512-bit blocks as are in the message.

The four variables are copied into different variables: a gets A, b gets B, c gets C, and d gets D.

The main loop has four rounds (MD4 had only three rounds), all very similar. Each round uses a different operation 16 times. Each operation performs a nonlinear func-

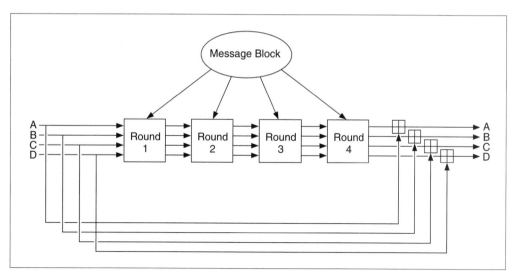

Figure 18.5   MD5 main loop.

tion on three of *a*, *b*, *c*, and *d*. Then it adds that result to the fourth variable, a sub-block of the text and a constant. Then it rotates that result to the right a variable number of bits and adds the result to one of *a*, *b*, *c*, or *d*. Finally the result replaces one of *a*, *b*, *c*, or *d*. See Figures 18.5 and 18.6.

There are four nonlinear functions, one used in each operation (a different one for each round).

$$F(X,Y,Z) = (X \wedge Y) \vee ((\neg X) \wedge Z)$$
$$G(X,Y,Z) = (X \wedge Z) \vee (Y \wedge (\neg Z))$$
$$H(X,Y,Z) = X \oplus Y \oplus Z$$
$$I(X,Y,Z) = Y \oplus (X \vee (\neg Z))$$

($\oplus$ is XOR, $\wedge$ is AND, $\vee$ is OR, and $\neg$ is NOT.)

These functions are designed so that if the corresponding bits of *X*, *Y*, and *Z* are independent and unbiased, then each bit of the result will also be independent and unbiased. The function F is the bit-wise conditional: If *X* then *Y* else *Z*. The function H is the bit-wise parity operator.

If M_j represents the *j*th sub-block of the message (from 0 to 15), and <<<*s* represents a left circular shift of *s* bits, the four operations are:

$$FF(a,b,c,d,M_j,s,t_i) \text{ denotes } a = b + ((a + F(b,c,d) + M_j + t_i) <<< s)$$
$$GG(a,b,c,d,M_j,s,t_i) \text{ denotes } a = b + ((a + G(b,c,d) + M_j + t_i) <<< s)$$
$$HH(a,b,c,d,M_j,s,t_i) \text{ denotes } a = b + ((a + H(b,c,d) + M_j + t_i) <<< s)$$
$$II(a,b,c,d,M_j,s,t_i) \text{ denotes } a = b + ((a + I(b,c,d) + M_j + t_i) <<< s)$$

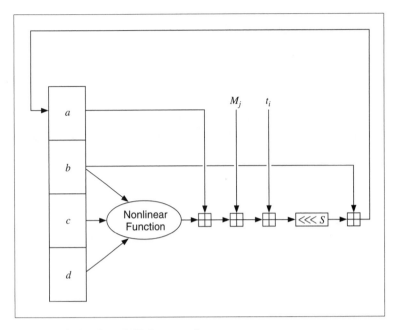

Figure 18.6   One MD5 operation.

The four rounds (64 steps) look like:

Round 1:

FF $(a, b, c, d, M_0, 7, 0xd76aa478)$

FF $(d, a, b, c, M_1, 12, 0xe8c7b756)$

FF $(c, d, a, b, M_2, 17, 0x242070db)$

FF $(b, c, d, a, M_3, 22, 0xc1bdceee)$

FF $(a, b, c, d, M_4, 7, 0xf57c0faf)$

FF $(d, a, b, c, M_5, 12, 0x4787c62a)$

FF $(c, d, a, b, M_6, 17, 0xa8304613)$

FF $(b, c, d, a, M_7, 22, 0xfd469501)$

FF $(a, b, c, d, M_8, 7, 0x698098d8)$

FF $(d, a, b, c, M_9, 12, 0x8b44f7af)$

FF $(c, d, a, b, M_{10}, 17, 0xffff5bb1)$

FF $(b, c, d, a, M_{11}, 22, 0x895cd7be)$

FF $(a, b, c, d, M_{12}, 7, 0x6b901122)$

FF $(d, a, b, c, M_{13}, 12, 0xfd987193)$

FF $(c, d, a, b, M_{14}, 17, 0xa679438e)$

FF $(b, c, d, a, M_{15}, 22, 0x49b40821)$

Round 2:

GG (a, b, c, d, M_1, 5, 0xf61e2562)
GG (d, a, b, c, M_6, 9, 0xc040b340)
GG (c, d, a, b, M_{11}, 14, 0x265e5a51)
GG (b, c, d, a, M_0, 20, 0xe9b6c7aa)
GG (a, b, c, d, M_5, 5, 0xd62f105d)
GG (d, a, b, c, M_{10}, 9, 0x02441453)
GG (c, d, a, b, M_{15}, 14, 0xd8a1e681)
GG (b, c, d, a, M_4, 20, 0xe7d3fbc8)
GG (a, b, c, d, M_9, 5, 0x21e1cde6)
GG (d, a, b, c, M_{14}, 9, 0xc33707d6)
GG (c, d, a, b, M_3, 14, 0xf4d50d87)
GG (b, c, d, a, M_8, 20, 0x455a14ed)
GG (a, b, c, d, M_{13}, 5, 0xa9e3e905)
GG (d, a, b, c, M_2, 9, 0xfcefa3f8)
GG (c, d, a, b, M_7, 14, 0x676f02d9)
GG (b, c, d, a, M_{12}, 20, 0x8d2a4c8a)

Round 3:

HH (a, b, c, d, M_5, 4, 0xfffa3942)
HH (d, a, b, c, M_8, 11, 0x8771f681)
HH (c, d, a, b, M_{11}, 16, 0x6d9d6122)
HH (b, c, d, a, M_{14}, 23, 0xfde5380c)
HH (a, b, c, d, M_1, 4, 0xa4beea44)
HH (d, a, b, c, M_4, 11, 0x4bdecfa9)
HH (c, d, a, b, M_7, 16, 0xf6bb4b60)
HH (b, c, d, a, M_{10}, 23, 0xbebfbc70)
HH (a, b, c, d, M_{13}, 4, 0x289b7ec6)
HH (d, a, b, c, M_0, 11, 0xeaa127fa)
HH (c, d, a, b, M_3, 16, 0xd4ef3085)
HH (b, c, d, a, M_6, 23, 0x04881d05)
HH (a, b, c, d, M_9, 4, 0xd9d4d039)
HH (d, a, b, c, M_{12}, 11, 0xe6db99e5)
HH (c, d, a, b, M_{15}, 16, 0x1fa27cf8)
HH (b, c, d, a, M_2, 23, 0xc4ac5665)

Round 4:

II $(a, b, c, d, M_0, 6, \text{0xf4292244})$

II $(d, a, b, c, M_7, 10, \text{0x432aff97})$

II $(c, d, a, b, M_{14}, 15, \text{0xab9423a7})$

II $(b, c, d, a, M_5, 21, \text{0xfc93a039})$

II $(a, b, c, d, M_{12}, 6, \text{0x655b59c3})$

II $(d, a, b, c, M_3, 10, \text{0x8f0ccc92})$

II $(c, d, a, b, M_{10}, 15, \text{0xffeff47d})$

II $(b, c, d, a, M_1, 21, \text{0x85845dd1})$

II $(a, b, c, d, M_8, 6, \text{0x6fa87e4f})$

II $(d, a, b, c, M_{15}, 10, \text{0xfe2ce6e0})$

II $(c, d, a, b, M_6, 15, \text{0xa3014314})$

II $(b, c, d, a, M_{13}, 21, \text{0x4e0811a1})$

II $(a, b, c, d, M_4, 6, \text{0xf7537e82})$

II $(d, a, b, c, M_{11}, 10, \text{0xbd3af235})$

II $(c, d, a, b, M_2, 15, \text{0x2ad7d2bb})$

II $(b, c, d, a, M_9, 21, \text{0xeb86d391})$

Those constants, t_i, were chosen as follows:

In step i, t_i is the integer part of $2^{32} * \text{abs}(\sin(i))$, where i is in radians.

After all of this, a, b, c, and d are added to A, B, C, D, respectively, and the algorithm continues with the next block of data. The final output is the concatenation of A, B, C, and D.

Security of MD5

Ron Rivest outlined the improvements of MD5 over MD4 [1322]:

1. A fourth round has been added.

2. Each step now has a unique additive constant.

3. The function G in round 2 was changed from $((X \wedge Y) \vee (X \wedge Z) \vee (Y \wedge Z))$ to $((X \wedge Z) \vee (Y \wedge \neg Z))$ to make G less symmetric.

4. Each step now adds in the result of the previous step. This promotes a faster avalanche effect.

5. The order in which message sub-blocks are accessed in rounds 2 and 3 is changed, to make these patterns less alike.

6. The left circular shift amounts in each round have been approximately optimized, to yield a faster avalanche effect. The four shifts used in each round are different from the ones used in other rounds.

Tom Berson attempted to use differential cryptanalysis against a single round of MD5 [144], but his attack is ineffective against all four rounds. A more successful attack by den Boer and Bosselaers produces collisions using the compression function in MD5 [203,1331,1336]. This does not lend itself to attacks against MD5 in practical applications, and it does not affect the use of MD5 in Luby-Rackoff-like encryption algorithms (see Section 14.11). It does mean that one of the basic design principles of MD5—to design a collision-resistant compression function—has been violated. Although it is true that "there seems to be a weakness in the compression function, but it has no practical impact on the security of the hash function" [1336], I am wary of using MD5.

18.6   MD2

MD2 is another 128-bit one-way hash function designed by Ron Rivest [801,1335]. It, along with MD5, is used in the PEM protocols (see Section 24.10). The security of MD2 is dependent on a random permutation of bytes. This permutation is fixed, and depends on the digits of π. $S_0, S_1, S_2, \ldots, S_{255}$ is the permutation. To hash a message M:

(1) Pad the message with i bytes of value i so that the resulting message is a multiple of 16 bytes long.

(2) Append a 16-byte checksum to the message.

(3) Initialize a 48-byte block: $X_0, X_1, X_2, \ldots, X_{47}$. Set the first 16 bytes of X to be 0, the second 16 bytes of X to be the first 16 bytes of the message, and the third 16 bytes of X to be the XOR of the first 16 bytes of X and the second 16 bytes of X.

(4) This is the compression function:

$$t = 0$$
$$\text{For } j = 0 \text{ to } 17$$
$$\quad \text{For } k = 0 \text{ to } 47$$
$$\quad\quad t = X_k \text{ XOR } S_t$$
$$\quad\quad X_k = t$$
$$\quad t = (t + j) \text{ mod } 256$$

(5) Set the second 16 bytes of X to be the second 16 bytes of the message, and the third 16 bytes of X to be the XOR of the first 16 bytes of X and the second 16 bytes of X. Do step (4). Repeat steps (5) and (4) with every 16 bytes of the message, in turn.

(6) The output is the first 16 bytes of X.

Although no weaknesses in MD2 have been found (see [1262]), it is slower than most other suggested hash functions.

18.7 SECURE HASH ALGORITHM (SHA)

NIST, along with the NSA, designed the Secure Hash Algorithm (SHA) for use with the Digital Signature Standard (see Section 20.2) [1154]. (The standard is the Secure Hash Standard (SHS); SHA is the algorithm used in the standard.)
According to the *Federal Register* [539]:

> A Federal Information Processing Standard (FIPS) for Secure Hash Standard (SHS) is being proposed. This proposed standard specified a Secure Hash Algorithm (SHA) for use with the proposed Digital Signature Standard . . .. Additionally, for applications not requiring a digital signature, the SHA is to be used whenever a secure hash algorithm is required for Federal applications.

And

> This Standard specifies a Secure Hash Algorithm (SHA), which is necessary to ensure the security of the Digital Signature Algorithm (DSA). When a message of any length $< 2^{64}$ bits is input, the SHA produces a 160-bit output called a message digest. The message digest is then input to the DSA, which computes the signature for the message. Signing the message digest rather than the message often improves the efficiency of the process, because the message digest is usually much smaller than the message. The same message digest should be obtained by the verifier of the signature when the received version of the message is used as input to SHA. The SHA is called secure because it is designed to be computationally infeasible to recover a message corresponding to a given message digest, or to find two different messages which produce the same message digest. Any change to a message in transit will, with a very high probability, result in a different message digest, and the signature will fail to verify. The SHA is based on principles similar to those used by Professor Ronald L. Rivest of MIT when designing the MD4 message digest algorithm [1319], and is closely modelled after that algorithm.

SHA produces a 160-bit hash, longer than MD5.

Description of SHA

First, the message is padded to make it a multiple of 512 bits long. Padding is exactly the same as in MD5: First append a one, then as many zeros as necessary to make it 64 bits short of a multiple of 512, and finally a 64-bit representation of the length of the message before padding.

Five 32-bit variables (MD5 has four variables, but this algorithm needs to produce a 160-bit hash) are initialized as follows:

$$A = 0x67452301$$
$$B = 0xefcdab89$$
$$C = 0x98badcfe$$
$$D = 0x10325476$$
$$E = 0xc3d2e1f0$$

The main loop of the algorithm then begins. It processes the message 512 bits at a time and continues for as many 512-bit blocks as are in the message.

First the five variables are copied into different variables: a gets A, b gets B, c gets C, d gets D, and e gets E.

The main loop has four rounds of 20 operations each (MD5 has four rounds of 16 operations each). Each operation performs a nonlinear function on three of a, b, c, d, and e, and then does shifting and adding similar to MD5.

SHA's set of nonlinear functions is:

$$f_t(X,Y,Z) = (X \wedge Y) \vee ((\neg X) \wedge Z), \text{ for } t = 0 \text{ to } 19.$$

$$f_t(X,Y,Z) = X \oplus Y \oplus Z, \text{ for } t = 20 \text{ to } 39.$$

$$f_t(X,Y,Z) = (X \wedge Y) \vee (X \wedge Z) \vee (Y \wedge Z), \text{ for } t = 40 \text{ to } 59.$$

$$f_t(X,Y,Z) = X \oplus Y \oplus Z, \text{ for } t = 60 \text{ to } 79.$$

Four constants are used in the algorithm:

$$K_t = 0x5a827999, \text{ for } t = 0 \text{ to } 19.$$

$$K_t = 0x6ed9eba1, \text{ for } t = 20 \text{ to } 39.$$

$$K_t = 0x8f1bbcdc, \text{ for } t = 40 \text{ to } 59.$$

$$K_t = 0xca62c1d6, \text{ for } t = 60 \text{ to } 79.$$

(If you wonder where those numbers came from: $0x5a827999 = 2^{1/2}/4$, $0x6ed9eba1 = 3^{1/2}/4$, $0x8f1bbcdc = 5^{1/2}/4$, and $0xca62c1d6 = 10^{1/2}/4$; all times 2^{32}.)

The message block is transformed from 16 32-bit words (M_0 to M_{15}) to 80 32-bit words (W_0 to W_{79}) using the following algorithm:

$$W_t = M_t, \text{ for } t = 0 \text{ to } 15$$

$$W_t = (W_{t-3} \oplus W_{t-8} \oplus W_{t-14} \oplus W_{t-16}) <<< 1, \text{ for } t = 16 \text{ to } 79.$$

(As an interesting aside, the original SHA specification did not have the left circular shift. The change "corrects a technical flaw that made the standard less secure than had been thought" [543]. The NSA has refused to elaborate on the exact nature of the flaw.)

If t is the operation number (from 0 to 79), W_t represents the tth sub-block of the expanded message, and $<<< s$ represents a left circular shift of s bits, then the main loop looks like:

```
FOR t = 0 to 79
    TEMP = (a <<< 5) + f_t(b,c,d) + e + W_t + K_t
    e = d
    d = c
    c = b <<< 30
    b = a
    a = TEMP
```

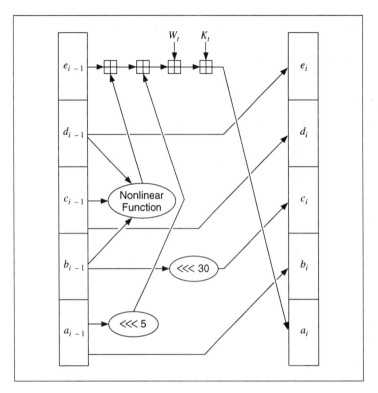

Figure 18.7   One SHA operation.

Figure 18.7 shows one operation. Shifting the variables accomplishes the same thing as MD5 does by using different variables in different locations.

After all of this, a, b, c, d, and e are added to A, B, C, D, and E respectively, and the algorithm continues with the next block of data. The final output is the concatenation of A, B, C, D, and E.

Security of SHA

SHA is very similar to MD4, but has a 160-bit hash value. The main changes are the addition of an expand transformation and the addition of the previous step's output into the next step for a faster avalanche effect. Ron Rivest made public the design decisions behind MD5, but SHA's designers did not. Here are Rivest's MD5 improvements to MD4 and how they compare with SHA's:

1. "A fourth round has been added." SHA does this, too. However, in SHA the fourth round uses the same f function as the second round.

2. "Each step now has a unique additive constant." SHA keeps the MD4 scheme where it reuses the constants for each group of 20 rounds.

3. "The function G in round 2 was changed from $((X \wedge Y) \vee (X \wedge Z) \vee (Y \wedge Z))$ to $((X \wedge Z) \vee (Y \wedge \neg (Z)))$ to make G less symmetric." SHA uses the MD4 version: $((X \wedge Y) \vee (X \wedge Z) \vee (Y \wedge Z))$.

4. "Each step now adds in the result of the previous step. This promotes a faster avalanche effect." This change has been made in SHA as well. The difference in SHA is that a fifth variable is added, and not b, c, or d, which is already used in f_t. This subtle change makes the den Boer-Bosselaers attack against MD5 impossible against SHA.

5. "The order in which message sub-blocks are accessed in rounds 2 and 3 is changed, to make these patterns less alike." SHA is completely different, since it uses a cyclic error-correcting code.

6. "The left circular shift amounts in each round have been approximately optimized, to yield a faster avalanche effect. The four shifts used in each round are different from the ones used in other rounds." SHA uses a constant shift amount in each round. This shift amount is relatively prime to the word size, as in MD4.

This leads to the following comparison: SHA is MD4 with the addition of an expand transformation, an extra round, and better avalanche effect; MD5 is MD4 with improved bit hashing, an extra round, and better avalanche effect.

There are no known cryptographic attacks against SHA. Because it produces a 160-bit hash, it is more resistant to brute-force attacks (including birthday attacks) than 128-bit hash functions covered in this chapter.

18.8 RIPE-MD

RIPE-MD was developed for the European Community's RIPE project [1305] (see Section 25.7). The algorithm is a variation of MD4, designed to resist known cryptanalytic attacks, and produce a 128-bit hash value. The rotations and the order of the message words are modified. Additionally, two instances of the algorithm, differing only in the constants, run in parallel. After each block, the output of both instances are added to the chaining variables. This seems to make the algorithm highly resistant to cryptanalysis.

18.9 HAVAL

HAVAL is a variable-length one-way hash function [1646]. It is a modification of MD5. HAVAL processes messages in blocks of 1024 bits, twice those of MD5. It has eight 32-bit chaining variables, twice those of MD5. It has a variable number of rounds, from three to five (each of which has 16 steps), and it can produce a hash length of 128, 160, 192, 224, or 256 bits.

HAVAL replaces MD5's simple nonlinear functions with highly nonlinear 7-variable functions, each of which satisfies the strict avalanche criterion. Each round uses a single function, but in every step a different permutation is applied to the inputs. It has a new message order and every step (except those in the first round) uses a different additive constant. The algorithm also has two rotations.

The core of the algorithm is

$$TEMP = (f(j,A,B,C,D,E,F,G) <<< 7) + (H <<< 11) + M[i][r(j)] + K(j)$$
$$H = G;\ G = F;\ F = E;\ E = D;\ D = C;\ C = B;\ B = A;\ A = TEMP$$

The variable number of rounds and variable-length output mean there are 15 versions of this algorithm. Den Boer's and Bosselaers's attack against MD5 [203] does not apply to HAVAL because of the rotation of H.

18.10 Other One-Way Hash Functions

MD3 is yet another hash function designed by Ron Rivest. It had several flaws and never really made it out of the laboratory, although a description was recently published in [1335].

A group of researchers at the University of Waterloo have proposed a one-way hash function based on iterated exponentiation in $GF(2^{593})$ [22]. In this scheme, a message is divided into 593-bit blocks; beginning with the first block, the blocks are successively exponentiated. Each exponent is the result of the computation with the previous block; the first exponent is given by an IV.

Ivan Damgård designed a one-way hash function based on the knapsack problem (see Section 19.2) [414]; it can be broken in about 2^{32} operations [290,1232,787].

Steve Wolfram's cellular automata [1608] have been proposed as a basis for one-way hash functions. An early implementation [414] is insecure [1052,404]. Another one-way hash function, Cellhash [384,404], and an improved version, Subhash [384,402,405], are based on cellular automata; both are designed for hardware. Boognish mixes the design principles of Cellhash with those of MD4 [402,407]. StepRightUp can be implemented as a hash function as well [402].

Claus Schnorr proposed a one-way hash function based on the discrete Fourier transform, called FFT-Hash, in the summer of 1991 [1399]; it was broken a few months later by two independent groups [403,84]. Schnorr proposed a revised version, called FFT-Hash II (the previous version was renamed FFT-Hash I) [1400], which was broken a few weeks later [1567]. Schnorr has proposed further modifications [1402,1403] but, as it stands, the algorithm is much slower than the others in this chapter. Another hash function, called SL_2 [1526], is insecure [315].

Additional theoretical work on constructing one-way hash functions from one-way functions and one-way permutations can be found in [412,1138,1342].

18.11 One-Way Hash Functions Using Symmetric Block Algorithms

It is possible to use a symmetric block cipher algorithm as a one-way hash function. The idea is that if the block algorithm is secure, then the one-way hash function will also be secure.

The most obvious method is to encrypt the message with the algorithm in CBC or CFB mode, a fixed key, and IV; the last ciphertext block is the hash value. These methods are described in various standards using DES: both modes in [1143], CFB in [1145], CBC in [55,56,54]. This just isn't good enough for one-way hash functions, although it will work for a MAC (see Section 18.14) [29].

A cleverer approach uses the message block as the key, the previous hash value as the input, and the current hash value as the output.

The actual hash functions proposed are even more complex. The block size is usually the key length, and the size of the hash value is the block size. Since most block algorithms are 64 bits, several schemes are designed around a hash that is twice the block size.

Assuming the hash function is correct, the security of the scheme is based on the security of the underlying block function. There are exceptions, though. Differential cryptanalysis is easier against block functions in hash functions than against block functions used for encryption: The key is known, so several tricks can be applied; only one right pair is needed for success; and you can generate as much chosen plaintext as you want. Some work on these lines is [1263,858,1313].

What follows is a summary of the various hash functions that have appeared in the literature [925,1465,1262]. Statements about attacks against these schemes assume that the underlying block cipher is secure; that is, the best attack against them is brute force.

One useful measure for hash functions based on block ciphers is the **hash rate**, or the number of n-bit messages blocks, where n is the block size of the algorithm, processed per encryption. The higher the hash rate, the faster the algorithm. (This measure was given the opposite definition in [1262], but the definition given here is more intuitive and is more widely used. This can be confusing.)

Schemes Where the Hash Length Equals the Block Size

The general scheme is as follows (see Figure 18.8):

$$H_0 = I_H, \text{ where } I_H \text{ is a random initial value}$$
$$H_i = E_A(B) \oplus C$$

where A, B, and C can be either M_i, H_{i-1}, $(M_i \oplus H_{i-1})$, or a constant (assumed to be 0). H_0 is some random initial value: I_H. The message is divided up into block-size chunks, M_i, and processed individually. And there is some kind of MD-strengthening, perhaps the same padding procedure used in MD5 and SHA.

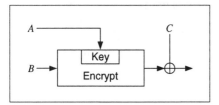

Figure 18.8   General hash function where the hash length equals the block size.

Table 18.1
Secure Hash Functions Where the
Block Length Equals the Hash Size

$$H_i = E_{H_{i-1}}(M_i) \oplus M_i$$
$$H_i = E_{H_{i-1}}(M_i \oplus H_{i-1}) \oplus M_i \oplus H_{i-1}$$
$$H_i = E_{H_{i-1}}(M_i) \oplus H_{i-1} \oplus M_i$$
$$H_i = E_{H_{i-1}}(M_i \oplus H_{i-1}) \oplus M_i$$
$$H_i = E_{M_i}(H_{i-1}) \oplus H_{i-1}$$
$$H_i = E_{M_i}(M_i \oplus H_{i-1}) \oplus M_i \oplus H_{i-1}$$
$$H_i = E_{M_i}(H_{i-1}) \oplus M_i \oplus H_{i-1}$$
$$H_i = E_{M_i}(M_i \oplus H_{i-1}) \oplus H_{i-1}$$
$$H_i = E_{M_i \oplus H_{i-1}}(M_i) \oplus M_i$$
$$H_i = E_{M_i \oplus H_{i-1}}(H_{i-1}) \oplus H_{i-1}$$
$$H_i = E_{M_i \oplus H_{i-1}}(M_i) \oplus H_{i-1}$$
$$H_i = E_{M_i \oplus H_{i-1}}(H_{i-1}) \oplus M_i$$

The three different variables can take on one of four possible values, so there are 64 total schemes of this type. Bart Preneel studied them all [1262].

Fifteen are trivially weak because the result does not depend on one of the inputs. Thirty-seven are insecure for more subtle reasons. Table 18.1 lists the 12 secure schemes remaining: The first 4 are secure against all attacks (see Figure 18.9) and the last 8 are secure against all but a fixed-point attack, which is not really worth worrying about.

The first scheme was described in [1028]. The third scheme was described in [1555,1105,1106] and was proposed as an ISO standard [766]. The fifth scheme was proposed by Carl Meyer, but is commonly called Davies-Meyer in the literature [1606,1607,434,1028]. The tenth scheme was proposed as a hash-function mode for LOKI [273].

The first, second, third, fourth, ninth, and eleventh schemes have a hash rate of 1; the key length equals the block length. The others have a rate of k/n, where k is the key length. This means that if the key length is shorter than the block length, then the message block can only be the length of the key. It is not recommended that the message block be longer than the key length, even if the encryption algorithm's key length is longer than the block length.

If the block algorithm has a DES-like complementation property and DES-like weak keys, there is an additional attack that is possible against all 12 schemes. The attack isn't very dangerous and not really worth worrying about. However, you can solve it by fixing bits 2 and 3 of the key to "01" or "10" [1081,1107]. Of course, this reduces the length of k from 56 bits to 54 bits (in DES, for example) and decreases the hash rate.

The following schemes, proposed in the literature, have been shown to be insecure.

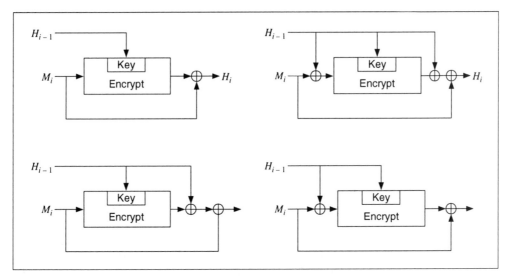

Figure 18.9 The four secure hash functions where the block length equals the hash size.

This scheme [1282] was broken in [369]:

$$H_i = E_{M_i}(H_{i-1})$$

Davies and Price proposed a variant which cycles the entire message through the algorithm twice [432,433]. Coppersmith's attack works on this variant with not much larger computational requirements [369].

Another scheme [432,458] was shown insecure in [1606]:

$$H_i = E_{M_i \oplus H_{i-1}}(H_{i-1})$$

This scheme was shown insecure in [1028] (*c* is a constant):

$$H_i = E_c(M_i \oplus H_{i-1}) \oplus M_i \oplus H_{i-1}$$

Modified Davies-Meyer

Lai and Massey modified the Davies-Meyer technique to work with the IDEA cipher [930,925]. IDEA has a 64-bit block size and 128-bit key size. Their scheme is

$$H_0 = I_H, \text{ where } I_H \text{ is a random initial value}$$
$$H_i = E_{H_{i-1}, M_i}(H_{i-1})$$

This function hashes the message in blocks of 64 bits and produces a 64-bit hash value (See Figure 18.10).

No known attack on this scheme is easier than brute force.

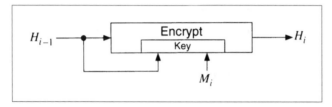

Figure 18.10   Modified Davies-Meyer.

Preneel-Bosselaers-Govaerts-Vandewalle

This hash function, first proposed in [1266], produces a hash value twice the block length of the encryption algorithm: A 64-bit algorithm produces a 128-bit hash.

With a 64-bit block algorithm, the scheme produces two 64-bit hash values, G_i and H_i, which are concatenated to produce the 128-bit hash. With most block algorithms, the block size is 64 bits. Two adjacent message blocks, L_i and R_i, each the size of the block length, are hashed together.

$G_0 = I_G$, where I_G is a random initial value

$H_0 = I_H$, where I_H is another random initial value

$G_i = E_{L_i \oplus H_{i-1}}(R_i \oplus G_{i-1}) \oplus R_i \oplus G_{i-1} \oplus H_{i-1}$

$H_i = E_{L_i \oplus R_i}(H_{i-1} \oplus G_{i-1}) \oplus L_i \oplus G_{i-1} \oplus H_{i-1}$

Lai demonstrates attacks against this scheme that, in some instances, make the birthday attack trivially solvable [925,926]. Preneel [1262] and Coppersmith [372] also have successful attacks against this scheme. Do not use it.

Quisquater-Girault

This scheme, first proposed in [1279], generates a hash that is twice the block length and has a hash rate of 1. It has two hash values, G_i and H_i, and two blocks, L_i and R_i, are hashed together.

$G_0 = I_G$, where I_G is a random initial value

$H_0 = I_H$, where I_H is another random initial value

$W_i = E_{L_i}(G_{i-1} \oplus R_i) \oplus R_i \oplus H_{i-1}$

$G_i = E_{R_i}(W_i \oplus L_i) \oplus G_{i-1} \oplus H_{i-1} \oplus L_i$

$H_i = W_i \oplus G_{i-1}$

This scheme appeared in a 1989 draft ISO standard [764], but was dropped in a later version [765]. Security problems with this scheme were identified in [1107,925, 1262,372]. (Actually, the version in the proceedings was strengthened after the version presented at the conference was attacked.) In some instances the birthday attack is solvable with a complexity of 2^{39}, not 2^{64}, through brute force. Do not use this scheme.

LOKI Double-Block

This algorithm is a modification of Quisquater-Girault, specifically designed to work with LOKI [273]. All parameters are as in Quisquater-Girault.

$G_0 = I_G$, where I_G is a random initial value

$H_0 = I_H$, where I_H is another random initial value

$W_i = E_{L_i \oplus G_{i-1}}(G_{i-1} \oplus R_i) \oplus R_i \oplus H_{i-1}$

$G_i = E_{R_i \oplus H_{i-1}}(W_i \oplus L_i) \oplus G_{i-1} \oplus H_{i-1} \oplus L_i$

$H_i = W_i \oplus G_{i-1}$

Again, in some instances the birthday attack is trivially solvable [925,926,1262, 372,736]. Do not use this scheme.

Parallel Davies-Meyer

This is yet another attempt at an algorithm with a hash rate of 1 that produces a hash twice the block length [736].

$G_0 = I_G$, where I_G is a random initial value

$H_0 = I_H$, where I_H is another random initial value

$G_i = E_{L_i \oplus R_i}(G_{i-1} \oplus L_i) \oplus L_i \oplus H_{i-1}$

$H_i = E_{L_i}(H_{i-1} \oplus R_i) \oplus R_i \oplus H_{i-1}$

Unfortunately, this scheme isn't secure either [928,861]. As it turns out, a double-length hash function with a hash rate of 1 cannot be more secure than Davies-Meyer [861].

Tandem and Abreast Davies-Meyer

Another way around the inherent limitations of a block cipher with a 64-bit key uses an algorithm, like IDEA (see Section 13.9), with a 64-bit block and a 128-bit key. These two schemes produce a 128-bit hash value and have a hash rate of ½ [930,925].

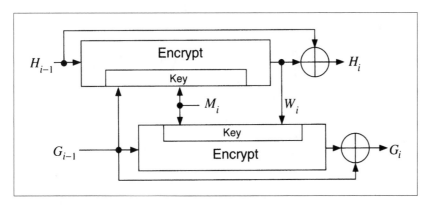

Figure 18.11   Tandem Davies-Meyer.

In this first scheme, two modified Davies-Meyer functions work in tandem (see Figure 18.11).

$$G_0 = I_G, \text{ where } I_G \text{ is some random initial value}$$
$$H_0 = I_H, \text{ where } I_H \text{ is some other random initial value}$$
$$W_i = E_{G_{i-1}, M_i}(H_{i-1})$$
$$G_i = G_{i-1} \oplus E_{M_i, W_i}(G_{i-1})$$
$$H_i = W_i \oplus H_{i-1}$$

The following scheme uses two modified Davies-Meyer functions side-by-side (see Figure 18.12).

$$G_0 = I_G, \text{ where } I_G \text{ is some random initial value}$$
$$H_0 = I_H, \text{ where } I_H \text{ is some other random initial value}$$
$$G_i = G_{i-1} \oplus E_{M_i, H_{i-1}}(\neg G_{i-1})$$
$$H_i = H_{i-1} \oplus E_{G_{i-1}, M_i}(H_{i-1})$$

In both schemes, the two 64-bit hash values G_i and H_i are concatenated to produce a single 128-bit hash.

As far as anyone knows, these algorithms have ideal security for a 128-bit hash function: Finding a message that hashes to a given hash value requires 2^{128} attempts, and finding two random messages that hash to the same value requires 2^{64} attempts—assuming that there is no better way to attack the block algorithm than by using brute force.

MDC-2 and MDC-4

MDC-2 and MDC-4 were first developed at IBM [1081,1079]. MDC-2, sometimes called Meyer-Schilling, is under consideration as an ANSI and ISO standard [61,765]; a variant was proposed in [762]. MDC-4 is specified for the RIPE project [1305] (see Section 25.7). The specifications use DES as the block function, although in theory any encryption algorithm could be used.

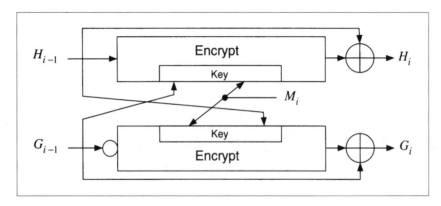

Figure 18.12   Abreast Davies-Meyer.

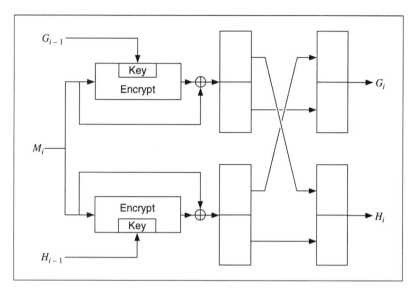

Figure 18.13   MDC-2.

MDC-2 has a hash rate of ½, and produces a hash value twice the length of the block size. It is shown in Figure 18.13. MDC-4 also produces a hash value twice the length of the block size, and has a hash rate of ¼ (see Figure 18.14).

These schemes have been analyzed in [925,1262]. They are secure against current computing power, but they are not nearly as secure as the designers have estimated. If the block algorithm is DES, they have been looked at with respect to differential cryptanalysis [1262].

Both MDC-2 and MDC-4 are patented [223].

AR Hash Function

The AR hash function was developed by Algorithmic Research, Ltd. and has been distributed by the ISO for information purposes only [767]. Its basic structure is a variant of the underlying block cipher (DES in the reference) in CBC mode. The last two ciphertext blocks and a constant are XORed to the current message block and encrypted by the algorithm. The hash is the last two ciphertext blocks computed. The message is processed twice, with two different keys, so the hash function has a hash rate of ½. The first key is 0x0000000000000000, the second key is 0x2a4152 2f4446502a, and c is 0x0123456789abcdef. The result is compressed to a single 128-bit hash value. See [750] for the details.

$$H_i = E_K(M_i \oplus H_{i-1} \oplus H_{i-2} \oplus c) \oplus M_i$$

This sounds interesting, but it is insecure. After considerable preprocessing, it is possible to find collisions for this hash function easily [416].

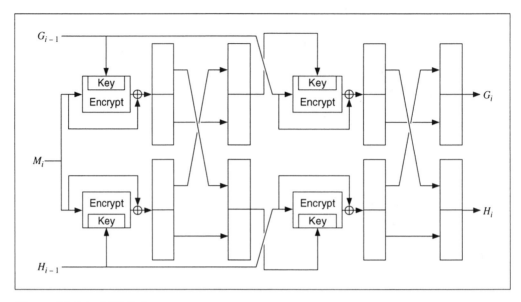

Figure 18.14   MDC-4.

GOST Hash Function

This hash function comes from Russia, and is specified in the standard GOST R 34.11-94 [657]. It uses the GOST block algorithm (see Section 14.1), although in theory it could use any block algorithm with a 64-bit block size and a 256-bit key. The function produces a 256-bit hash value.

The compression function, $H_i = f(M_i, H_{i-1})$ (both operands are 256-bit quantities) is defined as follows:

    (1) Generate four GOST encryption keys by some linear mixing of M_i, H_{i-1}, and some constants.

    (2) Use each key to encrypt a different 64 bits of H_{i-1} in ECB mode. Store the resulting 256 bits into a temporary variable, S.

    (3) H_i is a complex, although linear, function of S, M_i, and H_{i-1}.

The final hash of M is not the hash of the last block. There are actually three chaining variables: H_n is the hash of the last message block, Z is the sum mod 2^{256} of all the message blocks, and L is the length of the message. Given those variables and the padded last block, M', the final hash value is:

$$H = f(Z \oplus M', f(L, f(M', H_n)))$$

The documentation is a bit confusing (and in Russian), but I think all that is correct. In any case, this hash function is specified for use with the Russian Digital Signature Standard (see Section 20.3).

Other Schemes

Ralph Merkle proposed a scheme using DES, but it's slow; it only processes seven message bits per iteration and each iteration involves two DES encryptions [1065, 1069]. Another scheme [1642,1645] is insecure [1267]; it was once proposed as an ISO standard.

18.12 USING PUBLIC-KEY ALGORITHMS

It is possible to use a public-key encryption algorithm in a block chaining mode as a one-way hash function. If you then throw away the private key, breaking the hash would be as difficult as reading the message without the private key.

Here's an example using RSA. If M is the message to be hashed, n is the product of two primes p and q, and e is another large number relatively prime to $(p - 1)(q - 1)$, then the hash function, H(M), would be

$$H(M) = M^e \bmod n$$

An even easier solution would be to use a single strong prime as the modulus p. Then:

$$H(M) = M^e \bmod p$$

Breaking this problem is probably as difficult as finding the discrete logarithm of e. The problem with this algorithm is that it's far slower than any others discussed here. I don't recommend it for that reason.

18.13 CHOOSING A ONE-WAY HASH FUNCTION

The contenders seem to be SHA, MD5, and constructions based on block ciphers; the others really haven't been studied enough to be in the running. I vote for SHA. It has a longer hash value than MD5, is faster than the various block-cipher constructions, and was developed by the NSA. I trust the NSA's abilities at cryptanalysis, even if they don't make their results public.

Table 18.2 gives timing measurements for some hash functions. They are meant for comparison purposes only.

18.14 MESSAGE AUTHENTICATION CODES

A message authentication code, or MAC, is a key-dependent one-way hash function. MACs have the same properties as the one-way hash functions discussed previously, but they also include a key. Only someone with the identical key can verify the hash. They are very useful to provide authenticity without secrecy.

MACs can be used to authenticate files between users. They can also be used by a single user to determine if his files have been altered, perhaps by a virus. A user could compute the MAC of his files and store that value in a table. If the user used

Table 18.2
Speeds of Some Hash Functions on a 33 MHz 486SX

Algorithm	Hash Length	Encryption Speed (kilobytes/second)
Abreast Davies-Meyer (with IDEA)	128	22
Davies-Meyer (with DES)	64	9
GOST Hash	256	11
HAVAL (3 passes)	variable	168
HAVAL (4 passes)	variable	118
HAVAL (5 passes)	variable	95
MD2	128	23
MD4	128	236
MD5	128	174
N-HASH (12 rounds)	128	29
N-HASH (15 rounds)	128	24
RIPE-MD	128	182
SHA	160	75
SNEFRU (4 passes)	128	48
SNEFRU (8 passes)	128	23

instead a one-way hash function, then the virus could compute the new hash value after infection and replace the table entry. A virus could not do that with a MAC, because the virus does not know the key.

An easy way to turn a one-way hash function into a MAC is to encrypt the hash value with a symmetric algorithm. Any MAC can be turned into a one-way hash function by making the key public.

CBC-MAC

The simplest way to make a key-dependent one-way hash function is to encrypt a message with a block algorithm in CBC or CFB modes. The hash is the last encrypted block, encrypted once more in CBC or CFB modes. The CBC method is specified in ANSI X9.9 [54], ANSI X9.19 [56], ISO 8731-1 [759], ISO 9797 [763], and an Australian standard [1496]. Differential cryptanalysis can break this scheme with reduced-round DES or FEAL as the underlying block algorithms [1197].

The potential security problem with this method is that the receiver must have the key, and that key allows him to generate messages with the same hash value as a given message by decrypting in the reverse direction.

Message Authenticator Algorithm (MAA)

This algorithm is an ISO standard [760]. It produces a 32-bit hash, and was designed for mainframe computers with a fast multiply instruction [428].

$$v = v <<< 1$$
$$e = v \oplus w$$
$$x = ((((e + y) \bmod 2^{32}) \vee A \wedge C) \star (x \oplus M_i)) \bmod 2^{32} - 1$$
$$y = ((((e + x) \bmod 2^{32}) \vee B \wedge D) \star (y \oplus M_i)) \bmod 2^{32} - 2$$

Iterate these for each message block, M_i, and the resultant hash is the XOR of x and y. The variables v and e are determined from the key. A, B, C, and D are constants.

This algorithm is probably in wide use, but I can't believe it is all that secure. It was designed a long time ago, and isn't very complicated.

Bidirectional MAC

This MAC produces a hash value twice the length of the block algorithm [978]. First, compute the CBC-MAC of the message. Then, compute the CBC-MAC of the message with the blocks in reverse order. The bidirectional MAC value is simply the concatenation of the two. Unfortunately, this construction is insecure [1097].

Jueneman's Methods

This MAC is also called a quadratic congruential manipulation detection code (QCMDC) [792,789]. First, divide the message into m-bit blocks. Then:

$H_0 = I_H$, where I_H is the secret key

$H_i = (H_{i-1} + M_i)^2 \bmod p$, where p is a prime less than $2^m - 1$
and + denotes integer addition

Jueneman suggests $n = 16$ and $p = 2^{31} - 1$. In [792] he also suggests that an additional key be used as H_1, with the actual message starting at H_2.

Because of a variety of birthday-type attacks discovered in conjunction with Don Coppersmith, Jueneman suggested computing the QCMDC four times, using the result of one iteration as the IV for the next iteration, and then concatenating the results to obtain a 128-bit hash value [793]. This was further strengthened by doing the four iterations in parallel and cross-linking them [790,791]. This scheme was broken by Coppersmith [376].

Another variant [432,434] replaced the addition operation with an XOR and used message blocks significantly smaller than p. H_0 was also set, making it a keyless one-way hash function. After this scheme was attacked [612], it was strengthened as part of the European Open Shop Information-TeleTrust project [1221], quoted in CCITT X.509 [304], and adopted in ISO 10118 [764,765]. Unfortunately, Coppersmith has broken this scheme as well [376]. There has been some research using exponents other than 2 [603], but none of it has been promising.

RIPE-MAC

RIPE-MAC was invented by Bart Preneel [1262] and adopted by the RIPE project [1305] (see Section 18.8). It is based on ISO 9797 [763], and uses DES as a block encryption function. RIPE-MAC has two flavors: one using normal DES, called

RIPE-MAC1, and another using triple-DES for even greater security, called RIPE-MAC3. RIPE-MAC1 uses one DES encryption per 64-bit message block; RIPE-MAC3 uses three.

The algorithm consists of three parts. First, the message is expanded to a length that is a multiple of 64 bits. Next, the expanded message is divided up into 64-bit blocks. A keyed compression function is used to hash these blocks, under the control of a secret key, into a single block of 64 bits. This is the step that uses either DES or triple-DES. Finally, the output of this compression is subjected to another DES-based encryption with a different key, derived from the key used in the compression. See [1305] for details.

IBC-Hash

IBC-Hash is another MAC adopted by the RIPE project [1305] (see Section 18.8). It is interesting because it is provably secure; the chance of successful attack can be quantified. Unfortunately, every message must be hashed with a different key. The chosen level of security puts constraints on the maximum message size that can be hashed—something no other function in this chapter does. Given these considerations, the RIPE report recommends that IBC-Hash be used only for long, infrequently sent messages.

The heart of the function is

$$h_i = ((M_i \bmod p) + v) \bmod 2^n$$

The secret key is the pair p and v, where p is an n-bit prime and v is a random number less than 2^n. The M_i values are derived by a carefully specified padding procedure. The probabilities of breaking both the one-wayness and the collision-resistance can be quantified, and users can choose their security level by changing the parameters.

One-Way Hash Function MAC

A one-way hash function can also be used as a MAC [1537]. Assume Alice and Bob share a key K, and Alice wants to send Bob a MAC for message M. Alice concatenates K and M, and computes the one-way hash of the concatenation: $H(K,M)$. This hash is the MAC. Since Bob knows K, he can reproduce Alice's result. Mallory, who does not know K, can't.

This method works with MD-strengthening techniques, but has serious problems. Mallory can always add new blocks to the end of the message and compute a valid MAC. This attack can be thwarted if you put the message length at the beginning, but Preneel is suspicious of this scheme [1265]. It is better to put the key at the end of the message, $H(M,K)$, but this has some problems as well [1265]. If H is one-way but not collision-free, Mallory can forge messages. Still better is $H(K,M,K)$, or $H(K_1,M,K_2)$, where K_1 and K_2 are different [1537]. Preneel is still suspicious [1265].

The following constructions seem secure:

$H(K_1, H(K_2,M))$

$H(K, H(K,M))$

$H(K,p,M,K)$, where p pads K to a full message block.

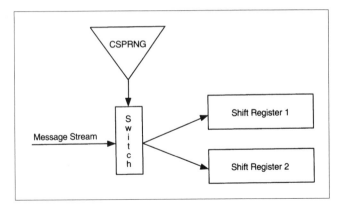

Figure 18.15   Stream cipher MAC.

The best approach is to concatenate at least 64 bits of the key with each message block. This makes the one-way hash function less efficient, because the message blocks are smaller, but it is much more secure [1265].

Alternatively, use a one-way hash function and a symmetric algorithm. Hash the file, then encrypt the hash. This is more secure than first encrypting the file and then hashing the encrypted file, but it is vulnerable to the same attack as the $H(M,K)$ approach [1265].

Stream Cipher MAC

This MAC scheme uses stream ciphers (see Figure 18.15) [932]. A cryptographically secure pseudo-random-bit generator demultiplexes the message stream into two substreams. If the output bit of the bit generator k_i, is 1, then the current message bit m_i, is routed to the first substream; if the k_i is 0, the m_i is routed to the second substream. The substreams are each fed into a different LFSR (see Section 16.2). The output of the MAC is simply the final states of the shift registers.

Unfortunately, this method is not secure against small changes in the message [1523]. For example, if you alter the last bit of the message, then only 2 bits in the corresponding MAC value need to be altered to create a fake MAC; this can be done with reasonable probability. The author presents a more secure, and more complicated, alternative.

CHAPTER   19

Public-Key Algorithms

19.1 BACKGROUND

The concept of public-key cryptography was invented by Whitfield Diffie and Martin Hellman, and independently by Ralph Merkle. Their contribution to cryptography was the notion that keys could come in pairs—an encryption key and a decryption key—and that it could be infeasible to generate one key from the other (see Section 2.5). Diffie and Hellman first presented this concept at the 1976 National Computer Conference [495]; a few months later, their seminal paper "New Directions in Cryptography" was published [496]. (Due to a glacial publishing process, Merkle's first contribution to the field didn't appear until 1978 [1064].)

Since 1976, numerous public-key cryptography algorithms have been proposed. Many of these are insecure. Of those still considered secure, many are impractical. Either they have too large a key or the ciphertext is much larger than the plaintext.

Only a few algorithms are both secure and practical. These algorithms are generally based on one of the hard problems discussed in Section 11.2. Of these secure and practical public-key algorithms, some are only suitable for key distribution. Others are suitable for encryption (and by extension for key distribution). Still others are only useful for digital signatures. Only three algorithms work well for both encryption and digital signatures: RSA, ElGamal, and Rabin. All of these algorithms are slow. They encrypt and decrypt data much more slowly than symmetric algorithms; usually that's too slow to support bulk data encryption.

Hybrid cryptosystems (see Section 2.5) speed things up: A symmetric algorithm with a random session key is used to encrypt the message, and a public-key algorithm is used to encrypt the random session key.

Security of Public-Key Algorithms

Since a cryptanalyst has access to the public key, he can always choose any message to encrypt. This means that a cryptanalyst, given $C = E_K(P)$, can guess the value of P and easily check his guess. This is a serious problem if the number of possible plaintext messages is small enough to allow exhaustive search, but can be solved by padding messages with a string of random bits. This makes identical plaintext messages encrypt to different ciphertext messages. (For more about this concept, see Section 23.15.)

This is especially important if a public-key algorithm is used to encrypt a session key. Eve can generate a database of all possible session keys encrypted with Bob's public key. Sure, this requires a large amount of time and memory, but for a 40-bit exportable key or a 56-bit DES key, it's a whole lot less time and memory than breaking Bob's public key. Once Eve has generated the database, she will have his key and can read his mail at will.

Public-key algorithms are designed to resist chosen-plaintext attacks; their security is based both on the difficulty of deducing the secret key from the public key and the difficulty of deducing the plaintext from the ciphertext. However, most public-key algorithms are particularly susceptible to a chosen-ciphertext attack (see Section 1.1).

In systems where the digital signature operation is the inverse of the encryption operation, this attack is impossible to prevent unless different keys are used for encryption and signatures.

Consequently, it is important to look at the whole system and not just at the individual parts. Good public-key protocols are designed so that the various parties can't decrypt arbitrary messages generated by other parties—the proof-of-identity protocols are a good example (see Section 5.2).

19.2 Knapsack Algorithms

The first algorithm for generalized public-key encryption was the knapsack algorithm developed by Ralph Merkle and Martin Hellman [713,1074]. It could only be used for encryption, although Adi Shamir later adapted the system for digital signatures [1413]. Knapsack algorithms get their security from the knapsack problem, an **NP-complete** problem. Although this algorithm was later found to be insecure, it is worth examining because it demonstrates how an **NP-complete** problem can be used for public-key cryptography.

The knapsack problem is a simple one. Given a pile of items, each with different weights, is it possible to put some of those items into a knapsack so that the knapsack weighs a given amount? More formally: Given a set of values $M_1, M_2, \ldots, M_n$, and a sum S, compute the values of b_i such that

$$S = b_1M_1 + b_2M_2 + \ldots + b_nM_n$$

The values of b_i can be either zero or one. A one indicates that the item is in the knapsack; a zero indicates that it isn't.

For example, the items might have weights of 1, 5, 6, 11, 14, and 20. You could pack a knapsack that weighs 22; use weights 5, 6, and 11. You could not pack a knapsack that weighs 24. In general, the time required to solve this problem seems to grow exponentially with the number of items in the pile.

The idea behind the Merkle-Hellman knapsack algorithm is to encode a message as a solution to a series of knapsack problems. A block of plaintext equal in length to the number of items in the pile would select the items in the knapsack (plaintext bits corresponding to the *b* values), and the ciphertext would be the resulting sum. Figure 19.1 shows a plaintext encrypted with a sample knapsack problem.

The trick is that there are actually two different knapsack problems, one solvable in linear time and the other believed not to be. The easy knapsack can be modified to create the hard knapsack. The public key is the hard knapsack, which can easily be used to encrypt but cannot be used to decrypt messages. The private key is the easy knapsack, which gives an easy way to decrypt messages. People who don't know the private key are forced to try to solve the hard knapsack problem.

Superincreasing Knapsacks

What is the easy knapsack problem? If the list of weights is a **superincreasing sequence**, then the resulting knapsack problem is easy to solve. A superincreasing sequence is a sequence in which every term is greater than the sum of all the previous terms. For example, {1,3,6,13,27,52} is a superincreasing sequence, but {1,3,4,9, 15,25} is not.

The solution to a **superincreasing knapsack** is easy to find. Take the total weight and compare it with the largest number in the sequence. If the total weight is less than the number, then it is not in the knapsack. If the total weight is greater than or equal to the number, then it is in the knapsack. Reduce the weight of the knapsack by the value and move to the next largest number in the sequence. Repeat until finished. If the total weight has been brought to zero, then there is a solution. If the total weight has not, there isn't.

For example, consider a total knapsack weight of 70 and a sequence of weights of {2,3,6,13,27,52}. The largest weight, 52, is less than 70, so 52 is in the knapsack. Subtracting 52 from 70 leaves 18. The next weight, 27, is greater than 18, so 27 is not in the knapsack. The next weight, 13, is less than 18, so 13 is in the knapsack. Subtracting 13 from 18 leaves 5. The next weight, 6, is greater than 5, so 6 is not in the knapsack. Continuing this process will show that both 2 and 3 are in the knapsack and the total weight is brought to 0, which indicates that a solution has been found. Were this a Merkle-Hellman knapsack encryption block, the plaintext that resulted from a ciphertext value of 70 would be 110101.

Non-superincreasing, or normal, knapsacks are hard problems; they have no known quick algorithm. The only known way to determine which items are in the

Plaintext:	1 1 1 0 0 1	0 1 0 1 1 0	0 0 0 0 0 0	0 1 1 0 0 0
Knapsack:	1 5 6 11 14 20	1 5 6 11 14 20	1 5 6 11 14 20	1 5 6 11 14 20
Ciphertext:	1+5+6+20=	5+11+14=	0=	5+6 =
	32	30	0	11

Figure 19.1 Encryption with knapsacks.

knapsack is to methodically test possible solutions until you stumble on the correct one. The fastest algorithms, taking into account the various heuristics, grow exponentially with the number of possible weights in the knapsack. Add one item to the sequence of weights, and it takes twice as long to find the solution. This is much more difficult than a superincreasing knapsack where, if you add one more weight to the sequence, it simply takes another operation to find the solution.

The Merkle-Hellman algorithm is based on this property. The private key is a sequence of weights for a superincreasing knapsack problem. The public key is a sequence of weights for a normal knapsack problem with the same solution. Merkle and Hellman developed a technique for converting a superincreasing knapsack problem into a normal knapsack problem. They did this using modular arithmetic.

Creating the Public Key from the Private Key

Without going into the number theory, this is how the algorithm works: To get a normal knapsack sequence, take a superincreasing knapsack sequence, for example {2,3,6,13,27,52}, and multiply all of the values by a number n, mod m. The modulus should be a number greater than the sum of all the numbers in the sequence: for example, 105. The multiplier should have no factors in common with the modulus: for example, 31. The normal knapsack sequence would then be

$$2 * 31 \bmod 105 = 62$$
$$3 * 31 \bmod 105 = 93$$
$$6 * 31 \bmod 105 = 81$$
$$13 * 31 \bmod 105 = 88$$
$$27 * 31 \bmod 105 = 102$$
$$52 * 31 \bmod 105 = 37$$

The knapsack would then be {62,93,81,88,102,37}.

The superincreasing knapsack sequence is the private key. The normal knapsack sequence is the public key.

Encryption

To encrypt a binary message, first break it up into blocks equal to the number of items in the knapsack sequence. Then, allowing a one to indicate the item is present and a zero to indicate that the item is absent, compute the total weights of the knapsacks—one for every message block.

For example, if the message were 011000110101101110 in binary, encryption using the previous knapsack would proceed like this:

$$message = 011000\ 110101\ 101110$$

011000 corresponds to 93 + 81 = 174
110101 corresponds to 62 + 93 + 88 + 37 = 280
101110 corresponds to 62 + 81 + 88 + 102 = 333

The ciphertext would be

174,280,333

Decryption

A legitimate recipient of this message knows the private key: the original super-increasing knapsack, as well as the values of n and m used to transform it into a normal knapsack. To decrypt the message, the recipient must first determine n^{-1} such that $n(n^{-1}) \equiv 1 \pmod{m}$. Multiply each of the ciphertext values by $n^{-1} \bmod m$, and then partition with the private knapsack to get the plaintext values.

In our example, the superincreasing knapsack is $\{2,3,6,13,27,52\}$, m is equal to 105, and n is equal to 31. The ciphertext message is 174,280,333. In this case n^{-1} is equal to 61, so the ciphertext values must be multiplied by 61 mod 105.

$$174 * 61 \bmod 105 = 9 = 3 + 6, \text{ which corresponds to } 011000$$
$$280 * 61 \bmod 105 = 70 = 2 + 3 + 13 + 52, \text{ which corresponds to } 110101$$
$$333 * 61 \bmod 105 = 48 = 2 + 6 + 13 + 27, \text{ which corresponds to } 101110$$

The recovered plaintext is 011000 110101 101110.

Practical Implementations

With a knapsack sequence of only six items, it's not hard to solve the problem even if it isn't superincreasing. Real knapsacks should contain at least 250 items. The value for each term in the superincreasing knapsack should be somewhere between 200 and 400 bits long, and the modulus should be somewhere between 100 to 200 bits long. Real implementations of the algorithm use random-sequence generators to produce these values.

With knapsacks like that, it's futile to try to solve them by brute force. If a computer could try a million possibilities per second, trying all possible knapsack values would take over 10^{46} years. Even a million machines working in parallel wouldn't solve this problem before the sun went nova.

Security of Knapsacks

It wasn't a million machines that broke the knapsack cryptosystem, but a pair of cryptographers. First a single bit of plaintext was recovered [725]. Then, Shamir showed that knapsacks can be broken in certain circumstances [1415,1416]. There were other results—[1428,38,754,516,488]—but no one could break the general Merkle-Hellman system. Finally, Shamir and Zippel [1418,1419,1421] found flaws in the transformation that allowed them to reconstruct the superincreasing knapsack from the normal knapsack. The exact arguments are beyond the scope of this book, but a nice summary of them can be found in [1233,1244]. At the conference where the results were presented, the attack was demonstrated on stage using an Apple II computer [492,494].

Knapsack Variants

Since the original Merkle-Hellman scheme was broken, many other knapsack systems have been proposed: multiple iterated knapsacks, Graham-Shamir knapsacks, and others. These have all been analyzed and broken, generally using the same cryptographic techniques, and litter the cryptographic highway [260,253,269,921,15,919, 920,922,366,254,263,255]. Good overviews of these systems and their cryptanalyses can be found in [267,479,257,268].

Other algorithms have been proposed that use ideas similar to those used in knapsack cryptosystems, but these too have been broken. The Lu-Lee cryptosystem [990,13] was broken in [20,614,873]; a modification [507] is also insecure [1620]. Attacks on the Goodman-McAuley cryptosystem are in [646,647,267,268]. The Pieprzyk cryptosystem [1246] can be broken by similar attacks. The Niemi cryptosystem [1169], based on modular knapsacks, was broken in [345,788]. A newer multistage knapsack [747] has not yet been broken, but I am not optimistic. Another variant is [294].

While a variation of the knapsack algorithm is currently secure—the Chor-Rivest knapsack [356], despite a "specialized attack" [743]—the amount of computation required makes it far less useful than the other algorithms discussed here. A variant, called the Powerline System, is not secure [958]. Most important, considering the ease with which all the other variations fell, it doesn't seem prudent to trust them.

Patents

The original Merkle-Hellman algorithm is patented in the United States [720] and worldwide (see Table 19.1). Public Key Partners (PKP) licenses the patent, along with other public-key cryptography patents (see Section 25.5). The U.S. patent will expire on August 19, 1997.

19.3 RSA

Soon after Merkle's knapsack algorithm came the first full-fledged public-key algorithm, one that works for encryption and digital signatures: RSA [1328,1329]. Of all the public-key algorithms proposed over the years, RSA is by far the easiest to understand and implement. (Martin Gardner published an early description of the algorithm in his "Mathematical Games" column in *Scientific American* [599].) It is

Table 19.1
Foreign Merkle-Hellman Knapsack Patents

Country	Number	Date of Issue
Belgium	871039	5 Apr 1979
Netherlands	7810063	10 Apr 1979
Great Britain	2006580	2 May 1979
Germany	2843583	10 May 1979
Sweden	7810478	14 May 1979
France	2405532	8 Jun 1979
Germany	2843583	3 Jun 1982
Germany	2857905	15 Jul 1982
Canada	1128159	20 Jul 1982
Great Britain	2006580	18 Aug 1982
Switzerland	63416114	14 Jan 1983
Italy	1099780	28 Sep 1985

also the most popular. Named after the three inventors—Ron Rivest, Adi Shamir, and Leonard Adleman—it has since withstood years of extensive cryptanalysis. Although the cryptanalysis neither proved nor disproved RSA's security, it does suggest a confidence level in the algorithm.

RSA gets its security from the difficulty of factoring large numbers. The public and private keys are functions of a pair of large (100 to 200 digits or even larger) prime numbers. Recovering the plaintext from the public key and the ciphertext is conjectured to be equivalent to factoring the product of the two primes.

To generate the two keys, choose two random large prime numbers, p and q. For maximum security, choose p and q of equal length. Compute the product:

$$n = pq$$

Then randomly choose the encryption key, e, such that e and $(p-1)(q-1)$ are relatively prime. Finally, use the extended Euclidean algorithm to compute the decryption key, d, such that

$$ed \equiv 1 \bmod (p-1)(q-1)$$

In other words,

$$d = e^{-1} \bmod ((p-1)(q-1))$$

Note that d and n are also relatively prime. The numbers e and n are the public key; the number d is the private key. The two primes, p and q, are no longer needed. They should be discarded, but never revealed.

To encrypt a message m, first divide it into numerical blocks smaller than n (with binary data, choose the largest power of 2 less than n). That is, if both p and q are 100-digit primes, then n will have just under 200 digits and each message block, m_i, should be just under 200 digits long. (If you need to encrypt a fixed number of blocks, you can pad them with a few zeros on the left to ensure that they will always be less than n.) The encrypted message, c, will be made up of similarly sized message blocks, c_i, of about the same length. The encryption formula is simply

$$c_i = m_i^e \bmod n$$

To decrypt a message, take each encrypted block c_i and compute

$$m_i = c_i^d \bmod n$$

Since

$$c_i^d = (m_i^e)^d = m_i^{ed} = m_i^{k(p-1)(q-1)+1} = m_i m_i^{k(p-1)(q-1)} = m_i \cdot 1 = m_i; \text{ all (mod } n)$$

the formula recovers the message. This is summarized in Table 19.2.

The message could just as easily have been encrypted with d and decrypted with e; the choice is arbitrary. I will spare you the number theory that proves why this works; most current texts on cryptography cover it in detail.

A short example will probably go a long way to making this clearer. If $p = 47$ and $q = 71$, then

Table 19.2
RSA Encryption

Public Key:

n product of two primes, p and q (p and q must remain secret)

e relatively prime to $(p-1)(q-1)$

Private Key:

d $e^{-1} \bmod ((p-1)(q-1))$

Encrypting:

$c = m^e \bmod n$

Decrypting:

$m = c^d \bmod n$

$$n = pq = 3337$$

The encryption key, e, must have no factors in common with

$$(p-1)(q-1) = 46 \star 70 = 3220$$

Choose e (at random) to be 79. In that case

$$d = 79^{-1} \bmod 3220 = 1019$$

This number was calculated using the extended Euclidean algorithm (see Section 11.3). Publish e and n, and keep d secret. Discard p and q.

To encrypt the message

$$m = 6882326879666683$$

first break it into small blocks. Three-digit blocks work nicely in this case. The message is split into six blocks, m_i, in which

$$m_1 = 688$$
$$m_2 = 232$$
$$m_3 = 687$$
$$m_4 = 966$$
$$m_5 = 668$$
$$m_6 = 003$$

The first block is encrypted as

$$688^{79} \bmod 3337 = 1570 = c_1$$

Performing the same operation on the subsequent blocks generates an encrypted message:

$$c = 1570 \ 2756 \ 2091 \ 2276 \ 2423 \ 158$$

Decrypting the message requires performing the same exponentiation using the decryption key of 1019, so

$$1570^{1019} \bmod 3337 = 688 = m_1$$

The rest of the message can be recovered in this manner.

RSA in Hardware

Much has been written on the subject of hardware implementations of RSA [1314, 1474,1456,1316,1485,874,1222,87,1410,1409,1343,998,367,1429,523,772]. Good survey articles are [258,872]. Many different chips perform RSA encryption [1310,252, 1101,1317,874,69,737,594,1275,1563,509,1223]. A partial list of currently available RSA chips, from [150,258], is listed in Table 19.3. Not all are available on the open market.

Speed of RSA

In hardware, RSA is about 1000 times slower than DES. The fastest VLSI hardware implementation for RSA with a 512-bit modulus has a throughput of 64 kilobits per second [258]. There are also chips that perform 1024-bit RSA encryption. Currently chips are being planned that will approach 1 megabit per second using a 512-bit modulus; they will probably be available in 1995. Manufacturers have also implemented RSA in smart cards; these implementations are slower.

In software, DES is about 100 times faster than RSA. These numbers may change slightly as technology changes, but RSA will never approach the speed of symmetric algorithms. Table 19.4 gives sample software speeds of RSA [918].

Software Speedups

RSA encryption goes much faster if you're smart about choosing a value of e. The three most common choices are 3, 17, and 65537 ($2^{16} + 1$). (The binary representation of 65537 has only two ones, so it takes only 17 multiplications to exponentiate.) X.509 recommends 65537 [304], PEM recommends 3 [76], and PKCS #1 (see Section 24.14) recommends 3 or 65537 [1345]. There are no security problems with using

Table 19.3
Existing RSA Chips

Company	Clock Speed	Baud Rate Per 512 Bits	Clock Cycles Per 512 Bit Encryption	Technology	Bits per Chip	Number of Transistors
Alpha Techn.	25 MHz	13 K	.98 M	2 micron	1024	180,000
AT&T	15 MHz	19 K	.4 M	1.5 micron	298	100,000
British Telecom	10 MHz	5.1 K	1 M	2.5 micron	256	——
Business Sim. Ltd.	5 MHz	3.8 K	.67 M	Gate Array	32	——
Calmos Syst. Inc.	20 MHz	28 K	.36 M	2 micron	593	95,000
CNET	25 MHz	5.3 K	2.3 M	1 micron	1024	100,000
Cryptech	14 MHz	17 K	.4 M	Gate Array	120	33,000
Cylink	30 MHz	6.8 K	1.2 M	1.5 micron	1024	150,000
GEC Marconi	25 MHz	10.2 K	.67 M	1.4 micron	512	160,000
Pijnenburg	25 MHz	50 K	.256 M	1 micron	1024	400,000
Sandia	8 MHz	10 K	.4 M	2 micron	272	86,000
Siemens	5 MHz	8.5 K	.3 M	1 micron	512	60,000

Table 19.4
RSA Speeds for Different Modulus Lengths
with an 8-bit Public Key (on a SPARC II)

	512 bits	768 bits	1,024 bits
Encrypt	0.03 sec	0.05 sec	0.08 sec
Decrypt	0.16 sec	0.48 sec	0.93 sec
Sign	0.16 sec	0.52 sec	0.97 sec
Verify	0.02 sec	0.07 sec	0.08 sec

any of these three values for e (assuming you pad messages with random values—see later section), even if a whole group of users uses the same value for e.

Private key operations can be speeded up with the Chinese remainder theorem if you save the values of p and q, and additional values such as $d \bmod (p - 1)$, $d \bmod (q - 1)$, and $q^{-1} \bmod p$ [1283,1276]. These additional numbers can easily be calculated from the private and public keys.

Security of RSA

The security of RSA depends wholly on the problem of factoring large numbers. Technically, that's a lie. It is *conjectured* that the security of RSA depends on the problem of factoring large numbers. It has never been mathematically proven that you need to factor n to calculate m from c and e. It is conceivable that an entirely different way to cryptanalyze RSA might be discovered. However, if this new way allows the cryptanalyst to deduce d, it could also be used as a new way to factor large numbers. I wouldn't worry about it too much.

It is also possible to attack RSA by guessing the value of $(p - 1)(q - 1)$. This attack is no easier than factoring n [1616].

For the ultraskeptical, some RSA variants have been proved to be as difficult as factoring (see Section 19.5). Also look at [36], which shows that recovering even certain bits of information from an RSA-encrypted ciphertext is as hard as decrypting the entire message.

Factoring n is the most obvious means of attack. Any adversary will have the public key, e, and the modulus, n. To find the decryption key, d, he has to factor n. Section 11.4 discusses the current state of factoring technology. Currently, a 129-decimal-digit modulus is at the edge of factoring technology. So, n must be larger than that. Read Section 7.2 on public key length.

It is certainly possible for a cryptanalyst to try every possible d until he stumbles on the correct one. This brute-force attack is even less efficient than trying to factor n.

From time to time, people claim to have found easy ways to break RSA, but to date no such claim has held up. For example, in 1993 a draft paper by William Payne proposed a method based on Fermat's little theorem [1234]. Unfortunately, this method is also slower than factoring the modulus.

There's another worry. Most common algorithms for computing primes p and q are probabilistic; what happens if p or q is composite? Well, first you can make the odds of that happening as small as you want. And if it does happen, the odds are that encryption and decryption won't work properly—you'll notice right away. There are a few numbers, called Carmichael numbers, which certain probabilistic primality algorithms will fail to detect. These are exceedingly rare, but they are insecure [746]. Honestly, I wouldn't worry about it.

Chosen Ciphertext Attack against RSA

Some attacks work against the implementation of RSA. These are not attacks against the basic algorithm, but against the protocol. It's important to realize that it's not enough to use RSA. Details matter.

Scenario 1: Eve, listening in on Alice's communications, manages to collect a ciphertext message, c, encrypted with RSA in her public key. Eve wants to be able to read the message. Mathematically, she wants m, in which

$$m = c^d$$

To recover m, she first chooses a random number, r, such that r is less than n. She gets Alice's public key, e. Then she computes

$$x = r^e \bmod n$$

$$y = xc \bmod n$$

$$t = r^{-1} \bmod n$$

If $x = r^e \bmod n$, then $r = x^d \bmod n$.

Now, Eve gets Alice to sign y with her private key, thereby decrypting y. (Alice has to sign the message, not the hash of the message.) Remember, Alice has never seen y before. Alice sends Eve

$$u = y^d \bmod n$$

Now, Eve computes

$$tu \bmod n = r^{-1}y^d \bmod n = r^{-1}x^dc^d \bmod n = c^d \bmod n = m$$

Eve now has m.

Scenario 2: Trent is a computer notary public. If Alice wants a document notarized, she sends it to Trent. Trent signs it with an RSA digital signature and sends it back. (No one-way hash functions are used here; Trent encrypts the entire message with his private key.)

Mallory wants Trent to sign a message he otherwise wouldn't. Maybe it has a phony timestamp; maybe it purports to be from another person. Whatever the reason, Trent would never sign it if he had a choice. Let's call this message m'.

First, Mallory chooses an arbitrary value x and computes $y = x^e \bmod n$. He can easily get e; it's Trent's public key and must be public to verify his signatures. Then he computes $m = ym' \bmod n$, and sends m to Trent to sign. Trent returns $m'^d \bmod n$. Now Mallory calculates $(m^d \bmod n)x^{-1} \bmod n$, which equals $n'^d \bmod n$ and is the signature of m'.

Actually, Mallory can use several methods to accomplish these same things [423,458,486]. The weakness they all exploit is that exponentiation preserves the multiplicative structure of the input. That is:

$$(xm)^d \bmod n = x^dm^d \bmod n$$

Scenario 3: Eve wants Alice to sign m_3. She generates two messages, m_1 and m_2, such that

$$m_3 \equiv m_1 m_2 \pmod{n}$$

If Eve can get Alice to sign m_1 and m_2, she can calculate m_3:

$$m_3{}^d = (m_1{}^d \bmod n)(m_2{}^d \bmod n)$$

Moral: Never use RSA to sign a random document presented to you by a stranger. Always use a one-way hash function first. The ISO 9796 block format prevents this attack.

Common Modulus Attack on RSA

A possible RSA implementation gives everyone the same n, but different values for the exponents e and d. Unfortunately, this doesn't work. The most obvious problem is that if the same message is ever encrypted with two different exponents (both having the same modulus), and those two exponents are relatively prime (which they generally would be), then the plaintext can be recovered without either of the decryption exponents [1457].

Let m be the plaintext message. The two encryption keys are e_1 and e_2. The common modulus is n. The two ciphertext messages are:

$$c_1 = m^{e_1} \bmod n$$
$$c_2 = m^{e_2} \bmod n$$

The cryptanalyst knows n, e_1, e_2, c_1, and c_2. Here's how he recovers m.

Since e_1 and e_2 are relatively prime, the extended Euclidean algorithm can find r and s, such that

$$r e_1 + s e_2 = 1$$

Assuming r is negative (either r or s has to be, so just call the negative one r), then the extended Euclidean algorithm can be used again to calculate c_1^{-1}. Then

$$(c_1^{-1})^{-r} \star C_2{}^s = m \bmod n$$

There are two other, more subtle, attacks against this type of system. One attack uses a probabilistic method for factoring n. The other uses a deterministic algorithm for calculating someone's secret key without factoring the modulus. Both attacks are described in detail in [449].

Moral: Don't share a common n among a group of users.

Low Encryption Exponent Attack against RSA

RSA encryption and signature verification are faster if you use a low value for e, but that can also be insecure [704]. If you encrypt $e(e + 1)/2$ linearly dependent messages with different public keys having the same value of e, there is an attack against the system. If there are fewer than that many messages, or if the messages are unrelated, there is no problem. If the messages are identical, then e messages are enough. The easiest solution is to pad messages with independent random values.

This also ensures that $m^e \bmod n \neq m^e$. Most real-world RSA implementations—PEM and PGP (see Sections 24.10 and 24.12), for example—do this.

Moral: Pad messages with random values before encrypting them; make sure m is about the same size as n.

Low Decryption Exponent Attack against RSA

Another attack, this one by Michael Wiener, will recover d, when d is up to one quarter the size of n and e is less than n [1596]. This rarely occurs if e and d are chosen at random, and cannot occur if e has a small value.

Moral: Choose a large value for d.

Lessons Learned

Judith Moore lists several restrictions on the use of RSA, based on the success of these attacks [1114,1115]:

— Knowledge of one encryption/decryption pair of exponents for a given modulus enables an attacker to factor the modulus.

— Knowledge of one encryption/decryption pair of exponents for a given modulus enables an attacker to calculate other encryption/ decryption pairs without having to factor n.

— A common modulus should not be used in a protocol using RSA in a communications network. (This should be obvious from the previous two points.)

— Messages should be padded with random values to prevent attacks on low encryption exponents.

— The decryption exponent should be large.

Remember, it is not enough to have a secure cryptographic algorithm. The entire cryptosystem must be secure, and the cryptographic protocol must be secure. A failure in any of those three areas makes the overall system insecure.

Attack on Encrypting and Signing with RSA

It makes sense to sign a message before encrypting it (see Section 2.7), but not everyone follows this practice. With RSA, there is an attack against protocols that encrypt before signing [48].

Alice wants to send a message to Bob. First she encrypts it with Bob's public key; then she signs it with her private key. Her encrypted and signed message looks like:

$$(m^{e_B} \bmod n_B)^{d_A} \bmod n_A$$

Here's how Bob can claim that Alice sent him m' and not m. Realize that since Bob knows the factorization of n_B (it's his modulus), he can calculate discrete logarithms with respect to n_B. Therefore, all he has to do is to find an x such that

$$m'^x = m \bmod n_B$$

Then, if he can publish xe_B as his new public exponent and keep n_B as his modulus, he can claim that Alice sent him message m' encrypted in this new exponent.

This is a particularly nasty attack in some circumstances. Note that hash functions don't solve the problem. However, forcing a fixed encryption exponent for every user does.

Standards

RSA is a *de facto* standard in much of the world. The ISO almost, but not quite, created an RSA digital-signature standard; RSA is in an information annex to ISO 9796 [762]. The French banking community standardized on RSA [525], as have the Australians [1498]. The United States currently has no standard for public-key encryption, because of pressure from the NSA and patent issues. Many U.S. companies use PKCS (see Section 24.14), written by RSA Data Security, Inc. A draft ANSI banking standard specifies RSA [61].

Patents

The RSA algorithm is patented in the United States [1330], but not in any other country. PKP licenses the patent, along with other public-key cryptography patents (see Section 25.5). The U.S. patent will expire on September 20, 2000.

19.4 Pohlig-Hellman

The Pohlig-Hellman encryption scheme [1253] is similar to RSA. It is not a symmetric algorithm, because different keys are used for encryption and decryption. It is not a public-key scheme, because the keys are easily derivable from each other; both the encryption and decryption keys must be kept secret.

Like RSA,

$$C = P^e \bmod n$$
$$P = C^d \bmod n$$

where

$$ed \equiv 1 \text{ (mod some complicated number)}$$

Unlike RSA, n is not defined in terms of two large primes, it must remain part of the secret key. If someone had e and n, they could calculate d. Without knowledge of e or d, an adversary would be forced to calculate

$$e = \log_P C \bmod n$$

We have already seen that this is a hard problem.

Patents

The Pohlig-Hellman algorithm is patented in the United States [722] and also in Canada. PKP licenses the patent, along with other public-key cryptography patents (see Section 25.5).

19.5 RABIN

Rabin's scheme [1283,1601] gets its security from the difficulty of finding square roots modulo a composite number. This problem is equivalent to factoring. Here is one implementation of this scheme.

First choose two primes, p and q, both congruent to 3 mod 4. These primes are the private key; the product $n = pq$ is the public key.

To encrypt a message, M (M must be less than n), simply compute

$$C = M^2 \bmod n$$

Decrypting the message is just as easy, but slightly more annoying. Since the receiver knows p and q, he can solve the two congruences using the Chinese remainder theorem. Compute

$$m_1 = C^{(p + 1)/4} \bmod p$$
$$m_2 = (p - C^{(p + 1)/4}) \bmod p$$
$$m_3 = C^{(q + 1)/4} \bmod q$$
$$m_4 = (q - C^{(q + 1)/4}) \bmod q$$

Then choose an integer $a = q(q^{-1} \bmod p)$ and a integer $b = p(p^{-1} \bmod q)$. The four possible solutions are:

$$M_1 = (am_1 + bm_3) \bmod n$$
$$M_2 = (am_1 + bm_4) \bmod n$$
$$M_3 = (am_2 + bm_3) \bmod n$$
$$M_4 = (am_2 + bm_4) \bmod n$$

One of those four results, M_1, M_2, M_3, or M_4, equals M. If the message is English text, it should be easy to choose the correct M_i. On the other hand, if the message is a random-bit stream (say, for key generation or a digital signature), there is no way to determine which M_i is correct. One way to solve this problem is to add a known header to the message before encrypting.

Williams

Hugh Williams redefined Rabin's schemes to eliminate these shortcomings [1601]. In his scheme, p and q are selected such that

$$p \equiv 3 \bmod 8$$
$$q \equiv 7 \bmod 8$$

and

$$N = pq$$

Also, there is a small integer, S, such that $J(S,N) = -1$. (J is the Jacobi symbol—see Section 11.3). N and S are public. The secret key is k, such that

$$k = 1/2 \ast (1/4 \ast (p - 1) \ast (q - 1) + 1)$$

To encrypt a message M, compute c_1 such that $J(M,N) = (-1)^{c_1}$. Then, compute $M' = (S^{c_1} \star M) \bmod N$. Like Rabin's scheme, $C = M'^2 \bmod N$. And $c_2 = M' \bmod 2$. The final ciphertext message is the triple:

$$(C, c_1, c_2)$$

To decrypt C, the receiver computes M'' using

$$C^k \equiv \pm M'' \pmod{N}$$

The proper sign of M'' is given by c_2. Finally,

$$M = (S^{c_1} \star (-1)^{c_1} \star M'') \bmod N$$

Williams refined this scheme further in [1603,1604,1605]. Instead of squaring the plaintext message, cube it. The large primes must be congruent to 1 mod 3; otherwise the public and private keys are the same. Even better, there is only one unique decryption for each encryption.

Both Rabin and Williams have an advantage over RSA in that they are provably as secure as factoring. However, they are completely insecure against a chosen-ciphertext attack. If you are going to use these schemes in instances where an attacker can mount this attack (for example, as a digital signature algorithm where an attacker can choose messages to be signed), be sure to use a one-way hash function before signing. Rabin suggested another way of defeating this attack: Append a different random string to each message before hashing and signing. Unfortunately, once you add a one-way hash function to the system it is no longer provably as secure as factoring [628], although adding hashing cannot weaken the system in any practical sense.

Other Rabin variants are [972,909,696,697,1439,989]. A two-dimensional variant is in [866,889].

19.6 ELGAMAL

The ElGamal scheme [518,519] can be used for both digital signatures and encryption; it gets its security from the difficulty of calculating discrete logarithms in a finite field.

To generate a key pair, first choose a prime, p, and two random numbers, g and x, such that both g and x are less than p. Then calculate

$$y = g^x \bmod p$$

The public key is y, g, and p. Both g and p can be shared among a group of users. The private key is x.

ElGamal Signatures

To sign a message, M, first choose a random number, k, such that k is relatively prime to $p - 1$. Then compute

$$a = g^k \bmod p$$

and use the extended Euclidean algorithm to solve for b in the following equation:

$$M = (xa + kb) \bmod (p - 1)$$

The signature is the pair: a and b. The random value, k, must be kept secret. To verify a signature, confirm that

$$y^a a^b \bmod p = g^M \bmod p$$

Each ElGamal signature or encryption requires a new value of k, and that value must be chosen randomly. If Eve ever recovers a k that Alice used, she can recover Alice's private key, x. If Eve ever gets two messages signed or encrypted using the same k, even if she doesn't know what it is, she can recover x.

This is summarized in Table 19.5.

For example, choose $p = 11$ and $g = 2$. Choose private key $x = 8$. Calculate

$$y = g^x \bmod p = 2^8 \bmod 11 = 3$$

The public key is $y = 3$, $g = 2$, and $p = 11$.

To authenticate $M = 5$, first choose a random number $k = 9$. Confirm that $\gcd(9,10) = 1$. Compute

$$a = g^k \bmod p = 2^9 \bmod 11 = 6$$

and use the extended Euclidean algorithm to solve for b:

$$M = (ax + kb) \bmod (p - 1)$$
$$5 = (8 \star 6 + 9 \star b) \bmod 10$$

The solution is $b = 3$, and the signature is the pair: $a = 6$ and $b = 3$.

Table 19.5
ElGamal Signatures

Public Key:
p prime (can be shared among a group of users)
g $< p$ (can be shared among a group of users)
y $= g^x \bmod p$

Private Key:
x $< p$

Signing:
k choose at random, relatively prime to $p - 1$
a (signature) $= g^k \bmod p$
b (signature) such that $M = (xa + kb) \bmod (p - 1)$

Verifying:
Accept as valid if $y^a a^b \bmod p = g^M \bmod p$

To verify a signature, confirm that

$$y^a a^b \bmod p = g^M \bmod p$$
$$3^6 6^3 \bmod 11 = 2^5 \bmod 11$$

A variant of ElGamal for signatures is in [1377]. Thomas Beth invented a variant of the ElGamal scheme suitable for proofs of identity [146]. There are variants for password authentication [312], and for key exchange [773]. And there are thousands more (see Section 20.4).

ElGamal Encryption

A modification of ElGamal can encrypt messages. To encrypt message M, first choose a random k, such that k is relatively prime to $p-1$. Then compute

$$a = g^k \bmod p$$
$$b = y^k M \bmod p$$

The pair, a and b, is the ciphertext. Note that the ciphertext is twice the size of the plaintext.

To decrypt a and b, compute

$$M = b/a^x \bmod p$$

Since $a^x \equiv g^{kx} \pmod p$, and $b/a^x \equiv y^k M/a^x \equiv g^{xk} M/g^{xk} \equiv M \pmod p$, this all works (see Table 19.6). This is really the same as Diffie-Hellman key exchange (see Section 22.1), except that y is part of the key, and the encryption is multiplied by y^k.

Speed

Table 19.7 gives sample software speeds of ElGamal [918].

Table 19.6
ElGamal Encryption

Public Key:
p prime (can be shared among a group of users)
g $< p$ (can be shared among a group of users)
y $= g^x \bmod p$

Private Key:
x $< p$

Encrypting:
k choose at random, relatively prime to $p-1$.
a (ciphertext) $= g^k \bmod p$
b (ciphertext) $= y^k M \bmod p$

Decrypting:
M (plaintext) $= b/a^x \bmod p$

Patents

ElGamal is unpatented. But, before you go ahead and implement the algorithm, realize that PKP feels that this algorithm is covered under the Diffie-Hellman patent [718]. However, the Diffie-Hellman patent will expire on April 29, 1997, making ElGamal the first public-key cryptography algorithm suitable for encryption and digital signatures unencumbered by patents in the United States. I can hardly wait.

19.7 McEliece

In 1978 Robert McEliece developed a public-key cryptosystem based on algebraic coding theory [1041]. The algorithm makes use of the existence of a class of error-correcting codes, known as **Goppa codes**. His idea was to construct a Goppa code and disguise it as a general linear code. There is a fast algorithm for decoding Goppa codes, but the general problem of finding a code word of a given weight in a linear binary code is **NP-complete**. A good description of this algorithm can be found in [1233]; see also [1562]. Following is just a quick summary.

Let $d_H(x,y)$ denote the Hamming distance between x and y. The numbers n, k, and t are system parameters.

The private key has three parts: G' is a $k * n$ generator matrix for a Goppa code that can correct t errors. P is an $n * n$ permutation matrix. S is a $k * k$ nonsingular matrix.

The public key is a $k * n$ matrix $G: G = SG'P$.

Plaintext messages are strings of k bits, in the form of k-element vectors over GF(2).

To encrypt a message, choose a random n-element vector over GF(2), z, with Hamming distance less than or equal to t.

$$c = mG + z$$

To decrypt the ciphertext, first compute $c' = cP^{-1}$. Then, using the decoding algorithm for the Goppa code, find m' such that $d_H(m'G, c')$ is less than or equal to t. Finally, compute $m = m'S^{-1}$.

In his original paper, McEliece suggested that $n = 1024$, $t = 50$, and $k = 524$. These are the minimum values required for security.

Table 19.7
ElGamal Speeds for Different
Modulus Lengths with a 160-bit
Exponent (on a SPARC II)

	512 bits	768 bits	1024 bits
Encrypt	0.33 sec	0.80 sec	1.09 sec
Decrypt	0.24 sec	0.58 sec	0.77 sec
Sign	0.25 sec	0.47 sec	0.63 sec
Verify	1.37 sec	5.12 sec	9.30 sec

Although the algorithm was one of the first public-key algorithms, and there were no successful cryptanalytic results against the algorithm, it has never gained wide acceptance in the cryptographic community. The scheme is two to three orders of magnitude faster than RSA, but has some problems. The public key is enormous: 2^{19} bits long. The data expansion is large: The ciphertext is twice as long as the plaintext.

Some attempts at cryptanalysis of this system can be found in [8,943,1559,306]. None of these were successful in the general case, although the similarity between the McEliece algorithm and knapsacks worried some.

In 1991, two Russian cryptographers claimed to have broken the McEliece system with some parameters [882]. Their paper contained no evidence to substantiate their claim, and most cryptographers discount the result. Another Russian attack, one that cannot be used directly against the McEliece system, is in [1447,1448]. Extensions to McEliece can be found in [424,1227,976].

Other Algorithms Based on Linear Error-Correcting Codes

The Niederreiter algorithm [1167] is closely related to the McEliece algorithm, and assumes that the public key is a random parity-check matrix of an error-correcting code. The private key is an efficient decoding algorithm for this matrix.

Another algorithm, used for identification and digital signatures, is based on syndrome decoding [1501]; see [306] for comments. An algorithm based on error-correcting codes [1621] is insecure [698,33,31,1560,32].

19.8 Elliptic Curve Cryptosystems

Elliptic curves have been studied for many years and there is an enormous amount of literature on the subject. In 1985, Neal Koblitz and V. S. Miller independently proposed using them for public-key cryptosystems [867,1095]. They did not invent a new cryptographic algorithm with elliptic curves over finite fields, but they implemented existing public-key algorithms, like Diffie-Hellman, using elliptic curves.

Elliptic curves are interesting because they provide a way of constructing "elements" and "rules of combining" that produce groups. These groups have enough familiar properties to build cryptographic algorithms, but they don't have certain properties that may facilitate cryptanalysis. For example, there is no good notion of "smooth" with elliptic curves. That is, there is no set of small elements in terms of which a random element has a good chance of being expressed by a simple algorithm. Hence, index calculus discrete logarithm algorithms do not work. See [1095] for more details.

Elliptic curves over the finite field GF(2^n) are particularly interesting. The arithmetic processors for the underlying field are easy to construct and are relatively simple to implement for n in the range of 130 to 200. They have the potential to provide faster public-key cryptosystems with smaller key sizes. Many public-key algorithms, like Diffie-Hellman, ElGamal, and Schnorr, can be implemented in elliptic curves over finite fields.

The mathematics here are complex and beyond the scope of this book. Those interested in this topic are invited to read the two references previously mentioned, and the excellent book by Alfred Menezes [1059]. Two analogues of RSA work in elliptic curves [890,454]. Other papers are [23,119,1062,869,152,871,892,25,895,353, 1061,26,913,914,915]. Elliptic curve cryptosystems with small key lengths are discussed in [701]. Next Computer Inc.'s Fast Elliptic Encryption (FEE) algorithm also uses elliptic curves [388]. FEE has the nice feature that the private key can be any easy-to-remember string. There are proposed public-key cryptosystems using hyperelliptic curves [868,870,1441,1214].

19.9 LUC

Some cryptographers have developed generalizations of RSA that use various permutation polynomials instead of exponentiation. A variation called Kravitz-Reed, using irreducible binary polynomials [898], is insecure [451,589]. Winfried Müller and Wilfried Nöbauer use Dickson polynomials [1127,1128,965]. Rudolph Lidl and Müller generalized this approach in [966,1126] (a variant is called the Réidi scheme), and Nöbauer looked at its security in [1172,1173]. (Comments on prime generation with Lucas functions are in [969,967,968,598].) Despite all of this prior art, a group of researchers from New Zealand managed to patent this scheme in 1993, calling it LUC [1486,521,1487].

The nth Lucas number, $V_n(P,1)$, is defined as

$$V_n(P,1) = PV_{n-1}(P,1) - V_{n-2}(P,1)$$

There's a lot more theory to Lucas numbers; I'm ignoring all of it. A good theoretical treatment of Lucas sequences is in [1307,1308]. A particularly nice description of the mathematics of LUC is in [1494,708].

In any case, to generate a public-key/private-key key pair, first choose two large primes, p and q. Calculate n, the product of p and q. The encryption key, e, is a random number that is relatively prime to $p - 1$, $q - 1$, $p + 1$, and $q + 1$.

There are four possible decryption keys,

$$d = e^{-1} \bmod (\mathrm{lcm}((p + 1), (q + 1)))$$
$$d = e^{-1} \bmod (\mathrm{lcm}((p + 1), (q - 1)))$$
$$d = e^{-1} \bmod (\mathrm{lcm}((p - 1), (q + 1)))$$
$$d = e^{-1} \bmod (\mathrm{lcm}((p - 1), (q - 1)))$$

where lcm is the least common multiple.

The public key is d and n; the private key is e and n. Discard p and q.

To encrypt a message, P (P must be less than n), calculate

$$C = V_e(P,1) \pmod{n}$$

And to decrypt:

$$P = V_d(P,1) \pmod{n}, \text{ with the proper } d$$

At best, LUC is no more secure than RSA. And recent, still-unpublished results show how to break LUC in at least some implementations. I just don't trust it.

19.10 FINITE AUTOMATON PUBLIC-KEY CRYPTOSYSTEMS

Chinese cryptographer Tao Renji has developed a public-key algorithm based on finite automata [1301,1302,1303,1300,1304,666]. Just as it is hard to factor the product of two large primes, it is also hard to factor the composition of two finite automata. This is especially so if one or both of them is nonlinear.

Much of this research took place in China in the 1980s and was published in Chinese. Renji is starting to write in English. His main result was that certain nonlinear automata (the quasilinear automata) possess weak inverses if, and only if, they have a certain echelon matrix structure. This property disappears if they are composed with another automaton (even a linear one). In the public-key algorithm, the secret key is an invertible quasilinear automaton and a linear automaton, and the corresponding public key can be derived by multiplying them out term by term. Data is encrypted by passing it through the public automaton, and decrypted by passing it through the inverses of its components (in some cases provided they have been set to a suitable initial state). This scheme works for both encryption and digital signatures.

The performance of such systems can be summed up by saying that like McEliece's system, they run much faster than RSA, but require longer keys. The keylength thought to give similar security to 512-bit RSA is 2792 bits, and to 1024-bit RSA is 4152 bits. For the former case, the system encrypts data at 20,869 bytes/sec and decrypts data at 17,117 bytes/sec, running on a 33 MHz 80486.

Renji has published three algorithms. The first is FAPKC0. This is a weak system which uses linear components, and is primarily illustrative. Two serious systems, FAPKC1 and FAPKC2, use one linear and one nonlinear component each. The latter is more complex, and was developed in order to support identity-based operation.

As for their strength, quite a lot of work has been done on them in China (where there are now over 30 institutes publishing cryptography and security papers). One can see from the considerable Chinese language literature that the problem has been studied.

One possible attraction of FAPKC1 and FAPKC2 is that they are not encumbered by any U.S. patents. Thus, once the Diffie-Hellman patent expires in 1997, they will unquestionably be in the public domain.

Chapter 20

Public-Key Digital Signature Algorithms

20.1 Digital Signature Algorithm (DSA)

In August 1991, The National Institute of Standards and Technology (NIST) proposed the Digital Signature Algorithm (DSA) for use in their Digital Signature Standard (DSS). According to the *Federal Register* [538]:

> A Federal Information Processing Standard (FIPS) for Digital Signature Standard (DSS) is being proposed. This proposed standard specifies a public-key digital signature algorithm (DSA) appropriate for Federal digital signature applications. The proposed DSS uses a public key to verify to a recipient the integrity of data and identity of the sender of the data. The DSS can also be used by a third party to ascertain the authenticity of a signature and the data associated with it.
>
> This proposed standard adopts a public-key signature scheme that uses a pair of transformations to generate and verify a digital value called a signature.

And:

> This proposed FIPS is the result of evaluating a number of alternative digital signature techniques. In making the selection NIST has followed the mandate contained in section 2 of the Computer Security Act of 1987 that NIST develop standards to "... assure the cost-effective security and privacy of Federal information and, among technologies offering comparable protection, on selecting the option with the most desirable operating and use characteristics."
>
> Among the factors that were considered during this process were the level of security provided, the ease of implementation in both hardware and software, the ease of export from the U.S., the applicability of patents, impact on national security and law enforcement and the level of efficiency in both the signing and verification functions. A number of techniques were deemed to provide appropriate protection for Federal systems. The technique selected has the following desirable characteristics:

NIST expects it to be available on a royalty-free basis. Broader use of this technique resulting from public availability should be an economic benefit to the government and the public.

The technique selected provides for efficient implementation of the signature operations in smart card applications. In these applications the signing operations are performed in the computationally modest environment of the smart card while the verification process is implemented in a more computationally rich environment such as a personal computer, a hardware cryptographic module, or a mainframe computer.

Before it gets too confusing, let me review the nomenclature: DSA is the algorithm; the DSS is the standard. The standard employs the algorithm. The algorithm is part of the standard.

Reaction to the Announcement

NIST's announcement created a maelstrom of criticisms and accusations. Unfortunately, it was more political than academic. RSA Data Security, Inc., purveyors of the RSA algorithm, led the criticism against DSS. They wanted RSA, and not another algorithm, used as the standard. RSADSI makes a lot of money licensing the RSA algorithm, and a royalty-free digital signature standard would directly affect their bottom line. (Note: DSA is not necessarily free of patent infringements; I'll discuss that later.)

Before the algorithm was announced, RSADSI campaigned against a "common modulus," which might have given the government the ability to forge signatures. When the algorithm was announced without this common modulus, they attacked it on other grounds [154], both in letters to NIST and statements to the press. (Four letters to NIST appeared in [1326]. When reading them, keep in mind that at least two of the authors, Rivest and Hellman, had a financial interest in DSS's not being approved.)

Many large software companies that already licensed the RSA algorithm came out against the DSS. In 1982, the government had solicited public-key algorithms for a standard [537]. After that, there wasn't a peep out of NIST for nine years. Companies such as IBM, Apple, Novell, Lotus, Northern Telecom, Microsoft, DEC, and Sun had already spent large amounts of money implementing the RSA algorithm. They were not interested in losing their investment.

In all, NIST received 109 comments by the end of the first comment period on February 28, 1992.

Let's look at the criticisms against DSA, one by one.

1. DSA cannot be used for encryption or key distribution.

     True, but not the point of the standard. This is a signature standard. NIST should have a standard for public-key encryption. NIST is committing a grave injustice to the American people by not implementing a public-key encryption standard. It is suspicious that this proposed digital signature standard cannot be used for encryption. (As it turns out, though, it can—see Section 23.3.) That does not mean that a signature standard is useless.

2. DSA was developed by the NSA, and there may be a trapdoor in the algorithm.

Much of the initial comments were just paranoia: "NIST's denial of information with no apparent justification does not inspire confidence in DSS, but intensifies concern that there is a hidden agenda, such as laying the groundwork for a national public-key cryptosystem that is in fact vulnerable to being broken by NIST and/or NSA" [154]. One serious question about the security of DSA was raised by Arjen Lenstra and Stuart Haber at Bellcore. This will be discussed later.

3. DSA is slower than RSA [800].

True, more or less. Signature generation speeds are the same, but signature verification can be 10 to 40 times slower with DSA. Key generation, however, is faster. But key generation is irrelevant; a user rarely does it. On the other hand, signature verification is the most common operation.

The problem with this criticism is that there are many ways to play with the test parameters, depending on the results you want. Precomputations can speed up DSA signature generation, but don't always apply. Proponents of RSA use numbers optimized to make their calculations easier; proponents of DSA use their own optimizations. In any case, computers are getting faster all the time. While there is a speed difference, it will not be noticeable in most applications.

4. RSA is a *de facto* standard.

Here are two examples of this complaint. From Robert Follett, the program director of standards at IBM [570]:

> IBM is concerned that NIST has proposed a standard with a different digital signature scheme rather than adopting the international standard. We have been convinced by users and user organizations that the international standards using RSA will be a prerequisite to the sales of security products in the very near future.

From Les Shroyer, vice president and director, corporate MIS and telecommunications, at Motorola [1444]:

> We must have a single, robust, politically-accepted digital signature standard that is usable throughout the world, between both U.S. and non-U.S., and Motorola and non-Motorola entities. The lack of other viable digital signature technology for the last eight years has made RSA a de facto standard. . . . Motorola and many other companies . . . have committed millions of dollars to RSA. We have concern over the interoperability and support of two different standards, as that situation will lead to added costs, delays in deployment, and complication. . . .

Many companies wanted NIST to adopt the ISO 9796, the international digital signature standard that uses RSA [762]. While this is a valid complaint, it is not a sufficient justification to make it a standard. A royalty-free standard would better serve the U.S. public interest.

5. The DSA selection process was not public; sufficient time for analysis has not been provided.

First NIST claimed that they designed the DSA; then they admitted that NSA helped them. Finally, they confirmed that NSA designed the algorithm. This worries many people; the NSA doesn't inspire trust. Even so, the algorithm is public and available for analysis; and NIST extended the time for analysis and comment.

6. DSA may infringe on other patents.

It may. This will be discussed in the section on patent issues.

7. The key size is too small.

This was the only valid criticism of DSS. The original implementation set the modulus at 512 bits [1149]. Since the algorithm gets its security from the difficulty of computing discrete logs in that modulus, this worried most cryptographers. There have since been advances in the problem of calculating discrete logarithms in a finite field, and 512 bits is too short for long-term security (see Section 7.2). According to Brian LaMacchia and Andrew Odlyzko, "... even 512-bit primes appear to offer only marginal security ..." [934]. In response to this criticism, NIST made the key size variable, from 512 bits to 1024 bits. Not great, but better.

On May 19, 1994, the standard was finally issued [1154]. The issuing statement said [542]:

> This standard is applicable to all Federal departments and agencies for the protection of unclassified information. . . . This standard shall be used in designing and implementing public-key based signature schemes which Federal departments and agencies operate or which are operated for them under contract. Adoption and use of this standard is available to private and commercial organizations.

Before you run out and implement this standard in your next product, read the section on patent issues below.

Description of DSA

DSA is a variant of the Schnorr and ElGamal signature algorithms, and is fully described in [1154]. The algorithm uses the following parameters:

p = a prime number L bits long, when L ranges from 512 to 1024 and is a multiple of 64. (In the original standard, the size of p was fixed at 512 bits [1149]. This was the source of much criticism and was changed by NIST [1154].)

q = a 160-bit prime factor of $p - 1$.

$g = h^{(p-1)/q} \bmod p$, where h is any number less than $p - 1$ such that $h^{(p-1)/q} \bmod p$ is greater than 1.

x = a number less than q.

$y = g^x \bmod p$.

The algorithm also makes use of a one-way hash function: $H(m)$. The standard specifies the Secure Hash Algorithm, discussed in Section 18.7.

The first three parameters, p, q, and g, are public and can be common across a network of users. The private key is x; the public key is y.

To sign a message, m:

(1) Alice generates a random number, k, less than q.

(2) Alice generates

$$r = (g^k \bmod p) \bmod q$$
$$s = (k^{-1} (H(m) + xr)) \bmod q$$

The parameters r and s are her signature; she sends these to Bob.

(3) Bob verifies the signature by computing

$$w = s^{-1} \bmod q$$
$$u_1 = (H(m) \star w) \bmod q$$
$$u_2 = (rw) \bmod q$$
$$v = ((g^{u_1} \star y^{u_2}) \bmod p) \bmod q$$

If $v = r$, then the signature is verified.

Proofs for the mathematical relationships are found in [1154]. Table 20.1 provides a summary.

Speed Precomputations

Table 20.2 gives sample software speeds of DSA [918].

Real-world implementations of DSA can often be speeded up through precomputations. Notice that the value r does not depend on the message. You can create a string of random k values, and then precompute r values for each of them. You can also precompute k^{-1} for each of those k values. Then, when a message comes along, you can compute s for a given r and k^{-1}.

This precomputation speeds up DSA considerably. Table 20.3 is a comparison of DSA and RSA computation times for a particular smart card implementation [1479].

Table 20.1
DSA Signatures

Public Key:

p 512-bit to 1024-bit prime (can be shared among a group of users)

q 160-bit prime factor of $p - 1$ (can be shared among a group of users)

g $= h^{(p-1)/q} \bmod p$, where h is less than $p - 1$ and $h^{(p-1)/q} \bmod p > 1$ (can be shared among a group of users)

y $= g^x \bmod p$ (a p-bit number)

Private Key:

x $< q$ (a 160-bit number)

Signing:

k choose at random, less than q

r (signature) $= (g^k \bmod p) \bmod q$

s (signature) $= (k^{-1} (H(m) + xr)) \bmod q$

Verifying:

$w = s^{-1} \bmod q$

$u_1 = (H(m) \star w) \bmod q$

$u_2 = (rw) \bmod q$

$v = ((g^{u_1} \star y^{u_2}) \bmod p) \bmod q$

If $v = r$, then the signature is verified.

DSA Prime Generation

Lenstra and Haber pointed out that certain moduli are much easier to crack than others [950]. If someone forced a network to use one of these "cooked" moduli, then their signatures would be easier to forge. This isn't a problem for two reasons: These moduli are easy to detect and they are so rare that the chances of using one when choosing a modulus randomly are almost negligible—smaller, in fact, than the chances of accidentally generating a composite number using a probabilistic prime generation routine.

In [1154] NIST recommended a specific method for generating the two primes, p and q, where q divides $p - 1$. The prime p is L bits long, between 512 and 1024 bits

Table 20.2
DSA Speeds for Different Modulus Lengths
with a 160-bit Exponent (on a SPARC II)

	512 bits	768 bits	1024 bits
Sign	0.20 sec	0.43 sec	0.57 sec
Verify	0.35 sec	0.80 sec	1.27 sec

Table 20.3
Comparison of RSA and DSA Computation Times

	DSA	RSA	DSA with Common p, q, g
Global Computations	Off-card (P)	N/A	Off-card (P)
Key Generation	14 sec	Off-card (S)	4 sec
Precomputation	14 sec	N/A	4 sec
Signature	.03 sec	15 sec	.03 sec
Verification	16 sec	1.5 sec	10 sec
	1–5 sec off-card (P)	1–3 sec off-card (P)	

Off-card computations were performed on an 80386 33 mHz, personal computer. (P) indicates public parameters off-card and (S) indicates secret parameters off-card. Both algorithms use a 512-bit modulus.

long, in some multiple of 64 bits. The prime q is 160 bits long. Let $L - 1 = 160n + b$, where L is the length of p, and n and b are two numbers and b is less than 160.

(1) Choose an arbitrary sequence of at least 160 bits and call it S. Let g be the length of S in bits.

(2) Compute $U = \text{SHA}(S) \oplus \text{SHA} ((S + 1) \bmod 2^g)$, where SHA is the Secure Hash Algorithm (see Section 18.7).

(3) Form q by setting the most significant bit and the least significant bit of U to 1.

(4) Check whether q is prime.

(5) If q is not prime, go back to step (1).

(6) Let $C = 0$ and $N = 2$.

(7) For $k = 0, 1, \ldots, n$, let $V_k = \text{SHA} ((S + N + k) \bmod 2^g)$

(8) Let W be the integer

$$W = V_0 + 2^{160}V_1 + \ldots + 2^{160(n-1)}V_{n-1} + 2^{160n}(V_n \bmod 2^b)$$

and let

$$X = W + 2^{L-1}$$

Note that X is an L-bit number.

(9) Let $p = X - ((X \bmod 2q) - 1)$. Note that p is congruent to 1 mod $2q$.

(10) If $p < 2^{L-1}$, then go to step (13).

(11) Check whether p is prime.

(12) If p is prime, go to step (15).

(13) Let $C = C + 1$ and $N = N + n + 1$.

(14) If $C = 4096$, then go to step (1). Otherwise, go to step (7).

(15) Save the value of S and the value of C used to generate p and q.

In [1154], the variable S is called the "seed," C is called the "counter," and N the "offset."

The point of this exercise is that there is a public means of generating p and q. For all practical purposes, this method prevents cooked values of p and q. If someone hands you a p and a q, you might wonder where that person got them. However, if someone hands you a value for S and C that generated the random p and q, you can go through this routine yourself. Using a one-way hash function, SHA in the standard, prevents someone from working backwards from a p and q to generate an S and C.

This security is better than what you get with RSA. In RSA, the prime numbers are kept secret. Someone could generate a fake prime or one of a special form that makes factoring easier. Unless you know the private key, you won't know that. Here, even if you don't know a person's private key, you can confirm that p and q have been generated randomly.

ElGamal Encryption with DSA

There have been allegations that the government likes the DSA because it is only a digital signature algorithm and can't be used for encryption. It is, however, possible to use the DSA function call to do ElGamal encryption.

Assume that the DSA algorithm is implemented with a single function call:

```
DSAsign (p,q,g,k,x,h,r,s)
```

You supply the numbers p, q, g, k, x, and h, and the function returns the signature parameters: r and s.

To do ElGamal encryption of message m with public key y, choose a random number, k, and call

```
DSAsign (p,p,g,k,0,0,r,s)
```

The value of r returned is a in the ElGamal scheme. Throw s away. Then, call

```
DSAsign (p,p,y,k,0,0,r,s)
```

Rename the value of r to be u; throw s away. Call

```
DSAsign (p,p,m,1,u,0,r,s)
```

Throw r away. The value of s returned is b in the ElGamal scheme. You now have the ciphertext, a and b.

Decryption is just as easy. Using secret key x, and ciphertext messages a and b, call

```
DSAsign (p,p,a,x,0,0,r,s)
```

The value r is $a^x \bmod p$. Call that e. Then call

```
DSAsign (p,p,1,e,b,0,r,s)
```

The value s is the plaintext message, m.

This method will not work with all implementations of DSA. Some may fix the values of p and q, or the lengths of some of the other parameters. Still, if the implementation is general enough, this is a way to encrypt using nothing more than digital signature function.

RSA Encryption with DSA

RSA encryption is even easier. With a modulus n, message m, and public key e, call

```
DSAsign (n,n,m,e,0,0,r,s)
```

The value of r returned is the ciphertext.

RSA decryption is the same thing. If d is the private key, then

```
DSAsign (n,n,m,d,0,0,r,s)
```

returns the plaintext as the value of r.

Security of DSA

At 512-bits, DSA wasn't strong enough for long-term security. At 1024 bits, it is.

The NSA, in its first public interview on the subject, commented to Joe Abernathy of *The Houston Chronicle* on allegations about a trapdoor in DSS [363]:

> Regarding the alleged trapdoor in the DSS. We find the term trapdoor somewhat misleading since it implies that the messages sent by the DSS are encrypted and with access via a trapdoor one could somehow decrypt (read) the message without the sender's knowledge.
>
> The DSS does not encrypt any data. The real issue is whether the DSS is susceptible to someone forging a signature and therefore discrediting the entire system. We state categorically that the chances of anyone—including NSA—forging a signature with the DSS when it is properly used and implemented is infinitesimally small.
>
> Furthermore, the alleged trapdoor vulnerability is true for *any* public key-based authentication system, including RSA. To imply somehow that this only affects the DSS (a popular argument in the press) is totally misleading. The issue is one of implementation and how one goes about selecting prime numbers. We call your attention to a recent EUROCRYPT conference which had a panel discussion on the issue of trapdoors in the DSS. Included on the panel was one of the Bellcore researchers who initially raised the trapdoor allegation, and our understanding is that the panel—including the person from Bellcore—concluded that the alleged trapdoor was not an issue for the DSS. Furthermore, the general consensus appeared to be that the trapdoor issue was trivial and had been overblown in the

press. However, to try to respond to the trapdoor allegation, at NIST's request, we have designed a prime generation process which will ensure that one can avoid selection of the relatively few weak primes which could lead to weakness in using the DSS. Additionally, NIST intends to allow for larger modulus sizes up to 1024 which effectively negates the need to even use the prime generation process to avoid weak primes. An additional very important point that is often overlooked is that with the DSS the primes are *public* and therefore can be subject to public examination. Not all public key systems provide for this same type of examination.

The integrity of any information security system requires attention to proper implementation. With the myriad of vulnerabilities possible given the differences among users, NSA has traditionally insisted on centralized trusted centers as a way to minimize risk to the system. While we have designed technical modifications to the DSS to meet NIST's requests for a more decentralized approach, we still would emphasize that portion of the *Federal Register* notice for the DSS which states:

> "While it is the intent of this standard to specify general security require-
> ments for generating digital signatures, conformance to this standard does
> not assure that a particular implementation is secure. The responsible
> authority in each agency or department shall assure that an overall imple-
> mentation provides an acceptable level of security. NIST will be working
> with government users to ensure appropriate implementations."

Finally, we have read all the arguments purporting insecurities with the DSS, and we remain unconvinced of their validity. The DSS has been subjected to intense evaluation within NSA which led to its being endorsed by our Director of Information Systems Security for use in signing unclassified data processed in certain intelligence systems and even for signing classified data in selected systems. We believe that this approval speaks to the lack of any credible attack on the integrity provided by the DSS given proper use and implementation. Based on the technical and security requirements of the U.S. government for digital signatures, we believe the DSS is the best choice. In fact, the DSS is being used in a pilot project for the Defense Message System to assure the authenticity of electronic messages of vital command and control information. This initial demonstration includes participation from the Joint Chiefs of Staff, the military services, and Defense Agencies and is being done in cooperation with NIST.

I'm not going to comment on the trustworthiness of the NSA. Take their comments for what you think they're worth.

Attacks against k

Each signature requires a new value of k, and that value must be chosen randomly. If Eve ever recovers a k that Alice used to sign a message, perhaps by exploiting some properties of the random-number generator that generated k, she can recover Alice's private key, x. If Eve ever gets two messages signed using the same k, even if she doesn't know what it is, she can recover x. And with x, Eve can generate undetectable forgeries of Alice's signature. In any implementation of the DSA, a good random-number generator is essential to the system's security [1468].

Dangers of a Common Modulus

Even though the DSS does not specify a common modulus to be shared by everyone, different implementations may. For example, the Internal Revenue Service is considering using the DSS for the electronic submission of tax returns. What if they require every taxpayer in the country to use a common p and q? Even though the standard doesn't require a common modulus, such an implementation accomplishes the same thing. A common modulus too easily becomes a tempting target for cryptanalysis. It is still too early to tell much about different DSS implementations, but there is some cause for concern.

Subliminal Channel in DSA

Gus Simmons discovered a subliminal channel in DSA [1468,1469] (see Section 23.3). This subliminal channel allows someone to embed a secret message in his signature that can only be read by another person who knows the key. According to Simmons, it is a "remarkable coincidence" that the "apparently inherent shortcomings of subliminal channels using the ElGamal scheme can all be overcome" in the DSS, and that the DSS "provides the most hospitable setting for subliminal communications discovered to date." NIST and NSA have not commented on this subliminal channel; no one knows if they even knew about it. Since this subliminal channel allows an unscrupulous implementer of DSS to leak a piece of the private key with each signature, it is important to never use an implementation of DSS if you don't trust the implementer.

Patents

David Kravitz, formerly of the NSA, holds a patent on DSA [897]. According to NIST [538]:

> NIST intends to make this DSS technique available world-wide on a royalty-free basis to the public interest. We believe this technique is patentable and that no other patents would apply to the DSS, but we cannot give firm assurances to such effect in advance of issuance of the patent.

Even so, three patent holders claim that the DSA infringes on their patents: Diffie-Hellman (see Section 22.1) [718], Merkle-Hellman (see Section 19.2) [720], and Schnorr (see Section 21.3) [1398]. The Schnorr patent is the most troublesome. The other two patents expire in 1997; the Schnorr patent is valid until 2008. The Schnorr algorithm was not developed with government money; unlike the PKP patents, the U.S. government has no rights to the Schnorr patent; and Schnorr patented his algorithm worldwide. Even if the U.S. courts rule in favor of DSA, it is unclear what other courts around the world would do. Is an international company going to adopt a standard that may be legal in some countries but infringes on a patent in others? This issue will take time to resolve; at the time of this writing it isn't even resolved in the United States.

In June 1993 NIST proposed to give PKP an exclusive patent license to DSA [541]. The agreement fell through after public outcry and the standard was issued without any deal. NIST said [542]:

... NIST has addressed the possible patent infringement claims, and has concluded that there are no valid claims.

So the standard is official, lawsuits are threatened, and no one knows what to do. NIST has said that it would help defend people sued for patent infringement, if they were using DSA to satisfy a government contract. Everyone else, it seems, is on their own. ANSI has a draft banking standard that uses DSA [60]. NIST is working to standardize DSA within the government. Shell Oil has made DSA their international standard. I know of no other proposed DSA standards.

20.2 DSA Variants

This variant makes computation easier on the signer by not forcing him to compute k^{-1} [1135]. All the parameters are as in DSA. To sign a message, m, Alice generates two random numbers, k and d, both less than q. The signature is

$$r = (g^k \bmod p) \bmod q$$
$$s = (H(m) + xr) \star d \bmod q$$
$$t = kd \bmod q$$

Bob verifies the signature by computing

$$w = t/s \bmod q$$
$$u_1 = (H(m) \star w) \bmod q$$
$$u_2 = (rw) \bmod q$$

If $r = ((g^{u_1} \star y^{u_2}) \bmod p) \bmod q$, then the signature is verified.

This next variant makes computation easier on the verifier [1040,1629]. All the parameters are as in DSA. To sign a message, m, Alice generates a random number, k, less than q. The signature is

$$r = (g^k \bmod p) \bmod q$$
$$s = k \star (H(m) + xr)^{-1} \bmod q$$

Bob verifies the signature by computing

$$u_1 = (H(m) \star s) \bmod q$$
$$u_2 = (sr) \bmod q$$

If $r = ((g^{u_1} \star y^{u_2}) \bmod p) \bmod q$, then the signature is verified.

Another DSA variant allows for batch verification; Bob can verify signatures in batches [1135]. If they are all valid, he is done. If one isn't valid, then he still has to find it. Unfortunately, it is not secure; either the signer or the verifier can easily create a set of bogus signatures that satisfy the batch criteria [974].

There is also a variant for DSA prime generation, one that embeds q and the parameters used to generate the primes within p. Whether this scheme reduces the security of DSA is still unknown.

(1) Choose an arbitrary sequence of at least 160 bits and call it S. Let g be the length of S in bits.

(2) Compute $U = \text{SHA}(S) \oplus \text{SHA}((S + 1) \bmod 2^g)$, where SHA is the Secure Hash Algorithm (see Section 18.7).

(3) Form q by setting the most significant bit and the least significant bit of U to 1.

(4) Check whether q is prime.

(5) Let p be the concatenation of q, S, C, and $\text{SHA}(S)$. C is set to 32 zero bits.

(6) $p = p - (p \bmod q) + 1$.

(7) $p = p + q$.

(8) If the C in p is 0x7fffffff, go to step (1).

(9) Check whether p is prime.

(10) If p is composite, go to step (7).

The neat thing about this variant is that you don't have to store the values of C and S used to generate p and q; they are embedded within p. For applications without a whole lot of memory, like smart cards, this can be a big deal.

20.3 GOST DIGITAL SIGNATURE ALGORITHM

This is a Russian digital signature standard, officially called GOST R 34.10-94 [656]. The algorithm is very similar to DSA, and uses the following parameters

p = a prime number, either between 509 and 512 bits long, or between 1020 and 1024 bits long.

q = a 254- to 256-bit prime factor of $p - 1$.

a = any number less than $p - 1$ such that $a^q \bmod p = 1$.

x = a number less than q.

$y = a^x \bmod p$.

The algorithm also makes use of a one-way hash function: $H(x)$. The standard specifies GOST R 34.11-94 (see Section 18.11), a function based on the GOST symmetric algorithm (see Section 14.1) [657].

The first three parameters, p, q, and a, are public and can be common across a network of users. The private key is x; the public key is y.

To sign a message, m

(1) Alice generates a random number, k, less than q

(2) Alice generates

$r = (a^k \bmod p) \bmod q$

$s = (xr + k(H(m))) \bmod q$

If $H(m) \bmod q = 0$, then set it equal to 1. If $r = 0$, then choose another k and start again. The signature is two numbers: $r \bmod 2^{256}$ and $s \bmod 2^{256}$. She sends these to Bob.

(3) Bob verifies the signature by computing

$$v = H(m)^{q-2} \bmod q$$
$$z_1 = (sv) \bmod q$$
$$z_2 = ((q - r) \star v) \bmod q$$
$$u = ((a^{z_1} \star y^{z_2}) \bmod p) \bmod q$$

If $u = r$, then the signature is verified.

The difference between this scheme and DSA is that with DSA $s = (xr + k^{-1}(H(m)))$ $\bmod q$, which leads to a different verification equation. Curious, though, is that q is 256 bits. Most Western cryptographers seem satisfied with a q of around 160 bits. Perhaps this is just a reflection of the Russian tendency to play it ultrasafe.

The standard has been in use since the beginning of 1995, and is not classified "for special use"—whatever that means.

20.4 Discrete Logarithm Signature Schemes

ElGamal, Schnorr (see Section 21.3), and DSA signature schemes are very similar. In fact, they are just three examples of a general digital signature scheme based on the Discrete Logarithm Problem. Along with thousands of other signature schemes, they are part of the same family [740,741,699,1184].

Choose p, a large prime number, and q, either $p - 1$ or a large prime factor of $p - 1$. Then choose g, a number between 1 and p such that $g^q \equiv 1 \pmod{p}$. All these numbers are public, and can be common to a group of users. The private key is x, less than q. The public key is $y = g^x \bmod p$.

To sign a message, m, first choose a random k less than and relatively prime to q. If q is also prime, any k less than q works. First compute

$$r = g^k \bmod p$$

The generalized **signature equation** now becomes

$$ak = b + cx \bmod q$$

The coefficients a, b, and c can be any of a variety of things. Each line in Table 20.4 gives six possibilities.

To verify the signature, the receiver must confirm that

$$r^a = g^b y^c \bmod p$$

This is called the **verification equation**.

Table 20.5 lists the signature and verifications possible from just the first line of potential values for a, b, and c, ignoring the effects of the $\pm$.

Table 20.4
Possible Permutations
of a, b, and c ($r' = r$ mod q)

$\pm r'$	$\pm s$	m
$\pm r'm$	$\pm s$	1
$\pm r'm$	$\pm ms$	1
$\pm mr'$	$\pm r's$	1
$\pm ms$	$\pm r's$	1

That's six different signature schemes. Adding the negative signs brings the total to 24. Using the other possible values listed for a, b, and c brings the total to 120.

ElGamal [518,519] and DSA [1154] are essentially based on equation (4). Other schemes are based on equation (2) [24,1629]. Schnorr [1396,1397] is closely related to equation (5), as is another scheme [1183]. And equation (1) can be modified to yield the scheme proposed in [1630]. The rest of the equations are new.

There's more. You can make any of these schemes more DSA-like by defining r as

$$r = (g^k \bmod p) \bmod q$$

Keep the same signature equation and make the verification equation

$$u_1 = a^{-1}b \bmod q$$
$$u_2 = a^{-1}c \bmod q$$
$$r = (g^{u_1}y^{u_2} \bmod p) \bmod q$$

There are two other possibilities along these lines [740,741]; you can do this with each of the 120 schemes, bringing the total to 480 discrete-logarithm-based digital signature schemes.

But wait—there's more. Additional generalizations and variations can generate more than 13,000 variants (not all of them terribly efficient) [740,741].

One of the nice things about using RSA for digital signatures is a feature called **message recovery**. When you verify an RSA signature you compute m. Then you compare the computed m with the message and see if the signature is valid for that

Table 20.5
Discrete Logarithm Signature Schemes

Signature Equation	Verification Equation
(1) $r'k = s + mx \bmod q$	$r^{r'} = g^s y^m \bmod p$
(2) $r'k = m + sx \bmod q$	$r^{r'} = g^m y^s \bmod p$
(3) $sk = r' + mx \bmod q$	$r^s = g^{r'} y^m \bmod p$
(4) $sk = m + r'x \bmod q$	$r^s = g^m y^{r'} \bmod p$
(5) $mk = s + r'x \bmod q$	$r^m = g^s y^{r'} \bmod p$
(6) $mk = r' + sx \bmod q$	$r^m = g^{r'} y^s \bmod p$

message. With the previous schemes, you can't recover m when you compute the signature; you need a candidate m that you use in a verification equation. Well, as it turns out it is possible to construct a message recovery variant for all the above signature schemes.

To sign, first compute

$$r = mg^k \bmod p$$

and replace m by 1 in the signature equation. Then you can reconstruct the verification equation such that m can be computed directly.

You can do the same with the DSA-like schemes:

$$r = (mg^k \bmod p) \bmod q$$

All the variants are equally secure, so it makes sense to choose a scheme that is easy to compute with. The requirement to compute inverses slows most of these schemes. As it turns out, a scheme in this pile allows computing both the signature equation and the verification equation without inverses and also gives message recovery. It is called the **p-NEW** scheme [1184].

$$r = mg^{-k} \bmod p$$
$$s = k - r'x \bmod q$$

And m is recovered (and the signature verified) by

$$m = g^s y^r r \bmod p$$

Some variants sign two and three message blocks at the same time [740]; other variants can be used for blind signatures [741].

This is a remarkable piece of research. All of the various discrete-logarithm-based digital signature schemes have been put in one coherent framework. In my opinion this finally puts to rest any patent dispute between Schnorr [1398] and DSA [897]: DSA is not a derivative of Schnorr, nor even of ElGamal. All three are examples of this general construction, and this general construction is unpatented.

20.5 ONG-SCHNORR-SHAMIR

This signature scheme uses polynomials modulo n [1219,1220]. Choose a large integer n (you need not know the factorization of n). Then choose a random integer, k, such that k and n are relatively prime. Calculate h such that

$$h = -k^{-2} \bmod n = -(k^{-1})^2 \bmod n$$

The public key is h and n; k is the private key.

To sign a message, M, first generate a random number, r, such that r and n are relatively prime. Then calculate:

$$S_1 = 1/2 \, \star \, (M/r + r) \bmod n$$
$$S_2 = k/2 \, \star \, (M/r - r) \bmod n$$

The pair, S_1 and S_2, is the signature.

To verify a signature, confirm that

$$S_1^2 + h \cdot S_2^2 \equiv M \pmod n$$

The version of the scheme described here is based on quadratic polynomials. When it was first proposed in [1217], a $100 reward was offered for successful crypt-analysis. It was proved insecure [1255,18], but its authors were not deterred. They proposed a modification of the algorithm based on cubic polynomials, which is also insecure [1255]. The authors then proposed a quartic version, which was also broken [524,1255]. A variant which fixes these problems is in [1134].

20.6 ESIGN

ESIGN is a digital signature scheme from NTT Japan [1205,583]. It is touted as being at least as secure and considerably faster than either RSA or DSA, with similar key and signature lengths.

The private key is a pair of large prime numbers, p and q. The public key is n, when

$$n = p^2 q$$

H is a hash function that operates on a message, m, such that $H(m)$ is between 0 and $n - 1$. There is also a security parameter, k, which will be discussed shortly.

(1) Alice picks a random number x, where x is less than pq.

(2) Alice computes:

> w, the least integer that is larger than or equal to
>
> $(H(m) - x^k \bmod n)/pq$
>
> $s = x + ((w/kx^{k-1}) \bmod p)pq$

(3) Alice sends s to Bob.

(4) To verify the signature, Bob computes $s^k \bmod n$. He also computes a, which is the least integer larger than or equal to two times the number of bits of n divided by 3. If $H(m)$ is less than or equal to $s^k \bmod n$, and if $s^k \bmod n$ is less than $H(m) + 2^a$, then the signature is considered valid.

This algorithm works faster with precomputation. This precomputation can be done at any time and has nothing to do with the message being signed. After pick-ing x, Alice could break step (2) into two partial steps. The first can be precomputed.

(2a) Alice computes:

> $u = x^k \bmod n$
>
> $v = 1/(kx^{k-1}) \bmod p$

(2b) Alice computes:

w = the least integer that is larger than or equal to

$(H(m) - u)/pq$

$s = x + (wv \bmod p)pq$

For the size of numbers generally used, this precomputation speeds up the signature process by a factor of 10. Almost all the hard work is done in the precomputation stage. A discussion of modular arithmetic operations to speed ESIGN can be found in [1625,1624]. This algorithm can also be extended to work with elliptic curves [1206].

Security of ESIGN

When this algorithm was originally proposed, k was set to 2 [1215]. This was quickly broken by Ernie Brickell and John DeLaurentis [261], who then extended their attack to $k = 3$. A modified version of this algorithm [1203] was broken by Shamir [1204]. The variant proposed in [1204] was broken in [1553]. ESIGN is the current incarnation of this family of algorithms. Another new attack [963] does not work against ESIGN.

The authors currently recommend these values for k: 8, 16, 32, 64, 128, 256, 512, and 1024. They also recommend that p and q each be of at least 192 bits, making n at least 576 bits long. (I think n should be twice that length.) With these parameters, the authors conjecture that ESIGN is as secure as RSA or Rabin. And their analysis shows favorable speed comparison to RSA, ElGamal, and DSA [582].

Patents

ESIGN is patented in the United States [1208], Canada, England, France, Germany, and Italy. Anyone who wishes to license the algorithm should contact Intellectual Property Department, NTT, 1–6 Uchisaiwai-cho, 1-chome, Chiyada-ku, 100 Japan.

20.7 Cellular Automata

A new and novel idea, studied by Papua Guam [665], is the use of cellular automata in public-key cryptosystems. This system is still far too new and has not been studied extensively, but a preliminary examination suggests that it may have a cryptographic weakness similar to one seen in other cases [562]. Still, this is a promising area of research. Cellular automata have the property that, even if they are invertible, it is impossible to calculate the predecessor of an arbitrary state by reversing the rule for finding the successor. This sounds a whole lot like a trapdoor one-way function.

20.8 Other Public-Key Algorithms

Many other public-key algorithms have been proposed and broken over the years. The Matsumoto-Imai algorithm [1021] was broken in [450]. The Cade algorithm was first proposed in 1985, broken in 1986 [774], and then strengthened in the same year [286]. In addition to these attacks, there are general attacks for decomposing polynomials over finite fields [605]. Any algorithm that gets its security from the composition of polynomials over a finite field should be looked upon with skepticism, if not outright suspicion.

The Yagisawa algorithm combines exponentiation mod p with arithmetic mod $p - 1$ [1623]; it was broken in [256]. Another public-key algorithm, Tsujii-Kurosawa-Itoh-Fujioka-Matsumoto [1548] is insecure [948]. A third system, Luccio-Mazzone [993], is insecure [717]. A signature scheme based on birational permutations [1425] was broken the day after it was presented [381]. Tatsuaki Okamoto has several signature schemes: one is provably as secure as the Discrete Logarithm Problem, and another is provably as secure as the Discrete Logarithm Problem *and* the Factoring Problem [1206]. Similar schemes are in [709].

Gustavus Simmons suggested J-algebras as a basis for public-key algorithms [1455,145]. This idea was abandoned after efficient methods for factoring polynomials were invented [951]. Special polynomial semigroups have also been studied [1619,962], but so far nothing has come of it. Harald Niederreiter proposed a public-key algorithm based on shift-register sequences [1166]. Another is based on Lyndon words [1476] and another on propositional calculus [817]. And a recent public-key algorithm gets its security from the matrix cover problem [82]. Tatsuaki Okamoto and Kazuo Ohta compare a number of digital signature schemes in [1212].

Prospects for creating radically new and different public-key cryptography algorithms seem dim. In 1988 Whitfield Diffie noted that most public-key algorithms are based on one of three hard problems [492,494]:

1. Knapsack: Given a set of unique numbers, find a subset whose sum is N.

2. Discrete logarithm: If p is a prime and g and M are integers, find x such that $g^x \equiv M \pmod{p}$.

3. Factoring: If N is the product of two primes, either
   a)   factor N,
   b)   given integers M and C, find d such that $M^d \equiv C \pmod{N}$,
   c)   given integers e and C, find M such that $M^e \equiv C \pmod{N}$, or
   d)   given an integer x, decide whether there exists an integer y such that $x \equiv y^2 \pmod{N}$.

According to Diffie [492,494], the Discrete Logarithm Problem was suggested by J. Gill, the Factoring Problem by Knuth, and the knapsack problem by Diffie himself.

This narrowness in the mathematical foundations of public-key cryptography is worrisome. A breakthrough in either the problem of factoring or of calculating discrete logarithms could render whole classes of public-key algorithms insecure. Diffie points out [492,494] that this risk is mitigated by two factors:

1. The operations on which public key cryptography currently depends—multiplying, exponentiating, and factoring—are all fundamental arithmetic phenom-

ena. They have been the subject of intense mathematical scrutiny for centuries and the increased attention that has resulted from their use in public key cryptosystems has on balance enhanced rather than diminished our confidence.

2. Our ability to carry out large arithmetic computations has grown steadily and now permits us to implement our systems with numbers sufficient in size to be vulnerable only to a dramatic breakthrough in factoring, logarithms, or root extraction.

As we have seen, not all public-key algorithms based on these problems are secure. The strength of any public-key algorithm depends on more than the computational complexity of the problem upon which it is based; a hard problem does not necessarily imply a strong algorithm. Adi Shamir listed three reasons why this is so [1415]:

1. Complexity theory usually deals with single isolated instances of a problem. A cryptanalyst often has a large collection of statistically related problems to solve—several ciphertexts encrypted with the same key.

2. The computational complexity of a problem is typically measured by its worst-case or average-case behavior. To be useful as a cipher, the problem must be hard to solve in almost all cases.

3. An arbitrarily difficult problem cannot necessarily be transformed into a cryptosystem, and it must be possible to insert trapdoor information into the problem so that a shortcut solution is possible with this information and only with this information.

CHAPTER 21

Identification Schemes

21.1 FEIGE-FIAT-SHAMIR

Amos Fiat's and Adi Shamir's authentication and digital signature scheme is discussed in [566,567]. Uriel Feige, Fiat, and Shamir modified the algorithm to a zero-knowledge proof of identity [544,545]. This is the best-known zero-knowledge proof of identity.

On July 9, 1986 the three authors submitted a U.S. patent application [1427]. Because of its potential military applications, the application was reviewed by the military. Occasionally the Patent Office responds not with a patent, but with something called a secrecy order. On January 6, 1987, three days before the end of their six-month period, the Patent Office imposed that order at the request of the Army. They stated that "... the disclosure or publication of the subject matter ... would be detrimental to the national security. ..." The authors were ordered to notify all Americans to whom the research had been disclosed that unauthorized disclosure could lead to two years' imprisonment, a $10,000 fine, or both. Furthermore, the authors had to inform the Commissioner of Patents and Trademarks of all foreign citizens to whom the information had been disclosed.

This was ludicrous. All through the second half of 1986, the authors had presented the work at conferences throughout Israel, Europe, and the United States. The authors weren't even American citizens, and all the work had been done at the Weizmann Institute in Israel.

Word spread through the academic community and the press. Within two days the secrecy order was rescinded; Shamir and others believe that the NSA pulled strings to rescind the order, although they officially had no comment. Further details of this bizarre story are in [936].

Simplified Feige-Fiat-Shamir Identification Scheme

Before issuing any private keys, the arbitrator chooses a random modulus, n, which is the product of two large primes. In real life, n should be at least 512 bits long and probably closer to 1024 bits. This n can be shared among a group of provers. (Choosing a Blum integer makes computation easier, but it is not required for security.)

To generate Peggy's public and private keys, a trusted arbitrator chooses a number, v, where v is a quadratic residue mod n. In other words, choose v such that $x^2 \equiv v \pmod{n}$ has a solution and v^{-1} mod n exists. This v is Peggy's public key. Then calculate the smallest s for which $s \equiv$ sqrt (v^{-1}) $\pmod{n}$. This is Peggy's private key.

The identification protocol can now proceed.

(1) Peggy picks a random r, where r is less then n. She then computes $x = r^2$ mod n, and sends x to Victor.

(2) Victor sends Peggy a random bit, b.

(3) If $b = 0$, then Peggy sends Victor r. If $b = 1$, then Peggy sends Victor $y = r \star s$ mod n.

(4) If $b = 0$, Victor verifies that $x = r^2$ mod n, proving that Peggy knows sqrt (x). If $b = 1$, Victor verifies that $x = y^2 \star v$ mod n, proving that Peggy knows sqrt (v^{-1}).

This is a single round—called an **accreditation**—of the protocol. Peggy and Victor repeat this protocol t times, until Victor is convinced that Peggy knows s. It's a cut-and-choose protocol. If Peggy doesn't know s, she can pick r such that she can fool Victor if he sends her a 0, or she can pick r such that she can fool Victor if he sends her a 1. She can't do both. The odds of her fooling Victor once are 50 percent. The odds of her fooling him t times are 1 in 2^t.

Another way for Victor to attack the protocol would be trying to impersonate Peggy. He could initiate the protocol with another verifier, Valerie. In step (1), instead of choosing a random r, he would just reuse an old r that he saw Peggy use. However, the odds of Valerie choosing the same value for b in step (2) that Victor did in the protocol with Peggy are 1 in 2. So, the odds of his fooling Valerie are 50 percent. The odds of his fooling her t times are 1 in 2^t.

For this to work, Peggy must not reuse an r, ever. If she did, and Victor sent Peggy the other random bit in step (2), then he would have both of Peggy's responses. Then, from even one of these, he can calculate s and it's all over for Peggy.

Feige-Fiat-Shamir Identification Scheme

In their papers [544,545], Feige, Fiat and Shamir show how parallel construction can increase the number of accreditations per round and reduce Peggy and Victor's interactions.

First generate n as in the previous example, the product of two large primes. To generate Peggy's public and private keys, first choose k different numbers: v_1, $v_2, \ldots, v_k$, where each v_i is a quadratic residue mod n. In other words, choose v_i such that $x^2 = v_i$ mod n has a solution and v_i^{-1} mod n exists. This string, $v_1, v_2, \ldots, v_k$, is the public key. Then calculate the smallest s_i such that $s_i =$ sqrt (v_i^{-1}) mod n. This string, $s_1, s_2, \ldots, s_k$, is the private key.

And the protocol is:

(1) Peggy picks a random r, when r is less than n. She then computes $x = r^2 \bmod n$, and sends x to Victor.

(2) Victor sends Peggy a random binary string k-bits long: b_1, b_2, . . . , b_k.

(3) Peggy computes $y = r * (s_1^{b_1} * s_2^{b_2} * \ldots * s_k^{b_k}) \bmod n$. (She multiplies together whichever values of s_i that correspond to $b_i = 1$. If Victor's first bit is a 1, then s_1 is part of the product; if Victor's first bit is a 0, then s_1 is not part of the product, and so on.) She sends y to Victor.

(4) Victor verifies that $x = y^2 * (v_1^{b_1} * v_2^{b_2} * \ldots * v_k^{b_k}) \bmod n$. (He multiplies together the values of v_i based on the random binary string. If his first bit is a 1, then v_1 is part of the product; if his first bit is a 0, then v_1 is not part of the product, and so on.)

Peggy and Victor repeat this protocol t times, until Victor is convinced that Peggy knows s_1, s_2, . . . , s_k.

The chance that Peggy can fool Victor is 1 in 2^{kt}. The authors recommend a 1 in 2^{20} chance of a cheater fooling Victor and suggest that $k = 5$ and $t = 4$. If you are more paranoid, increase these numbers.

An Example

Let's look at this protocol in action with small numbers.

If $n = 35$ (the two primes are 5 and 7), then the possible quadratic residues are:

> 1: $x^2 \equiv 1 \pmod{35}$ has the solutions: $x = 1, 6, 29,$ or 34.
>
> 4: $x^2 \equiv 4 \pmod{35}$ has the solutions: $x = 2, 12, 23,$ or 33.
>
> 9: $x^2 \equiv 9 \pmod{35}$ has the solutions: $x = 3, 17, 18,$ or 32.
>
> 11: $x^2 \equiv 11 \pmod{35}$ has the solutions: $x = 9, 16, 19,$ or 26.
>
> 14: $x^2 \equiv 14 \pmod{35}$ has the solutions: $x = 7$ or 28.
>
> 15: $x^2 \equiv 15 \pmod{35}$ has the solutions: $x = 15$ or 20.
>
> 16: $x^2 \equiv 16 \pmod{35}$ has the solutions: $x = 4, 11, 24,$ or 31.
>
> 21: $x^2 \equiv 21 \pmod{35}$ has the solutions: $x = 14$ or 21.
>
> 25: $x^2 \equiv 25 \pmod{35}$ has the solutions: $x = 5$ or 30.
>
> 29: $x^2 \equiv 29 \pmod{35}$ has the solutions: $x = 8, 13, 22$ or 27.
>
> 30: $x^2 \equiv 30 \pmod{35}$ has the solutions: $x = 10$ or 25.

The inverses (mod 35) and their square roots are:

v	v^{-1}	$s = \mathrm{sqrt}\,(v^{-1})$
1	1	1
4	9	3
9	4	2

11	16	4
16	11	9
29	29	8

Note that 14, 15, 21, 25, and 30 do not have inverses mod 35, because they are not relatively prime to 35. This makes sense, because there should be $(5 - 1) * (7 - 1)/4$ quadratic residues mod 35 relatively prime to 35: That is $gcd(x,35) = 1$ (see Section 11.3).

So, Peggy gets the public key consisting of $k = 4$ values: {4,11,16,29}. The corresponding private key is {3,4,9,8}. Here's one round of the protocol.

(1) Peggy chooses a random $r = 16$, computes $16^2 \bmod 35 = 11$, and sends it to Victor.

(2) Victor sends Peggy a random binary string {1,1,0,1}.

(3) Peggy computes $16 * ((3^1) * (4^1) * (9^0) * (8^1)) \bmod 35 = 31$ and sends it to Victor.

(4) Victor verifies that $31^2 * ((4^1) * (11^1) * (16^0) * (29^1)) \bmod 35 = 11$.

Peggy and Victor repeat the protocol t times, each time with a different random r, until Victor is satisfied.

With small values like these, there's no real security. But when n is 512 bits long or more, Victor cannot learn anything about Peggy's secret key except the fact that she knows it.

Enhancements

It is possible to embed identification information into the protocol. Assume that I is a binary string representing Peggy's identification: her name, address, social security number, hat size, preferred brand of soft drink, and other personal information. Use a one-way hash function $H(x)$ to compute $H(I,j)$, where j is a small number concatenated onto I. Find a set of js where $H(I,j)$ is a quadratic residue mod n. These $H(I,j)$s become $v_1, v_2, \ldots, v_k$ (the js need not be quadratic residues). Peggy's public key is now I and the list of js. She sends I and the list of js to Victor before step (1) of the protocol (or perhaps Victor downloads them from a public bulletin board someplace), and Victor generates $v_1, v_2, \ldots, v_k$ from $H(I,j)$.

Now, after Victor successfully completes the protocol with Peggy, he is assured that Trent, who knows the factorization of the modulus, has certified the association between I and Peggy by giving her the square roots of the v_i derived from I. (See Section 5.2 for background information.)

Feige, Fiat, and Shamir include the following implementation remarks [544,545]:

> For nonperfect hash functions, it may be advisable to randomize I by concatenating it with a long random string, R. This string is chosen by the arbitrator and is revealed to Victor along with I.
>
> In typical implementations, k should be between 1 and 18. Larger values of k can reduce the time and communication complexity by reducing the number of rounds.

The value n should be at least 512 bits long. (Of course, there has been considerable progress in factoring since then.)

If each user chooses his own n and publishes it in a public key file, they can dispense with the arbitrator. However, this RSA-like variant makes the scheme considerably less convenient.

Fiat-Shamir Signature Scheme

Turning this identification scheme into a signature scheme is basically a matter of turning Victor into a hash function. The primary benefit of the Fiat-Shamir digital signature scheme over RSA is speed: Fiat-Shamir requires only 1 percent to 4 percent of the modular multiplications of RSA. For this protocol, we'll bring back Alice and Bob.

The setup is the same as the identification scheme. Choose n to be the product of two large primes. Generate the public key, v_1, v_2, ..., v_k, and the private key, s_1, s_2, ..., s_k, such that $s_i = \mathrm{sqrt}\,(v_i^{-1}) \bmod n$.

(1) Alice picks t random integers between 1 and n: r_1, r_2, ..., r_t, and computes x_1, x_2, ..., x_t such that $x_i = r_i^2 \bmod n$.

(2) Alice hashes the concatenation of the message and the string of x_is to generate a bit stream: $H(m, x_1, x_2, \ldots, x_t)$. She uses the first $k * t$ bits of this string as values of b_{ij}, where i goes from 1 to t, and j goes from 1 to k.

(3) Alice computes y_1, y_2, ..., y_t, where

$$y_i = r_i * (s_1^{bi1} * s_2^{bi2} * \ldots * s_k^{bik}) \bmod n$$

(For each i, she multiplies together the values of the s_j based on the random $b_{i,\,j}$ values. If $b_{i,\,1}$ is a 1, then s_1 is multiplied; if $b_{i,\,1}$ is a 0, then s_1 is not multiplied.)

(4) Alice sends Bob m, all the bit values of $b_{i,\,j}$, and all the values of y_i. He already has Alice's public key: v_1, v_2, ..., v_k.

(5) Bob computes z_1, z_2, ..., z_t, where

$$z_i = y_i^2 * (v_1^{bi1} * v_2^{bi2} * \ldots * v_k^{bik}) \bmod n$$

(Again, Bob multiplies based on the $b_{i,\,j}$ values.) Also note that z_i should be equal to x_i.

(6) Bob verifies that the first $k * t$ bits of $H(m, z_1, z_2, \ldots, z_t)$ are the $b_{i,\,j}$ values that Alice sent him.

As with the identification scheme, the security of this signature scheme is proportional to $1/2^{kt}$. It also depends on the difficulty of factoring n. Fiat and Shamir pointed out that forging a signature is easier when the complexity of factoring n is considerably lower than 2^{kt}. And, because of birthday-type attacks (see Section 18.1), they recommend that $k * t$ be increased from 20 to at least 72. They suggest $k = 9$ and $t = 8$.

Improved Fiat-Shamir Signature Scheme

Silvio Micali and Adi Shamir improved the Fiat-Shamir protocol in [1088]. They chose $v_1, v_2, \ldots, v_k$ to be the first k prime numbers. So

$$v_1 = 2, v_2 = 3, v_3 = 5, \text{ and so on.}$$

This is the public key.

The private key, $s_1, s_2, \ldots, s_k$ is a random square root, determined by

$$s_i = \text{sqrt } (v_i^{-1}) \bmod n$$

In this version, every person must have a different n. The modification makes it easier to verify signatures. The time required to generate signatures, and the security of those signatures, is unaffected.

Other Enhancements

There is also an N-party identification scheme, based on the Fiat-Shamir algorithm [264]. Two other improvements to the Fiat-Shamir scheme are proposed in [1218]. Another variant is [1368].

Ohta-Okamoto Identification Scheme

This protocol is a modification of the Feige-Fiat-Shamir identification scheme and gets its security from the difficulty of factoring [1198,1199]. The same authors also wrote a multisignature scheme (see Section 23.1), by which a number of different people can sequentially sign a message [1200]. This scheme has been proposed for smart-card implementation [850].

Patents

Fiat-Shamir is patented [1427]. Anyone interested in licensing the algorithm should contact Yeda Research and Development, The Weizmann Institute of Science, Rehovot 76100, Israel.

21.2 GUILLOU-QUISQUATER

Feige-Fiat-Shamir was the first practical identity-based protocol. It minimized computation by increasing the number of iterations and accreditations per iteration. For some implementations, like smart cards, this is less than ideal. Exchanges with the outside world are time-consuming, and the storage required for each accreditation can strain the limited resources of the card.

Louis Guillou and Jean-Jacques Quisquater developed a zero-knowledge identification algorithm more suited to applications like these [670,1280]. The exchanges between Peggy and Victor and the parallel accreditations in each exchange are both kept to an absolute minimum: There is only one exchange of one accreditation for each proof. For the same level of security, the computation required by Guillou-Quisquater is greater than by Feige-Fiat-Shamir by a factor of three. And like Feige-Fiat-Shamir, this identification algorithm can be converted to a digital signature algorithm.

Guillou-Quisquater Identification Scheme

Peggy is a smart card who wants to prove her identity to Victor. Peggy's identity consists of a set of credentials: a data string consisting of the card's name, validity period, a bank account number, and whatever else the application warrants. This bit string is called J. (Actually, the credentials can be a longer string and hashed to a J value. This complexity does not modify the protocol in any way.) This is analogous to the public key. Other public information, shared by all "Peggys" who could use this application, is an exponent v and a modulus n, where n is the product of two secret primes. The private key is B, calculated such that $JB^v \equiv 1 \pmod{n}$.

Peggy sends Victor her credentials, J. Now, she wants to prove to Victor that those credentials are hers. To do this, she has to convince Victor that she knows B. Here's the protocol:

(1) Peggy picks a random integer r, such that r is between 1 and $n-1$. She computes $T = r^v \bmod n$ and sends it to Victor.

(2) Victor picks a random integer, d, such that d is between zero and $v-1$. He sends d to Peggy.

(3) Peggy computes $D = rB^d \bmod n$, and sends it to Victor.

(4) Victor computes $T' = D^v J^d \bmod n$. If $T \equiv T' \pmod{n}$, then the authentication succeeds.

The math isn't that complex:

$$T' = D^v J^d = (rB^d)^v J^d = r^v B^{dv} J^d = r^v (JB^v)^d = r^v \equiv T \pmod{n}$$

since B was constructed to satisfy

$$JB^v \equiv 1 \pmod{n}$$

Guillou-Quisquater Signature Scheme

This identification can be converted to a signature scheme, also suited for smart-card implementation [671,672].

The public and private key setup is the same as before. Here's the protocol:

(1) Alice picks a random integer r, such that r is between 1 and $n-1$. She computes $T = r^v \bmod n$.

(2) Alice computes $d = H(M,T)$, where M is the message being signed and $H(x)$ is a one-way hash function. The d produced by the hash function must be between 0 and $v-1$ [1280]. If the output of the hash function is not within this range, it must be reduced modulo v.

(3) Alice computes $D = rB^d \bmod n$. The signature consists of the message, M, the two calculated values, d and D, and her credentials, J. She sends this signature to Bob.

(4) Bob computes $T' = D^v J^d \bmod n$. He then computes $d' = H(M,T')$. If $d = d'$, then Alice must know B and the signature is valid.

Multiple Signatures

What if many people want to sign the same document? The easy solution has each of them signing separately, but this signature scheme can do better than that. Here Alice and Bob sign the same document and Carol verifies the signatures, but any number of people can be involved in the signature process. As before, Alice and Bob have their own unique J and B values: (J_A, B_A) and (J_B, B_B). The values n and v are common to the system.

(1) Alice picks a random integer, r_A, such that r_A is between 1 and $n - 1$. She computes $T_A = r_A^v \bmod n$ and sends T_A to Bob.

(2) Bob picks a random integer, r_B, such that r_B is between 1 and $n - 1$. He computes $T_B = r_B^v \bmod n$ and sends T_B to Alice.

(3) Alice and Bob each compute $T = (T_A T_B) \bmod n$.

(4) Alice and Bob each compute $d = H(M,T)$, where M is the message being signed and $H(x)$ is a one-way hash function. The d produced by the hash function must be between 0 and $v - 1$ [1280]. If the output of the hash function is not within this range, it must be reduced modulo v.

(5) Alice computes $D_A = r_A B_A^d \bmod n$ and sends D_A to Bob.

(6) Bob computes $D_B = r_B B_B^d \bmod n$ and sends D_B to Alice.

(7) Alice and Bob each compute $D = D_A D_B \bmod n$. The signature consists of the message, M, the two calculated values, d and D, and both of their credentials: J_A and J_B.

(8) Carol computes $J = J_A J_B \bmod n$.

(9) Carol computes $T' = D^v J^d \bmod n$. She then computes $d' = H(M,T')$. If $d \equiv d'$, then the multiple signature is valid.

This protocol can be extended to any number of people. For multiple people to sign, they all multiply their individual T_i values together in step (3), and their individual D_i values together in step (7). To verify a multiple signature, multiply all the signers J_i values together in step (8). Either all the signatures are valid or there is at least one invalid signature.

21.3 SCHNORR

Claus Schnorr's authentication and signature scheme [1396,1397] gets its security from the difficulty of calculating discrete logarithms. To generate a key pair, first choose two primes, p and q, such that q is a prime factor of $p - 1$. Then, choose an a not equal to 1, such that $a^q \equiv 1 \pmod p$. All these numbers can be common to a group of users and can be freely published.

To generate a particular public-key/private-key key pair, choose a random number less than q. This is the private key, s. Then calculate $v = a^{-s} \bmod p$. This is the public key.

Authentication Protocol

(1) Peggy picks a random number, r, less than q, and computes $x = a^r \bmod p$. This is the preprocessing stage and can be done long before Victor is present.

(2) Peggy sends x to Victor.

(3) Victor sends Peggy a random number, e, between 0 and $2^t - 1$. (I'll discuss t in a moment.)

(4) Peggy computes $y = (r + se) \bmod q$ and sends y to Victor.

(5) Victor verifies that $x = a^y v^e \bmod p$.

The security is based on the parameter t. The difficulty of breaking the algorithm is about 2^t. Schnorr recommended that p be about 512 bits, q be about 140 bits, and t be 72.

Digital Signature Protocol

Schnorr can also be used as a digital signature protocol on a message, M. The public-key/private-key key pair is the same, but we're now adding a one-way hash function, $H(M)$.

(1) Alice picks a random number, r, less than q, and computes $x = a^r \bmod p$. This computation is the preprocessing stage.

(2) Alice concatenates M and x, and hashes the result:

$$e = H(M,x)$$

(3) Alice computes $y = (r + se) \bmod q$. The signature is e and y; she sends these to Bob.

(4) Bob computes $x' = a^y v^e \bmod p$. He then confirms that the concatenation of M and x' hashes to e.

$$e = H(M,x')$$

If it does, he accepts the signature as valid.

In his paper, Schnorr cites these novel features of his algorithm:

Most of the computation for signature generation can be completed in a preprocessing stage, independent of the message being signed. Hence, it can be done during idle time and not affect the signature speed. An attack against this preprocessing stage is discussed in [475], but I don't think it's practical.

For the same level of security, the length of signatures is less for Schnorr than for RSA. For example, with a 140-bit q, signatures are only 212-bits long, less than half the length of RSA signatures. Schnorr's signatures are also much shorter than ElGamal signatures.

Of course, practical considerations may make even fewer bits suitable for a given scheme: For example, an identification scheme where the cheater must perform an on-line attack in only a few seconds, versus a signature scheme where the cheater can calculate for years off-line to come up with a forgery.

A modification of this algorithm, by Ernie Brickell and Kevin McCurley, enhances its security [265].

Patents

Schnorr is patented in the United States [1398] and in many other countries. In 1993, PKP acquired the worldwide rights to the patent (see Section 25.5). The U.S. patent expires on February 19, 2008.

21.4 CONVERTING IDENTIFICATION SCHEMES TO SIGNATURE SCHEMES

There is a standard method of converting an identification scheme into a signature scheme: Replace Victor with a one-way hash function. The message is not hashed before it is signed; instead the hashing is incorporated into the signing algorithm. In principle, this can be done with any identification scheme.

CHAPTER   22

Key-Exchange Algorithms

22.1   DIFFIE-HELLMAN

Diffie-Hellman was the first public-key algorithm ever invented, way back in 1976 [496]. It gets its security from the difficulty of calculating discrete logarithms in a finite field, as compared with the ease of calculating exponentiation in the same field. Diffie-Hellman can be used for key distribution—Alice and Bob can use this algorithm to generate a secret key—but it cannot be used to encrypt and decrypt messages.

The math is simple. First, Alice and Bob agree on a large prime, n and g, such that g is primitive mod n. These two integers don't have to be secret; Alice and Bob can agree to them over some insecure channel. They can even be common among a group of users. It doesn't matter.

Then, the protocol goes as follows:

(1) Alice chooses a random large integer x and sends Bob

$$X = g^x \bmod n$$

(2) Bob chooses a random large integer y and sends Alice

$$Y = g^y \bmod n$$

(3) Alice computes

$$k = Y^x \bmod n$$

(4) Bob computes

$$k' = X^y \bmod n$$

Both k and k' are equal to $g^{xy} \bmod n$. No one listening on the channel can compute that value; they only know n, g, X, and Y. Unless they can compute the discrete logarithm and recover x or y, they do not solve the problem. So, k is the secret key that both Alice and Bob computed independently.

The choice of g and n can have a substantial impact on the security of this system. The number $(n-1)/2$ should also be a prime [1253]. And most important, n should be large: The security of the system is based on the difficulty of factoring numbers the same size as n. You can choose any g, such that g is primitive mod n; there's no reason not to choose the smallest g you can—generally a one-digit number. (And actually, g does not have to be primitive; it just has to generate a large subgroup of the multiplicitive group mod n.)

Diffie-Hellman with Three or More Parties

The Diffie-Hellman key-exchange protocol can easily be extended to work with three or more people. In this example, Alice, Bob, and Carol together generate a secret key.

(1) Alice chooses a random large integer x and sends Bob

$$X = g^x \bmod n$$

(2) Bob chooses a random large integer y and sends Carol

$$Y = g^y \bmod n$$

(3) Carol chooses a random large integer z and sends Alice

$$Z = g^z \bmod n$$

(4) Alice sends Bob

$$Z' = Z^x \bmod n$$

(5) Bob sends Carol

$$X' = X^y \bmod n$$

(6) Carol sends Alice

$$Y' = Y^z \bmod n$$

(7) Alice computes

$$k = Y'^x \bmod n$$

(8) Bob computes

$$k = Z'^y \bmod n$$

(9) Carol computes

$$k = X'^z \bmod n$$

The secret key, k, is equal to $g^{xyz} \bmod n$, and no one else listening in on the communications can compute that value. The protocol can be easily extended to four or more people; just add more people and more rounds of computation.

Extended Diffie-Hellman

Diffie-Hellman also works in commutitive rings [1253]. Z. Shmuley and Kevin McCurley studied a variant of the algorithm where the modulus is a composite number [1442,1038]. V. S. Miller and Neal Koblitz extended this algorithm to elliptic curves [1095,867]. Taher ElGamal used the basic idea to develop an encryption and digital signature algorithm (see Section 19.6).

This algorithm also works in the Galois field GF(2^k) [1442,1038]. Some implementations take this approach [884,1631,1632], because the computation is much quicker. Similarly, cryptanalytic computation is equally fast, so it is important to carefully choose a field large enough to ensure security.

Hughes

This variant of Diffie-Hellman allows Alice to generate a key and send it to Bob [745].

(1)   Alice chooses a random large integer x and generates

$$k = g^x \bmod n$$

(2)   Bob chooses a random large integer y and sends Alice

$$Y = g^y \bmod n$$

(3)   Alice sends Bob

$$X = Y^x \bmod n$$

(4)   Bob computes

$$z = y^{-1}$$
$$k' = X^z \bmod n$$

If everything goes correctly, $k = k'$.

The advantage of this protocol over Diffie-Hellman is that k can be computed before any interaction, and Alice can encrypt a message using k prior to contacting Bob. She can send it to a variety of people and interact with them to exchange the key individually later.

Key Exchange Without Exchanging Keys

If you have a community of users, each could publish a public key, $X = g^x \bmod n$, in a common database. If Alice wants to communicate with Bob, she just has to retrieve Bob's public key and generate their shared secret key. She could then encrypt a message with that key and send it to Bob. Bob would retrieve Alice's public key to generate the shared secret key.

Each pair of users would have a unique secret key, and no prior communication between users is required. The public keys have to be certified to prevent spoofing attacks and should be changed regularly, but otherwise this is a pretty clever idea.

Patents

The Diffie-Hellman key-exchange algorithm is patented in the United States [718] and Canada [719]. A group called Public Key Partners (PKP) licenses the patent, along with other public-key cryptography patents (see Section 25.5). The U.S. patent will expire on April 29, 1997.

22.2 STATION-TO-STATION PROTOCOL

Diffie-Hellman key exchange is vulnerable to a man-in-the-middle attack. One way to prevent this problem is to have Alice and Bob sign their messages to each other [500].

This protocol assumes that Alice has a certificate with Bob's public key and that Bob has a certificate with Alice's public key. These certificates have been signed by some trusted authority outside this protocol. Here's how Alice and Bob generate a secret key, k.

(1) Alice generates a random number, x, and sends it to Bob.

(2) Bob generates a random number, y. Using the Diffie-Hellman protocol he computes their shared key based on x and y: k. He signs x and y, and encrypts the signature using k. He then sends that, along with y, to Alice.

$$y, E_k(S_B(x,y))$$

(3) Alice also computes k. She decrypts the rest of Bob's message and verifies his signature. Then she sends Bob a signed message consisting of x and y, encrypted in their shared key.

$$E_k(S_A(x,y))$$

(4) Bob decrypts the message and verifies Alice's signature.

22.3 SHAMIR'S THREE-PASS PROTOCOL

This protocol, invented by Adi Shamir but never published, enables Alice and Bob to communicate securely without any advance exchange of either secret keys or public keys [1008].

This assumes the existence of a symmetric cipher that is commutative, that is:

$$E_A(E_B(P)) = E_B(E_A(P))$$

Alice's secret key is A; Bob's secret key is B. Alice wants to send a message, M, to Bob. Here's the protocol.

(1) Alice encrypts M with her key and sends Bob

$$C_1 = E_A(M)$$

(2) Bob encrypts C_1 with his key and sends Alice

$$C_2 = E_B(E_A(M))$$

(3) Alice decrypts C_2 with her key and sends Bob

$$C_3 = D_A(E_B(E_A(M))) = D_A(E_A(E_B(M))) = E_B(M)$$

(4) Bob decrypts C_3 with his key to recover M.

One-time pads are commutative and have perfect secrecy, but they will not work with this protocol. With a one-time pad, the three ciphertext messages would be:

$$C_1 = P \oplus A$$
$$C_2 = P \oplus A \oplus B$$
$$C_3 = P \oplus B$$

Eve, who can record the three messages as they pass between Alice and Bob, simply XORs them together to retrieve the message:

$$C_1 \oplus C_2 \oplus C_3 = (P \oplus A) \oplus (P \oplus A \oplus B) \oplus (P \oplus B) = P$$

This clearly won't work.

Shamir (and independently, Jim Omura) described an encryption algorithm that will work with this protocol, one similar to RSA. Let p be a large prime for which $p - 1$ has a large prime factor. Choose an encryption key, e, such that e is relatively prime to $p - 1$. Calculate d such that $de \equiv 1 \pmod{p - 1}$.

To encrypt a message, calculate

$$C = M^e \bmod p$$

To decrypt a message, calculate

$$M = C^d \bmod p$$

There seems to be no way for Eve to recover M without solving the discrete logarithm problem, but this has never been proved.

Like Diffie-Hellman, this protocol allows Alice to initiate secure communication with Bob without knowing any of his keys. For Alice to use a public-key algorithm, she has to know his public key. With Shamir's three-pass protocol, she just sends him a ciphertext message. The same thing with a public-key algorithm looks like:

(1) Alice asks Bob (or a KDC) for his public key.
(2) Bob (or the KDC) sends Alice his public key.
(3) Alice encrypts M with Bob's public key and sends it to Bob.

Shamir's three-pass protocol will fall to a man-in-the-middle attack.

22.4 COMSET

COMSET (COMmunications SETup) is a mutual identification and key exchange protocol developed for the RIPE project [1305] (see Section 25.7). Using public-key cryptography, it allows Alice and Bob to identify themselves to each other and also to exchange a secret key.

The mathematical principle behind COMSET is Rabin's scheme [1283] (see Section 19.5). The scheme itself was originally proposed in [224]. See [1305] for details.

22.5 ENCRYPTED KEY EXCHANGE

The Encrypted Key Exchange (EKE) protocol was designed by Steve Bellovin and Michael Merritt [109]. It provides security and authentication on computer networks, using both symmetric and public-key cryptography in a novel way: A shared secret key is used to encrypt a randomly generated public key.

The Basic EKE Protocol

Alice and Bob (two users, a user and the host, or whoever) share a common password, P. Using this protocol, they can authenticate each other and generate a common session key, K.

(1) Alice generates a random public-key/private-key key pair. She encrypts the public key, K', using a symmetric algorithm and P as the key: $E_P(K')$. She sends Bob

$$A, E_P(K')$$

(2) Bob knows P. He decrypts the message to obtain K'. Then, he generates a random session key, K, and encrypts it with the public key he received from Alice and P as the key. He sends Alice

$$E_P(E_{K'}(K))$$

(3) Alice decrypts the message to obtain K. She generates a random string, R_A, encrypts it with K, and sends Bob

$$E_K(R_A)$$

(4) Bob decrypts the message to obtain R_A. He generates another random string, R_B, encrypts both strings with K, and sends Alice the result.

$$E_K(R_A, R_B)$$

(5) Alice decrypts the message to obtain R_A and R_B. Assuming the R_A she received from Bob is the same as the one she sent to Bob in step (3), she encrypts R_B with K and sends it to Bob.

$$E_K(R_B)$$

(6) Bob decrypts the message to obtain R_B. Assuming the R_B he received from Alice is the same one he sent to Alice in step (4), the protocol is complete. Both parties now communicate using K as the session key.

At step (3), both Alice and Bob know K' and K. K is the session key and can be used to encrypt all other messages between Alice and Bob. Eve, sitting between Alice and

Bob, only knows $E_P(K')$, $E_P(E_{K'}(K))$, and some messages encrypted with K. In other protocols, Eve could make guesses at P (people choose bad passwords all the time, and if Eve is clever she can make some good guesses) and then test her guesses. In this protocol, Eve cannot test her guess without cracking the public-key algorithm as well. And if both K' and K are chosen randomly, this can be an insurmountable problem.

The challenge-response portion of the protocol, steps (3) through (6), provides validation. Steps (3) through (5) prove to Alice that Bob knows K; steps (4) through (6) prove to Bob that Alice knows K. The Kerberos protocol timestamp exchange accomplishes the same thing.

EKE can be implemented with a variety of public-key algorithms: RSA, ElGamal, Diffie-Hellman. There are security problems with implementing EKE with a knapsack algorithm (aside from the inherent insecurity of knapsack algorithms): The normal distribution of the ciphertext messages negates the benefits of EKE.

Implementing EKE with RSA

The RSA algorithm seems perfect for this application, but there are some subtle problems. The authors recommend encrypting only the encryption exponent in step (1) and sending the modulus in the clear. An explanation of the reasoning behind this recommendation, as well as other subtleties involved in using RSA, is in [109].

Implementing EKE with ElGamal

Implementing EKE with the ElGamal algorithm is straightforward, and there is even a simplification of the basic protocol. Using the notation from Section 19.6, g and p are parts of the public key and are common to all users. The private key is a random number r. The public key is $g^r \bmod p$. The message Alice sends to Bob in step (1) becomes

$$\text{Alice, } g^r \bmod p$$

Note that this public key does not have to be encrypted with P. This is not true in general, but it is true for the ElGamal algorithm. Details are in [109].

Bob chooses a random number, R (for the ElGamal algorithm and independent of any random numbers chosen for EKE), and the message he sends to Alice in step (2) becomes

$$E_P(g^R \bmod p, Kg^{Rr} \bmod p)$$

Refer back to Section 19.6 for restrictions on choosing the variables for ElGamal.

Implementing EKE with Diffie-Hellman

With the Diffie-Hellman protocol, K is generated automatically. The final protocol is even simpler. A value for g and n is set for all users on the network.

(1) Alice picks a random number, r_A, and sends Bob

$$A, g^{r_A} \bmod n$$

With Diffie-Hellman, Alice does not have to encrypt her first message with P.

(2) Bob picks a random number, r_B, and calculates

$$K = g^{r_A \star r_B} \bmod n$$

He generates a random string R_B, then calculates and sends Alice:

$$E_P(g^{r_B} \bmod n), E_K(R_B)$$

(3) Alice decrypts the first half of Bob's message to obtain $g^{r_B} \bmod n$. Then she calculates K and uses K to decrypt R_B. She generates another random string, R_A, encrypts both strings with K, and sends Bob the result.

$$E_K(R_A, R_B)$$

(4) Bob decrypts the message to obtain R_A and R_B. Assuming the R_B he received from Alice is the same as the one he sent to Alice in step (2), he encrypts R_A with K and sends it to Alice.

$$E_K(R_A)$$

(5) Alice decrypts the message to maintain R_A. Assuming the R_A she received from Bob is the same as the one she sent to Bob in step (3), the protocol is complete. Both parties now communicate using K as the session key.

Strengthening EKE

Bellovin and Merritt suggest an enhancement of the challenge-and-response portion of the protocol—to prevent a possible attack if a cryptanalyst recovers an old K value.

Look at the basic EKE protocol. In step (3), Alice generates another random number, S_A, and sends Bob

$$E_K(R_A, S_A)$$

In step (4), Bob generates another random number, S_B, and sends Alice

$$E_K(R_A, R_B, S_B)$$

Alice and Bob now can both calculate the true session key, $S_A \oplus S_B$. This key is used for all future messages between Alice and Bob; K is just used as a key-exchange key.

Look at the levels of protection EKE provides. A recovered value of S gives Eve no information about P, because P is never used to encrypt anything that leads directly to S. A cryptanalytic attack on K is also not feasible; K is used only to encrypt random data, and S is never encrypted alone.

Augmented EKE

The EKE protocol suffers from one serious disadvantage: It requires that both parties possess the P. Most password-based authentication systems store a one-way hash of the user's password, not the password itself (see Section 3.2). The Augmented EKE (A-EKE) protocol uses a one-way hash of the user's password as the superencryption key in the Diffie-Hellman variant of EKE. The user then sends an extra message based on the original password; this message authenticates the newly chosen session key.

Here's how it works. As usual, Alice and Bob want to authenticate each other and generate a common key. They agree on some digital signature scheme where any number can serve as the private key, and where the public key is derived from the private key, rather than being generated along with it. The ElGamal and DSA algorithms work well for this. Alice's password P (or perhaps some simple hash of it) will serve as the private key and as P'.

(1) Alice picks her random exponent R_a and transmits

   $E_P(g^{R_A} \bmod n)$

(2) Bob, who knows only P' and cannot derive P from it, chooses R_b and sends

   $E_P(g^{R_A} \bmod n)$

(3) Both Alice and Bob calculate the shared session key $K = g^{r_A \cdot r_B} \bmod n$. Finally, Alice proves that she knows P itself, and not just P', by sending

   $E_K(S_P(K))$

Bob, who knows both K and P', can decrypt and validate the signature. Only Alice could have sent this message, since only she knows P; an intruder who obtains a copy of Bob's password file can try guessing at P, but cannot otherwise sign the session key.

The A-EKE scheme does not work with the public-key variant of EKE, since in it one party chooses the session key and imposes it on the other. This permits a man-in-the-middle attack by an attacker who has captured P'.

Applications of EKE

Bellovin and Merritt suggest using this protocol for secure public telephones [109]:

> Let us assume that encrypting public telephones are deployed. If someone wishes to use one of these phones, some sort of keying information must be provided. Conventional solutions . . . require that the caller possess a physical key. This is undesirable in many situations. EKE permits use of a short, keypad-entered password, but uses a much longer session key for the call.
>
> EKE would also be useful with cellular phones. Fraud has been a problem in the cellular industry; EKE can defend against it (and ensure the privacy of the call) by rendering a phone useless if a PIN has not been entered. Since the PIN is not stored within the phone, it is not possible to retrieve one from a stolen unit.

EKE's primary strength is that both symmetric and public-key cryptography work together in a manner that strengthens them both:

> From a general perspective, EKE functions as a *privacy amplifier*. That is, it can be used to strengthen comparatively weak symmetric and asymmetric systems

when used together. Consider, for example, the key size needed to maintain security when using exponential key exchange. As LaMacchia and Odlyzko have shown [934], even modulus sizes once believed to be safe (to wit, 192 bits) are vulnerable to an attack requiring only a few minutes of computer time. But their attack is not feasible if one must first guess a password before applying it.

Conversely, the difficulty of cracking exponential key exchange can be used to frustrate attempts at password-guessing. Password-guessing attacks are feasible because of how rapidly each guess may be verified. If performing such verification requires solving an exponential key exchange, the total time, if not the conceptual difficulty, increases dramatically.

EKE is patented [111].

22.6 FORTIFIED KEY NEGOTIATION

This scheme also protects key-negotiation schemes from poorly chosen passwords and man-in-the-middle attacks [47,983]. It uses a hash function of two variables that has a very special property: It has many collisions on the first variable while having effectively no collisions on the second variable.

$$H'(x, y) = H(H(k, x) \bmod 2^m, x),$$
where $H(k, x)$ is an ordinary hash function on k and x

Here's the protocol. Alice and Bob share a secret password, P, and have just exchanged a secret key, K, using Diffie-Hellman key exchange. They use P to check that their two session keys are the same (and that Eve is not attempting a man-in-the-middle attack), without giving P away to Eve.

(1) Alice sends Bob

$$H'(P, K)$$

(2) Bob computes $H'(P, K)$ and compares his result with what he received from Alice. If they match he sends Alice

$$H'(H(P, K))$$

(3) Alice computes $H'(H(P, K))$ and compares her result with what she received from Bob.

If Eve is trying a man-in-the-middle attack, she shares one key, K_1, with Alice, and another key, K_2, with Bob. To fool Bob in step (2), she has to figure out the shared password and then send Bob $H' * (P, K_2)$. With a normal hash function she can try common passwords until she guesses the correct one, and then successfully infiltrate the protocol. But with this hash function, many passwords are likely to produce the same value when hashed with K_1. So when she finds a match, she will probably have the wrong password, and hence Bob will not be fooled.

22.7 CONFERENCE KEY DISTRIBUTION AND SECRET BROADCASTING

Alice wants to broadcast a message, M, from a single transmitter. However, she doesn't want it to be intelligible by every listener. In fact, she only wants a select subset of listeners to be able to recover M. Everyone else should get nonsense.

Alice can share a different key (secret or public) with each listener. She encrypts the message in some random key, K. Then she encrypts a copy of K with each of the keys of her intended recipients. Finally, she broadcasts the encrypted message and then all of the encrypted Ks. Bob, who is listening, either tries to decrypt all the Ks with his secret key, looking for one that is correct, or, if Alice doesn't mind everyone knowing who her message is for, he looks for his name followed by an encrypted key. Multiple-key cryptography, previously discussed, also works.

Another method is suggested in [352]. First, each listener shares a secret key with Alice, one that is larger than any possible encrypted message. All of those keys should be pairwise prime. She encrypts the message in a random key, K. Then, she computes a single integer, R, such that R modulo a secret key is congruent to K when that secret key is supposed to decrypt the message, and R modulo a secret key is otherwise congruent to zero.

For example, if Alice wants the secret to be received by Bob, Carol, and Ellen, but not by Dave and Frank, she encrypts the message with K and then computes R such that

$$R \equiv K \pmod{K_B}$$
$$R \equiv K \pmod{K_C}$$
$$R \equiv 0 \pmod{K_D}$$
$$R \equiv K \pmod{K_E}$$
$$R \equiv 0 \pmod{K_F}$$

This is a straightforward algebra problem, one that Alice can solve easily. When listeners receive the broadcast, they compute the received key modulo their secret key. If they were intended to receive the message, they recover the key. Otherwise, they recover nothing.

Yet a third way, using a threshold scheme (see Section 3.7), is suggested in [141]. Like the others, every potential receiver gets a secret key. This key is a shadow in a yet-uncreated threshold scheme. Alice saves some secret keys for herself, adding some randomness to the system. Let's say there are k people out there.

Then, to broadcast M, Alice encrypts M with key K and does the following.

(1) Alice chooses a random number, j. This number serves to hide the number of recipients of the message. It doesn't have to be very large; it can be as small as 0.

(2) Alice creates a $(k + j + 1, 2k + j + 1)$ threshold scheme, with:

> K as the secret.
>
> The secret keys of the intended recipients as shadows.
>
> The secret keys of nonrecipients not as shadows.
>
> j randomly chosen shadows, not the same as any of the secret keys.

(3) Alice broadcasts $k + j$ randomly chosen shadows, none of which is any of the shadows listed in step (2).

(4) All listeners who receive the broadcast add their shadow to the $k + j$ shadows they received. If adding their shadow allows them to calculate the secret, then they have recovered the key. If it does not, then they haven't.

Another approach can be found in [885,886,1194]. For yet another approach, see [1000].

Conference Key Distribution

This protocol allows a group of n users to agree on a secret key using only insecure channels. The group shares two large primes, p and q, and a generator g the same size as q.

(1) User i, where i goes from 1 to n, chooses a random r_i less than q, and broadcasts

$$z_i = g^{r_i} \bmod p$$

(2) Every user verifies that $z_j{}^q \equiv 1 \pmod p$, for all i from 1 to n.

(3) User i broadcasts

$$x_i = (z_{i+1}/z_{i-1})^{r_i} \bmod p$$

(4) User i computes

$$K = (z_{i-1})^{nr_i} \star x_i{}^{n-1} \star x_{i+1}{}^{n-2} \star \ldots \star x_{i-2} \bmod p$$

All index computations in the above protocol—$i - 1$, $i - 2$, and $i + 1$—should be computed mod n. At the end of the protocol, all honest users have the same K. No one else gets anything. However, this protocol falls to a man-in-the-middle attack. Another protocol, not quite as pretty, is in [757].

Tatebayashi-Matsuzaki-Newman

This key distribution protocol is suitable for networks [1521]. Alice wants to generate a session key with Bob using Trent, the KDC. All parties know Trent's public key, n. Trent knows the two large primes that n factors to, and hence can easily take cube roots modulo n. A lot of the details are left out of the following protocol, but you get the idea.

(1) Alice chooses a random number, r_A, and sends Trent

$$r_A^3 \bmod n$$

(2) Trent tells Bob that someone wants to exchange a key with him.

(3) Bob chooses a random number, r_B, and sends Trent

$$r_B^3 \bmod n$$

(4) Trent uses his private key to recover r_A and r_B. He sends Alice

$$r_A \oplus r_B$$

(5) Alice calculates

$$(r_A \oplus r_B) \oplus r_A = r_B$$

She uses this r_B to communicate securely with Bob.

This protocol looks good, but it has a horrible flaw. Carol can listen in on step (3) and use that information, with the help of an unsuspecting Trent and another malicious user (Dave), to recover r_B [1472].

(1) Carol chooses a random number, r_C, and sends Trent

$$r_B^3 r_C^3 \bmod n$$

(2) Trent tells Dave that someone wants to exchange a key with him.

(3) Dave chooses a random number, r_D, and sends Trent

$$r_D^3 \bmod n$$

(4) Trent uses his private key to recover r_C and r_D. He sends Carol

$$(r_B r_C) \bmod n \oplus r_D$$

(5) Dave sends r_D to Carol.

(6) Carol uses r_C and r_D to recover r_B. She uses r_B to eavesdrop on Alice and Bob.

This is not good.

CHAPTER 23

Special Algorithms for Protocols

23.1 MULTIPLE-KEY PUBLIC-KEY CRYPTOGRAPHY

This is a generalization of RSA (see Section 19.3) [217,212]. The modulus, n, is the product of two primes, p and q. However, instead of choosing e and d such that $ed \equiv 1 \bmod ((p-1)(q-1))$, choose t keys, K_i, such that

$$K_1 \star K_2 \star \ldots \star K_t \equiv 1 \bmod ((p-1)(q-1))$$

Since

$$M^{K_1 \cdot K_2 \cdot \ldots \cdot K_t} = M$$

this is a multiple-key scheme as described in Section 3.5.

If, for example, there are five keys, a message encrypted with K_3 and K_5 can be decrypted with K_1, K_2, and K_4:

$$C = M^{K_3 \cdot K_5} \bmod n$$
$$M = C^{K_1 \cdot K_2 \cdot K_4} \bmod n$$

One use for this is multisignatures. Imagine a situation where both Alice and Bob have to sign a document for it to be valid. Use three keys: K_1, K_2, and K_3. The first two are issued one each to Alice and Bob, and the third is made public.

(1) First Alice signs M and sends it to Bob.

$$M' = M^{K_1} \bmod n$$

(2) Bob can recover M from M'.

$$M = M'^{K_2 \cdot K_3} \bmod n$$

(3) He can also add his signature.

$$M'' = M'^{K_2} \bmod n$$

(4) Anyone can verify the signature with K_3, the public key.

$$M = M''^{K_3} \bmod n$$

Note that a trusted party is needed to set this system up and distribute the keys to Alice and Bob. Another scheme with the same problem is [484]. Yet a third scheme is [695,830,700], but the effort in verification is proportional to the number of signers. Newer schemes [220,1200] based on zero-knowledge identification schemes solve both shortcomings of the previous systems.

23.2 SECRET-SHARING ALGORITHMS

Back in Section 3.7 I discussed the idea behind secret-sharing schemes. The four different algorithms that follow are all particular cases of a general theoretical framework [883].

LaGrange Interpolating Polynomial Scheme

Adi Shamir uses polynomial equations in a finite field to construct a threshold scheme [1414]. Choose a prime, p, which is both larger than the number of possible shadows and larger than the largest possible secret. To share a secret, generate an arbitrary polynomial of degree $m - 1$. For example, if you want to create a $(3,n)$-threshold scheme (three shadows are necessary to reconstruct M), generate a quadratic polynomial

$$(ax^2 + bx + M) \bmod p$$

where p is a random prime larger than any of the coefficients. The coefficients a and b are chosen randomly; they are kept secret and discarded after the shadows are handed out. M is the message. The prime must be made public.

The shadows are obtained by evaluating the polynomial at n different points:

$$k_i = F(x_i)$$

In other words, the first shadow could be the polynomial evaluated at $x = 1$, the second shadow could be the polynomial evaluated at $x = 2$, and so forth.

Since the quadratic polynomial has three unknown coefficients, a, b, and M, any three shadows can be used to create three equations. Two shadows cannot. One shadow cannot. Four or five shadows are redundant.

For example, let M be 11. To construct a $(3, 5)$-threshold scheme, where any three of five people can reconstruct M, first generate a quadratic equation (7 and 8 were chosen randomly):

$$F(x) = (7x^2 + 8x + 11) \bmod 13$$

The five shadows are:

$$k_1 = F(1) = 7 + 8 + 11 \equiv 0 \ (\bmod\ 13)$$
$$k_2 = F(2) = 28 + 16 + 11 \equiv 3 \ (\bmod\ 13)$$
$$k_3 = F(3) = 63 + 24 + 11 \equiv 7 \ (\bmod\ 13)$$

$$k_4 = F(4) = 112 + 32 + 11 \equiv 12 \ (\text{mod } 13)$$
$$k_5 = F(5) = 175 + 40 + 11 \equiv 5 \ (\text{mod } 13)$$

To reconstruct M from three of the shadows, for example k_2, k_3, and k_5, solve the set of linear equations:

$$a * 2^2 + b * 2 + M \equiv 3 \ (\text{mod } 13)$$
$$a * 3^2 + b * 3 + M \equiv 7 \ (\text{mod } 13)$$
$$a * 5^2 + b * 5 + M \equiv 5 \ (\text{mod } 13)$$

The solution will be $a = 7$, $b = 8$, and $M = 11$. So M is recovered.

This sharing scheme can be easily implemented for larger numbers. If you want to divide the message into 30 equal parts such that any six can get together and reproduce the message, give each of the 30 people the evaluation of a polynomial of degree 6.

$$F(x) = (ax^6 + bx^5 + cx^4 + dx^3 + ex^2 + fx + M) \bmod p$$

Six people can solve for the six unknowns (including M); five people cannot learn anything about M.

The most mind-boggling aspect of secret sharing is that if the coefficients are picked randomly, five people with infinite computing power can't learn anything more than the length of the message (which each of them knows anyway). This is as secure as a one-time pad; an attempt at exhaustive search (that is, trying all possible sixth shadows) will reveal that any conceivable message could be the secret. This is true for all the secret-sharing schemes presented here.

Vector Scheme

George Blakley invented a scheme using points in space [182]. The message is defined as a point in m-dimensional space. Each shadow is the equation of an $(m - 1)$-dimensional hyperplane that includes the point. The intersection of any m of the hyperplanes exactly determines the point.

For example, if three shadows are required to reconstruct the message, then it is a point in three-dimensional space. Each shadow is a different plane. With one shadow, you know the point is somewhere on the plane. With two shadows, you know the point is somewhere on the line formed where the two planes intersect. With three shadows, you can determine the point exactly: the intersection of the three planes.

Asmuth-Bloom

This scheme uses prime numbers [65]. For an (m, n)-threshold scheme, choose a large prime, p, greater than M. Then choose n numbers less than p, $d_1, d_2, \ldots, d_n$, such that:

1. The d values are in increasing order; $d_i < d_{i + 1}$
2. Each d_i is relatively prime to every other d_i
3. $d_1 * d_2 * \ldots * d_m > p * d_{n - m + 2} * d_{n - m + 3} * \ldots * d_n$

To distribute the shadows, first choose a random value r and compute

$$M' = M + rp$$

The shadows, k_i, are

$$k_i = M' \bmod d_i$$

Any m shadows can get together and reconstruct M using the Chinese remainder theorem, but any $m - 1$ cannot. See [65] for details.

Karnin-Greene-Hellman

This scheme uses matrix multiplication [818]. Choose $n + 1$ m-dimensional vectors, $V_0, V_1, \ldots, V_n$, such that any possible $m * m$ matrix formed out of those vectors has rank m. The vector U is a row vector of dimension $m + 1$.

M is the matrix product $U \cdot V_0$. The shadows are the products $U \cdot V_i$, where i is a number from 1 to n.

Any m shadows can be used to solve the $m * m$ system of linear equations, where the unknowns are the coefficients of U. UV_0 can be computed from U. Any $m - 1$ shadows cannot solve the system of linear equations and therefore cannot recover the secret.

Advanced Threshold Schemes

The previous examples illustrate only the simplest threshold schemes: Divide a secret into n shadows such that any m can be used to recover the secret. These algorithms can be used to create far more complicated schemes. The following examples will use Shamir's algorithm, although any of the others will work.

To create a scheme in which one person is more important than another, give that person more shadows. If it takes five shadows to recreate a secret and one person has three shadows while everyone else has only one, then that person and two other people can recreate the secret. Without that person, it takes five to recreate the secret.

Two or more people could get multiple shadows. Each person could have a different number of shadows. No matter how the shadows are distributed, any m of them can be used to reconstruct the secret. Someone with $m - 1$ shadows, be it one person or a roomful of people, cannot do it.

In other types of schemes, imagine a scenario with two hostile delegations. You can share the secret so that two people from the 7 in Delegation A and 3 people from the 12 in Delegation B are required to reconstruct the secret. Make a polynomial of degree 3 that is the product of a linear expression and a quadratic expression. Give everyone from Delegation A a shadow that is the result of an evaluation of the linear equation; give everyone from Delegation B a shadow that is the evaluation of the quadratic equation.

Any two shadows from Delegation A can be used to reconstruct the linear equation, but no matter how many other shadows the group has, they cannot get any information about the secret. The same is true for Delegation B: They can get three shadows together to reconstruct the quadratic equation, but they cannot get any more information necessary to reconstruct the secret. Only when the two delegations share their equations can they be multiplied to reconstruct the secret.

In general, any type of sharing scheme that can be imagined can be implemented. All you have to do is to envision a system of equations that corresponds to the particular scheme. Some excellent papers on generalized secret-sharing schemes are [1462,1463,1464].

Sharing a Secret with Cheaters

This algorithm modifies the standard (m, n)-threshold scheme to detect cheaters [1529]. I demonstrate this using the LaGrange scheme, although it works with the others as well.

Choose a prime, p, that is both larger than n and larger than

$$(s - 1) (m - 1)/e + m$$

where s is the largest possible secret and e is the probability of successful cheating. You can make e as small as you want; it just makes the computation more complex. Construct your shadows as before, except instead of using 1, 2, 3, . . . , n for x_i, choose random numbers between 1 and $p - 1$ for x_i.

Now, when Mallory sneaks into the secret reconstruction meeting with his false share, his share has a high probability of not being possible. An impossible secret is, of course, a fake secret. See [1529] for the math.

Unfortunately, while Mallory is exposed as a cheater, he still learns the secret (assuming that there are m other valid shares). Another protocol, from [1529,975], prevents that. The basic idea is to have a series of k secrets, such that none of the participants knows beforehand which is correct. Each secret is larger than the one before, except for the real secret. The participants combine their shadows to generate one secret after the other, until they create a secret that is less than the previous secret. That's the correct one.

This scheme will expose cheaters early, before the secret is generated. There are complications when the participants deliver their shadows one at a time; refer to the papers for details. Other papers on the detection and prevention of cheaters in threshold schemes are [355,114,270].

23.3   SUBLIMINAL CHANNEL

Ong-Schnorr-Shamir

This subliminal channel (see Section 4.2), designed by Gustavus Simmons [1458,1459,1460], uses the Ong-Schnorr-Shamir identification scheme (see Section 20.5). As in the original scheme, the sender (Alice) chooses a public modulus, n, and a private key, k, such that n and k are relatively prime. Unlike the original scheme, k is shared between Alice and Bob, the recipient of the subliminal message.

The public key is calculated:

$$h = -k^2 \bmod n$$

If Alice wants to send the subliminal message M by means of the innocuous message M', she first confirms that M' and n are relatively prime, and that M and n are relatively prime.

Alice calculates

$$S_1 = 1/2 * ((M'/M + M)) \bmod n$$
$$S_2 = k/2 * ((M'/M - M)) \bmod n$$

Together, the pair, S_1 and S_2, is the signature under the traditional Ong-Schnorr-Shamir scheme and the carrier of the subliminal message.

Walter the warden (remember him?) can authenticate the message as described by the Ong-Schnorr-Shamir signature scheme, but Bob can do better. He can authenticate the message (it is always possible that Walter can make his own messages). He confirms that

$$S_1{}^2 - S_2{}^2/k^2 \equiv M' \pmod n$$

If the message is authentic, the receiver can recover the subliminal message using this formula:

$$M = M'/(S_1 + S_2 k^{-1}) \bmod n$$

This works, but remember that the basic Ong-Schnorr-Shamir has been broken.

ElGamal

Simmons's second subliminal channel [1459], described in [1407,1473], is based on the ElGamal signature scheme (see Section 19.6).

Key generation is the same as the basic ElGamal signature scheme. First choose a prime, p, and two random numbers, g and r, such that both g and r are less than p. Then calculate

$$K = g^r \bmod p$$

The public key is K, g, and p. The private key is r. Besides Alice, Bob also knows r; it is the key that is used to send and read the subliminal message in addition to being the key used to sign the innocuous message.

To send a subliminal message M using the innocuous message M', M and p must be all relatively prime to each other, and M and $p - 1$ must be relatively prime. Alice calculates

$$X = g^M \bmod p$$

and solves the following equation for Y (using the extended Euclidean algorithm):

$$M' = rX + MY \bmod (p - 1)$$

As in the basic ElGamal scheme, the signature is the pair: X and Y.

Walter can verify the ElGamal signature. He confirms that

$$K^X X^Y \equiv g^{M'} \pmod p$$

Bob can recover the subliminal message. First he confirms that

$$(g^r)^X X^Y \equiv g^{M'} \pmod p$$

If it does, he accepts the message as genuine (not from Walter).

Then, to recover M, he computes

$$M = (Y^{-1}(M' - rX)) \bmod (p-1)$$

For example, let $p = 11$ and $g = 2$. The private key, r, is chosen to be 8. This means the public key, which Walter can use to verify the signature, is $g^r \bmod p = 2^8 \bmod 11 = 3$.

To send the subliminal message $M = 9$, using innocuous message $M' = 5$, Alice confirms that 9 and 11 are relatively prime and that 5 and 11 are relatively prime. She also confirms that 9 and $11 - 1 = 10$ are relatively prime. They are, so she calculates

$$X = g^M \bmod p = 2^9 \bmod 11 = 6$$

Then, she solves the following equation for Y:

$$5 = 8 \star 6 + 9 \star Y \bmod 10$$

$Y = 3$, so the signature is the pair, X and Y: 6 and 3.

Bob confirms that

$$(g^r)^X X^Y \equiv g^{M'} \pmod{p}$$
$$(2^8)^6 6^3 \equiv 2^5 \pmod{11}$$

It does (do the math yourself if you don't trust me), so he then recovers the subliminal message by calculating

$$M = (Y^{-1}(M' - rX)) \bmod (p-1) = 3^{-1}(5 - 8 \star 6) \bmod 10 = 7(7) \bmod 10 =$$
$49 \bmod 10 = 9$

ESIGN

A subliminal channel can be added to ESIGN [1460] (see Section 20.6).

In ESIGN, the secret key is a pair of large prime numbers, p and q, and the public key is $n = p^2 q$. With a subliminal channel, the private key is three primes, p, q, and r, and the public key is n, such that

$$n = p^2 q r$$

The variable, r, is the extra piece of information that Bob needs to read the subliminal message.

To sign a normal message, Alice first picks a random number, x, such that x is less than pqr and computes:

w, the least integer that is larger than $(H(m) - x^k \bmod n)/pqr$

$s = x + ((w/kx^{k-1}) \bmod p)pqr$

$H(m)$ is the hash of the message; k is a security parameter. The value s is the signature.

To verify the signature, Bob computes $s^k \bmod n$. He also computes a, which is the least integer larger than the number of bits of n divided by 3. If $H(m)$ is less than or equal to $s^k \bmod n$, and if $s^k \bmod n$ is less than $H(m) + 2^a$, then the signature is considered valid.

To send a subliminal message, M, using the innocuous message, M', Alice calculates s using M in place of $H(m)$. This means that the message must be smaller than p^2qr. She then chooses a random value, u, and calculates

$$x' = M' + ur$$

Then, use this x' value as the "random number" x to sign M'. This second s value is sent as a signature.

Walter can verify that s (the second s) is a valid signature of M'.

Bob can also authenticate the message in the same way. But, since he also knows r, he can calculate

$$s = x' + ypqr = M + ur + ypqr \equiv M \pmod{r}$$

This implementation of a subliminal channel is far better than the previous two. In the Ong-Schnorr-Shamir and ElGamal implementations, Bob has Alice's private key. Besides being able to read subliminal messages from Alice, Bob can impersonate Alice and sign normal documents. Alice can do nothing about this; she must trust Bob to set up this subliminal channel.

The ESIGN scheme doesn't suffer from this problem. Alice's private key is the set of three primes: p, q, and r. Bob's secret key is just r. He knows $n = p^2qr$, but to recover p and q he has to factor that number. If the primes are large enough, Bob has just as much trouble impersonating Alice as would Walter or anyone else.

DSA

There is also a subliminal channel in DSA (see Section 20.1) [1468,1469,1473]. In fact, there are several. The simplest subliminal channel involves the choice of k. It is supposed to be a 160-bit random number. However, if Alice chooses a particular k, then Bob, who also knows Alice's private key, can recover it. Alice can send Bob a 160-bit subliminal message in each DSA signature; everyone else simply verifies Alice's signature. Another complication: Since k should be random, Alice and Bob need to share a one-time pad and encrypt the subliminal message with the one-time pad to generate a k.

DSA has subliminal channels that do not require Bob to know Alice's private key. These also involve choosing particular values of k, but cannot be used to send 160 bits of information. This scheme, presented in [1468,1469], allows Alice and Bob to exchange one bit of subliminal information per signed message.

(1) Alice and Bob agree on a random prime, P (different from the parameter p in the signature scheme). This is their secret key for the subliminal channel.

(2) Alice signs an innocuous message, M. If she wants to send Bob the subliminal bit, 1, she makes sure the r parameter of the signature is a quadratic residue modulo P. If she wants to send him a 0, she makes sure the r parameter is a quadratic nonresidue modulo P. She does this by signing the message with random k values until she gets a signature with an r with the requisite property. Since quadratic residues and quadratic nonresidues are equally likely, this shouldn't be too difficult.

(3) Alice sends the signed message to Bob.

(4) Bob verifies the signature to make sure the message is authentic. Then he checks whether r is a quadratic residue or a quadratic nonresidue modulo P and recovers the subliminal bit.

Sending multiple bits via this method involves making r either a quadratic residue or a quadratic nonresidue modulo a variety of parameters. See [1468,1469] for details.

This scheme can be easily extended to send multiple subliminal bits per signature. If Alice and Bob agree on two random primes, P and Q, Alice can send two bits by choosing a random k such that r is either a quadratic residue mod P or a quadratic nonresidue mod P, and either a quadratic residue mod Q or a quadratic nonresidue mod Q. A random value of k has a 25 percent chance of producing an r of the correct form.

Here's how Mallory, an unscrupulous implementer of DSA, can have the algorithm leak 10 bits of Alice's private key every time she signs a document.

(1) Mallory puts his implementation of DSA in a tamperproof VLSI chip, so that no one can examine its inner workings. He creates a 14-bit subliminal channel in his implementation of DSA. That is, he chooses 14 random primes, and has the chip choose a value of k such that r is either a quadratic residue or a quadratic nonresidue modulo each of those 14 primes, depending on the subliminal message.

(2) Mallory distributes the chips to Alice, Bob, and everyone else who wants them.

(3) Alice signs a message normally, using her 160-bit private key, x.

(4) The chip randomly chooses a 10-bit block of x: the first 10 bits, the second 10 bits, and so on. Since there are 16 possible 10-bit blocks, a 4-bit number can identify which block it is. This 4-bit identifier, plus the 10 bits of the key, is the 14-bit subliminal message.

(5) The chip tries random values of k until it finds one that has the correct quadratic residue properties to send the subliminal message. The odds of a random k being of the correct form are 1 in 16,384. Assuming the chip can test 10,000 values of k per second, it will find one in less than two seconds. This computation does not involve the message and can be performed offline, before Alice wants to sign a message.

(6) The chip signs the message normally, using the value of k chosen in step (5).

(7) Alice sends the digital signature to Bob, or publishes it on the network, or whatever.

(8) Mallory recovers r and, because he knows the 14 primes, decrypts the subliminal message.

It's scary that even if Alice knows what is happening, she cannot prove it. As long as those 14 secret primes stay secret, Mallory is safe.

Foiling the DSA Subliminal Channel

The subliminal channel relies on the fact that Alice can choose k to transmit subliminal information. To foil the subliminal channel, Alice cannot be allowed to choose k. However, neither can anyone else; if someone else were allowed to choose k, it would allow that person to forge Alice's signature. The only solution is for Alice to jointly generate k with another party, call him Bob, in such a way that Alice cannot control a single bit of k and Bob cannot know a single bit of k. At the end of the protocol, Bob should be able to verify that Alice used the k that they jointly generated.

Here's the protocol [1470,1472,1473]:

(1) Alice chooses k' and sends Bob

$$u = g^{k'} \bmod p$$

(2) Bob chooses k'' and sends it to Alice.

(3) Alice calculates $k = k'k'' \bmod (p - 1)$. She uses k to sign her message, M, with the DSA and sends Bob the signature: r and s.

(4) Bob verifies that

$$((u^{k''} \bmod p) \bmod q) = r$$

If it does, he knows that k was used to sign M.

After step (4), Bob knows that no subliminal information can be embedded in r. If he is a trusted party, he can certify that Alice's signature is subliminal-free. Others will have to trust his certification; Bob cannot prove this fact to a third party with a transcript of the protocol.

A surprising result is that if Bob wants to, he can use this protocol to create his own subliminal channel. Bob can embed a subliminal message in one of Alice's signatures by choosing k'' with certain characteristics. When Simmons discovered this, he dubbed it the "Cuckoo's Channel." Details on how the Cuckoo's Channel works, and a three-pass protocol for generating k that prevents it, are discussed in [1471,1473].

Other Schemes

Any signature scheme can be converted into a subliminal channel [1458,1460, 1406]. A protocol for embedding a subliminal channel in the Fiat-Shamir and Feige-Fiat-Shamir protocols, as well as possible abuses of the subliminal channel, can be found in [485].

23.4 Undeniable Digital Signatures

This undeniable signature algorithm (see Section 4.3) is by David Chaum [343,327]. First, a large prime, p, and a primitive element, g, are made public, and used by a group of signers. Alice has a private key, x, and a public key, $g^x \bmod p$.

To sign a message, Alice computes $z = m^x \bmod p$. That's all she has to do. Verification is a little more complicated.

(1) Bob chooses two random numbers, a and b, both less than p, and sends Alice:

$$c = z^a(g^x)^b \bmod p$$

(2) Alice computes $t = x^{-1} \bmod (p-1)$, and sends Bob:

$$d = c^t \bmod p$$

(3) Bob confirms that

$$d \equiv m^a g^b \pmod p$$

If it is, he accepts the signature as genuine.

Imagine that Alice and Bob went through this protocol, and Bob is now convinced that Alice signed the message. Bob wants to convince Carol, so he shows her a transcript of the protocol. Dave, however, wants to convince Carol that some other person signed the document. He creates a fake transcript of the protocol. First he generates the message in step (1). Then in step (3) he generates d and the fake transmission from this other person in step (2). Finally, he creates the message in step (2). To Carol, both Bob's and Dave's transcripts are identical. She cannot be convinced of the signature's validity unless she goes through the protocol herself.

Of course, if she were watching over Bob's shoulder as he completed the protocol, she would be convinced. Carol has to see the steps done in order, just as Bob does.

There may be a problem with this signature scheme, but I know of no details. Please pay attention to the literature before you use it.

Another protocol not only has a confirmation protocol—Alice can convince Bob that her signature is valid—but it also has a disavowal protocol; Alice can use a zero-knowledge interactive protocol to convince him that the signature is not valid, if it is not [329].

Like the previous protocol, a group of signers use a shared public large prime, p, and a primitive element, g. Alice has a unique private key, x, and a public key, $g^x \bmod p$. To sign a message, Alice computes $z = m^x \bmod p$.

To verify a signature:

(1) Bob chooses two random numbers, a and b, both less than p, and sends Alice:

$$c = m^a g^b \bmod p$$

(2) Alice chooses a random number, q, less than p, and computes and sends to Bob:

$$s_1 = cg^q \bmod p, \; s_2 = (cg^q)^x \bmod p$$

(3) Bob sends Alice a and b, so that Alice can confirm that Bob did not cheat in step (1).

(4) Alice sends Bob q, so that Bob can use m^x and reconstruct s_1 and s_2. If

$$s_1 \equiv cg^q \pmod{p}$$
$$s_2 \equiv (g^x)^{b\,+\,q}z^a \pmod{p}$$

then the signature is valid.

Alice can also disavow a signature, z, for a message, m. See [329] for details.

Additional protocols for undeniable signatures can be found in [584,344]. Lein Harn and Shoubao Yang proposed a group undeniable signature scheme [700].

Convertible Undeniable Signatures

An algorithm for a **convertible undeniable signature**, which can be verified, disavowed, and also converted to a conventional digital signature is given in [213]. It's based on the ElGamal digital signature algorithm.

Like ElGamal, first choose two primes, p and q, such that q divides $p - 1$. Now you have to create a number, g, less than q. First choose a random number, h, between 2 and $p - 1$. Calculate

$$g = h^{(p\,-\,1)/q} \bmod p$$

If g equals the 1, choose another random h. If it doesn't, stick with the g you have.

The private keys are two different random numbers, x and z, both less than q. The public keys are p, q, g, y, and u, where

$$y = g^x \bmod p$$
$$u = g^z \bmod p$$

To compute the convertible undeniable signature of message m (which is actually the hash of a message), first choose a random number, t, between 1 and $q - 1$. Then compute

$$T = g^t \bmod p$$

and

$$m' = Ttzm \bmod q.$$

Now, compute the standard ElGamal signature on m'. Choose a random number, R, such that R is less than and relatively prime to $p - 1$. Then compute $r = g^R \bmod p$, and use the extended Euclidean algorithm to compute s, such that

$$m' \equiv rx + Rs \pmod{q}$$

The signature is the ElGamal signature (r, s), and T.

Here's how Alice verifies her signature to Bob:

(1) Bob generates two random numbers, a and b. He computes $c = T^{Tma}g^b \bmod p$ and sends that to Alice.

(2) Alice generates a random number, k, and computes $h_1 = cg^k \bmod p$, and $h_2 = h_1{}^z \bmod p$, and sends both of those numbers to Bob.

(3) Bob sends Alice a and b.

(4) Alice verifies that $c = T^{Tma}g^{b} \bmod p$. She sends k to Bob.

(5) Bob verifies that $h_1 = T^{Tma}g^{b + k} \bmod p$, and that $h_2 = y^{ta}r^{sa}u^{b + k} \bmod p$.

Alice can convert all of her undeniable signatures to normal signatures by publishing z. Now, anyone can verify her signature without her help.

Undeniable signature schemes can be combined with secret-sharing schemes to create **distributed convertible undeniable signatures** [1235]. Someone can sign a message, then distribute the ability to confirm that the signature is valid. He might, for example, require three out of five people to participate in the protocol in order to convince Bob that the signature is valid. Improvements on this notion deleted the requirement for a trusted dealer [700,1369].

23.5 DESIGNATED CONFIRMER SIGNATURES

Here's how Alice can sign a message and Bob can verify it, such that Carol can verify Alice's signature at some later time to Dave (see Section 4.4) [333].

First, a large prime, p, and a primitive element, g, are made public and used by a group of users. The product of two primes, n, is also public. Carol has a private key, z, and a public key is $h = g^x \bmod p$.

In this protocol Alice can sign m such that Bob is convinced that the signature is valid, but cannot convince a third party.

(1) Alice chooses a random x and computes

$$a = g^x \bmod p$$
$$b = h^x \bmod p$$

She computes the hash of m, $H(m)$, and the hash of a and b concatenated, $H(a,b)$. She then computes

$$j = (H(m) \oplus H(a, b))^{1/3} \bmod n$$

and sends a, b, and j to Bob.

(2) Bob chooses two random numbers, s and t, both less than p, and sends Alice

$$c = g^s h^t \bmod p$$

(3) Alice chooses a random q less than p, and sends Bob

$$d = g^q \bmod p$$
$$e = (cd)^x \bmod p$$

(4) Bob sends Alice s and t.

(5) Alice confirms that

$$g^s h^t \equiv c \ (\bmod \ p)$$

Then she sends Bob q.

(6) Bob confirms

$$d \equiv g^q \;(\text{mod } p)$$
$$e/a^q \equiv a^s b^t \;(\text{mod } p)$$
$$H(m) \oplus H(a, b) \equiv j^{1/3} \text{ mod } n$$

If they all check out, he accepts the signature as genuine.

Bob cannot use a transcript of this proof to convince Dave that the signature is genuine, but Dave can conduct a protocol with Alice's designated confirmer, Carol. Here's how Carol convinces Dave that a and b constitute a valid signature.

(1) Dave chooses a random u and v, both less than p, and sends Carol

$$k = g^u a^v \text{ mod } p$$

(2) Carol chooses a random w, less than p, and sends Dave

$$l = g^w \text{ mod } p$$
$$y = (kl)^z \text{ mod } p$$

(3) Dave sends Carol u and v.

(4) Carol confirms that

$$g^u a^v \equiv k \;(\text{mod } p)$$

Then she sends Dave w.

(5) Dave confirms that

$$g^w \equiv l \;(\text{mod } p)$$
$$y/h^w \equiv h^u b^v \;(\text{mod } p)$$

If they both check out, he accepts the signature as genuine.

In another protocol Carol can convert the designated-confirmer protocol into a conventional digital signature. See [333] for details.

23.6 COMPUTING WITH ENCRYPTED DATA

The Discrete Logarithm Problem

There is a large prime, p, and a generator, g. Alice has a particular value for x, and wants to know e, such that

$$g^e \equiv x \;(\text{mod } p)$$

This is a hard problem, and Alice lacks the computational power to compute the result. Bob has the power to solve the problem—he represents the government, or a large computing organization, or whatever. Here's how Bob can do it without Alice revealing x [547,4]:

(1) Alice chooses a random number, r, less than p.

(2) Alice computes

$$x' = xg^r \bmod p$$

(3) Alice asks Bob to solve

$$g^{e'} \equiv x' \pmod p$$

(5) Bob computes e' and sends it to Alice.

(6) Alice recovers e by computing

$$e = (e' - r) \bmod (p - 1)$$

Similar protocols for the quadratic residuosity problem and for the primitive root problem are in [3,4]. (See also Section 4.8.)

23.7 FAIR COIN FLIPS

The following protocols allow Alice and Bob to flip a fair coin over a data network (see Section 4.9) [194]. This is an example of flipping a coin into a well (see Section 4.10). At first, only Bob knows the result of the coin toss and tells it to Alice. Later, Alice may check to make sure that Bob told her the correct outcome of the toss.

Coin Flipping Using Square Roots

Coin-flip subprotocol:

(1) Alice chooses two large primes, p and q, and sends their product, n to Bob.

(2) Bob chooses a random positive integer, r, such that r is less than $n/2$. Bob computes

$$z = r^2 \bmod n$$

and sends z to Alice.

(3) Alice computes the four square roots of $z \pmod n$. She can do this because she knows the factorization of n. Let's call them $+x$, $-x$, $+y$, and $-y$. Call x' the smaller of these two numbers:

   $x \bmod n$

   $-x \bmod n$

Similarly, call y' the smaller of these two numbers:

   $y \bmod n$

   $-y \bmod n$

Note that r is equal either to x' or y'.

(4) Alice guesses whether $r = x'$ or $r = y'$, and sends her guess to Bob.

(5) If Alice's guess is correct, the result of the coin flip is heads. If Alice's guess is incorrect, the result of the coin flip is tails. Bob announces the result of the coin flip.

Verification subprotocol:

(6) Alice sends p and q to Bob.
(7) Bob computes x' and y' and sends them to Alice.
(8) Alice calculates r.

Alice has no way of knowing r, so her guess is real. She only tells Bob one bit of her guess in step (4) to prevent Bob from getting both x' and y'. If Bob has both of those numbers, he can change r after step (4).

Coin Flipping Using Exponentiation Modulo p

Exponentiation modulo a prime number, p, is used as a one-way function in this protocol [1306]:

Coin-flip subprotocol:

(1) Alice chooses a prime number, p, in such a way that the factorization of $p - 1$ is known and contains at least one large prime.
(2) Bob selects two primitive elements, h and t, in GF(p). He sends them to Alice.
(3) Alice checks that h and t are primitive and then chooses a random integer x, relatively prime to $p - 1$. She then computes one of the two values:

$$y = h^x \bmod p, \text{ or } y = t^x \bmod p$$

She sends y to Bob.

(4) Bob guesses whether Alice calculated y as a function of h or t, and sends his guess to Alice.
(5) If Bob's guess is correct, the result of the coin flip is heads. If Bob's guess is incorrect, the result of the coin flip is tails. Alice announces the result of the coin flip.

Verification subprotocol:

(6) Alice reveals x to Bob. Bob computes $h^x \bmod p$ and $t^x \bmod p$, to confirm that Alice has played fairly and to verify the result of the toss. He also checks that x and $p - 1$ are relatively prime.

For Alice to cheat, she has to know two integers, x and x', such that $h^x \equiv t^{x'} \pmod{p}$. If she knew those values, she would be able to calculate:

$$\log_t h = x'x^{-1} \bmod p - 1 \text{ and } \log_t h = x^{-1}x' \bmod p - 1$$

These are hard problems.

Alice would be able to do this if she knew $\log_t h$, but Bob chooses h and t in step (2). Alice has no other recourse except to try to compute the discrete logarithm. Alice could also attempt to cheat by choosing an x that is not relatively prime to $p - 1$, but Bob will detect that in step (6).

Bob can cheat if h and t are not primitive in GF(p), but Alice can easily check that after step (2) because she knows the prime factorization of $p - 1$.

One nice thing about this protocol is that if Alice and Bob want to flip multiple coins, they can use the same values for p, h, and t. Alice just generates a new x, and the protocol continues from step (3).

Coin Flipping Using Blum Integers

Blum integers can be used in a coin-flipping protocol.

(1) Alice generates a Blum integer, n, a random x relatively prime to n, $x_0 = x^2 \bmod n$, and $x_1 = x_0^2 \bmod n$. She sends n and x_1 to Bob.

(2) Bob guesses whether x_0 is even or odd.

(3) Alice sends x to Bob.

(4) Bob checks that n is a Blum integer (Alice would have to give Bob the factors of n and proofs of their primality, or execute some zero-knowledge protocol to convince him that n is a Blum integer), and he verifies that $x_0 = x^2 \bmod n$ and $x_1 = x_0^2 \bmod n$. If all this checks out, Bob wins the flip if he guessed correctly.

It is crucial that n be a Blum integer. Otherwise, Alice may be able to find an x'_0 such that $x'_0{}^2 \bmod n = x_0^2 \bmod n = x_1$, where x'_0 is also a quadratic residue. If x_0 were even and x'_0 were odd (or vice versa), Alice could freely cheat.

23.8 ONE-WAY ACCUMULATORS

There is a simple one-way accumulator function [116] (see Section 4.12):

$$A(x_i, y) = x_{i-1}{}^y \bmod n$$

The numbers n (n is the product of two primes) and x_0 must be agreed upon in advance. Then, the accumulation of y_1, y_2, and y_3 would be

$$((x_0^{y_1} \bmod n)^{y_2} \bmod n)^{y_3} \bmod n$$

This computation is independent of the order of y_1, y_2, and y_3.

23.9 ALL-OR-NOTHING DISCLOSURE OF SECRETS

This protocol allows multiple parties (at least two are required for the protocol to work) to buy individual secrets from a single seller (see Section 4.13) [1374,1175]. First, here's a definition. Take two bit strings, x and y. The **fixed bit index** (**FBI**) of x and y are the bits where the ith bit of x equals the ith bit of y.

For example:

$$x = 110101001011$$

$$y = 101010000110$$

FBI$(x, y) = \{1, 4, 5, 11\}$
(We're reading the bits from right to left, with the right-most bit as zero.)

Now, here's the protocol. Alice is the seller. Bob and Carol are buyers. Alice has k n-bit secrets: $S_1, S_2, \ldots, S_k$. Bob wants to buy secret S_b; Carol wants to buy secret S_c.

(1) Alice generates a public-key/private-key key pair and tells Bob (but not Carol) the public key. She generates another public-key/private-key key pair and tells Carol (but not Bob) the public key.

(2) Bob generates k n-bit random numbers, $B_1, B_2, \ldots, B_k$, and tells them to Carol. Carol generates k n-bit random numbers, $C_1, C_2, \ldots, C_k$, and tells them to Bob.

(3) Bob encrypts C_b (remember, S_b is the secret he wants to buy) with the public key from Alice. He computes the FBI of C_b and the result he just encrypted. He sends this FBI to Carol.

   Carol encrypts B_c (remember, S_c is the secret she wants to buy) with the public key from Alice. She computes the FBI of B_c and the result she just encrypted. She sends this FBI to Bob.

(4) Bob takes each of the n-bit numbers $B_1, B_2, \ldots, B_k$, and replaces every bit whose index is not in the FBI he received from Carol with its complement. He sends this new list of n-bit numbers, $B'_1, B'_2, \ldots, B'_k$, to Alice.

   Carol takes each of the n-bit numbers $C_1, C_2, \ldots, C_k$, and replaces every bit whose index is not in the FBI she received from Bob with its complement. She sends this new list of n-bit numbers, $C'_1, C'_2, \ldots, C'_k$, to Alice.

(5) Alice decrypts all C'_i with Bob's private key, giving her k n-bit numbers: $C''_1, C''_2, \ldots, C''_k$. She computes $S_i \oplus C''_i$, for $i = 1$ to k, and sends the results to Bob.

   Alice decrypts all B'_i with Carol's private key, giving her k n-bit numbers: $B''_1, B''_2, \ldots, B''_k$. She computes $S_i \oplus B''_i$, for $i = 1$ to k, and sends the results to Carol.

(6) Bob computes S_b by XORing C_b and the bth number he received from Alice.

   Carol computes S_c by XORing B_c and the cth number she received from Alice.

This is complicated. An example will go a long way to help.

Alice has the following eight 12-bit secrets for sale: $S_1 = 1990$, $S_2 = 471$, $S_3 = 3860$, $S_4 = 1487$, $S_5 = 2235$, $S_6 = 3751$, $S_7 = 2546$, and $S_8 = 4043$. Bob wants to buy S_7. Carol wants to buy S_2.

(1) Alice uses the RSA algorithm. The key pair she will use with Bob is: $n = 7387$, $e = 5145$, and $d = 777$. The key pair she will use with Carol is: $n = 2747$, $e = 1421$, and $d = 2261$. She tells Bob and Carol each their public key.

(2) Bob generates eight 12-bit random numbers, $B_1 = 743$, $B_2 = 1988$, $B_3 = 4001$, $B_4 = 2942$, $B_5 = 3421$, $B_6 = 2210$, $B_7 = 2306$, and $B_8 = 222$, and tells them to Carol. Carol generates eight 12-bit random numbers, $C_1 = 1708$, $C_2 = 711$, $C_3 = 1969$, $C_4 = 3112$, $C_5 = 4014$, $C_6 = 2308$, $C_7 = 2212$, and $C_8 = 222$, and tells them to Bob.

(3) Bob wants to buy S_7, so he encrypts C_7 with the public key that Alice gave him.

$$2212^{5145} \bmod 7387 = 5928$$

Now:

$$2212 = 0100010100100$$
$$5928 = 1011100101000$$

So, the FBI of those two numbers is {0, 1, 4, 5, 6}. He sends this to Carol.

Carol wants to buy S_2, so she encrypts B_2 with the public key that Alice gave her and computes the FBI of B_2 with the result of her encryption. She sends {0, 1, 2, 6, 9, 10} to Bob.

(4) Bob takes B_1, B_2, ..., B_8, and replaces every bit whose index is not in the set {0, 1, 2, 6, 9, 10} with its complement. For example:

$$B_2 = 111111000100 = 1988$$
$$B'_2 = 011001111100 = 1660$$

He sends B'_1, B'_2, ..., B'_8, to Alice.

Carol takes C_1, C_2, ..., C_8, and replaces every bit whose index is not in the set {0, 1, 4, 5, 6} with its complement. For example:

$$C_7 = 0100010100100 = 2212$$
$$C'_7 = 1011100101000 = 5928$$

She sends C'_1, C'_2, ..., C'_8, to Alice.

(5) Alice decrypts all C'_i with Bob's private key and XORs the results with S_i. For example, for $i = 7$:

$$5928^{777} \bmod 7387 = 2212; 2546 \oplus 2212 = 342$$

She sends the results to Bob.

Alice decrypts all B'_i with Carol's private key and XORs the results with S_i. For example, for $i = 2$:

$$1660^{2261} \ (\bmod \ 2747) = 1988; 471 \oplus 1988 = 1555$$

She sends the results to Carol.

(6) Bob computes S_7 by XORing C_7 and the seventh number he received from Alice:

$$2212 \oplus 342 = 2546$$

Carol computes S_2 by XORing B_2 and the second number she received from Alice.

$$1988 \oplus 1555 = 471$$

The protocol works for any number of buyers. If Bob, Carol, and Dave want to buy secrets, Alice gives each buyer two public keys, one for each of the others. Each buyer gets a set of numbers from each other buyer. Then, they complete the protocol with Alice for each of their sets of numbers and XOR all of their final results from Alice to get their secret. More details are in [1374,1175].

Unfortunately, a pair of dishonest parties can cheat. Alice and Carol, working together, can easily find out what secret Bob is getting: If they know the FBI of C_b and Bob's encryption algorithm, they can find b such that C_b has the right FBI. And Bob and Carol, working together, can easily get all the secrets from Alice.

If you assume honest parties, there's an easier protocol [389].

(1) Alice encrypts all of the secrets with RSA and sends them to Bob:

$$C_i = S_i^e \bmod n$$

(2) Bob chooses his secret C_b, picks a random r, and sends C' to Alice.

$$C' = C_b r^e \bmod n$$

(3) Alice sends Bob P'.

$$P' = C'^d \bmod n$$

(4) Bob calculates S_b.

$$S_b = P'r^{-1} \bmod n$$

If the parties may be dishonest, Bob can prove in zero-knowledge that he knows some r such that $C' = C_b r^e \bmod n$ and keep b secret until Alice gives him P' in step (3) [246].

23.10 FAIR AND FAILSAFE CRYPTOSYSTEMS

Fair Diffie-Hellman

Fair cryptosystems are a way to do key escrowing in software (see Section 4.14). This example is from Silvio Micali [1084,1085]. It is patented [1086,1087].

In the basic Diffie-Hellman scheme, a group of users share a prime, p, and a generator, g. Alice's private key is s, and her public key is $t = g^s \bmod p$.

Here's how to make Diffie-Hellman fair (this example uses five trustees).

(1) Alice chooses five integers, s_1, s_2, s_3, s_4, and s_5, each less than $p - 1$. Alice's private key is

$$s = (s_1 + s_2 + s_3 + s_4 + s_5) \bmod p - 1$$

and her public key is

$$t = g^s \bmod p$$

Alice also computes

$$t_i = g^{s_i} \bmod p, \text{ for } i = 1 \text{ to } 5$$

Alice's public shares are t_i, and her private shares are s_i.

(2)   Alice sends a private piece and corresponding public piece to each trustee. For example, she sends s_1 and t_1 to trustee 1. She sends t to the KDC.

(3)   Each trustee verifies that

$$t_i = g^{s_i} \bmod p$$

If it does, the trustee signs t_i and sends it to the KDC. The trustee stores s_i in a secure place.

(4)   After receiving all five public pieces, the KDC verifies that

$$t = (t_1 \star t_2 \star t_3 \star t_4 \star t_5) \bmod p$$

If it does, the KDC approves the public key.

At this point, the KDC knows that the trustees each have a valid piece, and that they can reconstruct the private key if required. However, neither the KDC nor any four of the trustees working together can reconstruct Alice's private key.

Micali's papers [1084,1085] also contain a procedure for making RSA fair and for combining a threshold scheme with the fair cryptosystem, so that m out of n trustees can reconstruct the private key.

Failsafe Diffie-Hellman

Like the previous protocol, a group of users share a prime, p, and a generator, g. Alice's private key is s, and her public key is $t = g^s \bmod p$.

(1)   The KDC chooses a random number, B, between 0 and $p - 2$, and commits to B using a bit-commitment protocol (see Section 4.9).

(2)   Alice chooses a random number, A, between 0 and $p - 2$. She sends $g^A \bmod p$ to the KDC.

(3)   The user "shares" A with each trustee using a verifiable secret-sharing scheme (see Section 3.7).

(4)   The KDC reveals B to Alice.

(5)   Alice verifies the commitment from step (1). Then she sets her public key as

$$t = (g^A)g^B \bmod p$$

She sets her private key as

$$s = (A + B) \bmod (p - 1)$$

The trustees can reconstruct A. Since the KDC knows B, this is enough to reconstruct s. And Alice cannot make use of any subliminal channels to send unauthorized information. This protocol, discussed in [946,833] is being patented.

23.11 ZERO-KNOWLEDGE PROOFS OF KNOWLEDGE

Zero-Knowledge Proof of a Discrete Logarithm

Peggy wants to prove to Victor that she knows an x that satisfies

$$A^x \equiv B \;(\mathrm{mod}\; p)$$

where p is a prime, and x is a random number relatively prime to $p - 1$. The numbers A, B, and p are public, and x is secret. Here's how Peggy can prove she knows x without revealing it (see Section 5.1) [338,337].

(1) Peggy generates t random numbers, $r_1, r_2, \ldots, r_t$, where all r_i are less than $p - 1$.

(2) Peggy computes $h_i = A^{r_i} \bmod p$, for all values of i, and sends them to Victor.

(3) Peggy and Victor engage in a coin-flipping protocol to generate t bits: b_1, $b_2, \ldots, b_t$.

(4) For all t bits, Peggy does one of the following:

    a) If $b_i = 0$, she sends Victor r_i

    b) If $b_i = 1$, she sends Victor $s_i = (r_i - r_j) \bmod (p - 1)$, where j is the lowest value for which $b_j = 1$

(5) For all t bits, Victor confirms one of the following:

    a) If $b_i = 0$, that $A^{r_i} \equiv h_i \;(\mathrm{mod}\; p)$

    b) If $b_i = 1$, that $A^{s_i} \equiv h_i h_j^{-1} \;(\mathrm{mod}\; p)$

(6) Peggy sends Victor Z, where

$$Z = (x - r_j) \bmod (p - 1)$$

(7) Victor confirms that

$$A^Z \equiv B h_j^{-1} \;(\mathrm{mod}\; p)$$

Peggy's probability of successfully cheating is 2^{-t}.

Zero-Knowledge Proof of the Ability to Break RSA

Alice knows Carol's private key. Maybe she has broken RSA; maybe she has broken into Carol's house and stolen the key. Alice wants to convince Bob that she knows Carol's key. However, she doesn't want to tell Bob the key or even decrypt one of Carol's messages for Bob. Here's a zero-knowledge protocol by which Alice convinces Bob that she knows Carol's private key [888].

Carol's public key is e, her private key is d, and the RSA modulus is n.

(1) Alice and Bob agree on a random k and an m such that

$$km \equiv e \ (\mathrm{mod}\ n)$$

They should choose the numbers randomly, using a coin-flip protocol to generate k and then computing m. If both k and m are greater than 3, the protocol continues. Otherwise, they choose again.

(2) Alice and Bob generate a random ciphertext, C. Again, they should use a coin-flip protocol.

(3) Alice, using Carol's private key, computes

$$M = C^d \ \mathrm{mod}\ n$$

She then computes

$$X = M^k \ \mathrm{mod}\ n$$

and sends X to Bob.

(4) Bob confirms that $X^m \ \mathrm{mod}\ n = C$. If it does, he believes Alice.

A similar protocol can be used to demonstrate the ability to break a discrete logarithm problem [888].

Zero-Knowledge Proof that n Is a Blum Integer

There are no known truly practical zero-knowledge proofs that $n = pq$, where p and q are primes congruent to 3 modulo 4. However, if you allow n to be of the form $p^r q^s$, where r and s are odd, then the properties which make Blum integers useful in cryptography still hold. And there exists a zero-knowledge proof that n is of that form.

Assume Alice knows the factorization of the Blum integer n, where n is of the form previously discussed. Here's how she can prove to Bob that n is of that form [660].

(1) Alice sends Bob a number u which has a Jacobi symbol -1 modulo n.

(2) Alice and Bob jointly agree on random bits: $b_1, b_2, \ldots, b_k$.

(3) Alice and Bob jointly agree on random numbers: $x_1, x_2, \ldots, x_k$.

(4) For each $i = 1, 2, \ldots, k$, Alice sends Bob a square root modulo n, of one of the four numbers: $x_i, -x_i, ux_i, -ux_i$. The square root must have the Jacobi symbol b_i.

The odds of Alice successfully cheating are one in 2^k.

23.12   BLIND SIGNATURES

The notion of blind signatures (see Section 5.3) was invented by David Chaum [317,323], who also invented their first implementation [318]. It uses the RSA algorithm.

Bob has a public key, *e*, a private key, *d*, and a public modulus, *n*. Alice wants Bob to sign message *m* blindly.

(1) Alice chooses a random value, *k*, between 1 and *n*. Then she blinds *m* by computing

$$t = mk^e \bmod n$$

(2) Bob signs *t*

$$t^d = (mk^e)^d \bmod n$$

(3) Alice unblinds t^d by computing

$$s = t^d/k \bmod n$$

(4) And the result is

$$s = m^d \bmod n$$

This can easily be shown

$$t^d \equiv (mk^e)^d \equiv m^d k \pmod{n}, \text{ so } t^d/k = m^d k/k \equiv m^d \pmod{n}.$$

Chaum invented a family of more complicated blind signature algorithms in [320,324], called blind unanticipated signatures. These signatures are more complex in construction, but more flexible.

23.13   OBLIVIOUS TRANSFER

In this protocol by Michael Rabin [1286], Alice has a 50 percent chance of sending Bob two primes, *p*, and *q*. Alice will not know whether the transfer is successful. (See Section 5.5.) (This protocol can be used to send Bob any message with a 50 percent success rate if *p* and *q* reveal an RSA private key.)

(1) Alice sends Bob the product of the two primes: *n = pq*.
(2) Bob chooses a random *x* less than *n*, such that *x* is relatively prime to *n*. He sends Alice:

$$a = x^2 \bmod n$$

(3) Alice, knowing *p* and *q*, computes the four roots of *a*: *x*, *n − x*, *y*, and *n − y*. She chooses one of these roots at random and sends it to Bob.
(4) If Bob receives *y* or *n − y*, he can compute the greatest common divisor of *x + y* and *n*, which is either *p* or *q*. Then, of course, *n/p = q*.
    If Bob receives *x* or *n − x*, he can't compute anything.

This protocol may have a weakness: It might be the case that Bob can compute a number *a* such that given the square root of *a* you can calculate a factor of *n* all the time.

23.14   SECURE MULTIPARTY COMPUTATION

This protocol is from [1373]. Alice knows the integer i; Bob knows the integer j. Alice and Bob together wish to know whether $i \leq j$ or if $i > j$, but neither Alice nor Bob wish to reveal the integer each knows. This special case of secure multiparty computation (see Section 6.2) is sometimes known as **Yao's millionaire problem** [1627].

For this example, assume that i and j range from 1 to 100. Bob has a public key and a private key.

(1) Alice chooses a large random number, x, and encrypts it in Bob's public key.

$$c = E_B(x)$$

(2) Alice computes $c - i$ and sends the result to Bob.

(3) Bob computes the following 100 numbers:

$$y_u = D_B(c - i + u), \text{ for } 1 \leq u \leq 100$$

D_B is the decryption algorithm with Bob's private key.

He chooses a large random prime, p. (The size of p should be somewhat smaller than x. Bob doesn't know x, but Alice could easily tell him the size of x.) He then computes the following 100 numbers:

$$z_u = (y_u \bmod p), \text{ for } 1 \leq u \leq 100$$

He then verifies that, for all $u \neq v$

$$|z_u - z_v| \geq 2$$

and that for all u

$$0 < z_u < p - 1$$

If this is not true, Bob chooses another prime and tries again.

(4) Bob sends Alice this sequence of numbers in this exact order:

$$z_1, z_2, \ldots, z_j, z_{j+1} + 1, z_{j+2} + 1, \ldots, z_{100} + 1, p$$

(5) Alice checks whether the ith number in the sequence is congruent to $x \bmod p$. If it is, she concludes that $i \leq j$. If it is not, she concludes that $i > j$.

(6) Alice tells Bob the conclusion.

All the verification that Bob goes through in step (3) is to guarantee that no number appears twice in the sequence generated in step (4). Otherwise, if $z_a = z_b$, Alice knows that $a \leq j < b$.

The one drawback to this protocol is that Alice learns the result of the computation before Bob does. Nothing stops her from completing the protocol up to step (5) and then refusing to tell Bob the results in step (6). She could even lie to Bob in step (6).

Example of the Protocol

Assume they're using RSA. Bob's public key is 7 and his private key is 23; $n = 55$. Alice's secret value, i, is 4; Bob's secret value, j, is 2. (Assume that only the values 1, 2, 3, and 4 are possible for i and j.)

(1) Alice chooses $x = 39$, and $c = E_B(39) = 19$.

(2) Alice computes $c - i = 19 - 4 = 15$. She sends 15 to Bob.

(3) Bob computes the following 4 numbers:

$$y_1 = D_B(15 + 1) = 26$$
$$y_2 = D_B(15 + 2) = 18$$
$$y_3 = D_B(15 + 3) = 2$$
$$y_4 = D_B(15 + 4) = 39$$

He chooses $p = 31$ and calculates:

$$z_1 = (26 \bmod 31) = 26$$
$$z_2 = (18 \bmod 31) = 18$$
$$z_3 = (2 \bmod 31) = 2$$
$$z_4 = (39 \bmod 31) = 8$$

He does all the verifications and confirms that the sequence is fine.

(4) Bob sends Alice this sequence of numbers in this exact order:

$$26, 18, 2 + 1, 8 + 1, 31 = 26, 18, 3, 9, 31$$

(5) Alice checks whether the 4th number in the sequence is congruent to $x \bmod p$. Since $9 \not\equiv 39 \pmod{31}$, then $i > j$.

(6) Alice tells Bob.

This protocol can be used to create far more complicated protocols. A group of people can conduct a secret auction over a computer network. They arrange themselves in a logical circle, and through individual pairwise comparisons, determine which is offering the highest price. In order to prevent people from changing their bids in mid-auction, some sort of bit-commitment protocol could also be used. If the auction is a Dutch auction, then the highest bidder gets the item for his highest price. If it is an English auction, then he gets the item for the second-highest price. (This can be determined by a second round of pairwise comparisons.) Similar ideas have applications in bargaining, negotiations, and arbitration.

23.15 PROBABILISTIC ENCRYPTION

The notion of **probabilistic encryption** was invented by Shafi Goldwasser and Silvio Micali [624]. Although its theory makes it the most secure cryptosystem invented, its early implementation was impractical [625]. More recent implementations have changed that.

The point behind probabilistic encryption is to eliminate any information leaked with public-key cryptography. Because a cryptanalyst can always encrypt random messages with a public key, he can get some information. Assuming he has ciphertext $C = E_K(M)$ and is trying to recover plaintext message M, he can pick a random message M' and encrypt it: $C' = E_K(M')$. If $C' = C$, then he guessed the correct plaintext. If it's wrong, he just guesses again.

Also, no partial information is leaked about the original message. With public-key cryptography, sometimes a cryptanalyst can learn things about the bits: The XOR of bits 5, 17, and 39 is 1, and so on. With probabilistic encryption, even this type of information remains hidden.

Not a whole lot of information is to be gained here, but there are potential problems with allowing a cryptanalyst to encrypt random messages with your public key. Some information is being leaked to the cryptanalyst every time he encrypts a message. No one really knows how much.

Probabilistic encryption tries to eliminate that leakage. The goal is that no computation on the ciphertext, or on any other trial plaintexts, can give the cryptanalyst any information about the corresponding plaintext.

In probabilistic encryption, the encrypting algorithm is probabilistic rather than deterministic. In other words, a large number of ciphertexts will decrypt to a given plaintext, and the particular ciphertext used in any given encryption is randomly chosen.

$$C_1 = E_K(M), \ C_2 = E_K(M), \ C_3 = E_K(M), \ \ldots, \ C_i = E_K(M)$$
$$M = D_K(C_1) = D_K(C_2) = D_K(C_3) = \ldots = D_K(C_i)$$

With probabilistic encryption, a cryptanalyst can no longer encrypt random plaintexts looking for the correct ciphertext. To illustrate, assume the cryptanalyst has ciphertext $C_i = E_K(M)$. Even if he guesses M correctly, when he encrypts $E_K(M)$, the result will be a completely different C: C_j. He cannot compare C_i and C_j, and so cannot know that he has guessed the message correctly.

This is amazingly cool stuff. Even if a cryptanalyst has the public encryption key, the plaintext, and the ciphertext, he cannot prove that the ciphertext is the encryption of the plaintext without the private decryption key. Even if he tries exhaustive search, he can only prove that every conceivable plaintext is a possible plaintext.

Under this scheme, the ciphertext will always be larger than the plaintext. You can't get around this; it's a result of the fact that many ciphertexts decrypt to the same plaintexts. The first probabilistic encryption scheme [625] resulted in a ciphertext so much larger than the plaintext that it was unusable.

However, Manual Blum and Goldwasser have an efficient implementation of probabilistic encryption using the Blum Blum Shub (BBS) random-bit generator described in Section 17.9 [199].

The BBS generator is based on the theory of quadratic residues. In English, there are two primes, p and q, that are congruent to 3 modulo 4. That's the private key. Their product, $pq = n$, is the public key. (Mind your ps and qs; the security of this scheme rests in the difficulty of factoring n.)

To encrypt a message, M, first choose some random x, relatively prime to n. Then compute

$$x_0 = x^2 \bmod n$$

Use x_0 as the seed of the BBS pseudo-random-bit generator and use the output of the generator as a stream cipher. XOR M, one bit at a time, with the output of the generator. The generator spits out bits b_i (the least-significant bit of x_i, where $x_i = x_{i-1}^2 \bmod n$), so

$$M = M_1, M_2, M_3, \ldots, M_t$$
$$C = M_1 \oplus b_1, M_2 \oplus b_2, M_3 \oplus b_3, \ldots, M_t \oplus b_t$$

where t is the length of the plaintext

Append the last computed value, x_t, to the end of the message and you're done.

The only way to decrypt this message is to recover x_0 and then set up the same BBS generator to XOR with the ciphertext. Because the BBS generator is secure to the left, the value x_t is of no use to the cryptanalyst. Only someone who knows p and q can decrypt the message.

In C, the algorithm to recover x_0 from x_t is:

```
int x0 (int p, int q, int n, int t, int xt)
{
    int a, b, u, v, w, z;

    /* we already know that gcd(p, q) == 1 */
    (void)extended_euclidian(p, q, &a, &b);
    u = modexp ((p+1)/4, t, p-1);
    v = modexp ((q+1)/4, t, q-1);
    w = modexp (xt%p, u, p);
    z = modexp (xt%q, v, q);
    return (b*q*w + a*p*z) % n;
}
```

Once you have x_0, decryption is easy. Just set up the BBS generator and XOR the output with the ciphertext.

You can make this scheme go even faster by using all the known secure bits of x_i, not just the least significant bit. With this improvement, Blum-Goldwasser probabilistic encryption is faster than RSA while leaking no partial information about the plaintext. You can also prove that the difficulty of breaking this scheme is the same as the difficulty of factoring n.

On the other hand, this scheme is totally insecure against a chosen-ciphertext attack. From the least significant bits of the right quadratic residues, it is possible to calculate the square root of any quadratic residue. If you can do this, then you can factor. For details, consult [1570,1571,35,36].

23.16 QUANTUM CRYPTOGRAPHY

Quantum cryptography taps the natural uncertainty of the quantum world. With it, you can create a communications channel where it is impossible to eavesdrop without disturbing the transmission. The laws of physics secure this quantum channel: even if the eavesdropper can do whatever he wants, even if the eavesdropper has unlimited computing power, even if **P** = **NP**. Charles Bennett, Gilles Brassard, Claude Crépeau, and others have expanded on this idea, describing quantum key distribution, quantum coin flipping, quantum bit commitment, quantum oblivious transfer, and quantum secure multiparty computation. Their work is described in [128,129,123,124,125,133,126,394,134,392,243,517,132,130,244,393,396]. The best overview of quantum cryptography can be found in [131]; [1651] is another good nontechnical overview. A complete bibliography of quantum cryptography is [237].

This would still be on the lunatic fringe of cryptography, but Bennett and Brassard actually went and built a working model of the thing [127,121,122]. Now we have *experimental* quantum cryptography.

So sit back, get yourself something to drink, and relax. I'm going to explain what this is all about.

According to quantum mechanics, particles don't actually exist in any single place. They exist in several places at once, with probabilities of being in different places if someone looks. However, it isn't until a scientist comes along and measures the particle that it "collapses" into a single location. But you can't measure every aspect (for example, position and velocity) of a particle at the same time. If you measure one of those two quantities, the very act of measuring it destroys any possibility of measuring the other quantity. The quantum world has a fundamental uncertainty and there's no way to avoid it.

That uncertainty can be used to generate a secret key. As they travel, photons vibrate in some direction; up and down, left to right, or more likely at some angle. Normal sunlight is unpolarized; the photons vibrate every which way. When a large group of photons vibrate in the same direction they are **polarized**. Polarization filters allow only photons that are polarized in a certain direction through; the rest are blocked. For example, a horizontal polarization filter only allows horizontally polarized photons through. Turn that filter 90 degrees, and only vertically polarized photons can come through.

Let's say you have a pulse of horizontally polarized photons. If they try to pass through a horizontally polarized filter, they all get through. Slowly turn that filter 90 degrees; the number of photons getting through gets smaller and smaller, until none get through. This is counterintuitive. You'd think that turning the filter just a little will block all the photons, since the photons are horizontally polarized. But in quantum mechanics, each particle has a probability of suddenly switching its polarization to match the filter. If the angle is a little bit off, it has a high probability. If the angle is 90 degrees off, it has zero probability. And if the angle is 45 degrees off, it has a 50 percent probability of passing through the filter.

Polarization can be measured in any **basis**: two directions at right angles. An example basis is rectilinear: horizontal and vertical. Another is diagonal: left-diagonal and right-diagonal. If a photon pulse is polarized in a given basis and you measure it in the same basis, you learn the polarization. If you measure it in the wrong basis, you get a random result. We're going to use this property to generate a secret key:

(1) Alice sends Bob a string of photon pulses. Each of the pulses is randomly polarized in one of four directions: horizontal, vertical, left-diagonal, and right-diagonal.

For example, Alice sends Bob:

| | / — — \ — | — /

(2) Bob has a polarization detector. He can set his detector to measure recti-linear polarization or he can set his detector to measure diagonal polariza-tion. He can't do both; quantum mechanics won't let him. Measuring one destroys any possibility of measuring the other. So, he sets his detectors at random, for example:

× + + × × + × + +

Now, when Bob sets his detector correctly, he will record the correct polar-ization. If he sets his detector to measure rectilinear polarization and the pulse is polarized rectilinearly, he will learn which way Alice polarized the photon. If he sets his detector to measure diagonal polarization and the pulse is polarized rectilinearly, he will get a random measurement. He won't know the difference. In this example, he might get the result:

/ | — \ / \ — / — |

(3) Bob tells Alice, over an insecure channel, what settings he used.

(4) Alice tells Bob which settings were correct. In our example, the detector was correctly set for pulses 2, 6, 7, and 9.

(5) Alice and Bob keep only those polarizations that were correctly measured. In our example, they keep:

* | * * * \ — * — *

Using a prearranged code, Alice and Bob each translate those polarization measurements into bits. For example, horizontal and left-diagonal might equal one, and vertical and right-diagonal might equal zero. In our exam-ple, they both have:

0 0 1 1

So, Alice and Bob have generated four bits. They can generate as many as they like using this system. On the average, Bob will guess the correct setting 50 percent of the time, so Alice has to send $2n$ photon pulses to generate n bits. They can use these bits as a secret key for a symmetric algorithm or they can guarantee perfect secrecy and generate enough bits for a one-time pad.

The really cool thing is that Eve cannot eavesdrop. Just like Bob, she has to guess which type of polarization to measure; and like Bob, half of her guesses will be wrong. Since wrong guesses change the polarization of the photons, she can't help introducing errors in the pulses as she eavesdrops. If she does, Alice and Bob will end up with different bit strings. So, Alice and Bob finish the protocol like this:

(6) Alice and Bob compare a few bits in their strings. If there are discrepancies, they know they are being bugged. If there are none, they discard the bits they used for comparison and use the rest.

Enhancements to this protocol allow Alice and Bob to use their bits even in the presence of Eve [133,134,192]. They could compare only the parity of subsets of the bits. Then, if no discrepancies are found, they only have to discard one bit of the subset. This detects eavesdropping with only a 50 percent probability, but if they do this with n different subsets Eve's probability of eavesdropping without detection is only 1 in 2^n.

There's no such thing as passive eavesdropping in the quantum world. If Eve tries to recover all the bits, she will necessarily disrupt the communications.

Bennett and Brassard built a working model of quantum key distribution and have exchanged secure bits on a laser table. The latest I heard, some folks at British Telecom were sending bits over a 10-kilometer fiber-optic link [276,1245,1533]. They figure 50 kilometers is feasible. The mind boggles.

PART IV

THE REAL WORLD

CHAPTER 24

Example Implementations

It's one thing to design protocols and algorithms, but another thing to field them in operational systems. In theory, theory and practice are the same; in practice they are different. Often ideas that look good on paper don't work in real life. Maybe the bandwidth requirements are too large; maybe the protocol is too slow. Chapter 10 discusses some of the issues related to using cryptography; this chapter gives examples of how it has been done in practice.

24.1 IBM SECRET-KEY MANAGEMENT PROTOCOL

In the late 1970s IBM developed a complete key management system for communications and file security on a computer network, using only symmetric cryptography [515,1027]. This protocol is less important in the actual mechanisms and more in its overall philosophy: By automating the generation, distribution, installation, storage, changing, and destruction of keys, the protocol went a long way to ensure the security of the underlying cryptographic algorithms.

This protocol provides three things: secure communications between a server and several terminals, secure file storage at the server, and secure communication among servers. The protocol doesn't really provide for direct terminal-to-terminal communication, although it can be modified to do that.

Each server on the network is attached to a cryptographic facility, which does all of the encrypting and decrypting. Each server has a **Master Key**, KM_0, and two variants, KM_1 and KM_2, both of which are simple variants of KM_0. These keys are used to encrypt other keys and to generate new keys. Each terminal has a **Master Terminal Key**, KMT, which is used to exchange keys with other terminals.

The servers store KMT, encrypted with KM_1. All other keys, such as those used to encrypt files of keys (called KNF), are stored in encrypted form under KM_2. The master key, KM_0, is stored in some nonvolatile security module. Today that could be either a ROM key or a magnetic card, or it could be typed in by the user (probably as a text string and then key crunched). KM_1 and KM_2 are not stored anywhere in the system, but are computed from KM_0 whenever they are needed. Session keys, for communication among servers, are generated with a pseudo-random process in the server. Keys to encrypt files for storage (KNF) are generated in the same manner.

The heart of the protocol is a tamper-resistant module, called a **cryptographic facility**. At both the server and the terminal, all encryption and decryption takes place within this facility. The most important keys, those used to generate the actual encryption keys, are stored in this module. These keys can never be read once they are stored. And they are tagged by use: A key dedicated for one purpose cannot accidentally be used for another. This concept of **key control vectors** is probably the most significant contribution of this system. Donald Davies and William Price discuss this key management protocol in detail [435].

A Variation

A variation on this scheme of master and session keys can be found in [1478]. It's built around network nodes with key notarization facilities that serve local terminals. It is designed to:

— Secure two-way communication between any two terminal users.
— Secure communications using encrypted mail.
— Provide personal file protection.
— Provide a digital signature capability.

For communication and file transfer among users, the scheme uses keys generated in the key notarization facility and sent to the users encrypted under a master key. The identities of the users are incorporated with the key, to provide evidence that the session key has been used between a particular pair of users. This **key notarization** feature is central to the system. Although the system does not use public-key cryptography, it has a digital-signature-like capability: A key could have only come from a particular source and could only be read at a particular destination.

24.2 MITRENET

One of the earliest implementations of public-key cryptography was the experimental system MEMO (MITRE Encrypted Mail Office). MITRE is a DoD contractor, a government think tank, and an all-around bunch of smart guys. MEMO was a secure electronic mail system for users in the MITRENET network, using public-key cryptography for key exchange and DES for file encryption.

In the MEMO system, all public keys are stored in a Public Key Distribution Center, which is a separate node on the network. They are stored in an EPROM to prevent anyone from changing them. Private keys are generated by users or by the system.

For a user to send secure messages, the system first establishes a secure communications path with the Public Key Distribution Center. The user requests a file of all public keys from the Center. If the user passes an identification test using his private key, the Center sends this list to the user's workstation. The list is encrypted using DES to ensure file integrity.

The implementation uses DES to encrypt messages. The system generates a random DES key for file encryption; the user encrypts the file with the DES key and encrypts the DES key with the recipient's public key. Both the DES-encrypted file and the public-key-encrypted key are sent to the recipient.

MEMO makes no provision for lost keys. There is some provision for integrity checking of the messages, using checksums. No authentication is built into the system.

The particular public-key implementation used for this system—Diffie-Hellman key exchange over $GF(2^{127})$—was proven insecure before the system was implemented (see Section 11.6), although it is easy to modify the system to use larger numbers. MEMO was intended mainly for experimental purposes and was never made operational on the real MITRENET system.

24.3 ISDN

Bell-Northern Research developed a prototype secure Integrated Services Digital Network (ISDN) telephone terminal [499,1192,493,500]. As a telephone, it was never developed beyond prototype. The resulting product was the Packet Data Security Overlay. The terminal uses Diffie-Hellman key exchange, RSA digital signatures, and DES data encryption; it can transmit and receive voice and data at 64 kilobits per second.

Keys

A long-term public-key/private-key key pair is embedded in the phone. The private key is stored in a tamper-resistant area of the phone. The public key serves as the identification of the phone. These keys are part of the phone itself and cannot be altered in any way.

Additionally, two other public keys are stored in the phone. One of these keys is the owner's public key. This key is used to authenticate commands from the owner and can be changed via a command signed by the owner. In this way an owner can transfer ownership of the phone to someone else.

The public key of the network is also stored in the phone. This key is used to authenticate commands from the network's key management facility and to authenticate calls from other users on the network. This key can also be changed via a signed command from the owner. This permits the owner to move his phone from one network to another.

These keys are considered long-term keys: rarely, if ever, changed. A short-term public-key/private-key key pair is also stored on the phone. These are encapsulated in a certificate signed by the key management facility. When two phones set up a call, they exchange certificates. The public key of the network authenticates these certificates.

This exchange and verification of certificates only sets up a secure call from phone to phone. To set up a secure call from person to person, the protocol has an additional piece. The owner's private key is stored on a hardware **ignition key**, which is inserted into the telephone by the owner. This ignition key contains the owner's private key, encrypted under a secret password known only by the owner (not by the phone, not by the network's key management facility, not by anybody). It also contains a certificate signed by the network's key management facility that contains the owner's public key and some identifying information (name, company, job title, security clearance, favorite pizza toppings, sexual preference, or whatever). This is also encrypted. To decrypt this information and enter it into the phone, the owner types his secret password on the phone's keypad. After the phone uses this information to set up calls, it is erased after the owner removes his ignition key.

The phone also stores a set of certificates from the network's key management facility. These certificates authorize particular users to use particular phones.

Calling

A call from Alice to Bob works as follows.

(1) Alice inserts her ignition key into the phone and enters her password.

(2) The phone interrogates the ignition key to determine Alice's identity and gives Alice a dial tone.

(3) The phone checks its set of certificates to ensure that Alice is authorized to use the particular phone.

(4) Alice dials the number; the phone places the call.

(5) The two telephones use a public-key cryptography key-exchange protocol to generate a unique and random session key. All subsequent protocol steps are encrypted using this key.

(6) Alice's phone transmits its certificate and user authentication.

(7) Bob's phone authenticates the signatures on both the certificate and the user authentication using the network's public key.

(8) Bob's phone initiates a challenge-and-reply sequence. It demands real-time signed responses to time-dependent challenges. (This prevents an adversary from using certificates copied from a previous exchange.) One response must be signed by Alice's phone's private key; another must be signed by Alice's private key.

(9) Bob's phone rings, unless he is already on the phone.

(10) If Bob is home, he inserts his ignition key into the phone. His phone interrogates the ignition key and checks Bob's certificate as in steps (2) and (3).

(11) Bob transmits his certificate and user authentication.

(12) Alice's phone authenticates Bob's signatures as in step (7), and initiates a challenge-and-reply sequence as in step (8).

(13) Both phones display the identity of the other user and phone on their displays.

(14) The secure conversation begins.

(15) When one party hangs up, the session key is deleted, as are the certificates Bob's phone received from Alice's phone and the certificates Alice's phone received from Bob's phone.

Each DES key is unique to each call. It exists only inside the two phones for the duration of the call and is destroyed immediately afterward. If an adversary captures one or both of the phones involved in the call, he will not be able to decrypt any previous call between the two phones.

24.4 STU-III

STU stands for "Secure Telephone Unit," an NSA-designed secure phone. The unit is about the size and shape of a conventional telephone, and can be used as such. The phones are also tamper-resistant, enough so that they are unclassified if unkeyed. They also have a data port and can be used to secure modem traffic as well as voice [1133].

Whitfield Diffie described the STU-III in [494]:

> To make a call with a STU-III, the caller first places an ordinary call to another STU-III, then inserts a key-shaped device containing a cryptographic variable and pushes a "go secure" button. After an approximately 15-second wait for cryptographic setup, each phone shows information about the identity and clearance of the other party on its display and the call can proceed.

> In an unprecedented move, Walter Deeley, NSA's deputy director for communications security, announced the STU-III or Future Secure Voice System in an exclusive interview given to *The New York Times* [282]. The objective of the new system was primarily to provide secure voice and low-speed data communications for the U.S. Defense Department and its contractors. The interview didn't say much about how it was going to work, but gradually the word began to leak out. The new system was using public key.

> The new approach to key management was reported early on [68] and one article spoke of phones being "reprogrammed once a year by secure telephone link," a turn of phrase strongly suggestive of a certificate passing protocol, similar to that described [in Section 24.3], that minimizes the need for phones to talk to the key management center. Recent reports have been more forthcoming, speaking of a key management system called FIREFLY that [1341] "evolved from public key

technology and is used to establish pair-wise traffic encryption keys." Both this description and testimony submitted to the U.S. Congress by Lee Neuwirth of Cylink [1164] suggest a combination of key exchange and certificates similar to that used in the ISDN secure phone and it is plausible that FIREFLY too is based on exponentiation.

STU-IIIs are manufactured by AT&T and GE. Somewhere between 300,000 and 400,000 have been fielded through 1994. A new version, the Secure Terminal Equipment (STE), will work on ISDN lines.

24.5 KERBEROS

Kerberos is a trusted third-party authentication protocol designed for TCP/IP networks. A Kerberos service, sitting on the network, acts as a trusted arbitrator. Kerberos provides secure network authentication, allowing a person to access different machines on the network. Kerberos is based on symmetric cryptography (DES as implemented, but other algorithms could be used instead). Kerberos shares a different secret key with every entity on the network and knowledge of that secret key equals proof of identity.

Kerberos was originally developed at MIT for Project Athena. The Kerberos model is based on Needham-Schroeder's trusted third-party protocol (see Section 3.3) [1159]. The original version of Kerberos, Version 4, is specified in [1094,1499]. (Versions 1 through 3 were internal development versions.) Version 5, modified from Version 4, is specified in [876,877,878]. The best overview of Kerberos is [1163]. Other survey articles are [1384,1493], and two good articles on using Kerberos in the real world are [781,782].

The Kerberos Model

The basic Kerberos protocol was outlined in Section 3.3. In the Kerberos model, there are entities—clients and servers—sitting on the network. Clients can be users, but can also be independent software programs that need to do things: download files, send messages, access databases, access printers, obtain administrative privileges, whatever.

Kerberos keeps a database of clients and their secret keys. For a human user, the secret key is an encrypted password. Network services requiring authentication, as well as clients who wish to use these services, register their secret key with Kerberos.

Because Kerberos knows everyone's secret key, it can create messages that convince one entity of another entity's identity. Kerberos also creates session keys which are given to a client and a server (or to two clients) and no one else. A session key is used to encrypt messages between the two parties, after which it is destroyed.

Kerberos uses DES for encryption. Kerberos Version 4 provided a nonstandard mode for authentication. This mode is weak: It fails to detect certain changes to the ciphertext (see Section 9.10). Kerberos Version 5 uses CBC mode.

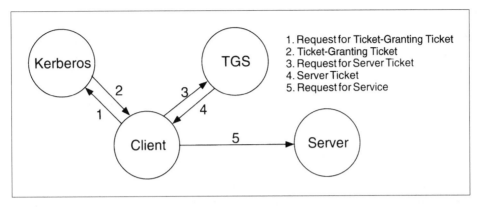

Figure 24.1   Kerberos authentication steps.

How Kerberos Works

This section discusses Kerberos Version 5. I will outline the differences between Version 4 and Version 5 further on. The Kerberos protocol is straightforward (see Figure 24.1). A client requests a ticket for a **Ticket-Granting Service (TGS)** from Kerberos. This ticket is sent to the client, encrypted in the client's secret key. To use a particular server, the client requests a ticket for that server from the TGS. Assuming everything is in order, the TGS sends the ticket back to the client. The client then presents this ticket to the server along with an authenticator. Again, if there's nothing wrong with the client's credentials, the server lets the client have access to the service.

Table 24.1
Kerberos Table of Abbreviations

c	= client
s	= server
a	= client's network address
v	= beginning and ending validity time for a ticket
t	= timestamp
K_x	= x's secret key
$K_{x, y}$	= session key for x and y
$\{m\}K_x$	= m encrypted in x's secret key
$T_{x, y}$	= x's ticket to use y
$A_{x, y}$	= authenticator from x to y

Credentials

Kerberos uses two types of credentials: **tickets** and **authenticators**. (The rest of this section uses the notation used in Kerberos documents—see Table 24.1.) A ticket is used to pass securely to the server the identity of the client for whom the ticket was issued. It also contains information that the server can use to ensure that the client using the ticket is the same client to whom the ticket was issued. An authenticator is an additional credential, presented with the ticket.

A Kerberos ticket takes this form:

$$T_{c,s} = s, \{c, a, v, K_{c,s}\}K_s$$

A ticket is good for a single server and a single client. It contains the client's name and network address, the server's name, a timestamp, and a session key. This information is encrypted with the server's secret key. Once the client gets this ticket, she can use it multiple times to access the server—until the ticket expires. The client cannot decrypt the ticket (she does not know the server's secret key), but she can present it to the server in its encrypted form. No one listening on the network can read or modify the ticket as it passes through the network.

A Kerberos authenticator takes this form:

$$A_{c,s} = \{c, t, key\}K_{c,s}$$

The client generates it every time she wishes to use a service on the server. The authenticator contains the client's name, a timestamp, and an optional additional session key, all encrypted with the session key shared between the client and the server. Unlike a ticket, it can only be used once. However, since the client can generate authenticators as needed (it knows the shared secret key), this is not a problem.

The authenticator serves two purposes. First, it contains some plaintext encrypted in the session key. This proves that it also knows the key. Just as important, the sealed plaintext includes the timestamp. An eavesdropper who records both the ticket and the authenticator can't replay them two days later.

Kerberos Version 5 Messages

Kerberos Version 5 has five messages (see Figure 24.1):

1. Client to Kerberos: c, tgs
2. Kerberos to client: $\{K_{c,tgs}\}K_c, \{T_{c,tgs}\}K_{tgs}$
3. Client to TGS: $\{A_{c,s}\}K_{c,tgs}, \{T_{c,tgs}\}K_{tgs}$
4. TGS to client: $\{K_{c,s}\}K_{c,tgs}, \{T_{c,s}\}K_s$
5. Client to server: $\{A_{c,s}\}K_{c,s}, \{T_{c,s}\}K_s$

These will now be discussed in detail.

Getting an Initial Ticket

The client has one piece of information that proves her identity: her password. Obviously we don't want her to send this password over the network. The Kerberos protocol minimizes the chance that this password will be compromised, while at the same time not allowing a user to properly authenticate herself unless she knows the password.

The client sends a message containing her name and the name of her TGS server to the Kerberos authentication server. (There can be many TGS servers.) In reality, the user probably just enters her name into the system and the login program sends the request.

The Kerberos authentication server looks up the client in his database. If the client is in the database, Kerberos generates a session key to be used between her and the TGS. This is called a **Ticket Granting Ticket** (**TGT**). Kerberos encrypts that session key with the client's secret key. Then it creates a TGT for the client to authenticate herself to the TGS, and encrypts that in the TGS's secret key. The authentication server sends both of these encrypted messages back to the client.

The client now decrypts the first message and retrieves the session key. The secret key is a one-way hash of her password, so a legitimate user will have no trouble doing this. If the user were an imposter, he would not know the correct password and therefore could not decrypt the response from the Kerberos authentication server. Access would be denied and he wouldn't be able to get the ticket or the session key.

The client saves the TGT and session key and erases the password and the one-way hash. This information is erased to reduce the chance of compromise. If an adversary manages to copy the client's memory, he will only get the TGT and the session key. These are valuable pieces of information, but only during the lifetime of the TGT. After the TGT expires, they will be worthless.

The client can now prove her identity to the TGS for the lifetime of the TGT.

Getting Server Tickets

A client has to obtain a separate ticket for each service she wants to use. The TGS grants tickets for individual servers.

When a client needs a ticket that she does not already have, she sends a request to the TGS. (In reality, the program would do this automatically, and it would be invisible to the user.)

The TGS, upon receiving the request, decrypts the TGT with his secret key. Then he uses the session key included in the TGT to decrypt the authenticator. Finally, he compares the information in the authenticator with the information in the ticket, the client's network address with the address the request was sent from, and the timestamp with the current time. If everything matches, he allows the request to proceed.

Checking timestamps assumes that all machines have synchronized clocks, at least to within several minutes. If the time in the request is too far in the future or the past, the TGS treats the request as an attempt to replay a previous request. The TGS should also keep track of all live authenticators, because past requests can have timestamps that are still valid. Another request with the same ticket and time-stamp as one already received can be ignored.

The TGS responds to a valid request by returning a valid ticket for the client to present to the server. The TGS also creates a new session key for the client and the server, encrypted with the session key shared by the client and the TGS. Both of these messages are then sent back to the client. The client decrypts the message and extracts the session key.

Requesting a Service

Now the client is ready to authenticate herself to the server. She creates a message very similar to the one sent to the TGS (which makes sense, since the TGS is a service).

The client creates an authenticator, consisting of her name and network address, and a timestamp, encrypted with the session key for her and the server that the TGS generated. The request consists of the ticket received from Kerberos (already encrypted with the server's secret key) and the encrypted authenticator.

The server decrypts and checks the ticket and the authenticator, as discussed previously, and also checks the client's address and the timestamp. If everything checks out, the server knows that, according to Kerberos, the client is who she says she is.

For applications that require mutual authentication, the server sends the client back a message consisting of the timestamp, encrypted with the session key. This proves that the server knew his secret key and could decrypt the ticket and therefore the authenticator.

The client and the server can encrypt future messages with the shared key, if desired. Since only they share this key, they both can assume that a recent message encrypted in that key originated with the other party.

Kerberos Version 4

The previous sections discussed Kerberos Version 5. In the messages and the construction of the tickets and authenticators, Version 4 is slightly different.

In Kerberos Version 4, the five messages looked like:

1. Client to Kerberos: c, tgs
2. Kerberos to client: $\{K_{c,\ tgs}, \{T_{c,\ tgs}\}K_{tgs}\}K_c$
3. Client to TGS: $\{A_{c,\ s}\}K_{c,\ tgs}, \{T_{c,\ tgs}\}K_{tgs}, s$
4. TGS to client: $\{K_{c,\ s}, \{T_{c,\ s}\}K_s\}K_{c,\ tgs}$
5. Client to server: $\{A_{c,\ s}\}K_{c,\ s}, \{T_{c,\ s}\}K_s$

$$T_{c,\ s} = \{s, c, a, v, l, K_{c,\ s}\}K_s$$
$$A_{c,\ s} = \{c, a, t\}K_{c,\ s}$$

Messages 1, 3, and 5 are identical. The double encryption of the ticket in steps 2 and 4 has been removed in Version 5. The Version 5 ticket adds the possibility of multiple addresses, and it replaces a "lifetime" field, *l*, with a beginning and ending time. The Version 5 authenticator adds the option of including an additional key.

Security of Kerberos

Steve Bellovin and Michael Merritt discussed several potential security vulnerabilities of Kerberos [108]. Although this paper was written about the Version 4 protocols, many of their comments also apply to Version 5.

It may be possible to cache and replay old authenticators. Although timestamps are supposed to prevent this, replays can be done during the lifetime of the ticket. Servers are supposed to store all valid tickets to prevent replays, but this is not always possible. And ticket lifetimes can be long; eight hours is typical.

Authenticators rely on the fact that all the clocks in the network are more or less synchronized. If a host can be fooled about the correct time, then an old authenticator can be replayed without any problem. Most network time protocols are insecure, so this can be a serious problem.

Kerberos is also vulnerable to password-guessing attacks. An intruder can collect tickets and then try to decrypt them. Remember that the average user doesn't usually choose good passwords. If Mallory collects enough tickets, his chances of recovering a password are good.

Perhaps the most serious attack involves malicious software. The Kerberos protocols rely on the fact that the Kerberos software is trustworthy. There's nothing to stop Mallory from surreptitiously replacing all client Kerberos software with a version that, in addition to completing the Kerberos protocols, records passwords. This is a problem with any cryptographic software package on an insecure computer, but the widespread use of Kerberos in these environments makes it a particularly tempting target.

Enhancements to Kerberos are in the works, including an implementation of public-key cryptography and a smart-card interface for key management.

Licenses

Kerberos is not in the public domain, but MIT's code is freely available. Actually implementing it into a working UNIX environment is another story. Several companies sell versions of Kerberos, but you can get a good version free from Cygnus Support, 814 University Ave., Palo Alto, CA, 94301; (415) 322-3811; fax: (415) 322-3270.

24.6   KryptoKnight

KryptoKnight (Kryptonite—get it?) is an authentication and key distribution system designed by IBM. It is a secret-key protocol and uses either DES in CBC mode (see Section 9.3) or a modified version of MD5 (see Section 18.5).

KryptoKnight supports four security services:

— User authentication (called single sign-on)
— Two-party authentication
— Key distribution
— Authentication of data origin and content

From a user's perspective, KryptoKnight is similar to Kerberos. Some differences are:

— KryptoKnight uses a hash function for authentication and encrypting tickets.
— KryptoKnight does not rely on synchronized clocks; it uses nonces for challenges (see Section 3.3).
— If Alice wishes to communicate with Bob, KryptoKnight has the option of allowing Alice to send a message to Bob and then for Bob to initiate the key exchange protocol.

KryptoKnight has tickets and authenticators, just like Kerberos. It has TGSs, but KryptoKnight calls them authentication servers. KryptoKnight's designers spent considerable effort minimizing the number of messages, lengths of messages, and amount of encryption. For further information on KryptoKnight, read [1110,173,174,175].

24.7 SESAME

SESAME stands for Secure European System for Applications in a Multivendor Environment. It's a European Community security project, 50 percent funded by RACE (see Section 25.7), whose primary objective is producing technology for user authentication with distributed access control. Think of it as kind of a European version of Kerberos. It's a two-part project: Stage one is a basic prototype of the architecture, and stage two is a set of commercial projects. The three companies with the greatest hand in development are ICL in the United Kingdom, Siemens in Germany, and Bull in France.

SESAME is an authentication and key-exchange system [361,1248,797,1043]. It uses the Needham-Schroeder protocol, with public-key cryptography to communicate between different security domains. The system is seriously flawed in several respects. Instead of using a real encryption algorithm, they use XOR with a 64-bit key size. Even worse, they use XOR in CBC mode, which leaves half the plaintext unencrypted. In their defense, they planned on using DES until the French government complained; they validated the code with DES but then removed it, and expect people to add it back. I am unimpressed nonetheless.

Authentication in SESAME is a function on the first block of a message, not on the entire message. This has the effect of authenticating "Dear Sir" and not the body of a letter. Key generation consists of two calls to the UNIX rand function, which isn't very random. SESAME uses crc32 and MD5 as one-way hash functions. And of course, SESAME is vulnerable to Kerberos-like password-guessing.

24.8   IBM COMMON CRYPTOGRAPHIC ARCHITECTURE

The Common Cryptographic Architecture (CCA) was designed and developed by IBM to provide cryptographic primitives for confidentiality, integrity, key management, and personal identification number (PIN) processing [751,784,1025,1026, 940,752]. Keys are managed by control vectors (CVs) (see Section 8.5). Every key has a CV XORed with it and is never separated from the vector unless inside secure hardware. The CV is a data structure providing an intuitive understanding of the privileges associated with a particular key.

The individual bits of the CV are defined to have specific meanings for using and handling each key managed by CCA. The CV is carried with the encrypted key in data structures called key tokens. Internal key tokens are used locally and contain keys encrypted under the local master key (MK). External key tokens are used to export and import encrypted keys between systems. Keys in external key tokens are encrypted under key-encrypting keys (KEK). The KEKs are managed in internal key tokens. Keys are separated according to their permitted uses.

Key length is also specified and enforced using bits in the CV. Single length keys are 56 bits and are used for such functions as privacy and message authentication. Double length keys are 112 bits and are used for key management, PIN functions, and other special uses. Keys can be required to be DOUBLE-ONLY in which both the left and right halves of the key must be different, DOUBLE in which the halves are permitted to be equal by chance, SINGLE-REPLICATED in which the left and right halves are equal, or SINGLE which contains only 56 bits. The CCA functions specify hardware enforcement of certain key types to be used for some operations.

The CV is checked in a secure hardware processor: It must conform to the permitted CCA rules for each CCA function. If the CV successfully passes the test requirements, a variant of the KEK or MK is obtained by the XOR of the KEK or MK with the CV, and the plaintext target key is recovered for use internally with the CCA function. When new keys are generated, the CV specifies the uses of the generated key. Those combinations of key types that could be used in attacking the system are not generated or imported into a CCA-compliant system.

CCA uses a combination of public-key cryptography and secret-key cryptography for key distribution. The KDC shares a secret master key with each user and encrypts session keys using that master key. Master keys are distributed using public-key cryptography.

The system's designers chose this hybrid approach for two reasons. The first is performance. Public-key cryptography is computationally intensive; if session keys are distributed using public-key cryptography, the system might bog down. The second is backwards compatibility; this system can be overlaid on existing secret-key schemes with minimal disruption.

CCA systems are designed to be interoperable. For systems that are non-CCA compliant, a Control Vector Translate (CVXLT) function permits keys to be passed between the two implementations. Initialization of the CVXLT function requires dual control. Two individuals must set up the required translation tables independently. Such dual control provides a high degree of assurance concerning the integrity and pedigree of any keys introduced into the system.

A key of type DATA is provided for compatibility with other systems. A DATA key is stored with a CV that identifies the key as a DATA key. DATA keys can have broad uses and as such must be regarded with suspicion and used with care. DATA keys may not be used for any key management functions.

The Commercial Data Masking Facility (CDMF) provides an exportable version of CCA. It has a special feature that reduces DES keys to an effective 40 bits for export (see Section 15.5) [785].

24.9 ISO Authentication Framework

Public-key cryptography has been recommended for use with the ISO authentication framework, also known as the X.509 protocols [304]. This framework provides for authentication across networks. Although no particular algorithms are specified for either security or authentication, the specification recommends RSA. There are

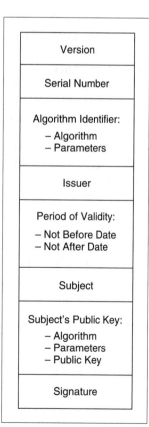

Figure 24.2   *An X.509 certificate.*

provisions, however, for multiple algorithms and hash functions. X.509 was initially issued in 1988. After public review and comment, it was revised in 1993 to correct some security problems [1100,750].

Certificates

The most important part of X.509 is its structure for public-key certificates. Each user has a distinct name. A trusted Certification Authority (CA) assigns a unique name to each user and issues a signed certificate containing the name and the user's public key. Figure 24.2 shows an X.509 certificate [304].

The version field identifies the certificate format. The serial number is unique within the CA. The next field identifies the algorithm used to sign the certificate, together with any necessary parameters. Issuer is the name of the CA. The period of validity is a pair of dates; the certificate is valid during the time period between the two. Subject is the name of the user. The subject's public key information includes the algorithm name, any necessary parameters, and the public key. The last field is the CA's signature.

If Alice wants to communicate with Bob, she first gets his certificate from a database. Then she verifies its authenticity. If both share the same CA, this is easy. Alice simply verifies the CA's signature on Bob's certificate.

If they use different CAs, it's more complicated. Think of a tree structure, with different CAs certifying other CAs and users. On the top is one master CA. Each CA has a certificate signed by the CA above it, and by the CAs below it. Alice uses these certificates to verify Bob's certificate.

Figure 24.3 illustrates this. Alice's certificate is certified by CA_A; Bob's is certified by CA_B. Alice knows CA_A's public key. CA_C has a certificate signed by CA_A, so Alice

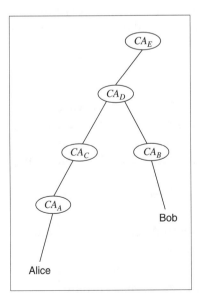

Figure 24.3   Sample certification hierarchy.

can verify that. CA_D has a certificate signed by CA_C. CA_B has a certificate signed by CA_D. And Bob's certificate is signed by CA_B. By moving up the certification tree to a common point, in this case CA_D, and then down to Bob, Alice can verify Bob's certificate.

Certificates can be stored on databases around the network. Users can send them to each other. When a certificate expires, it should be removed from any public directories. The issuing CA, however, should maintain a copy of the certificate. Should a dispute arise later, it will be required.

Certificates can also be revoked, either because the user's key has been compromised, the CA's key has been compromised, or because the CA no longer wants to certify the user. Each CA must maintain a list of all revoked but not expired certificates. When Alice receives a new certificate, she should check to see if it has been revoked. She can check a database of revoked keys on the network, but more likely she will check a locally cached list of revoked certificates. There are certainly possible abuses to this system; key revocation is probably its weakest part.

Authentication Protocols

Alice wants to communicate with Bob. First she goes to a database and obtains what is called a **certification path** from Alice to Bob, and Bob's public key. At this point Alice can initiate either a one-way, two-way, or three-way authentication protocol.

The one-way protocol is a single communication from Alice to Bob. It establishes the identities of both Alice and Bob and the integrity of any information communicated by Alice to Bob. It also prevents any replay attacks on the communication.

The two-way protocol adds a reply from Bob. It establishes that Bob, and not an imposter, sent the reply. It also establishes the secrecy of both communications and prevents replay attacks.

Both the one-way and two-way protocols use timestamps. A three-way protocol adds another message from Alice to Bob and obviates the need for timestamps (and therefore authenticated time).

The one-way protocol is:

(1) Alice generates a random number, R_A.

(2) Alice constructs a message, $M = (T_A, R_A, I_B, d)$, where T_A is Alice's timestamp, I_B is Bob's identity, and d is an arbitrary piece of data. The data may be encrypted with Bob's public key, E_B, for security.

(3) Alice sends $(C_A, D_A(M))$ to Bob. (C_A is Alice's certificate; D_A is Alice's private key.)

(4) Bob verifies C_A and obtains E_A. He makes sure these keys have not expired. (E_A is Alice's public key.)

(5) Bob uses E_A to decrypt $D_A(M)$. This verifies both Alice's signature and the integrity of the signed information.

(6) Bob checks the I_B in M for accuracy.

(7) Bob checks the T_A in M and confirms that the message is current.

(8) As an option, Bob can check R_A in M against a database of old random numbers to ensure the message is not an old one being replayed.

The two-way protocol consists of the one-way protocol and then a similar one-way protocol from Bob to Alice. After executing steps (1) through (8) of the one-way protocol, the two-way protocol continues with:

(9) Bob generates another random number, R_B.

(10) Bob constructs a message $M' = (T_B, R_B, I_A, R_A, d)$, where T_B is Bob's time-stamp, I_A is the identity of Alice and d is arbitrary data. The data may be encrypted with Alice's public key, E_A, for security. R_A is the random number Alice generated in step (1).

(11) Bob sends $D_B(M')$ to Alice.

(12) Alice uses E_B to decrypt $D_B(M')$. This verifies both Bob's signature and the integrity of the signed information.

(13) Alice checks the I_A in M' for accuracy.

(14) Alice checks the T_B in M' and confirms that the message is current.

(15) As an option, Alice can check the R_B in M' to ensure the message is not an old one being replayed.

The three-way protocol accomplishes the same thing as the two-way protocol, but without timestamps. Steps (1) through (15) are identical to the two-way protocol, with $T_A = T_B = 0$.

(16) Alice checks the received version of R_A against the R_A she sent to Bob in step (3).

(17) Alice sends $D_A(R_B)$ to Bob.

(18) Bob uses E_A to decrypt $D_A(R_B)$. This verifies both Alice's signature and the integrity of the signed information.

(19) Bob checks the received version of R_B against the R_B he sent to Alice in step (10).

24.10 PRIVACY-ENHANCED MAIL (PEM)

PEM is the Internet Privacy-Enhanced Mail standard, adopted by the Internet Architecture Board (IAB) to provide secure electronic mail over the Internet. It was initially designed by the Internet Research Task Force (IRTF) Privacy and Security Research Group (PSRG), and then handed over to the Internet Engineering Task Force (IETF) PEM Working Group. The PEM protocols provide for encryption, authentication, message integrity, and key management.

The complete PEM protocols were initially detailed in a series of RFCs (Requests for Comment) in [977] and then revised in [978]. The third iteration of the protocols [979,827,980] is summarized in [177,178]. The protocols were modified and improved, and the final protocols are detailed in another series of RFCs [981,825,76,802]. Another paper by Matthew Bishop [179] details the changes. Reports of attempts to implement PEM include [602,1505,1522,74,351,1366, 1367]. See also [1394].

PEM is an inclusive standard. The PEM procedures and protocols are intended to be compatible with a wide range of key-management approaches, including both symmetric and public-key schemes to encrypt data-encrypting keys. Symmetric cryptography is used for message-text encryption. Cryptographic hash algorithms are used for message integrity. Other documents support key-management mechanisms using public-key certificates; algorithms, modes, and associated identifiers; and paper and electronic format details and procedures for the key-management infrastructure to support these services.

PEM supports only certain algorithms, but allows for different suites of algorithms to be specified later. Messages are encrypted with DES in CBC mode. Authentication, provided by something called a **Message Integrity Check** (**MIC**), uses either MD2 or MD5. Symmetric key management can use either DES in ECB mode or triple-DES using two keys (called EDE mode). PEM also supports public-key certificates for key management, using the RSA algorithm (key length up to 1024 bits) and the X.509 standard for certificate structure.

PEM provides three privacy-enhancement services: confidentiality, authentication, and message integrity. No special processing requirements are imposed on the electronic mail system. PEM can be incorporated selectively, by site or by user, without affecting the rest of the network.

PEM Documents

The specifications for PEM come from four documents:

— RFC 1421: Part I, Message Encryption and Authentication Procedures. This document defines message encryption and authentication procedures in order to provide privacy-enhanced mail services for electronic mail transfer on the Internet.

— RFC 1422: Part II, Certificate-Based Key Management. This document defines a supporting key management architecture and infrastructure, based on public-key certificate techniques to provide keying information to message originators and recipients.

— RFC 1423: Part III, Algorithms, Modes, and Identifiers. This document provides definitions, formats, references, and citations for cryptographic algorithms, usage modes, and associated identifiers and parameters.

— RFC 1424: Part IV, Key Certification and Related Services. This document describes three types of service in support of PEM: key certification, certificate revocation list (CRL) storage, and CRL retrieval.

Certificates

PEM is compatible with the authentication framework described in [304]; see also [826]. PEM is a superset of X.509; it establishes procedures and conventions for a key-management infrastructure for use with PEM and with other protocols (from both the TCP/IP and OSI suites) in the future.

The key-management infrastructure establishes a single root for all Internet certification. The Internet Policy Registration Authority (IPRA) establishes global policies that apply to all certification under this hierarchy. Beneath the IPRA root are Policy Certification Authorities (PCAs), each of which establishes and publishes its policies for registering users or organizations. Each PCA is certified by the IPRA. Below PCAs, CAs certify users and subordinate organizational entities (such as departments, offices, subsidiaries). Initially, the majority of users are expected to be registered with some organization.

Some PCAs are expected to provide certification for users who wish to register independent of any organization. For users who wish anonymity while taking advantage of PEM privacy facilities, one or more PCAs are expected to be established with policies that allow for registration of users who do not wish to disclose their identities.

PEM Messages

PEM's heart is its message format. Figure 24.4 shows an encrypted message using symmetric key management, Figure 24.5 shows an authenticated and encrypted message using public-key key management, and Figure 24.6 shows an authenticated (but unencrypted) message using public-key key management.

The first field is "Proc-Type," and identifies the type of processing performed on the message. There are three possible types of messages. The "ENCRYPTED" spec-

```
       -----BEGIN PRIVACY-ENHANCED MESSAGE-----
       Proc-Type: 4,ENCRYPTED
       Content-Domain: RFC822
       DEK-Info: DES-CBC,F8143EDE5960C597
       Originator-ID-Symmetric: schneier@counterpane.com,,
       Recipient-ID-Symmetric: schneier@chinet.com,ptf-kmc,3
       Key-Info:
DES-ECB,RSA-MD2,9FD3AAD2F2691B9A,B70665BB9BF7CBCDA60195DB94F727D3
       Recipient-ID-Symmetric: pem-dev@tis.com,ptf-kmc,4
       Key-Info:
DES-ECB,RSA-MD2,161A3F75DC82EF26,E2EF532C65CBCFF79F83A2658132DB47
       LLrHBOeJzyhP+/fSStdW8okeEnv47jxe7SJ/iN72ohNcUk2jHEUSoH1nvNSIWL9M
       8tEjmF/zxB+bATMtPjCUWbz8Lr9wloXIkjHUlBLpvXROUrUzYbkNpkOagV2IzUpk
       J6UiRRGcDSvzrsoK+oNvqu6z7Xs5Xfz5rDquUcMlK1Z6720dcBWGGsDLpTpSCnpot
       dXd/H5LMDWnonNvPCwQUHt==
       -----END PRIVACY-ENHANCED MESSAGE-----
```

Figure 24.4   Example of an encapsulated message (symmetric case).

```
    -----BEGIN PRIVACY-ENHANCED MESSAGE-----
    Proc-Type: 4,ENCRYPTED
    Content-Domain: RFC822
    DEK-Info: DES-CBC,BFF968AA74691AC1
    Originator-Certificate:
MIIBlTCCAScCAWUwDQYJKoZIhvcNAQECBQAwUTELMAkGA1UEBhMCVVMxIDAeBgNV
BAoTF1JTQSBEYXRhIFNlY3VyaXR5LCBJbmMuMQ8wDQYDVQQLEwZCZXRhIDExDzAN
BgNVBAsTBk5PVEFSWTAeFw05MTA5MDQxODM4MTdaFw05MzA5MDMxODM4MTZaMEUx
CzAJBgNVBAYTAlVTMSAwHgYDVQQKExdSU0EgRGF0YSBTZWN1cml0eSwgSW5jLjEU
MBIGA1UEAxMLVGVzdCBVc2VyIDEwWTAKBgRVCAEBAgICAANLADBIAkEAwHZHl7i+
yJcqDtjJCowzTdBJrdAiLAnSC+CnnjOJELyuQiBgkGrgIh3j8/xOfM+YrsyFlu3F
LZPVtzlndhYFJQIDAQABMAOGCSqGSIb3DQEBAgUAA1kACKr0PqphJYwlj+YPtcIq
iWlFPuN5jJ79Khfg7ASFxskYkEMjRNZV/HZDZQEhtVaU7Jxfzs2wfX5byMp2X3U/
    5XUXGx7qusDgHQGs7Jk9W8CW1fuSWUgN4w==
    Key-Info: RSA,
I3rRIGXUGWAF8js5wCzRTkdhO34PTHdRZY9TuvmO3M+NM7fx6qc5udixps2LngO+
    wGrtiUm/ovtKdinz6ZQ/aQ==
    Issuer-Certificate:
MIIB3DCCAUgCAQowDQYJKoZIhvcNAQECBQAwTzELMAkGA1UEBhMCVVMxIDAeBgNV
BAoTF1JTQSBEYXRhIFNlY3VyaXR5LCBJbmMuMQ8wDQYDVQQLEwZCZXRhIDExDTAL
BgNVBAsTBFRMQOEwHhcNOTEwOTAxMDgwMDAwWhcNOTIwOTAxMDc1OTU5WjBRMQsw
CQYDVQQGEwJVUzEgMB4GA1UEChMXUlNBIERhdGEgU2VjdXJpdHksIEluYy4xDzAN
BgNVBAsTBkJldEGEgMTEPMAOGA1UECxMGTk9UQVJZMHAwCgYEVQgBAQICArwDYgAw
XwJYCsnp6lQCxYykNlODwutF/jMJ3kL+3PjYyHOwk+/9rLg6X65B/LD4bJHtO5XW
cqAz/7R7XhjYCmOPcqbdzoACZtIlETrKrcJiDYoP+DkZ8k1gCk7hQHpbIwIDAQAB
MAOGCSqGSIb3DQEBAgUAA38AAICPv4f9Gx/tY4+p+4DB7MV+tKZnvBoy8zgoMGOx
dD2jMZ/3HsyWKWgSFOeH/AJB3qr9zosG47pyMnTf3aSy2nBO7CMxpUWRBcXUpE+x
EREZd9++32ofGBIXaialnOgVUnOOzSYgugiQO77nJLDUjOhQehCizEs5wUJ35a5h
    MIC-Info: RSA-MD5,RSA,
UdFJR8u/TIGhfH65ieewe21OW4tooa3vZCvVNGBZirf/7nrgzWDABz8w9NsXSexv
    AjRFbHoNPzBuxwmOAFeAOHJszL4yBvhG
    Recipient-ID-Asymmetric:
MFExCzAJBgNVBAYTAlVTMSAwHgYDVQQKExdSU0EgRGF0YSBTZWN1cml0eSwgSW5j
    LjEPMAOGA1UECxMGQmVOYSAxMQ8wDQYDVQQLEwZOT1RBUlk=,
    66
    Key-Info: RSA,
O6BS1ww9CTyHPtS3bMLD+LOhejdvX6Qv1HK2ds2sQPEaXhX8EhvVphHYTjwekdWv
    7x0Z3Jx2vTAhOYHMcqqCjA==
qeWlj/YJ2Uf5ng9yznPbtDOmYloSwIuV9FRYx+gzY+8iXd/NQrXHfi6/MhPfPF3d
    jIqCJAxvld2xgqQimUzoS1a4r7kQQ5c/Iua4LqKeq3ciFzEv/MbZhA==
    -----END PRIVACY-ENHANCED MESSAGE-----
```

Figure 24.5   Example of an encapsulated ENCRYPTED message (asymmetric case).

ifier says that the message is encrypted and signed. The "MIC-ONLY" and "MIC-CLEAR" specifiers would indicate that the message is signed, but not encrypted. MIC-CLEAR messages are not encoded and can be read using non-PEM software. MIC-ONLY messages need PEM software to transform them to a human-readable form. A PEM message is always signed; it is optionally encrypted.

The next field, "Content-Domain," specifies the type of mail message. It has nothing to do with security. The "DEK-Info" field gives information on the **Data Exchange Key** (**DEK**), the encryption algorithm used to encrypt the text, and any parameters associated with the encryption algorithm. Only DES in CBC mode is currently specified, or "DES-CBC." The second subfield specifies the IV. Other algorithms may be specified by PEM in the future; their use will be noted in DEK-Info and in other fields that identify algorithms.

For messages with symmetric key management (see Figure 24.4), the next field is "Originator-ID-Symmetric" with three subfields. The first subfield identifies the sender by a unique electronic mail address. The second subfield is optional and identifies the authority that issued the interchange key. The third is an optional Version/Expiration subfield.

Continuing with the symmetric key-management case, each recipient has two fields: "Recipient-ID-Symmetric" and "Key-Info." The "Recipient-ID-Symmetric" field has three subfields; these identify the receiver in the same way that "Originator-ID-Symmetric" identified the sender.

The "Key-Info" field specifies the key-management parameters. This field has four subfields. The first subfield gives the algorithm used to encrypt the DEK. Since the key management in this message is symmetric, the sender and receiver have to share a common key. This is called the **Interchange Key** (**IK**), which is used to encrypt the DEK. The DEK can be either encrypted using DES in ECB (denoted by "DES-ECB") or triple-DES (which would be denoted "DES-EDE"). The second subfield specifies the MIC algorithm. It can be either MD2 (denoted by "RSA-MD2") or MD5 (which would be denoted "RSA-MD5"). The third subfield, the DEK, and the fourth field, the MIC, are both encrypted with the IK.

Figures 24.5 and 24.6 show messages with public-key key management (called "asymmetric" in PEM nomenclature). The headers are different. In ENCRYPTED messages, after the "DEK-Info" field comes the "Originator-Certificate" field. The certificate follows the X.509 standard (see Section 24.9). The next field is "Key-Info" with two subfields. The first subfield specifies the public-key algorithm used to encrypt the DEK; currently only RSA is supported. The next subfield is the DEK, encrypted in the originator's public key. This is an optional field, intended to permit the originator to decrypt his own message in the event that it is returned by the mail system. The next field "Issuer-Certificate," is the certificate of whomever signed the Originator-Certificate.

Continuing with the asymmetric key-management case, the next field is "MIC-Info." The first subfield gives the algorithm under which the MIC was computed. The second subfield shows the algorithm under which the MIC was signed. The third subfield consists of the MIC, signed by the sender's private key.

```
-----BEGIN PRIVACY-ENHANCED MESSAGE-----
Proc-Type: 4,MIC-ONLY
Content-Domain: RFC822
Originator-Certificate:
MIIB1TCCAScCAWUwDQYJKoZIhvcNAQECBQAwUTELMAkGA1UEBhMCVVMxIDAeBgNV
BAoTF1JTQSBEYXRhIFN1Y3VyaXR5LCBJbmMuMQ8wDQYDVQQLEwZCZXRhIDExDzAN
BgNVBAsTBk5PVEFSWTAeFw05MTA5MDQxODM4MTdaFw05MzA5MDMxODM4MTZaMEUx
CzAJBgNVBAYTA1VTMSAwHgYDVQQKExdSU0EgRGF0YSBTZWN1cm10eSwgSW5jLjEU
MBIGA1UEAxMLVGVzdCBVc2VyIDEwWTAKBgRVCAEBAgICAANLADBIAkEAwHZH17i+
yJcqDtjJCowzTdBJrdAiLAnSC+CnnjOJELyuQiBgkGrgIh3j8/xOfM+YrsyFlu3F
LZPVtzlndhYFJQIDAQABMAOGCSqGSIb3DQEBAgUAA1kACKrOPqphJYw1j+YPtcIq
iWlFPuN5jJ79Khfg7ASFxskYkEMjRNZV/HZDZQEhtVaU7Jxfzs2wfX5byMp2X3U/
5XUXGx7qusDgHQGs7Jk9W8CW1fuSWUgN4w==
Issuer-Certificate:
MIIB3DCCAUgCAQowDQYJKoZIhvcNAQECBQAwTzELMAkGA1UEBhMCVVMxIDAeBgNV
BAoTF1JTQSBEYXRhIFN1Y3VyaXR5LCBJbmMuMQ8wDQYDVQQLEwZCZXRhIDExDTAL
BgNVBAsTBFRMQQEwHhcNOTEwOTAxMDgwMDAwWhcNOTIwOTAxMDc1OTU5WjBRMQsw
CQYDVQQGEwJVUzEgMB4GA1UEChMXU1NBIERhdGEgU2VjdXJpdHksIEluYy4xDzAN
BgNVBAsTBkJldGEgMTEPMAOGA1UECxMGTk9UQVJZMHAwCgYEVQgBAQICArwDYgAw
XwJYCsnp61QCxYykN1ODwutF/jMJ3kL+3PjYyHOwk+/9rLg6X65B/LD4bJHtO5XW
cqAz/7R7XhjYCmOPcqbdzoACZtI1ETrKrcJiDYoP+DkZ8k1gCk7hQHpbIwIDAQAB
MAOGCSqGSIb3DQEBAgUAA38AAICPv4f9Gx/tY4+p+4DB7MV+tKZnvBoy8zgoMGOx
dD2jMZ/3HsyWKWgSFOeH/AJB3qr9zosG47pyMnTf3aSy2nBO7CMxpUWRBcXUpE+x
EREZd9++32ofGBIXaialnOgVUnOOzSYgugiQ077nJLDUjOhQehCizEs5wUJ35a5h
MIC-Info: RSA-MD5,RSA,
jV2OfH+nnXHU8bnL8kPAad/mSQ1TDZ1bVuxvZAOVRZ5q5+Ej15bQvqNeqOUNQjr6
EtE7K2QDeVMCyXsdJ1A8fA==
LSBBIG11c3NhZ2UgZm9yIHVzZSBpbiBOZXN0aW5nLgOKLSBGb2xsb3dpbmcaXMg
YSBibGFuayBsaW5lOgOKDQpUaGlzIG1zIHRoZSBlbmQuDQo=
-----END PRIVACY-ENHANCED MESSAGE-----
```

Figure 24.6   Example of an encapsulated MIC-ONLY message (asymmetric case).

Still continuing with asymmetric key management, the next fields deal with the recipients. There are two fields for each recipient: "Recipient-ID-Asymmetric" and "Key-Info." The "Recipient-ID-Asymmetric" field has two subfields. The first identifies the authority that issued the receiver's public key; the second is an optional Version/Expiration subfield. The "Key-Info" field specifies the key management parameters: The first subfield identifies the algorithm used to encrypt the message and the second subfield is the DEK encrypted with the receiver's public key.

Security of PEM

RSA keys in PEM can range from 508 bits to 1024 bits. This should be long enough for anyone's security needs. A more likely attack would be against the key-management protocols. Mallory could steal your private key—don't write it down anywhere—or attempt to fool you into accepting a bogus public key. The key certification provisions of PEM make this unlikely if everyone follows proper procedures, but people have been known to be sloppy.

A more insidious attack would be for Mallory to modify the PEM implementation running on your system. This modified implementation could surreptitiously send Mallory all of your mail, encrypted with his public key. It could even send him a copy of your private key. If the modified implementation works well, you will never know what is happening.

There's no real way to prevent this kind of attack. You could use a one-way hash function and fingerprint the PEM code. Then, each time you run it, you could check the fingerprint for modification. But Mallory could modify the fingerprint code at the same time he modifies the PEM code. You could fingerprint the fingerprint code, but Mallory could modify that as well. If Mallory can get access to your machine, he can subvert the security of PEM.

The moral is that you can never really trust a piece of software if you cannot trust the hardware it is running on. For most people, this kind of paranoia is unwarranted. For some, it is very real.

TIS/PEM

Trusted Information Systems, partially supported by the U.S. government Advanced Research Projects Agency, has designed and implemented a reference implementation of PEM (TIS/PEM). Developed for UNIX-based platforms, it has also been ported to VMS, DOS, and Windows.

Although the PEM specifications indicate a single certification hierarchy for use by the Internet, TIS/PEM supports the existence of multiple certification hierarchies. Sites may specify a set of certificates that are to be considered valid, including all certificates issued by them. A site need not join the Internet hierarchy in order to use TIS/PEM.

TIS/PEM is currently available to all U.S. and Canadian organizations and citizens upon request. It will be distributed in source code form. Interested parties should contact: Privacy-Enhanced Mail, Trusted Information Systems, Inc., 3060 Washington Road (Rte. 97), Glenwood, MD 21738; (301) 854-6889; fax: (301) 854-5363; Internet: pem-info@tis.com.

RIPEM

RIPEM is a program, written by Mark Riordan, that implements the PEM protocols. Although technically not public domain, the program is publicly available and can be used royalty-free for personal, noncommercial applications. A license for its use is included with the documentation.

The code cannot be exported. Of course, U.S. government laws don't apply outside the United States, and some people have ignored the export rules. RIPEM code is available on bulletin boards worldwide. Something called RIPEM/SIG, which only does digital signatures, is exportable.

At this writing, RIPEM is not a complete implementation of the PEM protocols; it does not implement certificates for authenticating keys.

Before writing RIPEM, Riordan wrote a similar program called RPEM. This was intended to be a public-domain electronic-mail encryption program. To try to avoid patent issues, Riordan used Rabin's algorithm (see Section 19.5). Public Key Partners claimed that their patents were broad enough to cover all of public-key cryptography and threatened to sue; Riordan stopped distributing the program.

RPEM isn't really used anymore. It is not compatible with RIPEM. Since RIPEM can be used with the full blessing of Public Key Partners, there is no reason to use RPEM instead.

24.11 MESSAGE SECURITY PROTOCOL (MSP)

The Message Security Protocol (MSP) is the military equivalent of PEM. It was developed by the NSA in the late 1980s under the Secure Data Network System (SDNS) program. It is an X.400-compatible application-level protocol for securing electronic mail. MSP will be used for signing and encrypting messages in the Department of Defense's planned Defense Message System (DMS) network.

The Preliminary Message Security Protocol (PMSP), to be used for "unclassified but sensitive" messages, is a version of MSP adapted for use with both X.400 and TCP/IP. This protocol is also called Mosaic.

Like PEM, MSP and PMSP software applications are flexible and designed to accommodate a variety of algorithms for security functions including signing, hashing, and encryption. PSMP will work with the Capstone chip (see Section 24.17).

24.12 PRETTY GOOD PRIVACY (PGP)

Pretty Good Privacy (PGP) is a freeware electronic-mail security program, originally designed by Philip Zimmermann [1652]. It uses IDEA for data encryption, RSA (with keys up to 2047 bits) for key management and digital signatures, and MD5 as a one-way hash function.

PGP's random public keys use a probabilistic primality tester, and get their initial seeds from measuring the user's keyboard latency while typing. PGP generates random IDEA keys using the method delineated in ANSI X9.17, Appendix C (see Section 8.1) [55], with IDEA as the symmetric algorithm instead of DES. PGP also encrypts the user's private key using a hashed pass phrase instead of a password.

PGP-encrypted messages have layered security. The only thing a cryptanalyst can learn about an encrypted message is who the recipient is, assuming he knows the recipient's key ID. Only after the recipient decrypts the message does he learn who signed the message, if it is signed. Contrast this approach with PEM, which leaves quite a bit of information about the sender, recipient, and message in the unencrypted header.

The most interesting aspect of PGP is its distributed approach to key management (see Section 8.12). There are no key certification authorities; PGP instead supports a "web of trust." Every user generates and distributes his own public key. Users sign each other's public keys, creating an interconnected community of PGP users.

For example, Alice might physically give her public key to Bob. Bob knows Alice, so he signs her public key. He then gives the signed key back to her and keeps a copy for himself. When Alice wants to communicate with Carol, Alice sends Carol a copy of the key Bob signed. Carol, who already has Bob's public key (she got it at some other time) and trusts Bob to certify other people's keys, verifies his signature on Alice's key and accepts it as valid. Bob has introduced Alice to Carol.

PGP does not specify a policy for establishing trust; users are free to decide who they trust and who they do not. PGP provides mechanisms for associating trust with public keys and for using trust. Each user keeps a collection of signed public keys in a file called a **public-key ring**. Each key in the ring has a key legitimacy field that indicates the degree to which the particular user trusts the validity of the key. The higher the trust level, the more the user believes the key is legitimate. A signature trust field measures how far the user trusts the signer to certify the public keys of other users. And finally, an owner trust field indicates the degree to which the particular user trusts the key's owner to sign other public keys; this field is set manually by the user. PGP continuously updates these fields as users supply new information.

Figure 24.7 shows how this model might look for a particular user, Alice. Alice's key is at the top, and the owner trust value is ultimate trust. Alice has signed Bob's, Carol's, Dave's, Ellen's, and Frank's keys. She trusts Bob and Carol to sign other people's public keys, and she partially trusts Dave and Ellen to sign other people's public keys. And she trusts Gail to sign other people's public keys, even though she has not signed Gail's key herself.

Two partially trusted signatures may be sufficient to certify a key. Alice believes that Kurt's key is legitimate because both Dave and Ellen have signed it. This is not automatic in PGP; Alice can set her own paranoia level.

Just because Alice believes a key to be valid, she does not have to trust it to sign other people's keys. She does not trust Frank to sign other people's public keys, even though she signed his key herself. And she does not trust Ivan's signature on Martin's key, or Kurt's signature on Nancy's key.

Owen's key doesn't fit into the web anywhere; perhaps Alice got it from a key server. PGP does not assume that the key is valid; Alice must either declare the key valid or decide to trust one of the key's signers.

Of course, nothing prevents Alice from using keys she does not trust. PGP's job is to alert Alice that the key is not trusted, not to prevent communications.

The weakest link of this whole system is key revocation: It is impossible to guarantee that no one will use a compromised key. If Alice's private key is stolen she can send out something called a **key revocation certificate**, but since key distribution is *ad hoc* and largely word of mouth there is no guarantee that it will reach

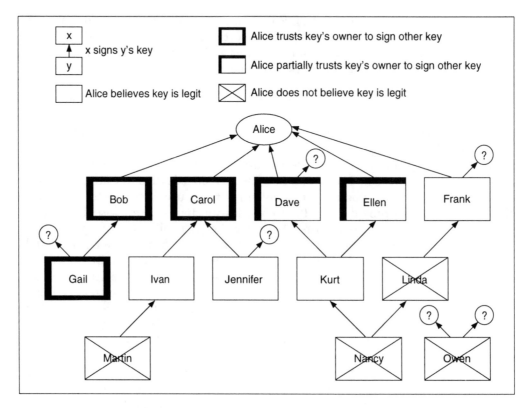

Figure 24.7   PGP trust model.

everyone who has her public key on his key ring. And as Alice has to sign the key revocation certificate with her private key; if she loses the key altogether she cannot revoke it.

The current version of PGP is 2.6.2. A new version of PGP, PGP 3.0, is scheduled for release by the end of 1995. Changes in 3.0 include options for triple-DES, SHA, and other public-key algorithms, a split of the encryption and signature public-key/private-key key pairs, enhanced procedures for key revocation, improved key-ring management functions, an API for integrating PGP in other programs, and a completely rewritten code base.

PGP is available for MS-DOS, UNIX, Macintosh, Amiga, and Atari. It is free for personal, noncommercial use, and is available from many ftp sites on the Internet. To ftp PGP from MIT, telnet to net-dist.mit.edu, log in as getpgp, answer the questions, then ftp to net-dist.mit.edu and change to the directory named in the telnet session. It is also available from ftp.ox.ac.uk, ftp.dsi.unimi.it, ftp.funet.fi, ftp.demon.co.uk, Compuserve, AOL, and elsewhere. For U.S. commercial users, PGP can be bought—complete with licenses—for about $100 from a company called ViaCrypt, 9033 N 24th Ave., Phoenix, AZ, 85021; (602) 944-0773; viacrypt@acm.org. Several shareware front-ends are available to help integrate PGP into MS-DOS, Microsoft Windows, Macintosh, and UNIX.

There are several books about PGP [601,1394,1495]. The source code has even been published in book form [1653] in an attempt to frustrate the U.S. Department of State, which continues to maintain that source code is exportable on paper but not electronically. Assuming you trust IDEA, PGP is the closest you're likely to get to military-grade encryption.

24.13   SMART CARDS

A smart card is a plastic card, the size and shape of a credit card, with an embedded computer chip. It's an old idea—the first patents were filed 20 years ago—but practical limitations made them feasible only five or so years ago. Since then they have taken off, mostly in Europe. Many countries use smart cards for pay telephones. There are also smart credit cards, smart cash cards, smart everything cards. The U.S. credit-card companies are looking at the technology, and within a few years even backwards Americans will have smart cards in their wallets.

A smart card contains a small computer (usually an 8-bit microprocessor), RAM (about a quarter kilobyte), ROM (about 6 or 8 kilobytes), and either EPROM or EEP-ROM (a few kilobytes). Future-generation smart cards will undoubtedly have more capacity, but some physical limitations on smart cards make expansion difficult. The card has its own operating system, programs, and data. (What it doesn't have is power; that comes when the card is plugged in to a reader.) And it is secure. In a world where you might not trust someone else's computer or telephone or whatever, you can still trust a card that you keep with you in your wallet.

Smart cards can have different cryptographic protocols and algorithms programmed into them. They might be configured as an electronic purse, and be able to spend and receive digital cash. They may be able to perform zero-knowledge authentication protocols; they may have their own encryption keys. They might be able to sign documents, or unlock applications on a computer.

Some smart cards are assumed to be tamperproof; this often protects the institution that issues the cards. A bank wouldn't want you to be able to hack their smart card to give yourself more money.

There is a lot of interest in smart cards, and a lot of information about them is available. A good survey article on the cryptography in smart cards is [672]. CARTES is a conference held in Paris every October; and CardTech is held in Washington, D.C. every April. The proceedings of two other smart-card conferences are [342, 382]. There are hundreds of smart-card patents, mostly owned by European companies. An interesting paper on possible future applications—integrity checking, audit trails, copy protection, digital cash, secure postage meters—is [1628].

24.14   PUBLIC-KEY CRYPTOGRAPHY STANDARDS (PKCS)

The Public-Key Cryptography Standards (PKCS) are RSA Data Security, Inc.'s attempt to provide an industry standard interface for public-key cryptography. Traditionally, this sort of thing would be handled by ANSI, but, considering the current situation in cryptography politics, RSADSI figured that they had better do it on their own. Working with a variety of companies, they developed a series of standards. Some are compatible with other standards and some are not.

These are not standards in the traditional sense of the word; no standards body convened and voted on PKCS. According to its own materials, RSADSI will "retain sole decision-making authority on what each standard is" and will "publish revised standards when appropriate" [803].

Even so, there is a lot of good stuff here. If you're not sure what kind of syntax and data structures to use when programming public-key cryptography, these standards are probably as good as anything else you can come up with. And, since they're not really standards, you can tailor them to suit your needs.

Following is a short description of each PKCS (PKCS #2 and PKCS #4 have been incorporated into PKCS #1).

PKCS #1 [1345] describes a method for RSA encryption and decryption, primarily for constructing the digital signatures and digital envelopes described in PKCS #7. For digital signatures, the message is hashed and then the hash is encrypted with the private key of the signer. Both message and hash are represented together as detailed in PKCS #7. For digital envelopes (encrypted messages), the message is first encrypted with a symmetric algorithm, and then the message key is encrypted with the public key of the recipient. The encrypted message and encrypted key are represented together according to the syntax of PKCS #7. Both of these methods are compatible with PEM standards. PKCS #1 also describes a syntax, identical to the syntax in X.509 and PEM, for RSA public and private keys and three signature algorithms—MD2 and RSA, MD4 and RSA, and MD5 and RSA—for signing certificates and the like.

PKCS #3 [1346] describes a method for implementing Diffie-Hellman key exchange.

PKCS #5 [1347] describes a method for encrypting messages with a secret key derived from a password. It uses either MD2 or MD5 to derive the key from the password, and encrypts with DES in CBC mode. The method is intended primarily to encrypt private keys when transferring them from one computer system to another, but can be used to encrypt messages.

PKCS #6 [1348] describes a standard syntax for public key certificates. The syntax is a superset of an X.509 certificate, so that X.509 certificates can be extracted if necessary. Over and above the X.509 set, additional attributes extend the certification process beyond just the public key. These include other information, such as electronic mail address.

PKCS # 7 [1349] is a general syntax for data that may be encrypted or signed, such as digital envelopes or digital signatures. The syntax is recursive, so that envelopes can be nested, or someone can sign some previously encrypted data. The syntax also allows other attributes, such as timestamps, to be authenticated along with the message content. PKCS #7 is compatible with PEM so that signed and encrypted messages can be converted to PEM messages without any cryptographic operations, and vice versa. PKCS #7 can support a variety of architectures—PEM is one—for certificate-based key management.

PKCS #8 [1350] describes a syntax for private key information—including a private key and a set of attributes—and a syntax for encrypted private keys. PKCS #5 can be used to encrypt the private key information.

PKCS #9 [1351] defines selected attribute types for PKCS #6 extended certificates, PKCS #7 digitally signed messages, and PKCS #8 private-key information.

PKCS #10 [1352] describes a standard syntax for certification requests. A certification comprises a distinguished name, a public key, and (optionally) a set of attributes, collectively signed by the person requesting certification. Certification requests are sent to a certification authority, who either transforms the request into an X.509 public-key certificate or a PKCS #6 certificate.

PKCS #11 [1353], the Cryptographic Token API Standard, specifies a programming interface called "Cryptoki" for portable cryptographic devices of all kinds. Cryptoki presents a common logical model, enabling applications to perform cryptographic operations on portable devices without knowing details of the underlying technology. The standard also defines application profiles: sets of algorithms that a device may support.

PKCS #12 [1354] describes syntax for storing in software a user's public keys, protected private keys, certificates, and other related cryptographic information. The goal is to standardize on a single key file for use among a variety of applications.

These standards are comprehensive, but not exhaustive. Many things are outside their scope: the problem of naming, noncryptographic issues surrounding certification, key lengths, and conditions on various parameters. What the PKCS provide are a format for transferring data based on public-key cryptography and an infrastructure to support that transfer.

24.15 Universal Electronic Payment System (UEPS)

The UEPS is a smart-card banking application initially developed for rural South Africa, but later adopted by all of that country's major banking groups. About 2 million cards were issued in that country by early 1995. It has also been adopted in Namibia, and is also being deployed by at least one bank in Russia.

The system provides a secure debit card suitable for regions where poor telephone service make on-line verification impossible. Both customers and merchants have cards; customers can use their cards to transfer money to merchants. Merchants can then take their cards to a telephone and deposit the money in their bank account; customers can take their cards to a telephone and have money moved onto their card. There is no intention to provide anonymity, only to prevent fraud.

Here is the communications protocol between customer Alice and merchant Bob. (Actually, Alice and Bob just plug their cards into a machine and wait for it to complete the transaction.) When Alice first gets her card, she is given a key pair, K_1 and K_2; the bank calculates them from her name and some secret function. Only the merchant cards have the secrets necessary to work out these customer keys.

(1) Alice sends Bob her name, A, his name, B, and a random number, R_A, encrypted using DES: first with K_2 and then with K_1. She also sends her name in the clear.

$$A, E_{K_1}(E_{K_2}(A, B, R_A))$$

(2) Bob calculates K_1 and K_2 from Alice's name. He decrypts the message, confirms that A and B are correct, then encrypts Alice's unencrypted second message with K_2.

$$E_{K_2}(A, B, R_A)$$

Bob does not send this message to Alice; 56 bits of the ciphertext become K_3. Bob then sends Alice his name, her name, and another random number, R_B, encrypted using DES: first with K_3 and then with K_1.

$$E_{K_1}(E_{K_3}(B, A, R_B))$$

(3) Alice computes K_3 in the same manner Bob did. She decrypts Bob's message, confirms that B and A are correct, then encrypts Bob's unencrypted message with K_3.

$$E_{K_3}(B, A, R_B)$$

Alice does not send this message to Bob; 56 bits of the ciphertext become K_4. Alice then sends Bob her name, his name, and the digital check, C. This check contains the names of the sender and recipient, a date, a check number, an amount, and two MACs, all encrypted using DES: first with K_4 and then with K_1. One of the MACs can be verified by Alice's bank, and the other can only be verified by the clearing center. Alice debits her account by the correct amount.

$$E_{K_1}(E_{K_4}(A, B, C))$$

(4) Bob computes K_4 in the same manner Alice did. Assuming all the names match and the check is correctly formed, he accepts it for payment.

A really clever thing about this protocol is that the encryption key for each message depends on the previous message. Each message doubles as an authenticator for *all* previous messages. This means that someone can't replay an old message; the receiver could never decrypt it. I am impressed with this idea and expect that it will see wider use once it becomes widely known.

Another clever thing about this protocol is that it enforces correct implementation. If the application developer doesn't implement this protocol correctly, it just won't work.

Both cards store records of every transaction. When the cards eventually go online to communicate with the bank—the merchant to deposit his money and the customer to get more money—the bank uploads these records for auditing purposes.

Tamperproof hardware prevents either participant from messing with the data; Alice cannot change the value of her card. Extensive audit trails provide data to identify and prosecute fraudulent transactions. There are universal secrets in the cards—MAC keys in the customer cards, functions to convert customer names to K_1 and K_2 in the merchant cards—but these are assumed to be difficult to reverse-engineer.

This scheme is not meant to be perfect, only more secure than either paper checks or traditional debit cards. The threat of fraud is not from rival militaries, but from opportunistic customers and merchants. UEPS protects against that kind of abuse.

The message exchange is an excellent example of a robust protocol: Every message names both parties, includes unique information to ensure freshness, and depends explicitly on all the messages that came before it.

24.16   CLIPPER

The Clipper chip (also known as the MYK-78T) is an NSA-designed, tamper-resistant VLSI chip designed for encrypting voice conversations; it is one of the two chips that implements the U.S. government's Escrowed Encryption Standard (EES) [1153]. VLSI Technologies, Inc. manufactures the chip, and Mykotronx, Inc. programs it. Initially, the Clipper chip will be available in the AT&T Model 3600 Telephone Security Device (see Section 24.18). The chip implements the Skipjack encryption algorithm (see Section 13.12), an NSA-designed classified secret-key encryption algorithm, in OFB only.

The most controversial aspect of the Clipper chip, and the entire EES, is the key-escrow protocol (see Section 4.14). Each chip has a special key, not needed for messages. This key is used to encrypt a copy of each user's message key. As part of the synchronization process, the sending Clipper chip generates and sends a **Law Enforcement Access Field** (**LEAF**) to the receiving Clipper chip. The LEAF contains a copy of the current session key, encrypted with a special key (called the **unit key**). This allows a government eavesdropper to recover the session key, and then recover the plaintext of the conversation.

According to the director of NIST [812]:

> A "key-escrow" system is envisioned that would ensure that the "Clipper Chip" is used to protect the privacy of law-abiding Americans. Each device containing the chip will have two unique "keys," numbers that will be needed by authorized government agencies to decode messages encoded by the device. When the device is manufactured, the two keys would be deposited separately in two "key-escrow" databases established by the attorney general. Access to these keys would be limited to government officials with legal authorization to conduct a wiretap.

The government also wants to encourage the sale of telephones with these devices abroad; no one knows what might happen to those key-escrow databases.

Politics aside, the internal structure of the LEAF is worth discussing [812,1154, 1594,459,107,462]. The LEAF is a 128-bit string containing enough information to allow law enforcement to recover the session key, K_S, assuming the two **escrow agencies** in charge of those key-escrow databases cooperate. The LEAF contains a 32-bit unit identifier, U, unique to the Clipper chip. It also contains the current 80-bit session key encrypted with the chip's unique unit key, K_U, and a 16-bit checksum, C, called an escrow identifier. This checksum is a function of the session key, the IV, and possibly other information. These three fields are encrypted with a fixed family key, K_F, shared by all interoperable Clipper chips. The family key, the encryption modes used, the details of the checksum, and the exact structure of the LEAF are all secret. It probably looks something like this:

$$E_{K_F}(U, {}_{K_U}(K_S, C))$$

K_U is programmed into Clipper chips at the factory. This key is then split (see Section 3.6) and stored in two different key-escrow databases, guarded by two different escrow agencies.

For Eve to recover K_S from the LEAF, she first has to decrypt the LEAF with K_F and recover U. Then she has to take a court order to each escrow agency, who each return half of K_U for the given U. Eve XORs the two halves together to recover K_U, then she uses K_U to recover K_S, and K_S to eavesdrop on the conversation.

The checksum is designed to prevent someone from circumventing this scheme; the receiving Clipper chip won't decrypt if the checksum doesn't check. However, there are only 2^{16} possible checksum values, and a bogus LEAF with the right checksum but the wrong key can be found in about 42 minutes [187]. This isn't much help for Clipper voice conversations. Because the key exchange protocol is not part of the Clipper chip, the 42-minute brute-force attack must occur after key exchange; it cannot be done before making the telephone call. This attack may work for facsimile transmission or with the Fortezza card (see Section 24.17).

Supposedly, the Clipper chip will resist reverse-engineering by "a very sophisticated, well-funded adversary" [1154], but rumors are that Sandia National Laboratories successfully reverse-engineered one. Even if those rumors aren't true, I suspect that the largest chip manufacturers in the world can reverse-engineer Clipper; it's just a matter of time before someone with the right combination of resources and ethics comes along.

Enormous privacy issues are associated with this scheme. Numerous civil liberty advocacy groups are actively campaigning against any key-escrow mechanism that gives the government the right to eavesdrop on citizens. But the sneaky thing is that this idea never went through Congress; NIST published the Escrowed Encryption Standard as a FIPS [1153], bypassing that irritating legislative process. Right now it looks like the EES is dying a slow and quiet death, but standards have a way of creeping up on you.

Anyway, Table 24.2 lists the different agencies participating in this program. Anyone want to do a threat analysis on having both escrow agents in the executive branch? Or on having escrow agents who really don't know anything about the wiretap requests, and can do no more than blindly approve them? Or on having the government impose a secret algorithm as a commercial standard?

In any case, implementing Clipper raises enough problems to question its value in court. Remember, Clipper only works in OFB mode. Despite what you may have been told to the contrary, this does not provide integrity or authentication. Imagine that Alice is on trial, and a Clipper-encrypted telephone call is part of the evidence. Alice claims that she never made the call; the voice is not hers. The phone's compression algorithm is so bad that it is hard to recognize Alice's voice, but the prosecution argues that since only Alice's escrowed key will decipher the call it must have been made from her telephone.

Alice argues that the call was forged like so [984,1339]: Given the ciphertext and the plaintext, it is possible to XOR them to get the keystream. This keystream can then be XORed with an entirely different plaintext to form a forged ciphertext, which can then be converted to forged plaintext when fed into the Clipper decryptor. True or not, this argument could easily put enough doubt in a jury's mind to disregard the telephone call as evidence.

Another attack, called the Squeeze attack, allows Alice to frame Bob. Here's how [575]: Alice calls Bob using Clipper. She saves a copy of his LEAF as well as the session key. Then, she calls Carol (who she knows is being wiretapped). During the key setup, Alice forces the session key to be identical to the one she used with Bob; this requires hacking the phone, but it is not hard. Then, instead of sending her LEAF she sends Bob's. It's a valid LEAF, so Carol's phone will not notice. Now she can say whatever she wants to Carol; when the police decrypt the LEAF, they will find that it is Bob's. Even if Bob wasn't framed by Alice, the mere fact that he can claim this in court undermines the purpose of the scheme.

The law enforcement authorities of the United States should not be in the business of collecting information in criminal investigations that is useless in court. Even if key escrow were a good idea, Clipper is a bad way of implementing it.

24.17   CAPSTONE

Capstone (also known as the MYK-80) is the other NSA-developed VLSI cryptographic chip that implements the U.S. government's Escrowed Encryption Standard [1153]. Capstone includes the following functions [1155,462]:

Table 24.2
EES Participating Agencies

Justice—System Sponsor and Family Key Agent
NIST—Program Manager and Escrow Agent
FBI—Decrypt User and Family Key Agent
Treasury—Escrow Agent
NSA—Program Developer

— The Skipjack algorithm in any of the four basic modes: ECB, CBC, CFB, and OFB.

— A public-key Key Exchange Algorithm (KEA), probably Diffie-Hellman.

— The Digital Signature Algorithm (DSA).

— The Secure Hash Algorithm (SHA).

— A general purpose exponentiation algorithm.

— A general purpose, random-number generator that uses a pure noise source.

Capstone provides the cryptographic functionality needed for secure electronic commerce and other computer-based applications. The first application of Capstone is in a PCMCIA card called Fortezza. (It was originally called Tessera until a company called Tessera, Inc. complained.)

NSA had considered lengthening Capstone's LEAF checksum in production versions for use in Fortezza cards, in order to foil the brute-force attack against the LEAF previously discussed. Instead, they added a feature that reset the card after 10 incorrect LEAFs. This only increases the time required to find a fake but valid LEAF by 10 percent, to 46 minutes. I am not impressed.

24.18 AT&T MODEL 3600 TELEPHONE SECURITY DEVICE (TSD)

The AT&T Telephone Security Device (TSD) is the Clipper phone. Actually, there are four models of the TSD. One contains the Clipper chip, another contains an exportable proprietary AT&T encryption algorithm, the third contains a proprietary algorithm for domestic use plus the exportable algorithm, and the fourth contains the Clipper, domestic, and exportable algorithms.

TSDs use a different session key for each telephone call. A pair of TSDs generate a session key using Diffie-Hellman key exchange, independent of the Clipper chip. Since Diffie-Hellman incorporates no authentication, the TSD has two methods to thwart a man-in-the-middle attack.

The first is a screen. The TSD hashes the session key and displays that hash on a small screen as four Hex digits. The conversants should confirm that their screens show the same digits. The voice quality is good enough that they can recognize each other's voice.

Eve still has a possible attack. Imagine her in the middle of Alice and Bob's conversation. She uses one TSD on the line with Alice and a modified TSD on the line with Bob; in the middle she bridges the two phone calls. Alice tries to go secure. She generates a key as normal, except that Eve is acting as Bob. Eve recovers the key, and using the modified TSD, forces the key she generates with Bob to have the same hash value. This attack may not sound very likely, but the TSD uses a variant of the interlock protocol to prevent it.

The TSD generates random numbers using a noise source and a chaotic amplifier with digital feedback. This generates a bit stream, which is fed through a post-whitening filter using the digital signal processor.

Despite all of this, the TSD manual does not mention security at all. In fact, it says [70]:

> AT&T makes no warranty that the TSD will prevent cryptanalytic attack on any encrypted transmission by any government agency, its agents, or any third party. Furthermore, AT&T makes no warranty that the TSD will prevent any attack on any communication by methods which bypass encryption.

CHAPTER 25

Politics

25.1 NATIONAL SECURITY AGENCY (NSA)

The NSA is the National Security Agency (once called "No Such Agency" or "Never Say Anything," but they've been more open recently), the official security body of the U.S. government. President Harry Truman created the agency in 1952 under the Department of Defense, and for many years its very existence was kept secret. The NSA is concerned with signals intelligence; its mandate is to listen in on and decode all foreign communications of interest to the security of the United States.

The following paragraphs are excerpted from NSA's original charter, signed by President Truman in 1952, and classified for many years thereafter [1535]:

> The COMINT mission of the National Security Agency (NSA) shall be to provide an effective, unified organization and control of the communications intelligence activities of the United States conducted against foreign governments, to provide for integrated operational policies and procedures pertaining thereto. As used in this directive, the terms "communications intelligence" or "COMINT" shall be construed to mean all procedures and methods used in the interception of communications other than foreign press and propaganda broadcasts and the obtaining of information from such communications by other than intended recipients, but shall exclude censorship and the production and dissemination of finished intelligence.
>
> The special nature of COMINT actives requires that they be treated in all respects as being outside the framework of other or general intelligence activities. Orders, directives, policies, or recommendations of any authority of the Executive Branch relating to the collection, production, security, handling, dissemination, or utilization of intelligence, and/or classified material, shall not be applicable to COMINT actives, unless specifically so stated and issued by competent department or agency authority represented on the Board. Other National Security

Council Intelligence Directives to the Director of Central Intelligence and related implementing directives issued by the Director of Central Intelligence shall be construed as non-applicable to COMINT activities, unless the National Security Council has made its directive specifically applicable to COMINT.

NSA conducts research in cryptology, both in designing secure algorithms to protect U.S. communications and in designing cryptanalytic techniques to listen in on non-U.S. communications. The NSA is known to be the largest employer of mathematicians in the world; it is also the largest purchaser of computer hardware in the world. The NSA probably possesses cryptographic expertise many years ahead of the public state of the art (in algorithms, but probably not in protocols) and can undoubtedly break many of the systems used in practice. But, for reasons of national security, almost all information about the NSA—even its budget—is classified. (Its budget is rumored to be $13 billion per year—including military funding of NSA projects and personnel—and it is rumored to employ 16,000 people.)

The NSA uses its power to restrict the public availability of cryptography, so as to prevent national enemies from employing encryption methods too strong for the NSA to break. James Massey discusses this struggle between academic and military research in cryptography [1007]:

> If one regards cryptology as the prerogative of government, one accepts that most cryptologic research will be conducted behind closed doors. Without doubt, the number of workers engaged today in such secret research in cryptology far exceeds that of those engaged in open research in cryptology. For only about 10 years has there in fact been widespread open research in cryptology. There have been, and will continue to be, conflicts between these two research communities. Open research is a common quest for knowledge that depends for its vitality on the open exchange of ideas via conference presentations and publications in scholarly journals. But can a government agency, charged with responsibilities of breaking the ciphers of other nations, countenance the publication of a cipher that it cannot break? Can a researcher in good conscience publish such a cipher that might undermine the effectiveness of his own government's code-breakers? One might argue that publication of a provably secure cipher would force all governments to behave like Stimson's "gentlemen," but one must be aware that open research in cryptography is fraught with political and ethical considerations of a severity more than in most scientific fields. The wonder is not that some conflicts have occurred between government agencies and open researchers in cryptology, but rather that these conflicts (at least those of which we are aware) have been so few and so mild.

James Bamford wrote a fascinating book about the NSA: *The Puzzle Palace* [79], recently updated by Bamford and Wayne Madsen [80].

The Commercial COMSEC Endorsement Program (CCEP)

The Commercial COMSEC Endorsement Program (CCEP), codenamed Overtake, is a 1984 NSA initiative to facilitate the development of computer and communications products with embedded cryptography [85,1165]. The military had always paid for this kind of thing for themselves, and it was very expensive. The NSA figured that if companies could sell equipment to both the military and to corporate users, even overseas, costs would go down and everyone would benefit. They would no longer endorse equipment as complying with Federal Standard 1027, and then CCEP would provide government-endorsed cryptographic equipment [419].

NSA developed a series of cryptographic modules for different purposes. Different algorithms would be used in the modules for different applications, and manufacturers would be able to pull one module out and plug in another depending on the customer. There were modules for military use (Type I), modules for "unclassified but sensitive" government use (Type II), modules for corporate use (Type III), and modules for export (Type IV). Table 25.1 summarizes the different modules, applications, and names.

This program is still around, but never became popular outside the government. All the modules were tamperproof, all the algorithms were classified, and you had to get your keys from NSA. Corporations never really bought into the idea of using classified algorithms dictated by the government. You'd think the NSA would have learned from this lesson and not even bothered with Clipper, Skipjack, and escrowed encryption chips.

25.2   NATIONAL COMPUTER SECURITY CENTER (NCSC)

The National Computer Security Center, a branch of the NSA, is responsible for the government's trusted computer program. Currently, the center evaluates commercial security products (both hardware and software), sponsors and publishes research, develops technical guidelines, and generally provides advice, support, and training.

The NCSC publishes the infamous "Orange Book" [465]. Its actual title is the *Department of Defense Trusted Computer System Evaluation Criteria*, but that's a mouthful to say and the book has an orange cover. The Orange Book attempts to define security requirements, gives computer manufacturers an objective way to measure the security of their systems, and guides them as to what to build into their secure products. It focuses on computer security and doesn't really say a lot about cryptography.

The Orange Book defines four broad divisions of security protection. It also defines classes of protection within some of those divisions. They are summarized in Table 25.2.

Table 25.1
CCEP Modules

Application	Type I	Type II
Voice/low-speed data	Winster	Edgeshot
Computer	Tepache	Bulletproof
High-speed data	Foresee	Brushstroke
Next Generation	Countersign I	Countersign II

Sometimes manufacturers say things like "we have C2 security." This is what they're talking about. For more information on this, read [1365]. The computer security model used in these criteria is called the Bell-LaPadula model [100,101,102,103].

The NCSC has published a whole series of books on computer security, sometimes called the Rainbow Books (all the covers have different colors). For example, *Trusted Network Interpretation of the Trusted Computer System Evaluation Criteria* [1146], sometimes called the "Red Book," interprets the Orange Book for networks and network equipment. The *Trusted Database Management System Interpretation of the Trusted Computer System Evaluation Criteria* [1147]—I can't even begin to describe the color of that cover—does the same for databases. There are now over 30 of these books, some with hideously colored covers.

For a complete set of the Rainbow Books, write Director, National Security Agency, INFOSEC Awareness, Attention: C81, 9800 Savage Road, Fort George G. Meade, MD 20755-6000; (410) 766-8729. Don't tell them I sent you.

25.3 NATIONAL INSTITUTE OF STANDARDS AND TECHNOLOGY (NIST)

The NIST is the National Institute of Standards and Technology, a division of the U.S. Department of Commerce. Formerly the NBS (National Bureau of Standards), it changed its name in 1988. Through its Computer Systems Laboratory (CSL), NIST promotes open standards and interoperability that it hopes will spur the economic development of computer-based industries. To this end, NIST issues standards and guidelines that it hopes will be adopted by all computer systems in the United States. Official standards are published as FIPS (Federal Information Processing Standards) publications.

If you want copies of any FIPS (or any other NIST publication), contact National Technical Information Service (NTIS), U.S. Department of Commerce, 5285 Port Royal Road, Springfield, VA 22161; (703) 487-4650; or visit gopher://csrc.ncsl.nist.gov.

When Congress passed the Computer Security Act of 1987, NIST was mandated to define standards for ensuring the security of sensitive but unclassified informa-

Table 25.2
Orange Book Classifications

D: Minimal Security
C: Discretionary Protection
    C1: Discretionary Security Protection
    C2: Controlled Access Protection
B: Mandatory Protection
    B1: Labeled Security Protection
    B2: Structured Protection
    B3: Security Domains
A: Verified Protection
    A1: Verified Design

tion in government computer systems. (Classified information and Warner Amendment data are under the jurisdiction of the NSA.) The Act authorizes NIST to work with other government agencies and private industry in evaluating proposed technology standards.

NIST issues standards for cryptographic functions. U.S. government agencies are required to use them for sensitive but unclassified information. Often the private sector adopts these standards as well. NIST issued DES, DSS, SHS, and EES.

All these algorithms were developed with some help from the NSA, ranging from analyzing DES to designing DSS, SHS, and the Skipjack algorithm in EES. Some people have criticized NIST for allowing the NSA to have too much control over these standards, since the NSA's interests may not coincide with those of NIST. It is unclear how much actual influence NSA has on the design and development of the algorithms. Given NIST's limited staff, budget, and resources, NSA's involvement is probably considerable. NSA has significant resources to contribute, including a computer facility second-to-none.

The official "Memorandum of Understanding" (MOU) between the two agencies reads:

MEMORANDUM OF UNDERSTANDING BETWEEN THE DIRECTOR OF THE NATIONAL INSTITUTE OF STANDARDS AND TECHNOLOGY AND THE DIRECTOR OF THE NATIONAL SECURITY AGENCY CONCERNING THE IMPLEMENTATION OF PUBLIC LAW 100-235

Recognizing that:

A. Under Section 2 of the Computer Security Act of 1987 (Public Law 100-235), (the Act), the National Institute of Standards and Technology (NIST) has the responsibility within the Federal Government for:

1. Developing technical, management, physical, and administrative standards and guidelines for the cost-effective security and privacy of sensitive information in Federal computer systems as defined in the Act; and,

2. Drawing on the computer system technical security guidelines of the National Security Agency (NSA) in this regard where appropriate.

B. Under Section 3 of the Act, the NIST is to coordinate closely with other agencies and offices, including the NSA, to assure:

1. Maximum use of all existing and planned programs, materials, studies, and reports relating to computer systems security and privacy, in order to avoid unnecessary and costly duplication of effort; and,

2. To the maximum extent feasible, that standards developed by the NIST under the Act are consistent and compatible with standards and procedures developed for the protection of classified information in Federal computer systems.

C. Under the Act, the Secretary of Commerce has the responsibility, which he has delegated to the Director of NIST, for appointing the members of the Computer System Security and Privacy Advisory Board, at least one of whom shall be from the NSA.

Therefore, in furtherance of the purposes of this MOU, the Director of the NIST and the Director of the NSA hereby agree as follows:

I. The NIST will:

1. Appoint to the Computer Security and Privacy Advisory Board at least one representative nominated by the Director of the NSA.

2. Draw upon computer system technical security guidelines developed by the NSA to the extent that the NIST determines that such guidelines are consistent with the requirements for protecting sensitive information in Federal computer systems.

3. Recognize the NSA-certified rating of evaluated trusted systems under the Trusted Computer Security Evaluation Criteria Program without requiring additional evaluation.

4. Develop telecommunications security standards for protecting sensitive unclassified computer data, drawing upon the expertise and products of the National Security Agency, to the greatest extent possible, in meeting these responsibilities in a timely and cost-effective manner.

5. Avoid duplication where possible in entering into mutually agreeable arrangements with the NSA for the NSA support.

6. Request the NSA's assistance on all matters related to cryptographic algorithms and cryptographic techniques including but not limited to research, development evaluation, or endorsement.

II. The NSA will:

1. Provide the NIST with technical guidelines in trusted technology, telecommunications security, and personal identification that may be used in cost-effective systems for protecting sensitive computer data.

2. Conduct or initiate research and development programs in trusted technology, telecommunications security, cryptographic techniques and personal identification methods.

3. Be responsive to the NIST's requests for assistance in respect to all matters related to cryptographic algorithms and cryptographic techniques including but not limited to research, development, evaluation, or endorsement.

4. Establish the standards and endorse products for application to secure systems covered in 10 USC Section 2315 (the Warner Amendment).

5. Upon request by Federal agencies, their contractors and other government-sponsored entities, conduct assessments of the hostile intelligence threat to federal information systems, and provide technical assistance and recommend endorsed products for application to secure systems against that threat.

III. The NIST and the NSA shall:

1. Jointly review agency plans for the security and privacy of computer systems submitted to NIST and NSA pursuant to section 6(b) of the Act.

2. Exchange technical standards and guidelines as necessary to achieve the purposes of the Act.

3. Work together to achieve the purposes of this memorandum with the greatest efficiency possible, avoiding unnecessary duplication of effort.

4. Maintain an on-going open dialogue to ensure that each organization remains abreast of emerging technologies and issues affecting automated information system security in computer-based systems.

5. Establish a Technical Working Group to review and analyze issues of mutual interest pertinent to protection of systems that process sensitive or other unclassified information. The Group shall be composed of six federal employees, three each selected by NIST and NSA and to be augmented as necessary by representatives of other agencies. Issues may be referred to the group by either the NSA Deputy Director for Information Security or the NIST Deputy Director or may be generated and addressed by the group upon approval by the NSA DDI or NIST Deputy Director. Within days of the referral of an issue to the Group by either the NSA Deputy Director for Information Security or the NIST Deputy Director, the Group will respond with a progress report and plan for further analysis, if any.

6. Exchange work plans on an annual basis on all research and development projects pertinent to protection of systems that process sensitive or other unclassified information, including trusted technology, for protecting the integrity and availability of data, telecommunications security and personal identification methods. Project updates will be exchanged quarterly, and project reviews will be provided by either party upon request of the other party.

7. Ensure the Technical Working Group reviews prior to public disclosure all matters regarding technical systems security techniques to be developed for use in protecting sensitive information in federal computer systems to ensure they are consistent with the national security of the United States. If NIST and NSA are unable to resolve such an issue within 60 days, either agency may elect to raise the issue to the Secretary of Defense and the Secretary of Commerce. It is recognized that such an issue may be referred to the President through the NSC for resolution. No action shall be taken on such an issue until it is resolved.

8. Specify additional operational agreements in annexes to this MOU as they are agreed to by NSA and NIST.

IV. Either party may elect to terminate this MOU upon six months' written notice. This MOU is effective upon approval of both signatories.
/signed/

RAYMOND G. KAMMER
Acting Director, National Institute of Standards and Technology, 24 March 1989

W. O. STUDEMAN
Vice Admiral, U.S. Navy; Director, National Security Agency, 23 March 1989

25.4   RSA Data Security, Inc.

RSA Data Security, Inc. (RSADSI) was founded in 1982 to develop, license, and market the RSA patent. It has some commercial products, including a standalone e-mail security package, and various cryptographic libraries (available in either source or object form). RSADSI also markets the RC2 and RC4 symmetric algorithms (see Section 11.8). RSA Laboratories, a research lab associated with RSADSI, performs basic cryptographic research and provides consulting services.

Anyone interested in either their patents or products should contact Director of Sales, RSA Data Security, Inc., 100 Marine Parkway, Redwood City, CA 94065; (415) 595-8782; fax: (415) 595-1873.

25.5 PUBLIC KEY PARTNERS

The five patents in Table 25.3 are held by Public Key Partners (PKP) of Sunnyvale, California, a partnership between RSADSI and Caro-Kahn, Inc.—the parent company of Cylink. (RSADSI gets 65 percent of the profits and Caro-Kahn gets 35 percent.) PKP claims that these patents, and 4,218,582 in particular, apply to *all uses* of public-key cryptography.

In [574], PKP wrote:

> These patents [4,200,770, 4,218,582, 4,405,829, and 4,424,414] cover all known methods of practicing the art of Public Key, including the variations collectively known as ElGamal.
>
> Due to the broad acceptance of RSA digital signatures throughout the international community, Public Key Partners strongly endorses its incorporation in a digital signature standard. We assure all interested parties that Public Key Partners will comply with all of the policies of ANSI and the IEEE concerning the availability of licenses to practice this art. Specifically, in support of any RSA signature standard which may be adopted, Public Key Partners hereby gives its assurance that licenses to practice RSA signatures will be available under reasonable terms and conditions on a nondiscriminatory basis.

Whether this is true depends on who you talk to. PKP's licenses have mostly been secret, so there is no way to check if the licenses are standard. Although they claim to have never denied a license to anyone, at least two companies claim to have been denied a license. PKP guards its patents closely, threatening anyone who tries to use public-key cryptography without a license. In part, this is a reaction to U.S. patent law. If you hold a patent and fail to prosecute an infringement, you can lose your patent. There has been much talk about whether the patents are legal, but so far it has all been talk. All legal challenges to PKP's patents have been settled before judgment.

Table 25.3
Public Key Partners' Patents

Patent #	Date	Inventors	Patent Covers
4,200,770	4/29/80	Hellman, Diffie, Merkle	Diffie-Hellman Key Exchange
4,218,582	8/19/80	Hellman, Merkle	Merkle-Hellman Knapsacks
4,405,829	9/20/83	Rivest, Shamir, Adleman	RSA
4,424,414	3/3/84	Hellman, Pohlig	Pohlig-Hellman
4,995,082	2/19/91	Schnorr	Schnorr Signatures

I am not going to dispense legal advice in this book. Maybe the RSA patent will not hold up in court. Maybe the patents do not apply to the entirety of public-key cryptography. (Honestly, I can't see how they cover ElGamal or elliptic curve cryptosystems.) Perhaps someone will eventually win a suit against PKP or RSADSI. But keep in mind that corporations with large legal departments like IBM, Microsoft, Lotus, Apple, Novell, Digital, National Semiconductor, AT&T, and Sun have all licensed RSA for use in their products rather than fight them in court. And Boeing, Shell Oil, DuPont, Raytheon, and Citicorp have all licensed RSA for their own internal use.

In one case, PKP brought suit against TRW Corporation for using the ElGamal algorithm without a license. TRW claimed they did not need a license. PKP and TRW reached a settlement in June 1992. The details of the settlement are unknown, but they included an agreement by TRW to license the patents. This does not bode well. TRW can afford good lawyers; I can only assume that if they thought they could win the suit without spending an unreasonable amount of money, they would have fought.

Meanwhile, PKP is having its own internal problems. In June 1994 Caro-Kahn sued RSADSI alleging, among other things, that the RSA patent is invalid and unenforceable [401]. Both partners are trying to have the partnership dissolved. Are the patents valid or not? Will users have to get a license from Caro-Kahn to use the RSA algorithm? Who will own the Schnorr patent? The matter will probably be sorted out by the time this book sees publication.

Patents are good for only 17 years, and cannot be renewed. On April 29, 1997, Diffie-Hellman key exchange (and the ElGamal algorithm) will enter the public domain. On September 20, 2000, RSA will enter the public domain. Mark your calendars.

25.6 International Association for Cryptologic Research (IACR)

The International Association for Cryptologic Research is the worldwide cryptographic research organization. Its stated purpose is to advance the theory and practice of cryptology and related fields. Membership is open to any person. The association sponsors two annual conferences, Crypto (held in Santa Barbara in August) and Eurocrypt (held in Europe in May), and publishes quarterly *The Journal of Cryptology* and the *IACR Newsletter*.

The address of the IACR Business Office changes whenever the president does. The current address is: IACR Business Office, Aarhus Science Park, Gustav Wieds Vej 10, DK-8000 Aarhus C, Denmark.

25.7 RACE Integrity Primitives Evaluation (RIPE)

The Research and Development in Advanced Communication Technologies in Europe (RACE) program was launched by the European Community to support pre-competitive and pre-normative work in communications standards and technologies to support Integrated Broadband Communication (IBC). As part of that effort, RACE established the RACE Integrity Primitives Evaluation (RIPE) to put together a portfolio of techniques to meet the anticipated security requirements of IBC.

Six leading European cryptography research groups made up the RIPE consortium: Center for Mathematics and Computer Science, Amsterdam; Siemens AG; Philips Crypto BV; Royal PTT Nederland NV, PTT Research; Katholieke Universiteit Leuven; and Aarhus Universitet. After calls for algorithms in 1989 and 1991 [1564], 32 submissions from around the world, and a 350 man-month evaluation project, the consortium published *RIPE Integrity Primitives* [1305,1332]. The report included an introduction and some basic integrity concepts, and these primitives: MDC-4 (see Section 18.11), RIPE-MD (see Section 18.8), RIPE-MAC (see Section 18.14), IBC-HASH, SKID (see Section 3.2), RSA, COMSET (see Section 16.1), and RSA key generation.

25.8 CONDITIONAL ACCESS FOR EUROPE (CAFE)

Conditional Access for Europe (CAFE) is a project in the European Community's ESPRIT program [204,205]. Work began in December 1992 and is scheduled to be finished by the end of 1995. The consortium involved consists of groups for social and market studies (Cardware, Institut für Sozialforschung), software and hardware manufacturers (DigiCash, Gemplus, Ingenico, Siemens), and cryptographers (CWI Amsterdam, PTT Research Netherlands, SPET, Sintef Delab Trondheim, Universities of Århus, Hildesheim and Leuven).

The goal is to develop systems for conditional access, particularly digital payment systems. Payment systems must give legal certainty to everybody at all times and require as little trust as possible—this certainty should not depend on the tamper-resistance of any devices.

The basic device for CAFE is an electronic wallet: a small computer that looks something like a pocket calculator. It has a battery, keyboard, screen, and an infrared channel for communicating with other wallets. Every user owns and uses his own wallet, which administers his rights and guarantees his security.

A device with a keyboard and screen has an advantage over a smart card; it can operate independent of a terminal. A user can directly enter his password and the amount of the payment. The user does not have to give his wallet up to complete a transaction, unlike the current situation with credit cards.

Additional features are:

— Offline transactions. The purpose of the system is to replace small cash transactions; an online system would be too cumbersome.

— Loss tolerance. If a user loses his wallet, or if it breaks or is stolen, he can recover his money.

— Support for different currencies.

— An open architecture and open system. A user should be able to pay for arbitrary services, such as shopping, telephone, and public transport, by a range of service providers. The system should be interoperable between any number of electronic money issuers, and between different wallet types and manufacturers.

— Low cost.

At this writing there is a software version of the system, and the consortium is hard at work on a hardware prototype.

25.9 ISO/IEC 9979

In the mid-80s, the ISO tried to standardize DES, which by then was already a FIPS and an ANSI standard. After some political wrangling, the ISO decided not to standardize cryptographic algorithms, but instead to register algorithms. Only encryption algorithms can be registered; hash functions and signature schemes cannot. Any national body can submit an algorithm for registration.

Currently only three algorithms have been submitted (see Table 25.4). A submission includes information about applications, parameters, implementations, modes, and test vectors. A detailed description is optional; it is possible to submit secret algorithms for registration.

The fact that an algorithm is registered does not imply anything about its quality, nor is registration an approval of the algorithm by the ISO/IEC. Registration merely indicates that a single national body wants to register the algorithm, based on whatever criteria that body uses.

I am not impressed with this idea. Registration obstructs the standardization process. Rather than agreeing on a few algorithms, the ISO is allowing any algorithm to be registered. With so little control over what is registered, stating that an algorithm is "ISO/IEC 9979 Registered" sounds a whole lot better than it is. In any case, the registry is maintained by the National Computer Centre Ltd., Oxford Road, Manchester, M1 7ED, United Kingdom.

Table 25.4
ISO/IEC 9979
Registered Algorithms

Name	Registration Number
B-CRYPT	0001
IDEA	0002
LUC	0003

25.10   PROFESSIONAL, CIVIL LIBERTIES, AND INDUSTRY GROUPS

Electronic Privacy Information Center (EPIC)

EPIC was established in 1994 to focus public attention on emerging privacy issues relating to the National Information Infrastructure, such as the Clipper chip, the Digital Telephony proposal, national identity numbers and systems, medical records privacy, and the sale of consumer data. EPIC conducts litigation, sponsors conferences, produces reports, publishes the *EPIC Alert*, and leads campaigns on privacy issues. Anyone interested in joining should contact Electronic Privacy Information Center, 666 Pennsylvania Avenue SE, Suite 301, Washington, D.C. 20003; (202) 544-9240; fax: (202) 547-5482; Internet: info@epic.org.

Electronic Frontier Foundation (EFF)

The EFF is dedicated to protecting civil rights in cyberspace. With respect to cryptographic policy in the United States, they believe that information and access to cryptography are fundamental rights, and therefore should be free of government restriction. They organized the Digital Privacy and Security Working Group, a coalition of 50 organizations. The group opposed the Digital Telephony bill and the Clipper initiative. The EFF is also helping in a lawsuit against cryptography export controls [143]. Anyone interested in joining the EFF should contact Electronic Frontier Foundation, 1001 G Street NW, Suite 950E, Washington, D.C. 20001; (202) 347-5400; fax: (202) 393-5509; Internet: eff@eff.org.

Association for Computing Machinery (ACM)

The ACM is an international computer industry organization. In 1994 the U.S. ACM Public Policy Committee produced an excellent report on U.S. cryptography policy [935]. This should be required reading for anyone interested in the politics of cryptography. It is available via anonymous ftp from info.acm.org in /reports/acm_crypto/acm_crypto_study.ps.

Institute of Electrical and Electronics Engineers (IEEE)

The IEEE is another professional organization. The U.S. office investigates and makes recommendations on privacy-related issues including encryption policy, identity numbers, and privacy protections on the Internet.

Software Publishers Association (SPA)

The SPA is a trade association of over 1000 personal computer software companies. They have lobbied for relaxation of export controls on cryptography, and maintain a list of commercially available foreign cryptography products.

25.11   SCI.CRYPT

Sci.crypt is the Usenet newsgroup for cryptology. It is read by an estimated 100,000 people worldwide. Most of the posts are nonsense, bickering, or both; some are political, and most of the rest are requests for information or basic questions. Occasionally nuggets of new and useful information are posted to this newsgroup. If you follow sci.crypt regularly, you will learn how to use something called a kill file.

Another Usenet newsgroup is sci.crypt.research, a moderated newsgroup devoted to discussions about cryptology research. There are fewer posts and they are more interesting.

25.12   CYPHERPUNKS

The Cypherpunks are an informal group of people interested in teaching and learning about cryptography. They also experiment with cryptography and try to put it into use. In their opinion, all the cryptographic research in the world doesn't do society any good unless it gets used.

In "A Cypherpunk's Manifesto," Eric Hughes writes [744]:

> We the Cypherpunks are dedicated to building anonymous systems. We are defending our privacy with cryptography, with anonymous mail forwarding systems, with digital signatures, and with electronic money.
>
> Cypherpunks write code. We know that someone has to write software to defend privacy, and since we can't get privacy unless we all do, we're going to write it. We publish our code so that our fellow Cypherpunks may practice and play with it. Our code is free for all to use, worldwide. We don't care much if you don't approve of the software we write. We know that software can't be destroyed and that widely dispersed systems can't be shut down.

People interested in joining the cypherpunks mailing list on the Internet should send mail to majordomo@toad.com. The mailing list is archived at ftp.csua. berkeley.edu in /pub/cypherpunks.

25.13   PATENTS

Software patents are an issue much larger than the scope of this book. Whether they're good or bad, they exist. Algorithms, cryptographic algorithms included, can be patented in the United States. IBM owned the DES patents [514]. IDEA is patented. Almost every public-key algorithm is patented. NIST even has a patent for the DSA. Some cryptography patents have been blocked by intervention from the NSA, under the authority of the Invention Secrecy Act of 1940 and the National Security Act of 1947. This means that instead of a patent, the inventor gets a secrecy order and is prohibited from discussing his invention with anybody.

The NSA has special dispensation when it comes to patents. They can apply for a patent and then block its issuance. It's a secrecy order again, but here the NSA is both the inventor and the issuer of the order. When, at some later date, the secrecy order is removed, the Patent Office issues the patent good for the standard 17 years. This rather clearly protects the invention while keeping it secret. If someone else invents the same thing, the NSA has already filed for the patent. If no one else invents it, then it remains secret.

Not only does this fly directly in the face of the patent process, which is supposed to disclose as well as protect inventions, it allows the NSA to keep a patent for more than 17 years. The 17-year clock starts ticking after the patent is issued, not when it is filed. How this will change, now that the United States has ratified the GATT treaty, is unclear.

25.14 U.S. Export Rules

According to the U.S. government, cryptography can be a munition. This means it is covered under the same rules as a TOW missile or an M1 Abrams tank. If you sell cryptography overseas without the proper export license, then you are an international arms smuggler. Unless you think time in a federal penitentiary would look good on your résumé, pay attention to the rules.

With the advent of the Cold War in 1949, all of the NATO countries (except Iceland), and later Australia, Japan, and Spain, formed CoCom, the Coordinating Committee for Multilateral Export Controls. This is an unofficial nontreaty organization, chartered to coordinate national restrictions on the export of sensitive military technologies to the Soviet Union, other Warsaw Pact countries, and the People's Republic of China. Examples of controlled technologies are computers, milling machinery, and cryptography. The goal here was to slow technology transfer into those countries, and thereby keep their militaries inferior.

Since the end of the Cold War, the CoCom countries realized that many of their controls were obsolete. They are supposedly in the process of defining something called the "New Forum," another multinational organization designed to stop the flow of military technologies to countries the members don't particularly like.

In any case, U.S. export policy on strategic goods is defined by the Export Administration Act, the Arms Export Control Act, the Atomic Energy Act, and the Nuclear Non-Proliferation Act. The controls established by all this legislation are implemented through a number of statutes, none of them coordinated with each other. Over a dozen agencies including the military services administer controls; often their regulatory programs overlap and contradict.

Controlled technologies appear on several lists. Cryptography has traditionally been classified as a munition and appears on the U.S. Munitions List (USML), the International Munitions List (IML), the Commerce Control List (CCL), and the International Industrial List (IIL). The Department of State is responsible for the USML; it is published as part of the International Traffic in Arms Regulations (ITAR) [466,467].

Two U.S. government agencies control export of cryptography. One is the Bureau of Export Administration (BXA) in the Department of Commerce, authorized by the Export Administration Regulations (EAR). The other is the Office of Defense Trade Controls (DTC) in the State Department, authorized by the ITAR. As a rule of thumb, the Commerce Department's BXA has far less stringent requirements, but

State Department's DTC (which takes technical and national security advice from the NSA, and always seems to follow that advice) sees all cryptography exports first and can refuse to transfer jurisdiction to BXA.

The ITAR regulates this stuff. (Before 1990 the Office of Defense Trade Controls was called the Office of Munitions Controls; presumably this public relations effort is designed to help us forget that we're dealing with guns and bombs.) Historically, the DTC has been reluctant to grant export licenses for encryption products stronger than a certain level—not that they have ever been public about exactly what that level is.

The following sections are excerpted from the ITAR [466,467]:

§ 120.10 Technical data.

Technical data means, for purposes of this subchapter:

(1) Information, other than software as defined in 120.10(d), which is required for the design, development, production, processing, manufacture, assembly, operation, repair, maintenance or modification of defense articles. This includes, for example, information in the form of blueprints, drawings, photographs, plans, instructions and documentation;

(2) Classified information relating to defense articles and defense services;

(3) Information covered by an invention secrecy order;

(4) Software as defined in Sec. 121.8(f) directly related to defense articles;

(5) This definition does not include information concerning general scientific, mathematical or engineering principles commonly taught in schools, colleges and universities in the public domain as defined in § 120.11. It also does not include basic marketing information on function or purpose or general system descriptions of defense articles.

§ 120.11 Public domain.

Public domain means information which is published and which is generally accessible or available to the public:

(1) Through sales at newsstands and bookstores;

(2) Through subscriptions which are available without restriction to any individual who desires to obtain or purchase the published information;

(3) Through second class mailing privileges granted by the U.S. Government;

(4) At libraries open to the public or from which the public can obtain documents;

(5) Through patents available at any patent office;

(6) Through unlimited distribution at a conference, meeting, seminar, trade show or exhibition, generally accessible to the public, in the United States;

(7) Through public release (i.e., unlimited distribution) in any form (e.g., not necessarily in published form) after approval by the cognizant U.S. government department or agency (see also § 125.4(b)(13));

(8) Through fundamental research in science and engineering at accredited institutions of higher learning in the U.S., where the resulting information is ordinarily published and shared broadly in the scientific community. Fundamental research is defined to mean basic and applied research in science and engineering where the

resulting information is ordinarily published and shared broadly within the scientific community, as distinguished from research the results of which are restricted for proprietary reasons or specific U.S. Government access and dissemination controls. University research will not be considered fundamental research if:

(i) The University or its researchers accept other restrictions on publication of scientific and technical information resulting from the project or activity, or

(ii) The research is funded by the U.S. Government and specific access and dissemination controls protecting information resulting from the research are applicable.

§ 120.17 Export.

Export means:

(1) Sending or taking defense articles out of the United States in any manner, except by mere travel outside of the United States by a person whose personal knowledge includes technical data; or

(2) Transferring registration, control or ownership to a foreign person of any aircraft, vessel, or satellite covered by the U.S. Munitions List, whether in the United States or abroad; or

(3) Disclosing (including oral or visual disclosure) or transferring in the United States any defense articles to an embassy, any agency or subdivision of a foreign government (e.g., diplomatic missions); or

(4) Disclosing (including oral or visual disclosure) or transferring technical data to a foreign person, whether in the United States or abroad; or

(5) Performing a defense service on behalf of, or for the benefit of, a foreign person, whether in the United States or abroad.

(6) A launch vehicle or payload shall not, by the launching of such vehicle, be considered export for the purposes of this subchapter. However, for certain limited purposes (see § 126.1 of this subchapter), the controls of this subchapter apply to sales and other transfers of defense articles or defense services.

Part 121—The United States Munitions List

§ 121.1 General. The United States Munitions List

Category XIII—Auxiliary Military Equipment

(1) Cryptographic (including key management) systems, equipment, assemblies, modules, integrated circuits, components or software with the capability of maintaining secrecy or confidentiality of information or information systems, except cryptographic equipment and software as follows:

(i) Restricted to decryption functions specifically designed to allow the execution of copy protected software, provided the decryption functions are not user-accessible.

(ii) Specifically designed, developed or modified for use in machines for banking or money transactions, and restricted to use only in such transactions. Machines for banking or money transactions include automatic teller machines, self-service statement printers, point of sale terminals or equipment for the encryption of interbanking transactions.

(iii) Employing only analog techniques to provide the cryptographic processing that ensures information security in the following applications. . . .

(iv) Personalized smart cards using cryptography restricted for use only in equipment or systems exempted from the controls of the USML.

(v) Limited to access control, such as automatic teller machines, self-service statement printers or point of sale terminals, which protects passwords or personal identification numbers (PIN) or similar data to prevent unauthorized access to facilities but does not allow for encryption or files or text, except as directly related to the password of PIN protection.

(vi) Limited to data authentication which calculates a Message Authentication Code (MAC) or similar result to ensure no alteration of text has taken place, or authenticate users, but does not allow for encryption of data, text or other media other than that needed for the authentication.

(vii) Restricted for fixed data compression or coding techniques.

(viii) Limited to receiving for radio broadcast, pay television or similar restricted audience television of the consumer type, without digital encryption and where digital decryption is limited to video, audio or management functions.

(ix) Software designed or modified to protect against malicious computer damage, (e.g., viruses).

(2) Cryptographic (including key management) systems, equipment, assemblies, modules, integrated circuits, components or software which have the capability of generating spreading or hopping codes for spread spectrum systems or equipment.

(3) Cryptographic systems, equipment, assemblies, modules, integrated circuits, components or software.

§ 125.2 Exports of unclassified technical data.

(a) General. A license (DSP-5) is required for the export of unclassified technical data unless the export is exempt from the licensing requirements of this subchapter. In the case of a plant visit, details of the proposed discussions must be transmitted to the Office of Defense Trade Controls for an appraisal of the technical data. Seven copies of the technical data or the details of the discussions must be provided.

(b) Patents. A license issued by the Office of Defense Trade Controls is required for the export of technical data whenever the data exceeds that which is used to support a domestic filing of a patent application or to support a foreign filing of a patent application whenever no domestic application has been filed. Requests for the filing of patent applications in a foreign country, and requests for the filing of amendments, modifications or supplements to such patents, should follow the regulations of the U.S. Patent and Trademark Office in accordance with 37 CFR part 5. The export of technical data to support the filing and processing of patent applications in foreign countries is subject to regulations issued by the U.S. Patent and Trademark Office pursuant to 35 U.S.C. 184.

(c) Disclosures. Unless otherwise expressly exempted in this subchapter, a license is required for the oral, visual or documentary disclosure of technical data by U.S. persons to foreign persons. A license is required regardless of the manner in which the technical data is transmitted (e.g., in person, by telephone, correspondence, electronic means, etc.). A license is required for such disclosures by U.S. persons in connection with visits to foreign diplomatic missions and consular offices.

And so on. There's a lot more information in this document. If you're going to try to export cryptography, I suggest you get a copy of the entire thing and a lawyer who speaks the language.

In reality, the NSA has control over the export of cryptographic products. If you want a Commodity Jurisdiction (CJ), you must submit your product to the NSA for approval and submit the CJ application to the State Department. After State Department approval, the matter moves under the jurisdiction of the Commerce Department, which has never cared much about the export of cryptography. However, the State Department will never grant a CJ without NSA approval.

In 1977 an NSA employee named Joseph A. Meyer wrote a letter—unauthorized, according to the official story of the incident—to the IEEE, warning them that the scheduled presentation of the original RSA paper would violate the ITAR. From *The Puzzle Palace:*

> He had a point. The ITAR did cover any "unclassified information that can be used, or adapted for use, in the design, production, manufacture, repair, overhaul, processing, engineering, development, operation, maintenance, or reconstruction" of the listed materials, as well as "any technology which advances the state-of-the-art or establishes a new art in an area of significant military applicability in the United States." And export did include transferring the information both by writing and by either oral or visual means, including briefings and symposia in which foreign nationals are present.
>
> But followed literally, the vague, overly broad regulations would seem to require that anyone planning to write or speak out publicly on a topic touching the Munitions List must first get approval from the State Department—a chilling prospect clearly at odds with the First Amendment and one as yet untested by the Supreme Court.

In the end NSA disavowed Meyer's actions and the RSA paper was presented as planned. No actions were taken against any of the inventors, although their work arguably enhanced foreign cryptography capabilities more than anything released since.

The following statement by NSA discusses the export of cryptography [363]:

> Cryptographic technology is deemed vital to national security interests. This includes economic, military, and foreign policy interests.
>
> We do not agree with the implications from the House Judiciary Committee hearing of 7 May 1992 and recent news articles that allege that U.S. export laws prevent U.S. firms' manufacture and use of top encryption equipment. We are unaware of any case where a U.S. firm has been prevented from manufacturing and using encryption equipment within this country or for use by the U.S. firm or

its subsidiaries in locations outside the U.S. because of U.S. export restrictions. In fact, NSA has always supported the use of encryption by U.S. businesses operating domestically and overseas to protect sensitive information.

For export to foreign countries, NSA as a component of the Department of Defense (along with the Department of State and the Department of Commerce) reviews export licenses for information security technologies controlled by the Export Administration Regulations or the International Traffic in Arms Regulations. Similar export control systems are in effect in all the Coordinating Committee for Multilateral Export Controls (CoCom) countries as well as many non-CoCom countries as these technologies are universally considered as sensitive. Such technologies are not banned from export and are reviewed on a case-by-case basis. As part of the export review process, licenses may be required for these systems and are reviewed to determine the effect such export could have on national security interests—including economic, military, and political security interests. Export licenses are approved or denied based upon the type of equipment involved, the proposed end use and the end user.

Our analysis indicates that the U.S. leads the world in the manufacture and export of information security technologies. Of those cryptologic products referred to NSA by the Department of State for export licenses, we consistently approve over 90%. Export licenses for information security products under the jurisdiction of the Department of Commerce are processed and approved without referral to NSA or DoD. This includes products using such techniques as the DSS and RSA which provide authentication and access control to computers or networks. In fact, in the past NSA has played a major role in successfully advocating the relaxation of export controls on RSA and related technologies for authentication purposes. Such techniques are extremely valuable against the hacker problem and unauthorized use of resources.

It is the stated policy of the NSA not to restrict the export of authentication products, only encryption products. If you want to export an authentication-only product, approval may merely be a matter of showing that your product cannot easily be used for encryption. Furthermore, the bureaucratic procedures are much simpler for authentication products than for encryption products. An authentication product needs State Department approval only once for a CJ; an encryption product may require approval for every product revision or even every sale.

Without a CJ, you must request export approval every time you wish to export the product. The State Department does not approve the export of products with strong encryption, even those using DES. Isolated exceptions include export to U.S. subsidiaries for the purposes of communicating to the U.S., exports for some banking applications, and export to appropriate U.S. military users. The Software Publishers Association (SPA) has been negotiating with the government to ease export license restrictions. A 1992 agreement between them and the State Department eased the export license rules for two algorithms, RC2 and RC4, as long as the key size is 40 bits or less. Refer to Section 7.1 for more information.

In 1993, Rep. Maria Cantwell (D-WA) introduced a bill at the behest of the software industry to relax export controls on encryption software. Sen. Patty Murray

(D-WA) introduced a companion bill in the Senate. The Cantwell Bill was appended to the general export control legislation going through Congress, but was deleted by the House Intelligence Committee after a massive lobbying effort by the NSA. Whatever the NSA did, it was impressive; the committee voted unanimously to delete the wording. I can't remember the last time a bunch of legislators voted unanimously to do anything.

In 1995 Dan Bernstein, with the help of the EFF, sued the U.S. government, seeking to bar the government from restricting publication of cryptographic documents and software [143]. The suit claimed that the export control laws are unconstitutional, an "impermissible prior restraint on speech, in violation of the First Amendment." Specifically, the lawsuit charges that the current export control process:

— Allows bureaucrats to restrict publication without ever going to court.

— Provides too few procedural safeguards for First Amendment rights.

— Requires publishers to register with the government, creating in effect a "licensed press."

— Disallows general publication by requiring recipients to be individually identified.

— Is sufficiently vague that ordinary people cannot know what conduct is allowed and what conduct is prohibited.

— Is overbroad because it prohibits conduct that is clearly protected (such as speaking to foreigners within the United States).

— Is applied too broadly, by prohibiting export of software that contains no cryptography, on the theory that cryptography could be added to it later.

— Egregiously violates the First Amendment by prohibiting private speech on cryptography because the government wishes its own opinions on cryptography to guide the public instead.

— Exceeds the authority granted by Congress in the export control laws in many ways, as well as exceeding the authority granted by the Constitution.

Everyone anticipates that the case will take several years to settle, and no one has any idea how it will come out.

Meanwhile, the Computer Security and Privacy Advisory Board, an official advisory board to NIST, voted in March 1992 to recommend a national policy review of cryptographic issues, including export policy. They said that export policy is decided solely by agencies concerned with national security, without input from agencies concerned with encouraging commerce. Those agencies concerned with national security are doing everything possible to make sure this doesn't change, but eventually it has to.

25.15 FOREIGN IMPORT AND EXPORT OF CRYPTOGRAPHY

Other countries have their own import and export rules [311]. This summary is incomplete and probably out of date. Countries could have rules and ignore them, or could have no rules but restrict import, export, and use anyway.

— Australia requires an import certificate for cryptography only upon request from the exporting country.

— Canada has no import controls, and export controls are similar to those of the United States. The exportation of items from Canada may be subject to restriction if they are included on the Export Control List pursuant to the Export and Import Permits Act. Canada follows the CoCom regulations in the regulation of cryptographic technology. Encryption devices are outlined in category five, part two of Canada's export regulations. These provisions are similar to U.S. category five in the Export Administration Regulations.

— China has a licensing scheme for importing commodities; exporters must file an application with the Ministry of Foreign Trade. Based on China's List of Prohibited and Restricted Imports and Exports enacted in 1987, China restricts the import and export of voice-encoding devices.

— France has no special rules for the import of cryptography, but they have rules regarding the sale and use of cryptography in their country. All products must be certified: Either they must meet a published specification, or the company proprietary specification must be provided to the government. The government may also ask for two units for their own use. Companies must have a license to sell cryptography within France; the license specifies the target market. Users must have a license to buy and use cryptography; the license includes a statement to the effect that users must be prepared to give up their keys to the government up to four months after use. This restriction may be waived in some cases: for banks, large companies, and so on. And there is no use license requirement for cryptography exportable from the U.S.

— Germany follows the CoCom guidelines, requiring a license to export cryptography. They specifically maintain control of public-domain and mass-market cryptography software.

— Israel has import restrictions, but no one seems to know what they are.

— Belgium, Italy, Japan, Netherlands, and the United Kingdom follow the CoCom guidelines on cryptography, requiring a license for export.

— Brazil, India, Mexico, Russia, Saudi Arabia, Spain, South Africa, Sweden, and Switzerland have no import or export controls on cryptography.

25.16 LEGAL ISSUES

Are digital signatures real signatures? Will they stand up in court? Some preliminary legal research has resulted in the opinion that digital signatures would meet the requirements of legally binding signatures for most purposes, including commercial use as defined in the Uniform Commercial Code (UCC). A GAO (General Accounting Office) decision, made at the request of NIST, opines that digital signatures will meet the legal standards of handwritten signatures [362].

The Utah Digital Signature Act went into effect on May 1, 1995, providing a legal framework for the use of digital signatures in the judicial system. California has a bill pending, while Oregon and Washington are still writing theirs. Texas and Florida are right behind. By this book's publication, more states will have followed suit.

The American Bar Association (EDI and Information Technology Division of the Science and Technology Section) produced a model act for states to use for their own legislation. The act attempts to incorporate digital signatures into the existing legal infrastructure for signatures: the Uniform Commercial Code, the United States Federal Reserve regulations, common law of contracts and signatures, the United Nations Convention on Contracts for the International Sale of Goods, and the United Nations Convention on International Bills of Exchange and International Promissory Committees. Included in the act are responsibilities and obligations of certification authorities, issues of liability, and limits and policies.

In the United States, laws about signatures, contracts, and commercial transactions are state laws, so this model act is designed for states. The eventual goal is a federal act, but if this all begins at the state level there is less chance of the NSA mucking up the works.

Even so, the validity of digital signatures has not been challenged in court; their legal status is still undefined. In order for digital signatures to carry the same authority as handwritten signatures, they must first be used to sign a legally binding document, and then be challenged in court by one party. The court would then consider the security of the signature scheme and issue a ruling. Over time, as this happened repeatedly, a body of precedent rulings would emerge regarding which digital signature methods and what key sizes are required for a digital signature to be legally binding. This is likely to take years.

Until then, if two people wish to use digital signatures for contracts (or purchase requests, or work orders, or whatever), it is recommended that they sign a paper contract in which they agree in the future to be bound by any documents digitally signed by them [1099]. This document would specify algorithm, key size, and any other parameters; it should also delineate how disputes would be resolved.

Afterword
by Matt Blaze

One of the most dangerous aspects of cryptology (and, by extension, of this book), is that you can almost measure it. Knowledge of key lengths, factoring methods, and cryptanalytic techniques makes it possible to estimate (in the absence of a real theory of cipher design) the "work factor" required to break a particular cipher. It's all too tempting to misuse these estimates as if they were overall security metrics for the systems in which they are used. The real world offers the attacker a richer menu of options than mere cryptanalysis. Often more worrisome are protocol attacks, Trojan horses, viruses, electromagnetic monitoring, physical compromise, blackmail and intimidation of key holders, operating system bugs, application program bugs, hardware bugs, user errors, physical eavesdropping, social engineering, and dumpster diving, to name just a few.

High-quality ciphers and protocols are important tools, but by themselves make poor substitutes for realistic, critical thinking about what is actually being protected and how various defenses might fail (attackers, after all, rarely restrict themselves to the clean, well-defined threat models of the academic world). Ross Anderson gives examples of cryptographically strong systems (in the banking industry) that fail when exposed to the threats of the real world [43,44]. Even when the attacker has access only to ciphertext, seemingly minor breaches in other parts of the system can leak enough information to render good cryptosystems useless. The Allies in World War II broke the German Enigma traffic largely by carefully exploiting operator errors [1587].

An NSA-employed acquaintance, when asked whether the government can crack DES traffic, quipped that real systems are so insecure that they never need to bother. Unfortunately, there are no easy recipes for making a system secure, no substitute for careful design and critical, ongoing scrutiny. Good cryptosystems have the nice property of making life much harder for the attacker than for the legitimate user; this is not the case for almost every other aspect of computer and communication security. Consider the following (quite incomplete) "Top Ten Threats to Security in Real Systems" list; all are easier to exploit than to prevent.

1. The sorry state of software. Everyone knows that nobody knows how to write software. Modern systems are complex, with hundreds of thousands of lines of code; any one of them has the chance to compromise security. Fatal bugs may even be far-removed from the security portion of the software.

2. Ineffective protection against denial-of-service attacks. Some cryptographic protocols allow anonymity. It may be especially dangerous to deploy anonymous protocols if they increase the opportunities for unidentified vandals to disrupt service; anonymous systems therefore need to be especially resistant to denial-of-service attacks. Robust networks can more easily support anonymity; consider that hardly anyone worries very much about the millions of anonymous entry points to more robust networks like the telephone system or the postal service, where it's relatively difficult (or expensive) for an individual to cause large-scale failures.

3. No place to store secrets. Cryptosystems protect large secrets with smaller ones (keys). Unfortunately, modern computers aren't especially good at protecting even the smallest secrets. Multi-user networked workstations can be broken into and their memories compromised. Standalone, single-user machines can be stolen or compromised through viruses that leak secrets asynchronously. Remote servers, where there may be no user available to enter a passphrase (but see threat #5), are an especially hard problem.

4. Poor random-number generation. Keys and session variables need good sources of unpredictable bits. A running computer has a lot of entropy in it but rarely provides applications with a convenient or reliable way to exploit it. A number of techniques have been proposed for getting true random numbers in software (taking advantage of unpredictability in things like I/O interarrival timing, clock and timer skew, and even air turbulence inside disk enclosures), but all these are very sensitive to slight changes in the environments in which they are used.

5. Weak passphrases. Most cryptographic software addresses the key storage and key generation problems by relying on user-generated passphrase strings, which are presumed to be unpredictable enough to produce good key material and are also easy enough to remember that they do not require secure storage. While dictionary attacks are a well-known problem with short passwords, much less is known about lines of attack against user-selected passphrase-based keys. Shannon tells us that English text has only just over 1 bit of entropy per character, which would seem to leave most passphrases well within reach of brute-force search. Less is known, however, about good techniques for enumerating passphrases in order to exploit this. Until we have a better understanding of how to attack passphrases, we really have no idea how weak or strong they are.

6. Mismatched trust. Almost all currently available cryptographic software assumes that the user is in direct control over the systems on which it runs and has a secure path to it. For example, the interfaces to programs like PGP assume that their passphrase input always comes from the user over a secure path like the local console. This is not always the case, of course; consider the problem of reading your encrypted mail when logged in over a network connection. What the system designer assumes is trusted may not match the needs or expectations of the real users, especially when software can be controlled remotely over insecure networks.

7. Poorly understood protocol and service interactions. As systems get bigger and more complex, benign features frequently come back to haunt us, and it's hard to know even where to look when things fail. The Internet worm was propagated via an obscure and innocent-looking feature in the sendmail program; how many more features in how many more programs have unexpected consequences just waiting to be discovered?

8. Unrealistic threat and risks assessment. Security experts tend to focus on the threats they know how to model and prevent. Unfortunately, attackers focus on what they know how to exploit, and the two are rarely exactly the same. Too many "secure" systems are designed without considering what the attacker is actually likely to do.

9. Interfaces that make security expensive and special. If security features are to be used, they must be convenient and transparent enough that people actually turn them on. It's easy to design encryption mechanisms that come only at the expense of performance or ease of use, and even easier to design mechanisms that invite mistakes. Security should be harder to turn off than on; unfortunately, few systems actually work this way.

10. Little broad-based demand for security. This is a well-known problem among almost everyone who has tied his or her fortune to selling security products and services. Until there is widespread demand for transparent security, the tools and infrastructure needed to support it will be expensive and inaccessible to many applications. This is partly a problem of understanding and exposing the threats and risks in real applications and partly a problem of not designing systems that include security as a basic feature rather than as a later add-on.

A more complete list and discussion of these kinds of threats could easily fill a book of this size and barely scratch the surface. What makes them especially difficult and dangerous is that there are no magic techniques, beyond good engineering and ongoing scrutiny, for avoiding them. The lesson for the aspiring cryptographer is to respect the limits of the art.

Matt Blaze
New York, NY

PART V

SOURCE CODE

1. DES

2. LOKI91

3. IDEA

4. GOST

5. BLOWFISH

6. 3-Way

7. RC5

8. A5

9. SEAL

DES

```
#define EN0    0      /* MODE == encrypt */
#define DE1    1      /* MODE == decrypt */

typedef struct {
        unsigned long ek[32];
        unsigned long dk[32];
} des_ctx;

extern void deskey(unsigned char *, short);
/*                 hexkey[8]     MODE
 * Sets the internal key register according to the hexadecimal
 * key contained in the 8 bytes of hexkey, according to the DES,
 * for encryption or decryption according to MODE.
 */

extern void usekey(unsigned long *);
/*                 cookedkey[32]
```

```
 * Loads the internal key register with the data in cookedkey.
 */

extern void cpkey(unsigned long *);
/*                cookedkey[32]
 * Copies the contents of the internal key register into the storage
 * located at &cookedkey[0].
 */

extern void des(unsigned char *, unsigned char *);
/*                from[8]          to[8]
 * Encrypts/Decrypts (according to the key currently loaded in the
 * internal key register) one block of eight bytes at address 'from'
 * into the block at address 'to'.  They can be the same.
 */

static void scrunch(unsigned char *, unsigned long *);
static void unscrun(unsigned long *, unsigned char *);
static void desfunc(unsigned long *, unsigned long *);
static void cookey(unsigned long *);

static unsigned long KnL[32] = { 0L };
static unsigned long KnR[32] = { 0L };
static unsigned long Kn3[32] = { 0L };
static unsigned char Df_Key[24] = {
        0x01,0x23,0x45,0x67,0x89,0xab,0xcd,0xef,
        0xfe,0xdc,0xba,0x98,0x76,0x54,0x32,0x10,
        0x89,0xab,0xcd,0xef,0x01,0x23,0x45,0x67 };

static unsigned short bytebit[8]    = {
        0200, 0100, 040, 020, 010, 04, 02, 01 };

static unsigned long bigbyte[24] = {
        0x800000L,    0x400000L,    0x200000L,    0x100000L,
        0x80000L,     0x40000L,     0x20000L,     0x10000L,
        0x8000L,      0x4000L,      0x2000L,      0x1000L,
        0x800L,             0x400L,             0x200L,             0x100L,
        0x80L,              0x40L,              0x20L,              0x10L,
        0x8L,         0x4L,         0x2L,         0x1L   };

/* Use the key schedule specified in the Standard (ANSI X3.92-1981). */

static unsigned char pc1[56] = {
        56, 48, 40, 32, 24, 16,  8,   0, 57, 49, 41, 33, 25, 17,
         9,  1, 58, 50, 42, 34, 26,  18, 10,  2, 59, 51, 43, 35,
        62, 54, 46, 38, 30, 22, 14,   6, 61, 53, 45, 37, 29, 21,
        13,  5, 60, 52, 44, 36, 28,  20, 12,  4, 27, 19, 11,  3 };

static unsigned char totrot[16] = {
        1,2,4,6,8,10,12,14,15,17,19,21,23,25,27,28 };

static unsigned char pc2[48] = {
        13, 16, 10, 23,  0,  4,   2, 27, 14,  5, 20,  9,
        22, 18, 11,  3, 25,  7,  15,  6, 26, 19, 12,  1,
        40, 51, 30, 36, 46, 54,  29, 39, 50, 44, 32, 47,
        43, 48, 38, 55, 33, 52,  45, 41, 49, 35, 28, 31 };
```

```
void deskey(key, edf)          /* Thanks to James Gillogly & Phil Karn! */
unsigned char *key;
short edf;
{
      register int i, j, l, m, n;
      unsigned char pc1m[56], pcr[56];
      unsigned long kn[32];

      for ( j = 0; j < 56; j++ ) {
            l = pc1[j];
            m = l & 07;
            pc1m[j] = (key[l >> 3] & bytebit[m]) ? 1 : 0;
            }
      for( i = 0; i < 16; i++ ) {
            if( edf == DE1 ) m = (15 - i) << 1;
            else m = i << 1;
            n = m + 1;
            kn[m] = kn[n] = 0L;
            for( j = 0; j < 28; j++ ) {
                  l = j + totrot[i];
                  if( l < 28 ) pcr[j] = pc1m[l];
                  else pcr[j] = pc1m[l - 28];
                  }
            for( j = 28; j < 56; j++ ) {
                l = j + totrot[i];
                if( l < 56 ) pcr[j] = pc1m[l];
                else pcr[j] = pc1m[l - 28];
                }
            for( j = 0; j < 24; j++ ) {
                  if( pcr[pc2[j]] ) kn[m] |= bigbyte[j];
                  if( pcr[pc2[j+24]] ) kn[n] |= bigbyte[j];
                  }
            }
      cookey(kn);
      return;
}


static void cookey(raw1)
register unsigned long *raw1;
{
      register unsigned long *cook, *raw0;
      unsigned long dough[32];
      register int i;

      cook = dough;
      for( i = 0; i < 16; i++, raw1++ ) {
            raw0 = raw1++;
            *cook   = (*raw0 & 0x00fc0000L) << 6;
            *cook  |= (*raw0 & 0x00000fc0L) << 10;
            *cook  |= (*raw1 & 0x00fc0000L) >> 10;
            *cook++        |= (*raw1 & 0x00000fc0L) >> 6;
            *cook   = (*raw0 & 0x0003f000L) << 12;
            *cook  |= (*raw0 & 0x0000003fL) << 16;
            *cook  |= (*raw1 & 0x0003f000L) >> 4;
            *cook++        |= (*raw1 & 0x0000003fL);
```

```
                }
        usekey(dough);
        return;
}

void cpkey(into)
register unsigned long *into;
{
        register unsigned long *from, *endp;

        from = KnL, endp = &KnL[32];
        while( from < endp ) *into++ = *from++;
        return;
}

void usekey(from)
register unsigned long *from;
{
        register unsigned long *to, *endp;

        to = KnL, endp = &KnL[32];
        while( to < endp ) *to++ = *from++;
        return;
}

void des(inblock, outblock)
unsigned char *inblock, *outblock;
{
        unsigned long work[2];

        scrunch(inblock, work);
        desfunc(work, KnL);
        unscrun(work, outblock);
        return;
}

static void scrunch(outof, into)
register unsigned char *outof;
register unsigned long *into;
{
        *into    = (*outof++ & 0xffL) << 24;
        *into   |= (*outof++ & 0xffL) << 16;
        *into   |= (*outof++ & 0xffL) << 8;
        *into++ |= (*outof++ & 0xffL);
        *into    = (*outof++ & 0xffL) << 24;
        *into   |= (*outof++ & 0xffL) << 16;
        *into   |= (*outof++ & 0xffL) << 8;
        *into   |= (*outof    & 0xffL);
        return;
}

static void unscrun(outof, into)
register unsigned long *outof;
register unsigned char *into;
{
```

```
        *into++ = (*outof >> 24) & 0xffL;
        *into++ = (*outof >> 16) & 0xffL;
        *into++ = (*outof >>  8) & 0xffL;
        *into++ =  *outof++           & 0xffL;
        *into++ = (*outof >> 24) & 0xffL;
        *into++ = (*outof >> 16) & 0xffL;
        *into++ = (*outof >>  8) & 0xffL;
        *into   =  *outof     & 0xffL;
        return;
}

static unsigned long SP1[64] = {
        0x01010400L, 0x00000000L, 0x00010000L, 0x01010404L,
        0x01010004L, 0x00010404L, 0x00000004L, 0x00010000L,
        0x00000400L, 0x01010400L, 0x01010404L, 0x00000400L,
        0x01000404L, 0x01010004L, 0x01000000L, 0x00000004L,
        0x00000404L, 0x01000400L, 0x01000400L, 0x00010400L,
        0x00010400L, 0x01010000L, 0x01010000L, 0x01000404L,
        0x00010004L, 0x01000004L, 0x01000004L, 0x00010004L,
        0x00000000L, 0x00000404L, 0x00010404L, 0x01000000L,
        0x00010000L, 0x01010404L, 0x00000004L, 0x01010000L,
        0x01010400L, 0x01000000L, 0x01000000L, 0x00000400L,
        0x01010004L, 0x00010000L, 0x00010400L, 0x01000004L,
        0x00000400L, 0x00000004L, 0x01000404L, 0x00010404L,
        0x01010404L, 0x00010004L, 0x01010000L, 0x01000404L,
        0x01000004L, 0x00000404L, 0x00010404L, 0x01010400L,
        0x00000404L, 0x01000400L, 0x01000400L, 0x00000000L,
        0x00010004L, 0x00010400L, 0x00000000L, 0x01010004L };

static unsigned long SP2[64] = {
        0x80108020L, 0x80008000L, 0x00008000L, 0x00108020L,
        0x00100000L, 0x00000020L, 0x80100020L, 0x80008020L,
        0x80000020L, 0x80108020L, 0x80108000L, 0x80000000L,
        0x80008000L, 0x00100000L, 0x00000020L, 0x80100020L,
        0x00108000L, 0x00100020L, 0x80008020L, 0x00000000L,
        0x80000000L, 0x00008000L, 0x00108020L, 0x80100000L,
        0x00100020L, 0x80000020L, 0x00000000L, 0x00108000L,
        0x00008020L, 0x80108000L, 0x80100000L, 0x00008020L,
        0x00000000L, 0x00108020L, 0x80100020L, 0x00100000L,
        0x80008020L, 0x80100000L, 0x80108000L, 0x00008000L,
        0x80100000L, 0x80008000L, 0x00000020L, 0x80108020L,
        0x00108020L, 0x00000020L, 0x00008000L, 0x80000000L,
        0x00008020L, 0x80108000L, 0x00100000L, 0x80000020L,
        0x00100020L, 0x80008020L, 0x80000020L, 0x00100020L,
        0x00108000L, 0x00000000L, 0x80008000L, 0x00008020L,
        0x80000000L, 0x80100020L, 0x80108020L, 0x00108000L };

static unsigned long SP3[64] = {
        0x00000208L, 0x08020200L, 0x00000000L, 0x08020008L,
        0x08000200L, 0x00000000L, 0x00020208L, 0x08000200L,
        0x00020008L, 0x08000008L, 0x08000008L, 0x00020000L,
        0x08020208L, 0x00020008L, 0x08020000L, 0x00000208L,
        0x08000000L, 0x00000008L, 0x08020200L, 0x00000200L,
        0x00020200L, 0x08020000L, 0x08020008L, 0x00020208L,
```

```
        0x08000208L, 0x00020200L, 0x00020000L, 0x08000208L,
        0x00000008L, 0x08020208L, 0x00000200L, 0x08000000L,
        0x08020200L, 0x08000000L, 0x00020008L, 0x00000208L,
        0x00020000L, 0x08020200L, 0x08000200L, 0x00000000L,
        0x00000200L, 0x00020008L, 0x08020208L, 0x08000200L,
        0x08000008L, 0x00000200L, 0x00000000L, 0x08020008L,
        0x08000208L, 0x00020000L, 0x08000000L, 0x08020208L,
        0x00000008L, 0x00020208L, 0x00020200L, 0x08000008L,
        0x08020000L, 0x08000208L, 0x00000208L, 0x08020000L,
        0x00020208L, 0x00000008L, 0x08020008L, 0x00020200L };

static unsigned long SP4[64] = {
        0x00802001L, 0x00002081L, 0x00002081L, 0x00000080L,
        0x00802080L, 0x00800081L, 0x00800001L, 0x00002001L,
        0x00000000L, 0x00802000L, 0x00802000L, 0x00802081L,
        0x00000081L, 0x00000000L, 0x00800080L, 0x00800001L,
        0x00000001L, 0x00002000L, 0x00800000L, 0x00802001L,
        0x00000080L, 0x00800000L, 0x00002001L, 0x00002080L,
        0x00800081L, 0x00000001L, 0x00002080L, 0x00800080L,
        0x00002000L, 0x00802080L, 0x00802081L, 0x00000081L,
        0x00800080L, 0x00800001L, 0x00802000L, 0x00802081L,
        0x00000081L, 0x00000000L, 0x00000000L, 0x00802000L,
        0x00002080L, 0x00800080L, 0x00800081L, 0x00000001L,
        0x00802001L, 0x00002081L, 0x00002081L, 0x00000080L,
        0x00802081L, 0x00000081L, 0x00000001L, 0x00002000L,
        0x00800001L, 0x00002001L, 0x00802080L, 0x00800081L,
        0x00002001L, 0x00002080L, 0x00800000L, 0x00802001L,
        0x00000080L, 0x00800000L, 0x00002000L, 0x00802080L };

static unsigned long SP5[64] = {
        0x00000100L, 0x02080100L, 0x02080000L, 0x42000100L,
        0x00080000L, 0x00000100L, 0x40000000L, 0x02080000L,
        0x40080100L, 0x00080000L, 0x02000100L, 0x40080100L,
        0x42000100L, 0x42080000L, 0x00080100L, 0x40000000L,
        0x02000000L, 0x40080000L, 0x40080000L, 0x00000000L,
        0x40000100L, 0x42080100L, 0x42080100L, 0x02000100L,
        0x42080000L, 0x40000100L, 0x00000000L, 0x42000000L,
        0x02080100L, 0x02000000L, 0x42000000L, 0x00080100L,
        0x00080000L, 0x42000100L, 0x00000100L, 0x02000000L,
        0x40000000L, 0x02080000L, 0x42000100L, 0x40080100L,
        0x02000100L, 0x40000000L, 0x42080000L, 0x02080100L,
        0x40080100L, 0x00000100L, 0x02000000L, 0x42080000L,
        0x42080100L, 0x00080100L, 0x42000000L, 0x42080100L,
        0x02080000L, 0x00000000L, 0x40080000L, 0x42000000L,
        0x00080100L, 0x02000100L, 0x40000100L, 0x00080000L,
        0x00000000L, 0x40080000L, 0x02080100L, 0x40000100L };

static unsigned long SP6[64] = {
        0x20000010L, 0x20400000L, 0x00004000L, 0x20404010L,
        0x20400000L, 0x00000010L, 0x20404010L, 0x00400000L,
        0x20004000L, 0x00404010L, 0x00400000L, 0x20000010L,
        0x00400010L, 0x20004000L, 0x20000000L, 0x00004010L,
        0x00000000L, 0x00400010L, 0x20004010L, 0x00004000L,
        0x00404000L, 0x20004010L, 0x00000010L, 0x20400010L,
```

```
        0x20400010L, 0x00000000L, 0x00404010L, 0x20404000L,
        0x00004010L, 0x00404000L, 0x20404000L, 0x20000000L,
        0x20004000L, 0x00000010L, 0x20400010L, 0x00404000L,
        0x20404010L, 0x00400000L, 0x00004010L, 0x20000010L,
        0x00400000L, 0x20004000L, 0x20000000L, 0x00004010L,
        0x20000010L, 0x20404010L, 0x00404000L, 0x20400000L,
        0x00404010L, 0x20404000L, 0x00000000L, 0x20400010L,
        0x00000010L, 0x00004000L, 0x20400000L, 0x00404010L,
        0x00004000L, 0x00400010L, 0x20004010L, 0x00000000L,
        0x20404000L, 0x20000000L, 0x00400010L, 0x20004010L };

static unsigned long SP7[64] = {
        0x00200000L, 0x04200002L, 0x04000802L, 0x00000000L,
        0x00000800L, 0x04000802L, 0x00200802L, 0x04200800L,
        0x04200802L, 0x00200000L, 0x00000000L, 0x04000002L,
        0x00000002L, 0x04000000L, 0x04200002L, 0x00000802L,
        0x04000800L, 0x00200802L, 0x00200002L, 0x04000800L,
        0x04000002L, 0x04200000L, 0x04200800L, 0x00200002L,
        0x04200000L, 0x00000800L, 0x00000802L, 0x04200802L,
        0x00200800L, 0x00000002L, 0x04000000L, 0x00200800L,
        0x04000000L, 0x00200800L, 0x00200000L, 0x04000802L,
        0x04000802L, 0x04200002L, 0x04200002L, 0x00000002L,
        0x00200002L, 0x04000000L, 0x04000800L, 0x00200000L,
        0x04200800L, 0x00000802L, 0x00200802L, 0x04200800L,
        0x00000802L, 0x04000002L, 0x04200802L, 0x04200000L,
        0x00200800L, 0x00000000L, 0x00000002L, 0x04200802L,
        0x00000000L, 0x00200802L, 0x04200000L, 0x00000800L,
        0x04000002L, 0x04000800L, 0x00000800L, 0x00200002L };

static unsigned long SP8[64] = {
        0x10001040L, 0x00001000L, 0x00040000L, 0x10041040L,
        0x10000000L, 0x10001040L, 0x00000040L, 0x10000000L,
        0x00040040L, 0x10040000L, 0x10041040L, 0x00041000L,
        0x10041000L, 0x00041040L, 0x00001000L, 0x00000040L,
        0x10040000L, 0x10000040L, 0x10001000L, 0x00001040L,
        0x00041000L, 0x00040040L, 0x10040040L, 0x10041000L,
        0x00001040L, 0x00000000L, 0x00000000L, 0x10040040L,
        0x10000040L, 0x10001000L, 0x00041040L, 0x00040000L,
        0x00041040L, 0x00040000L, 0x10041000L, 0x00001000L,
        0x00000040L, 0x10040040L, 0x00001000L, 0x00041040L,
        0x10001000L, 0x00000040L, 0x10000040L, 0x10040000L,
        0x10040040L, 0x10000000L, 0x00040000L, 0x10001040L,
        0x00000000L, 0x10041040L, 0x00040040L, 0x10000040L,
        0x10040000L, 0x10001000L, 0x10001040L, 0x00000000L,
        0x10041040L, 0x00041000L, 0x00041000L, 0x00001040L,
        0x00001040L, 0x00040040L, 0x10000000L, 0x10041000L };

static void desfunc(block, keys)
register unsigned long *block, *keys;
{
        register unsigned long fval, work, right, leftt;
        register int round;

        leftt = block[0];
```

```
right = block[1];
work = ((leftt >> 4) ^ right) & 0x0f0f0f0fL;
right ^= work;
leftt ^= (work << 4);
work = ((leftt >> 16) ^ right) & 0x0000ffffL;
right ^= work;
leftt ^= (work << 16);
work = ((right >> 2) ^ leftt) & 0x33333333L;
leftt ^= work;
right ^= (work << 2);
work = ((right >> 8) ^ leftt) & 0x00ff00ffL;
leftt ^= work;
right ^= (work << 8);
right = ((right << 1) | ((right >> 31) & 1L)) & 0xffffffffL;
work = (leftt ^ right) & 0xaaaaaaaaL;
leftt ^= work;
right ^= work;
leftt = ((leftt << 1) | ((leftt >> 31) & 1L)) & 0xffffffffL;

for( round = 0; round < 8; round++ ) {
        work  = (right << 28) | (right >> 4);
        work ^= *keys++;
        fval  = SP7[ work              & 0x3fL];
        fval |= SP5[(work >>  8) & 0x3fL];
        fval |= SP3[(work >> 16) & 0x3fL];
        fval |= SP1[(work >> 24) & 0x3fL];
        work  = right ^ *keys++;
        fval |= SP8[ work              & 0x3fL];
        fval |= SP6[(work >>  8) & 0x3fL];
        fval |= SP4[(work >> 16) & 0x3fL];
        fval |= SP2[(work >> 24) & 0x3fL];
        leftt ^= fval;
        work  = (leftt << 28) | (leftt >> 4);
        work ^= *keys++;
        fval  = SP7[ work              & 0x3fL];
        fval |= SP5[(work >>  8) & 0x3fL];
        fval |= SP3[(work >> 16) & 0x3fL];
        fval |= SP1[(work >> 24) & 0x3fL];
        work  = leftt ^ *keys++;
        fval |= SP8[ work              & 0x3fL];
        fval |= SP6[(work >>  8) & 0x3fL];
        fval |= SP4[(work >> 16) & 0x3fL];
        fval |= SP2[(work >> 24) & 0x3fL];
        right ^= fval;
        }

right = (right << 31) | (right >> 1);
work = (leftt ^ right) & 0xaaaaaaaaL;
leftt ^= work;
right ^= work;
leftt = (leftt << 31) | (leftt >> 1);
work = ((leftt >> 8) ^ right) & 0x00ff00ffL;
right ^= work;
leftt ^= (work << 8);
```

```
            work = ((leftt >> 2) ^ right) & 0x33333333L;
            right ^= work;
            leftt ^= (work << 2);
            work = ((right >> 16) ^ leftt) & 0x0000ffffL;
            leftt ^= work;
            right ^= (work << 16);
            work = ((right >> 4) ^ leftt) & 0x0f0f0f0fL;
            leftt ^= work;
            right ^= (work << 4);
            *block++ = right;
            *block = leftt;
            return;
}

/* Validation sets:
 *
 * Single-length key, single-length plaintext -
 * Key    : 0123 4567 89ab cdef
 * Plain  : 0123 4567 89ab cde7
 * Cipher : c957 4425 6a5e d31d
 *
 ********************************************************************/

void des_key(des_ctx *dc, unsigned char *key){
        deskey(key,EN0);
        cpkey(dc->ek);
        deskey(key,DE1);
        cpkey(dc->dk);
}

/* Encrypt several blocks in ECB mode.  Caller is responsible for
   short blocks. */
void des_enc(des_ctx *dc, unsigned char *data, int blocks){
        unsigned long work[2];
        int i;
        unsigned char *cp;

        cp = data;
        for(i=0;i<blocks;i++){
                scrunch(cp,work);
                desfunc(work,dc->ek);
                unscrun(work,cp);
                cp+=8;
        }
}

void des_dec(des_ctx *dc, unsigned char *data, int blocks){
        unsigned long work[2];
        int i;
        unsigned char *cp;

        cp = data;
        for(i=0;i<blocks;i++){
                scrunch(cp,work);
                desfunc(work,dc->dk);
```

```
                unscrun(work,cp);
                cp+=8;
        }
}

void main(void){
        des_ctx dc;
        int i;
        unsigned long data[10];
        char *cp,key[8] = {0x01,0x23,0x45,0x67,0x89,0xab,0xcd,0xef};
        char x[8] = {0x01,0x23,0x45,0x67,0x89,0xab,0xcd,0xe7};

        cp = x;

        des_key(&dc,key);
        des_enc(&dc,cp,1);
        printf("Enc(0..7,0..7) = ");
        for(i=0;i<8;i++) printf("%02x ", ((unsigned int) cp[i])&0x00ff);
        printf("\n");

        des_dec(&dc,cp,1);

        printf("Dec(above,0..7) = ");
        for(i=0;i<8;i++) printf("%02x ",((unsigned int)cp[i])&0x00ff);
        printf("\n");

        cp = (char *) data;
        for(i=0;i<10;i++)data[i]=i;

        des_enc(&dc,cp,5); /* Enc 5 blocks. */
        for(i=0;i<10;i+=2) printf("Block %01d = %08lx %08lx.\n",
                        i/2,data[i],data[i+1]);

        des_dec(&dc,cp,1);
        des_dec(&dc,cp+8,4);
        for(i=0;i<10;i+=2) printf("Block %01d = %08lx %08lx.\n",
                        i/2,data[i],data[i+1]);

}
```

LOKI91

```
#include <stdio.h>

#define LOKIBLK      8               /* No of bytes in a LOKI data-block        */
#define ROUNDS       16              /* No of LOKI rounds                       */

typedef unsigned long         Long;  /* type specification for aligned LOKI blocks
*/

extern Long    lokikey[2];    /* 64-bit key used by LOKI routines         */
extern char    *loki_lib_ver; /* String with version no. & copyright      */

#ifdef __STDC__               /* declare prototypes for library functions */
extern void enloki(char *b);
```

```
extern void deloki(char *b);
extern void setlokikey(char key[LOKIBLK]);
#else                           /* else just declare library functions extern */
extern void enloki(), deloki(), setlokikey();
#endif __STDC__

char P[32] = {
        31, 23, 15, 7, 30, 22, 14, 6,
        29, 21, 13, 5, 28, 20, 12, 4,
        27, 19, 11, 3, 26, 18, 10, 2,
        25, 17, 9, 1, 24, 16, 8, 0
        };

typedef         struct {
        short   gen;            /* irreducible polynomial used in this field */
        short   exp;            /* exponent used to generate this s function */
        } sfn_desc;

sfn_desc sfn[] = {
        { /* 101110111 */ 375, 31}, { /* 101111011 */ 379, 31},
        { /* 110000111 */ 391, 31}, { /* 110001011 */ 395, 31},
        { /* 110001101 */ 397, 31}, { /* 110011111 */ 415, 31},
        { /* 110100011 */ 419, 31}, { /* 110101001 */ 425, 31},
        { /* 110110001 */ 433, 31}, { /* 110111101 */ 445, 31},
        { /* 111000011 */ 451, 31}, { /* 111001111 */ 463, 31},
        { /* 111010111 */ 471, 31}, { /* 111011101 */ 477, 31},
        { /* 111100111 */ 487, 31}, { /* 111110011 */ 499, 31},
        { 00, 00}       };

typedef struct {
        Long loki_subkeys[ROUNDS];
} loki_ctx;

static Long     f();                    /* declare LOKI function f */
static short    s();                    /* declare LOKI S-box fn s */

#define ROL12(b) b = ((b << 12) | (b >> 20));
#define ROL13(b) b = ((b << 13) | (b >> 19));

#ifdef  LITTLE_ENDIAN
#define bswap(cb) {                                     \
        register char   c;                              \
        c = cb[0]; cb[0] = cb[3]; cb[3] = c;            \
        c = cb[1]; cb[1] = cb[2]; cb[2] = c;            \
        c = cb[4]; cb[4] = cb[7]; cb[7] = c;            \
        c = cb[5]; cb[5] = cb[6]; cb[6] = c;            \
}
#endif

void
setlokikey(loki_ctx *c, char *key)
{
        register        i;
        register Long   KL, KR;
```

```
#ifdef LITTLE_ENDIAN
        bswap(key);                         /* swap bytes round if little-endian */
#endif
        KL = ((Long *)key)[0];
        KR = ((Long *)key)[1];

        for (i=0; i<ROUNDS; i+=4) {         /* Generate the 16 subkeys */
            c->loki_subkeys[i] = KL;
            ROL12 (KL);
            c->loki_subkeys[i+1] = KL;
            ROL13 (KL);
            c->loki_subkeys[i+2] = KR;
            ROL12 (KR);
            c->loki_subkeys[i+3] = KR;
            ROL13 (KR);
        }
#ifdef LITTLE_ENDIAN
        bswap(key);                         /* swap bytes back if little-endian */
#endif
}

void
enloki (loki_ctx *c, char *b)
{
        register       i;
        register Long  L, R;        /* left & right data halves  */

#ifdef LITTLE_ENDIAN
        bswap(b);                           /* swap bytes round if little-endian */
#endif

        L = ((Long *)b)[0];
        R = ((Long *)b)[1];

        for (i=0; i<ROUNDS; i+=2) {         /* Encrypt with the 16 subkeys */
            L ^= f (R, c->loki_subkeys[i]);
            R ^= f (L, c->loki_subkeys[i+1]);
        }

        ((Long *)b)[0] = R;                 /* Y = swap(LR) */
        ((Long *)b)[1] = L;

#ifdef LITTLE_ENDIAN
        bswap(b);                           /* swap bytes round if little-endian */
#endif
}

void
deloki(loki_ctx *c, char *b)
{
        register       i;
        register Long  L, R;                /* left & right data halves  */

#ifdef LITTLE_ENDIAN
```

```
        bswap(b);                        /* swap bytes round if little-endian */
#endif

        L = ((Long *)b)[0];                 /* LR = X XOR K */
        R = ((Long *)b)[1];

        for (i=ROUNDS; i>0; i-=2) {                 /* subkeys in reverse order */
            L ^= f(R, c->loki_subkeys[i-1]);
            R ^= f(L, c->loki_subkeys[i-2]);
        }

        ((Long *)b)[0] = R;                 /* Y = LR XOR K */
        ((Long *)b)[1] = L;
}

#define MASK12          0x0fff              /* 12 bit mask for expansion E */

static Long
f(r, k)
register Long  r;       /* Data value R(i-1) */
Long           k;       /* Key      K(i)   */
{
        Long   a, b, c;             /* 32 bit S-box output, & P output */

        a = r ^ k;                  /* A = R(i-1) XOR K(i) */

        /* want to use slow speed/small size version */
        b = ((Long)s((a            & MASK12))       ) | /* B = S(E(R(i-1))^K(i)) */
            ((Long)s(((a >>  8) & MASK12)) <<  8) |
            ((Long)s(((a >> 16) & MASK12)) << 16) |
            ((Long)s((((a >> 24) | (a << 8)) & MASK12)) << 24);

        perm32(&c, &b, P);          /* C = P(S( E(R(i-1)) XOR K(i))) */

        return(c);                  /* f returns the result C */
}

static short s(i)
register Long i;        /* return S-box value for input i */
{
        register short r, c, v, t;
        short  exp8();                 /* exponentiation routine for GF(2^8) */

        r = ((i>>8) & 0xc) | (i & 0x3);             /* row value-top 2 & bottom 2 */
        c = (i>>2) & 0xff;                          /* column value-middle 8 bits */
        t = (c + ((r * 17) ^ 0xff)) & 0xff;         /* base value for Sfn */
        v = exp8(t, sfn[r].exp, sfn[r].gen);        /* Sfn[r] = t ^ exp mod gen */
        return(v);
}

#define       MSB    0x80000000L          /* MSB of 32-bit word */

perm32(out, in , perm)
Long    *out;           /* Output 32-bit block to be permuted              */
```

```
Long    *in;            /* Input  32-bit block after permutation       */
char    perm[32];       /* Permutation array                           */
{
        Long    mask = MSB;                     /* mask used to set bit in output   */
        register int   i, o, b;         /* input bit no, output bit no, value */
        register char  *p = perm;       /* ptr to permutation array  */

        *out = 0;                       /* clear output block */
        for (o=0; o<32; o++) {          /* For each output bit position o */
                i =(int)*p++;           /* get input bit permuted to output o */
                b = (*in >> i) & 01;            /* value of input bit i */
                if (b)                  /* If the input bit i is set */
                        *out |= mask;           /*  OR in mask to output i */
                mask >>= 1;                     /* Shift mask to next bit      */
        }
}

#define SIZE 256                /* 256 elements in GF(2^8) */

short mult8(a, b, gen)
short   a, b;           /* operands for multiply */
short   gen;            /* irreducible polynomial generating Galois Field */
{
        short   product = 0;            /* result of multiplication */

        while(b != 0) {                         /* while multiplier is non-zero */
                if (b & 01)
                        product ^= a;           /*    add multiplicand if LSB of b set */
                a <<= 1;                /*   shift multiplicand one place */
                if (a >= SIZE)
                        a ^= gen;       /*   and modulo reduce if needed */
                b >>= 1;                /*   shift multiplier one place   */
        }
        return(product);
}

short exp8(base, exponent, gen)
short   base;           /* base of exponentiation      */
short   exponent;       /* exponent                    */
short   gen;            /* irreducible polynomial generating Galois Field */
{
        short   accum = base;           /* superincreasing sequence of base */
        short   result = 1;     /* result of exponentiation       */

        if (base == 0)                  /* if zero base specified then     */
                return(0);      /* the result is "0" if base = 0    */

        while (exponent != 0) {         /* repeat while exponent non-zero */
                if (( exponent & 0x0001) == 0x0001)             /* multiply if exp 1 */
                        result = mult8(result, accum, gen);
                exponent >>= 1;                 /* shift exponent to next digit */
                accum = mult8(accum, accum, gen);                       /* & square  */
        }
        return(result);
}
```

```c
void loki_key(loki_ctx *c, unsigned char *key){
        setlokikey(c,key);
}

void loki_enc(loki_ctx *c, unsigned char *data, int blocks){
        unsigned char *cp;
        int i;

        cp = data;
        for(i=0;i<blocks;i++){
                enloki(c,cp);
                cp+=8;
        }
}

void loki_dec(loki_ctx *c, unsigned char *data, int blocks){
        unsigned char *cp;
        int i;

        cp = data;
        for(i=0;i<blocks;i++){
                deloki(c,cp);
                cp+=8;
        }
}

void main(void){
        loki_ctx lc;
        unsigned long data[10];
        unsigned char *cp;
        unsigned char key[] = {0,1,2,3,4,5,6,7};
        int i;

        for(i=0;i<10;i++) data[i]=i;

        loki_key(&lc,key);

        cp = (char *)data;
        loki_enc(&lc,cp,5);
        for(i=0;i<10;i+=2) printf("Block %01d = %08lx %08lx\n",
                        i/2,data[i],data[i+1]);
        loki_dec(&lc,cp,1);
        loki_dec(&lc,cp+8,4);
        for(i=0;i<10;i+=2) printf("Block %01d = %08lx %08lx\n",
                        i/2,data[i],data[i+1]);

}
```

IDEA

```c
typedef unsigned char boolean;     /* values are TRUE or FALSE */
typedef unsigned char byte; /* values are 0-255 */
typedef byte *byteptr;       /* pointer to byte */
```

```
typedef char *string;/* pointer to ASCII character string */
typedef unsigned short word16;        /* values are 0-65535 */
typedef unsigned long word32;         /* values are 0-4294967295 */

#ifndef TRUE
#define FALSE 0
#define TRUE (!FALSE)
#endif /* if TRUE not already defined */

#ifndef min    /* if min macro not already defined */
#define min(a,b) ( (a)<(b) ? (a) : (b) )
#define max(a,b) ( (a)>(b) ? (a) : (b) )
#endif /* if min macro not already defined */

#define IDEAKEYSIZE 16
#define IDEABLOCKSIZE 8

#define IDEAROUNDS 8
#define IDEAKEYLEN (6*IDEAROUNDS+4)

typedef struct{
       word16 ek[IDEAKEYLEN],dk[IDEAKEYLEN];
}idea_ctx;

/* End includes for IDEA.C */
#ifdef IDEA32        /* Use >16-bit temporaries */
#define low16(x) ((x) & 0xFFFF)
typedef unsigned int uint16;/* at LEAST 16 bits, maybe more */
#else
#define low16(x) (x) /* this is only ever applied to uint16's */
typedef word16 uint16;
#endif

#ifdef SMALL_CACHE
static uint16
mul(register uint16 a, register uint16 b)
{
       register word32 p;

       p = (word32)a * b;
       if (p) {
               b = low16(p);
               a = p>>16;
               return (b - a) + (b < a);
       } else if (a) {
               return 1-b;
       } else {
               return 1-a;
       }
} /* mul */
#endif /* SMALL_CACHE */

static uint16
mulInv(uint16 x)
{
```

```
        uint16 t0, t1;
        uint16 q, y;

        if (x <= 1)
                return x;       /* 0 and 1 are self-inverse */
        t1 = 0x10001L / x;   /* Since x >= 2, this fits into 16 bits */
        y = 0x10001L % x;
        if (y == 1)
                return low16(1-t1);
        t0 = 1;
        do {
                q = x / y;
                x = x % y;
                t0 += q * t1;
                if (x == 1)
                        return t0;
                q = y / x;
                y = y % x;
                t1 += q * t0;
        } while (y != 1);
        return low16(1-t1);
} /* mulInv */


static void
ideaExpandKey(byte const *userkey, word16 *EK)
{
        int i,j;

        for (j=0; j<8; j++) {
                EK[j] = (userkey[0]<<8) + userkey[1];
                userkey += 2;
        }
        for (i=0; j < IDEAKEYLEN; j++) {
                i++;
                EK[i+7] = EK[i & 7] << 9 | EK[i+1 & 7] >> 7;
                EK += i & 8;
                i &= 7;
        }
} /* ideaExpandKey */


static void
ideaInvertKey(word16 const *EK, word16 DK[IDEAKEYLEN])
{
        int i;
        uint16 t1, t2, t3;
        word16 temp[IDEAKEYLEN];
        word16 *p = temp + IDEAKEYLEN;

        t1 = mulInv(*EK++);
        t2 = -*EK++;
        t3 = -*EK++;
        *--p = mulInv(*EK++);
        *--p = t3;
        *--p = t2;
```

```
        *--p = t1;

        for (i = 0; i < IDEAROUNDS-1; i++) {
                t1 = *EK++;
                *--p = *EK++;
                *--p = t1;

                t1 = mulInv(*EK++);
                t2 = -*EK++;
                t3 = -*EK++;
                *--p = mulInv(*EK++);
                *--p = t2;
                *--p = t3;
                *--p = t1;
        }
        t1 = *EK++;
        *--p = *EK++;
        *--p = t1;

        t1 = mulInv(*EK++);
        t2 = -*EK++;
        t3 = -*EK++;
        *--p = mulInv(*EK++);
        *--p = t3;
        *--p = t2;
        *--p = t1;
/* Copy and destroy temp copy */
        memcpy(DK, temp, sizeof(temp));
        for(i=0;i<IDEAKEYLEN;i++)temp[i]=0;
} /* ideaInvertKey */

#ifdef SMALL_CACHE
#define MUL(x,y) (x = mul(low16(x),y))
#else /* !SMALL_CACHE */
#ifdef AVOID_JUMPS
#define MUL(x,y) (x = low16(x-1), t16 = low16((y)-1), \
                t32 = (word32)x*t16 + x + t16 + 1, x = low16(t32), \
                t16 = t32>>16, x = (x-t16) + (x<t16) )
#else /* !AVOID_JUMPS (default) */
#define MUL(x,y) \
        ((t16 = (y)) ? \
                (x=low16(x)) ? \
                        t32 = (word32)x*t16, \
                        x = low16(t32), \
                        t16 = t32>>16, \
                        x = (x-t16)+(x<t16) \
                : \
                        (x = 1-t16) \
        : \
                (x = 1-x))
#endif
#endif

static void
```

```
ideaCipher(byte *inbuf, byte *outbuf, word16 *key)
{
        register uint16 x1, x2, x3, x4, s2, s3;
        word16 *in, *out;
#ifndef SMALL_CACHE
        register uint16 t16; /* Temporaries needed by MUL macro */
        register word32 t32;
#endif
        int r = IDEAROUNDS;

        in = (word16 *)inbuf;
        x1 = *in++;   x2 = *in++;
        x3 = *in++;   x4 = *in;
#ifndef HIGHFIRST
        x1 = (x1 >>8) | (x1<<8);
        x2 = (x2 >>8) | (x2<<8);
        x3 = (x3 >>8) | (x3<<8);
        x4 = (x4 >>8) | (x4<<8);
#endif
        do {
                MUL(x1,*key++);
                x2 += *key++;
                x3 += *key++;
                MUL(x4, *key++);

                s3 = x3;
                x3 ^= x1;
                MUL(x3, *key++);
                s2 = x2;
                x2 ^= x4;
                x2 += x3;
                MUL(x2, *key++);
                x3 += x2;

                x1 ^= x2;   x4 ^= x3;

                x2 ^= s3;   x3 ^= s2;
        } while (--r);
        MUL(x1, *key++);
        x3 += *key++;
        x2 += *key++;
        MUL(x4, *key);

        out = (word16 *)outbuf;
#ifdef HIGHFIRST
        *out++ = x1;
        *out++ = x3;
        *out++ = x2;
        *out = x4;
#else /* !HIGHFIRST */
        *out++ = (x1 >>8) | (x1<<8);
        *out++ = (x3 >>8) | (x3<<8);
        *out++ = (x2 >>8) | (x2<<8);
        *out = (x4 >>8) | (x4<<8);
```

```
#endif
} /* ideaCipher */

void idea_key(idea_ctx *c, unsigned char *key){
        ideaExpandKey(key,c->ek);
        ideaInvertKey(c->ek,c->dk);
}

void idea_enc(idea_ctx *c, unsigned char *data, int blocks){
        int i;
        unsigned char *d = data;

        for(i=0;i<blocks;i++){
                ideaCipher(d,d,c->ek);
                d+=8;
        }
}

void idea_dec(idea_ctx *c, unsigned char *data, int blocks){
        int i;
        unsigned char *d = data;

        for(i=0;i<blocks;i++){
                ideaCipher(d,d,c->dk);
                d+=8;
        }
}

#include <stdio.h>

#ifndef BLOCKS
#ifndef KBYTES
#define KBYTES 1024
#endif
#define BLOCKS (64*KBYTES)
#endif

int
main(void)
{       /* Test driver for IDEA cipher */
        int i, j, k;
        idea_ctx c;
        byte userkey[16];
        word16 EK[IDEAKEYLEN], DK[IDEAKEYLEN];
        byte XX[8], YY[8], ZZ[8];
        word32 long_block[10]; /* 5 blocks */
        long l;
        char *lbp;

        /* Make a sample user key for testing... */
        for(i=0; i<16; i++)
                userkey[i] = i+1;

        idea_key(&c,userkey);

        /* Make a sample plaintext pattern for testing... */
```

```
        for (k=0; k<8; k++)
                XX[k] = k;

        idea_enc(&c,XX,1); /* encrypt */

        lbp = (unsigned char *) long_block;
        for(i=0;i<10;i++) long_block[i] = i;
        idea_enc(&c,lbp,5);
        for(i=0;i<10;i+=2) printf("Block %01d = %081x %081x.\n",
                             i/2,long_block[i],long_block[i+1]);

        idea_dec(&c,lbp,3);
        idea_dec(&c,lbp+24,2);

        for(i=0;i<10;i+=2) printf("Block %01d = %081x %081x.\n",
                             i/2,long_block[i],long_block[i+1]);

        return 0;          /* normal exit */
} /* main */
```

GOST

```
typedef unsigned long u4;
typedef unsigned char byte;

typedef struct {
        u4 k[8];
        /* Constant s-boxes -- set up in gost_init(). */
        char k87[256],k65[256],k43[256],k21[256];
} gost_ctx;

/* Note:  encrypt and decrypt expect full blocks--padding blocks is
          caller's responsibility.  All bulk encryption is done in
          ECB mode by these calls.  Other modes may be added easily
          enough.                                                    */
void gost_enc(gost_ctx *, u4 *, int);
void gost_dec(gost_ctx *, u4 *, int);
void gost_key(gost_ctx *, u4 *);
void gost_init(gost_ctx *);
void gost_destroy(gost_ctx *);

#ifdef __alpha  /* Any other 64-bit machines? */
typedef unsigned int word32;
#else
typedef unsigned long word32;
#endif

kboxinit(gost_ctx *c)
{
        int i;

        byte k8[16] = {14,  4, 13,  1,  2, 15, 11,  8,  3, 10,  6,
                       12,  5,  9,  0,  7 };
        byte k7[16] = {15,  1,  8, 14,  6, 11,  3,  4,  9,  7,  2,
```

```
                          13, 12,  0,  5, 10 };
           byte k6[16] = {10,  0,  9, 14,  6,  3, 15,  5,  1, 13, 12,
                           7, 11,  4,  2,  8 };
           byte k5[16] = { 7, 13, 14,  3,  0,  6,  9, 10,  1,  2,  8,
                           5, 11, 12,  4, 15 };
           byte k4[16] = { 2, 12,  4,  1,  7, 10, 11,  6,  8,  5,  3,
                          15, 13,  0, 14,  9 };
           byte k3[16] = {12,  1, 10, 15,  9,  2,  6,  8,  0, 13,  3,
                           4, 14,  7,  5, 11 };
           byte k2[16] = { 4, 11,  2, 14, 15,  0,  8, 13,  3, 12,  9,
                           7,  5, 10,  6,  1 };
           byte k1[16] = {13,  2,  8,  4,  6, 15, 11,  1, 10,  9,  3,
                          14,  5,  0, 12,  7 };

       for (i = 0; i < 256; i++) {
               c->k87[i] = k8[i >> 4] << 4 | k7[i & 15];
               c->k65[i] = k6[i >> 4] << 4 | k5[i & 15];
               c->k43[i] = k4[i >> 4] << 4 | k3[i & 15];
               c->k21[i] = k2[i >> 4] << 4 | k1[i & 15];
       }
}

static word32
f(gost_ctx *c,word32 x)
{
       x = c->k87[x>>24 & 255] << 24 | c->k65[x>>16 & 255] << 16 |
           c->k43[x>> 8 & 255] <<  8 | c->k21[x & 255];

       /* Rotate left 11 bits */
       return x<<11 | x>>(32-11);
}

void gostcrypt(gost_ctx *c, word32 *d){
     register word32 n1, n2; /* As named in the GOST */

       n1 = d[0];
       n2 = d[1];

     /* Instead of swapping halves, swap names each round */
       n2 ^= f(c,n1+c->k[0]); n1 ^= f(c,n2+c->k[1]);
       n2 ^= f(c,n1+c->k[2]); n1 ^= f(c,n2+c->k[3]);
       n2 ^= f(c,n1+c->k[4]); n1 ^= f(c,n2+c->k[5]);
       n2 ^= f(c,n1+c->k[6]); n1 ^= f(c,n2+c->k[7]);

       n2 ^= f(c,n1+c->k[0]); n1 ^= f(c,n2+c->k[1]);
       n2 ^= f(c,n1+c->k[2]); n1 ^= f(c,n2+c->k[3]);
       n2 ^= f(c,n1+c->k[4]); n1 ^= f(c,n2+c->k[5]);
       n2 ^= f(c,n1+c->k[6]); n1 ^= f(c,n2+c->k[7]);

       n2 ^= f(c,n1+c->k[0]); n1 ^= f(c,n2+c->k[1]);
       n2 ^= f(c,n1+c->k[2]); n1 ^= f(c,n2+c->k[3]);
       n2 ^= f(c,n1+c->k[4]); n1 ^= f(c,n2+c->k[5]);
       n2 ^= f(c,n1+c->k[6]); n1 ^= f(c,n2+c->k[7]);

       n2 ^= f(c,n1+c->k[7]); n1 ^= f(c,n2+c->k[6]);
       n2 ^= f(c,n1+c->k[5]); n1 ^= f(c,n2+c->k[4]);
```

```
                n2 ^= f(c,n1+c->k[3]); n1 ^= f(c,n2+c->k[2]);
                n2 ^= f(c,n1+c->k[1]); n1 ^= f(c,n2+c->k[0]);

                d[0] = n2; d[1] = n1;
        }

void
gostdecrypt(gost_ctx *c, u4 *d){
        register word32 n1, n2; /* As named in the GOST */

                n1 = d[0]; n2 = d[1];

                n2 ^= f(c,n1+c->k[0]); n1 ^= f(c,n2+c->k[1]);
                n2 ^= f(c,n1+c->k[2]); n1 ^= f(c,n2+c->k[3]);
                n2 ^= f(c,n1+c->k[4]); n1 ^= f(c,n2+c->k[5]);
                n2 ^= f(c,n1+c->k[6]); n1 ^= f(c,n2+c->k[7]);

                n2 ^= f(c,n1+c->k[7]); n1 ^= f(c,n2+c->k[6]);
                n2 ^= f(c,n1+c->k[5]); n1 ^= f(c,n2+c->k[4]);
                n2 ^= f(c,n1+c->k[3]); n1 ^= f(c,n2+c->k[2]);
                n2 ^= f(c,n1+c->k[1]); n1 ^= f(c,n2+c->k[0]);

                n2 ^= f(c,n1+c->k[7]); n1 ^= f(c,n2+c->k[6]);
                n2 ^= f(c,n1+c->k[5]); n1 ^= f(c,n2+c->k[4]);
                n2 ^= f(c,n1+c->k[3]); n1 ^= f(c,n2+c->k[2]);
                n2 ^= f(c,n1+c->k[1]); n1 ^= f(c,n2+c->k[0]);

                n2 ^= f(c,n1+c->k[7]); n1 ^= f(c,n2+c->k[6]);
                n2 ^= f(c,n1+c->k[5]); n1 ^= f(c,n2+c->k[4]);
                n2 ^= f(c,n1+c->k[3]); n1 ^= f(c,n2+c->k[2]);
                n2 ^= f(c,n1+c->k[1]); n1 ^= f(c,n2+c->k[0]);

                d[0] = n2; d[1] = n1;
        }

void gost_enc(gost_ctx *c, u4 *d, int blocks){
        int i;

        for(i=0;i<blocks;i++){
                gostcrypt(c,d);
                d+=2;
        }
}

void gost_dec(gost_ctx *c, u4 *d, int blocks){
        int i;

        for(i=0;i<blocks;i++){
                gostdecrypt(c,d);
                d+=2;
        }
}

void gost_key(gost_ctx *c, u4 *k){
        int i;
        for(i=0;i<8;i++) c->k[i]=k[i];
```

```
}

void gost_init(gost_ctx *c){
        kboxinit(c);
}

void gost_destroy(gost_ctx *c){
        int i;
        for(i=0;i<8;i++) c->k[i]=0;
}

void main(void){
        gost_ctx gc;
        u4 k[8],data[10];
        int i;

        /* Initialize GOST context. */
        gost_init(&gc);

        /* Prepare key--a simple key should be OK, with this many rounds! */
        for(i=0;i<8;i++) k[i] = i;
        gost_key(&gc,k);

        /* Try some test vectors. */
        data[0] = 0; data[1] = 0;
        gostcrypt(&gc,data);
        printf("Enc of zero vector:  %08lx %08lx\n",data[0],data[1]);
        gostcrypt(&gc,data);
        printf("Enc of above:        %08lx %08lx\n",data[0],data[1]);
        data[0] = 0xffffffff; data[1] = 0xffffffff;
        gostcrypt(&gc,data);
        printf("Enc of ones vector:  %08lx %08lx\n",data[0],data[1]);
        gostcrypt(&gc,data);
        printf("Enc of above:        %08lx %08lx\n",data[0],data[1]);

        /* Does gost_dec() properly reverse gost_enc()?  Do
           we deal OK with single-block lengths passed in gost_dec()?
           Do we deal OK with different lengths passed in? */

        /* Init data */
        for(i=0;i<10;i++) data[i]=i;

        /* Encrypt data as 5 blocks. */
        gost_enc(&gc,data,5);

        /* Display encrypted data. */
        for(i=0;i<10;i+=2) printf("Block %02d = %08lx %08lx\n",
                                  i/2,data[i],data[i+1]);

        /* Decrypt in different sized chunks. */
        gost_dec(&gc,data,1);
        gost_dec(&gc,data+2,4);
        printf("\n");

        /* Display decrypted data. */
```

```
        for(i=0;i<10;i+=2) printf("Block %02d = %08lx %08lx\n",
                                i/2,data[i],data[i+1]);

        gost_destroy(&gc);
}
```

BLOWFISH

```c
#include <math.h>
#include <stdio.h>
#include <stdlib.h>
#include <time.h>

#ifdef little_endian    /* Eg: Intel */
    #include <alloc.h>
#endif

#include <ctype.h>

#ifdef little_endian    /* Eg: Intel */
    #include <dir.h>
    #include <bios.h>
#endif

#ifdef big_endian
    #include <Types.h>
#endif

typedef struct {
        unsigned long S[4][256],P[18];
} blf_ctx;

#define MAXKEYBYTES 56          /* 448 bits */
// #define little_endian 1              /* Eg: Intel */
#define big_endian 1            /* Eg: Motorola */

void Blowfish_encipher(blf_ctx *,unsigned long *xl, unsigned long *xr);
void Blowfish_decipher(blf_ctx *,unsigned long *xl, unsigned long *xr);

#define N               16
#define noErr           0
#define DATAERROR         -1
#define KEYBYTES        8

FILE*       SubkeyFile;

unsigned long F(blf_ctx *bc, unsigned long x)
{
    unsigned short a;
    unsigned short b;
    unsigned short c;
    unsigned short d;
    unsigned long  y;
```

```
    d = x & 0x00FF;
    x >>= 8;
    c = x & 0x00FF;
    x >>= 8;
    b = x & 0x00FF;
    x >>= 8;
    a = x & 0x00FF;
    //y = ((S[0][a] + S[1][b]) ^ S[2][c]) + S[3][d];
    y = bc->S[0][a] + bc->S[1][b];
    y = y ^ bc->S[2][c];
    y = y + bc->S[3][d];

    return y;
}
void Blowfish_encipher(blf_ctx *c,unsigned long *xl, unsigned long *xr)
{
    unsigned long  Xl;
    unsigned long  Xr;
    unsigned long  temp;
    short          i;

    Xl = *xl;
    Xr = *xr;

    for (i = 0; i < N; ++i) {
        Xl = Xl ^ c->P[i];
        Xr = F(c,Xl) ^ Xr;

        temp = Xl;
        Xl = Xr;
        Xr = temp;
    }

    temp = Xl;
    Xl = Xr;
    Xr = temp;

    Xr = Xr ^ c->P[N];
    Xl = Xl ^ c->P[N + 1];

    *xl = Xl;
    *xr = Xr;
}

void Blowfish_decipher(blf_ctx *c, unsigned long *xl, unsigned long *xr)
{
    unsigned long  Xl;
    unsigned long  Xr;
    unsigned long  temp;
    short          i;

    Xl = *xl;
    Xr = *xr;
```

```
    for (i = N + 1; i > 1; --i) {
       Xl = Xl ^ c->P[i];
       Xr = F(c,Xl) ^ Xr;

       /* Exchange Xl and Xr */
       temp = Xl;
       Xl = Xr;
       Xr = temp;
    }

    /* Exchange Xl and Xr */
    temp = Xl;
    Xl = Xr;
    Xr = temp;

    Xr = Xr ^ c->P[1];
    Xl = Xl ^ c->P[0];

    *xl = Xl;
    *xr = Xr;
}

short InitializeBlowfish(blf_ctx *c, char key[], short keybytes)
{
    short          i;
    short          j;
    short          k;
    short          error;
    short          numread;
    unsigned long  data;
    unsigned long  datal;
    unsigned long  datar;

unsigned long ks0[] = {
0xd1310ba6, 0x98dfb5ac, 0x2ffd72db, 0xd01adfb7, 0xb8e1afed, 0x6a267e96,
0xba7c9045, 0xf12c7f99, 0x24a19947, 0xb3916cf7, 0x0801f2e2, 0x858efc16,
0x636920d8, 0x71574e69, 0xa458fea3, 0xf4933d7e, 0x0d95748f, 0x728eb658,
0x718bcd58, 0x82154aee, 0x7b54a41d, 0xc25a59b5, 0x9c30d539, 0x2af26013,
0xc5d1b023, 0x286085f0, 0xca417918, 0xb8db38ef, 0x8e79dcb0, 0x603a180e,
0x6c9e0e8b, 0xb01e8a3e, 0xd71577c1, 0xbd314b27, 0x78af2fda, 0x55605c60,
0xe65525f3, 0xaa55ab94, 0x57489862, 0x63e81440, 0x55ca396a, 0x2aab10b6,
0xb4cc5c34, 0x1141e8ce, 0xa15486af, 0x7c72e993, 0xb3ee1411, 0x636fbc2a,
0x2ba9c55d, 0x741831f6, 0xce5c3e16, 0x9b87931e, 0xafd6ba33, 0x6c24cf5c,
0x7a325381, 0x28958677, 0x3b8f4898, 0x6b4bb9af, 0xc4bfe81b, 0x66282193,
0x61d809cc, 0xfb21a991, 0x487cac60, 0x5dec8032, 0xef845d5d, 0xe98575b1,
0xdc262302, 0xeb651b88, 0x23893e81, 0xd396acc5, 0x0f6d6ff3, 0x83f44239,
0x2e0b4482, 0xa4842004, 0x69c8f04a, 0x9e1f9b5e, 0x21c66842, 0xf6e96c9a,
0x670c9c61, 0xabd388f0, 0x6a51a0d2, 0xd8542f68, 0x960fa728, 0xab5133a3,
0x6eef0b6c, 0x137a3be4, 0xba3bf050, 0x7efb2a98, 0xa1f1651d, 0x39af0176,
0x66ca593e, 0x82430e88, 0x8cee8619, 0x456f9fb4, 0x7d84a5c3, 0x3b8b5ebe,
0xe06f75d8, 0x85c12073, 0x401a449f, 0x56c16aa6, 0x4ed3aa62, 0x363f7706,
0x1bfedf72, 0x429b023d, 0x37d0d724, 0xd00a1248, 0xdb0fead3, 0x49f1c09b,
0x075372c9, 0x80991b7b, 0x25d479d8, 0xf6e8def7, 0xe3fe501a, 0xb6794c3b,
```

```
0x976ce0bd, 0x04c006ba, 0xc1a94fb6, 0x409f60c4, 0x5e5c9ec2, 0x196a2463,
0x68fb6faf, 0x3e6c53b5, 0x1339b2eb, 0x3b52ec6f, 0x6dfc511f, 0x9b30952c,
0xcc814544, 0xaf5ebd09, 0xbee3d004, 0xde334afd, 0x660f2807, 0x192e4bb3,
0xc0cba857, 0x45c8740f, 0xd20b5f39, 0xb9d3fbdb, 0x5579c0bd, 0x1a60320a,
0xd6a100c6, 0x402c7279, 0x679f25fe, 0xfb1fa3cc, 0x8ea5e9f8, 0xdb3222f8,
0x3c7516df, 0xfd616b15, 0x2f501ec8, 0xad0552ab, 0x323db5fa, 0xfd238760,
0x53317b48, 0x3e00df82, 0x9e5c57bb, 0xca6f8ca0, 0x1a87562e, 0xdf1769db,
0xd542a8f6, 0x287effc3, 0xac6732c6, 0x8c4f5573, 0x695b27b0, 0xbbca58c8,
0xe1ffa35d, 0xb8f011a0, 0x10fa3d98, 0xfd2183b8, 0x4afcb56c, 0x2dd1d35b,
0x9a53e479, 0xb6f84565, 0xd28e49bc, 0x4bfb9790, 0xe1ddf2da, 0xa4cb7e33,
0x62fb1341, 0xcee4c6e8, 0xef20cada, 0x36774c01, 0xd07e9efe, 0x2bf11fb4,
0x95dbda4d, 0xae909198, 0xeaad8e71, 0x6b93d5a0, 0xd08ed1d0, 0xafc725e0,
0x8e3c5b2f, 0x8e7594b7, 0x8ff6e2fb, 0xf2122b64, 0x8888b812, 0x900df01c,
0x4fad5ea0, 0x688fc31c, 0xd1cff191, 0xb3a8c1ad, 0x2f2f2218, 0xbe0e1777,
0xea752dfe, 0x8b021fa1, 0xe5a0cc0f, 0xb56f74e8, 0x18acf3d6, 0xce89e299,
0xb4a84fe0, 0xfd13e0b7, 0x7cc43b81, 0xd2ada8d9, 0x165fa266, 0x80957705,
0x93cc7314, 0x211a1477, 0xe6ad2065, 0x77b5fa86, 0xc75442f5, 0xfb9d35cf,
0xebcdaf0c, 0x7b3e89a0, 0xd6411bd3, 0xae1e7e49, 0x00250e2d, 0x2071b35e,
0x226800bb, 0x57b8e0af, 0x2464369b, 0xf009b91e, 0x5563911d, 0x59dfa6aa,
0x78c14389, 0xd95a537f, 0x207d5ba2, 0x02e5b9c5, 0x83260376, 0x6295cfa9,
0x11c81968, 0x4e734a41, 0xb3472dca, 0x7b14a94a, 0x1b510052, 0x9a532915,
0xd60f573f, 0xbc9bc6e4, 0x2b60a476, 0x81e67400, 0x08ba6fb5, 0x571be91f,
0xf296ec6b, 0x2a0dd915, 0xb6636521, 0xe7b9f9b6, 0xff34052e, 0xc5855664,
0x53b02d5d, 0xa99f8fa1, 0x08ba4799, 0x6e85076a};
unsigned long ks1[] = {
0x4b7a70e9, 0xb5b32944, 0xdb75092e, 0xc4192623, 0xad6ea6b0, 0x49a7df7d,
0x9cee60b8, 0x8fedb266, 0xecaa8c71, 0x699a17ff, 0x5664526c, 0xc2b19ee1,
0x193602a5, 0x75094c29, 0xa0591340, 0xe4183a3e, 0x3f54989a, 0x5b429d65,
0x6b8fe4d6, 0x99f73fd6, 0xa1d29c07, 0xefe830f5, 0x4d2d38e6, 0xf0255dc1,
0x4cdd2086, 0x8470eb26, 0x6382e9c6, 0x021ecc5e, 0x09686b3f, 0x3ebaefc9,
0x3c971814, 0x6b6a70a1, 0x687f3584, 0x52a0e286, 0xb79c5305, 0xaa500737,
0x3e07841c, 0x7fdeae5c, 0x8e7d44ec, 0x5716f2b8, 0xb03ada37, 0xf0500c0d,
0xf01c1f04, 0x0200b3ff, 0xae0cf51a, 0x3cb574b2, 0x25837a58, 0xdc0921bd,
0xd19113f9, 0x7ca92ff6, 0x94324773, 0x22f54701, 0x3ae5e581, 0x37c2dadc,
0xc8b57634, 0x9af3dda7, 0xa9446146, 0x0fd0030e, 0xecc8c73e, 0xa4751e41,
0xe238cd99, 0x3bea0e2f, 0x3280bba1, 0x183eb331, 0x4e548b38, 0x4f6db908,
0x6f420d03, 0xf60a04bf, 0x2cb81290, 0x24977c79, 0x5679b072, 0xbcaf89af,
0xde9a771f, 0xd9930810, 0xb38bae12, 0xdccf3f2e, 0x5512721f, 0x2e6b7124,
0x501adde6, 0x9f84cd87, 0x7a584718, 0x7408da17, 0xbc9f9abc, 0xe94b7d8c,
0xec7aec3a, 0xdb851dfa, 0x63094366, 0xc464c3d2, 0xef1c1847, 0x3215d908,
0xdd433b37, 0x24c2ba16, 0x12a14d43, 0x2a65c451, 0x50940002, 0x133ae4dd,
0x71dff89e, 0x10314e55, 0x81ac77d6, 0x5f11199b, 0x043556f1, 0xd7a3c76b,
0x3c11183b, 0x5924a509, 0xf28fe6ed, 0x97f1fbfa, 0x9ebabf2c, 0x1e153c6e,
0x86e34570, 0xeae96fb1, 0x860e5e0a, 0x5a3e2ab3, 0x771fe71c, 0x4e3d06fa,
0x2965dcb9, 0x99e71d0f, 0x803e89d6, 0x5266c825, 0x2e4cc978, 0x9c10b36a,
0xc6150eba, 0x94e2ea78, 0xa5fc3c53, 0x1e0a2df4, 0xf2f74ea7, 0x361d2b3d,
0x1939260f, 0x19c27960, 0x5223a708, 0xf71312b6, 0xebadfe6e, 0xeac31f66,
0xe3bc4595, 0xa67bc883, 0xb17f37d1, 0x018cff28, 0xc332ddef, 0xbe6c5aa5,
0x65582185, 0x68ab9802, 0xeececea50f, 0xdb2f953b, 0x2aef7dad, 0x5b6e2f84,
0x1521b628, 0x29076170, 0xecdd4775, 0x619f1510, 0x13cca830, 0xeb61bd96,
0x0334fe1e, 0xaa0363cf, 0xb5735c90, 0x4c70a239, 0xd59e9e0b, 0xcbaade14,
0xeecc86bc, 0x60622ca7, 0x9cab5cab, 0xb2f3846e, 0x648b1eaf, 0x19bdf0ca,
0xa02369b9, 0x655abb50, 0x40685a32, 0x3c2ab4b3, 0x319ee9d5, 0xc021b8f7,
0x9b540b19, 0x875fa099, 0x95f7997e, 0x623d7da8, 0xf837889a, 0x97e32d77,
```

```
0x11ed935f, 0x16681281, 0x0e358829, 0xc7e61fd6, 0x96dedfa1, 0x7858ba99,
0x57f584a5, 0x1b227263, 0x9b83c3ff, 0x1ac24696, 0xcdb30aeb, 0x532e3054,
0x8fd948e4, 0x6dbc3128, 0x58ebf2ef, 0x34c6ffea, 0xfe28ed61, 0xee7c3c73,
0x5d4a14d9, 0xe864b7e3, 0x42105d14, 0x203e13e0, 0x45eee2b6, 0xa3aaabea,
0xdb6c4f15, 0xfacb4fd0, 0xc742f442, 0xef6abbb5, 0x654f3b1d, 0x41cd2105,
0xd81e799e, 0x86854dc7, 0xe44b476a, 0x3d816250, 0xcf62a1f2, 0x5b8d2646,
0xfc8883a0, 0xc1c7b6a3, 0x7f1524c3, 0x69cb7492, 0x47848a0b, 0x5692b285,
0x095bbf00, 0xad19489d, 0x1462b174, 0x23820e00, 0x58428d2a, 0x0c55f5ea,
0x1dadf43e, 0x233f7061, 0x3372f092, 0x8d937e41, 0xd65fecf1, 0x6c223bdb,
0x7cde3759, 0xcbee7460, 0x4085f2a7, 0xce77326e, 0xa6078084, 0x19f8509e,
0xe8efd855, 0x61d99735, 0xa969a7aa, 0xc50c06c2, 0x5a04abfc, 0x800bcadc,
0x9e447a2e, 0xc3453484, 0xfdd56705, 0x0e1e9ec9, 0xdb73dbd3, 0x105588cd,
0x675fda79, 0xe3674340, 0xc5c43465, 0x713e38d8, 0x3d28f89e, 0xf16dff20,
0x153e21e7, 0x8fb03d4a, 0xe6e39f2b, 0xdb83adf7};
unsigned long ks2[] = {
0xe93d5a68, 0x948140f7, 0xf64c261c, 0x94692934, 0x411520f7, 0x7602d4f7,
0xbcf46b2e, 0xd4a20068, 0xd4082471, 0x3320f46a, 0x43b7d4b7, 0x500061af,
0x1e39f62e, 0x97244546, 0x14214f74, 0xbf8b8840, 0x4d95fc1d, 0x96b591af,
0x70f4ddd3, 0x66a02f45, 0xbfbc09ec, 0x03bd9785, 0x7fac6dd0, 0x31cb8504,
0x96eb27b3, 0x55fd3941, 0xda2547e6, 0xabca0a9a, 0x28507825, 0x530429f4,
0x0a2c86da, 0xe9b66dfb, 0x68dc1462, 0xd7486900, 0x680ec0a4, 0x27a18dee,
0x4f3ffea2, 0xe887ad8c, 0xb58ce006, 0x7af4d6b6, 0xaace1e7c, 0xd3375fec,
0xce78a399, 0x406b2a42, 0x20fe9e35, 0xd9f385b9, 0xee39d7ab, 0x3b124e8b,
0x1dc9faf7, 0x4b6d1856, 0x26a36631, 0xeae397b2, 0x3a6efa74, 0xdd5b4332,
0x6841e7f7, 0xca7820fb, 0xfb0af54e, 0xd8feb397, 0x454056ac, 0xba489527,
0x55533a3a, 0x20838d87, 0xfe6ba9b7, 0xd096954b, 0x55a867bc, 0xa1159a58,
0xcca92963, 0x99e1db33, 0xa62a4a56, 0x3f3125f9, 0x5ef47e1c, 0x9029317c,
0xfdf8e802, 0x04272f70, 0x80bb155c, 0x05282ce3, 0x95c11548, 0xe4c66d22,
0x48c1133f, 0xc70f86dc, 0x07f9c9ee, 0x41041f0f, 0x404779a4, 0x5d886e17,
0x325f51eb, 0xd59bc0d1, 0xf2bcc18f, 0x41113564, 0x257b7834, 0x602a9c60,
0xdff8e8a3, 0x1f636c1b, 0x0e12b4c2, 0x02e1329e, 0xaf664fd1, 0xcad18115,
0x6b2395e0, 0x333e92e1, 0x3b240b62, 0xeebeb922, 0x85b2a20e, 0xe6ba0d99,
0xde720c8c, 0x2da2f728, 0xd0127845, 0x95b794fd, 0x647d0862, 0xe7ccf5f0,
0x5449a36f, 0x877d48fa, 0xc39dfd27, 0xf33e8d1e, 0x0a476341, 0x992eff74,
0x3a6f6eab, 0xf4f8fd37, 0xa812dc60, 0xa1ebddf8, 0x991be14c, 0xdb6e6b0d,
0xc67b5510, 0x6d672c37, 0x2765d43b, 0xdcd0e804, 0xf1290dc7, 0xcc00ffa3,
0xb5390f92, 0x690fed0b, 0x667b9ffb, 0xcedb7d9c, 0xa091cf0b, 0xd9155ea3,
0xbb132f88, 0x515bad24, 0x7b9479bf, 0x763bd6eb, 0x37392eb3, 0xcc115979,
0x8026e297, 0xf42e312d, 0x6842ada7, 0xc66a2b3b, 0x12754ccc, 0x782ef11c,
0x6a124237, 0xb79251e7, 0x06a1bbe6, 0x4bfb6350, 0x1a6b1018, 0x11caedfa,
0x3d25bdd8, 0xe2e1c3c9, 0x44421659, 0x0a121386, 0xd90cec6e, 0xd5abea2a,
0x64af674e, 0xda86a85f, 0xbebfe988, 0x64e4c3fe, 0x9dbc8057, 0xf0f7c086,
0x60787bf8, 0x6003604d, 0xd1fd8346, 0xf6381fb0, 0x7745ae04, 0xd736fccc,
0x83426b33, 0xf01eab71, 0xb0804187, 0x3c005e5f, 0x77a057be, 0xbde8ae24,
0x55464299, 0xbf582e61, 0x4e58f48f, 0xf2ddfda2, 0xf474ef38, 0x8789bdc2,
0x5366f9c3, 0xc8b38e74, 0xb475f255, 0x46fcd9b9, 0x7aeb2661, 0x8b1ddf84,
0x846a0e79, 0x915f95e2, 0x466e598e, 0x20b45770, 0x8cd55591, 0xc902de4c,
0xb90bace1, 0xbb8205d0, 0x11a86248, 0x7574a99e, 0xb77f19b6, 0xe0a9dc09,
0x662d09a1, 0xc4324633, 0xe85a1f02, 0x09f0be8c, 0x4a99a025, 0x1d6efe10,
0x1ab93d1d, 0x0ba5a4df, 0xa186f20f, 0x2868f169, 0xdcb7da83, 0x573906fe,
0xa1e2ce9b, 0x4fcd7f52, 0x50115e01, 0xa70683fa, 0xa002b5c4, 0x0de6d027,
0x9af88c27, 0x773f8641, 0xc3604c06, 0x61a806b5, 0xf0177a28, 0xc0f586e0,
0x006058aa, 0x30dc7d62, 0x11e69ed7, 0x2338ea63, 0x53c2dd94, 0xc2c21634,
0xbbbcbee56, 0x90bcb6de, 0xebfc7da1, 0xce591d76, 0x6f05e409, 0x4b7c0188,
```

```
0x39720a3d, 0x7c927c24, 0x86e3725f, 0x724d9db9, 0x1ac15bb4, 0xd39eb8fc,
0xed545578, 0x08fca5b5, 0xd83d7cd3, 0x4dad0fc4, 0x1e50ef5e, 0xb161e6f8,
0xa28514d9, 0x6c51133c, 0x6fd5c7e7, 0x56e14ec4, 0x362abfce, 0xddc6c837,
0xd79a3234, 0x92638212, 0x670efa8e, 0x406000e0};
unsigned long ks3[] = {
0x3a39ce37, 0xd3faf5cf, 0xabc27737, 0x5ac52d1b, 0x5cb0679e, 0x4fa33742,
0xd3822740, 0x99bc9bbe, 0xd5118e9d, 0xbf0f7315, 0xd62d1c7e, 0xc700c47b,
0xb78c1b6b, 0x21a19045, 0xb26eb1be, 0x6a366eb4, 0x5748ab2f, 0xbc946e79,
0xc6a376d2, 0x6549c2c8, 0x530ff8ee, 0x468dde7d, 0xd5730a1d, 0x4cd04dc6,
0x2939bbdb, 0xa9ba4650, 0xac9526e8, 0xbe5ee304, 0xa1fad5f0, 0x6a2d519a,
0x63ef8ce2, 0x9a86ee22, 0xc089c2b8, 0x43242ef6, 0xa51e03aa, 0x9cf2d0a4,
0x83c061ba, 0x9be96a4d, 0x8fe51550, 0xba645bd6, 0x2826a2f9, 0xa73a3ae1,
0x4ba99586, 0xef5562e9, 0xc72fefd3, 0xf752f7da, 0x3f046f69, 0x77fa0a59,
0x80e4a915, 0x87b08601, 0x9b09e6ad, 0x3b3ee593, 0xe990fd5a, 0x9e34d797,
0x2cf0b7d9, 0x022b8b51, 0x96d5ac3a, 0x017da67d, 0xd1cf3ed6, 0x7c7d2d28,
0x1f9f25cf, 0xadf2b89b, 0x5ad6b472, 0x5a88f54c, 0xe029ac71, 0xe019a5e6,
0x47b0acfd, 0xed93fa9b, 0xe8d3c48d, 0x283b57cc, 0xf8d56629, 0x79132e28,
0x785f0191, 0xed756055, 0xf7960e44, 0xe3d35e8c, 0x15056dd4, 0x88f46dba,
0x03a16125, 0x0564f0bd, 0xc3eb9e15, 0x3c9057a2, 0x97271aec, 0xa93a072a,
0x1b3f6d9b, 0x1e6321f5, 0xf59c66fb, 0x26dcf319, 0x7533d928, 0xb155fdf5,
0x03563482, 0x8aba3cbb, 0x28517711, 0xc20ad9f8, 0xabcc5167, 0xccad925f,
0x4de81751, 0x3830dc8e, 0x379d5862, 0x9320f991, 0xea7a90c2, 0xfb3e7bce,
0x5121ce64, 0x774fbe32, 0xa8b6e37e, 0xc3293d46, 0x48de5369, 0x6413e680,
0xa2ae0810, 0xdd6db224, 0x69852dfd, 0x09072166, 0xb39a460a, 0x6445c0dd,
0x586cdecf, 0x1c20c8ae, 0x5bbef7dd, 0x1b588d40, 0xccd2017f, 0x6bb4e3bb,
0xdda26a7e, 0x3a59ff45, 0x3e350a44, 0xbcb4cdd5, 0x72eacea8, 0xfa6484bb,
0x8d6612ae, 0xbf3c6f47, 0xd29be463, 0x542f5d9e, 0xaec2771b, 0xf64e6370,
0x740e0d8d, 0xe75b1357, 0xf8721671, 0xaf537d5d, 0x4040cb08, 0x4eb4e2cc,
0x34d2466a, 0x0115af84, 0xe1b00428, 0x95983a1d, 0x06b89fb4, 0xce6ea048,
0x6f3f3b82, 0x3520ab82, 0x011a1d4b, 0x277227f8, 0x611560b1, 0xe7933fdc,
0xbb3a792b, 0x344525bd, 0xa08839e1, 0x51ce794b, 0x2f32c9b7, 0xa01fbac9,
0xe01cc87e, 0xbcc7d1f6, 0xcf0111c3, 0xa1e8aac7, 0x1a908749, 0xd44fbd9a,
0xd0dadecb, 0xd50ada38, 0x0339c32a, 0xc6913667, 0x8df9317c, 0xe0b12b4f,
0xf79e59b7, 0x43f5bb3a, 0xf2d519ff, 0x27d9459c, 0xbf97222c, 0x15e6fc2a,
0x0f91fc71, 0x9b941525, 0xfae59361, 0xceb69ceb, 0xc2a86459, 0x12baa8d1,
0xb6c1075e, 0xe3056a0c, 0x10d25065, 0xcb03a442, 0xe0ec6e0e, 0x1698db3b,
0x4c98a0be, 0x3278e964, 0x9f1f9532, 0xe0d392df, 0xd3a0342b, 0x8971f21e,
0x1b0a7441, 0x4ba3348c, 0xc5be7120, 0xc37632d8, 0xdf359f8d, 0x9b992f2e,
0xe60b6f47, 0x0fe3f11d, 0xe54cda54, 0x1edad891, 0xce6279cf, 0xcd3e7e6f,
0x1618b166, 0xfd2c1d05, 0x848fd2c5, 0xf6fb2299, 0xf523f357, 0xa6327623,
0x93a83531, 0x56cccd02, 0xacf08162, 0x5a75ebb5, 0x6e163697, 0x88d273cc,
0xde966292, 0x81b949d0, 0x4c50901b, 0x71c65614, 0xe6c6c7bd, 0x327a140a,
0x45e1d006, 0xc3f27b9a, 0xc9aa53fd, 0x62a80f00, 0xbb25bfe2, 0x35bdd2f6,
0x71126905, 0xb2040222, 0xb6cbcf7c, 0xcd769c2b, 0x53113ec0, 0x1640e3d3,
0x38abbd60, 0x2547adf0, 0xba38209c, 0xf746ce76, 0x77afa1c5, 0x20756060,
0x85cbfe4e, 0x8ae88dd8, 0x7aaaf9b0, 0x4cf9aa7e, 0x1948c25c, 0x02fb8a8c,
0x01c36ae4, 0xd6ebe1f9, 0x90d4f869, 0xa65cdea0, 0x3f09252d, 0xc208e69f,
0xb74e6132, 0xce77e25b, 0x578fdfe3, 0x3ac372e6};

/* Initialize s-boxes without file read. */
        for(i=0;i<256;i++){
                c->S[0][i] = ks0[i];
                c->S[1][i] = ks1[i];
                c->S[2][i] = ks2[i];
```

```
                        c->S[3][i] = ks3[i];
            }

        j = 0;
        for (i = 0; i < N + 2; ++i) {
                data = 0x00000000;
                for (k = 0; k < 4; ++k) {
                        data = (data << 8) | key[j];
                        j = j + 1;
                        if (j >= keybytes) {
                                j = 0;
                        }
                }
        c->P[i] = c->P[i] ^ data;
        }

    datal = 0x00000000;
    datar = 0x00000000;

    for (i = 0; i < N + 2; i += 2) {
            Blowfish_encipher(c,&datal, &datar);

            c->P[i] = datal;
            c->P[i + 1] = datar;
    }

    for (i = 0; i < 4; ++i) {
            for (j = 0; j < 256; j += 2) {

                    Blowfish_encipher(c,&datal, &datar);

                    c->S[i][j] = datal;
                    c->S[i][j + 1] = datar;

            }

    }
}

void blf_key(blf_ctx *c, char *k, int len){
        InitializeBlowfish(c,k,len);
}

void blf_enc(blf_ctx *c, unsigned long *data, int blocks){
        unsigned long *d;
        int i;

        d = data;
        for(i=0;i<blocks;i++){
                Blowfish_encipher(c,d,d+1);
                d += 2;
        }
}

void blf_dec(blf_ctx *c, unsigned long *data, int blocks){
        unsigned long *d;
        int i;
```

```
        d = data;
        for(i=0;i<blocks;i++){
                Blowfish_decipher(c,d,d+1);
                d += 2;
        }
}

void main(void){
        blf_ctx c;
        char key[]="AAAAA";
        unsigned long data[10];
        int i;

        for(i=0;i<10;i++) data[i] = i;

        blf_key(&c,key,5);
        blf_enc(&c,data,5);
        blf_dec(&c,data,1);
        blf_dec(&c,data+2,4);
        for(i=0;i<10;i+=2) printf("Block %01d decrypts to: %08lx %08lx.\n",
                                i/2,data[i],data[i+1]);
}
```

3-Way

```
#define    STRT_E    0x0b0b /* round constant of first encryption round */
#define    STRT_D    0xb1b1 /* round constant of first decryption round */
#define    NMBR        11 /* number of rounds is 11                    */

typedef    unsigned long int  word32 ;
                    /* the program only works correctly if long = 32bits */
typedef unsigned long u4;
typedef unsigned char u1;

typedef struct {
        u4 k[3],ki[3], ercon[NMBR+1],drcon[NMBR+1];
} twy_ctx;

/* Note:  encrypt and decrypt expect full blocks--padding blocks is
          caller's responsibility.  All bulk encryption is done in
          ECB mode by these calls.  Other modes may be added easily
          enough.                                                    */

/* destroy:  Context. */
/* Scrub context of all sensitive data. */
void twy_destroy(twy_ctx *);

/* encrypt:  Context, ptr to data block, # of blocks. */
void twy_enc(twy_ctx *, u4 *, int);

/* decrypt:  Context, ptr to data block, # of blocks. */
void twy_dec(twy_ctx *, u4 *, int);
```

```
/* key:  Context, ptr to key data. */
void twy_key(twy_ctx *, u4 *);

/* ACCODE------------------------------------------------------------ */
/* End of AC code prototypes and structures.                          */
/* ------------------------------------------------------------------ */

void mu(word32 *a)          /* inverts the order of the bits of a */
{
int i ;
word32 b[3] ;

b[0] = b[1] = b[2] = 0 ;
for( i=0 ; i<32 ; i++ )
   {
   b[0] <<= 1 ; b[1] <<= 1 ; b[2] <<= 1 ;
   if(a[0]&1) b[2] |= 1 ;
   if(a[1]&1) b[1] |= 1 ;
   if(a[2]&1) b[0] |= 1 ;
   a[0] >>= 1 ; a[1] >>= 1 ; a[2] >>= 1 ;
   }

a[0] = b[0] ;     a[1] = b[1] ;     a[2] = b[2] ;
}

void gamma(word32 *a)   /* the nonlinear step */
{
word32 b[3] ;

b[0] = a[0] ^ (a[1]|(~a[2])) ;
b[1] = a[1] ^ (a[2]|(~a[0])) ;
b[2] = a[2] ^ (a[0]|(~a[1])) ;

a[0] = b[0] ;     a[1] = b[1] ;     a[2] = b[2] ;
}

void theta(word32 *a)    /* the linear step */
{
word32 b[3];

b[0] = a[0] ^  (a[0]>>16) ^ (a[1]<<16) ^    (a[1]>>16) ^ (a[2]<<16) ^
               (a[1]>>24) ^ (a[2]<<8)  ^    (a[2]>>8)  ^ (a[0]<<24) ^
               (a[2]>>16) ^ (a[0]<<16) ^    (a[2]>>24) ^ (a[0]<<8)  ;
b[1] = a[1] ^  (a[1]>>16) ^ (a[2]<<16) ^    (a[2]>>16) ^ (a[0]<<16) ^
               (a[2]>>24) ^ (a[0]<<8)  ^    (a[0]>>8)  ^ (a[1]<<24) ^
               (a[0]>>16) ^ (a[1]<<16) ^    (a[0]>>24) ^ (a[1]<<8)  ;
b[2] = a[2] ^  (a[2]>>16) ^ (a[0]<<16) ^    (a[0]>>16) ^ (a[1]<<16) ^
               (a[0]>>24) ^ (a[1]<<8)  ^    (a[1]>>8)  ^ (a[2]<<24) ^
               (a[1]>>16) ^ (a[2]<<16) ^    (a[1]>>24) ^ (a[2]<<8)  ;

a[0] = b[0] ;     a[1] = b[1] ;     a[2] = b[2] ;
}

void pi_1(word32 *a)
```

```
{
a[0] = (a[0]>>10) ^ (a[0]<<22);
a[2] = (a[2]<<1)  ^ (a[2]>>31);
}

void pi_2(word32 *a)
{
a[0] = (a[0]<<1)  ^ (a[0]>>31);
a[2] = (a[2]>>10) ^ (a[2]<<22);
}

void rho(word32 *a)     /* the round function        */
{
theta(a) ;
pi_1(a) ;
gamma(a) ;
pi_2(a) ;
}

void rndcon_gen(word32 strt,word32 *rtab)
{                            /* generates the round constants */
int i ;

for(i=0 ; i<=NMBR ; i++ )
    {
    rtab[i] = strt ;
    strt <<= 1 ;
    if( strt&0x10000 ) strt ^= 0x11011 ;
    }
}

/* Modified slightly to fit the caller's needs. */
void encrypt(twy_ctx *c, word32 *a)
{
char i ;
for( i=0 ; i<NMBR ; i++ )
    {
    a[0] ^= c->k[0] ^ (c->ercon[i]<<16) ;
    a[1] ^= c->k[1] ;
    a[2] ^= c->k[2] ^ c->ercon[i] ;
    rho(a) ;
    }
a[0] ^= c->k[0] ^ (c->ercon[NMBR]<<16) ;
a[1] ^= c->k[1] ;
a[2] ^= c->k[2] ^ c->ercon[NMBR] ;
theta(a) ;
}

/* Modified slightly to meet caller's needs. */
void decrypt(twy_ctx *c, word32 *a)
{
char i ;

mu(a) ;
```

```
for( i=0 ; i<NMBR ; i++ )
   {
   a[0] ^= c->ki[0] ^ (c->drcon[i]<<16) ;
   a[1] ^= c->ki[1] ;
   a[2] ^= c->ki[2] ^ c->drcon[i] ;
   rho(a) ;
   }
a[0] ^= c->ki[0] ^ (c->drcon[NMBR]<<16) ;
a[1] ^= c->ki[1] ;
a[2] ^= c->ki[2] ^ c->drcon[NMBR] ;
theta(a) ;
mu(a) ;
}

void twy_key(twy_ctx *c, u4 *key){
        c->ki[0] = c->k[0] = key[0];
        c->ki[1] = c->k[1] = key[1];
        c->ki[2] = c->k[2] = key[2];
        theta(c->ki);
        mu(c->ki);
        rndcon_gen(STRT_E,c->ercon);
        rndcon_gen(STRT_D,c->drcon);

}

/* Encrypt in ECB mode. */
void twy_enc(twy_ctx *c, u4 *data, int blkcnt){
        u4 *d;
        int i;

        d = data;
        for(i=0;i<blkcnt;i++) {
                encrypt(c,d);
                d +=3;
        }
}

/* Decrypt in ECB mode. */
void twy_dec(twy_ctx *c, u4 *data, int blkcnt){
        u4 *d;
        int i;

        d = data;
        for(i=0;i<blkcnt;i++){
                decrypt(c,d);
                d+=3;
        }
}

/* Scrub sensitive values from memory before deallocating. */
void twy_destroy(twy_ctx *c){
        int i;

        for(i=0;i<3;i++) c->k[i] = c->ki[i] = 0;
```

```
        }

        void printvec(char *chrs, word32 *d){
                printf("%20s : %081x %081x %081x \n",chrs,d[2],d[1],d[0]);
        }

        main()
        {
        twy_ctx gc;
        word32 a[9],k[3];
        int i;

        /* Test vector 1. */

        k[0]=k[1]=k[2]=0;
        a[0]=a[1]=a[2]=1;
        twy_key(&gc,k);

        printf("**********\n");
        printvec("KEY = ",k);
        printvec("PLAIN = ",a);
        encrypt(&gc,a);
        printvec("CIPHER = ",a);

        /* Test vector 2. */

        k[0]=6;k[1]=5;k[2]=4;
        a[0]=3;a[1]=2;a[2]=1;
        twy_key(&gc,k);

        printf("**********\n");
        printvec("KEY = ",k);
        printvec("PLAIN = ",a);
        encrypt(&gc,a);
        printvec("CIPHER = ",a);

        /* Test vector 3. */

        k[2]=0xbcdef012;k[1]=0x456789ab;k[0]=0xdef01234;
        a[2]=0x01234567;a[1]=0x9abcdef0;a[0]=0x23456789;
        twy_key(&gc,k);

        printf("**********\n");
        printvec("KEY = ",k);
        printvec("PLAIN = ",a);
        encrypt(&gc,a);
        printvec("CIPHER = ",a);

        /* Test vector 4. */

        k[2]=0xcab920cd;k[1]=0xd6144138;k[0]=0xd2f05b5e;
        a[2]=0xad21ecf7;a[1]=0x83ae9dc4;a[0]=0x4059c76e;
        twy_key(&gc,k);

        printf("**********\n");
```

```
printvec("KEY = ",k);
printvec("PLAIN = ",a);
encrypt(&gc,a);
printvec("CIPHER = ",a);

/*  TEST VALUES

key        : 00000000 00000000 00000000
plaintext  : 00000001 00000001 00000001
ciphertext : ad21ecf7 83ae9dc4 4059c76e

key        : 00000004 00000005 00000006
plaintext  : 00000001 00000002 00000003
ciphertext : cab920cd d6144138 d2f05b5e

key        : bcdef012 456789ab def01234
plaintext  : 01234567 9abcdef0 23456789
ciphertext : 7cdb76b2 9cdddb6d 0aa55dbb

key        : cab920cd d6144138 d2f05b5e
plaintext  : ad21ecf7 83ae9dc4 4059c76e
ciphertext : 15b155ed 6b13f17c 478ea871

*/

/* Enc/dec test: */
for(i=0;i<9;i++) a[i]=i;
twy_enc(&gc,a,3);
for(i=0;i<9;i+=3) printf("Block %01d encrypts to %081x %081x %081x\n",
                    i/3,a[i],a[i+1],a[i+2]);

twy_dec(&gc,a,2);
twy_dec(&gc,a+6,1);

 for(i=0;i<9;i+=3) printf("Block %01d decrypts to %081x %081x %081x\n",
                    i/3,a[i],a[i+1],a[i+2]);
}
```

RC5

```
#include <stdio.h>

/* An RC5 context needs to know how many rounds it has, and its subkeys. */
typedef struct {
        u4 *xk;
        int nr;
} rc5_ctx;

/* Where possible, these should be replaced with actual rotate instructions.
   For Turbo C++, this is done with _lrotl and _lrotr. */

#define ROTL32(X,C) (((X)<<(C))|((X)>>(32-(C))))
#define ROTR32(X,C) (((X)>>(C))|((X)<<(32-(C))))
```

```
/* Function prototypes for dealing with RC5 basic operations. */
void rc5_init(rc5_ctx *, int);
void rc5_destroy(rc5_ctx *);
void rc5_key(rc5_ctx *, u1 *, int);
void rc5_encrypt(rc5_ctx *, u4 *, int);
void rc5_decrypt(rc5_ctx *, u4 *, int);

/* Function implementations for RC5. */

/* Scrub out all sensitive values. */
void rc5_destroy(rc5_ctx *c){
        int i;
     for(i=0;i<(c->nr)*2+2;i++) c->xk[i]=0;
     free(c->xk);
}


/* Allocate memory for rc5 context's xk and such. */
void rc5_init(rc5_ctx *c, int rounds){
     c->nr = rounds;
     c->xk = (u4 *) malloc(4*(rounds*2+2));
}


void rc5_encrypt(rc5_ctx *c, u4 *data, int blocks){
        u4 *d,*sk;
        int h,i,rc;

     d = data;
        sk = (c->xk)+2;
        for(h=0;h<blocks;h++){
                d[0] += c->xk[0];
                d[1] += c->xk[1];
                for(i=0;i<c->nr*2;i+=2){
                        d[0] ^= d[1];
                        rc = d[1] & 31;
                        d[0] = ROTL32(d[0],rc);
                        d[0] += sk[i];
                  d[1] ^= d[0];
                        rc = d[0] & 31;
                        d[1] = ROTL32(d[1],rc);
                        d[1] += sk[i+1];
/*printf("Round %03d : %08lx %08lx  sk= %08lx %08lx\n",i/2,
                                d[0],d[1],sk[i],sk[i+1]);*/
                }
           d+=2;
         }
}

void rc5_decrypt(rc5_ctx *c, u4 *data, int blocks){
     u4 *d,*sk;
        int h,i,rc;

     d = data;
        sk = (c->xk)+2;
     for(h=0;h<blocks;h++){
                for(i=c->nr*2-2;i>=0;i-=2){
```

```
/*printf("Round %03d: %08lx %08lx  sk: %08lx %08lx\n",
        i/2,d[0],d[1],sk[i],sk[i+1]); */
                        d[1] -= sk[i+1];
                        rc = d[0] & 31;
                        d[1] = ROTR32(d[1],rc);
                        d[1] ^= d[0];

                        d[0] -= sk[i];
                        rc = d[1] & 31;
                        d[0] = ROTR32(d[0],rc);
                d[0] ^= d[1];
                }
                d[0] -= c->xk[0];
                d[1] -= c->xk[1];
        d+=2;
    }
}

void rc5_key(rc5_ctx *c, u1 *key, int keylen){
    u4 *pk,A,B; /* padded key */
    int xk_len, pk_len, i, num_steps,rc;
    u1 *cp;

    xk_len = c->nr*2 + 2;
    pk_len = keylen/4;
    if((keylen%4)!=0) pk_len += 1;

    pk = (u4 *) malloc(pk_len * 4);
    if(pk==NULL) {
        printf("An error occurred!\n");
        exit(-1);
    }

    /* Initialize pk -- this should work on Intel machines, anyway.... */
    for(i=0;i<pk_len;i++) pk[i]=0;
    cp = (u1 *)pk;
    for(i=0;i<keylen;i++) cp[i]=key[i];

    /* Initialize xk. */
    c->xk[0] = 0xb7e15163; /* P32 */
    for(i=1;i<xk_len;i++) c->xk[i] = c->xk[i-1] + 0x9e3779b9; /* Q32 */

    /* TESTING */
    A = B = 0;
    for(i=0;i<xk_len;i++) {
        A = A + c->xk[i];
        B = B ^ c->xk[i];
    }

    /* Expand key into xk. */
    if(pk_len>xk_len) num_steps = 3*pk_len;else num_steps = 3*xk_len;

    A = B = 0;
    for(i=0;i<num_steps;i++){
        A = c->xk[i%xk_len] = ROTL32(c->xk[i%xk_len] + A + B,3);
        rc = (A+B) & 31;
```

```
            B = pk[i%pk_len] = ROTL32(pk[i%pk_len] + A + B,rc);

    }

    /* Clobber sensitive data before deallocating memory. */
    for(i=0;i<pk_len;i++) pk[i] =0;

    free(pk);
}

void main(void){
    rc5_ctx c;
    u4 data[8];
    char key[] = "ABCDE";
    int i;

    printf("-------------------------------------------------\n");

        for(i=0;i<8;i++) data[i] = i;
    rc5_init(&c,10); /* 10 rounds */
    rc5_key(&c,key,5);

        rc5_encrypt(&c,data,4);
        printf("Encryptions:\n");
        for(i=0;i<8;i+=2) printf("Block %01d = %081x %081x\n",
                                  i/2,data[i],data[i+1]);
        rc5_decrypt(&c,data,2);
    rc5_decrypt(&c,data+4,2);
        printf("Decryptions:\n");
        for(i=0;i<8;i+=2) printf("Block %01d = %081x %081x\n",
                                  i/2,data[i],data[i+1]);

}
```

A5

```
typedef struct {
        unsigned long r1,r2,r3;
} a5_ctx;

static int threshold(r1, r2, r3)
unsigned int r1;
unsigned int r2;
unsigned int r3;
{
int total;

  total = (((r1 >>  9) & 0x1) == 1) +
          (((r2 >> 11) & 0x1) == 1) +
          (((r3 >> 11) & 0x1) == 1);

  if (total > 1)
    return (0);
```

```
  else
    return (1);
}

unsigned long clock_r1(ctl, r1)
int ctl;
unsigned long r1;
{
unsigned long feedback;

  ctl ^= ((r1 >> 9) & 0x1);
  if (ctl)
  {
    feedback = (r1 >> 18) ^ (r1 >> 17) ^ (r1 >> 16) ^ (r1 >> 13);
    r1 = (r1 << 1) & 0x7ffff;
    if (feedback & 0x01)
      r1 ^= 0x01;
  }
  return (r1);
}

unsigned long clock_r2(ctl, r2)
int ctl;
unsigned long r2;
{
unsigned long feedback;

  ctl ^= ((r2 >> 11) & 0x1);
  if (ctl)
  {
    feedback = (r2 >> 21) ^ (r2 >> 20) ^ (r2 >> 16) ^ (r2 >> 12);
    r2 = (r2 << 1) & 0x3fffff;
    if (feedback & 0x01)
      r2 ^= 0x01;
  }
  return (r2);
}

unsigned long clock_r3(ctl, r3)
int ctl;
unsigned long r3;
{
unsigned long feedback;

  ctl ^= ((r3 >> 11) & 0x1);
  if (ctl)
  {
    feedback = (r3 >> 22) ^ (r3 >> 21) ^ (r3 >> 18) ^ (r3 >> 17);
    r3 = (r3 << 1) & 0x7fffff;
    if (feedback & 0x01)
      r3 ^= 0x01;
  }
  return (r3);
}
```

```
int keystream(key, frame, alice, bob)
unsigned char *key;     /* 64 bit session key              */
unsigned long frame;    /* 22 bit frame sequence number    */
unsigned char *alice;   /* 114 bit Alice to Bob key stream */
unsigned char *bob;     /* 114 bit Bob to Alice key stream */
{
unsigned long r1;    /* 19 bit shift register */
unsigned long r2;    /* 22 bit shift register */
unsigned long r3;    /* 23 bit shift register */
int i;               /* counter for loops      */
int clock_ctl;       /* xored with clock enable on each shift register */
unsigned char *ptr;  /* current position in keystream */
unsigned char byte;  /* byte of keystream being assembled */
unsigned int bits;   /* number of bits of keystream in byte */
unsigned int bit;    /* bit output from keystream generator */

   /* Initialise shift registers from session key */

   r1 = (key[0] | (key[1] << 8) | (key[2] << 16) ) & 0x7ffff;
   r2 = ((key[2] >> 3) | (key[3] << 5) | (key[4] << 13) | (key[5] << 21)) &
0x3fffff;
   r3 = ((key[5] >> 1) | (key[6] << 7) | (key[7] << 15) ) & 0x7fffff;

   /* Merge frame sequence number into shift register state, by xor'ing it
    * into the feedback path
    */

   for (i=0;i<22;i++)
   {
     clock_ctl = threshold(r1, r2, r2);
     r1 = clock_r1(clock_ctl, r1);
     r2 = clock_r2(clock_ctl, r2);
     r3 = clock_r3(clock_ctl, r3);
     if (frame & 1)
     {
       r1 ^= 1;
       r2 ^= 1;
       r3 ^= 1;
     }
     frame = frame >> 1;
   }

   /* Run shift registers for 100 clock ticks to allow frame number to
    * be diffused into all the bits of the shift registers
    */

   for (i=0;i<100;i++)
   {
     clock_ctl = threshold(r1, r2, r2);
     r1 = clock_r1(clock_ctl, r1);
     r2 = clock_r2(clock_ctl, r2);
     r3 = clock_r3(clock_ctl, r3);
   }

   /* Produce 114 bits of Alice->Bob key stream */
```

```
ptr = alice;
bits = 0;
byte = 0;
for (i=0;i<114;i++)
{
  clock_ctl = threshold(r1, r2, r2);
  r1 = clock_r1(clock_ctl, r1);
  r2 = clock_r2(clock_ctl, r2);
  r3 = clock_r3(clock_ctl, r3);

  bit = ((r1 >> 18) ^ (r2 >> 21) ^ (r3 >> 22)) & 0x01;
  byte = (byte << 1) | bit;
  bits++;
  if (bits == 8)
  {
    *ptr = byte;
    ptr++;
    bits = 0;
    byte = 0;
  }
}
if (bits)
  *ptr = byte;

/* Run shift registers for another 100 bits to hide relationship between
 * Alice->Bob key stream and Bob->Alice key stream.
 */

for (i=0;i<100;i++)
{
  clock_ctl = threshold(r1, r2, r2);
  r1 = clock_r1(clock_ctl, r1);
  r2 = clock_r2(clock_ctl, r2);
  r3 = clock_r3(clock_ctl, r3);
}

/* Produce 114 bits of Bob->Alice key stream */

ptr = bob;
bits = 0;
byte = 0;
for (i=0;i<114;i++)
{
  clock_ctl = threshold(r1, r2, r2);
  r1 = clock_r1(clock_ctl, r1);
  r2 = clock_r2(clock_ctl, r2);
  r3 = clock_r3(clock_ctl, r3);

  bit = ((r1 >> 18) ^ (r2 >> 21) ^ (r3 >> 22)) & 0x01;
  byte = (byte << 1) | bit;
  bits++;
  if (bits == 8)
  {
    *ptr = byte;
```

```
      ptr++;
      bits = 0;
      byte = 0;
    }
  }
  if (bits)
    *ptr = byte;

  return (0);

}

void a5_key(a5_ctx *c, char *k){
      c->r1 = k[0]<<11|k[1]<<3 | k[2]>>5           ; /* 19 */
      c->r2 = k[2]<<17|k[3]<<9 | k[4]<<1 | k[5]>>7; /* 22 */
      c->r3 = k[5]<<15|k[6]<<8 | k[7]              ; /* 23 */
}

/* Step one bit in A5, return 0 or 1 as output bit. */
int a5_step(a5_ctx *c){
      int control;
      control = threshold(c->r1,c->r2,c->r3);
      c->r1 = clock_r1(control,c->r1);
      c->r2 = clock_r2(control,c->r2);
      c->r3 = clock_r3(control,c->r3);
      return( (c->r1^c->r2^c->r3)&1);
}

/* Encrypts a buffer of len bytes. */
void a5_encrypt(a5_ctx *c, char *data, int len){
      int i,j;
      char t;

      for(i=0;i<len;i++){
            for(j=0;j<8;j++) t = t<<1 | a5_step(c);
            data[i]^=t;
      }
}

void a5_decrypt(a5_ctx *c, char *data, int len){
      a5_encrypt(c,data,len);
}

void main(void){
      a5_ctx c;
      char data[100];
      char key[] = {1,2,3,4,5,6,7,8};
      int i,flag;

      for(i=0;i<100;i++) data[i] = i;

      a5_key(&c,key);
      a5_encrypt(&c,data,100);

      a5_key(&c,key);
```

```
            a5_decrypt(&c,data,1);
            a5_decrypt(&c,data+1,99);

            flag = 0;
            for(i=0;i<100;i++) if(data[i]!=i)flag = 1;
            if(flag)printf("Decrypt failed\n"); else printf("Decrypt succeeded\n");
}
```

SEAL

```
#undef SEAL_DEBUG

#define ALG_OK 0
#define ALG_NOTOK 1
#define WORDS_PER_SEAL_CALL 1024

typedef struct {
      unsigned long t[520]; /* 512 rounded up to a multiple of 5 + 5*/
      unsigned long s[265]; /* 256 rounded up to a multiple of 5 + 5*/
      unsigned long r[20];  /* 16 rounded up to multiple of 5 */
        unsigned long counter; /* 32-bit synch value. */
        unsigned long ks_buf[WORDS_PER_SEAL_CALL];
        int ks_pos;
} seal_ctx;

#define ROT2(x)  (((x) >> 2) | ((x) << 30))
#define ROT9(x)  (((x) >> 9) | ((x) << 23))
#define ROT8(x)  (((x) >> 8) | ((x) << 24))
#define ROT16(x) (((x) >> 16) | ((x) << 16))
#define ROT24(x) (((x) >> 24) | ((x) << 8))
#define ROT27(x) (((x) >> 27) | ((x) << 5))

#define WORD(cp)  ((cp[0] << 24)|(cp[1] << 16)|(cp[2] << 8)|(cp[3]))

#define F1(x, y, z) (((x) & (y)) | ((~(x)) & (z)))
#define F2(x, y, z) ((x)^(y)^(z))
#define F3(x, y, z) (((x) & (y)) | ((x) & (z)) | ((y) & (z)))
#define F4(x, y, z) ((x)^(y)^(z))

int g(in, i, h)
unsigned char *in;
int i;
unsigned long *h;
{
unsigned long h0;
unsigned long h1;
unsigned long h2;
unsigned long h3;
unsigned long h4;
unsigned long a;
unsigned long b;
unsigned long c;
unsigned long d;
unsigned long e;
```

```
unsigned char *kp;
unsigned long w[80];
unsigned long temp;

    kp = in;
    h0 = WORD(kp); kp += 4;
    h1 = WORD(kp); kp += 4;
    h2 = WORD(kp); kp += 4;
    h3 = WORD(kp); kp += 4;
    h4 = WORD(kp); kp += 4;

    w[0] = i;
    for (i=1;i<16;i++)
        w[i] = 0;
    for (i=16;i<80;i++)
        w[i] = w[i-3]^w[i-8]^w[i-14]^w[i-16];

    a = h0;
    b = h1;
    c = h2;
    d = h3;
    e = h4;

    for (i=0;i<20;i++)
    {
        temp = ROT27(a) + F1(b, c, d) + e + w[i] + 0x5a827999;
        e = d;
        d = c;
        c = ROT2(b);
        b = a;
        a = temp;
    }
    for (i=20;i<40;i++)
    {
        temp = ROT27(a) + F2(b, c, d) + e + w[i] + 0x6ed9eba1;
        e = d;
        d = c;
        c = ROT2(b);
        b = a;
        a = temp;
    }
    for (i=40;i<60;i++)
    {
        temp = ROT27(a) + F3(b, c, d) + e + w[i] + 0x8f1bbcdc;
        e = d;
        d = c;
        c = ROT2(b);
        b = a;
        a = temp;
    }
    for (i=60;i<80;i++)
    {
        temp = ROT27(a) + F4(b, c, d) + e + w[i] + 0xca62c1d6;
        e = d;
        d = c;
```

```
            c = ROT2(b);
            b = a;
            a = temp;
        }
    h[0] = h0+a;
    h[1] = h1+b;
    h[2] = h2+c;
    h[3] = h3+d;
    h[4] = h4+e;

    return (ALG_OK);
}

unsigned long gamma(a, i)
unsigned char *a;
int i;
{
unsigned long h[5];

    (void) g(a, i/5, h);
    return h[i % 5];
}

int  seal_init(seal_ctx *result, unsigned char *key)
{
int i;
unsigned long h[5];

    for (i=0;i<510;i+=5)
        g(key, i/5, &(result->t[i]));
    /* horrible special case for the end */
    g(key, 510/5, h);
    for (i=510;i<512;i++)
        result->t[i] = h[i-510];
    /* 0x1000 mod 5 is +1, so have horrible special case for the start */
    g(key, (-1+0x1000)/5, h);
    for (i=0;i<4;i++)
        result->s[i] = h[i+1];
    for (i=4;i<254;i+=5)
        g(key, (i+0x1000)/5, &(result->s[i]));
    /* horrible special case for the end */
    g(key, (254+0x1000)/5, h);
    for (i=254;i<256;i++)
        result->s[i] = h[i-254];
    /* 0x2000 mod 5 is +2, so have horrible special case at the start */
    g(key, (-2+0x2000)/5, h);
    for (i=0;i<3;i++)
        result->r[i] = h[i+2];
    for (i=3;i<13;i+=5)
        g(key, (i+0x2000)/5, &(result->r[i]));
    /* horrible special case for the end */
    g(key, (13+0x2000)/5, h);
    for (i=13;i<16;i++)
        result->r[i] = h[i-13];
    return (ALG_OK);
```

```
}

int seal(seal_ctx *key, unsigned long in, unsigned long *out)
{
int i;
int j;
int l;
unsigned long a;
unsigned long b;
unsigned long c;
unsigned long d;
unsigned short p;
unsigned short q;
unsigned long n1;
unsigned long n2;
unsigned long n3;
unsigned long n4;
unsigned long *wp;

     wp = out;

     for (l=0;l<4;l++)
     {
          a = in ^ key->r[4*l];
          b = ROT8(in) ^ key->r[4*l+1];
          c = ROT16(in) ^ key->r[4*l+2];
          d = ROT24(in) ^ key->r[4*l+3];

          for (j=0;j<2;j++)
          {
               p = a & 0x7fc;
               b += key->t[p/4];
               a = ROT9(a);

               p = b & 0x7fc;
               c += key->t[p/4];
               b = ROT9(b);

               p = c & 0x7fc;
               d += key->t[p/4];
               c = ROT9(c);

               p = d & 0x7fc;
               a += key->t[p/4];
               d = ROT9(d);
          }
          n1 = d;
          n2 = b;
          n3 = a;
          n4 = c;

          p = a & 0x7fc;
          b += key->t[p/4];
```

```
    a = ROT9(a);

    p = b & 0x7fc;
    c += key->t[p/4];
    b = ROT9(b);

    p = c & 0x7fc;
    d += key->t[p/4];
    c = ROT9(c);

    p = d & 0x7fc;
    a += key->t[p/4];
    d = ROT9(d);

/* This generates 64 32-bit words, or 256 bytes of keystream. */
    for (i=0;i<64;i++)
    {
        p = a & 0x7fc;
        b += key->t[p/4];
        a = ROT9(a);
        b ^= a;

        q = b & 0x7fc;
        c ^= key->t[q/4];
        b = ROT9(b);
        c += b;

        p = (p+c) & 0x7fc;
        d += key->t[p/4];
        c = ROT9(c);
        d ^= c;

        q = (q+d) & 0x7fc;
        a ^= key->t[q/4];
        d = ROT9(d);
        a += d;

        p = (p+a) & 0x7fc;
        b ^= key->t[p/4];
        a = ROT9(a);

        q = (q+b) & 0x7fc;
        c += key->t[q/4];
        b = ROT9(b);

        p = (p+c) & 0x7fc;
        d ^= key->t[p/4];
        c = ROT9(c);

        q = (q+d) & 0x7fc;
        a += key->t[q/4];
        d = ROT9(d);

        *wp = b + key->s[4*i];
```

```
                wp++;
                *wp = c ^ key->s[4*i+1];
                wp++;
                *wp = d + key->s[4*i+2];
                wp++;
                *wp = a ^ key->s[4*i+3];
                wp++;

                if (i & 1)
                {
                    a += n3;
                    c += n4;
                }
                else
                {
                    a += n1;
                    c += n2;
                }


            }
        }
        return (ALG_OK);
}

/* Added call to refill ks_buf and reset counter and ks_pos. */
void seal_refill_buffer(seal_ctx *c){
        seal(c,c->counter,c->ks_buf);
        c->counter++;
        c->ks_pos = 0;
}

void seal_key(seal_ctx *c, unsigned char *key){
        seal_init(c,key);
        c->counter = 0;  /* By default, init to zero. */
        c->ks_pos = WORDS_PER_SEAL_CALL;
                /* Refill keystream buffer on next call. */
}

/* This encrypts the next w words with SEAL. */
void seal_encrypt(seal_ctx *c, unsigned long *data_ptr, int w){
        int i;

        for(i=0;i<w;i++){
                if(c->ks_pos>=WORDS_PER_SEAL_CALL) seal_refill_buffer(c);
                data_ptr[i]^=c->ks_buf[c->ks_pos];
                c->ks_pos++;
        }
}

void seal_decrypt(seal_ctx *c, unsigned long *data_ptr, int w) {
        seal_encrypt(c,data_ptr,w);
}

void seal_resynch(seal_ctx *c, unsigned long synch_word){
        c->counter = synch_word;
```

```
        c->ks_pos = WORDS_PER_SEAL_CALL;
}

void main(void){
        seal_ctx sc;
        unsigned long buf[1000],t;
        int i,flag;
        unsigned char key[] =
                {0,1,2,3,4,5,6,7,8,9,10,11,12,13,14,15,16,17,18,19};

        printf("1\n");
        seal_key(&sc,key);

        printf("2\n");
        for(i=0;i<1000;i++) buf[i]=0;
        printf("3\n");
        seal_encrypt(&sc,buf,1000);
        printf("4\n");
        t = 0;
        for(i=0;i<1000;i++) t = t ^ buf[i];
                printf("XOR of buf is %08lx.\n",t);

        seal_key(&sc,key);
        seal_decrypt(&sc,buf,1);
        seal_decrypt(&sc,buf+1,999);
        flag = 0;
        for(i=0;i<1000;i++) if(buf[i]!=0)flag=1;
        if(flag) printf("Decrypt failed.\n");
        else printf("Decrypt succeeded.\n");

}
```

References

1. ABA Bank Card Standard, "Management and Use of Personal Information Numbers," Aids from ABA, Catalog no. 207213, American Bankers Association, 1979.

2. ABA Document 4.3, "Key Management Standard," American Bankers Association, 1980.

3. M. Abadi, J. Feigenbaum, and J. Kilian, "On Hiding Information from an Oracle," *Proceedings of the 19th ACM Symposium on the Theory of Computing*, 1987, pp. 195–203.

4. M. Abadi, J. Feigenbaum, and J. Kilian, "On Hiding Information from an Oracle," *Journal of Computer and System Sciences*, v. 39, n. 1, Aug 1989, pp. 21–50.

5. M. Abadi and R. Needham, "Prudent Engineering Practice for Cryptographic Protocols," Research Report 125, Digital Equipment Corp Systems Research Center, Jun 1994.

6. C.M. Adams, "On Immunity Against Biham and Shamir's 'Differential Cryptanalysis,'" *Information Processing Letters*, v. 41, 14 Feb 1992, pp. 77–80.

7. C.M. Adams, "Simple and Effective Key Scheduling for Symmetric Ciphers," *Workshop on Selected Areas in Cryptography—Workshop Record*, Kingston, Ontario, 5–6 May 1994, pp. 129–133.

8. C.M. Adams and H. Meijer, "Security-Related Comments Regarding McEliece's Public-Key Cryptosystem," *Advances in Cryptology—CRYPTO '87 Proceedings*, Springer-Verlag, 1988, pp. 224–230.

9. C.M. Adams and S.E. Tavares, "The Structured Design of Cryptographically Good S-Boxes," *Journal of Cryptology*, v. 3, n. 1, 1990, pp. 27–41.

10. C.M. Adams and S.E. Tavares, "Designing S-Boxes for Ciphers Resistant to Differential Cryptanalysis," *Proceedings of the 3rd Symposium on State and Progress of Research in Cryptography*, Rome, Italy, 15–16 Feb 1993, pp. 181–190.

11. W. Adams and D. Shanks, "Strong Primality Tests That Are Not Sufficient," *Mathematics of Computation*, v. 39, 1982, pp. 255–300.

12. W.W. Adams and L.J. Goldstein, *Introduction to Number Theory*, Englewood Cliffs, N.J.: Prentice-Hall, 1976.

13. B.S. Adiga and P. Shankar, "Modified Lu-Lee Cryptosystem," *Electronics Letters*, v. 21, n. 18, 29 Aug 1985, pp. 794–795.

14. L.M. Adleman, "A Subexponential Algorithm for the Discrete Logarithm Problem with Applications to Cryptography," *Proceedings of the IEEE 20th Annual Symposium of Foundations of Computer Science*, 1979, pp. 55–60.

15. L.M. Adleman, "On Breaking Generalized Knapsack Public Key Cryptosystems," *Proceedings of the 15th ACM Symposium on Theory of Computing*, 1983, pp. 402–412.

16. L.M. Adleman, "Factoring Numbers Using Singular Integers," *Proceedings of the 23rd Annual ACM Symposium on the Theory of Computing*, 1991, pp. 64–71.

17. L.M. Adleman, "Molecular Computation of Solutions to Combinatorial Problems," *Science*, v. 266, n. 11, Nov 1994, p. 1021.

18. L.M. Adleman, D. Estes, and K. McCurley, "Solving Bivariate Quadratic Congruences in Random Polynomial Time," *Mathematics of Computation*, v. 48, n. 177, Jan 1987, pp. 17–28.

19. L.M. Adleman, C. Pomerance, and R.S. Rumeley, "On Distinguishing Prime Numbers from Composite Numbers," *Annals of Mathematics*, v. 117, n. 1, 1983, pp. 173–206.

20. L.M. Adleman and R.L. Rivest, "How to Break the Lu-Lee (COMSAT) Public-Key Cryptosystem," MIT Laboratory for Computer Science, Jul 1979.

21. G.B. Agnew, "Random Sources for Cryptographic Systems," *Advances in Cryptology—EUROCRYPT '87 Proceedings*, Springer-Verlag, 1988, pp. 77–81.

22. G.B. Agnew, R.C. Mullin, I.M. Onyszchuk, and S.A. Vanstone, "An Implementation for a Fast Public-Key Cryptosystem," *Journal of Cryptology*, v. 3, n. 2, 1991, pp. 63–79.

23. G.B. Agnew, R.C. Mullin, and S.A. Vanstone, "A Fast Elliptic Curve Cryptosystem," *Advances in Cryptology—EUROCRYPT '89 Proceedings*, Springer-Verlag, 1990, pp. 706–708.

24. G.B. Agnew, R.C. Mullin, and S.A. Vanstone, "Improved Digital Signature Scheme Based on Discrete Exponentiation," *Electronics Letters*, v. 26, n. 14, 5 Jul 1990, pp. 1024–1025.

25. G.B. Agnew, R.C. Mullin, and S.A. Vanstone, "On the Development of a Fast Elliptic Curve Cryptosystem," *Advances in Cryptology—EUROCRYPT '92 Proceedings*, Springer-Verlag, 1993, pp. 482–287.

26. G.B. Agnew, R.C. Mullin, and S.A. Vanstone, "An Implementation of Elliptic Curve Cryptosystems over F_2155," *IEEE Selected Areas of Communications*, v. 11, n. 5, Jun 1993, pp. 804–813.

27. A. Aho, J. Hopcroft, and J. Ullman, *The Design and Analysis of Computer Algorithms*, Addison-Wesley, 1974.

28. S.G. Akl, "Digital Signatures: A Tutorial Survey," *Computer*, v. 16, n. 2, Feb 1983, pp. 15–24.

29. S.G. Akl, "On the Security of Compressed Encodings," *Advances in Cryptology: Proceedings of Crypto 83*, Plenum Press, 1984, pp. 209–230.

30. S.G. Akl and H. Meijer, "A Fast Pseudo-Random Permutation Generator with Applications to Cryptology," *Advances in Cryptology: Proceedings of CRYPTO 84*, Springer-Verlag, 1985, pp. 269–275.

31. M. Alabbadi and S.B. Wicker, "Security of Xinmei Digital Signature Scheme," *Electronics Letters*, v. 28, n. 9, 23 Apr 1992, pp. 890–891.

32. M. Alabbadi and S.B. Wicker, "Digital Signature Schemes Based on Error-Correcting Codes," *Proceedings of the 1993 IEEE-ISIT*, IEEE Press, 1993, p. 199.

33. M. Alabbadi and S.B. Wicker, "Cryptanalysis of the Harn and Wang Modification of the Xinmei Digital Signature Scheme," *Electronics Letters*, v. 28, n. 18, 27 Aug 1992, pp. 1756–1758.

34. K. Alagappan and J. Tardo, "SPX Guide: Prototype Public Key Authentication Service," Digital Equipment Corp., May 1991.

35. W. Alexi, B.-Z. Chor, O. Goldreich, and C.P. Schnorr, "RSA and Rabin Functions: Certain Parts Are as Hard as the Whole," *Proceedings of the 25th IEEE Symposium on the Foundations of Computer Science*, 1984, pp. 449–457.

36. W. Alexi, B.-Z. Chor, O. Goldreich, and C.P. Schnorr, "RSA and Rabin Functions: Certain Parts are as Hard as the Whole," *SIAM Journal on Computing*, v. 17, n. 2, Apr 1988, pp. 194–209.

37. Ameritech Mobile Communications et al., "Cellular Digital Packet Data System Specifications: Part 406: Airlink Security," CDPD Industry Input Coordinator, Costa Mesa, Calif., Jul 1993.

38. H.R. Amirazizi, E.D. Karnin, and J.M. Reyneri, "Compact Knapsacks are Polynomial Solvable," *ACM SIGACT News*, v. 15, 1983, pp. 20–22.

39. R.J. Anderson, "Solving a Class of Stream Ciphers," *Cryptologia*, v. 14, n. 3, Jul 1990, pp. 285–288.

40. R.J. Anderson, "A Second Generation Electronic Wallet," *ESORICS 92, Proceedings of the Second European Symposium on*

Research in Computer Security, Springer-Verlag, 1992, pp. 411–418.

41. R.J. Anderson, "Faster Attack on Certain Stream Ciphers," *Electronics Letters*, v. 29, n. 15, 22 Jul 1993, pp. 1322–1323.

42. R.J. Anderson, "Derived Sequence Attacks on Stream Ciphers," presented at the rump session of CRYPTO '93, Aug 1993.

43. R.J. Anderson, "Why Cryptosystems Fail," *1st ACM Conference on Computer and Communications Security*, ACM Press, 1993, pp. 215–227.

44. R.J. Anderson, "Why Cryptosystems Fail," *Communications of the ACM*, v. 37, n. 11, Nov 1994, pp. 32–40.

45. R.J. Anderson, "On Fibonacci Keystream Generators," *K.U. Leuven Workshop on Cryptographic Algorithms*, Springer-Verlag, 1995, to appear.

46. R.J. Anderson, "Searching for the Optimum Correlation Attack," *K.U. Leuven Workshop on Cryptographic Algorithms*, Springer-Verlag, 1995, to appear.

47. R.J. Anderson and T.M.A. Lomas, "Fortifying Key Negotiation Schemes with Poorly Chosen Passwords," *Electronics Letters*, v. 30, n. 13, 23 Jun 1994, pp. 1040–1041.

48. R.J. Anderson and R. Needham, "Robustness Principles for Public Key Protocols," *Advances in Cryptology—CRYPTO '95 Proceedings*, Springer-Verlag, 1995, to appear.

49. D. Andleman and J. Reeds, "On the Cryptanalysis of Rotor Machines and Substitution-Permutation Networks," *IEEE Transactions on Information Theory*, v. IT-28, n. 4, Jul 1982, pp. 578–584.

50. ANSI X3.92, "American National Standard for Data Encryption Algorithm (DEA)," American National Standards Institute, 1981.

51. ANSI X3.105, "American National Standard for Information Systems—Data Link Encryption," American National Standards Institute, 1983.

52. ANSI X3.106, "American National Standard for Information Systems—Data Encryption Algorithm—Modes of Operation," American National Standards Institute, 1983.

53. ANSI X9.8, "American National Standard for Personal Information Number (PIN) Management and Security," American Bankers Association, 1982.

54. ANSI X9.9 (Revised), "American National Standard for Financial Institution Message Authentication (Wholesale)," American Bankers Association, 1986.

55. ANSI X9.17 (Revised), "American National Standard for Financial Institution Key Management (Wholesale)," American Bankers Association, 1985.

56. ANSI X9.19, "American National Standard for Retail Message Authentication," American Bankers Association, 1985.

57. ANSI X9.23, "American National Standard for Financial Institution Message Encryption," American Bankers Association, 1988.

58. ANSI X9.24, "Draft Proposed American National Standard for Retail Key Management," American Bankers Association, 1988.

59. ANSI X9.26 (Revised), "American National Standard for Financial Institution Sign-On Authentication for Wholesale Financial Transaction," American Bankers Association, 1990.

60. ANSI X9.30, "Working Draft: Public Key Cryptography Using Irreversible Algorithms for the Financial Services Industry," American Bankers Association, Aug 1994.

61. ANSI X9.31, "Working Draft: Public Key Cryptography Using Reversible Algorithms for the Financial Services Industry," American Bankers Association, Mar 1993.

62. K. Aoki and K. Ohta, "Differential-Linear Cryptanalysis of FEAL-8," *Proceedings of the 1995 Symposium on Cryptography and Information Security (SCIS 95)*, Inuyama, Japan, 24–27 Jan 1995, pp. A3.4.1-11. (In Japanese.)

63. K. Araki and T. Sekine, "On the Conspiracy Problem of the Generalized Tanaka's Cryptosystem," *IEICE Transactions*, v. E74, n. 8, Aug 1991, pp. 2176–2178.

64. S. Araki, K. Aoki, and K. Ohta, "The Best Linear Expression Search for FEAL," *Proceedings of the 1995 Symposium on Cryptography and Information Security (SCIS 95)*, Inuyama, Japan, 24–27 Jan 1995, pp. A4.4.1-10.

65. C. Asmuth and J. Bloom, "A Modular Approach to Key Safeguarding," *IEEE Transactions on Information Theory*, v. IT-29, n. 2, Mar 1983, pp. 208–210.

66. D. Atkins, M. Graff, A.K. Lenstra, and P.C. Leyland, "The Magic Words are Squeamish Ossifrage," *Advances in Cryptology—ASIACRYPT '94 Proceedings*, Springer-Verlag, 1995, pp. 263–277.

67. AT&T, "T7001 Random Number Generator," Data Sheet, Aug 1986.

68. AT&T, "AT&T Readying New Spy-Proof Phone for Big Military and Civilian Markets," *The Report on AT&T*, 2 Jun 1986, pp. 6–7.

69. AT&T, "T7002/T7003 Bit Slice Multiplier," product announcement, 1987.

70. AT&T, "Telephone Security Device TSD 3600—User's Manual," AT&T, 20 Sep 1992.

71. Y. Aumann and U. Feige, "On Message Proof Systems with Known Space Verifiers," *Advances in Cryptology—CRYPTO '93 Proceedings*, Springer-Verlag, 1994, pp. 85–99.

72. R.G. Ayoub, *An Introduction to the Theory of Numbers*, Providence, RI: American Mathematical Society, 1963.

73. A. Aziz and W. Diffie, "Privacy and Authentication for Wireless Local Area Networks," *IEEE Personal Communications*, v. 1, n. 1, 1994, pp. 25–31.

74. A. Bahreman and J.D. Tygar, "Certified Electronic Mail," *Proceedings of the Internet Society 1994 Workshop on Network and Distributed System Security*, The Internet Society, 1994, pp. 3–19.

75. D. Balenson, "Automated Distribution of Cryptographic Keys Using the Financial Institution Key Management Standard," *IEEE Communications Magazine*, v. 23, n. 9, Sep 1985, pp. 41–46.

76. D. Balenson, "Privacy Enhancement for Internet Electronic Mail: Part III: Algorithms, Modes, and Identifiers," RFC 1423, Feb 1993.

77. D. Balenson, C.M. Ellison, S.B. Lipner, and S.T. Walker, "A New Approach to Software Key Escrow Encryption," TIS Report #520, Trusted Information Systems, Aug 94.

78. R. Ball, *Mathematical Recreations and Essays*, New York: MacMillan, 1960.

79. J. Bamford, *The Puzzle Palace*, Boston: Houghton Mifflin, 1982.

80. J. Bamford and W. Madsen, *The Puzzle Palace*, Second Edition, Penguin Books, 1995.

81. S.K. Banerjee, "High Speed Implementation of DES," *Computers & Security*, v. 1, 1982, pp. 261–267.

82. Z. Baodong, "MC-Veiled Linear Transform Public Key Cryptosystem," *Acta Electronica Sinica*, v. 20, n. 4, Apr 1992, pp. 21–24. (In Chinese.)

83. P.H. Bardell, "Analysis of Cellular Automata Used as Pseudorandom Pattern Generators," *Proceedings of 1990 International Test Conference*, pp. 762–768.

84. T. Baritaud, H. Gilbert, and M. Girault, "FFT Hashing is not Collision-Free," *Advances in Cryptology—EUROCRYPT '92 Proceedings*, Springer-Verlag, 1993, pp. 35–44.

85. C. Barker, "An Industry Perspective of the CCEP," *2nd Annual AIAA Computer Security Conference Proceedings*, 1986.

86. W.G. Barker, *Cryptanalysis of the Hagelin Cryptograph*, Aegean Park Press, 1977.

87. P. Barrett, "Implementing the Rivest Shamir and Adleman Public Key Encryption Algorithm on a Standard Digital Signal Processor," *Advances in Cryptology—CRYPTO '86 Proceedings*, Springer-Verlag, 1987, pp. 311–323.

88. T.C. Bartee and D.I. Schneider, "Computation with Finite Fields," *Information and Control*, v. 6, n. 2, Jun 1963, pp. 79–98.

89. U. Baum and S. Blackburn, "Clock-Controlled Pseudorandom Generators on Finite Groups," *K.U. Leuven Workshop on Cryptographic Algorithms*, Springer-Verlag, 1995, to appear.

90. K.R. Bauer, T.A. Bersen, and R.J. Feiertag, "A Key Distribution Protocol Using Event Markers," *ACM Transactions on Computer Systems*, v. 1, n. 3, 1983, pp. 249–255.

91. F. Bauspiess and F. Damm, "Requirements for Cryptographic Hash Functions," *Computers & Security*, v. 11, n. 5, Sep 1992, pp. 427–437.

92. D. Bayer, S. Haber, and W.S. Stornetta, "Improving the Efficiency and Reliability of Digital Time-Stamping," *Sequences '91: Methods in Communication, Security, and Computer Science*, Springer-Verlag, 1992, pp. 329–334.

93. R. Bayer and J.K. Metzger, "On the Encipherment of Search Trees and Random Access Files," *ACM Transactions on Database Systems*, v. 1, n. 1, Mar 1976, pp. 37–52.

94. M. Beale and M.F. Monaghan, "Encrytion Using Random Boolean Functions," *Cryptography and Coding*, H.J. Beker and F.C. Piper, eds., Oxford: Clarendon Press, 1989, pp. 219–230.

95. P. Beauchemin and G. Brassard, "A Generalization of Hellman's Extension to Shannon's Approach to Cryptography," *Journal of Cryptology*, v. 1, n. 2, 1988, pp. 129–132.

96. P. Beauchemin, G. Brassard, C. Crépeau, C. Goutier, and C. Pomerance, "The Generation of Random Numbers that are Probably Prime," *Journal of Cryptology*, v. 1, n. 1, 1988, pp. 53–64.

97. D. Beaver, J. Feigenbaum, and V. Shoup, "Hiding Instances in Zero-Knowledge Proofs," *Advances in Cryptology—CRYPTO '90 Proceedings*, Springer-Verlag, 1991, pp. 326–338.

98. H. Beker, J. Friend, and P. Halliden, "Simplifying Key Management in Electronic Funds Transfer Points of Sale Systems," *Electronics Letters*, v. 19, n. 12, Jun 1983, pp. 442–444.

99. H. Beker and F. Piper, *Cipher Systems: The Protection of Communications*, London: Northwood Books, 1982.

100. D.E. Bell and L.J. LaPadula, "Secure Computer Systems: Mathematical Foundations," Report ESD-TR-73-275, MITRE Corp., 1973.

101. D.E. Bell and L.J. LaPadula, "Secure Computer Systems: A Mathematical Model," Report MTR-2547, MITRE Corp., 1973.

102. D.E. Bell and L.J. LaPadula, "Secure Computer Systems: A Refinement of the Mathematical Model," Report ESD-TR-73-278, MITRE Corp., 1974.

103. D.E. Bell and L.J. LaPadula, "Secure Computer Systems: Unified Exposition and Multics Interpretation," Report ESD-TR-75-306, MITRE Corp., 1976.

104. M. Bellare and S. Goldwasser, "New Paradigms for Digital Signatures and Message Authentication Based on Non-Interactive Zero Knowledge Proofs," *Advances in Cryptology—CRYPTO '89 Proceedings*, Springer-Verlag, 1990, pp. 194–211.

105. M. Bellare and S. Micali, "Non-Interactive Oblivious Transfer and Applications," *Advances in Cryptology—CRYPTO '89 Proceedings*, Springer-Verlag, 1990, pp. 547–557.

106. M. Bellare, S. Micali, and R. Ostrovsky, "Perfect Zero-Knowledge in Constant Rounds," *Proceedings of the 22nd ACM Symposium on the Theory of Computing*, 1990, pp. 482–493.

107. S.M. Bellovin, "A Preliminary Technical Analysis of Clipper and Skipjack," unpublished manuscript, 20 Apr 1993.

108. S.M. Bellovin and M. Merritt, "Limitations of the Kerberos Protocol," *Winter 1991 USENIX Conference Proceedings*, USENIX Association, 1991, pp. 253–267.

109. S.M. Bellovin and M. Merritt, "Encrypted Key Exchange: Password-Based Protocols Secure Against Dictionary Attacks," *Proceedings of the 1992 IEEE Computer Society Conference on Research in Security and Privacy*, 1992, pp. 72–84.

110. S.M. Bellovin and M. Merritt, "An Attack on the Interlock Protocol When Used for Authentication," *IEEE Transactions on Information Theory*, v. 40, n. 1, Jan 1994, pp. 273–275.

111. S.M. Bellovin and M. Merritt, "Cryptographic Protocol for Secure Communications," U.S. Patent #5,241,599, 31 Aug 93.

112. I. Ben-Aroya and E. Biham, "Differential Cryptanalysis of Lucifer," *Advances in Cryptology—CRYPTO '93 Proceedings*, Springer-Verlag, 1994, pp. 187–199.

113. J.C. Benaloh, "Cryptographic Capsules: A Disjunctive Primitive for Interactive Protocols," *Advances in Cryptology—CRYPTO '86 Proceedings*, Springer-Verlag, 1987, 213–222.

114. J.C. Benaloh, "Secret Sharing Homorphisms: Keeping Shares of a Secret Secret," *Advances in Cryptology—CRYPTO '86 Proceedings*, Springer-Verlag, 1987, pp. 251–260.

115. J.C. Benaloh, "Verifiable Secret-Ballot Elections," Ph.D. dissertation, Yale University, YALEU/DCS/TR-561, Dec 1987.

116. J.C. Benaloh and M. de Mare, "One-Way Accumulators: A Decentralized Alternative to Digital Signatures," *Advances in Cryptology—EUROCRYPT '93 Proceedings*, Springer-Verlag, 1994, pp. 274–285.

117. J.C. Benaloh and D. Tuinstra, "Receipt-Free Secret Ballot Elections," *Proceedings of the 26th ACM Symposium on the Theory of Computing*, 1994, pp. 544–553.

118. J.C. Benaloh and M. Yung, "Distributing the Power of a Government to Enhance

the Privacy of Voters," *Proceedings of the 5th ACM Symposium on the Principles in Distributed Computing*, 1986, pp. 52–62.

119. A. Bender and G. Castagnoli, "On the Implementation of Elliptic Curve Cryptosystems," *Advances in Cryptology—CRYPTO '89 Proceedings*, Springer-Verlag, 1990, pp. 186–192.

120. S. Bengio, G. Brassard, Y.G. Desmedt, C. Goutier, and J.-J. Quisquater, "Secure Implementation of Identification Systems," *Journal of Cryptology*, v. 4, n. 3, 1991, pp. 175–184.

121. C.H. Bennett, F. Bessette, G. Brassard, L. Salvail, and J. Smolin, "Experimental Quantum Cryptography," *Advances in Cryptology—EUROCRYPT '90 Proceedings*, Springer-Verlag, 1991, pp. 253–265.

122. C.H. Bennett, F. Bessette, G. Brassard, L. Salvail, and J. Smolin, "Experimental Quantum Cryptography," *Journal of Cryptology*, v. 5, n. 1, 1992, pp. 3–28.

123. C.H. Bennett and G. Brassard, "Quantum Cryptography: Public Key Distribution and Coin Tossing," *Proceedings of the IEEE International Conference on Computers, Systems, and Signal Processing*, Banjalore, India, Dec 1984, pp. 175–179.

124. C.H. Bennett and G. Brassard, "An Update on Quantum Cryptography," *Advances in Cryptology: Proceedings of CRYPTO 84*, Springer-Verlag, 1985, pp. 475–480.

125. C.H. Bennett and G. Brassard, "Quantum Public-Key Distribution System," *IBM Technical Disclosure Bulletin*, v. 28, 1985, pp. 3153–3163.

126. C.H. Bennett and G. Brassard, "Quantum Public Key Distribution Reinvented," *SIGACT News*, v. 18, n. 4, 1987, pp. 51–53.

127. C.H. Bennett and G. Brassard, "The Dawn of a New Era for Quantum Cryptography: The Experimental Prototype is Working!" *SIGACT News*, v. 20, n. 4, Fall 1989, pp. 78–82.

128. C.H. Bennett, G. Brassard, and S. Breidbart, *Quantum Cryptography II: How to Re-Use a One-Time Pad Safely Even if P=NP*, unpublished manuscript, Nov 1982.

129. C.H. Bennett, G. Brassard, S. Breidbart, and S. Weisner, "Quantum Cryptography, or Unforgeable Subway Tokens," *Advances in Cryptology: Proceedings of Crypto 82*, Plenum Press, 1983, pp. 267–275.

130. C.H. Bennett, G. Brassard, C. Crépeau, and M.-H. Skubiszewska, "Practical Quantum Oblivious Transfer," *Advances in Cryptology—CRYPTO '91 Proceedings*, Springer-Verlag, 1992, pp. 351–366.

131. C.H. Bennett, G. Brassard, and A.K. Ekert, "Quantum Cryptography," *Scientific American*, v. 267, n. 4, Oct 1992, pp. 50–57.

132. C.H. Bennett, G. Brassard, and N.D. Mermin, "Quantum Cryptography Without Bell's Theorem," *Physical Review Letters*, v. 68, n. 5, 3 Feb 1992, pp. 557–559.

133. C.H. Bennett, G. Brassard, and J.-M. Robert, "How to Reduce Your Enemy's Information," *Advances in Cryptology—CRYPTO '85 Proceedings*, Springer-Verlag, 1986, pp. 468–476.

134. C.H. Bennett, G. Brassard, and J.-M. Robert, "Privacy Amplification by Public Discussion," *SIAM Journal on Computing*, v. 17, n. 2, Apr 1988, pp. 210–229.

135. J. Bennett, "Analysis of the Encryption Algorithm Used in WordPerfect Word Processing Program," *Cryptologia*, v. 11, n. 4, Oct 1987, pp. 206–210.

136. M. Ben-Or, S. Goldwasser, and A. Wigderson, "Completeness Theorems for Non-Cryptographic Fault-Tolerant Distributed Computation," *Proceedings of the 20th ACM Symposium on the Theory of Computing*, 1988, pp. 1–10.

137. M. Ben-Or, O. Goldreich, S. Goldwasser, J. Håstad, J. Kilian, S. Micali, and P. Rogaway, "Everything Provable is Provable in Zero-Knowledge," *Advances in Cryptology—CRYPTO '88 Proceedings*, Springer-Verlag, 1990, pp. 37–56.

138. M. Ben-Or, O. Goldreich, S. Micali, and R.L. Rivest, "A Fair Protocol for Signing Contracts," *IEEE Transactions on Information Theory*, v. 36, n. 1, Jan 1990, pp. 40–46.

139. H.A. Bergen and W.J. Caelli, "File Security in WordPerfect 5.0," *Cryptologia*, v. 15, n. 1, Jan 1991, pp. 57–66.

140. E.R. Berlekamp, *Algebraic Coding Theory*, Aegean Park Press, 1984.

141. S. Berkovits, "How to Broadcast a Secret," *Advances in Cryptology—EUROCRYPT '91 Proceedings*, Springer-Verlag, 1991, pp. 535–541.

142. S. Berkovits, J. Kowalchuk, and B. Schanning, "Implementing Public-Key Scheme," *IEEE Communications Magazine*, v. 17, n. 3, May 1979, pp. 2–3.

143. D.J. Bernstein, Bernstein vs. U.S. Department of State et al., Civil Action No. C95-0582-MHP, United States District Court for the Northern District of California, 21 Feb 1995.

144. T. Berson, "Differential Cryptanalysis Mod 2^{32} with Applications to MD5," *Advances in Cryptology—EUROCRYPT '92 Proceedings*, 1992, pp. 71–80.

145. T. Beth, *Verfahren der schnellen Fourier-Transformation*, Teubner, Stuttgart, 1984. (In German.)

146. T. Beth, "Efficient Zero-Knowledge Identification Scheme for Smart Cards," *Advances in Cryptology—EUROCRYPT '88 Proceedings*, Springer-Verlag, 1988, pp. 77–84.

147. T. Beth, B.M. Cook, and D. Gollmann, "Architectures for Exponentiation in $GF(2^n)$," *Advances in Cryptology—CRYPTO '86 Proceedings*, Springer-Verlag, 1987, pp. 302–310.

148. T. Beth and Y. Desmedt, "Identification Tokens—or: Solving the Chess Grandmaster Problem," *Advances in Cryptology—CRYPTO '90 Proceedings*, Springer-Verlag, 1991, pp. 169–176.

149. T. Beth and C. Ding, "On Almost Nonlinear Permutations," *Advances in Cryptology—EUROCRYPT '93 Proceedings*, Springer-Verlag, 1994, pp. 65–76.

150. T. Beth, M. Frisch, and G.J. Simmons, eds., *Lecture Notes in Computer Science 578; Public Key Cryptography: State of the Art and Future Directions*, Springer-Verlag, 1992.

151. T. Beth and F.C. Piper, "The Stop-and-Go Generator," *Advances in Cryptology: Proceedings of EUROCRYPT 84*, Springer-Verlag, 1984, pp. 88–92.

152. T. Beth and F. Schaefer, "Non Supersingular Elliptic Curves for Public Key Cryptosystems," *Advances in Cryptology—EUROCRYPT '91 Proceedings*, Springer-Verlag, 1991, pp. 316–327.

153. A. Beutelspacher, "How to Say 'No'," *Advances in Cryptology—EUROCRYPT '89 Proceedings*, Springer-Verlag, 1990, pp. 491–496.

154. J. Bidzos, letter to NIST regarding DSS, 20 Sep 1991.

155. J. Bidzos, personal communication, 1993.

156. P. Bieber, "A Logic of Communication in a Hostile Environment," *Proceedings of the Computer Security Foundations Workshop III*, IEEE Computer Society Press, 1990, pp. 14–22.

157. E. Biham, "Cryptanalysis of the Chaotic-Map Cryptosystem Suggested at EUROCRYPT '91," *Advances in Cryptology—EUROCRYPT '91 Proceedings*, Springer-Verlag, 1991, pp. 532–534.

158. E. Biham, "New Types of Cryptanalytic Attacks Using Related Keys," Technical Report #753, Computer Science Department, Technion—Israel Institute of Technology, Sep 1992.

159. E. Biham, "On the Applicability of Differential Cryptanalysis to Hash Functions," lecture at EIES Workshop on Cryptographic Hash Functions, Mar 1992.

160. E. Biham, personal communication, 1993.

161. E. Biham, "Higher Order Differential Cryptanalysis," unpublished manuscript, Jan 1994.

162. E. Biham, "On Modes of Operation," *Fast Software Encryption, Cambridge Security Workshop Proceedings*, Springer-Verlag, 1994, pp. 116–120.

163. E. Biham, "New Types of Cryptanalytic Attacks Using Related Keys," *Journal of Cryptology*, v. 7, n. 4, 1994, pp. 229–246.

164. E. Biham, "On Matsui's Linear Cryptanalysis," *Advances in Cryptology—EUROCRYPT '94 Proceedings*, Springer-Verlag, 1995, pp. 398–412.

165. E. Biham and A. Biryukov, "How to Strengthen DES Using Existing Hardware," *Advances in Cryptology—ASIACRYPT '94 Proceedings*, Springer-Verlag, 1995, to appear.

166. E. Biham and P.C. Kocher, "A Known Plaintext Attack on the PKZIP Encryption," *K.U. Leuven Workshop on Cryptographic Algorithms*, Springer-Verlag, 1995, to appear.

167. E. Biham and A. Shamir, "Differential Cryptanalysis of DES-like Cryptosystems," *Advances in Cryptology—CRYPTO '90 Proceedings*, Springer-Verlag, 1991, pp. 2–21.

168. E. Biham and A. Shamir, "Differential Cryptanalysis of DES-like Cryptosystems," *Journal of Cryptology*, v. 4, n. 1, 1991, pp 3–72.

169. E. Biham and A. Shamir, "Differential Cryptanalysis of Feal and N-Hash," *Advances in Cryptology—EUROCRYPT*

'91 Proceedings, Springer-Verlag, 1991, pp. 1–16.

170. E. Biham and A. Shamir, "Differential Cryptanalysis of Snefru, Khafre, REDOC-II, LOKI, and Lucifer," *Advances in Cryptology—CRYPTO '91 Proceedings*, 1992, pp. 156–171.

171. E. Biham and A. Shamir, "Differential Cryptanalysis of the Full 16-Round DES," *Advances in Cryptology—CRYPTO '92 Proceedings*, Springer-Verlag, 1993, 487–496.

172. E. Biham and A. Shamir, *Differential Cryptanalysis of the Data Encryption Standard*, Springer-Verlag, 1993.

173. R. Bird, I. Gopal, A. Herzberg, P. Janson, S. Kutten, R. Molva, and M. Yung, "Systematic Design of Two-Party Authentication Protocols," *Advances in Cryptology—CRYPTO '91 Proceedings*, Springer-Verlag, 1992, pp. 44–61.

174. R. Bird, I. Gopal, A. Herzberg, P. Janson, S. Kutten, R. Molva, and M. Yung, "Systematic Design of a Family of Attack-Resistant Authentication Protocols," *IEEE Journal of Selected Areas in Communication*, to appear.

175. R. Bird, I. Gopal, A. Herzberg, P. Janson, S. Kutten, R. Molva, and M. Yung, "A Modular Family of Secure Protocols for Authentication and Key Distribution," *IEEE/ACM Transactions on Networking*, to appear.

176. M. Bishop, "An Application for a Fast Data Encryption Standard Implementation," *Computing Systems*, v. 1, n. 3, 1988, pp. 221–254.

177. M. Bishop, "Privacy-Enhanced Electronic Mail," *Distributed Computing and Cryptography*, J. Feigenbaum and M. Merritt, eds., American Mathematical Society, 1991, pp. 93–106.

178. M. Bishop, "Privacy-Enhanced Electronic Mail," *Internetworking: Research and Experience*, v. 2, n. 4, Dec 1991, pp. 199–233.

179. M. Bishop, "Recent Changes to Privacy Enhanced Electronic Mail," *Internetworking: Research and Experience*, v. 4, n. 1, Mar 1993, pp. 47–59.

180. I.F. Blake, R. Fuji-Hara, R.C. Mullin, and S.A. Vanstone, "Computing Logarithms in Finite Fields of Characteristic Two," *SIAM Journal on Algebraic Discrete Methods*, v. 5, 1984, pp. 276–285.

181. I.F. Blake, R.C. Mullin, and S.A. Vanstone, "Computing Logarithms in GF (2^n)," *Advances in Cryptology: Proceedings of CRYPTO 84*, Springer-Verlag, 1985, pp. 73–82.

182. G.R. Blakley, "Safeguarding Cryptographic Keys," *Proceedings of the National Computer Conference, 1979*, American Federation of Information Processing Societies, v. 48, 1979, pp. 313–317.

183. G.R. Blakley, "One-Time Pads are Key Safeguarding Schemes, Not Cryptosystems—Fast Key Safeguarding Schemes (Threshold Schemes) Exist," *Proceedings of the 1980 Symposium on Security and Privacy*, IEEE Computer Society, Apr 1980, pp. 108–113.

184. G.R. Blakley and I. Borosh, "Rivest-Shamir-Adleman Public Key Cryptosystems Do Not Always Conceal Messages," *Computers and Mathematics with Applications*, v. 5, n. 3, 1979, pp. 169–178.

185. G.R. Blakley and C. Meadows, "A Database Encryption Scheme which Allows the Computation of Statistics Using Encrypted Data," *Proceedings of the 1985 Symposium on Security and Privacy*, IEEE Computer Society, Apr 1985, pp. 116–122.

186. M. Blaze, "A Cryptographic File System for UNIX," *1st ACM Conference on Computer and Communications Security*, ACM Press, 1993, pp. 9–16.

187. M. Blaze, "Protocol Failure in the Escrowed Encryption Standard," *2nd ACM Conference on Computer and Communications Security*, ACM Press, 1994, pp. 59–67.

188. M. Blaze, "Key Management in an Encrypting File System," *Proceedings of the Summer 94 USENIX Conference*, USENIX Association, 1994, pp. 27–35.

189. M. Blaze and B. Schneier, "The MacGuffin Block Cipher Algorithm," *K.U. Leuven Workshop on Cryptographic Algorithms*, Springer-Verlag, 1995, to appear.

190. U. Blöcher and M. Dichtl, "Fish: A Fast Software Stream Cipher," *Fast Software Encryption, Cambridge Security Workshop Proceedings*, Springer-Verlag, 1994, pp. 41–44.

191. R. Blom, "Non-Public Key Distribution," *Advances in Cryptology: Proceedings of Crypto 82*, Plenum Press, 1983, pp. 231–236.

192. K.J. Blow and S.J.D. Phoenix, "On a Fundamental Theorem of Quantum Cryptography," *Journal of Modern Optics*, v. 40, n. 1, Jan 1993, pp. 33–36.

193. L. Blum, M. Blum, and M. Shub, "A Simple Unpredictable Pseudo-Random Number Generator," *SIAM Journal on Computing*, v. 15, n. 2, 1986, pp. 364–383.

194. M. Blum, "Coin Flipping by Telephone: A Protocol for Solving Impossible Problems," *Proceedings of the 24th IEEE Computer Conference (CompCon)*, 1982, pp. 133–137.

195. M. Blum, "How to Exchange (Secret) Keys," *ACM Transactions on Computer Systems*, v. 1, n. 2, May 1983, pp. 175–193.

196. M. Blum, "How to Prove a Theorem So No One Else Can Claim It," *Proceedings of the International Congress of Mathematicians*, Berkeley, CA, 1986, pp. 1444–1451.

197. M. Blum, A. De Santis, S. Micali, and G. Persiano, "Noninteractive Zero-Knowledge," *SIAM Journal on Computing*, v. 20, n. 6, Dec 1991, pp. 1084–1118.

198. M. Blum, P. Feldman, and S. Micali, "Non-Interactive Zero-Knowledge and Its Applications," *Proceedings of the 20th ACM Symposium on Theory of Computing*, 1988, pp. 103–112.

199. M. Blum and S. Goldwasser, "An *Efficient* Probabilistic Public-Key Encryption Scheme Which Hides All Partial Information," *Advances in Cryptology: Proceedings of CRYPTO 84*, Springer-Verlag, 1985, pp. 289–299.

200. M. Blum and S. Micali, "How to Generate Cryptographically-Strong Sequences of Pseudo-Random Bits," *SIAM Journal on Computing*, v. 13, n. 4, Nov 1984, pp. 850–864.

201. B. den Boer, "Cryptanalysis of F.E.A.L.," *Advances in Cryptology—EUROCRYPT '88 Proceedings*, Springer-Verlag, 1988, pp. 293–300.

202. B. den Boer and A. Bosselaers, "An Attack on the Last Two Rounds of MD4," *Advances in Cryptology—CRYPTO '91 Proceedings*, Springer-Verlag, 1992, pp. 194–203.

203. B. den Boer and A. Bosselaers, "Collisions for the Compression Function of MD5," *Advances in Cryptology—EUROCRYPT '93 Proceedings*, Springer-Verlag, 1994, pp. 293–304.

204. J.-P. Boly, A. Bosselaers, R. Cramer, R. Michelsen, S. Mjølsnes, F. Muller, T. Pedersen, B. Pfitzmann, P. de Rooij, B. Schoenmakers, M. Schunter, L. Vallée, and M. Waidner, "Digital Payment Systems in the ESPRIT Project CAFE," *Securicom 94*, Paris, France, 2–6 Jan 1994, pp. 35–45.

205. J.-P. Boly, A. Bosselaers, R. Cramer, R. Michelsen, S. Mjølsnes, F. Muller, T. Pedersen, B. Pfitzmann, P. de Rooij, B. Schoenmakers, M. Schunter, L. Vallée, and M. Waidner, "The ESPRIT Project CAFE— High Security Digital Payment System," *Computer Security—ESORICS 94*, Springer-Verlag, 1994, pp. 217–230.

206. D.J. Bond, "Practical Primality Testing," *Proceedings of IEE International Conference on Secure Communications Systems*, 22–23 Feb 1984, pp. 50–53.

207. H. Bonnenberg, *Secure Testing of VSLI Cryptographic Equipment*, Series in Microelectronics, Vol. 25, Konstanz: Hartung Gorre Verlag, 1993.

208. H. Bonnenberg, A. Curiger, N. Felber, H. Kaeslin, and X. Lai, "VLSI Implementation of a New Block Cipher," *Proceedings of the IEEE International Conference on Computer Design: VLSI in Computers and Processors (ICCD 91)*, Oct 1991, pp. 510–513.

209. K.S. Booth, "Authentication of Signatures Using Public Key Encryption," *Communications of the ACM*, v. 24, n. 11, Nov 1981, pp. 772–774.

210. A. Bosselaers, R. Govaerts, and J. Vanderwalle, *Advances in Cryptology—CRYPTO '93 Proceedings*, Springer-Verlag, 1994, pp. 175–186.

211. D.P. Bovet and P. Crescenzi, *Introduction to the Theory of Complexity*, Englewood Cliffs, N.J.: Prentice-Hall, 1994.

212. J. Boyar, "Inferring Sequences Produced by a Linear Congruential Generator Missing Low-Order Bits," *Journal of Cryptology*, v. 1, n. 3, 1989, pp. 177–184.

213. J. Boyar, D. Chaum, and I. Damgård, "Convertible Undeniable Signatures," *Advances in Cryptology—CRYPTO '90 Proceedings*, Springer-Verlag, 1991, pp. 189–205.

214. J. Boyar, K. Friedl, and C. Lund, "Practical Zero-Knowledge Proofs: Giving Hints and Using Deficiencies," *Advances in Cryptology—EUROCRYPT '89 Proceedings*, Springer-Verlag, 1990, pp. 155–172.

215. J. Boyar, C. Lund, and R. Peralta, "On the Communication Complexity of Zero-Knowledge Proofs," *Journal of Cryptology*, v. 6, n. 2, 1993, pp. 65–85.

216. J. Boyar and R. Peralta, "On the Concrete Complexity of Zero-Knowledge Proofs," *Advances in Cryptology—CRYPTO '89 Proceedings*, Springer-Verlag, 1990, pp. 507–525.

217. C. Boyd, "Some Applications of Multiple Key Ciphers," *Advances in Cryptology—EUROCRYPT '88 Proceedings*, Springer-Verlag, 1988, pp. 455–467.

218. C. Boyd, "Digital Multisignatures," *Cryptography and Coding*, H.J. Beker and F.C. Piper, eds., Oxford: Clarendon Press, 1989, pp. 241–246.

219. C. Boyd, "A New Multiple Key Cipher and an Improved Voting Scheme," *Advances in Cryptology—EUROCRYPT '89 Proceedings*, Springer-Verlag, 1990, pp. 617–625.

220. C. Boyd, "Multisignatures Revisited," *Cryptography and Coding III*, M.J. Ganley, ed., Oxford: Clarendon Press, 1993, pp. 21–30.

221. C. Boyd and W. Mao, "On the Limitation of BAN Logic," *Advances in Cryptology—EUROCRYPT '93 Proceedings*, Springer-Verlag, 1994, pp. 240–247.

222. C. Boyd and W. Mao, "Designing Secure Key Exchange Protocols," *Computer Security—ESORICS 94*, Springer-Verlag, 1994, pp. 217–230.

223. B.O. Brachtl, D. Coppersmith, M.M. Hyden, S.M. Matyas, C.H. Meyer, J. Oseas, S. Pilpel, and M. Schilling, "Data Authentication Using Modification Detection Codes Based on a Public One Way Function," U.S. Patent #4,908,861, 13 Mar 1990.

224. J. Brandt, I.B. Damgård, P. Landrock, and T. Pederson, "Zero-Knowledge Authentication Scheme with Secret Key Exchange," *Advances in Cryptology—CRYPTO '88*, Springer-Verlag, 1990, pp. 583–588.

225. S.A. Brands, "An Efficient Off-Line Electronic Cash System Based on the Representation Problem," Report CS-R9323, Computer Science/Department of Algorithms and Architecture, CWI, Mar 1993.

226. S.A. Brands, "Untraceable Off-line Cash in Wallet with Observers," *Advances in Cryptology—CRYPTO '93*, Springer-Verlag, 1994, pp. 302–318.

227. S.A. Brands, "Electronic Cash on the Internet," *Proceedings of the Internet Society 1995 Symposium on Network and Distributed Systems Security*, IEEE Computer Society Press 1995, pp 64–84.

228. D.K. Branstad, "Hellman's Data Does Not Support His Conclusion," *IEEE Spectrum*, v. 16, n. 7, Jul 1979, p. 39.

229. D.K. Branstad, J. Gait, and S. Katzke, "Report on the Workshop on Cryptography in Support of Computer Security," NBSIR 77-1291, National Bureau of Standards, Sep 21–22, 1976, September 1977.

230. G. Brassard, "A Note on the Complexity of Cryptography," *IEEE Transactions on Information Theory*, v. IT-25, n. 2, Mar 1979, pp. 232–233.

231. G. Brassard, "Relativized Cryptography," *Proceedings of the IEEE 20th Annual Symposium on the Foundations of Computer Science*, 1979, pp. 383–391.

232. G. Brassard, "A Time-Luck Tradeoff in Relativized Cryptography," *Proceedings of the IEEE 21st Annual Symposium on the Foundations of Computer Science*, 1980, pp. 380–386.

233. G. Brassard, "A Time-Luck Tradeoff in Relativized Cryptography," *Journal of Computer and System Sciences*, v. 22, n. 3, Jun 1981, pp. 280–311.

234. G. Brassard, "An Optimally Secure Relativized Cryptosystem," *SIGACT News*, v. 15, n. 1, 1983, pp. 28–33.

235. G. Brassard, "Relativized Cryptography," *IEEE Transactions on Information Theory*, v. IT-29, n. 6, Nov 1983, pp. 877–894.

236. G. Brassard, *Modern Cryptology: A Tutorial*, Springer-Verlag, 1988.

237. G. Brassard, "Quantum Cryptography: A Bibliography," *SIGACT News*, v. 24, n. 3, Oct 1993, pp. 16–20.

238. G. Brassard, D. Chaum, and C. Crépeau, "An Introduction to Minimum Disclosure," *CWI Quarterly*, v. 1, 1988, pp. 3–17.

239. G. Brassard, D. Chaum, and C. Crépeau, "Minimum Disclosure Proofs of Knowledge," *Journal of Computer and System Sciences*, v. 37, n. 2, Oct 1988, pp. 156–189.

240. G. Brassard and C. Crépeau, "Non-Transitive Transfer of Confidence: A *Perfect* Zero-Knowledge Interactive Protocol for SAT and Beyond," *Proceedings of the 27th IEEE Symposium on Foundations of Computer Science*, 1986, pp. 188–195.

241. G. Brassard and C. Crépeau, "Zero-Knowledge Simulation of Boolean Circuits," *Advances in Cryptology—CRYPTO '86 Proceedings*, Springer-Verlag, 1987, pp. 223–233.

242. G. Brassard and C. Crépeau, "Sorting Out Zero-Knowledge," *Advances in Cryptology—EUROCRYPT '89 Proceedings*, Springer-Verlag, 1990, pp. 181–191.

243. G. Brassard and C. Crépeau, "Quantum Bit Commitment and Coin Tossing Protocols," *Advances in Cryptology—CRYPTO '90 Proceedings*, Springer-Verlag, 1991, pp. 49–61.

244. G. Brassard, C. Crépeau, R. Jozsa, and D. Langlois, "A Quantum Bit Commitment Scheme Provably Unbreakable by Both Parties," *Proceedings of the 34th IEEE Symposium on Foundations of Computer Science*, 1993, pp. 362–371.

245. G. Brassard, C. Crépeau, and J.-M. Robert, "Information Theoretic Reductions Among Disclosure Problems," *Proceedings of the 27th IEEE Symposium on Foundations of Computer Science*, 1986, pp. 168–173.

246. G. Brassard, C. Crépeau, and J.-M. Robert, "All-or-Nothing Disclosure of Secrets," *Advances in Cryptology—CRYPTO '86 Proceedings*, Springer-Verlag, 1987, pp. 234–238.

247. G. Brassard, C. Crépeau, and M. Yung, "Everything in **NP** Can Be Argued in Perfect Zero-Knowledge in a Bounded Number of Rounds," *Proceedings on the 16th International Colloquium on Automata, Languages, and Programming*, Springer-Verlag, 1989, pp. 123–136.

248. R.P. Brent, "An Improved Monte-Carlo Factorization Algorithm," *BIT*, v. 20, n. 2, 1980, pp. 176–184.

249. R.P. Brent, "On the Periods of Generalized Fibonacci Recurrences, *Mathematics of Computation*, v. 63, n. 207, Jul 1994, pp. 389–401.

250. R.P. Brent, "Parallel Algorithms for Integer Factorization," Research Report CMA-R49-89, Computer Science Laboratory, The Australian National University, Oct 1989.

251. D.M. Bressoud, *Factorization and Primality Testing*, Springer-Verlag, 1989.

252. E.F. Brickell, "A Fast Modular Multiplication Algorithm with Applications to Two

Key Cryptography," *Advances in Cryptology: Proceedings of Crypto 82*, Plenum Press, 1982, pp. 51–60.

253. E.F. Brickell, "Are Most Low Density Polynomial Knapsacks Solvable in Polynomial Time?" *Proceedings of the 14th Southeastern Conference on Combinatorics, Graph Theory, and Computing*, 1983.

254. E.F. Brickell, "Solving Low Density Knapsacks," *Advances in Cryptology: Proceedings of Crypto 83*, Plenum Press, 1984, pp. 25–37.

255. E.F. Brickell, "Breaking Iterated Knapsacks," *Advances in Cryptology: Proceedings of Crypto 84*, Springer-Verlag, 1985, pp. 342–358.

256. E.F. Brickell, "Cryptanalysis of the Uagisawa Public Key Cryptosystem," *Abstracts of Papers, EUROCRYPT '86*, 20–22 May 1986.

257. E.F. Brickell, "The Cryptanalysis of Knapsack Cryptosystems," *Applications of Discrete Mathematics*, R.D. Ringeisen and F.S. Roberts, eds., Society for Industrial and Applied Mathematics, Philadelphia, 1988, pp. 3–23.

258. E.F. Brickell, "Survey of Hardware Implementations of RSA," *Advances in Cryptology—CRYPTO '89 Proceedings*, Springer-Verlag, 1990, pp. 368–370.

259. E.F. Brickell, D. Chaum, I.B. Damgård, and J. van de Graff, "Gradual and Verifiable Release of a Secret," *Advances in Cryptology—CRYPTO '87 Proceedings*, Springer-Verlag, 1988, pp. 156–166.

260. E.F. Brickell, J.A. Davis, and G.J. Simmons, "A Preliminary Report on the Cryptanalysis of Merkle-Hellman Knapsack," *Advances in Cryptology: Proceedings of Crypto 82*, Plenum Press, 1983, pp. 289–303.

261. E.F. Brickell and J. DeLaurentis, "An Attack on a Signature Scheme Proposed by Okamoto and Shiraishi," *Advances in Cryptology—CRYPTO '85 Proceedings*, Springer-Verlag, 1986, pp. 28–32.

262. E.F. Brickell, D.E. Denning, S.T. Kent, D.P. Maher, and W. Tuchman, "SKIPJACK Review—Interim Report," unpublished manuscript, 28 Jul 1993.

263. E.F. Brickell, J.C. Lagarias, and A.M. Odlyzko, "Evaluation of the Adleman Attack of Multiple Iterated Knapsack Cryptosystems," *Advances in Cryptology:*

Proceedings of Crypto 83, Plenum Press, 1984, pp. 39–42.

264. E.F. Brickell, P.J. Lee, and Y. Yacobi, "Secure Audio Teleconference," *Advances in Cryptology—CRYPTO '87 Proceedings*, Springer-Verlag, 1988, pp. 418–426.

265. E.F. Brickell and K.S. McCurley, "An Interactive Identification Scheme Based on Discrete Logarithms and Factoring," *Advances in Cryptology—EUROCRYPT '90 Proceedings*, Springer-Verlag, 1991, pp. 63–71.

266. E.F. Brickell, J.H. Moore, and M.R. Purtill, "Structure in the S-Boxes of the DES," *Advances in Cryptology—CRYPTO '86 Proceedings*, Springer-Verlag, 1987, pp. 3–8.

267. E.F. Brickell and A.M. Odlyzko, "Cryptanalysis: A Survey of Recent Results," *Proceedings of the IEEE*, v. 76, n. 5, May 1988, pp. 578–593.

268. E.F. Brickell and A.M. Odlyzko, "Cryptanalysis: A Survey of Recent Results," *Contemporary Cryptology: The Science of Information Integrity*, G.J. Simmons, ed., IEEE Press, 1991, pp. 501–540.

269. E.F. Brickell and G.J. Simmons, "A Status Report on Knapsack Based Public Key Cryptosystems," *Congressus Numerantium*, v. 7, 1983, pp. 3–72.

270. E.F. Brickell and D.R. Stinson, "The Detection of Cheaters in Threshold Schemes," *Advances in Cryptology—CRYPTO '88 Proceedings*, Springer-Verlag, 1990, pp. 564–577.

271. A.G. Broscius and J.M. Smith, "Exploiting Parallelism in Hardware Implementation of the DES," *Advances in Cryptology—CRYPTO '91 Proceedings*, Springer-Verlag, 1992, pp. 367–376.

272. L. Brown, M. Kwan, J. Pieprzyk, and J. Seberry, "Improving Resistance to Differential Cryptanalysis and the Redesign of LOKI," *Advances in Cryptology—ASIACRYPT '91 Proceedings*, Springer-Verlag, 1993, pp. 36–50.

273. L. Brown, J. Pieprzyk, and J. Seberry, "LOKI: A Cryptographic Primitive for Authentication and Secrecy Applications," *Advances in Cryptology—AUSCRYPT '90 Proceedings*, Springer-Verlag, 1990, pp. 229–236.

274. L. Brown, J. Pieprzyk, and J. Seberry, "Key Scheduling in DES Type Cryptosystems,"

Advances in Cryptology—AUSCRYPT '90 Proceedings, Springer-Verlag, 1990, pp. 221–228.

275. L. Brown and J. Seberry, "On the Design of Permutation P in DES Type Cryptosystems," *Advances in Cryptology—EUROCRYPT '89 Proceedings*, Springer-Verlag, 1990, pp. 696–705.

276. W. Brown, "A Quantum Leap in Secret Communications," *New Scientist*, n. 1585, 30 Jan 1993, p. 21.

277. J.O. Brüer, "On Pseudo Random Sequences as Crypto Generators," *Proceedings of the International Zurich Seminar on Digital Communication*, Switzerland, 1984.

278. L. Brynielsson "On the Linear Complexity of Combined Shift Register Sequences," *Advances in Cryptology—EUROCRYPT '85*, Springer-Verlag, 1986, pp. 156–166.

279. J. Buchmann, J. Loho, and J. Zayer, "An Implementation of the General Number Field Sieve," *Advances in Cryptology—CRYPTO '93 Proceedings*, Springer-Verlag, 1994, pp. 159–165.

280. M. Burmester and Y. Desmedt, "Broadcast Interactive Proofs," *Advances in Cryptology—EUROCRYPT '91 Proceedings*, Springer-Verlag, 1991, pp. 81–95.

281. M. Burmester and Y. Desmedt, "A Secure and Efficient Conference Key Distribution System," *Advances in Cryptology—EUROCRYPT '94 Proceedings*, Springer-Verlag, 1995, to appear.

282. D. Burnham, "NSA Seeking 500,000 'Secure' Telephones," *The New York Times*, 6 Oct 1994.

283. M. Burrows, M. Abadi, and R. Needham, "A Logic of Authentication," Research Report 39, Digital Equipment Corp. Systems Research Center, Feb 1989.

284. M. Burrows, M. Abadi, and R. Needham, "A Logic of Authentication," *ACM Transactions on Computer Systems*, v. 8, n. 1, Feb 1990, pp. 18–36.

285. M. Burrows, M. Abadi, and R. Needham, "Rejoinder to Nessett," *Operating System Review*, v. 20, n. 2, Apr 1990, pp. 39–40.

286. J.J. Cade, "A Modification of a Broken Public-Key Cipher," *Advances in Cryptology—CRYPTO '86 Proceedings*, Springer-Verlag, 1987, pp. 64–83.

287. T.R. Cain and A.T. Sherman, "How to Break Gifford's Cipher," *Proceedings of the 2nd Annual ACM Conference on*

Computer and Communications Security, ACM Press, 1994, pp. 198–209.

288. C. Calvelli and V. Varadharajan, "An Analysis of Some Delegation Protocols for Distributed Systems," *Proceedings of the Computer Security Foundations Workshop V*, IEEE Computer Society Press, 1992, pp. 92–110.

289. J.L. Camenisch, J.-M. Piveteau, and M.A. Stadler, "An Efficient Electronic Payment System Protecting Privacy," *Computer Security—ESORICS 94*, Springer-Verlag, 1994, pp. 207–215.

290. P. Camion and J. Patarin, "The Knapsack Hash Function Proposed at Crypto '89 Can Be Broken," *Advances in Cryptology—EUROCRYPT '91*, Springer-Verlag, 1991, pp. 39–53.

291. C.M. Campbell, "Design and Specification of Cryptographic Capabilities," *IEEE Computer Society Magazine*, v. 16, n. 6, Nov 1978, pp. 15–19.

292. E.A. Campbell, R. Safavi-Naini, and P.A. Pleasants, "Partial Belief and Probabilistic Reasoning in the Analysis of Secure Protocols," *Proceedings of the Computer Security Foundations Workshop V*, IEEE Computer Society Press, 1992, pp. 92–110.

293. K.W. Campbell and M.J. Wiener, "DES Is Not a Group," *Advances in Cryptology—CRYPTO '92 Proceedings*, Springer-Verlag, pp. 512–520.

294. Z.F. Cao and G. Zhao, "Some New MC Knapsack Cryptosystems," *CHINACRYPT '94*, Xidian, China, 11–15 Nov 1994, pp. 70–75. (In Chinese).

295. C. Carlet, "Partially-Bent Functions," *Advances in Cryptology—CRYPTO '92 Proceedings*, Springer-Verlag, 1993, pp. 280–291.

296. C. Carlet, "Partially Bent Functions," *Designs, Codes and Cryptography*, v. 3, 1993, pp. 135–145.

297. C. Carlet, "Two New Classes of Bent Functions" *Advances in Cryptology—EUROCRYPT '93 Proceedings*, Springer-Verlag, 1994, pp. 77–101.

298. C. Carlet, J. Seberry, and X.M. Zhang, "Comments on 'Generating and Counting Binary Bent Sequences,'" *IEEE Transactions on Information Theory*, v. IT-40, n. 2, Mar 1994, p. 600.

299. J.M. Carroll, *Computer Security*, 2nd edition, Butterworths, 1987.

300. J.M. Carroll, "The Three Faces of Information Security," *Advances in Cryptology—AUSCRYPT '90 Proceedings*, Springer-Verlag, 1990, pp. 433–450.

301. J.M. Carroll, "'Do-it-yourself' Cryptography," *Computers & Security*, v. 9, n. 7, Nov 1990, pp. 613–619.

302. T.R. Caron and R.D. Silverman, "Parallel Implementation of the Quadratic Scheme," *Journal of Supercomputing*, v. 1, n. 3, 1988, pp. 273–290.

303. CCITT, Draft Recommendation X.509, "The Directory—Authentication Framework," Consultation Committee, International Telephone and Telegraph, International Telecommunications Union, Geneva, 1987.

304. CCITT, Recommendation X.509, "The Directory—Authentication Framework," Consultation Committee, International Telephone and Telegraph, International Telecommunications Union, Geneva, 1989.

305. CCITT, Recommendation X.800, "Security Architecture for Open Systems Interconnection for CCITT Applications," International Telephone and Telegraph, International Telecommunications Union, Geneva, 1991.

306. F. Chabaud, "On the Security of Some Cryptosystems Based on Error-Correcting Codes," *Advances in Cryptology—EUROCRYPT '94 Proceedings*, Springer-Verlag, 1995, to appear.

307. F. Chabaud and S. Vaudenay, "Links Between Differential and Linear Cryptanalysis," *Advances in Cryptology—EUROCRYPT '94 Proceedings*, Springer-Verlag, 1995, to appear.

308. W.G. Chambers and D. Gollmann, "Generators for Sequences with Near-Maximal Linear Equivalence," *IEE Proceedings*, V. 135, Pt. E, n. 1, Jan 1988, pp. 67–69.

309. W.G. Chambers and D. Gollmann, "Lock-In Effect in Cascades of Clock-Controlled Shirt Registers," *Advances in Cryptology—EUROCRYPT '88 Proceedings*, Springer-Verlag, 1988, pp. 331–343.

310. A. Chan and R. Games, "On the Linear Span of Binary Sequences from Finite Geometries," *Advances in Cryptology—CRYPTO '86 Proceedings*, Springer-Verlag, 1987, pp. 405–417.

311. J.P. Chandler, D.C. Arrington, D.R. Berkelhammer, and W.L. Gill, "Identification and

Analysis of Foreign Laws and Regulations Pertaining to the Use of Commercial Encryption Products for Voice and Data Communications," National Intellectual Property Law Institute, George Washington University, Washington, D.C., Jan 1994.

312. C.C. Chang and S.J. Hwang, "Cryptographic Authentication of Passwords," *Proceedings of the 25th Annual 1991 IEEE International Carnahan Conference on Security Technology*, Taipei, Taiwan, 1–3 Oct 1991, pp. 126–130.

313. C.C. Chang and S.J. Hwang, "A Strategy for Transforming Public-Key Cryptosystems into Identity-Based Cryptosystems," *Proceedings of the 25th Annual 1991 IEEE International Carnahan Conference on Security Technology*, Taipei, Taiwan, 1–3 Oct 1991, pp. 68–72.

314. C.C. Chang and C.H. Lin, "An ID-Based Signature Scheme Based upon Rabin's Public Key Cryptosystem," *Proceedings of the 25th Annual 1991 IEEE International Carnahan Conference on Security Technology*, Taipei, Taiwan, 1–3 Oct 1991, pp. 139–141.

315. C. Charnes and J. Pieprzyk, "Attacking the SL_2 Hashing Scheme," *Advances in Cryptology—ASIACRYPT '94 Proceedings*, Springer-Verlag, 1995, pp. 322–330.

316. D. Chaum, "Untraceable Electronic Mail, Return Addresses, and Digital Pseudonyms," *Communications of the ACM*, v. 24, n. 2, Feb 1981, pp. 84–88.

317. D. Chaum, "Blind Signatures for Untraceable Payments," *Advances in Cryptology: Proceedings of Crypto 82*, Plenum Press, 1983, pp. 199–203.

318. D. Chaum, "Security Without Identification: Transaction Systems to Make Big Brother Obsolete," *Communications of the ACM*, v. 28, n. 10, Oct 1985, pp. 1030–1044.

319. D. Chaum, "Demonstrating that a Public Predicate Can Be Satisfied without Revealing Any Information about How," *Advances in Cryptology—CRYPTO '86 Proceedings*, Springer-Verlag, 1987, pp. 159–199.

320. D. Chaum, "Blinding for Unanticipated Signatures," *Advances in Cryptology—EUROCRYPT '87 Proceedings*, Springer-Verlag, 1988, pp. 227–233.

321. D. Chaum, "The Dining Cryptographers Problem: Unconditional Sender and Receiver Untraceability," *Journal of Cryptology*, v. 1, n. 1, 1988, pp. 65–75.

322. D. Chaum, "Elections with Unconditionally Secret Ballots and Disruptions Equivalent to Breaking RSA," *Advances in Cryptology—EUROCRYPT '88 Proceedings*, Springer-Verlag, 1988, pp. 177–181.

323. D. Chaum, "Blind Signature Systems," U.S. Patent #4,759,063, 19 Jul 1988.

324. D. Chaum, "Blind Unanticipated Signature Systems," U.S. Patent #4,759,064, 19 Jul 1988.

325. D. Chaum, "Online Cash Checks," *Advances in Cryptology—EUROCRYPT '89 Proceedings*, Springer-Verlag, 1990, pp. 288–293.

326. D. Chaum, "One-Show Blind Signature Systems," U.S. Patent #4,914,698, 3 Apr 1990.

327. D. Chaum, "Undeniable Signature Systems," U.S. Patent #4,947,430, 7 Aug 1990.

328. D. Chaum, "Returned-Value Blind Signature Systems," U.S. Patent #4,949,380, 14 Aug 1990.

329. D. Chaum, "Zero-Knowledge Undeniable Signatures," *Advances in Cryptology—EUROCRYPT '90 Proceedings*, Springer-Verlag, 1991, pp. 458–464.

330. D. Chaum, "Group Signatures," *Advances in Cryptology—EUROCRYPT '91 Proceedings*, Springer-Verlag, 1991, pp. 257–265.

331. D. Chaum, "Unpredictable Blind Signature Systems," U.S. Patent #4,991,210, 5 Feb 1991.

332. D. Chaum, "Achieving Electronic Privacy," *Scientific American*, v. 267, n. 2, Aug 1992, pp. 96–101.

333. D. Chaum, "Designated Confirmer Signatures," *Advances in Cryptology—EUROCRYPT '94 Proceedings*, Springer-Verlag, 1995, to appear.

334. D. Chaum, C. Crépeau, and I.B. Damgård, "Multiparty Unconditionally Secure Protocols," *Proceedings of the 20th ACM Symposium on the Theory of Computing*, 1988, pp. 11–19.

335. D. Chaum, B. den Boer, E. van Heyst, S. Mjølsnes, and A. Steenbeek, "Efficient Offline Electronic Checks," *Advances in Cryptology—EUROCRYPT '89 Proceedings*, Springer-Verlag, 1990, pp. 294–301.

336. D. Chaum and J.-H. Evertse, "Cryptanalysis of DES with a Reduced Number of Rounds; Sequences of Linear Factors in Block Ciphers," *Advances in Cryptology—CRYPTO '85 Proceedings*, Springer-Verlag, 1986, pp. 192–211.

337. D. Chaum, J.-H. Evertse, and J. van de Graff, "An Improved Protocol for Demonstrating Possession of Discrete Logarithms and Some Generalizations," *Advances in Cryptology—EUROCRYPT '87 Proceedings*, Springer-Verlag, 1988, pp. 127–141.

338. D. Chaum, J.-H. Evertse, J. van de Graff, and R. Peralta, "Demonstrating Possession of a Discrete Logarithm without Revealing It," *Advances in Cryptology—CRYPTO '86 Proceedings*, Springer-Verlag, 1987, pp. 200–212.

339. D. Chaum, A. Fiat, and M. Naor, "Untraceable Electronic Cash," *Advances in Cryptology—CRYPTO '88 Proceedings*, Springer-Verlag, 1990, pp. 319–327.

340. D. Chaum and T. Pedersen, "Transferred Cash Grows in Size," *Advances in Cryptology—EUROCRYPT '92 Proceedings*, Springer-Verlag, 1993, pp. 391–407.

341. D. Chaum and T. Pedersen, "Wallet Databases with Observers," *Advances in Cryptology—CRYPTO '92 Proceedings*, Springer-Verlag, 1993, pp. 89–105.

342. D. Chaum and I. Schaumuller-Bichel, eds., *Smart Card 2000*, North Holland: Elsevier Science Publishers, 1989.

343. D. Chaum and H. van Antwerpen, "Undeniable Signatures," *Advances in Cryptology—CRYPTO '89 Proceedings*, Springer-Verlag, 1990, pp. 212–216.

344. D. Chaum, E. van Heijst, and B. Pfitzmann, "Cryptographically Strong Undeniable Signatures, Unconditionally Secure for the Signer," *Advances in Cryptology—CRYPTO '91 Proceedings*, Springer-Verlag, 1992, pp. 470–484.

345. T.M. Chee, "The Cryptanalysis of a New Public-Key Cryptosystem Based on Modular Knapsacks," *Advances in Cryptology—CRYPTO '91 Proceedings*, Springer-Verlag, 1992, pp. 204–212.

346. L. Chen, "Oblivious Signatures," *Computer Security—ESORICS 94*, Springer-Verlag, 1994, pp. 161–172.

347. L. Chen and M. Burminster, "A Practical Secret Voting Scheme which Allows Voters to Abstain," *CHINACRYPT '94*, Xidian, China, 11–15 Nov 1994, pp. 100–107.

348. L. Chen and T.P. Pedersen "New Group Signature Schemes," *Advances in Cryptology—EUROCRYPT '94 Proceedings*, Springer-Verlag, 1995, to appear.

349. J. Chenhui, "Spectral Characteristics of Partially-Bent Functions," *CHINACRYPT '94*, Xidian, China, 11–15 Nov 1994, pp. 48–51.

350. V. Chepyzhov and B. Smeets, "On a Fast Correlation Attack on Certain Stream Ciphers," *Advances in Cryptology—EUROCRYPT '91 Proceedings*, Springer-Verlag, 1991, pp. 176–185.

351. T.C. Cheung, "Management of PEM Public Key Certificates Using X.500 Directory Service: Some Problems and Solutions," *Proceedings of the Internet Society 1994 Workshop on Network and Distributed System Security*, The Internet Society, 1994, pp. 35–42.

352. G.C. Chiou and W.C. Chen, "Secure Broadcasting Using the Secure Lock," *IEEE Transactions on Software Engineering*, v. SE-15, n. 8, Aug 1989, pp. 929–934.

353. Y.J. Choie and H.S. Hwoang, "On the Cryptosystem Using Elliptic Curves," *Proceedings of the 1993 Korea-Japan Workshop on Information Security and Cryptography*, Seoul, Korea, 24–26 Oct 1993, pp. 105–113.

354. B. Chor and O. Goldreich, "RSA/Rabin Least Significant Bits are $1/2+1/\mathrm{poly}(\log N)$ Secure," *Advances in Cryptology: Proceedings of CRYPTO 84*, Springer-Verlag, 1985, pp. 303–313.

355. B. Chor, S. Goldwasser, S. Micali, and B. Awerbuch, "Verifiable Secret Sharing and Achieving Simultaneity in the Presence of Faults," *Proceedings of the 26th Annual IEEE Symposium on the Foundations of Computer Science*, 1985, pp. 383–395.

356. B. Chor and R.L. Rivest, "A Knapsack Type Public Key Cryptosystem Based on Arithmetic in Finite Fields," *Advances in Cryptology: Proceedings of CRYPTO 84*, Springer-Verlag, 1985, pp. 54–65.

357. P. Christoffersson, S.-A. Ekahll, V. Fåk, S. Herda, P. Mattila, W. Price, and H.-O. Widman, *Crypto Users' Handbook: A Guide for Implementors of Cryptographic Protection in Computer Systems*, North Holland: Elsevier Science Publishers, 1988.

358. R. Cleve, "Controlled Gradual Disclosure Schemes for Random Bits and Their Applications," *Advances in Cryptology—CRYPTO '89 Proceedings*, Springer-Verlag, 1990, pp. 572–588.

359. J.D. Cohen, "Improving Privacy in Cryptographic Elections," Yale University Computer Science Department Technical Report YALEU/DCS/TR-454, Feb 1986.

360. J.D. Cohen and M.H. Fischer, "A Robust and Verifiable Cryptographically Secure Election Scheme," *Proceedings of the 26th Annual IEEE Symposium on the Foundations of Computer Science*, 1985, pp. 372–382.

361. R. Cole, "A Model for Security in Distributed Systems," *Computers and Security*, v. 9, n. 4, Apr 1990, pp. 319–330.

362. Comptroller General of the United States, "Matter of National Institute of Standards and Technology—Use of Electronic Data Interchange Technology to Create Valid Obligations," File B-245714, 13 Dec 1991.

363. M.S. Conn, letter to Joe Abernathy, National Security Agency, Ser: Q43-111-92, 10 Jun 1992.

364. C. Connell, "An Analysis of NewDES: A Modified Version of DES," *Cryptologia*, v. 14, n. 3, Jul 1990, pp. 217–223.

365. S.A. Cook, "The Complexity of Theorem-Proving Procedures," *Proceedings of the 3rd Annual ACM Symposium on the Theory of Computing*, 1971, pp. 151–158.

366. R.H. Cooper and W. Patterson, "A Generalization of the Knapsack Method Using Galois Fields," *Cryptologia*, v. 8, n. 4, Oct 1984, pp. 343–347.

367. R.H. Cooper and W. Patterson, "RSA as a Benchmark for Multiprocessor Machines," *Advances in Cryptology—AUSCRYPT '90 Proceedings*, Springer-Verlag, 1990, pp. 356–359.

368. D. Coppersmith, "Fast Evaluation of Logarithms in Fields of Characteristic Two," *IEEE Transactions on Information Theory*, v. 30, n. 4, Jul 1984, pp. 587–594.

369. D. Coppersmith, "Another Birthday Attack," *Advances in Cryptology—CRYPTO '85 Proceedings*, Springer-Verlag, 1986, pp. 14–17.

370. D. Coppersmith, "Cheating at Mental Poker," *Advances in Cryptology—CRYPTO '85 Proceedings*, Springer-Verlag, 1986, pp. 104–107.

371. D. Coppersmith, "The Real Reason for Rivest's Phenomenon," *Advances in Cryptology—CRYPTO '85 Proceedings*, Springer-Verlag, 1986, pp. 535–536.

372. D. Coppersmith, "Two Broken Hash Functions," Research Report RD 18397, IBM T.J. Watson Center, Oct 1992.

373. D. Coppersmith, "The Data Encryption Standard (DES) and Its Strength against Attacks," Technical Report RC 18613, IBM T.J. Watson Center, Dec 1992.

374. D. Coppersmith, "The Data Encryption Standard (DES) and its Strength against Attacks," *IBM Journal of Research and Development*, v. 38, n. 3, May 1994, pp. 243–250.

375. D. Coppersmith, "Attack on the Cryptographic Scheme NIKS-TAS," *Advances in Cryptology—CRYPTO '94 Proceedings*, Springer-Verlag, 1994, pp. 294–307.

376. D. Coppersmith, personal communication, 1994.

377. D. Coppersmith and E. Grossman, "Generators for Certain Alternating Groups with Applications to Cryptography," *SIAM Journal on Applied Mathematics*, v. 29, n. 4, Dec 1975, pp. 624–627.

378. D. Coppersmith, H. Krawczyk, and Y. Mansour, "The Shrinking Generator," *Advances in Cryptology—CRYPTO '93 Proceedings*, Springer-Verlag, 1994, pp. 22–39.

379. D. Coppersmith, A. Odlykzo, and R. Schroeppel, "Discrete Logarithms in $GF(p)$," *Algorithmica*, v. 1, n. 1, 1986, pp. 1–16.

380. D. Coppersmith and P. Rogaway, "Software Efficient Pseudo Random Function and the Use Thereof for Encryption," U.S. Patent pending, 1995.

381. D. Coppersmith, J. Stern, and S. Vaudenay, "Attacks on the Birational Signature Schemes," *Advances in Cryptology—CRYPTO '93 Proceedings*, Springer-Verlag, 1994, pp. 435–443.

382. V. Cordonnier and J.-J. Quisquater, eds., *CARDIS '94—Proceedings of the First Smart Card Research and Advanced Application Conference*, Lille, France, 24–26 Oct 1994.

383. C. Couvreur and J.-J. Quisquater, "An Introduction to Fast Generation of Large Prime Numbers," *Philips Journal Research*, v. 37, n. 5–6, 1982, pp. 231–264.

384. C. Couvreur and J.-J. Quisquater, "An Introduction to Fast Generation of Large Prime Numbers," *Philips Journal Research*, v. 38, 1983, p. 77.

385. C. Coveyou and R.D. MacPherson, "Fourier Analysis of Uniform Random Number Generators," *Journal of the ACM*, v. 14, n. 1, 1967, pp. 100–119.

386. T.M. Cover and R.C. King, "A Convergent Gambling Estimate of the Entropy of English," *IEEE Transactions on Information Theory*, v. IT-24, n. 4, Jul 1978, pp. 413–421.

387. R.J.F. Cramer and T.P. Pedersen, "Improved Privacy in Wallets with Observers," *Advances in Cryptology—EUROCRYPT '93 Proceedings*, Springer-Verlag, 1994, pp. 329–343.

388. R.E. Crandell, "Method and Apparatus for Public Key Exchange in a Cryptographic System," U.S. Patent #5,159,632, 27 Oct 1992.

389. C. Crépeau, "A Secure Poker Protocol That Minimizes the Effect of Player Coalitions," *Advances in Cryptology—CRYPTO '85 Proceedings*, Springer-Verlag, 1986, pp. 73–86.

390. C. Crépeau, "A Zero-Knowledge Poker Protocol that Achieves Confidentiality of the Players' Strategy, *or* How to Achieve an Electronic Poker Face," *Advances in Cryptology—CRYPTO '86 Proceedings*, Springer-Verlag, 1987, pp. 239–247.

391. C. Crépeau, "Equivalence Between Two Flavours of Oblivious Transfer," *Advances in Cryptology—CRYPTO '87 Proceedings*, Springer-Verlag, 1988, pp. 350–354.

392. C. Crépeau, "Correct and Private Reductions among Oblivious Transfers," Ph.D. dissertation, Department of Electrical Engineering and Computer Science, Massachusetts Institute of Technology, 1990.

393. C. Crépeau, "Quantum Oblivious Transfer," *Journal of Modern Optics*, v. 41, n. 12, Dec 1994, pp. 2445–2454.

394. C. Crépeau and J. Kilian, "Achieving Oblivious Transfer Using Weakened Security Assumptions," *Proceedings of the 29th Annual Symposium on the Foundations of Computer Science*, 1988, pp. 42–52.

395. C. Crépeau and J. Kilian, "Weakening Security Assumptions and Oblivious Transfer," *Advances in Cryptology—*

396. C. Crépeau and L. Salvail, "Quantum Oblivious Mutual Identification," *Advances in Cryptology—EUROCRYPT '95 Proceedings*, Springer-Verlag, 1995, pp. 133–146.

397. A. Curiger, H. Bonnenberg, R. Zimmermann, N. Felber, H. Kaeslin and W. Fichtner, "VINCI: VLSI Implementation of the New Block Cipher IDEA," *Proceedings of IEEE CICC '93*, San Diego, CA, May 1993, pp. 15.5.1–15.5.4.

398. A. Curiger and B. Stuber, "Specification for the IDEA Chip," Technical Report No. 92/03, Institut für Integrierte Systeme, ETH Zurich, Feb 1992.

399. T. Cusick, "Boolean Functions Satisfying a Higher Order Strict Avalanche Criterion," *Advances in Cryptology—EUROCRYPT '93 Proceedings*, Springer-Verlag, 1994, pp. 102–117.

400. T.W. Cusick and M.C. Wood, "The REDOC-II Cryptosystem," *Advances in Cryptology—CRYPTO '90 Proceedings*, Springer-Verlag, 1991, pp. 545–563.

401. Cylink Corporation, Cylink Corporation vs. RSA Data Security, Inc., Civil Action No. C94-02332-CW, United States District Court for the Northern District of California, 30 Jun 1994.

402. J. Daeman, "Cipher and Hash Function Design," Ph.D. Thesis, Katholieke Universiteit Leuven, Mar 95.

403. J. Daeman, A. Bosselaers, R. Govaerts, and J. Vandewalle, "Collisions for Schnorr's Hash Function FFT-Hash Presented at Crypto '91," *Advances in Cryptology—ASIACRYPT '91 Proceedings*, Springer-Verlag, 1993, pp. 477–480.

404. J. Daeman, R. Govaerts, and J. Vandewalle, "A Framework for the Design of One-Way Hash Functions Including Cryptanalysis of Damgård's One-Way Function Based on Cellular Automata," *Advances in Cryptology—ASIACRYPT '91 Proceedings*, Springer-Verlag, 1993, pp. 82–96.

405. J. Daeman, R. Govaerts, and J. Vandewalle, "A Hardware Design Model for Cryptographic Algorithms," *ESORICS 92, Proceedings of the Second European Symposium on Research in Computer Security*, Springer-Verlag, 1992, pp. 419–434.

406. J. Daemen, R. Govaerts, and J. Vandewalle, "Block Ciphers Based on Modular Arith-

CRYPTO '88 Proceedings*, Springer-Verlag, 1990, pp. 2–7.

metic," *Proceedings of the 3rd Symposium on State and Progress of Research in Cryptography*, Rome, Italy, 15–16 Feb 1993, pp. 80–89.

407. J. Daemen, R. Govaerts, and J. Vandewalle, "Fast Hashing Both in Hardware and Software," presented at the rump session of CRYPTO '93, Aug 1993.

408. J. Daeman, R. Govaerts, and J. Vandewalle, "Resynchronization Weaknesses in Synchronous Stream Ciphers," *Advances in Cryptology—EUROCRYPT '93 Proceedings*, Springer-Verlag, 1994, pp. 159–167.

409. J. Daemen, R. Govaerts, and J. Vandewalle, "Weak Keys for IDEA," *Advances in Cryptology—CRYPTO '93 Proceedings*, Springer-Verlag, 1994, pp. 224–230.

410. J. Daemen, R. Govaerts, and J. Vandewalle, "A New Approach to Block Cipher Design," *Fast Software Encryption, Cambridge Security Workshop Proceedings*, Springer-Verlag, 1994, pp. 18–32.

411. Z.-D. Dai, "Proof of Rueppel's Linear Complexity Conjecture," *IEEE Transactions on Information Theory*, v. IT-32, n. 3, May 1986, pp. 440–443.

412. I.B. Damgård, "Collision Free Hash Functions and Public Key Signature Schemes," *Advances in Cryptology—EUROCRYPT '87 Proceedings*, Springer-Verlag, 1988, pp. 203–216.

413. I.B. Damgård, "Payment Systems and Credential Mechanisms with Provable Security Against Abuse by Individuals," *Advances in Cryptology—CRYPTO '88 Proceedings*, Springer-Verlag, 1990, pp. 328–335.

414. I.B. Damgård, "A Design Principle for Hash Functions," *Advances in Cryptology—CRYPTO '89 Proceedings*, Springer-Verlag, 1990, pp. 416–427.

415. I.B. Damgård, "Practical and Provably Secure Release of a Secret and Exchange of Signatures," *Advances in Cryptology—EUROCRYPT '93 Proceedings*, Springer-Verlag, 1994, pp. 200–217.

416. I.B. Damgård and L.R. Knudsen, "The Breaking of the AR Hash Function," *Advances in Cryptology—EUROCRYPT '93 Proceedings*, Springer-Verlag, 1994, pp. 286–292.

417. I.B. Damgård and P. Landrock, "Improved Bounds for the Rabin Primality Test," *Cryptography and Coding III*, M.J. Ganley,

ed., Oxford: Clarendon Press, 1993, pp. 117–128.

418. I.B. Damgård, P. Landrock and C. Pomerance, "Average Case Error Estimates for the Strong Probable Prime Test," *Mathematics of Computation*, v. 61, n. 203, Jul 1993, pp. 177–194.

419. H.E. Daniels, Jr., letter to Datapro Research Corporation regarding CCEP, 23 Dec 1985.

420. H. Davenport, *The Higher Arithmetic*, Dover Books, 1983.

421. G.I. Davida, "Inverse of Elements of a Galois Field," *Electronics Letters*, v. 8, n. 21, 19 Oct 1972, pp. 518–520.

422. G.I. Davida, "Hellman's Scheme Breaks DES in Its Basic Form," *IEEE Spectrum*, v. 16, n. 7, Jul 1979, p. 39.

423. G.I. Davida, "Chosen Signature Cryptanalysis of the RSA (MIT) Public Key Cryptosystem," *Technical Report TR-CS-82-2*, Department of EECS, University of Wisconsin, 1982.

424. G.I. Davida and G.G. Walter, "A Public Key Analog Cryptosystem," *Advances in Cryptology—EUROCRYPT '87 Proceedings*, Springer-Verlag, 1988, pp. 143–147.

425. G.I. Davida, D. Wells, and J. Kam, "A Database Encryption System with Subkeys," *ACM Transactions on Database Systems*, v. 6, n. 2, Jun 1981, pp. 312–328.

426. D.W. Davies, "Applying the RSA Digital Signature to Electronic Mail," *Computer*, v. 16, n. 2, Feb 1983, pp. 55–62.

427. D.W. Davies, "Some Regular Properties of the DES," *Advances in Cryptology: Proceedings of Crypto 82*, Plenum Press, 1983, pp. 89–96.

428. D.W. Davies, "A Message Authentication Algorithm Suitable for a Mainframe Computer," *Advances in Cryptology: Proceedings of Crypto 82*, Springer-Verlag, 1985, pp. 393–400.

429. D.W. Davies and S. Murphy, "Pairs and Triplets of DES S-boxes," *Cryptologia*, v. 8, n. 1, 1995, pp. 1–25.

430. D.W. Davies and G.I.P. Parkin, "The Average Size of the Key Stream in Output Feedback Encipherment," *Cryptography, Proceedings of the Workshop on Cryptography, Burg Feuerstein, Germany, March 29–April 2, 1982*, Springer-Verlag, 1983, pp. 263–279.

431. D.W. Davies and G.I.P. Parkin, "The Average Size of the Key Stream in Output Feed-

back Mode," *Advances in Cryptology: Proceedings of Crypto 82*, Plenum Press, 1983, pp. 97–98.

432. D.W. Davies and W.L. Price, "The Application of Digital Signatures Based on Public-Key Cryptosystems," *Proceedings of the Fifth International Computer Communications Conference*, Oct 1980, pp. 525–530.

433. D.W. Davies and W.L. Price, "The Application of Digital Signatures Based on Public-Key Cryptosystems," National Physical Laboratory Report DNACS 39/80, Dec 1980.

434. D.W. Davies and W.L. Price, "Digital Signature—An Update," *Proceedings of International Conference on Computer Communications, Sydney, Oct 1984*, North Holland: Elsevier, 1985, pp. 843–847.

435. D.W. Davies and W.L. Price, *Security for Computer Networks*, second edition, John Wiley & Sons, 1989.

436. M. Davio, Y. Desmedt, M. Fosseprez, R. Govaerts, J. Hulsbrosch, P. Neutjens, P. Piret, J.-J. Quisquater, J. Vandewalle, and S. Wouters, "Analytical Characteristics of the Data Encryption Standard," *Advances in Cryptology: Proceedings of Crypto 83*, Plenum Press, 1984, pp. 171–202.

437. M. Davio, Y. Desmedt, J. Goubert, F. Hoornaert, and J.-J. Quisquater, "Efficient Hardware and Software Implementation of the DES," *Advances in Cryptology: Proceedings of CRYPTO 84*, Springer-Verlag, 1985, pp. 144–146.

438. M. Davio, Y. Desmedt, and J.-J. Quisquater, "Propagation Characteristics of the DES," *Advances in Cryptology: Proceedings of EUROCRYPT 84*, Springer-Verlag, 1985, 62–73.

439. D. Davis, R. Ihaka, and P. Fenstermacher, "Cryptographic Randomness from Air Turbulence in Disk Drives," *Advances in Cryptology—CRYPTO '94 Proceedings*, Springer-Verlag, 1994, pp. 114–120.

440. J.A. Davis, D.B. Holdbridge, and G.J. Simmons, "Status Report on Factoring (at the Sandia National Laboratories)," *Advances in Cryptology: Proceedings of CRYPTO 84*, Springer-Verlag, 1985, pp. 183–215.

441. R.M. Davis, "The Data Encryption Standard in Perspective," *Computer Security and the Data Encryption Standard*, National Bureau of Standards Special Publication 500-27, Feb 1978.

442. E. Dawson and A. Clark, "Cryptanalysis of Universal Logic Sequences," *Advances in Cryptology—EUROCRYPT '93 Proceedings*, Springer-Verlag, to appear.

443. M.H. Dawson and S.E. Tavares, "An Expanded Set of Design Criteria for Substitution Boxes and Their Use in Strengthening DES-Like Cryptosystems," *IEEE Pacific Rim Conference on Communications, Computers, and Signal Processing*, Victoria, BC, Canada, 9–10 May 1991, pp. 191–195.

444. M.H. Dawson and S.E. Tavares, "An Expanded Set of S-Box Design Criteria Based on Information Theory and Its Relation to Differential-like Attacks," *Advances in Cryptology—EUROCRYPT '91 Proceedings*, Springer-Verlag, 1991, pp. 352–367.

445. C.A. Deavours, "Unicity Points in Cryptanalysis," *Cryptologia*, v. 1, n. 1, 1977, pp. 46–68.

446. C.A. Deavours, "The Black Chamber: A Column; How the British Broke Enigma," *Cryptologia*, v. 4, n. 3, Jul 1980, pp. 129–132.

447. C.A. Deavours, "The Black Chamber: A Column; La Méthode des Bâtons," *Cryptologia*, v. 4, n. 4, Oct 1980, pp. 240–247.

448. C.A. Deavours and L. Kruh, *Machine Cryptography and Modern Cryptanalysis*, Norwood MA: Artech House, 1985.

449. J.M. DeLaurentis, "A Further Weakness in the Common Modulus Protocol for the RSA Cryptosystem," *Cryptologia*, v. 8, n. 3, Jul 1984, pp. 253–259.

450. P. Delsarte, Y. Desmedt, A. Odlyzko, and P. Piret, "Fast Cryptanalysis of the Matsumoto-Imai Public-Key Scheme," *Advances in Cryptology: Proceedings of EUROCRYPT 84*, Springer-Verlag, 1985, pp. 142–149.

451. P. Delsarte and P. Piret, "Comment on 'Extension of RSA Cryptostructure: A Galois Approach'," *Electronics Letters*, v. 18, n. 13, 24 Jun 1982, pp. 582–583.

452. R. DeMillo, N. Lynch, and M. Merritt, "Cryptographic Protocols," *Proceedings of the 14th Annual Symposium on the Theory of Computing*, 1982, pp. 383–400.

453. R. DeMillo and M. Merritt, "Protocols for Data Security," *Computer*, v. 16, n. 2, Feb 1983, pp. 39–50.

454. N. Demytko, "A New Elliptic Curve Based Analogue of RSA," *Advances in Cryptol-*

ogy—*EUROCRYPT '93 Proceedings*, Springer-Verlag, 1994, pp. 40–49.

455. D.E. Denning, "Secure Personal Computing in an Insecure Network," *Communications of the ACM*, v. 22, n. 8, Aug 1979, pp. 476–482.

456. D.E. Denning, *Cryptography and Data Security*, Addison-Wesley, 1982.

457. D.E. Denning, "Protecting Public Keys and Signature Keys," *Computer*, v. 16, n. 2, Feb 1983, pp. 27–35.

458. D.E. Denning, "Digital Signatures with RSA and Other Public-Key Cryptosystems," *Communications of the ACM*, v. 27, n. 4, Apr 1984, pp. 388–392.

459. D.E. Denning, "The Data Encryption Standard: Fifteen Years of Public Scrutiny," *Proceedings of the Sixth Annual Computer Security Applications Conference*, IEEE Computer Society Press, 1990.

460. D.E. Denning, "The Clipper Chip: A Technical Summary," unpublished manuscript, 21 Apr 1993.

461. D.E. Denning and G.M. Sacco, "Timestamps in Key Distribution Protocols," *Communications of the ACM*, v. 24, n. 8, Aug 1981, pp. 533–536.

462. D.E. Denning and M. Smid, "Key Escrowing Today," *IEEE Communications Magazine*, v. 32, n. 9, Sep 1994, pp. 58–68.

463. T. Denny, B. Dodson, A.K. Lenstra, and M.S. Manasse, "On the Factorization of RSA-120," *Advances in Cryptology—CRYPTO '93 Proceedings*, Springer-Verlag, 1994, pp. 166–174.

464. W.F. Denny, "Encryptions Using Linear and Non-Linear Codes: Implementations and Security Considerations," Ph.D. dissertation, The Center for Advanced Computer Studies, University of Southern Louisiana, Spring 1988.

465. Department of Defense, "Department of Defense Trusted Computer System Evaluation Criteria," DOD 5200.28-STD, Dec 1985.

466. Department of State, "International Traffic in Arms Regulations (ITAR)," 22 CFR 120–130, Office of Munitions Control, Nov 1989.

467. Department of State, "Defense Trade Regulations," 22 CFR 120–130, Office of Defense Trade Controls, May 1992.

468. Department of the Treasury, "Electronic Funds and Securities Transfer Policy," Department of the Treasury Directives Manual, Chapter TD 81, Section 80, Department of the Treasury, 16 Aug 1984.

469. Department of the Treasury, "Criteria and Procedures for Testing, Evaluating, and Certifying Message Authentication Decisions for Federal E.F.T. Use," Department of the Treasury, 1 May 1985.

470. Department of the Treasury, "Electronic Funds and Securities Transfer Policy—Message Authentication and Enhanced Security," Order No. 106-09, Department of the Treasury, 2 Oct 1986.

471. H. Dobbertin, "A Survey on the Construction of Bent Functions," *K.U. Leuven Workshop on Cryptographic Algorithms*, Springer-Verlag, 1995, to appear.

472. B. Dodson and A.K. Lenstra, "NFS with Four Large Primes: An Explosive Experiment," draft manuscript.

473. D. Dolev and A. Yao, "On the Security of Public-Key Protocols," *Communications of the ACM*, v. 29, n. 8, Aug 1983, pp. 198–208.

474. J. Domingo-Ferrer, "Probabilistic Authentication Analysis," *CARDIS 94—Proceedings of the First Smart Card Research and Applications Conference*, Lille, France, 24–26 Oct 1994, pp. 49–60.

475. P. de Rooij, "On the Security of the Schnorr Scheme Using Preprocessing," *Advances in Cryptology—EUROCRYPT '91 Proceedings*, Springer-Verlag, 1991, pp. 71–80.

476. A. De Santis, G. Di Crescenzo, and G. Persiano, "Secret Sharing and Perfect Zero Knowledge," *Advances in Cryptology—CRYPTO '93 Proceedings*, Springer-Verlag, 1994, pp. 73–84.

477. A. De Santis, S. Micali, and G. Persiano, "Non-Interactive Zero-Knowledge Proof Systems," *Advances in Cryptology—CRYPTO '87 Proceedings*, Springer-Verlag, 1988, pp. 52–72.

478. A. De Santis, S. Micali, and G. Persiano, "Non-Interactive Zero-Knowledge with Preprocessing," *Advances in Cryptology—CRYPTO '88 Proceedings*, Springer-Verlag, 1990, pp. 269–282.

479. Y. Desmedt, "What Happened with Knapsack Cryptographic Schemes" *Performance Limits in Communication, Theory and Practice*, NATO ASI Series E: Applied Sciences, v. 142, Kluwer Academic Publishers, 1988, pp. 113–134.

480. Y. Desmedt, "Subliminal-Free Authentication and Signature," *Advances in Cryptol-*

ogy—*EUROCRYPT '88 Proceedings*, Springer-Verlag, 1988, pp. 23–33.

481. Y. Desmedt, "Abuses in Cryptography and How to Fight Them," *Advances in Cryptology—CRYPTO '88 Proceedings*, Springer-Verlag, 1990, pp. 375–389.

482. Y. Desmedt and M. Burmester, "An Efficient Zero-Knowledge Scheme for the Discrete Logarithm Based on Smooth Numbers," *Advances in Cryptology—ASIACRYPT '91 Proceedings*, Springer-Verlag, 1993, pp. 360–367.

483. Y. Desmedt and Y. Frankel, "Threshold Cryptosystems," *Advances in Cryptology—CRYPTO '89 Proceedings*, Springer-Verlag, 1990, pp. 307–315.

484. Y. Desmedt and Y. Frankel, "Shared Generation of Authentication and Signatures," *Advances in Cryptology—CRYPTO '91 Proceedings*, Springer-Verlag, 1992, pp. 457–469.

485. Y. Desmedt, C. Goutier, and S. Bengio, "Special Uses and Abuses of the Fiat-Shamir Passport Protocol," *Advances in Cryptology—CRYPTO '87 Proceedings*, Springer-Verlag, 1988, pp. 21–39.

486. Y. Desmedt and A.M. Odlykzo, "A Chosen Text Attack on the RSA Cryptosystem and Some Discrete Logarithm Problems," *Advances in Cryptology—CRYPTO '85 Proceedings*, Springer-Verlag, 1986, pp. 516–522.

487. Y. Desmedt, J.-J. Quisquater, and M. Davio, "Dependence of Output on Input in DES: Small Avalanche Characteristics," *Advances in Cryptology: Proceedings of CRYPTO 84*, Springer-Verlag, 1985, pp. 359–376.

488. Y. Desmedt, J. Vandewalle, and R. Govaerts, "Critical Analysis of the Security of Knapsack Public Key Algorithms," *IEEE Transactions on Information Theory*, v. IT-30, n. 4, Jul 1984, pp. 601–611.

489. Y. Desmedt and M. Yung, "Weaknesses of Undeniable Signature Schemes," *Advances in Cryptology—EUROCRYPT '91 Proceedings*, Springer-Verlag, 1991, pp. 205–220.

490. W. Diffie, lecture at IEEE Information Theory Workshop, Ithaca, N.Y., 1977.

491. W. Diffie, "Cryptographic Technology: Fifteen Year Forecast," BNR Inc., Jan 1981.

492. W. Diffie, "The First Ten Years of Public-Key Cryptography," *Proceedings of the IEEE*, v. 76, n. 5, May 1988, pp. 560–577.

493. W. Diffie, "Authenticated Key Exchange and Secure Interactive Communication," *Proceedings of SECURICOM '90*, 1990.

494. W. Diffie, "The First Ten Years of Public-Key Cryptography," in *Contemporary Cryptology: The Science of Information Integrity*, G.J. Simmons, ed., IEEE Press, 1992, pp. 135–175.

495. W. Diffie and M.E. Hellman, "Multiuser Cryptographic Techniques," *Proceedings of AFIPS National Computer Conference*, 1976, pp. 109–112.

496. W. Diffie and M.E. Hellman, "New Directions in Cryptography," *IEEE Transactions on Information Theory*, v. IT-22, n. 6, Nov 1976, pp. 644–654.

497. W. Diffie and M.E. Hellman, "Exhaustive Cryptanalysis of the NBS Data Encryption Standard," *Computer*, v. 10, n. 6, Jun 1977, pp. 74–84.

498. W. Diffie and M.E. Hellman, "Privacy and Authentication: An Introduction to Cryptography," *Proceedings of the IEEE*, v. 67, n. 3, Mar 1979, pp. 397–427.

499. W. Diffie, L. Strawczynski, B. O'Higgins, and D. Steer, "An ISDN Secure Telephone Unit," *Proceedings of the National Telecommunications Forum*, v. 41, n. 1, 1987, pp. 473–477.

500. W. Diffie, P.C. van Oorschot, and M.J. Wiener, "Authentication and Authenticated Key Exchanges," *Designs, Codes and Cryptography*, v. 2, 1992, 107–125.

501. C. Ding, "The Differential Cryptanalysis and Design of Natural Stream Ciphers," *Fast Software Encryption, Cambridge Security Workshop Proceedings*, Springer-Verlag, 1994, pp. 101–115.

502. C. Ding, G. Xiao, and W. Shan, *The Stability Theory of Stream Ciphers*, Springer-Verlag, 1991.

503. A. Di Porto and W. Wolfowicz, "VINO: A Block Cipher Including Variable Permutations," *Fast Software Encryption, Cambridge Security Workshop Proceedings*, Springer-Verlag, 1994, pp. 205–210.

504. B. Dixon and A.K. Lenstra, "Factoring Integers Using SIMD Sieves," *Advances in Cryptology—EUROCRYPT '93 Proceedings*, Springer-Verlag, 1994, pp. 28–39.

505. J.D. Dixon, "Factorization and Primality Tests," *American Mathematical Monthly*, v. 91, n. 6, 1984, pp. 333–352.

506. D. Dolev and A. Yao, "On the Security of Public Key Protocols," *Proceedings of the*

22nd Annual Symposium on the Foundations of Computer Science, 1981, pp. 350–357.

507. L.X. Duan and C.C. Nian, "Modified Lu-Lee Cryptosystems," *Electronics Letters*, v. 25, n. 13, 22 Jun 1989, p. 826.

508. R. Durstenfeld, "Algorithm 235: Random Permutation," *Communications of the ACM*, v. 7, n. 7, Jul 1964, p. 420.

509. S. Dussé and B. Kaliski, Jr., "A Cryptographic Library for the Motorola DSP56000," *Advances in Cryptology—EUROCRYPT '90 Proceedings*, Springer-Verlag, 1991, pp. 230–244.

510. C. Dwork and L. Stockmeyer, "Zero-Knowledge with Finite State Verifiers," *Advances in Cryptology—CRYPTO '88 Proceedings*, Springer-Verlag, 1990, pp. 71–75.

511. D.E. Eastlake, S.D. Crocker, and J.I. Schiller, "Randomness Requirements for Security," RFC 1750, Dec 1994.

512. H. Eberle, "A High-Speed DES Implementation for Network Applications," *Advances in Cryptology—CRYPTO '92 Proceedings*, Springer-Verlag, pp. 521–539.

513. J. Edwards, "Implementing Electronic Poker: A Practical Exercise in Zero-Knowledge Interactive Proofs," Master's thesis, Department of Computer Science, University of Kentucky, May 1994.

514. W.F. Ehrsam, C.H.W. Meyer, R.L. Powers, J.L. Smith, and W.L. Tuchman, "Product Block Cipher for Data Security," U.S. Patent #3,962,539, 8 Jun 1976.

515. W.F. Ehrsam, C.H.W. Meyer, and W.L. Tuchman, "A Cryptographic Key Management Scheme for Implementing the Data Encryption Standard," *IBM Systems Journal*, v. 17, n. 2, 1978, pp. 106–125.

516. R. Eier and H. Lagger, "Trapdoors in Knapsack Cryptosystems," *Lecture Notes in Computer Science 149; Cryptography—Proceedings, Burg Feuerstein 1982*, Springer-Verlag, 1983, pp. 316–322.

517. A.K. Ekert, "Quantum Cryptography Based on Bell's Theorem," *Physical Review Letters*, v. 67, n. 6, Aug 1991, pp. 661–663.

518. T. ElGamal, "A Public-Key Cryptosystem and a Signature Scheme Based on Discrete Logarithms," *Advances in Cryptology: Proceedings of CRYPTO 84*, Springer-Verlag, 1985, pp. 10–18.

519. T. ElGamal, "A Public-Key Cryptosystem and a Signature Scheme Based on Discrete Logarithms," *IEEE Transactions on Information Theory*, v. IT-31, n. 4, 1985, pp. 469–472.

520. T. ElGamal, "On Computing Logarithms Over Finite Fields," *Advances in Cryptology—CRYPTO '85 Proceedings*, Springer-Verlag, 1986, pp. 396–402.

521. T. ElGamal and B. Kaliski, letter to the editor regarding LUC, *Dr. Dobb's Journal*, v. 18, n. 5, May 1993, p. 10.

522. T. Eng and T. Okamoto, "Single-Term Divisible Electronic Coins," *Advances in Cryptology—EUROCRYPT '94 Proceedings*, Springer-Verlag, 1995, to appear.

523. M.H. Er, D.J. Wong, A.A. Sethu, and K.S. Ngeow, "Design and Implementation of RSA Cryptosystem Using Multiple DSP Chips," *1991 IEEE International Symposium on Circuits and Systems*, v. 1, Singapore, 11–14 Jun 1991, pp. 49–52.

524. D. Estes, L.M. Adleman, K. Konpella, K.S. McCurley, and G.L. Miller, "Breaking the Ong-Schnorr-Shamir Signature Schemes for Quadratic Number Fields," *Advances in Cryptology—CRYPTO '85 Proceedings*, Springer-Verlag, 1986, pp. 3–13.

525. ETEBAC, "Échanges Télématiques Entre Les Banques et Leurs Clients," Standard ETEBAC 5, *Comité Français d'Organisation et de Normalisation Bancaires*, Apr 1989. (In French.)

526. A. Evans, W. Kantrowitz, and E. Weiss, "A User Identification Scheme Not Requiring Secrecy in the Computer," *Communications of the ACM*, v. 17, n. 8, Aug 1974, pp. 437–472.

527. S. Even and O. Goldreich, "DES-Like Functions Can Generate the Alternating Group," *IEEE Transactions on Information Theory*, v. IT-29, n. 6, Nov 1983, pp. 863–865.

528. S. Even and O. Goldreich, "On the Power of Cascade Ciphers," *ACM Transactions on Computer Systems*, v. 3, n. 2, May 1985, pp. 108–116.

529. S. Even, O. Goldreich, and A. Lempel, "A Randomizing Protocol for Signing Contracts," *Communications of the ACM*, v. 28, n. 6, Jun 1985, pp. 637–647.

530. S. Even and Y. Yacobi, "Cryptography and **NP**-Completeness," *Proceedings of the 7th International Colloquium on Automata,*

Languages, and Programming, Springer-Verlag, 1980, pp. 195–207.

531. H.-H. Evertse, "Linear Structures in Block Ciphers," *Advances in Cryptology—EUROCRYPT '87 Proceedings*, Springer-Verlag, 1988, pp. 249–266.

532. P. Fahn and M.J.B. Robshaw, "Results from the RSA Factoring Challenge," Technical Report TR-501, Version 1.3, RSA Laboratories, Jan 1995.

533. R.C. Fairfield, A. Matusevich, and J. Plany, "An LSI Digital Encryption Processor (DEP)," *Advances in Cryptology: Proceedings of CRYPTO 84*, Springer-Verlag, 1985, pp. 115–143.

534. R.C. Fairfield, A. Matusevich, and J. Plany, "An LSI Digital Encryption Processor (DEP)," *IEEE Communications*, v. 23, n. 7, Jul 1985, pp. 30–41.

535. R.C. Fairfield, R.L. Mortenson, and K.B. Koulthart, "An LSI Random Number Generator (RNG)," *Advances in Cryptology: Proceedings of CRYPTO 84*, Springer-Verlag, 1985, pp. 203–230.

536. "International Business Machines Corp. License Under Patents," *Federal Register*, v. 40, n. 52, 17 Mar 1975, p. 12067.

537. "Solicitation for Public Key Cryptographic Algorithms," *Federal Register*, v. 47, n. 126, 30 Jun 1982, p. 28445.

538. "Proposed Federal Information Processing Standard for Digital Signature Standard (DSS)," *Federal Register*, v. 56, n. 169, 30 Aug 1991, pp. 42980–42982.

539. "Proposed Federal Information Processing Standard for Secure Hash Standard," *Federal Register*, v. 57, n. 21, 31 Jan 1992, pp. 3747–3749.

540. "Proposed Reaffirmation of Federal Information Processing Standard (FIPS) 46-1, Data Encryption Standard (DES)," *Federal Register*, v. 57, n. 177, 11 Sep 1992, p. 41727.

541. "Notice of Proposal for Grant of Exclusive Patent License," *Federal Register*, v. 58, n. 108, 8 Jun 1993, pp. 23105–23106.

542. "Approval of Federal Information Processing Standards Publication 186, Digital Signature Standard (DSS)," *Federal Register*, v. 58, n. 96, 19 May 1994, pp. 26208–26211.

543. "Proposed Revision of Federal Information Processing Standard (FIPS) 180, Secure Hash Standard," *Federal Register*, v. 59, n. 131, 11 Jul 1994, pp. 35317–35318.

544. U. Feige, A. Fiat, and A. Shamir, "Zero Knowledge Proofs of Identity," *Proceedings of the 19th Annual ACM Symposium on the Theory of Computing*, 1987, pp. 210–217.

545. U. Feige, A. Fiat, and A. Shamir, "Zero Knowledge Proofs of Identity," *Journal of Cryptology*, v. 1, n. 2, 1988, pp. 77–94.

546. U. Feige and A. Shamir, "Zero Knowledge Proofs of Knowledge in Two Rounds," *Advances in Cryptology—CRYPTO '89 Proceedings*, Springer-Verlag, 1990, pp. 526–544.

547. J. Feigenbaum, "Encrypting Problem Instances, or, . . . , Can You Take Advantage of Someone Without Having to Trust Him," *Advances in Cryptology—CRYPTO '85 Proceedings*, Springer-Verlag, 1986, pp. 477–488.

548. J. Feigenbaum, "Overview of Interactive Proof Systems and Zero-Knowledge," in *Contemporary Cryptology: The Science of Information Integrity*, G.J. Simmons, ed., IEEE Press, 1992, pp. 423–439.

549. J. Feigenbaum, M.Y. Liberman, E. Grosse, and J.A. Reeds, "Cryptographic Protection of Membership Lists," *Newsletter of the International Association of Cryptologic Research*, v. 9, 1992, pp. 16–20.

550. J. Feigenbaum, M.Y. Liverman, and R.N. Wright, "Cryptographic Protection of Databases and Software," *Distributed Computing and Cryptography*, J. Feigenbaum and M. Merritt, eds., American Mathematical Society, 1991, pp. 161–172.

551. H. Feistel, "Cryptographic Coding for Data-Bank Privacy," RC 2827, Yorktown Heights, NY: IBM Research, Mar 1970.

552. H. Feistel, "Cryptography and Computer Privacy," *Scientific American*, v. 228, n. 5, May 1973, pp. 15–23.

553. H. Feistel, "Block Cipher Cryptographic System," U.S. Patent #3,798,359, 19 Mar 1974.

554. H. Feistel, "Step Code Ciphering System," U.S. Patent #3,798,360, 19 Mar 1974.

555. H. Feistel, "Centralized Verification System," U.S. Patent #3,798,605, 19 Mar 1974.

556. H. Feistel, W.A. Notz, and J.L. Smith, "Cryptographic Techniques for Machine to Machine Data Communications," RC 3663, Yorktown Heights, N.Y.: IBM Research, Dec 1971.

557. H. Feistel, W.A. Notz, and J.L. Smith, "Some Cryptographic Techniques for Machine to Machine Data Communications," *Proceedings of the IEEE*, v. 63, n. 11, Nov 1975, pp. 1545–1554.

558. P. Feldman, "A Practical Scheme for Noninteractive Verifiable Secret Sharing," *Proceedings of the 28th Annual Symposium on the Foundations of Computer Science*, 1987, pp. 427–437.

559. R.A. Feldman, "Fast Spectral Test for Measuring Nonrandomness and the DES," *Advances in Cryptology—CRYPTO '87 Proceedings*, Springer-Verlag, 1988, pp. 243–254.

560. R.A. Feldman, "A New Spectral Test for Nonrandomness and the DES," *IEEE Transactions on Software Engineering*, v. 16, n. 3, Mar 1990, pp. 261–267.

561. D.C. Feldmeier and P.R. Karn, "UNIX Password Security—Ten Years Later," *Advances in Cryptology—CRYPTO '89 Proceedings*, Springer-Verlag, 1990, pp. 44–63.

562. H. Fell and W. Diffie, "Analysis of a Public Key Approach Based on Polynomial Substitution," *Advances in Cryptology—CRYPTO '85 Proceedings*, Springer-Verlag, 1986, pp. 427–437.

563. N.T. Ferguson, "Single Term Off-Line Coins," Report CS-R9318, Computer Science/Department of Algorithms and Architecture, CWI, Mar 1993.

564. N.T. Ferguson, "Single Term Off-Line Coins," *Advances in Cryptology—EUROCRYPT '93 Proceedings*, Springer-Verlag, 1994, pp. 318–328.

565. N.T. Ferguson, "Extensions of Single-term Coins," *Advances in Cryptology—CRYPTO '93 Proceedings*, Springer-Verlag, 1994, pp. 292–301.

566. A. Fiat and A. Shamir, "How to Prove Yourself: Practical Solutions to Identification and Signature Problems," *Advances in Cryptology—CRYPTO '86 Proceedings*, Springer-Verlag, 1987, pp. 186–194.

567. A. Fiat and A. Shamir, "Unforgeable Proofs of Identity," *Proceedings of Securicom 87*, Paris, 1987, pp. 147–153.

568. P. Finch, "A Study of the Blowfish Encryption Algorithm," Ph.D. dissertation, Department of Computer Science, City University of New York Graduate School and University Center, Feb 1995.

569. R. Flynn and A.S. Campasano, "Data Dependent Keys for Selective Encryption Terminal," *Proceedings of NCC, vol. 47*, AFIPS Press, 1978, pp. 1127–1129.

570. R.H. Follett, letter to NIST regarding DSS, 25 Nov 1991.

571. R. Forré, "The Strict Avalanche Criterion: Spectral Properties and an Extended Definition," *Advances in Cryptology—CRYPTO '88 Proceedings*, Springer-Verlag, 1990, pp. 450–468.

572. R. Forré, "A Fast Correlation Attack on Nonlinearity Feedforward Filtered Shift Register Sequences," *Advances in Cryptology—CRYPTO '89 Proceedings*, Springer-Verlag, 1990, pp. 568–595.

573. S. Fortune and M. Merritt, "Poker Protocols," *Advances in Cryptology: Proceedings of CRYPTO 84*, Springer-Verlag, 1985, pp. 454–464.

574. R.B. Fougner, "Public Key Standards and Licenses," RFC 1170, Jan 1991.

575. Y. Frankel and M. Yung, "Escrowed Encryption Systems Visited: Threats, Attacks, Analysis and Designs," *Advances in Cryptology—CRYPTO '95 Proceedings*, Springer-Verlag, 1995, to appear.

576. W.F. Friedman, *Methods for the Solution of Running-Key Ciphers*, Riverbank Publication No. 16, Riverbank Labs, 1918.

577. W.F. Friedman, *The Index of Coincidence and Its Applications in Cryptography*, Riverbank Publication No. 22, Riverbank Labs, 1920. Reprinted by Aegean Park Press, 1987.

578. W.F. Friedman, *Elements of Cryptanalysis*, Laguna Hills, CA: Aegean Park Press, 1976.

579. W.F. Friedman, "Cryptology," *Encyclopedia Britannica*, v. 6, pp. 844–851, 1967.

580. A.M. Frieze, J. Hastad, R. Kannan, J.C. Lagarias, and A. Shamir, "Reconstructing Truncated Integer Variables Satisfying Linear Congruences," *SIAM Journal on Computing*, v. 17, n. 2, Apr 1988, pp. 262–280.

581. A.M. Frieze, R. Kannan, and J.C. Lagarias, "Linear Congruential Generators Do not Produce Random Sequences," *Proceedings of the 25th IEEE Symposium on Foundations of Computer Science*, 1984, pp. 480–484.

582. E. Fujiaski and T. Okamoto, "On Comparison of Practical Digitial Signature Schemes," *Proceedings of the 1992 Sym-*

posium on Cryptography and Information Security (SCIS 92), Tateshina, Japan, 2–4 Apr 1994, pp. 1A.1–12.

583. A. Fujioka, T. Okamoto, and S. Miyaguchi, "ESIGN: An Efficient Digital Signature Implementation for Smart Cards," *Advances in Cryptology—EUROCRYPT '91 Proceedings*, Springer-Verlag, 1991, pp. 446–457.

584. A. Fujioka, T. Okamoto, and K. Ohta, "Interactive Bi-Proof Systems and Undeniable Signature Schemes," *Advances in Cryptology—EUROCRYPT '91 Proceedings*, Springer-Verlag, 1991, pp. 243–256.

585. A. Fujioka, T. Okamoto, and K. Ohta, "A Practical Secret Voting Scheme for Large Scale Elections," *Advances in Cryptology—AUSCRYPT '92 Proceedings*, Springer-Verlag, 1993, pp. 244–251.

586. K. Gaardner and E. Snekkenes, "Applying a Formal Analysis Technique to the CCITT X.509 Strong Two-Way Authentication Protocol," *Journal of Cryptology*, v. 3, n. 2, 1991, pp. 81–98.

587. H.F. Gaines, *Cryptanalysis*, American Photographic Press, 1937. (Reprinted by Dover Publications, 1956.)

588. J. Gait, "A New Nonlinear Pseudorandom Number Generator," *IEEE Transactions on Software Engineering*, v. SE-3, n. 5, Sep 1977, pp. 359–363.

589. J. Gait, "Short Cycling in the Kravitz-Reed Public Key Encryption System," *Electronics Letters*, v. 18, n. 16, 5 Aug 1982, pp. 706–707.

590. Z. Galil, S. Haber, and M. Yung, "A Private Interactive Test of a Boolean Predicate and Minimum-Knowledge Public-Key Cryptosystems," *Proceedings of the 26th IEEE Symposium on Foundations of Computer Science*, 1985, pp. 360–371.

591. Z. Galil, S. Haber, and M. Yung, "Cryptographic Computation: Secure Fault-Tolerant Protocols and the Public-Key Model," *Advances in Cryptology—CRYPTO '87 Proceedings*, Springer-Verlag, 1988, pp. 135–155.

592. Z. Galil, S. Haber, and M. Yung, "Minimum-Knowledge Interactive Proofs for Decision Problems," *SIAM Journal on Computing*, v. 18, n. 4, 1989, pp. 711–739.

593. R.G. Gallager, *Information Theory and Reliable Communications*, New York: John Wiley & Sons, 1968.

594. P. Gallay and E. Depret, "A Cryptography Microprocessor," *1988 IEEE International Solid-State Circuits Conference Digest of Technical Papers*, 1988, pp. 148–149.

595. R.A. Games, "There are no de Bruijn Sequences of Span n with Complexity $2^{n-1} + n + 1$," *Journal of Combinatorical Theory*, Series A, v. 34, n. 2, Mar 1983, pp. 248–251.

596. R.A. Games and A.H. Chan, "A Fast Algorithm for Determining the Complexity of a Binary Sequence with 2^n," *IEEE Transactions on Information Theory*, v. IT-29, n. 1, Jan 1983, pp. 144–146.

597. R.A. Games, A.H. Chan, and E.L. Key, "On the Complexity of de Bruijn Sequences," *Journal of Combinatorical Theory*, Series A, v. 33, n. 1, Nov 1982, pp. 233–246.

598. S.H. Gao and G.L. Mullen, "Dickson Polynomials and Irreducible Polynomials over Finite Fields," *Journal of Number Theory*, v. 49, n. 1, Oct 1994, pp. 18–132.

599. M. Gardner, "A New Kind of Cipher That Would Take Millions of Years to Break," *Scientific American*, v. 237, n. 8, Aug 1977, pp. 120–124.

600. M.R. Garey and D.S. Johnson, *Computers and Intractability: A Guide to the Theory of NP-Completeness*, W.H. Freeman and Co., 1979.

601. S.L. Garfinkel, *PGP: Pretty Good Privacy*, Sebastopol, CA: O'Reilly and Associates, 1995.

602. C.W. Gardiner, "Distributed Public Key Certificate Management," *Proceedings of the Privacy and Security Research Group 1993 Workshop on Network and Distributed System Security*, The Internet Society, 1993, pp. 69–73.

603. G. Garon and R. Outerbridge, "DES Watch: An Examination of the Sufficiency of the Data Encryption Standard for Financial Institution Information Security in the 1990's," *Cryptologia*, v. 15, n. 3, Jul 1991, pp. 177–193.

604. M. Gasser, A. Goldstein, C. Kaufman, and B. Lampson, "The Digital Distributed Systems Security Architecture," *Proceedings of the 12th National Computer Security Conference*, NIST, 1989, pp. 305–319.

605. J. von zur Gathen, D. Kozen, and S. Landau, "Functional Decomposition of Polynomials," *Proceedings of the 28th IEEE Symposium on the Foundations of Com-

puter Science, IEEE Press, 1987, pp. 127–131.

606. P.R. Geffe, "How to Protect Data With Ciphers That are Really Hard to Break," *Electronics*, v. 46, n. 1, Jan 1973, pp. 99–101.

607. D.K. Gifford, D. Heitmann, D.A. Segal, R.G. Cote, K. Tanacea, and D.E. Burmaster, "Boston Community Information System 1986 Experimental Test Results," MIT/LCS/TR-397, MIT Laboratory for Computer Science, Aug 1987.

608. D.K. Gifford, J.M. Lucassen, and S.T. Berlin, "The Application of Digital Broadcast Communication to Large Scale Information Systems," *IEEE Journal on Selected Areas in Communications*, v. 3, n. 3, May 1985, pp. 457–467.

609. D.K. Gifford and D.A. Segal, "Boston Community Information System 1987–1988 Experimental Test Results," MIT/LCS/TR-422, MIT Laboratory for Computer Science, May 1989.

610. H. Gilbert and G. Chase, "A Statistical Attack on the Feal-8 Cryptosystem," *Advances in Cryptology—CRYPTO '90 Proceedings*, Springer-Verlag, 1991, pp. 22–33.

611. H. Gilbert and P. Chauvaud, "A Chosen Plaintext Attack of the 16-Round Khufu Cryptosystem," *Advances in Cryptology—CRYPTO '94 Proceedings*, Springer-Verlag, 1994, pp. 259–268.

612. M. Girault, "Hash-Functions Using Modulo-*N* Operations," *Advances in Cryptology—EUROCRYPT '87 Proceedings*, Springer-Verlag, 1988, pp. 217–226.

613. J. Gleick, "A New Approach to Protecting Secrets is Discovered," *The New York Times*, 18 Feb 1987, pp. C1 and C3.

614. J.-M. Goethals and C. Couvreur, "A Cryptanalytic Attack on the Lu-Lee Public-Key Cryptosystem," *Philips Journal of Research*, v. 35, 1980, pp. 301–306.

615. O. Goldreich, "A Uniform-Complexity Treatment of Encryption and Zero-Knowledge, *Journal of Cryptology*, v. 6, n. 1, 1993, pp. 21–53.

616. O. Goldreich and H. Krawczyk, "On the Composition of Zero Knowledge Proof Systems," *Proceedings on the 17th International Colloquium on Automata, Languages, and Programming*, Springer-Verlag, 1990, pp. 268–282.

617. O. Goldreich and E. Kushilevitz, "A Perfect Zero-Knowledge Proof for a Problem Equivalent to Discrete Logarithm," *Advances in Cryptology—CRYPTO '88 Proceedings*, Springer-Verlag, 1990, pp. 58–70.

618. O. Goldreich and E. Kushilevitz, "A Perfect Zero-Knowledge Proof for a Problem Equivalent to Discrete Logarithm," *Journal of Cryptology*, v. 6, n. 2, 1993, pp. 97–116.

619. O. Goldreich, S. Micali, and A. Wigderson, "Proofs That Yield Nothing but Their Validity and a Methodology of Cryptographic Protocol Design," *Proceedings of the 27th IEEE Symposium on the Foundations of Computer Science*, 1986, pp. 174–187.

620. O. Goldreich, S. Micali, and A. Wigderson, "How to Prove All **NP** Statements in Zero Knowledge and a Methodology of Cryptographic Protocol Design," *Advances in Cryptology—CRYPTO '86 Proceedings*, Springer-Verlag, 1987, pp. 171–185.

621. O. Goldreich, S. Micali, and A. Wigderson, "How to Play Any Mental Game," *Proceedings of the 19th ACM Symposium on the Theory of Computing*, 1987, pp. 218–229.

622. O. Goldreich, S. Micali, and A. Wigderson, "Proofs That Yield Nothing but Their Validity and a Methodology of Cryptographic Protocol Design," *Journal of the ACM*, v. 38, n. 1, Jul 1991, pp. 691–729.

623. S. Goldwasser and J. Kilian, "Almost All Primes Can Be Quickly Certified," *Proceedings of the 18th ACM Symposium on the Theory of Computing*, 1986, pp. 316–329.

624. S. Goldwasser and S. Micali, "Probabilistic Encryption and How to Play Mental Poker Keeping Secret All Partial Information," *Proceedings of the 14th ACM Symposium on the Theory of Computing*, 1982, pp. 270–299.

625. S. Goldwasser and S. Micali, "Probabilistic Encryption," *Journal of Computer and System Sciences*, v. 28, n. 2, Apr 1984, pp. 270–299.

626. S. Goldwasser, S. Micali, and C. Rackoff, "The Knowledge Complexity of Interactive Proof Systems," *Proceedings of the 17th ACM Symposium on Theory of Computing*, 1985, pp. 291–304.

627. S. Goldwasser, S. Micali, and C. Rackoff, "The Knowledge Complexity of Interactive Proof Systems," *SIAM Journal on Computing*, v. 18, n. 1, Feb 1989, pp. 186–208.

628. S. Goldwasser, S. Micali, and R.L. Rivest, "A Digital Signature Scheme Secure Against Adaptive Chosen-Message Attacks," *SIAM Journal on Computing*, v. 17, n. 2, Apr 1988, pp. 281–308.

629. S. Goldwasser, S. Micali, and A.C. Yao, "On Signatures and Authentication," *Advances in Cryptology: Proceedings of Crypto 82*, Plenum Press, 1983, pp. 211–215.

630. J.D. Golić, "On the Linear Complexity of Functions of Periodic GF(q) Sequences," *IEEE Transactions on Information Theory*, v. IT-35, n. 1, Jan 1989, pp. 69–75.

631. J.D. Golić, "Linear Cryptanalysis of Stream Ciphers," *K.U. Leuven Workshop on Cryptographic Algorithms*, Springer-Verlag, 1995, pp. 262–282.

632. J.D. Golić, "Towards Fast Correlation Attacks on Irregularly Clocked Shift Registers," *Advances in Cryptology—EUROCRYPT '95 Proceedings*, Springer-Verlag, 1995, to appear.

633. J.D. Golić and M.J. Mihajlević, "A Generalized Correlation Attack on a Class of Stream Ciphers Based on the Levenshtein Distance," *Journal of Cryptology*, v. 3, n. 3, 1991, pp. 201–212.

634. J.D. Golić and L. O'Connor, "Embedding and Probabilistic Correlation Attacks on Clock-Controlled Shift Registers," *Advances in Cryptology—EUROCRYPT '94 Proceedings*, Springer-Verlag, 1995, to appear.

635. R. Golliver, A.K. Lenstra, K.S. McCurley, "Lattice Sieving and Trial Division," *Proceedings of the Algorithmic Number Theory Symposium*, Cornell, 1994, to appear.

636. D. Gollmann, "Kaskadenschaltungen taktgesteuerter Schieberegister als Pseudozufallszahlengeneratoren," Ph.D. dissertation, Universität Linz, 1983. (In German.)

637. D. Gollmann, "Pseudo Random Properties of Cascade Connections of Clock Controlled Shift Registers," *Advances in Cryptology: Proceedings of EUROCRYPT 84*, Springer-Verlag, 1985, pp. 93–98.

638. D. Gollmann, "Correlation Analysis of Cascaded Sequences," *Cryptography and Coding*, H.J. Beker and F.C. Piper, eds., Oxford: Clarendon Press, 1989, pp. 289–297.

639. D. Gollmann, "Transformation Matrices of Clock-Controlled Shift Registers," *Cryptography and Coding III*, M.J. Ganley, ed., Oxford: Clarendon Press, 1993, pp. 197–210.

640. D. Gollmann and W.G. Chambers, "Lock-In Effect in Cascades of Clock-Controlled Shift-Registers," *Advances in Cryptology—EUROCRYPT '88 Proceedings*, Springer-Verlag, 1988, pp. 331–343.

641. D. Gollmann and W.G. Chambers, "Clock-Controlled Shift Registers: A Review," *IEEE Journal on Selected Areas in Communications*, v. 7, n. 4, May 1989, pp. 525–533.

642. D. Gollmann and W.G. Chambers, "A Cryptanalysis of Step$_{k,m}$-cascades," *Advances in Cryptology—EUROCRYPT '89 Proceedings*, Springer-Verlag, 1990, pp. 680–687.

643. S.W. Golomb, *Shift Register Sequences*, San Francisco: Holden-Day, 1967. (Reprinted by Aegean Park Press, 1982.)

644. L. Gong, "A Security Risk of Depending on Synchronized Clocks," *Operating Systems Review*, v. 26, n. 1, Jan 1992, pp. 49–53.

645. L. Gong, R. Needham, and R. Yahalom, "Reasoning About Belief in Cryptographic Protocols," *Proceedings of the 1991 IEEE Computer Society Symposium on Research in Security and Privacy*, 1991, pp. 234–248.

646. R.M. Goodman and A.J. McAuley, "A New Trapdoor Knapsack Public Key Cryptosystem," *Advances in Cryptology: Proceedings of EUROCRYPT 84*, Springer-Verlag, 1985, pp. 150–158.

647. R.M. Goodman and A.J. McAuley, "A New Trapdoor Knapsack Public Key Cryptosystem," *IEE Proceedings*, v. 132, pt. E, n. 6, Nov 1985, pp. 289–292.

648. D.M. Gordon, "Discrete Logarithms Using the Number Field Sieve," Preprint, 28 Mar 1991.

649. D.M. Gordon and K.S. McCurley, "Computation of Discrete Logarithms in Fields of Characteristic Two," presented at the rump session of CRYPTO '91, Aug 1991.

650. D.M. Gordon and K.S. McCurley, "Massively Parallel Computation of Discrete Logarithms," *Advances in Cryptology—*

CRYPTO '92 Proceedings, Springer-Verlag, 1993, pp. 312–323.

651. J.A. Gordon, "Strong Primes are Easy to Find," *Advances in Cryptology: Proceedings of EUROCRYPT 84*, Springer-Verlag, 1985, pp. 216–223.

652. J.A. Gordon, "Very Simple Method to Find the Minimal Polynomial of an Arbitrary Non-Zero Element of a Finite Field," *Electronics Letters*, v. 12, n. 25, 9 Dec 1976, pp. 663–664.

653. J.A. Gordon and R. Retkin, "Are Big S-Boxes Best?" *Cryptography, Proceedings of the Workshop on Cryptography, Burg Feuerstein, Germany, March 29–April 2, 1982*, Springer-Verlag, 1983, pp. 257–262.

654. M. Goresky and A. Klapper, "Feedback Registers Based on Ramified Extension of the 2-adic Numbers," *Advances in Cryptology—EUROCRYPT '94 Proceedings*, Springer-Verlag, 1995, to appear.

655. GOST, Gosudarstvennyi Standard 28147-89, "Cryptographic Protection for Data Processing Systems," Government Committee of the USSR for Standards, 1989. (In Russian.)

656. GOST R 34.10-94, Gosudarstvennyi Standard of Russian Federation, "Information technology. Cryptographic Data Security. Produce and check procedures of Electronic Digital Signature based on Asymmetric Cryptographic Algorithm." Government Committee of the Russia for Standards, 1994. (In Russian.)

657. GOST R 34.11-94, Gosudarstvennyi Standard of Russian Federation, "Information technology. Cryptographic Data Security. Hashing function." Government Committee of the Russia for Standards, 1994. (In Russian.)

658. R. Göttfert and H. Niederreiter, "On the Linear Complexity of Products of Shift-Register Sequences," *Advances in Cryptology—EUROCRYPT '93 Proceedings*, Springer-Verlag, 1994, pp. 151–158.

659. R. Göttfert and H. Niederreiter, "A General Lower Bound for the Linear Complexity of the Product of Shift-Register Sequences," *Advances in Cryptology—EUROCRYPT '94 Proceedings*, Springer-Verlag, 1995, to appear.

660. J. van de Graaf and R. Peralta, "A Simple and Secure Way to Show the Validity of Your Public Key," *Advances in Cryptology—CRYPTO '87 Proceedings*, Springer-Verlag, 1988, pp. 128–134.

661. J. Grollman and A.L. Selman, "Complexity Measures for Public-Key Cryptosystems," *Proceedings of the 25th IEEE Symposium on the Foundations of Computer Science*, 1984, pp. 495–503.

662. GSA Federal Standard 1026, "Telecommunications: General Security Requirements for Equipment Using the Data Encryption Standard," General Services Administration, Apr 1982.

663. GSA Federal Standard 1027, "Telecommunications: Interoperability and Security Requirements for Use of the Data Encryption Standard in the Physical and Data Link Layers of Data Communications," General Services Administration, Jan 1983.

664. GSA Federal Standard 1028, "Interoperability and Security Requirements for Use of the Data Encryption Standard with CCITT Group 3 Facsimile Equipment," General Services Administration, Apr 1985.

665. P. Guam, "Cellular Automaton Public Key Cryptosystems," *Complex Systems*, v. 1, 1987, pp. 51–56.

666. H. Guan, "An Analysis of the Finite Automata Public Key Algorithm," *CHINACRYPT '94*, Xidian, China, 11–15 Nov 1994, pp. 120–126. (In Chinese.)

667. G. Guanella, "Means for and Method for Secret Signalling," U.S. Patent #2,405,500, 6 Aug 1946.

668. M. Gude, "Concept for a High-Performance Random Number Generator Based on Physical Random Phenomena," *Frequenz*, v. 39, 1985, pp. 187–190.

669. M. Gude, "Ein quasi-idealer Gleichverteilungsgenerator basierend auf physikalischen Zufallsphänomenen," Ph.D. dissertation, Aachen University of Technology, 1987. (In German.)

670. L.C. Guillou and J.-J. Quisquater, "A Practical Zero-Knowledge Protocol Fitted to Security Microprocessor Minimizing Both Transmission and Memory," *Advances in Cryptology—EUROCRYPT '88 Proceedings*, Springer-Verlag, 1988, pp. 123–128.

671. L.C. Guillou and J.-J. Quisquater, "A 'Paradoxical' Identity-Based Signature Scheme Resulting from Zero-Knowledge," *Advances in Cryptology—CRYPTO '88 Proceedings*, Springer-Verlag, 1990, pp. 216–231.

672. L.C. Guillou, M. Ugon, and J.-J. Quisquater, "The Smart Card: A Standardized

Security Device Dedicated to Public Cryptology," *Contemporary Cryptology: The Science of Information Integrity*, G. Simmons, ed., IEEE Press, 1992, pp. 561–613.

673. C.G. Günther, "Alternating Step Generators Controlled by de Bruijn Sequences," *Advances in Cryptology—EUROCRYPT '87 Proceedings*, Springer-Verlag, 1988, pp. 5–14.

674. C.G. Günther, "An Identity-based Key-exchange Protocol," *Advances in Cryptology—EUROCRYPT '89 Proceedings*, Springer-Verlag, 1990, pp. 29–37.

675. H. Gustafson, E. Dawson, and B. Caelli, "Comparison of Block Ciphers," *Advances in Cryptology—AUSCRYPT '90 Proceedings*, Springer-Verlag, 1990, pp. 208–220.

676. P. Gutmann, personal communication, 1993.

677. H. Gutowitz, "A Cellular Automaton Cryptosystem: Specification and Call for Attack," unpublished manuscript, Aug 1992.

678. H. Gutowitz, "Method and Apparatus for Encryption, Decryption, and Authentication Using Dynamical Systems," U.S. Patent #5,365,589, 15 Nov 1994.

679. H. Gutowitz, "Cryptography with Dynamical Systems," *Cellular Automata and Cooperative Phenomenon*, Kluwer Academic Press, 1993.

680. R.K. Guy, "How to Factor a Number," *Fifth Manitoba Conference on Numeral Mathematics Congressus Numerantium*, v. 16, 1976, pp. 49–89.

681. R.K. Guy, *Unsolved Problems in Number Theory*, Springer-Verlag, 1981.

682. S. Haber and W.S. Stornetta, "How to Time-Stamp a Digital Document," *Advances in Cryptology—CRYPTO '90 Proceedings*, Springer-Verlag, 1991, pp. 437–455.

683. S. Haber and W.S. Stornetta, "How to Time-Stamp a Digital Document," *Journal of Cryptology*, v. 3, n. 2, 1991, pp. 99–112.

684. S. Haber and W.S. Stornetta, "Digital Document Time-Stamping with Catenate Certificate," U.S. Patent #5,136,646, 4 Aug 1992.

685. S. Haber and W.S. Stornetta, "Method for Secure Time-Stamping of Digital Documents," U.S. Patent #5,136,647, 4 Aug 1992.

686. S. Haber and W.S. Stornetta, "Method of Extending the Validity of a Cryptographic Certificate," U.S. Patent #5,373,561, 13 Dec 1994.

687. T. Habutsu, Y. Nishio, I. Sasase, and S. Mori, "A Secret Key Cryptosystem by Iterating a Chaotic Map," *Transactions of the Institute of Electronics, Information, and Communication Engineers*, v. E73, n. 7, Jul 1990, pp. 1041–1044.

688. T. Habutsu, Y. Nishio, I. Sasase, and S. Mori, "A Secret Key Cryptosystem by Iterating a Chaotic Map," *Advances in Cryptology—EUROCRYPT '91 Proceedings*, Springer-Verlag, 1991, pp. 127–140.

689. S. Hada and H. Tanaka, "An Improvement Scheme of DES against Differential Cryptanalysis," *Proceedings of the 1994 Symposium on Cryptography and Information Security (SCIS 94)*, Lake Biwa, Japan, 27–29 Jan 1994, pp 14A.1–11. (In Japanese.)

690. B.C.W. Hagelin, "The Story of the Hagelin Cryptos," *Cryptologia*, v. 18, n. 3, Jul 1994, pp. 204–242.

691. T. Hansen and G.L. Mullen, "Primitive Polynomials over Finite Fields," *Mathematics of Computation*, v. 59, n. 200, Oct 1992, pp. 639–643.

692. S. Harada and S. Kasahara, "An ID-Based Key Sharing Scheme Without Preliminary Communication," IEICE Japan, Technical Report, ISEC89-38, 1989. (In Japanese.)

693. S. Harari, "A Correlation Cryptographic Scheme," *EUROCODE '90—International Symposium on Coding Theory*, Springer-Verlag, 1991, pp. 180–192.

694. T. Hardjono and J. Seberry, "Authentication via Multi-Service Tickets in the Kuperee Server," *Computer Security—ESORICS 94*, Springer-Verlag, 1994, pp. 144–160.

695. L. Harn and T. Kiesler, "New Scheme for Digital Multisignatures," *Electronics Letters*, v. 25, n. 15, 20 Jul 1989, pp. 1002–1003.

696. L. Harn and T. Kiesler, "Improved Rabin's Scheme with High Efficiency," *Electronics Letters*, v. 25, n. 15, 20 Jul 1989, p. 1016.

697. L. Harn and T. Kiesler, "Two New Efficient Cryptosystems Based on Rabin's Scheme," *Fifth Annual Computer Security Applications Conference*, IEEE Computer Society Press, 1990, pp. 263–270.

698. L. Harn and D.-C. Wang, "Cryptanalysis and Modification of Digital Signature Scheme Based on Error-Correcting Codes," *Electronics Letters*, v. 28, n. 2, 10 Jan 1992, p. 157–159.

699. L. Harn and Y. Xu, "Design of Generalized ElGamal Type Digital Signature Schemes Based on Discrete Logarithm," *Electronics Letters*, v. 30, n. 24, 24 Nov 1994, p. 2025–2026.

700. L. Harn and S. Yang, "Group-Oriented Undeniable Signature Schemes without the Assistance of a Mutually Trusted Party," *Advances in Cryptology— AUSCRYPT '92 Proceedings*, Springer-Verlag, 1993, pp. 133–142.

701. G. Harper, A. Menezes, and S. Vanstone, "Public-Key Cryptosystems with Very Small Key Lengths," *Advances in Cryptology—EUROCRYPT '92 Proceedings*, Springer-Verlag, 1993, pp. 163–173.

702. C. Harpes, "Notes on High Order Differential Cryptanalysis of DES," internal report, Signal and Information Processing Laboratory, Swiss Federal Institute of Technology, Aug 1993.

703. G.W. Hart, "To Decode Short Cryptograms," *Communications of the ACM*, v. 37, n. 9, Sep 1994, pp. 102–108.

704. J. Hastad, "On Using RSA with Low Exponent in a Public Key Network," *Advances in Cryptology—CRYPTO '85 Proceedings*, Springer-Verlag, 1986, pp. 403–408.

705. J. Hastad and A. Shamir, "The Cryptographic Security of Truncated Linearly Related Variables," *Proceedings of the 17th Annual ACM Symposium on the Theory of Computing*, 1985, pp. 356–362.

706. R.C. Hauser and E.S. Lee, "Verification and Modelling of Authentication Protocols," *ESORICS 92, Proceedings of the Second European Symposium on Research in Computer Security*, Springer-Verlag, 1992, pp. 131–154.

707. B. Hayes, "Anonymous One-Time Signatures and Flexible Untraceable Electronic Cash," *Advances in Cryptology— AUSCRYPT '90 Proceedings*, Springer-Verlag, 1990, pp. 294–305.

708. D.K. He, "LUC Public Key Cryptosystem and its Properties," *CHINACRYPT '94*, Xidian, China, 11–15 Nov 1994, pp. 60–69. (In Chinese.)

709. J. He and T. Kiesler, "Enhancing the Security of ElGamal's Signature Scheme," *IEE Proceedings on Computers and Digital Techniques*, v. 141, n. 3, 1994, pp. 193–195.

710. E.H. Hebern, "Electronic Coding Machine," U.S. Patent #1,510,441, 30 Sep 1924.

711. N. Heintze and J.D. Tygar, "A Model for Secure Protocols and their Compositions," *Proceedings of the 1994 IEEE Computer Society Symposium on Research in Security and Privacy*, 1994, pp. 2–13.

712. M.E. Hellman, "An Extension of the Shannon Theory Approach to Cryptography," *IEEE Transactions on Information Theory*, v. IT-23, n. 3, May 1977, pp. 289–294.

713. M.E. Hellman, "The Mathematics of Public-Key Cryptography," *Scientific American*, v. 241, n. 8, Aug 1979, pp. 146–157.

714. M.E. Hellman, "DES Will Be Totally Insecure within Ten Years," *IEEE Spectrum*, v. 16, n. 7, Jul 1979, pp. 32–39.

715. M.E. Hellman, "On DES-Based Synchronous Encryption," Dept. of Electrical Engineering, Stanford University, 1980.

716. M.E. Hellman, "A Cryptanalytic Time-Memory Trade Off," *IEEE Transactions on Information Theory*, v. 26, n. 4, Jul 1980, pp. 401–406.

717. M.E. Hellman, "Another Cryptanalytic Attack on 'A Cryptosystem for Multiple Communications'," *Information Processing Letters*, v. 12, 1981, pp. 182–183.

718. M.E. Hellman, W. Diffie, and R.C. Merkle, "Cryptographic Apparatus and Method," U.S. Patent #4,200,770, 29 Apr 1980.

719. M.E. Hellman, W. Diffie, and R.C. Merkle, "Cryptographic Apparatus and Method," Canada Patent #1,121,480, 6 Apr 1982.

720. M.E. Hellman and R.C. Merkle, "Public Key Cryptographic Apparatus and Method," U.S. Patent #4,218,582, 19 Aug 1980.

721. M.E. Hellman, R. Merkle, R. Schroeppel, L. Washington, W. Diffie, S. Pohlig, and P. Schweitzer, "Results of an Initial Attempt to Cryptanalyze the NBS Data Encryption Standard," Technical Report SEL 76-042, Information Systems Lab, Department of Electrical Engineering, Stanford University, 1976.

722. M.E. Hellman and S.C. Pohlig, "Exponentiation Cryptographic Apparatus and Method," U.S. Patent #4,424,414, 3 Jan 1984.

723. M.E. Hellman and J.M. Reyneri, "Distribution of Drainage in the DES," *Advances in Cryptology: Proceedings of Crypto 82*, Plenum Press, 1983, pp. 129–131.

724. F. Hendessi and M.R. Aref, "A Successful Attack Against the DES," *Third Canadian*

Workshop on Information Theory and Applications, Springer-Verlag, 1994, pp. 78–90.

725. T. Herlestam, "Critical Remarks on Some Public-Key Cryptosystems," *BIT,* v. 18, 1978, pp. 493–496.

726. T. Herlestam, "On Functions of Linear Shift Register Sequences", *Advances in Cryptology—EUROCRYPT '85,* Springer-Verlag, 1986, pp. 119–129.

727. T. Herlestam and R. Johannesson, "On Computing Logarithms over $GF(2^p)$," *BIT,* v. 21, 1981, pp. 326–334.

728. H.M. Heys and S.E. Tavares, "On the Security of the CAST Encryption Algorithm," *Proceedings of the Canadian Conference on Electrical and Computer Engineering,* Halifax, Nova Scotia, Sep 1994, pp. 332–335.

729. H.M. Heys and S.E. Tavares, "The Design of Substitution-Permutation Networks Resistant to Differential and Linear Cryptanalysis," *Proceedings of the 2nd Annual ACM Conference on Computer and Communications Security,* ACM Press, 1994, pp. 148–155.

730. E. Heyst and T.P. Pederson, "How to Make Fail-Stop Signatures," *Advances in Cryptology—EUROCRYPT '92 Proceedings,* Springer-Verlag, 1993, pp. 366–377.

731. E. Heyst, T.P. Pederson, and B. Pfitzmann, "New Construction of Fail-Stop Signatures and Lower Bounds," *Advances in Cryptology—CRYPTO '92 Proceedings,* Springer-Verlag, 1993, pp. 15–30.

732. L.S. Hill, "Cryptography in an Algebraic Alphabet," *American Mathematical Monthly,* v. 36, Jun–Jul 1929, pp. 306–312.

733. P.J.M. Hin, "Channel-Error-Correcting Privacy Cryptosystems," Ph.D. dissertation, Delft University of Technology, 1986. (In Dutch.)

734. R. Hirschfeld, "Making Electronic Refunds Safer," *Advances in Cryptology—CRYPTO '92 Proceedings,* Springer-Verlag, 1993, pp. 106–112.

735. A. Hodges, *Alan Turing: The Enigma of Intelligence,* Simon and Schuster, 1983.

736. W. Hohl, X. Lai, T. Meier, and C. Waldvogel, "Security of Iterated Hash Functions Based on Block Ciphers," *Advances in Cryptology—CRYPTO '93 Proceedings,* Springer-Verlag, 1994, pp. 379–390.

737. F. Hoornaert, M. Decroos, J. Vandewalle, and R. Govaerts, "Fast RSA-Hardware:

Dream or Reality?" *Advances in Cryptology—EUROCRYPT '88 Proceedings,* Springer-Verlag, 1988, pp. 257–264.

738. F. Hoornaert, J. Goubert, and Y. Desmedt, "Efficient Hardware Implementation of the DES," *Advances in Cryptology: Proceedings of CRYPTO 84,* Springer-Verlag, 1985, pp. 147–173.

739. E. Horowitz and S. Sahni, *Fundamentals of Computer Algorithms,* Rockville, MD: Computer Science Press, 1978.

740. P. Horster, H. Petersen, and M. Michels, "Meta-ElGamal Signature Schemes," *Proceedings of the 2nd Annual ACM Conference on Computer and Communications Security,* ACM Press, 1994, pp. 96–107.

741. P. Horster, H. Petersen, and M. Michels, "Meta Message Recovery and Meta Blind Signature Schemes Based on the Discrete Logarithm Problem and their Applications," *Advances in Cryptology—ASIACRYPT '94 Proceedings,* Springer-Verlag, 1995, pp. 224–237.

742. L.K. Hua, *Introduction to Number Theory,* Springer-Verlag, 1982.

743. K. Huber, "Specialized Attack on Chor-Rivest Public Key Cryptosystem," *Electronics Letters,* v. 27, n. 23, 7 Nov 1991, pp. 2130–2131.

744. E. Hughes, "A Cypherpunk's Manifesto," 9 Mar 1993.

745. E. Hughes, "An Encrypted Key Transmission Protocol," presented at the rump session of CRYPTO '94, Aug 1994.

746. H. Hule and W.B. Müller, "On the RSA-Cryptosystem with Wrong Keys," *Contributions to General Algebra 6,* Vienna: Verlag Hölder-Pichler-Tempsky, 1988, pp. 103–109.

747. H.A. Hussain, J.W.A. Sada, and S.M. Kalipha, "New Multistage Knapsack Public-Key Cryptosystem," *International Journal of Systems Science,* v. 22, n. 11, Nov 1991, pp. 2313–2320.

748. T. Hwang, "Attacks on Okamoto and Tanaka's One-Way ID-Based Key Distribution System," *Information Processing Letters,* v. 43, n. 2, Aug 1992, pp. 83–86.

749. T. Hwang and T.R.N. Rao, "Secret Error-Correcting Codes (SECC)," *Advances in Cryptology—CRYPTO '88 Proceedings,* Springer-Verlag, 1990, pp. 540–563.

750. C. I'Anson and C. Mitchell, "Security Defects in CCITT Recommendation

X.509—the Directory Authentication Framework," *Computer Communications Review*, v. 20, n. 2, Apr 1990, pp. 30–34.

751. IBM, "Common Cryptographic Architecture: Cryptographic Application Programming Interface Reference," SC40-1675-1, IBM Corp., Nov 1990.

752. IBM, "Common Cryptographic Architecture: Cryptographic Application Programming Interface Reference—Public Key Algorithm," IBM Corp., Mar 1993.

753. R. Impagliazzo and M. Yung, "Direct Minimum-Knowledge Computations," *Advances in Cryptology—CRYPTO '87 Proceedings*, Springer-Verlag, 1988, pp. 40–51.

754. I. Ingemarsson, "A New Algorithm for the Solution of the Knapsack Problem," *Lecture Notes in Computer Science 149*; *Cryptography: Proceedings of the Workshop on Cryptography*, Springer-Verlag, 1983, pp. 309–315.

755. I. Ingemarsson, "Delay Estimation for Truly Random Binary Sequences or How to Measure the Length of Rip van Winkle's Sleep," *Communications and Cryptography: Two Sides of One Tapestry*, R.E. Blahut et al., eds., Kluwer Adademic Publishers, 1994, pp. 179–186.

756. I. Ingemarsson and G.J. Simmons, "A Protocol to Set Up Shared Secret Schemes without the Assistance of a Mutually Trusted Party," *Advances in Cryptology—EUROCRYPT '90 Proceedings*, Springer-Verlag, 1991, pp. 266–282.

757. I. Ingemarsson, D.T. Tang, and C.K. Wong, "A Conference Key Distribution System," *IEEE Transactions on Information Theory*, v. IT-28, n. 5, Sep 1982, pp. 714–720.

758. ISO DIS 8730, "Banking—Requirements for Message Authentication (Wholesale)," Association for Payment Clearing Services, London, Jul 1987.

759. ISO DIS 8731-1, "Banking—Approved Algorithms for Message Authentication—Part 1: DEA," Association for Payment Clearing Services, London, 1987.

760. ISO DIS 8731-2, "Banking—Approved Algorithms for Message Authentication—Part 2: Message Authenticator Algorithm," Association for Payment Clearing Services, London, 1987.

761. ISO DIS 8732, "Banking—Key Management (Wholesale)," Association for Payment Clearing Services, London, Dec 1987.

762. ISO/IEC 9796, "Information Technology—Security Techniques—Digital Signature Scheme Giving Message Recovery," International Organization for Standardization, Jul 1991.

763. ISO/IEC 9797, "Data Cryptographic Techniques—Data Integrity Mechanism Using a Cryptographic Check Function Employing a Block Cipher Algorithm," International Organization for Standardization, 1989.

764. ISO DIS 10118 DRAFT, "Information Technology—Security Techniques—Hash Functions," International Organization for Standardization, 1989.

765. ISO DIS 10118 DRAFT, "Information Technology—Security Techniques—Hash Functions," International Organization for Standardization, April 1991.

766. ISO N98, "Hash Functions Using a Pseudo Random Algorithm," working document, ISO-IEC/JTC1/SC27/WG2, International Organization for Standardization, 1992.

767. ISO N179, "AR Fingerprint Function," working document, ISO-IEC/JTC1/SC27/WG2, International Organization for Standardization, 1992.

768. ISO/IEC 10118, "Information Technology—Security Techniques—Hash Functions—Part 1: General and Part 2: Hash-Functions Using an n-Bit Block Cipher Algorithm," International Organization for Standardization, 1993.

769. K. Ito, S. Kondo, and Y. Mitsuoka, "SXAL8/MBAL Algorithm," Technical Report, ISEC93-68, IEICE Japan, 1993. (In Japanese.)

770. K.R. Iversen, "The Application of Cryptographic Zero-Knowledge Techniques in Computerized Secret Ballot Election Schemes," Ph.D. dissertation, IDT-report 1991:3, Norwegian Institute of Technology, Feb 1991.

771. K.R. Iversen, "A Cryptographic Scheme for Computerized General Elections," *Advances in Cryptology—CRYPTO '91 Proceedings*, Springer-Verlag, 1992, pp. 405–419.

772. K. Iwamura, T. Matsumoto, and H. Imai, "An Implementation Method for RSA Cryptosystem with Parallel Processing," *Transactions of the Institute of Electronics, Information, and Communication Engineers*, v. J75-A, n. 8, Aug 1992, pp. 1301–1311.

773. W.J. Jaburek, "A Generalization of ElGamal's Public Key Cryptosystem," *Advances in Cryptology—EUROCRYPT '89 Proceedings*, 1990, Springer-Verlag, pp. 23–28.

774. N.S. James, R. Lidi, and H. Niederreiter, "Breaking the Cade Cipher," *Advances in Cryptology—CRYPTO '86 Proceedings*, 1987, Springer-Verlag, pp. 60–63.

775. C.J.A. Jansen, "On the Key Storage Requirements for Secure Terminals," *Computers and Security*, v. 5, n. 2, Jun 1986, pp. 145–149.

776. C.J.A. Jansen, "Investigations on Nonlinear Streamcipher Systems: Construction and Evaluation Methods," Ph.D. dissertation, Technical University of Delft, 1989.

777. C.J.A. Jansen and D.E. Boekee, "Modes of Blockcipher Algorithms and their Protection against Active Eavesdropping," *Advances in Cryptology—EUROCRYPT '87 Proceedings*, Springer-Verlag, 1988, pp. 281–286.

778. S.M. Jennings, "A Special Class of Binary Sequences," Ph.D. dissertation, University of London, 1980.

779. S.M. Jennings, "Multiplexed Sequences: Some Properties of the Minimum Polynomial," *Lecture Notes in Computer Science 149; Cryptography: Proceedings of the Workshop on Cryptography*, Springer-Verlag, 1983, pp. 189–206.

780. S.M. Jennings, "Autocorrelation Function of the Multiplexed Sequence," *IEE Proceedings*, v. 131, n. 2, Apr 1984, pp. 169–172.

781. T. Jin, "Care and Feeding of Your Three-Headed Dog," Document Number IAG-90-011, Hewlett-Packard, May 1990.

782. T. Jin, "Living with Your Three-Headed Dog," Document Number IAG-90-012, Hewlett-Packard, May 1990.

783. A. Jiwa, J. Seberry, and Y. Zheng, "Beacon Based Authentication," *Computer Security—ESORICS 94*, Springer-Verlag, 1994, pp. 125–141.

784. D.B. Johnson, G.M. Dolan, M.J. Kelly, A.V. Le, and S.M. Matyas, "Common Cryptographic Architecture Cryptographic Application Programming Interface," *IBM Systems Journal*, v. 30, n. 2, 1991, pp. 130–150.

785. D.B. Johnson, S.M. Matyas, A.V. Le, and J.D. Wilkins, "Design of the Commercial Data Masking Facility Data Privacy Algorithm," *1st ACM Conference on Computer and Communications Security*, ACM Press, 1993, pp. 93–96.

786. J.P. Jordan, "A Variant of a Public-Key Cryptosystem Based on Goppa Codes," *Sigact News*, v. 15, n. 1, 1983, pp. 61–66.

787. A. Joux and L. Granboulan, "A Practical Attack Against Knapsack Based Hash Functions," *Advances in Cryptology—EUROCRYPT '94 Proceedings*, Springer-Verlag, 1995, to appear.

788. A. Joux and J. Stern, "Cryptanalysis of Another Knapsack Cryptosystem," *Advances in Cryptology—ASIACRYPT '91 Proceedings*, Springer-Verlag, 1993, pp. 470–476.

789. R.R. Jueneman, "Analysis of Certain Aspects of Output-Feedback Mode," *Advances in Cryptology: Proceedings of Crypto 82*, Plenum Press, 1983, pp. 99–127.

790. R.R. Jueneman, "Electronic Document Authentication," *IEEE Network Magazine*, v. 1, n. 2, Apr 1978, pp. 17–23.

791. R.R. Jueneman, "A High Speed Manipulation Detection Code," *Advances in Cryptology—CRYPTO '86 Proceedings*, Springer-Verlag, 1987, pp. 327–346.

792. R.R. Jueneman, S.M. Matyas, and C.H. Meyer, "Message Authentication with Manipulation Detection Codes," *Proceedings of the 1983 IEEE Computer Society Symposium on Research in Security and Privacy*, 1983, pp. 733–54.

793. R.R. Jueneman, S.M. Matyas, and C.H. Meyer, "Message Authentication," *IEEE Communications Magazine*, v. 23, n. 9, Sep 1985, pp. 29–40.

794. D. Kahn, *The Codebreakers: The Story of Secret Writing*, New York: Macmillan Publishing Co., 1967.

795. D. Kahn, *Kahn on Codes*, New York: Macmillan Publishing Co., 1983.

796. D. Kahn, *Seizing the Enigma*, Boston: Houghton Mifflin Co., 1991.

797. P. Kaijser, T. Parker, and D. Pinkas, "SESAME: The Solution to Security for Open Distributed Systems," *Journal of Computer Communications*, v. 17, n. 4, Jul 1994, pp. 501–518.

798. R. Kailar and V.D. Gilgor, "On Belief Evolution in Authentication Protocols," *Proceedings of the Computer Security Foundations Workshop IV*, IEEE Computer Society Press, 1991, pp. 102–116.

799. B.S. Kaliski, "A Pseudo Random Bit Generator Based on Elliptic Logarithms," Master's thesis, Massachusetts Institute of Technology, 1987.

800. B.S. Kaliski, letter to NIST regarding DSS, 4 Nov 1991.

801. B.S. Kaliski, "The MD2 Message Digest Algorithm," RFC 1319, Apr 1992.

802. B.S. Kaliski, "Privacy Enhancement for Internet Electronic Mail: Part IV: Key Certificates and Related Services," RFC 1424, Feb 1993.

803. B.S. Kaliski, "An Overview of the PKCS Standards," RSA Laboratories, Nov 1993.

804. B.S. Kaliski, "A Survey of Encryption Standards, *IEEE Micro*, v. 13, n. 6, Dec 1993, pp. 74–81.

805. B.S. Kaliski, personal communication, 1993.

806. B.S. Kaliski, "On the Security and Performance of Several Triple-DES Modes," RSA Laboratories, draft manuscript, Jan 1994.

807. B.S. Kaliski, R.L. Rivest, and A.T. Sherman, "Is the Data Encryption Standard a Group?", *Advances in Cryptology—EUROCRYPT '85*, Springer-Verlag, 1986, pp. 81–95.

808. B.S. Kaliski, R.L. Rivest, and A.T. Sherman, "Is the Data Encryption Standard a Pure Cipher? (Results of More Cycling Experiments in DES)," *Advances in Cryptology—CRYPTO '85 Proceedings*, Springer-Verlag, 1986, pp. 212–226.

809. B.S. Kaliski, R.L. Rivest, and A.T. Sherman, "Is the Data Encryption Standard a Group? (Results of Cycling Experiments on DES)," *Journal of Cryptology*, v. 1, n. 1, 1988, pp. 3–36.

810. B.S. Kaliski and M.J.B. Robshaw, "Fast Block Cipher Proposal," *Fast Software Encryption, Cambridge Security Workshop Proceedings*, Springer-Verlag, 1994, pp. 33–40.

811. B.S. Kaliski and M.J.B. Robshaw, "Linear Cryptanalysis Using Multiple Approximations," *Advances in Cryptology—CRYPTO '94 Proceedings*, Springer-Verlag, 1994, pp. 26–39.

812. B.S. Kaliski and M.J.B. Robshaw, "Linear Cryptanalysis Using Multiple Approximations and FEAL," *K.U. Leuven Workshop on Cryptographic Algorithms*, Springer-Verlag, 1995, to appear.

813. R.G. Kammer, statement before the U.S. government Subcommittee on Telecommunications and Finance, Committee on Energy and Commerce, 29 Apr 1993.

814. T. Kaneko, K. Koyama, and R. Terada, "Dynamic Swapping Schemes and Differential Cryptanalysis, *Proceedings of the 1993 Korea-Japan Workshop on Information Security and Cryptography*, Seoul, Korea, 24–26 Oct 1993, pp. 292–301.

815. T. Kaneko, K. Koyama, and R. Terada, "Dynamic Swapping Schemes and Differential Cryptanalysis," *Transactions of the Institute of Electronics, Information, and Communication Engineers*, v. E77-A, n. 8, Aug 1994, pp. 1328–1336.

816. T. Kaneko and H. Miyano, "A Study on the Strength Evaluation of Randomized DES-Like Cryptosystems against Chosen Plaintext Attacks," *Proceedings of the 1993 Symposium on Cryptography and Information Security (SCIS 93)*, Shuzenji, Japan, 28–30 Jan 1993, pp. 15C.1–10.

817. J. Kari, "A Cryptosystem Based on Propositional Logic," *Machines, Languages, and Complexity: 5th International Meeting of Young Computer Scientists, Selected Contributions*, Springer-Verlag, 1989, pp. 210–219.

818. E.D. Karnin, J.W. Greene, and M.E. Hellman, "On Sharing Secret Systems," *IEEE Transactions on Information Theory*, v. IT-29, 1983, pp. 35–41.

819. F.W. Kasiski, *Die Geheimschriften und die Dechiffrir-kunst*, E.S. Miller und Sohn, 1863. (In German.)

820. A. Kehne, J. Schonwalder, and H. Langendorfer, "A Nonce-Based Protocol for Multiple Authentications," *Operating Systems Review*, v. 26, n. 4, Oct 1992, pp. 84–89.

821. J. Kelsey, personal communication, 1994.

822. R. Kemmerer, "Analyzing Encryption Protocols Using Formal Verification Techniques," *IEEE Journal on Selected Areas in Communications*, v. 7, n. 4, May 1989, pp. 448–457.

823. R. Kemmerer, C.A. Meadows, and J. Millen, "Three Systems for Cryptographic Protocol Analysis," *Journal of Cryptology*, v. 7, n. 2, 1994, pp. 79–130.

824. S.T. Kent, "Encryption-Based Protection Protocols for Interactive User-Computer Communications," MIT/LCS/TR-162,

MIT Laboratory for Computer Science, May 1976.

825. S.T. Kent, "Privacy Enhancement for Internet Electronic Mail: Part II: Certificate-Based Key Management," RFC 1422, Feb 1993.

826. S.T. Kent, "Understanding the Internet Certification System," *Proceedings of INET '93*, The Internet Society, 1993, pp. BAB1-BAB10.

827. S.T. Kent and J. Linn, "Privacy Enhancement for Internet Electronic Mail: Part II: Certificate-Based Key Management," RFC 1114, Aug 1989.

828. V. Kessler and G. Wedel, "AUTOLOG—An Advanced Logic of Authentication," *Proceedings of the Computer Security Foundations Workshop VII*, IEEE Computer Society Press, 1994, pp. 90–99.

829. E.L. Key, "An Analysis of the Structure and Complexity of Nonlinear Binary Sequence Generators," *IEEE Transactions on Information Theory*, v. IT-22, n. 6, Nov 1976, pp. 732–736.

830. T. Kiesler and L. Harn, "RSA Blocking and Multisignature Schemes with No Bit Expansion," *Electronics Letters*, v. 26, n. 18, 30 Aug 1990, pp. 1490–1491.

831. J. Kilian, *Uses of Randomness in Algorithms and Protocols*, MIT Press, 1990.

832. J. Kilian, "Achieving Zero-Knowledge Robustly," *Advances in Cryptology—CRYPTO '90 Proceedings*, Springer-Verlag, 1991, pp. 313–325.

833. J. Kilian and T. Leighton, "Failsafe Key Escrow," MIT/LCS/TR-636, MIT Laboratory for Computer Science, Aug 1994.

834. K. Kim, "Construction of DES-Like S-Boxes Based on Boolean Functions Satisfying the SAC," *Advances in Cryptology—ASIACRYPT '91 Proceedings*, Springer-Verlag, 1993, pp. 59–72.

835. K. Kim, S. Lee, and S. Park, "Necessary Conditions to Strengthen DES S-Boxes Against Linear Cryptanalysis," *Proceedings of the 1994 Symposium on Cryptography and Information Security (SCIS 94)*, Lake Biwa, Japan, 27–29 Jan 1994, pp. 15D.1–9.

836. K. Kim, S. Lee, and S. Park, "How to Strengthen DES against Differential Attack," unpublished manuscript, 1994.

837. K. Kim, S. Lee, S. Park, and D. Lee, "DES Can Be Immune to Differential Cryptanaly-

sis," *Workshop on Selected Areas in Cryptography—Workshop Record*, Kingston, Ontario, 5–6 May 1994, pp. 70–81.

838. K. Kim, S. Park, and S. Lee, "How to Strengthen DES against Two Robust Attacks," *Proceedings of the 1995 Japan-Korea Workshop on Information Security and Cryptography*, Inuyama, Japan, 24–27 Jan 1995, 173–182.

839. K. Kim, S. Park, and S. Lee, "Reconstruction of s^2DES S-Boxes and their Immunity to Differential Cryptanalysis," *Proceedings of the 1993 Korea-Japan Workshop on Information Security and Cryptography*, Seoul, Korea, 24–26 Oct 1993, pp. 282–291.

840. S. Kim and B.S. Um, "A Multipurpose Membership Proof System Based on Discrete Logarithm," *Proceedings of the 1993 Korea-Japan Workshop on Information Security and Cryptography*, Seoul, Korea, 24–26 Oct 1993, pp. 177–183.

841. P. Kinnucan, "Data Encryption Gurus: Tuchman and Meyer," *Cryptologia*, v. 2, n. 4, Oct 1978.

842. A. Klapper, "The Vulnerability of Geometric Sequences Based on Fields of Odd Characteristic," *Journal of Cryptology*, v. 7, n. 1, 1994, pp. 33–52.

843. A. Klapper, "Feedback with Carry Shift Registers over Finite Fields," *K.U. Leuven Workshop on Cryptographic Algorithms*, Springer-Verlag, 1995, to appear.

844. A. Klapper and M. Goresky, "2-adic Shift Registers," *Fast Software Encryption, Cambridge Security Workshop Proceedings*, Springer-Verlag, 1994, pp. 174–178.

845. A. Klapper and M. Goresky, "2-adic Shift Registers," Technical Report #239-93, Department of Computer Science, University of Kentucky, 19 Apr 1994.

846. A. Klapper and M. Goresky, "Large Period Nearly de Bruijn FCSR Sequences," *Advances in Cryptology—EUROCRYPT '95 Proceedings*, Springer-Verlag, 1995, pp. 263–273.

847. D.V. Klein, " 'Foiling the Cracker': A Survey of, and Implications to, Password Security," *Proceedings of the USENIX UNIX Security Workshop*, Aug 1990, pp. 5–14.

848. D.V. Klein, personal communication, 1994.

849. C.S. Kline and G.J. Popek, "Public Key vs. Conventional Key Cryptosystems," *Pro-*

ceedings of AFIPS National Computer Conference, pp. 831–837.

850. H.-J. Knobloch, "A Smart Card Implementation of the Fiat-Shamir Identification Scheme," Advances in Cryptology—EUROCRPYT '88 Proceedings, Springer-Verlag, 1988, pp. 87–95.

851. T. Knoph, J. Frößl, W. Beller, and T. Giesler, "A Hardware Implementation of a Modified DES Algorithm," Microprocessing and Microprogramming, v. 30, 1990, pp. 59–66.

852. L.R. Knudsen, "Cryptanalysis of LOKI," Advances in Cryptology—ASIACRYPT '91 Proceedings, Springer-Verlag, 1993, pp. 22–35.

853. L.R. Knudsen, "Cryptanalysis of LOKI," Cryptography and Coding III, M.J. Ganley, ed., Oxford: Clarendon Press, 1993, pp. 223–236.

854. L.R. Knudsen, "Cryptanalysis of LOKI91," Advances in Cryptology—AUSCRYPT '92 Proceedings, Springer-Verlag, 1993, pp. 196–208.

855. L.R. Knudsen, "Iterative Characteristics of DES and s^2DES," Advances in Cryptology—CRYPTO '92, Springer-Verlag, 1993, pp. 497–511.

856. L.R. Knudsen, "An Analysis of Kim, Park, and Lee's DES-Like S-Boxes," unpublished manuscript, 1993.

857. L.R. Knudsen, "Practically Secure Feistel Ciphers," Fast Software Encryption, Cambridge Security Workshop Proceedings, Springer-Verlag, 1994, pp. 211–221.

858. L.R. Knudsen, "Block Ciphers—Analysis, Design, Applications," Ph.D. dissertation, Aarhus University, Nov 1994.

859. L.R. Knudsen, personal communication, 1994.

860. L.R. Knudsen, "Applications of Higher Order Differentials and Partial Differentials," K.U. Leuven Workshop on Cryptographic Algorithms, Springer-Verlag, 1995, to appear.

861. L.R. Knudsen and X. Lai, "New Attacks on All Double Block Length Hash Functions of Hash Rate 1, Including the Parallel-DM," Advances in Cryptology—EUROCRYPT '94 Proceedings, Springer-Verlag, 1995, to appear.

862. L.R. Knudsen, "A Weakness in SAFER K-64," Advances in Cryptology–CRYPTO

'95 Proceedings, Springer-Verlag, 1995, to appear.

863. D. Knuth, The Art of Computer Programming: Volume 2, Seminumerical Algorithms, 2nd edition, Addison-Wesley, 1981.

864. D. Knuth, "Deciphering a Linear Congruential Encryption," IEEE Transactions on Information Theory, v. IT-31, n. 1, Jan 1985, pp. 49–52.

865. K. Kobayashi and L. Aoki, "On Linear Cryptanalysis of MBAL," Proceedings of the 1995 Symposium on Cryptography and Information Security (SCIS 95), Inuyama, Japan, 24–27 Jan 1995, pp. A4.2.1–9.

866. K. Kobayashi, K. Tamura, and Y. Nemoto, "Two-dimensional Modified Rabin Cryptosystem," Transactions of the Institute of Electronics, Information, and Communication Engineers, v. J72-D, n. 5, May 1989, pp. 850–851. (In Japanese.)

867. N. Koblitz, "Elliptic Curve Cryptosystems," Mathematics of Computation, v. 48, n. 177, 1987, pp. 203–209.

868. N. Koblitz, "A Family of Jacobians Suitable for Discrete Log Cryptosystems," Advances in Cryptology—CRYPTO '88 Proceedings, Springer-Verlag, 1990, pp. 94–99.

869. N. Koblitz, "Constructing Elliptic Curve Cryptosystems in Characteristic 2," Advances in Cryptology—CRYPTO '90 Proceedings, Springer-Verlag, 1991, pp. 156–167.

870. N. Koblitz, "Hyperelliptic Cryptosystems," Journal of Cryptology, v. 1, n. 3, 1989, pp. 129–150.

871. N. Koblitz, "CM-Curves with Good Cryptographic Properties," Advances in Cryptology—CRYPTO '91 Proceedings, Springer-Verlag, 1992, pp. 279–287.

872. Ç.K. Koç, "High-Speed RSA Implementation," Version 2.0, RSA Laboratories, Nov 1994.

873. M.J. Kochanski, "Remarks on Lu and Lee's Proposals," Cryptologia, v. 4, n. 4, 1980, pp. 204–207.

874. M.J. Kochanski, "Developing an RSA Chip," Advances in Cryptology—CRYPTO '85 Proceedings, Springer-Verlag, 1986, pp. 350–357.

875. J.T. Kohl, "The Use of Encryption in Kerberos for Network Authentication," Advances in Cryptology—CRYPTO '89 Proceedings, Springer-Verlag, 1990, pp. 35–43.

876. J.T. Kohl, "The Evolution of the Kerberos Authentication Service," *EurOpen Conference Proceedings*, May 1991, pp. 295–313.

877. J.T. Kohl and B.C. Neuman, "The Kerberos Network Authentication Service," RFC 1510, Sep 1993.

878. J.T. Kohl, B.C. Neuman, and T. Ts'o, "The Evolution of the Kerberos Authentication System," *Distributed Open Systems*, IEEE Computer Society Press, 1994, pp. 78–94.

879. Kohnfelder, "Toward a Practical Public Key Cryptosystem," Bachelor's thesis, MIT Department of Electrical Engineering, May 1978.

880. A.G. Konheim, *Cryptography: A Primer*, New York: John Wiley & Sons, 1981.

881. A.G. Konheim, M.H. Mack, R.K. McNeill, B. Tuckerman, and G. Waldbaum, "The IPS Cryptographic Programs," *IBM Systems Journal*, v. 19, n. 2, 1980, pp. 253–283.

882. V.I. Korzhik and A.I. Turkin, "Cryptanalysis of McEliece's Public-Key Cryptosystem," *Advances in Cryptology—EUROCRYPT '91 Proceedings*, Springer-Verlag, 1991, pp. 68–70.

883. S.C. Kothari, "Generalized Linear Threshold Scheme," *Advances in Cryptology: Proceedings of CRYPTO 84*, Springer-Verlag, 1985, pp. 231–241.

884. J. Kowalchuk, B.P. Schanning, and S. Powers, "Communication Privacy: Integration of Public and Secret Key Cryptography," *Proceedings of the National Telecommunication Conference*, IEEE Press, 1980, pp. 49.1.1–49.1.5.

885. K. Koyama, "A Master Key for the RSA Public-Key Cryptosystem," *Transactions of the Institute of Electronics, Information, and Communication Engineers*, v. J65-D, n. 2, Feb 1982, pp. 163–170.

886. K. Koyama, "A Cryptosystem Using the Master Key for Multi-Address Communications," *Transactions of the Institute of Electronics, Information, and Communication Engineers*, v. J65-D, n. 9, Sep 1982, pp. 1151–1158.

887. K. Koyama, "Demonstrating Membership of a Group Using the Shizuya-Koyama-Itoh (SKI) Protocol," *Proceedings of the 1989 Symposium on Cryptography and Information Security (SCIS 89)*, Gotenba, Japan, 1989.

888. K. Koyama, "Direct Demonstration of the Power to Break Public-Key Cryptosystems," *Advances in Cryptology—AUSCRYPT '90 Proceedings*, Springer-Verlag, 1990, pp. 14–21.

889. K. Koyama, "Security and Unique Decipherability of Two-dimensional Public Key Cryptosystems," *Transactions of the Institute of Electronics, Information, and Communication Engineers*, v. E73, n. 7, Jul 1990, pp. 1057–1067.

890. K. Koyama, U.M. Maurer, T. Okamoto, and S.A. Vanstone, "New Public-Key Schemes Based on Elliptic Curves over the Ring Z_n," *Advances in Cryptology—CRYPTO '91 Proceedings*, Springer-Verlag, 1992, pp. 252–266.

891. K. Koyama and K. Ohta, "Identity-based Conference Key Distribution System," *Advances in Cryptology—CRYPTO '87 Proceedings*, Springer-Verlag, 1988, pp. 175–184.

892. K. Koyama and T. Okamoto, "Elliptic Curve Cryptosystems and Their Applications," *IEICE Transactions on Information and Systems*, v. E75-D, n. 1, Jan 1992, pp. 50–57.

893. K. Koyama and R. Terada, "How to Strengthen DES-Like Cryptosystems against Differential Cryptanalysis," *Transactions of the Institute of Electronics, Information, and Communication Engineers*, v. E76-A, n. 1, Jan 1993, pp. 63–69.

894. K. Koyama and R. Terada, "Probabilistic Swapping Schemes to Strengthen DES against Differential Cryptanalysis," *Proceedings of the 1993 Symposium on Cryptography and Information Security (SCIS 93)*, Shuzenji, Japan, 28–30 Jan 1993, pp. 15D.1–12.

895. K. Koyama and Y. Tsuruoka, "Speeding up Elliptic Cryptosystems Using a Singled Binary Window Method," *Advances in Cryptology—CRYPTO '92 Proceedings*, Springer-Verlag, 1993, pp. 345–357.

896. E. Kranakis, *Primality and Cryptography*, Wiler-Teubner Series in Computer Science, 1986.

897. D. Kravitz, "Digital Signature Algorithm," U.S. Patent #5,231,668, 27 Jul 1993.

898. D. Kravitz and I. Reed, "Extension of RSA Cryptostructure: A Galois Approach," *Electronics Letters*, v. 18, n. 6, 18 Mar 1982, pp. 255–256.

899. H. Krawczyk, "How to Predict Congruential Generators," *Advances in Cryptology—CRYPTO '89 Proceedings*, Springer-Verlag, 1990, pp. 138–153.

900. H. Krawczyk, "How to Predict Congruential Generators," *Journal of Algorithms*, v. 13, n. 4, Dec 1992, pp. 527–545.

901. H. Krawczyk, "The Shrinking Generator: Some Practical Considerations," *Fast Software Encryption, Cambridge Security Workshop Proceedings*, Springer-Verlag, 1994, pp. 45–46.

902. G.J. Kühn, "Algorithms for Self-Synchronizing Ciphers," *Proceedings of COMSIG 88*, 1988.

903. G.J. Kühn, F. Bruwer, and W. Smit, "'n Vinnige Veeldoelige Enkripsievlokkie," *Proceedings of Infosec 90*, 1990. (In Afrikaans.)

904. S. Kullback, *Statistical Methods in Cryptanalysis*, U.S. Government Printing Office, 1935. Reprinted by Aegean Park Press, 1976.

905. P.V. Kumar, R.A. Scholtz, and L.R. Welch, "Generalized Bent Functions and their Properties," *Journal of Combinational Theory*, Series A, v. 40, n. 1, Sep 1985, pp. 90–107.

906. M. Kurosaki, T. Matsumoto, and H. Imai, "Simple Methods for Multipurpose Certification," *Proceedings of the 1989 Symposium on Cryptography and Information Security (SCIS 89)*, Gotenba, Japan, 1989.

907. M. Kurosaki, T. Matsumoto, and H. Imai, "Proving that You Belong to at Least One of the Specified Groups," *Proceedings of the 1990 Symposium on Cryptography and Information Security (SCIS 90)*, Hihondaira, Japan, 1990.

908. K. Kurosawa, "Key Changeable ID-Based Cryptosystem," *Electronics Letters*, v. 25, n. 9, 27 Apr 1989, pp. 577–578.

909. K. Kurosawa, T. Ito, and M. Takeuchi, "Public Key Cryptosystem Using a Reciprocal Number with the Same Intractability as Factoring a Large Number," *Cryptologia*, v. 12, n. 4, Oct 1988, pp. 225–233.

910. K. Kurosawa, C. Park, and K. Sakano, "Group Signer/Verifier Separation Scheme," *Proceedings of the 1995 Japan-Korea Workshop on Information Security and Cryptography*, Inuyama, Japan, 24–27 Jan 1995, 134–143.

911. G.C. Kurtz, D. Shanks, and H.C. Williams, "Fast Primality Tests for Numbers Less than $50*10^9$," *Mathematics of Computation*, v. 46, n. 174, Apr 1986, pp. 691–701.

912. K. Kusuda and T. Matsumoto, "Optimization of the Time-Memory Trade-Off Cryptanalysis and Its Application to Block Ciphers," *Proceedings of the 1995 Symposium on Cryptography and Information Security (SCIS 95)*, Inuyama, Japan, 24–27 Jan 1995, pp. A3.2.1–11. (In Japanese.)

913. H. Kuwakado and K. Koyama, "Security of RSA-Type Cryptosystems Over Elliptic Curves against Hastad Attack," *Electronics Letters*, v. 30, n. 22, 27 Oct 1994, pp. 1843–1844.

914. H. Kuwakado and K. Koyama, "A New RSA-Type Cryptosystem over Singular Elliptic Curves," *IMA Conference on Applications of Finite Fields*, Oxford University Press, to appear.

915. H. Kuwakado and K. Koyama, "A New RSA-Type Scheme Based on Singular Cubic Curves," *Proceedings of the 1995 Japan-Korea Workshop on Information Security and Cryptography*, Inuyama, Japan, 24–27 Jan 1995, pp. 144–151.

916. M. Kwan, "An Eight Bit Weakness in the LOKI Cryptosystem," technical report, Australian Defense Force Academy, Apr 1991.

917. M. Kwan and J. Pieprzyk, "A General Purpose Technique for Locating Key Scheduling Weakness in DES-Like Cryptosystems," *Advances in Cryptology—ASIACRYPT '91 Proceedings*, Springer-Verlag, 1991, pp. 237–246.

918. J.B. Lacy, D.P. Mitchell, and W.M. Schell, "CryptoLib: Cryptography in Software," *UNIX Security Symposium IV Proceedings*, USENIX Association, 1993, pp. 1–17.

919. J.C. Lagarias, "Knapsack Public Key Cryptosystems and Diophantine Approximations," *Advances in Cryptology: Proceedings of Crypto 83*, Plenum Press, 1984, pp. 3–23.

920. J.C. Lagarias, "Performance Analysis of Shamir's Attack on the Basic Merkle-Hellman Knapsack Cryptosystem," *Lecture Notes in Computer Science 172; Proceedings of the 11th International Colloquium on Automata, Languages, and Programming (ICALP)*, Springer-Verlag, 1984, pp. 312–323.

921. J.C. Lagarias and A.M. Odlyzko, "Solving Low-Density Subset Sum Problems," *Proceedings of the 24th IEEE Symposium on Foundations of Computer Science*, 1983, pp. 1–10.

922. J.C. Lagarias and A.M. Odlyzko, "Solving Low-Density Subset Sum Problems," *Journal of the ACM*, v. 32, n. 1, Jan 1985, pp. 229–246.

923. J.C. Lagarias and J. Reeds, "Unique Extrapolation of Polynomial Recurrences," *SIAM Journal on Computing*, v. 17, n. 2, Apr 1988, pp. 342–362.

924. X. Lai, *Detailed Description and a Software Implementation of the IPES Cipher*, unpublished manuscript, 8 Nov 1991.

925. X. Lai, *On the Design and Security of Block Ciphers*, ETH Series in Information Processing, v. 1, Konstanz: Hartung-Gorre Verlag, 1992.

926. X. Lai, personal communication, 1993.

927. X. Lai, "Higher Order Derivatives and Differential Cryptanalysis," *Communications and Cryptography: Two Sides of One Tapestry*, R.E. Blahut et al., eds., Kluwer Adademic Publishers, 1994, pp. 227–233.

928. X. Lai and L. Knudsen, "Attacks on Double Block Length Hash Functions," *Fast Software Encryption, Cambridge Security Workshop Proceedings*, Springer-Verlag, 1994, pp. 157–165.

929. X. Lai and J. Massey, "A Proposal for a New Block Encryption Standard," *Advances in Cryptology—EUROCRYPT '90 Proceedings*, Springer-Verlag, 1991, pp. 389–404.

930. X. Lai and J. Massey, "Hash Functions Based on Block Ciphers," *Advances in Cryptology—EUROCRYPT '92 Proceedings*, Springer-Verlag, 1992, pp. 55–70.

931. X. Lai, J. Massey, and S. Murphy, "Markov Ciphers and Differential Cryptanalysis," *Advances in Cryptology—EUROCRYPT '91 Proceedings*, Springer-Verlag, 1991, pp. 17–38.

932. X. Lai, R.A. Rueppel, and J. Woollven, "A Fast Cryptographic Checksum Algorithm Based on Stream Ciphers," *Advances in Cryptology—AUSCRYPT '92 Proceedings*, Springer-Verlag, 1993, pp. 339–348.

933. C.S. Laih, J.Y. Lee, C.H. Chen, and L. Harn, "A New Scheme for ID-based Cryptosystems and Signatures," *Journal of the Chinese Institute of Engineers*, v. 15, n. 2, Sep 1992, pp. 605–610.

934. B.A. LaMacchia and A.M. Odlyzko, "Computation of Discrete Logarithms in Prime Fields," *Designs, Codes, and Cryptography*, v. 1, 1991, pp. 46–62.

935. L. Lamport, "Password Identification with Insecure Communications," *Communications of the ACM*, v. 24, n. 11, Nov 1981, pp. 770–772.

936. S. Landau, "Zero-Knowledge and the Department of Defense," *Notices of the American Mathematical Society*, v. 35, n. 1, Jan 1988, pp. 5–12.

937. S. Landau, S. Kent, C. Brooks, S. Charney, D. Denning, W. Diffie, A. Lauck, D. Mikker, P. Neumann, and D. Sobel, "Codes, Keys, and Conflicts: Issues in U.S. Crypto Policy," Report of a Special Panel of the ACM U.S. Public Policy Committee (USACM), Association for Computing Machinery, Jun 1994.

938. S.K. Langford and M.E. Hellman, "Cryptanalysis of DES," presented at 1994 RSA Data Security conference, Redwood Shores, CA, 12–14 Jan 1994.

939. D. Lapidot and A. Shamir, "Publicly Verifiable Non-Interactive Zero-Knowledge Proofs," *Advances in Cryptology—CRYPTO '90 Proceedings*, Springer-Verlag, 1991, pp. 353–365.

940. A.V. Le, S.M. Matyas, D.B. Johnson, and J.D. Wilkins, "A Public-Key Extension to the Common Cryptographic Architecture," *IBM Systems Journal*, v. 32, n. 3, 1993, pp. 461–485.

941. P. L'Ecuyer, "Efficient and Portable Combined Random Number Generators," *Communications of the ACM*, v. 31, n. 6, Jun 1988, pp. 742–749, 774.

942. P. L'Ecuyer, "Random Numbers for Simulation," *Communications of the ACM*, v. 33, n. 10, Oct 1990, pp. 85–97.

943. P.J. Lee and E.F. Brickell, "An Observation on the Security of McEliece's Public-Key Cryptosystem," *Advances in Cryptology—EUROCRYPT '88 Proceedings*, Springer-Verlag, 1988, pp. 275–280.

944. S. Lee, S. Sung, and K. Kim, "An Efficient Method to Find the Linear Expressions for Linear Cryptanalysis," *Proceedings of the 1995 Korea-Japan Workshop on Information Security and Cryptography*, Inuyama, Japan, 24–26 Jan 1995, pp. 183–190.

945. D.J. Lehmann, "On Primality Tests," *SIAM Journal on Computing*, v. 11, n. 2, May 1982, pp. 374–375.

946. T. Leighton, "Failsafe Key Escrow Systems," Technical Memo 483, MIT Laboratory for Computer Science, Aug 1994.

947. A. Lempel and M. Cohn, "Maximal Families of Bent Sequences," *IEEE Transactions on Information Theory*, v. IT-28, n. 6, Nov 1982, pp. 865–868.

948. A.K. Lenstra, "Factoring Multivariate Polynomials Over Finite Fields," *Journal of Computer System Science*, v. 30, n. 2, Apr 1985, pp. 235–248.

949. A.K. Lenstra, personal communication, 1995.

950. A.K. Lenstra and S. Haber, letter to NIST Regarding DSS, 26 Nov 1991.

951. A.K. Lenstra, H.W. Lenstra Jr., and L. Lovácz, "Factoring Polynomials with Rational Coefficients," *Mathematische Annalen*, v. 261, n. 4, 1982, pp. 515–534.

952. A.K. Lenstra, H.W. Lenstra, Jr., M.S. Manasse, and J.M. Pollard, "The Number Field Sieve," *Proceedings of the 22nd ACM Symposium on the Theory of Computing*, 1990, pp. 574–572.

953. A.K. Lenstra and H.W. Lenstra, Jr., eds., *Lecture Notes in Mathematics 1554: The Development of the Number Field Sieve*, Springer-Verlag, 1993.

954. A.K. Lenstra, H.W. Lenstra, Jr., M.S. Manasse, and J.M. Pollard, "The Factorization of the Ninth Fermat Number," *Mathematics of Computation*, v. 61, n. 203, 1993, pp. 319–349.

955. A.K. Lenstra and M.S. Manasse, "Factoring by Electronic Mail," *Advances in Cryptology—EUROCRYPT '89 Proceedings*, Springer-Verlag, 1990, pp. 355–371.

956. A.K. Lenstra and M.S. Manasse, "Factoring with Two Large Primes," *Advances in Cryptology—EUROCRYPT '90 Proceedings*, Springer-Verlag, 1991, pp. 72–82.

957. H.W. Lenstra Jr. "Elliptic Curves and Number-Theoretic Algorithms," Report 86-19, Mathematisch Instituut, Universiteit van Amsterdam, 1986.

958. H.W. Lenstra Jr. "On the Chor-Rivest Knapsack Cryptosystem," *Journal of Cryptology*, v. 3, n. 3, 1991, pp. 149–155.

959. W.J. LeVeque, *Fundamentals of Number Theory*, Addison-Wesley, 1977.

960. L.A. Levin, "One-Way Functions and Pseudo-Random Generators," *Proceedings of the 17th ACM Symposium on Theory of Computing*, 1985, pp. 363–365.

961. Lexar Corporation, "An Evaluation of the DES," Sep 1976.

962. D.-X. Li, "Cryptanalysis of Public-Key Distribution Systems Based on Dickson Polynomials," *Electronics Letters*, v. 27, n. 3, 1991, pp. 228–229.

963. F.-X. Li, "How to Break Okamoto's Cryptosystems by Continued Fraction Algorithm," *ASIACRYPT '91 Abstracts*, 1991, pp. 285–289.

964. Y.X. Li and X.M. Wang, "A Joint Authentication and Encryption Scheme Based on Algebraic Coding Theory," *Applied Algebra, Algebraic Algorithms and Error Correcting Codes 9*, Springer-Verlag, 1991, pp. 241–245.

965. R. Lidl, G.L. Mullen, and G. Turwald, *Pitman Monographs and Surveys in Pure and Applied Mathematics 65: Dickson Polynomials*, London: Longman Scientific and Technical, 1993.

966. R. Lidl and W.B. Müller, "Permutation Polynomials in RSA-Cryptosystems," *Advances in Cryptology: Proceedings of Crypto 83*, Plenum Press, 1984, pp. 293–301.

967. R. Lidl and W.B. Müller, "Generalizations of the Fibonacci Pseudoprimes Test," *Discrete Mathematics*, v. 92, 1991, pp. 211–220.

968. R. Lidl and W.B. Müller, "Primality Testing with Lucas Functions," *Advances in Cryptology—AUSCRYPT '92 Proceedings*, Springer-Verlag, 1993, pp. 539–542.

969. R. Lidl, W.B. Müller, and A. Oswald, "Some Remarks on Strong Fibonacci Pseudoprimes," *Applicable Algebra in Engineering, Communication and Computing*, v. 1, n. 1, 1990, pp. 59–65.

970. R. Lidl and H. Niederreiter, "Finite Fields," *Encyclopedia of Mathematics and its Applications*, v. 20, Addison-Wesley, 1983.

971. R. Lidl and H. Niederreiter, *Introduction to Finite Fields and Their Applications*, London: Cambridge University Press, 1986.

972. K. Lieberherr, "Uniform Complexity and Digital Signatures," *Theoretical Computer Science*, v. 16, n. 1, Oct 1981, pp. 99–110.

973. C.H. Lim and P.J. Lee, "A Practical Electronic Cash System for Smart Cards," *Proceedings of the 1993 Korea-Japan Workshop on Information Security and Cryptography*, Seoul, Korea, 24–26 Oct 1993, pp. 34–47.

974. C.H. Lim and P.J. Lee, "Security of Interactive DSA Batch Verification," *Electronics Letters*, v. 30, n. 19, 15 Sep 1994, pp. 1592–1593.

975. H.-Y. Lin and L. Harn, "A Generalized Secret Sharing Scheme with Cheater Detection," *Advances in Cryptology—ASIACRYPT '91 Proceedings*, Springer-Verlag, 1993, pp. 149–158.

976. M.-C. Lin, T.-C. Chang, and H.-L. Fu, "Information Rate of McEliece's Public-key Cryptosystem," *Electronics Letters*, v. 26, n. 1, 4 Jan 1990, pp. 16–18.

977. J. Linn, "Privacy Enhancement for Internet Electronic Mail: Part I—Message Encipherment and Authentication Procedures," RFC 989, Feb 1987.

978. J. Linn, "Privacy Enhancement for Internet Electronic Mail: Part I—Message Encipherment and Authentication Procedures," RFC 1040, Jan 1988.

979. J. Linn, "Privacy Enhancement for Internet Electronic Mail: Part I—Message Encipherment and Authentication Procedures," RFC 1113, Aug 1989.

980. J. Linn, "Privacy Enhancement for Internet Electronic Mail: Part III—Algorithms, Modes, and Identifiers," RFC 1115, Aug 1989.

981. J. Linn, "Privacy Enhancement for Internet Electronic Mail: Part I—Message Encipherment and Authentication Procedures," RFC 1421, Feb 1993.

982. S. Lloyd, "Counting Binary Functions with Certain Cryptographic Properties," *Journal of Cryptology*, v. 5, n. 2, 1992, pp. 107–131.

983. T.M.A. Lomas, "Collision-Freedom, Considered Harmful, or How to Boot a Computer," *Proceedings of the 1995 Korea-Japan Workshop on Information Security and Cryptography*, Inuyama, Japan, 24–26 Jan 1995, pp. 35–42.

984. T.M.A. Lomas and M. Roe, "Forging a Clipper Message," *Communications of the ACM*, v. 37, n. 12, 1994, p. 12.

985. D.L. Long, "The Security of Bits in the Discrete Logarithm," Ph.D. dissertation, Princeton University, Jan 1984.

986. D.L. Long and A. Wigderson, "How Discrete Is the Discrete Log," *Proceedings of the 15th Annual ACM Syposium on the Theory of Computing*, Apr 1983.

987. D. Longley and S. Rigby, "An Automatic Search for Security Flaws in Key Management Schemes," *Computers and Security*, v. 11, n. 1, Jan 1992. pp. 75–89.

988. S.H. Low, N.F. Maxemchuk, and S. Paul, "Anonymous Credit Cards," *Proceedings of the 2nd Annual ACM Conference on Computer and Communications Security*, ACM Press, 1994, pp. 108–117.

989. J.H. Loxton, D.S.P. Khoo, G.J. Bird, and J. Seberry, "A Cubic RSA Code Equivalent to Factorization," *Journal of Cryptology*, v. 5, n. 2, 1992, pp. 139–150.

990. S.C. Lu and L.N. Lee, "A Simple and Effective Public-Key Cryptosystem," *COMSAT Technical Review*, 1979, pp. 15–24.

991. M. Luby, S. Micali, and C. Rackoff, "How to Simultaneously Exchange a Secret Bit by Flipping a Symmetrically-Biased Coin," *Proceedings of the 24nd Annual Symposium on the Foundations of Computer Science*, 1983, pp. 11–22.

992. M. Luby and C. Rackoff, "How to Construct Pseudo-Random Permutations from Pseudorandom Functions," *SIAM Journal on Computing*, Apr 1988, pp. 373–386.

993. F. Luccio and S. Mazzone, "A Cryptosystem for Multiple Communications," *Information Processing Letters*, v. 10, 1980, pp. 180–183.

994. V. Luchangco and K. Koyama, "An Attack on an ID-Based Key Sharing System, *Proceedings of the 1993 Korea-Japan Workshop on Information Security and Cryptography*, Seoul, Korea, 24–26 Oct 1993, pp. 262–271.

995. D.J.C. MacKay, "A Free Energy Minimization Framework for Inferring the State of a Shift Register Given the Noisy Output Sequence," *K.U. Leuven Workshop on Cryptographic Algorithms*, Springer-Verlag, 1995, to appear.

996. M.D. MacLaren and G. Marsaglia, "Uniform Random Number Generators," *Journal of the ACM* v. 12, n. 1, Jan 1965, pp. 83–89.

997. D. MacMillan, "Single Chip Encrypts Data at 14Mb/s," *Electronics*, v. 54, n. 12, 16 June 1981, pp. 161–165.

998. R. Madhavan and L.E. Peppard, "A Multiprocessor GaAs RSA Cryptosystem," *Proceedings CCVLSI-89: Canadian Conference on Very Large Scale Integration*, Vancouver, BC, Canada, 22–24 Oct 1989, pp. 115–122.

999. W.E. Madryga, "A High Performance Encryption Algorithm," *Computer Security: A Global Challenge*, Elsevier Science Publishers, 1984, pp. 557–570.

1000. M. Mambo, A. Nishikawa, S. Tsujii, and E. Okamoto, "Efficient Secure Broadcast

Communication System," *Proceedings of the 1993 Korea-Japan Workshop on Information Security and Cryptography*, Seoul, Korea, 24–26 Oct 1993, pp. 23–33.

1001. M. Mambo, K. Usuda, and E. Okamoto, "Proxy Signatures," *Proceedings of the 1995 Symposium on Cryptography and Information Security (SCIS 95)*, Inuyama, Japan, 24–27 Jan 1995, pp. B1.1.1–17.

1002. W. Mao and C. Boyd, "Towards Formal Analysis of Security Protocols," *Proceedings of the Computer Security Foundations Workshop VI*, IEEE Computer Society Press, 1993, pp. 147–158.

1003. G. Marsaglia and T.A. Bray, "On-Line Random Number Generators and their Use in Combinations," *Communications of the ACM*, v. 11, n. 11, Nov 1968, p. 757–759.

1004. K.M. Martin, "Untrustworthy Participants in Perfect Secret Sharing Schemes," *Cryptography and Coding III*, M.J. Ganley, ed., Oxford: Clarendon Press, 1993, pp. 255–264.

1005. J.L. Massey, "Shift-Register Synthesis and BCH Decoding," *IEEE Transactions on Information Theory*, v. IT-15, n. 1, Jan 1969, pp. 122–127.

1006. J.L. Massey, "Cryptography and System Theory," *Proceedings of the 24th Allerton Conference on Communication, Control, and Computers*, 1–3 Oct 1986, pp. 1–8.

1007. J.L. Massey, "An Introduction to Contemporary Cryptology," *Proceedings of the IEEE*, v. 76, n. 5., May 1988, pp. 533–549.

1008. J.L. Massey, "Contemporary Cryptology: An Introduction," in *Contemporary Cryptology: The Science of Information Integrity*, G.J. Simmons, ed., IEEE Press, 1992, pp. 1–39.

1009. J.L. Massey, "SAFER K-64: A Byte-Oriented Block-Ciphering Algorithm," *Fast Software Encryption, Cambridge Security Workshop Proceedings*, Springer-Verlag, 1994, pp. 1–17.

1010. J.L. Massey, "SAFER K-64: One Year Later," *K.U. Leuven Workshop on Cryptographic Algorithms*, Springer-Verlag, 1995, to appear.

1011. J.L. Massey and I. Ingemarsson, "The Rip Van Winkle Cipher—A Simple and Provably Computationally Secure Cipher with a Finite Key," *IEEE International Symposium on Information Theory*, Brighton, UK, May 1985.

1012. J.L. Massey and X. Lai, "Device for Converting a Digital Block and the Use Thereof," International Patent PCT/CH91/00117, 28 Nov 1991.

1013. J.L. Massey and X. Lai, "Device for the Conversion of a Digital Block and Use of Same," U.S. Patent #5,214,703, 25 May 1993.

1014. J.L. Massey and R.A. Rueppel, "Linear Ciphers and Random Sequence Generators with Multiple Clocks," *Advances in Cryptology: Proceedings of EUROCRYPT 84*, Springer-Verlag, 1985, pp. 74–87.

1015. M. Matsui, "Linear Cryptanalysis Method for DES Cipher," *Advances in Cryptology—EUROCRYPT '93 Proceedings*, Springer-Verlag, 1994, pp. 386–397.

1016. M. Matsui, "Linear Cryptanalysis of DES Cipher (I)," *Proceedings of the 1993 Symposium on Cryptography and Information Security (SCIS 93)*, Shuzenji, Japan, 28–30 Jan 1993, pp. 3C.1–14. (In Japanese.)

1017. M. Matsui, "Linear Cryptanalysis Method for DES Cipher (III)," *Proceedings of the 1994 Symposium on Cryptography and Information Security (SCIS 94)*, Lake Biwa, Japan, 27–29 Jan 1994, pp. 4A.1–11. (In Japanese.)

1018. M. Matsui, "On Correlation Between the Order of the S-Boxes and the Strength of DES," *Advances in Cryptology—EUROCRYPT '94 Proceedings*, Springer-Verlag, 1995, to appear.

1019. M. Matsui, "The First Experimental Cryptanalysis of the Data Encryption Standard," *Advances in Cryptology—CRYPTO '94 Proceedings*, Springer-Verlag, 1994, pp. 1–11.

1020. M. Matsui and A. Yamagishi, "A New Method for Known Plaintext Attack of FEAL Cipher," *Advances in Cryptology—EUROCRYPT '92 Proceedings*, Springer-Verlag, 1993, pp. 81–91.

1021. T. Matsumoto and H. Imai, "A Class of Asymmetric Crypto-Systems Based on Polynomials Over Finite Rings," *IEEE International Symposium on Information Theory*, 1983, pp. 131–132.

1022. T. Matsumoto and H. Imai, "On the Key Production System: A Practical Solution to the Key Distribution Problem," *Advances in Cryptology—CRYPTO '87 Proceedings*, Springer-Verlag, 1988, pp. 185–193.

1023. T. Matsumoto and H. Imai, "On the Security of Some Key Sharing Schemes (Part

2)," IEICE Japan, Technical Report, ISEC90-28, 1990.

1024. S.M. Matyas, "Digital Signatures—An Overview," *Computer Networks*, v. 3, n. 2, Apr 1979, pp. 87–94.

1025. S.M. Matyas, "Key Handling with Control Vectors," *IBM Systems Journal*, v. 30, n. 2, 1991, pp. 151–174.

1026. S.M. Matyas, A.V. Le, and D.G. Abraham, "A Key Management Scheme Based on Control Vectors," *IBM Systems Journal*, v. 30, n. 2, 1991, pp. 175–191.

1027. S.M. Matyas and C.H. Meyer, "Generation, Distribution, and Installation of Cryptographic Keys," *IBM Systems Journal*, v. 17, n. 2, 1978, pp. 126–137.

1028. S.M. Matyas, C.H. Meyer, and J. Oseas, "Generating Strong One-Way Functions with Cryptographic Algorithm," *IBM Technical Disclosure Bulletin*, v. 27, n. 10A, Mar 1985, pp. 5658–5659.

1029. U.M. Maurer, "Provable Security in Cryptography," Ph.D. dissertation, ETH No. 9260, Swiss Federal Institute of Technology, Zürich, 1990.

1030. U.M. Maurer, "A Provable-Secure Strongly-Randomized Cipher," *Advances in Cryptology—EUROCRYPT '90 Proceedings*, Springer-Verlag, 1990, pp. 361–373.

1031. U.M. Maurer, "A Universal Statistical Test for Random Bit Generators," *Advances in Cryptology—CRYPTO '90 Proceedings*, Springer-Verlag, 1991, pp. 409–420.

1032. U.M. Maurer, "A Universal Statistical Test for Random Bit Generators," *Journal of Cryptology*, v. 5, n. 2, 1992, pp. 89–106.

1033. U.M. Maurer and J.L. Massey, "Cascade Ciphers: The Importance of Being First," *Journal of Cryptology*, v. 6, n. 1, 1993, pp. 55–61.

1034. U.M. Maurer and J.L. Massey, "Perfect Local Randomness in Pseudo-Random Sequences," *Advances in Cryptology—CRYPTO '89 Proceedings*, Springer-Verlag, 1990, pp. 110–112.

1035. U.M. Maurer and Y. Yacobi, "Non-interactive Public Key Cryptography," *Advances in Cryptology—EUROCRYPT '91 Proceedings*, Springer-Verlag, 1991, pp. 498–507.

1036. G. Mayhew, "A Low Cost, High Speed Encryption System and Method," *Proceed-ings of the 1994 IEEE Computer Society Symposium on Research in Security and Privacy*, 1994, pp. 147–154.

1037. G. Mayhew, R. Frazee, and M. Bianco, "The Kinetic Protection Device," *Proceedings of the 15th National Computer Security Conference*, NIST, 1994, pp. 147–154.

1038. K.S. McCurley, "A Key Distribution System Equivalent to Factoring," *Journal of Cryptology*, v. 1, n. 2, 1988, pp. 95–106.

1039. K.S. McCurley, "The Discrete Logarithm Problem," *Cryptography and Computational Number Theory* (*Proceedings of the Symposium on Applied Mathematics*), American Mathematics Society, 1990, pp. 49–74.

1040. K.S. McCurley, open letter from the Sandia National Laboratories on the DSA of the NIST, 7 Nov 1991.

1041. R.J. McEliece, "A Public-Key Cryptosystem Based on Algebraic Coding Theory," Deep Space Network Progress Report 42–44, Jet Propulsion Laboratory, California Institute of Technology, 1978, pp. 114–116.

1042. R.J. McEliece, *Finite Fields for Computer Scientists and Engineers*, Boston: Kluwer Academic Publishers, 1987.

1043. P. McMahon, "SESAME V2 Public Key and Authorization Extensions to Kerberos," *Proceedings of the Internet Society 1995 Symposium on Network and Distributed Systems Security*, IEEE Computer Society Press, 1995, pp. 114–131.

1044. C.A. Meadows, "A System for the Specification and Analysis of Key Management Protocols," *Proceedings of the 1991 IEEE Computer Society Symposium on Research in Security and Privacy*, 1991, pp. 182–195.

1045. C.A. Meadows, "Applying Formal Methods to the Analysis of a Key Management Protocol," *Journal of Computer Security*, v. 1, n. 1, 1992, pp. 5–35.

1046. C.A. Meadows, "A Model of Computation for the NRL Protocol Analyzer," *Proceedings of the Computer Security Foundations Workshop VII*, IEEE Computer Society Press, 1994, pp. 84–89.

1047. C.A. Meadows, "Formal Verification of Cryptographic Protocols: A Survey," *Advances in Cryptology—ASIACRYPT '94 Proceedings*, Springer-Verlag, 1995, pp. 133–150.

1048. G. Medvinsky and B.C. Neuman, "Net-Cash: A Design for Practical Electronic Currency on the Internet," *Proceedings of the 1st Annual ACM Conference on Computer and Communications Security*, ACM Press, 1993, pp. 102–106.

1049. G. Medvinsky and B.C. Neuman, "Electronic Currency for the Internet," *Electronic Markets*, v. 3, n. 9/10, Oct 1993, pp. 23–24.

1050. W. Meier, "On the Security of the IDEA Block Cipher," *Advances in Cryptology—EUROCRYPT '93 Proceedings*, Springer-Verlag, 1994, pp. 371–385.

1051. W. Meier and O. Staffelbach, "Fast Correlation Attacks on Stream Ciphers," *Journal of Cryptology*, v. 1, n. 3, 1989, pp. 159–176.

1052. W. Meier and O. Staffelbach, "Analysis of Pseudo Random Sequences Generated by Cellular Automata," *Advances in Cryptology—EUROCRYPT '91 Proceedings*, Springer-Verlag, 1991, pp. 186–199.

1053. W. Meier and O. Staffelbach, "Correlation Properties of Combiners with Memory in Stream Ciphers," *Advances in Cryptology—EUROCRYPT '90 Proceedings*, Springer-Verlag, 1991, pp. 204–213.

1054. W. Meier and O. Staffelbach, "Correlation Properties of Combiners with Memory in Stream Ciphers," *Journal of Cryptology*, v. 5, n. 1, 1992, pp. 67–86.

1055. W. Meier and O. Staffelbach, "The Self-Shrinking Generator," *Communications and Cryptography: Two Sides of One Tapestry*, R.E. Blahut et al., eds., Kluwer Adademic Publishers, 1994, pp. 287–295.

1056. J. Meijers, "Algebraic-Coded Cryptosystems," Master's thesis, Technical University Eindhoven, 1990.

1057. J. Meijers and J. van Tilburg, "On the Rao-Nam Private-Key Cryptosystem Using Linear Codes," *International Symposium on Information Theory*, Budapest, Hungary, 1991.

1058. J. Meijers and J. van Tilburg, "An Improved ST-Attack on the Rao-Nam Private-Key Cryptosystem," *International Conference on Finite Fields, Coding Theory, and Advances in Communications and Computing*, Las Vegas, NV, 1991.

1059. A. Menezes, *Elliptic Curve Public Key Cryptosystems*, Kluwer Academic Publishers, 1993.

1060. A. Menezes, ed., *Applications of Finite Fields*, Kluwer Academic Publishers, 1993.

1061. A. Menezes and S.A. Vanstone, "Elliptic Curve Cryptosystems and Their Implementations," *Journal of Cryptology*, v. 6, n. 4, 1993, pp. 209–224.

1062. A. Menezes and S.A. Vanstone, "The Implementation of Elliptic Curve Cryptosystems," *Advances in Cryptology—AUSCRYPT '90 Proceedings*, Springer-Verlag, 1990, pp. 2–13.

1063. R. Menicocci, "Short Gollmann Cascade Generators May Be Insecure," *Codes and Ciphers*, Institute of Mathematics and its Applications, 1995, pp. 281–297.

1064. R.C. Merkle, "Secure Communication Over Insecure Channels," *Communications of the ACM*, v. 21, n. 4, 1978, pp. 294–299.

1065. R.C. Merkle, "Secrecy, Authentication, and Public Key Systems," Ph.D. dissertation, Stanford University, 1979.

1066. R.C. Merkle, "Method of Providing Digital Signatures," U.S. Patent #4,309,569, 5 Jan 1982.

1067. R.C. Merkle, "A Digital Signature Based on a Conventional Encryption Function," *Advances in Cryptology—CRYPTO '87 Proceedings*, Springer-Verlag, 1988, pp. 369–378.

1068. R.C. Merkle, "A Certified Digital Signature," *Advances in Cryptology—CRYPTO '89 Proceedings*, Springer-Verlag, 1990, pp. 218–238.

1069. R.C. Merkle, "One Way Hash Functions and DES," *Advances in Cryptology—CRYPTO '89 Proceedings*, Springer-Verlag, 1990, pp. 428–446.

1070. R.C. Merkle, "A Fast Software One-Way Hash Function," *Journal of Cryptology*, v. 3, n. 1, 1990, pp. 43–58.

1071. R.C. Merkle, "Fast Software Encryption Functions," *Advances in Cryptology—CRYPTO '90 Proceedings*, Springer-Verlag, 1991, pp. 476–501.

1072. R.C. Merkle, "Method and Apparatus for Data Encryption," U.S. Patent #5,003,597, 26 Mar 1991.

1073. R.C. Merkle, personal communication, 1993.

1074. R.C. Merkle and M. Hellman, "Hiding Information and Signatures in Trapdoor Knapsacks," *IEEE Transactions on Infor-*

mation Theory, v. 24, n. 5, Sep 1978, pp. 525–530.

1075. R.C. Merkle and M. Hellman, "On the Security of Multiple Encryption," *Communications of the ACM*, v. 24, n. 7, 1981, pp. 465–467.

1076. M. Merritt, "Cryptographic Protocols," Ph.D. dissertation, Georgia Institute of Technology, GIT-ICS-83/6, Feb 1983.

1077. M. Merritt, "Towards a Theory of Cryptographic Systems: A Critique of Crypto-Complexity," *Distributed Computing and Cryptography*, J. Feigenbaum and M. Merritt, eds., American Mathematical Society, 1991, pp. 203–212.

1078. C.H. Meyer, "Ciphertext/Plaintext and Ciphertext/Key Dependencies vs. Number of Rounds for Data Encryption Standard," *AFIPS Conference Proceedings*, 47, 1978, pp. 1119–1126.

1079. C.H. Meyer, "Cryptography—A State of the Art Review," *Proceedings of Compeuro '89, VLSI and Computer Peripherals, 3rd Annual European Computer Conference*, IEEE Press, 1989, pp. 150–154.

1080. C.H. Meyer and S.M. Matyas, *Cryptography: A New Dimension in Computer Data Security*, New York: John Wiley & Sons, 1982.

1081. C.H. Meyer and M. Schilling, "Secure Program Load with Manipulation Detection Code," *Proceedings of Securicom '88*, 1988, pp. 111–130.

1082. C.H. Meyer and W.L. Tuchman, "Pseudo-Random Codes Can Be Cracked," *Electronic Design*, v. 23, Nov 1972.

1083. C.H. Meyer and W.L. Tuchman, "Design Considerations for Cryptography," *Proceedings of the NCC*, v. 42, Montvale, NJ: AFIPS Press, Nov 1979, pp. 594–597.

1084. S. Micali, "Fair Public-Key Cryptosystems," *Advances in Cryptology—CRYPTO '92 Proceedings*, Springer-Verlag, 1993, pp. 113–138.

1085. S. Micali, "Fair Cryptosystems," MIT/LCS/TR-579.b, MIT Laboratory for Computer Science, Nov 1993.

1086. S. Micali, "Fair Cryptosystems and Methods for Use," U.S. Patent #5,276,737, 4 Jan 1994.

1087. S. Micali, "Fair Cryptosystems and Methods for Use," U.S. Patent #5,315,658, 24 May 1994.

1088. S. Micali and A. Shamir, "An Improvement on the Fiat-Shamir Identification and Signature Scheme," *Advances in Cryptology—CRYPTO '88 Proceedings*, Springer-Verlag, 1990, pp. 244–247.

1089. M.J. Mihajlević, "A Correlation Attack on the Binary Sequence Generators with Time-Varying Output Function," *Advances in Cryptology—ASIACRYPT '94 Proceedings*, Springer-Verlag, 1995, pp. 67–79.

1090. M.J. Mihajlević and J.D. Golić, "A Fast Iterative Algorithm for a Shift Register Internal State Reconstruction Given the Noisy Output Sequence," *Advances in Cryptology—AUSCRYPT '90 Proceedings*, Springer-Verlag, 1990, pp. 165–175.

1091. M.J. Mihajlević and J.D. Golić, "Convergence of a Bayesian Iterative Error-Correction Procedure to a Noisy Shift Register Sequence," *Advances in Cryptology—EUROCRYPT '92 Proceedings*, Springer-Verlag, 1993, pp. 124–137.

1092. J.K. Millen, S.C. Clark, and S.B. Freedman, "The Interrogator: Protocol Security Analysis," *IEEE Transactions on Software Engineering*, v. SE-13, n. 2, Feb 1987, pp. 274–288.

1093. G.L. Miller, "Riemann's Hypothesis and Tests for Primality," *Journal of Computer Systems Science*, v. 13, n. 3, Dec 1976, pp. 300–317.

1094. S.P. Miller, B.C. Neuman, J.I. Schiller, and J.H. Saltzer, "Section E.2.1: Kerberos Authentication and Authorization System," MIT Project Athena, Dec 1987.

1095. V.S. Miller, "Use of Elliptic Curves in Cryptography," *Advances in Cryptology—CRYPTO '85 Proceedings*, Springer-Verlag, 1986, pp. 417–426.

1096. M. Minsky, *Computation: Finite and Infinite Machines*, Englewood Cliffs, NJ: Prentice-Hall, 1967.

1097. C.J. Mitchell, "Authenticating Multi-Cast Internet Electronic Mail Messages Using a Bidirectional MAC Is Insecure," draft manuscript, 1990.

1098. C.J. Mitchell, "Enumerating Boolean Functions of Cryptographic Significance," *Journal of Cryptology*, v. 2, n. 3, 1990, pp. 155–170.

1099. C.J. Mitchell, F. Piper, and P. Wild, "Digital Signatures," *Contemporary Cryptology: The Science of Information Integrity*, G.J. Simmons, ed., IEEE Press, 1991, pp. 325–378.

1100. C.J. Mitchell, M. Walker, and D. Rush, "CCITT/ISO Standards for Secure Message

Handling," *IEEE Journal on Selected Areas in Communications*, v. 7, n. 4, May 1989, pp. 517–524.

1101. S. Miyaguchi, "Fast Encryption Algorithm for the RSA Cryptographic System," *Proceedings of Compcon 82*, IEEE Press, pp. 672–678.

1102. S. Miyaguchi, "The FEAL-8 Cryptosystem and Call for Attack," *Advances in Cryptology—CRYPTO '89 Proceedings*, Springer-Verlag, 1990, pp. 624–627.

1103. S. Miyaguchi, "Expansion of the FEAL Cipher," *NTT Review*, v. 2, n. 6, Nov 1990.

1104. S. Miyaguchi, "The FEAL Cipher Family," *Advances in Cryptology—CRYPTO '90 Proceedings*, Springer-Verlag, 1991, pp. 627–638.

1105. S. Miyaguchi, K. Ohta, and M. Iwata, "128-bit Hash Function (*N*-Hash)," *Proceedings of SECURICOM '90*, 1990, pp. 127–137.

1106. S. Miyaguchi, K. Ohta, and M. Iwata, "128-bit Hash Function (*N*-Hash)," *NTT Review*, v. 2, n. 6, Nov 1990, pp. 128–132.

1107. S. Miyaguchi, K. Ohta, and M. Iwata, "Confirmation that Some Hash Functions Are Not Collision Free," *Advances in Cryptology—EUROCRYPT '90 Proceedings*, Springer-Verlag, 1991, pp. 326–343.

1108. S. Miyaguchi, A. Shiraishi, and A. Shimizu, "Fast Data Encipherment Algorithm FEAL-8," *Review of the Electrical Communication Laboratories*, v. 36, n. 4, 1988.

1109. H. Miyano, "Differential Cryptanalysis on CALC and Its Evaluation," *Proceedings of the 1992 Symposium on Cryptography and Information Security (SCIS 92)*, Tateshina, Japan, 2–4 Apr 1992, pp. 7B.1–8.

1110. R. Molva, G. Tsudik, E. van Herreweghen, and S. Zatti, "KryptoKnight Authentication and Key Distribution System," *Proceedings of European Symposium on Research in Computer Security*, Toulouse, France, Nov 1992.

1111. P.L. Montgomery, "Modular Multiplication without Trial Division," *Mathematics of Computation*, v. 44, n. 170, 1985, pp. 519–521.

1112. P.L. Montgomery, "Speeding the Pollard and Elliptic Curve Methods of Factorization," *Mathematics of Computation*, v. 48, n. 177, Jan 1987, pp. 243–264.

1113. P.L. Montgomery and R. Silverman, "An FFT Extension to the *p*-1 Factoring Algorithm," *Mathematics of Computation*, v. 54, n. 190, 1990, pp. 839–854.

1114. J.H. Moore, "Protocol Failures in Cryptosystems," *Proceedings of the IEEE*, v. 76, n. 5, May 1988.

1115. J.H. Moore, "Protocol Failures in Cryptosystems," in *Contemporary Cryptology: The Science of Information Integrity*, G.J. Simmons, ed., IEEE Press, 1992, pp. 541–558.

1116. J.H. Moore and G.J. Simmons, "Cycle Structure of the DES with Weak and Semi-Weak Keys," *Advances in Cryptology—CRYPTO '86 Proceedings*, Springer-Verlag, 1987, pp. 3–32.

1117. T. Moriyasu, M. Morii, and M. Kasahara, "Nonlinear Pseudorandom Number Generator with Dynamic Structure and Its Properties," *Proceedings of the 1994 Symposium on Cryptography and Information Security (SCIS 94)*, Biwako, Japan, 27–29 Jan 1994, pp. 8A.1–11.

1118. R. Morris, "The Data Encryption Standard—Retrospective and Prospects," *IEEE Communications Magazine*, v. 16, n. 6, Nov 1978, pp. 11–14.

1119. R. Morris, remarks at the 1993 Cambridge Protocols Workshop, 1993.

1120. R. Morris, N.J.A. Sloane, and A.D. Wyner, "Assessment of the NBS Proposed Data Encryption Standard," *Cryptologia*, v. 1, n. 3, Jul 1977, pp. 281–291.

1121. R. Morris and K. Thompson, "Password Security: A Case History," *Communications of the ACM*, v. 22, n. 11, Nov 1979, pp. 594–597.

1122. S.B. Morris, "Escrow Encryption," lecture at MIT Laboratory for Computer Science, 2 Jun 1994.

1123. M.N. Morrison and J. Brillhart, "A Method of Factoring and the Factorization of F_7," *Mathematics of Computation*, v. 29, n. 129, Jan 1975, pp. 183–205.

1124. L.E. Moser, "A Logic of Knowledge and Belief for Reasoning About Computer Security," *Proceedings of the Computer Security Foundations Workshop II*, IEEE Computer Society Press, 1989, pp. 57–63.

1125. Motorola Government Electronics Division, *Advanced Techniques in Network Security*, Scottsdale, AZ, 1977.

1126. W.B. Müller, "Polynomial Functions in Modern Cryptology," *Contributions to General Algebra 3: Proceedings of the*

Vienna Conference, Vienna: Verlag Hölder-Pichler-Tempsky, 1985, pp. 7–32.

1127. W.B. Müller and W. Nöbauer, "Some Remarks on Public-Key Cryptography," *Studia Scientiarum Mathematicarum Hungarica,* v. 16, 1981, pp. 71–76.

1128. W.B. Müller and W. Nöbauer, "Cryptanalysis of the Dickson Scheme," *Advances in Cryptology—EUROCRYPT '85 Proceedings,* Springer-Verlag, 1986, pp. 50–61.

1129. C. Muller-Scholer, "A Microprocessor-Based Cryptoprocessor," *IEEE Micro,* Oct 1983, pp. 5–15.

1130. R.C. Mullin, E. Nemeth, and N. Weidenhofer, "Will Public Key Cryptosystems Live Up to Their Expectations?—HEP Implementation of the Discrete Log Codebreaker," *ICPP 85,* pp. 193–196.

1131. Y. Murakami and S. Kasahara, "An ID-Based Key Distribution Scheme," IEICE Japan, Technical Report, ISEC90-26, 1990.

1132. S. Murphy, "The Cryptanalysis of FEAL-4 with 20 Chosen Plaintexts," *Journal of Cryptology,* v. 2, n. 3, 1990, pp. 145–154.

1133. E.D. Myers, "STU-III—Multilevel Secure Computer Interface," *Proceedings of the Tenth Annual Computer Security Applications Conference,* IEEE Computer Society Press, 1994, pp. 170–179.

1134. D. Naccache, "Can O.S.S. be Repaired? Proposal for a New Practical Signature Scheme," *Advances in Cryptology—EUROCRYPT '93 Proceedings,* Springer-Verlag, 1994, pp. 233–239.

1135. D. Naccache, D. M'Raïhi, D. Raphaeli, and S. Vaudenay, "Can D.S.A. be Improved? Complexity Trade-Offs with the Digital Signature Standard," *Advances in Cryptology—EUROCRYPT '94 Proceedings,* Springer-Verlag, 1995, to appear.

1136. Y. Nakao, T. Kaneko, K. Koyama, and R. Terada, "A Study on the Security of RDES-1 Cryptosystem against Linear Cryptanalysis," *Proceedings of the 1995 Japan-Korea Workshop on Information Security and Cryptography,* Inuyama, Japan, 24–27 Jan 1995, pp. 163–172.

1137. M. Naor, "Bit Commitment Using Pseudo-Randomness," *Advances in Cryptology—CRYPTO '89 Proceedings,* Springer-Verlag, 1990, pp. 128–136.

1138. M. Naor and M. Yung, "Universal One-Way Hash Functions and Their Cryptographic Application," *Proceedings of the 21st Annual ACM Symposium on the Theory of Computing,* 1989, pp. 33–43.

1139. National Bureau of Standards, "Report of the Workshop on Estimation of Significant Advances in Computer Technology," NBSIR76-1189, National Bureau of Standards, U.S. Department of Commerce, 21–22 Sep 1976, Dec 1977.

1140. National Bureau of Standards, NBS FIPS PUB 46, "Data Encryption Standard," National Bureau of Standards, U.S. Department of Commerce, Jan 1977.

1141. National Bureau of Standards, NBS FIPS PUB 46-1, "Data Encryption Standard," U.S. Department of Commerce, Jan 1988.

1142. National Bureau of Standards, NBS FIPS PUB 74, "Guidelines for Implementing and Using the NBS Data Encryption Standard," U.S. Department of Commerce, Apr 1981.

1143. National Bureau of Standards, NBS FIPS PUB 81, "DES Modes of Operation," U.S. Department of Commerce, Dec 1980.

1144. National Bureau of Standards, NBS FIPS PUB 112, "Password Usage," U.S. Department of Commerce, May 1985.

1145. National Bureau of Standards, NBS FIPS PUB 113, "Computer Data Authentication," U.S. Department of Commerce, May 1985.

1146. National Computer Security Center, "Trusted Network Interpretation of the Trusted Computer System Evaluation Criteria," NCSC-TG-005 Version 1, Jul 1987.

1147. National Computer Security Center, "Trusted Database Management System Interpretation of the Trusted Computer System Evaluation Criteria," NCSC-TG-021 Version 1, Apr 1991.

1148. National Computer Security Center, "A Guide to Understanding Data Remberance in Automated Information Systems," NCSC-TG-025 Version 2, Sep 1991.

1149. National Institute of Standards and Technology, NIST FIPS PUB XX, "Digital Signature Standard," U.S. Department of Commerce, DRAFT, 19 Aug 1991.

1150. National Institute of Standards and Technology, NIST FIPS PUB 46-2, "Data Encryption Standard," U.S. Department of Commerce, Dec 93.

1151. National Institute of Standards and Technology, NIST FIPS PUB 171, "Key Management Using X9.17," U.S. Department of Commerce, Apr 92.

1152. National Institute of Standards and Technology, NIST FIPS PUB 180, "Secure Hash Standard," U.S. Department of Commerce, May 93.

1153. National Institute of Standards and Technology, NIST FIPS PUB 185, "Escrowed Encryption Standard," U.S. Department of Commerce, Feb 94.

1154. National Institute of Standards and Technology, NIST FIPS PUB 186, "Digital Signature Standard," U.S. Department of Commerce, May 1994.

1155. National Institute of Standards and Technology, "Clipper Chip Technology," 30 Apr 1993.

1156. National Institute of Standards and Technology, "Capstone Chip Technology," 30 Apr 1993.

1157. J. Nechvatal, "Public Key Cryptography," NIST Special Publication 800-2, National Institute of Standards and Technology, U.S. Department of Commerce, Apr 1991.

1158. J. Nechvatal, "Public Key Cryptography," *Contemporary Cryptology: The Science of Information Integrity*, G.J. Simmons, ed., IEEE Press, 1992, pp. 177–288.

1159. R.M. Needham and M.D. Schroeder, "Using Encryption for Authentication in Large Networks of Computers," *Communications of the ACM*, v. 21, n. 12, Dec 1978, pp. 993–999.

1160. R.M. Needham and M.D. Schroeder, "Authentication Revisited," *Operating Systems Review*, v. 21, n. 1, 1987, p. 7.

1161. D.M. Nessett, "A Critique of the Burrows, Abadi, and Needham Logic," *Operating System Review*, v. 20, n. 2, Apr 1990, pp. 35–38.

1162. B.C. Neuman and S. Stubblebine, "A Note on the Use of Timestamps as Nonces," *Operating Systems Review*, v. 27, n. 2, Apr 1993, pp. 10–14.

1163. B.C. Neuman and T. Ts'o, "Kerberos: An Authentication Service for Computer Networks," *IEEE Communications Magazine*, v. 32, n. 9, Sep 1994, pp. 33–38.

1164. L. Neuwirth, "Statement of Lee Neuwirth of Cylink on HR145," submitted to congressional committees considering HR145, Feb 1987.

1165. D.B. Newman, Jr. and R.L. Pickholtz, "Cryptography in the Private Sector," *IEEE Communications Magazine*, v. 24, n. 8, Aug 1986, pp. 7–10.

1166. H. Niederreiter, "A Public-Key Cryptosystem Based on Shift Register Sequences," *Advances in Cryptology—EUROCRYPT '85 Proceedings*, Springer-Verlag, 1986, pp. 35–39.

1167. H. Niederreiter, "Knapsack-Type Cryptosystems and Algebraic Coding Theory," *Problems of Control and Information Theory*, v. 15, n. 2, 1986, pp. 159–166.

1168. H. Niederreiter, "The Linear Complexity Profile and the Jump Complexity of Keystream Sequences," *Advances in Cryptology—EUROCRYPT '90 Proceedings*, Springer-Verlag, 1991, pp. 174–188.

1169. V. Niemi, "A New Trapdoor in Knapsacks," *Advances in Cryptology—EUROCRYPT '90 Proceedings*, Springer-Verlag, 1991, pp. 405–411.

1170. V. Niemi and A. Renvall, "How to Prevent Buying of Voters in Computer Elections," *Advances in Cryptology—ASIACRYPT '94 Proceedings*, Springer-Verlag, 1995, pp. 164–170.

1171. I. Niven and H.A. Zuckerman, *An Introduction to the Theory of Numbers*, New York: John Wiley & Sons, 1972.

1172. R. Nöbauer, "Cryptanalysis of the Rédei Scheme," *Contributions to General Algebra 3: Proceedings of the Vienna Conference*, Verlag Hölder-Pichler-Tempsky, Vienna, 1985, pp. 255–264.

1173. R. Nöbauer, "Cryptanalysis of a Public-Key Cryptosystem Based on Dickson-Polynomials," *Mathematica Slovaca*, v. 38, n. 4, 1988, pp. 309–323.

1174. K. Noguchi, H. Ashiya, Y. Sano, and T. Kaneko, "A Study on Differential Attack of MBAL Cryptosystem," *Proceedings of the 1994 Symposium on Cryptography and Information Security (SCIS 94)*, Lake Biwa, Japan, 27–29 Jan 1994, pp. 14B.1–7. (In Japanese.)

1175. H. Nurmi, A. Salomaa, and L. Santean, "Secret Ballot Elections in Computer Networks," *Computers & Security*, v. 10, 1991, pp. 553–560.

1176. K. Nyberg, "Construction of Bent Functions and Difference Sets," *Advances in Cryptology—EUROCRYPT '91 Proceedings*, Springer-Verlag, 1991, pp. 151–160.

1177. K. Nyberg, "Perfect Nonlinear S-Boxes," *Advances in Cryptology—EUROCRYPT '91 Proceedings*, Springer-Verlag, 1991, pp. 378–386.

1178. K. Nyberg, "On the Construction of Highly Nonlinear Permutations," *Advances in Cryptology—EUROCRYPT '92 Proceedings*, Springer-Verlag, 1991, pp. 92–98.

1179. K. Nyberg, "Differentially Uniform Mappings for Cryptography," *Advances in Cryptology—EUROCRYPT '93 Proceedings*, Springer-Verlag, 1994, pp. 55–64.

1180. K. Nyberg, "Provable Security against Differential Cryptanalysis," presented at the rump session of Eurocrypt '94, May 1994.

1181. K. Nyberg and L.R. Knudsen, "Provable Security against Differential Cryptanalysis," *Advances in Cryptology—CRYPTO '92 Proceedings*, Springer-Verlag, 1993, pp. 566–574.

1182. K. Nyberg and L.R. Knudsen, "Provable Security against Differential Cryptanalysis," *Journal of Cryptology*, v. 8, n. 1, 1995, pp. 27–37.

1183. K. Nyberg and R.A. Rueppel, "A New Signature Scheme Based on the DSA Giving Message Recovery," *1st ACM Conference on Computer and Communications Security*, ACM Press, 1993, pp. 58–61.

1184. K. Nyberg and R.A. Rueppel, "Message Recovery for Signature Schemes Based on the Discrete Logarithm Problem," *Advances in Cryptology—EUROCRYPT '94 Proceedings*, Springer-Verlag, 1995, to appear.

1185. L. O'Connor, "Enumerating Nondegenerate Permutations," *Advances in Cryptology—EUROCRYPT '93 Proceedings*, Springer-Verlag, 1994, pp. 368–377.

1186. L. O'Connor, "On the Distribution of Characteristics in Bijective Mappings," *Advances in Cryptology—EUROCRYPT '93 Proceedings*, Springer-Verlag, 1994, pp. 360–370.

1187. L. O'Connor, "On the Distribution of Characteristics in Composite Permutations," *Advances in Cryptology—CRYPTO '93 Proceedings*, Springer-Verlag, 1994, pp. 403–412.

1188. L. O'Connor and A. Klapper, "Algebraic Nonlinearity and Its Application to Cryptography," *Journal of Cryptology*, v. 7, n. 3, 1994, pp. 133–151.

1189. A. Odlyzko, "Discrete Logarithms in Finite Fields and Their Cryptographic Significance," *Advances in Cryptology: Proceedings of EUROCRYPT 84*, Springer-Verlag, 1985, pp. 224–314.

1190. A. Odlyzko, "Progress in Integer Factorization and Discrete Logarithms," unpublished manuscript, Feb 1995.

1191. Office of Technology Assessment, U.S. Congress, "Defending Secrets, Sharing Data: New Locks and Keys for Electronic Communication," OTA-CIT-310, Washington, D.C.: U.S. Government Printing Office, Oct 1987.

1192. B. O'Higgins, W. Diffie, L. Strawczynski, and R. de Hoog, "Encryption and ISDN—a Natural Fit," *Proceedings of the 1987 International Switching Symposium*, 1987, pp. 863–869.

1193. Y. Ohnishi, "A Study on Data Security," Master's thesis, Tohuku University, Japan, 1988. (In Japanese.)

1194. K. Ohta, "A Secure and Efficient Encrypted Broadcast Communication System Using a Public Master Key," *Transactions of the Institute of Electronics, Information, and Communication Engineers*, v. J70-D, n. 8, Aug 1987, pp. 1616–1624.

1195. K. Ohta, "An Electrical Voting Scheme Using a Single Administrator," *IEICE Spring National Convention*, A-294, 1988, v. 1, p. 296. (In Japanese.)

1196. K. Ohta, "Identity-based Authentication Schemes Using the RSA Cryptosystem," *Transactions of the Institute of Electronics, Information, and Communication Engineers*, v. J72D-II, n. 8, Aug 1989, pp. 612–620.

1197. K. Ohta and M. Matsui, "Differential Attack on Message Authentication Codes," *Advances in Cryptology—CRYPTO '93 Proceedings*, Springer-Verlag, 1994, pp. 200–223.

1198. K. Ohta and T. Okamoto, "Practical Extension of Fiat-Shamir Scheme," *Electronics Letters*, v. 24, n. 15, 1988, pp. 955–956.

1199. K. Ohta and T. Okamoto, "A Modification of the Fiat-Shamir Scheme," *Advances in Cryptology—CRYPTO '88 Proceedings*, Springer-Verlag, 1990, pp. 232–243.

1200. K. Ohta and T. Okamoto, "A Digital Multisignature Scheme Based on the Fiat-Shamir Scheme," *Advances in Cryptology—ASIACRYPT '91 Proceedings*, Springer-Verlag, 1993, pp. 139–148.

1201. K. Ohta, T. Okamoto and K. Koyama, "Membership Authentication for Hierarchy Multigroups Using the Extended Fiat-Shamir Scheme," *Advances in Cryptol-*

ogy—EUROCRYPT '90 Proceedings, Springer-Verlag, 1991, pp. 446–457.

1202. E. Okamoto and K. Tanaka, "Key Distribution Based on Identification Information," IEEE Journal on Selected Areas in Communication, v. 7, n. 4, May 1989, pp. 481–485.

1203. T. Okamoto, "Fast Public-Key Cryptosystems Using Congruent Polynomial Equations," Electronics Letters, v. 22, n. 11, 1986, pp. 581–582.

1204. T. Okamoto, "Modification of a Public-Key Cryptosystem," Electronics Letters, v. 23, n. 16, 1987, pp. 814–815.

1205. T. Okamoto, "A Fast Signature Scheme Based on Congruential Polynomial Operations," IEEE Transactions on Information Theory, v. 36, n. 1, 1990, pp. 47–53.

1206. T. Okamoto, "Provably Secure and Practical Identification Schemes and Corresponding Signature Schemes," Advances in Cryptology—CRYPTO '92 Proceedings, Springer-Verlag, 1993, pp. 31–53.

1207. T. Okamoto, A. Fujioka, and E. Fujisaki, "An Efficient Digital Signature Scheme Based on Elliptic Curve over the Ring Z_n," Advances in Cryptology—CRYPTO '92 Proceedings, Springer-Verlag, 1993, pp. 54–65.

1208. T. Okamoto, S. Miyaguchi, A. Shiraishi, and T. Kawaoka, "Signed Document Transmission System," U.S. Patent #4,625,076, 25 Nov 1986.

1209. T. Okamoto and K. Ohta, "Disposable Zero-Knowledge Authentication and Their Applications to Untraceable Electronic Cash," Advances in Cryptology—CRYPTO '89 Proceedings, Springer-Verlag, 1990, pp. 134–149.

1210. T. Okamoto and K. Ohta, "How to Utilize the Randomness of Zero-Knowledge Proofs," Advances in Cryptology—CRYPTO '90 Proceedings, Springer-Verlag, 1991, pp. 456–475.

1211. T. Okamoto and K. Ohta, "Universal Electronic Cash," Advances in Cryptology—CRYPTO '91 Proceedings, Springer-Verlag, 1992, pp. 324–337.

1212. T. Okamoto and K. Ohta, "Survey of Digital Signature Schemes," Proceedings of the Third Symposium on State and Progress of Research in Cryptography, Fondazone Ugo Bordoni, Rome, 1993, pp. 17–29.

1213. T. Okamoto and K. Ohta, "Designated Confirmer Signatures Using Trapdoor Functions," Proceedings of the 1994 Symposium on Cryptography and Information Security (SCIS 94), Lake Biwa, Japan, 27–29 Jan 1994, pp. 16B.1–11.

1214. T. Okamoto and K. Sakurai, "Efficient Algorithms for the Construction of Hyperelliptic Cryptosystems," Advances in Cryptology—CRYPTO '91 Proceedings, Springer-Verlag, 1992, pp. 267–278.

1215. T. Okamoto and A. Shiraishi, "A Fast Signature Scheme Based on Quadratic Inequalities," Proceedings of the 1985 Symposium on Security and Privacy, IEEE, Apr 1985, pp. 123–132.

1216. J.D. Olsen, R.A. Scholtz, and L.R. Welch, "Bent Function Sequences," IEEE Transactions on Information Theory, v. IT-28, n. 6, Nov 1982, pp. 858–864.

1217. H. Ong and C.P. Schnorr, "Signatures through Approximate Representations by Quadratic Forms," Advances in Cryptology: Proceedings of Crypto 83, Plenum Press, 1984.

1218. H. Ong and C.P. Schnorr, "Fast Signature Generation with a Fiat Shamir-Like Scheme," Advances in Cryptology—EUROCRYPT '90 Proceedings, Springer-Verlag, 1991, pp. 432–440.

1219. H. Ong, C.P. Schnorr, and A. Shamir, "An Efficient Signature Scheme Based on Polynomial Equations," Proceedings of the 16th Annual Symposium on the Theory of Computing, 1984, pp. 208–216.

1220. H. Ong, C.P. Schnorr, and A. Shamir, "Efficient Signature Schemes Based on Polynomial Equations," Advances in Cryptology: Proceedings of CRYPTO 84, Springer-Verlag, 1985, pp. 37–46.

1221. Open Shop Information Services, OSIS Security Aspects, OSIS European Working Group, WG1, final report, Oct 1985.

1222. G.A. Orton, M.P. Roy, P.A. Scott, L.E. Peppard, and S.E. Tavares, "VLSI Implementation of Public-Key Encryption Algorithms," Advances in Cryptology—CRYPTO '86 Proceedings, Springer-Verlag, 1987, pp. 277–301.

1223. H. Orup, E. Svendsen, and E. Andreasen, "VICTOR—An Efficient RSA Hardware Implementation," Advances in Cryptology—EUROCRYPT '90 Proceedings, Springer-Verlag, 1991, pp. 245–252.

1224. D. Otway and O. Rees, "Efficient and Timely Mutual Authentication," Operating Systems Review, v. 21, n. 1, 1987, pp. 8–10.

1225. G. Pagels-Fick, "Implementation Issues for Master Key Distribution and Protected Keyload Procedures," *Computers and Security: A Global Challenge, Proceedings of IFIP/SEC '83*, North Holland: Elsevier Science Publishers, 1984, pp. 381–390.

1226. C.M. Papadimitriou, *Computational Complexity*, Addison-Wesley, 1994.

1227. C.S. Park, "Improving Code Rate of McEliece's Public-key Cryptosystem," *Electronics Letters*, v. 25, n. 21, 12 Oct 1989, pp. 1466–1467.

1228. S. Park, Y. Kim, S. Lee, and K. Kim, "Attacks on Tanaka's Non-interactive Key Sharing Scheme," *Proceedings of the 1995 Symposium on Cryptography and Information Security (SCIS 95)*, Inuyama, Japan, 24–27 Jan 1995, pp. B3.4.1–4.

1229. S.J. Park, K.H. Lee, and D.H. Won, "An Entrusted Undeniable Signature," *Proceedings of the 1995 Japan-Korea Workshop on Information Security and Cryptography*, Inuyama, Japan, 24–27 Jan 1995, pp. 120–126.

1230. S.J. Park, K.H. Lee, and D.H. Won, "A Practical Group Signature," *Proceedings of the 1995 Japan-Korea Workshop on Information Security and Cryptography*, Inuyama, Japan, 24–27 Jan 1995, pp. 127–133.

1231. S.K. Park and K.W. Miller, "Random Number Generators: Good Ones Are Hard to Find," *Communications of the ACM*, v. 31, n. 10, Oct 1988, pp. 1192–1201.

1232. J. Patarin, "How to Find and Avoid Collisions for the Knapsack Hash Function," *Advances in Cryptology—EUROCRYPT '93 Proceedings*, Springer-Verlag, 1994, pp. 305–317.

1233. W. Patterson, *Mathematical Cryptology for Computer Scientists and Mathematicians*, Totowa, N.J.: Rowman & Littlefield, 1987.

1234. W.H. Payne, "Public Key Cryptography Is Easy to Break," William H. Payne, unpublished manuscript, 16 Oct 90.

1235. T.P. Pederson, "Distributed Provers with Applications to Undeniable Signatures," *Advances in Cryptology—EUROCRYPT '91 Proceedings*, Springer-Verlag, 1991, pp. 221–242.

1236. S. Peleg and A. Rosenfield, "Breaking Substitution Ciphers Using a Relaxation Algorithm," *Communications of the ACM*, v. 22, n. 11, Nov 1979, pp. 598–605.

1237. R. Peralta, "Simultaneous Security of Bits in the Discrete Log," *Advances in Cryptology—EUROCRYPT '85*, Springer-Verlag, 1986, pp. 62–72.

1238. I. Peterson, "Monte Carlo Physics: A Cautionary Lesson," *Science News*, v. 142, n. 25, 19 Dec 1992, p. 422.

1239. B. Pfitzmann, "Fail-Stop Signatures: Principles and Applications," *Proceedings of COMPUSEC '91, Eighth World Conference on Computer Security, Audit, and Control*, Elsevier Science Publishers, 1991, pp. 125–134.

1240. B. Pfitzmann and M. Waidner, "Formal Aspects of Fail-Stop Signatures," Fakultät für Informatik, University Karlsruhe, Report 22/90, 1990.

1241. B. Pfitzmann and M. Waidner, "Fail-Stop Signatures and Their Application," *Securicom '91*, 1991, pp. 145–160.

1242. B. Pfitzmann and M. Waidner, "Unconditional Concealment with Cryptographic Ruggedness," *VIS '91 Verlassliche Informationsysteme Proceedings*, Darmstadt, Germany, 13–15 March 1991, pp. 3-2-320. (In German.)

1243. B. Pfitzmann and M. Waidner, "How to Break and Repair a 'Provably Secure' Untraceable Payment System," *Advances in Cryptology—CRYPTO '91 Proceedings*, Springer-Verlag, 1992, pp. 338–350.

1244. C.P. Pfleeger, *Security in Computing*, Englewood Cliffs, N.J.: Prentice-Hall, 1989.

1245. S.J.D. Phoenix and P.D. Townsend, "Quantum Cryptography and Secure Optical Communication," *BT Technology Journal*, v. 11, n. 2, Apr 1993, pp. 65–75.

1246. J. Pieprzyk, "On Public-Key Cryptosystems Built Using Polynomial Rings," *Advances in Cryptology—EUROCRYPT '85*, Springer-Verlag, 1986, pp. 73–80.

1247. J. Pieprzyk, "Error Propagation Property and Applications in Cryptography," *IEE Proceedings-E, Computers and Digital Techniques*, v. 136, n. 4, Jul 1989, pp. 262–270.

1248. D. Pinkas, T. Parker, and P. Kaijser, "SESAME: An Introduction," Issue 1.2, Bull, ICL, and SNI, Sep 1993.

1249. F. Piper, "Stream Ciphers," *Elektrotechnic und Maschinenbau*, v. 104, n. 12, 1987, pp. 564–568.

1250. V.S. Pless, "Encryption Schemes for Computer Confidentiality," *IEEE Transactions on Computing*, v. C-26, n. 11, Nov 1977, pp. 1133–1136.

1251. J.B. Plumstead, "Inferring a Sequence Generated by a Linear Congruence," *Proceedings of the 23rd IEEE Symposium on the Foundations of Computer Science*, 1982, pp. 153–159.

1252. R. Poet, "The Design of Special Purpose Hardware to Factor Large Integers," *Computer Physics Communications*, v. 37, 1985, pp. 337–341.

1253. S.C. Pohlig and M.E. Hellman, "An Improved Algorithm for Computing Logarithms in GF(p) and Its Cryptographic Significance," *IEEE Transactions on Information Theory*, v. 24, n. 1, Jan 1978, pp. 106–111.

1254. J.M. Pollard, "A Monte Carlo Method for Factorization," *BIT*, v. 15, 1975, pp. 331–334.

1255. J.M. Pollard and C.P. Schnorr, "An Efficient Solution of the Congruence $x^2 + ky^2 = m \pmod{n}$," *IEEE Transactions on Information Theory*, v. IT-33, n. 5, Sep 1987, pp. 702–709.

1256. C. Pomerance, "Recent Developments in Primality Testing," *The Mathematical Intelligencer*, v. 3, n. 3, 1981, pp. 97–105.

1257. C. Pomerance, "The Quadratic Sieve Factoring Algorithm," *Advances in Cryptology: Proceedings of EUROCRYPT 84*, Springer-Verlag, 1985, 169–182.

1258. C. Pomerance, "Fast, Rigorous Factorization and Discrete Logarithm Algorithms," *Discrete Algorithms and Complexity*, New York: Academic Press, 1987, pp. 119–143.

1259. C. Pomerance, J.W. Smith, and R. Tuler, "A Pipe-Line Architecture for Factoring Large Integers with the Quadratic Sieve Algorithm," *SIAM Journal on Computing*, v. 17, n. 2, Apr 1988, pp. 387–403.

1260. G.J. Popek and C.S. Kline, "Encryption and Secure Computer Networks," *ACM Computing Surveys*, v. 11, n. 4, Dec 1979, pp. 331–356.

1261. F. Pratt, *Secret and Urgent*, Blue Ribbon Books, 1942.

1262. B. Preneel, "Analysis and Design of Cryptographic Hash Functions," Ph.D. dissertation, Katholieke Universiteit Leuven, Jan 1993.

1263. B. Preneel, "Differential Cryptanalysis of Hash Functions Based on Block Ciphers," *Proceedings of the 1st ACM Conference on Computer and Communications Security*, 1993, pp. 183–188.

1264. B. Preneel, "Cryptographic Hash Functions," *European Transactions on Telecommunications*, v 5, n. 4, Jul/Aug 1994, pp. 431–448.

1265. B. Preneel, personal communication, 1995.

1266. B. Preneel, A. Bosselaers, R. Govaerts, and J. Vandewalle, "Collision-Free Hash Functions Based on Block Cipher Algorithms," *Proceedings of the 1989 Carnahan Conference on Security Technology*, 1989, pp. 203–210.

1267. B. Preneel, R. Govaerts, and J. Vandewalle, "An Attack on Two Hash Functions by Zheng-Matsumoto-Imai," *Advances in Cryptology—ASIACRYPT '92 Proceedings*, Springer-Verlag, 1993, pp. 535–538.

1268. B. Preneel, R. Govaerts, and J. Vandewalle, "Hash Functions Based on Block Ciphers: A Synthetic Approach," *Advances in Cryptology—CRYPTO '93 Proceedings*, Springer-Verlag, 1994, pp. 368–378.

1269. B. Preneel, M. Nuttin, V. Rijmen, and J. Buelens, "Cryptanalysis of the CFB mode of the DES with a Reduced Number of Rounds," *Advances in Cryptology—CRYPTO '93 Proceedings*, Springer-Verlag, 1994, pp. 212–223.

1270. B. Preneel and V. Rijmen, "On Using Maximum Likelihood to Optimize Recent Cryptanalytic Techniques," presented at the rump session of EUROCRYPT '94, May 1994.

1271. B. Preneel, W. Van Leekwijck, L. Van Linden, R. Govaerts, and J. Vandewalle, "Propagation Characteristics of Boolean Functions," *Advances in Cryptology—EUROCRYPT '90 Proceedings*, Springer-Verlag, 1991, pp. 161–173.

1272. W.H. Press, B.P. Flannery, S.A. Teukolsky, and W.T. Vetterling, *Numerical Recipes in C: The Art of Scientific Computing*, Cambridge University Press, 1988.

1273. W. Price, "Key Management for Data Encipherment," *Security: Proceedings of IFIP/SEC '83*, North Holland: Elsevier Science Publishers, 1983.

1274. G.P. Purdy, "A High-Security Log-in Procedure," *Communications of the ACM*, v. 17, n. 8, Aug 1974, pp. 442–445.

1275. J.-J. Quisquater, "Announcing the Smart Card with RSA Capability," *Proceedings of the Conference: IC Cards and Applications, Today and Tomorrow*, Amsterdam, 1989.

1276. J.-J. Quisquater and C. Couvreur, "Fast Decipherment Algorithm for RSA Public-Key Cryptosystem," *Electronic Letters*, v. 18, 1982, pp. 155–168.

1277. J.-J. Quisquater and J.-P. Delescaille, "Other Cycling Tests for DES," *Advances in Cryptology—CRYPTO '87 Proceedings*, Springer-Verlag, 1988, pp. 255–256.

1278. J.-J. Quisquater and Y.G. Desmedt, "Chinese Lotto as an Exhaustive Code-Breaking Machine," *Computer*, v. 24, n. 11, Nov 1991, pp. 14–22.

1279. J.-J. Quisquater and M. Girault, "2n-bit Hash Functions Using n-bit Symmetric Block Cipher Algorithms, *Advances in Cryptology—EUROCRYPT '89 Proceedings*, Springer-Verlag, 1990, pp. 102–109.

1280. J.-J. Quisquater and L.C. Guillou, "Des Procédés d'Authentification Basés sur une Publication de Problèmes Complexes et Personnalisés dont les Solutions Maintenues Secrètes Constituent autant d'Accréditations," *Proceedings of SECURICOM '89: 7th Worldwide Congress on Computer and Communications Security and Protection*, Société d'Édition et d'Organisation d'Expositions Professionnelles, 1989, pp. 149–158. (In French.)

1281. J.-J., Myriam, Muriel, and Michaël Quisquater; L., Marie Annick, Gaïd, Anna, Gwenolé, and Soazig Guillou; and T. Berson, "How to Explain Zero-Knowledge Protocols to Your Children," *Advances in Cryptology—CRYPTO '89 Proceedings*, Springer-Verlag, 1990, pp. 628–631.

1282. M.O. Rabin, "Digital Signatures," *Foundations of Secure Communication*, New York: Academic Press, 1978, pp. 155–168.

1283. M.O. Rabin, "Digital Signatures and Public-Key Functions as Intractable as Factorization," MIT Laboratory for Computer Science, Technical Report, MIT/LCS/TR-212, Jan 1979.

1284. M.O. Rabin, "Probabilistic Algorithm for Testing Primality," *Journal of Number Theory*, v. 12, n. 1, Feb 1980, pp. 128–138.

1285. M.O. Rabin, "Probabilistic Algorithms in Finite Fields," *SIAM Journal on Computing*, v. 9, n. 2, May 1980, pp. 273–280.

1286. M.O. Rabin, "How to Exchange Secrets by Oblivious Transfer," Technical Memo TR-81, Aiken Computer Laboratory, Harvard University, 1981.

1287. M.O. Rabin, "Fingerprinting by Random Polynomials," Technical Report TR-15-81, Center for Research in Computing Technology, Harvard University, 1981.

1288. T. Rabin and M. Ben-Or, "Verifiable Secret Sharing and Multiparty Protocols with Honest Majority," *Proceedings of the 21st ACM Symposium on the Theory of Computing*, 1989, pp. 73–85.

1289. RAND Corporation, *A Million Random Digits with 100,000 Normal Deviates*, Glencoe, IL: Free Press Publishers, 1955.

1290. T.R.N. Rao, "Cryposystems Using Algebraic Codes," *International Conference on Computer Systems and Signal Processing*, Bangalore, India, Dec 1984.

1291. T.R.N. Rao, "On Struit-Tilburg Cryptanalysis of Rao-Nam Scheme," *Advances in Cryptology—CRYPTO '87 Proceedings*, Springer-Verlag, 1988, pp. 458–460.

1292. T.R.N. Rao and K.H. Nam, "Private-Key Algebraic-Coded Cryptosystems," *Advances in Cryptology—CRYPTO '86 Proceedings*, Springer-Verlag, 1987, pp. 35–48.

1293. T.R.N. Rao and K.H. Nam, "Private-Key Algebraic-Code Encryptions," *IEEE Transactions on Information Theory*, v. 35, n. 4, Jul 1989, pp. 829–833.

1294. J.A. Reeds, "Cracking Random Number Generator," *Cryptologia*, v. 1, n. 1, Jan 1977, pp. 20–26.

1295. J.A. Reeds, "Cracking a Multiplicative Congruential Encryption Algorithm," in *Information Linkage Between Applied Mathematics and Industry*, P.C.C. Wang, ed., Academic Press, 1979, pp. 467–472.

1296. J.A. Reeds, "Solution of Challenge Cipher," *Cryptologia*, v. 3, n. 2, Apr 1979, pp. 83–95.

1297. J.A. Reeds and J.L. Manferdelli, "DES Has No Per Round Linear Factors," *Advances in Cryptology: Proceedings of CRYPTO 84*, Springer-Verlag, 1985, pp. 377–389.

1298. J.A. Reeds and N.J.A. Sloane, "Shift Register Synthesis (Modulo m)," *SIAM Journal on Computing*, v. 14, n. 3, Aug 1985, pp. 505–513.

1299. J.A. Reeds and P.J. Weinberger, "File Security and the UNIX Crypt Command," *AT&T Technical Journal*, v. 63, n. 8, Oct 1984, pp. 1673–1683.

1300. T. Renji, "On Finite Automaton One-Key Cryptosystems," *Fast Software Encryption*,

Cambridge Security Workshop Proceedings, Springer-Verlag, 1994, pp. 135–148.

1301. T. Renji and C. Shihua, "A Finite Automaton Public Key Cryptosystems and Digital Signature," *Chinese Journal of Computers*, v. 8, 1985, pp. 401–409. (In Chinese.)

1302. T. Renji and C. Shihua, "Two Varieties of Finite Automaton Public Key Cryptosystems and Digital Signature," *Journal of Computer Science and Tecnology*, v. 1, 1986, pp. 9–18. (In Chinese.)

1303. T. Renji and C. Shihua, "An Implementation of Identity-based Cryptosystems and Signature Schemes by Finite Automaton Public Key Cryptosystems," *Advances in Cryptology—CHINACRYPT '92*, Bejing: Science Press, 1992, pp. 87–104. (In Chinese.)

1304. T. Renji and C. Shihua, "Note on Finite Automaton Public Key Cryptosystems," *CHINACRYPT '94*, Xidian, China, 11–15 Nov 1994, pp. 76–80.

1305. Research and Development in Advanced Communication Technologies in Europe, *RIPE Integrity Primitives: Final Report of RACE Integrity Primitives Evaluation (R1040)*, RACE, June 1992.

1306. J.M. Reyneri and E.D. Karnin, "Coin Flipping by Telephone," *IEEE Transactions on Information Theory*, v. IT-30, n. 5, Sep 1984, pp. 775–776.

1307. P. Ribenboim, *The Book of Prime Number Records*, Springer-Verlag, 1988.

1308. P. Ribenboim, *The Little Book of Big Primes*, Springer-Verlag, 1991.

1309. M. Richter, "Ein Rauschgenerator zur Gewinnung won quasi-idealen Zufallszahlen für die stochastische Simulation," Ph.D. dissertation, Aachen University of Technology, 1992. (In German.)

1310. R.F. Rieden, J.B. Snyder, R.J. Widman, and W.J. Barnard, "A Two-Chip Implementation of the RSA Public Encryption Algorithm," *Proceedings of GOMAC (Government Microcircuit Applications Conference)*, Nov 1982, pp. 24–27.

1311. H. Riesel, *Prime Numbers and Computer Methods for Factorization*, Boston: Birkhaüser, 1985.

1312. K. Rihaczek, "Data Interchange and Legal Security—Signature Surrogates," *Computers & Security*, v. 13, n. 4, Sep 1994, pp. 287–293.

1313. V. Rijmen and B. Preneel, "Improved Characteristics for Differential Crypt-analysis of Hash Functions Based on Block Ciphers," *K.U. Leuven Workshop on Cryptographic Algorithms*, Springer-Verlag, 1995, to appear.

1314. R.L. Rivest, "A Description of a Single-Chip Implementation of the RSA Cipher," *LAMBDA Magazine*, v. 1, n. 3, Fall 1980, pp. 14–18.

1315. R.L. Rivest, "Statistical Analysis of the Hagelin Cryptograph," *Cryptologia*, v. 5, n. 1, Jan 1981, pp. 27–32.

1316. R.L. Rivest, "A Short Report on the RSA Chip," *Advances in Cryptology: Proceedings of Crypto 82*, Plenum Press, 1983, p. 327.

1317. R.L. Rivest, "RSA Chips (Past/Present/Future)," *Advances in Cryptology: Proceedings of EUROCRYPT 84*, Springer-Verlag, 1985, pp. 159–168.

1318. R.L. Rivest, "The MD4 Message Digest Algorithm," RFC 1186, Oct 1990.

1319. R.L. Rivest, "The MD4 Message Digest Algorithm," *Advances in Cryptology—CRYPTO '90 Proceedings*, Springer-Verlag, 1991, pp. 303–311.

1320. R.L. Rivest, "The RC4 Encryption Algorithm," RSA Data Security, Inc., Mar 1992.

1321. R.L. Rivest, "The MD4 Message Digest Algorithm," RFC 1320, Apr 1992.

1322. R.L. Rivest, "The MD5 Message Digest Algorithm," RFC 1321, Apr 1992.

1323. R.L. Rivest, "Dr. Ron Rivest on the Difficulty of Factoring," *Ciphertext: The RSA Newsletter*, v. 1, n. 1, Fall 1993, pp. 6, 8.

1324. R.L. Rivest, "The RC5 Encryption Algorithm," *Dr. Dobb's Journal*, v. 20, n. 1, Jan 95, pp. 146–148.

1325. R.L. Rivest, "The RC5 Encryption Algorithm," *K.U. Leuven Workshop on Cryptographic Algorithms*, Springer-Verlag, 1995, to appear.

1326. R.L. Rivest, M.E. Hellman, J.C. Anderson, and J.W. Lyons, "Responses to NIST's Proposal," *Communications of the ACM*, v. 35, n. 7, Jul 1992, pp. 41–54.

1327. R.L. Rivest and A. Shamir, "How to Expose an Eavesdropper," *Communications of the ACM*, v. 27, n. 4, Apr 1984, pp. 393–395.

1328. R.L. Rivest, A. Shamir, and L.M. Adleman, "A Method for Obtaining Digital Signatures and Public-Key Cryptosystems," *Communications of the ACM*, v. 21, n. 2, Feb 1978, pp. 120–126.

1329. R.L. Rivest, A. Shamir, and L.M. Adleman, "On Digital Signatures and Public Key

Cryptosystems," MIT Laboratory for Computer Science, Technical Report, MIT/LCS/TR-212, Jan 1979.

1330. R.L. Rivest, A. Shamir, and L.M. Adleman, "Cryptographic Communications System and Method," U.S. Patent #4,405,829, 20 Sep 1983.

1331. M.J.B. Robshaw, "Implementations of the Search for Pseudo-Collisions in MD5," Technical Report TR-103, Version 2.0, RSA Laboratories, Nov 1993.

1332. M.J.B. Robshaw, "The Final Report of RACE 1040: A Technical Summary," Technical Report TR-9001, Version 1.0, RSA Laboratories, Jul 1993.

1333. M.J.B. Robshaw, "On Evaluating the Linear Complexity of a Sequence of Least Period 2^n," *Designs, Codes and Cryptography*, v. 4, n. 3, 1994, pp. 263–269.

1334. M.J.B. Robshaw, "Block Ciphers," Technical Report TR-601, RSA Laboratories, Jul 1994.

1335. M.J.B. Robshaw, "MD2, MD4, MD5, SHA, and Other Hash Functions," Technical Report TR-101, Version 3.0, RSA Laboratories, Jul 1994.

1336. M.J.B. Robshaw, "On Pseudo-Collisions in MD5," Technical Report TR-102, Version 1.1, RSA Laboratories, Jul 1994.

1337. M.J.B. Robshaw, "Security of RC4," Technical Report TR-401, RSA Laboratories, Jul 1994.

1338. M.J.B. Robshaw, personal communication, 1995.

1339. M. Roe, "Reverse Engineering of an EES Device," *K.U. Leuven Workshop on Cryptographic Algorithms*, Springer-Verlag, 1995, to appear.

1340. P. Rogaway and D. Coppersmith, "A Software-Oriented Encryption Algorithm," *Fast Software Encryption, Cambridge Security Workshop Proceedings*, Springer-Verlag, 1994, pp. 56–63.

1341. H.L. Rogers, "An Overview of the Candware Program," *Proceedings of the 3rd Annual Symposium on Physical/Electronic Security*, Armed Forces Communications and Electronics Association, paper 31, Aug 1987.

1342. J. Rompel, "One-Way Functions Are Necessary and Sufficient for Secure Signatures," *Proceedings of the 22nd Annual ACM Symposium on the Theory of Computing*, 1990, pp. 387–394.

1343. T. Rosati, "A High Speed Data Encryption Processor for Public Key Cryptography," *Proceedings of the IEEE Custom Integrated Circuits Conference*, 1989, pp. 12.3.1–12.3.5.

1344. O.S. Rothaus, "On 'Bent' Functions," *Journal of Combinatorial Theory*, Series A, v. 20, n. 3, 1976, pp. 300–305.

1345. RSA Laboratories, "PKCS #1: RSA Encryption Standard," version 1.5, Nov 1993.

1346. RSA Laboratories, "PKCS #3: Diffie-Hellman Key-Agreement Standard," version 1.4, Nov 1993.

1347. RSA Laboratories, "PKCS #5: Password-Based Encryption Standard," version 1.5, Nov 1993.

1348. RSA Laboratories, "PKCS #6: Extended-Certificate Syntax Standard," version 1.5, Nov 1993.

1349. RSA Laboratories, "PKCS #7: Cryptographic Message Syntax Standard," version 1.5, Nov 1993.

1350. RSA Laboratories, "PKCS #8: Private Key Information Syntax Standard," version 1.2, Nov 1993.

1351. RSA Laboratories, "PKCS #9: Selected Attribute Types," version 1.1, Nov 1993.

1352. RSA Laboratories, "PKCS #10: Certification Request Syntax Standard," version 1.0, Nov 1993.

1353. RSA Laboratories, "PKCS #11: Cryptographic Token Interface Standard," version 1.0, Apr 95.

1354. RSA Laboratories, "PKCS #12: Public Key User Information Syntax Standard," version 1.0, 1995.

1355. A.D. Rubin and P. Honeyman, "Formal Methods for the Analysis of Authentication Protocols," draft manuscript, 1994.

1356. F. Rubin, "Decrypting a Stream Cipher Based on J-K Flip-Flops," *IEEE Transactions on Computing*, v. C-28, n. 7, Jul 1979, pp. 483–487.

1357. R.A. Rueppel, *Analysis and Design of Stream Ciphers*, Springer-Verlag, 1986.

1358. R.A. Rueppel, "Correlation Immunity and the Summation Combiner," *Advances in Cryptology—EUROCRYPT '85*, Springer-Verlag, 1986, pp. 260–272.

1359. R.A. Rueppel, "When Shift Registers Clock Themselves," *Advances in Cryptology—EUROCRYPT '87 Proceedings*, Springer-Verlag, 1987, pp. 53–64.

1360. R.A. Rueppel, "Security Models and Notions for Stream Ciphers," *Cryptogra-*

phy and Coding II, C. Mitchell, ed., Oxford: Clarendon Press, 1992, pp. 213–230.

1361. R.A. Rueppel, "On the Security of Schnorr's Pseudo-Random Sequence Generator," *Advances in Cryptology—EUROCRYPT '89 Proceedings*, Springer-Verlag, 1990, pp. 423–428.

1362. R.A. Rueppel, "Stream Ciphers," *Contemporary Cryptology: The Science of Information Integrity*, G.J. Simmons, ed., IEEE Press, 1992, pp. 65–134.

1363. R.A. Rueppel and J.L. Massey, "The Knapsack as a Nonlinear Function," *IEEE International Symposium on Information Theory*, Brighton, UK, May 1985.

1364. R.A. Rueppel and O.J. Staffelbach, "Products of Linear Recurring Sequences with Maximum Complexity," *IEEE Transactions on Information Theory*, v. IT-33, n. 1, Jan 1987, pp. 124–131.

1365. D. Russell and G.T. Gangemi, *Computer Security Basics*, O'Reilly and Associates, Inc., 1991.

1366. S. Russell and P. Craig, "Privacy Enhanced Mail Modules for ELM," *Proceedings of the Internet Society 1994 Workshop on Network and Distributed System Security*, The Internet Society, 1994, pp. 21–34.

1367. D.F.H. Sadok and J. Kelner, "Privacy Enhanced Mail Design and Implementation Perspectives," *Computer Communications Review*, v. 24, n. 3, Jul 1994, pp. 38–46.

1368. K. Sakano, "Digital Signatures with User-Flexible Reliability," *Proceedings of the 1993 Symposium on Cryptography and Information Security (SCIS 93)*, Shuzenji, Japan, 28–30 Jan 1993, pp. 5C.1–8.

1369. K. Sakano, C. Park, and K. Kurosawa, "(*k,n*) Threshold Undeniable Signature Scheme," *Proceedings of the 1993 Korea-Japan Workshop on Information Security and Cryptography*, Seoul, Korea, 24–26 Oct 1993, pp. 184–193.

1370. K. Sako, "Electronic Voting Schemes Allowing Open Objection to the Tally," *Transactions of the Institute of Electronics, Information, and Communication Engineers*, v. E77-A, n. 1, 1994, pp. 24–30.

1371. K. Sako and J. Kilian, "Secure Voting Using Partially Compatible Homomorphisms," *Advances in Cryptology—CRYPTO '94 Proceedings*, Springer-Verlag, 1994, p. 411–424.

1372. K. Sako and J. Kilian, "Receipt-Free Mix-Type Voting Scheme—A Practical Solution to the Implementation of a Voting Booth," *Advances in Cryptology—EUROCRYPT '95 Proceedings*, Springer-Verlag, 1995, pp. 393–403.

1373. A. Salomaa, *Public-Key Cryptography*, Springer-Verlag, 1990.

1374. A. Salomaa and L. Santean, "Secret Selling of Secrets with Many Buyers," *ETACS Bulletin*, v. 42, 1990, pp. 178–186.

1375. M. Sántha and U.V. Vazirani, "Generating Quasi-Random Sequences from Slightly Random Sources," *Proceedings of the 25th Annual Symposium on the Foundations of Computer Science*, 1984, pp. 434–440.

1376. M. Sántha and U.V. Vazirani, "Generating Quasi-Random Sequences from Slightly Random Sources," *Journal of Computer and System Sciences*, v. 33, 1986, pp. 75–87.

1377. S. Saryazdi, "An Extension to ElGamal Public Key Cryptosystem with a New Signature Scheme," *Proceedings of the 1990 Bilkent International Conference on New Trends in Communication, Control, and Signal Processing*, North Holland: Elsevier Science Publishers, 1990, pp. 195–198.

1378. J.E. Savage, "Some Simple Self-Synchronizing Digital Data Scramblers," *Bell System Technical Journal*, v. 46, n. 2, Feb 1967, pp. 448–487.

1379. B.P. Schanning, "Applying Public Key Distribution to Local Area Networks," *Computers & Security*, v. 1, n. 3, Nov 1982, pp. 268–274.

1380. B.P. Schanning, S.A. Powers, and J. Kowalchuk, "MEMO: Privacy and Authentication for the Automated Office," *Proceedings of the 5th Conference on Local Computer Networks*, IEEE Press, 1980, pp. 21–30.

1381. Schaumuller-Bichl, "Zur Analyse des Data Encryption Standard und Synthese Verwandter Chiffriersysteme," Ph.D. dissertation, Linz University, May 1981. (In German.)

1382. Schaumuller-Bichl, "On the Design and Analysis of New Cipher Systems Related to the DES," Technical Report, Linz University, 1983.

1383. A. Scherbius, "Ciphering Machine," U.S. Patent #1,657,411, 24 Jan 1928.

1384. J.I. Schiller, "Secure Distributed Computing," *Scientific American*, v. 271, n. 5, Nov 1994, pp. 72–76.

1385. R. Schlafly, "Complaint Against Exclusive Federal Patent License," Civil Action File No. C-93 20450, United States District Court for the Northern District of California.

1386. B. Schneier, "One-Way Hash Functions," *Dr. Dobb's Journal*, v. 16, n. 9, Sep 1991, pp. 148–151.

1387. B. Schneier, "Data Guardians," *MacWorld*, v. 10, n. 2, Feb 1993, pp. 145–151.

1388. B. Schneier, "Description of a New Variable-Length Key, 64-Bit Block Cipher (Blowfish)," *Fast Software Encryption, Cambridge Security Workshop Proceedings*, Springer-Verlag, 1994, pp. 191–204.

1389. B. Schneier, "The Blowfish Encryption Algorithm," *Dr. Dobb's Journal*, v. 19, n. 4, Apr 1994, pp. 38–40.

1390. B. Schneier, *Protect Your Macintosh*, Peachpit Press, 1994.

1391. B. Schneier, "Designing Encryption Algorithms for Real People," *Proceedings of the 1994 ACM SIGSAC New Security Paradigms Workshop*, IEEE Computer Society Press, 1994, pp. 63–71.

1392. B. Schneier, "A Primer on Authentication and Digital Signatures," *Computer Security Journal*, v. 10, n. 2, 1994, pp. 38–40.

1393. B. Schneier, "The GOST Encryption Algorithm," *Dr. Dobb's Journal*, v. 20, n. 1, Jan 95, pp. 123–124.

1394. B. Schneier, *E-Mail Security* (with PGP and PEM) New York: John Wiley & Sons, 1995.

1395. C.P. Schnorr, "On the Construction of Random Number Generators and Random Function Generators," *Advances in Cryptology—EUROCRYPT '88 Proceedings*, Springer-Verlag, 1988, pp. 225–232.

1396. C.P. Schnorr, "Efficient Signature Generation for Smart Cards," *Advances in Cryptology—CRYPTO '89 Proceedings*, Springer-Verlag, 1990, pp. 239–252.

1397. C.P. Schnorr, "Efficient Signature Generation for Smart Cards," *Journal of Cryptology*, v. 4, n. 3, 1991, pp. 161–174.

1398. C.P. Schnorr, "Method for Identifying Subscribers and for Generating and Verifying Electronic Signatures in a Data Exchange System," U.S. Patent #4,995,082, 19 Feb 1991.

1399. C.P. Schnorr, "An Efficient Cryptographic Hash Function," presented at the rump session of CRYPTO '91, Aug 1991.

1400. C.P. Schnorr, "FFT-Hash II, Efficient Cryptographic Hashing," *Advances in Cryptology—EUROCRYPT '92 Proceedings*, Springer-Verlag, 1993, pp. 45–54.

1401. C.P. Schnorr and W. Alexi, "RSA-bits are $0.5 + \varepsilon$ Secure," *Advances in Cryptology: Proceedings of EUROCRYPT 84*, Springer-Verlag, 1985, pp. 113–126.

1402. C.P. Schnorr and S. Vaudenay, "Parallel FFT-Hashing," *Fast Software Encryption, Cambridge Security Workshop Proceedings*, Springer-Verlag, 1994, pp. 149–156.

1403. C.P. Schnorr and S. Vaudenay, "Black Box Cryptanalysis of Hash Networks Based on Multipermutations," *Advances in Cryptology—EUROCRYPT '94 Proceedings*, Springer-Verlag, 1995, to appear.

1404. W. Schwartau, *Information Warfare: Chaos on the Electronic Superhighway*, New York: Thunders Mouth Press, 1994.

1405. R. Scott, "Wide Open Encryption Design Offers Flexible Implementations," *Cryptologia*, v. 9, n. 1, Jan 1985, pp. 75–90.

1406. J. Seberry, "A Subliminal Channel in Codes for Authentication without Secrecy," *Ars Combinatorica*, v. 19A, 1985, pp. 337–342.

1407. J. Seberry and J. Pieprzyk, *Cryptography: An Introduction to Computer Security*, Englewood Cliffs, N.J.: Prentice-Hall, 1989.

1408. J. Seberry, X.-M. Zhang, and Y. Zheng, "Nonlinearly Balanced Boolean Functions and Their Propagation Characteristics," *Advances in Cryptology—EUROCRYPT '91 Proceedings*, Springer-Verlag, 1994, pp. 49–60.

1409. H. Sedlack, "The RSA Cryptography Processor: The First High Speed One-Chip Solution," *Advances in Cryptology—EUROCRYPT '87 Proceedings*, Springer-Verlag, 1988, pp. 95–105.

1410. H. Sedlack and U. Golze, "An RSA Cryptography Processor," *Microprocessing and Microprogramming*, v. 18, 1986, pp. 583–590.

1411. E.S. Selmer, *Linear Recurrence over Finite Field*, University of Bergen, Norway, 1966.

1412. J.O. Shallit, "On the Worst Case of Three Algorithms for Computing the Jacobi Symbol," *Journal of Symbolic Computation,* v. 10, n. 6, Dec 1990, pp. 593–610.

1413. A. Shamir, "A Fast Signature Scheme," MIT Laboratory for Computer Science, Technical Memorandum, MIT/LCS/TM-107, Massachusetts Institute of Technology, Jul 1978.

1414. A. Shamir, "How to Share a Secret," *Communications of the ACM,* v. 24, n. 11, Nov 1979, pp. 612–613.

1415. A. Shamir, "On the Cryptocomplexity of Knapsack Systems," *Proceedings of the 11th ACM Symposium on the Theory of Computing,* 1979, pp. 118–129.

1416. A. Shamir, "The Cryptographic Security of Compact Knapsacks," MIT Library for Computer Science, Technical Memorandum, MIT/LCS/TM-164, Massachusetts Institute of Technology, 1980.

1417. A. Shamir, "On the Generation of Cryptographically Strong Pseudo-Random Sequences," *Lecture Notes in Computer Science 62: 8th International Colloquium on Automata, Languages, and Programming,* Springer-Verlag, 1981.

1418. A. Shamir, "A Polynomial Time Algorithm for Breaking the Basic Merkle-Hellman Cryptosystem," *Advances in Cryptology: Proceedings of Crypto 82,* Plenum Press, 1983, pp. 279–288.

1419. A. Shamir, "A Polynomial Time Algorithm for Breaking the Basic Merkle-Hellman Cryptosystem," *Proceedings of the 23rd IEEE Symposium on the Foundations of Computer Science,* 1982, pp. 145–152.

1420. A. Shamir, "On the Generation of Cryptographically Strong Pseudo-Random Sequences," *ACM Transactions on Computer Systems,* v. 1, n. 1, Feb 1983, pp. 38–44.

1421. A. Shamir, "A Polynomial Time Algorithm for Breaking the Basic Merkle-Hellman Cryptosystem," *IEEE Transactions on Information Theory,* v. IT-30, n. 5, Sep 1984, pp. 699–704.

1422. A. Shamir, "Identity-Based Cryptosystems and Signature Schemes," *Advances in Cryptology: Proceedings of CRYPTO 84,* Springer-Verlag, 1985, pp. 47–53.

1423. A. Shamir, "On the Security of DES," *Advances in Cryptology—CRYPTO '85 Proceedings,* Springer-Verlag, 1986, pp. 280–281.

1424. A. Shamir, lecture at SECURICOM '89.

1425. A. Shamir, "Efficient Signature Schemes Based on Birational Permutations," *Advances in Cryptology—CRYPTO '93 Proceedings,* Springer-Verlag, 1994, pp. 1–12.

1426. A. Shamir, personal communication, 1993.

1427. A. Shamir and A. Fiat, "Method, Apparatus and Article for Identification and Signature," U.S. Patent #4,748,668, 31 May 1988.

1428. A. Shamir and R. Zippel, "On the Security of the Merkle-Hellman Cryptographic Scheme," *IEEE Transactions on Information Theory,* v. 26, n. 3, May 1980, pp. 339–340.

1429. M. Shand, P. Bertin, and J. Vuillemin, "Hardware Speedups in Long Integer Multiplication," *Proceedings of the 2nd Annual ACM Symposium on Parallel Algorithms and Architectures,* 1990, pp. 138–145.

1430. D. Shanks, *Solved and Unsolved Problems in Number Theory,* Washington D.C.: Spartan, 1962.

1431. C.E. Shannon, "A Mathematical Theory of Communication," *Bell System Technical Journal,* v. 27, n. 4, 1948, pp. 379–423, 623–656.

1432. C.E. Shannon, "Communication Theory of Secrecy Systems," *Bell System Technical Journal,* v. 28, n. 4, 1949, pp. 656–715.

1433. C.E. Shannon, *Collected Papers: Claude Elmwood Shannon,* N.J.A. Sloane and A.D. Wyner, eds., New York: IEEE Press, 1993.

1434. C.E. Shannon, "Predication and Entropy in Printed English," *Bell System Technical Journal,* v. 30, n. 1, 1951, pp. 50–64.

1435. A. Shimizu and S. Miyaguchi, "Fast Data Encipherment Algorithm FEAL," *Transactions of IEICE of Japan,* v. J70-D, n. 7, Jul 87, pp. 1413–1423. (In Japanese.)

1436. A. Shimizu and S. Miyaguchi, "Fast Data Encipherment Algorithm FEAL," *Advances in Cryptology—EUROCRYPT '87 Proceedings,* Springer-Verlag, 1988, pp. 267–278.

1437. A. Shimizu and S. Miyaguchi, "FEAL—Fast Data Encipherment Algorithm," *Systems and Computers in Japan,* v. 19, n. 7, 1988, pp. 20–34, 104–106.

1438. A. Shimizu and S. Miyaguchi, "Data Randomization Equipment," U.S. Patent #4,850,019, 18 Jul 1989.

1439. M. Shimada, "Another Practical Public-key Cryptosystem," *Electronics Letters*, v. 28, n. 23, 5 Nov 1992, pp. 2146–2147.

1440. K. Shirriff, personal communication, 1993.

1441. H. Shizuya, T. Itoh, and K. Sakurai, "On the Complexity of Hyperelliptic Discrete Logarithm Problem," *Advances in Cryptology—EUROCRYPT '91 Proceedings*, Springer-Verlag, 1991, pp. 337–351.

1442. Z. Shmuley, "Composite Diffie-Hellman Public-Key Generating Systems Are Hard to Break," Computer Science Department, Technion, Haifa, Israel, Technical Report 356, Feb 1985.

1443. P.W. Shor, "Algorithms for Quantum Computation: Discrete Log and Factoring," *Proceedings of the 35th Symposium on Foundations of Computer Science*, 1994, pp. 124–134.

1444. L. Shroyer, letter to NIST regarding DSS, 17 Feb 1992.

1445. C. Shu, T. Matsumoto, and H. Imai, "A Multi-Purpose Proof System, *Transactions of the Institute of Electronics, Information, and Communication Engineers*, v. E75-A, n. 6, Jun 1992, pp. 735–743.

1446. E.H. Sibley, "Random Number Generators: Good Ones Are Hard to Find," *Communications of the ACM*, v. 31, n. 10, Oct 1988, pp. 1192–1201.

1447. V.M. Sidenikov and S.O. Shestakov, "On Encryption Based on Generalized Reed-Solomon Codes," *Diskretnaya Math*, v. 4, 1992, pp. 57–63. (In Russian.)

1448. V.M. Sidenikov and S.O. Shestakov, "On Insecurity of Cryptosystems Based on Generalized Reed-Solomon Codes," unpublished manuscript, 1992.

1449. D.P. Sidhu, "Authentication Protocols for Computer Networks," *Computer Networks and ISDN Systems*, v. 11, n. 4, Apr 1986, pp. 297–310.

1450. T. Siegenthaler, "Correlation-Immunity of Nonlinear Combining Functions for Cryptographic Applications," *IEEE Transactions on Information Theory*, v. IT-30, n. 5, Sep 1984, pp. 776–780.

1451. T. Siegenthaler, "Decrypting a Class of Stream Ciphers Using Ciphertext Only," *IEEE Transactions on Computing*, v. C-34, Jan 1985, pp. 81–85.

1452. T. Siegenthaler, "Cryptanalyst's Representation of Nonlinearity Filtered *ml*-sequences," *Advances in Cryptology—EUROCRYPT '85*, Springer-Verlag, 1986, pp. 103–110.

1453. R.D. Silverman, "The Multiple Polynomial Quadratic Sieve," *Mathematics of Computation*, v. 48, n. 177, Jan 1987, pp. 329–339.

1454. G.J. Simmons, "Authentication without Secrecy: A Secure Communication Problem Uniquely Solvable by Asymmetric Encryption Techniques," *Proceedings of IEEE EASCON '79*, 1979, pp. 661–662.

1455. G.J. Simmons, "Some Number Theoretic Questions Arising in Asymmetric Encryption Techniques," *Annual Meeting of the American Mathematical Society*, AMS Abstract 763.94.1, 1979, pp. 136–151.

1456. G.J. Simmons, "High Speed Arithmetic Using Redundant Number Systems," *Proceedings of the National Telecommunications Conference*, 1980, pp. 49.3.1–49.3.2.

1457. G.J. Simmons, "A 'Weak' Privacy Protocol Using the RSA Cryptosystem," *Cryptologia*, v. 7, n. 2, Apr 1983, pp. 180–182.

1458. G.J. Simmons, "The Prisoner's Problem and the Subliminal Channel," *Advances in Cryptology: Proceedings of CRYPTO '83*, Plenum Press, 1984, pp. 51–67.

1459. G.J. Simmons, "The Subliminal Channel and Digital Signatures," *Advances in Cryptology: Proceedings of EUROCRYPT 84*, Springer-Verlag, 1985, pp. 364–378.

1460. G.J. Simmons, "A Secure Subliminal Channel (?)," *Advances in Cryptology—CRYPTO '85 Proceedings*, Springer-Verlag, 1986, pp. 33–41.

1461. G.J. Simmons, "Cryptology," *Encyclopedia Britannica*, 16th edition, 1986, pp. 913–924B.

1462. G.J. Simmons, "How to (Really) Share a Secret," *Advances in Cryptology—CRYPTO '88 Proceedings*, Springer-Verlag, 1990, pp. 390–448.

1463. G.J. Simmons, "Prepositioned Secret Sharing Schemes and/or Shared Control Schemes," *Advances in Cryptology—EUROCRYPT '89 Proceedings*, Springer-Verlag, 1990, pp. 436–467.

1464. G.J. Simmons, "Geometric Shares Secret and/or Shared Control Schemes," *Advances in Cryptology—CRYPTO '90 Proceedings*, Springer-Verlag, 1991, pp. 216–241.

1465. G.J. Simmons, ed., *Contemporary Cryptology: The Science of Information Integrity*, IEEE Press, 1992.

1466. G.J. Simmons, "An Introduction to Shared Secret and/or Shared Control Schemes and Their Application," in *Contemporary Cryptology: The Science of Information Integrity*, G.J. Simmons, ed., IEEE Press, 1992, pp. 441–497.

1467. G.J. Simmons, "How to Insure that Data Acquired to Verify Treaty Compliance Are Trustworthy," in *Contemporary Cryptology: The Science of Information Integrity*, G.J. Simmons, ed., IEEE Press, 1992, pp. 615–630.

1468. G.J. Simmons, "The Subliminal Channels of the U.S. Digital Signature Algorithm (DSA)," *Proceedings of the Third Symposium on: State and Progress of Research in Cryptography*, Rome: Fondazone Ugo Bordoni, 1993, pp. 35–54.

1469. G.J. Simmons, "Subliminal Communication is Easy Using the DSA," *Advances in Cryptology—EUROCRYPT '93 Proceedings*, Springer-Verlag, 1994, pp. 218–232.

1470. G.J. Simmons, "An Introduction to the Mathematics of Trust in Security Protocols," *Proceedings: Computer Security Foundations Workshop VI*, IEEE Computer Society Press, 1993, pp. 121–127.

1471. G.J. Simmons, "Protocols that Ensure Fairness," *Codes and Ciphers*, Institute of Mathematics and its Applications, 1995, pp. 383–394.

1472. G.J. Simmons, "Cryptanalysis and Protocol Failures," *Communications of the ACM*, v. 37, n. 11, Nov 1994, pp. 56–65.

1473. G.J. Simmons, "Subliminal Channels: Past and Present," *European Transactions on Telecommuncations*, v. 4, n. 4, Jul/Aug 1994, pp. 459–473.

1474. G.J. Simmons and M.J. Norris, *How to Cipher Fast Using Redundant Number Systems*, SAND-80-1886, Sandia National Laboratories, Aug 1980.

1475. A. Sinkov, *Elementary Cryptanalysis*, Mathematical Association of America, 1966.

1476. R. Siromoney and L. Matthew, "A Public Key Cryptosystem Based on Lyndon Words," *Information Processing Letters*, v. 35, n. 1, 15 Jun 1990, pp. 33–36.

1477. B. Smeets, "A Note on Sequences Generated by Clock-Controlled Shift Registers," *Advances in Cryptology—EUROCRYPT '85*, Springer-Verlag, 1986, pp. 40–42.

1478. M.E. Smid, "A Key Notarization System for Computer Networks," NBS Special Report 500-54, U.S. Department of Commerce, Oct 1979.

1479. M.E. Smid, "The DSS and the SHS," *Federal Digital Signature Applications Symposium*, Rockville, MD, 17–18 Feb 1993.

1480. M.E. Smid and D.K. Branstad, "The Data Encryption Standard: Past and Future," *Proceedings of the IEEE*, v. 76, n. 5., May 1988, pp. 550–559.

1481. M.E. Smid and D.K. Branstad, "The Data Encryption Standard: Past and Future," in *Contemporary Cryptology: The Science of Information Integrity*, G.J. Simmons, ed., IEEE Press, 1992, pp. 43–64.

1482. J.L. Smith, "The Design of Lucifer, A Cryptographic Device for Data Communications," IBM Research Report RC3326, 1971.

1483. J.L. Smith, "Recirculating Block Cipher Cryptographic System," U.S. Patent #3,796,830, 12 Mar 1974.

1484. J.L. Smith, W.A. Notz, and P.R. Osseck, "An Experimental Application of Cryptography to a Remotely Accessed Data System," *Proceedings of the ACM Annual Conference*, Aug 1972, pp. 282–290.

1485. K. Smith, "Watch Out Hackers, Public Encryption Chips Are Coming," *Electronics Week*, 20 May 1985, pp. 30–31.

1486. P. Smith, "LUC Public-Key Encryption," *Dr. Dobb's Journal*, v. 18, n. 1, Jan 1993, pp. 44–49.

1487. P. Smith and M. Lennon, "LUC: A New Public Key System," *Proceedings of the Ninth International Conference on Information Security, IFIP/Sec 1993*, North Holland: Elsevier Science Publishers, 1993, pp. 91–111.

1488. E. Snekkenes, "Exploring the BAN Approach to Protocol Analysis," *Proceedings of the 1991 IEEE Computer Society Symposium on Research in Security and Privacy*, 1991, pp. 171–181.

1489. B. Snow, "Multiple Independent Binary Bit Stream Generator," U.S. Patent #5,237,615, 17 Aug 1993.

1490. R. Solovay and V. Strassen, "A Fast Monte-Carlo Test for Primality," *SIAM Journal on Computing*, v. 6, Mar 1977, pp. 84–85; erratum in ibid, v. 7, 1978, p. 118.

1491. T. Sorimachi, T. Tokita, and M. Matsui, "On a Cipher Evaluation Method Based on Differential Cryptanalysis," *Proceedings of the 1994 Symposium on Cryptography* and *Information Security (SCIS 94)*, Lake Biwa, Japan, 27–29 Jan 1994, pp. 4C.1–9. (In Japanese.)

1492. A. Sorkin, "Lucifer, a Cryptographic Algorithm," *Cryptologia*, v. 8, n. 1, Jan 1984, pp. 22–41.

1493. W. Stallings, "Kerberos Keeps the Ethernet Secure," *Data Communications*, Oct 1994, pp. 103–111.

1494. W. Stallings, *Network and Internetwork Security*, Englewood Cliffs, N.J.: Prentice-Hall, 1995.

1495. W. Stallings, *Protect Your Privacy: A Guide for PGP Users*, Englewood Cliffs, N.J.: Prentice-Hall, 1995.

1496. Standards Association of Australia, "Australian Standard 2805.4 1985: Electronic Funds Transfer—Requirements for Interfaces: Part 4—Message Authentication," SAA, North Sydney, NSW, 1985.

1497. Standards Association of Australia, "Australian Standard 2805.5 1985: Electronic Funds Transfer—Requirements for Interfaces: Part 5—Data Encipherment Algorithm," SAA, North Sydney, NSW, 1985.

1498. Standards Association of Australia, "Australian Standard 2805.5.3: Electronic Data Transfer—Requirements for Interfaces: Part 5.3—Data Encipherment Algorithm 2," SAA, North Sydney, NSW, 1992.

1499. J.G. Steiner, B.C. Neuman, and J.I. Schiller, "Kerberos: An Authentication Service for Open Network Systems," *USENIX Conference Proceedings*, Feb 1988, pp. 191–202.

1500. J. Stern, "Secret Linear Congruential Generators Are Not Cryptographically Secure," *Proceedings of the 28th Symposium on Foundations of Computer Science*, 1987, pp. 421–426.

1501. J. Stern, "A New Identification Scheme Based on Syndrome Decoding," *Advances in Cryptology—CRYPTO '93 Proceedings*, Springer-Verlag, 1994, pp. 13–21.

1502. A. Stevens, "Hacks, Spooks, and Data Encryption," *Dr. Dobb's Journal*, v. 15, n. 9, Sep 1990, pp. 127–134, 147–149.

1503. R. Struik, "On the Rao-Nam Private-Key Cryptosystem Using Non-Linear Codes," *IEEE 1991 Symposium on Information Theory*, Budapest, Hungary, 1991.

1504. R. Struik and J. van Tilburg, "The Rao-Nam Scheme Is Insecure against a Chosen-Plaintext Attack," *Advances in Cryp-*

tology—CRYPTO '87 Proceedings, Springer-Verlag, 1988, pp. 445–457.

1505. S.G. Stubblebine and V.G. Gligor, "Protecting the Integrity of Privacy-Enhanced Mail with DES-Based Authentication Codes," *Proceedings of the Privacy and Security Research Group 1993 Workshop on Network and Distributed System Security*, The Internet Society, 1993, pp. 75–80.

1506. R. Sugarman, "On Foiling Computer Crime," *IEEE Spectrum*, v. 16, n. 7, Jul 79, pp. 31–32.

1507. H.N. Sun and T. Hwang, "Public-key ID-Based Cryptosystem," *Proceedings of the 25th Annual 1991 IEEE International Carnahan Conference on Security Technology*, Taipei, Taiwan, 1–3 Oct 1991, pp. 142–144.

1508. P.F. Syverson, "Formal Semantics for Logics of Computer Protocols," *Proceedings of the Computer Security Foundations Workshop III*, IEEE Computer Society Press, 1990, pp. 32–41.

1509. P.F. Syverson, "The Use of Logic in the Analysis of Cryptographic Protocols," *Proceedings of the 1991 IEEE Computer Society Symposium on Research in Security and Privacy*, 1991, pp. 156–170.

1510. P.F. Syverson, "Knowledge, Belief, and Semantics in the Analysis of Cryptographic Protocols," *Journal of Computer Security*, v. 1, n. 3, 1992, pp. 317–334.

1511. P.F. Syverson, "Adding Time to a Logic Authentication," *1st ACM Conference on Computer and Communications Security*, ACM Press, 1993, pp. 97–106.

1512. P.F. Syverson and C.A. Meadows, "A Logical Language for Specifying Cryptographic Protocol Requirements," *Proceedings of the 1993 IEEE Computer Society Symposium on Research in Security and Privacy*, 1993, pp. 14–28.

1513. P.F. Syverson and C.A. Meadows, "Formal Requirements for Key Distribution Protocols," *Advances in Cryptology—EUROCRYPT '94 Proceedings*, Springer-Verlag, 1995, to appear.

1514. P.F. Syverson and P.C. van Oorschot, "On Unifying Some Cryptographic Protocol Logics," *Proceedings of the 1994 IEEE Computer Society Symposium on Research in Security and Privacy*, 1994, pp. 165–177.

1515. H. Tanaka, "A Realization Scheme for the Identity-Based Cryptosystem," *Advances in Cryptology—CRYPTO '87 Proceedings*, Springer-Verlag, 1988, pp. 340–349.

1516. H. Tanaka, "A Realization Scheme for the Identity-Based Cryptosystem," *Electronics and Communications in Japan, Part 3 (Fundamental Electronic Science)*, v. 73, n. 5, May 1990, pp. 1–7.

1517. H. Tanaka, "Identity-Based Noninteractive Common-Key Generation and Its Application to Cryptosystems," *Transactions of the Institute of Electronics, Information, and Communication Engineers*, v. J75-A, n. 4, Apr 1992, pp. 796–800.

1518. J. Tardo and K. Alagappan, "SPX: Global Authentication Using Public Key Certificates," *Proceedings of the 1991 IEEE Computer Society Symposium on Security and Privacy*, 1991, pp. 232–244.

1519. J. Tardo, K. Alagappan, and R. Pitkin, "Public Key Based Authentication Using Internet Certificates," *USENIX Security II Workshop Proceedings*, 1990, pp. 121–123.

1520. A. Tardy-Corfdir and H. Gilbert, "A Known Plaintext Attack of FEAL-4 and FEAL-6," *Advances in Cryptology—CRYPTO '91 Proceedings*, Springer-Verlag, 1992, pp. 172–182.

1521. M. Tatebayashi, N. Matsuzaki, and D.B. Newman, "Key Distribution Protocol for Digital Mobile Communication System," *Advances in Cryptology—CRYPTO '89 Proceedings*, Springer-Verlag, 1990, pp. 324–333.

1522. M. Taylor, "Implementing Privacy Enhanced Mail on VMS," *Proceedings of the Privacy and Security Research Group 1993 Workshop on Network and Distributed System Security*, The Internet Society, 1993, pp. 63–68.

1523. R. Taylor, "An Integrity Check Value Algorithm for Stream Ciphers," *Advances in Cryptology—CRYPTO '93 Proceedings*, Springer-Verlag, 1994, pp. 40–48.

1524. T. Tedrick, "Fair Exchange of Secrets," *Advances in Cryptology: Proceedings of CRYPTO '84*, Springer-Verlag, 1985, pp. 434–438.

1525. R. Terada and P.G. Pinheiro, "How to Strengthen FEAL against Differential Cryptanalysis," *Proceedings of the 1995 Japan-Korea Workshop on Information Security and Cryptography*, Inuyama, Japan, 24–27 Jan 1995, pp. 153–162.

1526. J.-P. Tillich and G. Zémor, "Hashing with SI_2," *Advances in Cryptology—CRYPTO '94 Proceedings*, Springer-Verlag, 1994, pp. 40–49.

1527. T. Tokita, T. Sorimachi, and M. Matsui, "An Efficient Search Algorithm for the Best Expression on Linear Cryptanalysis," *IEICE Japan, Technical Report*, ISEC93-97, 1994.

1528. M. Tompa and H. Woll, "Random Self-Reducibility and Zero-Knowledge Interactive Proofs of Possession of Information," *Proceedings of the 28th IEEE Symposium on the Foundations of Computer Science*, 1987, pp. 472–482.

1529. M. Tompa and H. Woll, "How to Share a Secret with Cheaters," *Journal of Cryptology*, v. 1, n. 2, 1988, pp. 133–138.

1530. M.-J. Toussaint, "Verification of Cryptographic Protocols," Ph.D. dissertation, Université de Liège, 1991.

1531. M.-J. Toussaint, "Deriving the Complete Knowledge of Participants in Cryptographic Protocols," *Advances in Cryptology—CRYPTO '91 Proceedings*, Springer-Verlag, 1992, pp. 24–43.

1532. M.-J. Toussaint, "Separating the Specification and Implementation Phases in Cryptology," *ESORICS 92, Proceedings of the Second European Symposium on Research in Computer Security*, Springer-Verlag, 1992, pp. 77–101.

1533. P.D. Townsend, J.G. Rarity, and P.R. Tapster, "Enhanced Single Photon Fringe Visibility in a 10 km-Long Prototype Quantum Cryptography Channel," *Electronics Letters*, v. 28, n. 14, 8 Jul 1993, pp. 1291–1293.

1534. S.A. Tretter, "Properties of PN^2 Sequences," *IEEE Transactions on Information Theory*, v. IT-20, n. 2, Mar 1974, pp. 295–297.

1535. H. Truman, "Memorandum for: The Secretary of State, The Secretary of Defense," A 20707 5/4/54/OSO, NSA TS CONTL. NO 73-00405, 24 Oct 1952.

1536. Y.W. Tsai and T. Hwang, "ID Based Public Key Cryptosystem Based on Okamoto and Tanaka's ID Based One-Way Communications Scheme," *Electronics Letters*, v. 26, n. 10, 1 May 1990, pp. 666–668.

1537. G. Tsudik, "Message Authentication with One-Way Hash Functions," *ACM Computer Communications Review*, v. 22, n. 5, 1992, pp. 29–38.

1538. S. Tsujii and K. Araki, "A Rebuttal to Coppersmith's Attacking Method," memorandum presented at Crypto '94, Aug 1994.

1539. S. Tsujii, K. Araki, J. Chao, T. Sekine, and Y. Matsuzaki, "ID-Based Key Sharing Scheme—Cancellation of Random Numbers by Iterative Addition," IEICE Japan, Technical Report, ISEC 92-47, Oct 1992.

1540. S. Tsujii, K. Araki, and T. Sekine, "A New Scheme of Noninteractive ID-Based Key Sharing with Explosively High Degree of Separability," Technical Report, Department of Computer Science, Tokyo Institute of Technology, 93TR-0016, May 1993.

1541. S. Tsujii, K. Araki, and T. Sekine, "A New Scheme of Non Interactive ID-Based key Sharing with Explosively High Degree of Separability (Second Version)," Technical Report, Department of Computer Science, Tokyo Institute of Technology, 93TR-0020, Jul 1993.

1542. S. Tsujii, K. Araki, T. Sekine, and K. Tanada, "A New Scheme of Non Interactive ID-Based Key Sharing with Explosively High Degree of Separability," *Proceedings of the 1993 Korea-Japan Workshop on Information Security and Cryptography*, Seoul, Korea, 24–26 Oct 1993, pp. 49–58.

1543. S. Tsujii, K. Araki, H. Tanaki, J. Chao, T. Sekine, and Y. Matsuzaki, "ID-Based Key Sharing Scheme—Reply to Tanaka's Comment," IEICE Japan, Technical Report, ISEC 92-60, Dec 1992.

1544. S. Tsujii and J. Chao, "A New ID-based Key Sharing System," *Advances in Cryptology—CRYPTO '91 Proceedings*, Springer-Verlag, 1992, pp. 288–299.

1545. S. Tsujii, J. Chao, and K. Araki, "A Simple ID-Based Scheme for Key Sharing," IEICE Japan, Technical Report, ISEC 92-25, Aug 1992.

1546. S. Tsujii and T. Itoh, "An ID-Based Cryptosystem Based on the Discrete Logarithm Problem," *IEEE Journal on Selected Areas in Communication*, v. 7, n. 4, May 1989, pp. 467–473.

1547. S. Tsujii and T. Itoh, "An ID-Based Cryptosystem Based on the Discrete Logarithm Problem," *Electronics Letters*, v. 23, n. 24, Nov 1989, pp. 1318–1320.

1548. S. Tsujii, K. Kurosawa, T. Itoh, A. Fujioka, and T. Matsumoto, "A Public-Key Cryptosystem Based on the Difficulty of Solving a System of Non-Linear Equations," TSUJII Laboratory Technical Memorandum, n. 1, 1986.

1549. Y. Tsunoo, E. Okamoto, and H. Doi, "Analytical Known Plain-Text Attack for FEAL-4 and Its Improvement," *Proceedings of the 1994 Symposium on Cryptography and Information Security (SCIS 93)*, 1993.

1550. Y. Tsunoo, E. Okamoto, T. Uyematsu, and M. Mambo, "Analytical Known Plain-Text Attack for FEAL-6" *Proceedings of the 1993 Korea-Japan Workshop on Information Security and Cryptography*, Seoul, Korea, 24–26 Oct 1993, pp. 253–261.

1551. W. Tuchman, "Hellman Presents No Shortcut Solutions to DES," *IEEE Spectrum*, v. 16, n. 7, July 1979, pp. 40–41.

1552. U.S. Senate Select Committee on Intelligence, "Unclassified Summary: Involvement of NSA in the Development of the Data Encryption Standard," *IEEE Communications Magazine*, v. 16, n. 6, Nov 1978, pp. 53–55.

1553. B. Vallée, M. Girault, and P. Toffin, "How to Break Okamoto's Cryptosystem by Reducing Lattice Values," *Advances in Cryptology—EUROCRYPT '88 Proceedings*, Springer-Verlag, 1988, p. 281–291.

1554. H. Van Antwerpen, "Electronic Cash," Master's thesis, CWI, Netherlands, 1990.

1555. K. Van Espen and J. Van Mieghem, "Evaluatie en Implementatie van Authentiseringsalgoritmen," graduate thesis, ESAT Laboratorium, Katholieke Universiteit Leuven, 1989. (In Dutch.)

1556. P.C. van Oorschot, "Extending Cryptographic Logics of Belief to Key Agreement Protocols," *Proceedings of the 1st Annual ACM Conference on Computer and Communications Security*, 1993, pp. 232–243.

1557. P.C. van Oorschot, "An Alternate Explanation for Two BAN-logic 'Failures,' " *Advances in Cryptology—EUROCRYPT '93 Proceedings*, Springer-Verlag, 1994, pp. 443–447.

1558. P.C. van Oorschot and M.J. Wiener, "A Known-Plaintext Attack on Two-Key Triple Encryption," *Advances in Cryptology—EUROCRYPT '90 Proceedings*, Springer-Verlag, 1991, pp. 318–325.

1559. J. van Tilburg, "On the McEliece Cryptosystem," *Advances in Cryptology—*

CRYPTO '88 Proceedings, Springer-Verlag, 1990, pp. 119–131.

1560. J. van Tilburg, "Cryptanalysis of the Xinmei Digital Signature Scheme," *Electronics Letters*, v. 28, n. 20, 24 Sep 1992, pp. 1935–1938.

1561. J. van Tilburg, "Two Chosen-Plaintext Attacks on the Li Wang Joing Authentication and Encryption Scheme," *Applied Algebra, Algebraic Algorithms and Error Correcting Codes 10*, Springer-Verlag, 1993, pp. 332–343.

1562. J. van Tilburg, "Security-Analysis of a Class of Cryptosystems Based on Linear Error-Correcting Codes," Ph.D. dissertation, Technical University Eindhoven, 1994.

1563. A. Vandemeulebroecke, E. Vanzieleghem, T. Denayer, and P.G. Jespers, "A Single Chip 1024 Bits RSA Processor," *Advances in Cryptology—EUROCRYPT '89 Proceedings*, Springer-Verlag, 1990, pp. 219–236.

1564. J. Vanderwalle, D. Chaum, W. Fumy, C. Jansen, P. Landrock, and G. Roelofsen, "A European Call for Cryptographic Algorithms: RIPE; RACE Integrity Primitives Evaluation," *Advances in Cryptology—EUROCRYPT '89 Proceedings*, Springer-Verlag, 1990, pp. 267–271.

1565. V. Varadharajan, "Verification of Network Security Protocols," *Computers and Security*, v. 8, n. 8, Aug 1989, pp. 693–708.

1566. V. Varadharajan, "Use of a Formal Description Technique in the Specification of Authentication Protocols," *Computer Standards and Interfaces*, v. 9, 1990, pp. 203–215.

1567. S. Vaudenay, "FFT-Hash-II Is not Yet Collision-Free," *Advances in Cryptology—CRYPTO '92 Proceedings*, Springer-Verlag, pp. 587–593.

1568. S. Vaudenay, "Differential Cryptanalysis of Blowfish," unpublished manuscript, 1995.

1569. U.V. Vazirani and V.V. Vazirani, "Trapdoor Pseudo-Random Number Generators with Applications to Protocol Design," *Proceedings of the 24th IEEE Symposium on the Foundations of Computer Science*, 1983, pp. 23–30.

1570. U.V. Vazirani and V.V. Vazirani, "Efficient and Secure Pseudo-Random Number Generation," *Proceedings of the 25th IEEE Symposium on the Foundations of Computer Science*, 1984, pp. 458–463.

1571. U.V. Vazirani and V.V. Vazirani, "Efficient and Secure Pseudo-Random Number Generation," *Advances in Cryptology: Proceedings of CRYPTO '84*, Springer-Verlag, 1985, pp. 193–202.

1572. I. Verbauwhede, F. Hoornaert, J. Vanderwalle, and H. De Man, "ASIC Cryptographical Processor Based on DES," *Euro ASIC '91 Proceedings*, 1991, pp. 292–295.

1573. I. Verbauwhede, F. Hoornaert, J. Vanderwalle, H. De Man, and R. Govaerts, "Security Considerations in the Design and Implementation of a New DES Chip," *Advances in Cryptology—EUROCRYPT '87 Proceedings*, Springer-Verlag, 1988, pp. 287–300.

1574. R. Vogel, "On the Linear Complexity of Cascaded Sequences," *Advances in Cryptology: Proceedings of EUROCRYPT 84*, Springer-Verlag, 1985, pp. 99–109.

1575. S. von Solms and D. Naccache, "On Blind Signatures and Perfect Crimes," *Computers & Security*, v. 11, 1992, pp. 581–583.

1576. V.L. Voydock and S.T. Kent, "Security Mechanisms in High-Level Networks," *ACM Computing Surveys*, v. 15, n. 2, Jun 1983, pp. 135–171.

1577. N.R. Wagner, P.S. Putter, and M.R. Cain, "Large-Scale Randomization Techniques," *Advances in Cryptology—CRYPTO '86 Proceedings*, Springer-Verlag, 1987, pp. 393–404.

1578. M. Waidner and B. Pfitzmann, "The Dining Cryptographers in the Disco: Unconditional Sender and Recipient Untraceability with Computationally Secure Serviceability," *Advances in Cryptology—EUROCRYPT '89 Proceedings*, Springer-Verlag, 1990, p. 690.

1579. S.T. Walker, "Software Key Escrow—A Better Solution for Law Enforcement's Needs?" TIS Report #533, Trusted Information Systems, Aug 1994.

1580. S.T. Walker, "Thoughts on Key Escrow Acceptability," TIS Report #534D, Trusted Information Systems, Nov 1994.

1581. S.T. Walker, S.B. Lipner, C.M. Ellison, D.K. Branstad, and D.M. Balenson, "Commercial Key Escrow—Something for Everyone—Now and for the Future," TIS Report #541, Trusted Information Systems, Jan 1995.

1582. M.Z. Wang and J.L. Massey, "The Characteristics of All Binary Sequences with Perfect Linear Complexity Profiles,"

Abstracts of Papers, EUROCRYPT '86, 20–22 May 1986.

1583. E.J. Watson, "Primitive Polynomials (Mod 2)," *Mathematics of Computation,* v. 16, 1962, p. 368.

1584. P. Wayner, "Mimic Functions," *Cryptologia,* v. 16, n. 3, Jul 1992, pp. 193–214.

1585. P. Wayner, "Mimic Functions and Tractability," draft manuscript, 1993.

1586. A.F. Webster and S.E. Tavares, "On the Design of S-Boxes," *Advances in Cryptology—CRYPTO '85 Proceedings,* Springer-Verlag, 1986, pp. 523–534.

1587. G. Welchman, *The Hut Six Story: Breaking the Enigma Codes,* New York: McGraw-Hill, 1982.

1588. A.L. Wells Jr., "A Polynomial Form for Logarithms Modulo a Prime," *IEEE Transactions on Information Theory,* Nov 1984, pp. 845–846.

1589. D.J. Wheeler, "A Bulk Data Encryption Algorithm," *Fast Software Encryption, Cambridge Security Workshop Proceedings,* Springer-Verlag, 1994, pp. 127–134.

1590. D.J. Wheeler, personal communication, 1994.

1591. D.J. Wheeler and R. Needham, "A Large Block DES-Like Algorithm," Technical Report 355, "Two Cryptographic Notes," Computer Laboratory, University of Cambridge, Dec 1994, pp. 1–3.

1592. D.J. Wheeler and R. Needham, "TEA, A Tiny Encryption Algorithm," Technical Report 355, "Two Cryptographic Notes," Computer Laboratory, University of Cambridge, Dec 1994, pp. 1–3.

1593. S.R. White, "Covert Distributed Processing with Computer Viruses," *Advances in Cryptology—CRYPTO '89 Proceedings,* Springer-Verlag, 1990, pp. 616–619.

1594. White House, Office of the Press Secretary, "Statement by the Press Secretary," 16 Apr 1993.

1595. B.A. Wichman and I.D. Hill, "An Efficient and Portable Pseudo-Random Number Generator," *Applied Statistics,* v. 31, 1982, pp. 188–190.

1596. M.J. Wiener, "Cryptanalysis of Short RSA Secret Exponents," *IEEE Transactions on Information Theory,* v. 36, n. 3, May 1990, pp. 553–558.

1597. M.J. Wiener, "Efficient DES Key Search," presented at the rump session of CRYPTO '93, Aug 1993.

1598. M.J. Wiener, "Efficient DES Key Search," TR-244, School of Computer Science, Carleton University, May 1994.

1599. M.V. Wilkes, *Time-Sharing Computer Systems,* New York: American Elsevier, 1968.

1600. E.A. Williams, *An Invitation to Cryptograms,* New York: Simon and Schuster, 1959.

1601. H.C. Williams, "A Modification of the RSA Public-Key Encryption Procedure," *IEEE Transactions on Information Theory,* v. IT-26, n. 6, Nov 1980, pp. 726–729.

1602. H.C. Williams, "An Overview of Factoring," *Advances in Cryptology: Proceedings of Crypto 83,* Plenum Press, 1984, pp. 71–80.

1603. H.C. Williams, "Some Public-Key Crypto-Functions as Intractable as Factorization," *Advances in Cryptology: Proceedings of CRYPTO 84,* Springer-Verlag, 1985, pp. 66–70.

1604. H.C. Williams, "Some Public-Key Crypto-Functions as Intractable as Factorization," *Cryptologia,* v. 9, n. 3, Jul 1985, pp. 223–237.

1605. H.C. Williams, "An M^3 Public-Key Encryption Scheme," *Advances in Cryptology—CRYPTO '85,* Springer-Verlag, 1986, pp. 358–368.

1606. R.S. Winternitz, "Producing One-Way Hash Functions from DES," *Advances in Cryptology: Proceedings of Crypto 83,* Plenum Press, 1984, pp. 203–207.

1607. R.S. Winternitz, "A Secure One-Way Hash Function Built from DES," *Proceedings of the 1984 Symposium on Security and Privacy,* 1984, pp. 88–90.

1608. S. Wolfram, "Random Sequence Generation by Cellular Automata," *Advances in Applied Mathematics,* v. 7, 1986, pp. 123–169.

1609. S. Wolfram, "Cryptography with Cellular Automata," *Advances in Cryptology—CRYPTO '85 Proceedings,* Springer-Verlag, 1986, pp. 429–432.

1610. T.Y.C. Woo and S.S. Lam, "Authentication for Distributed Systems," *Computer,* v. 25, n. 1, Jan 1992, pp. 39–52.

1611. T.Y.C. Woo and S.S. Lam, " 'Authentication' Revisited," *Computer,* v. 25, n. 3, Mar 1992, p. 10.

1612. T.Y.C. Woo and S.S. Lam, "A Semantic Model for Authentication Protocols," *Proceedings of the 1993 IEEE Computer Soci-*

ety *Symposium on Research in Security and Privacy*, 1993, pp. 178–194.

1613. M.C. Wood, technical report, Cryptech, Inc., Jamestown, NY, Jul 1990.

1614. M.C. Wood, "Method of Cryptographically Transforming Electronic Digital Data from One Form to Another," U.S. Patent #5,003,596, 26 Mar 1991.

1615. M.C. Wood, personal communication, 1993.

1616. C.K. Wu and X.M. Wang, "Determination of the True Value of the Euler Totient Function in the RSA Cryptosystem from a Set of Possibilities," *Electronics Letters*, v. 29, n. 1, 7 Jan 1993, pp. 84–85.

1617. M.C. Wunderlich, "Recent Advances in the Design and Implementation of Large Integer Factorization Algorithms," *Proceedings of 1983 Symposium on Security and Privacy*, IEEE Computer Society Press, 1983, pp. 67–71.

1618. Xerox Network System (XNS) Authentication Protocol, XSIS 098404, Xerox Corporation, Apr 1984.

1619. Y.Y. Xian, "New Public Key Distribution System," *Electronics Letters*, v. 23, n. 11, 1987, pp. 560–561.

1620. L.D. Xing and L.G. Sheng, "Cryptanalysis of New Modified Lu-Lee Cryptosystems," *Electronics Letters*, v. 26, n. 19, 13 Sep 1990, p. 1601–1602.

1621. W. Xinmei, "Digital Signature Scheme Based on Error-Correcting Codes," *Electronics Letters*, v. 26, n. 13, 21 Jun 1990, p. 898–899.

1622. S.B. Xu, D.K. He, and X.M. Wang, "An Implementation of the GSM General Data Encryption Algorithm A5," *CHINACRYPT '94*, Xidian, China, 11–15 Nov 1994, pp. 287–291. (In Chinese.)

1623. M. Yagisawa, "A New Method for Realizing Public-Key Cryptosystem," *Cryptologia*, v. 9, n. 4, Oct 1985, pp. 360–380.

1624. C.H. Yang, "Modular Arithmetic Algorithms for Smart Cards," IEICE Japan, Technical Report, ISEC92-16, 1992.

1625. C.H. Yang and H. Morita, "An Efficient Modular-Multiplication Algorithm for Smart-Card Software Implementation," IEICE Japan, Technical Report, ISEC91-58, 1991.

1626. J.H. Yang, K.C. Zeng, and Q.B. Di, "On the Construction of Large S-Boxes," *CHINACRYPT '94*, Xidian, China, 11–15 Nov 1994, pp. 24–32. (In Chinese.)

1627. A.C.-C. Yao, "Protocols for Secure Computations," *Proceedings of the 23rd IEEE Symposium on the Foundations of Computer Science*, 1982, pp. 160–164.

1628. B. Yee, "Using Secure Coprocessors," Ph.D. dissertation, School of Computer Science, Carnegie Mellon University, May 1994.

1629. S.-M. Yen, "Design and Computation of Public Key Cryptosystems," Ph.D. dissertation, National Cheng Hung University, Apr 1994.

1630. S.-M. Yen and C.-S. Lai, "New Digital Signature Scheme Based on the Discrete Logarithm," *Electronics Letters*, v. 29, n. 12, 1993, pp. 1120–1121.

1631. K. Yiu and K. Peterson, "A Single-Chip VLSI Implementation of the Discrete Exponential Public-Key Distribution System," *IBM Systems Journal*, v. 15, n. 1, 1982, pp. 102–116.

1632. K. Yiu and K. Peterson, "A Single-Chip VLSI Implementation of the Discrete Exponential Public-Key Distribution System," *Proceedings of Government Microcircuit Applications Conference*, 1982, pp. 18–23.

1633. H.Y. Youm, S.L. Lee, and M.Y. Rhee, "Practical Protocols for Electronic Cash," *Proceedings of the 1993 Korea-Japan Workshop on Information Security and Cryptography*, Seoul, Korea, 24–26 Oct 1993, pp. 10–22.

1634. M. Yung, "Cryptoprotocols: Subscriptions to a Public Key, the Secret Blocking, and the Multi-Player Mental Poker Game," *Advances in Cryptology: Proceedings of CRYPTO 84*, Springer-Verlag, 1985, 439–453.

1635. G. Yuval, "How to Swindle Rabin," *Cryptologia*, v. 3, n. 3, Jul 1979, pp. 187–190.

1636. K.C. Zeng and M. Huang, "On the Linear Syndrome Method in Cryptanalysis," *Advances in Cryptology—CRYPTO '88 Proceedings*, Springer-Verlag, 1990, pp. 469–478.

1637. K.C. Zeng, M. Huang, and T.R.N. Rao, "An Improved Linear Algorithm in Cryptanalysis with Applications," *Advances in Cryptology—CRYPTO '90 Proceedings*, Springer-Verlag, 1991, pp. 34–47.

1638. K.C. Zeng, C.-H. Yang, and T.R.N. Rao, "On the Linear Consistency Test (LCT) in Cryptanalysis with Applications," *Advances in Cryptology—CRYPTO '89*

Proceedings, Springer-Verlag, 1990, pp. 164–174.

1639. K.C. Zeng, C.-H. Yang, D.-Y. Wei, and T.R.N. Rao, "Pseudorandom Bit Generators in Stream-Cipher Cryptography," *IEEE Computer*, v. 24, n. 2, Feb 1991, pp. 8–17.

1640. M. Zhang, S.E. Tavares, and L.L. Campbell, "Information Leakage of Boolean Functions and Its Relationship to Other Cryptographic Criteria," *Proceedings of the 2nd Annual ACM Conference on Computer and Communications Security*, ACM Press, 1994, pp. 156–165.

1641. M. Zhang and G. Xiao, "A Modified Design Criterion for Stream Ciphers," *CHINACRYPT '94*, Xidian, China, 11–15 Nov 1994, pp. 201–209. (In Chinese.)

1642. Y. Zheng, T. Matsumoto, and H. Imai, "Duality between two Cryptographic Primitives," *Papers of Technical Group for Information Security*, IEICE of Japan, Mar 1989, pp. 47–57.

1643. Y. Zheng, T. Matsumoto, and H. Imai, "Impossibility and Optimality Results in Constructing Pseudorandom Permutations," *Advances in Cryptology—EUROCRYPT '89 Proceedings*, Springer-Verlag, 1990, pp. 412–422.

1644. Y. Zheng, T. Matsumoto, and H. Imai, "On the Construction of Block Ciphers Provably Secure and Not Relying on Any Unproved Hypotheses," *Advances in*

Cryptology—CRYPTO '89 Proceedings, Springer-Verlag, 1990, pp. 461–480.

1645. Y. Zheng, T. Matsumoto, and H. Imai, "Duality between two Cryptographic Primitives," *Proceedings of the 8th International Conference on Applied Algebra, Algebraic Algorithms and Error-Correcting Codes*, Springer-Verlag, 1991, pp. 379–390.

1646. Y. Zheng, J. Pieprzyk, and J. Seberry, "HAVAL—A One-Way Hashing Algorithm with Variable Length of Output," *Advances in Crytology—AUSCRYPT '92 Proceedings*, Springer-Verlag, 1993, pp. 83–104.

1647. N. Zierler, "Linear Recurring Sequences," *Journal Soc. Indust. Appl. Math.*, v. 7, n. 1, Mar 1959, pp. 31–48.

1648. N. Zierler, "Primitive Trinomials Whose Degree Is a Mersenne Exponent," *Information and Control*, v. 15, 1969, pp. 67–69.

1649. N. Zierler and J. Brillhart, "On Primitive Trinomials (mod 2)," *Information and Control*, v. 13, n. 6, Dec 1968, pp. 541–544.

1650. N. Zierler and W.H. Mills, "Products of Linear Recurring Sequences," *Journal of Algebra*, v. 27, n. 1, Oct 1973, pp. 147–157.

1651. C. Zimmer, "Perfect Gibberish," *Discover*, v. 13, n. 12, Dec 1992, pp. 92–99.

1652. P.R. Zimmermann, *The Official PGP User's Guide*, Boston: MIT Press, 1995.

1653. P.R. Zimmermann, *PGP Source Code and Internals*, Boston: MIT Press, 1995.

Index

A5, 389, 662–667
Abadi, Martin, 66
Absolute rate, of language, 234
Accreditation, 103
Active attacks, 27
Active cheaters, 27
Adams, Carlisle, 334
Adaptive-chosen-plaintext attack, 6
Addition chaining, 244
Additive generators, 390–392
Adjudicated protocol, 26, 71
Adjudicator, 26
Adleman, Leonard M., 163–164, 467
Adler, Roy, 266
Agnew, G. B., 423
Algebraic structure, DES, 282–283
Algorithm M, 393–394
Algorithms, 2–4, 17
    all-or-nothing disclosure of secrets, 543–546
    Asmuth-Bloom, 529–530
    Barrett's, 244
    Berlekamp-Massey algorithm, 380, 404
    block
        chain mode, 206–207
        choosing, 354–355
        replay, 191–193
    breaking, 8
    CAST, 334–335
    choosing, 214–216

cipher block chaining mode, 193–197, 208–210
cipher block chaining of plaintext difference mode, 208
cipher block chaining with checksum, 207–208
cipher-feedback mode, 200–202, 208–210
cipher mode
    choosing, 208–210
    summary, 209
classes, 217
coin flipping
    using Blum integers, 543
    using exponentiation modulo p, 542–543
    using square roots, 541–542
complexity, 237–239
constant, 238
convertible undeniable signatures, 538–539
counter mode, 205–206, 209
cubic, 238
data compression, 226
designated confirmer signatures, 539–540
Diffie-Hellman, fair, 546–547
digital signatures, 39
exponential, 238
for export, 215–216
extended Euclidean, 246–248
factoring, 256
ISO/IEC 9979 registered, 607
Karnin-Greene-Hellman, 530

Khafre, 317–318
Khufu, 317
linear, 238
linear syndrome, 381
modes, DES, 277–278
multiple block
    cascading, 367–368
    combining, 368
multiple-key public-key cryptography, 527–528
oblivious transfer, 550
one-way accumulators, 543
output-feedback mode, 203–205, 208–210
output feedback with a non-linear function, 208
plaintext block chaining mode, 208
plaintext feedback mode, 208
polynomial, 238
polynomial-time, 238
probabilistic encryption, 552–554
propagating cipher block chaining mode, 207
public-key, 4–5, 33
quadratic, 238
quantum cryptography, 554–557
restricted, 3
running times, 238–239
secret-sharing algorithms, 528–531
secure multiparty computation, 551–552

Algorithms (*Cont.*)
  security, 8–9
  self-synchronizing stream
    cipher, 198–199
  stream ciphers, 197–198
  subliminal-channel signature,
    79
  superpolynomial, 238
  symmetric, 4
  synchronous stream cipher,
    202–203
  TEA, 346
  types, 189
  unconditionally secure, 8
  undeniable digital signatures,
    536–539
  using, 213–229
  vector scheme, 529
  zero-knowledge proofs,
    548–550
  See also Block ciphers;
    Stream ciphers
All-or-nothing disclosure of
  secrets, 96, 543–546
  voting with a single central
    facility, 128–130
Alternating stop-and-go generator, 383, 385, 410–411
American National Standards
  Institute, DES approval,
  267–268
Anderson, Ross, 391
ANDOS, *see* All-or-nothing dis-
  closure of secrets
Anonymous message broadcast,
  137–139
ANSI X3.105, 267
ANSI X3.106, 267
ANSI X9.8, 267
ANSI X9.17, 268, 359
  key generation, 175
ANSI X9.19, 267
ANSI X9.26, 268
Arbitrated protocol, 23–26
Arbitration, timestamping,
  75–76
Arbitrator, 23
  document signing with,
    35–37
  group signatures with, 84–85
AR hash function, 453
Arithmetic, modular, 242–245
Arms Export Control Act, 610
Asmuth-Bloom scheme,
  529–530
Association for Computing
  Machinery, 608

Asymmetric algorithms, *see*
  Public-key algorithms
Atomic Energy Act, 610
Attack, 5
AT&T Model 3600 Telephone
  Security Device, 594–
  595
Authentication, 2, 52–56
  DASS, 62
  Denning-Sacco protocol, 63
  dictionary attacks, 52
  ISO framework, 574–577
  Kerberos, 60
  message, 56
  Needham-Schroeder protocol,
    58–59
  Neuman-Stubblebine proto-
    col, 60–62
  Otway-Rees protocol, 59–60
  protocols, formal analysis,
    65–68
  salt, 52–53
  Schnorr, 511
  SESAME, 572
  SKEY, 53
  SKID, 55–56
  using interlock protocol,
    54–55
  using one-way functions, 52
  using public-key cryptogra-
    phy, 53–54
  Wide-Mouth Frog protocol,
    56–57
  Woo-Lam protocol, 63–64
  Yahalom, 57–58
Authenticators, 568
Avalanche effect, 273

Backup keys, 181–182
BAN logic, 66–67
Barrett's algorithm, 244
BaseKing, 346
Basis, polarization measure-
  ment, 555
Battista, Leon, 11
BBS generator, 417
  add to spelled out, 553–554
Beacons, 89
Bellovin, Steve, 518, 520–521,
  571
Bennett, Charles, 555, 557
Berlekamp-Massey algorithm,
  380, 404
Bernstein, Dan, 616
Berson, Tom, 441
Best affine approximation
  attack, 381

Beth-Piper stop-and-go generator, 383–384
Bias, 425
Bidirectional message authenti-
  cation codes, 457
Biham, Eli, 284–285, 288, 296,
  301, 303, 306, 308,
  311–312, 314, 316, 319,
  354, 361, 434
Bilateral stop-and-go generator,
  384–385
Binary trees, 78
Biotechnology, as cryptanalysis
  tool, 156–157
Birthday attack, 165–166, 430
Bit commitment, 86–88
  using one-way functions,
    87–88
  using pseudo-random-
    sequence generators, 88
  using symmetric cryptogra-
    phy, 86–87
Blakley, George, 72, 529
Blaze, Matt, 346, 364
Blinding factor, 112
Blind signatures, 112–115,
  549–550
  patents, 115
  voting with, 126–127
Blobs, 88
Block algorithms, 4
Block chain mode, 206–207
Block ciphers, 4, 189
  Blowfish, 336–339
  CA-1.1, 327–328
  cascading algorithms,
    367–368
  CAST, 334–335
  CDMF key shortening, 366
  choosing algorithms, 354–355
  combining algorithms, 368
  counter mode, 205–206, 209
  Crab, 342–344
  CRYPTO-MECCANO, 346
  designing, 351
  design theory, 346–351
    Feistel networks, 347
    group structure, 348
    S-box, 349–351
    simple relations, 347–348
    strength against differential
      and linear cryptanalysis,
      348–349
    weak keys, 348
  double encryption, 357–358
  double OFB/counter, 363–364
  doubling length, 363

electronic codebook mode, 189–191, 208–210
encryption speeds, 355
FEAL, 308–312
feedback, 193
GOST, 331–334
IDEA, 319–325
iterated, 347
Li-Wang algorithm, 346
LOKI, 314–316
Lucifer, 303–304
Madryga, 304–306
McEliece algorithm, 346
MMB, 325–327
multiple encryption, 357
NewDES, 306–308
Rao-Nam algorithm, 346
RC2, 318–319
RC5, 344–346
REDOC II, 311–313
REDOC III, 313
SAFER K-64, 339–341
security, based on one-way hash functions, 353–354
Skipjack, 328–329
versus stream ciphers, 210–211
SXAL8/MBAL, 344
triple encryption, 358–363
3–Way, 341–342
using one-way hash functions, 351–354
whitening, 366–367
$xDES^1$, 365–366
Block length, doubling, 363
Block replay, 191–193
Blocks, 4
Blowfish, 336–339, 354, 647–654
Blum, Manuel, 89, 105, 108
Blum, Blum, and Shub generator, 417–418
Blum integers, 253
coin flipping, 543
zero-knowledge proofs, 549
Blum-Micali generator, 416–417
Boolean functions, in S-boxes, 350
Bosselaers, Antoon, 436, 441
Boyar, Joan, 369
Brassard, Gilles, 555, 557
Broadcasting:
anonymous, 137–139
secret, 523–524
Brute-force attack, 8, 151–152
software-based, 154–155
time and cost estimates, 152–154

Bureau of Export Administration, 610–611
Burrows, Michael, 66

CA-1.1, 327–328
Cade algorithm, 500–501
Caesar Cipher, 11
CAFE, 606–607
CALC, 346
Cantwell Bill, 615–616
Capstone, 593–594
Cascade generators, 405
Cascades, Gollmann, 387–388
Cascading:
multiple block algorithms, 367–368
multiple stream ciphers, 419–420
Cash, digital, *see* Digital cash
Cassells, Ian, 381
CAST, 334–335
S-boxes, 349
CBC, *see* Cipher block chaining mode
CCEP, 269, 598–599
CDMF, 366, 574
Cellhash, 446
Cellular automata, 500
Cellular automaton generator, 414
Certificates:
Privacy-Enhanced Mail, 579
public-key, 185–187
X.509, 574–575
Certification authority, 186
Certification path, 576
Certified mail, digital, 122–123
Chaining variables, 436
Chambers, Bill, 385–386
Characteristics, 286–288
Chaum, David, 84, 115, 133, 137, 536, 549
Cheater, 27
sharing secrets with, 531
Chess Grandmaster Problem, 109
Chinese Lottery, 156–157
Chinese remainder theorem, 249–250, 470
Chor-Rivest knapsack, 466
Chosen-ciphertext attack, 6–7, 471–472
Chosen-key attack, 7
Chosen-plaintext attack, 6–7, 359
Chosen-text attack, 7

Cipher:
substitution, 10–12
transposition, 12
Cipher block chaining mode, 193–197, 208–210
DES, 277–278
error extension, 196
error propagation, 195–196
initialization vector, 194
message authentication codes, 456
padding, 195
security, 196–197
self-recovering, 196
triple encryption, 360–361
Cipher block chaining of plaintext difference mode, 208
Cipher block chaining with checksum, 207–208
Cipher-feedback mode, 200–202, 208–210
DES, 277
error propagation, 201–202
initialization vector, 201
Cipher mode:
choosing, 208–210
summary, 208–210
Ciphertext, 1–2
auto key, 198
hiding in ciphertext, 227–228
pairs, differential cryptanalysis, 285
stealing, 191
Ciphertext-only attack, 5–6
Cleartext, *see* Plaintext
Clipper chip, 591–593
Clipper key-escrow, 328
Clipper phone, 594
Clock-controlled generators, 381
Clocking, 381
CoCom, 610
Code, 9
Coefficients, solving for, 248
Coin flipping, 89–92
fair, 541–543
into a well, 92
key generation, 92
using Blum integers, 543
using one-way functions, 90
using public-key cryptography, 90–91
using square roots, 541–542
Collision, 166
Collision-free, 30
Collision-resistance, 429
Combination generator, 381

Combining function, 381
Commercial COMSEC Endorsement Program, 269, 598–599
Commercial Data Masking Facility, 366, 574
Common Cryptographic Architecture, 573–574
Common modulus, dangers of, 493
Common modulus attack, RSA, 472
Communications:
  using public-key cryptography, 31–34
  using symmetric cryptography, 28–29
Communications channels, encryption, 216–220
Communications Setup, 517–518
Complementation property, 281
Complement keys, DES, 281–282
Completely blind signatures, 112–113
Complete set of residues, 242
Complexity-theoretic approach, stream ciphers, 415–418
Complexity theory, 237–242
  algorithms, 237–239
  complexity of problems, 239–241
Compression, 226
Compression function, 431
Compression permutation, 273–274
Compromise, 5
Compromised keys, 182–183
Computational complexity, 237
Computationally secure, 8
Computer algorithms, 17
Computer clock, as random-sequence generator, 424
Computer Security Act of 1987, 600–601
Computing, with encrypted data, 85–86, 540–541
COMSET, 517–518
Conditional Access for Europe, 606–607
Conference key distribution, 524
Confusion, 237, 346–347
Congruent, 242
Connection integer, 403
  feedback with carry shift registers, maximal-period, 406–407

Continued fraction algorithm, 256
Contract signing, simultaneous:
  with an arbitrator, 118
  without an arbitrator
    face-to-face, 118–119
    not face-to-face, 119–120
    using cryptography, 120–122
Control Vector, 180
Convertible undeniable signatures, 538–539
Coppersmith, Don, 94, 266, 280, 283, 293, 398, 457
Coppersmith's algorithm, 263
Correlation attack, 380
Correlation immunity, stream ciphers, 380
Correlations, random-sequence generators, 425
Counter mode, 205–206, 209
Counting coincidences, 14
Crab, 342–344
Credit cards, anonymous, 147
Crepeau, Claude, 555
Crypt(1), 414
CRYPT(3), 296
Cryptanalysis, 1, 5–8
  differential, *see* Differential cryptanalysis
  FEAL, 311–312
  GOST, 333–334
  IDEA, 323
  linear, 290–293
  LOKI91, 316
  Madryga, 306
  N-Hash, 434–435
  related-key, 290
  Snefru, 432
  types, 5–7
Cryptanalysts, 1
Crypt Breakers Workbench, 414
Cryptographers, 1
Cryptographic algorithm, *see* Cipher
Cryptographically secure pseudo-random, 45
Cryptographic facility, 562
Cryptographic mode, 189
Cryptographic protection, databases, 73–74
Cryptographic protocol, 22
Cryptography, 1
CRYPTO-LEGGO, 414
Cryptologists, 1
Cryptology, 1
CRYPTO-MECCANO, 346

Cryptosystems, 4
  fair, 97
  finite automaton public-key, 482
  hybrid, 32–34
  security, 234–235
  weak, 97
Cusick, Thomas, 312
Cut and choose, 103
Cypherpunks, 609

Daemen, Joan, 325, 341, 349, 414
Damgard, Ivan, 446
Damm, Arvid Gerhard, 13
Data, encrypted:
  computing with, 85–86, 540–541
  discrete logarithm problem, 540–541
  for storage, 220–222
Databases, cryptographic protection, 73–74
Data complexity, 9
Data Encryption Algorithm, *see* Data Encryption Standard
Data Encryption Standard, 17, 265–301
  adoption, 267–268
  algorithm, brute-force attack efficiency, 152–153
  characteristics, 286–288
  commercial chips, 279
  compared to GOST, 333–334
  compression permutation, 273–274
  CRYPT(3), 296
  decryption, 277
  description, 270
  DESX, 295
  development, 265–267
  differential cryptanalysis, 284–290
    DES variants, 298
  expansion permutation, 273–275
  final permutation, 277
  generalized, 296–297
  hardware and software implementation, 278–279
  with independent subkeys, 295
  initial permutation, 271
  iterated block cipher, 347
  key transformation, 272–273
  linear cryptanalysis, 290–293
  modes, 277–278

multiple, 294–295
1987 review, 268–269
1993 review, 269–270
outline of algorithm, 270–272
P-boxes
  design criteria, 294
  permutation, 275, 277
RDES, 297–298
related-key cryptanalysis, 290
RIPE-MAC, 457–458
S-boxes, 349
  alternate, 296–298
  design criteria, 294
  key-dependent, 298, 300,
    354
  substitution, 274–276
security, 278, 280–285
  algebraic structure,
    282–283
  complement keys, 281–282
  current, 300–301
  key length, 283–284
  number of rounds, 284
  possibly weak keys,
    281–282
  S-box design, 284–285
  semiweak keys, 280–281
  weak keys, 280–281
s^nDES, 298–299
source code, 623–632
speeds on microprocessors
  and computers, 279
validation and certification of
  equipment, 268
Data Exchange Key, 581
Data Keys, 176
Davies, Donald, 562
Davies-Meyer, 448
  abreast, 452
  modified, 449–450
  parallel, 451
  tandem, 451–452
Davies-Price, 358
Decoherence, 165
Decryption, 1
  DES, 277
  key, 3
  key-error detection, 179
  knapsack algorithms, 465
  with a public key, 39
  with symmetric algorithm, 4
den Boer, Bert, 434, 436, 441
Denning-Sacco protocol, 63
Dense, 378
Dereferencing keys, 221–222
Derived sequence attack, 381
Designated confirmer signa-
  tures, 82–83, 539–540

Desmedt, Yvo, 81
DES, *see* Data Encryption Standard
Destruction:
  information, 228–229
  of keys, 184–185
DESX, 295
Dictionary attack, 52, 171–173
Differential cryptanalysis,
  284–290
  attacks against
    DES, 288–290
    DES variants, 298
    Lucifer, 303
  extending to higher-order dif-
    ferentials, 293
  strength against, block cipher
    design theory, 348–349
Differential-linear cryptanalysis, 293
Diffie, Whitfield, 31, 37, 122,
  216, 283, 419, 461, 501,
  565
Diffie-Hellman:
  EKE implementation,
    519–520
  extended, 515
  failsafe, 547–548
  fair, 546–547
  Hughes variant, 515
  key exchange without
    exchanging keys, 515
  patents, 516
  with three or more parties, 514
Diffie's randomized stream
  cipher, 419
Diffusion, 237, 346–347
Digital card, properties, 146
Digital cash, 139–147
  anonymous, 139
    credit cards, 147
    money orders, 140
  double spending problem,
    140–141
  off-line systems, 146
  on-line systems, 145–146
  other protocols, 145–147
  perfect crime, 145
  practical, 145
  secret splitting, 142–145
Digital certified mail, 122–123
Digital Notary System, 78
Digital Signature Algorithm,
  17, 483–494
  attacks against k, 492
  computation time compari-
    son with RSA, 489
  criticisms, 484–486

dangers of common modulus,
  493
description, 486–488
ElGamal encryption with,
  490–491
patents, 493–494
prime generation, 488–490
proposal for NIST standard,
  483–486
RSA encryption with, 491
security, 491–492
speed precomputations,
  487–488
subliminal channel, 493,
  534–536
  foiling, 536
variants, 494–495
Digital signatures, 34–41
  algorithms, 39
  applications, 41
  blind, 112–115, 549–550
  convertible undeniable signa-
    tures, 538–539
  converting identification
    schemes to, 512
  definition, 39
  designated confirmer signa-
    tures, 82–83, 539–540
  ElGamal, 476–478
  with encryption, 41–44
  entrusted undeniable, 82
  fail-stop, 85
  Fiat-Shamir signature
    scheme, 507–508
  group signatures, 84–85
  Guillou-Quisquater signature
    scheme, 509–510
  improved arbitrated solution,
    76
  key exchange with, 50
  multiple, 39–40
    Guillou-Quisquater, 510
  nonrepudiation, 40
  oblivious, 117
  protocol, 40
  proxy, 83
  public-key algorithms,
    483–502
    Cade algorithm, 500–501
    cellular automata, 500
    Digital Signature Algo-
      rithm, *see* Digital Signa-
      ture Algorithm
    discrete logarithm signa-
      ture schemes, 496–498
    ESIGN, 499–500
    GOST digital signature
      algorithm, 495–496

Digital signatures (*Cont.*)
  public-key algorithms (*Cont.*)
    Matsumoto-Imai algo-
      rithm, 500
    Ong-Schnorr-Shamir,
      498–499
    public-key cryptography,
      37–38
    attacks against, 43–44
    one-way hash functions
      and, 38–39
    resend attack, foiling, 43
    RSA, 473–474
    Schnorr signature scheme,
      511–512
    subliminal-free, 80
    with symmetric cryptosys-
      tems and arbitrator,
      35–37
    terminology, 39
    timestamps, 38
    trees, 37
    undeniable, 81–82, 536–539
Dining Cryptographers Prob-
  lem, 137
Discrete logarithm, 245
  in finite field, 261–263
  zero-knowledge proofs, 548
Discrete Logarithm Problem,
  501, 540–541
Discrete logarithm signature
  schemes, 496–498
Distributed Authentication
  Security Service, 62
Distributed convertible undeni-
  able signatures, 539
Distributed key management,
  187
DNA computing, 163–164
DNRSG, 387
DoD key generation, 175
Double encryption, 357–358
Double OFB/counter, 363–364
Double spending problem,
  140–141
Driver-level encryption, 222–223
DSA, *see* Digital Signature
  Algorithm
Dynamic random-sequence gen-
  erator, 387

E-box, 273
ECB, *see* Electronic codebook
  mode
Electronic checks, 146
Electronic codebook mode,
  189–191, 208–210
  combined with OFB, 364

DES, 277–278
  padding, 190–191
  triple encryption, 362–363
Electronic coins, 146
Electronic Frontier Foundation,
  608
Electronic-funds transfer, DES
  adoption, 268
Electronic Privacy Information
  Center, 608
ElGamal, 532–533
  EKE implementation, 519
  encryption, 478
    with DSA, 490–491
  patents, 479
  signatures, 476–478
  speed, 478–479
ElGamal, Taher, 263
Elliptic curve cryptosystems,
  480–481
Elliptic curve method, 256
Ellison, Carl, 362
Encoding, 226
Encrypt-decrypt-encrypt mode,
  359
Encrypted Key Exchange:
  applications, 521–522
  augmented, 520–521
  basic protocol, 518–519
  implementation with
    Diffie-Hellman, 519–520
    ElGamal, 519
    RSA, 519
  strengthening, 520
Encryption, 1
  communication channels,
    216–220
    combining link-by-link and
      end-to-end, 219–221
  with compression and error
    control, 226
  data, for storage, 220–222
  detection, 226–227
  digital signatures with, 41–44
  driver-level versus file-level,
    222–223
  ElGamal, 478
    with DSA, 490–491
  end-to-end, 217–220
  with interleaving, 210–211
  key, 3
  knapsack algorithms, 464
  link-by-link, 216–218
  multiple, 357
  with a private key, 39
  probabilistic, 552–554
  RSA, 468
    with DSA, 491

with symmetric algorithm, 4
  using public key, 5
End-to-end encryption, 217–220
  combined with link-by-link,
    219–221
Enigma, 13, 414
Entropy, 233–234
Entrusted undeniable signature,
  82
Error detection:
  during decryption, 179
  during transmission, 178
Error extension, cipher block
  chaining mode, 196
Error propagation:
  cipher block chaining mode,
    195–196
  cipher-feedback mode,
    201–202
  output-feedback mode, 204
Escrow agencies, 592
Escrowed Encryption Standard,
  97, 593
ESIGN, 499–500, 533–534
Euclid's algorithm, 245
Euler totient function, 248–249
Expansion permutation,
  273–275, 315
Export:
  of algorithms, 215–216,
    610–616
  foreign, 617
Exportable Protection Device,
  389
Export Administration Act, 610
EXPTIME, 241
Extended Euclidean algorithm,
  246–248

Factoring, 255–258
  general number field sieve,
    159–160
  long-range predictions, 162
  public-key encryption algo-
    rithms, 158–159
  special number field sieve,
    160–161
  using quadratic sieve, 159
Factoring Problem, 501
Failsafe:
  Diffie-Hellman, 547–548
  key escrowing, 98
Fail-stop digital signatures, 85
Fair cryptosystems, 97
Fait-Shamir, 508
FAPKC0, 482
FAPKC1, 482
FAPKC2, 482

FEAL, 308–312
  cryptanalysis, 311–312
  description, 308–10
  patents, 311
Feedback:
  cipher block chaining mode,
    193, 195
  internal, output-feedback
    mode, 203
Feedback function, 373
Feedback shift register, 373
Feedback with carry shift regis-
    ters, 402–404
  combining generators, 405,
    410
  maximal-length, tap
    sequences, 408–409
  maximal-period, connection
    integers, 406–407
Feedforward, cipher block
    chaining mode, 195
Feige, Uriel, 503–504
Feige-Fiat-Shamir, 503–508
  enhancements, 506–507
  identification scheme,
    504–505
  simplified, 503–504
Feistel, Horst, 266, 303
Feistel network, 347
  Blowfish, 337
  practically secure, 349
Fermat's little theorem, 248
  Euler's generalization, 248
FFT-Hash, 446
Fiat, Amos, 503–504
Fiat-Shamir signature scheme,
    507–508
Fibonacci configuration, 373,
    379
Fibonacci shrinking generator,
    391
File-level encryption, 222–223
Filter generator, 381
Finite field, 254
  discrete logarithms, 261–263
FIPS PUB 46, 267
FIPS PUB 74, 267
FIPS PUB 81, 267
FIPS PUB 112, 267
Fish, 391
Fixed bit index, 543
Flat keyspace, 176
Flipping coins, *see* Coin flipping
Fortified key negotiation, 522

Galois configuration, linear
    feedback shift registers,
    378–379

Galois field, computing in,
    254–255
Garey, Michael, 241
Gatekeeper, 278
Geffe generator, 382–383
General number field sieve,
    159–160, 256
General Services Administra-
    tion, DES adoption, 268
Generators, 253–254
Gifford, 392–393
Gifford, David, 392
Gill, J., 501
Global deduction, 8
Goldwasser, Shafi, 94, 552
Gollmann, Dieter, 386
Gollmann cascade, 387–388
Goodman-McAuley cryptosys-
    tem, 466
Goresky, Mark, 404
GOST, 331–334, 354
  source code, 643–647
GOST digital signature algo-
    rithm, 495–496
GOST hash function, 454
GOST R 34.10–94, 495
Gosudarstvennyi Standard
    Soyuza SSR, 331–334
Graham-Shamir knapsacks, 465
Graph isomorphism, 104–105
Greatest common divisor,
    245–246
Grossman, Edna, 266
Group signatures, 84–85
Group Special Mobile, 389
Group structure, block ciphers
    design theory, 348
GSM, 389
Guillou, Louis, 102, 508
Guillou-Quisquater:
  identification scheme,
    508–510
  signature scheme, 509–510
Gutmann, Peter, 353
Guy, Richard, 159

Haber, Stuart, 75, 485, 488
Hamiltonian cycles, 105–106
Hard drive, encrypted, provid-
    ing random access to,
    222
Hardware:
  DES implementation,
    278–279
  encryption, 223–225
  RSA, 469
Hash functions, *see* One-way
    hash functions

Hash value, 30
HAVAL, 445–446
Hellman, Martin, 31–32, 37,
    262, 283, 293, 358–359,
    461–462
Hiding information from an
    oracle, 86
Historical terms, 9
Homophonic substitution
    cipher, 10–11
Hughes, 515
Hughes, Eric, 609
Hughes XPD/KPD, 389–390
Hybrid cryptosystems, 32–34,
    461

IBC-Hash, 458
IBM Common Cryptographic
    Architecture, 573–574
IBM secret-key management
    protocol, 561–562
IDEA, 319–325, 354
  cryptanalysis, 323
  description, 320–322
  modes of operation, 323–
    325
  overview, 320–321
  patents, 325
  S-boxes, 349
  source code, 637–643
  speed, 322–323
  strength against differential
    cryptanalysis, 348
  variants, 325
Ideal secrecy, 236
Identification schemes:
  converting to signature
    schemes, 512
  Feige-Fiat-Shamir, 503–508
  Guillou-Quisquater, 508–
    510
  Ohta-Okamoto, 508
  Schnorr authentication and
    signature scheme,
    510–512
Identity-based cryptosystems,
    115
Ignition key, 564
Import, foreign, 617
Index of coincidence, 14
Information:
  amount, information theory
    definition, 233
  deduction, 8
  destruction, 228–229
Information-theoretic approach,
    418
  stream ciphers, 415

Information theory, 233–237
  cryptosystem security,
    234–235
  entropy and uncertainty,
    233–234
  in practice, 236–237
  rate of the language, 234
  unicity distance, 235–236
Ingemarsson, Ingemar, 418
Initialization vector:
  cipher block chaining mode,
    194
  cipher-feedback mode, 201
  output-feedback mode, 204
Inner-CBC, 360, 363
Insertion attack, synchronous
    stream ciphers, 203
Instance deduction, 8
Institute of Electrical and Elec-
    tronics Engineers, 608
Integrated Services Digital Net-
    work, 563–565
Integrity, 2
Interactive protocol, 103
Interchange Key, 581
Interleave, 210–211
Interlock protocol, mutual
    authentication using,
    54–55
Internal feedback, 203
International Association for
    Cryptologic Research,
    605
International Standards Organi-
    zation:
  authentication framework,
    574–577
  DES adoption, 268
International Traffic in Arms
    Regulations, 610–614
Internet, Privacy-Enhanced
    Mail, 577–584
Introducers, 187
Inverses modulo a number,
    246–248
IPES, 319
ISDN, 563–565
ISO 8732, 359
ISO 9796, 472, 474, 486
ISO/IEC 9979, 607
ISO X.509 protocols, 574–577
Iterated block cipher, 347

Jacobi symbol, 252–253
J-algebras, 501
Jam, 414
Jennings generator, 383–384

Johnson, David, 241
Jueneman's methods, 457

Kaliski, Burt, 342
Karn, 351–352
Karn, Phil, 351
Karnin-Greene-Hellman, 530
Kerberos, 60, 566–571
  abbreviations, 567
  authentication steps, 567
  credentials, 568
  getting initial ticket, 569
  getting server tickets,
    569–570
  licenses, 571
  model, 566
  requesting services, 570
  security, 571
  Version 4, 570–571
  Version 5 messages, 568
Kerckhoffs, A., 5
Kerckhoffs's assumption, 7
Key, 3
  backup, 181–182
  CDMF shortening, 366
  complement, DES, 281–282
  compromised, 182–183
  controlling usage, 180
  dereferencing, 221–222
  destroying, 184–185
  distribution in large net-
    works, 177
  generating, 170–175
    ANSI X9.17 standard, 175
    DoD, 175
    pass phrases, 174–175
    poor choices, 171–173
    random keys, 173–174
    reduced keyspaces, 170–171
  ISDN, 563–564
  lifetime, 183–184
  possibly weak, DES, 281–282
  semiweak, DES, 280–281
  session, 33, 180
  storing, 180–181
  transferring, 176–177
  transmission, error detection,
    178
  updating, 180
  using, 179–180
  verification, 178–179
  weak
    block ciphers design theory,
      348
    DES, 280–281
Key and message broadcast,
  51–52

Key and message transmission,
  51
Key Auto-Key, 202
Keyboard latency, as random-
    sequence generator,
    424–425
Key Certification Authority, 43
Key control vectors, 562
Key distribution:
  anonymous, 94–95
  conference, 524
Key Distribution Center, 43–44
Key-Encryption Keys, 176, 184
Key escrow, 97–100, 181–182,
    591
  politics, 98–100
Key exchange, 47–52
  DASS, 62
  Denning-Sacco protocol, 63
  with digital signatures, 50
  interlock protocol, 49–50
  Kerberos, 60
  key and message broadcast,
    51–52
  key and message transmis-
    sion, 51
  man-in-the-middle attack,
    48–49
  Needham-Schroeder protocol,
    58–59
  Neuman-Stubblebine proto-
    col, 60–62
  Otway-Rees protocol, 59–60
  protocols, formal analysis,
    65–68
  with public-key cryptography,
    48
  with symmetric cryptogra-
    phy, 47–48
  Wide-Mouth Frog protocol,
    56–57
  without exchanging keys, 515
  Woo-Lam protocol, 63–64
  Yahalom, 57–58
Key-exchange algorithms:
  COMSET, 517–518
  conference key distribution
    and secret broadcasting,
    523–525
  Diffie-Hellman, 513–516
  Encrypted Key Exchange,
    518–522
  fortified key negotiation, 522
  Shamir's three-pass protocol,
    516–517
  station-to-station protocol,
    516

Tatebayashi-Matsuzaki-Newman, 524–525
Key generation, using coin flipping, 92
Key length:
  comparing symmetric and public-key, 165–166
  deciding on, 166–167
  DES, 283–284
  public-key, 158–165
    DNA computing, 163–164
    quantum computing, 164–165
    recommended lengths, 161–163
  symmetric, 151–158
    biotechnology as cryptanalysis tool, 156–157
    brute-force attack, 151–154
    Chinese Lottery, 156–157
    neural networks, 155
    software-based brute-force attacks, 154–155
    thermodynamic limitations on brute-force attacks, 157–158
    using viruses to spread cracking program, 155–156
Key management, 169–187
  distributed, 187
  public-key, 185–187
Key negotiation, fortified, 522
Key notarization, 562
Key revocation certificate, 585
Keyspace, 3
  flat, 176
  nonlinear, 175–176
  reduced, 170–171
Keystream generator, 197–198
  counter mode, 206
  periodic, 202
Khafre, 317–318, 349
Khufu, 317, 349
Kilian, Joe, 116
Kim, Kwangjo, 298, 350
Kinetic Protection Device, 389–390
Klapper, Andy, 404
Klein, Daniel, 53, 171
Knapsack algorithms, 462–466
  decryption, 465
  encryption, 464
  implementations, 465
  patents, 466
  public key created from private key, 464

security, 465
  superincreasing, 463–464
  variants, 465–466
Knapsack problem, 501
Known-plaintext attack, 6–7, 151, 359
Knudsen, Lars, 8, 293, 314, 316, 348–349
Knuth, 393, 501
Koblitz, Neal, 480
Konheim, Alan, 266, 280
Kravitz, David, 493
Kravitz-Reed, 481
KryptoKnight, 571–572

Lagged Fibonacci generators, 390
LaGrange interpolating polynomial scheme, 528–529
Lai, Xuejia, 319, 449
Langford, Susan, 293
Law Enforcement Access Field, 591
Legal issues, 618
Legendre symbol, 251
Lehmann, 259
Lehmann algorithm, 259
Length, shift register, 373
Lenstra, Arjen, 159, 162, 257, 485, 488
LFSR/FCSR summation/parity cascade, 410–411
Lidl, Rudolph, 481
Linear complexity:
  profile, 380
  stream ciphers, 380
Linear congruential generators, 369–372
  combining, 371–372
  constants, 370
Linear consistency test, 381
Linear cryptanalysis:
  DES, 290–293
  strength against, block cipher design theory, 348–349
Linear error-correcting codes, algorithms based on, 480
Linear feedback shift registers, 372–379
  Galois, 378–379
  primitive polynomials mod 2, 376–377
  software, 378–379
  stream ciphers using, *see* Stream ciphers
Linear syndrome algorithm, 381

Link-by-link encryption, 216–218
  combined with end-to-end, 219–221
Linking protocol, timestamping, 76–77
Li-Wang algorithm, 346
Local deduction, 8
Lock-in, 388
Logarithms, discrete, *see* Discrete logarithm
LOKI, 314–316
  S-boxes, 349
  source code, 632–637
LOKI Double-Block, 451
Low decryption exponent attack, RSA, 473
Low encryption exponent attack, RSA, 472–473
Luby, Michael, 352
Luby-Rackoff, 352–353
  $xDES^1$, 365
LUC, 481
Lucas number, 481
Luccio-Mazzone, 501
Lucifer, 266, 303–304
Lu-Lee cryptosystem, 466
Lyndon words, 501

MacGuffin, 346
Madryga, W. E., 304
Mafia Fraud, 110
Magic numbers, 423
Manasse, Mark, 159, 257
Man-in-the-middle attack, 48–49
Masks, REDOC II, 312
Massey, James, 319, 339, 386, 418, 449
Master Key, 561
Master Terminal Key, 561
Matsui, Mitsuru, 290–291
Matsumoto-Imai algorithm, 500
Mauborgne, Joseph, 15
Maurer, Ueli, 419
Maurer's randomized stream cipher, 419
Maximal period generator, 369
MBAL, 344
McEliece, Robert, 479
McEliece algorithm, 346, 479–480
MD2, 441
MD3, 446
MD4, 435–436
MD5, 436–441
MDC, 353–354

MDC-2, 452–453
MDC-4, 452–454
MD-strengthening, 431
Meet-in-the-middle attack, 358, 381
Mental poker, 92–95
Merkle, Ralph, 34, 316–318, 358–359, 432, 455, 461–462
Merkle's puzzles, 34
Merritt, Michael, 67, 518, 520–521, 571
Message:
  authentication, 56
  broadcasting, 69
  Privacy-Enhanced Mail, 579–582
  recovery, 497–498
  resending as receipt, 42–43
Message authentication codes, 31, 455–459
  bidirectional, 457
  CBC-MAC, 456
  IBC-Hash, 458
  Jueneman's methods, 457
  message authenticator algorithm, 456–457
  one-way hash functions as, 458–459
  RIPE-MAC, 457–458
  stream ciphers, 459
Message authenticator algorithm, 456–457
Message broadcast, anonymous, 137–139
Message Digest, 435–436
Message Digest Cipher, 353
Message Integrity Check, 578
Message-meaning rule, 66
Message Security Protocol, 584
Meyer, Carl, 266, 278
Meyer, Joseph A., 614
Meyer-Schilling, 452
Micali, Silvio, 94, 508, 546–547, 552
Miller, Gary, 259
Miller, V. S., 480
Mimic functions, 10
Minimum-disclosure proofs, 108
MITRENET, 562–563
Miyaguchi, Shoji, 308
MMB, 325–327
m*n-bit S box, 349
Modular arithmetic, 242–245
Modular Multiplication-based Block cipher, 325–327
Modular reduction, 242

Modulo, inverses, 246–248
Monoalphabetic cipher, 10
Montgomery's method, 244
Moore's Law, 153
m-sequence, 374
MSP, 584
Muller, Winfried, 481
Multiparty unconditionally secure protocols, 137
Multiple-bit generator, 421
Multiple encryption, 357
  quintuple, 366
Multiple Identity Fraud, 111
Multiple-key public-key cryptography, 527–528
Multiple signatures, 39–40
Multiplier, 369
Multispeed inner-product generator, 386–387
Mush, 392
Mutual shrinking generator, 392
MYK-80, 593–594
Mykotronx Clipper chip, 328
MYK-78T, 591–593

Nanoteq, 390
National Bureau of Standards, *see* National Institute of Standards and Technology
National Computer Security Center, 599–600
National Institute of Standards and Technology, 600–603
  DES development, 265–267
  Memorandum of Understanding, 601–603
National Security Agency, 597–599
  DES development, 266–267
  export of cryptography, 614–615
  Memorandum of Understanding, 601–603
  S-box development role, 278, 280
Navy Research Laboratory, protocol analyzer, 67–68
Needham, Roger, 58, 66, 216
Needham-Schroeder protocol, 58–59
Networks, large, key distribution, 177
Neuman-Stubblebine protocol, 60–62
Neural networks, breaking algorithms, 155
NewDES, 306–308

N-Hash, 433–435
Niederreiter, Harald, 501
Niederreiter algorithm, 480
Niemi cryptosystem, 466
Nobauer, Wilfried, 481
Noise, random, using as random-sequence generator, 423–424
Nonce-verification rule, 66
Non-Interactive Key Sharing systems, 115
Nonlinear-feedback shift registers, 412–413
Nonlinear keyspace, 175–176
Nonrepudiation, 2
Notz, Bill, 266
NP-complete problem, 240–242
  graph isomorphism, 104
  knapsack algorithms, 462
  McEliece algorithm, 479
  solving, 163–164
NRL Protocol Analyzer, 67–68
NSDD-145, 268
Nuclear Non-Proliferation Act, 610
Number field sieve, 256
Numbers:
  2–adic, 404
  large, 17–18
Number theory, 242–255
  Barrett's algorithm, 244
  Blum integers, 253
  Chinese remainder theorem, 249–250
  Euclid's algorithm, 245
  Euler totient function, 248–249
  extended Euclidean algorithm, 246–248
  Fermat's little theorem, 248
  Galois field, computing in, 254–255
  generators, 253–254
  greatest common divisor, 245–246
  inverses modulo a number, 246–248
  Jacobi symbol, 252–253
  Legendre symbol, 251
  modular arithmetic, 242–245
  Montgomery's method, 244
  prime numbers, 245
  quadratic residues, 250–251
  solving for coefficients, 248
Nyberg, Kaisa, 348

Oblivious transfer, 116–117, 550

Oblivous signatures, 117
OFB, *see* Output-feedback mode
Ohta, Kazuo, 146, 501
Ohta-Okamoto identification
    scheme, 508
Okamoto, Tatsuaki, 146, 501
1/p generator, 414
One-time pad, 15–17
    hiding ciphertext in cipher-
        text, 227–228
One-time tape, 418
One-way accumulators, 95–96,
    543
One-way function, 29–30
    authentication using, 52
    bit commitment using, 87–88
    coin flipping using, 90
    trap-door, 158
One-way hash functions, 30–31,
    351–354
    background, 429–431
    birthday attacks, 165–166,
        430
    choosing, 455
    cipher security, 353–354
    compression function, 431
    encryption speeds, 456
    HAVAL, 445–446
    improved arbitrated solution,
        76
    Karn, 351–352
    length, 430–431
    Luby-Rackoff, 352–353
    MD2, 441
    MD3, 446
    MD4, 435–436
    MD5, 436–441
    MD-strengthening, 431
    message authentication
        codes, 455–459
    Message Digest Cipher,
        353–354
    multiple signatures, 40
    N-Hash, 433–435
    RIPE-MD, 445
    Secure Hash Algorithm,
        442–445
    signing documents with,
        38–39
    Snefru, 432
    as unbiased random-bit gener-
        ator, 107
    using public-key algorithms,
        455
    using symmetric block algo-
        rithms, 446–455
        AR hash function, 453
        GOST hash function, 454

hash length equals block
    size, 447–449
    LOKI Double-Block, 451
    MDC-2 and MDC-4,
        452–454
    modified Davies-Meyer,
        449–450
    parallel Davies-Meyer, 451
    Preneel-Bosselaers-
        Govaerts-Vandewalle, 450
    Quisquater-Girault, 450
    tandem and abreast Davies-
        Meyer, 451–452
Ong-Schnorr-Shamir, 498–499,
    531–532
Orange Book, 599–600
Otway-Rees protocol, 59–60
Outerbridge, Richard, 363
Outer-CBC, 360
Output-feedback mode,
    203–205, 208–210
    combined with ECB, 364
    DES, 277
    with a nonlinear function,
        208
Overtake, 598
Overwriting, 229

Padding:
    cipher block chaining mode,
        195
    electronic codebook mode,
        190–191
    MD5, 436
    Secure Hash Algorithm, 442
    triple encryption with, 362
Painvin, Georges, 12
Pass phrases, 174–175
Passive attack, 27
Passive cheaters, 27
Patents, 609–610; *See also* spe-
    cific algorithms
P-boxes:
    design criteria, 294
    permutation, 275, 277, 316
PEM, *see* Privacy-Enhanced
    Mail
Perfect secrecy, 235
Period, 11
    shift register, 373
Permutation, 237
    key, DES, 272–273
PES, 319, 324
Pike, 391–392
PKZIP, 394–395
Plaintext, 1–2
Plaintext block chaining mode,
    208

Plaintext feedback mode, 208
Plaintext pair, right and wrong
    pairs, 287
Pless generator, 413–414
p-NEW scheme, 498
Pohlig, Stephen, 262
Pohlig-Hellman encryption
    scheme, 474
Polarized photons, 555
Pollard's Monte Carlo algo-
    rithm, 256
Polyalphabetic substitution
    cipher, 10–11
Polygram substitution cipher,
    10–11
Polynomials:
    degree, shift register length,
        374
    dense, 378
    irreducible, 255, 481
    sparse, 378
Pomerance, Carl, 257
Powerline System, 466
Pre-image, 30
Preneel, Bart, 457
Preneel-Bosselaers-Govaerts-
    Vandewalle, 450
Pretty Good Privacy, 584–587
Price, William, 562
Prime numbers, 245
    generation, 258–261
        DSA, 488–490
        practical considerations,
            260–260
    relatively prime, 245
    strong, 261
Primitive, 253
Principal square root, 251
Privacy-Enhanced Mail,
    577–584
    certificates, 579
    documents, 578
    messages, 579–582
    RIPEM, 583–584
    security, 582–583
    TIS/PEM, 583
Private key, 5
    creating public key from, 464
    for public-key cryptography,
        lifetime, 184
Probabilistic encryption,
    552–554
Problems:
    complexity, 239–241
    EXPTIME, 241
    hard, 239
    intractable, 239
    PSPACE, 241

Problems (*Cont.*)
  tractable, 239
  undecidable, 240
  See also NP-complete prob-
    lem
Processing complexity, 9
Product cipher, 347
Proofs of Membership, 111
Propagating cipher block chaining mode, 207
Proposed Encryption Standard,
  319
Protocols, 21, 47
  adjudicated, 26, 70–71
  all-or-nothing disclosure of
    secrets, 96
  analysis, approaches, 65–66
  anonymous message broad-
    cast, 137–139
  arbitrated, 23–26
  attacks against, 27
  authentication, 576–577
  authentication and key-
    exchange, formal analy-
    sis, 65–68
  BAN logic, 66–67
  basic zero-knowledge,
    102–104
  bit commitment, 86–88
  blind signatures, 112–115
  characteristics, 21
  cryptographic, 22
  DASS, 62
  definition, 21
  Denning-Sacco, 63
  digital cash, *see* Digital cash
  digital certified mail, 122–123
  digital signatures, 40
  distributed, timestamping,
    77–78
  fair coin flips, 89–92
  IBM Common Cryptographic
    Architecture, 573–574
  IBM secret-key management,
    561–562
  identity-based public-key
    cryptography, 115
  interactive, 103
  interlock, 49–50, 54–55
  Kerberos, 60, 566–571
  key escrow, 97–100
  key exchange, 47–52
  KryptoKnight, 571–572
  lessons, 64–65
  mental poker, 92–95
  multiparty unconditionally
    secure, 137
  Needham-Schroeder, 58

Neuman-Stubblebine, 60–62
  oblivious signatures, 117
  oblivious transfer, 116–117
  one-way accumulators, 95–96
  Otway-Rees, 59–60
  purpose, 22–23
  secret splitting, 70–71
  secure circuit evaluation, 137
  secure elections, *see* Secure
    elections
  secure multiparty computa-
    tion, 134–137
  self-enforcing, 26–27
  SESAME, 572
  simultaneous contract sign-
    ing, 118–122
  simultaneous exchange of
    secrets, 123–124
  subliminal channel, 79–80
  timestamping, 75–79
  types, 24
  Wide-Mouth Frog, 56–57
  Woo-Lam, 63–64
  Yahalom, 57–58
  See also Authentication;
    Zero-knowledge proofs
Pseudo-Hadamard Transform,
  340
Pseudo-random function family,
  SEAL, 398–399
Pseudo-random-number generator, 78, 416
Pseudo-random sequence,
  44–45
Pseudo-random-sequence generator, 44
  bit commitment using, 88
  generating multiple streams,
    420–421
  linear congruential genera-
    tors, 369–372
  linear feedback shift registers,
    372–379
PSPACE, 241
Public key, 5
  certificates, 185–187
  creating from private key, 464
  key length, 158–165
    recommended lengths,
      161–163
  key management, 185–187
Public-key algorithms, 4–5, 33,
  500–502
  background, 461–462
  based on linear error-correct-
    ing codes, 480
  Diffie-Hellman, 513
  ElGamal, 476–479

elliptic curve cryptosystems,
  480–481
  finite automaton cryptosys-
    tems, 482
  knapsack algorithms,
    462–466
  LUC, 481
  McEliece, 479–480
  one-way hash functions
    using, 455
  Pohlig-Hellman, 474
  Rabin, 475–476
  RSA, *see* RSA
  security, 461–462
  strength, 502
Public-key cryptography:
  attacks against, 43–44
  authentication using, 53–54
  coin flipping using, 90–91
  communications using, 31–34
  identity-based, 115
  key exchange with, 48
  multiple-key, 68–69
  private keys, lifetime, 184
  signing documents with,
    37–38
  one-way hash functions,
    38–39
  versus symmetric cryptogra-
    phy, 216–217
Public-Key Cryptography Standards, 588–589
Public Key Partners, 604–605
Public-key ring, 585
Purchase-key attack, 7

Quadratic nonresidues, 251
Quadratic residues, 250–251
  generator, 417
Quadratic sieve, 256
  factoring, 159
Quantum computing, 164–
  165
Quantum cryptography,
  554–557
Quintuple encryption, 366
Quisquater, Jean-Jacques, 102,
  508
Quisquater-Girault, 450

Rabin, 475–476
Rabin, Michael, 103, 259, 518,
  550
Rabin-Miller algorithm,
  259–260
RACE Integrity Primitives Eval-
  uation, 605–606
Rackoff, Charles, 352

Rainbow Books, 600
Rambutan, 390
Random keys, 173–174
Random noise, as random-
    sequence generator,
    423–424
Random-number generation, 44
Random-sequence generators,
    421–428
    biases and correlations,
        425–426
    computer clock, 424
    distilling randomness,
        426–428
    keyboard latency measure-
        ment, 424–425
    RAND tables, 422–423
    using random noise, 423–424
Random sequences, real, 45–46
Randomized approach, stream
    ciphers, 415
Randomized stream cipher,
    419
Randomness, distilling,
    426–428
RAND tables, 422–423
Rao-Nam algorithm, 346
Rate of the language, 234
RC2, 318–319
RC4, 319, 397–398
RC5, 344–346
    source code, 659–662
RDES, 297–298
Receipt, resending message as,
    42–43
REDOC II, 311–313
REDOC III, 313
Redundancy, of language, 234
Reeds, Jim, 369
Related-key cryptanalysis, 290
Renji, Tao, 482
Renting Passports, 111
Replay attacks, 58–59
Research and Development in
    Advanced Communica-
    tion Technologies,
    Integrity Primitives Eval-
    uation, 605–606
Resend attack, foiling, 43
Residue, 242
    quadratic, 250–251
    reduced set, 248
Restricted algorithms, 3
RFC 1421, 578
RFC 1422, 578
RFC 1423, 578
RFC 1424, 578
Richter, Manfield, 423

Riordan, Mark, 583–584
RIPE, 605–606
RIPEM, 583–584
RIPE-MAC, 457–458
RIPE-MD, 445
Rip van Winkle cipher, 418–419
Rivest, Ron, 159, 163, 318–319,
    344, 397, 435, 440–441,
    444, 446, 467
Rivest Cipher, 318
Robshaw, Matt, 342
Rogaway, Phil, 398
ROM key, 181
ROT13, 11
Rotor machines, 12–13
RSA, 17, 466–474
    ability to break, zero-knowl-
        edge proofs, 548–549
    attack on encrypting and
        signing with, 473–474
    blind signatures, 548
    chosen ciphertext attack,
        471–472
    common modulus attack,
        472
    compared to DSA, 485
    computation time compari-
        son with DSA, 489
    as de facto standard, 485–486
    EKE implementation, 519
    encryption, 468
        with DSA, 491
    in hardware, 469
    low decryption exponent
        attack, 473
    low encryption exponent
        attack, 472–473
    patents, 474
    restrictions on use, 473
    security, 470–471
    speed, 469
    standards, 474
RSA Data Security, Inc., 295,
    603–604
RSA Factoring Challenge, 257
RSA generator, 417
Rubber-hose cryptanalysis, 7
Rueppel, Ranier, 385–386
Running-key cipher, 12

SAFER K-64, 339–341
SAFER K-128, 341
Salt, 52–53
S-boxes:
    alternate, DES, 296–298
    Blowfish, 336
    Boolean functions in, 350
    DES, key-dependent, 298, 300

design
    criteria, 294
    security questions, 284
    theory, 349–351
    Lucifer, 303
    NSA role, 278, 280
    substitution, 274–276
Scherbius, Arthur, 13
Schlafly, Roger, 394
Schneier, Bruce, 336, 346
Schnorr, Claus, 418, 446, 510
Schnorr authentication and sig-
    nature scheme, 510–
    512
Schroeder, Michael, 58, 216
Schwartau, Winn, 300
Sci.crypt, 608–609
Scott, Robert, 306
SEAL, 398–400
    source code, 667–673
Secrecy:
    ideal, 236
    perfect, 235
Secrets, simultaneous
    exchange, 123–124
Secret sharing, 71–73
    without adjudication, 72
    with cheaters, 72
    with disenrollment, 73
    without revealing shares, 73
    schemes with prevention, 73
    verifiable, 73
Secret-sharing algorithms,
    528–531
    advanced threshold schemes,
        530–531
    Asmuth-Bloom, 529–530
    cheater detection, 531
    Karnin-Greene-Hellman, 530
    LaGrange interpolating poly-
        nomial scheme, 528–529
    vector scheme, 529
Secret splitting, 70–71
    digital cash, 142–145
Secure and Fast Encryption
    Routine, 339
Secure circuit evaluation, 137
Secure elections, 125–134
    divided protocols, 133
    multiple-key ciphers, 133
    simplistic voting protocols,
        125–126
    voting with
        blind signatures, 126–127
        single central facility,
            128–130
        two central facilities,
            127–128

Secure elections (*Cont.*)
  voting without central tabulating facility, 130–133
Secure European System for Applications in a Multi-vendor Environment, 572
Secure Hash Algorithm, 442–445
Secure multiparty computation, 134–137, 551–552
Secure Telephone Unit, 565
Security:
  of algorithms, 8–9
  Blowfish, 339
  cipher block chaining mode, 196–197
  ciphers based on one-way hash functions, 353–354
  cryptosystem, 234–235
  DES, 278, 280–285
    algebraic structure, 282–283
    current, 300–301
    key length, 283–284
    weak keys, 280–281
  DSA, 491–492
  ESIGN, 500
  Kerberos, 571
  knapsack algorithms, 465
  MD5, 440–441
  MMB, 326–327
  output-feedback mode, 205
  PKZIP, 395
  Privacy-Enhanced Mail, 582–583
  requirements for different information, 167
  RSA, 470–471
  SEAL, 400
  Secure Hash Algorithm, 444–445
  self-synchronizing stream cipher, 199
Selector string, 143
Self-decimated generator, 385–387
Self-enforcing protocols, 26–27
Self-recovering, cipher block chaining mode, 196
Self-shrinking generator, 388
Self-synchronizing stream cipher, 198–199
Selmer, E. S., 381
Semiweak keys, DES, 280–281
SESAME, 572
Session keys, 33, 180
SHA, 442–445

Shadows, 71–72
Shamir, Adi, 72, 284–285, 288, 291, 296, 303, 311–312, 314, 319, 416, 434, 462, 467, 502–504, 508, 516, 528
Shamir's pseudo-random-number generator, 416
Shamir's three-pass protocol, 516–517
Shimizu, Akihiro, 308
Shor, Peter, 164
Shrinking generator, 388, 411–412
Signature equation, 496
Signatures, *see* Digital signatures
Silverman, Bob, 159
Simmons, Gustavus, 72, 79, 493, 501, 531
Simple columnar transposition cipher, 12
Simple relations, 347–348
Simple substitution cipher, 10–11
Simultaneous exchange of secrets, 123–124
Skew, 425
SKEY, 53
SKID, 55–56
Skipjack, 267, 328–329
Smart cards, 587
  observer, 146
  Universal Electronic Payment System, 589–591
Smith, Lynn, 266
s^nDES, 298–299
Snefru, 432
Software:
  DES implementation, 278–279
  encryption, 225
  linear feedback shift registers, 378–379
  RSA speedups, 469–470
Software-based brute-force attack, 154–155
Software Publishers Association, 608
Solovay, Robert, 259
Solovay-Strassen algorithm, 259
Space complexity, 237
Sparse, 378
Special number field sieve, 160–161
SP network, 347
Square roots:
  coin flipping using, 541–542
  modulo n, 258

Standards:
  public-key cryptography, 588–589
  RSA, 474
Station-to-station protocol, 516
Steganography, 9–10
StepRightUp, 414
Stereotyped beginnings, 190
Stereotyped endings, 190
Storage:
  data encryption for, 220–222
  keys, 180–181
  requirements, 9
Stornetta, W. Scott, 75
Straight permutation, 275
Strassen, Volker, 259
Stream algorithms, 4
Stream ciphers, 4, 189, 197–198
  A5, 389
  additive generators, 390–392
  Algorithm M, 393–394
  versus block ciphers, 210–211
  Blum, Blum, and Shub generator, 417–418
  Blum-Micali generator, 416–417
  cascading multiple, 419–420
  cellular automaton generator, 414
  choosing, 420
  complexity-theoretic approach, 415–418
  correlation immunity, 380
  counter mode, 206
  crypt(1), 414
  design and analysis, 379–381
  Diffie's randomized stream cipher, 419
  encryption speeds, 420
  feedback with carry shift registers, 402–404
  Fish, 391
  Gifford, 392–393
  Hughes XPD/KPD, 389–390
  information-theoretic approach, 418
  linear complexity, 380
  Maurer's randomized stream cipher, 419
  message authentication codes, 459
  multiple, generating from single pseudo-random-sequence generator, 420–421